Biographical Dictionary of

MODERN WORLD LEADERS

1900 to 1991

John C. Fredriksen

☑®

Facts On File, Inc.

Biographical Dictionary of Modern World Leaders: 1900 to 1991

Facts On File, Inc.
132 West 31st Street
New York NY 10001

Library of Congress Cataloging-in-Publication Data
  Biographical dictionary of modern world leaders: 1900–1991 / [compiled] by John C. Fredriksen.
       p. cm.
  Includes bibliographical references and indexes.
  ISBN 0-8160-5366-9
  1. Statesmen—Biography—Dictionaries. 2. Heads of state—Biography—Dictionaries. 3. Biography—20th century—Dictionaries. I. Fredriksen, John C.
D412.6.B52 2004
909.82′092′2—dc22
[B]   2003047293

Facts On File books are available at special discounts when purchased in bulk quantities for businesses, associations, institutions, or sales promotions. Please call our Special Sales Department in New York at (212) 967-8800 or (800) 322-8755.

You can find Facts On File on the World Wide Web at http://www.factsonfile.com

Text design by Joan M. Toro
Cover design by Cathy Rincon

Printed in the United States of America

VB FOF 10 9 8 7 6 5 4 3 2 1

This book is printed on acid-free paper.

CONTENTS

LIST OF ENTRIES

INTRODUCTION

The 20th century witnessed some of the most monumental events and political upheavals of human history. It began with a continuation of European colonialism throughout Europe and Asia while a relatively new world power, Japan, also sought expansion. However, the process began unraveling in the wake of World War I, which forever altered the map of modern Europe and gave birth to a new and virulent ideology—communism—upon the ruins of the Russian Empire. The new democracies of the world had scarcely consolidated themselves before they were battered and nearly uprooted by another global malady, the Great Depression of 1929. The ensuing hardships occasioned the rise of other antidemocratic strains of thought—fascism in Italy, Nazism in Germany, and ultranationalism in Japan. Competition with democracies for land and natural resources ultimately precipitated an even greater cataclysm, World War II, which destroyed both extreme right wing ideologies and the final vestiges of colonialism. Thereafter the rise of new nations closely paralleled a partitioning of the world into capitalistic and communistic camps. For nearly four decades the cold war kept the global community on the brink of a nuclear precipice, but the fall of the Soviet Union in 1991 signaled the final triumph of democracy and capitalism. Pundits subsequently hailed the beginning of a "new world order" holding the promise of international peace and prosperity, but this has since proved illusory. The book you hold chronicles leaders from around the world throughout this exciting period, their contributions to events, and the ramifications these engendered.

This title is identical in format to its predecessor, *Biographical Dictionary of Modern World Leaders, 1992 to the Present* (2003). As previously I employed a relatively conventional approach in writing these essays; they range in length between 750 and 1,500 words, contingent upon the subject. Again I touch upon such diverse considerations as ethnic background, religion, education level, party affiliation, and performance in office. Where possible I also cite a direct quotation to liven up an otherwise dour recital of facts and allow greater insights into the individual in question. In designing this reference book I also cast as wide a net as possible to promote global perspectives. Thus, entries cover the 132 nations extant at the time, along with the United Nations and the Holy See. My chronological limitations are sharply defined and restricted to heads of state who assumed power at the turn of the century up through 1991. These may have been elected to high office or acquired power through other means, but they must have been actual or de facto leaders of a nation.

The publishing market is full of biographical dictionaries of varying quality, but from the onset I sought to make mine distinct, particularly respecting bibliographic citations. For me a disturbing trend in biographical reference books is the tendency of authors to cite only newspaper essays or news journal articles pertaining to the given subject. While these are legitimate references, I find the methodology self-defeating because even relatively current citations can be accessed only through microfilm. Most students, particularly at the undergraduate level, usually lack the discipline and resolve to track down and retrieve such materials and, consequently, their research efforts are discouraged. To counter this, I chose to cite only books and scholarly journals that are likely to remain available in hard copy for years to come. This makes them readily accessible on the shelf or through interlibrary loan. Also, great emphasis was taken to cull only the very latest and most comprehensive works available. I relied almost exclusively upon on-line searching in such useful sites as the Library of Congress catalog and WorldCat to turn up requisite materials. These items include not only published data like books and articles but also unpublished works and rarely cited nuggets such as master's theses and doctoral dissertations. Thus users are exposed to the greatest possible range of political and biographical scholarship available. The inclusion of autobiographical matter or philosophical writings was another criterion for inclusion, but I also occasionally list national or political studies for greater context. In sum I consider this approach more utilitarian than chasing slender and hard-to-find newspaper citations on microfilm.

Another distinctive feature of this book is the methodology underlying its compilation. Because librarians and researchers live in an information age, we are obliged to utilize those databases offering the very latest information about a given person or event. Amazingly, this data is sometimes only a few clicks away and can be regularly updated during the compilation of any book. Therefore, for those individuals listed who are still alive or in office I regularly referred to such on-line miracles as CNN.com and BBC.com to keep abreast of recent news or obituaries. Databases such as Infotrac and EBSCO were also regularly combed to inculcate the latest developments, where relevant.

Like its companion volume, the *Biographical Dictionary of Modern World Leaders, 1900 to 1991* will go far in promoting research and awareness of global events, along with the varied individuals and political systems propelling them. No effort was spared in comprehensiveness of coverage or recency of scholarship so, as a biographical dictionary, it remains in a class by itself. And, because the bulk of materials cited are from the year 2000 or later, this is truly a reference book for the 21st century. Gratitude is extended to my editor, Owen Lancer, for allowing me to compose this companion volume. From an author's perspective it was arduous and time-consuming, but ultimately informative and enlightening. I earnestly hope that others find it as useful.

Adenauer, Konrad (1876–1967) *chancellor of West Germany*

Konrad Adenauer was born in Cologne, Germany, on January 5, 1876, the son of a minor civil servant. He overcame modest origins to attend the University of Freiburg and study law. After a brief legal practice, Adenauer immersed himself in politics by joining the Zentrum (Center) Party, a moderate, Catholic-oriented organization. Regarded as more diligent and hardworking than brilliant, he eventually gained election as lord mayor of Cologne in 1917, where he served 16 years. That same year Adenauer was appointed to the upper chamber of the Prussian legislature by Kaiser WILHELM II. He also survived a terrible car accident that left him permanently disfigured. World War I ended the following year with the defeat of imperial Germany and the occupation of the Rhineland by Allied forces. Adenauer worked successfully to maintain good relations with American, French, and British military authorities, while striving to enhance Cologne's industrial, economic, and cultural appeal. And, although stridently anticommunist, he refused to order the police and militia to fire on socialist demonstrators and rioters in the immediate postwar period. He gained a reputation as an efficient, scrupulously honest administrator, and represented the Zentrum in the Prussian legislature until 1933.

The rise of ADOLF HITLER and the National Socialist (Nazi) Party placed Adenauer in extreme political danger. Having opposed the Nazis vocally, he was forced to retire from office and accept a pension. He was subsequently arrested by authorities several times and in 1944 was almost deported to the Buchenwald concentration camp. By the time the Nazis were vanquished in May 1945, Germany was devastated, its industrial base in ruins, and large segments of its population displaced. Worse, the nation was occupied by vengeful Allied forces who partitioned it into American, British, French, and Soviet zones of occupation. Adenauer was called out of retirement and reinstated as mayor of Cologne in 1946. In this capacity he set about reconstructing his shattered city and also served with the Parliamentary Council entrusted to draw up a new constitution for the three Western zones of occupied Germany. Intent upon combating a rising tide of communism and socialism in Germany, Adenauer helped to found a new political organization, the Christian Democratic Union (CDU). This was a centrist organization not unlike the earlier Zentrum, but it differed in opening its ranks to numerous Protestant groups. As head of the CDU, Adenauer guided the party to victory in the first postwar free elections, held on August 14, 1948, and by winning a slight coalition majority he became the first chancellor of the newly arisen West Germany. He was then 69 years of age.

Adenauer assumed the difficult and unenviable task of rebuilding his nation and reintegrating it into the community of nations. This proved no mean feat, as Germany lay in ruins and, worse, had become the object of intense loathing of neighboring nations, the victims of Nazi aggression. However, Adenauer methodically and characteristically tackled the problem by seeking rapprochement with his estranged neighbors, especially France, to forestall any future wars. In 1963 he experienced considerable criticism at home for concluding a famous treaty of cooperation with French president CHARLES DE GAULLE, which forever buried two centuries of Franco-German competition and animosity. Friendly relations with France remain the cornerstone of German foreign policy to the present time. Adenauer was also quick to demonstrate his willingness to fully commit Germany to Western political and economic integration, thereby winning the trust of England and the United States. Assisted by economic adviser LUDWIG ERHARD, he enjoyed amazing success, and by 1955 the military occupation of Germany had ended, the nation was once again allowed to raise its own army, and it became a full partner within the NATO alliance. Such policies put Adenauer on a collision course with his Soviet-sponsored opposite, WALTER ULBRICHT of East Germany, but Adenauer felt that improving his country's economic and political standing momentarily superseded the quest for national unification.

Adenauer served successfully as West Germany's chancellor until the early 1960s, when aggressive Russian policies sponsored by Soviet premier NIKITA KHRUSHCHEV culminated in erection of the infamous Berlin Wall. This event, and the nonconfrontational policies of American president JOHN F. KENNEDY during the provocation, made Adenauer appear weak and out of touch with current events. Therefore, at the urging of party leaders, he resigned the chancellorship on October 15, 1963, although retaining his seat in the legislature. Adenauer died while still in office on April 19, 1967, a towering figure of Germany's successful postwar reconstruction. That his funeral was attended by no less than 25 heads of government is unprecedented for a German chancellor of any age.

Further Reading

Adenauer, Konrad. *Memoirs, 1945–1953*. Chicago: Regnery, 1966.

Konrad Adenauer *(Library of Congress)*

Frei, Norbert. *Adenauer's Germany and the Nazi Past: The Politics of Amnesty and Integration*. New York: Columbia University Press, 2002.

Granirei, Ronald J. *The Ambivalent Alliance: Konrad Adenauer, the CDU/CSU, and the West, 1949–1966*. New York: Berghahn Books, 2002.

Irving, Ronald E. M. *Adenauer*. London: Longman, 2002.

McAllister, James. *No Exit: America and the German Problem, 1943–1954*. Ithaca, N.Y.: Cornell University Press, 2002.

Williams, Charles. *Adenauer: The Father of the New Germany*. New York: Wiley, 2001.

Williamson, D. G. *Germany from Defeat to Partition, 1945–1963*. New York: Longman, 2001.

Ahidjo, Ahmandou (1924–1989) *president of Cameroon*

Ahmandou Ahidjo was born in Garoua, French Cameroon, on August 24, 1924, the son of a Muslim

Fulani chief. He received scant secondary education and joined the French civil service as a radio operator with the post office. After World War II, France extended greater political participation to its colonies, and in 1947 Ahidjo won a seat in the first territorial assembly. In 1953 he next gained election to the newly created Assembly for the French Union, when the drive for independence intensified. Cameroon achieved self-rule in 1957, and Ahidjo helped found the Democrates Camerounais Party to counter the rising tide of communist-inspired insurgency. When that organization grew increasingly radical in outlook, he switched to the new Union Camerounais and continued pursuing moderate policies. The territory's first prime minister, Andre Marie Mbida, was forced to resign from office in February 1958, and Ahidjo succeeded him without fanfare. Two years later, once Cameroon gained political independence on January 1, 1960, he was installed as the new nation's first president. Previously, Ahidjo, a studious political moderate, sought to unify the northern, French-speaking half of the country with the English-speaking Southern Cameroon by peaceful means. Accordingly, a national plebiscite was passed in October 1961, reunification was achieved, and the new, united nation of Cameroon arose. Thus, at the age of 37, Ahidjo had garnered a reputation as "father of his country."

Despite the peaceful transfer of power, Ahidjo, like all postcolonial leaders in Africa, had to negotiate the treacherous waters of independence. Cameroon, united in name, remained deeply divided linguistically between English- and French-speaking administrators and more than 100 regional dialects, and religiously in long-standing distrust between a Muslim north and a Christian south. Ahidjo, himself a devout Muslim, preached unity and tolerance, thereby setting the tone for national reconciliation and harmony. As president, his 24-year tenure in office was marked by prudent, moderate economic policies that spared Cameroon the disastrous socialist-inspired experiments of neighboring countries. Consequently, the nation enjoyed great political stability and considerable prosperity for a former colony. He was also insistent upon maintaining close and friendly ties to France, which he could depend upon for financial aid and military assistance.

On the downside, Ahidjo's outlook on government was authoritarian by nature. He consolidated his rule through establishment of a one-party state in

1966 by either banning competing factions or forcibly merging them into an umbrella organization, the Cameroon National Union (CNU), of which he was the head. The government also established a relatively poor record on human rights, having clamped down on dissent and freedom of the press. Nonetheless, Ahidjo enjoyed considerable popularity nationwide, and in 1965, 1972, and 1980, he was repeatedly reelected by wide margins.

Ahidjo remained a rather quiet, nondescript individual in power, never given to showy displays of pomp or power. Therefore, having ruled competently for more than two decades, he stunned political observers at home in November 1982 by resigning from office on the grounds of exhaustion. His prime minister, Paul Biya, was chosen to succeed him as president, while he retained control of the CNU. However, a contretemps developed between the two men as to exactly who would continue ruling the nation, and in 1983 Biya expelled Ahidjo as head of the CNU. In November 1984 President Biya accused him of conspiring to overthrow the government, at which point Ahidjo fled for France. Biya had the former executive tried in absentia and sentenced to death, although this was later commuted to indefinite detention. Ahidjo remained in exile for the last seven years of his life, dying in Dakar, Senegal, on November 30, 1989. While not a completely successful leader, his strong rule and intelligent policies gave Cameroon a stability and prosperity sadly lacking in many new African nations.

Further Reading

Amin, John A. "Cameroon's Foreign Policy towards the United States." *Revue française d'histoire d'outre-mer* 81, no. 1 (1999): 211–236.

Azevedo, Mario. "The Post-Ahidjo Era in Cameroon." *Current History* 86 (May 1987): 217–220.

Chem-Langhee, Bengten. "The Road to the Unitary State of Cameroon, 1959–1972." *Paideuma* 41 (1995): 17–25.

Chiabi, Emmanuel. *The Making of Modern Cameroon.* Lanham, Md.: University Press of America, 1997.

Stark, Frank N. "Persuasion and Power in Cameroon." *Canadian Journal of African Studies* 14, no. 2 (1980): 273–293.

Wolf, Hans-Georg. *English in Cameroon.* New York: Mouton de Gruyter, 2001.

Alemán Valdés, Miguel (1900–1983) *president of Mexico*

Miguel Alemán Valdés was born in Sayula, Veracruz, Mexico, on September 29, 1900, the son of a small shopkeeper and revolutionary general. He pursued a degree from the National School of Law in 1928 and commenced a legal practice specializing in labor affairs. Thereafter Alemán expressed interest in politics and rose through various civil positions. Following a stint with the Secretariat of Livestock and Agriculture, he was appointed a judge within the Higher Tribunal of Justice of the Federal District in 1930. Four years later he became a senator from Veracruz. In 1939 Alemán was elected governor of his home state, but served only three years before MANUEL ÁVILA CAMACHO chose him to run his presidential campaign in 1939. When Ávila succeeded, he appointed Alemán to the important post of secretary of the government, where he oversaw the detention of enemy aliens during World War II and the suppression of labor unrest. Ávila was quite impressed by Alemán's intelligence and political talents, so in 1945 he appointed him as his political successor. His victory is a significant turning point in the evolution of Mexican national politics, for Alemán became the first civilian president to lead the country since FRANCISCO MADERO.

Prior to Alemán's ascension, national politics had been dominated by military figures associated with the Mexican Revolution. His success represented a distinct break with the recent past and he took steps to further reduce the military's influence in the national arena. Furthermore, Alemán entered high office with a reformist agenda at hand and his first task was implementing sweeping changes to the existing political organization, the Partido de la Revolución Mexicana (PRM). In 1946 he created the new Partido Revolucionario Institucional (PRI), which would dominate the Mexican political landscape for nearly half a century. To that end, he lessened the party's reliance on peasants and laborers and opened its ranks to the small but increasingly influential business class. This had the immediate effect of reducing left-wing pressure on PRI's policies, and paved the way for adopting more conservative, business-friendly stances. He was also determined to strengthen the office of the presidency to the point where it was virtually unchallenged by other branches of government.

Alemán's primary concern throughout his tenure in office was industrialization of the country. In another departure from past precepts, he rigorously opened Mexico up to foreign investment and began a crash program of infrastructural development. Highways, factories, hydroelectric dams, and new university campuses sprang up around the countryside, ushering in a better lifestyle for the average Mexican. Electrical output tripled in six years, while thousands of arid acres in the north were cultivated, thanks to extensive irrigation programs. To further facilitate efforts, Alemán broke with tradition by becoming the first Mexican president to visit Washington, D.C., where he established a close relationship with President HARRY S. TRUMAN. By carefully parroting the American view of cold war world affairs, he assured his northern neighbor of close cooperation and was rewarded with extended credit and other trade concessions. The Mexican economy boomed accordingly, amid left-wing charges that Alemán had "sold out" to the country's traditional enemy. Nonetheless, by the time his term in office ended in 1952, Mexico had been irrevocably placed on the road toward political and economic reform. Senior political leadership ceased being drawn from former military leaders; college-trained professionals came to the fore. However, there was a price for drawing so close to the commercial elite: throughout Alemán's administration, corruption became widespread, almost pandemic. Alemán left office in 1953 and was succeeded by ADOLFO RUIZ CORTINES, an economist. Thereafter all Mexican national leaders were civilian, not military, by profession. Alemán subsequently served as the nominal head of PRI until 1958, when he gained appointment as head of the National Tourism Board. He functioned capably in this capacity until his death in Mexico City on May 14, 1983. His modernizing influence is still felt today.

Further Reading

Dominguez, Jorge, and Rafael Fernandez de Castro. *The United States and Mexico: Between Partnership and Conflict.* New York: Routledge, 2001.

Krauze, Enrique. *Mexico, Biography of Power: A History of Modern Mexico, 1810–1996.* New York: HarperCollins, 1997.

Levy, Daniel C., Kathleen Bruhn, and Emilio Zebadua. *Mexico: The Struggle for Democratic Development.* Berkeley: University of California Press, 2001.

Niblo, Stephen R. *Mexico in the 1940s: Modernity, Politics, and Corruption.* Wilmington, Del.: Scholarly Resources, 1999.

Preston, Julia. *Opening Mexico: A Country's Tumultuous Passage to Democracy.* New York: Farrar, Straus and Giroux, 2004.

Sabbah, Leslie S. "The Mexican Presidential Succession of 1946." Unpublished master's thesis, University of Florida, 1973.

Alessandri Palma, Arturo (1868–1950) *president of Chile*

Arturo Alessandri Palma was born in Linares, Chile, on December 20, 1868, the son of Italian immigrants. He graduated with a law degree in 1893, joined the Alianza Liberal (AL), the liberal party, and in 1897 gained election to the Chamber of Deputies. Alessandri, a stern, outgoing personality with a flare for oratory, was continually reelected until 1915, when he became a senator. His ability to defeat a local party boss for that office earned him the nickname "Lion of Tarapaca." Alessandri served capably until December 1920, when he was tapped to run as the AL presidential candidate. A close vote resulted and several months elapsed before he was finally sworn into office. Alessandri came to office with extensive reforms in mind, and he was especially keen to tax rich landowners to aid the poor and improve working conditions.

Unfortunately, Alessandri rose to power at a difficult period in Chile's history. The end of World War I led to a precipitous drop in the price of nitrate (used for explosives), and a national depression ensued. Worse, when Alessandri tried to force much-needed reform legislation through the legislature, he was perpetually blocked by opponents. The Chilean military was also hard-hit by failure to be paid, and at one point a group of young officers made a threatening protest in the halls of the legislature. Their intimidation allowed several pieces of reform legislation to pass, but when the military refused to punish those officers responsible, Alessandri resigned from the presidency in 1924 and entered self-imposed exile in Europe. Within months a second military coup, in January 1925, induced him to resume office, and he sponsored a new national constitution instituting a parliamentary system, formally separated church and state, and created a central bank.

In 1926 Alessandri resigned from office and was elected senator. But when Minister of War Carlos Ibáñez del Campo won the presidency that year, Alessandri resigned a second time and retreated back to Europe to await the outcome of events. By 1931 Ibáñez had been overthrown; Alessandri returned home and tossed his hat into the ring a third time. He ran as presidential candidate of the Democratic Party, but lost to the more radical Juan Esteban Montero. But popular unrest disposed of Montero's regime within months and new elections were held. In 1932 Alessandri gained the presidency a third time. As before, he came to power while the country was in the throes of economic distress, in this instance the Great Depression. However, this time he quickly asserted civilian supremacy over the military, and so forcefully that it went unchallenged until 1937. Next, he bullied the legislature to impose strict austerity measures to balance the budget, reduce inflation, and restore economic growth. Success here carried a stiff price, and many poor people, aided and abetted by leftist organizations, took to the streets in protest. Alessandri dealt with them harshly, as he did an aborted 1938 pro-Nazi coup attempt. By the time he left office a third time, he had restored the rule of law and some semblance of prosperity. But his crackdown on the radicals induced them to unite behind a single candidate in the 1938 elections, and Alessandri's hand-picked successor lost.

For many years thereafter Alessandri continued on as nominal head of the AL and as a senator despite his prior association with the Democratic Party. By 1944 he was serving as senate president and two years later was tapped to run for a fourth term as the AL candidate for president. But, sensing his age, Alessandri deferred running and threw his weight behind radical nominee Gabriel González Videla in exchange for several AL cabinet ministers. He died at Santiago on August 24, 1950. Despite two turbulent terms in office, he remains widely hailed as one of the most important Chilean leaders of the early 20th century. In 1958 his son, Jorge Alessandri Rodríguez, was also elected president.

Further Reading

Alexander, Robert J. *Arturo Alessandri: A Biography.* 2 vols. Ann Arbor, Mich.: University Microfilms International for the Latin American Institute, Rutgers University, 1977.

Bart-Melej, Patrick. *Reforming Chile: Cultural Politics, Nationalism, and the Rise of the Middle Class.* Chapel Hill: University of North Carolina Press, 2001.

Ciria, Alberto. "The Individual in History: Five Latin American Biographies." *Latin American Research Review* 20, no. 3 (1985): 247–267.

Davis, H. F. "The Presidency in Chile." *Presidential Studies Quarterly* 15 (fall 1985): 707–724.

Kofas, J. "The Politics of Foreign Debt: The IMF, the World Bank, and U.S. Foreign Policy in Chile, 1946–1952." *Journal of Developing Areas* 31 (winter 1997): 157–182.

Nunn, Frederick M. "A Latin American State within a State: The Politics of the Chilean Army, 1924–1927." *The Americas* 27, no. 1 (1970): 40–55.

Alfonsín, Raúl (1927–) *president of Argentina*

Raúl Ricardo Alfonsín was born in Chascomus, Argentina, on March 13, 1927, and he attended military academies in his youth. However, he forsook military service in favor of pursuing law, and in 1945 he joined the Unión Cívica Radical (UCR), the Radical Civic Union, a traditional party with strong roots in the democratic tradition. Over the next 20 years, Argentina was ruled by the Justicialist Party of JUAN PERÓN, periodically interrupted by military coups against the government. In 1958 Alfonsín was elected as a UCR provincial deputy, but his term was suspended four years later after the military again seized power. He was reinstated a year later, and by 1973 Alfonsín felt emboldened enough to seek the presidency as the UCR candidate. He was defeated in the primaries by Ricardo Balbín, who went on to lose the general election when the Peronists returned to power. In 1976 the government was again upended by the military, and a three-man junta next assumed control of the country. Their top priority now was waging a ruthless campaign against leftist guerrilla forces, the so-called Dirty War. The insurgency was contained with great brutality. Thousands of civilians simply disappeared and were assumed to have been murdered by soldiers. Political parties and activities were also summarily suspended. However, in the wake of General LEOPOLDO GALTIERI's botched 1983 Falkland Islands war against Great Britain, the military fell under increasing pressure to allow free elections. By that time in 1984, Alfonsín had established himself as a leading candidate with solidly democratic credentials.

Prior to being elected president, Alfonsín took the courageous step of publicly criticizing the military for their zealotry in pursuing guerrillas. He also founded a reform movement with the UCR to clean out the political deadwood and bring the party closer to its constituents. On October 30, 1983, the Argentine people elected him president with 52 percent of the vote, and also delivered control of the legislature to the UCR. He assumed office amid high public expectations but confronted by two nearly insurmountable tasks. The first was prosecution of military officers accused of human rights abuses, including murder. Once in office, Alfonsín repealed a blanket amnesty the military had voted for itself, and began jailing and trying senior military figures. Attempts to punish junior officers stimulated several military insurrections, however, so to preserve the peace Alfonsín prosecuted only senior officers who issued the actual orders. It was a compromise that failed to please everybody, especially mothers of the 5,000 *desaparecidos* (disappeared), but the army was placated. Argentina thus remains the only Latin American country to successfully try to imprison military leaders for crimes against civilians.

Alfonsín had much less success in confronting his next challenge: the economy. Eight years of military rule racked up an $85 billion national debt, which induced hyperinflation and deep recession. The president fought back by adopting extreme austerity measures, the so-called Austral Plan, which temporarily brought down inflation. But such was the magnitude of Argentina's economic malaise that necessary wage freezes and layoffs incited mass demonstrations. By May 1989 food prices were rising 30 percent every month, a condition that greatly reduced Alfonsín's chances for reelection. Consequently he was handily defeated by the Peronist candidate, Carlos Saúl Menem. To emphasize the gravity of the situation, Alfonsín surrendered his office six months ahead of schedule. For many years thereafter, he served as nominal head of the UCR and of the opposition. In 1999 he also experienced a severe car accident and has since retired from politics. Alfonsín's tenure in office was in many respects far from successful, but it marked Argentina's return to the rule of law and democracy.

Further Reading

Epstein, E. C., ed. *The New Argentine Democracy: The Search for a Successful Formula.* Westport, Conn.: Praeger, 1992.

Erro, Davide G. *Resolving the Argentine Paradox: Politics and Development, 1966–1992.* Boulder, Colo.: Lynne Rienner Pubs., 1993.

Fournier, Dominique. "The Alfonsín Administration and the Promotion of Democratic Values in the Southern Cone and Andes." *Journal of Latin American Studies* 31 (February 1999): 39–74.

Huser, Herbert C. "Civil-Military Relations in Argentina: The Alfonsín Years, 1983–1989." Unpublished Ph.D. diss., George Washington University, 1991.

Lewis, Colin M. "Argentina in the Crisis Years (1983–1990): From Alfonsín to Menem." *Journal of Latin American Studies* 27, no. 3 (1995): 737–799.

Pion-Berlin, David. "Between Confrontation and Accommodation: Military Government Policy in Democratic Argentina." *Journal of Latin American Studies* 23 (October 1991): 543–571.

Allende, Salvador (1908–1973) *president of Chile*

Salvador Allende Gossens was born in Valparaíso, Chile, on June 26, 1908, into an upper-middle-class family with long traditions of political activism. After completing a term of military service, Allende attended the University of Chile to study medicine. There he was fully exposed to the tenets of Marxism-Leninism and fully embraced socialism. He became active in political affairs on campus and was arrested several times for protesting the dictatorship of General Juan Carlos Ibáñez. In 1933 Allende solidified his political credentials by helping to found the Chilean Socialist Party and was elected to lead the Valparaíso branch. By 1937 he won a seat in the national House of Deputies, and the following year he became minister of health in the administration of Pedro Aguirre Cerda. In this capacity he moved to establish much-needed medical programs for the nation's poor and underprivileged. In 1945 Allende parlayed his popularity by winning election to the Senate, where he skillfully served for the next 25 years.

In the early 1950s various groups of Chilean leftists began coalescing into a single political bloc, the Front of the People. Allende, as head of the newly established Popular Socialist Party (Marxist), ran as its presidential candidate in 1952 and lost decisively. Six years later he ran again as head of the Popular Action Front and was only narrowly defeated. His third attempt in 1964 proved no more successful, and Allende lost to Christian Democrat EDUARDO FREI by large margins. But defeat did little to undermine Allende's reputation as a master parliamentarian, and in 1966 he rose to president of the senate. The turning point in his political fortunes—and Chile's—occurred during the 1970 presidential elections. The conservatives split their vote by running two candidates, while Allende, at the head of the Unidad Popular (Popular Unity), amassed a slim plurality of 36.3 percent. This placed him slightly ahead of his nearest rival, Jorge Alessandri, who garnered 34.9 percent, and the final choice was referred to the legislature. After much internal wrangling, and a vow by Allende to uphold democracy and freedom, Congress finally declared him the winner on October 24, 1970. He thus became the first freely elected Marxist leader in world history.

True to his deeply held precepts, Allende wanted to establish socialism in Chile to mitigate the plight of the poor. However, unlike many Marxist contemporaries who espoused violent revolution, Allende determined to achieve his goals peacefully, through legislation. He then embarked on an ambitious program to hike wages, freeze prices, and expropriate land for the peasants. Such moves elicited considerable applause from the poor but also occasioned great alarm among the middle and upper classes, who felt their position threatened. Allende also managed to alienate the United States by nationalizing assets of three companies that controlled the national copper mining industry. This tactic angered President RICHARD M. NIXON, who cut off all foreign aid to Chile's slowly unraveling economy. The stage was being set for a massive political upheaval.

By 1973 Allende's reforms had precipitated a major economic crisis. Foreign capital had fled the country, cash reserves were exhausted, industrial and agrarian output plummeted, and the nation was seized by crippling strikes. But the president remained adamant in pursuing the establishment of socialism. Political unrest soon permeated the ranks of the conservative-minded Chilean military and in June 1973 a major rebellion was suppressed by soldiers loyal to the regime. Allende was forced to replace army head General Carlos Pratt with a new leader, General AUGUSTO PINOCHET, which proved a fateful decision. Three months later as the country continued spiraling down into economic and social chaos, Pinochet demanded Allende's resignation and voluntary exile abroad. When he refused, military troops and aircraft attacked the presidential palace on September 11, 1973, and in the ensuing fracas Allende was killed. Chile's brief and disastrous flirtation with socialism had come to a violent and bloody end. Worse, Pinochet's coup ushered in a 16-year period of repressive military rule that would endure, without remission, until 1990.

Further Reading

Falcoff, Mark. *Modern Chile, 1970–1989: A Critical History.* New Brunswick, N.J.: Transaction Pubs., 1989.

Hite, Katherine. *When the Romance Ended: Leaders of the Chilean Left, 1968–1998.* New York: Columbia University Press, 2000.

Meller, Patricio, and Tim Ennis. *The Unidad Popular and the Pinochet Dictatorship: A Political Economy Analysis.* New York: St. Martin's Press, 2000.

Power, Margaret. "Class and Gender in the Anti-Allende Women's Movement: Chile, 1970–1973." *Social Politics* 7 (fall 2000): 289–308.

Sigmund, Paul E. *Chile, 1973–1998: The Coup and Its Consequences.* Princeton, N.J.: Princeton University Press in Latin American Studies, 1999.

Amanullah Khan (1892–1960) *king of Afghanistan*

Amanullah was born in Kabul, Afghanistan, on June 1, 1892, a son of Emir (prince) Habibullah, leader of that country. At the time of his father's assassination in February 1919, Amanullah was governor of Kabul, and he took immediate steps to secure the arsenal and the treasury. He was thus enabled to thwart competing claims to the throne by his uncle Nasrullah, whom he denounced as a usurper for complicity in his father's murder. After some minor fighting Amanullah assumed control of Afghanistan as emir, but in 1926 he installed himself as khan (king). At that time his nation was still under the sway of Great Britain, which exercised complete control over its foreign policy. Amanullah, stridently anti-British, determined to remove this last vestige of colonialism. On May 3, 1919, he unilaterally declared independence from Great Britain and ordered his army to harass and attack British outposts. England, still exhausted from its sacrifices in World War I, lacked the will and resources to conduct a distant frontier war and sought a negotiated peace. Once a treaty was signed

in Kabul, Afghanistan was finally free of British control and a sovereign nation once more.

Amanullah was a reformer by nature and took inspiration from contemporaries like MOHAMMAD REZA PAHLAVI in Iran and KEMAL ATATÜRK of Turkey. He therefore took immediate steps to break Afghanistan's traditional isolation and establish diplomatic relations with France, Germany, and the Soviet Union. He also established foreign-language schools to encourage the influx of modern technology and knowledge. But Amanullah's biggest changes occurred in the realm of politics. Intent upon casting off Afghanistan's medieval mind-set, he promulgated a new constitution that enshrined personal freedom and offered equal rights to all citizens. He also allowed a *loya jirga* (parliament) to convene that wielded meaningful authority over legislative matters. Amanullah next took steps to centralize his authority in this fractious land by creating a territorial hierarchy based upon subdistricts, districts, and provinces, all of which possessed consultative bodies answerable directly to the Crown. The ancient practice of tax-farming was also abolished and replaced by direct taxation paid in cash. Finally, the king allowed a free press and appointed responsible members of the intelligentsia to positions of authority within government. All told, his was a sweeping agenda intent upon bringing Afghanistan into the 20th century.

Taking westernization a step further, the king next attempted to mitigate the effects of Islam on society—a risky proposition in such a highly conservative society. He drew up new dress codes that allowed women to unveil and also encouraged government officials to wear Western-style dress. Amanullah's reforms were well-intentioned, but he clearly underestimated the resistance to change in this profoundly Muslim nation. Large sectors of the clergy and tribal population resented his attempts at female emancipation, which they regarded as overtly secular and un-Islamic. At length, resistance to his reign coalesced around a variety of religious figures and traditional clan leaders who resented the king's intrusion upon their authority. Moreover the military, entrusted with the defense of the kingdom, was angered by recent pay cuts and sympathetic to the rebels. In 1924 the Khost rebellion broke out and was put down by force. Amanullah then ventured to Europe in December 1927, which signaled the outbreak of an uprising of the Shinwari tribesmen. At length the rebellion gathered force as members of the army joined the rebels, and the king was forced to abdicate in favor of his brother by May 1929. A series of subsequent rulers canceled out most of his major reforms, and the movement toward modernization halted.

In the fall of 1929 Amanullah made an attempt to regain his throne by force but failed. Thereafter he entered self-imposed exile in Europe, where he remained for the rest of his life. He died in Zurich, Switzerland, on April 25, 1960, best remembered as the father of Afghanistan independence.

Further Reading

Adamec, Ludwig W. *Historical Dictionary of Afghanistan.* Lanham, Md.: Scarecrow Press, 2003.

Greenhut, Frederick A. "Afghanistan: A Vision of the Future Unfulfilled . . . Amanullah and the Era of Reform." *Manuscripts* 33, no. 3 (1981): 201–210.

Nawid, Senzil K. *Religious Response to Social Change in Afghanistan, 1919–29: King Aman-Allah and the Afghan Ulama.* Costa Mesa, Calif.: Mazda Publishers, 1999.

Poullada, Leon B. *Reform and Rebellion in Afghanistan, 1919–1929: King Amanullah's Failure to Modernize a Tribal Society.* Ithaca, N.Y.: Cornell University Press, 1973.

Richards, Donald S. *The Savage Frontier: A History of the Anglo-Afghan Wars.* London: Macmillan, 1990.

Stewart, Rhea T. *Fire in Afghanistan, 1914–1929: Faith, Hope, and the British Empire.* Garden City, N.Y.: Doubleday, 1973.

Amin, Idi (ca. 1924–2003) *president of Uganda*

Idi Amin Dada Oumee was born in West Nile, upper northwest Uganda, around 1924, a member of the small Muslim Kakwa tribe. After receiving a rudimentary education, he enlisted in the King's African Rifles, then part of the British colonial army, in 1946. He proved himself an exceptional soldier and performed well in the suppression of JOMO KENYATTA's Mau Mau movement in the 1950s. Amin was also physically striking; he towered six feet three inches tall and was heavily built and very imposing. An excellent athlete, he was the only African allowed to play on the otherwise all-white Nile rugby team. As Uganda rushed toward political independence in 1959, Amin received the coveted rank of *effendis,* the highest rank a black African could attain in the colonial army. After 1961 he became one of only two native Ugandans with regular army commissions, and he

struck up an abiding relationship with Prime Minister MILTON OBOTE. This connection served both men well, for in 1966 they successfully orchestrated a coup that toppled King Mutesa II. Consequently, Obote became president while Amin, his willing henchman, advanced to army commander. Obote ran a carefully controlled police state, in which opponents of the government were either killed outright or mysteriously disappeared. Amin was his right-hand man throughout these grim proceedings, but gradually Obote came to distrust his army chief. In 1970 Amin was "kicked upstairs" to a staff position while the president began devising plans against him. However, Amin, himself an old hand at intrigue, decided to strike first, and on January 26, 1971, his forces toppled the government while Obote was out of the country.

Once in power, Amin quickly gained a reputation as one of Africa's most quixotic and repressive dictators. His ascension was initially greeted with enthusiasm as a welcome change from Obote's regime. But as events unfolded, he proved himself every bit as brutal and despotic as his predecessor. Amin wasted no time in violently purging the military of soldiers of Acholi and Lango descent—the same group as Obote—and they were replaced by ethnic Kakwa troops and Libyan mercenaries. Within a year the list of victims mounted and included two government ministers and an Anglican archbishop. This brutality triggered a surge of support among Obote's followers in nearby Tanzania, and they invaded Uganda. Amin, supported by Libyan and Sudanese mercenaries, managed to contain the invasion and he survived. Emboldened by success, Amin declared himself "president for life" and extended his reign of terror to all facets of Ugandan society.

A fanatical nationalist, the crazed leader next aimed his sights at the thriving Asian Indian community in Uganda, which traditionally ran the national economy. In August 1972 he gave them 90 days to leave the country, after which he parceled out their business holdings to his cronies. He also broke formerly close ties to Israel (where he had trained as a paratrooper) and embraced the radical Palestinian cause. To that end he had a hand in the July 1976 hijacking of a French airliner with Israeli passengers on board; they were dramatically rescued on landing at Entebbe by Israeli commandos. Amin also declared Uganda an Islamic state, even though Muslims constitute but a small part of the population. This move was undertaken less for religious reasons than to secure financial aid from Libya and other Arabic states. Armed and supplied by foreign sources, Amin then unleashed one of Africa's bloodiest periods of repression. An estimated 300,000 Ugandans are believed to have been murdered by government thugs before the regime finally and dramatically overplayed its hand.

In October 1978 Amin suddenly decided that the Kagera Salient in neighboring Tanzania rightfully belonged to Uganda, so he launched an invasion. He was met head on by forces under President JULIUS NYERERE and handily defeated. Tanzanian troops, their ranks swelled by anti-Amin Ugandans, advanced toward the capital of Kampala, and Amin fled first to Libya and then Saudi Arabia in April 1979. Uganda's national nightmare had finally ended, although its society and economy lay in tatters. Amin has since been confined to a mansion in Saudi Arabia. In January 1989 he unsuccessfully and inexplicably tried to return home while on a visit to Zaire and was quickly hustled back aboard his plane. The Saudis kept him under luxurious house arrest, surrounded by his several wives and 42 children. Amin died there on August 16, 2003, one of Africa's most notorious and bloodthirsty tyrants.

Further Reading

Apter, David E. *The Political Kingdom in Uganda: A Study in Bureaucratic Nationalism.* Essex, England: Frank Cass, 1997.

Decalo, Samuel. *Psychoses of Power: African Personal Dictatorships.* Gainesville, Fla.: FAP Books, 1998.

Jamison, Martin. *Idi Amin and Uganda: An Annotated Bibliography.* Westport, Conn.: Greenwood Press, 1992.

Measures, Bob, and Tony Walker. *Amin's Uganda.* Atlanta: Minerva Press, 1998.

Moody, Christopher L. *The Wit and Wisdom of Idi Amin.* Reno, Nev.: Great Basin Press, 1977.

Nyeko, Balam. "Exile Politics and Resistance to Dictatorship: The Uganda Anti-Amin Organizations in Zambia, 1972–1979." *African Affairs* 96, no. 382 (1997): 95–108.

Omara-Otunnu, Amii. *Politics and the Military in Uganda, 1890–1985.* New York: St. Martin's Press, 1985.

Spiller, Robert J. "Idi Amin: Colonial and African Legacy." Unpublished master's thesis, University of Virginia, 1990.

Andropov, Yuri (1914–1984) *general secretary of the Communist Party of the Soviet Union*

Yuri Vladimirovich Andropov was born in Stavropol, Russia, on June 15, 1914, the son of a railroad worker. He matured as the Communist-run Soviet Union arose, and in 1936 he joined the Young Communists (Komsomol League). Intelligent and gifted with a knack for organization, he quickly rose through the Komsomol ranks in the newly acquired region of Karelia, annexed from Finland in 1940. Throughout World War II Andropov fought as a partisan in the Karelian region and emerged with a credible reputation for bravery and efficiency. After the war he served as a senior administrator and was allowed to join the Communist Party. In 1953 Andropov advanced his political fortunes by passing into the Soviet diplomatic service as ambassador to the newly acquired satellite state of Hungary. From the Soviet embassy in Budapest, he proved instrumental in arranging the dismissal of Stalinist leader MÁTYÁS RÁKOSI and his replacement by a reform-minded leader, IMRE NAGY. By 1956 Nagy's reforms had pushed Hungary into open revolt against the Soviet Union, but Andropov continually assured the Hungarian government that the Soviets had no desire to interfere. That illusion quickly vanished in 1956 when Nagy's experiment was brutally crushed by Soviet tanks, while the prime minister was arrested and executed—despite Andropov's assurances of clemency. However, he secured the grudging approval of General Secretary NIKITA KHRUSHCHEV to allow another reform-minded leader, JÁNOS KÁDÁR, to succeed him. The Hungarian affair was a debacle for Soviet public relations worldwide but reflected the greatest credit on Andropov for effectively preserving Soviet interests. Accordingly, he was summoned to Moscow in 1957 and placed in charge of relations between Russia and Communist parties around the world. He served capably in this capacity until 1967, when LEONID BREZHNEV appointed him head of the Committee for State Security, the dreaded KGB. Andropov used his influence to arrange the promotion of his reform-minded protégé, MIKHAIL GORBACHEV, within the Communist Party.

Andropov's tenure as head of the Soviet secret police was one of that organization's most notorious and successful periods. He dismissed the crude and callous tactics of JOSEPH STALIN in favor of more subtle but equally effective means of oppression. As previously, the primary role of the KGB and other security agencies was stifling political dissent at home. Andropov introduced confinement in psychiatric wards for dissidents, instead of executing them outright. He also saw to it that political criminals were given mind-altering drugs and treated as mentally disturbed patients. His new tactics were cruelly effective, and within a few years the KGB had all but silenced its most vocal domestic critics. Andropov heightened the efficiency of Soviet spying and intelligence gathering operations around the world, and also used security agents to crack down on corruption and abuse at home. His 15 years of success as intelligence chief resulted in a seat on the party Politburo, the country's leading political body, and a chance to lead the Soviet Union as general secretary.

When Brezhnev died in November 1982, there was a scramble among senior party officials to succeed him. Andropov managed to outmaneuver the head of the Brezhnev faction, KONSTANTIN CHERNENKO, and became general secretary on November 12, 1982. Once in charge, Andropov instituted a concerted campaign to eliminate alcoholism and indolence, which were rampant and impeded economic growth. Efforts against official corruption were also renewed, although most culprits simply continued their deviances in a less visible manner. Andropov also sought to implement reform-minded policies by recruiting younger members like Gorbachev to the inner circles of power. Results were mixed at best, and strategic conditions further eroded through increasing tensions with United States president RONALD REAGAN, an avowed anticommunist. When Reagan announced his decision to commence work on a new strategic anti-missile defense system ("Star Wars") against Soviet missiles and to deploy short-range, nuclear cruise missiles in Western Europe to counter new Soviet weapons, the old spy master tried orchestrating a worldwide propaganda campaign against them. However, when Soviet fighters shot down a Korean airliner that inadvertently strayed into Russian airspace on September 1, 1983, the incident proved a disaster for Russian public relations. By this time, Andropov was ailing from kidney disease and becoming less and less visible on the national scene. He died on February 9, 1984, after 15 months in office, and was succeeded by Chernenko. Andropov had one of the shortest reigns of any Soviet leader, and he departed before the full weight of his reforms could affect a stagnant and long-suffering Soviet society.

Further Reading

Andropov, Yuri. *Speeches and Writings*. New York: Pergamon Press, 1983.

Hahn, Gordon M. *Russia's Revolution from Above, 1985–1989: Reform, Transition, and Devolution in the Fall of the Soviet Communist Regime*. New Brunswick, N.J.: Transaction Pubs., 2001.

Kagan, Frederick. "The Secret History of Perestroika." *National Interest* no. 23 (1991): 33–42.

Gooding, John. *Socialism in Russia: Lenin and His Legacy, 1890–1991*. New York: Palgrave, 2001.

Kotkin, Stephen. *Armageddon Averted: The Soviet Collapse, 1970–2000*. Oxford, England: Oxford University Press, 2001.

Medvedev, Zhores A. *Andropov*. New York: W. W. Norton, 1983.

Shlapentokh, Vladimir. *A Normal Totalitarian Society: How the Soviet Union Functioned and How It Collapsed*. Armonk, N.Y.: M. E. Sharpe, 2001.

Aoun, Michel (1935–) *prime minister of Lebanon*

Michel Aoun was born in Beirut, Lebanon, on September 30, 1935, into a Maronite Christian family. This placed him in the minority among his population, for Muslims constitute the nation's largest religious grouping. After receiving his secondary education, he entered the Beirut Military Academy in 1955 and graduated four years later. Aoun then pursued the life of a career military officer, and throughout the 1960s he received advanced training in the United States and France. He then assumed a minor role in the much fractured Lebanese army, wracked by religious and political dissent. Aoun, however, was a Lebanese patriot who worked easily with Christians and Muslims alike. Moreover, in 1982 he was the only ranking officer to oppose the massive Israeli incursion into southern Lebanon until ordered to stand down by President ELIAS SARKIS. Aoun also criticized the presence of thousands of Palestinian fighters in his country, along with an equally large Syrian army sent by President Hafez al-Assad. The country was then badly shaken by an internecine civil war along religious lines, pitting Christian soldiers and militia against their Muslim counterparts. Nonetheless, Aoun dutifully performed all his assignments, and in June 1984, President AMIN GEMAYEL appointed him the youngest commander of the much reduced Lebanese army.

That same year the Lebanese government proved unable to choose a successor for Gemayel, which further exacerbated political and religious tensions. Since 1943 there existed an unwritten power-sharing agreement stipulating that, in every government, the president would be a Maronite Christian, the prime minister a Sunni Muslim, and the speaker of the National Assembly a Shi'ite. When President Gemayel could not find a suitable Muslim to fill the role of prime minister, he appointed Aoun instead. This act not only antagonized Muslim sentiments, it also angered Syrian president Assad, who wished to personally select the next government. Consequently, neither the Muslim community nor the Syrian government recognized Aoun's political legitimacy. Despite repeated overtures for reconciliation, fighting erupted as Druze and Shi'ite militias faced off against Aoun's Christians in the Beirut area. Though outnumbered, Aoun skillfully fought them to a standstill. He also realized that Assad was the power actually manipulating Lebanese Muslims against him, so on March 14, 1989, he unilaterally declared war on Syria.

Aoun's rashness proved his own undoing. Not only was the Syrian army well-trained and -equipped compared to his rag-tag force, the move failed to evoke any great sympathy from Western governments. Only France, with long-standing interests in the region, offered humanitarian assistance. By September 1989, Assad's forces had reduced Aoun to all but the confines of Beirut. Worse still, a large meeting of Lebanese delegates in Saudi Arabia convened to reach a political settlement and end the civil war. In September 1989 the Taiif Accord called for replacing the Lebanese presidential system with a cabinet-based one, with increased Shi'ite representation. Aoun had no objection to the agreement until he realized that it lacked a timetable for the withdrawal of Syrian forces. Accordingly his Christian militia continued fighting Syrians, as well as Lebanese Muslims, and even other Christian forces until he had alienated virtually every armed force in the country. In the end, Aoun was defeated by Syrian firepower and he fled to the French embassy seeking asylum. At first the new, Syrian-backed government refused to allow him to leave the country, but in August 1991 the former prime minister was pardoned and allowed to flee to France.

Aoun continued residing in France for a decade until January 2001, when the Lebanese government offered him a complete pardon. This change in attitude is probably the result of attempts by the new Syrian president, Bashar al-Assad, to deflate rising discontent over the continuing occupation of Lebanon by his forces. The general expressed interest in coming home, but only after receiving immunity from prosecution for corruption.

Further Reading

Deeb, Marius. *Syria's Terrorist War on Lebanon and the Peace Process.* New York: Palgrave, 2003.

El-Khazen, Farid. *The Breakdown of the State in Lebanon, 1967–1976.* Cambridge, Mass.: Harvard University Press, 2000.

Fisk, Robert. *Pity the Nation: Lebanon at War.* New York: Oxford University Press, 2001.

Johnson, Michael. *All Honorable Men: The Social Origins of War in Lebanon.* New York: I. B. Tauris, 2001.

Khalaf, Samir. *Civil and Uncivil Violence: A History of the Internationalization of Communal Conflict in Lebanon.* New York: Columbia University Press, 2002.

O'Ballance, Edgar. *Civil War in Lebanon, 1975–1992.* Basingstoke, England: Palgrave, 1998.

Apithy, Sourou Migan (1913–1989) *president of Dahomey*

Sourou Migan Apithy was born in Porto-Novo, Dahomey (now Benin), on April 8, 1913, a member of that French colony's Goun tribe. He was well educated at mission schools and studied advanced economics in France at a time when few Africans were allowed abroad. Apithy lived there many years while working as an accountant, and in 1946 he gained election to the new Constituent Assembly and National Assembly. After representing Dahomey for several years, he returned home and commenced an active political career by joining the Rassemblement Démocratique Africain. When he disagreed with their increasingly Marxist line, Apithy switched alliances to another organization, the Parti Républicain Dahoméen (PRD), inspired by Senegal's LÉOPOLD SÉDAR SENGHOR. He soon became one of the colony's most recognized political voices, and in 1956 he gained election as mayor of Porto-Novo. But by 1957 two significant rivals had also emerged: Justin Ahomadégbé of the Union Démocratique Dahomée and HUBERT MAGA of the northern-based Mouvement

Démocratique Dahoméen. However, in assembly elections the following year, the PRD prevailed and Apithy was elected prime minister. In this capacity he entertained notions of joining the French-inspired Mali Federation in West Africa, but was blocked by political opposition at home and abroad. In 1959 Apithy's party again carried the territorial elections, amid cries of fraud. To avert violence he was forced to step down and allow Maga to serve as prime minister until Dahomey achieved political independence in 1960.

Apithy waited on the sidelines while Maga served as the nation's first president, but he subsequently received appointments as finance minister and vice president. With relatively little to do at home, he spent most of his time in Europe as a roving ambassador. However, the new administration failed to address rising inflation and unemployment, so Maga was overthrown by a military coup in 1963. The officers then restored civilian rule the following year, and Apithy fulfilled his lifelong ambition by becoming Dahomey's second president while Ahomadégbé served as vice president. However, his administration was equally unsuccessful at resolving deep-seated economic problems, which were exacerbated by regional and tribal factionalism. The two leaders openly squabbled over the impending appointment of a supreme court justice, which further polarized the nation. Conditions continued deteriorating to the point where, in 1965, the military again intervened and forced the three competing men, Apithy, Maga, and Ahomadégbé, to cooperate. When this failed and a military regime took over, Apithy left for exile in France.

Dahomey continued suffering from a continuous series of coups until December 1969, when civilian rule was finally restored. Apithy then returned home to tender his services to the country, along with Maga and Ahomadégbé. New elections were held and Apithy finished third, but the military annulled the results to prevent civil war. Further squabbling among the leaders was averted through adoption of a power-sharing arrangement—the Presidential Council. Here each man would serve as president for a period of two years before rotating the chair to his successor. Maga had completed his term and Ahomadégbé had only commenced his when the government was overthrown by Major Mathieu Kerekou in October 1972. The military then placed Apithy and his two consorts under house arrest where they remained for several years. Languishing in poor health, Apithy was finally allowed to immigrate to France in 1981, and he settled in Paris to compose his memoirs. Death concluded his stormy, 25-year political career on November 12, 1989. Kerekou, meanwhile, consolidated his rule and bequeathed to the country its present name of Benin.

Further Reading

Heilbrunn, John R. "Authority, Property, and Politics in Benin and Togo." Unpublished Ph.D. diss., University of California–Los Angeles, 1994.

Houngnikpo, Mathurin C. *Determinants of Democratization in Africa: A Comparative Study of Benin and Togo.* Lanham, Md.: University Press of America, 2001.

Magnusson, Bruce A. "The Politics of Democratic Regime Legitimation in Benin: Institutions, Social Policy, and Security." Unpublished Ph.D. diss., University of Wisconsin–Madison, 1994.

Manning, Patrick. *Slavery, Colonialism, and Economic Growth in Dahomey, 1640–1960.* Cambridge: Cambridge University Press, 2002.

Seely, Jennifer C. "Transitions to Democracy in Comparative Perspective: The National Conferences in Benin and Togo." Unpublished Ph.D. diss., Washington University, 2001.

Aquino, Corazon (1933–) *president of the Philippines*

Maria Corazon (Cory) Cojuangco was born in Tarlac Province, the Philippines, on January 25, 1933, into a family of wealthy sugar planters. She attended elite academies before arriving in New York to study at the College of Mount Saint Vincent in New York City. Having returned to the Philippines in 1953, she next enrolled at Far Eastern University in Manila to study law and met her future husband, Benigno "Ninoy" Aquino. They married and Aquino spent the next two decades raising the couple's five children while Benigno established himself as one of the Philippines's rising politicians. As the country's youngest senator, he was an outspoken critic of President FERDINAND MARCOS, who had declared martial law in 1972 and remained in power for another 13 years. Marcos proved intolerant of any such opposition and had the senator jailed on several occasions. In 1980 he offered the Aquinos amnesty provided they exile themselves to the United States, which they did. However, in 1983 Benigno decided to return home and help organize opposition forces. As he stepped off the plane on August 20, 1983, he was shot dead by a soldier—ostensibly on Marcos's orders. Public outrage followed.

The senator's death galvanized the much-divided opposition forces and they now united in their determination to oust Marcos. Salvador Laurel, head of the largest opposition faction, Unido, was intended to be their presidential candidate, but public opinion and enthusiasm began coalescing around Aquino. After prayer and contemplation, she accepted the nomination and appointed Laurel her vice presidential candidate. Aquino stridently portrayed her late husband as a martyr and herself a victim of the regime's oppression. Marcos was forced by illness to call for snap elections on February 7, 1986, feeling he should not grant opposition forces more time to organize. Government auditors then declared him the winner by a wide margin, but the accusations of fraud so enraged the electorate they took to the street en masse. Aquino, a loyal Roman Catholic, also enjoyed the support of the church hierarchy under Cardinal Jaime Sin. They were further buttressed by dissent in the military, and several bases broke into open revolt. When Marcos ordered troops against the mutineers at their base, they confronted a cordon of a million civilians surrounding them. This display of "people power" had an unnerving effect upon senior military leaders, most notably army chief of staff Fidel Ramos, who demanded that Marcos step down. Sensing the futility of his position, Marcos obliged and fled the country for Hawaii on February 25, 1986, the very day Aquino was inaugurated. At a single stroke she had become the seventh president of the Philippines and the first woman to rule the country.

Aquino took office with a reform agenda in hand, determined to undo the legacy of brutality and oppression perpetuated by her predecessor. Civil rights were restored along with freedom of speech and the press, and almost 500 political prisoners were released. More important, she authorized a constitutional commission to draw up a new body of laws ensuring a presidential system with term limits and a bicameral legislature. All told, her ascension ushered in the peaceful re-democratization of the Philippines after nearly two decades of tyranny. However, once in power, Aquino had to face the deep-seated institutional and economic shortcomings of the nation. Corruption was rife, poverty pandemic, and the countryside ablaze with communist- and Muslim-inspired insurrections. Furthermore, Aquino faced entrenched opposition from Marcos sympathizers and other factions in the legislature. Her reform package was subsequently watered down to facilitate passage, but made inadequate to the task of bringing badly needed change. She did manage to dissuade the United States from maintaining military bases on Philippine soil by not renewing their leases, thereby removing a major point of contention between the two countries.

Aquino came to office wielding tremendous moral authority, but her six-year tenure yielded mixed results. Democracy had been restored, but the nation remained mired in economic stagnation, grinding poverty, and guerrilla war. Conservative elements within the military establishment were also far from pleased with her attempts at land redistribution, and the president endured no less than seven attempted coups against her. The largest and most serious of these, in December 1989, required American military assistance to be contained. Therefore, Aquino decided to keep her legacy a bright one by declining to seek a second term. She stepped down on July 27, 1992. She was succeeded by Fidel Ramos, who had been Aquino's defense minister, the individual most responsible for her victory over Marcos. Aquino has since retired to private life, but in June 1998 she led a large public protest over the reburial in his homeland of the dictator Marcos, who had died overseas.

Further Reading

Bedell, Clifford H. "'Madam President': The Ascension of Corazon Aquino to the Philippine Presidency." Unpublished master's thesis, University of Georgia, 1989.

Budd, Eric N. "Towards an Uncertain Future: Oligarchy, Patrimony, and Democracy in the Transition from Marcos to Aquino." Unpublished Ph.D. diss., University of Chicago, 1993.

Crisostomo, Isabelo T. *Cory—Profile of a President.* Brookline Village, Mass.: Branden Pub. Co., 1987.

Gullas, Cecilia K. *Corazon Aquino: The Miracle of a President.* New York: Cultural House, 1987.

Reid, Robert H. *Corazon Aquino and the Brushfire Revolution.* Baton Rouge: Louisiana State University Press, 1995.

Thompson, Mark R. "Off the Endangered List: Philippine Democratization in Comparative Perspective." *Comparative Politics* 28 (June 1996): 179–206.

Arbenz Guzmán, Jacobo (1913–1971) *president of Guatemala*

Jacobo Arbenz Guzmán was born in Quetzaltenango, Guatemala, on September 14, 1913, the son of a Swiss immigrant pharmacist. In 1934 he passed through the Escuela Politécnica, the national military academy, with distinction and went on to become one of the army's most promising young officers. Most individuals affiliated with this group were invariably wedded to the business-oriented conservative elite, but in 1939 Arbenz married María Cristina Vilanova, a wealthy social activist. Under her influence Arbenz became increasingly sympathetic toward the tenets of state-sponsored socialism. Guatemala at that time was controlled by General JORGE UBICO, and Arbenz joined the conspiracy that overthrew him in July 1944. Democracy was then restored, and new elections resulted in the ascent of a noted leftist, Juan José Arévalo Bermejo, who appointed Arbenz his defense minister. More elections were scheduled for 1950, with the left-leaning Arbenz and a conservative candidate, Francisco

Javier Arana, as the leading contenders. A close contest was expected until Arana was suddenly assassinated on July 18, 1949. Arbenz, the principal beneficiary, was long suspected of eliminating his opponent, but it was never proven. Though Guatemala was growing increasingly polarized over matters of ideology, Arbenz was swept into power in November 1950 with 60 percent of the vote. The United States State Department, given its concern about Soviet penetration of Central America, noticed his success with trepidation.

Arbenz was a left-wing nationalist; he employed the small Communist Party whenever it was to his advantage, but his policies remained socialistic. He undertook measures to assist the poor through improved education and access to medicine, which in many cases was absolutely justified. However, he earned American ire by sponsoring Decree 900, a bill promoting appropriation of fallow (unused) land for redistribution to landless peasants. In a country where poverty was grinding and only 19 percent of the population owned 87 percent of the land, such a response was to be anticipated. What was not expected, however, was Arbenz's insistence that compensation be paid at the same rate that owners declared for tax purposes. Hence, the American-based United Fruit Company, threatened with the loss of nearly three-quarters of the 550,000 acres they controlled, were offered only $1.1 million. When the company demanded that they receive the market value, around $15 million, Arbenz refused. Corporate executives then began complaining to State Department officials that Arbenz was instituting "Marxist" reforms at their expense. Furthermore, they warned that his actions were establishing a "beachhead" for communism throughout the region.

The newly elected administration of President DWIGHT D. EISENHOWER decided to take immediate steps against what it perceived as a potential Soviet coup. Arbenz's decision to form a "people's militia," separate from the military and armed with weapons from communist Czechoslovakia, seemed to confirm this trend. In 1954 the State Department authorized the Central Intelligence Agency (CIA) to recruit and arm a guerrilla band of exiled Guatemalans under former army officer Carlos Castillo Armas. On June 18, 1954, Castillo's rag-tag force entered Guatemala unopposed from Honduras, assisted by aircraft flown by CIA operatives. When the conservative-minded army refused to resist the invaders as ordered, Arbenz judged

Jacobo Arbenz Guzmán *(Library of Congress)*

his time in office had ended. He thereupon sought refuge in the Mexican embassy while Castillo triumphantly installed himself as president. Eisenhower's collusion triggered a spell of anti-American demonstrations throughout Latin America, but it also eliminated communist activity in Guatemala for many years. Arbenz, for his part, relocated to Switzerland and Czechoslovakia before finally settling down in Mexico City, a disillusioned man. He died there on January 27, 1971, cited by Cuban dictator Fidel Castro as an example of how not to instigate a revolution.

Further Reading

Cullather, Nick. *Secret History of the CIA's Classified Account of Its Operations in Guatemala, 1952–1954.* Stanford, Calif.: Stanford University Press, 1999.

Gleijeses, Piero. *Shattered Hope: The Guatemalan Revolution and the United States, 1944–1954.* Princeton, N.J.: Princeton University Press, 1991.

Porter, Christopher F. "The United States' Role in the Overthrow of Jacobo Arbenz in Guatemala in 1954: Eisenhower's Latin American Policy." Unpublished master's thesis, California State University–Dominguez Hills, 1986.

Schlesinger, Stephen. *Bitter Fruit: The Story of an American Coup in Guatemala.* Cambridge, Mass.: Harvard University Press, 1999.

Trefzeger, Douglas W. "Guatemala's 1952 Agrarian Reform Law: A Critical Reassessment." *International Social Science Review* (spring-summer 2002): 32–47.

Arias Sánchez, Oscar (1941–) *president of Costa Rica*

Oscar Arias Sánchez was born in Heredia, Costa Rica, on September 13, 1941, into a wealthy coffee planting family. Costa Rica itself is unique among Central American nations in being steeped in democratic traditions and without standing military forces. Arias was well educated at private academies before pursuing medicine at Boston University in the United States in 1960. There he witnessed American politics firsthand and was greatly impressed by the candidacy of JOHN F. KENNEDY. He returned to Costa Rica shortly after, determined to pursue a life of public service. He joined the liberal Partido de Liberación Nacional (PLN), National Liberation Party, and struck up cordial relations with its leader, JOSÉ FIGUERES FERRER, who, as president in 1940,

abolished the nation's army. Arias supported the unsuccessful candidacy of Daniel Oduber, then traveled to England to pursue political science in 1969. Three years later he received his doctorate from the University of Essex and came home to serve in Figueres's administration as his minister of national planning, 1972–76. In this capacity he acquired a reputation for fairness and open-mindedness, and distanced himself from ideological platitudes of every persuasion. However, Arias was convinced that peace and economic growth were integral to Costa Rica's problems, which largely mirrored those of the rest of Central America. Between 1978 and 1981 Arias also served as a member of the National Assembly, while moving up the ranks of the PLN. By 1984 he was the party's secretary general and a viable candidate for the presidency. Campaigning with the mantra, "Roofs, jobs, and peace," he was narrowly elected and took the oath of office on May 8, 1986. Arias was the youngest government executive ever elected in Costa Rican history.

Arias's debut on the international scene proved fortuitous, for the region was wracked by communist-inspired insurgencies and American-supported antiguerrilla warfare. The new president expressed little admiration for the leftist dictatorship of DANIEL ORTEGA in Nicaragua but adamantly opposed President RONALD REAGAN's support for anticommunist "contras" operating on Costa Rican soil. He demanded that both they and the Central Intelligence Agency depart Costa Rica before embarking upon his major agenda: regional peace. This move angered the Americans as politically naive and they deprived Costa Rica of several million dollars in economic aid in retaliation. Unperturbed, Arias next summoned the leaders of Nicaragua, Guatemala, Honduras, and El Salvador to the town of Esquipulas where, on August 7, 1987, they signed the so-called Contadora peace plan. This agreement mandated respect for human rights and political freedom, and forbade the harboring of foreign forces for the purpose of overthrowing neighboring regimes. The plan did not achieve immediate peace, and Nicaragua accepted free elections only after mounting pressure from anticommunist contras, but Arias had enhanced his stature as an international statesman. He consequently received the 1987 Nobel Peace Prize for his efforts.

For the remainder of his term, Arias was occupied in addressing Costa Rica's widening social gulf between rich and poor and the peaceful redistribution of wealth to avoid civil strife. To that end he managed to raise taxes on the rich and middle class, and enacted programs to improve education and medical access for the poor. He also faced the task of reducing Costa Rica's burgeoning debt by acquiescing to austerity measures demanded by the International Monetary Fund (IMF). This entailed cutting social spending, freezing wages, and reducing government expenditures. Results proved mixed, and his administration also endured the taint of embarrassing corruption scandals. Arias stepped down in April 1990 after the PLN had been turned out of office by the more conservative Rafael Angel Calderón Fournier. As a private citizen, Arias became an active lecturer on the world circuit, and he gave speeches at Harvard University, the Jimmy Carter Center, the Mikhail Gorbachev Foundation, and the Oscar Arias Sánchez Foundation, which he founded to promote world peace. He remains firmly wedded to the notion of harmonious relations as the keystone to global prosperity.

Further Reading

Arias Sánchez, Oscar. *Ten Years After Esquipulas: Looking Forward to the Future.* Providence, R.I.: Academic Council on the United Nations System, 1997.

Janitschek, Hans. "Oscar Arias Sánchez." *Omni* 10 (July 1988): 76–82.

Kenworthy, Eldon. *America/Americas: Myth in the Making of U.S. Policy Towards Latin America.* University Park: Pennsylvania State University Press, 1995.

Mahoney, James. *The Legacies of Liberalism: Path Dependence and Political Regimes in Central America.* Baltimore: Johns Hopkins University Press, 2001.

Rolbein, Seth. *Nobel Costa Rica: A Timely Report on Our Peaceful, Pro-Yankee Central American Neighbor.* New York: St. Martin's Press, 1989.

Rojas Gomez, Claudia F. "Spiritualizing the Political: A Rhetorical Analysis of Oscar Arias' Discourse on Peace." Unpublished Ph.D. diss., Ohio University, 1992.

Asquith, Herbert Henry (first earl of Oxford and Asquith) (1852–1928) *prime minister of Great Britain*

Herbert Henry Asquith was born in Morley, Yorkshire, England, on September 12, 1852, the son of a mill owner. He lost his father at an early age and attended boarding schools in London where he excelled academically. Asquith subsequently studied at Balliol College, Oxford, on a scholarship, and displayed an impressive mastery of oratory. He joined the bar in 1876 and 10 years later was elected to the House of Commons as a Liberal Party member from East Fife, Scotland. He would hold this seat continuously for the next 32 years. Asquith continued distinguishing himself in a variety of legal and political capacities, so in 1895 Prime Minister William E. Gladstone appointed him home secretary. His first wife having died, he next married Margaret Tennant, a wealthy socialite whose position enhanced his social standing. The Liberals remained in the opposition for many years until the resignation of Prime Minister ARTHUR BALFOUR in December 1905, whereupon HENRY CAMPBELL-BANNERMAN led them back to power. Asquith assumed the important role of chancellor of the Exchequer, and used his influence to make the Liberal Party more receptive to the plight of the working poor. Asquith's popularity proved such that when Campbell-Bannerman died in office, he was chosen as his successor on April 3, 1908. One of his first acts was to appoint young and vigorous leaders like DAVID LLOYD GEORGE and WINSTON CHURCHILL to his cabinet.

England was then experiencing social dislocation brought on by the industrial revolution and modernization. Accordingly, Asquith fashioned a comprehensive package of social legislation aimed at improving the living and working conditions of citizens throughout the kingdom. In short order he managed to pass sweeping legislation like the Old Age Pension Act, the Labour Exchange Act, the Trade Boards Act, and the National Insurance Act. In 1911, when the aristocratic House of Lords vetoed the budget, Asquith conducted an intense and successful political campaign to reduce their legislative powers over budgetary matters. At one point he even approached King George V to create 500 new peers, entitled to serve in the House of Lords, so as to overwhelm all resistance. Hereafter, the landmark Parliamentary Act of 1911 enabled the Lords to delay, but not stop, fiscal legislation. However, Asquith also faced considerable opposition over his attempts to address widespread strikes for higher wages, women's suffrage, and home rule for Ireland. The country was consumed by the threat of street violence over the first two issues, and an outright mutiny by the army over the last. But before Asquith could bring his formidable political talents to bear, Europe was engulfed by the cataclysm of World War I.

As a Liberal, Asquith was committed to a peaceful resolution of conflict and did not join the initial rush toward war in the early summer months of 1914. However, once German armies violated Belgian neutrality that August, British troops were formally committed to the continent. No one could have anticipated the horror and bloodshed that followed, and for two years the British lost heavily without edging closer to victory. Asquith, though active and well-intentioned, seems to have been peculiarly detached from the sufferings of the nation, and conducted the war as he conducted the peace—in a detached, almost impersonal manner. When several military blunders occurred, political opinion started swinging against the Liberals. Lloyd George orchestrated a "palace coup" by forming a coalition with Conservatives, which removed Asquith from office and replaced him with Lloyd George. This betrayal led to a disastrous rift between the two leaders that fatally weakened the Liberals as a political force. Asquith continued on as head of the party and generally supported the war effort, but he continually sought to undermine Lloyd George's government. This left the Liberal Party badly split into warring factions, and in 1918 Asquith lost his seat and returned to private practice. By the time he returned to Parliament in 1922, the Liberal ascendency, so prominent before the war, had eroded in favor of the Conservatives and a new party—Labour.

Asquith's political fortunes, along with the Liberals, were now in eclipse. After losing his seat again in 1924, he retired with a peerage as earl of Oxford and Asquith, although he remained titular party leader until 1926. The former prime minister then retreated into relative obscurity to write his memoirs and died on his estate in Berkshire, England, on February 15, 1928. As a politician, the aloof and aristocratic Asquith remained somewhat underappreciated by the lower classes, despite the impressive litany of achievements accomplished on their behalf. In fact, the scope of his accomplishments anticipated FRANKLIN D. ROOSEVELT's "New Deal" legislation by several decades.

Further Reading

Adelman, Paul. *The Decline of the Liberal Party, 1910–1931.* New York: Longman, 1995.

Asquith, Herbert H. *Moments of Memory: Recollections and Impressions.* New York: Charles Scribner's Sons, 1938.

Cassar, George H. *Asquith as War Leader.* London: Hambledon, 1994.

Clifford, Colin. *The Asquiths.* London: John Murray, 2002.

Little, John G. "H. H. Asquith and Britain's Manpower Problem, 1914–1915." *History* 82 (July 1997): 397–409.

Lynch, Patricia. *The Liberal Party in Rural England, 1885–1910: Radicalism and Community.* New York: Oxford University Press, 2002.

Mead, Walter. "The Liberal Lion." *Foreign Affairs* 81 (May–June 2002): 151–156.

Atatürk, Kemal (1881–1938) *president of Turkey*

Kemal Atatürk was known simply as Mustafa at his birth on May 19, 1881, in Salonika, Greece, then part of the Ottoman Empire. His father, a minor bureaucrat, died while he was a child and the young man was sent to attend military schools. Young Mustafa excelled academically, and when his mathematics teacher dubbed him "Kemal" (the perfect one), he adopted it as his name. Kemal was commissioned in the Ottoman army in 1905 and immediately became involved with secret military societies. The most important of these was the Committee of Union and Progress (also known as the Young Turks), whose members were disgusted by the corrupt Ottoman sultanate and determined to either reform it or abolish it. In 1909 they orchestrated a coup that disposed of Sultan Abdul Hamid II, enthroned his brother, and resurrected the 1876 constitution allowing for a national legislature. Kemal, meanwhile, kept abreast of these revolutionary proceedings from afar, as he was variously deployed in Libya and the Balkans prior to World War I. Thereafter Kemal distinguished himself in combat against various Allied nations, defeating the English at Gallipoli in 1915 and the Russians in the Caucasus in 1916. However, the Ottoman Empire, having aligned itself with Germany and other Central European powers, was slated for dismemberment at war's end. Foreign contingents landed or invaded throughout the length and breadth of the empire, intending to seize as much territory as possible.

Kemal had utterly no sympathy for the fate of the Ottoman Empire but, as a Turkish nationalist, he was determined to defend his homeland at any cost. In May 1919 he attacked Ottoman forces in Constantinople,

Kemal Atatürk *(Library of Congress)*

driving the sultan off, and became president of a provisional government. He next defeated or stalemated a variety of Allied columns invading Turkey, and in 1922 drove Greek forces out of Western Anatolia completely. So successful were Kemal's activities that the Western powers finally abandoned their attempt to partition Turkey. With his borders now secured and peace at hand, Kemal convened the provisional government in Ankara on November 1, 1922, abolished the sultanate of Mehmed VI, and declare Turkey a republic. The following October the national legislature formally elected Kemal the nation's first president.

Having seized the reins of power, Kemal instituted sweeping, wide-ranging reforms aimed at bringing Turkey into the 20th century. He crystallized his governance into six different but interrelated principles known officially as the Six Arrows, but popularly dubbed "Kemalism": republicanism, nationalism, populism, reformism, statism, and secularism. These touched upon virtually every aspect of Turkish political, social, and economic life, and finally divested the country of its medieval trappings. Foremost among them was the deliberate decoupling of Islam as a state religion. This paved the way for secular, scientific education, the enfranchisement and social liberation of women, and an end to religious interference in politics. Moreover, he formally substituted the elaborate and overly ornate Arabic alphabet for the simple, effective Latin alphabet. Western dress, science, and thinking—heretofore alien in this predominantly Muslim land—now became the official norm. Turkey was thus the first Islamic country to declare itself a republic and embrace democratic principles.

In practice, Kemal was more of a dictator than a president. He frequently ruled by decree and consolidated his control by allowing only the Republican People's Party to exist. Kemal held office for 15 years without interruption or legitimate opposition, by which time Turkey had irrevocably passed down the road toward modernization. In 1923 he also adopted the surname Atatürk, or "father of Turks," and is still hailed as the father of his nation. Yet, for all the discipline and sense of purpose he imposed on Turkey, Atatürk's private life was much given to wild parties and heavy drinking. He died of cirrhosis of the liver on November 10, 1938, and was widely mourned. But the state he engineered survived his passing and it fell upon Turkey's second elected president, ISMET INÖNÜ, to finally allow multiparty politics. Despite the onset of Islamic fundamentalism throughout the Middle East, Turkey remains the most secular, stable, and westernized nation of the Muslim world.

Further Reading

Atabaki, Touraj, and Erik Jan Zurcher. *Men of Order: Authoritarian Modernization under Atatürk and Reza Shah.* London: I. B. Tauris, 2002.

Cooper, Malcolm. "The Legacy of Atatürk: Turkish Political Structures and Policy-making." *International Affairs* 78, no. 1 (2002): 115–128.

Kedourie, Sylvia, ed. *Seventy-Five Years of the Turkish Republic.* London: Frank Cass, 1999.

Mango, Andrew. *Atatürk: The Biography of the Founder of Modern Turkey.* New York: Overlook Press, 2000.

Sheldon, Garret W. *Jefferson and Atatürk: Political Philosophies.* New York: P. Lang, 2000.

Attlee, Clement (first earl Attlee) (1883–1967)

prime minister of Great Britain

Clement Richard Attlee was born in a plush suburb of London on January 3, 1883, the son of an attorney. He attended private schools before attending Oxford University to study law. After graduating he was called to the bar in 1905, but gradually forsook the legal profession in favor of social work. Having viewed firsthand the grinding poverty of London's East End, Attlee became a socialist by inclination and determined to improve the lives of the poor. After serving bravely throughout World War I, in which he was severely wounded, Attlee returned to London and entered politics as a member of the newly founded Labour Party. He was elected the first-ever mayor of Stepney in 1919 and three years later took a post as a Labour delegate to the House of Commons. Attlee's personal demeanor—calm, deliberate, and painfully polite—caused friends and enemies alike to underestimate him, but astute politicians recognized his abilities. RAMSAY MACDONALD, the first Labour prime minister, appointed him to various posts throughout the 1920s. His first chance for party leadership occurred in 1931 when MacDonald formed a coalition with the Conservatives, which Attlee considered a betrayal of party principles. He was subsequently voted deputy and then leader of the Labour Party in 1935, a post he held for the next 20 years.

Clement Attlee *(Library of Congress)*

While in opposition, Attlee differed markedly from many of his more dovish compatriots in recognizing the danger that BENITO MUSSOLINI and ADOLF HITLER posed to world peace. He strongly advocated British rearmament while most Labour leaders professed neutrality. Attlee also condemned Prime Minister NEVILLE CHAMBERLAIN's appeasement of Nazi aggression in 1938, anticipating that war was now inevitable. Once hostilities commenced and the conservatives elected WINSTON CHURCHILL as the new prime minister, Attlee was brought into a national unity government as deputy prime minister in 1942. Churchill was overly preoccupied by wartime strategies, so Attlee handled day-to-day operations of the country competently, clearly demonstrating his ability to serve as prime minister. Once Germany had been defeated, Churchill called for snap elections in July 1945, but Attlee scored a stunning upset by throwing out the Conservatives and giving Labour their first absolute majority in Parliament. He thus became the first Labour leader to actually control the reins of government and, in his quiet, unassuming manner, determined to enact great changes to the national landscape.

For many years into the 20th century, Britain had been gravitating to a government-sponsored welfare state, in which all basic services would be available to citizens free of charge. It was Attlee, however, who embodied these trends and brought them to fruition. Through a succession of bills he nationalized key sectors of the economy, established universal health care and a National Health Service, mandated full employment policies, and otherwise established cradle-to-grave socialism for the first time. However, Attlee was no radical, being steeped in the traditions of English law and democracy, and he insisted that socialism be achieved by peaceful—even piecemeal—means. Many of the programs enacted remain in place today and are hallmarks of everyday British life. Even so powerful and popular a Conservative as MARGARET THATCHER dared make only superficial adjustments to them.

Attlee was also determined to make his mark on the international scene. Being an anti-imperialist, he set in motion policies that granted political independence to large portions of the British Empire, including India, Pakistan, Ceylon (Sri Lanka), and Palestine. And while this may have pleased his left-wing cohorts, Attlee remained stridently anticommunist in his foreign policy. For many years he closely subscribed to the policies of U.S. president HARRY S. TRUMAN and, at his urging, began pursuing a British atomic bomb and membership in the North Atlantic Treaty Organization (NATO). Attlee also allowed British forces to be committed to the Korean War (1950–53) in support of the United Nations. These acts placed Britain in the forefront of "containment" of the Soviet Union, which may have angered purists in his party, but which rendered Great Britain a valuable ally in the cold war.

Attlee's sweeping changes to the economy carried a price. Britain's economy and treasury had been exhausted by World War II, and new taxes and regulations stifled economic growth. Public opinion eventually soured against the Labour Party, and in October 1951 Attlee was turned out of office by Churchill's Conservatives. However, his six-year tenure in office was among the most remarkable and productive in British political history, being orchestrated by a man reviled within his own party for blandness and painstaking deliberation. Attlee remained head of Labour until 1955, when he finally retired from public life. He died in London on October 8, 1967, a forgotten and somewhat embittered man. However, his success in erecting the long-sought welfare state was admirable, as was his orchestration of the peaceful transition from British Empire to British Commonwealth.

Further Reading

Allender, Paul. *What's Wrong with Labour? A Critical History of the Labour Party in the Twentieth Century.* London: Merlin, 2001.

Douglas, R. M. *The Labour Party, Nationalism and Internationalism, 1939–1951.* Portland, Ore.: Frank Cass, 2004.

Pearce, Robert D. *Attlee.* New York: Longman, 1997.

Smith, R., and J. Zametica. "The Cold Warrior: Clement Attlee Reconsidered, 1945–7." *International Affairs* 61 (spring 1985): 237–252.

Swift, John. *Labour in Crisis: Clement Attlee and the Labour Party in Opposition, 1931–1940.* New York: Palgrave, 2001.

Tomlinson, Jim. *Democratic Socialism and Economic Policy: The Attlee Years, 1945–1951.* Cambridge, England: Cambridge University Press, 1997.

Vickers, Rhiannon. *Manipulating Hegemony: State Power, Labour, and the Marshall Plan in Britain.* New York: St. Martin's Press, 2000.

Ávila Camacho, Manuel (1897–1955) *president of Mexico*

Manuel Ávila Camacho was born in Teziutlán, Puebla, Mexico, on April 24, 1897, into a family of ranchers. He studied accounting in college but was swept away by the fervor of the Mexican Revolution and joined the Constitutionalists under VENUSTIANO CARRANZA. Becoming closely associated with General LÁZARO CÁRDENAS, he rose quickly through the ranks, becoming brigadier general. Ávila Camacho fought with distinction in several actions and won the trust of Cárdenas. In 1933 he again served under him during a stint in the Secretariat of War and, once Cárdenas had become president, advanced to full secretary. Given his revolutionary credentials and close association with the popular executive, Ávila Camacho was a natural candidate for the Mexican presidency in 1940. Once nominated by the Partido de la Revolución Mexicana (PRM) to succeed Cárdenas, he engaged in a closely fought election with former general Juan Andreu Almazán of the more conservative Partido Revolucionario de Unificación Nacional (PRUN). Ávila Camacho easily trounced his opponent but only amid allegations of widespread voter fraud and violence. However, once Almazán exiled himself abroad, Ávila Camacho was sworn into office on December 1, 1940.

The new executive inherited a very divided nation in very dangerous times. Mexico was still restive under strict anticlerical laws militating against the Catholic Church, and socialistic policies that mandated land redistribution, a managed economy, and government-controlled education. In all these spheres, Ávila Camacho demonstrated political prowess as an enlightened conservative reformer. Far less revolutionary than his mentor Cárdenas, he took steps to terminate the official socialist-oriented education system in favor of basic literacy through private involvement ("Each One

Teach One"). Then, admitting to the political establishment that he was a practicing Catholic, he deliberately downplayed the more strident features of anticlericalism. Finally, Ávila Camacho scaled back revolutionary programs such as land distribution and focused his energies on stimulating Mexico's industrial base. In exchange for this deliberate swing to the right, the president also founded the Mexican Social Security System along with better access to health care. By all these expedients, he managed to bring feuding sectors of the Mexican polity closer together, and promoted much-needed national harmony. Perhaps his biggest contribution to domestic tranquillity was formally removing the military from politics and disbanding their faction within the official party.

Ávila Camacho's biggest challenge, however, was in managing Mexican affairs in World War II. He broke with all precedent by establishing close relations with the United States, an object of intense distrust since 1848, and conferred with President FRANKLIN D. ROOSEVELT in Veracruz on several occasions. He also marched in lockstep with Allied nations by declaring war on Germany, Italy, and Japan, and committed an aviation squadron to combat in the Pacific. In return, the Americans showered Mexico with billions of dollars of materiel and assistance, through which Ávila Camacho upgraded national defenses and laid the foundations for a modern industrial base. He even negotiated the famous "bracero" system with the United States, whereby thousands of poor Mexicans migrated north to harvest crops. Furthermore, Ávila Camacho also authorized the payment of compensation for American property that had been damaged during the Mexican Revolution and for oil fields that had been nationalized in the 1930s. By 1945 Mexican-American relations had reached a new and much-needed level of normalcy, which facilitated greater economic growth and trade over the next five decades.

Ávila Camacho stepped down from office in 1946 and was succeeded by MIGUEL ALEMÁN VALDÉS, who continued his conservative, business-oriented policies. The former executive then assumed a life of privacy on his ranch before dying in Mexico City on October 13, 1955. Although not appreciated at the time, Ávila Camacho's administration proved essential for Mexican rapprochement with the United States, and the good relations both countries enjoy today.

Further Reading

Canedo, Phillip J. "Mexico's War Years: The Administration of Manuel Ávila Camacho." Unpublished master's thesis, University of Oregon, 1972.

Glade, W. *Politics, Policies, and Economic Development in Latin America.* Stanford, Calif.: Hoover Institute Press, 1984.

Langston, Joy. "Breaking Out Is Hard to Do: Exit, Voice, and Loyalty in Mexico's One-Party Hegemonic Regime." *Latin American Politics and Society* 44 (fall 2002): 61–90.

Miller, Michael N. *Red, White, and Green: The Maturing of the Mexicanidad, 1940–1946.* El Paso: Texas Western Press, University of Texas at El Paso, 1998.

Niblo, Stephen R. *Mexico in the 1940s: Modernity, Politics, and Corruption.* Wilmington, Del.: Scholarly Resources, 1999.

Paz Salinas, Maria E. *Strategy, Security, and Spies: Mexico and the U.S. as Allies in World War II.* University Park: Pennsylvania State University Press, 1997.

Schuler, Friedrich. *Mexico between Hitler and Roosevelt: Mexican Foreign Relations in the Age of Lázaro Cárdenas, 1934–1940.* Albuquerque: University of New Mexico Press, 1998.

Ayub Khan, Mohammad (1907–1974) *president of Pakistan*

Mohammad Ayub Khan was born in the Hazara district of British India (modern northwest Pakistan) on May 14, 1907. Ethnically, his family was of Pathan Muslim descent and his father served as a cavalry sergeant in the British-controlled Indian army. Ayub was educated locally before attending the Muslim College at Aligarh in 1922, but eventually he was one of the few non-Europeans chosen to attend the prestigious British Military Academy at Sandhurst. He graduated in 1927 and was commissioned into the infantry. Ayub rose steadily through the ranks by dint of demonstrated ability, and in World War II he commanded a battalion in Burma. In 1947 the English government under Prime Minister CLEMENT ATTLEE granted the subcontinent independence, which resulted in creation of two new nations, India and Pakistan. Ayub, like many Muslim officers, transferred his allegiance to the newly founded Pakistani army, and in 1951 he became the nation's first non-European army commander. In this capacity, and much against his will, he was slowly drawn into the confusing world of Pakistani politics.

Pakistan had been beset by political instability since its inception, and by the late 1950s the nation seemed to be spinning out of control. On October 7, 1958, Ayub was asked by President Iskander Mirza to impose martial law to preserve order. Ayub, disgusted by politicians and the corruption they fostered, obediently obliged him—then exiled President Mirza to England. The coup was initially greeted with public enthusiasm, and Ayub set about imposing a comprehensive series of reforms to "clean up" his society. Foremost among these was the notion of "basic democracy," whereby 80,000 village headmen were enfranchised and enabled to vote in elections. He followed up in 1962 with a new constitution that mandated free elections for president within

Mohammad Ayub Khan *(Library of Congress)*

three years. Ayub was reelected by 65 percent of votes cast, easily beating off a strong challenge by Fatima Jinnah, sister of MOHAMMED ALI JINNAH, Pakistan's founding father. He also orchestrated programs for land reform, and government incentives for foreign investment and private enterprise. For a brief period the economy flourished, standards of living increased, and Ayub Khan reigned as the most popular politician in the country.

The Pakistani regime enjoyed less success in articulating its strategic concerns in foreign affairs. Ayub was friendly toward the United States and directed the country's entry into mutual defense treaties like the Central Treaty Organization (CENTO), in an attempt to contain communism. However, mounting border tensions with India over the state of Kashmir escalated to all-out war in 1965. The Pakistani military, which touted its invincibility, was fought to a draw and the government signed embarrassing concessions to restore the status quo. The settlement proved unpopular, for many Pakistanis believed that they never should have capitulated to their enemy. The war also resulted in a cutoff of greatly needed military assistance from the United States, whereupon Ayub turned to China and the Soviet Union for help.

Toward the end of his tenure in office, Ayub's regime had proved unable to address deep-seated social and infrastructural problems, and his popularity plummeted. His biggest problem became East Pakistan, separated by 1,000 miles from West Pakistan and caught up in the throes of an independence movement. A leading Pakistani military figure, MUJIBUR RAHMAN, began demanding greater autonomy to forestall a secessionist movement. But public discontent increased even further when it was revealed that members of Ayub's family had amassed fortunes through illegal influence peddling. As the economy began spiraling downward, domestic violence increased, and calls were made for Ayub's resignation. In a curious twist of fate, he was required to ask the military under General Yahya Khan to intercede and impose order. As in 1958, the military obliged but then deposed the president and assumed complete control of the country on March 25, 1969. Ayub returned to private life and remained in obscurity until his death on April 19, 1974. Try as he might, his modernizing policies could not overcome the traditional conservative nature of Pakistani society.

Further Reading

Ayub Khan, Mohammad. *Friends Not Masters: A Political Autobiography.* New York: Oxford University Press, 1967.

Cloughley, Brian. *A History of the Pakistan Army: Wars and Insurrections.* New York: Oxford University Press, 2000.

Ganguly, Sumit. *The Origins of War in South Asia: The Indo-Pakistani Conflicts Since 1947.* Boulder, Colo.: Westview Press, 1994.

Gauhar, Altaf. *Ayub Khan: Pakistan's First Military Leader.* New York: Oxford University Press, 1996.

Ziring, Lawrence. "Bureaucratic Politics and the Fall of Ayub Khan." *Asian Affairs* 8 (May 1981): 304–322.

Azcona Hoyo, José (1927–) *president of Honduras*

José Simón Azcona Hoyo was born in La Ceiba, Honduras, on January 26, 1927, the son of Spanish parents. He was raised and educated in Spain but fled that country to escape military service in 1949. Returning to Honduras, he was educated at the National Autonomous University, and then the Technological Institute for Superior Studies in Monterrey, Mexico. Early on, Azcona took an interest in Liberal Party politics, and was active from 1962 to 1974. He joined the party's central executive committee in 1977 and by 1978 was its general secretary. In this capacity he supported the candidacy of ROBERTO SUAZO CÓRDOVA for president in 1980 and joined his cabinet as secretary of state communications, public works, and transportation two years later. Urbane, articulate, and well-positioned politically, Azcona subsequently ran for the Honduran presidency as the Liberal Party candidate in December 1985. At that time, the government had adopted unique provisions for electing executive officers. Instead of popular tallies of candidates, presidents were selected from the party that garnered the greatest number of all-around votes, including those for state and municipal offices. Through this expedient, Azcona lost the popular vote to National Party candidate Rafael Leonardo Callejas Romero, yet won because the Liberals had accrued a larger aggregate. The results led to a questioning of Azcona's political legitimacy at a time when Honduras was sharply divided by domestic and international tensions. Yet his ascension marked the first time in recent

history that political power passed peacefully from one executive to another.

Once in office, Azcona was confronted by communist-inspired civil wars in Nicaragua and El Salvador. The Sandinista regime in Nicaragua under President DANIEL ORTEGA was clandestinely supplying guerrilla forces that were destabilizing the entire region. This drew an immediate and sharp response from American president RONALD REAGAN, who began arming a select group of Nicaraguan counterrevolutionaries, the so-called contras. These forces waged a steady but low-intensity guerrilla war against the Sandinistas until the latter agreed to internationally supervised democratic elections. In the pursuit of this objective, it fell upon Reagan to ask leaders of Central America to host the contras and allow them to use their countries as bases of operations. Azcona's predecessor, Suazo, complied at the insistence of the anticommunist Honduran military, and he was rewarded with a large influx of foreign aid. Not wishing to depart from this policy, Azcona also allowed the contras to operate unimpeded from Honduran soil, much to the satisfaction of the United States. Costa Rican president OSCAR ARIAS SÁNCHEZ eventually proposed a comprehensive peace settlement that Azcona only reluctantly signed, then ignored. In fact, contra forces mounted operations against Nicaragua until the government accepted free elections in 1990, when Ortega lost decisively. The role Honduras played in restoring democracy in Nicaragua was critical, a central factor in the Sandinista defeat.

In addition to wartime concerns, Azcona also had to confront a tottering economy at home. He had inherited a soaring national debt from his predecessor. Payment on the interest alone was swallowing up a quarter of the national budget, and his problems were further compounded by strict austerity measures imposed by the International Monetary Fund (IMF). Even with American assistance, the Honduran economy staggered along with nearly 25 percent unemployment. These problems remained unresolved throughout his tenure as president, and in January 1990 Azcona relinquished power to Rafael Callejas of the National Party, whom he had defeated four years earlier. This transfer represented a victory of sorts, it being only the second peaceful succession in a decade. Azcona returned to private life with little ceremony until March 1998, when the Honduran Attorney General's Office asked a court to begin proceedings against him for illegally extraditing a convicted drug lord to the United States. Because Honduran law does not allow for such procedures, Azcona's actions might constitute an abuse of presidential authority.

Further Reading

Hammond, Tony. "The Role of the Honduran Armed Forces in the Transition to Democracy." Unpublished master's thesis, University of Florida, 1991.

Karl, Terry Lynn. *Central America in the Twenty-first Century: The Prospects for a Democratic Region.* Notre Dame, Ind.: University of Notre Dame Press, 1994.

Mahoney, James. *The Legacies of Liberalism: Path Dependence and Political Regimes in Central America.* Baltimore: Johns Hopkins University Press, 2001.

Millet, Richard. "The Honduran Dilemma." *Current History* 86, no. 524 (1987): 409–412, 435–436.

Schultz, Donald E. *The United States, Honduras, and the Crisis in Central America.* Boulder, Colo.: Westview Press, 1994.

Tervo, Kathryn H. "Honduras and the Contras: Effects of the U.S.-sponsored Contra War on the Central American Republic of Honduras." Unpublished master's thesis, Central Connecticut State University, 1998.

Azhari, Ismail Sayyid al- (1902–1969) *president of Sudan*

Ismail Sayyid al-Azhari was born at Omdurman, Sudan, in 1902, the son of a noted Muslim cleric. He attended both Gordon College in Khartoum and American University in Beirut before returning home as a mathematics teacher. The Sudan at this time was administered by a joint British and Egyptian condominium government, and Azhari worked for them as an administrator. However, like many Sudanese, he resented poor treatment at the hands of foreigners and in 1938 he helped found the Graduates General Congress to agitate for independence. The onset of World War II caused the Sudanese nationalist movement to split, and Azhari took charge of the radical anti-British faction. By 1943 these efforts culminated in his founding of the Ashiqqa (Brothers) Party, the first such political organization in Sudan. As party president, Azhari espoused the two linchpins of Ashiqqa ideology: immediate independence from Great Britain and national unification with Egypt.

Such agitation led to his arrest and jailing in 1948, but British authorities eventually yielded to creation of a Sudanese territorial legislature. This move angered Egyptian king FAROUK, who then claimed unilateral control over the entire Sudan and damaged Azhari's platform for unification. But the move toward independence received greater impetus in 1952, when Farouk was overthrown by Arab nationalist GAMAL ABDEL NASSER. An antiforeign nationalist, Nasser was in complete sympathy with Sudanese aspirations and downplayed unification of the Nile region. Azhari also accelerated his political and nationalistic ambitions by founding the National Unionist Party (NUP) to seek independence from Great Britain at the earliest possible opportunity. National elections were held in 1953 and the NUP handily won, making Azhari Sudan's first prime minister.

With Sudanese independence virtually assured, Azhari made the most monumental political decision of his career. Having long touted unification of his country to Egypt as a precondition for severing ties to Great Britain, he suddenly did an about-face and opposed it. This reversal did little to diminish his political fortunes initially, and on January 1, 1956, Sudan became a sovereign nation with Azhari at its head. But soon after, intractable matters of governance manifested. Azhari's faction of the NUP sought to maintain a British-style parliamentary system while others sought a stronger presidential mode of leadership. He faced an even more daunting challenge from southern Sudan. Unlike the northern reaches of the country, preponderantly Arabic and Muslim, the southern section is overwhelmingly black African and Christian. This made national rule and reconciliation difficult, if not altogether elusive, especially for such a newly improvised government. When civil war broke out in the south, Azhari's inability to squelch it made him appear weak, and the NUP split up into feuding factions. Azhari tried reforming his administration into a coalition government "of all talents," but much too late. In July 1956 he lost a vote of confidence and was forced to resign. Azhari nonetheless continued as head of the opposition in a new regime headed by Abdullah Khalil.

Continued infighting between various factions led to the growth of instability and violence, so in November 1958 General Ibrahim Abboud overthrew the elected government and suspended all political activity. Azhari was briefly jailed and allowed to retire on a pension, but when democracy was restored in 1964 he returned to the political arena. In March 1965 Azhari became head of the Sudan within a five-man Supreme Council, which acted as a collective presidency. His was largely a ceremonial post with little actual authority, but it imparted some semblance of stability to the country. However, in May 1968 the civilian regime was again toppled by military forces under Colonel GAAFAR NIMEIRI. Azhari was once again seized and kept under house arrest. He died on August 26, 1969, still widely regarded as the father of his nation.

Further Reading

Holt, P. M., and M. W. Daly. *A History of the Sudan: From the Coming of Islam to the Present Day.* New York: Longman, 2000.

Idris, Amir H. *Sudan's Civil War: Slavery, Race, and the Formation of Identities.* Lewiston, N.Y.: Edwin Mellen Press, 2001.

Johnson, Douglas H. *The Root Causes of Sudan's Civil Wars.* Bloomington: Indiana University Press, 2003.

O'Balance, Edgar. *Sudan, Civil War, and Terrorism, 1956–1999.* New York: St. Martin's Press, 2000.

Spaulding, Jay, and Stephanie Beswick, eds. *White Nile, Black Blood: War, Leadership and Ethnicity from Khartoum to Kampala.* Lawrenceville, N.J.: Red Sea Press, 2000.

Azikiwe, Nnamdi (1904–1996) *president of Nigeria*

Nnamdi Azikiwe was born in Zungeru, northern Nigeria, on November 16, 1904, to parents of Ibo descent. Ibos are one of Nigeria's three major ethnic groups, the others being Yoruba and Hausa. Azikiwe was educated at missionary schools and briefly worked as a clerk before traveling to the United States in 1925. He subsequently earned a bachelor's degree from Howard University in Washington, D.C., in 1930 and a master's in anthropology from the University of Pennsylvania in 1932. He also encountered leading Pan-African spokesmen like Marcus Garvey in school, which converted his resentment against white colonial rule into burgeoning nationalism. Returning to Africa, Azikiwe found employment in the neighboring Gold Coast (Ghana) as a journalist and founded the *African Morning Post* in Accra. This became a mouthpiece for

anticolonial agitation, and in 1936 authorities closed the paper, arrested Azikiwe, and deported him back to Nigeria. Adversity only spurred his efforts to fan the flames of Pan-Africanism, and he established a new and even more influential publication, the *West African Pilot,* in Lagos. His editorials pointedly questioned the legitimacy of colonial rule and forcefully advocated moves toward independence. Azikiwe soon became the most renowned journalist in Nigeria, and he founded several regional papers to advance the cause of self-governance. He also dabbled in politics by joining the National Council of Nigeria and the Cameroons (NCNC), rising to president by 1946. To further foment independence from English influence, Azikiwe founded the African Commercial Bank in 1944, one of the earliest expressions of African economic nationalism.

After World War II the British Empire began granting greater autonomy to its colonies, and Azikiwe was at the forefront of Nigerian events. Through the late 1940s and well into the 1950s he visited London on several occasions to agitate for independence and changes to the colonial constitution. Back home, he rose through a succession of important posts, including minister of local government and premier of the Eastern Region by 1954. When Nigeria finally gained independence on October 1, 1960, Azikiwe threw his support behind ABUBAKAR TAFAWA BALEWA of the rival Nigerian People's Congress to serve as the nation's first prime minister. He himself functioned as governor general of Nigeria from 1960 to 1969, a largely symbolic post. However, when Nigeria turned its government into a federal republic on October 1, 1963, Azikiwe became Nigeria's first elected president. He held that post until January 1966, when civil unrest and economic hardship triggered a military coup that toppled his government and suspended all political activity.

In addition to political instability, Nigeria was also sharply cleft by ethnic and religious divisions that made good governance impractical. Azikiwe's Ibos, who formed the majority of the Eastern Region, were largely Christian, while the North and West were predominantly Muslim. Outnumbered and fearing persecution, the Ibos began a secessionist revolt under Colonel CHUKWUEMEKA OJUKWU and declared independence as the new state of Biafra in May 1967. Azikiwe, as a native Ibo, rallied behind the rebels and toured Africa on their behalf. However, as federal forces under General YAKUBU

GOWON edged closer to victory, the former journalist switched sides and began touting unification and reconciliation. With the war over and the ban on political parties lifted in 1978, Azikiwe returned to the arena as president of the Nigerian People's Party. After many years leading the opposition in parliament, he ran unsuccessfully for the presidency in 1979 and 1983, being defeated twice by Shehu Shagari of the National Party of Nigeria. Azikiwe finally retired from public life in 1986 after another military coup, still revered as Nigeria's foremost journalist and international statesman. "Zik," as he was affectionately known, died at Enugu, Nigeria, on May 11, 1996. He is regarded as the father of Nigerian nationalism and a guiding force toward fulfillment of independence. As a national leader, however, his main shortcoming was failure to reconcile Ibo regionalism with greater Nigerian nationalism.

Further Reading

Azikiwe, Nnamdi. *My Odyssey: An Autobiography.* New York: Praeger, 1970.

Echervo, Michael J. C. "Nnamdi Azikiwe and Nineteenth-Century Nigerian Thought." *Journal of Modern African Studies* 12 (July 1974): 245–263.

Flint, John E. "Managing Nationalism: The Colonial Office and Nnamdi Azikiwe, 1932–43." *Journal of Imperial and Commonwealth History* 27 (May 1999): 143–158.

Furlong, Patrick J. "Azikiwe and the National Church of Nigeria and the Cameroons: A Case Study of the Political Use of Religion in African Nationalism." *African Affairs* 91 (July 1992): 433–452.

Ulansky, Gene. "Nnamdi Azikiwe and the Myth of America." Unpublished Ph.D. diss., University of California–Berkeley, 1980.

B

Baldwin, Stanley (first earl Baldwin of Bewdley)
(1867–1947) *prime minister of Great Britain*
Stanley Baldwin was born in Bewdley, Worcestershire, England, on August 3, 1867, the son of an iron magnate and Conservative member of Parliament. He was well educated at private academies and Cambridge University before returning home to run the family industry. Baldwin twice ran unsuccessfully for a seat in Parliament, but after his father died in 1908, he managed to hold the family seat. For nearly a decade Baldwin did little to distinguish himself within the ranks of the Conservative Party until he became secretary under Chancellor of the Exchequer ANDREW BONAR LAW in 1916. With Bonar Law's patronage Baldwin was slowly drawn into the inner circles of power, and in 1917 he became financial secretary to the Treasury. He functioned in this capacity until 1922 when, at a meeting of Conservatives at the Carleton Club, Baldwin and others withdrew their support from the national coalition headed by DAVID LLOYD GEORGE of the Liberal Party. In the ensuing general election, the Conservatives won, Bonar Law became prime minister, and Baldwin was rewarded with the portfolio of chancellor of the Exchequer. In this capacity he ventured to the United States to negotiate payment of Great Britain's wartime debts and was roundly castigated for failing to secure better terms on his return. However, when illness forced Bonar Law from office in May 1923, Baldwin was chosen to succeed him. The new prime minister then spoke out for protectionist tariffs, called for elections in December 1923, and was swept out of office after six months. He was replaced by the first Labour Party administration, under RAMSAY MACDONALD.

Fortunately for the Conservatives, MacDonald called for new elections in November 1924, and Baldwin, having renounced protectionism and pledging a safe and dull government, was voted back to power. His greatest accomplishments over the next five years included signing the Locarno Agreement, in which Great Britain and Italy ensured existing Franco-German border arrangements. However, when he brought Britain's economy back to the gold standard at what was perceived as too high a rate, working-class wages spiraled downward. This in turn triggered the general strike of 1926, which threatened to bring the country to a standstill. Baldwin, however, remained firm in his denunciation of unions, rallied public support, and the strike collapsed in a matter of days. Moreover, Conservatives managed to pass the Trade Disputes Act, which outlawed coercive strikes and generally turned workers against the party. When general elections were called again in May 1929, the Conservatives again lost by a wide margin to the Labour Party under MacDonald.

By 1932 Britain's deteriorating economy forced MacDonald to usher in a coalition government, and Baldwin was appointed to the cabinet position of lord president of the council. Here he argued for and passed protective tariff legislation in an attempt to save the pound, discourage imports, and raise tax revenues. MacDonald's health declined, however, so in June 1935 he switched positions with Baldwin, who now began an unprecedented third term as prime minister. This time his political agenda was dominated by foreign events. Large parts of the British Empire, such as India, had begun pressing for greater autonomy, often in the face of fierce Conservative resistance. But Baldwin, who at heart was a moderate, managed to steer through legislation that placated the colonies while keeping the empire viable. He faced an even more daunting challenge, however, in the rise of totalitarian regimes in Italy, Germany, and Japan. In 1935 he was forced to scrap an unpopular plan that would have recognized BENITO MUSSOLINI's aggression in Ethiopia, followed the next year by ADOLF HITLER's seizure of the Rhineland. Cognizant of England's military weakness, he pushed strongly for general rearmament at a time when public opinion favored neutrality. He also weathered a constitutional crisis of sorts when King Edward VIII determined to marry Mrs. Wallis Simpson, a divorced American socialite. Baldwin prevailed upon the monarch to abdicate first, and he was replaced by his younger brother, George VI. By May 1937, Baldwin was exhausted and in ill health, so he resigned from office and appointed chancellor NEVILLE CHAMBERLAIN as his successor. He lived a quiet life in retirement and died on December 14, 1947, in Worcestershire, criticized for tardily rearming the nation and facilitating the outbreak of World War II. But historians have since revised their opinion of the stodgy, plain-spoken Baldwin; they see him providing steady leadership when the nation required it the most. Moderately disposed and politically flexible, he was much more popular nationally than with members of his own party.

Further Reading

Matthews, K. "Stanley Baldwin's 'Irish Question.'" *Historical Journal* 43 (December 2000): 1027–1049.

O'Riordan, Elspeth Y. *Britain and the Ruhr Crisis.* New York: Palgrave in Association with King's College London, 2001.

Ward-Smith, Gabrielle D. "Baldwin and Scotland: More than Englishness." *Contemporary British History* 15 (spring 2001): 61–82.

Watts, Duncan S. B. *Stanley Baldwin and the Search for Consensus.* London: Hodder & Stoughton, 1996.

Williamson, Philip. *Stanley Baldwin: Conservative Leadership and National Values.* New York: Cambridge University Press, 1999.

Williamson, Philip, and Edward Baldwin, eds. *A Conservative Prime Minister: Baldwin Papers, 1908–1947.* New York: Cambridge University Press, 2004.

Balewa, Alhaji Sir Abubakar Tafawa

(1912–1966) *prime minister of Nigeria*

Abubakar was born in Tafawa Balewa, northern Nigeria, in 1912, into the small Jere group. His father came from humble beginnings, but as the son of a clerk with the emir of Bauchi state, Abubakar received an excellent education by Nigerian standards. Having adopted, as was the custom, the name of his town of birth as a surname, Balewa studied at the Katsina Higher College and in 1928 received his teacher's certificate. In 1934 he published a novel, *Shaihu Umar,* which has since been dramatized on stage and in film. He rose successively through the district educational bureaucracy, rising to headmaster in 1944, and in 1945 received a scholarship to study at the Institute of Education of London University. Balewa obtained his advanced education certificate and returned to Nigeria in 1946, where profound political changes had unfolded.

After World War II Great Britain allowed greater autonomy within the empire and Nigeria received a new constitution allowing for a national legislature, and similar bodies in the East, West, and North regions of that colony. Balewa took an immediate liking to politics, and as early as 1943, he had founded the Bauchi General Improvement Group, which criticized colonial rule. He was next elected to the northern regional assembly in 1946, and the following year, became one of five delegates to the Central Legislative Council. As Britain granted Nigeria greater self-governance through a series of new constitutions, Balewa continued rising up the governing apparatus. He joined the national House of Representatives in 1952, and shortly after, went to London for constitutional discussions. He also served as vice president of the Muslim-oriented Northern People's Congress (NPC) under Ahmadu Bello, an influential emir and party president. After serving several years as minister of transport in the colony, Balewa was elected Nigeria's first prime minister on September 2, 1957. In this capacity he helped establish a timetable for independence, with the first national elections scheduled for December 1959. Balewa, a devout Muslim with a well-deserved reputation for honesty and intelligence, then formed a broad-based coalition government with several opposition parties to promote national unity. When independence was achieved on October 1, 1960, he was retained as prime minister while the office of governor general went to a respected southerner, NNAMDI AZIKIWE. In recognition of his efforts to peacefully promote Nigerian independence, Balewa received a knighthood from Queen Elizabeth II, and with it, the title Sir Bubakar.

The heady rush toward independence did not allow Nigeria time to address traditional and deep-seated fissures within its national polity. The country is strongly divided between a Christian south and a Muslim north, and further handicapped by 250 different tribal groupings and languages. Thus Balewa's tenure in office proved tenuous from the onset. A moderate by persuasion, he favored friendly ties to the West and a capitalistic approach to economics. He rejected the notion of Pan-Africanism as defined by KWAME NKRUMAH of Ghana. The possibility of governance was further challenged by imposition of a federal system that gave the three regions inordinate powers of autonomy at the central government's expense. Balewa endured his first crisis in 1962 when he charged Obafemi Awolowo of the Action Group (AG) party with conspiring to overthrow the government. Awolowo was then tried and imprisoned, but the western region reacted strongly against Balewa thereafter. The prime minister also had a difficult relationship with Azikiwe, now serving as president, amid charges of corruption and favoritism. As tensions mounted between the NPC and other parties, Balewa's coalition proved untenable and it split apart.

New elections held in 1964 returned Balewa as prime minister, but it took several months before President Azikiwe reappointed him. The following year adherents of jailed AG president Awolowo rioted for months on end, reducing the region to chaos. Further elections were held, which led to accusations of voter fraud, and the army was sent in to restore order. A disgruntled faction within the military seized the opportunity to overthrow the government, attacking Balewa's

house and killing him on January 15, 1966. He remains fondly regarded as a leading architect of Nigerian independence and the nation's first and finest prime minister.

Further Reading

Clark, Trevor. *A Right Honorable Gentleman: Abubakar from the Black Rock: A Narrative Chronicle of the Life and Times of Nigeria's Alhaji Sir Abubakar Tafawa Balewa.* London: Edward Arnold, 1991.

Mathews, Martin P. *Nigeria: Current Issues and Historical Background.* Hauppauge, N.Y.: Nova Science Publishers, 2002.

Reynolds, Jonathan T. *The Time of Politics (Zamanin Siyasa). Islam and the Politics of Legitimacy in Northern Nigeria, 1950–1966.* Lanham, Md.: University Press of America, 2001.

Vaughn, Olufemi. *Nigerian Chiefs: Traditional Power in Modern Politics.* Rochester, N.Y.: University of Rochester Press, 2000.

Yakubu, Alhaji M. "Coercing the Old Guard Emirs in Northern Nigeria: The Abdication of Yakubu III of Bauchi, 1954." *African Affairs* 92 (October, 1993): 593–605.

Balfour, Arthur (first earl of Balfour)

(1848–1930) *prime minister of Great Britain*

Arthur James Balfour was born in Whittinghame, East Lothian, Scotland, on July 25, 1848, the son of a wealthy landowner. His patrician origins afforded him opportunities for a splendid education and he passed through Eton and Cambridge University with distinction, majoring in philosophy. Over the course of a long lifetime he penned numerous tracts on religion and science, won many awards, and held the chancellorship of Cambridge University. However, acting upon the advice of his uncle, Lord Salisbury, himself a future prime minister, young Balfour entered politics. He won a seat in Parliament in 1874 as a Conservative and acquired a reputation as a brilliant debater. When Lord Salisbury became prime minister, Balfour joined his uncle's cabinet in several capacities, notably as chief secretary of Ireland (1887–91). Here Balfour suppressed civil unrest with a firm hand, but also took constructive measures to eliminate absentee landlordism and grant acreage to landless peasants. Given his intellect, social connections, and parliamentary skills, Balfour seemed destined for greatness, and by 1895 he was head of the House of

Commons. When Lord Salisbury resigned from office for health reasons in July 1902, Balfour succeeded him as prime minister.

Being intellectually inclined, Balfour operated more or less on the basis of moral principles. Politically he was loath to engage in backroom machinations that generally bring about compromise and consensus. Consequently, many of his programs, while successful, generated little party or public enthusiasm. His most important endeavor, the Education Act of 1902, completely overhauled English primary and secondary education and rendered it more efficient and timely. He then sponsored the Irish Land Purchase of 1903, which codified many of the reforms he had sponsored as Irish secretary. Balfour also was acutely interested in military affairs, having witnessed the often disastrous performance of British forces during the recent Boer War (1899–1902). The result was creation of the Committee of Imperial Defense in 1904, a body of experts who met to coordinate future strategic planning for the empire. Finally, mindful of rising militarism under Kaiser WILHELM II, Balfour concluded the Anglo-French Entente of 1904, which normalized relations between the two military powers and established an alliance against Germany if war erupted. Unfortunately, all these expedients bore fruit long after their author had left office, and none were appreciated at the time. Balfour eventually lost his prime ministership when the Conservatives split over the issue of trade protectionism in December 1905. Having failed to heal the rift between feuding factions, he resigned and called a general election, resoundingly won by the Liberals under HENRY CAMPBELL-BANNERMAN.

Out of power, Balfour resumed the role of head of the Conservative Party and adopted obstructionist modes of blocking Liberal budgets within the House of Lords. Consequently, in 1911 Prime Minister HERBERT HENRY ASQUITH pushed through laws that stripped the upper house of vetoing power in budgetary matters. It was an embarrassing defeat for the Conservatives, and Balfour resigned from politics altogether. However, during World War I Asquith brought him into the cabinet as first lord of the Admiralty to replace WINSTON CHURCHILL, and DAVID LLOYD GEORGE subsequently appointed him foreign secretary. His most notable accomplishment was the 1917 Balfour Declaration, made at the urging of Zionist CHAIM WEIZMANN, which committed Great Britain to creation of a Jewish state in British-controlled Palestine. It was a controversial document that muddied relations between Arabs, Jews, and the West to the present time, especially once the state of Israel emerged in 1948. After the war, Balfour attended the Paris Peace Conference and lent his acumen to negotiating the 1919 Treaty of Versailles. Two years later he represented Great Britain in the Washington naval conference of 1921, striking up cordial relations with his fellow scholar, President WOODROW WILSON. He was elevated to the peerage as Earl Balfour in 1922 and served as an elder statesman in the STANLEY BALDWIN administration before retiring to private life in June 1929, aged 80 years. His final act, the Balfour Report, provided an intellectual and constitutional framework for what would emerge as the British Commonwealth. Balfour died on March 19, 1930, in Surrey, England, not highly regarded as a prime minister or party leader, but widely respected as an intellectual and diplomat.

Further Reading

Balfour, Arthur J. *Retrospect: An Unfinished Autobiography, 1848–1886.* Boston: Houghton, Mifflin, 1930.

Hudson, David R. C. *The Ireland That We Make: Arthur and Gerard Balfour's Contributions to the Origins of Modern Ireland.* Akron, Ohio: University of Akron Press, 2002.

Marshall, Peter. "The Balfour Formula and the Evolution of the Commonwealth." *Round Table* no. 361 (September 2001): 541–553.

Rasor, Eugene L. *Arthur J. Balfour, 1848–1930: Historiography and Annotated Bibliography.* Westport, Conn.: Greenwood Press, 1998.

Renton, James E. "The Historiography and the Balfour Declaration: Towards a Multi-Causal Framework." *Journal of Israeli History* 19 (Summer 1998): 109–128.

Thornton, A. P. "Balfour and Zionism." *Queen's Quarterly* 105, no. 4 (1998): 556–576.

Tomes, Jason. *Balfour and Foreign Policy: The International Thought of a Conservative Statesman.* New York: Cambridge University Press, 1997.

Bandaranaike, Solomon West Ridgeway Dias

(1899–1959) *prime minister of Sri Lanka*

Solomon West Ridgeway Dias Bandaranaike was born in Veyangoda, Ceylon (modern Sri Lanka), on January 8,

1899, the son of a wealthy Christian landowner. This put him distinctly in a minority as the island was overwhelmingly Buddhist or Hindu. Bandaranaike was well educated at private schools and ultimately graduated from Oxford University in England in 1925. He was called to the bar at London but returned home to practice law. After several years he developed a taste for politics and ran for a seat on the State Council as member and secretary of the Ceylon National Congress (CNC). Finding this organization too conservative for his tastes, Bandaranaike converted to Buddhism and established a Sinhalese nationalist party, the Sinhala Maha Sabha, in 1937. A cornerstone of his policy was the belief that Sinhalese should be the island's official language, even at the expense of the minority Hindu Tamils occupying the northern reaches of the island. After Great Britain released Ceylon in 1947, Bandaranaike brought his group into the ranks of a new organization, the United National Party (UNP), which had long agitated for independence. That same year Bandaranaike gained election to the new House of Representatives, and the first prime minister, D. D. Senanayake, also appointed him minister of health and local government. In time Bandaranaike experienced a falling-out with the government, quit the UNP, and established the decidedly leftist Sri Lanka Freedom Party (SLFP) in July 1951. When Senanayake was killed in a car crash the following year he campaigned hard to succeed him, but was badly beaten by the UNP. The insurgents then regrouped while Bandaranaike served as head of the opposition in Parliament.

Unknown at the time, Bandaranaike's agitation had unleashed the forces of Sinhala nationalism on the island's political landscape. It flourished over the next four years, so that by the 1956 elections, more than 10,000 Buddhist priests campaigned door-to-door on Bandaranaike's behalf, canvassing votes and singing his praises. That year the SLFP won a resounding victory, and he became the island republic's fourth prime minister. Having renounced both Christianity and Western influences, he intended to govern strictly with the interests of his Buddhist/Sinhalese power base in mind. He initially took a hard line toward the British and demanded that they abandon their naval bases, which was accomplished, but he subsequently decided to remain within the Commonwealth. Consistent with his leftist philosophy, he joined the unaligned, or Third World, movement, which preached neutrality in the cold war. He also broke with political convention by

establishing diplomatic relations with the Soviet Union, China, and other communist nations.

On the domestic front, Bandaranaike nationalized many industries, redistributed land to the peasants and established generous welfare and medical programs for the poor. These acts won him much popularity but also drained the treasury and ruined the economy. Within months discontent arose over skyrocketing rates of unemployment. However, Bandaranaike deflected public anger through passage of his long-coveted Official Language Act, which enshrined Sinhalese as the island's official dialect. Such arrogance angered the sizable Tamil minority, who felt that they and their culture were being marginalized, but it pleased hard-line Buddhists in the SLFP. Disaffected Tamils then began a low-intensity terror campaign and the first stages of a secessionist movement. Bandaranaike apparently underestimated the anger his policies generated on both sides of the issue, and he met with high-ranking Tamils to discuss compromise. When the outlines of an agreement granting greater autonomy to the Tamils was reached, it outraged many Sinhalese nationalists in turn. On September 25, 1959, Bandaranaike was assassinated by a Buddhist monk for betraying the cause. The following year he was succeeded by his wife, Sirimavo Bandaranaike, who became the island's first woman prime minister and continued many of her late husband's policies. These, however, have continued to fuel Tamil violence against the Sinhalese majority to the present time.

Further Reading

Alles, A. C. *The Assassination of a Prime Minister.* New York: Vantage Press, 1986.

Gooneratne, Tilak E. *S. W. R. D. Bandaranaike, Prime Minister of Ceylon, April 1956–26 September 1959.* London: Third World Promoter, Ltd., 1995.

Gooneratne, Yasmine. *Relative Merits: A Personal Memoir of the Bandaranaike Family of Sri Lanka.* New York: St. Martin's Press, 1986.

Jayawardena, Kumari. *Nobodies to Somebodies: The Rise of the Colonial Bourgeoisie in Sri Lanka.* New York: Zed Books, 2002.

Manor, James. *The Expedient Utopian: Bandaranaike and Ceylon.* New York: Cambridge University Press, 1989.

Silva, K. "Sri Lanka: The Bandaranaikes in the Island's Politics and Public Life." *Round Table* no. 350 (April 1999): 241–280.

Barrientos Ortuño, René (1919–1969) *president of Bolivia*

René Barrientos Ortuño was born in Tunarí, Cochabamba, Bolivia, on May 30, 1919, the son of a Spanish-speaking father and an Indian peasant mother. While growing up he became fluent in Quechua, a major Indian dialect, and was deeply affected by the grinding poverty of the peasant classes. After graduating from high school, Barrientos enrolled at a nearby military academy but was briefly expelled for political activism. By 1943 he was commissioned a lieutenant in the Bolivian air force and also maintained close links to the newly formed Movimiento Nacionalista Revolucionario (MNR), National Revolutionary Movement, of VÍCTOR PAZ ESTENSSORO. In 1952 Paz Estenssoro came to power through a bloody coup with the tacit backing of many young military officers like Barrientos. The MNR then embarked on much needed reforms such as land redistribution to the Indians, better education for all classes, and economic growth. Barrientos, meanwhile, ventured to the United States for additional military training, where he absorbed the values of various "civic action" programs for indigenous poor people. Returning to Bolivia, he spent many years assisting the Indians of his native Cochabamba, winning their public support in return. His vocal support for MNR activities also resulted in his steady rise to general in Bolivia's small air force.

The turning point in Barrientos's career came in 1964 when Paz Estenssoro announced he was running for a third term. Growing politically ambitious, Barrientos prevailed upon the executive to accept him as a vice presidential running mate. Paz Estenssoro agreed, but only after insisting that Barrientos leave the military and campaign as a civilian. Accordingly, the general resigned his commission before barnstorming the countryside. Barrientos proved especially effective in addressing Indian peasants in their native tongue, promising them continuing reforms if elected. Consequently, Paz Estenssoro carried the popular vote by wide margins, and he was swept back into power in August 1964. However, only three months into his third term, Paz Estenssoro was suddenly toppled by Bolivia's 184th military coup. This had been engineered by Barrientos and General Alfredo Ovando Candía, and the two men agreed to run the country as a copresidency for the next two years. However, true to his word, Barrientos kept visiting the countryside, displaying great compassion for the poor Indians who com-pose the majority of Bolivia's population. They looked upon him as a father figure and he went to great lengths to craft a dominant political alliance, the Frente de la Revolución Boliviana (FRB), Bolivian Revolutionary Front, consisting of the military, business interests, conservative peasant organizations, and his own Popular Christian Movement. Having established his political base, Barrientos withdrew from the ruling junta and, in a quest for political legitimacy, sought the presidency as a civilian.

Throughout most of 1966, Barrientos conducted an American-style campaign, flying around the country in his helicopter and personally meeting with his constituents. The peasants returned his attention with massive support, and in July 1966 the FRB carried the day with 62 percent of votes cast. For the next three years Barrientos ruled with a benevolent, if iron, hand. He continued the policy of land distribution to the peasants and continued winning their support. This paid immediate dividends in 1967 when they assisted the army in capturing and killing the noted guerrilla Ernesto "Che" Guevara. But Barrientos was intolerant toward worker unrest, and he unflinchingly used military force to crush several strikes by miners. Within months, organized labor had ceased to be a factor in the political equation. Barrientos also proved adept at promoting growth through foreign investment and cultivating close personal ties with business classes and other elites. Bolivia was enjoying one of its brief periods of political stability and economic growth when Barrientos was killed in a helicopter crash on April 27, 1969. He was succeeded by Vice President Luis Adolfo Siles Salinas who, in turn, was overthrown by General Ovando five months later. Barrientos was unique in being a military populist who employed right-wing techniques to support left-wing programs.

Further Reading

Dunkerly, James. *Barrientos and Debray.* London: Institute of Latin American Studies, 1992.

Garcia, Arganaras Fernando. "Raison d'etat and Bolivia's Deadlock." Unpublished Ph.D. diss., Yale University, 1991.

Hendel, Fred. *Revolutions in Bolivia.* Ypsilanti, Mich.: Aventura Press, 1992.

Holtey, Joseph C. "Bolivia: The Era of René Barrientos Ortuño, 1964–1969." Unpublished master's thesis, University of Arizona, 1973.

Lussier, Virginia. "Barrientos and Beyond." *Contemporary Review* no. 215 (September 1969): 137–139.

Ruhl, M. J. "National Revolution to Revolution of National Restoration: Arms and Factional Politics in Bolivia." *Inter-American Economic Affairs* 39 (fall 1985): 63–80.

Barton, Edmund (1849–1920) *prime minister of Australia*

Edmund Barton was born in Sydney, New South Wales, on January 18, 1849, the son of a financier. Australia was then a British colony with a patchwork of scattered settlements across the length and breadth of a huge, largely uninhabited continent. With help from his father, Barton attended the University of Sydney, from which he graduated in 1870. He then decided to pursue legal studies, and in 1872 gained admission into the bar. Barton began his political career in 1877 when he unsuccessfully ran for a seat in the New South Wales legislative assembly. However, he was victorious two years later and, a consummate politician by nature, rose to become Speaker of the House by 1883. After 1887 Barton was a popular fixture in provincial politics, and he rose through a succession of important posts, including attorney general (1889–93). But, despite his obvious abilities, Barton gained an unsavory reputation for laziness and being smitten by unending pursuit of the "good life," his trademark slogan. It was not until 1889, when he heard Sir Henry Parkes give an impassioned speech on the subject of federation (or national unity) that his genuine talents emerged. Barton subsequently threw himself wholeheartedly into the quest for Australian statehood. This had long been the goal of Parkes, who in 1891 convened a political convention to promote federation, but failed. At length Barton was tapped to succeed him as head of the movement and, assisted by ALFRED DEAKIN of Victoria, he prevailed upon the New South Wales territorial legislature to accept federation. In 1897 he summoned another political convention, where delegates tasked him with drafting a constitution over continuing opposition from New South Wales and Western Australia. Certain amendments regarding local sovereignty were then implemented and a final draft was completed and circulated around the colony. By July 1900 the majority of voters approved adoption of this document, the Commonwealth Constitution Bill, which now required passage by the English Parliament to become law.

That year Barton headed a delegation to Great Britain to legalize the constitution and make Australia a nation. After continued wrangling, whereby it was agreed that England would still manage Australia's foreign affairs, the federal constitution won parliamentary approval in May 1900. It went into effect on January 1, 1901, and the new Commonwealth of Australia came into being. Given his popularity and the fact that he had done more for federation than any other individual, Barton gained appointment as Australia's first prime minister. He was knighted in 1902, while his ally Deakin served as the first attorney general.

Barton's two years in office were productive, if tempestuous. He intended to establish and maintain a protectionist regime to shelter the country's nascent industries but encountered heavy opposition from committed free traders in the new Parliament. Nonetheless, Barton won support for the nation's first tariff and also pushed through the Immigration Restriction Act that blocked Asian entry to Australia. Among his other accomplishments were organizing the machinery of federal governance and a high court, finalizing a Commonwealth Defense Force, and forcibly deporting Kanakas (native laborers) back to New Guinea. But after two years in high office Barton had grown weary of political bickering, so he tendered his resignation in favor of Deakin. Barton then took his seat on the Australian High Court from which he rendered several important decisions relative to federation. His judgment generally supported states' rights, but during World War I he lent his weight to government control of the economy pending the return of peace. Barton functioned effectively in this capacity for the next 17 years before dying suddenly at Medlow Bath, New South Wales, on January 7, 1920. He remains highly respected as the architect of Australian nationhood and its first national leader of note.

Further Reading

Birrell, Robert. *Federation: The Secret Story.* Sydney: Duffy and Snellgrove, 2001.

Bolton, Geoffrey. *Edmund Barton: One Man for the Job.* Sydney: Allen & Unwin, 2000.

Martin, Ged. *Australia, New Zealand, and Federation; 1883–1901.* London: Menzies Centre for Australian Studies, King's College, London, 2001.

Reynolds, John. *Edmund Barton.* Melbourne, Victoria: Bookman, 1999.

Simms, Marian, and John Bannon. *1901: The Forgotten Election.* St. Lucia, Queensland: University of Queensland Press, 2001.

Ward, John M. *The State and the People: Australian Federation and Nation-Making, 1870–1901.* Leichhardt, New South Wales: Federation Press, 2001.

Batista, Fulgencio (1901–1973) *president of Cuba*

Fulgencio Batista y Zaldívar was born in Banes, Cuba, on January 16, 1901, into a poor working-class family. He was educated at Quaker missionary schools and subsequently held down menial jobs. In 1921 Batista joined the Cuban army and rose quickly to sergeant/stenographer. This placed him within the inner circles of the military's power structure and he slyly absorbed how it operated. In August 1933 he and other disgruntled elements joined a movement that deposed dictator Gerardo Machado y Morales. Three weeks later Batista proved instrumental in organizing the so-called Sergeant's Revolt, which overthrew provisional president Carlos Manuel de Céspedes. Here they were supported by student groups, revolutionaries, and other malcontents, but by now Batista had emerged as a genuine power broker in Cuba. A new executive, Ramón Grau San Martín, appointed him colonel chief of staff, which only tightened his control over the military. Grau, a left-wing extremist, then embarked on sweeping social legislation and anti-American rhetoric. At the urging of the United States government, Batista suddenly toppled Grau in January 1934. However, rather than rule like a traditional Latin American caudillo (strongman) Batista remained out of the political arena. Instead, he chose to rule Cuba through a succession of puppet presidents over the next six years. He also allowed a surprising degree of progressive social legislation to pass, which improved the life of the average Cuban citizen. His popularity increased commensurately, so in 1940, Batista sought political legitimization by running for the presidency himself. He then bested Grau at the voting booth and won a four-year term.

In office, Batista continuing ruling with a strong hand over political dissent and economic policy, but he proved surprisingly liberal toward the poor. And because the advent of World War II coincided with his tenure in office, he received increasing attention from the administration of President FRANKLIN D. ROOSEVELT. The Americans badly needed bases in Cuba and acquisition of the island's large sugar crop, so Batista granted both in exchange for an influx of foreign aid. He even managed to buy off the upper and middle classes controlling sugar production, because prices were at an all-time high. Cuba basically thrived during his four years in office, and Batista and his cronies also profited enormously. However, he remained pragmatically nonideological, and in 1943 his government became the first in Latin America to employ communists at the cabinet level. In 1944 he even accepted Roosevelt's advice to observe strict term limitations in office and step down. Thereafter, when Grau was returned to office, Batista moved to self-imposed exile in Florida to enjoy his considerable wealth. He left behind a record of prosperity, but also one of increased corruption, which only intensified under Grau and his successor, Carlos Prío Socarrás. The stage was being set for a major social upheaval.

Batista ended his exile in 1948 by coming home and winning a seat in the Cuban senate. Four years later he announced his intention to run again for president and outwardly moved to establish his own party. Suddenly, on March 10, 1952, he overthrew the Prío regime with the help of army officers. The change was initially welcomed by Cubans, weary of corruption, but this time Batista ran the nation for the sole purpose of self-enrichment. Social legislation was neglected, while gangsterism and political cronyism became rampant. Worse, the regime responded to political dissidence with outright force and repression. Discontent eventually trickled up from the peasants to members of the middle class, including Fidel Castro. This former lawyer executed a botched attack on an army barracks on July 26, 1953, and was jailed. In one of his biggest political errors, Batista released Castro and exiled him to Mexico. From there Castro bided his time, reorganized his followers, and invaded Cuba again in 1956. He again suffered defeat, but he brought a nascent guerrilla movement into Cuba's Sierra Maestra, fueled by discontent over corruption, repression, and desire for change. Batista's response was to crack down harder, which only embarrassed the country internationally and swelled rebel ranks. By 1958 the tide of fighting had swung in Castro's favor and Batista's government was in such disarray that President DWIGHT D. EISENHOWER cut off all military aid. Unable to stem the insurgency, Batista fled Cuba for the Dominican Republic on January 1, 1959, while Castro entered Havana in triumph. Batista eventually made his way to Spain and luxurious exile. Thereafter he adopted a low profile and died in Guadalmina, Spain, on August 6, 1973. Despite the ignominious end of his government, Batista had been the most influential Cuban political figure for over two decades.

Further Reading

Gellman, Irwin F. *Roosevelt and Batista: Good Neighbor Diplomacy in Cuba, 1933–1945.* Albuquerque: University of New Mexico Press, 1973.

Halperin, Ernest. *Fidel Castro's Road to Power.* Cambridge, Mass.: Center for International Studies, 1970.

Hargrove, Claude. "Fulgencio Batista: Politics of the Electoral Process in Cuba, 1933–1944." Unpublished Ph.D. diss., Howard University, 1979.

Mallin, Jay. *Fulgencio Batista: Ousted Cuban Dictator.* Charlotteville, N.Y.: SamHar Press, 1974.

Perez, G. E. G. *Insurrection and Revolution: Armed Struggle in Cuba, 1952–1959.* Boulder, Colo.: Lynne Rienner Pubs., 1996.

Whitney, Robert. *State and Revolution in Cuba: Mass Mobilization and Political Change, 1920–1940.* Chapel Hill: University of North Carolina Press, 2001.

Batlle y Ordóñez, José (1856–1929) *president of Uruguay*

José Batlle y Ordóñez was born in Montevideo on May 21, 1856, the son of a former general and president of Uruguay. His family embraced a long tradition of political activism within the Colorado Party, a liberal organization based in the nation's urban centers. Their opponents, the Blancos, were rural conservatives who drew their strength from the agrarian countryside. Batlle attended the National University in 1873, but did not graduate and spent several months roaming about Paris. He returned home intending to work as a journalist on behalf of social causes and in 1886 briefly fought in an uprising against dictator Maximo Santos. He was captured but spared, owing to the reputation of his father, who served Uruguay well and retired without looting the treasury. Thereafter, Batlle intensified his efforts to reform the

nation through political means. He began by joining the Colorado Party, which was dispirited and in need of reorganization. In July 1886 he also founded the newspaper *El Día,* which became the party's partisan mouthpiece and the first mass-circulation paper in Uruguayan history. By 1890 he won his first election to the House of Deputies, and in 1897 advanced his fortunes by becoming a senator. However, not everybody in the Colorado Party appreciated Batlle's crusading spirit for fiscal reform, and his election as president of the Senate split that body deeply. Ultimately, hostile factions acting in concert with Blanco members forced him to concede his position. But Batlle gained many allies in his quest for social justice, and in March 1903 he was elected president of Uruguay for a four-year term.

Batlle assumed office with a reform agenda at hand, but his first years were preoccupied by waging civil war. Apparently, a conservative Blanco faction took up arms in the countryside and fought the government stubbornly for two years. The military finally prevailed after killing rebel leader Aparicio Saravia, and Batlle could finally address the nation's pressing social problems. He pursued this challenge hesitatingly at first, realizing the magnitude of political opposition against him. Nevertheless, he presided over such moderate, if landmark, reforms as reducing income taxes on public workers, building secondary schools in all cities, and granting women the right of divorce. Batlle was clearly disappointed by his inability to enact sweeping changes but he had established the groundwork for later, greater reform.

When Batlle's term in office expired he stepped down and spent several years in Europe studying contemporary social and political institutions. He was especially impressed by governance in Switzerland, which was headed by a plural presidency of several members. The former executive saw in this an opportunity to curb Uruguay's penchant for one-man dictatorships, and he returned home in 1911 determined to effect greater change. His columns in *El Día* began touting the outlines of a bold social and economic program intent on forever altering the nation's political landscape. The public readily absorbed Batlle's intentions, and in March 1911 he was reelected president by overwhelming margins. His second term was much more progressive and productive than the first. In 1912 Batlle managed to pass comprehensive life insurance for workers and also established an eight-hour working day and the right to strike. Moreover, the death penalty was abolished, women's rights expanded, and governmental stores created whereby subsidized essentials were purchased at reduced prices. In time, the entire package of legislation became popularly hailed as Batllismo, a government-sponsored policy aimed at fostering greater democracy and social justice. With time his values were indelibly imprinted on Uruguayan democracy, and are embraced to the present day.

Batlle failed, however, in his attempt to establish the much vaunted collective presidency, or *colegiado,* which was bitterly resisted from many quarters. At length he abandoned the quest, retiring from office in 1915 amid national popularity. Batlle nevertheless continued agitating among political allies for adoption of the scheme and in 1918, after warning the establishment that he might run a third time, the government adopted the *colegiado* in the new constitution. Thereafter, Uruguay was ruled by a single executive with reduced powers, assisted by eight elected assistants, the National Council of Administration. The scheme proved unwieldy and was abandoned during the Great Depression in 1933, but it ushered in a period of political stability that Uruguay had never previously enjoyed. Batlle, popularly known as "Don Pepe," continued fomenting reform for the rest of his life, cherished as the father of Uruguayan democracy. He died in Montevideo on October 20, 1929, having conducted one of the earliest effective reform programs in Latin American history. Unlike many of his predecessors, Batlle long held the reins of government, yet used his office to achieve social justice rather than personal gain.

Further Reading

Pazzina, Francisco. "Late Institutionalization and Early Modernization: The Emergence of Uruguay's Liberal Democratic Political Order." *Journal of Latin American Studies* 29 (October 1997): 667–691.

Struthers, David R. "The Batlle Era and Labor in Uruguay: U.S. Low-Intensity Conflict Policy in Latin America." Unpublished master's thesis, University of Texas–Austin, 1990.

Vanger, Milton I. *The Model Country: José Batlle y Ordóñez of Uruguay, 1907–1915.* Hanover, N.H.: University Press of New England, 1980.

Walker, Jack C. "Modernization and Secularization in Uruguay, 1880–1930." Unpublished master's thesis, Abilene Christian University, 1992.

Weinstein, Martin. *Uruguay Democracy at the Crossroads.* Boulder, Colo.: Westview Press, 1988.

Begin, Menachem (1913–1992) *prime minister of Israel*

Menachem Wolfovitch Begin was born in Brest-Litovsk, Russia (modern Belarus), on August 16, 1913, the son of a prominent Jewish activist. As he matured, his father enrolled him in a number of Zionist organizations whose ideology promoted resurrection of the ancient state of Israel. Begin flourished in the role of leader of Betar, a Zionist youth movement, and he became an important spokesman. When World War II commenced in September 1939, he fled to Lithuania to escape Nazi persecution but several family members were captured and killed. In 1940 the Soviet Union occupied Lithuania, arrested Begin for espionage, and sentenced him to an Arctic labor camp for several months. However, once Germany invaded Russia, he was released to join the Polish Free Army and made his way to British-controlled Palestine. His arrival brought within reach his pursuit of a new Jewish state, and Begin, physically small but possessed of steely resolve, refused to let adversity stand in his way.

Begin wasted no time organizing the Irgun Tzevai Leumi, a militant underground militia separate and distinct from the more moderate Haganah under DAVID BEN GURION. As commander, he refrained from attacking British forces occupying the Palestinian Mandate as long as war was waged against Germany. Afterward he commenced an orchestrated terrorist campaign against British and Arabs alike, especially the notorious bombing of the King David Hotel in 1946. On more than one occasion, Ben-Gurion ordered his own forces against the renegade Irgun, which nearly led to a Jewish civil war. At length Begin called off his attacks. Once Israel was established in 1948 with Ben-Gurion as prime minister, Begin founded a conservative party, Herut, and led it in opposition for many years. In 1965 Herut expanded into a coalition by joining with the Liberal Party to form Gahal. During the 1967 war Begin was finally brought into a government of national unity under Prime Minister GOLDA MEIR but, as strident as ever, he quit the coalition to protest peace initiatives sponsored by the United States. Israel had since conquered the West Bank of the Jordan River and with it, Jerusalem, so their retention became a cornerstone of Zionist political and religious ideology. To that end Begin's Gahal alliance with a variety of conservative and religious parties cobbled together a new umbrella organization, Likud (Unity), in 1973. They stridently opposed returning any captured Arab land for peace.

In May 1977 Begin became prime minister when his coalition garnered a majority of seats—the first nonsocialist government in Israeli history. But despite his firm commitment to Zionism, the new leader proved willing to negotiate with some of his more moderately disposed Arab counterparts. In November 1977 he welcomed Egyptian president ANWAR AL-SADAT to Jerusalem to commence peace talks. Discussions were long and tortuous, and had to be partially shepherded along by American president JIMMY CARTER. But perseverance paid off in March 1979 when all three leaders gathered in Washington, D.C., for the historic signing of the Camp David peace accords—the first such agreement between Israel and an Arab state. It stipulated that Begin would withdraw from the Sinai Peninsula, captured in 1967, in exchange for full diplomatic recognition and normalized relations. Both leaders consequently won the Nobel Peace Prize for 1978, although the final disposition of the Palestinian issue remains a burning issue to present times.

In June 1981 Knesset elections resulted in another victory for Likud, although Begin's second administration was viewed by many as counterproductive. In June 1981 he ordered the bombing of an Iraqi atomic power plant to prevent nuclear weapons from being manufactured there. The following year he ordered Israeli forces into Lebanon in an attempt to crush the Palestine Liberation Organization (PLO) under Yasser Arafat. Envisioned as an easy victory, the campaign quickly became bogged down in an endless guerrilla war with heavy losses to both sides. Worse, Begin was partly implicated in a massacre of Palestinian civilians by his Christian militia allies, and several of his cabinet members were forced to resign. Disenchanted by events, saddened by the loss of his wife, and ailing, Begin suddenly resigned from office on September 16, 1983, and was replaced by Yitzhak Shamir. He lived the remainder of his life in obscurity before dying in Tel Aviv on March 9, 1992, an uncompromising defender of Israel's right to exist and one of its most controversial leaders.

Further Reading

Begin, Menachem. *The Revolt: The Story of the Irgun.* New York: Nash Pub. Co., 1978.

Mahler, Gregory S., ed. *Israel After Begin.* Albany: State University of New York Press, 1990.

Rabinowitz, Stanley. "Who Is a Jew: Prime Minister Begin and the Jewish Question." *Judaism* 46 (summer 1997): 293–302.

Seidman, Hillel. *Menachem Begin: His Life and Legacy.* New York: Shengold, 1990.

Shindler, Colin. *Israel, Likud, and the Zionist Dream: Power, Politics, and Ideology from Begin to Netanyahu.* New York: Tauris, 1995.

Temko, Ned. *To Win or Die: A Personal Portrait of Menachem Begin.* New York: William Morrow, 1987.

Belaúnde Terry, Fernando (1912–2002) *president of Peru*

Fernando Belaúnde Terry was born in Lima, Peru, on October 7, 1912, into a distinguished family of aristocrats and public servants. His father, a former prime minister, was exiled abroad and Belaúnde spent his most formative years in Paris, France, studying architecture. He subsequently obtained a bachelor's degree in architecture from the University of Texas in 1935. Belaúnde then returned to Peru and practiced his craft with considerable success, becoming dean of the School of Architecture at Lima's Catholic University and founder of the Peruvian Urban Institute. He commenced politicking in 1945 by being elected to Congress with the National Democratic Front, a party of moderate reformers. When the government was overthrown by military forces under General MANUEL ODRÍA in 1948, he resumed his private practice and toured the country, touting much-needed national reforms. Democracy was finally restored in 1956 and Belaúnde's national reputation enabled him to run for the presidency, which he narrowly lost to Manuel Prado y Ugarteche. Six years later he tried again at the head of his own Acción Popular (AP), Popular Action party, and again was narrowly defeated by Victor Raúl Haya de la Torre. However, because neither man won an outright majority, the military invalidated the results and called for a new election. In 1963 Belaúnde finally triumphed by a substantial margin.

Once empowered, Belaúnde attempted to enact a package of sweeping social and economic reforms and projects. Foremost among these was his ambitious Andean jungle highway, aimed at accessing the vast natural resources of the interior. He also pushed through important legislation touching on health care and improved education, along with the Popular Cooperation program to distribute tools for constructing public works. For all his good intentions, however, Belaúnde was thwarted in implementing serious change by a majority coalition of opponents in Congress. These stymied his attempts to raise revenue through taxation, and he was forced into deficit spending to finance his many projects. This only fueled rising inflation at a time of high unemployment. Belaúnde also erred by attempting to establish comfortable relations with an American oil firm, the International Petroleum Company, after campaigning on a platform to nationalize it. When details of a generous compensation deal became known, a public uproar ensued. This tumult, combined with a sagging national economy, gave General JUAN VELASCO sufficient pretext for intervention, and on October 3, 1968, he ousted the civilian regime.

The former president returned to the United States in exile, where he lectured for many years at Harvard, Columbia, and Johns Hopkins Universities. He finally returned to Peru in 1975 after military rulers granted a general amnesty. Democracy was restored in 1980, and Belaúnde ran again for the presidency with the AP, winning with 45 percent of votes cast. It was an impressive encore, but in practice his second term in office proved as disappointing as his first. Peru by then was staggered by huge national debts and an unresponsive economy. Furthermore, inflation, natural disasters, and weak foreign markets all conspired to sink the country deeper into recession. But the greatest challenge facing Belaúnde—if not all Peruvians—was the rise of a Maoist guerrilla movement, the Shining Path, which waged a protracted terrorist war against military and civilians alike. Belaúnde responded with counterinsurgency measures, but the rebels acted with seeming immunity. Further crackdowns resulted in allegations of widespread abuse and human rights violations. Beset by turmoil and events beyond his control, Belaúnde ran against ALAN GARCÍA PÉREZ of the Alianza Popular Revolucionario Americana (APRA), American Revolutionary Popular Alliance, in April 1985 and lost with only 5 percent of the vote. However, he became the first civilian authority in Peru to peacefully transfer power to another party. The former executive remained in politics and served as a senator until 1992. Belaúnde died in Lima on June 6, 2002, enjoying more respect in death than he ever did as president.

Further Reading

Davila, Marai del Pilar. "The Peruvian Military in the 1960s: The Impact of Guerrilla Insurgency and Belaúnde's Failed Reforms." Unpublished master's thesis, University of Texas–Austin, 1990.

Gorman, Stephen M., ed. *Post-Revolutionary Peru: The Politics of Transformation.* Boulder, Colo.: Westview Press, 1982.

Kuczynski-Godard, Pedro-Pablo. *Peruvian Democracy under Economic Stress: An Account of the Belaúnde Administration, 1963–1968.* Princeton, N.J.: Princeton University Press, 1977.

Stern, Steve J., ed. *Shining and Other Paths: War and Society in Peru, 1980–1995.* Durham, N.C.: Duke University Press, 1998.

Weber, Cynthia. "Representing Debt: Peruvian Presidents Belaúnde's and García's Reading/Writing of Peruvian Debt." *International Studies Quarterly* 34 (September 1990): 353–365.

Werlich, D. P. "Debt, Democracy, and Terrorism in Peru." *Current History* 86 (January 1987): 29–32.

Ben Bella, Ahmed (1918–) *president of Algeria*
Ahmed Ben Bella was born in the town of Maghnia, Algeria, on December 25, 1918, the son of a farmer. His country being a French colonial possession, he received a Western-style education before returning to work on his father's farm. Young Ben Bella was outraged by the discriminatory policies of Europeans toward Muslims and he vowed one day to oppose them. In World War II Ben Bella was conscripted into the French army and fought with distinction, winning several medals. After the war he considered remaining with the military but was further angered when French authorities discharged him because he was Arabic. Ben Bella returned home by 1946 and joined several clandestine organizations to foment armed resistance against France. The most important of these, the Secret Organization, sought to strike directly at colonial assets and garrisons. In 1949 Ben Bella directed an attack on a post office but was subsequently arrested and jailed. He remained incarcerated until he staged a daring escape in 1952 and made his way to Egypt. There he found an ally in President

GAMAL ABDEL NASSER, another strident Arab nationalist, who sympathized with Ben Bella and other Algerian expatriates. He provided them with a safe haven, money, technical advice, and weapons to carry on their struggle.

Algerian resentment against colonial rule coalesced around several individuals, including Ben Bella, and they met in November 1954 to forge an armed organization called the Front de Libération National (FLN) to wage guerrilla warfare. France responded by pouring thousands of troops into Algeria, where they conducted a ruthless counterinsurgency campaign. Consequently, thousands of people died in one of history's most vicious colonial wars. Ben Bella, as the principal arms runner for the FLN, became a wanted man, and the French laid a trap to snare him. On August 20, 1956, two French pilots flying Ben Bella and others from discussions in Morocco suddenly diverted the craft to Algeria, where its occupants were arrested. Ben Bella subsequently endured six years of incarceration while the war for independence raged without him. But by 1962 France had conceded defeat and a referendum on independence passed overwhelmingly. Ben Bella and other political detainees were then freed and released to their transformed homeland.

While Ben Bella was absent, several strong leaders emerged to replace him, and friction ensued following his return. However, he secured a strategic alliance with Colonel HOUARI BOUMÉDIENNE, commander of the FLN's military wing, and established a rival government, the Political Bureau. The two then went on to intimidate and eliminate all potential rivals. In October 1962 national elections legitimized the new regime with Ben Bella as prime minister. The following year a new constitution was adopted, under which he became the first president of independent Algeria. Given his life experiences, the new executive was stridently anticolonial and prorevolutionary in outlook. He formed close ties with the Soviet Union and pushed for coordination with other developing nations in the Nonaligned Movement. Domestically, Ben Bella imposed stringent socialist policies upon the national economy while also touting a return to traditional Muslim values. He then consolidated his control by adopting one-party rule through the National Liberation Front and began cracking down on even minor dissent. The degree of oppression alarmed Boumédienne, his erstwhile ally, who suddenly overthrew Ben Bella in a bloodless coup on June 19, 1965. The deposed president remained under house arrest for the next 15 years without trial.

Ben Bella was finally released by President BENJEDID CHADLI in October 1980. He thereupon entered self-imposed exile in France for a decade, mixing with other dissidents and calling for creation of a pluralist democracy. He returned in 1990 only to witness the eruption of an Islamic-inspired civil war two years later. In 1995 the aged statesman was tapped to serve as a negotiator in Rome between the warring factions, but otherwise his impact on events has been null. Though marginalized politically, Ben Bella's reputation as one of the driving forces behind Algerian independence is secure.

Further Reading

Connelly, Matthew J. *A Diplomatic Revolution: Algeria's Fight for Independence and the Origins of the Post-Cold War Era.* New York: Oxford University Press, 2002.

Cook, James J., and Alf A. Heggoy. "The American Periodical Press and Ahmed Ben Bella." *Muslim World* 6, no. 4 (1971): 293–302.

Derradji, Abder-Rahmane. *A Concise History of Political Violence in Algeria, 1954–2000: Brothers in Faith, Enemies in Arms.* Lewiston, N.Y.: E. Mellen Press, 2002.

Gleijeses, Piero. "Cuba's First Venture in Africa: Algeria, 1961–1965," *Journal of Latin American Studies* 28 (February 1996): 159–196.

Gosnell, Jonathan K. *The Politics of Frenchness in Colonial Algeria, 1930–1954.* Rochester, N.Y.: University of Rochester Press, 2002.

Knauss, P. R. *The Persistence of Patriarchy: Class, Gender, and Ideology in Twentieth-Century Algeria.* New York: Praeger Publishers, 1987.

Beneš, Edvard (1884–1948) *president of Czechoslovakia*

Edvard Beneš was born in Kozlany, Bohemia, on May 28, 1884, one of 10 children from a peasant farmer family. Despite his poverty he thrived academically and attended various academies in Prague and Paris, earning advanced degrees. There he also befriended TOMÁŠ MASARYK, a leading Czech nationalist. Because Beneš's homeland constituted part of the Austro-Hungarian Empire, he was drafted during World War I, but an old leg injury precluded him from military service. Thereafter he joined the Maffia, a clandestine organiza-

Edvard Beneš *(Library of Congress)*

tion dedicated to overthrowing the tottering Hapsburg monarchy. In time he made his way to Paris to function as secretary general of the Czechoslovak National Council, which agitated for national independence. In 1918 the victorious Allies recognized the council as a government-in-exile, and even before the Austro-Hungarian Empire surrendered, the new nation of Czechoslovakia emerged on October 28, 1918. Masaryk was then installed as president, while Beneš gained appointment as foreign minister at the age of 34. He occupied this post with great distinction over the next 15 years.

Political independence for Czechoslovakia did not translate into national security, for the country was small and surrounded by larger, more powerful neighbors. Equally disconcerting, its population contained large swathes of minorities, including Germans, Hungarians, and Poles, forcibly separated from their homelands. It fell upon Beneš to secure defensive treaties with smaller countries to shore up Czechoslovakia's position. Fortunately, he proved adept

as a diplomat and successfully concluded the so-called Little Entente with Romania and Yugoslavia. This was envisioned as a counterweight to Hungary and Poland, and would forestall any territorial claims on minority-dominated sections of his country. In 1935 France also subscribed to the arrangement. So strongly did Beneš believe in treaties to deter aggression that he enthusiastically embraced U.S. president WOODROW WILSON's new League of Nations, created after World War I to circumvent future conflict. He soon gained international recognition as one of the world's most successful diplomats, and served as president of the league no less than six times. Ever the realist, Beneš acknowledged that he would sooner or later have to deal with the Soviet Union's JOSEPH STALIN. He thereupon concluded several mutual defense treaties with Russia and successfully campaigned for its entrance into the League of Nations, winning Stalin's trust.

By December 1935 the ailing Masaryk had resigned from office and Beneš was elected to succeed him. But now Europe faced the specter of a resurgent Germany under Chancellor ADOLF HITLER and his Nazi party. A major facet of Hitler's plans for conquest entailed absorption of all German-speaking parts of Europe. In the spring of 1938 the Nazis peacefully acquired Austria, and Hitler began agitating for acquisition of Czechoslovakia's Sudetenland, home to a sizable German minority. Beneš refused to negotiate with the Germans and fell back upon his defensive arrangements with France and Great Britain. Unknown to him, however, those governments were militarily weak and desperate to avoid another conflict with Germany. British prime minister NEVILLE CHAMBERLAIN then flew to Munich and, without consulting Beneš, agreed to the partitioning of Czechoslovakia. Beneš, betrayed by his allies, angrily resigned from office and exiled himself to the United States. Within a year Hitler had reneged on promises to respect the remnants of Czechoslovakia, absorbing the Czech part, while Slovakia became a fascist puppet ally.

Once World War II commenced in 1939, Beneš returned to England as head of the Czechoslovakian government-in-exile. The tide of war eventually swung in the Allies' favor, and he again ventured to Moscow to sign friendship and cooperation treaties with Stalin for the impending postwar period. On May 16, 1945, Beneš accompanied the Red Army back into Prague and was triumphantly reinstalled as president. In fact, he was the only prewar Eastern European politician allowed back into office, in recognition of his prior cooperation with the Soviet Union. With their help, Beneš undertook the most controversial aspect of his otherwise distinguished career; the forced repatriation of nearly 3 million Sudetenland Germans back to Germany. However, the communists then began a period of political consolidation in Czechoslovakia with a view toward taking over. Beneš, weakened by two strokes, did not have the strength to contest Communist Party chairman KLEMENT GOTTWALD's demands for a new constitution that assured communist domination of the country. But, rather than sign the document, Beneš again resigned from power on June 7, 1948. He subsequently died of a stroke in Sezimovo Usti, Bohemia, on September 3, 1948, while his country remained a hostage to cold war politics for nearly four decades.

Further Reading

Beneš, Edvard. *Memoirs: From Munich to New War and New Victory.* Boston: Houghton, Mifflin, 1954.

Berglund, Bruce R. "All Germans Are the Same: Czech and Sudeten German Exiles in Britain and the Transfer Plans." *National Identities,* nos. 2–3 (November 2000): 225–244.

Kalvoda, Joseph. "Munich: Beneš and the Soldiers." *Ukrainian Quarterly* 47 (summer 1991): 153–169.

Lukes, Igor. *Czechoslovakia Between Stalin and Hitler: The Diplomacy of Edvard Beneš in the 1930s.* New York: Oxford University Press, 1996.

Orzoff, Andrea R. "Battle for the Castle: The Friday Men and the Czech Republic, 1918–1938." Unpublished Ph.D. diss., Stanford University, 2001.

Vysny, Paul. *The Runciman Mission to Czechoslovakia, 1938: Prelude to Munich.* New York: Palgrave Macmillan, 2002.

Zeman, Zbynek, and Antonin Klimek. *The Life of Edvard Beneš, 1884–1948: Czechoslovakia in War and Peace.* New York: Oxford University Press, 1997.

Ben-Gurion, David (1886–1973) *prime minister of Israel*

David Joseph Gruen was born in Plonsk, in czarist Russia (modern Poland), on October 16, 1886, the son of a Jewish family prominently engaged in Zionist activities, namely, resurrection of the state of Israel.

After long association with Zionist youth movements he immigrated to Palestine to work as a farm laborer in 1906. Thereafter Gruen became a central player in events leading up to the establishment of the Jewish state. In 1910 he adopted the Hebraic surname of Ben-Gurion after a defender of Jerusalem from Roman times, a further indication of his devotion to Zionism. Ben-Gurion had planned to attend college in Turkey, but he was expelled following the onset of World War I and moved to the United States. There he helped organize recruits for the British Legion, a force of Jewish soldiers intending to fight the Turks. Ben-Gurion and many Zionists were particularly heartened in 1917 when Prime Minister ARTHUR BALFOUR issued his famous declaration espousing British support for creation of a Jewish homeland. When the Ottoman Empire was partitioned after the war, Great Britain received Palestine as a League of Nations mandate in 1920. Thereafter Ben-Gurion constantly harangued the British government for the partitioning of Palestine into Jewish and Arabic halves and in 1937 he was greatly encouraged by a Royal Commission that advocated as much. However, the advent of World War II forced the British government to suspend Jewish immigration to Palestine to placate Arabic public opinion. Thereafter Ben-Gurion advocated armed struggle against both British and Arab forces to attain his sacred goal. However, he carefully restrained guerrilla activity against Great Britain until the war against Nazi Germany concluded. In fact, he actively promoted Jewish participation in the war to both fight a hated oppressor and help Jews achieve military proficiency for the impending struggle.

In 1947, following repeated attacks by Jewish guerrillas controlled by Ben-Gurion and the fanatically zealous MENACHEM BEGIN, the British announced their decision to abandon Palestine altogether. This was the opportunity Ben-Gurion had waited for since 1906, so he declared restoration of the state of Israel on May 14, 1948. And, as the long-serving head of the Mapai (Labor Party), he was appointed prime minister while CHAIM WEIZMANN became president. Independence triggered a strong Arab reaction; seven hostile armies descended upon the nascent Jewish state. But the Jews, favored by luck and better training, defeated the invaders and a cease-fire ensued. Ben-Gurion then wasted no time implementing concerted policies to promote Jewish immigration to Israel from around the world, while simultaneously creating the basic machinery of government. Despite his socialist orientation, a parliamentary democracy was adopted through creation of the Knesset. Ben-Gurion then served as prime minister from 1948 to 1953, during which time Israel absorbed thousands of new citizens, established schools, hospitals, and universities, and created a modern industrialized state from virtually nothing. After 2,000 years in the wilderness, the Jews had come home.

Ben-Gurion resigned from office in 1953 for personal reasons, but he resumed high office in 1956 to impose order on warring factions in the Knesset. That year he joined in a coalition with France and Great Britain to wage war on Egyptian president GAMAL ABDEL NASSER, who nationalized the strategic Suez Canal. Israeli forces scored stunning victories in the Sinai desert but withdrew under pressure from the United States. However, this affair confirmed Jewish military superiority over neighboring states, which continues as a hallmark of Israeli defense policy. Ben-Gurion remained in office until 1963 when he resigned in the face of a political scandal. Thereafter he functioned as a senior Israeli spokesman and a living symbol of Jewish identity. He also continued writing and exhorted fellow Jews to study the Old Testament, speak Hebrew, and in every way affirm their religious identity. He also founded his own faction of the Labor Party, the Rafi, and maintained a seat in the Knesset until 1970. This astute world leader, part visionary, part Old Testament prophet, died on December 1, 1973. Israel's success as a nation and the survival of its people are directly linked to his determined leadership and the messianic zeal he applied to it.

Further Reading

Beckman, Morris. *The Jewish Brigade: An Army with Two Masters, 1944–45.* Rockville Center, N.Y.: Sarpedon, 1998.

Ben-Gurion, David. *My Talks with Arab Leaders.* New York: Third Press, 1973.

Heller, Joseph. *The Birth of Israel, 1945–1949: Ben-Gurion and His Critics.* Gainesville: University Press of Florida, 2000.

Shalom, Zakai. *David Ben-Gurion, the State of Israel, and the Arab World, 1949–1956.* Portland, Ore.: Sussex Academic, 2002.

Tal, David. *War in Palestine, 1948: Strategy and Diplomacy.* Portland, Ore.: Frank Cass, 2003.

Teveth, Shabtai. *Ben-Gurion and the Holocaust.* New York: Harcourt Brace, 1996.

Weitz, Yechiam. "Taking Leave of the 'Founding Father': Ben-Gurion's Resignation as Prime Minister in 1963." *Middle Eastern Studies* 37 (April 2000): 131–152.

———. "To Fantasy and Back: David Ben-Gurion's First Resignation, 1953." *Israel Affairs* 8 (autumn-winter 2002): 59–78.

Bennett, Richard Bedford (1870–1947) *prime minister of Canada*

Richard Bedford Bennett was born in Hopewell, New Brunswick, Canada, on July 3, 1870, with roots descending from Loyalist settlers. He studied law at Dalhousie University and began practicing in Nova Scotia. Having distinguished himself as a lawyer, Bennett moved west in 1897 and settled at Calgary in the soon-to-be-established province of Alberta. Bennett entered into a successful law partnership and also served as a solicitor for the Canadian Pacific Railway. He soon gained financial independence as a millionaire but never married. Bennett then was drawn to politics in the Conservative Party and, after several failed attempts, was elected to the House of Commons in 1911. He declined to run for reelection during World War I, preferring instead to serve as director of national service. Bennett returned to Parliament in 1921 when Prime Minister ARTHUR MEIGHEN appointed him minister of justice. Four years later he was elected to the Senate, and the following year Meighen named him minister of finance. Bennett advanced his political fortunes in 1927 when, following Meighen's resignation from politics, he became head of the Conservatives in opposition. He proved himself a forceful leader and debater, gaining national attention for political skill and personal integrity. Fate intervened in October 1929 when the world economy was shaken by the Great Depression, and Canada was severely hit. Surprisingly, Prime Minister WILLIAM LYON MACKENZIE KING declared that unemployment benefits would not be made available to provinces controlled by Conservatives. The result was national uproar, and elections held in August 1930 swept the Conservatives to power. Bennett had previously campaigned on a pledge to create jobs through public works programs and to shelter the Canadian economy through trade protectionism. But enacting such remedial measures, and achieving their anticipated beneficial results, proved much more difficult to realize.

Once in power, Bennett followed through on his pledge and erected high trade barriers. However, this had the effect of raising prices on Canadian exports, making them noncompetitive and further depressing the economy. He also attended several Imperial economic conferences and successfully argued for preferential trade arrangements within the British Empire. Bennett, a self-made millionaire with little understanding of the sufferings of average Canadians, honestly believed that only a period of belt tightening would be necessary to launch a recovery. But his aloofness, penchant for living in luxury, and inability to deliver on campaign promises made him one of the most unpopular politicians in the country. He became the subject of much public derision, and cars towed by horses because the owners could not afford to buy gasoline were disparagingly nicknamed "Bennett Buggies."

By 1934 discontent with Bennett's policies led to a minor revolt in the Conservative Party under H. H. Stevens and other like-minded reformers. Bennett, who was nothing if not a realist, concluded that dramatic action must be undertaken to save both his administration and Conservative political fortunes. Looking south, he was impressed by the popularity and success of New Deal legislation championed by President FRANKLIN D. ROOSEVELT and determined to enact his own Canadian version. Without consulting party leaders, Bennett took to the airwaves and announced a startling series of government programs to alleviate public distress. These included such decidedly non-Conservative practices as extending farm credits and unemployment compensation, establishment of national health insurance and minimum wages, and setting maximum hours in the workweek. However, it proved too little too late. The October 1935 elections were disastrous for Conservatives, and King returned to power with a large majority in Parliament. Worse, when the bulk of Bennett's proposed programs were declared unconstitutional, the Liberals made the necessary legal adjustments and coopted them as their own.

Bennett lingered on for three years as head of the Conservatives in Parliament, but his reputation never recovered. Angered by his diminished influence and the public's unforgiving attitude toward him, he quit

Canada altogether in 1938 and moved to England. There his friend Lord Beaverbrook helped him become Viscount Bennett of Mickleham, Calgary, and Hopewell, thereby granting him appointment to the House of Lords. He died in England on June 26, 1947, all but forgotten in his native land. In reality, nothing Bennett did could have mitigated the effects of the Great Depression on Canada, certainly not in time to salvage his reputation.

Further Reading

Beaverbrook, Max A. *Friends; Sixty Years of Intimate and Personal Relations with Richard Bedford Bennett.* London: Heinemann, 1959.

Glassford, Larry A. *Reaction and Reform: The Politics of the Conservative Party under R. B. Bennett, 1927–1938.* Toronto: University of Toronto Press, 1992.

Gray, James H. *R. B. Bennett: The Calgary Years.* Toronto: University of Toronto Press, 1991.

Nesmith, Thomas C. "R. B. Bennett and the Revival of the Conservative Party in Quebec, 1927–1930." Unpublished master's thesis, Queen's University, 1975.

Waite, Peter B. *The Loner: Three Sketches of the Personal Life and Ideas of Richard B. Bennett, 1870–1947.* Toronto: University of Toronto Press, 1992.

Betancourt, Rómulo (1908–1981) *president of Venezuela*

Rómulo Betancourt was born near Caracas, Venezuela, on February 22, 1908, the son of an accountant. He became politically active while studying law at the Central University of Venezuela, and in 1928 participated in violent demonstrations against the regime of dictator Juan Vicente Gómez. He was consequently exiled to Costa Rica for several years, where he briefly joined the Communist Party. After Gómez died in 1935, Betancourt was allowed back into the country and immediately resumed political agitation for change. He founded the Partido Democrático Nacional (PDN), National Democratic Party, which began calling for the overthrow of dictator Eleazar López Contreras. The government quickly cracked down on dissent, and Betancourt was forced into exile a second time. A new leader, President Isaias Medina Angarita, came to power in 1941 and he allowed dissidents to come home. Betancourt then legalized the PDN under a new name,

Acción Democrática (AD), Democratic Action, and in 1944 the party advanced a presidential candidate to oppose Medina. However, when the regime refused to allow for open elections, Betancourt and a group of disgruntled army officers overthrew Medina in October 1945. Control of the nation passed into the hands of a seven-man junta, in which Betancourt served as provisional president.

Over the next two years Betancourt enacted sweeping political and economic changes intended to place Venezuela on the path to democracy and modernization. Accordingly, peasant unions were legalized, universal male and female suffrage was adopted, land reform was enacted, and a new national assembly convened. Legislators then adopted a new constitution legalizing the right to strike, and also guaranteed civil rights. Betancourt then adopted legislation requiring that foreign oil companies pay 50 percent of their profits to the nation's coffers, where it was spent for the enhancement of schools, for teachers, and hospitals. More important, the first free and open presidential elections were finally scheduled, and on December 14, 1947, AD candidate Rómulo Gallegos was victorious. Betancourt then set an important precedent by peacefully stepping down. However, Gallegos held power for only 10 months before being overthrown in a military coup headed by General MARCOS PÉREZ JIMÉNEZ. Betancourt fled Venezuela a third time, spending 10 years abroad in Cuba, Puerto Rico, and Costa Rica. It was not until 1958 that the military regime was ousted by popular discontent, and he returned to run for the presidency. That year Betancourt was resoundingly elected the second AD president, with 48 percent of votes cast, and settled into a five-year term.

Betancourt assumed the mantle at a difficult period in Venezuela's history. The nation was wracked by profound economic recession, while the countryside was beset by an intractable communist insurgency. He nonetheless continued his reforming impulse by enhancing land reform, encouraging organized labor, and allowing for collective bargaining. The government also embarked on improving the national infrastructure by constructing roads, dams, highways, electrification, and other facets of a modern, industrialized state. He then proved instrumental in laying down the guidelines for what emerged as the Organization of Petroleum Exporting States, or OPEC, to better regulate the price of this valuable resource. On the international scene,

Betancourt also espoused a set of precepts, the "Betancourt Doctrine," stating that no Latin American country should recognize any government that achieved power by revolution or force. He thereupon broke off diplomatic relations with Fidel Castro's Cuba and encouraged members of the Organization of American States (OAS) to do the same. In 1960 Betancourt narrowly survived an assassination attempt orchestrated by RAFAEL TRUJILLO of the Dominican Republic, whose country he also boycotted. New elections held in 1963 resulted in yet another AD candidate, Raúl Leoni, becoming president. Betancourt thus became the first Venezuelan president to achieve power through democratic means and then peacefully surrender it to another official.

In 1964 Betancourt left the country so as not to infringe upon Leoni's administration, and he traveled and lectured abroad in Europe and the United States. He returned in 1973 to campaign for another successful AD candidate, Carlos Andrés Pérez Rodríguez. Betancourt died suddenly in New York City on September 28, 1981, widely recognized as the father of Venezuelan democracy and a champion of social benefits for the poor. His political success broke a series of military dictatorships that had plagued the Venezuelan nation since the early 19th century and substituted a stable, thriving democracy.

Further Reading

Alexander, Robert J. *Romulo Betancourt and the Transformation of Venezuela*. New Brunswick, N.J.: Transactions Books, 1992.

———. *The Venezuelan Democratic Revolution: A Profile of the Regime of Rómulo Betancourt*. New Brunswick, N.J.: Rutgers University Press, 1964.

———. *Venezuela's Voice for Democracy: Conversations and Correspondence with Rómulo Betancourt*. New York: Praeger Books, 1990.

Betancourt, Rómulo. *Venezuela, Oil and Politics*. Boston: Houghton, Mifflin, 1979.

Davila, Luis R. "Rómulo Betancourt and the Development of Venezuelan Nationalism." *Bulletin of Latin American Research* 12 (January 1993): 49–63.

Koeneke, Herbert. "Personal and Situational Components of Political Leadership: A Case Study of Romulo Betancourt." Unpublished Ph.D. diss., Tulane University, 1983.

Salazar-Carrillo, Jorge. *Oil and Development in Venezuela during the 20th Century.* Westport, Conn.: Praeger, 2004.

Schwartzberg, Steven. "Betancourt from a Communist Anti-Imperialist to a Social Democrat with United States Support." *Journal of Latin American Studies* 29 (October 1997): 613–665.

Betancur Cuartas, Belisario (1923–) *president of Colombia*

Belisario Betancur Cuartas was born in Amaga, Colombia, on February 4, 1923, the second of 22 children born to a poor farming family. He eked out a hardscrabble existence before managing to attend the Bolívar Pontifical University in Medellín to study law. Graduating in 1947, Betancur became a journalist for the Conservative Party before gaining election to the Constituent Assembly in 1950. In this capacity he agitated against the dictatorship of GUSTAVO ROJAS PINILLA and was repeatedly jailed. Eventually, political stability was restored through adoption of the National Front, whereby Conservative and Liberal candidates rotated through the presidency at prescribed intervals. Betancur was tapped to serve as minister of labor in 1963, and he first ran for the presidency in 1970, losing by a wide margin. After serving several years as ambassador to Spain, he endured another presidential failure in 1978 before striking up an alliance with disenchanted Liberals. Betancur finally won on his third attempt in May 1982, garnering 47 percent of the vote. True to his humble origins, he discarded all luxury vehicles from the presidential motor pool, ordered his driver to strictly observe downtown traffic signals and even opened the presidential palace to the public on weekends. And, because he represented the progressive wing of the Conservatives, Betancur broke with tradition by appointing women deputy ministers to every post in government.

Betancur had campaigned on a platform to reduce unemployment and inflation by proffering tax incentives and encouraging foreign investment. However, because coffee prices—Colombia's main export—remained high, he amassed sufficient capital to grow out of the recession. Latin America was then awash in national debt and the situation so imperiled political stability that Betancur established a debtor's cartel to demand better repayment conditions. The new executive was also part of the international Nonaligned Movement, and he made moves to establish diplomatic relations with Fidel Castro's Cuba. Moreover, and to the chagrin of the United States, he refused to see the social turmoil of South and Central America within a strict cold war context. For that reason Betancur proved instrumental in advancing the Contadora peace process in Central America, encouraging El Salvador and Nicaragua to settle their respective civil wars peacefully. Through all these expedients, he emerged as one of the most widely respected heads of state in Latin America.

Unfortunately for Colombia, Betancur enjoyed less success in resolving a protracted guerrilla war waged by various left-wing extremist groups. In fact, the countryside had been in turmoil for 30 years and the fighting had claimed the lives of at least 20,000 people. But once in power Betancur took the dramatic step of proposing a cease-fire and a general amnesty, whereby 4,000 insurgents came forward and laid down their arms. Betancur's success was predicated upon his willingness to seek dialogue with the rebels and their demands for social and economic reforms. His attempts seemed to be on the verge of success until December 1985, when the radical M-19 movement seized the Palace of Justice, taking more than 400 hostages. Betancur refused to negotiate with the rebels and sent the army in. Over 100 people were killed, including several ranking jurists, but the government displayed its determination not to be intimidated. The president also determined to confront another pressing problem, the rise of the notorious Colombian drug cartels. These frequently acted in concert with the guerrillas, exchanging military security for a part of the profits. When Betancur ordered a harsh crackdown on known dealers, they responded by assassinating his minister of justice in April 1984.

By the time Betancur's tenure in office expired, he had amassed a mixed record of success. Inflation was lowered and the national debt reduced, but unemployment and poverty continued growing. Nor was he able to defeat guerrillas and drug lords who had woven themselves into the very fabric of Colombian society. Consequently, Betancur left office with somewhat diminished popularity numbers, having accrued more respect overseas than at home.

Further Reading

Dudley, Steven. *Walking Ghosts: Murder and Guerrilla Politics in Colombia.* New York: Routledge, 2004.

Mendenhall, Warner. "Belisario Betancur's Peace Process, 1982–1986: Trauma and State Autonomy in Colombia." Unpublished master's thesis, Kent State University, 1996.

Richani, Nazih. *Systems of Violence: The Political Economy of War and Peace in Colombia.* Albany: New York State University Press, 2002.

Ruiz, Bert. *The Colombian Civil War.* Jefferson, N.C.: McFarland, 2001.

Sanders, Thomas G. *Colombia, Betancur, and the Challenge of 1984.* VESI Reports, South America, no. 24. Indianapolis: Universities Field Staff International, 1983.

Tokatlian, Juan G. "Colombia at War: The Search for a Peace Diplomacy." *International Journal of Politics, Culture, and Society* 14 (winter 2000): 333–362.

Bethmann Hollweg, Theobald von

(1856–1921) *chancellor of Germany*

Theobald Theodor Friedrich Alfred von Bethmann Hollweg was born in Hohenfinow, Prussia (modern Germany), on November 29, 1856, into an aristocratic family of landowners. Afforded an excellent education, he attended universities in Strassburg, Leipzig, and Berlin before joining the civil service in 1879. A competent administrator, Bethmann enjoyed a spectacular rise through the ranks of the bureaucracy, becoming minister of the interior in 1905. Like most Prussian aristocrats, he was staunchly conservative but also exhibited liberal-minded tendencies. In 1906, for example, he agitated for reforming the archaic Prussian three-class voter system that gave the aristocracy political influence far out of proportion to its numbers. The plan was rejected by the conservative-dominated Reichstag (legislature), but by 1907 Bethmann had advanced to state secretary of the interior, in line to become chancellor. He also gained a reputation for political flexibility, being able to rally a parliamentary majority of conservatives and centrists to counter the rising influence of the Social Democrats. Since Bethmann was viewed as politically reliable and predictable, following the resignation of BERNARD BULOW in July 1909 Kaiser WILHELM II appointed him chancellor of Imperial Germany.

Bethmann brought the strengths and experience of a veteran bureaucrat to the office, but he completely lacked the nuances of diplomacy and debating skills. He also acquired grave national responsibilities at a perilous time in German history. The aggressive policies of Wilhelm had alienated Germany from most of the world, and the nations of Europe suffered from an abundance of bellicose nationalism. It was a tinderbox situation awaiting the inevitable spark to set everything off. Bethmann, meanwhile, earnestly tried moderate reforms by adopting a liberal constitution for Alsace-Lorraine in 1911 and attempting to integrate left-wing Social Democrats into the mainstream of national politics. In 1912 he welcomed a British naval deputation in an attempt to resolve the arms race between their respective nations, but the scheme was torpedoed by Admiral Alfred von Tirpitz and other conservatives. Furthermore, Bethmann fumbled badly in July 1914 when Austrian archduke Ferdinand was assassinated in Serbia. Austria mobilized its forces for war and Bethmann, unwilling to lose Germany's last European ally, issued his famous "blank check" statement of unfettered approval. Russia then began mobilizing its army, and confronted equally by France and Great Britain, Germany went to war.

As the conflict progressed, Bethmann made additional errors by failing to stand up to the army militarists. He allowed diplomacy to be conducted for short-term military gains—acquiring Turkey and Bulgaria as allies, but losing Italy, Greece, and Romania. He also failed to take advantage of President WOODROW WILSON's attempt at mediation in October 1916, which meant that fighting dragged on to the detriment of Germany. By the spring of 1917, the war effort was led by Field Marshals PAUL VON HINDENBURG and Erich Ludendorff, who regarded resumption of unrestricted U-boat warfare as a means of knocking Britain out of the war. Bethmann dissented strongly against this policy, as it risked bringing the United States into hostilities against Germany, but in the end he consented. Three months later Wilson asked Congress for a declaration of war against Germany, fulfilling the chancellor's worst fears. He let himself be diverted by continual efforts at reforming the Prussian voting system in favor of universal suffrage, and dithered over a 1917 peace resolution advanced by a coalition of parties in the Reichstag. At length, Hindenburg could no longer tolerate Bethmann's indecisiveness, and on July 13, 1917, he demanded his resignation. The military now enjoyed nearly complete control of the country.

Out of office, Bethmann retired to seclusion on his private estate in Hohenfinow, dying there on January 1, 1921. While technically competent and not necessarily militaristic, he lacked the vision of a great statesman and the doggedness to fight for policies he thought essential. Well intentioned politically, his penchant for trying to balance left- and right-wing factions only antagonized both, making compromise impossible. Worse, by allowing the military to usurp more and more of his political prerogatives, Bethmann set the stage for the disastrous events of 1918 and the peace that followed. His tenure as chancellor is frequently cited by historians as a major cause of Germany's defeat in the First World War.

Further Reading

Bethmann Hollweg, Theobald von. *Reflections on the World War.* London: T. Butterworth, 1920.

Eley, Geoff, and James Retallack, eds. *Wilhelminism and Its Legacies: German Modernities, Imperialism, and the Meanings of Reform.* New York: Berghahn Books, 2003.

Jarausch, Konrad H. *The Enigmatic Chancellor: Bethmann-Hollweg and the Hubris of Imperial Germany.* New Haven, Conn.: Yale University Press, 1973.

———. "Revising German History: Bethmann-Hollweg Revisited." *Central European History* 21, no. 3 (1988): 224–243.

Kapp, Richard W. "Bethmann-Hollweg, Austria-Hungary, and Mitteleuropa, 1914–1915." *Austrian History Yearbook* 19–20 (1983–84): 215–236.

Taylor, John M. "Bethmann's War on Falkenhayn: The Campaign Against Germany's Second Wartime Chief of Staff." Unpublished master's thesis, University of Minnesota, 1992.

Bhutto, Zulfikar Ali (1928–1979) *prime minister of Pakistan*

Zulfikar Ali Bhutto was born in Larkana, Sindh Province, India (modern Pakistan), on January 5, 1928, the son of a prominent Muslim landowner. He was well educated at private schools in Bombay before pursuing advanced studies at the University of California–Berkeley and Oxford University, England. Having acquired a law degree in 1953, Bhutto came home to open a practice. In 1958 the civilian government was overthrown by General MOHAMMAD AYUB KHAN, who appointed Bhutto minister of fuel, power, and natural resources. He functioned capably, and in 1963 Ayub Khan reassigned him to head the foreign ministry. Here

Bhutto displayed considerable independence by closely aligning his country with Communist China, as a counterweight to giant India in the south. Relations between the South Asian neighbors deteriorated by 1965, and Bhutto conceived a scheme to infiltrate 5,000 armed guerrillas into Indian-controlled Kashmir, with a view toward fomenting a Muslim uprising. The result was a 17-day war in which Pakistan fared badly. Ayub Khan subsequently negotiated a cease-fire favorable to India, but Bhutto refused to support the resulting peace treaty signed in the Soviet city of Tashkent. He was subsequently dismissed from the cabinet in 1967. Unperturbed, Bhutto created his own political organization, the Pakistan People's Party (PPP), to further advance his ambitions. This was the nation's first mass-based political organization, which pledged to help end the suffering of the poor majority. Bhutto skillfully employed his minions in street demonstrations that finally brought down the regime of Ayub Khan in March 1969.

Zulfikar Ali Bhutto *(Library of Congress)*

In 1970 the new leader, General Asha Mohammad Yahya Khan, arranged for Pakistan's first national elections. The PPP, which espoused a blend of Islamic fundamentalism and socialism, easily carried the western section of the country, but the eastern half voted for the Awami League of Sheikh MUJIBUR RAHMAN, who refused to concede defeat. The following year a civil war raged in which East Pakistan seceded to form a new nation, Bangladesh. This defeat greatly embarrassed the military, forcing Yahya Khan from office, and in December 1971 Bhutto became president. True to his socialist precepts, he nationalized banks and industries, redistributed land to the poor, took Pakistan out of the British Commonwealth, and distanced himself from the United States. He believed that Pakistan's rightful place was as a leader of the Nonaligned Nations, and also a leader of the Muslim community. In 1972 he became the first Pakistani leader to visit India, and he signed a treaty of cooperation with Prime Minister INDIRA GANDHI. Two years later he extended diplomatic recognition to Bangladesh before hosting the yearly Islamic Summit at Lahore.

Despite poor economic performance, Bhutto enjoyed considerable public support and he convinced the assembly to adopt a new constitution in 1973 that made him prime minister. Armed with near-dictatorial powers, he embarked on further socialization of the economy while cracking down on dissent. Street protests increased as the economy faltered, so in March 1977 Bhutto sought to shore up his position with snap elections before the opposition could organize itself. Surprisingly, coalition forces of the Pakistan National Alliance (PNA) were prepared for such contingencies and scored well during the election. However, when Bhutto declared himself and the PPP the winners, rioting and daily street protests broke out. The prime minister responded with harsher measures and even imposed martial law in several cities. Before events could get even further out of hand, army chief of staff General MOHAMMAD ZIA UL-HAQ arrested Bhutto on July 5, 1977, and declared himself ruler. Bhutto was freed after a brief detention but the military, apparently after second thoughts about releasing such an effective firebrand, promptly rearrested him. Eventually, the former prime minister was accused of having arranged the assassination of a political opponent in 1974. He was tried, found guilty, and hanged in Rawalpindi on April 4, 1979, amid international outcries. Thus concluded

one of the most dynamic and unpredictable interludes of Pakistani political history. However, Bhutto extracted a measure of revenge from the grave in 1988 when his daughter, Benazir Bhutto, became the first woman prime minister of Pakistan.

Further Reading

Bhutto, Zulfikar. *The Myth of Independence.* London: Oxford University Press, 1969.

Hasan, Mubashir. *The Mirage of Power: An Inquiry into the Bhutto Years.* New York: Oxford University Press, 2000.

Lodi, Maleeha. "The Bhutto Faction in Pakistan Politics." *Contemporary Review* no. 247 (December 1985): 289–294.

Raza, Rafi. *Zulfikar Ali Bhutto, 1967–1977.* New York: Oxford University Press, 1997.

Syed, Anwar H. *The Discourse and Politics of Zulfikar Ali Bhutto.* New York: St. Martin's Press, 1992.

Wolf-Phillips, Leslie. "Z. A. Bhutto of Pakistan: A Biography." *Third World Quarterly* 15 (December 1994): 723–730.

Wolpert, Stanley. *Zulfi Bhutto of Pakistan: His Life and Times.* New York: Oxford University Press, 1993.

Bierut, Bolesław (1892–1956) *first secretary, Polish United Workers Party*

Bolesław Krasnodebski was born on April 18, 1892, in Rury Jezuickie, Poland, the son of a farmer. In his youth he became attracted to socialist thinking and joined the outlawed Communist Party in 1918. His subversive activities forced him underground, and he finally adopted the surname Bierut, from several aliases. He proved adept at organizing clandestine cells throughout eastern Europe and gained a reputation for complete political reliability. After two decades of clandestine organizing and arrests, Bierut fled Poland for the Soviet Union. There he met and became infatuated with dictator JOSEPH STALIN, developing into an ardent exponent of totalitarianism. During World War II he helped organize the Union of Polish Patriots, the political cadre of a future communist regime in Poland, and oversaw the liquidation of Trotskyists and other political renegades. As the Red Army advanced westward, Bierut was tapped to head the new Polish Committee of National Liberation, which served as a provisional government in Soviet-controlled territory. He accomplished this subversively by founding the Polish Worker's Party, representing it as a domestic socialist movement. Within months he consolidated his grip on power by establishing the quasi-legislative National Council of the Homeland, earning Stalin's complete trust. With Russian help he annexed the German provinces of Pomerania and Silesia to Poland, expelling 5 million Germans in the process. This was as compensation for the eastern third of Poland that Stalin had absorbed at his western border as a buffer zone in the event of a future war. Bierut complied as ordered and finally announced creation of an interim Polish government with himself as provisional president on June 28, 1945. At the Potsdam Conference the following month, Bierut assured British prime minister WINSTON CHURCHILL that the new Polish political system would evolve along democratic lines. Two years later he directed shamelessly rigged elections that formalized communist control over the country. By a vote of 408 to 24, the party-controlled legislature elected Bierut president for a seven-year term in office.

Finally in charge, Bierut rounded up and eliminated the last remnants of the noncommunist Polish Home Army, while also purging the polity of socialists and other leftists not sufficiently beholden to Stalin. Those not executed or imprisoned were forced to join the newly created Polish United Workers (Communist) Party, now the sole legitimate organization. He also began the forced Sovietization of his country with collectivized agriculture, centralized economic planning, and greater emphasis upon industrialization. To further augment Communist control of the social apparatus, laws were enacted against the Catholic Church while the party-dominated Polish Youth Movement was organized. When a leading politician, WŁADYSŁAW GOMUŁKA, dissented from such harsh measures, Bierut arranged his dismissal from the government. This deliberateness included a general purge of cadres to weed out potential Titoists, who sympathized with Yugoslavia's independence leader Josip Broz, MARSHAL TITO. So closely did Bierut adhere to Moscow's line, including adoption of his own personality cult, that he was widely regarded as the "Little Stalin."

Bierut, now firmly at the helm, ensured that Poland functioned as a loyal Soviet satellite. In 1949 he joined the Warsaw Pact, a defensive alliance intending to counter the newly organized North Atlantic Treaty Organization (NATO). Taking his cue from Moscow, he also refused to accept American aid in the form of the Marshall Plan, which communists feared might undermine their authority. In 1952 Bierut resigned as head of the Polish United Worker's Party to serve as the new prime minister. The turning point in his career came with the death of Stalin in 1953, when he was forced by more moderate interests to resign as head of state. A gradual process of de-Stalinization then swept Eastern Europe as hard-liners were invariably replaced by reformers. But Bierut remained loyal to his idolized leader to the end. In the spring of 1956 he traveled to Moscow to attend the Soviet Communist Party's Twentieth Congress, and was aghast at Premier NIKITA KHRUSHCHEV's secret speech denouncing Stalin. The age of political terror had finally passed and, as if on cue, Bierut died suddenly on March 12, 1956, three years after the tyrant that he had served so slavishly.

Further Reading

Dziewanowski, M. K. *The Communist Party of Poland: An Outline History.* Cambridge, Mass.: Harvard University Press, 1976.

Kemp-Welch, A. *Stalinism in Poland, 1944–1956.* New York: St. Martin's Press, 1999.

Kenney, Padraic. *Rebuilding Poland: Workers and Communists, 1945–1960.* Ithaca, N.Y.: Cornell University Press, 1997.

Kersten, Krystyna. *The Establishment of Communist Rule in Poland, 1943–1948.* Berkeley: University of California Press, 1991.

Simoncini, Gabriele. *The Communist Party of Poland, 1918–1929: A Study in Political Ideology.* Lewiston, N.Y.: E. Mellen Press, 1993.

Bishop, Maurice (1944–1983) *prime minister of Grenada*

Maurice Bishop was born on Aruba, Netherlands Antilles, on May 29, 1944, the son of Grenadian immigrants. He was raised on Grenada and became an exceptional student, eventually studying law at the University of London. Bishop became a lawyer in 1969 and commenced practicing in Grenada the following year. He was enamored of the American black power movement then in vogue, and gravitated toward Marxist politics. Grenada was then controlled by ERIC GAIRY, who ran the island as a personal fiefdom and ruthlessly suppressed all opposition. In time, Bishop became engaged in politics as an anti-Gairy activist. This brought him severe beatings at the hands of the Mongoose Gang, a paramilitary force of Gairy's followers, but he went on to found the Movement for the Assemblies of the People to address grievances. His father was murdered by government henchmen during a protest. In 1973, after several more arrests and beatings, Bishop merged his group with the Joint Endeavor for Welfare, Education, and Liberation (JEWEL) to start the New Jewel Movement on Grenada. Beyond decrying the harsh repressiveness of Gairy's regime, the group also opposed his moves to seek independence from Great Britain, formalized in February 1974. Bishop continued on as a leading opponent of Gairy, and in 1976 he successfully ran for a seat in Parliament. In concert with the Grenada National Party and United People's Party, Bishop organized a wide coalition, the People's Alliance, to further protest government tyranny.

Bishop's strident activism and his revolutionary rhetoric brought him accolades from the poverty-stricken masses, making him the island's most popular political figure. On March 13, 1979, he sponsored a bloodless coup while Gairy was out of the country and declared creation of a People's Revolutionary Government. Initially, the coup was greeted with wild enthusiasm from Grenadians of every class. Abandoning the parliamentary mode of governance, Bishop patterned his own regime on the Cuban model of Fidel Castro, with peasant and worker involvement at every level of administration. He also strove for improvements in health care, housing, and medical assistance to the island's poor majority. All these actions endeared him to the lower classes, but Bishop had no real intention of instituting even limited democracy. He continued delaying new elections, restricted press activity, and kept political prisoners of his own. More controversially, he invited Cuban and Soviet workers onto the island, ostensibly to construct a new international runway. He also took the precaution of making several trips to the United States to assure the government of his peaceful intentions.

Bishop's flirtation with communist regimes raised hackles in the United States, and in 1983 President RONALD REAGAN instituted a trade embargo. This greatly exacerbated Grenada's precarious economy and led to splits between Bishop and his hard-line vice premier, Bernard Coard. Tensions between the two increased and climaxed on October 12, 1983, when a meeting of the People's Revolutionary Government formally accused the prime minister of spreading false rumors of an assas-

sination plot. Bishop was then confronted at his home by Coard supporters and placed under house arrest. He lingered there a week until, on October 19, 1983, thousands of his followers massed into the street and released him. Bishop then led his throng to the military installation at Fort Rupert, which was subsequently stormed by Coard's soldiers. An estimated 100 civilians were killed before Bishop and several ministers were detained and executed in cold blood. A large number of American students studying at a nearby medical college were also taken hostage.

The Reagan administration used the murder of Bishop, the presence of Soviet advisers, and the taking of hostages as a pretext for eliminating communism on Grenada altogether. On October 25, 1983, American forces swooped onto the island, routed the Cuban garrison, and liberated Grenada. They also arrested Coard and his supporters, who were subsequently tried by the new government and found guilty of Bishop's murder. Under American supervision, freedom and democracy were finally restored to Grenada. But despite Bishop's repression and untimely demise, he still retains a measure of popularity with the island's poorer classes.

Further Reading

Adkin, Mark. *Urgent Fury: The Battle for Grenada.* Lexington, Mass.: Lexington Books, 1989.

Bishop, Maurice. *Maurice Bishop Speaks: The Grenada Revolution and Its Overthrow, 1979–1983.* New York: Pathfinder Press, 1983.

Coles, Romand. *Self/Power/Other: Political Theory and Dialogical Ethics.* Ithaca, N.Y.: Cornell University Press, 1992.

Payne, Anthony. *The International Crisis of the Caribbean.* Baltimore: Johns Hopkins University Press, 1984.

Williams, Gary. "Brief Encounter: Grenadian Prime Minister Maurice Bishop's Visit to Washington." *Latin American Studies* 34 (August 2002): 659–687.

———. "Prelude to an Intervention: Grenada, 1983." *Journal of Latin American Studies* 29 (February 1997): 131–169.

Blum, Léon (1872–1950) *prime minister of France*

Léon Blum was born in Paris on April 9, 1872, into a middle-class family of Jewish descent. A brilliant student, he attended the prestigious Ecole Normale

Supérieure on a scholarship and subsequently received a doctorate in law and philosophy from the Sorbonne. After working several years as an attorney for the Conseil d'Etat, a high administrative court, Blum became politically active during the trial of Alfred Dreyfus, a Jewish army officer wrongly accused of espionage. He then adopted the ideas of Jean Jaurès, founder of the French Socialist Party, and joined the group in 1902. Thereafter he unequivocally committed himself to the Enlightenment principles of justice, equality, and humanity. For nearly a decade Blum moved within intellectual circles, gaining fame as an accomplished literary and social critic. In the early days of World War I, his friend and mentor Jaurès was assassinated and Blum succeeded him as head of the Socialist Party, dutifully serving through the war years as part of the Union Sacré, a national unity government involving all political factions. In 1919 Blum gained election to the Chamber of Deputies, but the following year he indelibly left his imprint on national politics during the 1920 meeting of the Third Socialist International. More than two-thirds of the French socialists voted to break away and join the Communist Party controlled by Russian revolutionary VLADIMIR LENIN but, in an eloquent diatribe, Blum denounced violent revolution as the path to dictatorship. He also strongly reaffirmed French socialist principles of freedom and democracy. Afterward he took the remainder of the now greatly weakened Socialist Party and commenced a slow rebuilding process.

Over the next 15 years Blum served as leader of the opposition and emerged as one of France's most eloquent and socially conscious politicians. Given his great popularity, he had been invited to form a coalition government with various leftist groups, including communists, but he refused to serve in any regime where the socialists were not dominant. By the mid-1930s Europe was trembling from the onset of fascism, and right-wing riots in Paris convinced Blum to assemble a broad, left-wing coalition government. In concert with communists, socialists, and non-leftist radicals, he formed a popular front against fascism, winning a coalition majority in June 1936. Blum thus became France's first socialist prime minister and also the first Jewish chief executive. In this capacity he embarked on a revolutionary program of social and labor reform, including a 40-hour workweek, paid vacations for workers, nationalization of the Bank of France, and government control of the arms industry. However, while promulgating such sweeping reform he stoked the ire of industrialists and the right wing. Worse, when Blum refused overt aid to leftist Republicans during the Spanish civil war for fear of alienating Great Britain, he greatly angered communists and socialists in his own administration. The government became paralyzed, and when the Senate refused to grant Blum special financial powers, he resigned after only a year in office. In 1938 he would briefly reprise his role as prime minister, but with few tangible accomplishments. Moreover, he failed to initiate a significant rearmament program to counter the growing menace of ADOLF HITLER's Nazi Germany.

When World War II commenced in 1939, Blum had returned to the Chamber of Deputies. Here he became one of only 36 deputies to vote against granting PHILIPPE PÉTAIN special powers to rule unoccupied portions of France following Germany's victory in May 1940. The pro-Nazi Vichy regime then arrested Blum and put on a show trial in Riom on February 19, 1942, charging him with failure to prepare the nation for war. However, Blum defended himself and his actions brilliantly and the court was summarily adjourned. The former prime minister was then shipped off to the Buchenwald concentration camp with many other French Jews until American troops rescued them in May 1945. After the war, Blum tried to rebuild the Socialist Party as a counterweight to the newly invigorated communists, whom he still despised. He also became prime minister a second time to lead an all-socialist caretaker government that ushered in the Fourth Republic in 1947. Blum, now a respected elder statesman, then negotiated with the United States over a reduction of war debts before resigning from office in January 1947. To the end of his days, Blumremained an impassioned and articulate spokesman for his own unique brand of "socialism with a human face." He died suddenly in Paris on March 30, 1950, France's most influential left-wing politician of the early 20th century.

Further Reading

Blum, Leon. *For All Mankind.* New York: Viking Press, 1946.

Gallagher, M. D. "Leon Blum and the Spanish Civil War." *Journal of Contemporary History* 6, no. 3 (1971): 56–64.

Jordan, Nicole. *The Popular Front and Central Europe: The Dilemmas of French Impotence, 1918–1940.* New York: Cambridge University Press, 1992.

Judt, Tony. *The Burden of Responsibility: Blum, Aron, and the French Twentieth Century.* Chicago: University of Chicago Press, 1998.

Newman, Michael. "Leon Blum, French Socialism, and European Unity, 1940–1950." *History Journal* 24 (March 1981): 189–200.

Parry, D. L. L. "Passion, Politics, and the French Third Republic." *History Journal* 36 (March 1993): 217–223.

Weisberg, Richard. "Leon Blum in Vichy France." *Partisan Review* 63 (fall 1996): 553–571.

Bokassa, Jean-Bédel (1921–1996) *emperor of the Central African Empire*

Jean-Bédel Bokassa was born in Bangui, Ubangi-Shari, on February 22, 1921, the son of a Mbaka chief. He belonged to a politically active family, and was related to Barthélemy Boganda, a prominent figure in Ubangi-Shari's eventual independence. Orphaned at the age of six, Bokassa was raised in missionary schools until 1939, when he joined the French army. He fought with distinction in World War II and colonial ventures, retiring from the army in 1961 with a rank of captain. At that time the Central African Republic had recently achieved independence from France under the aegis of Bokassa's cousin, DAVID DACKO. When Dacko asked him to help constitute a new national army, he obliged and was promoted to commander-in-chief in 1963. However, as the government became hopelessly mired in corruption, Dacko's popularity declined, and Bokassa saw an opportunity for himself. On December 31, 1965, he engineered a bloodless coup, toppling the government and installing himself as president. Intent on consolidating power as quickly as possible, Bokassa also dissolved the national assembly and abrogated the constitution. Ironically, his succession was greeted favorably by the public and by the French government, both having high expectations for the new leader.

In power, Bokassa's leadership proved uneven, unpredictable, and bloodthirsty. He brooked absolutely no opposition to his rule. Numerous enemies, real or imagined, were summarily arrested and executed. Among his many victims was Colonel Alexandre Banza, his second-in-command, whom Bokassa suspected of treachery and personally murdered himself. In 1972 the president decreed that thieves should be publicly mutilated as punishment; his soldiers killed several. Despite his heavy-handed rule, the government of CHARLES DE GAULLE cultivated close ties to the Central African Republic, for it was France's only source of high-quality uranium for nuclear weapons. On the world stage, Bokassa portrayed himself as a whimsical buffoon, much given to humorous antics and lavish costumes. He struck up cordial relations with two other notorious tyrants, IDI AMIN of Uganda and FRANCISCO MACÍAS NGUEMA of Equatorial Guinea. Despite his repressive reputation, the new administration of VALÉRY GISCARD D'ESTAING continued the pattern of friendly and close relations.

In 1971 the increasingly megalomaniac Bokassa declared himself president for life and field marshal. In 1977 he institutionalized his absurdist tendencies by having the assembly adopt a new constitution declaring the tiny, impoverished Central African Republic an empire. Bokassa then arranged a lavish coronation for himself as its self-styled "emperor." The ceremony, consciously patterned after that of Emperor Napoleon I, whom Bokassa closely identified with, reputedly cost the nation $30 million. His diamond-studded crown alone was valued at $5 million. However, by 1979, many citizens were antagonized with Bokassa's inherent cruelty, corruption, and self-serving policies. At one point, when a crowd of schoolchildren protested buying uniforms from a factory owned by one of Bokassa's wives, they were fired on by soldiers. Bokassa himself was allegedly on hand and committed atrocities himself. Not surprisingly, several attempts were made to depose this despot, but Bokassa survived. He rounded up numerous conspirators, including his own son-in-law, and executed them all. At this juncture the United States and other donor nations began phasing out foreign aid to the quixotic dictatorship.

By now Bokassa's erratic behavior was simply too embarrassing for France to endure, and on September 20, 1979, French troops took over the country while he was on a state visit to Libya. They then reinstalled Dacko as president after a hiatus of 14 years. Bokassa, meanwhile, withdrew to the Côte d'Ivoire and then to France where he maintained a lavish chateau. Then, in November 1986, he suddenly flew into Bangui expecting to be greeted as a liberator. However, the former "emperor" was summarily arrested and charged with numerous crimes, including murder and cannibalism. Bokassa had been previously sentenced to death in absentia, but on February 29, 1988, the Central African Republic's new leader, General Andre Kolingba, commuted his sentence to life imprisonment. In September 1993 he was released and allowed to spend the rest of his life in obscurity. Bokassa died in Bangui on November 3, 1996, one of the most cruel and unpredictable dictators to ever rule an African nation.

Further Reading

Blumenthal, Susan. "Operation Bokassa." *African Report* 16, no. 9 (1971): 18–22.

Decalo, Samuel. *Psychoses of Power: African Personal Dictatorships.* Gainesville, Fla.: Florida Academic Press, 1998.

Kalck, Pierre. *Historical Dictionary of the Central African Republic.* Metuchen, N.J.: Scarecrow Press, 1992.

Shoumatoff, Alex. *African Madness.* New York: Vintage Press, 1990.

Titley, Brian. *Dark Age: The Political Odyssey of Emperor Bokassa.* Liverpool, England: Liverpool University Press, 1997.

Borden, Robert Laird (1854–1937) *prime minister of Canada*

Robert Laird Borden was born in Grand Pré, Nova Scotia, on June 26, 1854, the son of former New England immigrants. He was well educated and served as assistant master of his own school at the age of 14. As a young man Borden clerked at a local law firm before passing the bar exam and being called to the bar in 1890. He expressed no formal interest in politics until 1896, when he ran as a Conservative Party candidate from Halifax. That year the Conservatives under Sir Charles Tupper were badly beaten by the Liberals under WILFRID LAURIER, but Borden managed to capture his seat in Parliament. He was viewed as an exceptionally thorough and methodical individual, rather than brilliant, so when in 1901, following another defeat at the hands of Laurier, Tupper resigned, Borden—with great reluctance—became party head. This commenced a decade in the opposition for the Conservative leader, so effectively had the Liberals entrenched themselves in power. Never one to shirk a fight, Borden slowly and systematically rebuilt

the base of his party. He had to endure additional reverses in the 1904 and 1908 elections but his opportunity to shine finally arrived in 1911 when the Liberals were divided by internal opposition over Laurier's Naval Service Bill. Borden and the Conservatives denounced it as woefully inadequate for either assisting Great Britain or shoring up Canada's defenses. Laurier was also pummeled by the business community for negotiating the Reciprocity Agreement with the United States, which many feared would leave Canadian businesses overwhelmed by foreign competition. Borden carefully orchestrated his attacks upon the Liberals and their misguided policies, so the general election of 1911 swept the Conservatives back into power after 15 years in opposition.

For most of his tenure in office Borden's agenda was dominated by foreign events. In view of growing war clouds between Great Britain and Germany, he visited London in 1912 to proffer Canadian assistance for naval defense. His Naval Aid Bill promised to construct three battleships for British use as needed, but it was defeated in the Senate by Laurier and his Liberals. Borden's preoccupation with Europe reached a new urgency in August 1914 when World War I commenced. He was determined to stand by Great Britain, taking emergency steps to raise an army and increase Canada's level of industrialization. To do this he acquired emergency powers from the War Measures Act, levied the first national taxes upon Canadians, and founded the Canadian National Railway. Canadians fought with distinction in the air, on the sea, and especially on land, rendering valuable assistance to the hard-pressed British and French. By 1917, no less than 100,000 soldiers were deployed along the Western Front commanded—at Borden's insistence—by a Canadian general. That same year Borden was summoned to London by Prime Minister DAVID LLOYD GEORGE for deliberations in the Imperial War Cabinet. Impressed by the necessity of winning the war, he came home determined to resolve a long-standing problem in Canadian mobilization—manpower. As the pool of military volunteers slowly shrank through attrition, he managed to pass the nation's first draft law, the Military Service Bill, in July 1917. Like all conscription acts it proved highly unpopular and caused riots in French-speaking Quebec. The following year he also put through the Women's Franchise Bill of 1918, granting adult Canadian females the right to vote. All told, Borden's ceaseless efforts proved instrumental to Allied victory over Germany, and in 1919 he represented his country at the Paris peace talks. Canada thus enjoyed overseas representation for the first time.

Borden's wholehearted cooperation with Britain carried a price, however. He was indignant about the superior attitude shown by the mother country toward its colonies and determined that better treatment was necessary. He felt that if Canada could meet its military obligations to the empire it ought to have greater say in the management of imperial affairs affecting it. His efforts to upgrade the political status of all colonies laid the ideological foundation for a new power-sharing arrangement, the British Commonwealth, which emerged in the 1930s. Canada was thus enabled to join the new League of Nations as a sovereign nation and not simply an appendage of Great Britain. Borden remained in power until July 1920 when he resigned and was replaced by ARTHUR MEIGHEN. Thereafter, he led an active political life, lecturing widely on constitutional affairs and serving as chancellor of several leading universities. Borden died in Ottawa on June 10, 1937, having guided the Conservative Party from one of its darkest periods into its brightest political triumph. He also played a pivotal role in transforming the British Empire into the British Commonwealth for the benefit of its constituent members. Through hard work, hard bargaining, and determination he left Canada a mature nation with its own voice in global affairs, capable of shouldering international responsibilities.

Further Reading

Ballard, E. J. "Performance Ratings of Canadian Prime Ministers: Individual and Situational Factors." *Political Psychology* 9 (June 1988): 291–302.

Borden, Henry, ed. *Robert Laird Borden: His Memoirs.* 2 vols. Toronto: McClelland and Stewart, 1969.

Bothrell, R., and J. Bothrell. "The View From Inside Out: Canadian Diplomats and Their Public." *International Journal* 39 (winter 1984): 47–67.

Brown, Robert C. *Robert Laird Borden: A Biography.* 2 vols. Toronto: Macmillan of Canada, 1975–80.

English, John. *The Decline of Politics: The Conservatives and the Party System, 1901–1920.* Toronto: University of Toronto Press, 1993.

Morton, Desmond. *A Peculiar Kind of Politics: Canada's Overseas Ministry in the First World War.* Toronto: University of Toronto Press, 1982.

Bosch, Juan (1909–2001) *president of the Dominican Republic*

Juan Bosch Gaviño was born in La Vega, the Dominican Republic, on June 30, 1909, to lower-middle-class parents. He excelled academically and was drawn toward writing and publishing. His first collection of short stories emerged in 1933 and was widely acclaimed, but Bosch, an outspoken critic of Dominican dictator RAFAEL TRUJILLO, was arrested the following year. After working several months as a newspaper journalist Bosch entered voluntary exile in 1938 by moving to Cuba. There he helped to found the Partido Revolucionario Dominicano (PRD), Dominican Revolutionary Party, in exile, which agitated for an overthrow of Trujillo and a return to democracy. Eventually, he came to the attention of Cuban president Carlos Prío Socarrás, who made him his secretary. In 1947, with the help of a little-known leftist lawyer named Fidel Castro, Bosch helped organize the unsuccessful Cayo Confite expedition to topple Trujillo by force. It was not until Trujillo's assassination in 1961 that Bosch felt ready to come home, and he did so by organizing the PRD on Dominican soil and running for president. The ruling elite denounced him and his leftist ideology as Marxist, but on December 20, 1962, he won the island's first free elections since 1930.

Once inaugurated in February 1963, Bosch embarked on an ambitious campaign of land reform and other overt assistance to the poor majority. Such moves further alienated the landed gentry, the business classes, the Catholic Church hierarchy, and conservative military elements, who feared the rise of a home-grown Fidel Castro in their midst. Accordingly, he had been in power for only seven months before a military coup directed by General Elías Wessin y Wessin overthrew his regime. Bosch was then arrested and forcibly deported to the United States where he remained until 1966. Wessin installed a three-man civilian junta under Donald Reid Cabral, which clung to power until April 24, 1965, when it was overthrown by left-wing officers and military sympathizers. The rebels, self-styled "constitutionalists," wanted Bosch reinstalled as president along with the progressive policies he represented. Their actions roused the ire of American president LYNDON B. JOHNSON, who, fearing creation of another Marxist-dominated stronghold in the Caribbean, sent in marines to quell the disturbance in April 1965. Order was forcibly restored to the Dominican Republic, but the move was strongly denounced by most Latin American governments as yet another example of "gunboat diplomacy." Nevertheless, Johnson had made his point and had his way, and new Dominican presidential elections were scheduled for 1966.

After some criticism for not having returned home earlier to rally the "constitutionalists" fighting on his behalf, Bosch entered himself as the PRD's candidate for the presidency. His opponent was Joaquín Balaguer of the Reformist Party, who subsequently won the election by wide margins. This defeat initiated a 30-year rivalry between the two candidates, both being men of letters and embracing authoritarianism as a leadership style. Bosch continued running as the PRD candidate until 1973, when he broke with his allies to form a new organization, the Partido de la Liberación Dominicana (PLD), Dominican Liberation Party. The new group espoused an even stricter Marxist approach to politics and further contributed to Bosch's political alienation. By 1986 the PRD had disintegrated into several squabbling factions, while Bosch's PLD remained Balaguer's main opposition. In 1990 the two caudillos faced each other again, and Balaguer prevailed, although by the narrowest of margins. Bosch cried fraud and was determined to mount massive street protests but, dissuaded by President JIMMY CARTER, he accepted the results. He ran again in 1994, finishing a distant third, which effectively ended Bosch's political career. He nevertheless remained widely respected as a national hero and a figure of literary merit. Bosch died in Santo Domingo on November 1, 2001, a conspicuous figure in Dominican politics for 50 years.

Further Reading

Bosch, Juan. *The Unfinished Experiment: Democracy in the Dominican Republic.* New York: Praeger, 1965.

Chester, Eric T. *Rag-tags, Scum, Riff-raff, and Commies: The U.S. Intervention in the Dominican Republic, 1965–1966.* New York: Monthly Review Press, 2001.

Conklin, Deane. "Juan Bosch: His Literary Works and a Biographical Sketch." Unpublished Ph.D. diss., University of Southern California, 1972.

Lowenthal, Abraham L. "The Public Role of the Dominican Armed Forces: A Note on the 1963 Election of Juan Bosch and the 1965 Dominican Revolution." *Journal of Interamerican Studies and World Affairs* 15, no. 3 (1973): 355–361.

Wiarda, Pablo A. "The Democratic Process in the Dominican Republic: Some Fundamental Characteristics." *North-South* 4 (September 1994): 14–17.

Botha, Louis (1862–1919) *prime minister of South Africa*

Louis Botha was born in Greytown, Natal Province, South Africa, on September 27, 1862, the son of Afrikaner (Boer or Dutch) frontiersmen, or "Voortrekkers." Raised on a farm, he had little opportunity for higher education, but did become fluent in Zulu and other influential African dialects. Botha was also exposed to military training essential for frontier life and in 1884 he raised a commando (a troop of soldiers) that helped settle a succession dispute in the Zulu nation. Consequently, he was rewarded with a large tract of land, which Botha established as the New Republic. In 1884 this land was incorporated into the Transvaal, a large frontier community settled exclusively by Boers fleeing English domination of the coastal regions. South Africa was at that time an English colony and experiencing increased tensions between native Boers and newly arrived settlers. Botha, however, as a member of the Transvaal Volksraad (legislature), urged caution and conciliation when dealing with the English, who were many times more powerful than the scattered Afrikaners. His willingness to reach accord with the hated English caused much suspicion among his own people but, when the Boer War erupted in 1899, Botha threw his weight fully behind the fight for independence.

Botha proved himself a military commander of considerable merit and skillfully defeated larger British forces sent against him on three different occasions. At one point he counted among his captives the future English prime minister WINSTON CHURCHILL. By May 1900 Botha had emerged as commander in chief of the Transvaal region, aged but 38 years. Unfortunately, as the British continued pouring more men and resources into the campaign, the Afrikaners were forced back. Botha realized that the war was lost in a conventional sense, so he disbanded his commandos and engaged in a brilliant guerrilla war for nearly two years. The British remained inflexible in their determination to prevail, at which point Botha conceded that the war was lost and entered into peace negotiations. After several halting starts, the Treaty of Vereeniging was finally signed on

May 31, 1902, in which the Boers recognized British control over all South Africa. Thereafter, Botha supported reconciliation with Great Britain and amicable relations with all Afrikaners of European descent. To this end he founded the Het Volk Party in 1905 to promote harmonious governance.

Botha's efforts at fostering loyalty paid dividends in 1907 when the English government permitted self-government in the Transvaal. Botha, by dint of his immense wartime popularity, was easily elected prime minister on February 20, 1907, and ventured to an Imperial Conference in London. He initiated talks with the Crown for creation of a unified South African state that was loyal to the empire yet completely self-governing. His views were accepted by Parliament on May 31, 1910, when the four regions of Transvaal, the Orange Free State, Natal, and Capetown were unified into the Union of South Africa. Botha, at the head of his new South Africa Party, became the new nation's first prime minister. However, his willingness to negotiate with the English still occasioned resentment among hard-line elements in the Dutch-speaking community. One leader, James B. M. Hertzog, went on to form the decidedly anti-British National Party. Thereafter political friction between the two cliques was constant and disruptive.

As prime minister, Botha was faced with organizing his new country to function efficiently. He preached reconciliation as national policy, yet unflinchingly used military force to quell labor unrest by white miners. Worse, Botha, like many Afrikaners of his generation, looked unfavorably upon native black Africans and imported Indian laborers, and he enacted legislation to institutionalize second-class status for both groups. In June 1913 Parliament passed the Natives Land Act, which granted white Afrikaners 80 percent of South Africa's land. The majority populations, colored and mixed, were left to subsist on just 13 percent. Thousands of tribesmen were thus driven from their homelands into squatter camps, completely dependent upon whites for employment. This legislation was the genesis of official racial separation policies that reached their highest expression in the apartheid system of the 1950s. But Botha and others sincerely viewed such measures as the most rational way of preserving peace between the two groups, as long as whites remained intent upon securing control. It proved a most poisonous legacy.

When World War I commenced in August 1914, Botha loyally and vociferously supported Great Britain's war aims. This, in turn, resurrected old charges of betrayal to a hated conqueror from strident Boer factions. When Botha mobilized South African troops to invade German-held Southwest Africa (modern Namibia), radical elements rose in revolt and had to be quelled by force. In the spring of 1915 Botha successfully conquered the German colony for England and was allowed to represent South Africa at the 1919 Paris Peace Conference. In addition to securing rights to administer former German possessions, he also entreated the victors to be lenient with the defeated Germany. Botha died in Pretoria, Transvaal, on August 27, 1919, and was replaced by his close associate JAN SMUTS. He still is celebrated as the architect of his nation and for his willingness to accommodate English-speaking settlers, but reviled for the racial policies that sowed much discord later on.

Further Reading

Feinberg, Harvey M. "The 1913 Natives Land Act in South Africa: Politics, Race, and Segregation in the Early 20th Century." *International Journal of African Studies* 26, no. 1 (1993): 65–109.

Garson, N. G. "'Het-Volk': The Botha-Smuts Party in the Transvaal, 1904–11." *Historical Journal* 9 (1966): 101–132.

Hyam, Ronald. *The Lion and the Springbok: Britain and South Africa since the Boer War.* New York: Cambridge University Press, 2003.

Kalley, Jacqueline A. *South Africa's Treaties in Theory and Practice.* Lanham, Md.: Scarecrow Press, 2001.

Mawby, A. A. *Goldmining and Politics: Johannesburg, 1900–1907: The Origins of Old South Africa.* Lewiston, N.Y.: Edwin Mellen Press, 2001.

Meintjes, Johannes. *General Louis Botha: A Biography.* London: Cassell, 1970.

Botha, Willem (P. W. Botha) (1916–)

president of South Africa

P(ieter) W(illem) Botha was born in Paul Roux, Orange Free State, South Africa, on January 12, 1916, the son of Afrikaner farmers. His family had fought in the Boer War against England and were active in conservative Afrikaner politics. Not surprisingly, Botha attended the University of Orange Free State to study law but dropped out in 1935 to help found the white supremacist National Party. This organization was zealously committed to the separation of all Africans by their races, with political power exclusively reserved for whites. Botha initially sought work as a public information officer, and in 1948 he gained a seat in Parliament from the George district in Cape Province. He held it for the next 32 years. That same year the National Party was swept to power and immediately acted out its credo by establishing strict racial separation laws, known collectively as apartheid. South Africa had always known some degree of racial separation, but now barriers were codified and systematically enforced. Botha continued on as a party operative until 1958, when Prime Minister HENDRIK VERWOERD made him minister of the interior. Thereafter his sterling credentials served him well as he successively acquired important government portfolios.

Botha's rise to national prominence began in 1966 when he gained appointment as defense minister in the administration of BALTHAZAR VORSTER. In this capacity, he made indelible contributions to the maintenance and survival of apartheid in South Africa. Botha increased the defense budget 20-fold and acquired modern weapons systems for the military. Disregarding an international arms embargo against South Africa, Botha orchestrated programs to help the country become self-sufficient in military technology—including a small cache of nuclear weapons. The size of the armed forces was also enlarged through universal conscription of white males, and South Africa quickly emerged as a regional superpower south of the Sahara. As defense minister, Botha did not hesitate to employ preemptive strikes against neighboring states that harbored guerrillas from the banned African National Congress (ANC), a leftist resistance group. Namibia, Mozambique, Tanzania, and other frontline states were repeatedly attacked until governments there agreed to ban ANC activities on their soil. Botha, an avowed anticommunist, committed South African soldiers to Angola, where they fought with Cuban forces deployed by Fidel Castro. This aggressive combination of limited warfare and muscle flexing greatly buoyed Botha's national profile and popularity among white Afrikaners, so in 1978 he succeeded Vorster as prime minister.

Once in power, Botha displayed a distinct dichotomy to his leadership. Realizing that South Africa could not endure forever, he advised his countrymen to "adapt or die." He then implemented cosmetic changes to the apartheid system, dismantling some of its longstanding policies, like the ban on interracial marriage, authorizing of African trade unions, and allowing black Africans in urban centers to own property. Such tinkering led to howls of protest from extreme Afrikaner elements in the National Party and they split off to form the new, hardline Conservative Party. Undaunted, in 1982 Botha pushed through constitutional amendments creating a three-house (tricameral) legislature that allowed mixed race and Indian representation for the first time. The office of prime minister was then abolished and Botha was reinstated as president on September 14, 1984. However, no accommodation was made toward the black majority, and whites firmly controlled the reins of power.

Instead of fostering amity, Botha's reforms exacerbated black impatience at home and alienated world opinion abroad. New economic sanctions were enacted against South Africa while Africans took to the streets in violent protest. Botha's response was to unleash police and state security forces against them, and at one point an estimated 40,000 people were confined. Another 4,000 citizens died in confrontations with security forces. On the international scene, Botha did manage to negotiate a peaceful settlement to the ongoing conflicts in Angola and Namibia, but Western nations, joined now by the United States, refused to lift their embargos. When Botha fell ill in January 1989 party officials moved quickly to replace him with the more moderately disposed F. W. De Klerk. Botha resigned from public life on August 15, 1989, both admired and reviled as the "Old Crocodile" of South African politics. But by March 1992 the rule of apartheid ended as Nelson Mandela became South Africa's first black executive. As clever and ruthlessly determined as Botha was, even he could not forestall the eclipse of a violent, hated regime based solely on racial division.

In the mid-1990s, Botha was repeatedly summoned before the National Truth and Reconciliation Commission for frank discussion of his role in maintaining the apartheid state. Three times he blatantly ignored their subpoenas and was finally charged with contempt in 1998. However, old and ailing, he successfully appealed his conviction and no further action has been taken against him. Botha, true to his Afrikaner heritage, remains a strident critic of South Africa's new, multiracial government.

Further Reading

Botha, P. W. *P. W. Botha in His Own Words.* New York: Penguin, 1987.

Geldenhuys, Deon, and Koos Van Wyk. "South Africa in Crisis: A Comparison of the Vorster and Botha Eras." *South Africa International* 16, no. 3 (1986): 135–145.

Grundy, Kenneth W. "Race Politics in South Africa: Change and Revolt." *Current History* 85, no. 451 (1986): 197–200, 227–228.

Roherty, James M. *State Security in South Africa: Civil-Military Relations under P. W. Botha.* Armonk, N.Y.: M. E. Sharpe, 1992.

Shephard, Robert B., and Christopher H. Goldman. "P. W. Botha's Foreign Policy." *National Interest* 15 (1989): 68–78.

Vale, Peter. "Simple-mindedness and Repression: The Establishment Responds to South Africa's Woes." *Round Table* no. 303 (1987): 311–321.

Boumédienne, Houari (1932–1978) *president of Algeria*

Mohammed Ben Brahim Boukharouba was born in Clauzel, eastern Algeria, on August 23, 1932, the son of a poor farmer. He attended both French and Koranic schools as a child but, like many youths of his generation, Boukharouba became increasingly estranged from the colonial regime. In 1952 he fled Algeria to escape serving in the French army and settled in Cairo, Egypt, a hotbed of burgeoning Arab nationalism. While attending classes at the famous Al Azhar University, Boukharouba encountered another Algerian expatriate, AHMED BEN BELLA, and together they founded the Front de Libération Nationale (FLN), National Liberation Front, to end French rule in their homeland. Boukharouba then received military training from Egyptian president GAMAL ABDEL NASSER before joining the underground resistance in western Algeria. Commencing in 1954 the FLN conducted a concerted guerrilla war against French troops and civilians while the French countered with a brutal counterinsurgency campaign. An estimated 1 million Algerians and 40,000 French died in consequence. But by 1958 Boukharouba had risen through the FLN to the rank of colonel and chief of operations. He also adopted the name Houari Boumédienne, after two deceased Algerian patriots. After eight years of ruthless warfare in which

Boumédienne demonstrated skill as an organizer and guerrilla fighter, the French government finally accepted defeat as inevitable. In 1962 a public referendum on independence was overwhelmingly approved, and Algeria became a new nation.

No sooner had the FLN triumphed militarily than the political leadership began squabbling among themselves. When one faction of senior revolutionaries wanted to bring the military wing of the party entirely under their control, Boumédienne sided with Ben Bella, and their forces crushed the opposition on June 30, 1962. Consequently, Ben Bella became Algeria's first prime minister while Boumédienne was elevated to first vice minister and defense minister. The two men then set about a long-cherished goal of introducing modern socialism to their backward nation. For nearly three years Boumédienne watched as the flamboyant Ben Bella mishandled the economy trying to establish a Cuban-style economic revolution. Distrusting his defense secretary, he drew politically closer to Algeria's labor unions and Communist Party while taking steps to create a people's militia as a counterweight to the army. Boumédienne felt that moves against him were imminent and struck first on June 18, 1965. With Ben Bella removed from power he installed himself as the unofficial head of a council of officers. The march toward socialism continued.

In contrast to his outspoken predecessor, Boumédienne was austere, laconic, and rarely seen in public. Yet, by dint of sheer personality, he commanded the military's loyalty and survived a 1967 coup attempt with their help. For the next 16 years he ruled Algeria with an iron hand but never deviated from his goal of establishing a command economy. The oil industry was nationalized along with large sectors of industry. Greater emphasis was placed on construction of schools, hospitals, roads, electrification, and a better lifestyle for all citizens. Reforms were intelligently applied and diligently pursued so that in a few years Algeria enjoyed the most thriving economy of any developing nation. Boumédienne was determined to be a leader of the Nonaligned Movement of poor countries, distancing himself from France and the United States while cultivating closer ties with the Soviet Union and Arabic states. But, as an indication of his distaste for colonialism of any stripe, he did not allow the Russians to base their ships in Algerian ports. Boumédienne also fervently supported wars of national liberation against colonialism in the Maghreb (northwestern Africa), and gave arms and shelter to Polisario rebels fighting King MOHAMMED V of Morocco in the western Sahara. In 1967 he bitterly denounced Israeli conquests of Jerusalem and the Golan Heights and broke off diplomatic relations with the United States.

In December 1976, confident of his power base, Boumédienne sponsored a new constitution that institutionalized the FLN as Algeria's only legal party with himself as president. The measure passed overwhelmingly as an indication of his national popularity. His success lay partly in his approach to Islam in this rather conservative country; though secular by nature, Boumédienne treated creed and culture with diffidence and sought a rare union of religious practice with state-sponsored socialism. By the time he died of a rare blood ailment on December 27, 1978, he had transformed Algeria from a ravaged French colony to a thriving independent nation. However, his successor, CHADLI BENJEDID, systematically dismantled government control over the economy and implemented free market policies more attuned to Western nations.

Further Reading

Babinet, Bertrand. "Algeria: Boumédienne's Regime: Structures, Values, and Achievements." Unpublished master's thesis, American University, 1971.

Connelly, Matthew J. *A Diplomatic Revolution: Algeria's Fight for Independence and the Origins of the Post–Cold War Era.* New York: Oxford University Press, 2002.

Mortimer, R. "Algeria's New Sultan." *Current History* 80 (December 1981): 418–421, 433–434.

Pazzanita, Anthony G. "From Boumédienne to Benjedid: The Algerian Regime in Transition." *Journal of South Asian and Middle Eastern Studies* 15, no. 4 (1992): 51–70.

Ruf, Werner K. "The Flight of Rent: The Rise and Fall of a National Economy." *Journal of North African Studies* 2 (summer 1997): 1–15.

Salhi, Hamoud. "Hidden Liberalism in Boumédienne's Strategy of Development." Unpublished Ph.D. diss., University of Southern California, 1995.

Bourguiba, Habib Ben Ali (1903–2000)
president of Tunisia

Habib Ben Ali Bourguiba was born in Monastir, Tunisia, on August 3, 1903, into a modest family background. Well-educated at local French schools, he went on to pursue legal studies at the Sorbonne in Paris and returned in 1928 to practice law. Bourguiba, like many youths of his generation, strongly resented French colonial rule and he joined the Dustour, or Constitution, Party, to oppose them. Finding this group of aging and aristocratic elites too faint-hearted, he broke ranks in 1934 to form the more radical Neo-Dustour Party, calling for outright independence. French authorities responded by repeatedly arresting Bourguiba over the next few years, and in 1938 he was imprisoned in France. However, World War II intervened when occupying German forces released him in an attempt to solicit his cooperation. Bourguiba refused, however, and by 1943 he was back in Tunisia intent on ingratiating his party with the Allies. After the war ended two years later, he intensified his campaign for Tunisian independence and even promulgated a seven-point plan to achieve it, but the French opposed any such moves. After addressing the United Nations in 1951, Bourguiba was again arrested and detained by French authorities. However, by 1954 Pan-Arabic nationalism was in full play and Tunisia was beset by mass protests and rioting. The French government, preoccupied by a war raging in Algeria, felt it had no choice but to negotiate with the Neo-Dustour Party. Bourguiba was accordingly released in 1955 and commenced negotiations. His nine years of imprisonment on behalf of independence would pay off handsomely.

Bourguiba proved a skilled and patient negotiator, for he realized that time and events were on his side. By 1956 the French capitulated to Neo-Dustour demands for Tunisian freedom and the party won new legislative elections easily. Bourguiba became the nation's first prime minister, and in 1957 he convinced the national legislature to dissolve the monarchy, declare Tunisia a republic, and appoint him as president. By patient negotiations and guile, Bourguiba achieved his goals without the internecine violence that left Algeria in ruins. Moreover, being favorably disposed toward the West, the new executive was bent on enacting a modernizing agenda for his nation. His first act was to upgrade the status of women with voting rights and equality in divorce. He curtailed the influence of Islam on daily life, stressed secularized education, and placed many mosques under strict government control. All these accomplishments won Bourguiba plaudits from the West and rendered him the most popular politician in the country.

Unlike many Arab contemporaries, Bourguiba cultivated close ties to the West and strongly opposed communist penetration of North Africa. He also attacked the Pan-Arabic movement and its sponsor, Egyptian president GAMAL ABDEL NASSER, initiating a period of tense relations. Bourguiba was unusual in advocating a peaceful settlement of the Arab-Israeli dispute, and he distanced himself from more radical states such as Syria and Iraq. In 1961 Tunisian forces had a brief but costly war attempting to force the French from their last remaining outpost at Bizerte, but afterward he sought reconciliation and closer ties with his former adversaries. As a reward for his independent stance many Western nations, in particular the United States, supported Tunisia with generous financial assistance. Bourguiba remained a trusted Arab ally throughout most of the cold war, at a time when the Middle East was dangerously polarized.

Bourguiba remained head of state for 30 years, ruling Tunisia with an autocratic turn of mind that belied his polished, Western outlook. Declared president for life in 1976, his economic policies were socialist-oriented, and he enshrined the Neo-Dustour Party as the only legal outlet for political expression. Moreover, he stifled political dissent, especially Islamic fundamentalists who resented his modernizing efforts. When Tunisia's command economy began failing in the 1980s, Bourguiba unhesitatingly employed troops to maintain order, with several hundred deaths resulting. He also ruthlessly sacked ministers and prime ministers to prevent them from gaining popularity and potentially challenging his authority. But by 1987 Bourguiba's physical and mental health had declined to the point where onlookers began questioning his sanity. On November 7, 1987, General Zine al-Abidine Ben Ali deposed the president in a bloodless coup, thereby concluding a remarkable chapter in Tunisia's political history. Bourguiba remained under house arrest for 13 years until his death on April 6, 2000. Despite the oppression of his rule and the erratic behavior associated with his final years in power, he is fondly regarded as the father of modern Tunisia. In fact, the term "Bourguibaism" has been coined to describe his tactic of methodically and patiently achieving dramatic and otherwise unattainable political ends.

Further Reading

Brown, Carl L. "Bourguiba and Bourguibaism Revisited: Reflections and Interpretation." *Middle East Journal* 55 (winter 2001): 43–58.

Habib Bourguiba *(Library of Congress)*

Hopwood, Derek. *Habib Bourguiba of Tunisia: The Tragedy of Longevity.* New York: St. Martin's Press, 1992.

Murphy, Emma C. *Economic and Political Change in Tunisia: From Bourguiba to Ben Ali.* New York: St. Martin's Press, 1999.

———. "Women in Tunisia: A Survey of Achievements and Challenges." *Journal of North African Studies* 1 (autumn 1996): 138–156.

Salem, Norma. *Habib Bourguiba, Islam, and the Creation of Tunisia.* Dover, N.H.: Croom Helm, 1984.

Zouari, Abdel J. "The Effects of Ben Ali's Democratic Reforms in the Islamist Movement in Tunisia." Unpublished master's thesis, University of Washington, 1989.

Brandt, Willy (1913–1992) *chancellor of West Germany*

Karl Herbert Frahm was born in Lübeck, Germany, on December 18, 1913, the illegitimate son of a teenage store clerk. He endured a life of deprivation but proved an excellent student, winning a scholarship to a private high school. The greatest influence on his life was his grandfather, an old-time socialist who imparted leftist political values to him. Accordingly, Frahm was still a teenager when he became active in the Social Democratic Party (SPD), writing columns as an aspiring journalist under the pseudonym "Willy Brandt." By the 1930s, with ADOLF HITLER's Nazi Party on the rise, Frahm found the SPD too tame in its opposition, so he quit and joined the more radical Socialist Worker's Party (SWP). His political activism made him a wanted man, so he fled Germany for Norway to assist the flow of other refugees. Throughout 1936 Brandt continued making illicit trips back to Berlin to maintain political contacts, and the following year he covered the Spanish civil war for the party paper. He was somewhat disillusioned by the communist cadres he encountered. Brandt was living in Norway when Germany attacked in 1940, and subsequently he fled for Sweden. There he encountered two other determined socialists, OLOF PALME and BRUNO KREISKY, whom he befriended for life. Moreover, the experience of living in Scandinavia, where he witnessed moderate brands of socialism, forever altered his political perspectives. Thereafter, Brandt dedicated himself to mainstream, moderate policies, while denouncing the Marxist-Leninist subversion and tyranny of the far left.

After the defeat of Nazi Germany in 1945, Brandt returned home as a Norwegian journalist but found the lure of politics irresistible. Accordingly, he regained his German citizenship in 1948 and successfully ran for a seat in the Bundestag (legislature) as an SPD member. Over the next decade he worked conscientiously to advance his socialist agenda, although in a form acceptable to the new Federal Republic of West Germany. Germany was then partitioned between the Western powers and the Soviet Union, which created its own client state, the German Democratic Republic (East Germany). Brandt played a crucial role at the SPD congress in Bad Godesberg in 1959 in the party's formal renunciation of its former Marxist beliefs. In October 1957 Brandt was elected mayor of West Berlin, deep inside the Soviet sector. It was in this

Willy Brandt *(Library of Congress)*

capacity, on the front line of cold war politics, that he rose to international prominence. When Soviet premier NIKITA KHRUSHCHEV authorized construction of the Berlin Wall, effectively dividing the eastern and western halves of the city, Brandt bitterly denounced the act. He also became convinced, in the interest of keeping East German citizens from drifting away from the rest of the nation, that West Germany should adopt more conciliatory practices toward its communist neighbor.

In 1961 Brandt was the SPD candidate for chancellor, but he was easily defeated by KONRAD ADENAUER of the Christian Democratic Union. He ran again in 1965 against LUDWIG ERHARD, losing by a smaller margin. However, in 1966 the Free Democrats withdrew from the Christian Democratic coalition, and a new chancellor, KURT KIESINGER, invited the SPD in as a partner for the first time. Brandt thus became foreign minister and vice chancellor, eager to implement what he called his Ostpolitik (Eastern policy). This centered on friendly, normalized relations with the Soviet Union and its Warsaw Pact allies, including East Germany. The policy was well received publicly, and in September 1969 new elections gave the SPD a chance to form a coalition with the Free Democrats in the legislature. Brandt then became the nation's first socialist chancellor since the 1930s. He now accelerated the pace of Ostpolitik, signing a nonaggression pact with the Soviets in August 1970, and formally recognizing the new boundary between Germany and Poland (the Oder-Neisse Line) in December 1970. This paved the way for mutual recognition between East and West Germany, which began opening borders to each other's citizens in 1971. Brandt, mindful of the horrors of the Nazi past, was also determined to display German contrition over the war, and at one point he knelt before the Warsaw Memorial Ghetto. He also became the first German political executive to visit the state of Israel, largely created in the wake of Hitler's Holocaust against the Jews. Through these expedients, Brandt resurrected Germany onto the main stage of international politics. It proved a bravura performance that did much to defuse cold war tensions throughout central and Eastern Europe. For all his endeavors Brandt received the Nobel Peace Prize in 1971.

In May 1974 the cold war intruded on Brandt's political fortunes when it was revealed that a close personal aide was an East German spy. He resigned from office in favor of HELMUT SCHMIDT, but was allowed to remain as head of the SPD until 1987. Two years later he witnessed the fall of the hated Berlin Wall and the peaceful reunification of his homeland. Previously, in 1976, he had become leader of the Socialist Internationale (the worldwide socialist organization) and pushed for greater assistance to the Third World. Brandt also relished his role as an elder world statesman, and in 1991 he visited the Persian Gulf to negotiate the release of hostages held in Iraq. He also attempted to prevent civil war in the former Yugoslavia. Brandt died on October 9, 1992, in Bonn, greatly mourned by the German nation. For the previous five decades he worked hard at bona fide reconciliation between the Western and communist camps, with the purpose of reuniting Germany peacefully and restoring its standing as a civilized nation. That Germany today is a unified, pluralistic, and economically dominant nation testifies to Brandt's political skill and vision.

Further Reading

Allen, Debra J. *The Oder-Neisse Line: The U.S., Poland, and Germany in the Cold War.* Westport, Conn.: Praeger, 2003.

Bluth, Christopher. *The Two Germanies and Military Security in Europe.* New York: Palgrave Macmillan, 2002.

Brandt, Willy. *My Life in Politics.* New York: Viking, 1992.

Marshall, Barbara. *Willy Brandt: A Political Biography.* New York: St. Martin's Press, 1997.

Sarotte, M. E. "A Small Town in (East) Germany: The Erfurt Meeting of 1970 and the Dynamics of Cold War Detente." *Diplomatic History* 25, no. 1 (2001): 85–104.

Smyser, W. R. *From Yalta to Berlin: The Cold War Struggle Over Germany.* New York: St. Martin's Press, 1999.

Branting, Karl (1860–1925) *prime minister of Sweden*

Karl Hjalmar Branting was born in Stockholm, Sweden, on November 23, 1860, the son of a university professor. He was well educated at private schools, and in 1877 gained admittance to the University of Uppsala to study astronomy. Branting proved himself a talented student and a promising scientist, but in 1882 he dropped out of school to pursue journalism and politics. Specifically, he had become enamored of the tenets of labor socialism and contributed daily columns to labor newspapers. By 1889 Branting was well positioned among left-wing agitators to help found the Social Democratic Party (SDP), Sweden's first labor-oriented movement, serving as its first secretary. Seven years later he became the party's first parliamentary deputy by winning a seat in the Riksdag from Stockholm in 1896. Branting remained the SDP's sole representative until 1902, and in 1907 he advanced to party chairman.

Swedish socialism by then had diverged from most European models by distancing itself from violent revolution and striving to work from within the existing system. Branting, in essence, was determined to gradually reshape capitalist society rather than upend it, and he usually worked in alliance with reformist elements of the Liberal Party. Branting was largely responsible for peaceful transformation through the SDP. He and others had watched in horror as the Russian Revolution of 1905 unfolded in all its fury, and he maintained that extending universal suffrage to adults could circumvent similar violence. In 1906 he forcefully purged the party of violent anarchist and communist elements, thereby improving its respectability. By 1917 the SDP was the largest party in the legislature and well positioned to push for universal suffrage and an eight-hour working day. In concert with Liberals, Branting's efforts were successful. That year he was also tapped to serve as finance minister in the Liberal/socialist coalition government of Nils Eden, becoming the first SDP minister.

In March 1920 Eden resigned over policy differences, and Branting succeeded him, becoming Sweden's first socialist prime minister. His administration lasted only a few months but he established several commissions to investigate industrial democracy, nationalization of certain sectors of the economy, and socialization of natural resources. Elections of September 1921 were the first held under universal suffrage, and the SPD triumphed handily, assuring Branting's second term as prime minister. His legislative accomplishments were limited, as he lacked a working majority in the legislature and was further beset by labor disputes and unemployment. His government fell in April 1923 after a dispute with the Commission on Unemployment. The socialists then resumed power in October 1924, although Branting, by now an ailing man, was forced to resign in January 1925. All told, his three terms in office produced no legislative miracles or sweeping reforms, but did demonstrate that the SDP possessed the acumen to govern the nation competently and peacefully.

In addition to social democracy, Branting gained international renown as a pacifist. He was an outspoken proponent of the international peace movement and in 1905 worked diligently to maintain good relations between Sweden and Norway when the latter unilaterally opted for independence. When World War I erupted in August 1914 Branting argued strenuously for Swedish neutrality and spent the next four years trying to reach a negotiated settlement. In 1919 he served as the Swedish delegate to the Paris peace conference and denounced the Treaty of Versailles as too harsh toward Germany. In 1920 he visited London to broker a solution to the disputed ownership of the Aland Islands, jointly claimed by Sweden and Finland, and also helped arrange for the removal of British troops from Turkey following its diplomatic recognition in 1924. He was a staunch exponent of the newly organized League of Nations and served as the first Swedish representative in 1922. By this time, Branting was an internationally recognized figure, and in 1921 he shared the Nobel Peace Prize with his fellow Scandinavian, Christian L. Lange of Norway. Branting died in Stockholm on February 24, 1925. Having established the Social Democrats as a legitimate force in national politics, he also laid the groundwork for the famous welfare state that dominated and defined Swedish political culture for the next 70 years.

Further Reading

Berman, Sheri. *The Social Democratic Movement: Ideas and Politics in the Making of Interwar Europe.* Cambridge, Mass.: Harvard University Press, 1998.

Hurd, Madeline. *Public Spheres, Public Mores, and Democracy: Hamburg and Stockholm, 1870–1914.* Ann Arbor: University of Michigan Press, 2000.

Malmbourg, Mikael. *Neutrality and State-Building in Sweden.* New York: Palgrave, 2001.

Nordstrom, Byron J. *The History of Sweden.* Westport, Conn.: Greenwood Press, 2002.

Tilton, Timothy A. *The Political History of Swedish Social Democracy: Through the Welfare State to Socialism.* New York: Oxford University Press, 1990.

Brezhnev, Leonid (1906–1982) *general secretary of the Communist Party of the Soviet Union*

Leonid Ilyich Brezhnev was born in Kamenskoye, Ukraine, on December 19, 1906, the son of Russian immigrant parents. After training as a metallurgist, he joined the Communist Party in 1931 and commenced a slow but steady climb through the official hierarchy. In this process he was greatly assisted by NIKITA KHRUSHCHEV, who took him in as an understudy. During World War II Brezhnev served as a political commissar in the Red Army, rising to the rank of major general. Afterward he held party positions of increasing responsibility in Moldavia and Kazakhstan, and in 1952 he was summoned to Moscow by Soviet dictator JOSEPH STALIN as part of the Central Committee. After Stalin died in 1953, Brezhnev's career was briefly sidelined by political competitors, but by 1956 he had been rehabilitated by Khrushchev, himself now premier. By 1960 he had been promoted to nonvoting membership within the Politburo and was a chairperson of the Supreme

Soviet (legislature). However, when Khrushchev was summarily deposed in 1964 by conservative elements, Brezhnev sided with them. He then aligned himself with numerous leaders, including Aleksey Kosygin, but within two years, with backing from the military leaders, Brezhnev emerged as first among equals and de facto head of the vast Soviet Union.

Brezhnev inherited a nation with a large military-industrial complex, a respectable scientific community, and—thanks to Khrushchev—an economy tottering on collapse. To resolve this he quickly undid many of the latter's more liberalizing reforms and sought stability by reimposing state control over agriculture. He also clamped down on the arts, which had flourished under Khrushchev, and resumed a strict Communist orthodoxy with respect to creativity. Mindful of the recent Soviet humiliation by the United States during the 1962 Cuban missile crisis, Brezhnev vowed never to back down from his capitalist adversary for want of strength. Henceforth, the Soviet economy became heavily skewed toward heavy industry and the production of a colossal military establishment. Agricultural production, consumer goods, and health care were all slowly sacrificed in the Communist quest for strategic superiority over the United States. It was the biggest military outlay in history and transformed both the Soviet Union and its Warsaw Pact allies of Eastern Europe into the world's most formidably armed garrison states.

Concurrent with this buildup, Brezhnev also sent out peace feelers to the United States and its Western allies in an attempt to secure better, more harmonious relations. This process, known as detente, began in 1969 with the Strategic Arms Limitation Treaty (SALT), which was designed to place ceilings on nuclear arsenals. In 1972 he concluded the SALT I Treaty in Moscow, with President RICHARD M. NIXON, and subsequently negotiated a more extensive SALT II agreement with Presidents GERALD R. FORD and JIMMY CARTER. In 1975 Brezhnev reached the pinnacle of diplomatic success by concluding the Helsinki Accords, which finalized Western recognition of Soviet territorial gains made since 1945. Major provisions for respecting human rights, included in the accords, were consistently ignored. With the Soviet Union at peace and its economy briefly and temporarily reviving, the world seemed to be entering a new chapter in human cooperation. But, in keeping with the nature of the communist regime, Brezhnev's peace overtures were a smokescreen

for expanding Soviet subversion and influence around the world, which was accomplished primarily through armed proxies like Cuba and East Germany. The Soviets made significant gains in the Horn of Africa, Southeast Asia, and the Middle East, while the Western democracies dithered in response.

In 1968 Brezhnev announced a major new policy, the "Brezhnev Doctrine," whereby the Soviet Union reserved the right to intervene with any East European ally to preserve "socialism." This was starkly demonstrated in August 1968, when he crushed a reformist movement in Czechoslovakia under ALEXANDER DUBČEK. After failing to achieve a rapprochement with MAO ZEDONG of the People's Republic of China, Russian and Chinese forces clashed several times along their heavily armed border in 1969. But the Soviets otherwise remained committed to assisting "wars of liberation" waged by communist elements throughout the developing world. Domestically, Brezhnev greatly enhanced the size and authority of the KGB, the dreaded secret police, by granting YURI ANDROPOV carte blanche to crack down on dissent. However, the aging and ailing Communist erred badly in December 1979, when he dispatched several thousand Soviet troops to Afghanistan to install a communist regime under BABRAK KARMAL. Such overt aggression brought world condemnation and stimulated the rise of anticommunist stalwarts like RONALD REAGAN in the United States and MARGARET THATCHER in the United Kingdom. Reagan, in particular, was determined to roll back Soviet gains in Afghanistan, Nicaragua, and elsewhere. He initiated a two-track policy, matching the Soviet arms buildup while supplying covert aid to anticommunist freedom fighters. The results bogged down the Soviet Union in guerrilla wars it could not win, while forcing it to acquire more weapons at the expense of long-suffering citizens.

By 1982 the Soviet Union was nearing a state of collapse economically and could hardly feed its own people. Worse, the political stability and loyalty Brezhnev cultivated during his long tenure in power resulted in unprecedented corruption and graft, which contributed to dramatically declining standards of living. In his last years, Brezhnev seemed moribund and detached from events, being rarely seen at mandatory public festivities. He died in Moscow on November 10, 1982, and was replaced, surprisingly, by former KGB chief Yuri Andropov rather than his longtime protégé

KONSTANTIN CHERNENKO. But the Soviet Union, which he led longer than any other postwar Communist leader, proved every bit as ossified and dysfunctional as himself. It sputtered on until its final collapse under MIKHAIL GORBACHEV in 1991, a grim testimony to the folly of communism.

Further Reading

Anderson, Richard. *Public Politics in an Authoritarian State: Making Foreign Policy during the Brezhnev Years.* Ithaca, N.Y.: Cornell University Press, 1993.

Bacon, Edwin, and Mark Sandle. *Brezhnev Reconsidered.* New York: Palgrave, 2002.

Brezhnev, Leonid. *Memoirs.* Oxford, England: Pergamon Press, 1982.

Brezhnev, Luba. *The World I Left Behind: Pieces of the Past.* New York: Random House, 1995.

Dallin, Alexander. *The Khrushchev and Brezhnev Years.* New York: Garland, 1992.

Grogin, Robert C. *Natural Enemies: The United States and the Soviet Union in the Cold War, 1917–1991.* Lanham, Md.: Lexington Books, 2001.

Loth, Wilfried. *Overcoming the Cold War: A History of Detente, 1950–1991.* New York: Palgrave, 2002.

Ouimet, Matthew J. *The Rise and Fall of the Brezhnev Doctrine in Soviet Foreign Policy.* Chapel Hill: University of North Carolina Press, 2003.

Briand, Aristide (1862–1932) *prime minister of France*

Aristide Pierre Henri Briand was born in Nantes, France, on March 28, 1862, into a family of small shop owners. He studied law in Paris but was drawn to politics and union activism. Early in his life Briand was associated with radical socialism of one sort or another, pairing it with strict anticlericalism, but by the end of the century he moderated his militancy and joined the mainstream French Socialist Party. After repeated attempts Briand finally gained election to the House of Deputies in 1905, where he distinguished himself with fine oratory and a grasp of complicated issues. In 1906 he demonstrated his skill by finessing a bill mandating the separation of church and state, winning surprising support from both anticlericals and the Catholic Church. In 1908 Briand's fame was such that he gained appointment as minister of justice in the administration of GEORGES CLEMENCEAU. By this time he had also broken with the socialists and

served more or less as a conservative legislator. In 1909 he rose to become prime minister, the first of 11 times. He clearly demonstrated how far he had drifted from leftist politics by using military force to suppress striking railway workers in 1910. Briand also made it clear that even greater violence would be in the offing, for he deemed railroads essential to the well-being of France. Such posturing cost him what little socialist support remained in the Chamber of Deputies, and when the socialists withdrew from the coalition, he resigned from office, in February 1911. He returned briefly to power in 1913 and, true to his newfound conservative beliefs, extended military service from two to three years.

The onset of World War I brought Briand back into the headlines with more controversy. In October 1915 he again became prime minister and railed against the senior Allied leadership's obsession with the western front. Instead, he advocated a diversionary campaign into the Balkans to support Greece and Serbia, which was eventually done. Briand also extended peace feelers to Germany and Austria in an attempt to find a negotiated settlement, but these efforts failed. Moreover, he ran afoul of the formidable war leader Clemenceau over the issue of army performance, and in November 1917 he was forced from office a second time. His political eclipse was such that he played no role in the ensuing Paris Peace Conference of 1919 and the treaty that followed. For the next two years Briand ably plotted backroom machinations through which he maneuvered himself back into power. He enjoyed a brief stint as premier again in 1921, only to be ousted again the following year, but in 1924 Briand assumed the office that was to bring him renown, that of foreign minister.

Unlike many postwar contemporaries, Briand harbored little ill will toward Germany and realized that the harsh provisions in the Treaty of Versailles militated against long-term rapprochement. Therefore, in 1924 he entered into negotiations with German foreign secretary GUSTAV STRESEMANN for some much-needed diplomatic readjustments. The ensuing Locarno Pact, signed on October 16, 1925, was significant for reaffirming Germany's pledge to repay wartime reparations in exchange for membership in the newly organized League of Nations. In fact, Briand thought it essential that both nations strive for closer economic and political relations to rule out the possibility of a future war. For their diligent efforts, Briand and Stresemann shared the 1926 Nobel Peace Prize.

Aristide Briand (center) *(Library of Congress)*

In 1927 Briand sought to capitalize on his peace efforts by soliciting closer ties to the United States. Negotiations with American secretary of state Frank B. Kellogg produced the so-called Kellogg-Briand Pact, which essentially outlawed the use of war as a means for achieving foreign policy objectives. It was finalized on August 27, 1928, by over 50 signatories, but proved impractical to enforce. By the end of the decade, Briand, now a committed internationalist, sought to advance peace by proposing a European federal union, the United States of Europe. Such an organization would be closely integrated economically and militarily, thereby reducing the chances for war. The idea failed to garner wide acceptance at that time but, curiously, anticipated today's European Union (EU) by 50 years. To underscore his determination, Briand withdrew French troops from the German Rhineland in exchange for pledges to honor reparation payments. After completing his 11th stint as prime minister in 1929, Briand finally retired from public life. Active

and eloquent as ever, he was contemplating a run for the presidency of France before dying in Paris on March 7, 1932. Given his longevity in office and his pursuit of Franco-German amity—an unthinkable prospect for many after the horrors of World War I— he was one of the most farsighted statesmen of his generation.

Further Reading

Dutton, David. "A Nation of Shopkeepers in Search of a Suitable Frenchman: Britain and Briand, 1915–1930." *Modern and Contemporary France* 6, no. 4 (1998): 463–478.

Jones, Catharine. "The 1929 League of Nations Initiative: Aristide Briand's Plan for European Federation." *Journal of the Georgia Association of Historians* 19 (1998): 15–38.

Keeton, Edward D. *Briand's Locarno Policy: French Economics, Politics, and Diplomacy, 1925–1929.* New York: Garland, 1987.

Kneeshaw, Stephen J. *In Pursuit of Peace: The American Reaction to the Kellogg-Briand Pact, 1928–1929.* New York: Garland, 1991.

Martin, B. F. "Briand à la Barre: Aristide Briand and the Politics of Betrayal." *French Politics and Society* 15 (summer 1997): 57–64.

Navari, Cornelia. "The Origins of the Briand Plan." *Diplomacy and Statecraft* 3, no. 1 (1992): 74–104.

Bruce, Stanley (1883–1967) *prime minister of Australia*

Stanley Melbourne Bruce was born in Melbourne, Australia, on April 15, 1883, into an affluent mercantile family. Well-educated as a youth, he ventured to England in 1902 to attend Trinity College, Cambridge University, and read law. Bruce was called to the bar but elected to join a London business firm controlled by his father, where he made a fortune. When World War I commenced in August 1914, he joined the famous Royal Fusiliers as an officer and fought with distinction, earning many decorations. His wounds made him ineligible for further service, so after 15 years Bruce came home with the deportment and speech mannerisms of an English aristocrat. He became interested in politics and in 1918 was elected to Parliament with the National Party. He impressed contemporaries with his tact and ability, and in 1921 Prime Minister WILLIAM MORRIS HUGHES appointed him treasurer. Bruce fulfilled his duties capably until a coalition of National Party and Country Party members arranged Hughes's ouster in 1923. They anointed Bruce his successor. It was a startling development for a relatively inexperienced politician, although Bruce appeared well suited to lead the nation. But not in Australia.

In power Bruce was a quintessential English capitalist and an expert at promoting business interests. He adopted the slogan, "men, money, and markets," to foster Australia's economic development within its imperial setting. He placed great emphasis on immigration from Europe while scouting the English money markets for investment capital. As national infrastructure projects unfolded, more and more Australian farm products made their way back to British markets. For many years Bruce's policies produced a booming economy but he also subscribed to the tenet of a minimum wage to maintain a standard of living. Internationally, Bruce lent his weight to activities of the League of Nations and to preventing the squandering of Australian manpower in another European war. For many years his coalition government functioned smoothly until its policy of high farm prices drove down worker's wages. This occasioned a series of bitter strikes by unions to regain what had been lost. Bruce, who displayed little sympathy for organized labor, resorted to repressive measures to contain unrest. Moreover, his reputation for acting more as an insensitive Englishman than a native Australian alienated many voters, and his popularity dwindled. Though the Great Depression commenced in 1929, he continued on with his attacks on labor over the objections of imperiled politicians. On October 12, 1929, the Labour Party was swept back into power and Bruce became the first and only sitting prime minister to lose his seat. He regained it two years later representing the Australia United Party, but the consensus of political opinion found him too divisive a figure for national leadership. He never again held executive office.

Bruce was ideally suited, by dint of his education, training, and impeccable British background, to represent Australian interests abroad once the British Empire had slowly converted itself into a commonwealth. In 1932 he accepted appointment as Australian high commissioner in London where he remained successfully employed for 12 years. He enjoyed his greatest success during World War II, when he articulated Australia's wartime concerns and strategies. He proved especially forceful in convincing Prime Minister WINSTON CHURCHILL to keep the majority of Australia's fighting men at home to boost national morale and resist the Japanese. On two occasions, in 1939 and 1946, Bruce also sounded out the possibility of returning to Australian politics but found no enthusiasm at home. He therefore remained in England after the war, where he was far more culturally attuned, and in 1947 the government granted him the title of viscount. Bruce thus became the first Australian eligible to sit in the House of Lords. After serving as the first chancellor of the Australian National University, 1951–61, he died in London on August 25, 1967. Like CALVIN COOLIDGE, the American president to whom he has been most frequently compared, Bruce was well suited for high office and fully committed to his charge, but he failed to understand the priorities of differing socioeconomic backgrounds. Despite his overall ability, Bruce proved too much an Englishman for fellow Australians to tolerate.

Further Reading

Carment, David. "A Question of Conscience: Sir Littleton Groom, the Speakership, and the Fall of the Bruce-Page Government." *Australian Journal of Politics and History* 23, no. 1 (1977): 67–75.

Cumpston, I. M. *History of Australia's Foreign Policy, 1901–1991.* 2 vols. Deakin West, Canberra: I. M. Cumpston, 1995.

———. *Lord Bruce of Melbourne.* Melbourne: Longman, Cheshire, 1989.

Edwards, P. G. "S. M. Bruce, R. G. Menzies, and Australia's War Aims and Peace Aims, 1939–40." *Historical Studies* 17, no. 66 (1976): 1–14.

Grattan, Michelle. *Australian Prime Ministers.* Frenchs Forrest, New South Wales: New Holland, 2000.

Powell, Graeme. "Bruce, Latham, and the 1926 Industrial Powers Referendum." *ANU Historical Journal* 14 (1979–80): 20–36.

Brüning, Heinrich (1885–1970) *chancellor of Germany*

Heinrich Brüning was born in Munich, Westphalia, Germany, on November 26, 1885, the son of a Roman Catholic industrialist. He attended the University of Bonn to study history and philosophy, acquired his doctorate in 1915, and subsequently joined the German army. Brüning fought with distinction in World War I and received the Iron Cross. Afterward, he struck up a close association with the Catholic trade union movement, serving as its general secretary from 1920 to 1930. Brüning, a devout Catholic and a political conservative, also joined the Catholic Center Party, where he expressed the views of an ardent monarchist. He gained election to the Reichstag (parliament) in 1924 and served for nearly a decade as an expert on finance. When the grand Social Democratic coalition government collapsed in the spring of 1930, President PAUL VON HINDENBURG was obliged to find a new chancellor. Brüning, a quiet, reserved bachelor with few enemies and apparently fewer political aspirations, was chosen to serve as national executive on March 30, 1930. He was selected as much for his economic expertise as his admiration for Hindenburg and the military. At 44, Brüning was also the second-youngest German head of state since 1871.

Unfortunately, Brüning assumed power just as the Great Depression was eviscerating the German econo-my. Unemployment was high, productivity low, and the nation reeled from reparations payments levied under the 1919 Treaty of Versailles. Inflation began to skyrocket menacingly, and it was here that Brüning wielded his greatest impact. Intent on cutting expenditures and balancing the budget, he ruthlessly raised consumption taxes while reducing unemployment benefits and salaries. When the Reichstag rejected such measures as too draconian, he invoked Article 48 of the Weimar Constitution, which enabled him to dissolve the legislature, call for new elections, and rule by decree. Brüning's program did in fact bring spiraling inflation under control but contributed to rising unemployment and a growing sense of political instability. However, his measures enjoyed the tacit approval of arch-conservative Hindenburg, and he allowed Brüning to employ Article 48 and acquire whatever powers he needed, over the objections of the Reichstag. Thus the nation's only democratic body was marginalized to the point of impotence.

As the months rolled by the German economy sank deeper, and by the fall of 1930 the number of unemployed topped 6 million. Largely for this reason, elections that fall resulted in marked gains by communists and National Socialists (Nazis) under ADOLF HITLER. Brüning was then forced to depend upon support from his adversaries in the Reichstag, the Social Democrats, to get his measures through. When this expedient failed, he simply resorted to Article 48 to have his way. Ironically, Brüning enjoyed much better success on the international scene and, by citing Germany's economic distress, he managed to have war reparations canceled by the former Allies at the Lausanne Conference of 1932. But all his economic expertise could not resuscitate Germany's moribund economy, and the resulting tide of social unrest fueled the rise of Hitler and his Nazi movement.

The issue that finally broke Brüning's hold on power was his attempt to partition large, bankrupt estates in the eastern part of the country. Hindenburg, himself a large landowner, regarded such policies as "agrarian Bolshevism." On May 30, 1932, the aging and nearly senile president demanded Brüning's resignation from office and replaced him with FRANZ VON PAPEN. Brüning remained in the Reichstag as the Catholic Center leader until Hitler was elected chancellor in 1933. He then strenuously opposed the Enabling Act of 1933, which conferred near dictatorial powers on Hitler's cabinet. This resistance placed him on the Nazi harassment list and in May 1933 he resigned as head of the Catholic Center Party. The following July Brüning dissolved the party completely and fled to Switzerland, fearing for his life. Brüning eventually settled in the United States where he taught economics at Harvard University from 1939 to 1952. He returned to Germany to teach political science at Cologne University. Brüning died in Norwich, Vermont, on March 30, 1970, thoroughly if unfairly discredited. His arbitrary ruling by decree set a dangerous political precedent, for it anticipated the means of Hitler's ensuing dictatorship. However, historians have since conceded that no economic measure invoked by Brüning—or anyone else—would have improved Germany's economy enough to forestall the advent of Nazism.

Further Reading

Balderston, Theo. *Economics and Politics in the Weimar Republic.* New York: Cambridge University Press, 2002.

Dahlberg, Robert C. "Heinrich Brüning, the Center Party, and Germany's 'Middle Way': Political Economy and Foreign Policy in the Weimar Republic." Unpublished Ph.D. diss., Johns Hopkins University, 1984.

Housden, M. "Germany's First Republic." *Historical Journal* 44 (June 2000): 579–585.

Nicholls, Anthony J. *Weimar and the Rise of Hitler.* New York: St. Martin's Press, 2000.

Patch, William L. *Heinrich Brüning and the Dissolution of the Weimar Republic.* New York: Cambridge University Press, 1998.

Voth, Hans Joachim. "Wages, Investment, and the Fate of the Weimar Republic: A Long-Term Perspective." *German History* 11, no. 3 (1993): 265–292.

Bülow, Bernhard (1849–1929) *chancellor of Germany*

Bernhard Heinrich Martin von Bülow was born in Klein Flottbek, Germany, on May 3, 1849, the son of a senior Prussian diplomat. After studying at numerous universities in Berlin and Leipzig, he followed his father's example by joining the German diplomatic corps in 1874. Bülow performed capably in European capitals but his rise through the bureaucratic ranks owed more to friends and influence than innate talent. He was elevated to state secretary of the German Foreign Office in 1897 and struck up a close relationship with Kaiser WILHELM II. In time he functioned as a trusted adviser. Germany was still basking in the glow of its successful 1870 unification, which made it the strongest nation on the European continent. Consistent with those feelings, Bülow fully embraced the kaiser's Weltpolitik (world policy) declaration to achieve, in Bülow's phrase, Germany's "place in the sun" as a great power. Given this mindset, both the kaiser and his future chancellor resolved to pursue an aggressive course of expansionism to extend the empire overseas. As foreign secretary, Bülow managed to acquire such distant outposts as Kiaochow in China, the Caroline Islands and Samoa in the Pacific, and Togoland and Cameroon in Africa. But such aggressive colonizing, and Wilhelm's decision to acquire a large surface navy, placed Germany on a collision course with France, Great Britain, and other imperial interests. Bülow, as an experienced diplomat, should have foreseen the consequences but he remained unswervingly devoted to the kaiser. Their friendship culminated in his appointment as chancellor of Germany in October 1900, following the resignation of Prince Chlodwig Hohenlohe.

The rise of Germany as a world-class military power inevitably led to a new series of defensive alliances to constrain it. France, England, and Russia, all weaker by comparison, began treaty negotiations to form what eventually became known as the Triple Entente in 1907. Germany, meanwhile, remained closely allied to Austria and Italy in their own Triple Alliance. It was imperative for Bülow to stop the allies from drawing closer and encircling Germany militarily, but over the next nine years he mishandled several widely publicized incidents. In 1905 he antagonized France by his handling of the so-called Moroccan crisis and failed to block French expansion into North Africa. Germany had little national interest in the region, and the anxiety it generated further ruffled Gallic pride. In 1908 Bülow strongly supported Austria in its annexation of Bosnia-Herzegovina, which alienated Russia. He also failed to convince Admiral Alfred von Tirpitz that construction of a major surface navy was unsettling to England, whose mastery of the waves had never been challenged. All these moves were detrimental to German strategic interests, and Bülow's lack of vision and his aggressive diplomacy strengthened the military alliance he wanted to stop. The solidity of the Triple Entente in World War I became the major factor in Germany's defeat.

One of Bülow's more quixotic enterprises was his proposed construction of the Baghdad Railway, from central Turkey to the Persian Gulf, in 1902 to advance German influence in the region. In practice this only further alarmed Britain and Russia, who already possessed vested interests there. The Turkish part of the line was constructed with German money, but Bülow was forced to turn to the international marketplace for additional funding. When England and Russia refused to assist and leaned heavily on France to do likewise, the project collapsed. Bülow's machinations had accomplished little for German prestige, while further cementing the Triple Entente. His own decline was hastened by the *Daily Telegraph* affair of October 1908 in which the kaiser gave a forceful interview to a British newspaper, revealing his contemptuous policy toward Great Britain. Bülow, unfortunately, failed to approve the text beforehand, and when published it caused an uproar in both countries. After this, relations between the two men cooled considerably. By July 1909, the sheer expense of maintaining all of Germany's newly acquired colonies was bankrupting the nation, and Bülow requested the Reichstag to levy new taxes. When the legislators failed to comply, he tendered his resignation and was replaced by THEOBOLD VON BETHMANN HOLLWEG. Bülow subsequently retired to a large estate in Italy. His last diplomatic service to Germany came in 1915 when he failed to prevent Italy from joining the Allies in World War I. Bülow died in Rome on October 28, 1929, a forgotten architect of German imperialism—and a singular cause of its undoing.

Further Reading

Bülow, Bernhard von. *Memoirs.* 4 vols. New York: Putnam, 1931.

Eley, Geoff, and James Retullack, eds. *Wilhelminism and Its Legacies: German Modernities, and the Meanings of Reform, 1890–1930.* New York: Berghahn Books, 2003.

Feuchtwanger, E. J. *Imperial Germany, 1850–1918.* New York: Routledge, 2001.

Lerman, Katherine A. *The Chancellor as Courier: Bernhard Von Bülow and the Governance of Germany, 1900–1909.* New York: Cambridge University Press, 1990.

Mommsen, Wolfgang J. "Public Opinion and Foreign Policy in Wilhelmian Germany, 1897–1914." *Central European History* 24 (December 1991): 381–402.

Thompson, Alastair P. *Left Liberals, the State, and Popular Politics in Wilhelmine Germany.* New York: Oxford University Press, 2000.

Winzen, Peter. "Prince Bülow's Weltmachpolitik." *Australian Journal of Politics and History* 22, no. 2 (1976): 277–242.

Burnham, Forbes (1923–1985) *president of Guyana*

Linden Forbes Sampson Burnham was born in Kitty, British Guiana, on February 20, 1923, the son of a school headmaster. He belonged to the sizable African community inhabiting the coastal regions of the colony, distinct from East Indian laborers who populated most of the interior. His father gave him a sense of scholastic excellence, and in 1945 Burnham enrolled at the University of London. Two years later he acquired a law degree and returned home to start a practice. In England Burnham had been exposed to the tenets of socialism, so in 1950 he joined West Indian politician Cheddi Jagan in founding the People's Progressive Party (PPP). It espoused, beyond the usual Marxist-Leninist rhetoric, complete independence from Great Britain. Burnham also campaigned for leadership of the British Guiana Labor Union, the colony's strongest, and in 1951 he won a seat on the Georgetown City Council. When the colony held its first general election under universal suffrage in 1953, the PPP won handily and Jagan, now prime minister, appointed Burnham education minister. However, British prime minister WINSTON CHURCHILL, fearing the onset of a communist regime, summarily canceled the colony's constitution and sent in troops to restore order. Burnham was one of a handful of PPP leaders to avoid arrest during the next four years, and by 1957 he had split with Jagan over ideological differences.

Upon further reflection, Burnham scuttled his previous alliance with radicals like Jagan and adopted a moderate socialist line. To that end he founded the People's National Congress (PNC) in 1957, although he lost elections that year to Jagan. In 1961 the PNC was again bested by the PPP, although the United States, under President JOHN F. KENNEDY, committed the Central Intelligence Agency (CIA) to destabilizing Jagan's regime. By 1964 new voting rules allowing proportional representation had been adopted, and

Burnham, in conjunction with the smaller United Democratic Party, formed a coalition government and became prime minister. Two years later, in 1966, Britain granted independence to the colony, which renamed itself Guyana. Burnham, who would be firmly ensconced in power for the next 19 years, reversed course again and embarked on a program to develop his country into a cooperative, or socialist, republic.

True to its leftist inclinations, the government nationalized the country's natural resources along with the sugar and bauxite industries. Burnham developed the national economy along similar lines, while expanding social programs like education and health care for the poor. He converted most government agencies into extensions of the PNC to enhance his grip on power. His foreign relations were also radicalized: he became a strong proponent of Third World and Nonaligned movements, and established close relations with Cuba's Fidel Castro and Grenada's MAURICE BISHOP. But Burnham trod carefully with the West, maintaining diplomatic relations with both the United States and the British Commonwealth. More important, he addressed the deep-seated antipathy between Guyanans of African and East Indian descent by appointing Indians to government ministries. His policies were initially successful and did much to decrease high levels of unemployment among unskilled workers.

Toward the end of his tenure Burnham grew despotic, circumventing Parliament altogether by 1978 and circulating a referendum for new constitutional reforms. These, when passed, made him executive president of Guyana, with powers to dismiss the prime minister or veto any piece of legislation. He also assumed the mantle of commander-in-chief of the armed forces to ensure military backing. His power had been largely uncontested over the course of two decades and he intended to keep it that way, invoking any measure, including fraud, bribery, press intimidation, and even assassination, to keep it. Fortunately, he died suddenly in office on August 6, 1985, and was succeeded by Prime Minister Ptolemy Reid, who gradually dismantled his socialist policies. Burnham still remains something of a folk hero to the poor despite his autocratic tendencies.

Further Reading

Brotherson, Festus. "The Foreign Policy of Guyana, 1970–1985: Forbes Burnham's Search for Legitimacy." *Journal of Interamerican Studies and World Affairs* 31, no. 3 (1989): 9–35.

Burnham, Forbes. *A Destiny to Mould: Selected Speeches by the Prime Minister of Guyana.* New York: Africana Pub. Corp., 1970.

Caires, David. "Guyana after Burnham: A New Era?" *Caribbean Affairs* 1, no. 1 (1988): 183–198.

Griffith, Ivelaw L. "The Military and the Politics of Change in Guyana." *Journal of Interamerican Studies and World Affairs* 33 (summer 1991): 141–174.

Gibson, Kean. *The Cycle of Racial Oppression in Guyana.* Lanham, Md.: University Press of America, 2003.

Parekh, Hector J. "Subversion in British Guyana: Why and How the Kennedy Administration Got Rid of a Democratic Government." *Monthly Review* 51, no. 5 (1999): 50–58.

Bush, George H. W. (1924–   ) *president of the United States*

George Herbert Walker Bush was born in Milton, Massachusetts, on June 12, 1924, into an affluent New England family. His father, Prescott Bush, a noted Wall Street investor and U.S. senator from Connecticut (1952–62), educated him in private schools and in June 1942 he graduated from the elite Phillips Academy. Bush then joined the U.S. Navy for service in World War II, passed through flight school, and became the nation's youngest carrier pilot. On September 2, 1944, while flying from the carrier USS *San Jacinto* against the Japanese-held atoll of Chi Chi Jima, Bush's plane was shot down and he won the Distinguished Flying Cross. After the war he married, and attended Yale University in pursuit of a business degree, graduating Phi Beta Kappa in 1948. Bush then relocated to Texas to work in the burgeoning oil industry. He started several companies, became a successful entrepreneur and millionaire, and by 1964 was testing the waters to launch a political career.

In 1964 Bush first ran for public office as a conservative Republican by contesting a U.S. Senate seat held by Democrat Ralph Yarborough. He was defeated, but two years later became the first Republican ever elected to the House of Representatives from Houston. Bush was successively reelected until, at the urging of President RICHARD M. NIXON, he contested another Senate seat with Democrat Lloyd Bentsen in 1970, and lost again. However, Nixon rewarded his loyalty by appointing him U.S. ambassador to the United Nations. Despite a lack of foreign policy experience, Bush flourished in the role, and his two-year tenure is considered highly successful. By 1973, however, the Watergate political scandal had erupted, and Nixon asked Bush to serve as chairman of the Republican National Committee. Here he strongly defended the president against accusations of wrong-doing until Nixon resigned from office. In 1974 Nixon's successor, GERALD R. FORD, appointed Bush the U.S. liaison to the People's Republic of China, where he displayed a flair for personal diplomacy. He was suddenly recalled in 1975 by Ford, who wanted him to serve as director of the Central Intelligence Agency (CIA). That bureau had come under intense scrutiny for clandestine activities directed against other governments, but Bush ordered a wide-ranging reorganization and effectively countered the critics. Ford was defeated in 1976 by JIMMY CARTER, so Bush resumed his private life back in Texas to plan his own conquest of the White House.

Bush announced his candidacy for the Republican nomination in May 1979. This brought him in direct competition with California governor RONALD REAGAN, and an intense rivalry developed between the two men. Bush, portraying himself as a moderate, strongly questioned Reagan's grasp of business and labeled his proposals "voodoo economics." However, the charismatic governor went on to win the nomination in August 1980 and, wishing to unite the conservative and moderate wings of the Republican Party, he chose Bush as his running mate. Together they badly trounced Carter and the Democrats the following November, restoring Republican rule with a vengeance. As vice president, Bush was tasked with heading important panels on crime, drugs, and terrorism, all of which he handled with aplomb. When Reagan recuperated from an assassination attempt in 1981, Bush ran the country for several weeks as acting president. In November 1984 both men sought reelection and they routed Democratic contender and former vice president Walter Mondale, taking 49 states. This victory put a public stamp of approval on Reagan's brand of conservative populism and made Bush, who now embraced it, his ideological heir.

In 1988 Bush announced his candidacy for the highest office in the land. He campaigned on a familiar platform of conservative economics: a cut in the capital gains tax, increased defense spending, and the pledge,

"Read my lips, no new taxes." However, Bush was by no means as telegenic as his predecessor and he was ridiculed by the Democrats as incapable of existing outside of Reagan's shadow. They even invoked the old charge of "voodoo economics" against him in light of rising budget deficits. Bush was widely expected to lose to the Democratic contender, Massachusetts governor Michael Dukakis, but instead scored a stunning upset by carrying 40 states. But the Republicans failed to secure control of Congress from the Democrats, so Bush's efforts to pass his legislative agenda were thwarted from the onset. Still he was the first vice president elected directly to the presidency since Martin Van Buren in 1836.

Once in office, Bush exhibited a pronounced dichotomy to his political leadership. He seemed more at ease with international affairs, which gave him ample opportunities to display his leadership abilities. In December 1989, he ordered Operation Just Cause, which toppled the Panamanian dictator and drug lord MANUEL NORIEGA from power. He also conducted a series of skilled negotiations with Soviet premier

George H. W. Bush *(Library of Congress)*

MIKHAIL GORBACHEV, which reduced cold war tensions and accelerated the breakup of the Soviet Union. But in 1990 he faced his biggest challenge when Iraqi dictator Saddam Hussein invaded and annexed the oil-rich state of Kuwait, a United States ally. Bush, greatly incensed, orchestrated a carefully determined United Nations coalition against Hussein. By January 1991, when the Iraqis stubbornly refused to abandon their conquests, Bush authorized Operation Desert Storm. The ensuing rout liberated Kuwait in just under 100 hours and inflicted an estimated 100,000 Iraqi casualties. The nation had overcome its Vietnam War–era reluctance to employ military force abroad. Bush's approval rating reached 89%, and he appeared unbeatable in the following presidential election.

Despite Bush's spectacular successes abroad, his performance on the domestic front proved lackluster at best. The national economy, which boomed during the Reagan years, began tripping over huge budget deficits and a severe recession. In a sincere attempt to address the problem, Bush reneged on his "no new taxes" pledge, which cost him considerable Republican support. Moreover, the country was seized by a pervasive sense that it was headed in the wrong direction domestically. Bush, try as he might, was powerless to correct this sense of malaise. To many voters Bush, the child of privilege, seemed unable to connect with the daily struggles of average Americans. Thus in November 1992 he lost to Democratic contender Bill Clinton, who was assisted by the presence of independent Ross Perot. The electorate remained deeply divided and none of the candidates received 50 percent of the vote.

After 12 years in the political hot seat, Bush seemed generally relieved to be out of Washington, D.C. He retired to private life, while his two sons, Jeb and George W., were being groomed to succeed him. Both were elected governors, of Florida and Texas respectively, and in November 2000 the elder Bush enjoyed a measure of revenge when George W. defeated Al Gore, Clinton's vice president, for the White House. He thus became the first president to be succeeded by his son since John Quincy Adams followed John Adams in 1828.

Further Reading

Feldman, Leslie D., and Rosanna Perotti, eds. *Honor and Loyalty: Inside the Politics of the George H. W. Bush White House.* Westport, Conn.: Greenwood Press, 2002.

Greenstein, Fred I. "The Prudent Professionalism of George Herbert Walker Bush." *Journal of Interdisciplinary History* 31 (winter 2001): 385–392.

Hermann, Richard K., and Richard N. Lebow, eds. *Ending the Cold War.* New York: Palgrave Macmillan, 2004.

Herskowitz, Mickey. *Duty, Honor, Country: The Life and Legacy of Prescott Bush.* Nashville, Tenn.: Rutledge Hill Press, 2003.

Hess, Gary R. *Presidential Decisions for War: Korea, Vietnam, and the Persian Gulf.* Baltimore: Johns Hopkins University, 2001.

Thompson, Kenneth W. *The Bush Presidency: Ten Intimate Perspectives,* 2 vols. Lanham, Md.: University Press of America, 1997–98.

Wicker, Tom. *George Herbert Walker Bush.* New York: Lipper/Viking, 2004.

Busia, Kofi (1913–1978) *prime minister of Ghana*

Kofi Abrefa Busia was born in Wenchi, Gold Coast, a member of the influential Ashanti tribe. He was educated at missionary schools and received a scholarship to attend teacher's school. By 1936 he was on the staff of the Prince of Wales College in Achimota, from which he enrolled at Oxford University in England in 1939. Busia returned home two years later as one of the first Africans to serve as an administrative officer within the colonial service. After several years, he returned to Oxford in 1946 to pursue a doctorate in sociology. His dissertation, *The Position of the Chief in the Modern Political System of Ashanti,* was published as a standard text in 1951 and commenced a long and distinguished association with academia. Busia came home in 1949 when he secured a post as a lecturer at the University of Gold Coast; within two years he had become its first African professor. As demands grew for independence and greater political participation, Busia gained a seat in 1951 in the first territorial legislative council with the Ghana Congress Party (GCP). He did so largely in opposition to KWAME NKRUMAH of the radical Convention People's Party (CCP), and the two remained political adversaries for the rest of their lives.

Over the next six years Busia divided his time between politics, conducting government surveys, and teaching responsibilities. These proved conflicting demands that the avowed intellectual never really mastered. However, by 1956 there emerged a violent,

Ashanti-based National Liberation Movement (NLM) intending to rid the country of Nkrumah's radicals at any cost. Busia thought highly enough of the movement to quit teaching altogether and pursue politics full time. The following year he argued in Britain against granting the Gold Coast independence before its political foundations had stabilized. He was unsuccessful, and that year the nation terminated British dominance and renamed itself Ghana. Nkrumah, who enjoyed great popularity, became the nation's first prime minister and immediately reverted to dictatorial powers. One of his first targets was Busia, who in 1959 fled the country for his life. He spent the next eight years teaching at Leiden University in the Netherlands and at Oxford, awaiting an opportunity to come home. It was during his exile that Busia gained renown as a world-class lecturer on African social and political matters. He eventually published nine books and scores of essays. He was much in demand as a lecturer, and in 1966 he even addressed the U.S. Congress to discourage aid to Ghana.

Nkrumah was finally overthrown by the Ghanaian military in February 1966. Busia returned to conduct careful negotiations with the ruling National Liberation Council, advising them on constitutional matters. At length the council consented to restore democracy, with Busia as its favored candidate. In September 1969 he was easily elected Ghana's second prime minister by the national legislature as head of the new Progress Party (PP). Ghana was then in the midst of a deep financial and economic crisis; the new executive immediately imposed strict austerity measures. He abolished the powerful trade unions, purged the civil service of unproductive bureaucrats, and expelled large numbers of Nigerian aliens from the nation. When these expedients failed, Busia resorted to a 44 percent devaluation of the national currency. This triggered spiraling food costs, a major downturn in the economy, and a commensurate rise in public dissatisfaction. Busia, who brooked no dissent, was accused of being every bit as oppressive as his predecessor. To forestall the outbreak of mass violence, the military under General Ignatius Acheampong decisively intervened in 1972 while Busia was in England, deposing him bloodlessly.

Removed from power, Busia resumed the activity that he enjoyed best and proved most adept at—lecturing at universities. He regained his old post at Oxford

and remained there until his death on August 28, 1978. Though never highly regarded by Ghanaians as a political figure, he was accorded a state funeral in his native land.

Further Reading

Austin, Denis, and Robin Lockham, eds. *Politicians and Soldiers in Ghana, 1966–1972.* London: Frank Cass, 1975.

Busia, Kofi A. *Africa in Search of Democracy.* New York: Praeger, 1967.

Chazan, N. "Ethnicity and Politics in Ghana." *Political Quarterly* 97 (fall 1982): 461–486.

Danso-Boafa, A. K. "The Political Biography of Dr. Kofi Brefa Busia." Unpublished Ph.D. diss., Howard University, 1981.

Korang, Kwaku Larbi. *Writing Ghana, Imagining Africa: Nation and African Modernity.* Rochester, N.Y.: University of Rochester Press, 2004.

Le Vine, Victor T. "Autopsy on a Regime: Ghana's Civilian Interregnum, 1969–72." *Journal of Modern African Studies* 25 (March 1987): 169–178.

Wilson, Phyllis R. "Betwixt and Between: A Study of Three Ghanaian Intellectuals as Mediators between Tradition and Modernity." Unpublished Ph.D. diss., University of Chicago, 1974.

Bustamante, William (1884–1977) *prime minister of Jamaica*

William Alexander Clarke was born in Blenheim, Jamaica, on February 24, 1884, the son of an Irish immigrant planter and a black African mother. He eked out a poverty-stricken existence and in 1899 was adopted by a Spanish sailor named Bustamante, whose surname he took. After being educated in Spain, Bustamante joined the Spanish army and fought in North Africa. Discharged, he worked in such places as Panama and Cuba, holding a variety of governmental positions. By 1923 he arrived in New York City where, as a light-skinned black, he blended easily among the elite of Harlem. Bustamante worked several years as a dietitian in a Harlem hospital, acquiring a personal fortune through clever investments. He returned to Jamaica in 1934, a self-made man with a sense of destiny.

At that time, Jamaica was growing restless under the reign of the British colonial administration. Bustamante himself was taken aback by the poverty of the island's sugar plantation workers. He acquired a reputation as a fiery orator and organizer, wrote newspaper articles on behalf of the working class, and instigated numerous protests and strikes. In 1938 his popularity induced him to found the Bustamante Industrial Trade Union, which became the most powerful labor organization on the island and a ladder for his political ambitions. But Bustamante had intense competition from his cousin, Norman Michael Manley, founder of the People's National Party (PNP). Bustamante belonged to the PNP initially but found Manley's radical policies distasteful. Nonetheless the British authorities jailed him for several months for disrupting the island's economy with strikes during World War II. When Bustamante was released in 1943 he immediately founded the Jamaican Labour Party (JLP) to counter Manley's growing influence. By 1944 the British government reacted to mounting unrest by allowing internal self-governance, universal suffrage, and a new legislature. Elections were held and Bustamante, touting a conservative agenda that welded the island's sugar interests and upper classes to the JLP, defeated Manley's PNP by winning a majority of seats. In 1947 he became mayor of Kingston, the island's capital. The success of Bustamante and the JLP put them on a collision course with the charismatic Manley, and an intense political rivalry developed.

In 1953, under a changed constitution, Bustamante assumed the new post of chief minister. In 1955 he was knighted for his services to the Commonwealth by Queen Elizabeth II. Though Manley ousted him from power that same year, he remained a strident critic of British plans to include Jamaica in a proposed West Indies Federation. Bustamante feared that such a move would permanently relegate the island to minority status. Instead, he called for complete political independence from both Great Britain and any proposed federation. His message resonated with voters in 1962, when they returned him to power and he began negotiations for a new constitution.

Jamaica gained its independence in August 1962, whereupon Bustamante became the island's first prime minister. In contrast to the ever-radical Manley, Bustamante proved decidedly conservative in outlook and sought close political and economic ties to the United States and Great Britain. He also strongly condemned the communist regime of Fidel Castro in neighboring Cuba and solidly supported the West throughout the cold war. Bustamante's health began failing around 1967 and he declined to run for office that year. But such was his reputation that Manley did not return to power until 1972, and then only in the midst of severe economic distress. Bustamante had since retired from politics and contentedly served as the island's elder statesman. He died in Kingston on August 6, 1977, universally lauded as the father of Jamaican independence.

Further Reading

Eaton, George E. *Alexander Bustamante and Jamaica.* Kingston, Jamaica: Kingston Publishers, 1975.

Hamilton, B. L. St. John. *Bustamante: Anthology of a Hero.* Kingston, Jamaica: Produced for B. St. J. Hamilton by Publications and Productions, 1978.

Hill, Frank. *Bustamante and His Letters.* Kingston, Jamaica: Kingston Publishers, 1976.

Ranston, Jackie. *From We Were Boys: The Story of the Magnificent Cousins, the Rt. Excellent Sir William Alexander Bustamante and the Rt. Excellent Norman Washington Manley.* Kingston, Jamaica: Bustamante Institute of Public and International Affairs, 1989.

Shearer, Hugh L. *Alexander Bustamante: Portrait of a Hero.* Kingston, Jamaica: Kingston Publishers, 1978.

C

Cabral, Amilcar (1924–1973) *leader of Guinea-Bissau*

Amilcar Lopes Cabral was born in Bafatá, Portuguese Guinea, on September 12, 1924, the son of Cape Verdean parents. Because he was entitled to Portuguese citizenship Cabral attended local schools and distinguished himself academically. In the 1940s the Cape Verde Islands experienced a terrible drought in which an estimated 60,000 people were allowed to die. This seminal event turned Cabral against Portuguese colonialism, and he matured determined to resist whenever possible. In 1945 Cabral won a scholarship to attend college in Lisbon, five years later earning a degree in agricultural engineering from the Instituto Superior de Agronomia. He returned to Africa in 1951 charged with conducting the first detailed agricultural survey of Portuguese Guinea. Cabral then traveled extensively throughout the colony, meeting with peasants and assessing people's needs. This experience proved invaluable for his work as a revolutionary, for Cabral became intimately familiar with his fellow colonists. He knew what they possessed, what they lacked, and how they could best contribute to a revolution. By 1955 he was back in Lisbon working as an agricultural consultant, but during a brief visit to the colonies Cabral, in concert with his brother Luis, ARISTIDES PEREIRA, and others, founded the Partido Africano da Independência da Guinée Cabo Verde (PAIGC),

African Party for the Independence of Guinea and Cape Verde. Despite Marxist overtones, this was intended as a nonviolent association for organizing passive resistance to colonial oppression. Cabral, moreover, was never a communist. In fact, he always took deliberate measures to distance himself from Moscow-backed revolutionary movements in an extraordinary attempt to win sympathy and support from Western nations.

The turning point in PAIGC's history happened during the August 1959 strike by dock workers at Pidjiguiti. Portuguese troops responded brutally, killing at least 50 people. More than anything, this convinced Cabral and others that peaceful means could not solve Guinea-Bissau's quest for independence. PAIGC then grew more militant and dispatched its cadres to Libya, China, and Algeria for covert military training. By 1962 the guerrillas had infiltrated back to Guinea-Bissau where they commenced a low-intensity war against the Portuguese administration. Here Cabral was careful to solicit peasant support in the countryside by building schools, providing medical assistance, and trying to be as useful as possible. The result was overwhelming support for the revolution, and in 1965 PAIGC controlled two-thirds of the colony.

What made Cabral distinctive as a revolutionary agent was his carefully crafted ideology. He rejected the proletarian notion of Soviet-style "wars of liberation" as unsuitable for Africa's uneducated masses and selected a more Maoist approach to warfare. This involved bringing people in at every level of the struggle, particularly women, for Cabral insisted that females be given complete gender equality and rights to participate. Furthermore, Cabral did not denounce his African roots as inferior but rather embraced them. He strongly felt that denying one's culture, or adopting the culture of an oppressor, made it easier for colonies to be exploited. His calm, reasoned approach to liberation, combined with humane rules of engagement, routinely freeing captured Portuguese soldiers unharmed, won him respect and admiration from around the world. True to his intellectual bent, Cabral penned treatises on people's war highly esteemed throughout the developing world. He assisted AGOSTINHO NETO in setting up his own liberation movement in Angola. After addressing the United Nations on Guinea-Bissau in 1962, Cabral was recognized as the de facto leader of his party, his movement, and his nation.

As Cabral predicted, the rise of mass insurgencies throughout Portuguese West Africa severely compromised military efforts to defeat them. The strain on Portugal proved so inordinate that in 1974 the government was overthrown by leftist military officers who then granted the colonies independence. Cabral had successfully directed the liberation struggle for a decade but he failed to see his plans come to fruition. From the onset, PAIGC was beset by intense rivalry between leaders of Cape Verdean and native African stock. The Portuguese secret police used this schism to convince several dissident elements to turn against Cabral. On January 20, 1973, he was assassinated by a fellow member near his home. He was succeeded by his brother, Luis Cabral, who went on to become the first president of newly independent Guinea-Bissau. In light of his contributions to independence, Cabral's birthday was enshrined as a national holiday.

Further Reading

Cabral, Amilcar. *Unity and Struggle: Speeches and Writings.* New York: Monthly Review Press, 1979.
Chabal, Patrick. *Amilcar Cabral: Revolutionary Leadership and People's War.* New York: Cambridge University Press, 1983.
Chilcote, Ronald H. *Amilcar Cabral's Revolutionary Theory and Practice: A Critical Guide.* Boulder, Colo.: Lynne Rienner Publishers, 1991.
Davidson, Basil. "On Revolutionary Nationalism: The Legacy of Cabral." *Race and Class* 27 (winter 1986): 21–45.
Dhada, Mustafah. *Warriors at Work: How Guinea Was Really Set Free.* Niwot, Colo.: University Press of Colorado, 1993.
McCulloch, Jack. *In the Twilight of Revolution: The Political Theory of Amilcar Cabral.* Boston: Routledge and Kegan Paul, 1983.

Callaghan, James (baron Callaghan of Cardiff)

(1912–   ) *prime minister of Great Britain*

Leonard James Callaghan was born in Portsmouth, England, on March 27, 1912, the son of a Royal Navy petty officer. His father's early death resulted in a poverty-stricken childhood, so at the age of 17 Callaghan quit school, passed a governmental exam, and worked as a tax clerk. He also became active in the trade union movement and by 1938 had risen to assistant secretary. When World War II commenced in 1939 Callaghan joined the Royal Navy and worked as an intelligence analyst in the Far East. He returned home in 1945 to run as a Labour candidate and was elected to Parliament in the landslide victory that brought down the government of WINSTON CHURCHILL. Early on, Callaghan acquired a reputation as an affable figure nicknamed Sunny Jim, but he was an astute political operator. He held two minor posts in the Labour administration of CLEMENT ATTLEE, and by the mid-1950s had emerged as a national spokesman. However, because Callaghan hailed from the center-conservative wing of the party, he remained at odds with some of the more stridently left-wing personalities of the national leadership. Callaghan continued serving quietly and efficiently in Parliament until 1963, when he decided to run for party head. He finished respectably in third place, and the following year, when Labour returned to power under HAROLD WILSON, Callaghan gained appointment as chancellor of the Exchequer.

Once in power, both Wilson and Callaghan determined not to devalue the British pound to stimulate a sluggish economy. Instead, Callaghan imposed strict austerity measures to reduce government spending and bring inflation under control. However, by 1967 the economy only worsened and the pound was ultimately devalued by 14 percent. Callaghan did so only under duress, resigned from office, and was reappointed Home

Secretary. This gave rise to his most controversial deed in office. Many citizens expressed fear that the British Isles were being overrun by immigrants, so Callaghan shepherded the Immigration Act of 1968, which placed a freeze on passports. Though the measure was popular with Conservatives, it angered the radical left within the Labour Party. Callaghan also had to deal with the onset of sectarian violence in Northern Ireland. To curb mounting attacks against Roman Catholics he authorized deployment of several thousand British troops to maintain order. Labour subsequently lost the general elections of 1970. Callaghan remained in Parliament until 1974, when Wilson again became prime minister. This time he served as foreign secretary until Wilson suddenly resigned from office in March 1976. Callaghan then easily defeated the more radical Michael Foot to succeed Wilson, becoming the first prime minister to have occupied the three most important ministries: state, foreign affairs, and chancellor. In contrast with the party's core leadership, mostly educated at Oxford, Callaghan prided himself on his working-class background and his sense of the common touch.

For all his good nature and ability to deal with unions, Callaghan's grasp on power proved tenuous. Recent elections had reduced Labour to minority status in Parliament, and the party had to form a coalition with the small Liberal Party to retain power. In return the Liberals received the right to veto any financial legislation not to their liking. Callaghan also inherited a country suffering from economic stagnation and high unemployment. Prospects for recovery proved so unsettling that the government was forced to approach the International Monetary Fund (IMF) for a $2 billion loan, in exchange for strict austerity measures. By 1978 inflation had fallen to single digits, but Callaghan's attempts to revive prosperity were further compromised by union militancy. Throughout the winter of 1979 a series of nationwide strikes caused great dissatisfaction. Callaghan was forced to capitulate to the unions by granting inordinate pay raises to buy labor peace. Public anger over the settlement spilled over to the House of Commons, and on March 28, 1979, they passed a resolution of "no confidence" against the government. This was the first such vote since 1924 when Prime Minister RAMSAY MACDONALD was forced from power. Callaghan had no choice but to resign and call for new elections in May 1979. The resulting Conservative landslide brought MARGARET THATCHER to power.

Callaghan continued in Parliament, although leftists secured his resignation as party head. Nonetheless, he became "Father of the House of Commons" in 1983 for having served continuously since 1945. That year he attacked his party's stance on unilateral nuclear disarmament during parliamentary elections, which further antagonized left-wing advocates. Callaghan received a peerage in 1987, after which he resigned and transferred to the House of Lords. His tenure as prime minister had been unspectacular, but he managed to keep his party from splintering. After Callaghan vacated the party leadership and was succeeded by Foot, Labour assumed a far more radical stance on many issues and was badly beaten by Thatcher's Conservatives.

Further Reading

Black, Lawrence. *The Political Culture of the Left in Britain, 1951–1964: Old Labour, New Britain?* New York: Palgrave, 2002.

Callaghan, James. *Time and Chance.* London: Collins, 1987.

Hansen, R. "The Kenyan Asians, British Politics, and the Commonwealth Immigrants Act, 1968." *Historical Journal* 42 (September 1999): 809–834.

Jeffreys, Kevin, ed. *Leading Labour: From Keir Hardie to Tony Blair.* London: I. B. Tauris, 1999.

Morgan, Kenneth O. *Callaghan: A Life.* New York: Oxford University Press, 1997.

Seldon, Anthony, and Kevin Hickson, eds. *New Labour, Old Labour: The Wilson and Callaghan Governments, 1974–79.* New York: Routledge, 2004.

Calles, Plutarco Elías (1877–1945) *president of Mexico*

Plutarco Elías Calles was born in Guaymas, Sonora, Mexico, on September 25, 1877, the illegitimate son of a prominent landowner. Orphaned at three, he was raised by relatives and adopted their surname. He was relatively well educated and served briefly as a schoolteacher before farming and running a small business. In 1913 Calles's personal fortunes dramatically changed when the Mexican Revolution re-erupted after the assassination of President FRANCISCO MADERO by General VICTORIANO HUERTA. He joined the ranks of the Constitutionalists and fought several years as an officer under General ÁLVARO OBREGÓN. In August 1915 a new commander, VENUSTIANO CARRANZA, appointed Calles interim governor of Sonora. In this capacity he displayed a talent for administration and progressive reform, creating a minimum wage and new and better schools, and outlawing gambling and alcoholism. Consistent with the new Mexican constitution, Calles was one of very few leaders to strictly enforce anticlerical provisions against public prayer by the Catholic clergy. Nevertheless, Calles proved a popular and efficient governor, so in 1916 he was formally elected to the post. In May 1919, the new president of Mexico, his old commander Carranza, appointed him secretary of industries, trade, and labor.

Up to this point Calles had displayed little interest in national politics, but in 1920 he resigned from the government to champion the candidacy of Obregón for president. As Obregón's minister of the interior, Calles functioned efficiently for four years and actively enforced badly needed land reforms before declaring his own candidacy in 1924. A robust, popular figure, he was elected to succeed Obregón on December 1, 1924. His accession marked one of the most turbulent periods of postrevolutionary Mexico. Drawing upon his prior experiences as governor, Calles realized that Mexico was in dire need of infrastructural and fiscal modernization. To facilitate both reforms, he established the Bank of Mexico in September 1925, along with the National Bank of Agricultural Credit the following year. These institutions provided money for badly needed roads, dams, and schools, as well as assisting hard-pressed farmers. A former teacher, Calles was also acutely concerned with upgrading the level of education available to Mexico's peasantry. He therefore authorized construction of new schools throughout the land along with the hiring of teachers. His programs helped establish the Mexican government as a source of welcome assistance for years to come.

On the downside, Calles was confronted by certain intractable problems that had to be finessed with tact. First and foremost were relations with the United States, which had deteriorated because of his policy of nationalizing oil resources and foreign landholdings. It was not until the Mexican government suspended these practices that normalized relations became tenable. An even bigger problem remained the Catholic Church. Calles consistently enforced anticlerical laws to the letter, which led to spontaneous rebellions throughout Mexico by prochurch militants. The so-called Cristeros waged a vicious guerrilla campaign and were suppressed with equal brutality. But overall, Calles left his country in much better shape than when he acquired it. He prepared to leave office in 1928 following the reelection of Obregón to the presidency, but the nation was suddenly thrown into tumult following Obregón's unexpected death. This triggered a constitutional crisis, as no provision existed for a vice president to succeed him. Calles, however, saw an opportunity to relinquish the throne, yet remain in control. In 1928 he declared Mexico a one-party state with his creation of the Partido Revolucionario Nacional (PRN), National Revolutionary Party, which had sole responsibility to choose candidates. And because Calles was de facto head of the new organization, he personally selected three puppet candidates to occupy the executive office. In this manner he dominated the national agenda in a period popularly known as the Maximato.

Calles's undoing occurred in 1934 when he selected LÁZARO CÁRDENAS to succeed him. Not only did Cardenas prove independent of PRN control, but he also marshaled various forces of the left to combat Calles's increasingly conservative agenda. When the former president protested government labor policies he was summarily exiled to the United States in 1936. Calles lived in San Diego, California, until 1941 when President MANUEL ÁVILA CAMACHO invited him home. He took no further role in public life and died in obscurity on October 19, 1945. Calles may have been a harsh reformer and a political manipulator but his social, economic, and political reforms bequeathed a stability to subsequent administrations sadly lacking in earlier regimes. In many respects he was the father of modern Mexico.

Further Reading

Brown, James C. "Consolidation of the Mexican Revolution under Calles, 1924–1928: Politics, Modernization, and the Roots of the Revolutionary National Party." Unpublished Ph.D. diss., University of New Mexico, 1979.

Dooley, Francis P. "The Cristeros, Calles, and Mexican Catholicism." Unpublished Ph.D. diss., University of Maryland, 1972.

Farmer, Edward M. "Plutarco Elías Calles and the Revolutionary Government in Sonora, Mexico." Unpublished Ph.D. diss., Cambridge University, 1997.

Marcoux, Carl H. "Plutarco Elías Calles and the Partido Nacional Revolucionario: Mexican National and Regional Politics in 1928 and 1929." Unpublished Ph.D. diss., University of California–Riverside, 1994.

Maurer, Noel. *The Power and the Money: The Mexican Financial System, 1876–1932.* Stanford, Calif.: Stanford University Press, 2002.

McCullen, Christopher J. "Calles and the Diplomacy of Revolution: Mexican-American Relations, 1924–1928." Unpublished Ph.D. diss., Georgetown University, 1981.

Campbell-Bannerman, Sir Henry (1836–1908)

prime minister of Great Britain

Sir Henry Campbell-Bannerman was born in Glasgow, Scotland, on September 7, 1836, the son of a middle-class retail businessman. A talented student, he passed through Trinity College, Cambridge University, before running for Parliament in 1868 as a Liberal. After 1871, in accordance with a family will, he appended his mother's maiden name of Bannerman to his own. Campbell-Bannerman was soon recognized as a talented administrator despite his youth, and he held a series of important posts in the administrations of William Gladstone and the fifth earl of Rosebery. The most memorable was as secretary of state for war, when he tactfully but forcefully obtained the resignation of the aged duke of Cambridge, commander in chief of armed forces in 1895. The duke, who had occupied his office for 39 years, had consistently opposed military reforms, and the British army languished in near obsolescence. Campbell-Bannerman, an avowed reformer, wasted no time in modernizing both the army and the navy in the face of rising threats from Germany. His performance so delighted Queen Victoria that she knighted him, and in 1898 he rose to become head of the Liberal Party. Three years later the party unanimously reconfirmed his leadership position.

Campbell-Bannerman initially faced the unenviable task of unifying a party torn by intense emotional issues. When the Boer War erupted in 1899 he had to reconcile prowar Imperialists with the pro-Boer faction of which he was leader. In fact, Campbell-Bannerman vividly condemned the conduct of the war, denouncing it as barbaric, but he studiously refrained from criticizing the army itself. He so angered fellow Liberals that in

1905 several adversaries tried to have him elevated to the House of Lords, where he would be out of the way. Campbell-Bannerman faced an equally difficult time over the issue of Irish home rule, which further split the Liberals into Unionist and pro-Irish camps. But his easy charm and self-deprecating Scottish wit won over many critics and he kept the Liberal Party from fracturing. He proved so successful that it was the Conservative Party of ARTHUR BALFOUR that ultimately splintered over these same issues. In December 1905 Balfour resigned as prime minister without calling for elections, and King Edward VII authorized Campbell-Bannerman to form a minority government. He did so with relish and in new elections that followed in January 1906, the Liberals obtained an absolute majority in the House of Commons. Campbell-Bannerman's success is significant in that he came from a business background, rather than the traditional landed gentry, and was the first English prime minister who was not Anglican by faith. He had heretofore been scarcely viewed as a leader of national caliber, but now he embarked on one of the great reformist periods of British history.

As a Liberal, Campbell-Bannerman wished to completely overhaul certain aspects of society to improve the lot of the common people, and his cabinet included such future Liberal luminaries as HERBERT HENRY ASQUITH and DAVID LLOYD GEORGE. With his parliamentary majority he quickly passed important legislation touching upon education, Irish self-governance, and an enlarged voter franchise only to see it vetoed by the aristocratic House of Lords. However, he did prevail upon the Lords to enact the Trades Dispute Act, which for the first time recognized workers' rights to strike. On the international scene, Campbell-Bannerman pushed successfully for home rule in the Transvaal and Orange Free State of newly conquered South Africa. These moves subdued political discontent and made possible the creation of a republic there in 1910. Long-standing disputes with Russia over Persia and Afghanistan were also resolved and paved the way for a critical military alliance, the Entente. Campbell-Bannerman then extended an olive branch to the newly emergent Labour Party and successfully encouraged close cooperation on a number of pressing matters.

Campbell-Bannerman skillfully held the reins of power for only two years when ill health forced him to retire in April 1908 and he was replaced by Asquith. He died on April 22, 1908, one of the least known and least appreciated prime ministers. However, his legacy rests in keeping the Liberal Party intact and achieving its greatest period of ascendency. Moreover, the obstinacy he encountered from the House of Lords prompted Asquith to ultimately strip it of veto power in 1911.

Further Reading

Campbell-Bannerman, Henry. *Early Letters of Sir Henry Campbell-Bannerman to His Sister Louisia, 1850–1851.* London: T. F. Unwin, 1925.

Bernstein, George L. "Sir Henry Campbell-Bannerman and the Liberal Imperialists." *Journal of British Studies* 23, no. 1 (1983): 105–124.

Cook, Chris. *A Short History of the Liberal Party, 1900–2001.* New York: Palgrave, 2002.

Gutzke, David W. "Rosebery and Campbell-Bannerman: The Conflict over Leadership Reconsidered." *Institute of Historical Research Bulletin* 54 (November 1981): 241–250.

Hazlehurst, Cameron, and Jose F. Harris. "Campbell-Bannerman as Prime Minister." *History* 55 (October 1970): 360–383.

Johnson, Graham. *Social Democratic Politics in Britain, 1881–1911.* Lewiston, N.Y.: E. Mellen Press, 2003.

Wilson, John. *CB: A Life of Sir Henry Campbell-Bannerman.* New York: St. Martin's Press, 1974.

Cárdenas, Lázaro (1895–1970) *president of Mexico*

Lázaro Cárdenas del Río was born in Jiquilpan, Michoacán, Mexico, on May 21, 1895, the son of a shopkeeper. Indifferently educated, he worked as a tax clerk until the Mexican Revolution commenced in 1913, when he joined a group of rebels fighting the regime of VICTORIANO HUERTA. Cárdenas proved himself an able soldier, and at length he became closely associated with the military staff of General PLUTARCO ELÍAS CALLES. After much fighting, in 1920 Cárdenas was appointed governor general of Michoacán where he witnessed the arrogance and corrupting influence of foreign oil companies firsthand. He returned to the field several times to oppose rebellions and counterrevolutionary uprisings that plagued the postrevolutionary period. However, Cárdenas acquitted himself well and in 1928 he was formally elected governor of Michoacán. He went to great lengths fulfilling the ideals of the revolution: agrarian reform for landless peasants, new schools touting socialist education, and promotion of peasant and worker organizations. He was also tapped by former president Calles to serve as interim president of the new Partido Nacional Revolucionario (PNR), National Revolutionary Party, which institutionalized one-party rule in Mexico. Calles had left office in 1928, but he still wielded great influence through a succession of puppet executives. Thinking he enjoyed similar influence over Cárdenas, Calles arranged for the PNR to nominate him as the next presidential candidate.

Selection by the PNR hierarchy virtually assured Cárdenas's election, but he nonetheless campaigned vigorously for the office. Within a year he traveled 18,000 miles throughout Mexico, visiting groups of peasants, listening to their complaints, and promising swift action if elected. Such attention endeared him to the lower classes and he won overwhelmingly in 1934. Cárdenas came to office full of revolutionary vigor and quite determined to assist the poor majority of Mexicans. In fact, resurrecting the impassioned ideals of the Mexican Revolution became a personal crusade for him, seeing that his predecessors in office had grown wealthy and conservative in their governmental policies. Cárdenas was convinced that new and more radical solutions were necessary to address the nation's maldistribution of wealth and promote a better standard of living for all its citizens.

Once empowered, Cárdenas directly embraced the nascent Mexican labor movement and encouraged the use of strikes to gain results. His organizing of trade unions and peasant groups flew in the face of an enraged Calles, who began orchestrating campaigns against reform. But Cárdenas remained in charge of the situation, and in 1936 he ordered Calles out of the country for his own safety. With the labor movement firmly cornered, Cárdenas next turned his attention to agrarian reform. Accordingly, he instituted a sweeping redistribution of 4.5 million acres of land to 800,000 peasants. This was the largest and most successful such program in Latin American history and did much to improve the squalid existence of poor campesinos. On the education front the regime institutionalized the construction of thousands of new schools, and a modern curriculum emphasizing nationalism, socialism, and anticlericalism. Like Calles, Cárdenas was profoundly anti-Catholic in outlook but he differed in the degree to which he suppressed the clergy. Rather than

Lázaro Cárdenas *(Library of Congress)*

foment religious-based uprisings, he allowed church services to be conducted, but insisted that clergymen wear civilian clothes in public. Having adroitly conducted the mass mobilization of peasants and workers, Cárdenas further cultivated their loyalty by incorporating them into the new state organization, the Partido Revolucionario Mexicano (PRM), Mexican Revolution Party. In this manner he hoped to perpetuate their political alliance to the revolution long after he left office. The system he established did, in fact, dominate Mexican national politics for over 70 years.

Internationally, Cárdenas made headlines when he nationalized the assets of foreign-based oil companies after they refused to provide Mexican workers with better wages. In their place he erected a new state oil company, Pemex, to acquire oil and distribute it nationally. Such actions greatly angered the United States and Great Britain, which imposed crippling economic sanc-

tions until reparations were paid. Toward the end of his presidency, Cárdenas curbed his zeal for revolutionary reform and toed a more conciliatory line toward conservative forces, which in 1939 had established the Partido Acción Nacional (PAN), National Action Party, to oppose him. In July 1940 he anointed as his successor the moderate MANUEL ÁVILA CAMACHO, who continued this conservative drift. Thereafter Cárdenas remained out of power officially, but he wielded tremendous political and moral authority until his death in Mexico City on October 19, 1970. He remains a popular figure among leftist intellectual establishments, despite the fact that he was never a communist and openly dismissed Marxism as impractical for Mexico's needs. But more than anything else, Cárdenas is revered for revitalizing the people's faith in their own revolution.

Further Reading

Bantjes, Adrian A. *As If Jesus Walked on Earth: Cardenismo, Sonora, and the Mexican Revolution.* Wilmington, Del.: Scholarly Resources, 1998.

Becker, Marjorie. *Setting the Virgin on Fire: Lázaro Cárdenas, Michoacán Peasants, and the Redemption of the Mexican Revolution.* Berkeley: University of California Press, 1995.

Dwyer, John J. "Diplomatic Weapons of the Weak: Mexican Policymaking during the U.S.-Mexican Agrarian Dispute, 1934–1941." *Diplomatic History* 26 (summer 2002): 375–395.

Fallaw, Ben. *Cárdenas Compromised: The Failure of Reform in Postrevolutionary Yucatan, 1934–1940.* Durham, N.C.: Duke University Press, 2001.

Philip, George. "Populist Possibilities and Political Constraints in Mexico." *Bulletin of Latin American Research* 19 (April 2000): 207–221.

Schuler, Friedrich. *Mexico between Hitler and Roosevelt: Mexican Foreign Relations in the Age of Lázaro Cárdenas.* Albuquerque: University of New Mexico Press, 1998.

Carranza, Venustiano (1859–1920) *president of Mexico*

Venustiano Carranza was born in Cuatro Ciénegas, Coahuila, Mexico, on December 29, 1859, the scion of a wealthy, landowning family. He was well educated locally, and steeped in the nuances of 19th-century political liberalism, namely the necessity of constitutional rule. Carranza was politically active at an early age and held a number of local offices, including mayor, local deputy, and senator. By 1910 he had become a political disciple of FRANCISCO MADERO in his struggle against aging dictator PORFIRIO DÍAZ. Carranza was appointed governor of Coahuila and a member of Madero's presidential cabinet. However, when Madero was murdered by General VICTORIANO HUERTA in 1913, Carranza led a revolt in the north as the self-appointed chief of the new Constitutionalist Armies. More than anything, Carranza swore he would never recognize Huerta's legitimacy and intended to restore the rule of law. However, he was forced to deal with other local caudillos to lead a unified front against Huerta. Carranza's army clashed with leading figures such as Francisco "Pancho" Villa and Emiliano Zapata and their followers, but at length these disparate forces united and drove the usurper out of the country. By July 1914 Carranza, victorious in the north, led his army south to Mexico City and appointed himself interim president. But discontent over the political spoils soon split the Constitutionalists, and the competing generals were forced to hold a convention on October 4, 1914. There Carranza declared he would not relinquish power unless a new constitution had been drawn up and enacted. His primary goal was reestablishing order, not dramatic social reforms.

For the rest of 1914 Carranza consolidated his grip on power by quelling several rebellions. A significant uprising by Pancho Villa was defeated by General ÁLVARO OBREGÓN, a nominal Carranza ally. The new president was then free to continue writing his new constitution. A convention assembled at Aguascalientes in September 1916; several drafts were submitted. However, because the majority of delegates were more radically inclined than Carranza, the document they produced was far different from the one he envisioned. In fact the Constitution of 1917 enshrined the principle that material wealth in the form of private property could be expropriated for national benefit. The radicals went on to include anticlerical provisions against the Catholic Church as well as institutionalizing land and labor reform. The final document was more extremist than Carranza wished, but he relented in the interest of national harmony. In May 1917 he was officially installed as the first president of postrevolutionary Mexico. He also ordered the assassination of Zapata in 1919, which stained his reputation as a staunch upholder of law.

In office, Carranza used his basic conservatism to slow down and even halt constitutionally mandated courses of change. He experimented briefly with land reform but never fully implemented it. Nor did he crack down excessively on the church and clergy in an attempt to maintain religious peace. The biggest area of contention came in relations with the United States. In 1914 President WOODROW WILSON dispatched American troops to Veracruz to protect American property and citizens. He did not offer diplomatic recognition of the Carranza regime until 1915, and the two sides viewed each other with suspicion. The pace of confrontation quickened dramatically in 1916 when Villa attacked Columbus, New Mexico, and U.S. Army forces under General John Pershing were sent in pursuit. Carranza remonstrated angrily and considered the affair a gross violation of national sovereignty. Mexican troops were ordered to resist the incursion, which enhanced Carranza's reputation as a staunch nationalist. However, normal relations were restored once American soldiers departed Mexico in 1917.

Carranza left office in 1920 as planned, but he unexpectedly named a little-known civilian, Ignacio Bonillas, to succeed him. He apparently chose this puppet figure as a means of perpetuating his own influence. This deceptive move greatly angered General Obregón, who expected to be chosen. He declared war against Carranza. PLUTARCO ELÍAS CALLES joined him, and the former president was forced to flee Mexico City for Veracruz. On May 21, 1920, his train was attacked by Obregón sympathizers and Carranza was killed. His political legacy has been diminished by conservative tendencies that undermined the revolutionary principles of the very constitution he inspired. However, the fact that Carranza insisted on a strict legal framework for any new government gave subsequent Mexican leaders political legitimacy they would have otherwise lacked. Furthermore, the Constitution of 1917 he so distrusted remains in place to the present.

Further Reading

Gilderhus, Mark T. "Wilson, Carranza, and the Monroe Doctrine: A Question in Regional Organization." *Diplomatic History* 7, no. 2 (1983): 103–115.

Gonzales, Michael J. *The Mexican Revolution, 1910–1940.* Albuquerque, N.M.: University of New Mexico, 2002.

Richmond, Douglas W. *Venustiano Carranza's Nationalist Struggle, 1893–1920*. Lincoln: University of Nebraska Press, 1983.

Stout, Joseph A. *Border Conflict: Villistas, Carrancistas, and the Punitive Expedition, 1915–1920*. Fort Worth: Texas Christian University, 1999.

Tardanico, Richard. "Revolutionary Nationalism and State Building in Mexico." *Politics and Society* 10, no. 1 (1980): 59–86.

Carter, Jimmy (1924–) *president of the United States*

James Earl Carter was born in Plains, Georgia, on October 1, 1924, the son of a small farmer. After completing high school he briefly attended Georgia Southwestern College before transferring to the U.S. Naval Academy at Annapolis, Maryland. Carter graduated and was commissioned an ensign in 1946 with a specialty in electronics. His expertise led to an assignment with Admiral Hyman Rickover as the first American nuclear-powered submarines were built. Carter intended to make the navy his career, but he resigned his commission in 1953 following the death of his father, returning home to run the family farm. He eventually built a successful business farming peanuts, and in 1962 commenced his political career by running for a seat in the state senate. He was successful and gained reelection two years later. As a politician, Carter was unique in espousing a brand of political liberalism touching upon civil rights for African Americans and equality for women—a courageous stance in the South at the time. In 1966 he unsuccessfully ran for the governorship of Georgia and took solace in his religion, becoming an evangelical, "born again" Christian. Four years later he won handily and entered high office determined to use government for the benefit of all citizens. Despite roots in the Deep South, Carter embraced affirmative action and appointed more African Americans and women to positions of responsibility than any prior executive. He was also fiscally conservative, compressing over 300 state agencies into a mere 30 to curb expenses. His willingness to protect the environment and encourage openness in government made him extremely popular and, constitutionally denied a second term in office, he declared his candidacy for the U.S. presidency in 1976.

Conditions were then extremely favorable for Democrat Carter to seek high office. The nation still

Jimmy Carter *(Library of Congress)*

reeled from the Watergate scandal that forced Republican RICHARD M. NIXON from office, and his successor, GERALD R. FORD, had been unable to improve the economy. Carter, sensing that the polity welcomed change, deliberately campaigned as an "outsider," untainted by the Washington, D.C., political establishment. He also adopted a high moral tone for his campaign, declaring to the American people, "I will never lie to you." The national mood was indicative of change, and throughout the spring of 1976, Carter rolled up an impressive series of primary victories that culminated in his nomination that August. In the general election that fall, he campaigned hard on the message of honesty and integrity, leaving Ford with the stigma of having pardoned Nixon for his crimes. The race was closer than many pundits anticipated, but Carter managed to win with 48 percent of the votes cast. He thus became the first president from the Deep South since Zachary Taylor in 1848.

In office Carter adopted the high moral tone so central to his political philosophy. The centerpiece of his administration became human rights, and he held both allies and Communist-bloc nations accountable. He also established a new Department of Energy, issued a blanket pardon to Vietnam War draft dodgers, and stopped production of the controversial B-1 bomber (although testing was allowed to continue). Taking his principles overseas, he sought to win over Latin American opinion by signing a treaty with Panamanian strongman OMAR TORRIJOS that relinquished the contentious Panama Canal by 1999. Carter, deeply concerned with the Middle East, then interjected himself in the stalled peace process by inviting Egyptian president ANWAR SADAT and Israeli prime minister MENACHEM BEGIN to Washington for talks. The result was a diplomatic triumph, the Camp David peace accords signed in 1979, through which Israel gave up Egyptian land in exchange for diplomatic recognition. Carter then eagerly pursued nuclear arms reduction with the Soviet Union and signed the Strategic Arms Limitation Treaty (SALT II) with Premier LEONID BREZHNEV.

Unfortunately, Carter's success abroad was not duplicated at home. The economy remained in a deep recession while inflation spiraled to 15 percent. Carter's presidency began floundering. Part of his failure lay in an inability to work harmoniously with a Congress that, while Democratically controlled, basically ignored his economic initiatives. A bigger blow fell in November 1979 when Iranian militants, angered by Carter's decision to allow the ailing Shah MOHAMMAD REZA PAHLAVI into the United States for cancer treatment, stormed the American embassy in Teheran and took 52 hostages. They remained captive for 444 days while Carter attempted an ill-advised rescue mission that cost eight American lives. Carter's inability to influence events was further underscored in December 1979 when the Soviet Union suddenly invaded Afghanistan with thousands of troops, triggering fears of an escalating cold war. Carter then boycotted the 1980 Moscow Olympics and imposed a grain embargo against Russia, but this hurt only farming interests. The Senate also refused to ratify the SALT II agreement, clear evidence that the cold war was growing hotter. In the spring of 1980 Carter successfully battled Massachusetts senator Ted Kennedy for the Democratic nomination, which left the Democrats badly divided. That November, Carter was trounced by the Republicans under California governor RONALD REAGAN, signifying the first time an incumbent president was unseated since 1932. Carter, feeling genuinely despised by the American people, withdrew into private life back at Plains, Georgia. His polling numbers were then in the low 20s, about the same as WARREN G. HARDING's after he died in office.

Carter's self-imposed exile proved short-lived, for he remained strongly motivated by faith to help disadvantaged people. He became active with Habitat for Humanity, which erects low-cost housing for poor people, and also gained a degree of international notoriety as a roving goodwill ambassador. President Bill Clinton dispatched him to North Korea, Haiti, and Somalia, in the interest of promoting peace. In 1990 Carter also served as a United Nations monitor of free elections in Nicaragua, and implored Sandinista president DANIEL ORTEGA to accept defeat gracefully. In May 2002 he became the first American president to visit Fidel Castro's Cuba and called upon the United States to end its 40-year embargo. He also squarely challenged Castro to respect human rights and democracy. Carter's consistent defense of human rights around the world and his advocacy of peaceful resolution to armed conflict made him the most visible and popular ex-president in American history. In December 2002 he appeared in Stockholm, Sweden, to receive the Nobel Peace Prize for his efforts. Carter accepted the distinction with his usual modesty, declaring, "War may sometimes be a necessary evil. But no matter how necessary it is always an evil, never a good."

Further Reading

Biven, W. Carl. *Jimmy Carter's Economy: Policy in an Age of Limits.* Chapel Hill: University of North Carolina Press, 2002.

Brinkley, David. *The Unfinished Presidency: Jimmy Carter's Journey beyond the White House.* New York: Penguin Books, 1999.

Carter, Jimmy. *An Hour before Daylight: Memoirs of a Rural Boyhood.* New York: Simon and Schuster, 2001.

Garrison, Jean A. *Games Advisors Play: Foreign Policy in the Carter and Nixon Administrations.* College Station: Texas A & M University Press, 1999.

Strong, Robert A. *Working in the World: Jimmy Carter and the Making of American Foreign Policy.* Baton Rouge: Louisiana State University Press, 2000.

Castelo Branco, Humberto (1900–1967)
president of Brazil

Humberto de Alencar Castelo Branco was born in Fortaleza, Brazil, on September 20, 1900, scion of a long line of military officers. He passed through the Realengo Military Academy in 1921 and, though an officer, declined to join military uprisings against the government. A dedicated professional, he rose successively through the ranks and during World War II commanded the Brazilian Expeditionary Force in Italy. Even as a general, Castelo Branco maintained a strict legalistic outlook on politics, and in 1954 he was one of several officers who petitioned General GETÚLIO VARGAS to resign from the presidency and restore civilian rule. Castelo Branco's superior military record and lack of political ambition resulted in a promotion to four-star general in 1962. By this time, however, Brazil was being rocked by social unrest unleashed by President JÂNIO QUADROS and his replacement, the leftist João Goulart. Their governments had tendered diplomatic recognition to Fidel Castro's Communist Cuba and the People's Republic of China, much to the consternation of the officer corps. This led to a schism in the army, with Castelo Branco and the legalists wishing to maintain order while others sought military control of the country. As leftist-inspired unrest spread to the peasant population of Brazil, Castelo Branco, now chief of staff, conferred with Goulart to have him reverse many of his controversial policies. When this failed, Castelo Branco feared the onset of a communist-style revolution in Brazil, and he agreed to participate in action against the government. On March 31, 1964, the generals, seconded by numerous governors, congressmen, and business executives, struck swiftly and removed Goulart from office with little loss of life.

After internal wrangling among the coup leaders, Castelo Branco was selected to serve out the balance of Goulart's term in office as president and he was confirmed by Congress on April 11, 1964. Unlike in previous coups undertaken to unseat a popular regime, the military now sought to maintain power long enough to reshape the nation's political landscape. The new president's immediate priority was controlling runaway inflation, eliminating communism, and orchestrating economic development. To attack these issues he installed Roberto Campos in the new and powerful Ministry of Economic Planning, with near dictatorial powers for regulating the economy. The government then embarked on a 15-year program to promote capital formation, expand consumer markets, and stimulate foreign investment. Castelo Branco severed ties with Cuba and China, while instituting close political and economic relations with the United States. Eventually his programs produced the desired results and brought inflation down to single digits.

Other parts of Castelo Branco's national policies were less commendable. The hard-line faction in the officer corps insisted that he impose several "institutional acts" in 1964 and 1965. The first stripped former presidents like JUSCELINO KUBITSCHEK of their political rights. The second act, taken in response to state elections that went contrary to their wishes, disbanded all political parties and allowed presidents to be elected by Congress. Thereafter political activity was restricted to a pro-government party, the National Renovating Alliance (Arena), and the opposition Movimento Democrático Brasileiro (MDB), Brazilian Democratic Movement. The supreme court was also packed with jurists considered friendly to the military. Castelo Branco's control of government seemed secure by 1966 and he was ready to retire from office, but the junta suddenly extended his presidential term by another year. Castelo Branco hoped that a civilian would succeed him, but the military disagreed and appointed former war minister Artur da Costa e Silva as president on March 25, 1967. Castelo Branco then retired from public life, although he continued to exert a moderating influence on the junta. He died suddenly in a plane crash on July 18, 1967, the first in a line of military officers who ruled Brazil without interruption for 20 years.

Further Reading

Brown, Diana DeG. *Umbanda: Religion and Politics in Urban Brazil.* New York: Columbia University Press, 1994.

Ciria, Alberto. "The Individual as History: Five Latin American Biographies." *Latin American Research Review* 20, no. 3 (1985): 247–267.

Cohen, Youssef. *Radicals, Reformers, and Reactionaries: The Prisoner's Dilemma and the Collapse of Democracy in Latin America.* Chicago: University of Chicago Press, 1994.

Dulles, John F. *Castelo Branco: The Making of a Brazilian President.* College Station: Texas A & M University Press, 1978.

————. *President Castelo Branco: Brazilian Reformer.* College Station: Texas A & M University Press, 1980.

Johnson, Ollie A. *Brazilian Party Politics and the Coup of 1964.* Gainesville: University Press of Florida, 2001.

Ceauşescu, Nicolae (1918–1989) *president of Romania*

Nicolae Ceauşescu was born in Scornicesti, Romania, on January 26, 1918, into a peasant family. He was attracted to the Communist Party as a youth and spent several years alternating between underground activity and jail. By 1944 the approaching Red Army induced Romanian king MICHAEL I to abandon Nazi Germany and become a Soviet ally. Ceauşescu rose rapidly through the ranks of the new Romanian Worker's Party aided by his old cellmate, Gheorghe Gheorghiu-Dej, the new party secretary. Because neither man had spent any time in the Soviet Union, they were not regarded as politically reliable by Kremlin authorities. Nonetheless, Ceauşescu served as minister of agriculture, chief of political instruction for the military, and secretary to the party's central committee. He also worked hard cementing his relationship to Gheorghiu as heir apparent. After Gheorghiu died in 1965, Ceauşescu became secretary of the newly renamed Communist Party of Romania, although he submitted to a power-sharing arrangement with other senior leaders. A contest for supremacy ensued but by 1967 Ceauşescu managed to have himself crowned president of Romania's state council. In 1974 he further consolidated power by winning an "election" as president of Romania. Backed by his dreaded secret police, the Securitate, he completely controlled the nation and its destiny.

Early on Ceauşescu gained a well-earned reputation as a communist maverick in the mold of Yugoslavia's MARSHAL TITO. Like Tito he embraced communism politically but steered a course independent from the dictates of the Soviet Union. He was the only leader of the Warsaw Pact alliance to maintain diplomatic relations with Israel in the wake of the 1967 war. The following year he strongly condemned Premier LEONID BREZHNEV's invasion of Czechoslovakia and refused Soviet troops access to Romanian facilities. In 1989 Ceauşescu again attacked the Soviets for their invasion of Afghanistan. Naturally, such belligerence earned him plaudits from the West,

and Ceauşescu willingly struck up cordial relations with the United States. He also functioned as an intermediary between MAO ZEDONG and President RICHARD NIXON in talks that initiated diplomatic relations. In return Romania enjoyed closer economic ties and more financial aid from the West than any country in Eastern Europe.

Despite his seemingly enlightened foreign policy, Ceauşescu ran one of the world's most oppressive regimes. His contempt for Soviet methods was selective, for he closely copied the dictatorial methods of JOSEPH STALIN and administered his entire nation as a police state. Virtually every decision affecting the daily life of average Romanians was made either by Ceauşescu himself or his immediate circle. And, like Stalin, Ceauşescu subscribed to the notion of a centrally controlled economy emphasizing heavy industry to the exclusion of everything else. One of his more brutally enforced policies was that of "systematization," namely, bulldozing thousands of traditional Romanian villages in favor of concrete apartment complexes. Ceauşescu was quick to propagate cultural nationalism at the expense of Germans, the Romany (Gypsies), and the sizable Hungarian minority living there. None were allowed to speak or learn their native tongue publicly. His rigidly enforced policies resulted in dramatically declining standards of living, and the country became impoverished trying to pay off staggering national debts. Nepotism was also widely practiced by Ceauşescu; no less than 30 of his family members received high political sinecures. The nation slowly starved, but the family elite grew fabulously wealthy and lived in conspicuous luxury.

Ceauşescu's downfall can be traced to the 1980s after he concluded several trips to China and North Korea, the sole remaining bastions of Stalinism. He was impressed by the "cult of personality" surrounding Mao and Kim Il Sung, and he determined to emulate them at home. Statues of Ceauşescu sprang up around the country, while the media, arts, and literature were conscripted in an endless campaign to sing his praises. Resentment against this quixotic dictator peaked on December 17, 1989, when security forces fired on a demonstration and killed hundreds of people. The revolt quickly spread and was soon joined by the army. With his elaborate police state collapsing around him, Ceauşescu and his wife tried fleeing Bucharest by helicopter but were apprehended and placed on trial. Both were summarily executed on December 25, 1989, concluding one of the most brutal episodes in Romanian history.

Further Reading

Almond, Mark. *The Rise and Fall of Nicolae and Elena Ceauşescu.* London: Chapman, 1992.

Barnett, Thomas P. M. *Romanian and East German Policies in the Third World: Comparing the Strategies of Ceauşescu and Honecker.* Westport, Conn.: Praeger, 1992.

Behr, Edward. *Kiss the Hand You Cannot Bite: The Rise and Fall of the Ceauşescus.* New York: Villard Books, 1991.

Deletant, Dennis. *Ceauşescu and the Securitate: Coercion and Dissent in Romania, 1965–1989.* London: Hurst & Co., 1995.

Verdery, Katherine. *National Ideology under Socialism: Identity and Cultural Politics in Ceauşescu Romania.* Berkeley: University of California Press, 1991.

Cerezo Arévalo, Marco (1942–) *president of Guatemala*

Marco Vinicio Cerezo Arévalo was born in Guatemala City, Guatemala, on December 26, 1942, into a family noted for political activism. His father had been a justice on the Guatemalan Supreme Court while his grandfather was murdered for opposing dictator JORGE UBICO. Cerezo was educated locally and attended the University of San Carlos and Loyola University, New Orleans, to study law. He had witnessed the overthrow of left-wing president JACOBO ARBENZ GUZMÁN in 1954, and he became active in politics. Cerezo joined the Democracia Cristiana Guatemalteca (DCG), Christian Democratic Party, in the mid-1960s and he rose to become general secretary. He gained election to Congress in 1974, surviving three assassination attempts. For most of Cerezo's life, Guatemala was in the throes of a protracted civil war pitting left-wing insurgents against right-wing military and business interests. Moreover, the military persistently intervened in the political arena and tossed out any president they suspected of coddling the rebels. It was not until 1983, after 15 years of military rule, that the generals deposed EFRAÍN RÍOS MONTT and allowed democracy to return. By that time Cerezo had announced his candidacy for president. His opponent was Jorge Carpio Nicolle of the conservative Union of the National Center, who enjoyed strong ties to the business and military classes. Positioning himself as a man of the people, Cerezo campaigned on a platform of national reform and reconciliation, winning 68 percent of votes cast in a runoff election. He was inaugurated on January 14, 1986, amid high hopes for his war-weary nation.

Unfortunately for Cerezo, he inherited a country on the brink of chaos. Inflation was rampant, the national deficit soared, and unemployment hovered around 50 percent. He quickly enacted a neoliberal program that diversified exports, devalued the currency, and removed price controls to jump-start the economy. After five years Guatemala had improved economically but at the cost of reduced living standards for most citizens. Especially hard-hit were Indians, the majority population who remained poverty-stricken and were the source of most guerrilla recruits. Cerezo's reform programs also greatly angered the trade union movement, which launched crippling nationwide strikes in 1987, 1988, and 1989. Worse still, the military establishment felt that Cerezo was not pursuing counterinsurgency efforts with sufficient vigor, so in 1988 and 1989, he weathered two attempted coups against the government.

Cerezo remained overwhelmed by domestic problems throughout his tenure in office but did enjoy a measure of success with international diplomacy. In 1987 he reestablished diplomatic relations with Great Britain, which had been severed over the issue of independence for British Honduras (Belize). Cerezo was also a party to peace-making efforts in Central America that arose out of communist-inspired conflicts in Nicaragua and El Salvador. Despite diplomatic pressure from American president RONALD REAGAN, he steadfastly refused to allow Guatemala to be used as a base for Nicaraguan counterrevolutionary contra forces, suffering reduced foreign aid in return, though Cerezo was no friend to the Sandinista regime of DANIEL ORTEGA. He urged passage of the peace plan enunciated by Costa Rican president OSCAR ARIAS SÁNCHEZ, which mandated nonaggression and improved human rights throughout the region. Ironically, these issues were the major failure of Cerezo's administration. He tried negotiating with his own rebel groups in Madrid, but the Unidad Revolucionaria Nacional Guatemalteca (URNG), Guatemalan National Revolutionary Union, responded with increased attacks. This prompted savage reprisals from the military, especially toward the Indian population. Private death squads were particularly active, and a massacre of 14 Indian men and boys in December 1990 led to the suspension of all U.S. military aid. The beleaguered executive also endured charges of corruption and drug trafficking by the time his term expired.

The return of democracy under Cerezo did not bring about the changes anticipated and in some respects the nation was worse off than when he assumed office. Largely for that reason, his handpicked successor, Alfonso Cabrera, was soundly defeated by the more conservative Jorge Serrano Elias in December 1991. However, his departure marked the first peaceful transfer of power from one president to another in 151 years. Since leaving office Cerezo has resumed his place as a member of Congress and a leading elder spokesman.

Further Reading

Garcia, Robert. "Guatemala under Cerezo: A Democratic Opening." *SAIS Review* 6, no. 2 (1986): 69–81.
Jonas, S. "Contradictions of Guatemala's Political Opening." *Latin American Perspectives* 15 (summer 1988): 26–46.
Langevin, Mark S. "Christian Democrat Administrations Confront the Central American Cauldron." Unpublished master's thesis, University of Arizona, 1989.
Painter, James. *Guatemala: False Hope, False Freedom: The Rich, the Poor, and the Christian Democrats.* New York: Catholic Institute for International Relations, 1989.
Steigenga, Timothy J. *The Politics of the Spirit: The Political Implications of Pentacostalized Religion in Costa Rica and Guatemala.* Lanham, Md.: Lexington Books, 2001.

Chadli, Benjedid (1929–   ) *president of Algeria*

Benjedid Chadli was born in Bouteldja, Algeria, on April 14, 1929, into a peasant family. His nation was then a French protectorate and, like many youths of his generation, he embraced anticolonial activities. When fighting between Algerian nationalists and the French military erupted in 1954 Chadli joined the clandestine National Liberation Front (NLF). He proved himself an accomplished soldier and Colonel HOUARI BOUMÉDIENNE appointed him to the Northern Military Zone in 1961. Algeria won its independence from France in 1962 after a horrific conflict, and Chadli decided to remain in the military. He supported Boumédienne and AHMED BEN BELLA in their coup against the military junta and was rewarded with command of the Second Military District. Chadli subsequently supported Boumédienne's attempt to oust the erratic Ben Bella in 1965 and received a seat on the newly organized Council of the Revolution. However, he expressed little interest in politics or ideology and seemed content to endorse whatever action the council entertained. When Boumédienne unexpectedly died in December 1978, the council strove for a peaceful transfer of power to a successor, and Chadli became one of two main candidates. After a brief struggle his moderate faction of the NLF prevailed, and he was formally elected February 9, 1979.

Under Boumédienne Algeria had transformed itself from a tottering former colony into the most robust economy among developing countries. Chadli intended to continue pursuing state-sponsored socialism, although tempered by his own sense of moderate pragmatism. One of his first deeds was to release former president Ben Bella from the prison where he had languished for 14 years. Chadli touted his own reformist agenda, which sought to scale back some of the revolutionary excesses of his predecessors. He then set about consolidating his control by reducing the size of the Politburo and general staff, and appointing trusted figures with similar views. He also planned to upgrade the political status of women but ran afoul of rising Muslim fundamentalism, which thwarted his goal. On the international front, Chadli sought to maintain Algeria's high visibility as a leader of the nonaligned nations but with closer relationships to the United States and France. Chadi secretly assisted President JIMMY CARTER during attempts to release the American hostages from Iran in 1981. He tried to mediate the internecine war between Iran and Iraq, and performed similar work in 1990 when Iraq invaded Kuwait. His enlightened diplomacy and willingness to advocate moderate solutions in the Middle East and elsewhere made him a respected figure. He also tried arbitrating Algeria's long-standing dispute with Morocco over the occupation of Western Sahara, but the problem remained intractable.

Domestic affairs were less successful. In 1981 declining oil prices, on which Algeria was highly dependent, led to rising national deficits, inflation, and unemployment. When the state-controlled economy failed to improve by 1985, widespread strikes and riots resulted. Chadli then unleashed his security forces to maintain order, and several hundred demonstrators were killed.

Much of the unrest stemmed from the fact that Algeria was a democracy in name only, actually run as a one-party state headed by the NLF. But Chadli, wishing to circumvent more violence, felt that dramatic political reforms were needed. In February 1989 he promulgated a new constitution allowing multiparty democracy for the first time. It was a welcome departure from the political norm in Algeria but also held unforeseen consequences. In 1990 and 1991, local and national elections resulted in outright victories for the Front Islamique du Salut (FIS), the Islamic Salvation Front, which campaigned to roll back 30 years of progressive reforms and institute a conservative Islamic republic. Chadli was disillusioned by the result but also determined to abide by the popular will. But he failed to consider the military's response to this rising tide of religious militancy, and in January 1992, the generals ousted him. This act and the nullification of election results triggered a vicious civil war between secular and religious interests that persists to the present time. Chadli endured a spell of house arrest but continues on as a voice of moderation in this increasingly polarized society. It is ironic that the introduction of political pluralism to Algeria ushered in a state of extreme sectarian violence.

Further Reading

Derradji, Abder-Rahman. *A Concise History of Political Violence in Algeria, 1954–2000: Brothers in Faith, Enemies in Arms.* Lewiston, N.Y.: E. Mellen Press, 2002.

Farley, J. "Algeria: Democracy on Hold." *Contemporary Review* 262 (March 1993): 130–135.

Pazzanita, Anthony G. "From Boumédienne to Benjedid: The Algerian Regime in Transition." *Journal of South Asian and Middle Eastern Studies* 15 (April 1991): 51–70.

Tahi, M. "The Arduous Democratization Process in Algeria." *Journal of Modern African Studies* 30 (September 1992): 397–419.

Volpi, Frederic. *Islam and Democracy: The Failure of Dialogue in Algeria, 1988–2001.* Sterling, Va.: Pluto Press, 2002.

Chamberlain, Neville (1869–1940) *prime minister of Great Britain*

Arthur Neville Chamberlain was born in Birmingham, England, on March 18, 1869, the son of a noted politician. He was well educated locally before studying science at the University of Birmingham, but in 1890 his father dispatched him to run a family estate in the Bahamas. Chamberlain remained seven years, ultimately failing to convert hemp into a cash crop and returning to Birmingham in 1897 to business and politics. He proved adept at both, and in 1915 gained election as lord mayor. Chamberlain's administrative success brought him to the attention of Liberal prime minister DAVID LLOYD GEORGE, who appointed him director general of national service in December 1916. His office being poorly prepared for its assigned task, Chamberlain resigned within months, but he returned to public life as a Conservative member of Parliament in 1918. He declined to serve as a cabinet official under Lloyd George and waited until ANDREW BONAR LAW assumed power in 1922 before accepting successive appointments as postmaster general, paymaster general, minister of health, and finally chancellor of the Exchequer. In 1924 Prime Minister STANLEY BALDWIN reassigned Chamberlain to the ministry of health, where he made remarkable progress. A conservative by nature, Chamberlain nonetheless felt that government should take positive steps to assist those willing to help themselves. He then sponsored a comprehensive series of bills covering pensions, health care, unemployment, housing, and poor relief. In many respects he laid the groundwork for the British welfare state that emerged in the late 1940s. In 1931 Labour prime minister RAMSAY MACDONALD appointed Chamberlain chancellor of the Exchequer again, where he unceremoniously abandoned the 80-year-old policy of free trade, in favor of high tariffs. This was undertaken during the height of the Great Depression to protect British industry and jobs. He continued in the same post in the second Baldwin administration until he himself became prime minister in 1937.

Chamberlain previously enjoyed a reputation as one of the most far-sighted and efficient politicians in the Conservative Party, gifted with a flair for crafting and passing important social legislation. His tenure as prime minister, unfortunately, was singularly dominated by foreign affairs, for which he possessed little aptitude. Since the election of ADOLF HITLER in 1933 and the rise of an invigorated German military machine, dark clouds had been growing on Europe's horizon. Many in France and England recalled the horrors of World War I and were determined to avoid another military confrontation if possible. Chamberlain nonetheless recognized the threat posed by Nazism, strongly supporting Baldwin's efforts at national rearmament, and he continued these policies once in office. But the Allied powers were still weak by comparison and needed additional time to rearm. For this reason, Chamberlain engaged in appeasement, accepting Hitler's territorial ambitions in exchange for peace. World events climaxed in 1938 when Hitler, having forcibly absorbed Austria, now demanded annexation of the German-speaking Sudetenland region of Czechoslovakia. On September 30, 1938, Chamberlain flew to Munich, Germany, where, in concert with French premier ÉDOUARD DALADIER and Italian dictator BENITO MUSSOLINI, he signed a document recognizing Hitler's bloodless conquest. Hitler also pledged to stop his expansionist ploys and respect the remaining parts of Czechoslovakia. Chamberlain then flew home, dramatically waving the Munich Pact and declaring it "peace in our time." But British rearmament continued apace.

Chamberlain's appeasement policy, which enjoyed wide public support, ended suddenly in March 1939 when Hitler broke his promise and absorbed the remnants of Czechoslovakia. Perceiving his country as still too weak for war, he next sought defensive alliances that could contain Nazism through diplomacy. Treaties were accordingly signed with France, Poland, Romania, and Greece, pledging a British declaration of war should Hitler attack. In September 1939, Hitler did exactly that, invading Poland, and Chamberlain found himself a wartime prime minister. Completely out of his league, he did little to clarify a muddled strategy that discounted a German offensive in the west. In April 1940 Hitler astonished the world by his lightning conquest of Norway, and Chamberlain faced a revolt from Conservatives in Parliament. He consequently resigned from power on May 10, 1940, just as France was being overrun by German forces, and was replaced by WINSTON CHURCHILL. Chamberlain lingered on in government as lord president of the council until ill health forced his resignation four months later. He died in London on November 9, 1940, harshly judged and much derided for having appeased the Nazis. Historians have since reevaluated Chamberlain as an effective national leader; his diplomacy brought England a badly needed respite to enhance its defenses. His fault lay in taking Hitler at his word.

Further Reading

Chamberlain, Neville. *The Neville Chamberlain Diary Letters,* 2 vols. Burlington, Vt.: Ashgate Pub., 2000.

Dutton, David. *Neville Chamberlain.* London: Arnold, 2001.

Grayson, Richard S. *Liberals, International Relations, and Appeasement: The Liberal Party, 1919–1931.* Portland, Ore.: Frank Cass, 2001.

Imlay, Talbot C. *Facing the Second World War: Strategy, Politics, and Economics in Britain and France, 1938–1940.* New York: Oxford University Press, 2003.

Ruggiero, John. *Neville Chamberlain and British Rearmament: Pride, Prejudice, Politics.* Westport, Conn.: Greenwood Press, 1999.

Smart, Nick. *British Strategy and Politics During the Phony War: Before the Balloon Went Up.* Westport, Conn.: Praeger, 2003.

Stewart, Graham. *Burying Caesar: The Churchill-Chamberlain Rivalry.* New York: Overlook Press, 2001.

Witherell, Larry L. "Lord Salisbury's 'Watching Committee' and the Fall of Neville Chamberlain, May 1940." *English Historical Review* 116 (November 2001): 1134–1166.

Chamoun, Camille (1900–1987) *president of Lebanon*

Camille Chamoun was born in Deir al-Kamar, south Lebanon, on April 3, 1900, into a Maronite Christian family. In 1920 Lebanon became a French protectorate, and in 1925 he passed through Saint Joseph University with a degree in law. In 1934 he gained election to the national legislature as a member of Bishara al-Khuri's Constitutional Bloc and began pushing for national independence. A talented administrator with a knack for backroom machinations, Chamoun gained appointment as minister of finance in 1938. During World War II he developed several abiding political links to Great Britain and the United States, especially after Allied forces freed Lebanon from Vichy French control. Thereafter he played a prominent role in securing Lebanese independence in 1943, with Khuri serving as the new nation's first executive. Because of Lebanon's crazy-quilt assemblage of Maronite Christians, Druze, and Sunni and Shia Muslims, a constitutional agreement was worked out whereby a Christian became president, a Sunni served as prime minister, and a Shia would be speaker of the house. It seemed an unworkable arrangement given the region's reputation for secular intolerance, but it bought the country several years of peace and stability.

Chamoun served as a loyal Khuri ally for six years and fully expected to be chosen his successor. However, in 1952 the president began seeking constitutional changes that would extend his term in office by another six years. Chamoun then broke with the Constitutional Bloc and cemented an alliance with Druze leader Kamal Jumblatt of the Socialist Front to oppose Khuri. They accused him of institutionalized corruption, nepotism, and authoritarian tendencies. Throughout the summer of 1952 the two men also orchestrated an effective national strike that brought the country to a halt and induced Khuri to step down. On September 23, 1952, Chamoun was elected president by the legislature, securing many Muslim votes in the process. Despite his Christian background he proved ready and able to reach across to potential allies in the Muslim camp. This greatly angered former supporters in the Constitutional Bloc, who regarded such collaboration as treasonable. Nonetheless it gave Chamoun a working majority in the legislature, and he enacted several sweeping reforms. Among them were creation of an independent judiciary, voting rights for women, and liberalized trade policies. In fact, Chamoun's tenure in office was among the most prosperous in Lebanon's history.

The harmony of Chamoun's administration was suddenly shattered by the rise of radical Pan-Arabism, extolled by Egypt's GAMAL ABDEL NASSER. When Nasser nationalized the Suez Canal in 1956, the British and French committed military forces to seize it back. Such intervention inflamed Sunni and Shia Muslim passions in Lebanon, but Chamoun declined to break diplomatic relations with either country. He further incurred anger by refusing to allow Lebanon to join the Egyptian/Syrian United Arab Republic. Chamoun then deliberately sought close political and diplomatic ties with American president DWIGHT D. EISENHOWER and implored him to use force in Lebanon should civil war erupt. But Chamoun soon displayed similar tendencies to his predecessor, and charges of nepotism, corruption, and authoritarianism were leveled against him. In 1957 Chamoun ostensibly rigged parliamentary elections to pass constitutional reforms that would enable him to serve a second term. This proved too much for Muslim prime minister RASHID KARAMAI and civil war broke out

in 1958. Eisenhower obligingly dispatched the marines to Lebanon and order was restored, but only after Chamoun agreed to step down as planned.

Out of office, Chamoun determined to remain active in politics. In 1959 he founded his own National Liberation Party (NLP), with its own armed militia, the Tigers. He then maneuvered with other Christian blocs to arrange the election of Sulayman Franjiyya as president in 1970. When the Lebanese civil war commenced in 1975, Chamoun served as minister of the interior under President AMIN GEMAYEL. He attempted to revive his role as a power broker until he was defeated by a combination of Druse and Syrian-backed Muslim militias. When fighting temporarily stopped a decade later, he lent his support to a Government of National Unity as minister of finance and housing. He also served as a vocal proponent of Christian efforts to preserve Lebanon's religious and cultural pluralism in the face of Islamic fundamentalism. By now Chamoun, once widely respected, was powerless to influence the course of events. He died suddenly on August 7, 1987, a respected former president who guided Lebanon down the treacherous roads of independence and self-rule.

Further Reading

Attie, Caroline C. *Lebanon in the 1950s.* London: I. B. Tauris, 2002.

Khaalafi, Samir. *Civil and Uncivil Violence in Lebanon: A History of the Internationalization of Communal Contact.* New York: Columbia University Press, 2002.

Picard, Elizabeth. *Lebanon, a Shattered Country: Myths and Realities of the Wars in Lebanon.* New York: Holmes and Meier, 2002.

Zamir, Meir. *Lebanon's Quest: The Road to Statehood, 1926–1939.* New York: I. B. Tauris, 2000.

Zisser, Eyal. "The Downfall of the Khuri Administration: A Dubious Revolution." *Middle Eastern Studies* 30 (July 1994): 486–511.

Chernenko, Konstantin (1911–1985) *general secretary of the Communist Party of the Soviet Union*

Konstantin Ustinovich Chernenko was born in Bolshaya Tes, Siberia, imperial Russia, on September 24, 1911. Part of a large peasant family, he quit school at 12 to work as a farm laborer and did not resume his education for nearly two decades. The communists had seized power in 1917, and in 1929 Chernenko joined the Komsomol (Young Communist League), displaying a talent for organization. Following three years of army service, he formally joined the Communist Party in 1933 with a specialty in propaganda activities. He missed out on service in World War II and in 1943 was allowed to attend the Higher School for Party Organizers. After a series of routine assignments, he was appointed political officer to the Moldavian Republic in 1948. Two years later he befriended LEONID BREZHNEV, head of the Moldavian party, accompanying Brezhnev back to Moscow in 1956 to work in the party's central propaganda department. He labored there four years until Brezhnev became chairman of the Presidium in 1960, and Chernenko was appointed his chief of staff. Chernenko proved himself to be an ideal associate for the ambitious Brezhnev for he was modest, publicity-shy, and highly effective in his appointed role. His star continued to rise along with that of his mentor.

In 1964 Brezhnev helped topple Premier NIKITA KHRUSHCHEV and became de facto leader of the Soviet Union. Chernenko advanced alongside him, and by 1971 had risen to full member of the Central Committee. By 1978 the quiet, efficient Chernenko was promoted to a full voting member of the Politburo, the highest decision-making body in the country. This also made him a contender to succeed Brezhnev as general secretary. He gained additional stature in January 1982 with an appointment as chief ideologist and subsequently assumed control of the party's daily affairs. Brezhnev was visibly ailing by then and Chernenko was widely expected to succeed him. However, when the general secretary died on November 10, 1982, the Politburo surprisingly selected former KGB chief YURI ANDROPOV to lead the country. Chernenko, unassuming and unambitious as always, ignored the snub and continued working in the background. Andropov's rise is viewed as a victory for younger party members, who were tired of the innate corruption and cronyism of the Brezhnev era. Many also wished to quicken the pace of badly needed reform.

Andropov initiated a widespread anticorruption campaign aimed mostly at friends of the former general secretary. But his death 15 months later led to a temporary resurgence among the conservative elements in the Kremlin, and Chernenko was tapped to succeed him. Aged 72 years, he became the oldest man to ever govern the equally tottering Soviet Union. Moreover, Chernenko

was by training and disposition a doctrinaire communist and opposed to reform. His résumé was noticeably deficient in other important positions: he never ran a state enterprise, never headed a government agency, and never served as party secretary in any region of the country. His only claims to high office were as a career politician and a close associate of the now disgraced Brezhnev. As general secretary, Chernenko slowed Andropov's anticorruption efforts and disregarded all further attempts at economic revitalization.

In foreign affairs, Soviet relations with the United States had reached their nadir in consequence of new Russian missiles deployed in Europe, the invasion of Afghanistan, and the shooting down of a Korean airliner over Soviet airspace in 1983. When American president RONALD REAGAN countered by supplying covert aid to Afghan rebels and deploying Pershing II and cruise missiles to Western Europe, Chernenko—or those immediately around him—resurrected a hard propaganda line against the Americans with a shrillness not seen since the days of JOSEPH STALIN. But after boycotting the 1984 Olympic games in Los Angeles, Chernenko permitted long-suspended arms control agreements to resume in January 1985. After that his public appearances grew increasingly scarce, and it was generally assumed his health was failing.

By the time Chernenko died in Moscow on March 10, 1985, a corner had been turned in the history of the Communist Party. He represented the last of the Old Guard members who had dominated the country since World War II. His tenure as head of the Soviet Union—13 months—was the nation's briefest and passed almost unnoticed. Significantly, only four hours after Chernenko's demise, the Politburo elected the young and vigorous MIKHAIL GORBACHEV to advance the cause of badly needed reform.

Further Reading

Chernenko, K. V. *Speeches and Writings*. Oxford, England: Pergamon, 1985.

Parker, John W. *Kremlin in Transition*, Vol. 1, *From Brezhnev to Chernenko, 1978 to 1985*. Winchester, Mass.: Allen and Unwin, 1991.

Solov'ev, Vladimir. *Behind the High Kremlin Walls*. New York: Berkeley Books, 1987.

Xenakis, Christopher I. *What Happened to the Soviet Union? How and Why American Sovietologists Were Caught by Surprise*. Westport, Conn.: Praeger, 2002.

Zemtsov, Ilya. *Chernenko: The Last Bolshevik*. New Brunswick, N.J.: Transaction Publishers, 1989.

Chiang Ching-kuo (Jiang Jingguo) (1910–1988)
president of the Republic of China

Chiang Ching-kuo was born in Fengsha, Chekiang Province, China, on March 18, 1910, the son of General CHIANG KAI-SHEK. After a strict Buddhist upbringing by his grandmother he was sent to attend Western-style schools in Shanghai. During most of his youth Chiang rarely saw his father and the two remained quite detached. Chiang lived in relative seclusion from worldly events until 1925 when he was allowed to visit the Soviet Union and attend the Sun Yat-sen University in Moscow. While matriculating he studied Marxism and military science and received tentative membership in the Communist Party. However, after Chiang expressed sympathy for the pariah Leon Trotsky, JOSEPH STALIN canceled his membership and sent him to toil in Siberian mines. It was not until 1937, after a rapprochement between Stalin and General Chiang, that he was allowed to return home. His 12 years in the Soviet Union indelibly seared him, and after that he was incontrovertibly anticommunist. General Chiang initially viewed his son with some ambivalence for having denounced him as "an enemy of the people" while in Russia. Later he was convinced that such sentiments were coerced and granted his son a free rein within the Kuomintang (KMT or Nationalist) hierarchy. When China was gripped by a Japanese invasion, Chiang immediately assumed important political roles in the KMT army.

By 1938 Chiang was the political head of Kiangshi Province, where he forcefully instituted badly needed administrative and social reforms. Three years later he assumed responsibilities as head of the KMT youth league organization, tasked with recruiting and training future cadres for the party. Allied victory in 1945 granted China little respite, for General Chiang began girding for his final showdown with MAO ZEDONG's Chinese Communist Party (CCP). Chiang had helped earlier to negotiate the removal of Soviet forces from Manchuria. Civil war erupted in 1948 and it went badly for the Nationalists. Chiang was dispatched by his father to try stabilizing the economic situation in Shanghai, but the crisis proved beyond remedy and he failed. Within a year he accompanied his father and surviving KMT forces to the island of Taiwan and prepared to make a last stand. When the impending communist assault failed to materialize, Chiang helped his father consolidate political control over the island. He headed the secret police and employed methods similar to Stalinist Russia's for breaking up communist cells and punishing offenders. He proved himself a ruthless exponent of law and order, and his father rewarded him with a succession of high posts within the party.

By 1964 Chiang had risen to minister of defense and in 1975 he became premier. In this capacity Chiang again demonstrated simple-minded determination to enact social and economic reforms that he felt were essential to Taiwan's survival. He was the first KMT official to appoint native Taiwanese to high posts within the government. He also supervised spending on the island's infrastructure, including freeways, harbors, nuclear power plants, and modern shipyards. Chiang laid the groundwork for what was known as the Taiwanese "economic miracle." The island at that time was displaying growth rates of 9 percent annually, among the world's highest. When his father died in 1975 Chiang inherited the mantle of KMT leadership as party chairman. In 1978 he won election as president of the Republic of China, was reelected four years later, and continued on his path of progressive reforms. Chiang differed noticeably from his father in being less straitjacketed in political affairs, for he readily established a dialogue with communist officials in Beijing. He then granted Nationalist citizens the right to visit relatives on the mainland. Chiang was also more democratically inclined than his father. Martial law, which had been imposed since 1949, was lifted in 1987, and he encouraged the growth of multiparty political pluralism.

One of the biggest problems facing Taiwan was growing international isolation once Communist China gained admittance into the United Nations. He combated this economically by converting his little island into one of the four "Asian Tigers," whose outstanding performance in high technology and commerce could not be ignored. In 1986 Taiwan boasted a record surplus of $12 billion, second only to Japan. By the time Chiang died in Taipei on January 13, 1988, he had established a reputation as an earnest reformer and modernizer, strong-willed but benevolent. He selected as his successor the American-educated Lee Teng-hui, who continued his successful policies of democratization.

Quiet, austere, and modest by nature, Chiang is regarded as one of the most influential reformers of modern Chinese history.

Further Reading

Chow, Peter C. Y. *Taiwan's Modernization in Global Perspective.* Westport, Conn.: Praeger, 2002.

Harrison, Selig S. "Taiwan after Chiang Ching-kuo." *Foreign Affairs* 66, no. 4 (1988): 790–808.

Hsiung, James C. "Diplomacy against Adversity: Foreign Relations under Chiang Ching-kuo." *Asian Affairs* 27 (summer 2000): 111–123.

Leng, Shao-chen, ed. *Chiang Ching-kuo's Leadership in the Development of the Republic of China on Taiwan.* Lanham, Md.: University Press of America, 1993.

Roy, Denny. *Taiwan: A Political History.* Ithaca, N.Y.: Cornell University Press, 2003.

Taylor, Jay. *The Generalissimo's Son: Chiang Ching-Kuo and the Revolutions in China and Taiwan.* Cambridge, Mass.: Harvard University Press, 2000.

Chiang Kai-shek (Jiang Jieshi) (1887–1975)
president of the Republic of China

Chiang Kai-shek was born in Chekiang Province, China, on October 30, 1887, the son of a wealthy salt merchant. After receiving a classical Chinese education he attended military academies in China and Japan until SUN YAT-SEN's revolution of October 1911. Chiang then deserted the Japanese army and came home to fight under the new Kuomintang (KMT or Nationalist) banner. The Manchu (Qing) dynasty was quickly overthrown and the new Republic of China declared. However, in 1913 Chiang briefly took up arms against the northern warlord YUAN SHIKAI until the latter was appointed president of China. Thereafter Chiang migrated south to Shanghai and struck up cordial relations with the so-called Green Gang, an influential underworld society. In February 1923 he relocated to Canton to become Sun's chief of staff and also assumed duties as head of the newly created Wampoa Military Academy. This institution, created largely with help from the Soviet Union, was intended to provide a steady stream of military cadres for the KMT movement in its quest to unify China by force. The generally conservative KMT had also organized a united front against various warlords by allowing MAO ZEDONG's Communist Party to join its ranks. This proved an unholy alliance, however, and after Sun died in 1925 Chiang moved to purge the KMT of any communist-leaning opponents to his succession.

As de facto head of the KMT Chiang organized the Northern Expedition in July 1926 to bring the warlords into his fold. He was supported in the field by many communist forces. Within a year Chiang succeeded brilliantly and the contending private armies had either been defeated or sworn into allegiance with him. Then, on April 12, 1927, Chiang suddenly turned upon his communist allies and drove them from Shanghai. Chiang, meanwhile, further cemented his ties to the Chinese elite by marrying Soong Mei-ling, the Western-educated daughter of a leading Christian merchant. As part of the marriage agreement, Chiang became a devout, lifelong Methodist. Between 1927 and 1937 he made ceaseless efforts to consolidate his regime, enroll warlords into KMT ranks, and hound the communists out of existence. He may very well have triumphed, but fate intervened in

Chiang Kai-shek *(Library of Congress)*

September 1931 when Japanese forces seized Manchuria and established a puppet regime. Public opinion demanded war against Japan but Chiang, obsessed by defeating the communists first, refused. Instead he promulgated his "New Life Movement," a unique blend of Confucianism, fascism, and capitalism to cement the commercial elites to the KMT. The fact that it did little to address the sufferings of China's preponderantly peasant population was in stark contrast to the agrarian-based activities of the communists. Ultimately it proved a major cause of Chiang's defeat. The government was also unsuccessful at curbing rampant corruption, which further eroded support for Chiang's regime and placed additional hardships on the people.

An uneasy peace prevailed between the KMT government and Japan until December 1936 when the warlord Chang Hsueh-liang kidnapped Chiang and forced him back into a united front arrangement with the communists. Furthermore, when Japanese aggression developed into full-scale war in 1937, Chiang had no recourse but to fight. The badly outgunned Chinese fought bravely but gradually withdrew into the interior. This retreat was partly orchestrated by Chiang who remained determined to husband his strength for a final showdown with the communists. Mao, meanwhile, sensed an opportunity and readily fought the invaders to acquire a following among the peasantry. Chiang's war effort was further abetted by the United States and Great Britain after December 1941, but while welcoming aid, he refused to become closely engaged in fighting and settled upon a passive defense. The communists, meanwhile, continued gaining experience in guerrilla warfare and, with it, tremendous popular support. After 1945 President HARRY S. TRUMAN attempted to arrange a truce between Chiang and Mao, but ideological differences proved insurmountable. Civil war soon erupted, and the KMT, well-equipped but overconfident, were gradually and inexorably defeated by the communists. Chiang, eager for more American aid, agreed to further "democratize" his regime by adopting a new constitution on January 1, 1947, under which he served as president. However, such cosmetic changes did little to alter the military balance, and on December 10, 1949, Chiang and his surviving KMT forces sought refuge on the offshore island of Taiwan. Days later Mao victoriously announced creation of the new People's Republic of China.

From his island enclave Chiang set about consolidating control and bolstering his defenses for a final showdown. He declared martial law in 1949 but also instituted wide-ranging social and economic reforms that had eluded him on the mainland. He also declared himself the legitimate ruler of China and promised to re-invade one day and defeat the communists. His efforts were stoutly underwritten by the United States, which provided him with a defensive military alliance and millions of dollars in assistance. Taiwan remained a conservative dictatorship for the rest of Chiang's life, but it posted impressive economic gains, second only to Japan's. However, after President RICHARD M. NIXON visited Communist China in 1972, Taiwan lost its seat at the United Nations. But Chiang's strategy of improving the national economy now provided dividends for Taiwan's extensive trade arrangements with the rest of the world, and few countries were willing to sever diplomatic relations. In sum, Chiang could implement the changes and enjoy the success that eluded him in China. In May 1972 the aging ruler appointed his son CHIANG CHING-KUO to succeed him as president. He died in Taipei on April 5, 1975, a major force in the unification of China and its rise as a modern nation.

Further Reading
Bush, Richard C. *At Cross Purposes: U.S.-Taiwan Relations Since 1942.* Armonk, N.Y.: M.E. Sharpe, 2004.
Chiang Kai-shek. *China's Destiny.* New York: Macmillan, 1947.
Huang, Ray. *Chiang Kai-shek and His Diary as a Historical Source.* Armonk, N.Y.: M. E. Sharpe, 1996.
Lattimore, Owen. *China Memoirs: Chiang Kai-shek and the War against Japan.* Tokyo: University of Tokyo Press, 1990.
Loh Pichon Pei Yung. *The Early Chiang Kai-shek: A Study of His Personality and Politics, 1887–1924.* New York: Columbia University Press, 1988.
Phillips, Steven E. *Between Assimilation and Independence: The Taiwanese Encounter Nationalist China, 1945–1950.* Stanford, Calif.: Stanford University Press, 2003.
Wang, Shih-chen. "The Wampoa Military Academy and the Rise of Chiang Kai-shek." Unpublished master's thesis, University of Texas–Austin, 1991.

Chifley, Joseph (1885–1951) *prime minister of Australia*

Joseph Benedict ("Ben") Chifley was born in Bathurst, New South Wales (now Australia), on September 22, 1885, the son of a blacksmith. A devout Catholic, he was only irregularly educated before joining the railways at the age of 15. By 1917 Chifley was the youngest railroad engineer in the country before he was dismissed for supporting a transport strike. Once reinstated, he began organizing among his fellow workers and by 1920 had established the Australian Federated Union of Locomotive Enginemen. Success here whetted his appetite for politics, and Chifley made several unsuccessful runs for Parliament. His efforts were crowned by success in 1928, and two years later he became minister of defense in the Labor administration of JAMES HENRY SCULLIN. However, the Labor Party was wracked by dissent, and a rival movement sprang up in New South Wales headed by J. T. Lang. This split the vote nationally with the larger Federal Party and in December 1931, Labor was swept from power. Chifley was among many who lost their seats and he spent nearly a decade sharpening his skills in party politics. By 1936 he reentered the national scene as part of the Royal Commission on Banking and Monetary Reform, displaying a great command of fiscal matters and also advocating the nationalization of banks. In 1940 Chifley returned to Parliament. Following the onset of World War II, Prime Minister JOHN CURTIN appointed him director of labor regulation and supply with the Department of Munitions. The following year he advanced to treasurer and joined Curtin's war cabinet. Entrusted with fiscal matters on a national scale, Chifley displayed considerable acumen fulfilling his charge and greatly assisted the fiscal base of the war effort. His greatest accomplishment was the imposition of uniform taxation, giving the federal government responsibility for income taxes formerly collected by the states, and greatly increasing revenue resources for spending on social programs. Such was Curtin's trust in his abilities that in 1942 Chifley assumed an additional portfolio as minister of postwar reconstruction. Following Curtin's death in July 1945, Chifley, by an overwhelming vote, was made head of the Labor Party and the new prime minister. The following year the public confirmed his hold on public office in the general election.

Chifley assumed power with an extensive reform agenda and strove to reach what he called the "light on the hill." As a devout leftist organizer he was committed to full employment and to expanding the benefits of the welfare state. Among his many accomplishments were bills pertaining to national health care, labor arbitration, industrial development, and the founding of the Australian National University in Canberra. And, as an exponent of state-controlled economics, he ordered the nationalization of several airlines. In foreign affairs, Chifley differed from same of his predecessors in being proimmigration and pro-Asian in outlook. In 1948 he lent vocal support to the Dutch East Indies effort to throw off its colonial yoke, from which a new nation, Indonesia, arose. But despite his close association with Labor, Chifley proved intolerant toward unrest, and he unflinchingly deployed troops to counter striking coal miners. This proved a controversial action that split the Labor Party along ideological lines.

Chifley had advanced a socialist agenda further than any prime minister before him, but he tripped up over the issue of nationalized finance. In 1947 minor changes that he sought to control the state banking industry were deemed unconstitutional by the High Court, so he enacted legislation to nationalize the entire industry. This move prompted intense opposition from the business sector, and in 1949 the High Court again dismissed the legislation as illegal. Chifley was then criticized for seemingly cordial relations with the Australian Communist Party, which contributed to the perception that he was too far to the left. By 1949 voter discontent turned Labor out of office in favor of Liberal ROBERT GORDON MENZIES. Chifley continued on as head of the opposition in Parliament until his sudden death in Canberra on June 13, 1951. He still is a popular icon to the Labor Party and one of the most successful progressive leaders in Australian history.

Further Reading

Bennett, Scott C. *J. B. Chifley.* New York: Oxford University Press, 1973.

Day, David. *Chifley.* Pymble, New South Wales: HarperCollins, 2001.

Deery, Phillip. "Chifley, the Army, and the 1949 Coal Strike." *Labor History* 68 (1995): 80–97.

Johnson, Carol. "Social Harmony and Australian Labor: The Role of Private Industry in the Curtin and Chifley Government's Plans for Australian Economic Development." *Australian Journal of Politics and History* 32 (1986): 39–51.

Scalmer, Sean. "Labor's Golden Age and the Changing Forms of Worker's Representation in Australia." *Journal of the Royal Australian Historical Society* 84, no. 2 (1998): 180–198.

Sheridan, Tom. *Division of Labour: Industrial Relations in the Chifley Years, 1945–1949.* New York: Oxford University Press, 1989.

Chun Doo Hwan (1931–) *president of South Korea*

Chun Doo Hwan was born in Hapcheon, South Kyongsang Province, Korea, on January 18, 1931, the son of a soldier. Korea was then administered as part of the Japanese Empire, and Chun's family moved to Manchuria where he was partially educated. He returned to Korea in 1943 and attended Christian missionary schools in Taegu. After 1945 Korea had been divided into an American-sponsored democratic south and a Soviet-dominated communist north. In 1951 Chun was chosen to attend the newly formed Korean Military Academy, from which he graduated in 1955 with the first class. This proved an important event in Korean history, for many officers of the graduating class subsequently wielded inordinate influence on politics. Chun continued on as a distinguished military officer, being among the very first Koreans to receive special-forces training in the United States. Following the rise to power of General PARK CHUNG HEE in 1961, Chun formed a close relationship with him in the Supreme Council of National Reconstruction. In 1968 Chun proved instrumental in repelling a determined attack by Korean commandos on the presidential palace. He was promoted to lieutenant general of the 1st Army Infantry Division in 1973 and again made headlines by discovering underground tunnels dug by North Korea for infiltration. When President Park was assassinated on October 26, 1979, Chun led the investigation team that arrested General Chung Seong Hwa as a conspirator. A civilian, Choi Kyu Ha, then succeeded Park as president but Chun remained on as head of both the military and the Korean Central Intelligence Agency (KCIA).

In many respects Chun formed a shadow government behind the civilian regime. When a poor economy in 1980 resulted in massive civil unrest Chun imposed martial law and arrested several leading dissidents, including Kim Dae Jung, later elected president. This act precipitated mass student demonstrations in Kwangju Province, which were brutally suppressed by the military. President Choi announced his resignation on August 16, 1980, and Chun was declared interim president until confirmed by the newly installed electoral college 10 days later. Seeking to ingratiate himself with the public, he ordered martial law lifted and promulgated a new constitution forbidding all future presidents from serving beyond a seven-year term. Chun was then formally elected president on February 25, 1980, becoming the first executive of the Fifth Republic of Korea.

In power, Chun continued many policies of his predecessors. He clamped down on media and instituted severe press restrictions. However, he placed emphasis on jump-starting the stalled national economy through tax cuts and work programs, and by 1981 the nation rebounded with a 6.1 percent rate of growth. Prosperity ushered in a new sense of domestic tranquility and Chun felt free to pursue national interests abroad. That summer he spoke with President RONALD REAGAN in Washington, D.C., and became the first Korean executive to visit Kenya, Nigeria, Gabon, and Senegal. In 1983 Chun became the first Korean head of state to ever visit Japan, long regarded as an arch enemy. Closer to home he also traveled to all five countries of the Association of Southeast Asian Nations (ASEAN). Tragedy struck in October 1983 when a North Korean bomb, intended for Chun, killed several cabinet ministers. He nonetheless remained fixed in his determination to pursue better relations with the unpredictable dictator, Kim Il Sung, and offered to meet with him several times. His gestures for improved dialogue were greeted by silence, and the Korean peninsula remained an armed camp.

The high point in Chun's tenure was the 1988 Olympic Games, which gave South Korea an opportunity to showcase its impressive economic accomplishments. The country received a positive boost to its international profile, except for complaints about the authoritarian nature of Chun's regime. Indeed, when his handpicked successor, Roh Tae Woo, addressed the nation for the first time in June 1987, he declared his intention to resign immediately if Chun did not agree to widespread democratic reforms. Chun relented and left office in February 1988, which constituted the first peaceful transfer of political power in Korean history. Unfortunately, he remained haunted by the memory of the Kwangju massacre and allegations of widespread corruption by family members. Public pressure against him mounted, and in 1995 Kim Dae Jung, Korea's freely-elected president, had Chun arrested. He was tried on various charges, found guilty, and received a life sentence, but in 1997 Chun was paroled and released.

Further Reading

Clark, Donald N., ed. *The Kwangju Uprising: Shadows over the Regime in South Korea.* Boulder, Colo.: Westview Press, 1988.

Harrison, Selig S. "Dateline South Korea: A Divided Seoul." *Foreign Policy* 67 (1987): 154–175.

Kong, Tat Yan. *The State of Development in South Korea: A Fragile Miracle.* New York: Routledge, 2000.

Lewis, Linda S. *Laying Claim to the Memory of May: A Look Back at the Kwangju Uprising.* Honolulu: University of Hawaii Press, 2002.

Rhee, Steve Y. "The Role of the Military in South Korean Politics." *Journal of Third World Studies* 5, no. 1 (1988): 6–18.

Saxer, Carl J. *From Transition to Power Alternation: Democracy in South Korea, 1987–1997.* New York: Routledge, 2002.

Churchill, Sir Winston (1874–1965) *prime minister of Great Britain*

Winston Leonard Spencer Churchill was born in Blenheim Palace, Woodstock, England, on November 30, 1874, the son of a prominent British politician and an American mother. Indifferent as a student, he passed through Harrow before attending the Military Academy at Sandhurst. Churchill was commissioned in the cavalry and saw active service in Cuba, India, and South Africa, where he was taken prisoner by the Boers and staged a daring escape. He also supplemented his income by working as a war correspondent for various newspapers. In 1900 he gained election to Parliament as a member of the Conservative Party but he disagreed with Prime Minister ARTHUR BALFOUR's adoption of protectionist policies and switched to the free trade Liberals. He became undersecretary of state under HENRY CAMPBELL-BANNERMAN and subsequently served as president of the Board of Trade under reformist prime minister HERBERT HENRY ASQUITH. Despite his aristocratic background, Churchill took acute interest in the lives and well-being of working people, so he pioneered the introduction of labor exchanges and

other welfare benefits. However, he was intolerant of union militancy, and in 1910 he dispatched troops to crush a riot by striking miners in Wales. The following year Churchill gained appointment as first lord of the Admiralty and took energetic measures to improve and modernize the Royal Navy in anticipation of hostilities with Germany. Such foresight proved invaluable; throughout World War I Great Britain faced down a serious German naval threat and ruled the waves. However, his advocacy of an amphibious campaign in the Dardanelles in 1915 proved disastrous, and he was forced from office. After briefly serving as a colonel on the western front in 1916, Churchill returned to politics under Prime Minister DAVID LLOYD GEORGE, who offered him a portfolio as minister of munitions. By war's end, Churchill had functioned successively as secretary of war and secretary of the colonies,

Winston Churchill *(Library of Congress)*

negotiating establishment of the Irish Free State but also supporting Allied intervention against VLADIMIR LENIN's Bolshevik Russia.

For a man of Churchill's ambition, the interwar period was one of political setbacks and disappointments. He quit the Liberals in 1923 and was reelected as a Conservative the following year, but was never really trusted by that party again. He nonetheless served as chancellor of the Exchequer under Prime Minister STANLEY BALDWIN and orchestrated Britain's return to the gold standard. This only exacerbated the nation's economic troubles, and in 1926 Churchill further alienated himself from voters by deploying troops to defeat a nationwide general strike. His controversial nature and tempestuous disposition finally resulted in a 10-year exile to Parliament from the ministry. Here he preferred remaining in the House of Commons, which wielded real power, to serving in the aristocratic and largely symbolic House of Lords. Throughout the 1930s, Churchill further eroded his popularity by bitterly opposing home rule for India and for constant attacks upon Baldwin, a fellow Conservative. However, he became aware of the dangers posed by ADOLF HITLER long before it was expedient to do so. Moreover, Churchill railed against the appeasement policy adopted by Prime Minister NEVILLE CHAMBERLAIN and called for comprehensive national rearmament. Churchill, after two decades in the political wilderness, finally established his niche as a formidable spokesman for freedom and democracy. His vitriolic wit and classical elegance made him a symbol of British resistance to tyranny.

When World War II broke out in September 1939, Churchill joined Chamberlain's government as head of the Admiralty. Like many contemporaries he made his share of military blunders but his sheer doggedness inspired those around him. Following France's collapse in May 1940, Churchill took Chamberlain's place as prime minister. His ascent at this crucial time proved fortuitous for Great Britain and the free world. Hitler seemed unstoppable on land and was massing his forces for the inevitable assault upon England. But Churchill proved as indomitable as he was defiant. He rallied the British people throughout this bleak period in their history, ruthlessly appointed, fired, and reappointed military leaders based on their performance, and oversaw the miraculous evacuation of Dunkirk and the aerial Battle of Britain in 1940. These defeats negated Hitler's plans for invading Britain, and thereafter Churchill

brooked no delays in signing the important Lend-Lease Agreement with President FRANKLIN D. ROOSEVELT for navy destroyers and other armaments. He also weathered stormy relations with General CHARLES DE GAULLE, commander of the Free French forces. When the United States finally entered the war in December 1941, Churchill, Roosevelt, and the Soviet Union's JOSEPH STALIN formed the "Big Three" in the fight against fascism. Churchill personally loathed communism and distrusted Stalin, but he realized that the war could not be won without Russia. Churchill committed serious strategic blunders in the Mediterranean and sustained serious losses at the hands of imperial Japan, but otherwise the war went increasingly well for the Allies. Hitler was defeated in May 1945, and Churchill incessantly tried to convince Roosevelt of the dangers Stalin posed to the postwar world. However, in August 1945 the Conservatives were unceremoniously defeated by the Labour Party under CLEMENT ATTLEE. Churchill, one of the leading architects of victory, played virtually no role in settling the war he worked so hard to win.

For six years Churchill remained as head of the opposition in Parliament, but he was primarily concerned with publishing his memoirs and other historical treatises. In fact, he was regarded as an outstanding historian with a superb flair for writing; in 1953 he received the Nobel Prize for literature. Churchill continued warning about the danger of communism to world peace, and in 1946 he toured the United States declaring that an "Iron Curtain" had descended across Europe. The outbreak of the Korean War in 1950 confirmed this risk for British voters, and the following year they returned Churchill to power. Plagued by poor health, his second tenure in office was far less dramatic than his first, although the nation made marked strides in terms of economic recovery. Britain also began to acquire its own nuclear arsenal. But Churchill's plans for a united Europe and an end to the cold-war tensions met with disillusionment. He barely survived a third stroke at the age of 81 and was finally replaced by ANTHONY EDEN in April 1955. For his remaining life, Churchill concentrated on his writings and basking in the glow of international celebrity. He died in London on January 24, 1965, and was accorded a massive state funeral, attended by many heads of state from around the world. Churchill's career in public life had not been uniformly successful, and he endured defeats and setbacks that would have effectively ended the careers of lesser men. But he put his indelible imprint on human events by standing up to fascism in the 1940s and communism in the 1950s. In looks, temperament, and stubbornness Churchill was the personification of Britain's indomitable bulldog.

Further Reading

Cohen, Eliot A. *Supreme Command: Soldiers, Statesmen, and Leadership in Wartime.* London: Simon and Schuster, 2002.

Jenkins, Roy. *Churchill: A Biography.* New York: Farrar, Straus, and Giroux, 2001.

Keegan, John. *Churchill: A Life.* London: Weidenfeld and Nicolson, 2002.

Kimball, Warren F. *Forged in War: Roosevelt, Churchill, and the Second World War.* Chicago: I. R. Dee, 2003.

Larres, Klaus. *Churchill's Cold War: The Politics of Personal Diplomacy.* New Haven, Conn.: Yale University Press, 2002.

Lukacs, John. *Churchill: Visionary, Statesman, Historian.* New Haven, Conn.: Yale University Press, 2002.

Sandys, Celia. *Never Surrender: The Wisdom and Leadership of Winston Churchill.* New York: Portfolio, 2003.

Wood, Ian S. *Churchill.* Basingstoke, England: Macmillan, 2000.

Clark, Joe (1939–   ) *prime minister of Canada*

Charles Joseph (Joe) Clark was born in High River, Alberta, on June 5, 1939, the son of a newspaper editor. While attending the University of Alberta to study political science he became politically active within the youth wing of the Progressive Conservative Party (PC). Clark proved himself adept in a variety of party functions and successively worked as an organizer, strategist, and campaign manager. He successfully ran for a seat in Parliament in 1972 and held it for the next 21 years. At this time Canada was dominated by the Liberal Party of charismatic prime minister PIERRE TRUDEAU, and in July 1974 he scored his biggest election upset over the PC. Clark was lucky to hold onto his seat, but he displayed great talent for opposition parliamentary tactics. His rising popularity convinced others that he should become head of the party, and in February 1976 delegates selected Clark as their new leader. He thereafter campaigned on a theme of national decentralization to allow more local control. "We will not take this nation by storm, by stealth, or by surprise," he declared, "We will win it by work." National elections were then held in May 1979, and the PC, in concert with the New Democratic Party (NDP), eked out a narrow victory over Trudeau's Liberals. Clark thus became the 16th prime minister of Canada and, at 39, its youngest. He was also the first premier to originate from the western reaches of the country.

As the head of a minority coalition government, Clark enjoyed only a tenuous hold on power. However, he tried ruling Canada as if the PC were in the majority, which proved a strategic mistake. As a Conservative he was determined to scale back the size of government, rein in spending, and impose an austerity budget to bring deficits under control. His agenda included tax hikes on gasoline and liberalization of the economy, including the privatization of Petro-Canada, the national petroleum concern. However, the stridency of his plans proved too much for his allies, and in February 1980 the New Democrats forced a vote of "no confidence." The Liberals under Trudeau then resumed power, winning 148 seats to a PC tally of 101. Clark's tenure in office lasted only 272 days, the shortest in Canadian history. Humiliated by defeat and lampooned by the media for ineptitude, he continued on as leader of the opposition in Parliament.

Back on the floor, Clark again demonstrated his mastery of parliamentary tactics by delaying Trudeau's ambitious plan for constitutional reforms. He managed to stop all progress until a complete judicial review had been achieved and new federal-provincial compromises adopted. In light of his success, Clark tried to maintain his position as party head in June 1983 but was defeated on the fourth ballot by a dynamic newcomer, Brian Mulroney. Clark closed ranks with fellow Conservatives, and in September 1984 they routed the Liberals, capturing 211 of the 284 seats. Mulroney rewarded Clark for his loyalty by appointing him secretary of state for external affairs. For the next seven years, Clark made his presence felt at many international gatherings, pressing for an end to apartheid in South Africa and for the release of political prisoners in the Soviet Union. His presence was especially useful at the United Nations during the 1990 crisis over Kuwait, and Clark helped orchestrate the multilateral alliance, led by the United States, that drove Iraqi forces out. In June 1990 Clark was appointed constitutional affairs minister and tasked with drawing up a new document that would bring a rebellious Quebec back into the national fold. After arduous work and intense negotiations, the new Charlottetown Accord was approved by all the provincial premiers and put before the public as a referendum. In October 1992 the reforms were rejected, and Clark, exhausted and disappointed, withdrew from politics the following year.

In 1993 Clark accepted a teaching position at the University of California–Berkeley, and also worked as a political consultant. His political exile lasted until 1998 when, by a popular vote, he returned to Canadian government as head of the Progressive Conservatives and set about reviving the fortunes of his party. He followed up this success by winning a seat in Parliament in September 2000, thereby cementing his political comeback. It remains to be seen if Clark will run again for the prime ministership of his nation. For the time being he continues as one of Canada's most trusted elder statesmen and a highly respected international ambassador.

Further Reading

Clark, Joe. *A Nation Too Good to Lose: Renewing the Purpose of Canada.* Toronto: Key Books, 1994.

Dorey, James, and Peter Ward. *The Clark Team.* Don Mills, Ont.: Corpus, 1979.

Humphreys, David L. *Joe Clark: A Portrait.* Don Mills, Ont.: Totem Books, 1979.

MacIntosh, Donald, and Michael Hawes. *Sport and Canadian Diplomacy.* Montreal: McGill-Queen's University Press, 1994.

Nolan, Michael, and Ted Grant. *Joe Clark, the Emerging Leader.* Toronto: Fitzhenry and Whiteside, 1978.

Troyer, Warner. *200 Days: Joe Clark in Power; The Anatomy of the Rise and Fall of the 21st Government.* Toronto: Personal Library Publisher, 1980.

Clemenceau, Georges (1841–1929) *prime minister of France*

Georges Clemenceau was born in Mouilleron-en-Pareds, France, on September 28, 1841, the son of a country doctor. From his father he inherited a staunch atheism, anticlerical sentiments, and profound respect for democratic republicanism. He obtained his medical degree in Paris in 1865 but traveled to the United States to work as a journalist. Clemenceau returned home in 1869 and witnessed the disastrous Franco-Prussian War of the following year. In 1871 he gained election to the National Assembly and voted against the peace treaty

that ceded Alsace-Lorraine to Germany. Clemenceau subsequently served as mayor of Montmartre when the Paris Commune was bloodily suppressed by French troops. By 1876 he was serving in the Chamber of Deputies as a spokesman for the Radical Socialists and quickly established himself as an effective debater with a genius for caustic invective. He was particularly harsh toward numerous cabinet ministers, forced their resignations, and became widely feared as the "Tiger." For nearly two decades, Clemenceau flourished as a political gadfly and a no-nonsense destroyer of ministers until 1893, when he was implicated in the notorious Panama Canal scandal. He lost his seat, but over the next six years built up a national following as a journalist. He was outspoken in his defense of Captain Alfred Dreyfus, the Jewish officer wrongly accused of treason, and his agitation led to Dreyfus's retrial and acquittal. In 1902 Clemenceau returned to the public arena as a senator from Vars.

Back in power, Clemenceau was as relentless as ever in attacking government waste and incompetence. To silence him, the government named him minister of the interior in 1906 under Prime Minister Ferdinand Sarrien. Clemenceau, although a former radical, and sympathetic toward workers, quickly demonstrated his intolerance of illegal strikes or violence. He called in troops to put down numerous disturbances, which earned him the undying enmity of former allies on the left. His popularity was such that he was called upon to serve as prime minister. Clemenceau did so with relish, cracking down on illegal strikes with force while simultaneously warning the nation about rising German militarism. To that end, he actively pursued closer ties to Great Britain and refused to apologize to Germany over an armed confrontation in Morocco. Despite his forcefulness, Clemenceau was removed from office in July 1909 because of the poor condition of the French navy.

In the years preceding World War I, Clemenceau revived his journalism by publishing a daily paper called *L'Homme Libre* (The Free Man), in which he lambasted President RAYMOND POINCARÉ for military unpreparedness. After hostilities commenced in August 1914, Clemenceau acidly attacked key government members for incompetence and his paper was forcibly closed down. Over the next three years the war effort tottered badly and a spirit of defeatism gripped the land. But when it appeared that the government might arrange a negotiated settlement with Germany, the halls of the

Senate thundered with Clemenceau's remonstrances. Finally, in a bid to shore up his sagging administration, Poincaré overlooked Clemenceau's blistering personal attacks and appointed him prime minister for a second time on November 17, 1917. This proved a turning point in the conduct of allied military affairs for, as Clemenceau blithely declared, "I wage war." The 75-year-old executive quickly sacked incompetent, politically-appointed generals, visited troops in the field to raise their morale, executed spies and double agents, and arrested pacifist leaders for treason. He also arranged for Marshal Ferdinand Foch to serve as commander in chief of Allied armies, including the newly arriving Americans, to better coordinate the war effort. France was thus better prepared for the German offensive of March 1918, which drove to within 30 miles of Paris. Unyielding and defiant, Clemenceau, with his Gallic swagger, became a rallying point for the exhausted nation, and within months the tide of war had dramatically turned. That Germany agreed to an unconditional armistice on November 11, 1918, testifies to Clemenceau's unflinching resolve to win. Thereafter he was popularly hailed as the "father of victory."

Clemenceau's popularity mandated that he preside over the 1919 Paris Peace Conference, and he was determined to secure stronger frontiers for France. Alsace-Lorraine was handed back to France unconditionally, but the prime minister failed to secure a French-controlled Rhineland region or large fiscal reparations from Germany. He was persuaded by U.S. president WOODROW WILSON and British prime minister DAVID LLOYD GEORGE to accept more lenient terms for the vanquished than he would have imposed himself. In the interest of preserving Allied unity, Clemenceau agreed to the Treaty of Versailles, which settled none of France's security concerns. The "father of victory" suddenly found himself accused of caving in to Germany by conservatives, while socialists still despised him for his use of troops against strikers. Therefore, when Clemenceau tried to close his political career by becoming president of France, his opponents secured enough votes to defeat him. The 80-year-old hero then concluded five decades of controversial but always conscientious public service by retiring. Ironically, his heroic contributions to victory were nullified by the same brand of partisan shrillness that he pioneered and came to exemplify. Clemenceau died in Paris on November 24, 1929, one of the most influential national leaders of French history.

Further Reading

Clemenceau, Georges. *In the Evening of My Thought.* Garden City, N.Y.: Doubleday, Page, and Co., 1929.

Cohen, Eliot A. *Supreme Command: Soldiers, Statesmen, and Leadership in Wartime.* London: Simon and Schuster, 2002.

Corp, Edward. "Sir Eyre Crowe and Georges Clemenceau At the Paris Peace Conference, 1919–1920." *Diplomacy and Statecraft* 8, no. 1 (1997): 10–19.

Dallas, Gregor. *At the Heart of a Tiger: Clemenceau and His World, 1841–1929.* New York: Carroll and Graf, 1993.

Hanks, Robert K. "Georges Clemenceau and the English." *Historical Journal* 43 (March 2002): 53–77.

Macmillan, Margaret O. *Paris 1919: Six Months That Changed the World.* New York: Random House, 2002.

Newhall, David S. *Clemenceau: A Life at War.* Lewiston, N.Y.: E. Mellen, 1991.

Coolidge, Calvin (1872–1933) *president of the United States*

John Calvin Coolidge was born in Plymouth Notch, Vermont, on July 4, 1872, the son of a small farmer with family roots in New England's colonial past. In many respects Coolidge epitomized those very historical qualities, being taciturn, frugal, and straitlaced in outlook and behavior. He graduated from Amherst College with honors in 1895 and, unable to afford law school, he clerked at a local law office. Attentive to his duties, Coolidge was admitted to the bar and by 1897 had opened up a successful law practice in Northampton, Massachusetts. Coolidge was also pro-business by nature so he joined the Republican Party and took part in local politics. He then served two terms in the state house of representatives before successfully running for a senate seat in 1911. Despite his cool exterior, Coolidge was a skilled political operator and within two years he had risen to president of the state senate. In 1915 he advanced his political aspirations by being elected lieutenant governor, and three years later gained the governor's mansion. Conservative by nature, Coolidge displayed a considerable progressive streak by championing bills for woman suffrage, greater protection of child labor, and a state savings bank insurance system. He also worked earnestly as a mediator in bitter labor disputes, gaining a reputation for honesty and impartiality. In 1919 he garnered national attention by ordering the National Guard to quell a violent strike by Boston police. "There is no right to strike against the public safety by anybody, anywhere, any time," he declared, which boosted his popularity and led to his overwhelming reelection.

By 1920 Coolidge was viewed by many as an excellent vice presidential candidate and that year the Republican National Convention teamed him up with presidential nominee WARREN G. HARDING. A greater contrast in personality and style is harder to imagine: Harding was colorful, dynamic, and surrounded by a bevy of corrupt friends, while Coolidge was low key, modest, and ethically unimpeachable. Once in office, he assumed his limited responsibilities without complaint or comment, acquiring the derisive nickname Silent Cal. But his political fortunes turned dramatically on August 3, 1923, when Harding, besmirched by several scandals, suddenly died. Coolidge was vacationing at the time and was sworn into office by his father, a local notary, on the family Bible. He remained untainted by scandal, fulfilled the remainder of Harding's term, and then ran on his own under the slogan, "Keep Cool with Coolidge." Enjoying the advantages of incumbency in a time of great prosperity, he was easily reelected to his own term in office.

As an executive, Coolidge was guided by his firm belief that a president should enact legislation passed by Congress—and little else. Hence, throughout his tenure in office, he seemed more like an administrative caretaker than a chief executive. But despite his hands-off approach to governance, many useful policies were enacted under his administration, including regulations for the radio industry, advancement of commercial aviation, and the 1926 Railroad Labor Act for settling disputes peacefully. As a confirmed capitalist, Coolidge also advocated tax cuts to stimulate economic growth and installed pro-business appointees to regulatory commissions. In that respect, he had blind faith in his dictum that "America's business is business." On the international scene, Coolidge took little stock in the League of Nations and rejected American membership, but did lend support to the idealistic Kellogg-Briand Pact of 1929, which outlawed war. He also sought to quell the rising tide of anti-Americanism in Latin America by mending fences with Mexico and Nicaragua. Despite his reluctance to become engaged politically, Coolidge enjoyed high popularity ratings and could have easily won reelection. Then, on August 27, 1927, he laconically announced "I do not choose to run for president in 1928." The following year he was succeeded by his fellow Republican, HERBERT HOOVER.

Coolidge died suddenly in Northampton on January 5, 1933, only four years out of office. Ironically, his fondness for encouraging speculation in the stock market left the nation unprepared for the 1929 market crash, which ultimately precipitated the Great Depression. He also turned a blind eye to the rise of fascism in Europe and Asia, and took no diplomatic initiatives to forestall future aggression. But Coolidge was always content to run the country more as a business than a nation, and his presidency was highly successful. In many respects, Coolidge's New England simplicity, earnestness, and nondescript manner proved a reassuring counterpoint to the otherwise raucous and roaring 1920s.

Calvin Coolidge *(Library of Congress)*

Further Reading

Booraem, Hendrik. *The Provincial: Calvin Coolidge and His World, 1885–1895*. Lewisburg, Pa.: Bucknell University Press, 1994.

Coolidge, Calvin. *The Autobiography of Calvin Coolidge*. New York: Cosmopolitan Book Co., 1929.

Ferrell, Robert H. *The Presidency of Calvin Coolidge*. Lawrence: University Press of Kansas, 1998.

Fowler, Russell. "Calvin Coolidge and the Supreme Court." *Journal of Supreme Court History* 25, no. 3 (2000): 271–295.

Gilbert, Robert E. *The Tormented President: Calvin Coolidge and the Trauma of Death*. Westport, Conn.: Praeger, 2003.

Hannaford, Peter, ed. *The Quotable Calvin Coolidge: Sensible Words for a New Century*. Bennington, Vt.: Images from the Past, 2001.

Haynes, John E. *Calvin Coolidge and the Coolidge Era: Essays on the History of the 1920s*. Washington, D.C.: Library of Congress, 1998.

Cosgrave, Liam (1920–   ) *prime minister of Ireland*

Liam Cosgrave was born in Dublin, Ireland, on April 30, 1920, a son of WILLIAM T. COSGRAVE, the nation's first prime minister. He attended St. Vincent's College in Dublin, studied law at King's Inn, and was called to the Irish bar in 1943. That year Cosgrave gained election to the Dáil Éireann (Irish parliament) as a member of the conservative Fine Gael Party. Adept at backbench politics, he rose to become secretary of the minister for industry and commerce in 1948, following the historic victory over EAMON DE VALERA's Fianna Fáil Party. When Fine Gael resumed power in 1957 Cosgrave was appointed minister of external affairs, heading Ireland's first delegation to the United Nations General Assembly. By 1965 Cosgrave had become party leader and head of the opposition in parliament. At that time Irish political discussion revolved around Fianna Fáil's decision to forsake traditional policies of isolation and self-sufficiency in favor of modernization and membership in the global economy. They pushed hard and finally achieved Ireland's entrance into the European Economic Community (EEC) in 1973. Fine Gael, by comparison, toed a more progressive line by representing itself as an avatar of social justice and economic fairness. Cosgrave, who was much more conservative than many of the younger party members, worked assiduously at keeping liberal elements in line with more traditional members. Once Ireland entered the EEC in February 1973, voters decided it was time to put the brakes on change, and Fine Gael was swept back into power. Cosgrave accordingly became *taoiseach* (literally "chieftain" or prime minister) in a coalition with the small Labour Party. This also constituted the first non-Fianna Fáil government in 16 years.

Cosgrave had campaigned on a 14-point program that focused upon economic and social issues such as housing and unemployment. However, he had made his biggest impact in the field of foreign affairs relating to Northern Ireland. On December 6, 1973, Cosgrave signed onto the Sunningdale Agreement with British prime minister EDWARD HEATH. This document attempted to lessen sectarian violence between the Catholic south and Protestant north by creating a coalition, the Council of Ireland, jointly staffed by representatives from both. The agreement was basically nonbinding and required members only to address problems of mutual concern, but militant Protestant Unionists feared it as the first step in unification with the south. They initiated a crippling general strike that induced a new British prime minister, HAROLD WILSON, to scrap this power-sharing agreement altogether. Cosgrave had problems of his own when the militant Irish Republican Army (IRA) assassinated the British ambassador in July 1976. He consequently declared a state of emergency and enacted strict security measures to counter domestic terrorism. However, when Irish president Cearbhall O'Dalaigh referred these measures to the Supreme Court for constitutional review, he was denounced by many in Cosgrave's cabinet as a "thundering disgrace." The Irish presidency is a nonpolitical office traditionally above political scrutiny, but when the prime minister failed to dismiss the offending ministers, O'Dalaigh resigned. Rather than incur additional embarrassment Cosgrave did not oppose his Fianna Fáil replacement, Patrick Millery.

By 1977 the Irish economy floundered, thanks to the Arab oil embargo, and endured a spate of rising unemployment and inflation. Cosgrave could do little to ameliorate these difficulties and further alienated the public by voting against his own party's bill to liberalize Ireland's strict contraceptive laws. By June the voters turned Fine Gail out of power with a vengeance and granted Fianna Fáil its largest proportion of votes cast in four decades. Cosgrave was reduced to party head and leader of the opposition in parliament until his replacement by GARRETT FITZGERALD in 1981. He then retired from public life amid criticism that his only ambition was retaining power, not implementing policy. But while Cosgrave's tenure in office is regarded as less than successful, his Sunningdale Agreement broke important ground by establishing a precedent. Henceforth every peace agreement for Northern Ireland has recognized that moves toward unity are predicated upon the consent of the Protestant majority. This guiding precept remains the basis for all subsequent negotiations.

Further Reading

Collins, Stephen. *The Cosgrave Legacy.* Dublin: Blackwater Press, 1996.

Coogan, Tim Pat. *The IRA.* New York: Palgrave for St. Martin's Press, 2002.

Kerrigan, Gene. *Never Make a Promise You Can't Break: How to Succeed in Irish Politics.* Dublin: Gill and Macmillan, 2002.

Kissane, Bill. *Explaining Irish Democracy.* Dublin: University College Dublin Press, 2002.

Mac Ginty, Roger. *Guns and Government: The Management of the Northern Ireland Peace Process.* New York: Palgrave, 2002.

Tannam, Etain. *Cross-border Cooperation in the Republic of Ireland and Northern Ireland.* New York: St. Martin's Press, 1999.

Cosgrave, William T. (1880–1965) *president of Ireland*

William Thomas Cosgrave was born in Dublin, Ireland, on June 5, 1880, the son of a vintner. Ireland by that time had been a British possession for three centuries and was growing restive for independence. Cosgrave became politically active at the age of 25 when he helped found the Sinn Féin Party to oppose the continuance of British rule. In 1909 he was elected to the Dublin city council, remaining there until 1922. When the Irish finally rose against Great Britain during the famous Easter Rebellion of 1916, Cosgrave fought with the Irish Volunteers and was captured. Tried and sentenced to death, he was ultimately freed under a general amnesty in January 1917. Ireland then took its first perilous steps down the road to independence, but internal consolidation remained necessary. Cosgrave was subsequently elected to the British

Parliament from Kilkenny but refused to be seated. Meanwhile provisions had been made for a new legislative body, the Dáil Éireann, to arise. In 1919 the provisional government under EAMON DE VALERA appointed Cosgrave to serve as minister of local governments, and he used his influence to further the membership of Sinn Féin. When fighting against British forces broke out in the Black and Tan War of 1919–21, Cosgrave directed party affairs from underground. By 1921 Michael Collins had successfully negotiated a peace treaty with Great Britain, which stipulated that Ireland remain a dominion within the empire. De Valera and other hardliners violently rejected the settlement as insufficient. Cosgrave, however, viewed it as the basis upon which a nation could be built and cast the decisive vote in its favor. De Valera and other antitreaty members then stormed out of the Dáil and boycotted further legislative matters. More ominously, they also formed a paramilitary wing to Sinn Féin, the Irish Republican Army (IRA), to resist the provisional government by force.

Cosgrave continued on as minister of local governments, and in July 1922 he advanced to chairperson of the provisional government. However, when Michael Collins was assassinated in August 1922, he served as interim president until formally elected president of the Dáil on September 9, 1922. In this capacity Cosgrave introduced a new constitution, which was approved on September 21, 1922. The following December he became first president of the Executive Council of the new Irish Free State in the middle of a bloody civil war against the IRA. On December 7, 1922, two sitting members of the Dáil were assassinated. Cosgrave, knowing the political risk involved, summarily ordered the execution of four IRA captives and the assassinations ceased. With peace finally at hand, he commenced laying the foundations of a new republic and an intense period of nation building ensued. He modeled most public institutions along the lines of British counterparts and established a national bank. And because Cosgrave also held the portfolio of finance, he directed creation of numerous state-sponsored companies to stimulate the national economy. Desiring greater international recognition for his land, he next sponsored Irish membership in the League of Nations. Cosgrave also intended to reshape the British Empire, to which Ireland still technically belonged, by supporting the Statute of Westminster. This introduced the concept of the commonwealth with greater internal autonomy for all its dominions. He represented Ireland at the Imperial Conference of 1923, strongly backed by delegates from South Africa and Canada seeking greater sovereignty. Cosgrave's most conspicuous failure was his attempted reconciliation of the largely Catholic Republic of Ireland with Protestant-dominated Northern Ireland. Hard-line Protestant Unionists, intent on remaining part of Great Britain, violently rejected any notion of unification. The problem remains unresolved to the present day.

Cosgrave's judicious and moderate efforts bequeathed to his new nation the mechanisms for self-governance. However, a constitutional crisis ensued in July 1927 when Vice President Kevin O'Higgins was murdered. Cosgrave then enacted legislation requiring all members of the Dáil to take an oath of allegiance before being allowed to sit. He continued on as president until 1932 when De Valera, having reentered politics, swept the elections with his new Fianna Fáil Party. Cosgrave graciously accepted the will of the people and peacefully transferred power to his long-time adversary. For many years thereafter, he remained head of the opposition with his own Fine Gael Party. Cosgrave finally retired from public life in 1944 and died in Dublin on November 16, 1965. His skill as a politician brought stability to a nation wracked by dissension, and ensured its survival.

Further Reading

Collins, Stephen. *The Cosgrave Legacy.* Dublin: Blackwater Press, 1996.

Jackson, Alvin. *Home Rule: An Irish History, 1800–2000.* New York: Oxford University Press, 2004.

Keogh. Dermot. "The Catholic Church and the Irish Free State." *History of Ireland* 2, no. 1, (1994): 47–51.

Kissane, Bill. "Democratic Consolidation and Government Changeover in the Irish Free State." *Commonwealth and Contemporary Politics* 39 (March 2001): 1–22.

Ward, Alan. *The Easter Rising: Revolution and Irish Nationalism.* Wheeling, Ill.: Harland Davidson, 2003.

Craxi, Bettino (1934–2000) *prime minister of Italy*

Benedetto (Bettino) Craxi was born in Milan, Italy, on February 24, 1934, the son of a socialist lawyer. He became politically active at 14 by working for his father's unsuccessful election campaign for the legislature in 1948, and subsequently attended the University of Milan. He quit school to join the Socialist Party in 1952 as part of its youth movement. Over the years Craxi proved himself an astute political operator, and by 1960 he had won a seat on the Milan city council. The following year he served on the party executive committee, and in 1968 Craxi won his first national election, to the Chamber of Deputies. These were lean years for the Socialists as they found themselves ideologically subservient to the much larger and more radical Communist Party. Their status militated against their emergence as a force in national politics, and in 1976 they suffered their largest losses to date. That year Craxi was elected the new party general secretary, and he immediately set about revamping and revitalizing his charge. First and foremost, he completely distanced himself from the Moscow-oriented Communists and committed the party to ideological pragmatism and mainstream European socialism. Craxi then purged the Socialists of dogmatic leftists and dismissed Marxism-Leninism as impractical for Italian politics. He even went so far as to drop the party's hammer-and-sickle symbol for a new red carnation. Now comfortably ensconced in the center, Craxi and the Socialists spent the next two decades attacking their former allies on the left, thereby increasing their appeal to middle-class voters.

Craxi's reforms paid dividends in May 1978 when the party posted impressive gains and he advanced the candidacy of Socialist Sandro Pertini for president of Italy. He succeeded and in 1979 Pertini asked Craxi to form a government. He failed, owing to the reluctance of the Christian Democrats to join his coalition, but Craxi played an ever-increasing role in backroom machinations during the next four administrations. In August 1983 the Socialists again performed well enough at the polls to attempt a government, and Craxi became Italy's first Socialist prime minister, as well as its youngest. Once in power Craxi proved surprisingly pragmatic in economic and social matters. He cut taxes, eliminated automatic wage increases to fight inflation, and even concluded a new concordat with Pope John Paul II. This document formally erased all references to Roman Catholicism as Italy's official state religion.

In foreign affairs Craxi more or less touted a pro-Western, pro-American line, and in 1984 he conferred with President RONALD REAGAN at the White House. To underscore his firm commitment to NATO, he allowed deployment of controversial Pershing II and cruise missiles on Italian soil to counter new Soviet weapons in Eastern Europe. Craxi also committed his administration to deploying troops in Lebanon as peacekeepers and initiated severe crackdowns on organized crime. But the issue of combating international terrorism proved far more intricate. In 1985, the Americans captured four Palestinian terrorists accused of hijacking the Italian cruise liner *Achille Lauro* and killing an elderly American passenger. However, the plane carrying them landed in Sicily, a violation of Italian sovereignty, Craxi ordered the captives released. Several of the offenders have since been tried and sentenced in absentia. Craxi managed to retain power for three and a half years, longer than any incumbent in the postwar era. He finally resigned in March 1987 over differences within his five-party coalition. He then continued as head of the invigorated Socialist Party in the legislature for the next six years.

For all his skill as a politician, Craxi's reputation was undermined and indelibly stained by corruption charges. In 1992 a national investigation entitled "Operation Clean Hands" revealed widespread bribery and favoritism at virtually all levels of government. As the probe unfolded, Craxi became the principal target of one of the largest corruption scandals in Italian history The former prime minister and several members of his family were then indicted. Public pressure forced Craxi to resign as head of the Socialists in 1993 after 17 years. He decried all the allegations as false before suddenly immigrating to Tunisia to avoid trial. Craxi was subsequently convicted and sentenced to 13 years in prison by a Milanese court. In 1996 he received another eight-year sentence for fraud and three more years under a third conviction. He nonetheless proclaimed his innocence from abroad and remained in self-imposed exile before dying in Hammamet, Tunisia, on January 19, 2000. Craxi's successful career notwithstanding, he has come to exemplify everything wrong with Italian politics since 1945.

Further Reading

Allum, Percy. "The Craxi Government: Turning Point or Dead End?" *Political Quarterly* 55 (July/ September 1984): 314–320.

Bufacchi, Vittorio, and Simon Burgess. *Italy since 1989: Events and Interpretations.* New York: St. Martin's Press, 1998.

Craxi, Bettino. *In the World: Selected Speeches of Bettino Craxi.* New York: Vintage Press, 1996.

Daniels, Philip A. "The End of the Craxi Era? The Italian Parliamentary Elections of June 1987." *Parliamentary Affairs* 41, no. 2 (1988): 258–286.

Di Scala, Spencer M. *Renewing Italian Socialism: Nenni to Craxi.* New York: Oxford University Press, 1988.

Favretto, Ilaria. *The Long Search for a Third Way: The British Labour Party and the Italian Left since 1945.* New York: Palgrave Macmillan, 2002.

Gundle, Stephen, and Simon Parker, eds. *The New Italian Republic: From the Fall of the Berlin Wall to Berlusconi.* New York: Routledge, 1996.

Curtin, John (1885–1945) *prime minister of Australia*

John Joseph Curtin was born in Creswick, Victoria, Australia, on January 8, 1885, the son of Irish immigrants. Indifferently educated, he worked as a printer and became attracted to socialist policies as a youth before joining the Australian Labor Party. In 1911 he served as a local union secretary and, a committed pacifist, he opposed Prime Minister WILLIAM MORRIS HUGHES's attempts to make overseas service compulsory during World War I. To that end he joined the Anti-Conscription League in 1916 and also functioned as its secretary. That year Curtin relocated to Perth in Western Australia, where he edited a radical newspaper. Having run for office several times, in 1928 he finally succeeded in winning a seat in the House of Representatives. His eloquent speeches and firm convictions made him a rising star in the Labor Party; in 1935 he was elected its leader. The party at that time was riven by dissension, including a breakaway group in New South Wales, but Curtin slowly imposed unity and discipline on all ranks. Curtin's own climb to the top was less than meteoric, for he was sidelined several times by recurring bouts with alcoholism. But by the late 1930s he began distancing himself from his more socialist, doctrinaire stances on national defense. In 1938 he routinely lectured on the threat posed by Nazi Germany and urged greater military preparedness and an end to isolationism. Curtin's stance was less than enthusiastically received by many Laborites, most of whom subscribed to pacifism and international solidarity. The onset of World War II triggered a major reevaluation of these beliefs at the party level.

Initially, Curtin had been invited to join the all-party unity government of ROBERT GORDON MENZIES in 1939, but he served on the War Advisory Council instead. The Menzies administration collapsed within two years, and on October 7, 1941, Curtin was asked to form a government. Australia, as part of the British Commonwealth, was legally obliged to donate troops to the defense of the British Empire. This entailed deployment of troops as far away as North Africa, where they won laurels in combat. But after the Japanese attack on Pearl Harbor on December 7, 1941, the specter of war moved much closer to home. Curtin realized Australia's military weakness, and in the spring of 1942 he flatly refused Prime Minister WINSTON CHURCHILL's request for Australian troops to defend Burma. The Australian leader adamantly insisted that these men were better employed defending their own homeland. Moreover, Curtin realized that the balance of world power had shifted in favor of the United States, and he struck up a cordial working relationship with General Douglas MacArthur, supreme allied commander in the Southwest Pacific. "Without any inhibitions," he declared, "I make it quite clear that Australia looks to America, free of any pangs as to our traditional links or kinship with the United Kingdom." Over the next four years Curtin worked closely with MacArthur and supported his strategic decisions, over the objections of many Australian generals. He also prevailed on the Labor-controlled legislature to authorize higher conscription levels, and enable Australian forces to be legally deployed beyond their own borders. In 1945 he fully endorsed the concept of the United Nations, sought closer defensive ties to neighboring New Zealand, and called upon the Americans to play a greater role in Pacific security matters. By war's end Curtin was rightly regarded as a faithful American ally.

While Curtin may have altered his socialist stance respecting military affairs, he held true to its domestic tenets. In fact, he used the war as an opportunity to expand the role of government and enact many of his most cherished programs. Long before the war ended, he began planning postwar integration of military veterans back into society. He also made plans to pursue full employment, enlargement of state welfare benefits, and centralized economic planning. Curtin died suddenly in Canberra at the height of his political influence, on July 1, 1945, shortly before the war concluded, but his legacy was clear. Curtin had worked closely with the United States for four years throughout the difficult struggle with Japan and is regarded as an effective wartime leader. He was succeeded by JOSEPH CHIFLEY, who continued building upon the foundations of the welfare state established by his predecessor.

Further Reading

Curtin, John. *In His Own Words: John Curtin Speeches and Writings.* Bentley, Western Australia: Paradigm Books Curtin University, 1995.

Day, David. *John Curtin: A Life.* New York: HarperCollins, 1999.

Edwards, Peter. "Curtin, MacArthur, and the 'Surrender of Sovereignty': A Historiographical Assessment." *Australian Journal of International Affairs* 55 (July 2001): 175–185.

Johnson, Carol. "Social Harmony in Australian Labour: The Role of Private Industry in the Curtin and Chifley Government's Plans for Australian Economic Development." *Australian Journal of Politics and History* 32 (1986): 39–51.

Lloyd, Clem, and Richard Hall, eds. *Backroom Briefings: John Curtin's War.* Canberra: National Library of Australia, 1997.

Love, Peter. "Curtin, MacArthur, and Conscription, 1942–43." *Historical Studies* 17 (October 1977): 505–511.

D

Dacko, David (1930–2003) *president of the Central African Republic*

David Dacko was born in Bouchia, Oubangui-Chari, on March 24, 1930, the son of a night watchman. Educated as a teacher, he became headmaster of a primary school in Bangui and also served as head of a local teacher's trade union. Dacko began his political career in 1957 when he gained election to the Territorial Assembly with the Mouvement pour l'évolution sociale de l'Afrique noire (MESAN), Movement for the Social Evolution of Black Africa. That year MESAN founder Barthélémy Boganda, who was also Dacko's cousin, appointed him minister of agriculture during his interim administration. The following year he served as interior minister as the region drew closer toward independence from France. However, fate intervened in March 1959 when Boganda was killed in an airplane crash, and a political struggle ensued. Dacko clashed with Abel Goumba, Boganda's vice president, who reasonably demanded the right of succession. But Dacko used his family influence to have the Territorial Assembly declare him president on May 5, 1959, and he formed a new regime without Goumba. On August 13, 1960, Oubangui-Chari formally gained its independence as the Central African Republic with Dacko as its first president.

From the onset, Dacko fell into bickering with other MESAN officials over the final form of the new constitution. The president sought an office with strong executive powers but he was opposed by Goumba and his rival party, the Mouvement l'évolution démocratique d'Afrique centrale (MEDAC), Movement for the Evolution of Democratic Central Africa. In December 1960 Dacko felt sufficiently threatened to have Goumba arrested and his organization outlawed. Thereafter he ruled the Central African Republic as a one-party state. To preserve political power at any cost, he enlisted the support of elites from various regions in the country who benefited economically from the alliance. Dacko also quickly cultivated ties to France by giving foreign corporations free rein to exploit the country's natural resources. In exchange the French provided ongoing military and economic support. The Central African Republic thus toiled along for several years without economic growth or political pluralism. Dacko and his cronies continued enriching themselves at public expense until December 31, 1965, when he was suddenly overthrown by another cousin, Colonel JEAN-BÉDEL BOKASSA.

Dacko remained under house arrest for a decade, until 1976, when the erratic Bokassa released him to serve as a personal adviser. The nation, meanwhile, suffered greatly under the erratic rule of Bokassa, who crowned himself "emperor." When France could no longer endure such an embarrassment it dispatched troops to topple the regime on September 20, 1979. Dacko was then installed as president for a second time. The sense of relief among many citizens was sincere, but the president quickly slipped back into old habits of control. As previously, Dacko allied himself with regional elites in exchange for political and economic patronage. He also created a new party, the Union démocratique africain (UDC), Union of Democratic Central Africa, which would serve as the nation's only outlet for political expression. However, by February 1981 mounting dissatisfaction led to the adoption of a new constitution that made allowances for multiparty democracy. The following month Dacko "won" the presidential election with 50 percent of the vote, conveniently edging out Ange Felix Patasse for the office. This resulted in widespread unrest in various parts of the country, and French troops were called in to quell dissent. That May Dacko announced suspension of forthcoming legislative elections to circumvent further disorder. Disturbances continued, however, and Dacko dissolved the central trade union organization, banned opposition parties, and arrested several leaders. These escalating authoritarian measures were ample proof that Dacko had lost control of the situation, and he was deposed by General Andre Kolingba on September 1, 1981.

Dacko was exiled to France where he lived until 1991. He then returned home and announced his candidacy during the next round of presidential elections in August 1993. Dacko garnered only 20 percent of votes cast and finally assumed that his political career had ended. He died in Yaounde, the capital of Cameroon, where he had been sent when his health deteriorated, on November 21, 2003. Dacko is remembered primarily for having twice failed to establish either a representative democracy or coherent economic policies.

Further Reading

Delayen, Julie Ann. "Origins and Causes of Military Rule in the Central African Republic." Unpublished master's thesis, University of Florida, 1985.

Hill, Robert W. "The Christianization of the Central African Republic." Unpublished Ph.D. diss., Fuller Theological Seminary, 1969.

Kalck, Pierre. Central African Republic: A Failure in Decolonization. New York: Praeger, 1971.

———. Historical Dictionary of the Central African Republic. Metuchen, N.J.: Scarecrow Press, 1992.

O'Toole, Thomas. The Central African Republic: The Continent's Hidden Heart. Boulder, Colo.: Westview Press, 1986.

Daddah, Moktar Ould (1924–2003) *president of Mauritania*

Moktar Ould Daddah was born in Boutilimit, Mauritania, on December 25, 1924, into a family of Berber Islamic scholars. After attending elite Islamic academies, he worked for the French colonial administration as a translator. In 1948 Daddah ventured to France to study law at the University of Paris, and he was admitted to the bar at Dakar, Senegal, in 1955. By this time pressure was building for greater autonomy in French colonies, and Mauritania acquired its first Territorial Council. In 1957 Daddah won a seat on the council as part of the Union progressive Mauritanienne (UPM), Progressive Union of Mauritania, and quickly rose to vice chairman. His most dramatic action was to relocate the council from St. Louis, Senegal, to its present-day location at Nouakchott. By 1959 the UPM had merged with other parties to become the Parti de regroupement Mauritanien (PRM), Party of Mauritanian Regroupment, with Daddah as secretary. Mauritania achieved its independence from France on November 28, 1960, when the assembly elected Daddah prime minister. When a new constitution took effect in 1961, his title was changed to president.

The onset of independence did little to ameliorate Mauritania's deep ethnic divisions. Here the Islamic Moorish majority, populating the central and northern parts of the country, exuded undisguised antipathy for the black African south. As president, Daddah tried to heal old wounds by appointing blacks to high cabinet positions. However, despite earlier pretensions of political pluralism, Daddah imposed one-party rule by absorbing all political factions into the Parti du peuple Mauritanien (PPM), Mauritanian People's Party, which he controlled. In 1965 he sought to further consolidate control by declaring Arabic and French the official languages of Mauritania, which black Africans both resented and resisted. He also nationalized various sectors of the economy, especially the mining of copper and iron, the nation's principal exports.

Given the tumultuous history of the region, Daddah was by necessity acutely interested in foreign affairs. Morocco had always claimed Mauritania as part of its historic territory and refused to grant it diplomatic recognition for a decade. Daddah sought to cultivate close ties with the Muslim world by joining the Arab League in 1973 and mending his country's fences with Morocco by severing ties with the United States in the aftermath of the 1967 Arab-Israeli War, and taking a hard line in espousing the Palestinian cause. In a final assertion of national sovereignty, Daddah also withdrew from the French franc zone in 1973 and instituted a new currency, the ouguiya. This further eroded the national economy but established his credentials as a Pan-Arabic nationalist. Daddah also projected himself as a Pan-Africanist, and in 1971–72 he served as president of the Organization of African Unity (OAU).

Mauritania remained a poor nation under Daddah's regime, with pressing needs for internal improvement. However, in 1974 he became preoccupied with Spanish efforts to disengage from Western Sahara, which Mauritania and Morocco both claimed. He then ambitiously laid claim to the entire region but backed down in the face of armed intervention from his erstwhile ally. At length Daddah contented himself with acquiring the southern third of Western Sahara, but his problems had only begun. An indigenous liberation movement, the Polisario Front, sprang up to resist Mauritania and Morocco by force. These peerless desert warriors conducted a lengthy guerrilla campaign and raided Mauritania on several occasions. Daddah's determined prosecution of the war also incurred trouble at home, draining the treasury and creating dissension among the Africans in the south. Already a minority, the blacks felt they would be further marginalized by the inclusion of additional Berber peoples. Daddah continued losing support at home until, on July 10, 1978, he was overthrown by Colonel Mustapha Ould Mohamad Salek.

After a brief house arrest, Daddah was allowed to immigrate to France where he remained for the next 23 years. On July 18, 2001, he finally came home and was greeted by a cheering throng at Nouakchott airport. Daddah then expressed his disinterest in national affairs beyond serving as a political arbiter. He died on October 15, 2003, at a military hospital in Paris, France.

Further Reading

Gerteiny, Alfred G. *Islamic Influences on Politics in Mauritania.* Boston: African Studies Center, Boston University, 1971.

Goldensohn, Max D. "Bureaucracy and Development: A Case from Mauritania." Unpublished Ph.D. diss., Harvard University, 1978.

Hacene-Djaballah, Balkacem. "Conflict in Western Sahara: A Study of POLISARIO as an Insurgency Movement." Unpublished Ph.D. diss., 1985.

Harrell-Bond, Barbara E. *The Struggle for the Western Sahara.* Hanover, N.H.: American Universities Field Staff, 1981.

Pazzanita, Anthony. "The Origins and Evolution of Mauritania's Second Republic." *Journal of Modern African Studies* 34 (December 1996): 575–589.

Thompson, Virginia L. *The Western Saharans: Background to Conflict.* Totowa, N.J.: Barnes and Noble Books, 1980.

Daladier, Édouard (1884–1970) *prime minister of France*

Édouard Daladier was born in Carpentras, France, on June 18, 1884, a baker's son. He inherited from his activist father a passion for leftist politics, further abetted by his history teacher, EDOUARD HERRIOT, a future prime minister. In 1914 Daladier was elected mayor of his home town but he quit to join the army after the outbreak of World War I. He fought with distinction, was highly decorated, and returned home a war hero. In 1919, on Herriot's urging, he successfully ran for a seat in the Chamber of Deputies as part of the Radical Party. In June 1924 Prime Minister Herriot first assigned him a portfolio as colonial minister; he served in a variety of capacities over the next eight years. He also established himself as a leading republican figure of the interwar period, usually in concert with other noted leftists such as LÉON BLUM. In 1928 Daladier defeated his mentor Herriot in a bitter battle for control of the Radicals and in January 1933 he was called to form a government. This lasted only until October, but the following year he assembled another coalition while the country reeled from violent clashes between right- and left-wing extremists. On February 6, 1934, militant conservatives, angered by the dismissal of a popular police commissioner, nearly stormed the Chamber of Deputies. Daladier's grip on affairs appeared very tenuous, so he tendered his resignation after only four weeks in office. The following year he brought the Radical Party into the Popular Front in concert with socialists and communists under Blum, who appointed him minister of national defense in 1936. Over the next two years Daladier was responsible for a rearmament campaign to counter the rising militarism of ADOLF HITLER's Nazi Germany. His efforts were compromised by the effects of the Great Depression, which weakened the economy.

In April 1938 Daladier again assumed the premiership and was confronted by a grave international situation. Germany's rearmament campaign had far outstripped that of France and Great Britain, and Hitler began flexing his might abroad. Intent upon uniting all Germans into a single *reich,* he annexed Austria in March 1938. The Western democracies' reluctance to confront German expansion only encouraged his aggression, and Hitler next sought to annex the German-speaking Sudetenland region of Czechoslovakia. Daladier and British prime minister NEVILLE CHAMBERLAIN, cognizant of their own military weakness, sought to appease Hitler to buy time. In September 1938 they flew to Germany and signed the infamous Munich Pact to forestall future aggression, buying France and England a much needed respite to continue rearming. However, when Hitler attacked Poland on September 1, 1939, Daladier felt he had no recourse but to follow England's lead and declare war on Germany.

For several months into the war British and French forces sat idly engaged in a phony war while Germany conquered Poland and Norway. However, when JOSEPH STALIN's Soviet forces conquered Finland in March 1940, Daladier's government was criticized for failing to provide military support. He resigned from office and subsequently served as war minister under Paul Reynaud. German forces then successfully invaded France in May 1940 and Daladier boarded a ship to form a government in exile. However, his arrest was ordered by General PHILIPPE PÉTAIN, head of the new French regime in Vichy, and he was brought to trial at Riom. Daladier was then charged with failing to adequately prepare France for war, which he ably and dramatically refuted, and the proceedings were suspended. He was sent off to Germany, a prisoner of war, and remained in confinement until released by American troops in May 1945.

Back home Daladier became a pariah, blamed for the disaster that befell France. There was plenty of culpability to go around, and he ably resuscitated his reputation. He gained reelection as a deputy with the now nearly defunct Radicals and remained active in politics until 1958. His most notable accomplishment was steadfast opposition to CHARLES DE GAULLE's new constitution. Daladier died in Paris on October 10, 1970. Once a leading national figure in the 1930s, his passing went almost unnoticed.

Further Reading

Alexander, Martin S., and William J. Philpott, eds. *Anglo-French Defense Relations between the Wars.* New York: Palgrave, 2002.

Daladier, Édouard. *Prison Journal, 1940–1945.* Boulder, Colo.: Westview Press, 1995.

Davis, Richard. *Anglo-French Relations before the Second World War: Appeasement and Crisis.* New York: Palgrave in association with King's College, London, 2001.

Imlay, Talbot C. *Facing the Second World War: Strategy, Politics, and Economics in Britain, 1938–1940.* New York: Oxford University Press, 2003.

Jackson, Julian. *France: The Dark Years, 1940–1944.* New York: Oxford University Press, 2001.

Jackson, Peter. *France and the Nazi Menace: Intelligence and Policy Making.* New York: Oxford University Press, 2000.

Zahniser, Marvin R. *Then Came Disaster: France and the United States, 1918–1940.* Westport, Conn.: Praeger, 2002.

Deakin, Alfred (1856–1919) *prime minister of Australia*

Alfred Deakin was born in Melbourne, Victoria (in present-day Australia), on August 3, 1856, the son of English immigrant parents. He pursued a law degree at the University of Melbourne but forsook legal practice in favor of journalism. Deakin was eminently successful writing essays for the *Age,* a progressive newspaper, until his editor prevailed upon him to run for the state legislature in 1879. He was successful and commenced a wide-ranging political career. Possessed of a sharp mind and a friendly manner, Deakin quickly established a reputation as Affable Alfred. He served in several state ministries and visited California in 1884 to study advanced irrigation techniques. He then helped transplant them to Victoria through the 1886 Irrigation Act, for the benefit of farmers. Deakin subsequently represented Australia at the London Imperial Conference of 1887, where he became intrigued by the idea of federation. Australia was then a series of disparate colonies groping toward some kind of political union. After the Federal Convention of 1891 failed to have its proposal passed by colonial legislatures, he became a vocal proponent for federation. Deakin served as a delegate to the 1897 convention and drafted the constitution that made Australia a commonwealth. When this finally won approval by the states, Deakin again ventured to London in 1900 to shepherd its passage through the English Parliament.

In 1900 Deakin served as attorney general in the administration of Prime Minister EDMUND BARTON and proved instrumental in adopting tariff and other protectionist legislation. He succeeded Barton in 1903 but Deakin's Liberal ministry lasted only seven months until Labor withdrew its support. During this period he managed to pass the Defense Acts, which subjected eligible males to a military draft for the first time. He also enacted strict immigration laws to ban the migration of nonwhite peoples to Australia. Deakin subsequently patched up his differences with Labor in 1905 and formed a second government. By then his agenda focused on social matters, and the government enacted commercial laws and pensions for the elderly. In 1907 Deakin also imposed his New Protection doctrine, which mandated that only factories paying "fair and reasonable" wages should enjoy the benefits of tariff protection. This landmark legislation served as the basis for Australia's minimum-wage laws. The choice of Canberra as the site of the national capital was also settled. However, the Liberal Party was continually losing ground to Labor on the left and the Free Traders on the right, which made Deakin's grip on power increasingly untenable. Abandoned by Labor again in 1908, he resigned a second time to serve as head of the opposition in Parliament.

One year later Deakin returned to power a third time through the aegis of the "Fusion Party," an alliance between conservative Free Traders and Liberals. He continued passing legislation for the protection of workers and nascent Australian industries, but his biggest accomplishment was creation of the Royal Australian Navy in 1910. Deakin, like many Australians, was alarmed when Great Britain allowed France to establish naval facilities on nearby New Caledonia in 1906.

Fearing foreign threats and the fact that the Royal Navy was far too distant and too dispersed to offer help, he successfully argued for creation of a single Australian squadron. When Labor returned to power in 1910, Deakin resigned a third and final time. He remained in the House of Representatives until his retirement in 1913, and died in Melbourne on October 7, 1919. Deakin was an important force behind the quest for federation and the maturation of Australia. As prime minister he shaped many of the policies that guided the nation through most of the 20th century. Curiously the Liberal Party, which began the national age as the largest party, enacting much useful legislation, continually shrank throughout Deakin's tenure before finishing third behind Labor and the conservatives.

Further Reading

Crisp, L. F., and B. C. Atkinson. "Ramsay MacDonald, James Scullin and Alfred Deakin at Ballart: Imperial Standards, 1906." *Australian Journal of Politics and History* 17 (April 1971): 73–81.

Deakin, Alfred. *The Federal Story: An Inner History of the Federal Cause, 1880–1900.* Melbourne: Robertson and Mullens, 1944.

Gabay, Al. *The Mystic Life of Alfred Deakin.* New York: Cambridge University Press, 1992.

MacCullum, D. M. "Alfred Deakin, a Biography." *Journal of the Royal Australian Historical Society* 52, no. 3 (1966): 241–247.

Partington, Geoffrey. "Alfred Deakin and the Significant Past." *Journal of the Royal Australian Historical Society* 78, nos. 3–4 (1978): 108–199.

Rickard, John. *A Family Romance: The Deakins at Home.* Carlton South, Victoria: Melbourne University Press, 1996.

De Gasperi, Alcide (1881–1954) *prime minister of Italy*

Alcide De Gasperi was born in Pieve Tesino, Trento, then part of the Austro-Hungarian Empire, on April 3, 1881. As a youth he became active in the Social Christian movement, and its tenets guided his personal and political convictions through life. De Gasperi subsequently attended the University of Vienna where he further deepened his commitment to Christian social values and Italian nationalism. Having established the Trentino Popular Party he was elected to the Austrian legislature in 1911, and throughout World War I remained in the neutralist camp. After the war the Austro-Hungarian Empire was dismembered and Trento reverted to Italy. De Gasperi, now an Italian citizen, helped to found a new Christian organization, the Partito Populare Italiano (PPI), Italian Popular Party, and was elected to the Chamber of Deputies in 1921. Italy was then on the cusp of being ruled by BENITO MUSSOLINI's fascists, to whom he was unalterably opposed. In 1926 Mussolini ordered the PPI dissolved and De Gasperi, now general secretary, attempted to flee the country. However, he was caught and sentenced to jail, serving 18 months before gaining release. Thereafter De Gasperi found employment under Pope PIUS XII in the Vatican library and spent the next 14 years immersed in Catholic theology and social philosophy. He remained highly active in the underground press and printed what amounted to a political manifesto for new Christian-based organizations. By 1944 Italian fascism had been defeated, so De Gasperi founded the Democrazia Cristiana (DC), Christian Democratic Party, and served as the first secretary general.

After 1945 Italy embarked on the long and rocky road toward economic and social reconstruction, a feat greatly complicated by the popularity of the Italian Communist Party. De Gasperi held various portfolios in an interim administration, but in December 1945 he was elected the first postwar prime minister. He maintained his office for eight consecutive years, the longest tenure in the history of modern Italy. De Gasperi's first task was guiding the transition from a monarchy to a republic, which he accomplished through a public referendum in 1946. He was moderately disposed politically but also a pragmatist, who realized that he would have to deal with communists and socialists to achieve political stability. Therefore his first government included cabinet members from both parties. De Gasperi then visited Washington, D.C., to confer with President HARRY S. TRUMAN and became the first European head of state to sign onto the new Marshall Plan to secure economic assistance. He also agreed to drop all leftists from his administration. Thereafter De Gasperi relied upon a fluid coalition of Christian Democrats, Liberals, Social Democrats, and Republicans to govern Italy. The public apparently agreed with his approach, for in 1948 they handed the Christian Democrats their first electoral victory. The conservatives' control of government would last nearly five decades.

In the emerging cold war that followed, De Gasperi proved himself fully committed to the Western alliance. He eagerly joined the ranks of NATO in 1949 and integrated Italy closer into the economic fabric of Europe by joining the Council of Europe and the European Steel and Coal Community. Domestically he favored conservative fiscal policies, a mixed private and state-owned economy, and developing the poorer southern regions of the nation. But despite the conservative tenor of his administration De Gasperi refused all attempts to transform the DC into a Catholic party or to ally himself with neo-fascists as a bulwark against communism. Throughout his tenure he repeatedly cautioned his countrymen about supporting extremists on either end of the political spectrum and closely hewed to his centrist line. In this deliberate, cautious manner, the foundations of modern Italian democracy were established.

By 1953 the CD coalition failed to secure a clear parliamentary majority and, after much haggling, De Gasperi resigned as prime minister. He remained on as party secretary for another year until his death in Sella Valsugana on August 18, 1954. His significance to the postwar reconstruction of Italy was pivotal, for he prevented Italian communists—the largest such party in Europe—from taking power and sabotaging relations with the West. In doing so he brought Italy out of its wartime isolation and firmly back into the community of nations. In that sense De Gasperi remains highly regarded as one of the principal architects of modern Europe.

Further Reading

Brogi, Alessandro. *A Question of Self-Esteem: The United States and the Cold War Choices in France and Italy, 1944–1958.* Westport, Conn.: Praeger, 2002.

Carillo, Elisa A. "Alcide De Gasperi and the Fascist Regime, 1924–1929." *Review of Politics* 26, no. 4 (1964): 518–530.

———. "Alcide De Gasperi and the Lateran Pacts." *Catholic Historical Review* 49, no. 4 (1964): 532–539.

———. *Alcide De Gasperi; the Long Apprenticeship.* Notre Dame, Ind.: University of Notre Dame Press, 1965.

Keyserlingk, Robert W. *Fathers of Europe: Patriots of Peace.* Montreal: Palm Publishers, 1972.

Koff, Sandra Z., and Stephen P. Koff. *Italy, from the First to the Second Republic.* New York: Routledge, 2000.

de la Madrid, Miguel (1934–) *president of Mexico*

Miguel de la Madrid Hurtado was born on December 12, 1934, in Colima, Mexico, the son of a lawyer. He was educated in Mexico City at the National Autonomous University and subsequently pursued a graduate degree in public administration from Harvard University. Interested in economics, he accepted work in various Mexican businesses and government agencies after returning. He tested the political waters by joining the Partido Revolucionario Institucional (PRI), which had governed Mexico for 40 years. De la Madrid performed exceptionally well and came to the attention of President JOSÉ LÓPEZ PORTILLO, who appointed him to his cabinet in 1979. He received a portfolio as secretary of planning and programming, winning plaudits for his overall performance. In 1981 López Portillo nominated him as his successor in the upcoming presidential elections. Mexico being a tightly controlled one-party state, any PRI candidate was expected to win overwhelmingly, and in 1982 he became president. Being the first Mexican executive to have been educated outside the country and the first to possess an advanced degree, much was expected of him.

De la Madrid's accession to power coincided with a difficult period in Mexican history, for the nation reeled from economic mismanagement and faced imminent collapse. He inherited the worst economy since the Great Depression of the 1930s, with massive national debts topping $90 billion, and inflation rates approaching 100 percent. The problem was exacerbated by a worldwide oil glut, which reduced the prices of Mexico's most profitable export. The difficulties of finding work also triggered widespread social dislocation and a massive illegal immigration to the United States. The rise of drug trafficking along the international border also led to the murder of several tourists and a federal drug enforcement officer. Mexico's inability to control either its economy or population severely strained relations with U.S. president RONALD REAGAN, who demanded both reforms in exchange for financial assistance. De la Madrid's position was unenviable, but he was uniquely qualified to abandon traditional solutions in favor of newer ones. In fact, his generation of highly educated technocrats looked down upon establishment politicians and their cronies. The new generation's apparent independence and defiance caused tremendous strains with the established political order.

The economic crisis severely curtailed de la Madrid's political options, so he imposed strict austerity measures to bring spending under control and reduce the deficit. Salaries were cut, 50,000 government jobs were eliminated, and the peso devalued. These moves brought howls of protest from the bureaucracy, a loyal PRI constituency, but within a year inflation fell to 20 percent. Consistent with the dictates of the International Monetary Fund (IMF) and World Bank, de la Madrid also took steps to liberalize Mexico's state-run economy by selling off unprofitable state enterprises. The ensuing sacrifice proved great but creditors were sufficiently impressed to grant Mexico additional time to pay off skyrocketing debts. Over the next six years, growth proved marginal but the economy was no longer in free fall. De la Madrid proved no miracle worker yet his embrace of neoliberal economics prevented Mexico from slipping over the precipice.

When not absorbed by economic matters, de la Madrid confronted frosty relations with the United States. In addition to tensions arising from drugs and illegal immigration, there remained the question of war in Central America. De la Madrid, like many Latin American leaders, opposed Reagan's policy of arming counterrevolutionary guerrillas to fight the communist-backed regime in Nicaragua. In fact, he helped sponsor the Contadora peace initiative with six other nations to neutralize hostility without toppling any regimes. The Americans considered such an approach to be naive and kept a steady flow of arms and supplies to anticommunist forces until 1990. De la Madrid had also pledged himself to undertake a "moral renovation" of the country to root out deep-seated corruption within public and private institutions. He prosecuted several high-ranking officials from the previous administration but accomplished little to resolve institutionalized corruption. By the time he left office de la Madrid had stabilized the nation but little else. He was replaced by Carlos Salinas Gortari in 1989, who presided over the very economic disaster that de la Madrid sacrificed so much to stop. Out of office, de la Madrid became general manager of a large publishing house. His tenure in office proved constructive but produced more favorable ratings abroad than he ever received at home.

Further Reading

Babb, Sarah L. *Managing Mexico: Economists from Nationalism to Neoliberalism.* Princeton, N.J.: Princeton University Press, 2001.

Castaneda, Jorge. *Perpetuating Power: How Mexican Presidents Were Chosen.* New York: New Press, 2000.

Cornelius, Wayne A. *The Political Economy of Mexico under de la Madrid: The Crisis Deepens, 1985–1986.* La Jolla, Calif.: Center for U.S.-Mexican Studies, University of California–San Diego, 1986.

Eschbach, Cheryl. "Dilemmas of Sovereignty: Mexican Policy towards Central America under Presidents López Portillo and de la Madrid." Unpublished Ph.D. diss., Princeton University, 1989.

Morris, S. D. *Political Reformism in Mexico: An Overview of Contemporary Mexican Politics.* Boulder, Colo.: Lynne Rienner Publishers, 1995.

Schmidt, Henry C. "The Mexican Foreign Debt and the Sexennial Transition from López Portillo to de la Madrid." *Mexican Studies* 1, no. 2 (1985): 227–254.

De Valera, Eamon (1882–1975) *prime minister of Ireland*

Edward De Valera was born in New York City on October 14, 1882, the son of an Irish immigrant mother and a Spanish father. His father died while he was three, and he was sent back to live with relatives in County Limerick, Ireland. Poor and indifferently educated, De Valera displayed aptitude as a student and won a scholarship to Blackrock College in Dublin. After graduating, he taught mathematics at various colleges. Ireland was then chafing under 300 years of English rule, and resentment culminated in an Irish cultural renaissance. De Valera studied Gael (Irish), changed his name to Eamon, and in 1913 joined Sinn Féin, a paramilitary organization determined to resist the British. He fought well during the famous Easter Uprising of April 1916 and was captured. His death sentence was commuted the following year, and he was released. That same year De Valera won election as the Sinn Féin candidate for a seat in England's Parliament and refused to be seated. His Republican (nationalist) activities landed him in jail again in 1918 but he staged a daring escape and a year later became first minister of the newly created Dáil Éireann (Irish parliament). In this capacity he traveled to the United States to raise money for Republican causes. De Valera also began final peace negotiations with English prime minister DAVID LLOYD GEORGE, which were finished by Michael Collins. The resulting treaty recognized Irish independence, but only as a dominion within the British Empire. De Valera, who insisted upon complete independence, angrily denounced the treaty, and when it was passed under President WILLIAM T. COSGRAVE, a civil war commenced. He was briefly imprisoned in 1922 but refused to seat his Sinn Féin members in the legislature because of a loyalty oath to the English king. "Whenever I wanted to know what the Irish people wanted," he maintained, "I had only to examine my own heart." De Valera reveled in his role as a romantic Irish rebel.

De Valera remained head of Sinn Féin until 1926 when he founded the new Fianna Fáil party. This signaled his intention to work within the system, and upon being elected to the Dáil in 1927, he took the hated loyalty oath to the king. He maintained a strong influence in politics, and in 1932, when Cosgrave's

Eamon De Valera *(Library of Congress)*

coalition failed, De Valera was sworn in as prime minister. This victory ushered in a period of undisputed Fianna Fáil control for the next 23 years. He gained considerable international stature by becoming president of the League of Nations, but his activities centered upon severing the final links with Great Britain.

De Valera's first task was successfully removing the oath of allegiance for all Dáil members. He then engaged in an intense trade war with England and refused to pay land annuities until Great Britain relinquished control of all naval bases on Irish soil. He promulgated a new constitution in 1937 that made Ireland an independent republic in all but name. However, he failed in his attempts to have the six Protestant-dominated counties of Northern Ireland brought into the fold. These have stoutly resisted incorporation with the south to the present. For all his revolutionary nationalism, De Valera was extremely conservative in social matters, and he incorporated Catholic social doctrine as part of national policy. He also espoused traditional Irish positions on isolation and self-sufficiency. When World War II broke out in 1939, De Valera stuck to a closely prescribed policy of neutrality, ignoring tremendous diplomatic pressure from Prime Minister WINSTON CHURCHILL and American president FRANKLIN D. ROOSEVELT to enter on behalf of the Allies. The move proved popular at home, and Ireland emerged from the struggle with its economy free from devastation.

De Valera finally lost power in 1948 but he subsequently served as *taoiseach* (prime minister) in 1951 and 1957. By 1959 his health and eyesight were failing, so he accepted the ceremonial post of president of Ireland. His national popularity may be gauged by the fact that he remained in office until 1973 and retired only at the age of 91. De Valera died in Dublin on August 29, 1975, after dominating politics for four decades and indelibly stamping Ireland with his no-compromise approach to nationalism. He was a stubborn fighter for independence, a peerless cultural patriot, and a far-sighted politician.

Further Reading

Coogan, Tim Pat. *De Valera: The Man Who Was Ireland.* New York: HarperCollins, 1993.

De Valera, Eamon. *Speeches and Statements of Eamon De Valera.* New York: St. Martin's Press, 1980.

Dunphy, Richard. *The Making of Fianna Fáil Power in Ireland, 1923–1948.* New York: Oxford University Press, 1995.

English, Richard. *Armed Struggle: A History of the IRA.* New York: Oxford University Press, 2003.

Kautt, William H. *The Anglo-Irish War, 1916–1921: A People's War.* Westport, Conn.: Praeger, 1999.

Laffan, Michael. *The Resurrection of Ireland: The Sinn Féin Party, 1916–1923.* New York: Cambridge University Press, 1999.

O'Brien, Mark. *De Valera, Fianna Fáil, and the Irish Press.* Portland, Ore.: Irish Academic Press, 2001.

Wood, Ian S. *Ireland during the Second World War.* London: Caxton Editions, 2002.

Díaz, Porfirio (1830–1915) *president of Mexico*

Porfirio Díaz was born in Oaxaca, Mexico, on September 15, 1830, the son of a mixed Spanish-Indian (mestizo) family. He briefly studied at a nearby seminary but decided to pursue a legal career under Benito Juárez. However, Díaz was drawn toward military service during the war against the United States, 1846–48, and in the War of the Reform, 1858–61. He especially distinguished himself during the period of French intervention, 1862–67, when Emperor Napoleon III made Austrian archduke Maximilian emperor of Mexico. Díaz defeated French troops on several occasions, escaped from captivity, and ended up capturing Mexico City on behalf of Juárez, now president. He then returned to civilian life in Oaxaca until 1871, when Juárez decided to seek a fourth term in office. Díaz considered the move unconstitutional, and unsuccessfully ran against him. He raised the standard of revolt against his former benefactor, was defeated, but called a truce following Juárez's death in 1872. Díaz then ran and lost again to Sebastian Lerdo de Tejada, but in 1876 he launched a successful military campaign to oust him. Mexico by then was a nation in ruins after three decades of constant warfare. Upon assuming office Díaz promised the public he would not seek reelection. In 1880 he briefly stepped aside to allow General Manuel Gonzalez to run affairs, but by 1884 Díaz discarded his "no reelection" stance, seized the reins of power, and held them for the next 27 years.

In office Díaz took systematic steps to consolidate his control of the country. In fact he erected one of the longest-lasting political machines in Mexican history. His first task was restoring public order through establishment of the rural police, or *rurales*. This was a ruthless organization that enjoyed free rein in the countryside and answered only to him. The *rurales* did useful work eradicating bandit gangs that plagued the frontier, but they were notorious for brutalizing peasants and Indians into subservience. With order restored Díaz next needed a source of revenue to replenish Mexico's empty coffers. He turned to foreign investors for capital and offered them generous terms and high profits in exchange for their money. With funding now pouring into the country Díaz was free to conduct one of the most extensive modernization campaigns in Latin American history. An intricate network of railroads sprang up that connected distant parts of the country to the interior, which also abetted the rise of internal commerce and markets. Soon after, factories, mines, and farms arose along these routes along with the nation's first telegraph and electrical systems. Over the next three decades Mexico's economy boomed, giving rise to agricultural exports to the United States and elaborate consumer goods for the domestic market. By the turn of the century Díaz had transformed his country from a poverty-ridden enclave into Latin America's richest and most politically stable nation.

Financial success does not tell the entire story, unfortunately. The crux of Díaz's political system lay with political and economic patronage. He systematically recruited rural and regional elites into his government and enriched them in return for unbending political support. Thus only the national elites enjoyed the benefits arising from modernization, and they greatly enriched themselves. The vast majority of Mexicans living in the interior continued suffering under abject poverty and illiteracy. By 1910 wages for agricultural and trade workers had remained at the same level as in 1810, while consumer prices soared. Such glaring disparities created social and labor unrest, which Díaz and his cronies ruthlessly suppressed with violence and intimidation. Moreover, Díaz surrounded himself with a circle of European-trained intellectuals, the so-called Científicos, who were devoted to serving the white majority. Mixed races were to be kept strictly in place while native Indians, comprising nearly one-third of the population, were ignored altogether. But so far-reaching was Díaz's political apparatus, and so effectively did it control the tenor of Mexican life, that he ruled unchallenged for three and a half decades. Periodically Díaz made a show of being "elected" president without meaningful opposition, but otherwise his rule was absolute.

In the first decade of the 20th century, Mexico experienced periodic economic recessions that increased suffering among the masses and disillusioned many of the rising middle class. As widespread social discontent arose, Díaz's elaborate system of control began unraveling. In 1908 he made the mistake of announcing to an American journalist that Mexico was ready for democracy and that he was would not seek reelection. The interview sent shock waves around the nation and potential successors began marshaling their forces. But the 80-year-old Díaz had second thoughts and decided to run again in 1910. Disillusioned and outraged, many political and military leaders withdrew their unswerving support and began arming themselves. It fell upon FRANCISCO MADERO, a wealthy northern industrialist, to declare war against the Díaz regime. A period of intense fighting ensued, and the government collapsed like a house of cards. Díaz then fled the country in May 1911 and made for France. He died in luxurious exile on July 2, 1915, hailed by onlookers as a modernizing and stabilizing force in Mexico. Citizens who knew him better refused to allow his ashes to come home for burial—they remain in Paris to this day. But so pervasive an influence did Díaz wield over Mexico that the term *Porfiriato* was coined to describe his era in power.

Further Reading

Gardner, Paul H. *Porfirio Diaz.* New York: Longman, 2001.

Krauze, Enrique. *Mexico: Biography of Power: A History of Modern Mexico, 1810–1996.* New York: HarperCollins, 1997.

Macias Gonzalez, Victor M. "The Mexican Aristocracy and Porfirio Diaz, 1876–1911." Unpublished Ph.D. diss., Texas Christian University, 1999.

Maurer, Noel. *The Power and the Money: The Mexican Financial System, 1876–1932.* Stanford, Calif.: Stanford University Press, 2002.

Passananti, Thomas P. "Managing Finance and Financiers: The State and the Politics of Debt, Banking, and Money in Porfirian Mexico." Unpublished Ph.D. diss., University of Chicago, 2001.

Taylor, Lawrence D. "The Battle of Ciudad Juarez: Death Knell of the Porfirian Regime in Mexico." *New Mexico Historical Review* 72, no. 2 (1999): 179–207.

Weiner, Richard. *Race, Nation, and Market: Economic Culture in Porfirian Mexico.* Tucson: University of Arizona Press, 2004.

Díaz Ordaz, Gustavo (1911–1979) *president of Mexico*

Gustavo Díaz Ordaz was born in Puebla, Mexico, on March 11, 1911, the son of a government accountant. He briefly attended college in Mexico City before obtaining his law degree from the University of Puebla in 1937. Thereafter he devoted himself to a life of public service commencing with a stint as public prosecutor. In 1943 Díaz successfully ran for a seat in Mexico's Congress where he remained three years. He then acquired a seat in the Senate. A terse, authoritarian, but highly effective legislator, Díaz impressed many officials in Mexico's ruling party, the Partido Revolucionario Institucional (PRI), and he came to the attention of President ADOLFO LÓPEZ MATEOS. In 1953 López Mateos made Díaz director of the department of legal affairs, followed five years later by appointment as secretary of the government. Díaz demonstrated great sympathy for the business community, but otherwise he subscribed to a strict law-and-order philosophy of governance. He used army troops to suppress a railroad strike in 1959 and ordered the arrest of several noted leftist politicians. However, Díaz was an efficient administrator and a loyal party hand, so in 1964 he was selected by López Mateos to succeed him as president. Official endorsement by the PRI meant an assured election victory, and in 1964 Díaz was sworn in as Mexico's chief executive.

As president, Díaz carried through on the probusiness policies of his earlier career. To facilitate better control and planning of domestic investment, he modified tax laws and reduced public expenditures. He then invested heavily in Mexico's aging infrastructure by constructing dams, subways, and highways. The government placed renewed emphasis on education, building large numbers of schools, training new teachers, and increasing school enrollment among the poor. Díaz also continued the government policy of land distribution to peasants, releasing over 22 million acres. Through his deft handling of economic matters, Mexico's gross national product soared from $16 billion to $23 billion and, for the first time, the country became agriculturally self-sufficient. He even secured a small parcel of Mexican territory called Chamizal that was also claimed by the United States. Díaz sustained a 6 percent growth rate and low inflation throughout his presidency, making it among the most prosperous in Mexican history.

Economic success did not translate into domestic tranquility for Díaz, however, for Mexico was gripped by peasant disturbances and unrest among its burgeoning student population. For many young people, the political machine represented by PRI was little more than a self-serving oligarchy, impervious to change. Tensions were not defused when Díaz, an arch conservative, refused to introduce liberalizing reforms urged by his own party leaders. Consequently Díaz faced outbreaks of armed guerrilla resistance in Chihuahua and Mexico City, which were contained only by force. But the defining moment of his presidency occurred in May 1968, just prior to the Olympic Games in Mexico City. Many political opponents, including students, objected to his using the Olympics to showcase Mexican achievements, while distorting the actual state of domestic affairs. A student strike was called two weeks before the games in an attempt to have them canceled. With national prestige on the line, such defiance drew a sharp response from Díaz, and he ordered troops and riot police into the streets. The opposing forces converged upon the Plaza of Tlatelolco on October 1, 1968, and a bloody confrontation ensued. By the time the shooting stopped, nearly 200 students were dead and several thousand had been arrested. It was a poignant reminder to the world of just how authoritarian the Mexican regime really was.

Díaz secured order and the games were an international success, but his heavy-handed treatment of dissent diminished his prestige. By the time he yielded his office in 1970 to LUIS ECHEVERRÍA ÁLVAREZ, another hand-picked PRI successor, his success at handling the economy had largely been forgotten. The stigma of the 1968 Olympics continued stalking Díaz for the rest of his public life. In 1977 he was appointed ambassador to Spain but public furor triggered his resignation only four months later. Díaz then retired to Mexico City a bitter, disillusioned man. He died there on July 15, 1979, the last Mexican executive to enjoy continuous prosperity, but among the first to endure such public scorn. Fortunately, his mishandling of student unrest led to increased pressure within and without the PRI for political liberalization.

Further Reading

Hellman, Judith A. *Mexico in Crisis.* New York: Holmes and Meier, 1983.

Hofstader, Dan. *Mexico, 1946–73.* New York: Facts On File, 1974.

Niemeyer, E. Victor. "Personal Diplomacy: Lyndon B. Johnson and Mexico, 1963–1968." *Southwestern Historical Quarterly* 90 (October 1986): 159–186.

Preston, Julia. *Opening Mexico: A Country's Tumultuous Passage to Democracy.* New York: Farrar, Straus and Giroux, 2004.

Sloan, Julia L. "The 1968 Student Movement and the Crisis of Mexico's Institutionalized Revolution." Unpublished Ph.D. diss., University of Houston, 2001.

Wager, Steven J. "The Mexican Army, 1940–1982: The Country Comes First." Unpublished Ph.D. diss., Stanford University, 1992.

Diefenbaker, John (1895–1979) *prime minister of Canada*

John George Diefenbaker was born in Neustadt, Ontario, on September 18, 1895, the son of a schoolmaster. He relocated to Saskatchewan as a child and was imbued with the sense of "prairie populism" characterizing that region. After completing military service in World War I, Diefenbaker earned his law degree from the University of Saskatchewan and began a successful legal practice. He gained renown as a powerful and eloquent defense attorney, and as his interest in politics matured, he joined the Progressive Conservative Party. Commencing in 1928, Diefenbaker ran five unsuccessful campaigns for public office, even though he was elected head of the provincial party in 1938. It was not until 1940 that Diefenbaker finally won a seat in Parliament, where he again demonstrated formidable debating and oratorical skills. But it was not until 1956 that Diefenbaker became head of the Progressive Conservatives and the following year he scored an upset victory over Liberals under LOUIS ST. LAURENT. It was the first conservative administration in 22 years, though it governed as a minority coalition. A flurry of important social bills were enacted by Diefenbaker, who then dissolved Parliament and called for new elections. To everybody's surprise, the conservatives scored resoundingly, taking 208 of 265 seats—the most ever accorded a single party to that date.

With a firm working majority in his favor Diefenbaker set about enacting an ambitious legislative agenda, reflecting his unique blend of nationalism and populism. He pushed through the Canadian Bill of Rights, which for the first time extended a voting franchise to all native peoples. He also appointed the first female cabinet member in Canadian history. The government then promoted a "northern vision," which entailed economic development of Canada's farthest reaches. In international circles Diefenbaker was determined to have Canada's voice heard, especially within the British Commonwealth. In 1961 he so lambasted South Africa for its apartheid racial policies that the government in Pretoria withdrew its membership. Diefenbaker also angered British prime minister HAROLD MACMILLAN by criticizing his decision to enter the European Common Market. Finally, he flouted political convention by selling Canadian wheat to the People's Republic of China at a time when the United States refused China diplomatic recognition. During his five years in power Diefenbaker did much to enhance social and political affairs at home while projecting a distinct Canadian perspective on affairs abroad.

By 1962 the national economy had soured, so the Liberals made parliamentary gains that relegated the conservatives to a minority government and weakened Diefenbaker's ability to rule. That year he also entered into a bitter contretemps with American president JOHN F. KENNEDY over the issue of nuclear weapons. Previously, Canada had agreed in principle to the stationing of U.S. nuclear-tipped Bomarc missiles on Canadian soil with the caveat that the United States alone could authorize its warheads to be mounted. But during the 1961 Cuban missile crisis with the Soviet Union, when Kennedy ordered a mass mobilization of nuclear weapons, Diefenbaker refused to comply. The Liberals were quick to use this recalcitrance as proof of the prime minister's indecision and anti-Americanism. He had also acquired a reputation for being soft on national security measures by canceling the highly expensive Avro Arrow jet fighter in 1959 at the cost of 15,000 jobs. When elections were held in 1963, the Progressive Conservatives were badly defeated by Liberals under LESTER PEARSON, who became prime minister.

Back in the opposition Diefenbaker retained his role as head of the Progressive Conservatives though he was increasingly viewed as an electoral liability. He weathered several attempts to depose him but finally lost the leadership in 1967. Diefenbaker retained his seat in Parliament for another 12 years in this diminished capacity. He died in Ottawa, Ontario, on August 16, 1979, and his flag-draped coffin wended its way across the prairies by train. Historians still debate the relative merits of his administration and question the rationale behind his approach to nuclear weapons, but most conclude that his commitment to Canada and its citizens was beyond reproach.

Further Reading

Diefenbaker, John G. *One Canada: Memoir of the Right Honorable John G. Diefenbaker.* Toronto: Macmillan of Canada, 1975.

Glazov, Jamie. *Canadian Policy toward Khrushchev's Soviet Union.* Montreal: McGill-Queen's University Press, 2002.

Gloin, Kevin J. "Canada's Role in the United States National Security Policy: Strategic Materials in the Eisenhower-Diefenbaker Era." Unpublished master's thesis, University of Calgary, 1995.

McMahon, Patricia. "The Politics of Canada's Nuclear Policy, 1957–1963." Unpublished Ph.D. diss., University of Toronto, 1999.

Slade Arthur G. *John Diefenbaker: An Appointment with Destiny.* Montreal: XYZ Pub., 2001.

Smith, Denis. *Rogue Tory: The Life and Legend of John G. Diefenbaker.* Toronto: Macfarlane, Walter, and Ross, 1995.

Story, Donald C., and R. Bruce Shepard. *The Diefenbaker Legacy: Canadian Politics, Law, and Society since 1957.* Regina, Sask.: Canadian Plains Society Research Center, University of Regina, 1998.

Dimitrov, Georgi (1882–1949) *prime minister of Bulgaria*

Georgi Mikhailovich Dimitrov was born in Kovachevsti, Bulgaria, on June 18, 1882, the son of Macedonian immigrants. Poverty precluded any chance of his attending college, so Dimitrov began working as a printer while a teenager. He became active in union organizing and by 1903 had won a seat on the Sofia city council. Dimitrov's politics progressively took more radical turns. In 1913 he was elected to the Bulgarian legislature. In 1919 he helped found the Bulgarian Communist Party while serving on its Central Committee. After repeatedly being jailed for organizing and antiwar activities, Dimitrov ventured to the Soviet Union in 1921 to meet revolutionary leader VLADIMIR LENIN. This brought his political views more in line with orthodox Soviet-style communism, and he subsequently served with the executive committee of the Comintern. This organization was ostensibly created to foment revolutionary activity around the world, but in fact was intended to impose Russian control over all communist parties. In June 1923 Dimitrov and other communist leaders led an unsuccessful revolt against the government, and he fled to Yugoslavia. Sentenced to death in absentia, he did not return to Bulgaria until 1945, when JOSEPH STALIN entrusted Dimitrov to conduct Comintern activities in several European capitals, including Vienna and Berlin. In 1933 he was arrested by German authorities and falsely charged in the "communist plot" to burn down the Reichstag (legislature). However, he ably defended himself in a Nazi show trial, was acquitted and released in February 1934. A special plane flew him to Moscow, where he acquired Soviet citizenship.

Between 1935 and 1943 Dimitrov functioned as general secretary of the Comintern under Stalin's watchful eye. He managed to convince superiors that fascism had supplanted capitalism as the enemy of socialism. Dimitrov was consequently authorized to coordinate Comintern activities with antifascist movements throughout Europe. He officially altered his stance following the Nazi-Soviet Nonaggression Pact of 1939, but resumed it following Germany's invasion of Russia in 1941. In 1943 Stalin dissolved the Comintern and ordered Dimitrov to establish a Fatherland Front of antifascist elements in his native Bulgaria. After September 9, 1944, when Bulgaria left the Axis alliance and surrendered to the Allies, plans were developed to draw that nation into a Soviet orbit. Dimitrov arrived home in April 1945 and set about consolidating Communist control, assisted by the overwhelming presence of the Red Army. Under Dimitrov's guidance, the party arrested its former allies in the Fatherland Front and executed them. The remaining antifascist figures then withdrew from the coalition and boycotted the rigged October 1945 elections. Communist governance became a reality.

Now in power, Dimitrov orchestrated a public referendum in September 1946 that abolished the monarchy and elevated him as prime minister. Another rigged vote the following October gave the communists formal control of the Fatherland Front; the pace of Stalinization quickened dramatically. The government established numerous "people's courts" to eliminate all enemies of the state, real or perceived, and additional leaders were shot. Many of those purged were fellow communists who arose locally and who had not spent the war years in Moscow under Stalin's watchful eye. In 1947 Dimitrov consolidated control by promulgating a new constitution transforming Bulgaria into a "people's republic." This entailed the forced collectivization of agriculture, nationalization of private property, and renewed emphasis on heavy industry. However, in 1948 Dimitrov fell out with Stalin over a possible Balkan federation with MARSHAL TITO of Yugoslavia. Dimitrov immediately recanted but was summoned to Moscow for "talks." He died there under mysterious circumstances on July 2, 1949. As a tribute to Bulgaria's most stalwart communist, his body was embalmed and displayed in central Sofia until 1990.

Further Reading

Banac, Ivo, ed. *The Diary of Georgi Dimitrov.* New Haven, Conn.: Yale University Press, 2003.

Bell, John D. *The Bulgarian Communist Party from Blagoev to Zhivkov.* Stanford, Calif.: Hoover Institution Press, 1986.

Dallin, Alexander, and F. I. Firsov, eds. *Dimitrov and Stalin, 1934–1944: Letters from the Soviet Archives.* New Haven, Conn.: Yale University Press, 2000.

Devedjiev, Hristol. *Stalinization of the Bulgarian Society, 1949–1953.* Philadelphia: Dorrance, 1975.

Moser, Charles A. *Dimitrov of Bulgaria: A Political Biography of Dr. Georgi M. Dimitrov.* Thornwood, N.Y.: Caroline House, 1979.

Pundeff, Marin. "Dimitrov at Leipzig: Was There a Deal?" *Slavic Review* 45, no. 3 (1986): 545–549.

Diori, Hamani (1916–1989) *president of Niger*
El-Hadj Hamani Diori was born in Soudoure, French West Africa, on June 6, 1916, into the Djerma ethnic grouping. His father was a public health official working for the colonial administration and secured him an excellent education. After passing through the prestigious William Ponty School in Dakar (now Senegal), Diori worked as a teacher for many years. In 1936 he relocated to Paris to serve as a language instructor

teaching Hausa and Djerma at the Institute of Overseas Studies. A decade later he returned home as a headmaster in Niamey, but Diori also joined nationalist activities. In 1946 he cofounded the Parti Progressiste Nigerien (PPN), Progressive Party of Niger, as a regional branch of the larger African Democratic Rally based in the Ivory Coast. Because France then allowed limited African representation in its National Assembly, Diori was elected a deputy in 1946. He served for five years before being defeated for reelection by his cousin, Djibo Bakary. That year the African Democratic Rally also divested itself of communist elements, and the PPN split into competing factions: moderates under Diori and radicals under Bakary, who went on to found a new organization, Sawaba (Freedom). The division cost Diori his seat in the assembly, and he came home in 1951. A deep personal animosity festered between the two cousins for the rest of their lives. After teaching several more years, Diori returned to the National Assembly in 1956 where he became assistant speaker. He also won a seat in the Niger National Assembly. For many months this body debated the relative merits of independence from France, with Bakary's faction pushing hard for a complete separation. But Diori sought autonomy from France, not independence, and he solidified support from tribal chiefs who perceived Bakary's radicalism as a threat to traditional authority. In 1958 he was positioned to lead the PPN to victory in national elections and become prime minister. Niger gained independence from France anyway, in August 1960, and constitutional changes made Diori the nation's first president. He was reelected in 1965 and again in 1970.

Diori's first priority in office was consolidating political power to enhance national security. He did this by arresting top Sawaba leaders, including Bakary, and exiling them to Mali. From there they launched a lengthy guerrilla campaign to destabilize the Nigerois government, and in 1965 Diori was nearly assassinated in a mosque. However, when the guerrillas were finally defeated, Diori was free to turn his attention to the international scene. He emerged as a respected figure throughout West Africa for his attempts at mediating conflicts. In 1968 Diori was the leading spokesman for an attempted federation by French-speaking African states. No less than four nations asked him to represent their interests. He headed the African Entente from 1968 to 1974 and was chairperson of the West African Community, 1973–74. Diori also displayed diplomatic independence from France by establishing close ties to Soviet Bloc countries and by favoring the Nigerian government in its bloody civil war against Biafra. Relations with neighboring Ghana chilled when President KOFI BUSIA expelled 200,000 Niger workers for economic reasons.

Unfortunately, Diori's success in the international arena was not mirrored in events at home. For many years Niger was among the most stable nations in Africa, but Diori's many trips abroad left matters of state in the hands of corrupt subordinates. The economy tottered, and Diori was perceived as more interested in foreign affairs than in the domestic concerns of his people. Many also resented his increasingly authoritarian tone and prolonged mishandling of the economy. Diori's political standing plummeted in the wake of a prolonged drought that afflicted the region throughout the early 1970s. His administration apparently mishandled the influx of foreign aid, with much of it being siphoned off by government officials. On April 15, 1974, Diori was overthrown by Colonel Seyni Kountche and jailed. He was incarcerated for six years and under house arrest for another seven years before being encouraged to leave the country. Diori settled in Rabat, Morocco, where he died on April 23, 1989, an unappreciated founding father of Niger.

Further Reading

Baker, Geoffrey L. *Trade Winds on the Niger: The Saga of the Royal Niger Company, 1830–1971.* New York: Radcliffe Press, 1996.

Charlick, Robert B. *Niger: Personal Rule and Survival in the Sahel.* Boulder, Colo.: Westview Press, 1991.

Fuglestad, Finn. "The 1974 Coup d'Etat in Niger: Towards an Explanation." *Journal of Modern African Studies* 13 (September 1975): 383–398.

———. *A History of Niger, 1850–1960.* New York: Cambridge University Press, 1983.

Robinson, Pearl T. "African Traditional Rulers and the Modern State: The Linkage Role of Chiefs in the Republic of Niger." Unpublished master's thesis, Columbia University, 1975.

Doe, Samuel K. (1951–1990) *president of Liberia*

Samuel Kanyon Doe was born in Turzon, Liberia, on May 6, 1951, a member of the Krahn tribe. He joined the army after dropping out of high school and distinguished himself as a noncommissioned officer, rising to sergeant major in 1979, one of the few African soldiers to receive special forces training in the United States. In that year Liberia, Africa's oldest republic since 1847, was wracked by severe social upheavals. Since 1870 the nation had been governed by the True Whig Party, consisting of the descendants of freed African-American slaves who wielded power at the expense of tribes living in the interior. Doe, who had previously expressed no interest in politics, suddenly overthrew the regime of President William Tolbert on April 12, 1980. Tolbert was killed and, to underscore the brutality of things to come, Doe publicly executed 13 leading government officials. Thereafter he instituted rule through a People's Redemption Council (PRC), which consisted of other low-ranking soldiers like himself. The 133-year-old constitution, patterned after the American model, was then suspended along with all political activities. However, the majority of Liberians were tired of oligarchic rule and welcomed the change. Doe also promised to restore democracy to the country in a few months, spelling the end of Liberia's traditional one-party dominance.

Given the violence of his accession, Doe was initially shunned by most African governments, but he eventually made amends and established normal relations. Domestically, however, his regime was characterized by brutal repression, sporadic coup attempts, and bloody countermeasures. Doe fulfilled his promise of restoring democracy in 1985 when he promulgated a new constitution that was passed by a public referendum. The PRC was dissolved and ambitious plans for multiparty pluralism put into place. Not surprisingly, Doe and his new National Democratic Party won the contest with 50 percent of the vote in a process described as manifestly flawed. African countries and Liberia's biggest benefactor, the United States, overlooked the entire process and continued with normalized relations. Doe, in fact, became something of an international celebrity and, because of his anticommunist posturing, was invited to Washington to confer with American president RONALD REAGAN.

Doe's regime had proved every bit as extravagant as Tolbert's, and he practiced the same kind of ethnic favoritism. He recruited soldiers only from his own Krahn tribe, and the army repressed the 15 other tribal groups comprising Liberia. The Doe administration, having been deserted by the middle class, also proved remarkably inept at running the economy. Liberia was previously one of Africa's most prosperous nations and yet was run into the ground through incompetence and graft. By 1989 both the International Monetary Fund (IMF) and World Bank had cut off financial aid. But Doe was kept afloat for many years by the United States, which feared further communist inroads into Africa. In time, 50 percent unemployment, tribal favoritism, and political repression ignited a widespread revolt in the interior of the country among the Mano and Gio peoples. In December 1989 Charles Taylor led fighters of the National Patriot Front from the Ivory Coast to seize the capital of Monrovia. At length they were joined by soldiers from another group, headed by Prince Yormie Johnson, which further compromised Doe's grip on power. The presence of a Nigerian peace-keeping force in the vicinity did little to stabilize events, which had already cost 20,000 lives.

Liberia's army, badly trained and disciplined, responded to the fighting by indiscriminately murdering civilians. This only further enraged the populace, and the guerrillas continued advancing. Doe obtained a temporary respite when competing rebel camps started fighting each other outside the capital. Sensing an opportunity to negotiate a peaceful end to his regime, he approached the representatives from Johnson's group, who invited him across the lines to parley. On September 9, 1990, Doe's motorcade was ambushed, and he was wounded, captured, and tortured to death. This act concluded one of Africa's most brutal regimes and ushered in a prolonged period of civil war lasting another five years. Liberia, once one of Africa's most stable and prosperous nations, now lay in ruins. The only good to come from all this bloodshed was that the Americo-Liberians finally lost their stranglehold on political power.

Further Reading

Abango, George. "Political Gamble in Liberia: The Rise and Fall of Samuel Doe." *Towson State Journal of International Affairs* 29, no. 2 (1994): 14–19.

Ahmadu Sesay, Max. "Politics and Society in Postwar Liberia." *Journal of Modern African Studies* 34 (September 1996): 395–421.

Andrews, G. Henry. *Cry, Liberia, Cry!* New York: Vantage Press, 1993.

Dolo, Emmanuel. *Democracy Versus Dictatorship: The Quest for Freedom and Justice in Africa's Oldest Republic, Liberia.* Lanham, Md.: University Press of America, 1996.

Gifford, Paul. *Christianity and Politics in Doe's Liberia.* Cambridge, England: Cambridge University Press, 2002.

Givens, Willie A., ed. *Liberia: The Road to Democracy under the Leadership of Samuel Kanyon Doe.* Bourne End, Bucks., England: Kensal Press, 1986.

Lyons, T. "Liberia's Path from Anarchy to Elections." *Current History* 97 (May 1998): 229–233.

Dollfuss, Engelbert (1892–1934) *chancellor of Austria*

Engelbert Dollfuss was born in Texing, part of the Austro-Hungarian Empire, on October 4, 1892, the illegitimate son of a farmer. Like most peasants in this intensely Catholic country, Dollfuss was extremely conservative in his political outlook. He was raised by grandparents before passing through the University of Vienna to study law. During World War I the diminutive Dollfuss (around five feet tall) had trouble joining the army, but he eventually fought with distinction in Italy. Afterward he ventured to Germany and obtained an advanced law degree from the University of Berlin. World War I left the Austro-Hungarian Empire dismembered, and Austria, cut adrift from its imperial past, tried adjusting to parliamentary democracy as a small republic. Dollfuss entered politics in 1922 by joining the Lower Austria Chamber of Commerce and within five years served as its director. A skilled administrator, he advanced to president of the Federal Railway Board in 1930 and served as leader of the conservative Christian Social Party. The following year, drawing upon his lifelong experience as part of the Peasant League, Dollfuss became minister of agriculture. He rose unexpectedly to chancellor of Austria in 1932, thanks to a coalition of conservative groups dissatisfied with the nation's political instability. This made him the youngest head of state then in Europe.

Dollfuss assumed power at a difficult juncture in Austrian history, for the economy was reeling under the Great Depression. Worse, in 1933 the nation seethed with Nazi-inspired agitation after the election of ADOLF HITLER as chancellor of Germany. The rise of Nazism was something Dollfuss was determined to prevent. Ignoring public opinion, he refused to join a German customs union for fear it would serve as a platform for annexation. Instead he accepted a $9 million bank loan from the League of Nations, while striking up cordial relations with Italian fascist dictator BENITO MUSSOLINI. In this manner he hoped to revive the economy while playing German Nazism off against Italian fascism. It seemed to be all a small nation like Austria could do, and ultimately proved a Faustian deal.

As the Austrian economy tottered and the nation slipped into chaos and disorder, Dollfuss was required to call upon the paramilitary Home Guard and the Catholic Social Peasant League to maintain order. But he alienated the Social Democratic Party, the largest antifascist organization in Austria, by refusing to enter into a government with it. Dollfuss instead relied heavily on a coalition of conservative and right-wing parties, including the small Austrian Nazi Party. When competing agendas could not be harmonized, Dollfuss became increasingly authoritarian in outlook. In March 1933 he dissolved the legislature, outlawed all political parties, and effectively terminated the Austrian First Republic. That September he announced creation of a Fatherland Front to effectively rule the nation and govern by decree. Dollfuss did so only upon the insistence of Mussolini, who offered to buttress Austrian independence following creation of an Italian-style fascist state. Dollfuss hoped this arrangement would dissuade Hitler from coercing a political union between Germany and Austria. Left-wing elements were distressed over such moves, and in February 1934 the socialists and communists rebelled against the government. They were quickly crushed by the military. In May 1934 a new constitution formalized Dollfuss's dictatorial powers. Henceforth Austria was little more than an Italian client-state, which enjoyed ties to the Vatican. Dollfuss had squelched the last remnants of democracy in Austria but kept the nation free from Hitler.

The Austrian Nazis realized that they could never unite with Germany as long as Dollfuss remained in power and, backed by their German counterparts, they organized a putsch to overthrow the government by force. On July 25, 1934, a group of Nazis, disguised as soldiers, forced their way into government offices, confronted Dollfuss, and killed him. He was then replaced by the pro-Nazi German FRANZ VON PAPEN, who facilitated the path to unification. In February 1938 Austria was formally absorbed by Germany in a process known as Anschluss—the move that Dollfuss had feared most. By invoking extreme authoritarian measures to maintain order, he had inadvertently prepared his nation for the takeover.

Further Reading

Allinson, Mark. *Germany and Austria, 1814–2000.* New York: Oxford University Press, 2002.

Bischof, Gunter, Anton Pelinka, and Alexander Lassner, eds. *The Dollfuss/Schuschnigg Era in Austria: A Reassessment.* New Brunswick, N.J.: Transaction Publishers, 2003.

Lewis, Jill. *Fascism and the Working Class in Austria, 1918–1934: The Failure of Labour in the First Republic.* New York: St. Martin's Press, 1991.

Messner, Johannes. *Dollfuss: An Austrian Patriot.* Norfolk, Va.: Gates of Vienna Books, 2003.

Miller, James W. "Englebert Dollfuss and Austrian Agriculture: An Authoritarian Democrat and His Policies." Unpublished Ph.D. diss., University of Minnesota, 1985.

Rath, John R. "The Dollfuss Ministry: The Demise of the Nationalrat." *Austrian Yearbook* 32 (2001): 125–147.

Douglas-Home, Alexander (baron Home of the Hirsel) (1903–1995) *prime minister of Great Britain*

Alexander Frederick Douglas-Home was born in London on July 2, 1903, into an aristocratic Scottish family. As such he was tutored privately and attended the elite private school at Eton before passing through Oxford University. Against his father's wishes he decided upon a career in politics and was elected to the House of Commons in 1930 with the Conservative Party. Charming, urbane, and cool-headed, Douglas-Home became a popular figure in Parliament, and he quickly befriended NEVILLE CHAMBERLAIN, then chancellor of the Exchequer. Chamberlain appointed him his secretary and, when Chamberlain became prime minister, Douglas-Home served as his personal secretary. In this capacity he accompanied Chamberlain on his eventful trip to Munich in 1938 to sign a nonaggression pact with ADOLF HITLER. He fully supported the government's policy of appeasement at that time, although it was thoroughly discredited when World War II erupted the following year. Douglas-Home remained sidelined for the war due to back surgery, but in May 1945 Prime Minister Winston Churchill invited him into his caretaker government as foreign office minister. That summer he lost his seat in Parliament in the surprising Labour Party sweep and returned to his estate in Scotland. After the death of his father in 1951 Douglas-Home inherited the title of earl and was seated in the House of Lords. His easygoing manner made him a popular fixture in that gilded assembly, and he rose to become its leader.

When the Conservatives returned to power in 1951, Churchill appointed Douglas-Home his secretary for Scotland. In 1955 Prime Minister ANTHONY EDEN made him Commonwealth relations secretary. The world was then at the height of the cold war, and Douglas-Home, drawing upon his earlier mistake at Munich, emerged as a hard-liner in dealing with Soviet expansionism. Douglas-Home was regarded as an authority in foreign affairs, and he performed yeoman work by keeping the Commonwealth intact during Eden's ill-fated Suez Canal adventure in 1956. He directed the squelching by British troops of a communist uprising in Malaysia. Continuing into the administration of Prime Minister HAROLD MACMILLAN, he held the portfolio as foreign minister. In 1962 Douglas-Home finalized the Nassau Agreement with American president JOHN F. KENNEDY whereby England acquired its own Polaris nuclear missiles. However, he was pragmatic in dealing with problems dogging the Commonwealth and insisted that Great Britain acknowledge the forces of nationalism and grant the remaining colonies their independence. He also urged Rhodesia to accept a multiracial constitution as a solution to its rising guerrilla insurgency. This far-sighted solution, sadly ignored, would arise again.

By 1963 Macmillan, ill, racked by a spy scandal, and ready to leave, sought to have Douglas-Home succeed him in office. However, this would require him to renounce his titles and peerage in order to sit in the House of Commons. He readily complied and became the first aristocrat since 1902 to hold executive power. Much was expected of the urbane, cultured Douglas-Home, but his unfamiliarity with domestic politics—especially economics—proved his undoing. He was especially uncomfortable in front of a television camera and came across as weak and vacillating. His administration lasted only 12 months before the Conservatives were bested by HAROLD WILSON of the Labour Party. The Conservatives, then eager to shed their image as a party of aristocratic privilege, dumped

Douglas-Home as head in favor of the more populist EDWARD HEATH. The two men retained good relations, and when the Conservatives won in 1970 Douglas-Home functioned as Heath's foreign secretary. Still stridently anticommunist, he expelled 107 Soviet diplomats from Britain for spying in 1971, which created a major diplomatic incident. Douglas-Home also turned his attention to Rhodesia again and belatedly convinced Prime Minister IAN SMITH to adopt a racially balanced government to end the African nationalist insurgency there. He performed well in diplomatic spheres until the Conservatives were again ousted in 1974. Douglas-Home then received the title Baron Home of the Hirsel from Queen Elizabeth II and returned to the House of Lords as a respected elder statesman. The affable aristocrat died on his estate in Berwick, Scotland, on October 9, 1995. His tenure as prime minister may have been little more than a caretaker administration, but it was more than balanced by a lifetime of conscientious public service.

Further Reading

Ball, Stuart, ed. *The Conservative Party since 1945*. New York: Manchester University Press, 1998.

Francis, Martin. "Tears, Tantrums, and Bared Teeth: The Emotional Economy of Three Conservative Prime Ministers, 1951–1963." *Journal of British Studies* 41 (July 2002): 354–388.

Hennessy, Peter. *The PM: The Office and Its Holders since 1945*. New York: St. Martin's Press, 2001.

Home of the Hirsel, Alec Douglas-Home, Baron. *The Way the Wind Blows: An Autobiography*. New York: New York Times Book Co., 1976.

Lomas, Charles W. "Sir Alec Douglas-Home: Case Study in Rhetorical Failure." *Quarterly Journal of Speech* 56, no. 3 (1970): 296–303.

Thorpe, D. R. *Alec Douglas-Home*. London: Sinclair-Stevenson, 1996.

Duarte, José Napoleón (1925–1990) *president of El Salvador*

José Napoleón Duarte Fuentes was born in San Salvador, El Salvador, on November 23, 1925, the son of an affluent tailor. After receiving a strict Catholic education, he attended the University of Notre Dame in the United States and obtained his degree in civil engineering four years later. Back home, Duarte entered the family business and did not became politically active until 1960. That year the dictatorship of Colonel José María Lemus was overthrown by a leftist clique, a move prompting Duarte, with other middle-class adherents fearful of communism, to seek a political alternative. That year he helped found the Partido Democrática Cristiano (PDC), the Christian Democratic Party, which was moderately conservative yet beholden to the social teachings of the Catholic Church. In 1964 he was elected mayor of San Salvador and distinguished himself by erecting street lights in the poorer districts and forcing the rich to pay retroactive taxes for city services. Though denounced by right-wing elements as a communist, Duarte was reelected mayor in 1966 and 1968. By 1972 he felt ready to try for the presidency and headed the Unión Nacional Opositora (UNO), National Opposition Union. This coalition comprised the PDC and two small leftist parties. Initial election results suggested that Duarte handily defeated his conservative opponent, Arturo Armando Molina, but the military stopped counting ballots and declared their candidate victorious. Duarte subsequently backed a group of reform-minded officers whose coup attempt against the government failed, and he was arrested, beaten, and exiled to Venezuela. He still remained head of the Christian Democrats and coordinated party affairs from abroad.

Duarte remained overseas for seven years until October 1979, when a coup by reformist officers toppled the regime of Carlos Humberto Romero. In March 1980 he was invited to join the ruling junta and did so willingly. But this move alienated many leftist PDC supporters, who deserted the party and took up arms. Duarte, moreover, was convinced that no meaningful reforms could transpire without the tacit support of military moderates. In December 1980 the junta disbanded and elected Duarte provisional president of El Salvador. He then tried pushing through badly needed land and labor reforms but was perpetually thwarted by conservatives in the Constituent Assembly. However, he won major backing from the United States as the only candidate who could both promote democracy and defuse a communist guerrilla insurgency.

Since the mid-sixties El Salvador had been racked by the Frente Farabundo Martí para la Liberacíon Nacional (FMLN), Farabundo Marti National Liberation Front, which waged a pitiless guerrilla war against the government and its supporters. In 1979 its efforts were aided and abetted by the communist regime of DANIEL ORTEGA in neighboring Nicaragua. This subversion stimulated the rise of right-wing death squads, and 70,000 civilians were killed between the two groups. Duarte nonetheless resolved to establish dialogue with the guerrillas and achieve a peaceful settlement. This gained him the ire of the Alianza Republicana Nacionalista (Arena), National Republican Alliance, of army major Roberto d'Aubuisson, who controlled the legislature and who removed Duarte from office in 1982. But Duarte, motivated by a sense of destiny, commenced a two-year campaign to win back the presidency by a popular mandate. On May 6, 1984, he defeated d'Aubuisson in El Salvador's first democratic election in 50 years. His victory did much to promote the rise of political pluralism in El Salvador but FMLN guerrillas proved intractable, and conservatives were unwilling to compromise. Worse, El Salvador was beset by a devastating earthquake in 1986 that killed thousands and threw the economy into a tailspin. Only the continued financial assistance of President RONALD REAGAN allowed Duarte to hold the country together and the guerrillas at bay.

By the time his term in office ended, Duarte had failed in his quest for peace. Both the guerrillas and the death squads were as active as ever. His own daughter was kidnapped and he had to free 100 guerrilla prisoners to gain her release. Worse, when the army forbade the guerrillas to participate in the election, they launched a costly nationwide offensive. Duarte, meanwhile, offered continuing negotiations for a settlement, but the public's attitude hardened. On March 19, 1989, Arena candidate Alfredo Cristiani defeated the PDC nominee Fidel Chávez Mena, and the conservatives took control. Duarte thus became the first Salvadoran president to peacefully surrender power to another elected civilian. Disillusioned by failure and fatally stricken by cancer, Duarte took no further part in public life and died in San Salvador on February 23, 1990. His country remained badly divided between reformist, reactionary, and revolutionary factions until 1992 but the multiparty system he pioneered survives until the present day.

Further Reading

Duarte, Jose N. *My Story.* New York: Putnam, 1986.
Garcia, Jose Z. "Democratic Consolidation in El Salvador." *Current History* 87, no. 533 (1988): 421–424, 437–438.

Landau, Saul. *The Guerrilla Wars of Central America: Nicaragua, El Salvador, and Guatemala.* New York: St. Martin's Press, 1993.

Langevia, Mark S. "Christian Democratic Administrations Confront the Central American Caldron." Unpublished master's thesis, University of Arizona, 1989.

Mahoney, James. *The Legacies of Liberalism: Path Dependency and Political Regimes in Central America.* Baltimore: Johns Hopkins University Press, 2001.

Webre, Stephen. *José Napoleon Duarte and the Christian Democratic Party in Salvadorian Politics, 1960–1972.* Baton Rouge: Louisiana State University Press, 1979.

Dubček, Alexander (1921–1992) *first secretary of the Communist Party of Czechoslovakia*

Alexander Dubček was born in Uhrovec, Slovakia, on November 27, 1921, the son of a carpenter. His parents, both devoted communists, relocated to the Soviet Union where Dubček was educated. He returned to Czechoslovakia just as the Nazis annexed the Czech region, leaving Slovakia as a puppet ally. Dubček spent most of World War II working in a German-run munitions factory, although in 1944 he joined the Slovakian resistance and was wounded twice. In 1948 a Communist coup overthrew the democratic government of newly reunited Czechoslovakia, and Dubček, a lifelong party member, began ascending the hierarchy. After serving as a party official in Bratislava he was sent to Moscow and attended the Communist Party school in 1955, graduating three years later with honors. This accelerated his political prospects, and by 1962 he served on the party's central committee. At that time Czechoslovakia was torn by dissension over the government's ineffective response to national stagnation. When First Secretary Antonin Novotny, a hard-line, doctrinaire Stalinist, refused to implement the economic liberalization schemes of Premier NIKITA KHRUSHCHEV, protests sprang up around the nation. Slovaks were particularly incensed that he openly favored Czechs at their expense. In 1967 Dubček broke ranks with the communist hierarchy and denounced Novotny in the Central Committee, a move that endeared him to fellow Slovaks. Consequently when Novotny was ousted from the party in January 1968, Dubček became first secretary to succeed him. His appointment surprised many since, despite a lengthy career, he was little known outside of Slovakia.

In practice Dubček proved a loyal communist but a dedicated reformer. He sensed a need for dramatic change to save the system, and began espousing what he called "socialism with a human face." His new Action Program, proffered in April 1968, entailed granting free speech, rights of assembly, freedom of the press, and multiparty democracy—all under the aegis of the Communist Party. His reforming impulse was widely welcomed by intellectuals, who began pushing him toward even greater liberalization. The resulting political flowering has passed into history as the Prague Spring, and it appeared that Czechoslovakia was about to cast off its communist chains peacefully.

Dubček's reforms proved popular at home but they greatly alarmed the leaders of other Warsaw Pact nations, who feared a groundswell in their own countries. Nor did Premier LEONID BREZHNEV look kindly upon such revisionism, which he considered a threat to socialism—and Soviet control. Moscow authorities sent Dubček a series of veiled warnings and ordered him to rejoin the fold, but he refused. Curiously, at no time did Czechoslovakia's leadership threaten to leave the Warsaw Pact or denounce communism. Instead, Dubček pleaded with communist superiors to upgrade socialism and make it compatible with basic human freedoms. Dubček received his response in August 1968, when the Soviets orchestrated a massive invasion of Czechoslovakia with troops from Russia, Poland, Hungary, and East Germany. Dubček was taken prisoner and hauled back to Moscow for "consultations." He then signed a formal renunciation of all reform efforts. Dubček was allowed to return home safely, but the Soviets began engineering steps to remove him. In 1969 he resigned as first secretary and was replaced by hardliner GUSTÁV HUSÁK. Dubček briefly served as ambassador to Turkey before being recalled and permanently assigned work as a forest warden.

Dubček remained an official nonentity until 1989 when he publicly lauded reform efforts undertaken by Russian premier MIKHAIL GORBACHEV. Once Soviet troops were withdrawn from Czechoslovakia, the communist regime crumbled under the onslaught of the so-called Velvet Revolution. Poet Václav Havel became prime minister, and he helped arrange for Dubček to serve as president of the new National Assembly. Thirty years after the ill-fated Prague Spring, Dubček's reforms finally became a reality. He was hailed as a freedom fighter, winning the Andrei Sakharov Prize for Human Rights in 1992. Dubček continued in government until November 7, 1992, when he died from injuries received in a car crash. He remains a national hero to the Slovak people and symbolic of their quest for freedom and independence.

Further Reading

Dubček, Alexander. *Dubček Speaks.* New York: I. B. Tauris, 1990.

———. *Hope Dies Last: The Autobiography of Alexander Dubček.* London: HarperCollins, 1993.

Eyal, Gil. *The Origins of Postcommunist Elites: from Prague Spring to the Breakup of Czechoslovakia.* Minneapolis: University of Minnesota Press, 2003.

Hetnal, Adam A. "An Idealist and a True Believer in Spite of Everything: The Return of Alexander Dubček from Obscurity to Prominence." *Ukrainian Quarterly* 46, no. 4 (1990): 428–434.

Shawcross, William. *Dubček.* London: Hogarth Press, 1990.

William, Kieran. *The Prague Spring and Its Aftermath: Czechoslovak Politics, 1968–1970.* New York: Cambridge University Press, 1997.

Duvalier, François (1907–1971) *president of Haiti*

François Duvalier was born in Port-au-Prince, Haiti, on April 14, 1907, the son of a schoolteacher. He passed through the Haitian National University Medical School in 1934, specializing in rural medicine. While attending, Duvalier embraced Le Group de Griots, a circle of writers advocating voodoo (*vodou*) as an expression of African culture and spirituality. After graduating he worked many years among the island's poor majority and acquired considerable popularity. In 1946 he enhanced his reputation by figuring prominently in the U.S.-sponsored campaign to control malaria and other tropical diseases. Three years later Duvalier was made director of public health by President Dumarsais Estimé, with a subsequent appointment as secretary of labor. However, Estimé was removed in 1950 by Paul Magloire, head of the Haitian National Guard. Duvalier consequently lost his office and retired into the interior to practice medicine. While in seclusion he also clandestinely worked

for the overthrow of Magloire, which was accomplished in December 1956. Haiti then underwent political instability as six governments arose and collapsed over the next 10 months. At this juncture Duvalier presented himself as a candidate for the presidency and campaigned on the twin themes of black nationalism and social reform. He also steered clear of political endorsements and sought military backing instead. Duvalier consequently won in a rigged election and was inaugurated on October 22, 1957.

Haiti was long the Western Hemisphere's poorest nation, and much was expected of Duvalier's administration. However, for 14 years he governed the islands like a personal fiefdom, for his own enrichment. There were two fundamental aspects to Duvalier's control. The first was creation of a personal militia, the Tontons Macoutes (Bogeymen), an organization of thugs who operated above the law and were responsible only to Duvalier. Wearing dark hoods and striking late at night, they abducted, tortured, and killed all enemies of the regime, real or imagined. The second aspect of Duvalier's power was more intangible, but in the minds of his countrymen, very real. A practitioner of voodoo, he presented himself as the living embodiment of Haiti's spirit and openly claimed to possess supernatural powers. To many of his illiterate and superstitious countrymen, this afforded him another level of control while stoking the fires of his megalomania. Between 30,000 and 60,000 people were ultimately killed by Duvalier's security forces, with thousands more terrorized into submission. Nonetheless he always referred to himself as "Papa Doc" and was convinced he acted in the best interests of fellow Haitians.

As head of state Duvalier evinced no fixed political precepts beyond acquiring and retaining power. He thus ruled through a combination of intimidation, corruption, and patronage. To secure American support he adopted an anticommunist stance, which brought him millions of dollars until President JOHN F. KENNEDY broke diplomatic relations in 1961. Duvalier's black nationalism incurred the anger of President JUAN BOSCH of the neighboring Dominican Republic, who nearly mounted an invasion to depose him. He also harassed the Catholic Church, appointed his own bishops and clergy, and suffered excommunication by the pope. In 1961 Duvalier dissolved the National Assembly and held fraudulent elections to procure a rubber-stamp legislature amenable to his will. In 1964 a new constitution was likewise passed, making Duvalier "president for life." His 14-year reign was the longest in Haitian history and the most stable, but also the most repressive. Mismanagement of the economy and growing diplomatic isolation depressed the gross national product, until Haiti's was the lowest in the Western Hemisphere. But Duvalier's power remained unchallenged. "Papa Doc" died in Port-au-Prince on April 21, 1971, and was succeeded by his son, the equally nefarious JEAN-CLAUDE DUVALIER, or "Baby Doc."

Further Reading

Abbott, Elizabeth. *Haiti: The Duvaliers and Their Legacy.* New York: Simon and Schuster, 1988.

Diederich, Bernard, and Al Burt. *Papa Doc: Haiti and Its Dictator.* Maplewood, N.J.: Waterfront Press, 1991.

Ferguson, James. *Papa Doc, Baby Doc: Haiti and the Duvaliers.* Cambridge, Mass.: B. Blackwell, 1989.

Mackenzie, George W. "Voodoo as a Source of Political Control in Haiti, 1959–1971." *Michigan Journal of Political Science* 11 (winter 1989): 88–96.

McAlister, Elizabeth A. *Rara! Vodou, Power, and Performance in Haiti and Its Diaspora.* Berkeley: University of California Press, 2002.

Weinstein, Brian, and Aaron Segal. *Haiti: The Failure of Politics.* New York: Praeger, 1992.

Duvalier, Jean-Claude (1951–) *president of Haiti*

Jean-Claude Duvalier was born somewhere in the Haitian countryside on July 3, 1951, the son of rural doctor FRANÇOIS DUVALIER. His father, formerly the minister of labor, had been deposed by a coup and remained in hiding. But in 1957 he became president of Haiti and, as Papa Doc, ruled the country with an iron fist for 14 years. During this time the younger Duvalier lived in the lap of luxury, attended public school, and briefly studied law at the national university. His father managed to alter the national constitution prior to dying in April 1971 and appointed his son to succeed him as "president for life." Thus, aged but 19 years, "Baby Doc" Duvalier became the world's youngest head of state.

Unlike his father, who ran a tyrannical regime based upon terror and superstition, the younger Duvalier appeared less interested in power than money. He slowly unraveled the regime of terror instituted by the dreaded Tontons Macoutes and placed security in the hands of a regular army unit, the Leopard Battalion. He also eased press restrictions, permitted a degree of criticism, and also tolerated the formation of political parties. In this relaxed atmosphere the international community hoped that Haiti would rejoin the community of nations. Duvalier also attempted to upgrade Haitian primary schools and invested widely in education. And, when he evinced the same anti-communism as his father, President JIMMY CARTER resumed American financial assistance that had been terminated in 1961. This was followed by an influx of investment from foreign corporations, eager to avail themselves of low labor costs. It seemed like a promising enough beginning for the young administration, especially since Haiti suffered from a 90 percent illiteracy rate and grinding poverty.

The true nature of Baby Doc's regime manifested itself by 1978 after several attempted invasions from Florida by Haitian expatriates, who were rounded up and summarily executed. To forestall newspaper criticism, press restrictions were again imposed. Corruption at the highest levels was also rampant, and friends of the Duvalier family routinely embezzled millions of dollars from foreign investments. Duvalier himself seemed totally above the fray, contentedly riding around the island in expensive sports cars or sailing on his yachts. In December 1979, as if to underscore the fact that things had more or less returned to normal in Haiti, the island's first human rights rally was broken up by thugs.

Papa Doc had ruled Haiti by aligning himself with the largely dark-skinned poor and middle classes against the light-skinned commercial elites. Baby Doc, however, was beholden to no such allegiances, and he began drawing nearer to the mulattos for their money and influence. In 1980 he cemented his alliance by marrying Michelle Bennet, daughter of a leading businessman, in a ceremony estimated to cost $3 million—the most expensive wedding on record. His wife proved as accomplished a kleptomaniac as he was, maintaining an opulent lifestyle while the bulk of Haitians suffered. The island's plummeting economy led to a wave of refugees on Florida's beaches. The administration of President RONALD REAGAN, tired of rounding up aliens, cut off financial aid. The turning point in this comic opera affair was not reached until November 1985 when thugs murdered four schoolgirls. Large demonstrations spontaneously arose across the island, clamoring for change. When Baby Doc felt he could no longer control the situation he was flown from Haiti to France on an obliging American military transport. The 30-year reign of the Duvalier family, which occasioned such poverty and oppression to the Haitian people, had reached its ignominious end.

Prior to leaving, Duvalier looted the treasury and arrived in France with a fortune estimated at $200 million. The new Haitian government sued for the return of all expropriated funds while the ex-president and his family maintained their luxurious exile. By 1994 the seizure of money by the courts, coupled with a divorce and fiscal mismanagement, reduced Duvalier to poverty. He currently owns a small house in Vallauris, France, and lives in obscurity.

Further Reading

Abbott, Elizabeth. *Haiti: The Duvaliers and Their Legacy.* New York: Simon and Schuster, 1991.

Ferguson, James. *Papa Doc. Baby Doc: Haiti and the Duvaliers.* Cambridge, Mass.: B. Blackwell, 1989.

Martin, Ian. "Haiti: International Force and National Compromise." *Journal of Latin American Studies* 31 (October 1991): 711–734.

Matibag, Eugenio. *Haitian-Dominican Counterpoint: Nation, State, and Race in Hispaniola.* New York: Palgrave, 2002.

Trovillot, Michel-Rolph. *Haiti: State against Nation: The Origins of Duvalierism.* New York: Monthly Review Press, 1989.

Weinstein, Brian, and Aaron Segal. *Haiti: The Failure of Politics.* New York: Praeger, 1992.

E

Echeverría, Luis (1922–) *president of Mexico*

Luis Echeverría Álvarez was born in Mexico City, Mexico, on January 17, 1922, and received his law degree through the National Autonomous University in 1945. Like all individuals intent on pursuing politics, he joined the ranks of the ruling Partido Revolucionario Institucional (PRI). An able administrator, Echeverría rose swiftly through the ranks, and in 1957 he was appointed to the party's Central Executive Committee. Here he gained the confidence of GUSTAVO DÍAZ ORDAZ and in 1964 joined his presidential cabinet as government secretary. Echeverría thus became responsible for state security matters during a turbulent period in Mexico's history. Student and peasant unrest culminated in numerous demonstrations just prior to the Mexico City Olympic Games in 1968. Echeverría, apparently with President Díaz's consent, ordered in troops to subdue the protesters, and several hundred were killed in a bloody confrontation. Despite harsh criticism for his handling of events he received the party nod to succeed Díaz in 1969 and, like all PRI candidates, was overwhelmingly elected to office in 1970.

Once empowered, Echeverría contrasted markedly with his conservative forebear. In fact, he conducted the most left-wing administration since LÁZARO CÁRDENAS in the 1940s. His sympathies were especially pronounced in economic policy, where he deemphasized industrialization and reintroduced agrarian reform and land redistribution. The government purchased various business holdings and kept them at full employment regardless of inefficiency. Echeverría also went on a massive borrowing binge that increased the national debt and drove up interest rates. If through such expedients he was trying to make amends with students and progressive elements in Mexican society he was sadly mistaken, for protests continued. Mexican society was further rocked by the incursion of armed guerrillas and some high-profile kidnappings. As in 1968, Echeverría proved intolerant of dissent and he unloosed the military against the protesters. The uprisings were eventually crushed with brutality, and stability was restored. However, he incurred additional criticism for his rough handling of student demonstrations in June 1971 when hundreds of student and left-wing agitators died at the hands of paramilitaries. The president's sympathy for the left had distinct limitations.

In foreign policy Echeverría tried making his mark by demonstrating solidarity with socialist regimes around the world. He was particularly cordial with Chile's president, SALVADOR ALLENDE, and following the coup of 1973 he welcomed Allende's widow and hundreds of Chilean refugees. He also agitated for Communist China's admission to the United Nations and repeatedly denounced the U.S. economic blockade of Fidel Castro's Cuba. Understandably, his none-too-veiled criticism of the United States led to a chill in relations between the two neighbors. But Echeverría's friendly embrace of nationalism in developing countries could not overcome a rapidly deteriorating economy at home. As inflation and unemployment continued shrinking the gross national product, he gained the dubious distinction of devaluing the peso twice in two months. Significantly, by the time Echeverría left office in 1977 the Mexican economy, previously robust, teetered on the edge of collapse. He especially stirred resentment from the large business community, which began questioning their traditional alliance with PRI for the first time. Echeverría was succeeded in office by JOSÉ LÓPEZ PORTILLO, who spent his entire tenure cleaning up the mess he inherited. Thereafter the office of the presidency was indelibly weakened in the eyes of the public.

Echeverría, free from power, entertained hopes that he would be nominated as the next United Nations secretary general, but his sponsorship of Third World causes came to nothing. Instead he was appointed ambassador to Australia by López Portillo and then returned home as director of a private international studies institute. In 1995 Echeverría broke with established political norms by publicly criticizing the presidency of Carlos Salinas Gortari. However, in July 2002 the 80-year-old former executive appeared before a special prosecutor and was questioned about his role in the massacres of student protesters in 1968 and 1971. The investigation was ordered by President Vicente Fox in an attempt to have PRI atone for human rights abuses in the pursuit of political dominance.

Further Reading

Dooney, R. E. "Mexican Economic Performance During the Echeverría Administration; Bad Luck or Poor Planning?" *Bulletin of Latin American Research* 2 (May 1983): 56–68.

Elizondo, C. "In Search of Revenue: Tax Reform in Mexico under the Administrations of Echeverría and Salinas." *Journal of Latin American Studies* 20 (February 1994): 159–190.

Hall, Linda B. "Mexican Presidentialism from Diaz to Echeverría: An Interpretative Essay." *Social Science Journal* 17 (January 1980): 41–52.

Preston, Julia. *Opening Mexico: A Country's Tumultuous Passage to Democracy.* New York: Farrar, Straus and Giroux, 2004.

Ross, Stanley R. "The Administration of Luis Echeverría." *Texas Quarterly* 16, no. 2 (1973): 45–61.

Schmidt, Samuel. *The Deterioration of the Mexican Presidency: The Years of Luis Echeverría.* Tucson: University of Arizona Press, 1999.

Eden, Anthony (first earl of Avon) (1897–1967)
prime minister of Great Britain

Robert Anthony Eden was born in Windlestone, England, on June 12, 1897, the scion of an aristocratic family. Uninspired as a student, he attended the elite boarding school at Eton before joining the army in World War I. Eden was highly decorated in combat and returned a war hero. He subsequently passed through Christ Church College, Oxford University, majoring in Oriental languages. In 1923 friends prevailed on him to run for a seat in Parliament as a Conservative, and he lost handily but won the following year. Bright, articulate, and handsome, Eden then commenced a spectacular rise through the party hierarchy. Evincing interest and expertise in foreign affairs, he was appointed undersecretary to Foreign Minister Austen Chamberlain, and by 1935 Prime Minister STANLEY BALDWIN elevated him to minister for League of Nations affairs. Months later he became England's youngest-ever foreign affairs minister in the cabinet of NEVILLE CHAMBERLAIN. In this capacity he witnessed a world sliding toward war, with mounting aggression from Japan in Asia, Italy in Africa, and Germany in Europe. Eden was dispatched on several important missions abroad, despite his youth, and personally conferred with Italian dictator BENITO MUSSOLINI. He also initially supported Chamberlain's policy of appeasing ADOLF HITLER but resigned in 1938 when the prime minister conducted foreign affairs without consulting him.

World War II erupted in September 1939 and Eden rejoined the Chamberlain administration as secretary for dominion affairs. However, once WINSTON CHURCHILL assumed office in May 1940, his career received a resounding boost when he became foreign secretary a second time. Churchill, a harsh and irritable taskmaster, relied explicitly on Eden's good judgment, and the two made a formidable pair. Eden proved particularly farsighted in illustrating that JOSEPH STALIN's Red Army was essential to victory in Europe and that close cooperation with the Soviet Union was therefore essential. Eden was subsequently appalled by the extent of Stalin's influence in Eastern Europe after the war. He was nonetheless viewed as Churchill's potential successor when the Labour Party stormed back to power in August 1945. Eden then served as deputy leader of the opposition after Churchill. His notorious appetite for hard work greatly taxed both his health and his marriage, and he was divorced in 1950.

When Churchill's Conservatives returned to power in 1951, Eden followed him into office as deputy prime minister and foreign secretary for the third time. He served for three years and became de facto national leader while Churchill was recovering from two strokes. Eden performed capably as always and helped the newly organized North Atlantic Treaty Organization organize itself in a more rational fashion. He helped in resolving an oil dispute between Great Britain and Iranian leader MOHAMMAD MOSSADEGH and provided encouragement for France's decision to depart from Indochina. When Churchill resigned from public life in 1955, Eden fulfilled his lifelong ambition by occupying No. 10 Downing Street. He offered the public tax cuts as a campaign issue, and on April 6, 1956, became the only prime minister to actually gain seats in Parliament while in office. That year he also sought to reduce international tensions by hosting a state visit by Soviet premier NIKITA KHRUSHCHEV.

Despite his reputation as a consummate diplomat, Eden's performance was slowly being undermined by poor health, which seriously affected his judgment. In October 1956 Egyptian president GAMAL ABDEL NASSER confiscated the Suez Canal Company in which England and France shared controlling interest. Within days Eden overreacted to this display of Arab nationalism by ordering troops to seize the canal with help from France and Israel. The Suez crisis sparked world condemnation and nearly split the Commonwealth apart. It also damaged relations with Arab countries for over a decade. The problem was resolved only when American president DWIGHT D. EISENHOWER pressured England and France to withdraw their forces. The entire episode was a political disaster that cost Eden his credibility. Rather than face a storm of political invective, he resigned from office on January 9, 1957, citing poor health. He was replaced by HAROLD MACMILLAN.

Eden neither sought nor held political office again. He retired to his family estate and in 1961 was made earl of Avon by Queen Elizabeth II. Eden died in Alvediston, Wiltshire, on January 14, 1967, the first prime minister of the 20th century cognizant that Great Britain was no longer a world power.

Further Reading

Dutton, David. *Anthony Eden: A Life and Reputation.* New York: Arnold, 1997.

Eden, Anthony. *Facing the Dictators: The Memoirs of Anthony Eden, Earl of Avon.* Boston: Houghton, Mifflin, 1962.

Kelly, Saul, and Anthony Gorst, eds. *Whitehall and the Suez Crisis.* Portland, Ore.: Frank Cass, 2000.

Lawrence, Alan, and Peter Dodd. *Anthony Eden, 1897–1967: A Bibliography.* Westport, Conn.: Greenwood Press, 1995.

Mallet, Robert. "Fascist Foreign Policy and Official Italian Views of Anthony Eden in the 1930s." *Historical Journal* 43 (March 2000): 157–188.

Pearson, Jonathan. *Sir Anthony Eden and the Suez Crisis: Reluctant Gamble.* New York: Palgrave, 2002.

Thorpe, D. R. *Eden: The Life and Times of Anthony Eden, First Earl of Avon.* London: Chatto and Windus, 2003.

Woolner, David B. "The Frustrated Idealists: Cordell Hull, Anthony Eden, and the Search for Anglo-American cooperation, 1933–1938." Unpublished Ph.D. diss., McGill University, 1997.

Young, John W. "Whitehall and the Suez Crisis: Conclusions." *Contemporary British History* 13, no. 2 (1999): 221–231.

Eisenhower, Dwight D. (1890–1969) *president of the United States*

Dwight David Eisenhower was born in Denison, Texas, on October 14, 1890, the son of Mennonite pacifist parents. They were duly upset in 1911 when he was accepted into the U.S. Military Academy, West Point, from which he received a lieutenant's commission in 1915. He spent World War I stateside commanding a tank training school and establishing a reputation for cordiality and efficiency. These traits served him well in 1933 when he became secretary to army chief of staff General Douglas MacArthur and accompanied him to the Philippines. He returned home in 1940, and the following year gained national attention through brilliant handling of troops during the famous 1941 Louisiana war games. When the United States entered

World War II in December 1941, Eisenhower was serving as assistant to chief of staff General George C. Marshall. Marshall, a good judge of leadership, then appointed Eisenhower commander in chief of the Allied war effort in Europe, over the heads of 300 more senior leaders. It proved an unenviable position, for he had to contend with such strong personalities as WINSTON CHURCHILL and CHARLES DE GAULLE. But in this capacity Eisenhower devised and implemented successful Allied strategies that drove the Germans from North Africa in 1942. After conquering Sicily and southern Italy in 1943 he returned to London to plan a massive cross-channel invasion of Europe. On June 6, 1944, American, British, and Canadian forces splashed ashore at Normandy, took the Germans by surprise, and liberated Paris the following August. He then effectively countered the surprise German offensive in December 1944 and concluded the European phase of World War II by May 1945. Eisenhower was never highly regarded as a combat commander but he was probably the finest coalition leader in military history. His tact, willingness to listen to others, and steely determination greatly facilitated victory in the field.

Eisenhower returned home a national war hero in 1946, and he was lobbied by both the Democratic and Republican Parties as a presidential candidate. He remained disinterested in politics and functioned for several years as president of Columbia University, until President HARRY S. TRUMAN tapped him to serve as head of the newly created North Atlantic Treaty Organization (NATO) in 1950. Two years later he ran for the presidency as a Republican with vice presidential candidate RICHARD M. NIXON. Ike, as he was popularly known, cashed in on his enormous national popularity and handily defeated Democrat Adlai Stevenson. He came to power as the cold war confrontation with the Soviet Union was at its height. Previously, he had threatened to use nuclear weapons if JOSEPH STALIN and MAO ZEDONG did not agree to end hostilities in Korea, and an armistice was signed in June 1953. However, following the defeat of French forces in Indochina in 1954 Eisenhower refused to commit American forces to the Asian mainland. Instead, he gave economic and military aid to President NGO DINH DIEM of South Vietnam. In 1956 Egyptian president GAMAL ABDEL NASSER nationalized the Suez Canal, which prompted British, French, and Israeli intervention. Eisenhower leaned heavily upon British prime minister ANTHONY EDEN, and the

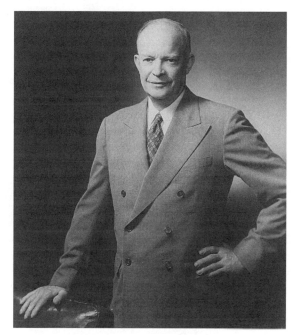

Dwight D. Eisenhower *(Library of Congress)*

coalition forces soon departed. In 1958 American marines landed in Lebanon to shore up the regime of President CAMILLE CHAMOUN. He then promulgated the "Eisenhower Doctrine," whereby American troops would be committed to any Middle Eastern nation threatened by communism. To shore up defenses in Southeast Asia he sponsored the South East Asia Treaty Organization (SEATO) in 1954, again to deter Soviet- or Chinese-inspired aggression. In 1957 his "Atoms for Peace" program induced the United Nations to establish the International Atomic Energy Agency.

Eisenhower was readily reelected over Stevenson again in 1956, but he had continually less success dealing with Soviet premier NIKITA KHRUSHCHEV. Eisenhower managed to reduce overall military spending by placing greater emphasis on nuclear deterrence and scaling back conventional forces. He did not intervene when Russian forces crushed a Hungarian uprising in 1956 but did allow clandestine overflights of the Soviet Union with new U-2 spy planes. One was shot down in May 1960, and Eisenhower tacitly admitted to illegal activities. This revelation caused Khrushchev to storm out of a 1960 Paris peace summit. Closer to home, in 1958 Eisenhower cut off military assistance to Cuban dictator FULGENCIO BATISTA, who was subsequently overthrown by guerrillas under Fidel Castro. Once Castro fell firmly into a Soviet orbit Eisenhower ended diplomatic relations in 1959 and imposed a trade embargo. Both policies remain in place to this day.

At home Eisenhower presided over a nation at peace and enjoying unprecedented prosperity. For this reason he remained somewhat detached from domestic policy and advanced no bold social agendas. In fact, having correctly gauged that the programs of President FRANKLIN D. ROOSEVELT were quite popular, he left them intact and even expanded Social Security benefits. But he became directly involved in the emerging civil rights struggle as of 1954 when the Supreme Court declared segregation in public schools unconstitutional. Eisenhower himself never strongly subscribed to the notion of integration, but he concluded it was inevitable and chose not to be an obstacle. In 1957 he committed federal troops to enforce the integration of schools in Little Rock, Arkansas, and supported creation of the Civil Rights Commission and the Department of Health, Education and Welfare. By the time Eisenhower left office in 1961, replaced by Democrat JOHN F. KENNEDY, he was one of the most popular figures in America. In his farewell address to the nation he cautioned his countrymen against the emerging "military-industrial complex" that wielded inordinate influence in the conduct of national affairs.

Eisenhower retired to a farm in Gettysburg, Pennsylvania, to write his memoirs and died there on March 28, 1969. Since then Ike has come to personify American prosperity in the 1950s, replete with rock and roll, cars with fins, and a contented middle class. His calm assurance, refusal to engage in military adventurism, and willingness to enforce social reforms render him one of the most effective chief executives in United States history.

Further Reading

Abbott, Philip. "Eisenhower, King Utopus, and the Fifties Decade in America." *Presidential Studies Quarterly* 32 (March 2002): 7–29.

Eisenhower, Dwight D. *The White House Years,* 2 vols. Garden City, N.Y.: Doubleday, 1963–65.

Geelhoud, E. Bruce. *Eisenhower, Macmillan, and Allied Unity, 1957–1961.* New York: Palgrave Macmillan, 2002.

Harting, William D. "Eisenhower's Warning: The Military-Industrial Complex Forty Years Later." *World Policy Journal* 18 (spring 2001): 39–44.

Kinnard, Douglas. *Eisenhower: Soldier-Statesman of the American Century.* Washington, D.C.: Brassey's, 2002.

Tal, David. "Eisenhower's Disarmament Dilemma: From Chance for Peace to Open Skies Proposal." *Diplomacy and Statecraft* 12 (June 2001): 175–196.

Wicker, Tom. *Dwight D. Eisenhower.* New York: Times Books, 2002.

Erhard, Ludwig (1897–1977) *chancellor of Germany*

Ludwig Erhard was born in Furth, Bavaria, on February 4, 1897. After distinguished service in the First World War he attended the University of Frankfurt to study economics and sociology. He received his doctorate and subsequently taught economics at the Nuremberg Business School from 1928 until 1942. Erhard was dismissed from his position for refusing to join the Nazi Party, whereupon he served as an economic consultant. Germany was gutted by World War II, and the western two-thirds of the country were occupied by British, French, and American forces. Erhard, untainted by a Nazi past, was consequently tapped by Allied authorities to assist in the massive rebuilding effort. He became economics minister for Bavaria in late 1945, impressed his superiors, and advanced as part of the occupation government's economic council. Here Erhard espoused pristine neoliberal policies and called for removal of price controls and a large tax cut to stimulate growth. However, he also sought creation of a "social market economy," in which the benefits of growth would be shared by all citizens. In 1947 Erhard prevailed upon General Lucius D. Clay, military governor of the U.S. zone, to reform the currency system, privatize state-owned enterprises, and eliminate all price controls. This was accomplished by August of 1948, when a new currency, the deutsche mark, was introduced while tax rates shrank from 85 percent to 18 percent.

Nobody exactly knew what to expect from the war-ravaged nation, but the results were impressive. Amazingly, within months the national economy totally rebounded, with food and consumer goods appearing on store shelves for the first time in years. Because workers were no longer required to forage for food, absenteeism from factories fell and production increased commensurately. Erhard's predictions for economic growth exceeded all expectations, and in 1949, when the new Federal Republic of Germany (or West Germany) was created, he became economics minister under Chancellor KONRAD ADENAUER. Erhard, nominally apolitical, was required to join Adenauer's Christian Democratic Union (CDU) and did so obligingly. Over the next decade Germany's economic miracle was in full play. It created a measure of prosperity that exceeded prewar levels, rendering it the strongest economy in Western Europe. Erhard received full recognition for his role in the postwar boom, and he became a popular national figure. Therefore, when Adenauer stepped down as chancellor in 1963, the portly, cigar-smoking Erhard, aptly symbolizing the new German prosperity, was elected to succeed him.

Erhard, not a politician by training or inclination, was uncomfortable as chancellor. However, he determined to cement the new German democracy to an American orbit because it was the only nation that could ensure European security. This put him on a collision course with Adenauer, who sought a "European" solution to security through closer ties with France. Erhard scoffed at embracing CHARLES DE GAULLE and, with his foreign minister, Gerhard Schroeder, he sought closer ties with American president LYNDON B. JOHNSON. He thus evinced support for American involvement in Vietnam and stood solidly in the ranks of the North Atlantic Treaty Organization (NATO) as a bulwark against Soviet communism. But Erhard proved pragmatic in his dealings with Eastern Europe, and at one point he tendered normalized relations to most nations of the Warsaw Pact. The offer fell through when he failed to extend recognition to WALTER ULBRICHT's communist-controlled East Germany. His biggest diplomatic accomplishment came with recognizing the Jewish state of Israel. His unease with national politics notwithstanding, the public resoundingly approved of his leadership, and in 1965 the conservatives handily defeated the Social Democrats under WILLY BRANDT.

Curiously Erhard lost his office in a row over economic policy. By 1966 Europe was seized by a mild recession, and the chancellor wanted to raise taxes slightly to ensure sustained growth. This caused the Christian Social Union (CSU) to bolt the coalition and it fell. Erhard was then replaced by KURT KIESINGER and withdrew from public life. He continued on as an elder

statesman until his death on May 5, 1977, revered as the architect of Germany's postwar miracle.

Further Reading

Erhard, Ludwig. *The Economics of Success.* Princeton, N.J.: Van Nostrand, 1963.

———. *Germany's Comeback in the World Market.* Westport, Conn.: Greenwood Press, 1976.

Grafin von Kageneck, Aglaia S. G. "Ludwig Erhard and European Integration, 1954–1958: Economic Principles Versus Political Goals." Unpublished master's thesis, Oxford University, 1999.

McAllister, James. *No Exit: America and the German Problem, 1943–1954.* Ithaca, N.Y.: Cornell University Press, 2002.

Tooze, J. Adam. *Statistics and the German State, 1900–1945: The Making of Modern Economic Knowledge.* New York: Cambridge University Press, 2001.

Van Hook, James C. "Rebuilding Germany: The Creation of a Social Market Economy, 1945–1957." Unpublished Ph.D. diss., University of Virginia, 1999.

Schlect, O. "Erhard's legacy: What Elements of the Social Market Economy Will Be Taken into the Next Century?" *Deutschland* 2 (April 1997): 14–17.

Erlander, Tage (1901–1985) *prime minister of Sweden*

Tage Erlander Fritiof was born in Ransater, Sweden, on June 13, 1901, the son of a schoolteacher. He graduated from Lund University in 1928 and acquired a degree in social science. Being from a lower-middle-class background, Erlander was attracted by the Social Democratic Party and in 1930 he gained election to the Lund city council. He soon came to the attention of local party leaders—principally because he was 6 feet 4 inches in height, outgoing, and gregarious. They encouraged him to seek a seat in the Riksdag (parliament) in 1933, which he accomplished. However, Erlander maintained a strong academic bent in his public life, and from 1932 to 1938 he also served as coeditor of a major encyclopedia. But his chief calling remained politics. He held a number of ministerial positions in the administration of Gustav Moller, and in 1944 joined a wartime coalition government as minister without portfolio. Moller, a leading architect of the nascent Swedish welfare state, indelibly altered Erlander's views on governance. When the Social Democrats resumed control of the government in 1945, Erlander became minister of ecclesiastical affairs, entrusted with educational reform. He was lauded by the governments of Denmark and Norway for clandestinely assisting refugees during the Nazi occupation.

Erlander came to national prominence in 1946 following the sudden death of Prime Minister Per Albin Hansson. He was elevated by party officials as a transition to the new generation of national leaders, despite the fact that Erlander was openly viewed as too young, too inexperienced, and too little known to succeed. The bookish new prime minister was hardly an inspiring or charismatic figure, but he possessed a common touch and loved mingling with the public. In fact, Erlander's greatest asset was his ability to summon strong-willed public figures from the unions, industry, and banking to his estate at Harpsund and wring consensus out of them on social policy. His successful tenure in office for the next 23 years, the longest in Swedish political history, is mute testimony to what it popularly known as "Harpsund democracy."

As a Social Democrat Erlander was ideologically committed to expanding the benefits of the welfare state to all segments of society. He deemed this approach the "strong society." He did so gradually, and over the next two decades established the most generous social system in the West. Foremost on his agenda were old-age pension reforms, a government-sponsored retirement pension program, modernization of the education system, and conduct of a generous foreign aid program. Of special interest to Erlander were the 1967 constitutional reforms replacing the bicameral legislature with a unilateral one. Moreover, this new body offered proportional representation for all parties receiving more than 4 percent of the popular vote, allowing the smallest political voices in Sweden to be heard. Over the next two decades, the Social Democrats largely controlled the legislature through clear majorities, but on occasion Erlander formed coalition governments with the Agrarian Party (now Center Party). As a rule he accepted votes from the small but vocal Communist Party only if no conditions were attached.

In terms of foreign policy Erlander was a clear-eyed realist. He distrusted the Soviet Union and was determined to maintain Swedish neutrality through a sizable military establishment. He felt so pressing a need for deterrence that in 1948 he halted progress on universal medical insurance to shore up Swedish defenses. Erlander also strongly embraced the new United Nations and the notion of collective security, along with the peaceful resolution of conflict. Moreover, despite his emphasis on building socialism, he repeatedly identified Sweden as one of the Western democracies and spoke out against Soviet activities when necessary. When Erlander retired from office in 1969, he concluded a spectacularly productive chapter in Sweden's political history and was replaced by his secretary, SVEN OLOF PALME. To the end of his life he remained active in politics and was especially fond of public gatherings and meeting with young people. Erlander died in Huddinge, Sweden, on June 21, 1985, a leading exponent of social welfare politics.

Further Reading

Aunesluoma, Juhana. *Britain, Sweden, and the Cold War, 1945–54: Understanding Neutrality.* New York: Palgrave Macmillan, 2003.

Malmborg, Mikael. *Neutrality and State Building in Sweden.* New York: Palgrave, 2001.

Ruin, Olaf. *Tage Erlander: Serving the Welfare State, 1946–1969.* Pittsburgh: University of Pittsburgh Press, 1990.

Sweason, Peter. *Capitalists Against Markets: The Making of Labor Markets and Welfare States in the United States and Sweden.* New York: Oxford University Press, 2002.

Tilton, Timothy A. *The Political Theory of Swedish Social Democracy: Through the Welfare State to Socialism.* New York: Oxford University Press, 1990.

Whyman, Philip. *Sweden and the 'Third Way': A Macroeconomic Evaluation.* Burlington, Vt.: Ashgate, 2003.

Ershad, Hussein Mohammad (1930–)

president of Bangladesh

Hussein Mohammad Ershad was born in Rangpur, North Bengal, on February 1, 1930, into an upper-class family. In 1947 British India was partitioned in the creation of Muslim-dominated Pakistan, which was itself subdivided into East Pakistan and West Pakistan, separated from each other by 1,000 miles. Ershad graduated from Dhaka University in 1950 and joined the newly created Pakistani army. Intelligent and well educated, he passed rapidly through the hierarchy and was serving in West Pakistan when East Pakistan declared its independence in 1971. Assisted by India's INDIRA GANDHI, East Pakistan won its freedom and was renamed Bangladesh. Following two years imprisonment Ershad was repatriated to his homeland to resume his military career. In 1975 ruling general Sheik MUJIBUR RAHMAN was assassinated by junior officers and succeeded by another military figure, General ZIAUR RAHMAN. Rahman promoted the youthful Ershad to chief of staff of the army due to his apparent indifference to politics. However, when Rahman was himself assassinated on May 31, 1981, Ershad defeated the coup attempt by force. He threw his support behind Abdul Sattar, a sitting judge and member of the ruling Bangladesh National Party (BNP), to be president. Sattar went on to win a landslide victory and was installed as the new chief executive, while Ershad, having seemingly embraced constitutional law, became a national hero.

Everything changed on March 24, 1982. Sattar was suddenly and bloodlessly overthrown by Ershad on the grounds of poor health. The chief of staff then declared himself president, dissolved parliament, declared martial law, and arrested several high-ranking cabinet ministers for corruption. He then founded the Jatiya Dal Party and ran for president in 1986 to seek political legitimization. When the opposition Awami Party under Khaleda Zia (widow of General Ziaur Rahman) was easily defeated, Ershad acquired the requisite mandate. He embarked on a scheme in 1987 to consolidate power by decentralizing all civil and judicial administration, and sponsored a constitutional amendment formalizing the military's role in government. When mass demonstrations erupted in April 1988, he did a sudden about-face and vetoed the bill. Ershad further ingratiated himself with voters by suspending martial law and promising the electorate major social and economic reforms.

Ershad ruled over Bangladesh with little difficulty until 1988, when the parliamentary elections were declared fraudulent and boycotted by opposition parties. This feat compromised Ershad's political legitimacy at home and abroad, and he experienced increasing pressure from the United States, a major source of financial assistance, to restore democratic institutions. Ershad adopted his usual pretense of upholding constitutional law, and in October 1990 he was reelected president. However, once the Awami League and other parties protested what they considered a rigged election, he reimposed martial law. Feeling that the end of his presidency neared, Ershad next secured a pledge of parliamentary immunity before repealing martial law in November. He then resigned from office to be replaced by Khaleda Zia, the nation's first woman executive. She voided his immunity from prosecution. Ershad was then summarily arrested, charged with corruption, and brought to trial. Found guilty, he served five years in prison before a judge reduced his sentence. He was released in 1995. The following year he was elected to parliament as head of the Jatiya Dal Party and served in a coalition government until 1998. Thereafter he was repeatedly charged with various offensives, briefly jailed, but never brought to trial.

When Zia returned to power in 2001 Ershad had left the country for England, ostensibly to seek medical treatment. His checkered past caught up with him again in February 2002, when he was summoned before a district court in Dhaka, charged with murdering the general who overthrew General Ziaur Rahman. The 72-year-old former executive flew home and appeared in court as ordered, denying all charges and dismissing speculation that he was retiring from politics. He anticipated that his Jatiya Dal Party would participate in upcoming elections and serve a constructive purpose in government.

Further Reading

Haider, Zagul. "Role of the Military in the Politics of Bangladesh: Mujib, Zia, and Ershad Regimes." *Journal of South Asian and Middle Eastern Studies* 22, no. 3 (1999): 57–82.

Maniruzzaman, Talukder. "The Fall of the Military Dictator: 1991 Elections and the Prospect of Civilian Rule in Bangladesh." *Pacific Affairs* 65 (summer 1992): 203–225.

Moten, A. Rashid. "Practices of Personal Rule: H. M. Ershad in Bangladesh." *Asian Thought and Society* 15, no. 44 (1990): 276–294.

Riyaja, Ali. *God Willing: The Politics of Islamism in Bangladesh.* Lanham, Md.: Rowman & Littlefield, 2004.

Ziring, Lawrence. *Bangladesh from Mujib to Ershad: An Interpretative Study.* New York: Oxford University Press, 1993.

Eshkol, Levi (1895–1969) *prime minister of Israel*

Levi Eshkol was born in Oratovo, Ukraine, in the Russian Empire, on October 25, 1895, and raised in a strict Jewish household. From his parents he absorbed the Zionist belief that Jews around the world were obliged to immigrate to Palestine and reinstitute the ancient state of Israel. Eshkol was educated locally and joined a Zionist organization for teenagers before arriving in Palestine in 1914. There he served as an agricultural laborer and acquired considerable expertise on the subject of irrigation and water control. In 1918 he joined the Jewish Legion and fought alongside British units against the Turks in World War I. After that he became completely immersed in his Zionist activities, founding a kibbutz (collective farm), joining the Histadrut (General Federation of Labor) in 1920, and venturing to Vienna to secure arms for the defense of Jewish settlements. By 1930 Eshkol was a driving force behind creation of the Labor (Mapai) Party and had applied himself to the study of economics and accounting. In 1933, following the rise of the Nazis, Eshkol visited Germany repeatedly to organize immigration and transfer funds to Palestine to establish settlement projects. As the decade wore on, Arab resentment against Jewish immigration led to constant attacks, which in turn led to creation of the Jewish Haganah or defense force. Eshkol joined as accounting officer and arms procurement expert. The Israeli war for independence was finally declared in 1948, and Eshkol served as deputy defense minister under DAVID BEN-GURION. In this capacity he founded Israel's nascent ordnance and arms industry—including, with American assistance, its own nuclear stockpile.

Eshkol played an active role in helping to organize and consolidate the new Jewish state. In 1949 he assumed control of the new Land Settlement Department, which found homes for a flood of European immigrants, and two years later he was elected to the Knesset (legislature). Ben-Gurion, a close associate, quickly made him minister of agriculture and development in October 1951. The following year he advanced to the important post of minister of finance and helped arrange reparation payments to Israel from the new West German government. He wisely redirected this funding into the development of industry and creation of a national merchant marine. Eshkol subsequently represented Israel at various meetings of the World Bank and International Monetary Fund.

When Ben-Gurion resigned from office in June 1963, Eshkol was tapped by the Labor Party to succeed him as Israel's third prime minister and defense minister. Soon after, a rift developed between the two friends over the Lavon Affair, a bungled spy caper in Egypt that was kept hidden from the government. Ben-Gurion demanded that Eshkol reopen the case, and when he refused, the former broke from Labor and formed his own party, the Rafi. He then challenged Eshkol for political dominance, but Labor won a surprisingly easy victory in November 1965. In June 1964, Eshkol had become the first Israeli head of state to visit the United States, when he conferred with American president LYNDON B. JOHNSON. He also conducted high-profile meetings with France's CHARLES DE GAULLE and England's HAROLD WILSON. Most important symbolically, Eshkol also presided over negotiations that restored diplomatic relations with West Germany in 1965, two decades after the genocidal Holocaust against the Jews had ended.

In May 1967 tensions between Israel and Egypt were escalating, and President GAMAL ABDEL NASSER ordered the United Nations to remove peace-keeping forces between the two antagonists. He also instituted a naval blockade of the Gulf of Elat, which further exacerbated the drift toward war. At this critical juncture, many in Labor were demanding the resignation of Eshkol, seen as a low-key, pacific figure, in favor of the more dynamic Moshe Dayan of Rafi. Surprisingly, Eshkol stood his ground and refused to resign, although he did tender Dayan the portfolio of defense minister. The ensuing 1967 Arab-Israeli War was a stunning success for Eshkol, who now led a government of national unity that encompassed a variety of small parties. He died in office on February 26, 1969, little appreciated at the time but now viewed as one of Israel's most accomplished leaders.

Further Reading

Cohen, Avner. "Israeli Nuclear History: The Untold Kennedy-Eshkol Dimona Correspondence." *Journal of Israeli History* 16, no. 2 (1995): 159–194.

Edmunds, June. *The Left and Israel: Party Policy Change and Internal Democracy.* Basingstoke, England: Macmillan, 2000.

Eshkol, Levi. *The State Papers of Levi Eshkol.* New York: Funk and Wagnalls, 1969.

Oren, Michael. *Six Days of War: June 1967 and the Making of the Modern Middle East.* Oxford: Oxford University Press, 2002.

Prittie, Terrence. *Eshkol of Israel: The Man and the Nation.* New York: Pitman Corp., 1969.

Shlaim, Avi. *The Iron Wall: Israel and the Arabs.* New York: W. W. Norton, 2000.

Evren, Kenan (1918–) *president of Turkey*

Kenan Evren was born in Alasehir, Turkey, in January 1918, the son of a civil servant. At that time the Ottoman Empire to which Turkey belonged experienced tremendous nationalistic pressures and broke into several independent countries. Turkey's new leader, KEMAL ATATÜRK, defied Muslim traditions by creating a secularized Western-style republic. Evren joined the military as a means of social mobility and he passed through the Turkish War College in 1942. Adept as an officer, he accepted a succession of important military commands and assignments at home and during the Korean War. His good conduct and performance culminated in promotion to general in 1964 and chief of the general staff in 1974. Turkey was then experiencing another stage of political and economic instability, and over the next 20 years the military deposed administrations they viewed as inept. They also mandated constitutional changes to restore order before allowing civilian rule. However, by 1980 the situation had grown critical with the onset of terrorism and political extremism. Bombings and assassinations were commonplace, the gross national product declined, and the country seemed on the verge of economic and social collapse. Again the Turkish military, viewing itself as the steward of Atatürk's republic, stood ready to intervene and save the nation.

On September 12, 1980, Evren ordered a bloodless coup that toppled the government, and installed a National Security Council staffed by high-ranking military officers. They then suspended the constitution, dissolved the legislature, banned political parties, and arrested hundreds of known extremists. The council then appointed Admiral Bulent Ulusu as prime minister and announced plans for drawing up a new constitution. The coup had its intended effect, for the rash of killings stopped and civil order prevailed. "We will not leave our present duty," Evren declared, "until we clean up all the country. As good soldiers we always keep our word." In light of the conditions that preceded it, the coup was hailed in the West as a means of restoring law and order. President RONALD REAGAN lifted an arms embargo against Turkey that had been in place since the invasion of Cyprus in 1974. On November 7, 1982, the new constitution appeared before the public in a referendum and was approved by 90 percent of votes cast. Evren now became president of Turkey with enhanced powers, entitled to a seven-year term.

With security restored, Evren's greatest priority was reviving the moribund economy. He applied austerity measures judiciously, and within two years of his coup, exports had doubled and the balance of trade improved significantly. Tax cuts and increased privatization led to annual growth rates of 4.4 percent, higher than in any European country. But despite this impressive performance Turkey still suffered from allegations of human rights abuses. The terror network had so ingrained itself in the social fabric that upward of 100,000 suspects were arrested—and some tortured—before the violence stopped. But Evren disarmed critics of his human rights policy by reminding them of conditions before he assumed control. "Then the most elementary human right—the right to live and work—was violated," he insisted. By April 1982, the government felt secure enough to lift its ban on political activity, although political parties required government approval before being allowed to form. The military then put its official weight behind Turgut Sunalp, a retired general, and his National Democratic Party. But when elections were held on November 5, 1983, the winner proved to be Turgut Ozal of the Motherland Party. Evren calmly accepted the outcome and allowed Ozal to become prime minister. "All freedoms provided by democracy are for those who believe in it," he announced upon retiring.

Evren continued on as president of Turkey for six more years, retaining a final say in defense, foreign policy, and security matters. All told he wielded a moderating, stabilizing influence on the conduct of Turkish affairs and fully cooperated with his prime minister. He finally stepped down from office on November 7, 1989, and retired to private life. The general remains a respected national figure for having restored Turkish democracy and respected the will of the people.

Further Reading

Abramowitz, Morton. *Turkey's Transformation and American Policy.* New York: Zed Books, 2000.

Heper, Metin, and Aylin Guney. "The Military and Democracy in the Third Turkish Republic." *Armed Forces and Society* 22 (summer 1996): 619–642.

Kinzer, Stephen. *Crescent and Star: Turkey between Two Worlds.* New York: Farrar, Straus and Giroux, 2001.

Liel, Alon. *Turkey in the Middle East: Oil, Islam, and Politics.* Boulder, Colo.: Lynne Rienner Publishers, 2001.

Ozbudun, Ergun. *Contemporary Turkish Politics: Challenges to Democratic Consolidation.* Boulder, Colo.: Lynne Rienner Publishers, 2000.

Rubin, Barry M., and Kemal Kirisci. *Turkey in World Politics: An Emerging Multi-Regional Power.* Boulder, Colo.: Lynne Rienner Publishers, 2001.

F

Faisal (1905–1975) *king of Saudi Arabia*

Faisal ibn Abdul Aziz ibn Abd al-Rahman al-Saud was born in Riyadh, Arabia, in 1905, a son of ABD AL-AZIZ IBN SAUD, founder of Saudi Arabia. His mother, who belonged to a family of prominent Islamic scholars, died in his infancy and young Faisal was raised by an uncle, a noted cleric. This upbringing profoundly influenced his life, for thereafter he was very pious and beholden to Islamic precepts and law. In 1926 he was appointed viceroy of Hejaz, a holding containing the holy city of Mecca, and in 1930 he gained appointment as foreign minister. Faisal held that appointment for the next 45 years, making him the longest-serving foreign minister of the 20th century. He quickly distinguished himself through tact and intelligence and was the first member of the family dispatched abroad to foreign countries. He visited the United States in 1945 and represented Saudi Arabia during inauguration of the new United Nations in San Francisco.

Shortly before King ibn Saud died in 1953, he appointed his eldest son, Saud, to succeed him. Faisal became crown prince to his brother in line of succession, while still functioning as foreign minister. However, Saud proved something of a wastrel, running up extravagant bills while pursuing a life of luxury. His lack of spending discipline nearly bankrupted the oil-rich kingdom by 1958, and Faisal was asked to make

the country solvent again. A council of family princes transferred authority to the crown prince, who completely rectified the situation within two years. Saud proved jealous of his success, and in 1960 he stripped Faisal of his authority. The Middle East was entering a period of profound destabilization with the onset of Arab nationalism and the encroachment of communism, and Saud was viewed as unfit to lead. On November 3, 1964, a family council prevailed upon him to abdicate, and the quiet, methodical Faisal became king in his place.

His deeply conservative and religious nature notwithstanding, Faisal was astute enough to realize that if Saudi Arabia were to survive it had to modernize both its institutions and its outlook. He therefore abolished slavery, expanded public education, and permitted girls to attend school for the first time. He also instituted sweeping social reforms such as subsidized housing, free college education, and comprehensive medical coverage to all inhabitants of the kingdom. Faisal's adroit social policies thus wedded modernity to traditional notions of Islam and transformed Saudi Arabia into the most stable Arab nation of the Middle East.

Faisal was equally artful in navigating the treacherous waters of foreign policy. He completely rejected the socialist-inspired Pan-Arabism of GAMAL ABDEL NASSER, and relations between the two countries chilled. When the king of neighboring Yemen was overthrown by a communist-inspired coup backed by Egyptian troops, Faisal intervened with financial and military assistance, and a stalemate ensued. But Saudi Arabia assumed a more mainstream Arab stance in its dealings with Israel. The disastrous outcome of the 1967 Arab-Israeli War, where Egyptian and Syrian armies were completely defeated, enabled Nasser and Faisal to achieve a rapprochement. Thereafter the king made Saudi Arabia the most influential nation in the Arab world, providing generous financial aid to regimes supporting a hard line against the Jewish state. Paradoxically he had to constantly balance this stance against friendly relations with the United States—Israel's staunchest ally. Faisal realized that only America could curtail Soviet policies in the world theater, and he maintained cordial relations. The 1973 Arab-Israeli War, another disastrous encounter, necessitated an oil embargo against the West and he convinced the Organization of Petroleum Exporting Countries (OPEC) to impose a boycott against the United States under President RICHARD M. NIXON. Within months, however, he quickly reinstated close ties with his chief benefactor. Faisal thus remained leader of the pro-Western bloc of Arab states, determined to thwart Soviet penetration of the Middle East. The United States greatly appreciated his support and friendship.

For all his far-sighted policies, the conservative nature of Faisal's regime alienated younger, more impatient members of the royal family. On March 25, 1975, the king was assassinated by a nephew, Prince Faisal ibn Musad. His reign marked an era in Saudi history when the reputation and influence of the desert kingdom was at its zenith. Faisal, more than any individual, was the architect of the modern Saudi state.

Further Reading

Aburish, Said K. *The Rise, Corruption, and Coming Fall of the House of Saud.* New York: St. Martin's Press, 1995.

Kechichian, Joseph A. *Succession in Saudi Arabia.* New York: Palgrave, 2001.

Osaimi, Mohammed al-. "The Persuasion of King Faisal Ibn Abd-al-Aziz: A Case Study in Contemporary Islamic Oratory." Unpublished Ph.D. diss., Indiana University, 1990.

Schwartz, Stephen. *The Two Faces of Islam: The House of Saud from Tradition to Terror.* New York: Doubleday, 2003.

King Faisal *(Library of Congress)*

Teitelbaum, Joshua. *Holier Than Thou: Saudi Arabia's Islamic Opposition.* Washington, D.C.: Washington Institute for Near East Policy, 2000.

Vassiliev, Alexei. *The History of Saudi Arabia.* New York: New York University Press, 2000.

Faisal I (1885–1933) *king of Iraq*

Faisal ibn Husayn was born near Mecca, Arabia, on May 20, 1885, the son of Husayn ibn Ali, a noted member of the Hashemite family. As such he could claim direct ancestry to the prophet Muhammad through the prophet's daughter Fatima. Faisal was raised by Bedouins, learning the art of diplomacy and guile in tribal affairs. He subsequently accompanied his father to Constantinople, capital of the Ottoman Empire, where the family was closely watched for their pro-Arabic sentiments. In 1908 they returned to Hejaz, site of the most holy shrines in Islam, where Husayn ruled as emir. Faisal, who had matured into an intelligent and forceful young man, gained election to the Ottoman parliament in 1913 from Jiddah. There he openly espoused Arabic interests but, after visiting Damascus, he also expanded contacts with underground Arab organizations plotting their independence from the empire. After World War I commenced in 1914 the elder Husayn contacted the British in nearby Egypt about a possible revolt against the Turks. Support proved forthcoming, and the "Arab revolt" was launched on June 10, 1916. Faisal took up arms in concert with Colonel Thomas E. Lawrence ("of Arabia"), and his mounted soldiers cut railways and captured the town of Aqaba. The British then encouraged him to enter Damascus in October 1918 and rally the population against the Ottomans. Faisal obliged and also set forth his own political agenda to become king of Syria.

In time Faisal's Pan-Arabist ambitions ran afoul of Western colonialism. France had been guaranteed possession of Syria and Lebanon through the Treaty of Paris, and viewed Faisal as little more than a British tool. The French were determined to remove him from power. Faisal had pressed his case for an independent kingdom with British backing, and had signed an accord with CHAIM WEIZMANN for the legal emigration of Jews from Europe to the Middle East. In March 1920 Faisal had the Syrian national congress proclaim him king, but four months later the French military forcibly evicted him from the throne. Faisal ended up in exile in London, where he conferred with the new colonial secretary, WINSTON CHURCHILL. The British, having acquired nearby Mesopotamia and Iraq, were eager to maintain the oil assets located there and needed a pliable figurehead to "reign but not govern." Faisal readily acquiesced to the scheme, and in August 1921 he was proclaimed king of Iraq by a plebiscite of local notables.

Unfortunately for British intentions, Faisal proved no puppet. Using consummate skill as a diplomat and a negotiator, he brought together diverse and mutually hostile elements such as Sunni and Shia Muslims, and Christian Assyrians, to present a united front against the British. His Pan-Arabic sentiments were favorably received and, in fact, Faisal acted as a brake upon the more nationalistic segments of the urban elite. A delicate balancing act ensued whereby the king enhanced his position domestically, while grudgingly consenting to British designs on the region. He sponsored a new constitution in 1925 and was increasingly able to assert himself diplomatically. By 1930 he forced his British overseers to conclude a new treaty granting de facto Iraqi independence, in exchange for a monopoly on oil production. In 1932 Iraq became the first modern Arab state to join the League of Nations.

Faisal never forgot the humiliation he endured in Syria, and he continued various machinations to combine Jordan, Lebanon, and Iraq into a major Arab power. When his brother Ali had been ousted from Hejaz by the Saudis, Faisal began touting him as the next king of Syria. His ambitions were again opposed by both France and Britain, who declined to promote Arab unity and independence at their own expense. Faisal nonetheless instituted a monarchist party in Syria, expecting to have his brother declared king. But this ultimately failed, as other leaders had emerged since 1920. In fact, Faisal never really overcame his reputation as an outsider in Iraq and, while his rule seemed undisputed, his popularity was questionable. In 1932 Faisal's failing health required him to visit Europe for medical treatment. In his absence, fighting broke out between Muslims and Christians, and he called for an end to hostilities. Religious restraint in this highly divisive atmosphere caused his popularity to plummet further, and many began calling for his resignation. Faisal died suddenly in Geneva on September 7, 1933, his dream for a unified Arab power unrealized. However, he is still regarded as the first regional nationalist, an astute politician, and a pristine Arabic patriot.

Further Reading

Erskine, Beatrice. *King Faisal of Iraq: An Authorized and Authentic Study.* London: Hutchinson, 1933.

Haj, Samira. *The Making of Iraq, 1900–1963: Capital, Power, and Ideology.* Albany: State University of New York Press, 1997.

Masalha, N. "Faisal's Pan-Arabism, 1921–1933." *Middle Eastern Studies* 27 (October 1991): 679–694.

Silverfarb, Daniel. *Britain's Informal Empire in the Middle East: A Case Study of Iraq, 1929–1941.* New York: Oxford University Press, 1986.

Simon, Reeva S. *Iraq between the Two World Wars: The Creation and Implementation of a Nationalist Ideology.* New York: Columbia University Press, 1986.

Tripp, Charles. *A History of Iraq.* New York: Cambridge University Press, 2002.

Farouk (1920–1965) *king of Egypt*

Farouk was born in Cairo, Egypt, on February 11, 1920, a son of Sultan (later King) Fuad I and part of the Alawid dynasty that had ruled since 1805. Egypt was partially occupied by Great Britain to preserve the strategic Suez Canal for its own use. Farouk was educated locally and sent to study at the Royal Military College in England. Before his graduation, his father died in April 1936, and he returned home. He was still too young to reign when appointed king on May 6, 1936, so power briefly passed into the hands of a regency council. A year later the young monarch assumed full control amid popular enthusiasm. He was handsome, urbane, and apparently willing to tilt Egypt against its British overseers. However, national politics were dominated by a decade-old struggle between the traditional throne and the liberal, modernizing Wafd Party. Farouk determined to continue this struggle even to the point of encouraging rival parties, like the violent Muslim Brotherhood, to take root.

World War II proved a defining time for Farouk's reign. Egypt was officially neutral, as Great Britain battled Germany and Italy for control of North Africa, but the young king and several of his ministers were pro-Axis in outlook. This caused consternation in British military circles, for loss of the Suez would prove disastrous to the empire. By the fall of 1941 Axis forces under the celebrated general Erwin Rommel were hurtling across the desert toward Egypt. The British, to shore up domestic support in the kingdom, requested Farouk to appoint the pro-British Wafd leader Mustafa Nahhas Pasha as prime minister. The king concurred initially but insisted that Nahhas preside over a coalition government of several parties. Nahhas then insisted upon a purely Wafd Party government or he would not take office. With Rommel fast approaching, the gravity of the situation required Britain to expedite matters by force. On February 4, 1942, a battalion of British tanks surrounded the royal palace and a deputation of officers approached the king. They then demanded that he either accept Nahhas as prime minister of a Wafd-dominated government or abdicate. The king reluctantly submitted to this coercion, which made him appear weak and was widely resented by the public. After the victory of El Alamein in the fall of 1942, the British were less willing to interfere in Egyptian affairs but the damage had been done. In 1944 Farouk summarily dismissed Nahhas, although, after his humiliation, he himself took less interest in public matters. In fact, the monarch acquired notoriety as a dilettante for gambling, womanizing, and drug use. His penchant for profligacy when the majority of citizens lived in abject poverty generated greater resentment against him.

The transition to the postwar period proved difficult for Egypt and other Arab countries, for their polity was strained by the twin forces of nationalism and Islamic fundamentalism. In 1948 the United Nations created the Jewish state of Israel on land previously occupied by Palestinians. Farouk, against the advice of his own generals, then committed the Egyptian army to battle, not so much to fight the Jews as to prevent the Hashemite kingdom of Jordan from expanding its territory. The result was a humiliating defeat for Arab forces, and many young officers held the king responsible. The Wafd Party formed a majority government in October 1951 and they promptly abrogated the Anglo-Egyptian treaty binding them as allies. It proved a popular move, but Farouk dismissed all Wafd ministers from the government. Civil unrest prevailed until July 22, 1952, when a group of military conspirators under Colonel GAMAL ABDEL NASSER forced Farouk to abdicate. He did so grudgingly and was allowed to leave the country with a small fortune in gold ingots. In August 1953 the monarchy was abolished and the Republic of Egypt established in its place.

Farouk lived a life of luxurious exile in Rome, where he frequented many of the most notorious nightclubs. He died there suddenly on March 18, 1965, little mourned by his countrymen. His remains nonetheless were transported home and interred in Egyptian soil.

Further Reading

Cooper, Artemis. *Cairo in the War.* London: Hamilton, 1989.

Cromer, Evelyn B. *Modern Egypt.* New York: Routledge, 2000.

Gershoni, Israel, and James P. Jankowski. *Redefining the Egyptian Nation, 1930–1945.* New York: Cambridge University Press, 2002.

Sabit, Adel M. *A King Betrayed: The Ill-fated Reign of Farouk of Egypt.* New York: Quartet, 1989.

Stadiem, William. *Too Rich: The High Life and Tragic Death of King Farouk.* New York: Carroll and Graf, 1991.

Thornhill, Michael T. "Britain and the Collapse of Egypt's Constitutional Order, 1950–52." *Diplomacy and Statecraft* 13 (March 2002): 121–152.

Figueiredo, João (1918–1999) *president of Brazil*

João Batista de Oliveira Figueiredo was born in Rio de Janeiro on January 15, 1918, the son of an army officer. His father, Colonel Euclides de Oliveira Figueiredo, was one of several who opposed the dictatorship of GETÚLIO VARGAS by force in 1932. Thus a traditional respect for constitutional government was established in this military family. The younger Figueiredo followed in his father's footsteps by attending the Escola Militar do Realengo, a military academy from which he graduated in 1937. Assigned to the cavalry, Figueiredo demonstrated talent as an officer and passed rapidly up through the ranks. By 1961 he was a staff member of the general staff school, and three years later, had risen to colonel. Figueiredo supported the military coup that brought down the unstable leftist regime of João Goulart in 1964, ushering in two decades of military rule. During this interval Figueiredo served with the newly created Servico Nacional de Informacoes (SNI), an intelligence gathering agency, until 1974 when President ERNESTO GEISEL appointed him director with the rank of general. Geisel, himself a former general, was impressed by the short, taciturn Figueiredo and began grooming him as a successor. By the time he was appointed president in March 1979, he was still relatively unknown to most Brazilians.

The new executive's first priority after taking power was addressing the ongoing economic crisis. Brazil was saddled with a $50 billion national deficit that drove inflation to 110 percent annually. This lowered productivity and repressed the wages of the poor and working classes. Unrelieved misery led to massive strikes countrywide, which were roughly handled by the military to maintain order. But Figueiredo finessed the crisis with discipline and precision. At his behest the government introduced a schedule of pay increases pegged to inflation and allowed collective bargaining to resume for the first time in 15 years. Figueiredo then devalued the currency and fixed interest rates to shore up the economy. Furthermore, when hard-pressed farmers in the north began illegally seizing land, the president authorized expropriation of 47,000 acres for redistribution. His deliberate attempts to ameliorate hardships of the lower classes brought a renewed sense of stability to Brazil and paved the way for political reforms. The government also embarked on an aggressive scheme of oil exploration and construction of hydroelectric dams to support anticipated growth.

Figueiredo assumed power vowing to "make this country a democracy," and he meant it. In fact he greatly expanded the process of *abertura* (opening) begun by Geisel. By degrees, he began liberalizing press restrictions and released 4,650 political prisoners under a general amnesty. Thousands more were invited to return from exile abroad. In November 1979, Figueiredo abolished the country's two legal political organizations and allowed for multiparty pluralism. He undertook this more out of a sense of cynicism than altruism, for the general rightly believed that his opponents would dilute their vote by splintering into factions. More important, the government conscientiously improved its human rights image abroad. Military authorities previously could arrest and torture suspected extremists at leisure, but new restrictions were imposed to rein in such abuses. In 1982 Figueiredo authorized the direct election of state governors for the first time in 15 years. The public was clearly ready for greater change, and by 1984 there were massive demonstrations for restoration of Brazil's democracy. True to his word, Figueiredo stepped aside, elections were held, and JOSE SARNEY became the first civilian executive in over two decades. Figueiredo's six-year transition from military to civilian control proved startlingly successful. While in office Figueiredo consistently declared his distaste for politics and wished that someone else had been chosen for the job. He then resumed his former obscurity to pursue his only passion in life, riding horses. He died in Rio de Janeiro on December 24, 1999, highly regarded as the general who restored democracy and political freedom to Brazil.

Further Reading

Brooke, J. "Dateline Brazil: Southern Superpower." *Foreign Policy* 44 (fall 1981): 167–180.

Castro, Celso. *The Military and Politics in Brazil, 1964–2000.* Center for Brazilian Studies, University of Oxford, 2000.

Dassin, J. R. "The Brazilian Press and the Politics of Abertura." *Journal of International American Studies* 26 (August 1984): 385–414.

Gall, Norman. *In the Name of Democracy: Brazil's Presidential Succession.* Hanover, N.H.: American Universities Field Staff, 1978.

Levine, Robert M. "Brazil: Democracy without Adjectives." *Current History* 78 (February 1980): 49–52.

Serbin, Ken. *Secret Dialogues: Church-State Relations, Torture, and Social Justice in Authoritarian Brazil.* Pittsburgh, Pa.: University of Pittsburgh Press, 2000.

Figueres Ferrer, José (1906–1990) *president of Costa Rica*

José Figueres Ferrer was born in San Ramón, Costa Rica, on September 25, 1906, the son of an immigrant Spanish doctor. He was indifferently educated and arrived in the United States to study electrical engineering at the Massachusetts Institute of Technology. In 1928 Figueres dropped out and returned home, having acquainted himself with American democratic practices. That year he established a farm to grow crops and produce rope. It proved a profitable enterprise, but Figueres distinguished himself from contemporaries by providing benefits to poor working peasants. In 1942 he criticized the regime of Rafael Angel Calderón Guardia for being overly dependent upon the Communist Party and was expelled to Mexico. While in exile Figueres helped found the so-called Caribbean Legion, a group of expatriates sworn to rid Central America of military despots. He was allowed back home in 1944 and immediately agitated for greater democracy. In 1948 Congress annulled the election of Otilio Ulate Blanco in favor of Calderón's ally, Teodoro Picado Michalski. Figueres led an armed insurrection that toppled the government in six weeks. On May 8, 1948, he assumed command of the new Founding Junta of the Second Republic as provisional president.

The junta ruled for only 18 months, but under Figueres's direction, it enacted dramatic political and social reforms. First and foremost, Costa Rica abolished its army in favor of a much-reduced police force. Next Figueres nationalized banking and instituted a 10 percent tax on the rich to fill the country's coffers. Women were allowed to vote for the first time. He then held new elections for a constituent assembly to draw up a new constitution, which was adopted in 1949. Figueres resigned in November 1948 and allowed Ulate Blanco to continue on as president. However, finding the new regime too conservative, Figueres founded the Partido de Liberación Nacional (PLN), National Liberation Party, in 1953 and ran for high office. He won resoundingly, and over the next four years continued his reforming agenda. He expanded the role of government to provide basic services, health care, banking, and insurance to all citizens. He also stimulated the economy through credits, price supports, and marketing facilities. Figueres proved something of a foreign policy maverick. Staunchly anticommunist, he nonetheless publicly denounced dictators such as ANASTASIO DEBAYLE SOMOZA, RAFAEL TRUJILLO, FULGENCIO BATISTA, and MARCOS PÉREZ JIMÉNEZ. He also offered sanctuary to refugees such as RÓMULO BETANCOURT and JUAN BOSCH. Somoza became so angered by his activity that he twice supported unsuccessful invasions of Costa Rica from Nicaragua.

Figueres stepped down in 1958 and was replaced by another PLN candidate. Having previously aided Fidel Castro with weapons, he now denounced him for aligning his island with the Soviet Union. Figueres had by then emerged as an unofficial spokesman for Central America and a champion of democracy and social reform. He avidly supported President JOHN F. KENNEDY's new Alliance for Progress in 1961, but his popularity declined following revelations that he had assisted the Central Intelligence Agency throughout the region. When the PLN lost the elections in 1965, Figueres reentered the political arena as a presidential candidate in 1970. He was elected again but this time had to weather several controversies. The first was his decision to establish diplomatic recognition of the Soviet Union to open additional markets for Costa Rican exports. This brought about mass demonstrations by right-wing interests, and accusations of his being a communist sympathizer. Figueres then allowed fugitive investor Robert Vesco into the country and refused to extradite him to the United States. When Vesco invested heavily in the president's ranch industries, a highly damaging scandal surfaced. Finally, when Figueres tried engineering constitutional changes that would allow him to serve another consecutive term, they were struck down by the courts. He stepped down a second time in 1975, having prepared the nation for a new generation of PLN leaders.

Figueres, affectionately known as "Don Pepe," died in San José, Costa Rica, on June 8, 1990. He was easily the most influential national leader of Costa Rica in the 20th century and bequeathed to his country degrees of peace and stability unheard of in Central America. Costa Rica consequently enjoys the highest standard of living and freest democracy in that strife-torn region. Such happy consequences are a testament to his farsighted policies and the resolve with which he pursued them.

Further Reading

Ameringer, Charles D. *Don Pepe: A Political Biography of José Figueres of Costa Rica.* Albuquerque: University of New Mexico Press, 1978.

Longley, Kyle. *The Sparrow and the Hawk: Costa Rica and the United States during the Rise of José Figueres.* Tuscaloosa: University of Alabama Press, 1997.

Mahoney, James. *The Legacies of Liberalism: Path Dependence and Political Regimes in Central America.* Baltimore: Johns Hopkins University Press, 2001.

Thomason, Mark W. "Costa Rican-Nicaraguan Relations, 1948–1955: José Figueres versus Anastasio Somoza and Rafael Calderón." Unpublished master's thesis, New Mexico State University, 1997.

Wolfe, Jefferson L. "José Figueres and the International Aspects of the 1948 Revolution in Costa Rica." Unpublished master's thesis, Bowling Green State University, 1995.

Zarate, Juan C. *Forging Democracy: A Comparative Study of the Effects of U.S. Foreign Policy on Central American Democratization.* Lanham, Md.: University Press of America, 1994.

FitzGerald, Garrett (1926–) *prime minister of Ireland*

Garrett FitzGerald was born in Dublin, Ireland, on February 9, 1926, to a Catholic father and a Protestant mother. Both parents had been active in the 1916 Irish uprising, and in 1922 his father, Desmond FitzGerald, served as minister of external affairs in the new Irish Free State. The younger FitzGerald was educated locally and ultimately received his Ph.D. from the University College, Dublin, in 1959. He was called to the Irish bar but declined law to work as an economics lecturer. FitzGerald gradually acquired a reputation as a jovial, if rather bookish, intellectual, which set him apart from most politicians of his generation. And because his family life straddled the religious divide between Ireland and Northern Ireland, he was far more progressive on sectarian issues than his contemporaries. In 1964 he joined the moderate Fine Gael Party and won appointment to the Senad, or senate. Five years later he was elected to the Dáil (parliament) and viewed as a liberal alternative to the Conservative Party leader LIAM COSGRAVE. When Fine Gael entered into a coalition arrangement with the Labour Party in 1973,

Cosgrave became *taoiseach* (prime minister) and FitzGerald his minister of foreign affairs. Fluent in French and knowledgeable about economics, he proved spectacularly successful while representing Ireland in the European Economic Community (EEC) council, where he served six months in 1975 as its first Irish president. FitzGerald also attended the ground-breaking Sunningdale Conference between England and Ireland in December 1973, which established a power-sharing arrangement between the two Irelands. Two years later Fine Gael lost control of the government, Cosgrave stepped down as party head, and FitzGerald succeeded him. He spent considerable time revamping and modernizing the party, and his efforts crested in June 1981 when he became prime minister under a new Fine Gael/Labour coalition.

Ireland was then besieged by a balky economy, and the first FitzGerald government collapsed within months over raising taxes. However, the coalition resumed power in December 1985 with a complete majority, and FitzGerald embarked upon what he considered his "constitutional crusade." Specifically, he wanted the Republic of Ireland to drop its traditional and stridently Catholic social policies and become more pluralistic. This was essential if the Catholic south was to ever peacefully unite with the Protestant north. But he failed to stop a 1983 referendum outlawing abortion, which enjoyed strong church backing. In 1986 another referendum stripping the constitutional ban on divorce was also defeated. For all his finely honed intellect and good intentions. FitzGerald misjudged the conservative nature of his fellow Catholics.

FitzGerald's real accomplishment was in the realm of foreign affairs. In 1983 he established the New Ireland Forum to discuss high-level policies and solutions to problems impeding Irish unity. On November 15, 1985, the forum promulgated the Anglo-Irish Agreement, which FitzGerald signed with British prime minister MARGARET THATCHER. This document stipulated creation of an Anglo-Irish Conference, a secretariat through which the Irish government would negotiate its positions on Northern Ireland with its British equivalent. Cooperation between the two governments, previously problematic, now became institutionalized. It also reaffirmed the principle that change to Northern Ireland could happen only with the consent of the majority. Militant Unionists in the north bitterly denounced the agreement as a sell-out, but it laid the foundation for greater political discourse and culminated in the landmark Downing Street Declaration of 1993. FitzGerald, the product of a mixed religious environment, was eager to placate both sides to achieve lasting peace.

In January 1987 the Fine Gael/Labour coalition broke up over the issue of budget austerity, and FitzGerald stepped down both as prime minister and party leader. He resigned from Parliament in 1993 to pursue the lecturing and publishing for which he was much in demand. In 1995 FitzGerald also received the prestigious Legion d'Honneur in recognition of his service to European unity.

Further Reading

Dooge, James, ed. *Ireland in the Contemporary World: Essays in Honor of Garrett FitzGerald.* Dublin: Gill and Macmillan, 1986.

FitzGerald, Garrett. *All in a Life: An Autobiography.* New York: Gill and Macmillan, 1991.

———. *Reflections on the Irish State.* Portland, Ore.: Irish Academic Press, 2002.

Kenny, Anthony J. P. *The Road to Hillsborough: The Shaping of the Anglo-Irish Agreement.* New York: Pergamon Press, 1986.

Maye, Brian. *Fine Gael, 1923–1987: A General History with Biographical Sketches of Leading Members.* Dublin: Blackwater Press, 1993.

O'Byrnes, Stephen. *Hiding behind a Face: Fine Gael under FitzGerald.* Dublin: Gill and Macmillan, 1986.

Ford, Gerald R. (1913–   ) *president of the United States*

Gerald Rudolph Ford (originally named Leslie Lynch King, Jr.) was born in Omaha, Nebraska, on July 14, 1913. His mother divorced his father while he was a child and married Gerald R. Ford, Sr., a paint store owner; her son assumed his stepfather's name. Ford graduated from high school with honors and was admitted to the University of Michigan on a football scholarship. From there he passed through the Yale University Law School in 1941, graduating in the top third of his class. Ford then served in the U.S. Navy during World War II and was discharged in 1946 as a lieutenant commander. After returning to practice law in Grand Rapids, Michigan, he was persuaded by friends to run for Congress as a Republican in 1948 and he easily defeated the incumbent Democrat. Ford served as a U.S. representative for the next 25 years. Moreover he gained a reputation for affability and pragmatism, which made him among that body's most popular and effective members. He was known to friends and the nation simply as Jerry Ford. By 1963 he functioned as chairman of the House Republican Conference and subsequently filled the role of minority leader. Here his agenda was dominated by two divisive issues; the Great Society measures promoted by President LYNDON B. JOHNSON and the Vietnam War. Ford, staunchly conservative, basically opposed the former and supported the latter. In 1968, after the election of RICHARD M. NIXON to the White House, he served as an important spokesman for GOP initiatives in Congress. Until that time he was viewed only as a highly loyal party activist. But Ford's political fortunes took an unforeseen turn in December 1973 when Nixon tapped him to succeed Spiro T. Agnew as vice president. "I am a Ford, not a Cadillac," he modestly informed the nation.

Ford, a low-key, unpretentious, and highly trusted figure, took the office when the nation was deeply engulfed by domestic dissension. The unpopular Vietnam War still raged as Nixon came under increasing scrutiny for his role in the notorious Watergate cover-up. Ford nonetheless toured the country on his behalf, refuting partisan charges and speaking up in his defense. Political attitudes hardened, and by the summer of 1974, the House voted three articles of impeachment against the president. Ford continued on as a Nixon loyalist even while many in his own party began withdrawing support. Rather than face trial and removal by the Senate, Nixon tendered his resignation on August 9, 1974. Ford was sworn in as chief executive with little ceremony. He thus became the only vice president and president who was never elected to either post.

Ford's ascension was initially greeted with sighs of relief, and it seemed that a national malady had finally ended. But the new executive surprised the pundits on September 8, 1974 when he granted Nixon a "free and absolute pardon" to shield him from prosecution. Ford's popularity plummeted but the turmoil of Watergate fell with it. "My fellow Americans," he declared on television, "our long national nightmare is over." For the next two years Ford grappled with the final phase of the Vietnam War and a sluggish economy, neither of which concluded satisfactorily. In 1975 the Democrat controlled Congress summarily ceased all aid to the South Vietnamese regime of NGUYEN VAN THIEU, and it fell to communist aggression. In May 1975, when Cambodian Khmer Rouge forces seized the American cargo ship *Mayaguez* in international waters, he ordered U.S. military forces into action. This cost the Americans 41 dead and a like number wounded but the ship and crew were retrieved and Ford's popularity recovered. He undertook this in defiance of the newly passed War Powers Act, which imposed legislative oversight on all military actions. Ford, and all presidents since, have regarded such measures as unconstitutional and ignored them. The president enjoyed greater diplomatic success in European affairs, and in 1975 he conferred with Soviet premier LEONID BREZHNEV over a new arms reduction treaty (SALT II) and the Helsinki Accords.

Ford enjoyed less success moderating the effects of a prolonged recession and high inflation. Part of this lay with his inability to pass legislation through a hostile, Democrat controlled Congress, which advanced its own agenda. Ford countered through extensive use of his presidential veto and effectively killed 48 out of 60 bills put before him. But such political posturing did little to ameliorate the hardships of a balky economy. In 1976 Ford initially hinted that he would decline to seek reelection but changed his mind and received the Republican nomination in August. He accomplished this only after defeating a serious challenge from California governor RONALD REAGAN. Ford then campaigned against JIMMY CARTER, the Democratic nominee, who enjoyed a large lead in the polls. Despite a series of lackluster missteps Ford dramatically closed the margin by election day, losing by only 48 percent to 50 percent. This concluded his political career and he retired into private life, becoming much in demand as a speaker. Ford remains unapologetic about his pardon of Nixon, although historians regard it as the single greatest cause for his defeat.

Ford avoided the public eye until the fall of 1998, when President Bill Clinton was weathering a controversy of his own. The Republican-controlled Congress began debating articles of impeachment against him for perjury and conspiracy in the Monica Lewinsky affair. Ford, however, entreated them to tread lightly. He felt the nation would be better served if Clinton were only rebuked instead of impeached, a position shared by former president Carter. "Let it be dignified, honest, and above all, cleansing," Ford said. "The result, I believe, would be the first moment of majesty in an otherwise squalid year." Ford continues on as a respected elder statesman. In August 2000 he was briefly hospitalized for a minor stroke but has since resumed his private affairs. Ford's tenure in office may have been brief and wrought with controversy, yet he served an important purpose by restoring a sense of normalcy to his strife-torn nation.

Gerald R. Ford *(Library of Congress)*

Further Reading

Deen, Rebecca E., and Laura W. Arnold. "Veto Threats as a Policy Tool: When to Threaten? *Presidential Studies Quarterly* 32, no. 1 (2002): 30–45.

Firestone, Bernard J., and Alexej Ugrinsky, eds. *Gerald R. Ford and the Politics of Post Watergate America.* Westport, Conn.: Greenwood Press, 1993.

Ford, Gerald R. *A Time to Heal: The Autobiography of Gerald R. Ford.* Norwalk, Conn.: Eastern Press, 1987.

Greene, John R. *The Presidency of Gerald R. Ford.* Lawrence: University of Kansas Press, 1995.

Jespersen, T. Christopher. "Kissinger, Ford, and Congress: The Very Bitter End in Vietnam." *Pacific Historical Review* 71 (August 2002): 439–474.

Lee, J. Edward, and Toby Haynsworth. *Nixon, Ford, and the Abandonment of South Vietnam.* Jefferson, N.C.: McFarland, 2002.

Rozell, M. "Executive Privilege in the Ford Administration: Prudence in the Exercise of Presidential Power." *Presidential Studies Quarterly* 18 (spring 1998): 286–298.

Franco, Francisco (1892–1975) *dictator of Spain*
Francisco Franco Bahamonde was born in El Ferrol, Spain, on December 4, 1892, the son of a debauched naval administrator. Intent upon a military career, he failed to secure a posting with the Naval Academy due to cutbacks, so he passed through the Infantry Academy at Toledo instead. After graduating in 1912 Franco was deployed overseas with troops suppressing the notorious Rif rebellion in Morocco. He quickly gained a reputation for bravery and efficiency surpassing many contemporaries, and in 1923 he accepted command of the elite Spanish Foreign Legion. Franco emerged from the conflict a national hero, and in 1926 he became Europe's youngest brigadier general. He served as director of the newly created General Military Academy until 1931, when the Spanish monarchy was overthrown and a republic declared. Franco accepted a temporary demobilization, but conservatives resumed power in 1934 and restored him as a full general. He brutally crushed a strike by Asturian miners, winning plaudits from the right and condemnation from the left. When the leftist Republicans regained control in 1936, he was exiled to the Canary Islands. Competition between monarchists and republicans subsequently spilled onto the streets, and the country edged closer to civil war. Franco, who had previously avoided political alliances or military conspiracies, felt that order must be imposed to keep the country solvent. On July 18, 1936, he airlifted troops from Morocco to southern Spain and commenced marching north toward Madrid—an act precipitating the Spanish civil war. He was appointed "generalissimo" of Nationalist (monarchist) forces, and was bolstered by arms and air support provided by the fascist regimes of BENITO MUSSOLINI and ADOLF HITLER. The Republicans resisted staunchly with covert assistance from JOSEPH STALIN and the Soviet Union but were steadily pushed back. On April 1, 1939, Franco's Nationalists finally triumphed and ushered in three and a half decades of military dictatorship.

Franco ruled like a traditional Spanish caudillo (strongman) and ruthlessly rounded up communists and republicans, executing them by the thousands. World War II broke out shortly thereafter but, while sympathetic to Hitler and Mussolini, both Franco and neighboring Portuguese dictator ANTONIO SALAZAR remained studiously neutral. By 1945, however, the newly created United Nations recommended that member states withhold diplomatic relations from Spain to keep it in isolation. Franco then further alienated himself from the West in 1948 by declaring Spain a monarchy—without a monarch. He would retain control of the government until further notice. However, attitudes shifted quickly following the onset of the cold war and Franco's sterling anticommunist credentials stood him in good stead. Diplomatic relations with the rest of the world slowly resumed, and in 1953 he reached a concordance with the Vatican and a defensive pact with the United States. Spain was also accorded full UN membership as of 1955. This move finally signaled Spain's reemergence into the community of nations, although

Francisco Franco *(Library of Congress)*

membership in NATO and the European Economic Community (EEC) lay decades ahead. As foreign aid filled Spanish coffers, Franco began a slow process of liberalizing his authoritarian regime.

Franco had long been reviled as the "last fascist dictator," but his governance was more military than political in nature and difficult to quantify. As army chief he had the last word on virtually every aspect of Spanish life, including religious matters, but he gradually allowed creation of small political parties. In fact, Franco openly despised politics and politicians, and he preferred running affairs through his hand-picked ministries. They were invariably chosen in such a manner as to pit one competing interest group against another, thereby preserving his own rule. Nor was he a doctrinaire fascist in the manner of Hitler or Mussolini. Franco maintained cordial relations with the Falange (Spanish fascists) only so long as he perceived them useful. In the late 1950s he discarded them completely from government. On the positive side, Spain's new stability led to rapid economic development. During the 1950s growth rates approached 7 percent annually—faster than most of Europe. By 1960 Spanish prosperity was assured and Franco continually relaxed controls of the media, while tightening police powers. Toward the end of his reign he was publicly viewed as much less a dictator than an elderly father figure.

Franco was determined that the changes he made to Spanish politics would survive his passing, so in 1969 he appointed Juan Carlos, nephew of deposed king Alfonso XIII, as the new king. Juan Carlos took a vow to preserve the existing political order but, after Franco's death on November 20, 1975, he began dismantling the authoritarian apparatus. Curiously and perhaps appropriately, the only head of state to attend Franco's funeral was Chilean dictator AUGUSTO PINOCHET. Within a few years, Spain had evolved into a constitutional monarchy and a full-fledged democracy, replete with NATO membership and a voice in the European Union (EU). Franco today seems but a distant and unpleasant memory—although many acknowledge that the stability he bequeathed to Spain laid the foundation for its present-day success.

Further Reading

Angel Vinas, Carlos. "Franco's Request to the Third Reich for Military Assistance." *European History* 11 (May 2002): 191–213.

De Meneses, Filipe R. *Franco and the Spanish Civil War.* New York: Routledge, 2001.

Hodges, Gabrielle A. *Franco: A Concise Biography.* New York: St. Martin's Press, 2002.

Jensen, Geoffrey. *Irrational Triumph: Cultural Despair, Military Nationalism, and the Ideological Origins of Franco's Spain.* Reno: University of Nevada Press, 2002.

Lewis, Paul H. *Latin Fascist Elites: The Mussolini, Franco, and Salazar Regimes.* Westport, Conn.: Praeger, 2003.

Palomares, Cristina. *The Quest for Survival after Franco: Moderate Francoism and the Slow Journey to the Polls, 1964–1977.* Portland, Ore.: Sussex Academic Press, 2004.

Southworth, Herbert R. *Conspiracy and the Spanish Civil War: The Brainwashing of Francisco Franco.* New York: Routledge, 2001.

Franz Joseph I (1830–1916) *emperor of Austria-Hungary*

Franz Joseph was born in Vienna, capital of the Austrian Empire, on August 18, 1830, a son of Archduke Franz Charles and Princess Sophie of Bavaria. He belonged to the Hapsburg dynasty, a leading European family that had influenced political events in Europe since the 10th century. Franz Joseph underwent the strict upbringing of a Hapsburg prince and, consequently, was imbued with a sense of piety and duty that he exhibited throughout his long life. He was also fastidiously attached to the ceremony and protocol surrounding the court. Furthermore, Franz Joseph's mindset proved so traditionalist that he refrained from using modern conveniences such as automobiles, typewriters, and elevators. In 1848 Central and Eastern Europe were engulfed by democratic upheavals and the Austrian Empire, led by the mentally unbalanced Ferdinand I, failed to respond effectively. Ferdinand was persuaded by family members to abdicate, and the 18-year-old Franz Joseph became the new emperor. The new monarch reacted energetically to the crisis and personally took command of the army. Then, by allying himself with Czar Nicholas I of Russia, he successfully crushed a large revolt in Hungary. Peace was restored and the empire preserved, at which point Franz Joseph contemplated constitutional reforms to liberalize his regime. But by 1850 he had changed his mind and reinstated an absolutist, highly centralized system intended to eliminate the last vestiges of ethnic nationalism and political liberalism. Austria, in light of events elsewhere in Europe, was on the verge of becoming a political anachronism.

If by cracking down on the 13 distinct ethnic groups comprising the Austrian Empire Franz Joseph hoped to preserve his charge, he was sadly deceived. These tensions remained unresolved and even intensified throughout most of the 19th century. At best, his heavy-handed response served as the rear guard of dynastic leadership that was out of touch with emerging political realities. Worse yet, Austria experienced a disastrous series of wars: in 1859 Franz Joseph fought with Napoleon III over possession of Italy and lost. In 1866 he was maneuvered into a disastrous confrontation with militaristic Prussia under Chancellor Otto von Bismarck and was tossed out of the German Confederation. The emperor then faced increasing unrest from the non-German state of Hungary and was forced to sign the Compromise (Ausgleich) of 1867. Thereafter Hungary held equal political status with Austria and considerable autonomy, while Franz Joseph presided over a Dual Monarchy as Austrian emperor and Hungarian king. The agreement engendered considerable peace between the two leading states but stoked the fires of nationalistic resentment among Czech, Polish, and Italian subjects who were denied political equality.

To compensate for his recent defeats Franz Joseph directed imperial ambitions toward southeastern Europe, the dominion of the Slavs. Serbian resentment against Austria had risen exponentially since the annexation of Bosnia Herzegovina in 1878, which severed Serb access to the Adriatic. Events in the region became even more complicated once the cause of Pan-Slavism was championed by the Russian czar. These developments led Franz Joseph to strike up a closer relationship with his erstwhile adversary Bismarck, and in 1879 they concluded the Dual Alliance. Russia responded by forging ties of its own with France and Great Britain. By the turn of the 20th century, all of Europe was a powder keg, tightly bound by innumerable defensive agreements and awaiting the inevitable match to ignite it. Franz Joseph by that time had become increasingly reclusive after the murder of his wife in 1898, the suicide of his son in 1889, and the death of his brother Maximilian before a Mexican firing squad in 1867.

The turning point in Hapsburg fortunes occurred in Sarajevo in June 1914, when Franz Joseph's heir and nephew, Franz Ferdinand, was assassinated by a Serbian nationalist. The 84-year-old emperor then issued an ultimatum for Serbian surrender of the suspects, backed by Kaiser WILHELM II of Germany. When Russian czar NICHOLAS II came to the rescue of his Balkan ally by mobilizing against Germany, World War I erupted in full force that August. The result was the final disaster for the Hapsburg monarchy. Poorly trained and racked by ethnic dissent, Austrian field forces fared badly and were repeatedly bolstered by German manpower. A bloody stalemate ensued for the next four years while the combined forces of nationalism and military defeat chipped away at the empire's solvency. Franz Joseph did not live to witness the denouement of the kingdom he loved so much and worked 68 years to preserve. He died in Vienna on November 21, 1916, and was succeeded by Charles I, who oversaw the dismantling of the empire three years later. Franz Joseph strove harder than any individual in Hapsburg history to preserve his hereditary charge. He maintained it probably longer than any other individual could have in his position but ultimately lost to the forces of modernity.

Further Reading

Baidins Valdis, F. J. "Kaisertreue and Loyalty in the Late Hapsburg Empire." Unpublished Ph.D. diss., University of Washington, 1999.

Beller, Steven. *Francis Joseph*. White Plains, N.Y.: Longman, 1996.

Cornwall, Mark. *The Last Years of Austria-Hungary: A Multi-national Experiment in Early Twentieth-Century Europe*. Exeter, England: University of Exeter Press, 2002.

Franz Joseph I. *The Incredible Friendship: The Letters of Emperor Franz Joseph to Frau Katharina Schratt*. Albany: State University of New York Press, 1966.

Gero, Andras. *Emperor Francis Joseph: King of the Hungarians*. Wayne, N.J.: Center for Hungarian Studies and Publ., 2001.

Sked, Alan. *The Decline and Fall of the Hapsburg Empire, 1815–1918*. New York: Longman, 2001.

Unowski, Daniel L. "The Pomp and Politics of Patriotism: Imperial Celebrations in Hapsburg Austria, 1848–1916." Unpublished Ph.D. diss., Columbia University, 2000.

Fraser, Malcolm (1930–) *prime minister of Australia*

John Malcolm Fraser was born in Melbourne, Australia, on May 31, 1930, the son of a wealthy grazier (sheep rancher). He was educated locally before attending Oxford University in England, from which he received a master's degree in 1952. Two years later he was prompted by friends to run for a seat in the House of Representatives as part of the Liberal (actually conservative) Party. Defeated, he tenaciously sought out the seat in 1955 and won, becoming the government's youngest representative. Before long Fraser acquired a reputation as an able politician, though one beset by a snarling, uncompromising disposition. He continued climbing through the party ranks by holding a variety of portfolios throughout the 1960s, including army, defense, and education and science. In all these capacities Fraser handled himself well and ferociously silenced criticism with well-aimed invective of his own. As army minister he incurred a degree of national controversy by strongly supporting Australian involvement in the American-led Vietnam War. Furthermore, his decision to resign from the government of Prime Minister JOHN GORTON caused the downfall of that leader and his replacement by William McMahon. But Fraser's dogged, outspoken nature convinced many in the Liberal Party that he could lead them to victory, so in March 1975 he replaced Bill Snedden as party head. Fraser then orchestrated a carefully scripted political coup that landed him in the prime minister's office. Because the Liberals controlled the upper house or Senate, Fraser could block Labor prime minister GOUGH WHITLAM from passing budgetary legislation. This precipitated an immediate constitutional crisis. But rather than allow the impasse to continue, Governor General Sir John Kerr dismissed Whitlam as prime minister. He then appointed Fraser to lead an interim government while new elections were pending. Fraser obliged, and to everybody's surprise the Liberals swept the election and gave the new government a mandate. It was an unorthodox manner of achieving high office, but it confirmed Fraser's leadership credentials as a fearless risk taker.

Fraser assumed power in the middle of the biggest economic recession in recent Australian history, compounded by high inflation and unemployment. Previously he had campaigned against Labor for enacting big-spending social programs that were at the root of the problem, and was determined to roll them back. Accordingly Fraser, a disciple of neoliberal economics, embarked on a major program of fiscal retrenchment. Numerous government programs were either scaled back or eliminated outright, to reduce the national debt and ease inflation. He then stimulated the private sector through tax cuts, while eliminating governmental departments, imposing staff ceilings, and reducing public service tenure. He was bitterly assailed by Labor for imposing undue hardships on Australia's working class but acidly countered that "life was not meant to be easy." Fraser's hard-bitten tactics went over well with the Australian public, for in 1977 and 1980 they returned the Liberals to power.

Fraser's success at reducing the size of government inspired British prime minister MARGARET THATCHER to attempt the same. He also railed against the activities of the Soviet Union in the Indian Ocean and boycotted the 1980 Moscow Olympics after the Soviet invasion of Afghanistan. In light of his sterling conservative philosophy, he also emerged as a favored ally of American president RONALD REAGAN, and was invited several times to the White House. The Liberals finally ran out of steam in 1983 when their much-vaunted reforms only marginally improved the economic climate. Fraser called early elections that March, and Labor came roaring back to power under ROBERT HAWKE. Fraser lost control of the Liberals to Andrew Peacock, so he withdrew from politics altogether. Nonetheless his eight years in office mark him as the most successful Liberal politician since ROBERT GORDON MENZIES.

Back in private life, the gruff-speaking Fraser continued on as a presence in national politics. In 1985 Hawke nominated him to represent Australia during Commonwealth talks on South African apartheid. Fraser outspokenly inveighed against the Australian practice of removing Aboriginal children from their families, which he considered genocidal. Finally, in July 2000, he defiantly came out against Australian participation in the proposed American missile defense program. "The needs and desires of the United States do not necessarily conform with what is necessary for the security and integrity of Australia," Fraser insisted.

Further Reading
Ayers, Philip. *Malcolm Fraser: A Biography.* Richmond, Victoria: W. Heinemann, 1987.

Campbell, Andrew. "Malcolm Fraser: Political Decadent." *National Observer* no. 52 (autumn 2002): 50–64.

Fraser, Malcolm. *Common Ground: Issues That Should Bind Us and Not Divide Us.* Campbell, Victoria: Viking, 2002.

Little, Graham. *Strong Leadership: Thatcher, Reagan, and an Eminent Person.* New York: Oxford University Press, 1988.

Schneider, Russell. *War Without Blood: Malcolm Fraser in Power.* London: Angus and Robertson, 1980.

Weller, Patrick M. *Malcolm Fraser, PM: A Study on Prime Ministerial Power.* New York: Penguin Books, 1989.

Frei, Eduardo (1911–1982) *president of Chile*

Eduardo Frei Montalva was born in Santiago, Chile, on January 16, 1911, to a Swiss immigrant father and a Chilean mother. He received a Catholic upbringing, studied law at the Catholic University of Chile in 1928 and graduated with honors four years later. Frei became politically active in the Catholic youth organizations of his day, which culminated in a 1934 pilgrimage to Rome and the Congress of Catholic Youth. Here he was indelibly impressed by the social teachings of Catholic scholars like Jacques Maritain and resolved to impart these values at home. Though part of the Conservative Party, he pressed for greater attention to Chile's poor and working class, but to no avail. In 1938 Frei broke with the Conservatives and founded a new party, the National Falange, which positioned itself as a "third way" between unbridled capitalism and dictatorial socialism. By 1940 Frei's activities landed him the post of labor law professor at Catholic University, where he was president of Falange. In 1943 he gained appointment as minister of public works under President Juan Antonio Ríos, but he resigned in 1946 following a bloody crackdown on demonstrators. In 1949 he gained election to the national Senate and was reelected again in 1957. The following year Frei combined the Falange with two other parties to found the Partido Demócrata Cristiano (PDC), Christian Democratic Party. He ran for president in 1958 under its banner and finished a respectable third with 21 percent of the vote. Congressional elections two years later established the PDC as the nation's fastest-growing party, a fact confirmed in 1964 when Frei bested socialist SALVADOR ALLENDE for the presidency with 56 percent of votes cast.

Frei had campaigned on the social platform central to his party, including agrarian reform and control of inflation. Specifically he sought a fairer distribution of wealth without violence or expropriation. However, the foremost item on his agenda was "Chileanization" of national copper mining, long controlled by foreign interests. Here he nationalized 51 percent of the industry in an attempt to assert sovereignty and acquire more profits. He proffered this as a peaceful alternative to the nationalization schemes of socialists for fear of the economic backlash it would engender. This, unfortunately, proved a middling solution that pleased no one. Furthermore, Frei's good intentions appeared dangerously leftist to the nation's business and right-wing interests. And although the PDC controlled the Chamber of Deputies, the conservatives banded together to stop or dilute the more progressive parts of Frei's agenda. Consequently, only 28,000 peasants received any land through redistribution, instead of the 100,000 he proposed. The government also proved unable to stimulate the economy to reduce unemployment, and remained dogged by high inflation. Discontent over Frei's policies led to a bitter split between liberals and conservatives within the PDC, and in the 1970 elections they each fielded their own presidential candidates. The socialists under Allende were thus enabled to achieve a slight plurality and come to power.

Frei had actively campaigned against Allende, warning that a socialist regime would end in "blood and horror." Few heeded his prophetic remarks. But he was shocked when the military, under General AUGUSTO PINOCHET, violently overthrew the government in 1973. Frei expected that the military would step aside and appoint him interim leader until democracy was restored, but to his disgust Pinochet sought retention of power indefinitely. For the next 12 years he served as the junta's most vocal opponent, protected only by his international reputation. Just prior to the coup Frei had been reelected to the Senate, and in 1978 he campaigned against constitutional reforms that would have legitimized Pinochet's rule. However, his reputation was tarnished following revelations of CIA assistance and funding during his 1964 presidential campaign, which made him appear a tool of the United States. During his final years in office Frei joined a global commission on international development chaired by former West German chancellor WILLY BRANDT, which further heightened his international prestige. Frei died in Santiago on

January 22, 1982, a dedicated reformer whose efforts polarized politics and occasioned the disaster he feared most. From 1994 to 2000, his son, Eduardo Frei Ruiz-Tagle, also served as president of Chile.

Further Reading

Edwards, Thomas L. *Economic Development and Reform in Chile: Progress under Frei, 1964–1970.* East Lansing: Latin American Studies Center, Michigan State University, 1972.

Falcoff, Mark. "Eduardo Frei Montalva (1911–1982)." *Review of Politics* 44 (July 1982): 323–327.

Fleet, Michael. *The Rise and Fall of Chilean Christian Democracy.* Princeton, N.J.: Princeton University Press, 1985.

Gross, Leonard. *The Last, Best Hope; Eduardo Frei and Chilean Democracy.* New York: Random House, 1967.

Peppe, Patrick V. *The Frei Government and the Chilean Labor Market.* New York: New York University Ibero-American Language and Area Center, 1974.

Wolff-Wilhemly, Manfred von. "Chilean Foreign Policy: The Frei Government, 1964–1970." Unpublished Ph.D. diss., Princeton University, 1973.

G

Gairy, Eric (1922–1997) *prime minister of Grenada*

Eric Matthew Gairy was born in Grenville, Grenada, on February 18, 1922, into a poor family of African descent. He had few options for education or career choices because the British colonial administration was effectively controlled by a handful of white and mulatto business elites. In 1942 Gairy relocated to nearby Aruba to work in a refinery and became active in trade union organizing. Dutch authorities expelled him in 1949, and he came home to found the Grenada United Labor Party (GULP), the island's first such organization. In 1951 Great Britain granted universal suffrage to all adult Grenadians, and Gairy, a charismatic leader, parlayed his personal popularity into politics. That year GULP captured six out of eight seats on the legislative council, and Gairy called a general strike that nearly brought the island to a standstill. He was by this time the recognized leader of Grenadian labor issues. However, the following year he was suspended from the council for riotous behavior, and two years later he lost his seat altogether. When GULP made an electoral comeback a few months later Gairy was reinstated, only to be suspended again in 1955 for disruptive behavior. Two years later he was disenfranchised for violating electoral laws, although after March 1961, when GULP carried eight of 10 council seats, he became an

unofficial "adviser to the government." That year Gairy returned to office as a council member and also served as minister of finance.

As Grenada began preparing for independence from Great Britain, Gairy increased his political profile on the island, intent upon becoming its first prime minister. His reputation, unfortunately, was punctuated by charges of fiscal and ethical impropriety. He also faced increasing competition from Herbert A. Blaize of the rival Grenada National Party (GNP), who in 1962 beat back a challenge from GULP and became chief minister. When the island received associated statehood in March 1967, acquiring greater internal self-rule, Gairy fought his way back into power by capturing seven of 10 seats for the premiership. Grenada gained its political independence from Great Britain in February 1974, and Gairy became its first prime minister. As a political figure, he spoke of redistributing land to peasants, but took no action and distanced himself from socialist programs. It soon became apparent that his sole ideological concern was acquiring power and keeping it.

From 1967 to 1979, Gairy ran Grenada as a personal fiefdom. His rule grew increasingly despotic and erratic as time went by, underscored by political violence. By the early 1970s he was overwhelmingly dependent on a private army of thugs, the notorious

"Mongoose Gang," who intimidated and murdered opposition figures. Intent on cracking dissent from any quarter, Gairy restricted the right of unions to strike in 1978 and then curtailed legislative powers so that the island's assembly became powerless. His tenure was marked by severe economic decline and massive electoral fraud. At length various dissident elements, including leftists, union leaders, and church leaders, began coalescing into an underground opposition movement. They waited until March 1979 to strike, when Gairy was in New York addressing the United Nations General Assembly about flying saucers. A bloodless coup ensued, and MAURICE BISHOP of the New Jewel Movement became prime minister.

Gairy remained in exile abroad until Bishop was murdered in a military coup in 1983. President RONALD REAGAN, fearing increased communist infiltration into the Caribbean, toppled the People's Revolutionary Government by force that November. Gairy returned home and tried resuscitating his political fortunes. When GULP captured only one seat out of 15, it effectively spelled the end of his political career. He ran again for high office in 1988, claiming to be an adherent of voodoo and African religion, but was again defeated. Gairy died on Grenada on August 24, 1997, in relative obscurity. He had nonetheless been a central figure in Grenada's campaign for independence, built the island's first mass movement, and dominated the political landscape for 30 years.

Further Reading

Archer, Ewart. "Gairyism, Revolution, and Reorganization: Three Decades of Turbulence in Grenada." *Journal of Commonwealth and Comparative Politics* 23 (July 1985): 91–111.

Henfrey, Colin. "Between Populism and Leninism: The Grenadian Experience." *Latin American Perspectives* 11 (summer 1984): 15–36.

Lent, John A. "Mass Media in Grenada: Three Lives in a Decade." *Journalism Quarterly* 62, no. 4 (1985): 755–862.

Noguera, Pedro A. "Charismatic Leadership and Popular Support: A Comparison of the Leadership Styles of Eric Gairy and Maurice Bishop." *Social and Economic Studies* 44, no. 1 (1995): 1–30.

———. *The Imperatives of Power: Political Change and the Social Basis of Regime Support in Grenada from 1951–1991.* New York: P. Lang, 1997.

Wagner, Geoffrey A. *Red Calypso: The Grenadian Revolution and Its Aftermath.* Washington, D.C.: Regnery Gateway, 1988.

Galtieri, Leopoldo (1926–2003) *president of Argentina*

Leopoldo Fortunato Galtieri was born in Caseros, Argentina, on July 15, 1926, the son of Italian immigrants. He graduated from the Argentine Military Academy in 1945, specializing in military engineering. Over the next three decades, Galtieri proved himself a capable officer and repeatedly visited the United States for advanced training. He gained promotion to brigadier general in 1972 and, being politically reliable, he seemed slated for high command. Argentina was then racked by a poor economy, high inflation, and violent urban guerrilla groups. Following the death of President JUAN PERÓN in 1974, his wife, Isabel, came to power but proved ineffectual at stabilizing national affairs. In 1976 the military decided it was necessary to intervene, and they deposed Perón in favor of a junta under General JORGE VIDELA. Galtieri, meanwhile, advanced to chief of staff for operations within the army general staff. He was partially responsible for the conduct of military affairs during Argentina's "Dirty War," in which upward of 30,000 suspected guerrillas were rounded up by security forces and executed. Their bodies were never found, and they were internationally known and mourned as the "disappeared." Galtieri's complicity in the deaths of civilians has never been clearly established.

In December 1979 Galtieri rose to lieutenant general and commander in chief of the armed forces. Two years later Videla's term as president expired, and the baton passed to General Roberto Viola. However, Viola was ill and incapable of improving the economy, so on December 29, 1981, he was replaced by Galtieri, who now served as both president and commander in chief. His primary concern was reducing the nation's triple-digit inflation and rising unemployment, which threatened the military's ability to govern. Galtieri froze public salaries and reduced government expenditures to curb hyperinflation. When this failed to produce results, the public mounted large demonstrations against the continuance of military rule. Galtieri, rather than risk social disorder, sought to decisively deflect public attention away from the economy. On April 1, 1982, he ordered military and naval units to attack the British-held Falkland Islands, 300 miles off the Argentine coast. His forces quickly overcame a small British garrison, and the public reacted with wild enthusiasm.

The Falklands, or Malvinas, as they are known in Latin America, have been a hotly contested diplomatic issue between Great Britain and Argentina since 1833. The British seized them by force and colonized them over Argentinean protests. The disputed territory is basically barren, windswept, and useful only for sheep grazing, but its retention was an enormous point of pride to the contenders. Galtieri, unfortunately, badly miscalculated in thinking that the British response would be confined to diplomacy. Prime Minister MARGARET THATCHER was enraged by such overt aggression and, with solid public support, she launched a full-scale military and naval expedition in May 1982. The ensuing struggle painfully demonstrated how inadequate Argentine military preparations had been, and culminated in the capture of the capital, Port Stanley, on June 15, 1982. The British killed around 700 Argentineans, netted 15,000 prisoners, and captured tons of military equipment. This national humiliation proved so great that spontaneous demonstrations broke out demanding Galtieri's ouster. "I'm going because the army did not give me backing to continue as commander and president of the nation," he confided two days after the surrender. Galtieri was subsequently replaced by General Benito Antonio Bignone, who took the first steps toward restoring civilian rule.

Within a year public pressure forced the military to relinquish control, and in 1983 RAÚL ALFONSÍN was elected president. Galtieri, meanwhile, had been cashiered, stripped of rank, and tried by a military court for human rights abuses in the Dirty War, and incompetence in the Malvinas. He was cleared of the former, found guilty of the latter, and sentenced to 12 years' imprisonment. However, President Carlos Menem pardoned him and other military figures in 1989 to promote national harmony. For many years it appeared that Galtieri would escape prosecution for culpability in human rights abuses, but in July 2002 he received a warrant issued 22 years earlier by Judge Claudio Bonadio for the deaths of 20 guerrilla captives. He was charged with kidnapping and arrested but, after complaining about heart problems, was released to his home. Argentine law requires any prisoner over the age of 70 to serve under house arrest, so Galtieri escaped real incar-

ceration, and died in Buenos Aires on January 12, 2003, little mourned.

Further Reading

Danchev, Alex. *International Perspectives on the Falklands Conflict: A Matter of Life and Death.* New York: St. Martin's Press, 1992.

Feldman, D. L. "The United States Role in the Malvinas Crisis, 1982: Misguidance and Misperception in Argentina's Decision to Go to War." *Journal of International American Studies* 27 (summer 1985): 1–22.

Guerra, Roger J. "Political Perception and Strategic Miscalculations: Argentina's Role in the Malvinas/Falkland War." Unpublished Ph.D. diss., University of Miami. 1990.

Lewis, Paul H. *Guerrillas and Generals: The 'Dirty War' in Argentina.* Westport, Conn.: Praeger, 2002.

Pang, Eul-Soo. *The International Political Economy of Transformation in Argentina, Brazil, and Chile since 1970.* New York: Palgrave Macmillan, 2002.

Spektorowski, Alberto. *The Origins of Argentina's Revolution of the Right.* Notre Dame, Ind.: University of Notre Dame Press, 2002.

Gandhi, Indira (1917–1984) *prime minister of India*

Indira Priyadarshini Nehru was born in Allahabad, India, on November 19, 1917, the only child of future prime minister JAWAHARLAL NEHRU. She endured a lonely childhood punctuated by intense political discussions with her father. Gandhi became politically active at the age of 12 by organizing the "monkey brigade," a children's auxiliary, to assist her father's National Congress Party. Since the party strongly agitated for Indian independence from Great Britain, her house was raided by British security forces on several occasions. She subsequently attended Oxford University in England until ill health forced her to return home. That year she married journalist Feroze Gandhi in a controversial love match that was not traditionally arranged. She and her husband remained politically active in the independence movement, and both were arrested and jailed. When India gained its independence in 1947, Nehru became prime minister, and Gandhi, following the death of her mother, became de facto first lady. She was also active in Congress Party affairs, rising to president by 1959.

Gandhi remained closely identified with her father's administration and she accompanied him overseas on various diplomatic missions. Following Nehru's death in 1964, the administration of Bahadur Shastri appointed her minister of information. She continued in that capacity until Shastri suddenly died on January 11, 1966. Gandhi was appointed prime minister to succeed him, the first woman to lead the world's most populous democracy.

As a leader, Gandhi proved herself clever, manipulative, and headstrong. The traits soon alienated her from the ruling circles of the Congress Party, and a break seemed inevitable. She was also far more accommodating toward socialist policies than conservative elements in the party were, especially after she nationalized banking. In 1969, when Gandhi threw her support to a presidential candidate who was not from the Congress Party, she was formally expelled. She then formed her own Congress (I[ndira]) Party and campaigned under the banner, "Abolish poverty." Her popularity soared, and in 1971 Congress (I) won resoundingly on a platform of continuing economic and social reform. That year foreign affairs intruded into the national arena. Pakistan, India's traditional adversary, was split by a secessionist movement in East Pakistan, and intense fighting resulted in 10 million refugees. Unable to support such an influx, Gandhi unexpectedly declared war and the Pakistanis were defeated in only two weeks. The new nation of Bangladesh emerged from East Pakistan; with its opponent now split in two, India was master of the subcontinent. In 1972 Gandhi won another landslide victory over her opponents.

Within months the euphoria surrounding the Pakistani war gave way to the realities of economic hardship. Oil prices had skyrocketed, and the nation was beset by sectarian violence between competing groups of Hindus, Muslims, and Sikhs. When the International Monetary Fund threatened to suspend aid, Gandhi was forced to adopt austerity measures that angered partisans within her own party. Worse, in June 1975 a high court ruled that Gandhi had violated election rules four years earlier and thus forfeited her seat in parliament. The court then banned her from politics for six years. But Gandhi countered by declaring a state of emergency, arrested thousands of political opponents, and suspended civil rights. She eventually relented and scheduled new elections for March 1977, but the Congress (I) Party lost heavily and she finally relinquished

Indira Gandhi *(Library of Congress)*

her office. The new Janata Party subsequently misruled India for three years before losing coalition support, and by 1980 Gandhi had again returned to power. However, she suffered an irreplaceable loss when her youngest son, Sanjay, then being grooming for succession, died in a 1980 plane crash.

Gandhi's second term provided additional controversies, mostly in foreign policy. She aligned herself closely with the Soviet Union to offset any possible alliance between Pakistan and China. For this reason she refused to condemn the 1979 Soviet invasion of Afghanistan, a ploy that angered the United States. By 1983 sectarian strife proved pandemic, with militant Sikhs demanding political autonomy for the Punjab region. In 1984 the Golden Temple of Amritsar, the holiest structure of the Sikh religion, was being used as a terrorist arsenal to store arms. In June of that year Gandhi ordered 30,000 Indian troops to storm the temple, causing several hundred deaths. The incident marked the first time in Indian history that military forces had turned their guns upon fellow citizens. Religious tensions and resentment ran high. On October 31 Gandhi was assassinated by Sikh members of her own bodyguard. The ensuing public outrage led to the massacre of several thousand Sikhs by enraged Hindus before her eldest son, RAJIV GANDHI, succeeded her to high office.

Further Reading

Dhar, P. N. *Indira Gandhi, the "Emergency," and Indian Democracy.* New York: Oxford University Press, 2000.

Frank, Katherine. *Indira: The Life of Indira Nehru Gandhi.* Boston: Houghton, Mifflin, 2001.

Gandhi, Indira. *My Truth.* New York: Grove Press, 1982.

Hasan, Zoya. *Parties and Party Politics in India.* New York: Oxford University Press, 2002.

Jayakar, Pupul. *Indira Gandhi: An Intimate Biography.* New York: Pantheon, 1993.

Saria, Rifu. *The Assassination of Indira Gandhi.* New York: Penguin Books, 1990.

Gandhi, Rajiv (1944–1991) *prime minister of India*

Rajiv Gandhi was born in Bombay, India, on August 20, 1944, a son of future prime minister INDIRA GANDHI and a grandson of JAWAHARLAL NEHRU. A scion to India's most prominent political family, he was raised in a politically active environment yet displayed little interest in politics. Gandhi was educated at numerous elite academies at home before attending Cambridge University in England to study mechanical engineering. He then returned home, obtained a pilot's license, and spent several years flying for Indian Airlines. Gandhi married an Italian woman, Sonia Manio, who has since become a naturalized Indian citizen. He remained aloof from politics until 1980 when his younger brother, Sanjay, groomed to succeed his mother, died in a plane crash. Indira Gandhi then prevailed upon her son to run for a seat in the Lok Sabha (the lower house of parliament) as part of her Congress (I) Party, and he won. Through his mother's influence he also became general secretary of the party and remained a trusted adviser on domestic affairs and foreign policy. As a political personality, Rajiv represented a complete departure from his domineering mother and ambitious younger brother. He was reticent, soft-spoken, and initially regarded as honest. Nonpolitical by nature, he parlayed his interests in high technology to a position as spokesman for India's nascent computer industry.

The rise of Indian sectarian violence reached its climax on October 31, 1984, when Indira Gandhi was killed by her own Sikh bodyguards. Rajiv was then sworn in as prime minister to succeed her and pleaded with the country not to direct anger against the Sikh minority. Nonetheless, an estimated 3,000 Sikhs were killed by vengeful Hindus in New Delhi alone. To prevent a repetition of such violence, Gandhi's earliest action was to negotiate with the rebellious state of Punjab for greater autonomy. Initially these talks held the promise of reducing ethnic strife, but Gandhi was ultimately forced to impose presidential rule to maintain order. The new prime minister also resolved to address the problem of endemic corruption within the Congress (I) Party, and he purged election lists of known offenders. The public appreciated his candor and in the December 1984 national elections Congress (I) won a resounding 401 out of 508 seats in parliament. Gandhi quickly discarded many of his mother's socialistic policies in favor of economic liberalization and free enterprise. He openly welcomed foreign investment and surrounded himself with younger, less doctrinaire party members. This move had the effect of alienating the older, more tradition-bound political establishment.

In 1987 Gandhi asserted India's role as a regional superpower by assisting in the Sri Lankan civil war. That year he dispatched 50,000 troops to help the Sinhalese end their bloody strife with the Tamil minority. Many deaths resulted and the policy ultimately failed, but worst of all, it antagonized the sizable Tamil community of south India. Two years later Gandhi engaged in a contretemps with President Zail Singh over the issues of corruption and incompetence. Singh resigned in consequence and became an outspoken adversary of the government. Relations worsened when Defense Minister V. P. Singh began investigating a major kickback scheme involving Gandhi's cabinet and the Swedish arms manufacturer Bofors. By 1989 the prime minister's political stock had all but collapsed. His attempts to end sectarian violence had failed, and he was seemingly unaware of social and economic problems confronting the country.

Gandhi's detachment from the political arena suggested incompetence, and his insistence upon advancing technology as a panacea underscored perceptions that he was simply out of touch. Elections held that November resulted in major losses to Congress (I), so Gandhi resigned from office. He remained head of the opposition in parliament, and after November 1989 he supported a coalition government that kept the contentious figure Chandra Shekhar in power. When this arrangement proved untenable after May 1991, new elections were called.

Once out of office Gandhi began methodically rebuilding his career and reputation. He campaigned tirelessly throughout the country until polls in 1991 suggested that Congress (I) would carry forthcoming elections by its biggest margins ever. Then, while visiting Tamil Nadu in south India on May 21, 1991, Gandhi was killed by a suicide terrorist. Thus ended a political dynasty that had dominated India's political landscape since 1947.

Further Reading

Dalal, Ramesh. *Rajiv Gandhi's Assassination: The Mystery Unfolds.* London: Sangam, 2001.

Kapur, Harish. "India's Foreign Policy under Rajiv Gandhi." *Round Table* no. 304 (1987): 469–480.

Kreisberg, Paul H. "Gandhi at Midterm." *Foreign Affairs* 65, no. 5 (1987): 1055–1076.

Mehta, Ved. *Rajiv Gandhi and Rama's Kingdom.* New Haven: Yale University Press, 1994.

Merchant, Minhaz. *Rajiv Gandhi, the End of a Dream.* New York: Viking, 1991.

Sen Gupta, Bhabani. *Rajiv Gandhi, a Political Study.* New York: Kennark, 1989.

Garcia, Carlos P. (1896–1971) *president of the Philippines*

Carlos Polestico Garcia was born on November 4, 1896, in Talibon, Bohol Province, the Philippines, the son of a municipal mayor. He attended Silliman University and read law at the Philippine Law School before being called to the bar in 1923. Garcia subsequently turned down a legal practice to teach high school, but in 1925 he successfully ran for congress from Bohol. After three terms in office he served as governor of Bohol Province, 1933–41. Garcia subsequently gained election to the Philippine senate but his career was interrupted by the Japanese invasion of December 1941. Following the American surrender of May 1942 Garcia was hunted by Japanese authorities because of his refusal to cooperate with their military occupation. He joined guerrilla forces until the end of World War II, and in August 1945 he resumed his senate career. Garcia then arrived in the United States to lobby for Philippine war damage claims and also served as a delegate to the newly constituted United Nations in San Francisco. Active in senate affairs at home, he rose to minority leader and chaired influential committees on government, the military, justice, and foreign affairs. Garcia was also active as vice president of the Nacionalista Party and expounded nationalistic views of defense, economics, and foreign policy.

In November 1953 Garcia was elected vice president of the Philippines with presidential candidate RAMÓN MAGSAYSAY and also held the portfolio of foreign affairs secretary. He did prodigious work in helping to define the role of the Philippines in postwar Asia. His most important accomplishment was in hammering out a peace treaty with Japan (still technically at war with the Philippines) and arranging a schedule for reparations. He also attended the Geneva Conference on Asian matters, attacking communists and supporting United States policy throughout the Far East. Back home, he continued finessing several foreign policy matters by presiding over the Southeast Asia Treaty Organization (SEATO) Conference in 1954, which resulted in an eight-member military alliance to dissuade communist expansion. Stridently anticommunist and fiercely nationalist in outlook, Garcia consistently supported better relations with the United States while simultaneously cultivating close ties to other Asian nations. The evolving cold war found the Philippines squarely in the Western camp and a stalwart ally in the struggle against communism.

Garcia's political career took an unexpected turn on March 17, 1957, when President Magsaysay died in a plane crash. He was sworn into office that same day, and in the scheduled elections the following November he handily defeated four other well-known candidates. To secure his victory Garcia took the politically unprecedented move of selecting vice presidential candidate DIOSDADO P. MACAPAGAL from the opposition Liberal Party. Once elected he maintained a strict program of austerity to weed out corruption, put the brakes on a thriving black market, and stimulated the economy. However, Garcia remains best known for promulgating the "Filipino First" policy to end foreign dominance of the economy. All foreign investors (mainly American) were restricted to less than a 51 percent interest in domestic companies. He also began a subtle shift away from near complete dependence on the United States as the guarantor of Philippine security and sought a new orientation toward other Asian states. These moves were not at all appreciated by the American government, but they accelerated the overall trend toward national sovereignty and economic independence. Garcia also worked to revive native cultural arts to reaffirm Filipino national identity.

In 1961 a sluggish economy and allegations of corruption led to Garcia's defeat at the hands of his own vice president, Macapagal. He then retired from politics altogether until 1971, when President FERDINAND MARCOS summoned him to head a new constitutional convention. Garcia died in Manila on June 14, 1971, before taking his post.

Further Reading

Gleeck, Lewis E. *Dissolving the Colonial Bond: American Ambassadors to the Philippines, 1946–1984.* Denver, Colo.: Academic Books, 2001.

Hedman, Eva-Lotta E. *Philippine Politics and Society in the Twentieth Century: Colonial Legacies, Post-Colonial Trajectories.* New York: Routledge, 2000.

McFerson, Hazel M. *Mixed Blessing: The Impact of the American Colonial Experience on Politics and Society in the Philippines.* Westport, Conn.: Greenwood Press, 2002.

Rodell, Paul A. *Culture and Customs of the Philippines.* Westport, Conn.: Greenwood Press, 2002.

García Pérez, Alan (1949–) *president of Peru*

Alan García Pérez was born in Lima, Peru, on May 23, 1949, into a politically active family. Both his parents were prominent in the Alianza Popular Revolucionaria Americana (APRA), American Revolutionary Popular Front, and his father had been imprisoned for opposing dictator MANUEL ODRÍA. García himself joined the youth wing of the party at the age of 11 and established himself as an understudy of APRA leader Víctor Raúl Haya de la Torre. He passed through the Catholic University in Lima before undertaking graduate study in Madrid and Paris. García received a doctorate in law from the Sorbonne, then returned home in 1977 to run for office. Over six feet tall, handsome, and charismatic, he had no trouble getting elected to the Constituent Assembly in 1978 and helped rewrite the new national constitution. This was undertaken to undo the effects of 12 years of military rule. Two years later he successfully ran for a seat in the Chamber of Deputies, and by 1984 he had been elected secretary general of APRA. García decided to run for the presidency in 1985, laboring mightily to remove the last vestiges of radicalism associated with his party. He constantly invoked themes of pragmatism, technical competence, and social responsibility. However, his policies were progressive, and he campaigned on a platform promising job creation, financial assistance, and limited wealth redistribution to assist the poor majority of the population. His message resonated with the populace, who elected him president by 48 percent of votes cast, the largest percentage ever received by a Peruvian candidate on the first ballot. On July 28, 1985, García donned the presidential sash given him by outgoing executive FERNANDO BELAÚNDE TERRY. He was the first APRA candidate in high office and represented the first peaceful transfer of power in four tumultuous decades. And, at 36, he was also Latin America's youngest chief executive.

García came to power during a period of acute economic crisis. In fact all Latin America was awash in debt. The previous administration had been unable to address Peru's structural deficiencies, which resulted in high unemployment and skyrocketing inflation. The main focus of García's economic program was restricting debt payments to no more than 10 percent of the value of exports. "We are faced with a dramatic choice," he insisted. "It is either debt or democracy." He anticipated resistance and punitive measures from the International Monetary Fund (IMF) and World Bank, but debt payments were suffocating Peru's economic vitality. His tough stance toward the global financial community thus won him plaudits at home and respect throughout Latin America. In 1986 he also proposed nationalizing the country's banking system, but this was badly received and precipitated a downturn as money began fleeing the country.

In addition to a weak economy García also inherited an internecine guerrilla war with several left-wing insurgent groups. The largest and most violent was the Shining Path (Sendero Luminoso), a Maoist-based movement comprised mainly of poor Indian peasants from the interior. Despite repeated army sweeps against them, they proved ruthless opponents who killed hundreds of civilian bystanders. García tried negotiating with the guerrillas, but when this failed he responded with additional force. In addition, the government faced large-scale drug cartels that raised coca, produced high-quality cocaine, and shipped it to the United States. The cartels acted with considerable sophistication and frequently paid the guerrillas for protection. By the time García's term ended in 1990 he, like his predecessor, had been unable to rectify Peru's problems. In fact, his free spending nearly bankrupted the nation: inflation for common commodities reached 7,000 percent annually. García was succeeded by Alberto Fujimori and retired to a seat in the senate, but in 1992 he fled the country to escape corruption charges.

The former president remained in self-imposed exile for nine years until 2001. That spring most charges against him were dropped and he came home to resuscitate his political fortunes. García's recovery was impressive, and in April 2001 he forced Alejandro Toledo into a run-off election scheduled for summer. But by June his hopes were dashed. He lost the final tally by 53 percent to 46 percent. García has since declared his intention to remain active in APRA affairs.

Further Reading

Crabtree, John. *Peru under García: An Opportunity Lost.* Pittsburgh: University of Pittsburgh Press, 1992.

Graham, Carol. *Peru's Apra: Parties, Politics, and the Elusive Quest for Democracy.* Boulder, Colo.: Lynne Rienner Publications, 1991.

Marks, Thomas A. *Maoist Insurgency since Vietnam.* Portland, Ore.: Frank Cass, 1996.

Poole, D. G. Renique. *Peru: Time of Fear.* New York: Monthly Review Press, 1992.

Rudolph, James D. *Peru: Evolution of a Crisis.* New York: Praeger, 1992.

Stern, Steven J. *Shining and Other Paths: War and Society in Peru, 1980–1995.* Durham, N.C.: Duke University Press, 1998.

Gaulle, Charles de (1890–1970) *president of France*

Charles-André-Marie-Joseph de Gaulle was born in Lille, France, on November 22, 1890, the son of a history teacher. He inherited from his father an intense love of history and a passionate French nationalism. Because his family had supplied the country with distinguished soldiers since the 13th century, de Gaulle entered the St. Cyr Military Academy in 1907 and graduated four years later as a second lieutenant. During World War I he served in the 33rd Infantry Regiment under Colonel PHILIPPE PÉTAIN, whom de Gaulle idolized as a father figure. He fought bravely in combat, was thrice wounded, and captured. De Gaulle returned to France in 1918, a heavily decorated war hero, and resumed his military career. However, over the next two decades he acquired a reputation as an acerbic outsider, quick to criticize superiors and prevailing military dogma. He also published several well-received treatises on military leadership and tactics, and one volume. *Towards a Modern Military,* that anticipated the rise of tank-driven armies. The correctness of de Gaulle's tactical insights was amply demonstrated in May 1940 when the German blitzkrieg rolled over static French defenses. De Gaulle,

Charles de Gaulle *(Library of Congress)*

then France's youngest brigadier general, scored one of France's few military victories at Montcornet. He then flew to England rather than surrender. On June 18, 1940, de Gaulle made a famous radio broadcast announcing creation of the Free French Army, which would carry on the struggle against Germany. His stiff-necked defiance in the face of disaster served as a national rallying point for many dispirited Frenchmen and announced the beginning of a legendary career.

Throughout World War II, de Gaulle symbolized the fighting spirit of France but his haughtiness, arrogance, and unwillingness to compromise made him powerful enemies. Foremost among these were Prime Minister WINSTON CHURCHILL and President FRANKLIN D. ROOSEVELT, both of whom would have preferred another leader to head the Free French. But de Gaulle proved as crafty as he was determined, so when Allied forces liberated Paris in August 1944 he remained in the van of events. Hailed as a national savior, de Gaulle functioned as president of a provisional government until national politics were sorted out through adoption of a new constitution. However, his harshly expressed beliefs that France could survive only in the hands of a strong executive officer put him at odds with a century-and-a-half-long tradition of republican (legislative) government. Various political interests united in opposition, and de Gaulle resigned from power in early 1946. In October of that year the French people passed a referendum authorizing a new constitution—and the Fourth Republic was born.

Back in private life, de Gaulle disparaged the new constitution as hopelessly parliamentarian and organized a new national movement, the Rally for the Republic, to change it. He enjoyed electoral success until 1953 before again retiring from the public arena. However, by 1958 the Fourth Republic was threatened by revolt in North Africa and by a severe economic recession. The inability of the three main political parties, the Christian Democrats, the Socialists, and the Communists, to advance meaningful legislation only underscored de Gaulle's criticisms. With civil war a growing possibility the nation turned to the former general to save France a second time. Accordingly, he was elected prime minister by the National Assembly and immediately promulgated constitutional reforms creating a strong presidential government. When this was approved in a plebiscite on December 21, 1958, de Gaulle became president of France and the Fifth Republic was born. One of his

first—and most controversial—deeds was disengaging from Algeria and allowing independence in 1962. This move angered many conservatives and colonialists, but de Gaulle realized the impossibility of holding on to colonies. It was more important for the nation that peace be restored. However, he was determined that France should reassert itself on the international stage. France thereupon pursued its own nuclear weapons program free from American or English interference. In fact, de Gaulle went to great lengths, or so it seemed, to antagonize his erstwhile allies by rejecting Great Britain's admission into the European Common Market and withdrawing France from the North Atlantic Treaty Organization (NATO). Furthermore he condemned America's growing involvement in Vietnam and, during a visit to Canada in 1967, he raised hackles by exhorting Quebec to secede.

Despite opposition claims that he sought a dictatorship, de Gaulle remained firmly in the democratic camp and sought legitimization by being elected through a popular vote. The assembly eventually agreed and in 1962 he became the fist French president since 1851 to gain power through a national election. De Gaulle enjoyed tremendous popularity at home and was hailed for having restored France to some semblance of international grandeur. But in May 1968 the Fifth Republic faced imminent political crisis from an uprising by students and workers demanding drastic changes in French society. De Gaulle greeted the unrest with his trademark, contemptuous defiance, and resoundingly secured the next round of elections. Order was restored but discontent continued. In 1969, when de Gaulle failed to pass a minor reform bill, he resigned from office and was replaced by GEORGES POMPIDOU. The former national savior then retired to Colombey-les-Deux-Églises to write his memoirs. He died there on November 9, 1970, widely mourned. De Gaulle may have been stubborn, arrogant, and even unrealistic in his obsession to return France to greatness, but in the minds of his compatriots, he succeeded with Gallic panache. He also bequeathed to his nation a far more stable political system than he inherited. For dominating the national landscape of France for 30 years de Gaulle is viewed as its most important political leader of the 20th century.

Further Reading

Bell, David S. *Presidential Power in Fifth Republic France.* New York: Berg, 2000.

Berthon, Simon. *Allies at War: The Bitter Rivalry between Churchill, Roosevelt, and De Gaulle*. New York: Carroll and Graf, 2001.

Bozo, Frederic. *Two Strategies, One Europe: De Gaulle, the United States, and the Atlantic Alliance*. Lantham, Md.: Rowman and Littlefield, 2001.

Chalaby, Jean K. *The De Gaulle Presidency and the Media: Statism and Public Communications*. New York: Palgrave, 2002.

Gaulle, Charles de. *Memoir of Hope: Renewal and Endeavor*. New York: Simon and Schuster, 1971.

Mahan, Erin R. *Kennedy, De Gaulle, and Western Europe*. New York: Palgrave Macmillan, 2002.

Mahoney, Daniel J. *De Gaulle: Statesmanship, Grandeur, and Modern Democracy*. New Brunswick, N.J.: Transaction Publishers, 2000.

Geisel, Ernesto (1908–1996) *president of Brazil*

Ernesto Geisel was born in Bento Gonçalves, Brazil, on August 3, 1908, the son of German Protestant immigrants. He entered the military in 1924 and graduated first in his class four years later. During the 1930 revolution Geisel joined the military clique supporting General GETÚLIO VARGAS. He proved himself an able officer and filled a variety of military and civilian offices before completing the general staff course in 1943. Geisel subsequently received advanced military training in the United States, and in October 1945 he played an important role in overthrowing Vargas's regime and restoring democracy. Geisel had acquired the reputation of a highly competent professional officer with little interest in politics. In 1957 he represented military interests on the board of the National Petroleum Council (Petrobras) and developed a long association with the petrochemical industry. He was promoted to general in May 1960 and assumed command of the military district of Brasília, the nation's capital. Brazil was in a political crisis brought on by the resignation of President JÂNIO QUADROS and his replacement by the leftist extremist João Goulart. The military stood by silently while Goulart ruined the economy through centralized planning, but in March 1964 Geisel and other ranking army figures bloodlessly deposed him. This act ushered in a period of 24 years of military rule from which a select group of general officers would be chosen as president.

Immediately after the coup, Geisel served as a judge on the Supreme Military Tribunal. But he soon became identified with the faction under General HUMBERTO CASTELO BRANCO, who sought restoration of democracy as soon as possible. However, both were repeatedly overruled by hard-line officers who saw military rule as the only way of restoring national stability. Geisel, who had retired from active service as a four-star general in 1969, was nominated by the "Castellistas" for president based upon his fine handling of Petrobras. Suffering from the effects of world recession and high oil prices, Brazil needed a leader versed in the nuances of global economics. Geisel was appointed president on March 15, 1974.

In office Geisel initially continued aspects of the military regime that ensured tight political and social control but he also initiated steps to liberalize the political arena. His policy became known as *distensão*, the gradual relaxation of controls in an orderly fashion. He met repeatedly with church and union leaders to explain his position and solicit their cooperation. By 1978 he felt secure enough to reinstate basic civil rights, a limited political opposition, and less censorship of the press. In economics Geisel subscribed to the notion of "pragmatic nationalism." He sought to maintain high levels of growth by borrowing heavily and erecting a massive new national infrastructure, including dams, highways, and atomic energy. He also opened up the country to foreign oil companies to promote increased prospecting for mineral wealth. In foreign affairs Geisel struck an independent line by seeking closer ties to Japan, Germany, Iran, and South Korea. He did this in response to remarks from American president JIMMY CARTER, who criticized Brazil's record on human rights—the very policy Geisel labored so hard to improve. He also angrily canceled a 25-year-old military alliance with the United States. However, by the time Geisel left office, Brazil was slowly but irrevocably headed down the road toward democratic reform. It did not appear so to onlookers at that time.

A major issue of contention during the last two years of Geisel's tenure was choosing a successor. Hard-line elements resented his moves toward liberalization and wanted one of their own members, army minister General Selvio Frota, to steer the country over the next five years. But Geisel and his brother, another four-star general, successfully arranged for JOÃO FIGUEIREDO to become president in March 1979. That officer continued the liberalizing precedents enacted by Geisel and ultimately restored civilian rule. Geisel had left the country in relatively good shape economically, although inflation ran at 42 percent and the national debt topped $43 billion. But Brazil also enjoyed the assets of a modern economic infrastructure, which laid the foundation for future national prosperity. Geisel served for many years as a prominent business leader before dying in Rio de Janeiro on September 12, 1996. His tenure as president, while not democratic, signifies an important and deliberate milestone in the nation's quest for normalcy.

Further Reading

Bacchus, Wilfred A. *Mission in Mufti: Brazil's Military Regime, 1964–1985.* New York: Greenwood Press, 1990.

Hunter, Wendy. *Eroding Military Influence in Brazil: Politicians against Soldiers.* Chapel Hill: University of North Carolina Press, 1997.

Kinzo, Maria D'Alva G. *Legal Opposition Politics under Authoritarian Rule in Brazil: The Case of the MDB, 1966–79.* New York: St. Martin's Press, 1988.

Nazario, Olga. "Pragmatism in Brazilian Foreign Policy: The Geisel Years." Unpublished Ph.D. diss., University of Miami, 1983.

Pang, Eul-Soo. *The International Political Economy of Transformation in Argentina, Brazil, and Chile since 1960.* New York: Palgrave Macmillan, 2002.

Skidmore, Thomas E. *The Politics of Military Rule in Brazil, 1964–1985.* New York: Oxford University Press, 1988.

Gemayel, Amin (1942–   ) *president of Lebanon*

Amin Gemayel (or Jumayyil) was born in Bikfaya, Lebanon, on November 10, 1942, into a Maronite Christian household. His father, Pierre Gemayel, was the founder of the Phalanges, a Christian political party backed by its own militia. However, the younger Gemayel eschewed both politics and the military service in favor of law. He received his degree from St. Joseph University in 1965 and commenced a successful legal practice. And unlike his more strident younger brother, Bashir Gemayel, he maintained friendly relations with Muslim leaders throughout Lebanon. This ability greatly facilitated his rise in this politically and religiously fractious nation. In 1970 Gemayel captured a seat in the legislature previously held by his uncle, becoming its youngest member. Lebanon's descent into civil war commenced in 1975 but he nonetheless expanded his contacts to include leaders of the Palestine Liberation Organization (PLO) and Syrian president Hafiz al-Assad. Gemayel, as a trained attorney, was interested in modifying those portions of the national constitution that gave Christians disproportional representation and power at Muslim expense. Above all Gemayel was an Arab nationalist who sought to preserve Lebanon's unique culture and identity. All these traits made him far less inclined to support Israel than other members of his family and party were.

Gemayel's political fortunes quickened in September 1982 when his brother Bashir, who had just been elected president of Lebanon, was assassinated. His father and other party elders prevailed on him to take his place. With Muslim help he was easily confirmed in the legislature by 78 votes to one. His only real opponent, the veteran former president CAMILLE CHAMOUN, bowed out before the vote was taken. Much was expected from the handsome, articulate, and charismatic Gemayel on all sides, but he was ultimately overwhelmed by the complexities of a divided country splintered by war. Lebanon at that time was occupied by two invading armies: Syrians to the north and Israelis to the south. The military situation was further muddled by the presence of armed militias in the Christian, Druze, Sunni Muslim, and Shia Muslim camps, none having great affection for the others. Under these circumstances little could be realistically accomplished, and no sooner had Gemayel taken office than events quickly went awry.

For the next six years Gemayel strove futilely for peace and unity among the nation's warring factions. Two National Reconciliation Conferences were held in Switzerland in 1983 and 1984 but nothing could be agreed upon. Worse, intense fighting erupted between the militias, once Israeli troops had decamped from south Lebanon. In their absence Syria enlarged and strengthened its hold on the nation, openly arming both Muslim forces and dissident Christians under Suleiman Franjieh. In February 1984 Gemayel ordered the Lebanese army into action against the Shias of West Beirut, but this act caused the military to splinter along religious lines. Fighting intensified as Christians and Muslims competed for newly vacated territory, and at one point Gemayel was shelled in the presidential palace. In March 1984 he assembled a government of national unity and appointed RASHID KARAMI, a Sunni Muslim, as his prime minister (as required by law). The following August, Pierre Gemayel, spiritual head of the

Phalangists, died, his absence further weakening the president's control over Christian forces, who began fighting among themselves.

Warfare continued sporadically well into Gemayel's last year in office. His attempts to have Syrian forces withdrawn were rebuffed by President Assad, who sought to control Lebanon as a buffer state against Israel. The Israelis also made no attempt to assist their erstwhile Christian allies. When Gemayel refused to enact constitutional reforms that would weaken presidential power—and further marginalize the Christian minority—angry demands for his dismissal arose from Muslim leaders, and fighting was renewed. Chaos prevented orderly elections from being held, so on September 22, 1988, Gemayel appointed General MICHAEL AOUN as prime minister and acting head of state until a new executive could be chosen. He then left for self-imposed exile in France to pursue business matters. Gemayel remained abroad for 12 years until July 2000, when he returned and began reasserting his control over the much-reduced Phalangists. A new generation of leaders greatly resented his authority, however, and on July 10, 2002 they formally evicted him from the party. Such discord is certain to weaken the already tenuous power base of Lebanon's Christian minority.

Further Reading

Dagher, Carole. *Bring Down the Walls: Lebanon's Postwar Challenge.* New York: St. Martin's Press, 2000.

El-Khazen, Farid. *The Breakdown of the State in Lebanon, 1967–1976.* Cambridge, Mass.: Harvard University Press, 2000.

Fisk, Robert. *Pity the Nation: Lebanon at War.* New York: Oxford University Press, 2001.

Jumayyil, Amin. *Peace and Unity: Major Speeches, 1982–1984.* Gerrards Cross, England: C. Smythe; distributed in North America by Medialink International, 1984.

———. *Rebuilding Lebanon.* Lanham, Md.: University Press of America, 1992.

Khalifah, Bassem. *The Rise and Fall of Christian Lebanon.* Toronto: York Press, 2001.

Gierek, Edward (1913–2001) *first secretary of the Polish United Workers Party*

Edward Gierek was born in Porabka, Poland, on January 6, 1913, the son of a coal miner. After his father died in an accident, his mother immigrated to France, and Gierek began working in mines at the age of 14. He joined the French Communist Party and was deported in 1934 for organizing sit-down strikes. Within a few years Gierek had relocated to Belgium, where he worked the mines and joined the Belgian Communist Party. During World War II he fought in the underground and led a group of Polish expatriates. However, Gierek returned to Poland in 1948 to join the Polish United Workers (Communist) Party in his native state of Katowice (Silesia). From there he built up a political power base that propelled him up through the party hierarchy. Gierek was conscientious in his responsibilities toward workers and fought to secure better wages and living conditions. While dealing with party matters, he attended the University of Kraków to obtain his doctorate in mine engineering. By 1954 Gierek had gained appointment as director of Poland's heavy industry department and two years later he was seated on the Politburo, Poland's highest decision-making body. Here he distinguished himself as a youthful technocrat. Distancing himself from subservience to Moscow's doctrinaire policies, he pursued a course of national reconciliation, whereby Marxism-Leninism was adapted to local and national circumstances. Gierek functioned well until December 1970, when sudden increases in food prices triggered violent rioting and the deaths of 40 people. First Secretary WŁADYSŁAW GOMUŁKA was consequently forced from office, and the popular Gierek was selected to succeed him.

Gierek used his credentials for innovation to improve the tottering communist system. He shook up the party structure, ejecting Gomułka's cronies, and stressing better managerial qualifications. Gierek next took the unprecedented steps of meeting with workers, explaining his own predicaments and soliciting trust and support. He also addressed declining living standards by placing greater emphasis on Western consumer goods. In 1971 he initiated a major program of economic recovery based on massive borrowing from the West. These funds were earmarked for modernizing Poland's outdated industrial base and other structural deficiencies. The initial results proved encouraging, and for a few years Poles enjoyed an assortment of goods and services not usually associated with a state-controlled economy. More important, Gierek loosened travel restrictions and allowed his citizens to travel freely to the West. For a generation of Poles raised under communism the first half of the 1970s was perhaps the most pleasant time of their lives.

Despite good intentions, even Gierek could not surmount the inherent flaws of socialized economics. The economy began slowing down in 1976, slowly crushed by the burden of a $40 billion national debt. In fact the majority of borrowed funds were conspicuously misspent or mishandled on unproductive government enterprises. Poland's plight became so pronounced that food prices suddenly and unexpectedly rose again. This occasioned angry protests that were brutally repressed by the army and led to the rise of the Worker's Defense Committee. Organized union and political opposition continued rising in direct proportion to hardships encountered. Communist control of politics further eroded after Pope John Paul II made a historic visit to his native homeland in 1979 that galvanized resistance to the regime. Massive strikes and marches continued into August 1980, when Gierek was forced to negotiate the creation of Solidarity, the Eastern Bloc's first free trade union.

Gierek had been under pressure from Moscow to resign as first secretary and he finally capitulated in September 1980. The following year he was formally expelled from the party, and General WOJCIECH JARUZELSKI had him arrested and imprisoned for corruption. Gierek was released shortly after, and he retired into obscurity to write his memoirs. He died in Cieszyn, Poland, on July 29, 2001, where his funeral was attended by 10,000 marchers. Gierek's attempts to reform the system were sincere, but his failure foretold the end of communism in Poland.

Further Reading

Lepak, Keith J. "Prelude to Crisis: Leadership Drift in Poland in the 1970s." *Journal of Communist Studies* 22 (spring 1989): 11–22.

———. *Prelude to Solidarity: Poland and the Politics of the Gierek Regime.* New York: Columbia University Press, 1988.

Lipski, J. J. *KOR: A History of the Worker's Defense Committee in Poland, 1976–1981.* Berkeley: University of California Press, 1985.

Reisinger, W. M. "The Brezhnev Doctrine and Polish-Soviet Bargaining, 1971." *Journal of Communist Studies* 3 (September 1987): 250–266.

Sperlich, Peter W. *Rotten Foundations: The Conceptual Basis of the Marxist-Leninist Regimes of East Germany and Other Countries of the Soviet Bloc.* Westport, Conn.: Praeger, 2002.

Wozniuk, V. *From Crisis to Crisis: Soviet-Polish Relations in the 1970s: A Case Study in Alliance Politics.* Charlottesville: University of Virginia Press, 1984.

Giolitti, Giovanni (1842–1928) *prime minister of Italy*

Giovanni Giolitti was born in Mondovi, kingdom of Piedmont, on October 27, 1842, the son of mountain peasants. Adept as a student, he attended the University of Turin for a law degree, then entered the civil service. He won a seat in the Chamber of Deputies in 1882 and thereafter held a succession of increasingly important posts, including minister of the treasury. Giolitti became prime minister for the first time in 1892, the first national politician not to have participated in the Risorgimento (war of unification) against Austria. His tenure in office lasted only 18 months before he was brought down by a banking scandal. Over the next two decades he slowly and methodically reconstructed his political career, acquiring a well-deserved reputation for craftiness and manipulation. In 1901 he gained appointment as minister of the interior, responsible for Italy's internal order. He nonetheless raised controversy by refusing to crack down on strikes and other social unrest. True to his liberal roots, Giolitti was sympathetic toward the working class and felt that government should not intervene in class conflicts. To silence critics he insisted that the best way of maintaining labor peace was by providing the lower classes with higher wages and better working conditions.

Giolitti formed his second administration in 1903 and embarked on a series of much-needed social reforms. He opened a dialogue with the labor movement, nationalized the railways, and authorized universal male suffrage. Conservative opposition to his program was intensive but Giolitti almost always prevailed owing to his mastery of *trasformismo,* a skillful balancing act between competing interests in the legislature. Giolitti continually made, dropped, and remade political alliances to suit his purpose. He brilliantly brought a disparate range of political interests, including socialists, Catholics, liberals, and radicals, in line for his most important policies. Giolitti's unscrupulous manipulation of political dialogue established him as the dominant political figure of early-20th-century Italy. Ironically, he is celebrated for both liberal reforms and his Machiavellian ways of achieving them.

In foreign policy Giolitti was decidedly cautious, conservative, and dedicated to maintaining the Triple Alliance among Italy, Austria, and Germany. But in 1911 he was forced by nationalists to embark on a costly war against the Ottoman Empire in Libya, which Italy acquired as a colony. As the war clouds gathered over Europe, Giolitti approached France for a possible alliance, but he otherwise pursued a neutral course. Once war erupted in August 1914, he fell under increasing pressure to enter the fighting on behalf of the Allies. But Giolitti was painfully aware of Italy's military weakness and, despite accusations of having Austrian sympathies, he eschewed confrontation. Furthermore, he cynically reasoned that Italy stood to gain much more by staying neutral and trading that stance for territorial concessions. When it became clear that the king and the liberal leadership were intent on war, he resigned in May 1915 and resumed his seat in the legislature. Italy entered World War I that same month, and Giolitti campaigned for a return to neutrality.

After the war the 78-year-old Giolitti hovered in the political background until June 1920, when he became prime minister for the fifth and final time. He performed useful work in negotiating the Treaty of Rapallo with Yugoslavia, which precluded Italian designs on the Dalmatian coast and angered nationalists. But he completely misjudged the rise of BENITO MUSSOLINI's fascists and the danger they posed to democracy. In fact Giolitti initially supported the fascists for their imposition of discipline. He mistakenly believed he could coopt them into the government like any other interest group. Giolitti thus adopted his usual lax attitude toward the newcomers and did not use state powers to constrain them. He resigned from power in 1921, and within a year Mussolini, backed by orchestrated street violence, had seized power. Giolitti then publicly denounced the fascists, and in 1924 he withdrew his party from the coalition government. He died in Cavour, Piedmont, on July 17, 1928, an outspoken critic of the fascist regime. But by failing to head off Mussolini from the onset, he inadvertently facilitated the rise of Italy's most notorious dictator— a conspicuous blot on a productive career spanning two decades, for which the term Giolittian Era was coined.

Further Reading

Conner, Paul. "The Road to Fascism: An Italian Sonderweg?" *Contemporary European History* 11, no. 2 (2002): 273–295.

De Grande, Alexander. "Giovanni Giolitti: A Pessimist as Modernizer." *Journal of Modern Italian Studies* 6 (spring 2001): 57–67.

———. *The Hunchback's Tailor: Giovanni Giolitti and Liberal Italy.* Westport, Conn.: Praeger, 2001.

De Grande, Alexander, and S. Di Scala. *Giolitti and the Socialists: Italian Socialism.* Amherst: University of Massachusetts Press, 1996.

Dunnage, Jonathan. "Law and Order in Giolitti Italy: A Case Study of the Province of Bologna." *European History Quarterly* 25 (July 1995): 381–408.

Giolitti, Giovanni. *Memoirs of My Life.* New York: Fertig, 1973.

Giscard d'Estaing, Valéry (1926–) *prime minister of France*

Valéry Giscard d'Estaing was born in Koblenz, Germany, on February 2, 1926, the son of a French civil servant. He belonged to an old aristocratic family from the Clermont-Ferrand region of central France, with long traditions of service to the state. Giscard was well educated at elite academies, but when World War II broke out he quit and joined the resistance at the age of 16. In 1946 he was admitted to the Ecole polytechnique and the Ecole nationale de l'administration, a training ground for future bureaucrats. Giscard proved adept as an administrator, and by 1952 he was operating as a financial inspector. Four years later he successfully ran for a seat in the parlement and commenced his meteoric climb in politics. In 1959 the Fifth Republic was organized under President CHARLES DE GAULLE, who promised a return to French grandeur. Giscard and many young technocrats welcomed the change for its promised modernization of the moribund French economy. That year he was made deputy finance minister, becoming the youngest member of de Gaulle's cabinet. However, Giscard felt alienated by the imperious, inward-looking Gaullist party, so in 1962 he founded a new organization, the independent Republicans. This group was as conservative as the Gaullists politically, but economically it embraced technology, modernity, and reform. In 1962 Giscard became minister of finance and economic affairs, but resigned four years later over a difference in government policy. However, in 1969 President GEORGES POMPIDOU reappointed him to the post, where he remained until Pompidou died in office. In 1974 Giscard ran for president as the Independent Republican candidate against Socialist François Mitterrand. He managed to win by a narrow margin, becoming third president of the Fifth Republic and ushering in another seven years of conservative rule.

While conservative in outlook, Giscard represented a new breed of technocrats, eager to break with the past and proud of their managerial competence. He openly advocated a freer, more pluralistic society with better social services and environmental protection. But Giscard also wanted to transform France's economy from one of relatively stagnant government control into a thriving world leader. He fully embraced liberalizing trends and free market policies to enhance competition and change. Giscard was also intent on promoting greater political and economic integration in Europe through closer ties to Germany. He struck up a working relationship with Chancellor HELMUT SCHMIDT, and the two laid the groundwork for the European Monetary System in 1979. Socially Giscard was instrumental in liberalizing access to abortion and contraception. All told, the Fifth Republic under Giscard became less beholden to ideology and more receptive to technocratic solutions for national governance.

Politically Giscard's term in office was hampered by several factors beyond his control. First, he could not shake his indelibly aristocratic mien, which made him appear stridently elitist. Second, he had to deal with other ambitious conservatives for power. His most notable adversary proved to be his own prime minister, Jacques Chirac, who constantly pigeonholed his policies. Friction on the right made his much-anticipated alliance with the center-left almost impossible. Chirac's criticism proved so unbearable that Giscard demanded his resignation and replaced him with Raymond Barre in 1976. There were other problems, as well. Many state controls were lifted toward the end of the decade, but these reforms failed to stop the onset of a deep recession. In this weakened condition Giscard ran for reelection against both Mitterrand and Chirac in 1981, a situation that split the conservative vote. Because no candidate received a majority a runoff election was required. Chirac, who finished third, continued damning Giscard with faint praise, and Mitterrand won, 51 percent to 48 percent.

Giscard returned to parlement in 1984 by winning his seat back, but it appeared his days as a national leader had ended. Nevertheless, in 1990 he founded a new conservative organization, l'Union pour la France (UPF), the Union for France, which remains a major force in French politics. Moreover Giscard found his niche as a leading spokesman for European unity. For a decade he worked laboriously for a better constitution for the European Union (EU), which he wanted replaced by an even stronger entity, the United States of Europe. This met with objections from newer members who entered the EU in 2004 and feared domination by the older, larger powers. But Giscard remains as haughty and unapologetic as ever. "Our proposal is to make things work in a more united way," he insisted. "Europe has become too complicated with too much hostility."

Further Reading

Cole, Alistair. "The Presidential Party and the Fifth Republic." *West European Politics* 16 (April 1993):49–67.

Frears, J. R. *France in the Giscard Presidency.* Winchester, Mass.: Allen and Unwin, 1981.

Giscard d'Estaing, Valéry. "New Challenges." *Foreign Affairs* 61, no. 1 (1983): 176–199.

———. *Towards a New Democracy.* London: Collins, 1977.

Ryan, W. Francis. "France under Giscard." *Current History* 80, no. 466 (1981): 201–204, 228–229.

Serfaty, S. "The Fifth Republic under Giscard d'Estaing: Steadfast or Changing?" *World Today* 32 (March 1976): 95–103.

Wright, Vincent. *Continuity and Change in France.* Boston: Allen and Unwin, 1984.

Gómez Castro, Laureano (1889–1965) *president of Colombia*

Laureano Eleuterio Gómez Castro was born in Bogotá, Colombia, on February 20, 1889, to middle-class parents. He obtained an engineering degree from the National University in 1909 but found his real calling in politics. Colombia's polity had been traditionally divided into two main parties, the Liberals and the Conservatives, whose animus was reciprocal and entrenched. Gómez joined the Conservatives at the age of 20 and established himself as a force within party affairs by editing *La Unidad,* a partisan newspaper. He gained election to the Chamber of Deputies in 1911, functioning as a Conservative gadfly. He had a flair for vehement polemics, and in 1923 Liberal president Marco Fidel Suarez resigned rather than tolerate his abuse. Gómez also proved himself a competent bureaucrat and held a succession of important governmental posts. In 1925 he functioned as minister of public works and advanced ambitious plans for enhancing the nation's infrastructure until they were vetoed by congress. In 1930 Gómez gained appointment as minister to Germany and returned the following year to win a seat in the senate. His political rise coincided with the onset of the Great Depression in Colombia, which heralded a period of Liberal ascendancy. Over the next 15 years Gómez viciously orchestrated editorial attacks on three liberal executives and established himself as de facto head of the Conservative Party. He also expressed glowing admiration for such right-wing authoritarian figures as ADOLF HITLER and FRANCISCO FRANCO. His nonstop invective contributed to a growing sense of national polarization, and in 1939 violence broke out between supporters of the two parties. At this juncture Gómez stridently urged Conservative adherents to arm themselves and prepare for civil war, which only added to the mounting tension.

By 1945 the Liberals had run their course and the Conservatives resumed power, under Mariano Ospina Pérez. Gómez was appointed foreign minister but as nominal party leader he wielded power behind the scenes. He authorized a purge of all Liberals from the government and may have played a role in the assassination of Jorge Eliécer Gaitán, a leading Liberal figure. This act initiated a period of outright war in the countryside, known as La Violencia, which continued unabated for several years. Gómez, feeling himself targeted by violence, fled to Spain in 1948, but the following year he returned and announced his candidacy for the presidency. Public violence had grown so pandemic that President Ospina declared a state of emergency and dissolved congress, at which point the Liberals boycotted the election. Consequently Gómez won and was sworn in as the new chief executive in 1950.

Once empowered, the full range of Gómez's authoritarian tendencies became apparent. He struck a close alliance between paramilitary groups and the Catholic Church, consistent with the Spanish tradition of caudillismo. He invariably sided with management against workers in labor disputes while inviting foreign trade and investment. To demonstrate his anticommunist credentials Gómez was the only Latin American head of state to commit troops to the United Nations war in Korea, 1950–53. This earned him plaudits from the United States and increased foreign aid. However, the president suffered a heart attack in 1951, and in his absence violence surged throughout the countryside. He tried pushing constitutional reforms that would have prolonged Conservative control indefinitely, which caused splits within his own tradition-bound party. Colombia grew so imperiled by instability that on June 13, 1953, General GUSTAVO ROJAS PINILLA overthrew the government in a bloodless coup. Gómez was summarily exiled to Spain.

For the next four years Gómez languished in exile until 1957, when the Liberals approached him to form a National Front against General Rojas. This was successfully accomplished, and democracy returned to Colombia in March 1958 through the election of Liberal ALBERTO LLERAS CAMARGO. The National Front established the principle of power sharing, whereby Liberals and Conservatives alternated control every four years. It proved an effective method of restoring national tranquility, which lasted until 1974. Gómez returned home in 1958 and lived a quiet existence until he died in Bogotá on July 13, 1965. He was one of the most extreme ideologues to head Colombia and presided over one of the bloodiest chapters in its history.

Further Reading

Gonzalo Sanchez, G., and Donny Meertens. *Bandits, Peasants, and Politics: The Case of 'La Violencia' in Colombia.* Austin: University of Texas Press, 2001.

Henderson, James D. *Conservative Thought in Twentieth Century Latin America: The Ideas of Laureano Gómez.* Athens: Ohio University Center for International Studies, 1988.

———. *Modernization in Colombia: The Laureano Gómez years, 1889–1965.* Gainesville: University Press of Florida, 2001.

Roldan, Mary. *Blood and Fire: La Violencia in Antioquia, Colombia, 1946–1953.* Durham, N.C.: Duke University Press, 2002.

Walthour, Douglas A. "Laureano Gómez and Colombia in the Korean War: Internal and External Factors in Foreign Policy Decision-making." Unpublished master's thesis, University of Texas–Austin, 1990.

Gomułka, Władysław (1905–1982) *first secretary of the Polish United Workers Party*

Władysław Gomułka was born in Krosno, Galicia, in Austria-Hungary, on February 6, 1905, the son of Polish workers. Poland at that time had been divided between Austria-Hungary, Germany, and Russia, and would not reemerge as a nation until 1919. His parents, strong socialists, had only recently returned from the United States, disillusioned by capitalism. Gomułka followed his father's lead in political activism, and in 1926 he joined the illegal Polish Communist Party. Active in strikes and organizing, he was repeatedly arrested and jailed until 1934, when he visited Moscow to attend the International Communist School. In 1936 Gomułka returned home for another spate of arrests that probably saved his life. Soviet dictator JOSEPH STALIN distrusted Polish communists, and between 1936 and 1939 he arrested and executed all those living in Russia. Gomułka nonetheless relocated to the Soviet-occupied zone of Poland after the start of World War II in 1939. By 1942 he was director of the Polish Workers Party and

Władysław Gomułka *(Library of Congress)*

was sent home to organize workers and fight in the resistance. Poland was occupied by Soviet troops after 1945, and Gomułka next served as deputy premier under BOLESŁAW BIERUT. In this capacity he ruthlessly suppressed the rival Polish Peasants Party and forced a union between the communists and socialists. However, his career was sidelined after 1949 when Stalin, distrustful of Poles as ever, accused him of "nationalistic deviance" from the official party line. In truth Gomułka was a nationalist who distanced himself from Soviet-style communism and sought a quasi-independent party. He openly resisted collectivization of agriculture and opposed creation of the Cominform to solidify Moscow's control of party affairs. Stalin was intolerant of such behavior so Gomułka was arrested, jailed, and expelled from the party in 1951. Stalin died two years later, and Gomułka's career was slowly rehabilitated by the new premier, NIKITA KHRUSHCHEV. But by 1956 Poland was racked by strikes and disorders brought on by economic and social stagnation. Gomułka accepted Khrushchev's invitation to become first secretary of the Polish United Workers (Communist) Party, but on the condition that he pursue a "Polish road to socialism" and conduct badly needed reforms. His appointment also convinced the Russians not to intervene and restore order by force as they did in Hungary.

Gomułka's appointment led to national celebration, as he was seen as the only Pole capable of standing up to Moscow. He began his regime with moderate reforms, intending to repair relations with the Catholic Church, and in January 1957 the communists overwhelmingly won the national parliamentary elections. Gomułka next turned to reforming the Communist Party, purging it of incompetents and opponents to reform. His hand thus strengthened, he turned back to his avowed goal of creating "Polish communism." But Gomułka's liberalizing trend proved transitory, for within a few years he was commanding the nation in an authoritarian manner. He remained a committed communist by nature, even if he felt that the Soviet model was unacceptable for his country. By 1968 he had alienated students, workers, and intellectuals, the very interests that had supported him so fervently in 1956. The economy was again stagnating and food shortages were endemic. But to demonstrate his loyalty to Soviet premier LEONID BREZHNEV, Gomułka dispatched Polish troops to crush the Czechoslovakian reform movement in

August 1968. So despite an earlier reputation as a reformist, Gomułka toward the end of his tenure was solidly backing Soviet conservatives. His only real success in office was in normalizing relations with West Germany in 1970 and acquiring international recognition of the postwar Oder-Neisse boundary.

Gomułka's regime ended in December 1970, when a disastrous economic performance triggered sudden and unexpected food price hikes. Widespread demonstrations then arose that provoked a national crisis. Despite severe crackdowns by police and military forces, Gomułka had lost control of the situation and was on the verge of requesting Soviet intervention. Fortunately he suffered a heart attack on December 19, 1970, and adversaries on the Central Committee arranged for his ouster. He was replaced by EDWARD GIEREK. Now shunned by the party, Gomułka, retired to a life of obscurity until his death in Warsaw on September 1, 1982. He had successfully balanced Polish nationalism with international communism but otherwise failed to make the system work.

Further Reading

Bethel, Nicholas W. *Gomułka and His Communism.* Harlow, England: Longman, 1969.

De Weydenthal, J. B. *The Communists of Poland: An Historical Outline.* Stanford, Calif: Hoover Institution Press, 1986.

Diskin, Hanna. *The Seeds of Triumph: Church and State in Gomułka's Poland.* Budapest and New York: Central Europe University Press, 2001.

Gluchowski, L. W. "Poland, 1956: Khrushchev, Gomułka, and the 'Polish October,'" *World International History Project Bulletin* 5, no. 1 (1995): 38–49.

Granville, Johanna. "To Invade or Not to Invade? A New Look at Gomułka, Nagy, and Soviet Foreign Policy in 1956." *Canadian Slavonic Papers* 43 (December 2001): 437–474.

Werblan, A. "Władysław Gomułka and the Dilemmas of Polish Communism." *Internal Political Science Review* 9 (April 1988): 143–158.

Gorbachev, Mikhail (1931–) *general secretary of the Communist Party of the Soviet Union*

Mikhail Sergeyevich Gorbachev was born in Privolnoye, Stavropol, Soviet Union, on March 2, 1931, into a peasant family. He drove farm machinery before enrolling at Moscow State University in 1952 to study law. Gorbachev also joined the Communist Party to enhance his political and personal fortunes. After graduating he returned to Stavropol to work within the Komsomol youth organization and advanced to regional leader. In this capacity he became acquainted with YURI ANDROPOV, a rising star within the party elite. By 1962 Gorbachev had been promoted to secretary of agriculture in Stavropol where he gained a reputation as a hardworking, intelligent young operative. At length Andropov prevailed upon ailing party secretary LEONID BREZHNEV to transfer Gorbachev to Moscow in 1978. There he functioned as agriculture secretary of the entire Soviet Union, but despite his best effort, failed to upgrade its performance. This convinced Gorbachev that deep-seated structural changes were necessary to improve the stagnating Soviet economy. After Andropov succeeded Brezhnev in January 1980, he adopted Gorbachev as his protégé and the two men began concerted efforts to stamp out corruption and alcoholism. For his good performance Gorbachev gained promotion as a full voting member of the Politburo, the highest decision-making body in the Soviet Union. However, his reputation as an ardent reformer alienated conservative party members, so that when Andropov died suddenly in 1982, hard-liner KONSTANTIN CHERNENKO advanced to succeed him. Gorbachev ignored the slight and continued cementing his reputation as a youthful and vigorous leader. After the ailing Chernenko died in March 1985, Gorbachev became first secretary of the Communist Party the following day.

Gorbachev embarked on an ambitious reform program to improve living and working conditions in the Soviet Union, which had declined dramatically since the 1970s. Thus were born the twin policies of glasnost (openness) and perestroika (restructuring), which addressed the last vestiges of Soviet totalitarianism. The affable and charismatic Gorbachev himself set the tone for his new administration by meeting ordinary citizens on the street and discussing their complaints. Such candor in the traditionally closed Russian society was as unprecedented as it was welcome. Freedom of expression, unthinkable in the days of JOSEPH STALIN, was also encouraged in the arts, literature, and the press. Furthermore, Gorbachev fostered the growth of political factions inside the dominant Communist Party, to entertain as wide a spectrum of political views as possible. In economic reforms, Gorbachev proved less bold, remaining firmly wedded to the notion of state control and centralized planning. He assented to the rise of private factories and farms to encourage personal incentive, growth, and competition. But his unwillingness to embrace more radical measures, backed by an unshakable belief that communism could be reformed, ensured that economic growth remained below expectations.

Gorbachev made his biggest impact in foreign affairs. The expansionist policies of his predecessors had caused tense relations with the United States, and the new first secretary was intent on mending fences. He met repeatedly with British prime minister MARGARET THATCHER and American president RONALD REAGAN, impressing both with his warmth, intelligence, and willingness to compromise. Several arms reduction treaties were concluded, including the destruction of all intermediate-range missiles stationed in Europe. He also ended the Soviet occupation of Afghanistan by withdrawing troops in 1989. More dramatically Gorbachev encouraged the downfall of hard-line communist regimes in East Germany, Hungary, Poland, and Romania. By 1989 all had been replaced by democratically elected governments, while Gorbachev committed himself to a phased withdrawal of Russian troops from Eastern Europe. When the Berlin Wall finally fell, Europe had undergone a transformation that was as remarkable as it had been peaceful. The 40-year-old cold war, which had engendered several brushes with nuclear warfare, was concluded without a shot. For his remarkable contributions to world stability, Gorbachev received the Nobel Peace Prize in 1990.

Back home, Gorbachev's reform efforts were being seriously compromised by conservatives in the Communist Party and the rising tide of nationalism. The Soviet Union comprised several ethnic republics, all of which began clamoring for greater autonomy from Moscow. This was especially true in the three Baltic states of Latvia, Estonia, and Lithuania, which agitated for complete independence. In 1990 Gorbachev utilized military force to maintain order in the republics, but the genie of nationalism had escaped its bottle, never to return. Gorbachev also faced increasing competition from Boris Yeltsin, an ex-communist now serving as president of the new Russian Republic. Yeltsin publicly railed against Gorbachev's reforms as inadequate and pressed for greater liberalization of the economy. Conservatives were equally distressed by what they considered the loss of Russian greatness, and they systematically blocked reform efforts. Events climaxed on August 19, 1991, when a group of hard-liners seized Gorbachev while he was on vacation. Back in Moscow, Yeltsin quickly rallied public resistance to the coup, which collapsed after three days. Gorbachev was released unharmed, but his political position had been fatally compromised. Yeltsin was clearly controlling events thereafter and he systematically dismantled the Soviet empire and removed the Communist Party from power. On December 25, 1991, the national legislature voted the Soviet Union out of existence. That dreaded totalitarian regime, spawned from blood, fire, and revolution, passed into history without a whimper.

Gorbachev next resumed the life of a private citizen in demand for lecturing and fund-raising. He established the Gorbachev Foundation to discuss and explore global policy issues. And as a member of the Green Cross, an organization dedicated to the destruction of the world's remaining stocks of chemical and biological weapons, he has been an outspoken proponent of continued disarmament. While visiting London in July 2002, he declared, "Our project is aimed at eliminating the environmental consequences of the Cold War and the arms race. It is a terrible legacy we are trying to deal with." Gorbachev's seven-year tenure in office proved a decisive turning point in world history for, by reforming the inherently flawed communist system, he inadvertently hastened its demise.

Further Reading

Arbel, David. *Western Intelligence and the Collapse of the Soviet Union, 1980–1990: Ten Years That Did Not Shake the World.* London: Frank Cass, 2003.

Beissinger, Mark R. *Nationalist Mobilization and the Collapse of the Soviet State.* New York: Cambridge University Press, 2002.

Breslauer, George W. *Gorbachev and Yeltsin as Leaders.* New York: Cambridge University Press, 2002.

Gorbachev, Mikhail. *On My Country and the World.* New York: Columbia University Press, 2000.

Kotkin, Stephen. *Armageddon Averted: The Soviet Collapse, 1970–2000.* Oxford: Oxford University Press, 2001.

March, Luke. *The Communist Party in Post-Soviet Russia.* Manchester, England: University of Manchester Press, 2002.

Mlynar, Zdenek. *Conversations with Gorbachev on Perestroika, the Prague Spring, and the Crossroads of Socialism.* New York: Columbia University Press, 2002.

Gorton, John (1911–2002) *prime minister of Australia*

John Grey Gorton was born in Melbourne, Australia, on September 11, 1911, to affluent English parents. He passed through several elite boarding schools before attending Oxford University in England for a history degree. Returning home in 1936 Gorton ran the family orchards for three years until the advent of World War II. He then joined the Royal Australian Air Force and served several years as a fighter pilot before being shot down in 1942. His face was seriously disfigured, and the need for repeated plastic surgery finally led to his discharge in 1944. Afterward Gorton became involved in local politics and joined the Liberal (actually conservative) Party in 1948. The following year he was elected to the Australian Senate during the election sweep of Prime Minister ROBERT GORDON MENZIES. For many years thereafter Gorton held a number of ministerial portfolios throughout various Liberal governments. By October 1967 his strong political skills led to an appointment as Senate leader, and he was also a conspicuous part of Prime Minister Sir Harold Holt's administration. However when Holt subsequently drowned in an accident, the Liberals were forced to elect a new leader. Gorton was viewed as a compromise candidate, and on January 10, 1968, he was sworn to high office. He thus became the first senator to be prime minister, for the majority of Australia's national leaders originate from the House of Representatives. Gorton corrected this anomaly by resigning from the Senate and winning the House seat previously occupied by Holt.

Despite the best of intentions Gorton proved a divisive figure for the Liberal Party. Earthy, self-effacing, and unorthodox, he portrayed himself as a larger-than-life nationalist with a robust appetite for the sporting and outdoor activities so loved by Australians. But Gorton's informal style alienated more stodgy members of his own administration and he acquired powerful enemies. He did little to ameliorate tensions by playing favorites in office and shifting potential rivals aside when it suited him. Gorton further estranged himself from the party establishment by attempting to strengthen the Commonwealth at the expense of states, alienating the powerful regional sections of the party. His inability to inspire loyalty, his penchant for fast living and being seen in public with women other than his wife provided additional grist for the political mills. In the end Gorton was far more popular among the Australian people than with his fellow Liberals.

In office Gorton was a pronounced moderate in his approach to national issues and less dogmatic than many party elders. He discouraged overseas investment, enlarged government's role in education, and asserted national priorities over states' rights. He was also caught up in a heated debate over the American war in Vietnam. Like his predecessor Gorton supported Australian involvement in the war, but he labored to limit the troops and resources committed. He also ushered through Congress an unpopular conscription bill for drafting young men into military service. His unorthodox style of leadership and a resurgence in Labor support translated into the loss of 18 seats during the November 1969 elections, at which point more ambitious members of his cabinet began distancing themselves from him. The most embarrassing moment occurred on March 31, 1971, when Defense Minister MALCOLM FRASER withdrew from the cabinet and denounced Gorton as disloyal to the party. This triggered a vote of "no confidence" in the House, which resulted in a 33-33 tie vote. Surprisingly, it fell upon Gorton to cast the deciding "no" vote, and he became the first Australian prime minister to vote himself out of office. He was then succeeded by William McMahon, who granted him the portfolio of defense minister.

Gorton's term as defense minister proved brief, for he began writing a series of scathing newspaper articles about the back-stabbing nature of his fellow Liberals. This prompted McMahon to fire him, and in 1972 he resigned from the party altogether. The quixotic old fighter pilot made a final stab at running as an independent senator in 1975 but was defeated. Thereafter Gorton remained in semiretirement from politics, emerging occasionally to make controversial statements to the press. He died in Sydney on May 19, 2002, unmourned by his party, perhaps, but very much "his own man."

Further Reading

Frankrum, Ronald B. *The United States and Australia in Vietnam, 1954–1968: Silent Partners.* Lewiston, N.Y.: Edwin Mellen Press, 2001.

Hancock, Ian. *John Gorton: He Did It His Way.* Sydney: Hodden Australia, 2002.

Griffen-Foley, Bridget. "Sir Frank Packer and the Leadership of the Liberal Party, 1967–71."

Australian Journal of Political Science 36 (November 2001): 499–513.

Reid, Alan D. *The Power Struggle.* Sydney: Shakespeare Head Press, 1969.

———. *The Gorton Experiment.* Sydney: Shakespeare Head Press, 1971.

Western, J. S., and Colin A. Hughes. "Hunting the PM: The Sequel." *Australian Quarterly* 44, no. 1 (1972): 30–41.

Gottwald, Klement (1896–1953) *president of Czechoslovakia*

Klement Gottwald was born in Dedice, Moravia (Austria-Hungary), on November 23, 1896, the illegitimate son of a peasant. He apprenticed as a carpenter in Vienna before being conscripted into the Austro-Hungarian army to fight in World War I. Gottwald served with distinction before deserting to Russia in 1917. There he witnessed firsthand the exciting transformations undertaken by VLADIMIR LENIN's Bolshevik Party and became committed to the cause. In 1918 he returned to the new nation of Czechoslovakia and joined the leftist Social Democratic Party. Largely through his agitation the left wing of the party split off in 1921 to form the Czechoslovakian Communist Party (CPC). Gottwald was extremely active as a party leader and newspaper editor, and by 1927 he functioned as secretary general. In this capacity he also gained election to the national legislature and continually railed against his bourgeois opponents. Gottwald's behavior proved so belligerent that in 1936 he was exiled to the Soviet Union where he pledged undying loyalty to JOSEPH STALIN. He returned two years later just as Czechoslovakia fell under increasing pressure from ADOLF HITLER to surrender the German-speaking Sudetenland. Gottwald spoke out strongly on behalf of national defense and extended his hand in friendship to former adversaries but after the infamous Munich Pact of September 1938 he fled to Moscow for his own safety. He spent most of World War II in front of a microphone, exhorting armed resistance to the German occupation. Gottwald had clearly won Stalin's favor, however, for in 1943 he conferred with Czechoslovakian president EDUARD BENEŠ to discuss a plan for postwar administration. Once the nation had been occupied by Russian troops, Gottwald arrived to bring it into the Soviet orbit.

Gottwald now entered into a motley coalition government, the National Front. In June 1946 the communists triumphed in free elections, winning 38 percent of votes cast and becoming the largest single party. At that juncture Beneš felt obliged to appoint Gottwald prime minister. He was initially viewed as a moderate and pledged himself to respect freedoms of speech and the press as outlined in the constitution. However, on orders from Stalin, Gottwald began hatching a plot to subvert the government and install a Soviet-style dictatorship. In February 1948 his plans were revealed by noncommunist members of the administration who then resigned from the coalition en masse. Gottwald, faced with impending defeat at the polls, organized street demonstrations, seized factories and schools, and threatened a general strike. Beneš proved powerless to oppose him, and on February 25, 1948, he allowed Gottwald to form a new government of communists and their allies. The coup succeeded brilliantly, and by May Beneš himself had been forced from the presidency. Once Gottwald took his place, a new constitution was enacted that legalized one-party rule under the communists. He then dropped all pretense of following an independent path to socialism. The official party mantra now became, "With the Soviet Union forever."

Gottwald proved himself an utterly ruthless exponent of "Stalinization." Private property was abolished, industry and public works nationalized, and agriculture collectivized. Worse, the country was watched by an effective secret police operating under wide-ranging powers of arrest. Freedom of expression was curtailed, civil rights suspended, and transgressors severely punished. As proof of his total subservience to Stalin, Gottwald was ordered to purge the Communist Party of any "potential Titoists" who might oppose Moscow's authority. He happily complied and arrested several hundred party members, including many of his closest friends. They were subjected to elaborate Stalinist "show trials," convicted on manufactured evidence, and executed. Czechoslovakia thus became a full-fledged Soviet satellite state behind the Iron Curtain. But Gottwald did not long enjoy his handiwork. Stalin died in March 1953, and Gottwald dutifully attended his funeral during the cold Russian winter. Subsequently he contracted pneumonia and died in Prague on March 14, 1953, just days after the tyrant he so dutifully served. In true Stalinist fashion, his body was embalmed and put on public display in Prague.

Further Reading

Cohen, Barry M. "Moscow at Munich: Did the Soviet Union Offer Unilateral Aid to Czechoslovakia?" *East European Quarterly* 12, no. 3 (1978): 341–348.

Kraus, Michael. "The Kremlin and the Slovak National Uprising, August–October, 1944." *Slovakia* 34, nos. 62–63 (1989–90): 50ff.

Kurze, Marsch. *The Short March: The Communist Takeover of Czechoslovakia, 1945–48.* London: C. Hurst, 1987.

Skilling, H. Gordon. "Gottwald and the Bolshivization of the Communist Party of Czechoslovakia." *Slavic Review* 20, no. 4 (1961): 641–655.

Gouled Aptidon, Hassan (1916–) *president of Djibouti*

Hassan Gouled Aptidon was born in Zeila, French Somaliland, on October 15, 1916, a son of Issa nomads. After working many years as a street vendor he entered politics and by 1952 had been elected to the French National Assembly. Gouled Aptidon allied himself with President CHARLES DE GAULLE and supported his policy of allowing colonial territories greater autonomy and aid instead of independence. He returned home in 1963 to serve as minister of education but became increasingly disillusioned by French favoritism shown toward the minority Afar people. By 1969 Gouled Aptidon was serving in the Territorial Assembly and had switched his political allegiance to François Mitterrand of the Socialist Party. He now agitated for complete independence from France and also founded the Ligue Populaire Africaine pour l'Indépendance (LPAI), African People's League for Independence, to propagate his anti-imperialist beliefs. By December 1975 France had declared its intention to withdraw from the Horn of Africa, and a 10-member governing council was established as a transition government. The council was carefully drawn up along ethnic lines and comprised six Issa and four Afar. Gouled Aptidon, as one of French Somaliland's most respected politicians, was appointed to a seat, and on June 24, 1977, he was voted president of the newly founded Republic of Djibouti. He retained power for the next 22 years.

Independence did little to mitigate deep-seated tribal tensions between the majority Issa and minority Afar, but Gouled Aptidon achieved an unexpected degree of consensus through a masterful juggling of ethnic priorities. The president deliberately cultivated friendly ties with Afar leaders, appointing several to positions of responsibility within his government, including prime minister. Furthermore, he downplayed traditional tribal rivalries while stressing their common Arabic heritage as a unifying factor. To further reduce ethnic competition in politics, he installed one-party rule through creation of the Rassemblement pour la République (RPR), Popular Rally for Progress, which replaced the LPAI in March 1979. In July 1981 Gouled Aptidon, running as the sole candidate, was overwhelmingly elected by popular vote to a second six-year term. He repeated this feat again on April 24, 1987, with 90 percent of votes cast.

As chief executive, Gouled Aptidon displayed considerable ingenuity in transforming Djibouti from a parched desert enclave into a center of high tech and commerce. He accomplished this by maintaining close ties to France, granting it naval facilities on the Red Sea, and receiving foreign aid in return. This assistance was channeled into badly needed irrigation programs, geothermal facilities, and oil exploration. Djibouti's port and rail facilities were also upgraded to handle increased trade with the interior. Consequently, the tiny nation emerged as one of the most stable and prosperous regions of the volatile Horn of Africa. And despite his affinity for the West, Gouled Aptidon joined the Arab League, establishing close ties to Egypt and Saudi Arabia, and receiving additional financial and technical backing in return.

A major concern of Gouled Aptidon's administration was relations with its two larger neighbors, Ethiopia and Somalia. Djibouti at one time or another was claimed by both, and its port facilities constituted Ethiopia's only access to the sea. But for many years these two countries battled for possession of the Ogaden region, resulting in millions of refugees. Djibouti dutifully absorbed and cared for the displaced populations, comprising the same Issa and Afar people dominating their country. The refugees caused a tremendous drain on national resources, however, and Gouled Aptidon worked as a regional mediator, promoting peace and dialogue between the warring parties. His efforts succeeded in April 1988, when Ethiopia and Somalia reestablished diplomatic relations and tensions eased. As an added measure of security, Gouled Aptidon also relied upon the presence of a 5,000-strong French garrison as a guarantor of Djibouti independence.

By the early 1990s Gouled Aptidon faced growing opposition to one-party rule from Afar-dominated guerrilla groups. In 1993 he permitted a return to multiparty elections, but the opposition boycotted the process. That same year the aging president easily triumphed over four opponents, winning 60 percent of the vote. In 1994 an accord was reached with the insurgents, and peace has prevailed ever since. Gouled Aptidon was more than 80 years old in February 1999 when he finally announced his retirement from public office. He was succeeded by a hand-picked nominee, Ismail Omar Guelleh. His tenure in office is viewed as a major stabilizing influence in the Horn of Africa, a conduit for national development.

Further Reading

Aboubaker, Alawan Daoud. *Historical Dictionary of Djibouti.* Lanham, Md.: Scarecrow Press, 2000.

Agonafrer, Fantu. "Djibouti's Three-Way Struggle for Independence, 1967–77." Unpublished master's thesis, University of Denver, 1979.

Cutbill, Catherine C. "A Postcolonial Predicament: Imagining Djibouti." Unpublished Ph.D. diss., University of Virginia, 1994.

"Djibouti." *The Courier* no. 153 (September–October 1995): 14–31.

Saint Vernon, Robert, and Virginia M. Thompson. *Djibouti, Pawn of the Horn of Africa.* Metuchen, N.J.: Scarecrow Press, 1981.

Schraeder, Peter J. "Ethnic Politics in Djibouti: From Eye of the Hurricane to Boiling Caldron." *African Affairs* 92 (April 1993): 203–222.

Gowon, Yakubu (1934–) *military head of state, Nigeria*

Yakubu Dan Yumma Gowon was born in Lur Pankshim, Plateau State, Nigeria, on October 19, 1934, the son of a Christian evangelist and a member of the minority Angas tribe. He was well educated at missionary schools before joining the army in 1954. Gowon proved competent as a soldier and received advanced military training in Ghana and at the Royal Military Academy, Sandhurst. Once home he had prominent roles in Nigerian peacekeeping efforts in the Congo, 1960–63, rising to lieutenant colonel. Gowon was absent from the country during a January 1966 military coup that killed the prime minister, ALHAJI SIR ABUBAKAR TAFAWA BALEWA, and installed General Aguiyi-Ironsi as president. The new leader then appointed Gowon army chief of staff with a rank of general. When northern ethnic officers staged a countercoup that July, in which Aguiyi-Ironsi died, the hunt for an acceptable successor led to Gowon, a northerner untainted by any conspiracies. On August 1, 1966, aged but 32 years, he became Africa's youngest head of state.

From the onset Gowon displayed moderate tendencies by releasing political prisoners and pledging to restore democracy as soon as practical. However, recurrent ethnic tensions resulted in large-scale massacres of Ibo people in the north. The 10-million-strong Ibo, who dominated the eastern third of the nation, undertook steps to secede. Gowon met repeatedly with their military leader, Colonel CHUKWUEMEKA OJUKWU, to forestall hostilities but to no avail. He declared a state of emergency, dividing the nation into 12 states to sever Ibo access to the sea. Ojukwu declared a new state of Biafra on May 27, 1967, starting an intense and costly civil war. Gowon, as military head of state, sought desperately to keep Nigeria functioning as a united nation. His conciliatory position became one of "no victors and no vanquished." Gowon ordered his troops into action against the rebels but issued a stern "Code of Conduct" to moderate their behavior. This required them to treat captured Biafrans as fellow Nigerians and not external enemies. To further demonstrate his intentions, Gowon allowed international observers to accompany military units in the field. He also turned a blind eye toward foreign food relief flights into the rebel areas, not wishing to starve civilians. After two and a half years of intense fighting and nearly 2 million deaths, federal forces reunited Biafra with the rest of Nigeria. Gowon, in a show of surprising magnanimity, eschewed punitive measures against Colonel Ojukwu and welcomed the Ibo back into the fold. It remains one of Africa's most peaceful acts of national reconciliation.

The restoration of peace did little to ameliorate Nigeria's pressing social and political problems. The country remained riven by corruption and ethnic tensions that could have erupted at any moment. In 1970 Gowon had optimistically predicted that he would be able to restore civilian rule, a new constitution, and new elections within six years. But by 1974 he felt obliged to delay the return of democracy until internal order had been consolidated. This reversal disappointed many civilians and also encouraged military opponents to lay their own plans. On July 27, 1975, while Gowon was attending the Organization for African Unity meeting in Uganda, he was toppled by military officers in a bloodless coup. General MURTALA RAMAT MUHAMMED, his successor, declared that Gowon was free to return at any time, but the former leader immigrated to England. There he enrolled at the University of Warwick to pursue a doctorate in sociology. In 1976 Gowon was implicated in an aborted coup against the government and declared an enemy of the state. The general denied any knowledge of the plot, insisting, "I give my word as an officer and a gentleman. I am not a plotter." However, it was not until 1981 that civilian president Shehu Shagari officially pardoned him; he came home the following year. In November 1987 Gowon's rank and titles were formally restored to him by President Ibrahim B. Babangida. He has since lived as a private citizen, but in 1999 Gowon emerged to campaign for the candidacy of fellow general Olusegun Obasanjo.

Further Reading

Abegunrin, Olayiwola. *Nigerian Foreign Policy under Military Rule, 1966–1999.* Westport, Conn.: Praeger, 2003.

Clarke, John D. *Yakubu Gowon: Faith in a United Nigeria.* Totowa, N.J.: Frank Cass, 1987.

Elaigwu, J. Isawa. *Gowon: The Biography of a Soldier-Statesman.* Ibadan, Nigeria: West Books Press, 1986: distributed in the U.S.A. and Canada by Humanities Press.

Forsyth, Frederick. *The Biafra Story: The Making of an African Legend.* London: Leo Cooper, 2001.

Oyovbaire, S. Egite. *Federalism in Nigeria: A Study in the Development of the Nigerian State.* New York: St. Martin's Press, 1985.

Peal, J. D. Y. "Two Northerners Contrasted in Their Visions of Nigerian Unity." *Canadian Journal of African Studies* 22, no. 1 (1988): 144–148.

Grósz, Karóly (1930–1996) *first secretary of the Socialist Workers Party of Hungary*

Karóly Grósz was born in Miskolc, Hungary, on August 1, 1930, into a working-class family. He trained as a printer and after 1945 joined the Hungarian Socialist Workers Party (HSWP). There he trained as a teacher for the Hungarian Young People's Federation and by 1954 had risen to membership on the Borsod County Committee. In 1956 Hungary was swept by an anti-Soviet revolution that ended with the execution of the reformers' prime minister, IMRE NAGY, and the rise of JÁNOS KÁDÁR. Grósz's role in this affair is not known, but he emerged from the chaos with his political career intact. After 1962 he was appointed secretary of the party committee at Hungarian Radio and Television, a choice propagandist position. He had acquired the reputation of a colorless but efficient apparatchik and continued rising quietly but steadily through the hierarchy. By 1985 he was first secretary of the Budapest HSWP central committee, and within two years gained national prominence to become prime minister over the heads of senior party officials. Hungary was then staggered by economic deterioration and social distress that threatened to unleash political instability. Grósz was now known as a hard-nosed reformer, loyal to the precepts of communism, but embracing liberalization as inevitable. He took the unprecedented steps of reviving the moribund economy by expanding the private sector and allowing for limited capitalism and private ownership. He also promoted a scheme of political pluralism by tolerating factions within the party as a prelude for alternative parties. These reforms were quite dramatic by communist standards, but they closely mirrored similar efforts by Soviet premier MIKHAIL GORBACHEV in Russia, and apparently received his blessing. Thanks to Grósz, an important corner had been rounded in the political history of communist Hungary; thereafter the country turned increasingly to the capitalist West for inspiration and investments.

Despite good intentions, Grósz restricted his reforms to halfway measures, which were politically acceptable but inadequate for modernizing Hungary. Another major reason for the lack of progress was the continuing presence of Kádár as general secretary of the HSWP, who acted as an ideological brake on reforms. By May 1988, however, the political situation had grown so untenable that an emergency meeting of the central committee removed Kádár and substituted the reform-minded Grósz. This was another milestone in Hungarian history, since Kádár had ruled unchecked since 1956. More important, the Communist Party was now wedded to the notion of democracy, and the pace of liberalization accelerated. Grósz proceeded to cement his credentials as a reformer by visiting various heads of state in the West. He singularly impressed British prime minister

MARGARET THATCHER on a state visit, and in July 1988 he paid a similar call upon American president RONALD REAGAN. Grósz thus became the first Hungarian leader to visit Washington in 42 years. In August 1988 he also met with fellow Communist NICOLAE CEAUŞESCU in a failed attempt to secure better treatment for the Hungarian minority living in Romania. But once home, Grósz fell under increasing pressure to open up the political process by returning to multiparty democracy. This would have spelled the end to communism in Hungary altogether—a move that Grósz was still either unable or unwilling to take. Events crested in the October 1989 meeting of the central committee, when the HSWP renamed itself the Hungarian Socialist Party and formally dedicated itself to democratic principles. Grósz remained aloof from events and, clinging to the past, he reestablished the HSWP in December 1989 with himself as party head. But the following March was the decisive moment, when Hungarians voted in their first free election since 1945 and the communists were completely defeated.

Perhaps Grósz's greatest contribution to the reform process was his peaceful surrender of power. Disillusioned by events, he left public life altogether and lived in relative obscurity. He died in Budapest on January 7, 1996, a political anachronism swept away by the tide of change.

Further Reading

Adair, Bianca L. "The Evolution of Hungarian Democracy: Antisystems in Communist Hungary." Unpublished Ph.D. diss., University of Alabama, 2000.

Bockman, Johanna K. "Economists and Social Change: Science, Professional Power, and Politics in Hungary, 1945–1995." Unpublished Ph.D. diss., University of California–San Diego, 2000.

Kurti, Lazlo. *Youth and State in Hungary: Capitalism, Communism, and Class.* Sterling, Va.: Pluto Press, 2002.

Meusburger, Peter, and Heike Jons, eds. *Transformations in Hungary: Essays in Economy and Society.* New York: Physica-Verlag, 2001.

Schopflin, George, Rudolf Tokes, and Ivan Volgyes. "Leadership Change and Crisis in Hungary." *Problems of Communism* 37, no. 5 (1988): 23–46.

H

Habré, Hissène (1942–) *president of Chad*

Hissène Habré was born in Faya Largeau, Chad, in 1942, to shepherd parents of the Toubou tribe. He was educated locally and began working for the French army as a clerk. A promising administrator, Habré was allowed to visit France to attend the Institut International des Hautes Etudes Administratives for advanced training before returning home in 1971. The following year President FRANÇOIS TOMBALBAYE commissioned him to negotiate with Abba Siddik, leader of Frolinat, a hostile opposition movement. However, Habré promptly switched sides and joined the rebels, fighting for many years with Goukouni Oueddei, an allied commander. In 1976 he took several European hostages and held them for ransom, an act that infuriated Siddik and caused Habré to form his own movement, Forces Armées du Nord (FAN), the Armed Forces of the North. As head of FAN, he concluded a peace treaty with new Chadian executive FÉLIX MALLOUM and was appointed prime minister on August 29, 1978. In a power struggle between the two leaders, Oueddei suddenly toppled Malloum and installed himself as president. Habré then served as defense minister under Oueddei until friction with his supporters led to open conflict. The rebels were defeated and Habré retreated to the Sudan to recuperate and regroup. Months later he conducted a brilliant counteroffensive that drove Oueddei completely from power. On October 21, 1982, Habré was sworn in as president, the first time in 17 years that Chad functioned under a single head of state.

In office Habré's only political philosophy was to hold onto power by any means. His repressive regime was responsible for the deaths of an estimated 40,000 civilians. A further 200,000 claimed to have been tortured. But because he was viewed as a stabilizing force by the Organization of African Unity and the United Nations, Habré enjoyed a degree of political legitimacy. He also brooked no challenges to his rule. Once his power base was consolidated, he moved north to dislodge the remnants of Oueddei's followers. They had been heavily reinforced by Libyan forces sent by Colonel Muammar Gadhafi and recaptured much lost ground. In 1983 Chadian forces failed to remove the rebels, and Habré successfully appealed for help from abroad. He then received troops from France and Niger, along with substantial American arms supplies. By 1986 the tide of fighting turned decisively, and Habré's forces had eliminated the rebels and Libyans from northern territories. In October 1988 Chad and Libya concluded a general cease-fire and hostilities stopped.

With his northern flank secure Habré returned to the problem of internal consolidation. In 1984 he founded a new national party, Union Nationale pour l'Indépendance et la Révolution (UNIR), the National Union for Independence and Revolution, to mend divisions between Christian southerners and Muslim northerners. Results were mixed and discord remained below the surface. In April 1989 several government ministers attempted a failed coup against Habré and were pursued out of the country. Colonel Idriss Deby, the most accomplished leader, took refuge in the Sudan to rebuild his forces. The following December Habré was overwhelmingly elected president as the sole candidate and gained another seven years in office. However, his sheer brutality had alienated popular support, and his grip on power remained tenuous. This intrinsic weakness was underscored in November 1990 when Habré personally led a large-scale invasion of Sudan to eliminate Deby's forces and was decisively defeated. Due to the oppressive nature of his regime, the French refused to extend him any assistance. In December 1990 Habré fled to exile in Cameroon and then Senegal, after Deby captured the capital at Ndjamena and became president. Only then was the full extent of Habré's excesses realized, with the discovery of mass graves filled with political victims. An estimated 10,000 people had been murdered within the confines of the presidential compound. But the bloody civil war in Chad had ended, and it was time for national reconciliation. In December 1994 President Deby announced a general amnesty for his political opponents—with the singular exception of Habré.

In Dakar Habré is a wanted man. The many victims of his misrule, and a number of human rights organizations, Amnesty International in particular, have been pressing for his extradition and trial in Chad. In April 2001 Senegalese president Abdoulaye Wade asked him to leave the country, but otherwise took no steps against him. Habré remains one of Africa's most wanted fugitives.

Further Reading

Boyd, Herb. "Chad: A Civil War without End?" *Journal of African Studies* 10, no. 4 (1983–84): 119–126.

Brody, R. "The Prosecution of Hissène Habré–an African Pinochet." *North East Law Review* 35 (2001): 321–336.

James, F. "Habre's Hour of Glory." *African Report* 32 (September-October 1987): 20–23.

Joffe, George. "Turmoil in Chad." *Current History* 89 (April 1990): 157–160, 175–177.

May, Roy, and Simon Massey. "Two Steps Forward, One Step Back: Chad's Protracted 'Transition' to Democracy." *Journal of Contemporary African Studies* 18, no. 1 (2000): 107–132.

Miles, William F. S. "Tragic Tradeoffs: Democracy and State Security in Chad." *Journal of Modern African Studies* 33, no. 1 (1995): 513–565.

Haile Selassie (1892–1975) *emperor of Ethiopia*

Lij Tafari Makonnen was born in Ejersa Goro, Ethiopia, on July 23, 1892, a son of Ras (prince) Makonnen, grand-nephew of reigning emperor Menelik II. As such he claimed a family lineage dating back to King Solomon and the Queen of Sheba in biblical times. Tafari, a Coptic Christian, was raised at the imperial court in Addis Ababa, educated by French monks, and became acutely versed in court intrigue. At the age of 17 he was appointed governor of Sidamo province and in 1916 he helped depose Menelik's Muslim-oriented grandson, Lij Yasu, from the throne. Thereafter he installed himself as crown prince and regent while Zawditu, the emperor's daughter, became empress. For the next 14 years Tafari was the real power behind the throne. He displayed great interest in modernizing his charge to improve living conditions but also sought to weaken the feudal nobility and centralize his authority. In 1923 he outlawed the slave trade, led Ethiopia's entrance into the League of Nations, and had himself crowned king. Following the death of Zawditu in 1930 he succeeded to the throne as emperor and assumed the name Haile Selassie ("Power of the Trinity"). True to his reforming tendencies the new emperor ordered the construction of schools, roads, and hospitals and even promulgated the nation's first constitution. This document created Ethiopia's first appointed legislature but also reserved most governmental powers to the emperor. In 1935 he was attacked by BENITO MUSSOLINI's Italian forces, which easily crushed the poorly equipped Ethiopian tribesmen. He fled the country and pleaded before the League of Nations for help in regaining his throne. A short man with intense eyes and regal bearing, Haile Selassie harangued member states and prophetically warned, "It is us today. It will be you tomorrow." When aid was not forthcoming he remained in England for six years until British forces recaptured Ethiopia in May 1941. The emperor then made a triumphal return to his capital and began strengthening his ties to the United States and other Western countries.

Haile Selassie *(Library of Congress)*

Back in power Haile Selassie resumed his course of national modernization. He overhauled the bureaucracy, rebuilt his army, and sought to extend further control over the church and government. In November 1955 he issued a new constitution that granted the nation's first democratic elections, although he still retained the bulk of executive powers. By this time, Haile Selassie's reformist tendencies had moderated somewhat and he became more interested in preserving his authority. Furthermore, his reluctance to modernize the political system became a source of unrest as citizens acquired more education and began questioning the existing political order.

By the 1960s Haile Selassie had emerged as a leading voice of African nationalism. In 1963 he helped found the Organization of African Unity (OAU) with headquarters in Addis Ababa. He was active in diplomacy and personally mediated many disputes between African neighbors. However, he fomented considerable regional unrest by annexing the predominantly Muslim province of Eritrea in 1952 to secure direct access to the Red Sea. This led to an ongoing secessionist crisis that pitted Christians against Muslims and lasted 40 years. Discontent with Haile Selassie's autocratic reign began manifesting itself in 1960 while he was on a state visit to Brazil. Disillusioned students and part of his imperial guard rebelled and had to be crushed by military forces still loyal to the emperor. But he ignored the unrest and enacted no political liberalization. By 1973 the nation was beset by a serious drought that the government proved unable to respond to. The emperor by then had been in power for more than six decades and had grown increasingly detached from events. In April 1974 a group of dissident military officers formed a military committee called the Dergue to oversee national affairs. After dismissing most government ministers they suddenly forced Haile Selassie to abdicate his throne on September 13, 1974. The emperor remained under house arrest for nearly a year before dying under mysterious circumstances on August 27, 1975. The Dergue then proclaimed Ethiopia a socialistic people's republic under the leadership of General MENGISTU HAILE MARIAM. Haile Selassie remained buried in an unmarked grave until 1992, when his remains were properly interred with honors befitting Ethiopia's last emperor. In longevity and impact he was probably the most influential African leader of the 20th century.

Further Reading

Haile Selassie. *My Life and Ethiopia's Progress, 1892–1937: The Autobiography of Emperor Haile Selassie.* New York: Oxford University Press, 1976.

Haile-Selassie, Teferra. *The Ethiopian Revolution, 1974–91: From a Monarchical Autocracy to a Military Oligarchy.* New York: Kegan Paul International, 1997.

Henze, Paul B. *Layers of Time: A History of Ethiopia.* London: Hurst, 2000.

Lefebvre, J. A. "The United States, Ethiopia, and the 1963 Somalia-Soviet Arms Deal." *Journal of Modern African Studies* 36 (December 1998): 611–644.

Marcus, Harold. *Haile Selassie I: The Formative Years, 1892–1936.* Lawrenceville, N.J.: Red Sea Press, 1998.

Mockler, Anthony. *Haile Selassie's War.* New York: Olive Branch Press, 2003.

Hammarskjöld, Dag (1905–1961) *secretary general of the United Nations*

Dag Hjalmar Agne Carl Hammarskjöld was born in Jonkoping, Sweden, on July 29, 1905, part of an old aristocratic family steeped in traditions of public service. He graduated from the University of Stockholm in 1935 with a doctorate in political economics and the following year worked for the department of finance. Following a stint as president of the National Bank, Hammerskjold was appointed a finance specialist in the foreign office in 1946, which granted him greater exposure to international affairs. Two years later he served as vice chairman of the Organization for European Economic Cooperation (OEEC), which assisted European nations administering the American-sponsored Marshall Plan for postwar recovery. Hammarskjöld, a brilliant, intense, and deeply committed individual, joined the United Nations General Assembly in 1951 as vice chairman of the Swedish delegation. That international body, created in 1945 to promote peaceful cooperation, was in a quandary over how to fulfill its charter on a global basis. Furthermore it was beset by intense bickering between member states. The gridlock proved so intractable that the first secretary general, TRYGVE LIE of Norway, tendered his resignation. The hunt for a successor began and Hammarskjöld, a member of neutral Sweden, replaced him in 1952. It proved a decisive turning point in the history of the United Nations.

Hammarskjöld assumed his post imbued with a sense of destiny and profound commitment to his charge. Intent upon doing things in a new way, he embarked on his own brand of personal "quiet diplomacy" as a conduit for conflict resolution. In 1955 he successfully secured the release of 15 Americans, held by Communist China, who had been captured during the Korean War. He also attempted mediating between Israeli president DAVID BEN-GURION and Egyptian president GAMAL ABDEL NASSER to prevent violence in the Middle East. However, when Nasser subsequently nationalized the strategic Suez Canal, prompting Israeli, French, and British intervention, he successfully negotiated a halt to hostilities. This was followed by the first imposition of armed UN peacekeepers and the withdrawal of foreign forces from Egypt. Around this time, Lebanon was racked by political instability occasioning the deployment of U.S. marines to the region. But once again Hammarskjöld managed to insert armed peacekeepers between the belligerents, facilitating the removal of American forces without incident. His actions displayed international cooperation of a very high order and established precedents for UN intervention to circumvent armed confrontations.

Despite his successes, Hammarskjöld was roundly attacked by Soviet premier NIKITA KHRUSHCHEV, who felt him too beholden to Western interests. Moreover Khrushchev wanted to replace the office of secretary general with a three-member panel consisting of representatives from the East, the West, and a neutral country. But Hammarskjöld enjoyed tremendous personal popularity among member nations and in September 1957 he was overwhelmingly elected to a second five-year term. He then felt free to expand United Nations operations to include financial assistance for developing nations in Asia, Latin America, and especially Africa, which he referred to as the Third World. Under his tutelage the UN emerged with new operating guidelines as an impartial body ready to act in the best interests of both peace and development. Africa in particular remained an area of concern to Hammarskjöld for the rest of his tenure in office. In 1960 he conducted an extensive 23-nation inspection that convinced him of the need for continuing assistance to emerging political systems. In 1961 the new nation of Congo experienced a secessionist crisis when Katanga Province rebelled under MOÏSE TSHOMBE, which induced Belgium to deploy troops there. Khrushchev loudly decried the move as imperialistic and pledged support to Congo prime minister PATRICE LUMUMBA, while the United States and its allies fell in behind pro-Western president JOSEPH KASAVUBU. Hammarskjöld felt the unfolding crisis was sufficiently threatening to intervene personally, and he flew to Africa to consult with the contenders. However, on September 18, 1961, his plane crashed in Ndola, Zambia, killing all on board. Hammarskjöld was greatly mourned and he was replaced by Thailand's U THANT, the United Nations' first non-European secretary.

Hammarskjöld was unquestionably the United Nations' most effective secretary general, and in 1961 he received a posthumous Nobel Peace Prize. In 1997 he was further honored through creation of the Hammarskjöld Medal, awarded to UN peacekeepers killed in the line of duty.

Further Reading

Gibbs, David M. "Dag Hammarskjöld, the United Nations, and the Congo Crisis of 1960–61: A

Reinterpretation." *Journal of Modern African Studies* 31 (March 1993): 163–174.

Hammarskjöld, Dag. *Markings.* New York: Knopf, 1964.

Heller, Peter B. *The United Nations under Dag Hammarskjöld.* Lanham. Md.: Scarecrow Press, 2001.

Hughes, M. "The Strange Death of Dag Hammarskjöld." *History Today* 51 (October 2001): 2–3.

Oren, Michael B. "Ambivalent Adversaries: David Ben-Gurion and Israel vs. the United Nations and Dag Hammarskjöld." *Journal of Contemporary History* 27 (January 1992): 89–127.

Rosio, Bengt. "The Ndola Crash and the Death of Dag Hammarskjöld." *Journal of Modern African Studies* 31 (December 1993): 661–671.

Harding, Warren G. (1865–1923) *president of the United States*

Warren Gamaliel Harding was born in Blooming Grove, Ohio, on November 2, 1865, the son of a farmer. Educated locally, he attended Ohio Central College before beginning a journalism career in 1884. In concert with his ambitious wife, Florence Kling De Wolfe, he transformed the ailing Marion *Star* into a successful newspaper and was gradually drawn into politics. At first glance, Harding seemed like a natural for elected office: he was handsome, affable, and a gifted orator. Unfortunately he lacked genuine intellectual capacity and was more concerned with getting along with people than crafting policies. In 1899 he was elected to the state senate as a Republican and subsequently served two terms as lieutenant governor. In 1910 and 1912 he lost two bids for the governorship but, at the behest of his wife, he continued circulating among the Old Guard or conservative wing of his party. In 1912 he was tapped to nominate WILLIAM H. TAFT at the party convention, and two years later Harding became the first popularly elected U.S. senator from Ohio.

By 1919 the nation was weary of the trauma of World War I and nostalgic for simpler times. Harding declared his candidacy for the presidency, promising his countrymen a "return to normalcy." He won the nomination as a compromise candidate after eight ballots and was teamed with the austere and relatively unknown CALVIN COOLIDGE as vice president. Harding eschewed national campaigning in favor of interviews given from his front porch to throngs of visitors at his Marion home. To many voters he embodied the spirit and values of hometown America, so in 1920 Harding was elected over Democrat James M. Cox by 60.3 percent of the vote—the largest winning margin recorded to that time.

In office Harding proved himself hard-working and personally scrupulous. But he recognized his own scholarly limitations and appointed a cabinet of strong-minded individuals. Two of these, Charles Evans Hughes as secretary of state and HERBERT HOOVER as secretary of commerce, proved outstanding. The director of the budget, Charles G. Dawes, was also an excellent administrator. Harding then made the mistake of appointing friends and cronies to positions of authority, including Harry Daugherty as attorney general and Albert B. Fall as secretary of the interior. He selected them as much to pay off political debts as anything else, yet he believed in them implicitly. As

Warren G. Harding *(Library of Congress)*

events demonstrated, his trust was misplaced and they were widely derogated as the "Ohio gang."

Harding had previously campaigned against American entry into the League of Nations, but he sought to relieve world tensions by sponsoring the Washington Naval Disarmament Conference in 1921. This concluded with the United States, Great Britain, Italy, France, and Japan all pledging to limit the construction of large warships. Harding also signed laws reducing the steel industry's workday to eight hours, imposing higher tariffs, lowering taxes on business, and reducing immigration. His legislative success reflected his immense national popularity at that time, but by 1923 events within his inner circle began going awry. The public became aware of scandals involving some of Harding's closest associates, including Charles Forbes of the Veterans Bureau, whom he allowed to leave the country to escape prosecution. Subsequent investigations induced several members of Forbes's staff to commit suicide rather than testify. More shocking were revelations that Interior Secretary Fall had acquired the naval oil reserves at Teapot Dome, Wyoming, and was selling exploration rights in return for kickbacks. Attorney General Daugherty himself was also implicated in several schemes and brought to trial. Harding grew so exasperated by the incessant stream of allegations that he quipped he could handle his enemies, it was his friends that he worried about.

Harding grew depressed over the rumor mill surrounding his presidency, although he himself was never implicated in any misconduct. By the summer of 1923 he sought to shore up political support by touring the nation and giving speeches. While visiting Alaska the president suddenly fell ill and was rushed to San Francisco. He died there on August 2, 1923, and was succeeded by Coolidge. Harding was a talented politician but a poor judge of character. For this reason he is regarded as America's least effective president.

Further Reading

Anthony, Carl S. *Florence Harding: The First Lady, the Jazz Age, and the Death of America's Most Scandalous President.* New York: W. Morrow, 1998.

Dean, John W. *Warren G. Harding.* New York: Times Books, 2004.

Ferrell, Robert H. *The Strange Death of President Harding.* Columbia: University of Missouri Press, 1996.

Frederick, Richard G. *Warren G. Harding: A Biography.* Westport, Conn.: Greenwood Press, 1992.

Grant, Philip. "President Warren G. Harding and the British War Debt Question, 1921–1923." *Presidential Studies Quarterly* 25 (summer 1995): 479–487.

Harding, Warren G. *Our Common Country: Mutual Good Will in America.* Edited by Warren G. Harding III. Columbia: University of Missouri Press, 2003.

Murray, Robert K. *The Harding Era: Warren G. Harding and His Administration.* Newtown, Conn.: American Political Biography, 2000.

Hatoyama Ichiro (1883–1959) *prime minister of Japan*

Ichiro Hatoyama was born in Tokyo, Japan, on January 1, 1883, the son of two noted educators. He graduated from Tokyo Imperial University in 1907 and entered politics by being elected to the Diet in 1915 with the conservative Seiyukai Party. He held down successive ministerial posts throughout the 1920s and 1930s, displaying pronounced conservative tendencies. He soon became identified with the rightist faction of ultranationalists and stirred controversy for proposing the death penalty for all opponents of "national polity," a byword for political control. Hatoyama was a vocal proponent of Japanese expansion onto the Asian mainland and supported the annexation of Manchuria. He also demanded an end to negotiations with Great Britain and the United States over naval arms limitations. In 1931 Hatoyama took charge of the ministry of education, where he instituted curbs on freedom of speech and textbook revisions to reflect strident nationalism. In May 1933 he dismissed a prominent faculty member of Kyoto Imperial University for noncompliance, which led to 36 other resignations in protest. Hatoyama himself was forced to resign from office in the wake of an income tax scandal in 1934. Three years later he accompanied Prince KONOE FUMIMARO on a tour of the United States to seek accord with President FRANKLIN D. ROOSEVELT's administration. He also wrote a book commenting favorably on the Nazis under ADOLF HITLER. But commencing in 1937 Hatoyama modified his tone and began opposing the more extreme measures of Prime Minister TOJO HIDEKI that had precipitated World War II in the Pacific. By the time of Japan's final defeat in 1945, Hatoyama's activities had solidified the perception that he supported the prewar militarist clique responsible for the war.

After Japan was forcibly occupied by the American military, democracy was slowly reintroduced. Hatoyama founded a new political organization, the Liberal Party, which scored impressive gains in the May 1946 elections. He was on the point of forming a coalition government with other factions and becoming prime minister when occupation authorities interceded and removed him from power. Having branded Hatoyama as a militarist and ultranationalist they forbade him from holding public office until further notice. A more acceptable candidate, YOSHIDA SHIGERU, was made prime minister in his stead. Hatoyama remained in the background until 1951, when the Americans prepared to end their military occupation. He resumed his seat in the Diet and formed a new organization, the Democratic Party, which consisted largely of his previous supporters whose defections forced Yoshida from office. So in December 1954, Hatoyama emerged as Japan's second postwar prime minister.

Though in power, Hatoyama's Democratic Party lacked a ruling majority, so he strove to unite all conservative factions under one umbrella organization. The result was the new Liberal Democratic Party, which completely dominated Japanese national politics from 1955 for the next four decades. As prime minister, Hatoyama still brimmed with nationalistic pride and sought to reduce Japan's overweening reliance upon the United States in defense and foreign policy matters. He therefore tried to modify the postwar constitutional articles forbidding Japan from rearming. But given the painful memories of the recent conflict, his efforts were overwhelmingly rejected. Hatoyama then embarked on his next major objective: pursuit of an independent foreign policy. He began by negotiating with the Soviet Union, with whom Japan was still technically at war, for normalized relations. By October 1956 diplomatic recognition was mutually exchanged and other talks were held respecting trade and fisheries issues. He also gained Japan's entry into the United Nations that same year. But Hatoyama failed to resolve the issue of the Kuril Islands, seized by the Soviets in 1945, which remain an emotional point of contention to present times.

Under Hatoyama's tutelage, Japan slowly emerged from under America's giant shadow. He accomplished much useful legislation, but his conservative approach toward restricting universal suffrage and repealing voting rights for women was not approved. Poor health forced him from office in December 1956 and he died in Tokyo on March 7, 1959. But his brief time in office created a direction in Japanese politics that led his country back to the international stage along its own independent path.

Further Reading

Beer, Lawrence W. *From Imperial Myth to Democracy: Japan's Two Constitutions, 1889–2001.* Boulder: University Press of Colorado, 2002.

Braddick, C. W. *Japan and the Sino-Soviet Alliance, 1950–1964: In the Shadow of the Monolith.* New York: Palgrave Macmillan, 2004.

Luther, Catherine A. *Press Images, National Identity, and Foreign Policy: A Case Study of U.S.–Japan Relations from 1955–1995.* New York: Routledge, 2001.

Rozman, Gilbert. *Japan and Russia: The Tortuous Path to Normalization, 1949–1999.* New York: St. Martin's Press, 2000.

Saito, Motohide. "The 'Highly Crucial' Decision Making Model for Postwar Japan and Prime Minister Hatoyama's Policy towards the USSR." Unpublished Ph.D. diss., Columbia University, 1987.

Stockwin, J. A. A. *Dictionary of the Modern Politics of Japan.* New York: Routledge, 2003.

Hatta, Mohammad (1902–1980) *vice president of Indonesia*

Mohammad Hatta was born in Bukittinggi, Dutch West Indies (modern Indonesia), on August 12, 1902, into a family of Minangkabu Muslim intellectuals. He was well educated in colonial schools, learned Dutch, and in 1922 attended the University of Rotterdam to study economics. Like many youths of his generation, Hatta resented Dutch colonial rule, and he began organizing anti-imperialist student groups. In 1927 he was arrested by Dutch authorities for publishing seditious articles. Hatta remained undeterred, and he ultimately emerged as an intellectual leader within the Indonesian nationalist movement. He struck up cordial relations with Indian activist JAWAHARLAL NEHRU, and the two remained lifelong friends. Hatta obtained his doctorate in 1932 and came home to pursue political agitation. He helped found the National Education Club and joined forces with another radical leader, SUKARNO, to foment a campaign for independence. This resulted in his imprisonment and internal exile for several years. However, in 1942 Hatta was freed by victorious Japanese forces, and he joined their provisional government. He also served as vice president of Putera, a popular organization created to imbue the public with political activism. The Japanese deliberately fostered nationalism among Indonesians to promote a sense of "Asia for the Asians"—if only to better allow them to secure the islands' natural resources. But by 1945 Japan had lost the war, and before withdrawing they heavily armed Indonesian resistance forces. This triggered an upswelling of nationalism, and Hatta and Sukarno were both kidnaped by young activists and coerced into declaring immediate independence. Accordingly, on August 17, 1945, they proclaimed creation of the new Republic of Indonesia. Sukarno and Hatta were designated president and vice president by the provisional government.

Over the next four years the Netherlands waged an unsuccessful campaign to regain its colony. Hatta, now prime minister, gained world renown as an articulate spokesman for his people and for his ease in dealing with European politicians. In 1948 he gained considerable favor in the West by helping crush a communist-inspired insurrection in Java. The following year he helped to lay out the final details of Indonesian independence at The Hague. Hatta consequently gained appointment as vice president in Sukarno's administration. Once in office Hatta was unflinchingly committed to promoting socialism and Islamic principles. He also felt that the best manner of addressing the nation's economic problems was the establishment of cooperatives and decentralized administration. Hatta remained deeply committed to the notion of popular democracy, which put him on a collision course with Sukarno and his increasingly autocratic tenor. It was hoped Hatta's moderate policies would counteract the government's aggressive nationalism, but in July 1956, when Sukarno formally abolished free elections in favor of "guided democracy," Hatta resigned from office in protest. He then assumed various university teaching positions until the government forced him into seclusion in 1960. He never held public office again.

Hatta remained in the political background until the Sukarno regime was upended by Suharto in 1967. Thereafter he lacked real influence but continued functioning as an elder statesman and national philosopher.

He came out of retirement in 1978 to chair the Foundation for the Institute of Constitutional Awareness, convened to express discontent over Suharto's regime. Hatta died in Jakarta on March 14, 1980, still serving in this capacity. Throughout a long life he never forsook his vision of a united, peaceful country, modernized through Western economics and democracy yet guided by the spiritual tenets of Islam. He remains highly regarded as one of the founding fathers of Indonesia.

Further Reading

Friend, Theodore. *Indonesian Destinies.* Cambridge, Mass.: Belknap Press of Harvard University Press, 2003.

Kingsbury, Damien. *The Politics of Indonesia.* New York: Oxford University Press, 2002.

Laffan, Michael F. *Islamic Nationhood and Colonial Indonesia: The Umma below the Winds.* New York: Routledge, 2002.

Porter, Donald J. *Managing Politics and Islam in Indonesia.* New York: Routledge Curzon, 2002.

Rose, Mavis. *Indonesia Free: A Political Biography of Mohammad Hatta.* Ithaca, N.Y.: Cornell Modern Indonesia Project, Southeast Asia Program, Cornell University, 1987.

Taylor, Jean G. *Indonesia: The People and the Histories.* New Haven, Conn.: Yale University Press, 2003.

Hawke, Robert (1929–) *prime minister of Australia*

Robert James Lee Hawke was born in Bordertown, South Australia, on December 9, 1929, the son of a Congregational minister. His mother, an intensely religious woman, imbued her son with a sense of purpose and destiny that shaped and defined his political ambitions. Hawke passed through the University of Western Australia with distinction, won a Rhodes scholarship, and subsequently attended Oxford University in 1953. He came home to pursue a doctorate in labor relations at the Australian National University but quit to take a position within the influential Australian Council of Trade Unions (ACTU). There Hawke gained a reputation as a brilliant labor advocate and union leader. He also took an interest in national politics within the Australian Labor Party (ALP), losing a 1963 election to the House of Representatives but winning a seat in

1980. As head of the ACTU from 1973 to 1978 he acquired national exposure and was regarded as one of Australia's most popular public figures. Hawke also stood out from most contemporaries by deliberately cultivating a larger-than-life image. Handsome, rakishly dressed, a heavy drinker, and openly emotional, he struck a chord with constituents as the embodiment of Australian manhood. In February 1983 he succeeded Robert Hayden as leader of the ALP, a move that induced Liberal prime minister MALCOLM FRASIER to call early elections before the opposition could consolidate. However, he underestimated Hawke's charisma and organizational ability, for the Labor Party won handily the following month. Hawke thus became prime minister after an exceedingly brief tenure as head of his party, a feat unprecedented in Australian political history.

Hawke enjoyed pristine credentials as a labor operative but, drawing upon his religious upbringing, he also proffered himself as a peacemaker and a conciliator. In fact his tendency toward consensus rule was viewed as a refreshing change after the autocratic persona of Frasier. Consequently he ushered in a new age of harmony between unions and management, and achieved striking economic reforms. The government successfully deregulated the financial and banking markets, the Australian dollar was floated to make the country more competitive, the public service was completely overhauled, and a national surplus achieved. Hawke's administration also initiated a unique role reversal for the ALP; heretofore party leaders set the national agenda and imposed it on the government. But under Hawke's leadership the reverse was true—he decided what policy paths the government should adopt and had the party endorse them. In this manner the traditional Labor platforms of social and political reform gave way to economic restructuring. His success at juggling the priorities of labor and business resulted in the 1983 wage accord that rolled back wages—with union consent—in order to promote global competitiveness. Many hard-liners within the ALP accused Hawke of selling out his principles and cozying up to big business, but on three occasions Hawke was reelected prime minister—a feat never duplicated in Australian politics.

Hawke also enjoyed a measure of success in international affairs. He struck up cordial relations with American president RONALD REAGAN and expressed commitment to the state of Israel after meeting with Prime Minister GOLDA MEIR. However, the Australian economy was slipping into a deep recession by 1991, and Hawke began distancing himself from his treasury minister, Paul Keating, who fully expected to be nominated as his successor. The two men had a falling-out, and in December 1991 Keating orchestrated Hawke's removal as party head, leading him to angrily resign from office while still one of Australia's most popular politicians. Hawke has since taken up a career in business, where he has proved successful. He also remains outspoken on national policy and is a recurring critic of Liberal prime minister John Howard. Regarding the latter's unequivocal support for American president George W. Bush and his hard-line stance against Saddam Hussein before the 2003 war with Iraq, Hawke insisted, "We should not be jumping ahead of the U.S. the way we are. It's wrong, it's against our interests, and it's not, I believe, in the interests of the community internationally or of the U.S. itself." In September 2002, the former prime minister visited Yinchuan, China, to promote the use of advanced technology in solar energy. Hawke also praised the city's environmental-protection efforts respecting lakes and wetlands, advocating that Australia learn from such practices.

Further Reading

Brennan, Geoffrey, and Francis G. Castles. *Australia Reshaped: 200 Years of Institutional Transformation.* New York: Cambridge University Press, 2002.

Campbell, Colin, and John Halligan. *Political Leadership in an Age of Constraints: The Australian Experience.* Pittsburgh: University of Pittsburgh Press, 1993.

Cox, D. "Critical Assessment of the Hawke Government's 1985 Code of Conduct for Australian Companies with Interests in the Republic of South Africa." *Australian Journal of Political Science* 29 (July 1994): 302–320.

Hawke, Robert. *The Hawke Memoirs.* Port Melbourne, Victoria: Heinemann Australia, 1994.

Mills, Stephen. *The Hawke Years: The Story from the Inside.* New York: Viking, 1993.

Heath, Sir Edward (1916–) *prime minister of Great Britain*

Edward Richard George Heath was born in Broadstairs, Kent, England, on July 9, 1916, the son of a carpenter.

Despite common origins he excelled academically and was admitted to Balliol College, Oxford University. Heath then became politically active by joining the Conservative Party and was outspoken in his denunciation of Prime Minister NEVILLE CHAMBERLAIN's policy of appeasement. He graduated in 1939 with a degree in politics and immediately entered the Royal Artillery. Heath compiled an impressive service record in World War II, and afterward he served as a bureaucrat with the ministry of civil aviation. By 1950 he had been elected to the House of Commons from Bexley, Kent, which seat he held for 40 years. Heath quickly established himself as a rising star within Conservative ranks; throughout the 1950s he served as the junior whip in Parliament and proved instrumental in keeping the party unified during the Suez Crisis of 1956. Three years later Prime Minister HAROLD MACMILLAN appointed him minister of labor and he subsequently served as assistant secretary of state for industry, trade, and regional development under ALEXANDER DOUGLAS-HOME. As a politician Heath was committed to European unity and he campaigned hard to have England admitted into the European Economic Community. He was appreciably embittered when French president CHARLES DE GAULLE vetoed Britain's application in January 1963. Two years later Heath succeeded Douglas-Home as head of the Conservatives, becoming the youngest leader of the party in a century and also the first commoner and the first elected by a popular vote. In 1966 Heath lost the general election to Labour's HAROLD WILSON, and he spent the next five years reorganizing the Conservatives and broadening their appeal. In 1970 he managed a narrow victory over Wilson and became prime minister.

Despite his conservative credentials Heath was moderately disposed in terms of policy and outlook. He was also determined to enter the Common Market, and in January 1973 he prevailed upon French president GEORGES POMPIDOU to allow British membership. This was the high mark of his administration and a genuine political triumph in the face of fierce opposition from Labour and Conservatives alike. Heath, however, enjoyed far less success on the domestic front. He originally pursued a "quiet revolution" through reduction of government controls, lower taxes, and overhauling the trade union law. But after 1973 the nation reeled from recession and rising oil prices brought on by the Arab oil embargo. England became strapped for energy, and Heath declared a national emergency, adopting a three-day workweek to conserve supplies. This crippling dependency on oil emboldened the miners' union, whose strikes nearly brought the nation to a standstill. Heath also angered Conservatives by executing numerous U-turns on well-established conservative principles. As unemployment approached the 1 million mark he was forced to bail out various lame duck industries, which, under normal circumstances, would have succumbed. Northern Ireland was also rocked by the onset of sectarian violence, culminating in "Bloody Sunday," on January 30 1972, when British troops killed 13 Catholic protesters. Peace talks were suspended and the British imposed direct rule on the province. Still, Heath's most conspicuous failure proved economic, and in February 1974 Labour won the general election. Heath surrendered his office to Wilson, and the Conservatives were trounced again the following October. At this point many concluded Heath was an electoral liability, and in January 1975 he lost his post as party head to neo-conservative MARGARET THATCHER. He thus enjoys the melancholy distinction of being the first Conservative leader ousted by a vote. Heath was not gracious in defeat, for he disliked Thatcher personally, and subsequently railed against her archconservative policies.

Heath may have proven an unpopular leader but he continued sitting in Parliament for the next two decades. Throughout 1990–91 he visited Iraq repeatedly and negotiated the release of British hostages from Saddam Hussein. He has since acquired an international reputation for negotiations and statecraft, but his past eventually came back to haunt him. In 1999 Prime Minister Tony Blair instituted a commission to investigate the events of Bloody Sunday as a sop to peace efforts in Northern Ireland. On June 10, 2002, Heath was summoned before the committee to answer questions as to his knowledge of matters pertaining to the massacre. The former prime minister insisted that he give testimony in London and not Londonderry, for he feared an assassination attempt by Irish militants.

Further Reading

Campbell, John. *Edward Heath: A Biography.* London: J. Cape, 1993.

Cowley, Philip, and Matthew Bailey. "Peasant's Uprising or Religious War? Reexamining the 1995 Conservative Leadership Contest." *British Journal of Political Science* 30 (October 2000): 599–629.

Crowson, N. J. *The Longman Companion to the Conservative Party since 1830.* New York: Longman, 2001.

Heath, Edward. *The Course of My Life.* London: Hodder and Stoughton, 1998.

Lord, Christopher. *British Entry into the European Community under the Heath Government, 1970–74.* Brookfield, Vt.: Dartmouth, 1993.

Seldon, Anthony, and Stuart Ball, eds. *The Heath Government, 1970–74: A Reappraisal.* New York: Longman, 1996.

Heng Samrin (1934–) *president of Cambodia*

Heng Samrin was born in Ponhea, Kompong Province, Cambodia, on May 25, 1934, the son of an affluent peasant. Little is known of his early years, but by 1951 he embraced the anticolonialist tide sweeping Southeast Asia, and joined the Khmer Peoples' Revolutionary Party (KPRP). This was a communist organization organized and financed by its North Vietnamese equivalent. Around 1954 Heng arrived in Hanoi for additional training and indoctrination. He returned home two years later as part of the Pracheachon, a leftist front opposing the regime of Prince Norodom Sihanouk. In 1960 the pace of insurgency quickened with the establishment of the Communist Party of Kampuchea (CPK), Cambodia Communist Party, by POL POT, who owed his political allegiance to Beijing, not Hanoi. Ultimately this group of guerrilla fighters gained international infamy as the dreaded Khmer Rouge. Heng, meanwhile, continued on as a mid-level party cadre and occasionally strengthened his ties to Hanoi through continuing visits there. It is not known exactly when he acquired CPK membership, but by 1968 he functioned as a divisional commander within the eastern zone. This placed him in close proximity to North Vietnamese forces infiltrating into South Vietnam during their conflict with the United States. When the Sihanouk regime was overthrown by General LON NOL in March 1970, the Cambodian guerrillas increased the tempo of their operations. By April 1975 the CPK had driven the general from power and Pol Pot assumed control of the nation, which he renamed Kampuchea.

Now in power, the Khmer Rouge instituted a heinous regime that uprooted and liquidated millions of people. Heng's complicity in this affair has never been ascertained but, as a low-level operative, he escaped a violent party purge conducted by Pol Pot loyalists. Friction between the two factions of Cambodian Communists—the Hanoi-led and the Beijing-led—grew more discordant as time and atrocities went on. At length the Hanoi faction under Heng and So Phim unsuccessfully rebelled against Pol Pot in May 1978 and then fled to Vietnam for their lives. There they formed the United Front for the National Salvation of Kampuchea, as an alternative to the detested Khmer Rouge. Heng, given his long record of subservience to Vietnam, was also appointed president of the Revolutionary People's Council in exile.

Not content with slaughtering his own subjects, Pol Pot began waging guerrilla warfare along the Vietnamese border to retake disputed land. This brought on a sharp reaction from Hanoi, which invaded Cambodia in overwhelming force. After heavy fighting the Khmer Rouge were driven from Phnom Penh in January 1979, and Heng was installed as the new leader. He immediately halted Pol Pot's genocidal practices and began rebuilding his devastated country. But because Heng assumed power in the wake of a Vietnamese invasion the international community considered him a puppet and isolated him diplomatically. The only recognition Kampuchea now received came from countries within the Soviet Bloc—allies of Vietnam. Moreover, China continued arming and equipping Pol Pot's guerrillas while the United States and Thailand assisted forces loyal to Prince Sihanouk. A protracted civil war ensued, coupled with Khmer Rouge efforts to drive out the Vietnamese invaders. Fighting continued until 1989 when the United Nations finally convinced Vietnam to withdraw from Kampuchea. New elections were held, and Heng, representing the Council of State, lost to Sihanouk in November 1991. It was a surprising end for a figure who wielded undisputed control for over a decade, but peace was finally restored to war-torn Cambodia.

Since 1993 Heng has continued to hold minor bureaucratic positions under Prime Minister Hun Sen, his former foreign minister. A major objective of the Cambodian government has been the arrest of former Pol Pot supporters to try them for war crimes. After intense negotiations a UN-backed tribunal was finally approved in April 2001. Heng, now serving as vice chairman of the National Assembly, was exultant but restrained. "I would like to appeal to our compatriots who were with the Khmer Rouge in the past, please do not be scared because we will try only the top leaders and the people who had direct responsibility for the genocide," he insisted.

Further Reading

Bizot, Francois. *The Gate.* New York: Knopf, 2003.

Clymer, Kenton J. *The United States and Cambodia, 1969–2000: A Troubled Relationship.* New York: Routledge, 2004.

Hughes, Caroline. *The Political Economy of Cambodia's Transition, 1991–2001.* New York: Routledge, 2002.

Kiernan, Ben. *The Pol Pot Regime: Race, Power, and Genocide in Cambodia.* New Haven, Conn.: Yale University Press, 1996.

Morris, Stephen. *Why Vietnam Invaded Cambodia: Political Culture and the Causes of War.* Stanford, Calif.: Stanford University Press, 1999.

Herriot, Édouard (1872–1957) *prime minister of France*

Édouard Herriot was born in Troyes, France, on July 5, 1872, the son of an army officer. An exceptional student, he performed brilliantly at the prestigious Ecole Normale Superieure and worked as a teacher for many years. While at school he absorbed the high ideals of French republicanism and in 1901 he joined the Radical Socialist Party. Herriot commenced his long political career by being elected mayor of Lyon in 1904, a post he would hold almost continuously through life. He next gained a seat in the French senate in 1912, and during World War I functioned as minister of public works in the administration of ARISTIDE BRIAND. Herriot demonstrated real brilliance as a debater and political writer, so in 1919 he was elected president of the Radical Socialists. That same year he successfully ran for a seat in the Chamber of Deputies, where he organized resistance to the Bloc National, a conservative alliance that took power after the war. By deft political maneuvering among socialists and communists Herriot rose to command a similar alliance, the Cartel des Gauches, and in June 1924 he became prime minister. He also served as his own foreign minister and broke new ground diplomatically by extending recognition to the Soviet Union. But from the onset Herriot's administration was beset by intractable economic problems and resistance from the influential French business community. His administration collapsed in April 1925, after which he assumed the role of minister of public instruction under conservative RAYMOND POINCARÉ. This move was resented by many in the Radical Party, and they ousted him as party leader in favor of ÉDOUARD DALADIER. Herriot remained a minister until 1928, and four years later he led another broad coalition of leftists to power and became prime minister again. As previously, he proved unable to surmount economic hardships, now intensified by the Great Depression. When the French senate refused to endorse his plan to pay war debts owed to the United States, he resigned again in January 1936.

In 1936 Herriot assumed his most influential role, that of president of the Chamber of Deputies. Over the next four years he played a crucial role in shaping left-wing policies and proved a useful ally to Prime Minister LEON BLUM and his Popular Front government. However, he steadfastly declined to serve in that administration, distrusting the communists there. In fact the tenor of national politics was becoming increasingly polarized between the right and left, and little was accomplished in preparing France for war. World War II broke out in September 1939, and Herriot argued for a vigorous prosecution. After the fall of France in June 1940 he abstained from a vote to give Marshal PHILIPPE PETAIN unlimited powers. This act ended the French Third Republic to which Herriot and so many radicals were deeply devoted. Thereafter he opposed collaborating with the Germans, and in 1944 he was arrested and deported. Freed by Soviet troops the following year, he returned to France to assume control of the greatly reduced and largely discredited radicals. He was nonetheless elected party president and determined to continue crusading on behalf of republican values.

In 1946 the 73-year-old Herriot was reelected to the new National Assembly, quickly emerging as an opponent of General CHARLES DE GAULLE's attempt to create the new Fourth Republic. However, he could not surmount the legacy of national weakness attached to the Third Republic, which was not revived. But Herriot's machinations and influence ensured that the new government closely resembled its predecessor as a parliamentary republic. Over the next 10 years he remained a powerful influence in national politics, opposing the centralizing tendencies of the right and the growing strength of the communists. He also railed against creation of the European Defense Community and the rearming of Germany. But by January 1954, it was apparent that the heyday of radical influence had passed. Herriot resigned from public office that year, although he remained president of the party. He spent his last years as a celebrated elder statesman, a living embodiment of French parliamentary republicanism. Declining health forced Herriot to resign as party leader in 1956 and he died in Lyon on March 26, 1957. He was thus spared from witnessing creation of the highly organized Fifth Republic with his antithesis, de Gaulle, as president.

Further Reading

Dutton, Paul V. *Origins of the French Welfare State, 1914–1947.* New York: Cambridge University Press, 2002.

Gildea, Robert. *Marianne in Chains: In Search of the German Occupation, 1940–1945.* London: Macmillan, 2002.

Herriot, Édouard. *Eastward from Paris.* London: V. Gollancz, 1934.

Jackson, Peter. *The Fall of France: The Nazi Invasion of 1940.* New York: Oxford University Press, 2003.

Jessner, Sabine. *Édouard Herriot: Patriarch of the Republic.* New York: Haskell House Publishers, 1974.

Moure, Kenneth. *The Gold Standard Illusion: France, the Bank of France, and the International Gold Standards, 1914–1939.* New York: Oxford University Press, 2002.

Zahniser, Marvin P. *Then Came Disaster: France and the United States, 1914–1940.* Westport, Conn.: Praeger, 2002.

Hindenburg, Paul von (1847–1934) *president of Germany*

Paul Ludwig Hans Anton von Beneckendorff und von Hindenburg was born in Posen, Prussia (modern Poznań, Poland), on October 2, 1847, the son of an aristocratic father and a commoner mother. His Junker family had provided soldiers to the Prussian state for centuries so Hindenburg, like his illustrious forebears, pursued a military career. He fought well in the Six Weeks' War against Austria in 1866 and the Franco-Prussian War of 1870–71, eventually rising to lieutenant general. Hindenburg retired from active service in 1911, concluding a career that was by far more competent than brilliant. However, in August 1914 he returned to the colors following the outbreak of World War I and was dispatched to the Eastern Front. There, in concert with General Erich von Ludendorff, he orchestrated decisive victories over larger Russian forces. These feats catapulted him to the status of national hero and, by 1916, he was able to remove Kaiser WILHELM II as director of the war effort. Furthermore Hindenburg and Ludendorff were convinced that the only way to win was by unrestricted submarine warfare to starve Great Britain into surrender. When Chancellor THEOBALD VON BETHMANN HOLLWEG objected on the grounds that it would bring the United States into the war, Hindenburg arranged his dismissal. In the spring and summer of 1918 the Germans launched an ambitious assault that rapped at the gates of Paris, but the arrival of American forces slowly drove them back. Hindenburg, now convinced that the war was lost, prevailed upon the kaiser to abdicate, then arranged for an armistice and Germany's unconditional surrender. He withdrew from public life a second time in June 1919, still the most popular figure in the nation.

After the war Hindenburg remained sequestered on his country estate in Neudeck and avoided politics. A committed monarchist, he despised the newly instituted Weimar Republic and distanced himself from it. But after the death of Friedrich Ebert, the republic's first president, a conservative clique of military and business figures convinced Hindenburg to run for the office. Hindenburg—displaying neither interest in nor aptitude for politics— complied only out of a sense of duty. In April 1925 he was narrowly elected and viewed his administration, regardless of what others thought, as simply a transitional government until Wilhelm II was restored to the throne. He was fortunate to be assisted in office by Chancellor GUSTAV STRESEMANN, who arranged Germany's entrance into the League of Nations in 1925. But neither leader was prepared for the Great Depression of 1929 and the tremendous social dislocation and chaos it occasioned. Out of this troubling period emerged ADOLF HITLER and his National Socialist (Nazi) Party, which wanted to restore order with an iron hand. Hindenburg initially dismissed Hitler as "that Bohemian corporal," appointed HEINRICH BRÜNING as chancellor, and granted him near dictatorial powers to confront the national emergency. The Reichstag (legislature) was dissolved in July 1930 (one of many times up to early 1933), and Germany was ruled by decree, marking the end of the Weimar Republic as a parliamentary entity. But no economic reform eased Germany's distress, and by 1932 unemployment had reached the 6 million mark. Hindenburg nonetheless ran for office again in April 1932, easily defeating Hitler and a communist candidate. Curiously, this time he had been deserted by his traditional conservative and nationalist allies, who now supported Hitler. Hindenburg won with an awkward alliance between the Social Democrat and the Catholic Center Parties; despite mounting turmoil and failure in Weimar politics, the aged leader was viewed by many Germans as a symbol of unity and calm reassurance. But as Germany's economy withered, Hitler's popularity rose.

By November 1932 the Nazis had emerged as the largest party in the Reichstag, and Hindenburg finally acknowledged that he would have to deal with Hitler. He was further angered by Brüning's attempts to appropriate landed estates for redistribution, and dismissed him from power. FRANZ VON PAPEN then became chancellor and brokered a deal between the president and Hitler by allowing the latter to become chancellor on January 30, 1933. Hindenburg and von Papen hoped that Hitler could be controlled by bringing him into government. Both were egregiously mistaken. For nearly two years Hitler paraded the aging and ailing president around at various public functions, exploiting his national stature to cultivate a veneer of legitimacy. Hindenburg was by now bordering on senility and proved incapable of resisting. Thus the fate of the Weimar Republic was sealed. After he died on August 2, 1934, Hitler arranged a national plebiscite allowing him to combine the powers of the presidency and chancellery into one office. Germany would remain a military dictatorship for the next 12 years. The stolid Hindenburg, completely out of his depth in the byzantine world of politics, had unwittingly served as a conduit for tyranny.

Further Reading

Asprey, Robert B. *The German High Command at War: Hindenburg and Ludendorff Conduct World War I.* New York: William Morrow, 1991.

Cary, Noel D. "The Making of the Reich President, 1925: German Conservatism and the Nomination of Paul von Hindenburg." *Central European History* 23 (June 1990): 179–204.

Dorpalen, Andreas. *Hindenburg and the Weimar Republic.* Princeton, N.J.: Princeton University Press, 1984.

Falter, Jurgen W. "The Two Hindenburg Elections of 1925 and 1932: A Total Reversal of Voter Coalitions." *Central European History* 23, nos. 2–3 (1990): 225–241.

Jones, Larry E. "Hindenburg and the Conservative Dilemma in the 1932 Presidential Elections." *German Studies Review* 20, no. 2 (1997): 235–259.

Nicholls, Anthony J. *Weimar and the Rise of Hitler.* New York: St. Martin's Press, 2000.

Hirohito (1901–1989) *emperor of Japan*

Michi no miya Hirohito was born in Tokyo, Japan, on April 29, 1901, a son of Yoshihito, the crown prince and future emperor Taisho. He was part of a ruling dynasty that claimed a lineage dating back 2,500 years to the mythical sun goddess Amaterasu Omikami. Hirohito experienced a traditional court upbringing, being separated from his parents early and trained by a councilor. Under these conditions he matured into a somewhat grave, somber individual, unswervingly devoted to his responsibilities. As a young man Hirohito displayed little faculty for history or politics, but excelled in marine biology. In 1918 he broke imperial precedent by marrying a princess outside the immediate Yamato clan. He also abolished the traditional system of court concubinage and remained happily monogamous for over 50 years. In 1921 Hirohito became the first Japanese crown prince to travel abroad and was especially impressed by the constitutional monarchy of Great Britain. Shortly after returning home he became regent to succeed his mentally ailing father, and on December 25, 1926, Hirohito succeeded him to the throne. His reign was known officially as "Showa," meaning enlightenment and peace.

Hirohito assumed power at a transitional point in Japanese history and politics. The nation had consciously copied Western politics and culture for almost four decades and Japan seemed fully receptive to the ethos of democracy. Hirohito was especially encouraged to pursue modernization and liberalization by his genro (senior adviser) SAIONJI KIMMOCHI. However, this sense of political stability and progress was slowly undermined by the rise of ultranationalism and militarism, which irrevocably committed Japan to a course of aggression in Asia. As emperor, Hirohito was theoretically the center of all political authority in Japan, but in practice he remained isolated from the world and was required only to consent to policies formatted by his ministers. However, on

February 26, 1936, he intervened definitively in the wake of a failed and bloody military coup and ordered the transgressors arrested and punished. But a year later, when the army commenced a war against China, he resumed his cloistered style of leadership. The policy continued over the protests of Prime Minister KONOE FUMIMARO and culminated in TOJO HIDEKI's decision to attack the American naval installation at Pearl Harbor, Hawaii, on December 7, 1941. Hirohito's culpability for the move has never been clearly established, but it resulted in the destruction of the Japanese Empire. In August 1945, following the atomic bombing of Hiroshima and Nagasaki, Hirohito again played a decisive role by ordering the military to surrender. He then took to the airwaves for the first time in his life, beseeching his countrymen to "endure the unendurable" and accept defeat gracefully. Japan was then occupied by foreign forces for the first time in its 2,000-year history.

After the war many Americans sought to punish the emperor as a war criminal, but General Douglas MacArthur, the supreme Allied commander, felt Hirohito would be infinitely more useful to occupation authorities on the throne. He was forced to renounce all claims to divinity and reduced to a symbol of state, but Hirohito, who was never comfortable as a "living god," willingly obliged. Thereafter he wholeheartedly cooperated with MacArthur and acquired considerable respect in return. Consistent with American demands to "democratize" his throne, he also became the first Japanese emperor to make himself accessible to the public. Hirohito proved himself somewhat awkward and shy while mingling with strangers, but the Japanese people nonetheless appreciated his sincerity. For the first time the emperor of Japan became a beloved public figure. When the military occupation ended in 1954, Japan had been disarmed, adopted a new Western-style constitution, and embarked on one of the great economic recoveries of the century. Hirohito subsequently symbolized the country's peaceful transformation into the world's second-largest economy. In 1971 he became the first Japanese monarch to travel abroad when he visited Europe, and four years later he became the first emperor to visit the United States. His role in politics and policy making was now virtually nil, and he devoted much of his time to writing books about marine biology. When Hirohito died in Tokyo on January 7, 1989, he concluded a reign of 63 years—the longest in Japanese history and among the most eventful. His funeral was attended by over 10,000 people and scores of foreign dignitaries, testimony to Japan's status as an economic superpower and an important world player.

Emperor Hirohito *(Library of Congress)*

Further Reading

Beer, Lawrence W. *From Imperial Myth to Democracy: Japan's Two Constitutions, 1889–2001.* Boulder: University Press of Colorado, 2002.

Bix, Herbert. *Hirohito and the Making of Modern Japan.* New York: HarperCollins, 2000.

Drea, Edward. "The Emperor's Duplicity." *Military History Quarterly* 12, no. 3. (2000): 28–40.

Hartoonian, Hirohito. "Hirohito redux." *Critical Asian Studies* 33, no. 4 (2001): 609–636.

Hellegers, Dale M. *We, the Japanese People: World War II and the Origins of the Japanese Constitution,* 2 vols. Stanford, Calif.: Stanford University Press, 2002.

Moore, Ray A. *Partners for Democracy: Crafting the New Japanese State under MacArthur.* New York: Oxford University Press, 2002.

Ruoff, Kenneth J. *The People's Emperor: Democracy and the Japanese Monarchy, 1945–1995.* Cambridge, Mass.: Harvard University Press, 2001.

Seagrave, Sterling. *The Yamato Dynasty: The Secret History of Japan's Imperial Family.* New York: Broadway Books, 1999.

Hitler, Adolf (1889–1945) *chancellor/president of Germany*

Adolf Hitler was born in Braunau am Inn, Austria-Hungary, on April 20, 1889, the son of a customs official. Sullen as a student, he dropped out of school to study art, yet failed to gain entrance into the Vienna Academy of Arts. In 1914 he joined the Bavarian army and fought with distinction during World War I, being twice wounded and decorated for bravery. Afterward he remained in Bavaria along with thousands of discontented military veterans, and in 1919 began his fateful association with the small German Worker's Party, a right-wing, anti-Semitic gathering of bullies and street toughs. By dint of amazing charisma and oratory, Hitler emerged as their uncontested leader by 1920, and he renamed the party the Nationalist Socialist German Workers Party, or Nazis. Taking inspiration from Fascist BENITO MUSSOLINI's March on Rome, Hitler tried organizing a similar effort against the Bavarian government on November 8, 1923. The coup failed; Hitler was arrested and sentenced to six years in Landsberg prison. During this interval he further refined and codified his beliefs into an infamous publication called *Mein Kampf* (My Struggle). Here he expounded his extreme hatred for Jews and communists, the need for Germany to cleanse itself of such malcontents and, furthermore, the utter necessity for acquiring additional living space (Lebensraum). Nobody took the treatise seriously at the time, but Hitler, for the remainder of his life, remained unswervingly devoted to its precepts.

Released after only a few months in prison Hitler rejoined the Nazis and reorganized them. But recruiting was slow and they remained a minor political entity until the onset of the Great Depression in 1929. This event completely gutted Germany's economy, swelling the unemployment ranks and contributing to a sense of political instability. Suddenly Hitler's talk of Germany rearming, of defying the 1919 Versailles Peace Treaty, and blaming Jews and communists for the nation's ills began resonating with the public. In 1932 Hitler finished a close second behind PAUL VON HINDENBURG during presidential elections and the reinvigorated Nazis emerged as the Reichstag's (legislature) biggest voting bloc. Hindenburg had contemptuously dismissed Hitler as "that Bohemian corporal" but, upon the advice of Vice Chancellor FRANZ VON PAPEN, he was persuaded to make him chancellor in January 1933. Hitler then convinced the Reichstag to pass the so-called Enabling Act, granting him dictatorial powers during the national emergency. Once Hindenburg died Hitler moved swiftly to combine the offices of chancellor and president into one; thereafter he was known as Germany's führer, or leader.

Adolf Hitler *(Library of Congress)*

True to his rantings Hitler took immediate steps to restore Germany to full employment by launching public works programs and massive national rearmament. The economy miraculously improved, Germany regained its reputation for technical proficiency, and the Nazis were viewed as saviors. Hitler then commenced a deliberate game of brinkmanship with the Western democracies over territorial expansion. In 1938 he ordered the assassination of Austrian chancellor ENGELBERT DOLLFUSS and forcibly joined that nation to Germany. Months later he leaned heavily upon Great Britain and France for annexation of the German-speaking Sudetenland region of Czechoslovakia. The führer deduced that the Allies would do anything to avoid war, a fact confirmed when British prime minister NEVILLE CHAMBERLAIN signed the notorious Munich Pact. This document allowed for the dismemberment of Czechoslovakia in return for pledges of nonaggression. But Hitler ultimately went back upon his word, absorbed the Czech lands entirely, and started making demands for Polish territory. When the Allies finally affirmed defensive commitments to the Poles, Hitler countered by signing a nonaggression pact with the Soviet Union's JOSEPH STALIN and the Tripartite Pact with Italy's Mussolini and Japan's TOJO HIDEKI. On September 1, 1939, Hitler ordered panzer forces into Poland, an act that plunged Europe into World War II.

The well-trained and -led German forces quickly overran most of Europe but were stopped at the English Channel in 1940. Great Britain then rallied under a new leader, WINSTON CHURCHILL, who cemented an alliance with American president FRANKLIN D. ROOSEVELT. In June 1941 Hitler made the fatal mistake of invading Russia before reaching a peace accord with the West, committing Germany to waging a two-front war that it lacked the resources to win. The United States entered the fray after the December 7, 1941, bombing of Pearl Harbor by Japanese forces and Hitler's dreams of conquest waned. By 1942 German forces were defeated in North Africa and at Stalingrad and began a long retreat that did not end until 1945. Meanwhile Hitler carried through on his threats against the Jews by rounding up millions of captives throughout Europe and deporting them to death camps in Eastern Europe. Six million Jews and 7 million others perished in the tragedy known as the Holocaust. It was a monstrous expression of genocide and racial hatred.

By the spring of 1945 Russian armies were invading eastern Germany in preparation for an attack on Berlin. Rather than flee, Hitler fortified himself in the gutted capital, hoping to stave off defeat through the invention of wonder weapons such as jets and rockets. None could turn the tide and on April 30, 1945, Hitler and his mistress Eva Braun committed suicide in their bunker. An ocean of blood had been spilled but the European side of World War II had finally reached its calamitous ending. Germany was divided among the Western Allies and the Soviet Union for the next 40 years. Along with Stalin and MAO ZEDONG, Hitler ranks as one of the bloodiest tyrants of the 20th century.

Further Reading

Dorpat, Theodore L. *Wounded Monster: Hitler's Path from Trauma to Malevolence.* Lanham, Md.: University Press of America, 2002.

Dunn, Walter S. *Heroes or Traitors: The German Replacement Army, the July Plot, and Adolph Hitler.* Westport, Conn.: Praeger, 2003.

Hitler, Adolph. *Mein Kampf.* Boston: Houghton Mifflin, 2002.

Mitchell, Charles P. *The Hitler Filmography: Worldwide Feature Film and Television Miniseries Portrayals, 1940 through 2000.* Jefferson, N.C.: McFarland, 2002.

Pauley, Bruce F. *Hitler, Stalin, and Mussolini: Totalitarianism in the Twentieth Century.* Wheeling, Ill.: Harlan Davidson, 2003.

Shore, Zachary. *What Hitler Knew: The Battle for Information in Nazi Foreign Policy.* New York: Oxford University Press, 2003.

Williamson, D. G. *The Third Reich.* New York: Longman, 2002.

Ho Chi Minh (1890–1969) *president of the Democratic Republic of Vietnam*

Ho Chi Minh was born Nguyen That Thanh in Kim Lien Province, French Indochina, on May 19, 1890, the son of a scholarly bureaucrat. He was educated locally and like many young men of his generation, Ho became active in anti-imperialist movements. Despite his youth he was profoundly nationalistic and railed against French colonial domination. Expelled from school by French authorities, Ho decided to visit Europe in 1911 to further his education. In 1917 he was living and

Ho Chi Minh *(Library of Congress)*

working in Paris and actively involved in the French Socialist Party. Ho worked constantly to gain sympathy for Vietnamese independence, and in 1920 he helped found the French Communist Party. Three years later he visited Moscow for further political indoctrination and ended up as a Soviet agent in south China. In February 1930 he founded the Indochina Communist Party in Hong Kong among the large community of Vietnamese expatriates living there. But it was not until the advent of the Pacific War in 1941 that he clandestinely returned to French Indochina after a 30-year hiatus. There he organized an independence league, the Viet Minh, and also adopted the name Ho Chi Minh (Enlightened One). Ho spent several years fighting Japanese occupation forces, who had temporarily displaced the French, and was assisted by the United States. His political career reached its turning point on September 2, 1945, when Ho formally declared Vietnam's independence from France. But he failed to gain recognition from the

Western world, and France announced its intention to reclaim Vietnam as a colony. Ho journeyed to Paris for negotiations to avert hostilities and even offered to keep Indochina an autonomous republic within the French Union, but talks failed. The First Indochina War erupted in December 1946 and raged for eight years.

Ho was a communist by persuasion, but he always couched his doctrines in nationalistic language to attract as wide a following as possible. His internecine guerrilla war ended in a decisive French defeat at Dien Bien Phu in 1954. A peace agreement concluded in Geneva recognized the Democratic Republic of Vietnam, with Ho as president. However, the southern half of the country remained independent under Ngo Dinh Diem until elections could be held in 1956. At this juncture the United States, fearing expansion of communism into Southeast Asia, obstructed the elections to keep the popular Ho from office. He remained undeterred by this setback, and in 1960 commenced a ruthless guerrilla campaign to subvert and conquer South Vietnam. This triggered a sharp response from the United States, and in 1961 President JOHN F. KENNEDY introduced 15,000 military advisers and the first special forces into the region. By 1964 it became apparent that a massive influx of aid was necessary to keep South Vietnam from falling, and a new U.S. president, LYNDON B. JOHNSON, deployed half a million troops and commenced full-scale bombardment of the north. The Vietnamese suffered frightful losses at the hands of their technologically superior adversaries, but Ho pursued his mission to unite the country with iron resolve. He even entered into peace talks with the Americans in Paris in 1968 to buy time and allow growing antiwar movements in the United States to influence events on his behalf.

Ho was also adept at juggling foreign affairs. He cleverly played off the Soviet Union, under LEONID BREZHNEV, against Red China, under MAO ZEDONG, to secure military assistance and political support. Together, these otherwise implacable adversaries supplied the North Vietnamese and Viet Cong (South Vietnamese communists) with ample food and weapons to wage war. By 1969 President RICHARD M. NIXON concluded that the war was unwinnable and began withdrawing American forces from the theater. But Ho could not savor his life's work: he died suddenly on September 3, 1969. The war to conquer South Vietnam, headed by NGUYEN VAN THIEU and NGUYEN CAO KY, dragged on another five years before the communists triumphed. In recognition of their leader's dedicated contributions to national reunification, the southern capital of Saigon was renamed Ho Chi Minh City in his honor. His efficacy as a leading figure in 20th-century anticolonialism is secure and forms an important chapter in Vietnam's thousand-year struggle to eliminate foreign influence.

Further Reading

Asselin, Pierre. *A Bitter Peace: Washington, Hanoi, and the Making of the Paris Agreement.* Chapel Hill: University of North Carolina Press, 2002.

De Caro, Peter A. *Rhetoric of Revolt: Ho Chi Minh's Discourse for Revolution.* Westport, Conn.: Praeger, 2002.

Duiker, William J. *Ho Chi Minh.* New York: Hyperion, 2000.

Ho Chi Minh. *On Revolution: Selected Writings, 1920–1966.* Boulder, Colo.: Westview Press, 1984.

Quinn-Judge, Sophie. *Ho Chi Minh: The Missing Years.* Berkeley: University of California Press, 2002.

Vo, Nghia M. *The Bamboo Gulag: Political Imprisonment in Communist Vietnam.* Jefferson, N.C.: McFarland, 2004.

Holyoake, Keith (1904–1983) *prime minister of New Zealand*

Keith Jacka Holyoake was born in Pahiatua, New Zealand, on February 11, 1904, the son of a small farmer. He quit school while young to work on the farm, and finished his education by correspondence. Holyoake excelled in athletics and became president of the local Farmer's Union. He commenced his political career by winning a seat in the House of Representatives in 1932 as a Reform Party member, becoming the nation's youngest politician. He subsequently joined the newly formed National Party, brought about by the union of several conservative groups. Holyoake lost his seat in 1938 and returned to farming for five years. He gained reelection from Pahiatua in 1943 and held this seat for the next 34 years. His political fortunes quickened in 1949 when the National Party took control of the government for the first time and Holyoake became both deputy prime minister and minister of agriculture. He successfully negotiated minimum prices for New Zealand beef and dairy products with his British counterparts. In 1957 he briefly succeeded Sir Sidney

Holland as prime minister just three months short of national elections but was ousted by the Labor Party. Over the next three years Holyoake functioned effectively as head of the opposition in Parliament, relentlessly attacking Labor's budgeting tactics and cementing his reputation as an astute operator. Perseverance paid off in 1960 when the National Party returned to power with a comfortable majority and Holyoake became prime minister a second time.

In office Holyoake proved himself among New Zealand's most effective executive officers. He held office for 11 consecutive years, the third longest tenure in national history, and triumphed in four direct elections. And despite an aloof, seemingly detached demeanor he was at heart a consensus builder and a pragmatist. True to his conservative leanings, the government now became less likely to interfere in the economy or the lives of private individuals. Fortunately for the National Party his administration coincided with a period of unprecedented prosperity and growth. The electorate was complacent, the economy boomed, and Holyoake basked in the glow of his campaign motto, "Steady does it." And because he concurrently held the portfolio of foreign minister, he was heavily involved in overseas travel to promote New Zealand products and perspectives.

The only contentious episode during the Holyoake years was New Zealand's involvement in the Vietnam War. As part of the ANZUS alliance with Australia and the United States, the country was obliged to commit forces to combat in the mid-1960s. The New Zealanders fought well, but the war proved unpopular. Holyoake was nonetheless determined to honor treaty commitments but he refused to increase manpower commitments when requested by the United States. Holyoake faced an economic crisis with Britain's impending entry into the European Economic Community (EEC) in 1971. New trade barriers now threatened to close out New Zealand exports entirely, a severe blow to his small nation. Holyoake recognized Britain's right to seek out new markets but successfully argued that all Commonwealth trading partners must be protected. When Holyoake stepped down as prime minister and head of the National Party in February 1972, he concluded one of the most successful political interludes in the nation's annals.

Holyoake remained active in politics as a member of Parliament and as a respected elder statesman once Labor returned to power in November 1972. The National Party reversed its fortunes in 1975 under

ROBERT MULDOON, and Holyoake then received the portfolio of minister of state. Two years later Muldoon promoted the aging politician to the largely ceremonial post of governor general of New Zealand, becoming the first native New Zealander to hold that office. This appointment engendered some controversy, for many public figures felt that a retired politician was not suited to represent the queen's interests. Holyoake nonetheless served impartially and competently over the next three years, and in 1980 Queen Elizabeth II conferred a knighthood upon him. He remains the only New Zealand citizen so honored. His death on December 8, 1983, closed a public career that spanned five decades. In Muldoon's estimation, he was "the greatest New Zealander of our time."

Further Reading

Clark, Margaret, ed. *Sir Keith Holyoake: Towards a Political Biography.* Palmerston North, New Zealand: Dumore Press, 1997.

Doughty, Ross A. *The Holyoake Years.* Fielding, New Zealand: R. Doughty, 1977.

Gustafson, Barry. *The First 50 Years: A History of the New Zealand National Party.* Auckland: Reed Methuen, 1986.

Macleod, Alexandra. "Sir Keith Holyoake Completes a Decade: Difficulties Thread." *Round Table* no. 241 (1971): 175–180.

Miller, Raymond, ed. *New Zealand: Government and Politics.* New York: Oxford University Press, 1997.

Honecker, Erich (1912–1994) *first secretary of the Socialist Unity Party of East Germany*

Erich Honecker was born in Neunkirchen, the Saar, Germany, on August 25, 1912, the son of a miner. Both his parents were devout communists, and their son became steeped in their ideology. Throughout his long life Honecker never questioned his belief that communism was the only solution for running a modern nation. He became active in party youth activities, and by 1928 had formally joined the Konservativen Deutschen Partei (KDP), German Communist Party. Two years later he received advanced political training at the Lenin School, in Moscow, reserved for only the most promising cadres, and returned home to foment political unrest. The Saar region had been separated from Germany by the terms of the 1919 Treaty of Versailles,

so Honecker's activities were legal. However, once ADOLF HITLER came to power and annexed the Saar in 1935, he outlawed the Communist Party, and Honecker was forced underground. He clandestinely headed communist youth activities in Berlin until he was arrested by the Gestapo and charged with treason in 1935. Honecker received a 10-year prison sentence, but in May 1945 he was freed by Soviet forces after Germany's surrender in World War II.

At war's end Germany was divided into two occupation zones, two-thirds of the country dominated by the Western Allies, the eastern third by the Soviet Union. For Honecker this situation represented the opportunity of a lifetime. He immediately parlayed his communist credentials into a viable political career and struck up cordial relations with party chief WALTER ULBRICHT. One of his first tasks was forcing a merger between German communists and Social Democrats to create a new entity, the Socialist Unity Party (Sozialistische Einheitspartei Deutschlands; SED). After the German Democratic Republic (GDR) was formally established as a one-party police state in 1949, the SED was the only legal source of political activity. Ulbricht proved himself an unrepentant Stalinist, and for many years Honecker functioned as his most loyal aide. When East German workers rose in revolt and were crushed by Soviet troops in 1953, he readily applauded the action. In 1955 Honecker returned to Moscow for additional training, and by 1960 he was a full member of the GDR Politburo. The following year he undertook his most controversial project, constructing the notorious Berlin Wall. Eventually a barbed-wire fence was erected that stretched 250 miles along the border with West Germany. This was intended to stop a steady hemorrhaging of freedom-seeking refugees to the West, whose flight seriously impeded East Germany's economy. Almost immediately the Berlin Wall became the most enduring and hated symbol of the cold war.

Honecker continued serving Ulbricht loyally until 1971 when, apparently with Soviet approval, he deposed the inflexible leader. He was then installed as first secretary and head of state, a change that ushered in hopes for increased freedom. Initially Honecker made moves to decrease tensions with neighboring West Germany and cooperated with Chancellor WILLY BRANDT's Ostpolitik. In 1972 he signed the Basic Treaty, through which diplomatic relations were established and some travel rights restored. Three years later Honecker acquired greater international recognition by signing the Helsinki Accords beside Chancellor HELMUT SCHMIDT. This agreement enshrined the principle of human rights, but in practice East Germany remained the most repressive member of the Warsaw Pact and a loyal ally of the Soviet Union. It boasted an impressive economy and industrial output by communist standards, but free speech and artistic expression were curtailed. As the Soviet grip on Eastern Europe slackened in the late 1980s, so too did Honecker's control of East Germany. He rejected Soviet premier MIKHAIL GORBACHEV's emphasis on openness and reform, and clung to orthodox communist solutions to address East Germany's mounting problems. By 1989 the economy was in a serious recession, and thousands of citizens fled the moment Hungary opened its borders to the West. Badly needed reforms were not forthcoming, and mass demonstrations broke out. Moreover the Politburo, disillusioned by Honecker's refusal to liberalize his rule, removed him as party head in October 1989 and appointed a new leader, EGON KRENZ. Honecker then fled to Moscow for his own safety. Several months later the two halves of Germany were reunited, and the cold war in Europe became a memory.

Honecker remained sequestered in the U.S.S.R. until it also collapsed in August 1991. When the new Russian leader, Boris Yeltsin, ordered him out of the country, he took temporary refuge in the Chilean embassy. However, in 1992 Honecker returned to Germany to face charges of abuse of power and responsibility for the deaths of citizens killed while crossing the Berlin Wall. His trial began in November 1992 but Honecker, stricken with cancer, was released on humanitarian grounds. He relocated to Santiago, Chile, and died there on May 29, 1994, an unrepentant communist to the last.

Further Reading

Caldwell, Peter C. *Dictatorship, Central Planning, and Social Theory in the German Democratic Republic.* New York: Cambridge University Press, 2003.

Gearson, John P. S., and Kori Schake, eds. *The Berlin Wall Crisis: Perspectives on Cold War Alliances.* New York: Palgrave Macmillan, 2002.

Honecker, Erich. *From My Life.* New York: Pergamon, 1981.

Metzler, John J. *Divided Dynamism: The Diplomacy of Separated Nations: Germany, Korea, China.* Lanham, Md.: University Press of America, 2001.

Rodden, John. *Repainting the Little Red Schoolhouse: A History of Eastern German Education, 1945–1995.* New York: Oxford University Press, 2002.

Ross, Corey. *The East German Dictatorship: Problems and Perspectives in the Interpretation of the GDR.* New York: Oxford University Press, 2002.

Hoover, Herbert (1874–1964) *president of the United States*

Herbert Clark Hoover was born in West Branch, Iowa, on August 10, 1874, the son of a blacksmith. Orphaned at an early age, he was raised by Quaker relatives and became deeply imbued with their sense of humanity—a trait he carried throughout life. He graduated from Stanford University in 1895 with a degree in mine engineering and two decades later retired a multimillionaire. Hoover was residing in London when World War I commenced in August 1914, and he proved instrumental in orchestrating relief efforts for thousands of stranded Americans. He also efficiently directed operations of the Commission for Relief in Belgium, a feat that prompted President WOODROW WILSON to appoint him U.S. food administrator for the duration of the war. Afterward Hoover displayed great acumen while heading the American Relief Agency and feeding thousands of dispossessed Europeans. He also shipped food to relieve the great famine in Germany and the Soviet Union in 1921–23. Hoover was a strict humanitarian by nature, and when criticized for assisting communists in Russia he responded, "Twenty million people are starving. Whatever their politics, they shall be fed." His high national visibility and popularity made him a possible presidential contender in 1920, but he subsequently accepted a position as secretary of commerce under President WARREN G. HARDING. Again, Hoover displayed genuine talent for administration and completely overhauled his charge. He continued his good work in the administration of CALVIN COOLIDGE, when such notable projects as Hoover Dam and the St. Lawrence Seaway were begun. Hoover's tenure as secretary of commerce coincided with one of the longest periods of growth and prosperity in American history. When Coolidge declined to seek a second term, Hoover was readily tapped to serve as the Republican Party nominee. In 1928 he handily defeated his Democrat challenger, Alfred E. Smith, by 444 electoral votes to 87, becoming the first and only sitting cabinet member to gain the presidency.

Hoover entered office with high expectations in the spring of 1929, being fully convinced he could eradicate poverty through economic growth. He also extended his altruism to international affairs by participating in the unsuccessful London Naval and Geneva Disarmament conferences for global arms reduction. However, the defining moment of his administration came with the stock market crash of October 1929, which precipitated the worldwide Great Depression. As the economy slowly unraveled, unemployment lines lengthened, homelessness became endemic and the country was seized by a sense of widespread anxiety. Hoover clearly sympathized with the plight of the unemployed and urged business leaders not to lay off workers or reduce wages. He also encouraged state and local governments to cooperate with charities to assist the swelling ranks of the poor. But for all his good intent, Hoover failed to comprehend that the sheer magnitude of the depression transcended simple solutions, and government intervention on a far larger scale was required. This, unfortunately, he was unwilling to do. Like many Republicans, Hoover felt that the federal government had no role in social programs beyond facilitating economic growth. Thus he refused to pass any bills authorizing direct monetary payments for the relief of hungry families. Worse, when a group of disgruntled army veterans organized the so-called Bonus March to demand promised benefits from Congress in 1932, Hoover sent General Douglas A. MacArthur to clear them from the capital. This was accomplished brutally and did little to enhance Hoover's public ratings. Having presided over the worst period of social dislocation in American history, he was soundly beaten by Democrat FRANKLIN D. ROOSEVELT in the November 1932 elections. He then retired to his home in California, ostensibly the most hated man in America. The Republican Party remained eclipsed at the executive level for the next two decades.

Hoover spent the next 12 years roundly criticizing the New Deal politics of the Roosevelt administration, despite their great popularity. A confirmed isolationist, he also opposed American entry into World War II until the advent of Pearl Harbor. Hoover then worked slowly but conscientiously to rehabilitate his reputation. He performed especially sterling work on presidential commissions authorized by HARRY S. TRUMAN and DWIGHT D. EISENHOWER, which modernized the national bureaucracy and improved efficiency. By the time he died in New

Herbert Hoover *(Library of Congress)*

York City on October 20, 1964, Hoover was once again regarded as a humane individual and a fine administrator. But given his inflexible approach to the role of government, nothing he contemplated would have mitigated the worst effects of the Great Depression.

Further Reading

Allen, Anne B. *An Independent Woman: The Life of Lou Henry Hoover.* Westport, Conn.: Greenwood Press, 2000.

Eisinger, Robert M. "Gauging Public Opinion in the Hoover White House: Understanding the Roots of Presidential Polling." *Presidential Studies Quarterly* 30 (December 2000): 643–661.

Gerdes, Louise I., ed. *The Crash of 1929.* San Diego, Calif.: Greenhaven Press, 2002.

Hoover, Herbert. *The Memoirs of Herbert Hoover,* 3 vols. New York: Garland Publishing, 1979.

Liebovich, Louis. *Bylines in Despair: Herbert Hoover, the Great Depression, and the U.S. News Media.* Westport, Conn.: Praeger, 1994.

Polsky, Andrew J., and Olesya Tkacheva. "Legacies versus Politics: Herbert Hoover, Partisan Conflict, and the Symbolic Appeal of Associationism in the 1920s." *International Journal of Politics, Culture, and Society* 16, no. 2 (2002): 207–235.

Horthy, Miklós (1868–1957) *regent of Hungary*

Miklós Horthy de Nagybánya was born in Kenderes, in the Austro-Hungarian Empire, on June 18, 1868, into an affluent Protestant family. He passed through the elite Naval Academy at Fiume in 1882 and acquired the reputation of a competent officer. A talented linguist, in 1909 Horthy also became an aide de camp to Emperor FRANZ JOSEPH I, whom he served until the outbreak of World War I. After 1914 Horthy commanded the heavy cruiser *Novara,* and conducted successful forays throughout the Adriatic Sea. In May 1917 he fought and won the Battle of Otranto, and the following year he was promoted to rear admiral. However, following the empire's capitulation and dismemberment in 1918, it became Horthy's melancholy duty to surrender his fleet to the new nation of Yugoslavia. He then returned home to his native Hungary, now an independent republic in the heart of eastern Europe. By the terms of the Treaty of Trianon, signed June 4, 1920, Hungary surrendered 72 percent of its territory and 28 percent of its population to Romania and the newly created states of Yugoslavia and Czechoslovakia. Such sacrifice incurred great national resentment, which lingers to the present day.

Horthy initially expressed little interest in politics, but he was by nature extremely religious, very conservative, and profoundly anticommunist. In 1919 revolutionary forces under Bela Kun installed a Bolshevik government in Budapest, and Horty was asked to lead a counterrevolution. Assisted by Romanian troops he reoccupied the capital that November, drove Kun's followers into Russia, and officially restored the monarchy. Thereafter he twice refused King Charles VI's attempts to reoccupy his throne and chose instead to run the country as regent. The legislature ratified his position on May 1, 1920, and he retained power for the next 24 years. Horthy initially remained detached from politics and delegated day-to-day affairs to his capable prime minister, Count Istvan Bethlen. When the onset of the Great Depression in 1929 precipitated an economic crisis, Horthy was forced to assume near dictatorial powers to maintain order. Worse, Hungary found itself increasingly dependent upon Germany to absorb its agricultural exports. The rise of ADOLF HITLER in 1933 induced Horthy to urge restraint in dealing with Germany, even though the country sympathized with Hungarian losses after World War I. A cat-and-mouse diplomatic game ensued whereby Horthy solicited military aid and diplomatic support for regaining Hungarian lands, while simultaneously cultivating friendly relations with Western powers. His pleas for assistance from France and England fell upon deaf ears, but Horthy remained studiously neutral toward German expansionism.

Following the onset of World War II in September 1939, Hungary fell under increasing pressure to support Hitler's territorial ambitions in the East. German forces invaded the Soviet Union in June 1941, and six months later Hungary followed suit, entering the conflict on behalf of the Axis. For the next three years Horthy maintained a difficult high-wire act, balancing German demands against Hungarian interests. He authorized token troop commitments to the eastern front and allowed German troop maneuvers across Hungarian soil, but otherwise Horthy proved a reluctant ally. Furthermore, he refused to cooperate with the Nazi policy of transporting Hungarian Jews to Germany for extermination. By 1944 Hitler was clearly losing the war and Horthy, determined to prevent a Soviet takeover of his country, tried negotiating a separate peace treaty with JOSEPH STALIN. The Russians held all the cards and were not interested. Moreover, Hitler resented Horthy's clandestine peace efforts and had him kidnapped by German special forces on October 15, 1944. He remained imprisoned until freed by American troops in May 1945.

After the war Horthy was rearrested as an Axis head of state and liable to face war crime charges. Curiously, he was released at Stalin's behest. Hungary by then was completely occupied by Soviet troops—Horthy's worst nightmare—and he elected not to return home. He subsequently settled in Estoril, Portugal, to write his memoirs and await events. Horthy died there on February 9, 1957, a skilled national leader faced with an impossible diplomatic situation. In 1993 his remains were relocated to his ancestral home and interred with honors.

Further Reading

Bán, András. *Hungary and Britain, 1939–1941: The Attempt to Maintain Relations.* Portland, Oreg.: Frank Cass, 2004.

Horthy, Miklós. *Admiral Miklós Horthy: Memoirs.* Safety Harbor, Fla.: Simon Publications, 2000.

Pritz, Pal. "Horthy and Edmund Veesenmayer: Hungarian-German Relations after March 1944." *Hungarian Studies Review* 23, nos. 1–2 (1996): 29–42.

Sakmyster, Thomas. *Hungary's Admiral on Horseback: Miklos Horthy, 1918–1944.* New York: East European Monographs, 1995.

Swanson, John C. *The Remnants of the Hapsburg Monarchy: The Shaping of Modern Austria and Hungary, 1918–1922.* Boulder, Colo.: Eastern European Monographs, 2001.

Vego, Milan N. *Austro-Hungarian Naval Policy, 1904–14.* Portland, Ore.: Frank Cass, 1996.

Hoxha, Enver (1908–1985) *first secretary of the Party of Labor of Albania*

Enver Hoxha was born in Gjirokastra, Albania, on October 16, 1908, the son of a Muslim cloth dealer. He was educated locally and attended the University of Montpelier, France, on a state scholarship. There he encountered Marxist-Leninist ideas and lost his scholarship after publishing essays critical of the Albanian government. He returned home in 1936 to teach French and also opened a small tobacco shop as a front for subversive activities. In April 1939 Albania was overrun by Italian forces, and Hoxha lost his teaching position after refusing to join the Fascist Party. Resistance to the invaders was scattered as the Albanian left was split by divided loyalties and petty jealousies. This changed after the brutal occupation of Albania by German forces in November 1941, and that month Hoxha founded the Communist Party of Albania with himself as general secretary. He then led an armed resistance movement that the invaders failed to squelch, and eventually formed the National Liberation Front as a provisional government. The guerrillas finally drove Axis forces from Albania in the fall of 1944, an impressive military feat accomplished without Allied assistance. Victory only enhanced Hoxha's reputation as a war hero, and in December 1945 he won 92 percent of the votes in a free and fair presidential election. This proved a turning point in the history of his country, for in January 1946 Hoxha proclaimed the People's Republic of Albania. The Communist Party under his control was also renamed the Party of Labor of Albania.

As a communist, Hoxha had long admired JOSEPH STALIN and he sought to create a socialist state along Stalinist lines. Private property was confiscated, agriculture collectivized, and political liberties extinguished. Worse, thousands of suspected opponents of the regime were summarily lined up and executed, especially known admirers of Yugoslavia's MARSHAL TITO. Hoxha had been alerted to Tito's schemes for bringing Albania into the Yugoslavian fold, and in 1948 he executed Koci Xoxe, minister of the interior, for alleged "Titoist" sympathies. Thereafter Albania settled firmly into a pro-Soviet orbit and broke off relations with Yugoslavia. After Stalin's death in 1953, however, Hoxha's opinion of the Soviet Union was also drastically revised. In 1956 Premier NIKITA KHRUSHCHEV denounced Stalin and embarked on political and economic liberalization. Hoxha regarded such practices as heretical, and during the 1961 international gathering of communists in Moscow he publicly assailed Khrushchev. The Russians were so angered by his criticism that they withdrew all diplomatic and technical assistance to his underdeveloped country. Hoxha remained undeterred and countered by establishing close relations with MAO ZEDONG and the People's Republic of China. He also instituted a Stalinist-style cult of personality around himself and began persecuting churches and mosques to create a truly atheist state.

Albania remained one of China's closest allies until 1971 when Mao began a rapprochement with the United States. An angry Hoxha denounced his erstwhile benefactors as "capitalists," whereupon China withdrew technical and diplomatic support. Albania had become the most isolated country in the world, but Hoxha was determined to steer his own course. He redoubled efforts to achieve economic self-sufficiency, increased religious persecutions, and publicly declared that "Albanianism"—a virulent form of Balkan nationalism—was the nation's sole religion. Critics of his regime were also purged and punished, and his control remained unchallenged. Albania by this time was among the most repressive states in the world, completely xenophobic in its hostility to other countries. Hoxha did manage to create the rudiments of industrialization, agricultural self-sufficiency, and an end to illiteracy, but at a terrible cost to the Albanian people. He died in Tirana on April 11, 1985, concluding 40 years of unfettered totalitarian rule—longer than any other European head of state. His successor, Ramiz Alia, immediately began dismantling this last bastion of Stalinist dictatorship.

Further Reading

Blumi, Isa. "Hoxha's Class War: The Cultural Revolution and State Reformation, 1961–1971." *East European Quarterly* 33, no. 3 (1999): 303–326.

———. "The Politics of Culture and Power: The Roots of Hoxha's Postwar State." *East European Quarterly* 31 no. 3 (1997): 379–398.

Hoxha, Enver. *With Stalin: Memories.* Toronto: Norman Bethune Institute, 1980.

Kola, Paulin. *The Myth of Greater Albania.* New York: New York University Press, 2001.

Lubenja, Fatos. "Privacy in a Totalitarian Regime." *Social Research* 68, no. 1 (2001): 237–254.

O'Donnell, James S. *A Coming of Age: Albania under Enver Hoxha.* Boulder, Colo.: East European Monographs, 1999.

Pipa, Arshi. *Albanian Stalinism: Ideo-political Aspects.* Boulder, Colo.: East European Monographs, 1990.

Hua Guofeng (1921–   ) *chairman of the Communist Party of China*

Hua Guofeng was born in Paifang, Shanxi Province, China, in 1921, the son of impoverished peasants. He joined the Red Army at the age of 15, survived the famous long march, and fought with distinction as a guerrilla in World War II. After MAO ZEDONG founded the People's Republic of China in 1949, Hua promoted land reform and collectivization in Hunan Province. He proved himself politically adept and continued advancing through the ranks of the Chinese Communist Party (CCP). By 1957 he served as head of the party's United Front Department for Hunan. During the cultural revolution of 1966–76 he was one of a few mid-level party members to survive a massive party purge, ostensibly because of his enthusiasm for Mao's revolutionary dictates. By 1971 Hua transferred to Beijing to serve under Premier Zhou Enlai in the State Council. In this capacity he became personally acquainted with Mao, who looked favorably upon his zealotry and ideological purity. In 1972 Hua was called upon to investigate activities of the disgraced Lin Biao and the following year he gained appointment to the Politburo, China's second-highest decision-making body. After Zhou died in January 1976 Hua was chosen to succeed him, over the more reform-minded Deng Xiaoping—the two men remained strict political adversaries after that. The following April Hua advanced to party vice chairman, making him—after

Mao—the second most powerful individual in China. "With you in charge," Mao reputedly told Hua, "I am at ease." Mao himself died on September 9, 1976, and Hua succeeded him as chairman of the CCP. He was now sole leader of the Chinese nation and also held the titles of premier, chairman of the Central Committee, and chairman of the Central Military Commission—a tremendous concentration of power in the hands of a single individual. Moreover, given his relative youth (56 years old) and obscurity outside Mao's inner circle, Hua's rise constituted an exceptional feat.

In power, Hua wasted no time confronting the radical faction responsible for the excesses of the cultural revolution. He promptly arrested and tried the so-called Gang of Four, including Mao's widow, Jiang Qing. Hua also allowed Deng to be released from prison and rehabilitated. But Deng had little regard for his youthful benefactor and began marshaling allies to oust him. In fact Hua represented the conservative strain of Chinese communism, and his unswerving devotion to whatever Mao preached led to his denigration as head of the "whatever" faction. There were other factors working against him as well. Hua, unlike, Mao, was less a charismatic leader than a well-intentioned sycophant. To address the problems of state or international relations, all he could draw upon were worn and discredited platitudes from the cultural revolution. Hua may have been a skilled party member, but his presence at the top struck many as more the result of happenstance than merit, and was widely resented. His lack of support from senior figures, the military, and the intellectuals assured his eventual fall.

Deng, a master conspirator, wasted little time easing Hua from power and began systematically stripping him of his offices. In September 1980 Hua lost the post of premier to ZHAO ZIYANG through Deng's machinations, and the following year HU YAOBANG supplanted him as CCP general secretary. By 1982 Deng himself succeeded Hua as chairman of the important Central Military Committee, at which point Hua became little more than a figurehead. He has remained in virtual obscurity ever since, a transitional figure in the long and tumultuous history of the Chinese Communist Party. Hua won applause at home for confronting radicals within the party and finally removing them from power. But he proved to be the final casualty in a struggle between a doctrinaire Maoist past and a pragmatic future dominated by Deng. If anything Hua will be remembered for a meteoric rise and an equally spectacular downfall.

Further Reading

Cook, Ian G. *China's Third Revolution: Tensions in the Transition Towards a Post-Communist China.* Richmond, Surrey: Curzon, 2001.

Fontana, Dorothy G. "Background to the Fall of Hua Guofeng." *Asian Survey* 22, no. 3 (1982): 237–260.

Forster, Keith. "China's Coup of October 1976." *Modern China* 18, no. 3 (1992): 263–303.

Holm, D. "Hua Guofeng and the Village Drama Movement in the Northwest Shanxi Base Area, 1943–1945." *China Quarterly* 84 (December 1980): 669–693.

Leung, Edwin Pak-wah. *Political Leaders of Modern China: A Biographical Dictionary.* Westport, Conn.: Greenwood Press, 2002.

Wang, Ting. *Chairman Hua, Leader of the Chinese Communists.* London: C. Hurst, 1980.

Huerta, Victoriano (1854–1916) *president of Mexico*

Victoriano Huerta was born in Colotlan, Jalisco, Mexico, on March 23, 1854, of mixed Spanish-Indian heritage. In 1876 he graduated from the National Military Academy and commenced a lengthy and distinguished career. Huerta gained renown for his skill in combat and was feared for his brutality toward civilians. He disavowed his own Indian origins and was especially vindictive toward Mayan rebels whenever he defeated them. Huerta repeatedly crushed revolts against the PORFIRIO DÍAZ regime and rose in 1901 to brigadier general. When Díaz was overthrown in 1911 Huerta escorted him to Veracruz for deportation to Europe. Up to this point he had been a competent, career-minded officer with little inclination toward politics. The ascent of FRANCISCO MADERO to the presidency in 1912 induced Huerta to retire from the military altogether. Madero recalled him to the colors in February 1913 to put down a revolt by Félix Díaz. Huerta then engineered what has become known as the "tragic ten days," after which most of Mexico City lay in ruins: Huerta colluded with Mexican conservatives and U.S. ambassador Henry Lane Wilson to dispose of Madero. He had the president and vice president arrested and summarily executed on February 22, 1913. The following October Huerta staged a transparently fraudulent election and declared himself president of Mexico.

Victoriano Huerta *(Library of Congress)*

As chief executive Huerta exhibited no ideology or political philosophy other than using government for self-enrichment. His first executive action was to dissolve congress. Next he assumed dictatorial powers. Nominally conservative, Huerta allowed some progressive land reforms to take place, but his regime was more preoccupied with fending off enemies. He ruled Mexico with an iron hand, ruthlessly executing political opponents, including several notable senators. Huerta also instituted a military draft for mobilizing society to support his armies. But the brutality of his usurpation had the effect of unifying disparate revolutionary forces that had been battling each other for supremacy. Madero, never popular while alive, ironically became a rallying point for rebels throughout Mexico. Initially VENUSTIANO CARRANZA raised the banner of revolt over the new Constitutionalist movement, and he was joined by the forces of Francisco

"Pancho" Villa, Emiliano Zapata, and ÁLVARO OBREGÓN. Huerta also acquired a powerful adversary in American president WOODROW WILSON, who abhorred Madero's murder. Wilson immediately recalled his ambassador from Mexico City and thereafter refused to extend diplomatic recognition. In April 1914, Wilson used the detention of American sailors in Veracruz as a pretext to bombard and seize the town, infringing upon Huerta's ability to import foreign arms. But if by seizing Veracruz Wilson hoped to reduce support for Huerta, he sadly miscalculated. This overt aggression rekindled simmering resentments against the United States, and thousands of Mexicans suddenly flocked to Huerta's army. Huerta then simply took his new recruits and deployed them against Constitutionalist armies advancing from the north.

At length Huerta confronted enemy forces on four fronts and lacked the resources and popular support to contain them. By July 1914 his forces were badly defeated outside Mexico City, and he decided to flee the country. Huerta exiled himself in London and Barcelona before relocating to the United States in March 1915. With German backing, he hoped to raise an insurgent force from anti-Carrancista forces and resume fighting. But on June 27, 1915, Huerta was arrested and detained by American authorities in El Paso, Texas. He died while in their custody on January 13, 1916, possibly from cirrhosis of the liver. Historians regard his administration as something of an aberration, for he was devoid of any ideals associated with the Mexican revolution. Huerta's tenure in office was simply a power-grabbing interlude displaying no political or social merit.

Further Reading

Benjamin, Thomas. *La Revolución: Mexico's Great Revolution in Memory, Myth, and History.* Austin: University of Texas Press, 2000.

Foreman, Michael A. "A Storm over Veracruz." *American History Illustrated* 29, no. 1 (1994): 28–37, 72.

Gonzalez, Michael J. *The Mexican Revolution, 1910–1940.* Albuquerque: University of New Mexico Press, 2002.

Henderson, Paul V. N. "Woodrow Wilson, Victoriano Huerta, and the Recognition Issue in Mexico." *Americas* 41, no. 2 (1984): 151–176.

Meyer, Michael C. *Huerta: a Political Portrait.* Lincoln: University of Nebraska Press, 1972.

Torres, Mark A. "Victoriano Huerta and the Conspiracy of 1915." Unpublished master's thesis. University of Texas–El Paso, 1997.

Hughes, William Morris (1862–1952) *prime minister of Australia*

William Morris Hughes was born in London, England, on September 25, 1862, the son of Welsh working-class parents. He immigrated to Australia in 1884, worked at several odd jobs, and began organizing maritime workers. Hughes joined the Labor Party and was elected to the New South Wales Assembly in 1894; he held this seat for the next 50 years. After 1901 Hughes functioned within the new, federal House of Representatives and, to make himself more politically competitive, he studied law and was admitted to the bar. As a politician Hughes was stridently loyal to Labor principles, although his forceful, prickly disposition occasioned him many enemies. He nonetheless performed competently as minister for external affairs under Prime Minister John Watson in 1904 and subsequently served as attorney general three times under Andrew Fisher. In October 1915, after Fisher resigned from office to serve as high commissioner in England, Hughes became both party leader and prime minister.

Australia was then embroiled in World War I, a conflict resulting in heavy loss of life to Commonwealth forces. Hughes nonetheless remained fully committed to the British Empire, and in January 1916 he visited England as part of the United Kingdom War Cabinet. However, trouble was brewing at home between the prime minister and his party over the issue of conscription. Hughes wanted to draft Australian men for service in Europe and the Middle East, but the Labor Party, consisting mostly of Irish workers with little sympathy for England, refused to support him. Hughes decided to put the issue through a public referendum, which was defeated, and his strident behavior so estranged fellow Labor members that they ejected him from the party. Angered by what he considered betrayal, Hughes quickly shuffled conservative Labor members into a new Nationalist Party. He then fashioned a coalition with the Liberal (actually conservative) Party and continued on in office. Determined to assist England, he put through another conscription referendum in December 1917, which was again rejected. Despite this national reluctance to deploy manpower abroad, Australian troops rendered sterling service to the empire and justified their nation's presence at the 1919 Versailles Peace Conference.

In light of Australian sacrifices Hughes was determined to advance Australian concerns for the Pacific region. He greatly irritated President WOODROW WILSON by disputing his desire to place the former German colony of Papua New Guinea under a League of Nations mandate. After hard bargaining he secured Australian administration of the territory. Hughes also defeated a Japanese-sponsored attempt to have racial equality declared throughout the Pacific, thereby nullifying concerns over non-white immigration to Australia. For his bullying performance, the diminutive Hughes won accolades at home as the Little Digger (soldier).

Hughes gradually lost his popularity over the issue of wage determinations passed by the Arbitration Court. By 1922 the Nationalist Party was forced into a coalition with the Country Party, which Hughes despised, and in 1923 he was ousted by STANLEY BRUCE. For the next six years he remained a vitriolic critic of Bruce's policies, and in 1929 he sided with Labor in yet another dispute over wage arbitration. The Nationalists were subsequently ejected from power and Hughes expelled from the party. Shortly after, he founded a new organization from discontented Labor and Nationalist elements, the United Australia Party. Over the next decade he served capably as minister for health and minister of foreign affairs in various administrations. For a while it appeared that Hughes might win back the prime ministership, but in April 1939 he narrowly lost the party's nomination to ROBERT GORDON MENZIES. During World War II Hughes served as minister of the navy and attorney general under Labor prime minister JOHN CURTIN. However, when the United Australia Party leadership ordered him to quit the Advisory War Council, Hughes refused, and he was expelled from his party for a third time. In 1944 he joined the new Liberal Party and continued serving in the House of Representatives until his death on October 28, 1952. Despite his cantankerous reputation, Billy Hughes made his mark on national politics for half a century and is regarded as one of Australia's most effective politicians. He was also the first Australian leader to gain a measure of international stature.

Further Reading

Booker, Malcolm. *The Great Professional: A Study of W. M. Hughes.* New York: McGraw-Hill, 1980.

Fitzhardinge, Lawrence F. *William Morris Hughes,* 2 vols. New York: Oxford University Press, 1964–79.

Hughes, William M. *Policies and Potentates.* Sydney: Angus and Robertson, 1950.

Moses, John A., and Christopher Pugsley, eds. *The German Empire and Britain's Pacific Dominions, 1871–1919: Essays on the Role of Imperialism.* Claremont, Calif.: Regina, 2000.

Sales, Peter M. "W. M. Hughes and the Chanal Crisis of 1922." *Australian Journal of Politics and History* 17, no. 3 (1971): 392–405.

Spartalis, Peter. *The Diplomatic Battles of Billy Hughes.* Sydney, New South Wales: Hale and Iremonger, 1983.

Tsokhas, Kosmas. "W. M. Hughes, the Imperial Wool Purchase, and the Pastoral Lobby, 1914–20." *Journal of Imperial and Commonwealth History* 17 (January 1989): 232–263.

Husák, Gustáv (1913–1991) *first secretary of the Communist Party of Czechoslovakia*

Gustáv Husák was born in Bratislava, Austria-Hungary, on January 10, 1913, the son of Slovak workers. He pursued a law degree at Comenius University and also became attracted to Marxism-Leninism while a student. Husák joined the Slovak Communist Party in 1934 and subsequently served as a lawyer. In 1938 Slovakia was separated from Czechoslovakia by ADOLF HITLER and governed by a fascist dictatorship. Husák, deputy chairman of the party, was arrested several times for political activity, and in 1944 he participated in the Slovak national uprising against Nazi Germany. The rebellion failed and Husák fled to the Soviet Union, returning a year later in the wake of the victorious Red Army. Afterward he served in numerous capacities under Prime Minister KLEMENT GOTTWALD, especially after the communists formally seized power in 1948. By turns chairman of the Slovak Board of Commissioners, the party Central Committee, and the National Assembly, Husák was viewed as a committed ideologue and a rising star in party politics. However, in 1951 Soviet dictator JOSEPH STALIN ordered his Eastern European satellites to purge all party members suspected of harboring sympathies for MARSHAL TITO of Yugoslavia. Husák, an outspoken proponent of Slovak nationalism, was among those rounded up and imprisoned. He was stripped of his party membership, received a life sentence for treason in

1954, and served six years before being released in 1960. Husák was formally rehabilitated by 1963 and resumed his ambitious climb up through the party hierarchy.

Czechoslovakia was then ruled by Antonin Novotny, a communist with arch-Stalinist tendencies. Husák was one of several "liberal" party members to criticize his inflexible policies, and by 1968 Novotny had been replaced by ALEXANDER DUBČEK. This act ushered in a broad period of political and cultural liberalization known as the Prague Spring. Many basic freedoms were allowed for the first time in decades, a trend that unduly alarmed communist officials in the Kremlin. As deputy prime minister, Husák initially supported liberalization but as complaints from Moscow grew, he urged caution. By the time Soviet and Warsaw Pact forces invaded Czechoslovakia on August 20, 1968, he completely reversed his position. Husák publicly thanked the Russians for their support and ingratiated himself with them. Consequently, when Dubček was finally purged from the inner circle in April 1969, Husák was appointed the new first secretary of the Communist Party of Czechoslovakia with Soviet blessings.

Once in power Husák reverted to orthodox Marxist policies and procedures. A police state was reinstated, dissidents rounded up and jailed, and freedom of expression suppressed. Moreover, the Communist Party was thoroughly purged of members suspected of complicity with reforms. Thereafter Czechoslovakia ceased being a maverick state and became a loyal puppet of Soviet foreign policy. Political control became quite brutal, and Charter 77, a leading human rights group, was among the first groups targeted for punishment. Among those arrested was a little-known playwright named Václav Havel. For the next 14 years Husák continued ruling his nation with an iron hand despite liberalizing trends in Eastern Europe as a whole. He adopted the title of president in 1975 to further consolidate his powers. But, true to his nationalist leanings, he pushed through a new constitution granting Slovakia greater cultural and political autonomy in January 1969. This did little to improve the steadily deteriorating national economy, a victim of state control and planning. Nonetheless Husák rejected overtures by Soviet premier MIKHAIL GORBACHEV to liberalize the nation, and Czechoslovakia remained among the most oppressive states of the Eastern Bloc. But by 1989 the groundswell toward democracy could not be restrained, and free elections were held. When the communists were soundly defeated

in the so-called velvet revolution, Husák resigned and turned over the reins of power to the former dissident Václav Havel.

Out of office Husák assumed a life of anonymity and died in Bratislava on November 18, 1991. Two years before, Slovakia had separated itself from the Czech Republic and became the independent nation he tried so faithfully to serve.

Further Reading

Eyal, Gil. *The Origins of Postcommunist Elites: From Prague Spring to the Breakup of Czechoslovakia.* Minneapolis: University of Minnesota Press, 2003.

Griffith, William E. "The Soviet Counter-revolution in Czechoslovakia in 1968: Causes, Course, and Aftermath." *Studies on the Soviet Union* 11, no. 4 (1971): 559–572.

Husák, Gustáv. *Speeches and Writings.* New York: Pergamon Press, 1986.

Roberts, Adam. "Socialist Conservatism in Czechoslovakia." *World Today* 26, no. 11 (1970): 478–488.

Taborsky, Edward. "Czechoslovakia under Husák." *Current History* 70 (March 1976): 114–118, 134.

Williams, Kiernan. *The Prague Spring and Its Aftermath: Czechoslovakian Politics, 1968–1970.* New York: Cambridge University Press, 1997.

Hussein, Abdullah ibn (1882–1951) *king of Jordan*

Abdullah ibn Hussein was born in the holy city of Mecca, Arabia, in 1882, a son of Hussein ibn Ali, a Hashemite whose family traced its descent from the prophet Mohammad. The Arab world was then controlled by the Turkish-based Ottoman Empire, and in 1891 his father brought his family to Constantinople. There Hussein immersed himself in the murky world of Ottoman politics and met Arab nationalists chafing under Turkish rule. In 1912 he joined the Ottoman legislature, but four years later Hussein joined his father in a revolt against the empire. Assisted by British forces, he drove the Turks away from Syria, and in 1920 his brother was appointed king as FAISAL I. Hussein himself sought the crown of Iraq to unite the region under the Hashemite family with British support. However, France contested British ambitions in the Middle East, and it forcefully deposed Faisal in July 1920. Thereafter

Faisal ruled as king of Iraq, while Hussein, after conferring with Colonial Secretary WINSTON CHURCHILL, was appointed emir of the Transjordan region (modern-day Jordan). But the neighboring territory of Palestine had been reserved by the League of Nations as a British mandate to serve as a possible "Jewish National Home"—a prospect upsetting to Arab nationalists. Hussein nonetheless agreed to the conditions and he spent the next three decades laying down the foundation of his state.

By 1923 Transjordan had evolved into an autonomous emirate, under British supervision, that kept Hussein firmly in Britain's corner with lucrative stipends. He also received aid for training the Arab Legion, an indigenous military force. A constitution that created a bicameral legislature was drawn up. However, the emir never abandoned the idea of unifying Transjordan, Syria, and Iraq into a single Arabic entity, despite opposition from leaders in Egypt and Saudi Arabia who favored the status quo for fear of losing their influence in the region. But Hussein also cultivated good relations with the leader of the Zionist movement, CHAIM WEIZMANN, and allowed limited Jewish migration to Palestine. He again was opposed by Arab nationalists who painted him as a puppet of England. Hussein nonetheless supported his British benefactors during World War II and helped drive out the Vichy French regime in Syria. Consequently, in May 1946 Hussein was enthroned as Abdullah I of the new Hashemite kingdom of Jordan.

After World War II the pace of Jewish immigration to the Middle East accelerated, and Abdullah still entertained notions of granting the immigrants a semi-independent state in Palestine under his rule. But once the first Arab-Israeli war commenced in May 1948, the king informed his secret contact, GOLDA MEIR, that he could not resist Arab pressure for military action. Still his forces were deployed only in Arab-held sectors of Palestine and, following a truce in April 1949, the king quickly resumed his contact with Jewish leaders. Hussein also occupied the left bank of the Jordan River by default. The war proved a complete disaster for the Arabs, and the new state of Israel was founded. This act greatly inflamed local passions, but Hussein nevertheless tried negotiating a formal peace treaty with the Jews. This prospect so enraged his cabinet that three prime ministers resigned rather than sign the document. Furthermore, a multitude of Arab states threatened to expel Jordan from the Arab League if the king signed a separate treaty with Israel. Abdullah then relented and received Arab recognition of his annexation of the east bank—and the holy city of Jerusalem—to Jordan.

Abdullah tried placating nationalist sentiments in Palestine by granting refugees citizenship and bringing local notables into his government. However, he was viewed as a traitor for his close ties to Britain and Israel, and as partly responsible for the loss of Arab lands. Moreover, the population, seething with nationalistic fervor, resisted his rule. Events climaxed on July 20, 1951, when the king was assassinated by a Palestinian extremist while entering Al-Aqsa Mosque in Jerusalem.

Further Reading

Abdullah, King of Jordan. *My Memoirs Completed.* New York: Longman, 1978.

Braizat, Musa S. *The Jordanian-Palestinian Relationship: The Bankruptcy of the Confederal Idea.* London: British Academic Press, 1998.

Karsh, Efraim, and P. R. Kumaraswamy, eds. *Israel, the Hashemites, and the Palestinians: The Fateful Triangle.* Portland, Ore.: Frank Cass, 2003.

Nevo, Joseph. *King Abdullah and Palestine: A Territorial Ambition.* Oxford, England: Oxford University Press, 1996.

Satloff, Robert B. *From Abdullah to Hussein: Jordan in Transition.* New York: Oxford University Press, 1994.

Wilson, Mary C. *King Abdullah, Britain, and the Making of Jordan.* New York: Cambridge University Press, 1987.

Hu Yaobang (1915–1989) *general secretary of the Communist Party of China*

Hu Yaobang was born in Liuyang, Hunan Province, China, on November 20, 1915, the son of poor parents. Virtually uneducated, Hu left home and joined the Chinese Communist Party (CCP) at the age of 14. He survived the arduous long march of 1934–35, and during World War II served as political commissar of the 2nd Field Army, striking up a close and abiding relationship with Deng Xiaoping. Afterward, their two careers became inextricably linked. Hu, headstrong and outspoken, rose through the party infrastructure, and by 1952 he was stationed in Beijing as head of the Young

Communist League. In 1966 party chairman MAO ZEDONG unleashed his cultural revolution against perceived reactionaries. Hu and Deng were both purged from the party and spent several years working cow pastures. But when Deng was rehabilitated for the second and final time in 1976, he became de facto head of state and appointed Hu director of the party's organization department and a Politburo member. And, unlike the older generation of revolutionaries who were dogmatic and grounded in beliefs, Deng and Hu were both reform-minded pragmatists. In time Hu proved to be the more radical of the two. His political fortunes crested in February 1980, when he rose to general secretary of the CCP and also joined the Politburo's Standing Committee. This placed him at the very center of political power. Hu used his influence to slowly displace HUA GUOFENG, Mao's hand-picked successor, as party chairman and then assumed his post. By 1982 he had the chairmanship and continued on as general secretary. But Deng remained the real power behind the throne, and a brake on Hu's liberalizing tendencies.

China began distancing itself from the ideological excesses and zealotry of Mao. As general secretary Hu instituted a new political outlook that stopped short of discrediting Chairman Mao's teachings and enacted more flexible policies. Later, greater emphasis was placed upon collective leadership, and Mao's cult of personality was discarded altogether. Hu regarded this policy as "seeking truth from facts" and implemented degrees of political and economic liberalization unthinkable only a few years before. Moreover, Hu systematically cleansed hard-line Maoists and corrupt incompetents from the party hierarchy, replacing them with younger, better-trained, and ideologically flexible cadres. He thus became the idol of the student movement and the intellectuals who sought a return to greater freedom.

In 1980 Hu took the unprecedented step of visiting Tibet, which had been annexed by China in 1959, and apologizing for Chinese excesses there. He then pledged to improve living conditions throughout the region and encouraged Chinese migrants to learn the language and culture. But Hu's reforms and the speed with which he enacted them only alienated conservative party elements, including his former mentor Deng. The turning point was reached in December 1986, when

students held massive demonstrations throughout China, demanding free speech, freedom of the press, and free elections. Hu took no action against the dissenters, and to critics he appeared to actually encourage the process. Deng himself attacked Hu for creating an atmosphere whereby the supremacy of the communist system was questioned. During the annual party congress in January 1987, Hu admitted to major mistakes on policy issues and was stripped of his post. He was replaced by hard-liner ZHAO ZIYANG, although he was allowed to retain his Politburo seat for appearance's sake. On the surface China's fling with liberalization seemed to have reached an ignominious end.

Ironically Hu's greatest impact on the course of Chinese politics occurred after he died on April 15, 1989. He was idolized by the large student community, and his passing induced prodemocracy demonstrations in Shanghai and Beijing. On April 21, 1989, 100,000 protesters encamped in Tiananmen Square in downtown Beijing, demanding the restoration of Hu's reputation and the granting of basic rights. Conservatives debated for several weeks on how to cope with this challenge to authority, and on June 4, 1989, military units were ordered to clear the area. Several thousand people were killed and underscored with their lives Hu's reputation as a popular reformer.

Further Reading

Bachman, David. "Varieties of Chinese Conservatism and the Fall of Hu Yaobang." *Journal of North East Asian Studies* 7, no. 1 (1988): 22–46.

Chan, Adrian. *Chinese Marxism.* New York: Continuum, 2002.

Chang, Parris H. "From Mao to Hua to Hu to Chao: Changes in the Chinese Communist Party Leadership and Its Rules of the Game." *Issues and Studies* 25, no. 1 (1989): 56–72.

Goldman, Merle. "Hu Yaobang's Intellectual Network and the Theory Conference of 1979." *China Quarterly* no. 126 (June 1991): 219–242.

———. *Sowing Seeds of Democracy in China: Political Reform in the Deng Xiaoping Era.* Cambridge, Mass.: Harvard University Press, 1994.

Yang, Zhong Mei. *Hu Yao Bang: A Chinese Biography.* Armonk, N.Y.: M. E. Sharpe, 1988.

I

Ikeda Hayato (1899–1965) *prime minister of Japan*

Ikeda Hayato was born in Yoshina, Japan, on December 3, 1899, into a family of wealthy brewers. He pursued law and economics while attending Kyoto Imperial University and in 1927 commenced his long association with the ministry of finance. Adept as an administrator, Ikeda worked as a taxation officer throughout the 1930s, and in 1945 he served as director of the national tax bureau. Japan was occupied by United States military forces at the end of World War II but, because he lacked the national stature of many senior bureaucrats, Ikeda was allowed to retain his position. In fact he was enlisted by occupation authorities to assist in rebuilding the war-shattered economy to curtail inflation. Ikeda, as a professional bureaucrat, had detailed knowledge of Japan's financial methods, along with the political views guiding them. Moreover, he was in a position to improve them. Ikeda successfully captured a seat in the Diet (legislature) in 1949, becoming a close associate of Prime Minister YOSHIDA SHIGERU. He next was appointed head of the finance ministry, where he had spent his professional career, and continued implementing his anti-inflationary policies. In 1951 Ikeda also helped negotiate a security treaty with the United States while the country rearmed. After 1955, when the Liberal Party merged with the Democrats to form the Liberal Democratic Party (LDP),

Ikeda was tapped to serve as finance minister. He subsequently became minister for international trade under Prime Minister Kishi Nobusuke. When that executive strongly pushed for resumption of the American security treaty, his high-handed behavior offended many factions within the party and caused a public furor. The LDP leadership concluded that retaining Kishi was a political liability so they acquired his resignation and appointed Ikeda to succeed him on July 18, 1960.

Ikeda's traditional brand of leadership was a welcome departure from the confrontational tactics of his predecessor. As an experienced Japanese bureaucrat, he well understood the value of compromise and consensus to get things done. He therefore sacrificed some of his leadership responsibilities and parceled out appointed posts to all factions within the LDP. This brought on a degree of unity and harmony that facilitated Ikeda's legislative agenda. In another bold departure from the previous administration the new prime minister proffered his "income doubling plan" to double Japan's gross national product within a decade. He sought to attain this by striking close alliances between business and government leaders to stimulate a closely managed high-growth period. The bulk of Ikeda's policy revolved around government spending to stimulate consumer demands, coupled with spending on national infrastructure and public service. Ikeda was so confident of success

216

that he increased fiscal outlays without raising taxes and relied upon increasing revenues to fill the gap. Ikeda consistently drew upon his familiarity with Japan's national bureaucracy to help shepherd the desired changes through quickly and efficiently. He also bridged the gap in understanding between bureaucrats and politicians to better coordinate national economic planning. The results proved spectacular: within only five years the national income doubled, spending increased further, and tax levels remained the same. Income for the average Japanese worker also tripled during the same period, thereby ensuring a higher standard of living.

Spectacularly effective on the home front. Ikeda also enjoyed success internationally. Good relations with the United States remained paramount, but Japan slowly showed greater diplomatic independence by initiating increased trade with Communist China and the Soviet Union. In 1964 Ikeda also managed to hold the Olympics in Tokyo, a perfect venue to showcase Japan's new-found prosperity. But Ikeda himself did not observe the bulk of his attainments. He resigned from office because of cancer in October 1964 and died on August 13, 1965. His tenure in office was brief, but it stimulated a culture of sustained growth lasting three decades. He is seen as a leading architect of Japan's vaunted "economic miracle."

Further Reading

Braddick, C. W. *Japan and the Sino-Soviet Alliance, 1950–1964: In the Shadow of the Monolith.* New York: Palgrave Macmillian, 2004.

Johnson, Stephen. *Opposition Politics in Japan: Strategies under a One-Party Dominant Regime.* New York: Routledge, 2000.

Kamibeppu, Takao. *History of Japanese Policies in Education Aid to Developing Countries, 1950s–1990s.* New York: Routledge, 2002.

Maga, Timothy. "The New Frontier and the New Japan: Kennedy, Ikeda, and the 'End of United States Protectionism,' 1961–63." *Diplomacy and Statecraft* 5, no. 2 (1991): 371–393.

Shinoda, Tomohito. *Leading Japan: The Role of the Prime Minister.* Westport, Conn.: Praeger, 2000.

Inönü, Ismet (1884–1973) *president of Turkey*

Ismet (his only given name) was born in Smyrna, in the Ottoman Empire, on September 24, 1884, the son of a judiciary official. After graduating from a military academy he passed through the Artillery School in 1903 and assumed an officer's career. The Ottoman military was then restive over the acute need for modernization, and young leaders like Ismet banded together and demanded reform. In 1908 a coup by the officer-oriented Union of Progress forced the sultan to accept much needed change. It also established the military as a force in politics. Ismet then resumed his career by fighting in Yemen, the Balkans, and throughout World War I. In 1916 he transferred to the Second Turkish Army in Anatolia under General KEMAL ATATÜRK. The two men, differing in temperament but united by a determination to save Turkey, struck up an abiding relationship. In 1918 Ismet was undersecretary of war, but the conflict ended unsuccessfully for the Ottomans. The victorious Western powers declared their intention to divide the empire among themselves. In 1919 a Greek army landed in western Anatolia, and it fell upon forces under Ismet to confront the invaders. He decisively defeated them at the two battles of Inönü in 1920–21 and subsequently adopted Inönü as his surname. He then led the Turkish delegation to negotiations at Lausanne, Switzerland, where the Allies recognized the new country's boundaries and those of the states that arose on the ashes of the defunct empire.

In October 1923 the Republic of Turkey was officially proclaimed with Atatürk as president and Inönü as prime minister. Over the next 15 years the two men worked closely to implement an ambitious agenda that would transform Turkey into a modern secular state. In many respects Inönü served as Atatürk's hatchet man, ruthlessly firing any public figures obstructing progress. But in contrast to his flamboyant and reckless superior, Inönü was decidedly cautious and conservative in outlook. When Atatürk died from overindulgence in November 1938, Inönü became Turkey's second president and chairman of the Republican People's Party (RPP), the country's sole outlet for political expression. Inönü then steered his country through the dangerous period of World War II when Germany put great pressure on Turkey to join the Axis alliance. Inönü nevertheless remained studiously neutral until war's end and sought closer relationships with the West. But Turkey fell under increasing criticism for its one-party rule and was then pressured to adopt political pluralism. Inönü felt that the nation's institutions were sufficiently mature for competition, so in 1946 he allowed creation of the

Democratic Party. He anticipated that the ruling RPP would have no problem remaining in power indefinitely, but in 1950 the Democratic Party handily won elections. Military conservatives then harangued him to remain in power, but Inönü gracefully stepped aside to become head of the opposition. His decision was roundly applauded in the West and resulted in increased commercial and diplomatic contacts.

Inönü remained in opposition for a decade, until the military intervened and ousted the regime of President Celal Bayar in May 1960. He was then asked to become prime minister and form a coalition government with several other groups. Inönü obliged, but none of the arrangements lasted long, and by 1965 Inönü was back in the opposition. Worse, continuing ideological cracks appeared in the ranks of the RPP, as conservative and radical factions exerted themselves. Inönü was thus unable to gather enough political support to become prime minister again. The RPP suffered two serious defeats in 1965 and 1969, which further diminished his influence. By 1972 he was supplanted by left-leaning Bulent Ecevit as party head. Inönü nonetheless continued on as a respected elder statesman until he died in Ankara on December 25, 1973. Along with his friend and mentor Atatürk, Inönü is considered one of the founding figures of modern Turkey and among its longest serving.

Further Reading

Deringil, Selim. *Turkish Foreign Policy during the Second World War: An "Active" Neutrality.* New York: Cambridge University Press, 1989.

Heper, Metin. *Ismet Inönü: The Making of a Turkish Statesman.* New York: E. J. Brill, 1998.

Kedourie, Sylvia, ed. *Seventy-five Years of the Turkish Republic.* Portland, Ore.: Frank Cass, 2000.

Logoglu, Osman F. "Ismet Inönü and the Political Modernization of Turkey, 1945–1966." Unpublished Ph.D. diss., Princeton University, 1970.

Psomiades, Harry J. *The Eastern Question: The Last Phase: A Study in Greek-Turkish Diplomacy.* New York: Pella Publishing Co., 2000.

Vander Lippe, John M. "Decade of Struggle: The Presidency of Ismet Inönü and Turkish Politics, 1938–1950." Unpublished Ph.D. diss., University of Texas–Austin, 1993.

J

Jaruzelski, Wojciech (1923–) *president of Poland*

Wojciech Jaruzelski was born in Kurow, eastern Poland, on July 6, 1923, the son of an army officer. He was educated at Jesuit schools until the German invasion of September 1939, when his family fled to Lithuania. However, in 1940 they were forcibly deported to Siberia by Soviet officials. Both of Jaruzelski's parents died during the internment, and he himself was impressed into the coal mines. After 1943 the Soviets raised an army of Polish expatriates, and he became an infantry officer. Jaruzelski fought with distinction, was heavily decorated for bravery, and after the war attended the Polish Higher Infantry School near Warsaw. In keeping with his sterling reputation for performance and loyalty, he joined the Polish United Worker's (Communist) Party in 1948, and by 1956 he had emerged as the nation's youngest brigadier general. When he became a major general in 1968, he was elected to the party's Central Committee, and also gained appointment as minister of national defense. Jaruzelski commanded Polish troops that invaded Czechoslovakia in August 1968 to crush the liberalizing regime of ALEXANDER DUBČEK. The event underscored for him Russia's determination to keep its Warsaw Pact allies in the communist fold by any measure. But within two years, worker discontent in Poland led to outbreaks of illegal strike activity in

Gdansk and other cities. Jaruzelski ordered troops in to restore order, but fighting broke out and 44 people died. He has since denied authorizing the use of deadly force against fellow Poles.

By 1971 Jaruzelski's reputation allowed him to be elected to the Politburo, Poland's senior decision-making body. By then the regime of WŁADYSŁAW GOMUŁKA had failed to improve the sagging national economy or eroding standards of living. Disturbances continued with increasing regularity and culminated with the founding of the Solidarity Labor Union under Lech Walesa in 1980. Walesa took a militant stand toward communist rule, led a series of crippling strikes, and made wage demands that the cash-strapped nation could not meet. Such defiance initiated a shake-up of the communist elite, and in 1981 Jaruzelski assumed the portfolios of prime minister and party first secretary, in addition to his military functions. This rendered him the single most powerful figure in the country. He tried negotiating with Walesa over worker's rights and living conditions, but compromise proved impossible. Worse, such large-scale unrest alarmed Soviet authorities in Moscow, and they demanded that communist supremacy be restored immediately. Jaruzelski, mindful of 250 Soviet divisions stationed outside Poland's border, felt he had little recourse but to comply and avert disaster. On December 31, 1981, he imposed martial law on

Poland, arrested Walesa and other Solidarity leaders, and clamped down on dissent.

Communist control of Poland was resumed within months, and in July 1983 martial law was lifted. Jaruzelski, meanwhile, attempted to improve the nation's flagging economy through minor tinkering, but to no avail. He then resigned as prime minister, to assume the largely ceremonial position of president, while directing defense and party matters. However, he completely lost control of events after 1988 when Soviet premier MIKHAIL GORBACHEV allowed noncommunist parties to form. Sensing the game was up, Jaruzelski entered negotiations with both Solidarity and church officials to establish a timetable for free elections. In April 1989 the government granted Solidarity legal status, and the first free elections in 50 years saw noncommunists swept to power under TADEUSZ MAZOWIECKI. Jaruzelski managed to retain the presidency by a single parliamentary vote. However, in December 1990 he too was ousted by Walesa and retired from office, the last communist leader of Poland. Since that time Jaruzelski has remained in seclusion, amid demands to try him for imposing martial law. In October 1996 the Polish legislature defeated those motions, but in May 2001 a court ordered his trial for the deaths of workers killed in 1970. Jaruzelski, old and infirm, denied any wrongdoing, and so far, has not been convicted. He remains a controversial figure but an essential player in the transition from a totalitarian system to a democratic one.

Further Reading

Berger, Manfred E. *Jaruzelski.* New York: Econ Verlag, 1990.

Jaruzelski, Wojciech. *Jaruzelski, Prime Minister of Poland: Selected Speeches.* New York: Oxford University Press, 1985.

Kramer, Mark. "Jaruzelski, the Soviet Union, and the Imposition of Martial Law in Poland: New Light on the Mystery of December 1981." *International History Project Bulletin* no. 11 (1998): 5–14.

Michta, Andrew A. *Red Eagle: The Army in Polish Politics, 1944–1988.* Stanford, Calif.: Hoover Institution Press, 1990.

Pelinka, Anton. *Politics of the Lesser Evil: Leadership, Democracy, and Jaruzelski's Poland.* New Brunswick, N.J.: Transaction Publishers, 1999.

Sharman, Jason C. *Repression and Resistance in Communist Europe.* New York: RoutledgeCurzon, 2003.

Jayewardene, Junius (1906–1996) *president of Sri Lanka*

Junius Richard Jayewardene was born in Colombo, Ceylon (Sri Lanka), on September 17, 1906, the son of a supreme court justice. He passed through the Ceylon Law College in 1932 and commenced a successful legal practice. However, in 1933 Jayewardene entered politics by joining the Ceylon National Congress (CNC), which agitated for independence from Great Britain. By dint of hard work he rose to party secretary in 1939. Jayewardene was elected to the island's legislature and, after Ceylon became an independent dominion within the British Commonwealth in 1947, he switched over to the newly formed United National Party (UNP). For many years thereafter, island politics were dominated by the figure of D. S. Senanayake, who appointed Jayewardene as his finance minister. He continued in this capacity when Dudley Senanayake, the leader's son, became prime minister. However, because Ceylon's economy was overwhelmingly dependent on tea and rubber exports, Jayewardene was repeatedly forced to cut back on government subsidies as market prices plunged. The island was in an extreme recession by 1956, when national elections were won by the rival Sri Lanka Freedom Party (SLFP) under S. W. R. D. BANDARANAIKE. Over the next decade Jayewardene reorganized the party, and by 1965 Senanayake returned as prime minister. Five years later the SLFP revived under Sirimavo Bandaranaike, and the UNP was reduced to a mere 17 seats in the legislature. Jayewardene again set about reorganizing the party and, following the death of Senanayake in 1973, succeeded him as party leader. He continued on as head of the opposition until 1977, when the UNP won a resounding electoral victory and Jayewardene became prime minister.

Jayewardene's first political priority was to discard the Westminister parliamentary system in favor of a French presidential system, accomplished in February 1978. His constitutional reforms mandated that the presidency become a strong executive office that combined the functions of head of state with head of government. This meant that chief executives would be chosen directly by a public vote. New elections were held in October 1982 and Jayewardene won handily. Thus strengthened he set about reversing the decades-old socialist economic policies enacted by his predecessors. Jayewardene was a strong exponent of free-market principles and undertook measures to liberalize the market and sell off government-owned industries. He adopted the highly successful Singapore model of national growth, whereby the government provided infrastructural facilities to attract private investment. Sri Lanka (so named since 1972) experienced unprecedented growth, which contributed to the popularity of Jayewardene and his party. He also moved the island away from its traditional nonaligned status and sought closer political and economic ties with Western democracies.

As president, Jayewardene enjoyed success in most of his endeavors. One conspicuous failure, which has haunted every Sri Lankan executive to present times, was the issue of Tamil separatism. The island's majority Sinhalese population is predominantly Buddhist, and its Tamil-speaking minority is Hindu. Violence had flared up since the Sinhalese language and Buddhism were institutionalized in the late 1950s, sparking armed resistance. Jayewardene originally campaigned on a platform espousing justice and equality for all Sri Lankans, the so-called "Dharmishtha Society," but the insurgents proved unwilling to compromise. Jayewardene then resorted to a carrot-and-stick approach to national security: he was willing to negotiate a peaceful settlement to the dispute but did not hesitate to use force to crush the guerrillas. The result was a bloody impasse that continued throughout his tenure in office. Jayewardene retired from public life in 1989, and died in Colombo on November 1, 1996. His successor was the SLFP's Chandrika Kumaratunga, daughter of the socialist Sirimavo Bandaranaike, but she allowed free-market policies to remain in place.

Further Reading

De Silva, K. M. J. R. *Jayewardene of Sri Lanka: A Political Biography,* 2 vols. Honolulu: University of Hawaii Press, 1988–94.

Jayewardene, Junius R. *Men and Memories: Autobiographical Recollections and Reflections.* New Delhi: Vikas Pub. House, 1992.

Krishna, Sankaram. "Producing Sri Lanka: J. R. Jayewardene and Post Colonial Identity." *Alternatives* 21 (July–September 1996): 303–320.

Lakshman, W. D. *Sri Lanka's Development since Independence.* Huntington, N.Y.: Nova Science Publishers, 2000.

Sabaratnam, Lakshmanan. *Ethnic Attachments in Sri Lanka: Social Change and Cultural Continuity.* New York: Palgrave, 2001.

Sivarajah, Ambalavanar. *Politics of Tamil Nationalism in Sri Lanka.* Denver, Colo.: iAcademic Books, 2000.

Jinnah, Mohammed Ali (1876–1948) *governor general of Pakistan*

Mohammed Ali Jinnah was born in Karachi, British India, on December 25, 1876, the son of a prosperous Muslim merchant. Educated locally he left for England in 1893 to train for business but found himself attracted to law. He enrolled at Lincoln's Inn and was called to the bar in 1895, the youngest Indian barrister in the country. Back home he established a lucrative legal practice in Bombay and gained renown as one of India's foremost lawyers. His country was growing restive under British rule, so in 1906 Jinnah joined the Hindu-dominated Indian National Congress Party to agitate for independence. While nominally a Muslim, he sought to foster unity and cooperation with the majority Hindu population to present a united front against a common oppressor. In 1910 Jinnah gained election to the Imperial Council from Bombay, where he held a seat for the next 37 years. He strove for greater unity among the Muslim community by joining the Muslim League in 1913 and serving as its president. Three years later he helped create the Congress-League Pact, which stipulated Indian independence with allowance for separate Muslim electorates. However, after 1920 the Congress Party fell increasingly under the sway of Mohandas Gandhi, who advocated a radical policy of noncooperation. Jinnah not only disagreed with this approach for gaining independence, but he also resented increasing Hindu stridency toward Muslims in general. He was eventually convinced that Muslims would never receive proper representation in a Hindu-dominated society. Jinnah, however, continued propagating the notion of Indian independence with high hopes for accommodating Muslims.

In 1930 Jinnah attended the Round Table Conference in London to discuss the possibility of Indian independence. He also proffered his "fourteen points" to ensure political protection for the Muslim minority, but his proposal was rejected by Congress leader JAWAHARLAL NEHRU. Jinnah was disillusioned by the Hindu-centric policies of the Congress Party and equally disheartened over disunity between warring Muslim communities. He thus remained in London to resume his legal practice until summoned back home by leading Muslims in 1934. Thereafter Jinnah increasingly embraced the notion of a new state, Pakistan, which would be created for and dominated by Muslims alone. National elections held in 1937 confirmed his belief that the Hindus intended to dominate the new nation, when they won all regional assemblies and refused Muslim representation of any kind. In 1940 the Muslim League issued the Lahore resolution, whereby Jinnah confronted the British with demands that any move toward independence must include creation of a separate Muslim state. He argued that the 100 million Muslims in South Asia constituted a viable nation in themselves, and could never expect equal treatment at the hands of the more numerous and increasingly nationalistic Hindus. The Congress Party, however, ridiculed the plan and opposed partitioning the subcontinent under any circumstances. The pace of events quickened after World War II as Great Britain made final preparations to withdraw from South Asia. Jinnah, by hard campaigning, managed to have Muslims win new elections in every district where they held a majority. He presented this as proof of the necessity for creating Pakistan to avert a bloody religious war. Violent rioting between Hindus and Muslims killed several hundred thousand people, which further underscored the urgency of his demands. British authorities reluctantly agreed, and on July 14, 1947, the British House of Commons authorized creation of two new entities, India and Pakistan. Jinnah's unflinching resolve and refusal to compromise finally paid dividends.

Jinnah, long hailed by Muslims as the Quaid-i-Azam (Great Leader), was immediately elected the first governor general of Pakistan, as well as president of the new Constituent Assembly. Pakistan itself constituted four provinces on the northwest frontier of India, along with another entity, East Pakistan, 1,000 miles distant on the Indian Ocean. But Jinnah was ailing and died in Karachi on September 11, 1948. In recognition of his contributions to nationhood his hometown of Karachi became the new capital of Pakistan. He is still revered as the father of his country.

Further Reading

Ahmed, Akbar S. *Jinnah, Pakistan, and Islamic Identity: The Search for Saladin.* New York: Routledge, 1997.

Bandopadhaya, Sailesh Kumar. *Quaid-i-Azam Mohammad Ali Jinnah and the Creation of Pakistan.* New Delhi: Sterling, 1991.

Burke, S. M. *Quaid-i-Azam Mohammad Ali Jinnah: His Personality and His Politics.* New York: Oxford University Press, 1997.

Jalal, Ayesha. *Self and Sovereignty: Individual and Community in South Asian Islam since 1850.* New York: Routledge, 2000.

Khairi, Saad R. *Jinnah Reinterpreted: The Journey from Indian Nationalism to Muslim Statehood.* New York: Oxford University Press, 1995.

Qureshi, Saleem, ed. *Jinnah, the Founder of Pakistan: In the Eyes of His Contemporaries and His Documentary Records at Lincoln's Inn.* Oxford: Oxford University Press, 1998.

Wolpert, Stanley A. *Jinnah of Pakistan.* New York: Oxford University Press, 1984.

John XXIII (Giuseppe Roncalli) (1881–1963)
pope of the Roman Catholic Church

Angelo Giuseppe Roncalli was born in Sotto il Monte, Bergamo, Italy, on November 25, 1881, one of 13 children in a farming family. He followed a religious calling as a young man and was ordained in August 1904. For many years Roncalli served as a secretary to the bishop of Bergamo, where he cultivated sensitivity toward the poor, along with the church's obligation to assist them. When Italy entered World War I in 1915 he joined the army as a chaplain, rising to lieutenant. Afterward Roncalli served as director of the Society for the Propagation of the Faith, which further honed his bureaucratic and diplomatic skills. Roncalli proved himself a model clergyman, so in March 1925 Pope Pius XI appointed him ambassador to Bulgaria with the rank of archbishop. This was a mission requiring considerable delicacy, as Bulgaria was predominantly Orthodox, but Roncalli handled church matters adroitly. After 1934 he performed similar work as Vatican ambassador to Turkey, a predominantly Muslim country. In 1944 Pope PIUS XII assigned him to serve as the papal nuncio to France, then recovering from wartime political and religious schisms. Roncalli nonetheless worked patiently and tactfully to heal old divisions and reconcile the church with its members. So effectively did Roncalli fulfill his responsibility that in January 1953, he was elevated to the college of cardinals. He also became patriarch of Venice and distinguished himself by mixing openly with parishioners, visiting jails and hospitals, and personally assisting the poor where necessary. After Pius

XII died in October 1958, the college of cardinals convened in Rome and chose Roncalli as pope. He took the name John XXIII, the first pontiff so named since the 14th century.

The new pope was relatively old and declining in health so pundits assumed that he would serve only as a transitional figure. But John XXIII had other ideas. Unlike previous popes, traditionally remote authoritarian figures, the new leader was sunnily disposed, openly loved humanity, and went to great lengths to interact with them. Nor did he forsake his role as a priest; he continued visiting hospitals and prisons on short notice. He also enlarged the college of cardinals by appointing 23 new cardinals from younger, more vigorous archbishops. In 1961 he next entered into the international arena by appealing to both American president JOHN F. KENNEDY and Soviet premier NIKITA KHRUSHCHEV to refrain from confrontation during the 1962 Cuban mis-

sile crisis. But John XXIII's most lasting legacy was in summoning a Vatican council, only the second convened since 1870. Advisers questioned the wisdom of such a dramatic gesture, for the church was not facing imminent crisis, but John XXIII saw matters differently. Ignoring complacency, he felt that the church was in dire need of updating its role and rituals to better conform with the modern world. The famous Vatican II convened in October 1962, attended by 2,400 bishops and scores of foreign observers. Under John XXIII's guidance, major changes were instituted within the Catholic Church, especially substitution of the local language for Latin during mass. The laity (church members) were also invited to play a more active role in church affairs and religious celebrations. The pope himself then submitted two encyclicals (letters) to the bishops that were among the most significant ever issued by the Holy See. The first, entitled "Peace on Earth," was addressed not simply to Catholics but also to Protestants and all people of good conscience, regardless of faith, and called upon them to strive for harmony and human rights. The second, "Mother and Teacher," reaffirmed the church's position on social justice. Here he reiterated the necessity for assisting the poor in their daily struggles, urging that rich nations must assist poorer neighbors by sharing their wealth. It also advocated greater ecumenism, or unity, between the various Christian denominations.

John XXIII's efforts led the Catholic Church to begin to adapt to the realities of a changing world. However, he did not live to see the success of his efforts. He died of cancer on June 3, 1963, and was mourned the world over. It fell upon his successor, PAUL VI, to complete the task of Vatican II, now regarded as the most important church gathering since the Middle Ages. It ushered in a period of renewal and opened new chapters in the 2,000-year history of the Catholic Church.

Further Reading

Cahill, Thomas. *Pope John XXIII.* New York: Viking Penguin, 2002.

Feldman, Christian. *Pope John XXIII: A Spiritual Biography.* New York: Crossroad, 2000.

Hebblethwaite, Peter. *Pope John XXIII: Shepherd of the Modern World.* New York: Doubleday, 1985.

John XXIII. *Journey of a Soul: The Autobiography of Pope John XXIII.* New York: Image Doubleday, 2000.

Pope John XXIII *(Library of Congress)*

Markey, John J. *Creating Communion: The Theology of the Constitutions of the Church.* Hyde Park, N.Y.: New City Press, 2003.

Wigginton, F. Peter. *The Popes of Vatican Council II.* Chicago: Franciscan Herald Press, 1983.

Johnson, Lyndon B. (1908–1973) *president of the United States*

Lyndon Baines Johnson was born in Johnson City, Texas, on August 27, 1908, the son of a state legislator. Politics was in his blood, and after teaching high school for several years he served as an aide to a Texas congressman. He met and idolized President FRANKLIN D. ROOSEVELT, further stoking his political ambitions. Johnson gained election to the U.S. House of Representatives in 1937 as a New Deal Democrat and closely allied himself to the Roosevelt administration. However, he narrowly lost election as a U.S. senator four years later and, following the Japanese attack on Pearl Harbor, joined the U.S. Navy. He won the Silver Star for gallantry before Roosevelt ordered all congressmen in uniform back to Washington, D.C., and he was reelected to the House. After 1945 Johnson adopted a more conservative approach to politics, a move reflecting the changing nature of his state. In 1948 he narrowly won election to the Senate by only 87 votes, earning the nickname "Landslide Lyndon." Johnson nonetheless established himself as a political force to reckon with, and by 1951 he became minority leader. Three years later, when the Democrats captured control of the Senate, he became the youngest majority leader ever. Here he worked closely with Republican president DWIGHT D. EISENHOWER, and in 1957 his influence proved critical for passing the first civil rights bill since 1867. This act established Johnson as among the most liberal of southern politicians, and through 1960 he threw his weight behind similar measures. That year Johnson also ran briefly to secure the Democratic nomination as president, but he was completely upstaged by the charismatic JOHN F. KENNEDY. Johnson accepted Kennedy's offer to run as his vice president, and he campaigned vigorously through the South. His efforts proved successful and provided the Democrats with a slim margin of victory over Republican contender RICHARD M. NIXON.

Johnson, a vigorous, forceful, self-possessed individual, was singularly unhappy in his role as vice president. He gracefully accepted token appointments as titular head of the space program and various diplomatic assignments, but he clearly missed being at the center of power. Worse, Johnson and Kennedy were at odds personally. Johnson, a poor man who had worked his way up the ladder of success, felt abused and ignored by the aristocratic Kennedy, who came to regard his vice president as a country bumpkin. All this changed in the wake of Kennedy's assassination on November 22, 1963. Johnson took his oath of office on Air Force One. Intent upon securing the murdered president's legacy, Johnson pushed through a major series of legislative reforms, including civil rights and a large tax cut. Both passed handily, over Republican opposition, and gave Johnson an air of political legitimacy, confirmed during the 1964 presidential elections, when Johnson trounced his opponent, Arizona senator Barry Goldwater, with 61 percent of votes cast. This remains the widest margin of

Lyndon B. Johnson *(Library of Congress)*

victory ever recorded by a winning presidential candidate.

Victory emboldened Johnson to pursue his reform agenda. In 1965 he sponsored the "Great Society," a comprehensive series of bills intending to enhance civil rights for African Americans, and spent millions of dollars to end poverty in the inner cities. The Voting Rights Act of 1965 proved a landmark piece of legislation that guaranteed, for the first time since the Civil War, the ability of minorities to take part in democratic elections. Other programs were enacted, such as Medicate for the elderly, and new departments created, including Housing and Urban Development, and Transportation. Furthermore Johnson outlined a vigorous "war on poverty" program offering food stamps, youth employment, Head Start for underprivileged children, and legal services to the poor. In sum Johnson promulgated the most ambitious overhaul of civil programs since Roosevelt's New Deal of the 1930s. The fact that he achieved such sweeping changes so quickly testifies to his abilities as a master politician.

For all his good intent Johnson's presidency was slowly undermined by his mishandling of foreign affairs. Like Kennedy, he was predisposed to use force when confronted by the specter of communist expansion. In 1965 he sent marines into the Dominican Republican to depose JUAN BOSCH; they stayed until democracy was restored a year later. But his downfall resulted from the entanglements he inherited from Kennedy in Vietnam. Communist leader HO CHI MINH was determined to unite his divided nation by any means necessary, and he launched an all-out guerrilla war to oust the regime of NGUYEN VAN THIEU in South Vietnam. Johnson responded by raising American troop levels from 20,000 in 1964 to half a million the following year. He also commenced a systematic aerial bombardment of North Vietnam's industrial base to dissuade Ho. The Vietnamese suffered horrendous losses but, by dint of clever guerrilla tactics, they could not be destroyed. In January 1968 they staged the surprise Tet Offensive, which further embarrassed the Americans and convinced Johnson that the war was unwinnable. At home he faced increasing political hostility to his Vietnam policies, which built into a massive antiwar movement. Resentment spilled over into politics and culminated in several challenges for his party's next presidential nomination. In February 1968 Johnson only narrowly prevailed over antiwar candidate Eugene McCarthy. But

the experience seared him politically and on March 31, 1968, the president declared in a televised speech his decision not to seek reelection. His withdrawal led to a divisive nomination convention in Chicago that summer, the nomination of Johnson's vice president, Hubert Humphrey, and loss of the White House to Republican RICHARD M. NIXON that fall. Johnson spent the balance of his last year in office trying to establish peace talks with North Vietnamese officials in Paris, after which he retired from politics altogether.

Johnson remained at his ranch in Johnson City, Texas, for the rest of his life, with no inclination to return to the political arena. He died there on January 22, 1973, one of the most unbeloved presidents of recent American history. But his failure respecting Vietnam has overshadowed his valuable work in the far-reaching realm of social reform and civil rights. Johnson's legislative achievements were concrete and establish him, next to Roosevelt, as one of the most influential Democratic executives of the 20th century.

Further Reading

Califiano, Joseph A. *The Triumph and Tragedy of Lyndon Johnson: The White House Years.* College Station: Texas A & M University Press, 2000.

Caro, Robert. *The Years of Lyndon Johnson,* 3 vols. New York: Knopf, 1982–2002.

Helsing, Jeffrey W. *Johnson's War/Johnson's Great Society: The Guns and Butter Trap.* Westport, Conn.: Praeger, 2000.

Hess, Gary J. *Presidential Decisions for War: Korea, Vietnam, and the Persian Gulf.* Baltimore: Johns Hopkins University Press, 2001.

Johnson, Lyndon B. *The Vantage Point; Perspectives of the Presidency, 1963–1969.* New York: Holt, Rinehart and Winston, 1971.

Kaiser, David E. *American Tragedy: Kennedy, Johnson, and the Origins of the Vietnam War.* Cambridge, Mass.: Belknap Press of Harvard University Press, 2000.

Schwartz, Thomas A. *Lyndon Johnson and Europe: In the Shadow of Vietnam.* Cambridge, Mass.: Harvard University Press, 2003.

Jonathan, Joseph Leabua (1914–1987) *prime minister of Lesotho*

Joseph Leabua Jonathan was born in Leribe, Basutoland, on October 30, 1914, the son of Chief

Jonathan Molapo and a grandson of Moshoeshoe I, founder of that nation. He was educated at mission schools before relocating to South Africa to clerk in the mining industry. In 1937 he came home at the urging of an uncle and joined the local civil service. Jonathan proved adept as a bureaucrat and he rose rapidly through the ranks. By 1951 he was assessor to Judicial Commissioner Patrick Duncan, who convinced him to enter politics. In 1956 Jonathan was elected to the National Council, receiving the rank of chief. Basutoland was chafing under British administration and began pressing for political independence. In 1959 Jonathan founded the Basutoland National Party (BNP) as a direct alternative to the ruling Basutoland Congress Party (BCP), which he found too left-leaning. He was appointed to the Legislative Council where he spoke out on behalf of civil rights for women and the sizable Indian community. Jonathan then ventured to London in 1964 as part of a delegation tasked with negotiating independence from England; the first steps toward responsible self-governance were taken the following year. The BNP carried the general elections in July 1965, although Jonathan failed in his own district. He subsequently won a by-election and, as head of the BNP, became prime minister with portfolios of external affairs, defense, and internal security. Basutoland became independent in October 1966 and renamed itself Lesotho.

As a political leader Jonathan was pragmatic and realistic. He was painfully aware that his little nation was entirely surrounded by the apartheid regime of South Africa, and harmonious relations were therefore paramount to survival. He thus became the first black leader to confer with Prime Minister BALTHAZAR VORSTER in 1967, despite criticism from fellow African states. Jonathan was accused of being a South African puppet by fellow citizens and at the next national elections in 1970, it became apparent that the BNP was going to lose. Jonathan abruptly halted the vote count, suspended the constitution, and instituted a state of emergency. He also had King Moshoeshoe II arrested for interfering in national politics and exiled to Holland. The king was allowed back home only after he agreed to accept a ceremonial role. The rival BCP leadership went underground, where they conducted a guerrilla insurgency for many years. But for the time being Jonathan's rule was absolute; he ruled by decree and remained in power for another 15 years.

Jonathan came to resent South Africa's arrogance toward Lesotho, and his pride stiffened. To display his independence from Pretoria, he established diplomatic relations with the Soviet Union, North Korea, and Communist China in 1982. He also began allowing political refugees from apartheid to settle in Lesotho. The South African government, which regarded such refugees as members of the outlawed African National Congress (ANC), began applying economic sanctions and blockades against Lesotho to encourage better behavior. When this failed to nudge Jonathan toward compliance, Pretoria launched punitive military raids against ANC guerrillas hiding there. Jonathan, once reviled as a puppet, suddenly gained new stature among leaders within the Organization of African Unity (OAU) for his defiance. But South Africa continued holding all the cards. After a spate of ANC guerrilla attacks in December 1985 South Africa imposed a complete economic blockade of Lesotho. The nation's economy was halted for three weeks, until the army intervened and deposed Jonathan in a bloodless coup on January 20, 1986. Military rule persisted until the return of constitutional law in 1994.

Out of power and closely watched, Jonathan retired to his farm and avoided public life. He died there on April 5, 1987, a leader who wielded enormous influence in his nation for 21 years.

Further Reading

Bardill, John E. *Lesotho: Dilemmas of Dependence in Southern Africa.* Boulder, Colo.: Westview Press, 1985.

Ferguson, James. *The Anti-Politics Machine: 'Development,' Democratization, and Bureaucratic Power in Lesotho.* Minneapolis: University of Minnesota Press, 1994.

Frank, Lawrence. "Khama and Jonathan: Leadership Strategies in Contemporary Southern Africa." *Journal of Developing Areas* 14, no. 2 (1981): 173–198.

Gay, John. *Citizen Perceptions of Democracy, Governance and Political Crisis in* Lesotho. East Lansing: Michigan State University, Department of Political Science, 2000.

Machobane, L. B. D. J. *Government and Change in Lesotho, 1880–1966: A Study of Political Institutions.* New York: St. Martin's Press, 1994.

K

Kádár, János (1912–1989) *general secretary of the Hungarian Socialist Worker's Party*

János Jozsef Csermancik was born in Fiume, Austria-Hungary, on May 25, 1912, the illegitimate son of a Hungarian servant girl. Spottily educated, he settled into an apprenticeship and became a mechanic. He also joined the illegal Hungarian Communist Party in 1931, assuming the alias of Kádár. Over the next decade he was repeatedly arrested and jailed by the conservative regime of Admiral MIKLÓS HORTHY. But during World War II he joined the underground resistance and in 1942 was admitted into the party's Central Committee. Kádár was captured and tortured by the Nazis in 1944 but he managed to escape. Hungary was occupied by Soviet troops in 1945, and he found work in the hard-line Stalinist regime of MÁTYÁS RÁKOSI as head of the Budapest secret police. In 1949 he rose to minister of the interior just as Soviet dictator JOSEPH STALIN ordered a purge of "national" communists not tutored in Moscow. To advance his reputation within the party, Kádár then committed the first of several treacherous acts by inducing his friend, the foreign minister and lifelong communist Laszlo Rajk, to confess to nonexistent crimes: he was then immediately executed. But Kádár himself faced charges of secretly sympathizing with Yugoslavia's MARSHAL TITO in 1951 and was imprisoned for three years. He gained release by 1954 as part of a de-Stalinization program and was politically rehabilitated. However, in May 1956 Rákosi was overthrown and a new leader, IMRE NAGY, embarked on a course of political liberalization. Kádár initially joined the new government but when it was about to be crushed by Soviet troops, he suddenly switched sides. Thousands of people died in the fighting and Nagy escaped to Romania after Kadar, now prime minister and party first secretary, offered him safe conduct. Nagy was then arrested, brought back to Hungary, and executed, along with 5,000 other freedom fighters. Kádár subsequently espoused slavish obedience to Moscow, which made him, in the eyes of fellow Hungarians, a traitor.

Kádár's first term as prime minister lasted until 1958, during which time he purged the party of malcontents and harshly reasserted communist control. But he also eliminated the last vestiges of Stalinism among the hierarchy. He was called back to power as premier in 1961 and surprised pundits by enacting a new reform-minded agenda. Kádár did so carefully, pledging to superiors in Moscow his loyalty in foreign policy while extracting promises of noninterference in domestic affairs. Thus situated, Kádár embarked on what was officially deemed the "New Economic Mechanism." He began a gradual drift toward a mixed economy that incorporated several features of free market capitalism. Heavy industry was downplayed in favor of greater emphasis on consumer goods. Kádár also allowed for limited freedom of expression among noncommunists, declaring, "Those who are not against us are for us." Under "goulash communism" Hungary ultimately enjoyed the most diverse and thriving economy of Eastern Europe, and Kádár became the most successful national leader after Tito behind the Iron Curtain.

Authorities in Moscow turned a blind eye to Kádár's reforms, provided he followed their cue on international matters. After the 1956 revolution he allowed Soviet troops to remain on Hungarian soil to ensure stability. In 1968 he dutifully sent Hungarian forces to invade Czechoslovakia and help crush the liberalization program of ALEXANDER DUBČEK. Unfortunately in the 1980s, Kádár's halfway compromises between capitalism and central planning broke down, and the economy stagnated. By 1988 reform elements under KAROLY GRÓSZ had seized the reins of power while Kádár was dismissed as general secretary and eased into the ceremonial post of president. In May 1989 he was purged from the Central Committee altogether and forced into retirement. Kádár died in Budapest on July 6, 1989, just months before communism collapsed throughout Eastern Europe. A ruthless political survivor, he played a key role in Hungary's ultimate transition from a Stalinist state to a social democracy. But most citizens never forgave him for his role in the deaths of Rajk, Nagy, and many others.

Further Reading

Dessewiffy, Tibor. "Speculated Travelers: The Political Construction of the Tourist in the Kádár Regime." *Cultural History* 16, no. 1 (2002): 44–62.

Felkay, Andrew. *Hungary and the USSR, 1956–1988: Kádár's Political Leadership.* Westport, Conn.: Greenwood Press, 1989.

Gati, Charles. *Hungary and the Soviet Bloc.* Durham, N.C.: Duke University Press, 1986.

Kádár, János. *Selected Speeches and Interviews.* New York: Pergamon, 1985.

Molnar, Miklos. *From Bela Kun to János Kádár: Seventy Years of Hungarian Communism.* New York: Berg, 1990.

Sharman, Jason C. *Repression and Resistance in Communist Europe.* New York: RoutledgeCurzon, 2003.

Karami, Rashid (1921–1987) *prime minister of Lebanon*

Rashid Karami was born in Tripoli, Lebanon, on December 30, 1921, into a wealthy Sunni Muslim family. His father, Abdul Hamid Karami, was a noted Islamic judge while Lebanon was administered as a League of Nations mandate by France. Karami attended French schools locally before studying law at Cairo University in Egypt. He came home in 1947 and commenced a successful law practice in Tripoli. However, in 1950 he was elected a deputy to the Lebanese legislature, taking the seat of his late father, and the following year he became minister of justice. Unlike many Sunni contemporaries, Karami was a radical who embraced the Pan-Arabism espoused by Egyptian president GAMAL ABDEL NASSER. He demanded that Lebanon break off diplomatic relations with France and Great Britain during the 1956 Suez Crisis, which made him a leader of the left-leaning Arab factions. Karami's radicalism also buoyed his national standing, and in 1955 he became prime minister. Under Lebanese custom, the prime minister can only be a Sunni Muslim, the speaker of the legislature a Shia Muslim, while the presidency is reserved for a Maronite Christian. In 1958 President CAMILLE CHAMOUN refused to step down and tried extending his term in office, a step that Karami opposed. A civil war erupted between Christians and Muslims that had to be contained through the intervention of U.S. Marines. Chamoun's resignation was then secured, and Karami remained prime minister. Over the next decade Karami served intermittently with several attempts at a "unity" government to ensure domestic peace. However, events outside of Lebanon kept destabilizing the delicate balance of internal affairs. After the 1967 Arab-Israeli war Karami fully embraced the goals and objectives of the radical Palestine Liberation Organization (PLO), which put him on a collision course with most Christians. In 1969 the Cairo Accord was signed, which legitimized PLO camps in southern Lebanon while also reaffirming Lebanese political sovereignty. Karami lent support to the agreement and also encouraged strong ties with Syrian president Hafez al-Assad to counter Israeli influence in south Lebanon.

Karami remained in office for a decade until April 1970, when friction between the PLO and the Lebanese army led to armed clashes, and he resigned. By 1975 the fractious Lebanese polity arose in civil war and Christian militias were pitted against their Sunni, Shia, and Druze equivalents. Alliances changed fast and furiously while all sides took turns battling with each other. That April President Suleiman Franjieh appointed Karami prime minister one more time, counting on his stature within the Muslim community to encourage peaceful relations. But even he could not stop the fighting at this juncture, and in December 1976 President ELIAS SARKIS replaced him with Salim Hoss. The militancy of Muslim factions increased after the April 1982 Israeli invasion of Lebanon. The following year President AMIN GEMAYEL signed a treaty with Israel to formalize Israel's occupation of the southern half of the country. Karami then became an outspoken opponent of Gemayel, and the following May he established the National Salvation Front to resist further Israeli encroachment. In 1984 he attended two national reconciliation conferences in Geneva and Lausanne, Switzerland, but accord proved elusive. Fighting continued unabated until 1985, when Karami helped broker the Tripartite Agreement among rival armed militias and religious groups. In May 1987 the Lebanese legislature revoked the 1983 treaty with Israel, along with the 1969 Cairo Accord. This legislation, which Gemayel touted as the "National Agreement to Solve the Lebanese Crisis," was crafted with minimal Sunni cooperation, and Karami, as prime minister, refused to sign it.

Karami's intransigence toward Gemayel only further strained relations between the Christian and Muslim communities, and in May 1987 Karami tendered his resignation. It was refused by Gemayel, for no Sunni politician of his stature could be found to replace him. Unfortunately, on June 1, 1987, the prime minister died when the helicopter he was riding in exploded. Since then, Samir Geagea of the Lebanese Forces Militia has been implicated in his murder. But Karami's 10 terms as Lebanon's prime minister is a record and establishes him as one of the nation's most enduring political figures.

Further Reading

Attie, Caroline. *Lebanon in the 1950s.* London: I. B. Tauris, 2002.

Dagher, Carole. *Bring Down the Walls: Lebanon's Postwar Challenge.* New York: St. Martin's Press, 2000.

Najem, Tom. *Lebanon: The Politics of a Penetrated Society.* London: Routledge, 2002.

Picard, Elizabeth. *Lebanon, a Shattered Country: Myths and Realities of the Wars in Lebanon.* New York: Holes and Meier, 2002.

Salem, Elie A. *Violence and Diplomacy in Lebanon: The Troubled Years, 1982–1988.* New York: I. B. Tauris, 1995.

Schultz, Kirsten F. *Israel's Covert Diplomacy in Lebanon.* New York: St. Martin's Press, 1998.

Karmal, Babrak (1929–1996) *president of Afghanistan*

Babrak Karmal was born in Kamari, Afghanistan, on January 6, 1929, the son of a leading army general. He was related by birth to future prime minister Mohammed Daoud and the reigning king, Mohammad Zahir Shah. Karmal was educated at German-language schools before gaining admittance to the University of Kabul in 1949. There he embraced Marxism and was subsequently arrested and jailed for political activity. His cellmate was Mir Akbar Khyber, a leading Marxist theorist, who refined his understanding of revolutionary politics. Released in 1956, Karmal continued his studies at the university before gaining employment with the ministry of education. By 1961 he had transferred to the ministry of planning where he was working when Prime Minister Daoud reduced Zahir Shah to a constitutional monarch in 1964. Karmal then left the government to concentrate on politics. The following year he helped found the People's Democratic Party of Afghanistan (PDPA), which immediately split into two factions. The largest, the Khalg (the Masses), under Nur Mohammed Taraki was Maoist-oriented, while the Parcham (the Banner) under Karmal retained a Soviet orientation. The factions maintained a tenuous truce, and in July 1973 they assisted Daoud in deposing the king and declaring a republic. However, on April 28, 1978, Marxists in the military killed Daoud and established the Democratic Republic of Afghanistan. Taraki, the new president, then purged the party of Parcham adherents. Karmal, serving as ambassador to Czechoslovakia, was ordered home to face trial but fled to Moscow. Taraki was then killed by his chief adviser, Hafizullah Amin, an act that convinced Soviet premier LEONID BREZHNEV to intervene directly with force.

On December 25, 1979, thousands of Soviet troops spilled over the border and Amin was killed. Two days later Karmal arrived in Kabul on a Soviet transport and was installed as the new president of Afghanistan. He also assumed the portfolios of prime minister, party general secretary, and commander in chief. With massive Russian backing Karmal moved quickly to consolidate his rule. He freed an estimated 2,000 Parcham political prisoners and replaced them with a like number of Khalq sympathizers. He also abolished the dreaded Afghan secret police, and installed a Soviet-style intelligence service to suppress discontent. For the next seven years Karmal and his Soviet allies battled to remain in power. But try as he might his administration elicited no loyalty beyond the capital of Kabul. In fact, the mass of conservative Muslim peasants viewed him as an atheist and a puppet of the Russians. As the conflict expanded, roughly a third of the country's population fled into the countryside or the relative security of neighboring Pakistan. Those remaining behind initiated a bloody, internecine guerrilla war, and thousands of Mujahid (Muslim) warriors sacrificed themselves to rid Afghanistan of the infidels. The primitive guerrillas were initially outgunned by sophisticated Soviet weaponry, but covert military aid provided by American president RONALD REAGAN and Pakistani dictator MOHAMMAD ZIA UL HAQ slowly turned the tide. The Soviets found themselves in an inextricable quagmire.

By 1986 the Soviet gamble was a costly failure. Afghanistan remained embroiled in its holy war against communism, and Karmal proved incapable of exerting any control beyond Kabul. On May 4, 1986, the Soviets suddenly eased him from power on account of "ill health." He was replaced by a former security chief, Najibullah, viewed as a compromise candidate who could negotiate with the rebels. Karmal was then exiled to Moscow where he remained until after the Soviets withdrew from Afghanistan in 1991. He declined to become involved in national politics and lived in obscurity. Karmal subsequently relocated to Moscow once again to receive cancer treatment and died on December 3, 1996. Najibullah, upon whom the Soviets placed great reliance, also failed to control the insurgency, and he was ultimately captured and executed by Muslim fighters.

Further Reading

Bradshear, Henry S. *Afghan Communism and Soviet Intervention.* New York: Oxford University Press, 1999.

Grau, Lester W., and Michael A. Gress. *The Soviet-Afghan War: How a Superpower Fought and Lost.* Lawrence: University Press of Kansas, 2002.

Lobato, Chantal. "Islam in Kabul: The Religious Politics of Babrak Karmal." *Central Asian Survey* 4, no. 4 (1985): 111–120.

Magnus, Ralph H. *Afghanistan: Mullah, Marx, and Mujahid.* Boulder, Colo.: Westview Press, 2000.

Rubin, Barnett R. *The Fragmentation of Afghanistan: State Formation and Collapse in the International System.* New Haven, Conn.: Yale University Press, 2002.

Saikai, Amin, and Beverly Male. *Regime Change in Afghanistan: Foreign Intervention and the Politics of Legitimacy.* Boulder, Colo.: Westview Press, 1991.

Kasavubu, Joseph (ca. 1913–1969) *president of the Republic of Congo*

Joseph Kasavubu was born in Tshela Province, Belgian Congo, around 1913, a member of the sizable Bakongo tribal grouping. He studied many years for the priesthood but quit in 1937 to join the civil service. Kasavubu became closely involved in Bakongo tribal and cultural matters, and after 1950 he was elected president of ABAKO, a Bakongo rights organization. Belgian colonial leaders did not permit formal political organizations for Africans but Kasavubu nonetheless transformed ABAKO into a forum for independence. In time he became closely identified with radical elements demanding freedom of the press and free speech if only for his fellow Bakongo. In 1957 Kasavubu parleyed his popularity into politics by being elected a town mayor in Leopoldville, and two years later was arrested in the wake of political rioting. But continuing unrest prompted the Belgians to convene the Round Table Conference in Brussels to commence negotiations for independence. Kasavubu, as a nationalist spokesman, was present and demanded that talks conclude no later than June 1960. He also pressed for imposition of a federal constitution that granted the Bakongo region considerable autonomy in any national government. But Kasavubu found competition in Moscow-trained PATRICE LUMUMBA of Mouvement National Congolais (MCN), National Congo Movement, who pushed for a strongly centralized regime. When national elections were held in May 1960, neither man won a clear majority so a coalition government was formed, making Kasavubu president and Lumumba prime minister.

The Congo gained independence on June 24, 1960, but its two executive leaders had a stormy relationship. Their competing visions for a national government inspired regional unrest, and two weeks after they took office the army mutinied and riots broke out. The Belgians then intervened with military force to protect their own citizens and property. Worse, in July the leader of Katanga Province, MOÏSE TSHOMBE, declared his independence from the Congo. The ensuing crisis prompted both Kasavubu and Lumumba to jointly request United Nations forces from Ghana to restore order. However, the two men distrusted each other and failed to reconcile their differences. Rumors also circulated that Lumumba had accepted a Soviet offer of troops to prop up his ailing regime. Kasavubu then took to the airwaves on September 5, 1960, declaring that Lumumba was dismissed as prime minister. Lumumba countered with a broadcast of his own, dismissing Kasavubu from the presidency. The chaos continued until a part of the army under Colonel Joseph Mobutu seized power in a bloodless coup and deposed both. Lumumba tried escaping to Stanleyville but was arrested by Tshombe's men and eventually murdered. The United Nations, meanwhile, adopted a resolution recognizing Kasavubu as the sole legitimate ruler of Congo, and he was reinstated in July 1961. He accepted a new constitution calling for a looser confederation of independent ethnic states.

For four years Kasavubu attempted to run national affairs through a succession of prime ministers that he seemingly appointed and dismissed at will. Part of his problem was his close identification with the Bakongo people, one of several hundred tribal factions, and he failed to cultivate a national following. When Tshombe refused to accept the new power arrangements in 1961, he was arrested and deported. Relations with Prime Minister Antoine Gizenga then broke down and he was discharged from office, while Tshombe was appointed to succeed him in October 1963. Two years later Kasavubu relieved Tshombe again on October 13, 1965, declaring the need for a new national government. A period of national instability ensued, at which point General Mobutu intervened a second time, deposing Kasavubu for good on November 25, 1965. Sensing that his political career was finally over, the former executive pledged allegiance to the military regime and was allowed to remain in politics as a senator. Kasavubu died at home while serving in that capacity on March 24, 1969. Considering the sheer chaos surrounding his tenure in office, it is a tribute to his political skill that he survived as long as he did.

Further Reading
Abi-Saab, Georges. *The United Nations Operations in the Congo, 1960–1964.* New York: Oxford University Press, 1978.
James, Alan. *Britain and the Congo Crisis, 1960–63.* New York: St. Martin's Press, 1996.
Lemarchand, Rene. *Political Awakening in the Belgian Congo.* Westport, Conn.: Greenwood Press, 1982.
Nzongola-Ntalaja, Georges. *The Congo from Leopold to Kabila: A People's History.* New York: Zed Books, 2002.
———. *Resistance and Repression in the Congo: Strengths and Weaknesses of the Democracy Movement, 1956–2000.* New York: Zed Books, 2001.
O'Ballance, Edgar. *The Congo-Zaire Experience, 1960–98.* New York: St. Martin's Press, 2000.

Kaunda, Kenneth (1924–   ) *president of Zambia*
Kenneth David Kaunda was born in Lubwa, Northern Rhodesia, on April 28, 1924, the son of missionaries and teachers from Malawi. After adapting to the culture and language of the Bemba people he followed in his parent's profession, rising to headmaster by 1943. Kaunda, however, became disenchanted by the racism of British colonial rule while working in Southern Rhodesia. Consequently in 1949 he helped found the Northern Rhodesia African National Congress (ANC), an early nationalist organization. Kaunda was a talented administrator and he soon rose to party secretary general behind President Harry Nkumbula. In this capacity he visited India in 1957, and was deeply impressed by the nonviolent traditions of Mahatma Gandhi. Kaunda then returned to Northern Rhodesia to start a campaign of political agitation, in which he would be routinely jailed and released. He was especially opposed to continuation of the Central African Federation, which had been created in 1953 by a union of Northern and Southern Rhodesia with Nyasaland (Malawi). This organization catered almost exclusively to white minority governments at the expense of the majority African population. Its imposition upon Central African residents convinced Kaunda that more radical tactics were necessary for change, so in 1958 he left the ANC to found his own group, the Zambia African National Congress. The following year he organized an election boycott and was again arrested. By the time he was released in 1960, Britain had recognized the futility of administering the

region and initiated decolonization procedures. Kaunda, as a leading nationalist figure, had a prominent role in negotiating independence from England, and in October 1962 he won a seat in the territorial assembly. He also founded a new political entity, the United National Independence Party (UNIP), to advance the cause of independence. New elections held in January 1964 made him the youngest prime minister within the British Commonwealth. The following October, Northern Rhodesia was transformed into the new nation of Zambia, with Kaunda as its first president.

The new executive officer inherited a multiplicity of problems associated with decolonization. Tribal friction was endemic, the economy weak, and national infrastructure lacking. Worse, Zambia's geographical location placed it in the heart of anticolonial wars and conflicts throughout the region. Kaunda found himself leading a front-line state in wars against white minority governments and racial supremacy. Worse, in 1965 Prime Minister IAN SMITH unilaterally declared independence from Great Britain under the flag of Rhodesia. His government controlled all of Zambia's railroad links to world markets and exerted a stranglehold. Over the next 15 years, Kaunda carefully juggled national priorities in supporting guerrillas while fending off attacks by vengeful colonial armies. His approach to the white-ruled apartheid regime of South Africa was also ambivalent, but pragmatic. He allowed guerrillas of Joshua Nkomo to station themselves in Zambia, and also permitted the ANC to operate an office in the capital of Lusaka. He then forbade South African investment in Zambia, but he did purchase food and other essential commodities from the apartheid regime when necessary. His perseverance paid off when the liberation struggles were successfully concluded, and in 1980 he brokered negotiations that transformed Rhodesia into the new nation of Zimbabwe. Kaunda's diplomatic success ensured his reputation as one of Africa's foremost nationalist statesmen.

Domestically Kaunda was less successful in creating general levels of prosperity. His socialist economic policies nationalized the copper industry and agriculture, and ran both into the ground. He refused financial assistance from the International Monetary Fund (IMF), because its austerity measures required too much sacrifice from the Zambian people. In the wake of rising tribal violence, Kaunda also outlawed all political parties other than the UNIP in 1973. For nearly two decades

he presided over a sinking national economy backed by mounting despotism. When growing international pressure forced him to accept a return to political pluralism in 1990, he did so only reluctantly. In November 1991 Kaunda was decisively defeated by Frederick Chiluba and peacefully stepped down. When Chiluba proved no more adept at improving the economy, Kaunda announced his candidacy for president in 1996. Chiluba preempted the attempt by passing a constitutional amendment allowing only native-born Zambians to hold high office. Worse, in 1997 Kaunda was jailed for his alleged role in an aborted coup attempt. He was released the following year and announced his retirement from politics. In July 2002 Kaunda emerged from retirement long enough to praise the new administration of President Levy Patrick Mwanawasa and its determination to try Chiluba for corruption. "I think it's the right thing for them to do," he stated, "very right indeed." Kaunda remains highly respected as an elder African statesman and among the most successful in the struggle against colonialism.

Further Reading

Burnell, P. "The Significance of the December 1998 Local Elections in Zambia and Their Aftermath." *Commonwealth and Comparative Politics* 38 (March 2000): 1–20.

Chan, Stephen. *Zambia and the Decline of Kaunda, 1984–1998.* Lewiston, N.Y.: Edwin Mellen Press, 2000.

———. *Kaunda and Southern Africa: Image and Reality in Foreign Policy.* New York: British Academic Press, 1992.

Herbert, Eugenia. *Twilight on the Zambezi: Late Colonialism in Central Africa.* New York: Palgrave, 2002.

Kaunda, Kenneth D. *Zambia Shall Be Free: An Autobiography.* New York: Praeger, 1963.

Simutanyi, Neo R. *Challenges to Democratic Consolidation in Zambia.* East Lansing: Michigan State University, Department of Political Science, 2002.

Kayibanda, Grégoire (1924–1976) *president of Rwanda*

Grégoire Kayibanda was born in Tare, Gritarana region, Rwanda, on May 1, 1924, as part of the Hutu tribal majority. The Tutsi minority had traditionally ruled

Rwanda as kings, and their special status had been enhanced by the Belgian colonial administration. Kayibanda was educated at Catholic missionary schools and subsequently studied at various seminaries, but after 1943 he turned toward a career in teaching and journalism. He briefly edited two Catholic newspapers and was also employed by the colonial civil service as inspector of schools. In the early 1950s, Kayibanda became politically active in advocating greater rights for the Hutu majority of Rwanda. In 1952 he founded a cooperative movement that evolved into a political party, the Muhutu Social Movement (MSM), for the same purpose. In 1958 Kayibanda was selected to visit Belgium to study journalism. That government was making preparations to grant Rwanda political independence, a move that many Hutus greeted with trepidation. Kayibanda felt that the Hutus had not mastered the skills necessary for political organization, and independence would lead only to further exploitation by the Tutsi. When Kayibanda returned to Rwanda in 1959, he found it in an ethnic uproar. The Tutsi king Mutara II had just been murdered, and Tutsi nationalists began rounding up Hutu leaders in response. Armed clashes turned into bloody battles between the two groups and wholesale massacres seemed imminent. What many Hutu leaders feared most began unfolding before them.

Kayibanda had failed to persuade the Belgian government to hold off granting independence to Rwanda. He therefore accelerated his own timetable by founding a new political party, Parmehutu, which was a nationalistic, ethnically based organization. Sensing what would follow, the Hutus began registering to vote in large numbers, and Parmehutu was swept to power in the 1960 national elections. Kayibanda, as party leader, became prime minister, and the monarchy was abolished. Further constitutional changes a year later made him executive president, and by 1962 Rwanda had finally become an independent nation. However, Hutu supremacy was resented by the displaced Tutsi, many of whom fled to neighboring countries to take up an armed insurgency. In 1963 a large Tutsi force almost captured the capital before being turned back. Their defeat triggered a spate of killings by vengeful Hutus, and an estimated 10,000 people died, while 150,000 became refugees. Much time elapsed before Kayibanda restored order and attempted to rule his nation as its first president and Hutu head of state.

Kayibanda could do little to rectify the sinking economy of Rwanda, a small country with scanty resources—and a burgeoning population. He was unable to promote growth. In practice Kayibanda gravitated toward despotism. After Parmehutu took all legislative seats in the 1965 elections, he outlawed opposition parties and instituted one-party rule. Furthermore his policies were ethnically tinged and clearly favored Hutus over Tutsis. He was also accused of favoring Hutus from the southern and central part of the nation at the expense of northerners. But despite this growing tendency toward authoritarianism, he was overwhelmingly reelected president in 1965 and 1969. When additional ethnic clashes erupted in February 1973, the defense minister, General Juvenal Habyarimana, seized the opportunity to depose the government in a bloodless coup on July 5, 1973. Kayibanda was then imprisoned, charged with stirring up racial animosities, and sentenced to death. The sentence was subsequently commuted to home arrest for life. Kayibanda died of a heart attack there on December 22, 1976.

Further Reading

Chretien, Jean-Pierre. *The Great Lakes of Africa: Two Thousand Years of History.* New York: Zone Books, 2003.

Forster, Peter G. *Race and Ethnicity in East Africa.* New York: St. Martin's Press, 2000.

Mamdani, Mahmood. *When Victims Become Killers: Colonialism, Nativism, and the Genocide in Rwanda.* Princeton, N.J.: Princeton University Press, 2001.

Mwakikagile, Godfrey. *Civil Wars in Rwanda and Burundi.* Huntington, N.Y.: Nova Science Publishers, 2001.

Newbury, Catharine E. *The Cohesion of Oppression: Clientship and Ethnicity in Rwanda, 1860–1960.* New York: Columbia University Press, 1988.

Wagoner, Fred E. "Nation-building in Africa: A Descriptive Analysis of the Development of Rwanda." Unpublished Ph.D. diss., University of Michigan, 1974.

Keita, Modibo (1915–1977) *president of Mali*

Modibo Keita was born in Bamako, capital of French Sudan, on June 4, 1915. He was descended from a family line that claimed kinship with rulers of the ancient empire of Mali. After receiving a good education in neighboring Senegal, Keita came home to work as a teacher. However, he was by nature an extreme left-wing anticolonialist, and sought an outlet for his political beliefs. In 1947 he became secretary of the Sudanese Union (US), which agitated for independence from France. That same year US struck up cordial relations with another anticolonial group, the Rassemblement Democratique Africain (RDA), which had chapters throughout francophone West Africa. As head of the coalition Keita was elected to French Sudan's first territorial assembly and solidified his credentials as a left-wing African nationalist. French colonial administrators considered Keita a communist and briefly imprisoned him in 1948. Two years later they exiled him into the interior to organize schools for nomadic dwellers. But Keita retained considerable popularity, and in 1952 he returned to the assembly and as mayor of Bamako. France at this time began allowing direct colonial representation in its own National Assembly, and in 1956 Keita won a seat; he eventually served as its first African vice president. He also held a cabinet post in France's Ministry of Overseas Territories. But none of these accomplishments mitigated his antipathy for imperialism and colonialism. He came home in November 1958, once French Sudan became a self-governing republic within the overseas French community. Keita was determined to effect radical change.

From the onset of his career, Keita was obsessed with the notion of a French-speaking, West African federation of several regional states. To that end he began negotiations with the governments of Senegal, Upper Volta, and Dahomey to found a new Mali Federation based upon the ancient empire. In 1959 the federation was formed, with Keita as president, but it just as quickly faded away. By 1960 only French Sudan and Senegal retained a federation, but disagreements between Keita and LÉOPOLD SÉDAR SENGHOR resulted in Senegal's departure in June 1960. Undeterred Keita became president of French Sudan on September 23, 1960, which promptly renamed itself Mali. He also remained head of the US party, now the only legal political organization.

Once in power Keita embarked on a strict regimen to develop the national economy along Marxist lines. The government nationalized key sectors of the economy and closely aligned itself with communist bloc nations. Keita also hastily withdrew from the French franc zone to further demonstrate his abhorrence for the colonial past. So closely did he adhere to the communist line that in 1963 the Soviet Union awarded him with the Lenin Peace Prize. That year he also helped to found the Organization of African Unity (OAU). Unfortunately, Soviet economics had little relevance in a desperately poor, underdeveloped nation like Mali, and the economy unraveled. In a desperate attempt to attract foreign capital Keita negotiated a return to the franc zone, a move that angered many radicals within the ruling circle. To placate critics, the president instituted a national purge, patterned after MAO ZEDONG's cultural revolution, in August 1967. The national assembly voted itself out of existence, and Keita assumed dictatorial control. He also created and unleashed the "popular militia" that ran roughshod over the countryside, arresting, harassing, and murdering perceived enemies of the state. "If it is necessary to ruin and kill men in order to stay independent, we shall do so without pity or regret," he warned. This systematic abuse eliminated Keita's once buoyant popularity and also alienated the military establishment. After an especially poor harvest, Colonel Moussa Traore stepped in and overthrew Keita on November 19, 1968. He was subsequently sentenced to life imprisonment in Bamako and died there on May 16, 1977. Keita was by that time an official nonentity, but his funeral was nonetheless well attended by peasants who fondly recalled his role in securing Mali's independence.

Further Reading

Binger, R. James, David Robinson, and John M. Staatz. *Democracy and Development in Mali.* East Lansing: Michigan State University Press, 2000.

Brenner, Louis. *Controlling Knowledge: Religious Power and Schooling in a West African Muslim Society.* Bloomington: Indiana University Press, 2001.

Flotz, William J. *From French West Africa to the Mali Federation.* New Haven, Conn.: Yale University Press, 1965.

Mann, Gregory. "The Tirailleur Elsewhere: Military Veterans in Colonial and Post Colonial Mali, 1918–1968." Unpublished Ph.D. diss., Northwestern University, 2000.

Snyder, Frank G. *One Party Government in Mali: Transition Towards Control.* New Haven, Conn.: Yale University Press, 1965.

———. "The Political Thought of Modibo Keita." *Journal of Modern African Studies* 5 (May 1967): 79–106.

Kekkonen, Urho (1900–1986) *president of Finland*

Urho Kaleva Kekkonen was born in Pielavesi, Finland, on September 3, 1900, the son of a lumberman. When the Russian Revolution broke out in 1917, Finland fought for independence under the leadership of Marshal CARL GUSTAV MANNERHEIM. Kekkonen served in the White Army as part of an execution squad, and became so traumatized that he forsook confrontation in favor of conciliation. He subsequently attended the University of Helsinki and obtained his doctorate in law by 1936. That year he joined the Agrarian Union Party and gained a seat in the Finnish legislature where he railed against profascist and procommunist groups in Finland and attempted to have both banned as a menace to democracy. When Soviet forces under JOSEPH STALIN attacked Finland in 1940, Kekkonen opposed the peace treaty that ceded land to the Russians. He also supported the German invasion of 1941–44 in order to reclaim lost territories, but after 1943 Kekkonen realized that Germany was losing. He was also aware of Finland's need to strike up amicable relations with Russia if it was to survive. In 1948 he helped negotiate the Finnish-Soviet Treaty of Friendship, Cooperation, and Mutual Assistance, which stipulated Russia's right to intervene in Finland's politics to prevent a hostile regime from taking power. Finnish awareness of Soviet security concerns thus provided a realistic basis for better relations and also raised Kekkonen's national profile. In 1950 he became prime minister for the first time, an office he held over the next six years. He worked closely with Finnish president Juho Kusti Paasikivi to further clarify relations with the Soviets, known domestically as the Paasikivi-Kekkonen Line. Western observers, however, derogated the entire process as "Finlandization," a voluntary submission to Soviet will and policy. Few Finns would disagree with that assessment, but it proved essential for securing the country's political independence.

In 1956 Kekkonen was elected president of Finland by a two-vote margin in the legislature. He held that office continuously for the next 25 years, indelibly shaping national policy toward the Soviet Union. In practice Kekkonen worked closely with Russian counterparts in foreign policy, insisting on a neutrality based upon Soviet concerns, not Scandinavian ones. This brought him cordial relations with Moscow and considerable trade activity. This arrangement also allowed Finland to freely pursue its own economic agenda throughout Western Europe, and the country experienced an impressive expansion and growth. Domestically he also sought support from a Soviet-controlled Communist Party and its socialist allies who, on orders from Moscow, unswervingly supported him. For this reason communists were openly incorporated into the political system. The most influential moment of Kekkonen's long tenure in office came in 1975 when he sponsored a Soviet-inspired Conference on Security and Cooperation in Europe. The resulting Helsinki Accord was significant for formalizing Western recognition of Warsaw Pact nations, while also holding them to standards of human rights. In 1980 Kekkonen received the Lenin Peace Prize from his grateful neighbors.

In a political sense Kekkonen was a strong executive entrusted with the wellbeing of his people. His approach to politics was sometimes dictatorial and unsavory for many opposing his policies in the legislature, but it proved resoundingly popular with the public. In 1962, 1968, and 1978, he was elected by increasingly larger margins. In 1978 the legislature extended his term in office an additional four years to placate the Soviets. However, Kekkonen suffered from poor health by then, and he retired in 1981, to be succeeded by MAUNO KOIVISTO. Having dominated national politics for a quarter century, Kekkonen died in Helsinki on August 31, 1986. He preserved Finnish independence through compromise, but his abiding sense of Realpolitik carefully juggled national and foreign priorities, kept the peace, and fulfilled his political mandate. Kekkonen remains the dominant Finnish politician of the 20th century.

Further Reading

Allison, Roy. *Finland's Relations with the Soviet Union, 1944–84.* New York: St. Martin's Press, 1985.

Hanhimaki, Jussi M. *Containing Coexistence: America, Russia, and the 'Finnish Solution.'* Kent: Ohio State University Press, 1997.

Kekkonen, Urho, *A President's View.* London: Heinemann, 1982.

Korhonen, Keijo. *Urho Kekkonen, a Statesman for Peace.* London: Heinemann, 1975.

Mouritzen, Hans. *Finlandization: Towards a General Theory of Adaptive Politics.* Brookfield, Vt.: Avebury, 1988.

Nevakivi, Jukka. "Kekkonen, the Soviet Union, and Scandinavia: Aspects of Policy in the Years 1948–1968." *Scandinavian Journal of History* 22, no. 2 (1997): 65–81.

Kennedy, John F. (1917–1963) *president of the United States*

John Fitzgerald Kennedy was born in Brookline, Massachusetts, May 29, 1917, a son of noted businessman and diplomat Joseph Kennedy. Descended from Irish immigrants, he was firmly rooted in Roman Catholicism and inherited his father's sense of public service. After a sickly childhood, Kennedy was admitted into Princeton University in 1936. Illness forced him to drop out and he subsequently attended Harvard University. He graduated in 1940 and published his senior thesis, *While England Slept,* as a best-selling book. Back injuries prevented him from joining the army in 1941 so he sought a naval commission to work as an intelligence officer. After the Japanese attack upon Pearl Harbor, Kennedy requested a combat assignment and transferred to a Patrol Torpedo Boat (PT) squadron. He then commanded the PT-109 boat in the Solomon Islands, and in August 1943 he was nearly killed when a Japanese destroyer rammed and sank his vessel. Kennedy heroically saved most of his crew, was rescued, and returned a decorated war hero.

After the war Kennedy went home to Massachusetts and commenced his political career as a Democrat. In 1946 he won a seat in the House of Representatives and six years later defeated an incumbent Republican for the Senate. He then married Washington, D.C., socialite Jacqueline Bouvier and penned a second best-selling title, *Profiles in Courage,* becoming one of the party's rising stars. He failed to gain the nomination for vice president in 1956, but two years later, coasted to an impressive reelection in the Senate. In January 1960 Kennedy declared his candidacy for the presidency, and handily defeated LYNDON B. JOHNSON for the nomination. That fall he appeared with Republican vice president RICHARD M. NIXON in the first ever televised political debates. Kennedy, handsome, articulate, and charming, bested his nervous opponent, and went on to narrowly win the general election in November, with Johnson as his running mate. Persistent doubts as to his youth and religion restricted his margin of victory to only 118,550 votes, one of the narrowest ever recorded for a presidential contest. At 43 he was the youngest individual elected to the White House, and the first Roman Catholic.

In office Kennedy exuded the persona of a new generation of American leadership, stylish, energetic, optimistic, and idealistic. "Ask not what your country can do for you," he challenged young Americans, "ask what you can do for your country." But he assumed power at a dangerous time, at the height of the cold war when relations with the Soviet Union were at their nadir. In April 1961 the new president backed a half-hearted attempt by the Central Intelligence Agency (CIA) to land Cuban refugees in Cuba and overthrow Fidel Castro. The ensuing Bay of Pigs fiasco cost Kennedy much credibility, especially after he declined to support the doomed effort with American forces. That same month he met with Soviet premier NIKITA KHRUSHCHEV at Vienna, and was warned of the Soviet intention to drive the Western allies out of West Berlin—by force, if necessary. Kennedy countered that such an act would mean war, and he pushed for an increase in defense spending once home. In August 1961 the East German government of WALTER ULBRICHT constructed the infamous Berlin Wall to cut off the exodus of freedom-seeking refugees. Both sides then rushed tanks and men to the construction site, but cooler heads prevailed and the crisis subsided. The Berlin Wall did not constitute an attack upon allied territory, so Kennedy felt compelled to let it stand. However, he recognized that the charged political atmosphere would not allow him to suffer accusations of being "soft on communism." In 1963, possibly against his better judgment, he committed 20,000 combat troops and military advisers to prop up the tottering regime of NGO DINH DIEM in South Vietnam. He also authorized creation of a new counterinsurgency force, the Green Berets, to face down communist guerrillas wherever they threatened American interests. The ramifications of these decisions would be felt most keenly by his successor, Lyndon Johnson.

Kennedy's finest hour was his handling of the Cuban Missile Crisis of October 1962. When apprised that Khrushchev had secretly shipped nuclear missiles to Fidel Castro's Cuba, he promptly erected a naval quarantine of the island, to prevent the missiles from

John F. Kennedy *(Library of Congress)*

But he was less bold respecting civil rights, despite pressure from African-American leaders to enact sweeping changes. Kennedy's reluctance to pursue civil rights is understandable considering his reliance upon southern white congressmen to get his legislation passed. But by 1962 he was finally prodded into dispatching federal troops to enforce desegregation of the University of Mississippi, and he also signed executive orders ending discrimination in federal housing. The changes were welcome, but monumental civil rights legislation did not materialize until after he left office.

More than anything, Kennedy enjoyed immense national popularity. In fact his presidency was compared with King Arthur's "Camelot," an idealistic setting for a youthful national leader. His family life became part of the nation's own, and, as an individual, John F. Kennedy became a truly beloved figure. The entire world was therefore shocked when the youthful executive was suddenly assassinated in Dallas, Texas, on November 22, 1963. Supreme Court chief justice Earl Warren conducted an exhaustive investigation that concluded that his death resulted from the actions of a single individual, Lee Harvey Oswald. But many theories and allegations of conspiracy dispute these findings and persist to the present day. Kennedy thus continues attracting as much high-profile attention in death as he did in life.

becoming operational. Khrushchev vowed he would break the blockade, an act of war, and dispatched vessels to reinforce Cuba. Tense days passed as Soviet warships approached the American demarcation line, and both countries placed their nuclear arsenals on full alert. Fortunately Khrushchev relented, and the blockade remained unchallenged. The Soviet leader agreed to dismantle his missile sites in exchange for Kennedy's word not to invade Cuba. Out of this potential holocaust emerged the Nuclear Test Ban Treaty of 1963, which eliminated air and water testing and restricted future tests to underground locations.

Domestically Kennedy was free to pursue his idealistic notions of public service. The Soviets roundly embarrassed the United States by putting the first man in Earth orbit in August 1961, and Kennedy boldly declared that the United States would put a man on the Moon by decade's end. He founded the Peace Corps as a means of involving young Americans in the war against global poverty, and established the Alliance for Progress to assist unsteady Latin American economies.

Further Reading

Ashton, Nigel J. *Kennedy, Macmillan, and the Cold War: The Story of Interdependence.* New York: Palgrave, 2002.

Freedman, Lawrence. *Kennedy's Wars: Berlin, Cuba, Laos, and Vietnam.* New York: Oxford University Press, 2000.

Niven, David. *The Politics of Injustice: The Kennedys, the Freedom Riders, and the Electoral Consequences of a Moral Compromise.* Knoxville: University of Tennessee Press, 2003.

Perret, Geoffrey. *Jack: A Life like No Other.* New York: Random House, 2003.

Rorabach, W. J. *Kennedy and the Promise of the Sixties.* New York: Cambridge University Press, 2002.

See, Jennifer. "An Uneasy Truce: John F. Kennedy and Soviet-American Detente, 1963." *Cold War History* 2 (January 2002): 161–194.

Smith, Sally B. *Grace and Power: The Private World of the Kennedy White House.* New York: Random House, 2004.

Kenyatta, Jomo (1891–1978) *president of Kenya*
Kamau wa Ngengi was born in Ichaweri, British East
Africa, on October 20, 1891, the son of a farmer. He
belonged to the large and influential Kikuyu tribe, the
largest ethnic grouping in what is today known as Kenya.
In 1916 Ngengi was baptized a Christian and adopted
the name Johnstone, although he subsequently went by
the nickname Jomo Kenyatta. Like many Kikuyus of his
generation, Kenyatta resented and protested the large-
scale seizure of tribal land by English colonists, an act
that fanned the growth of nationalist sentiments. In
1928 Kenyatta joined the Kikuyu Central Association
(KCA), a cultural group with political overtones, and
rose to be both secretary and editor of the organization
newsletter. In 1929 tribal authorities dispatched him to
London to air grievances against British policies, where
he won the right for Kikuyus to operate their own
schools. Two years later Kenyatta made another pilgrimage to England for identical reasons, but this time he
remained overseas for the next 15 years. During the
interval he took an English wife, studied for a year in
the Soviet Union, and also enrolled at the London
School of Economics. There he penned a significant
anthropological work, *Facing Mount Kenya* (1938),
which codified his complaints against British rule.
Kenyatta also embraced Pan-Africanism, and in 1945,
assisted by KWAME NKRUMAH and others, he helped
organize the Fifth Pan-African Congress in Manchester.
Through such activities Kenyatta became a folk hero, but
otherwise gained the reputation of a trouble maker. After
1946 he was watched closely by colonial authorities.

Once home, Kenyatta became vice principal of the
Independent Teacher's College at Githunguri, which he
used to further Kikuyu independence. That year he was
elected head of the Kenya Africa Union (KAU), a cultural organization that he enlarged into a nationally
based political forum. Kenyatta thus became a leading
spokesperson for his cause, although he never advocated
violence against the British or their supporters. But in
1948 more restless elements commenced a peasant
uprising known as the Mau Mau, which sparked a harsh
military reaction from British authorities. By the time
fighting died down in 1958, more than 200 white colo-
nials and 12,000 black Africans were killed. Kenyatta,
meanwhile, had been accused of fomenting violence in
1953, and imprisoned on manufactured evidence. He
received a six-year sentence to be served in the northern
desert region, but was released in 1959. Thereafter he
remained under house arrest, but his incarceration,
which many Kenyans viewed as illegal, only bolstered
his national standing.

By 1959 the colonial authorities deduced that their
control over British East Africa was ebbing, and
England took steps toward greater internal autonomy.
In 1960 a new political organization, the Kenya African
National Union (KANU) emerged, with Kenyatta as
honorary president—while under house arrest. But the
British refused to allow Kenyatta, whom they saw as a
dangerous radical, to serve. Nonetheless, when KANU
swept regional elections in 1963, they finally relented
and Kenyatta became prime minister. After constitutional changes the following year, he served as president
of the newly independent nation of Kenya. Much to the
surprise and relief of British inhabitants, Kenyatta
decried socialism and adopted a capitalistic, Western-
oriented attitude. He was extremely friendly to Britain,
despite past abuses heaped upon him. He also went so
far as to address white audiences to assure them of their
role in Kenyan society, and pledged to work with them
in a spirit of Harambee, a Kikuyu word for unity and
harmony.

Kenyatta's regime was despotic, but not athoritari-
an in nature. He brooked no dissent within KANU and
demanded obedience from party members. After 1974
Kenyatta outlawed all political parties except for
KANU, and several of his leading opponents died under
mysterious circumstances. But the majority of Kenyans
prospered under his free-market approach to economics.
He also steered clear of radical African states that ruined
themselves with socialist central planning. By the time
Kenyatta died in Mombasa on August 22, 1978, he left
behind a nation that was politically stable and relatively
prosperous. For 40 years he also functioned as an
endearing symbol of African nationalism and its determination to discard the colonial yoke.

Further Reading

Kenyatta, Jomo. *Harambee! The Prime Minister of Kenya's
Speeches, 1963–1964.* New York: Oxford University
Press, 1964.
Lewis, Joanna. *Empire State-building: War and Welfare in
Kenya, 1925–52.* Oxford, England: James Currey,
2000.
Odhiambo, E. S. Ateino, and John Lonsdale. *Mau Mau
and Manhood: Arms, Authority and Narration.*
Oxford, England: James Currey, 2003.

Oded, Arye. *Islam and Politics in Kenya.* Boulder, Colo.: Lynne Rienner Publishers, 2000.

Peterson, Derek R. *Creative Writing: Translation, Bookkeeping, and the Work of Imagination in Colonial Kenya.* Westport, Conn.: Praeger, 2004.

Sabar, Galia. *Church, State, and Society in Kenya: From Mediation to Opposition, 1963–1993.* Portland, Ore.: Frank Cass, 2002.

Throup, David, and Charles Hornsby. *Multi-party Politics in Kenya: The Kenyatta and Moi States.* Athens: Ohio University Press, 1998.

Kerensky, Aleksandr (1881–1970) *prime minister of Russia*

Aleksandr Fedorovich Kerensky was born in Simbirsk, Russia, on February 22, 1881, the son of a high-ranking education official. He entered St. Petersburg University in 1899 to study law and acquitted himself with distinction. Kerensky was also drawn to radical politics, and he flirted with socialist student groups protesting against the government of Czar NICHOLAS II. In 1904 he was admitted to the St. Petersburg bar and quickly gained a reputation as a brilliant attorney specializing in legal aid for the poor. In this capacity he also assisted in the legal defense for revolutionary figures. He commenced his political career in 1912 by successfully running for a seat in the Duma (legislature) that had been created in the wake of the 1905 revolution. Kerensky was identified with the moderately socialist Labor Party and he continued on as an outspoken champion of civil rights. The government considered him such a menace that by 1914 he was arrested twice for subversive activities. When World War I erupted in August 1914, Kerensky railed against Russian participation and publicly denounced it as fratricidal. The Russian army and people suffered terribly due to gross mismanagement, and by 1917 popular support for the czarist regime had all but collapsed. The ensuing February Revolution of that year finally toppled the imperial government, and a provisional administration was installed under Prince GEORGI LVOV. The stage was now being set for dramatic revolutionary activities by the Bolshevik faction under VLADIMIR LENIN.

During the initial phases of the revolution, Kerensky served as both a member of the Duma and as board member of the Petrograd Soviet (revolutionary council) of workers and soldiers. He also joined the Socialist Revolutionary Party, and so was uniquely positioned to work between the forces of moderation and revolution. That spring Lvov also appointed him to serve as minister of justice. However, within months dissatisfaction over the conduct of the war resulted in a spate of resignations, and Kerensky was offered the portfolio of minister of war and the navy. Reversing his earlier opposition to the war, he argued that Russia should remain active to secure the advantages of supporting the winning side. To that end he mustered and launched the ill-fated "Kerensky offensive" in June 1917, which utterly failed and incurred heavy losses. Defeat further alienated public opinion against both the war and the provisional government, so Lvov resigned in 1917.

Kerensky assumed the role of prime minister immediately following Lvov's departure, and played a pivotal role in events as they played out. He inherited a nation on the brink of political and military collapse, but he tackled the problems of leadership with characteristic energy and eloquence. His preoccupation with military affairs prevented him from addressing deep-seated problems, like the pressing need for land reform, which he felt must wait until after the war. But events seemed to gravitate toward stability after the exile of radical agitators like Lenin and Leon Trotsky, so Kerensky sought creation of a constituent assembly to formalize the transition to democratic rule. Unfortunately, this trend was upended by a reactionary revolt orchestrated by General Lavr G. Kornilov, which forced the government to rely upon the radical forces for its very survival. Shortly after, Lenin returned to Russia and, sensing that the time was right, began fomenting a communist revolution against the provisional government. Fighting commenced that November, and Kerensky, unable to find sufficient military forces to support him, was driven willy-nilly out of Petrograd. He then failed to retake the city and ended up fleeing Russia in the spring of 1918, while Lenin and the communists consolidated their grasp on power. He was only 36 years old at the time.

Kerensky exiled himself to various cities in Europe, where he wrote and lectured on his role in the provisional government for many years. He also tried and failed to marshal international opinion against the new Soviet Union. In 1940 he relocated to the United States and commenced an academic career at Stanford University, California. Kerensky died in New York City on June 11, 1970, a talented politician with a poor grasp of governance, and lacking the sheer ruthlessness necessary to contain violent revolutionaries like Lenin and his Bolsheviks.

Further Reading

Abraham, Richard. *Alexander Kerensky: The First Love of the Revolution.* New York: Columbia University Press, 1987.

Fitzpatrick, Sheila. *The Russian Revolution.* Oxford, England: Oxford University Press, 2001.

Holquist, Peter. *Making War, Forging Revolution: Russia's Continuum of Crisis, 1914–1921.* Cambridge, Mass.: Harvard University Press, 2002.

Jacoby, Robert B. "The August Coups: A Historical Comparison of the Kornilov Affair of August 1917 and the Putsch Attempt of August 1991 in Russia." Unpublished A.B. thesis, Harvard University, 1994.

Kerensky, Aleksandr F. *The Kerensky Memoirs: Russia and History's Turning Points.* London: Cassell, 1966.

Melancon, Michael S. *Rethinking Russia's February Revolution: Anonymous Spontaneity or Socialist Agenda?* Pittsburgh, Pa.: Center for Russian and East European Studies, University of Pittsburgh, 2000.

Sanborn, Joshua A. *Drafting the Russian Nation: Military Conscription, Total War, and Mass Politics, 1905–1925.* DeKalb: Northern Illinois University Press, 2003.

Khama, Seretse (1921–1980) *president of Botswana*

Seretse Khama was born in Serowe, Bechuanaland, on July 1, 1921, the son of a hereditary chief of the Bamangwato people. His grandfather, Khama III, was a great leader who repelled Boer invasions from South Africa and placed his kingdom under British protection. His own father died while he was an infant, and rule of Bechuanaland reverted to an uncle, Tshekedi Khama, who became regent. Young Khama attended missionary schools at home and received a college degree from Fort Hare College, South Africa, in 1944. But rather than return home for further grooming, he pursued a law degree at Oxford University, England. There he engendered considerable controversy by marrying an English woman, Ruth Williams, in September 1948. The marriage had to be performed as a civil ceremony, for no London church was willing to admit them. Furthermore, tribal elders were incensed that he would wed a woman outside of his tribe. The act also inflamed the apartheid regime in neighboring South Africa, which had specifically outlawed interracial unions. To placate all parties, the English detained Khama until he renounced all claims to his chieftaincy. He remained in exile, raising six children, and finally abandoned the throne in 1956. Once home in Bechuanaland, he became associated with nationalistic circles and entered politics the following year as a member of the Tribal Council.

At this time Britain was allowing Bechuanaland greater territorial autonomy in anticipation of granting independence. In 1960 Khama became one of five African members on the new legislative assembly, and two years later he advanced his political fortunes by founding the Bechuanaland Democratic Party (BDP). Consistent with his own beliefs, the BDP stood for racial tolerance and peaceful political pluralism. The party swept the first national elections, held in 1965, by taking 28 of 31 seats in the assembly. As party head Khama was appointed prime minister with all the powers previously denied him as chief. The pace of independence accelerated, and on September 20, 1966, Khama became the first president of the new nation of Botswana. That year he was also knighted by Queen Elizabeth II for exemplary service to the Commonwealth.

Once empowered, Khama fulfilled his party's mission by installing a multiracial democracy. In fact, compared to events in South Africa and elsewhere, the transition to self-rule was seamless and peaceful. Bostwana was then one of the world's poorest nations, with cattle grazing as its principal economic activity. It was also almost entirely dependent upon South Africa for the transportation of goods to market. Therefore Khama was forced to make hard choices relative to working with both the racist regime and radical African states demanding its ouster. He opted for pragmatism in dealing with Pretoria; overt criticism of apartheid was downplayed and South African technical expertise was welcomed into the country. He was especially keen on developing Botswana's vast, untapped mineral wealth, and was fortunate to uncover large diamond deposits. But Khama was no dupe. While he forbade guerrillas of the African National Congress (ANC) from basing themselves in Botswana, he permitted them transit rights into and out of Namibia.

Such compliance usually brought retaliatory raids from South Africa, but his economic ties remained intact. He also provided similar service for guerrillas fighting the white minority regime in Rhodesia. All told Khama walked a fine line during the struggle against apartheid, but he performed capably as the head of a front-line state. Not surprisingly he was successively reelected president four times.

Khama died of cancer on July 13, 1980, in Gabarone, Botswana, and was widely mourned. His 14-year tenure bequeathed to his people a legacy of freedom, racial harmony, and comparative prosperity that is still held as a model for developing nations everywhere. Khama remains one of Africa's most successful postcolonial leaders.

Further Reading

Good, Kenneth. *The Liberal Model and Africa: Elites against Democracy.* New York: Palgrave, 2002.
Henderson, Willie. "Seretse Khama: A Personal Appreciation." *African Affairs* 89, no. 354 (1990): 27–56.
Hope, Kempe R. *From Crisis to Renewal: Development Policy and Management in Africa.* Boston: Brill, 2002.
Hyam, Ronald. "The Political Consequences of Seretse Khama: Britain, the Bamangwato, and South Africa, 1948–1952." *Historical Journal* 29, no. 4 (1986): 921–947.
Khama, Seretse. *From the Frontline: Speeches of Sir Seretse Khama.* Stanford, Calif.: Hoover Institution Press, 1981.
Parsons, Neil. "The Impact of Seretse Khama on British Public Opinion, 1948, 1956, and 1978." *Immigrants and Minorities* 12, no. 3 (1993): 195–219.

Khomeini, Ruholla (1900–1989) *ayatollah of Iran*

Ruholla Hendi was born in Khomein, Persia, on September 24, 1900, into a religious family of Shia Muslim clerics tracing their ancestry back to the prophet Mohammed. His father was a noted religious scholar who was murdered while Ruholla was still a child. The young man received intense Koranic instruction and soon distinguished himself as a religious thinker of note. He also adopted the name Khomeini to honor the town

of his birth. Iran had then been under a monarchy of one sort or another for the past 2,500 years and Khomeini felt that kingship ran counter to the religious tenets of Islam. Drawing inspiration from Plato's *Republic,* he envisioned a pure Islamic state headed by an all-powerful theocracy. The theocrats would draw their moral authority from the Koran and therefore be infallible in judgment. He began espousing his ideas in numerous books and in 1940 attacked the rule of REZA SHAH PAHLAVI. Up through the 1950s Khomeini was primarily concerned with teaching religious students in the holy city of Qom. But, following the ascent of Shah MOHAMMAD REZA PAHLAVI, he became an outspoken exponent of Islamic revolution. He bitterly denounced the shah's modernization programs as un-Islamic, and in 1963 riots broke out against the shah. The following year Khomeini was deported to Turkey, and he eventually settled into a Shia theological school in Iraq. From there he continued railing against the shah's corruption, authoritarianism, and his close ties to the United States. He gained a wide following as public dissatisfaction in Iran escalated. The shah responded with greater repression and also pressured Iraqi president Saddam Hussein to deport Khomeini. The fiery cleric subsequently relocated to Paris, France, where he enjoyed complete access to Western media and exhorted followers of the faith to overthrow the shah. In January 1979 they accomplished exactly that and the following month Khomeini triumphantly returned to an adoring populace. On April 1, 1979, he crowned his achievements by declaring the creation of the Islamic Republic of Iran, with himself as ayatollah, the highest clerical rank in Shia Islam.

In practice Khomeini ruled over a theocratic dictatorship based upon Koranic principles and backed by armed fundamentalists. Media was heavily controlled and censored, non-Islamic books and ideas were banned, and all forms of Western entertainment and dress outlawed. Women were also stripped of political rights and forced to wear veils, religious attendance became compulsory, and non-Islamic groups were harassed and discriminated against. The new regime proved even more oppressive than its predecessor, and thousands of perceived opponents were summarily rounded up and executed. The state-controlled economy began sinking within months, but Khomeini distracted public attention by denouncing the United States as the "Great Satan" and encouraging militants to seize its embassy in Teheran. The 63 hostages remained captive for 444 days and were a major factor in the downfall of American president JIMMY CARTER. Khomeini was also intent upon exporting his brand of militant Islam throughout the world. Border tensions with Iraq exploded in September 1980, and for eight years badly equipped Iranian masses hurled themselves against the well-equipped armies of Saddam Hussein. In 1987 the Iranians illegally began mining the Persian Gulf to deny Iraq oil, which brought on a sharp and costly encounter with United States naval forces. A bloody and costly impasse ensued until 1988, when cabinet members finally convinced Khomeini that the war was lost. After accepting the United Nations-sponsored cease-fire he declared it "more deadly than drinking poison." The following year, the ayatollah further alienated himself from world opinion by declaring a death sentence on British author Salman Rushdie, whose 1988 novel the *Satanic Verses* was viewed as slanderous to Islam. Great Britain consequently broke off diplomatic relations with Iran, furthering its diplomatic isolation.

For all his radicalism and oppression, Khomeini was a skilled political player who consolidated his regime swiftly, ruled with an iron hand, and still maintained a huge following. It is difficult to account for such popularity, but his views on Islam apparently resonated in Iran and elsewhere. In fact Iranian oil money found its way into the hands of militant Shia groups throughout the Middle East, and they embarked on a campaign of terrorism against Israel. The Iranian economy never completely recovered from the aftermath of the revolution, but Khomeini was quick to blame its shortcomings on Zionist and American plots. When Khomeini died in Teheran on June 3, 1989, his funeral was accompanied by an emotional outpouring of grief. He was succeeded by Ayatollah Mohammed Ali Khamenei, who pledged to carry on with his predecessor's Islamic radicalism, and president Hashemi Rafsanjani, a more moderate figure. Khomeini's tenure as a religious head of state remains controversial but he is regarded as the most influential Muslim cleric of the 20th century.

Further Reading

Fischer, Michael M. J. *Iran: From Religious Dispute to Revolution.* Madison: University of Wisconsin Press, 2003.

Hoveyda, Fereydoun. *The Shah and the Ayatollah: Iranian Mythology and Islamic Revolution.* Westport, Conn.: Praeger, 2003.

Khomeini, Ruhollah. *Islam and Revolution: Writings and Declarations.* New York: Kegan Paul, 2002.

Martin, Vanessa. *Creating an Islamic State: Khomeini and the Making of a New Iran.* London: I. B. Tauris, 2000.

Moin, Baqer. *Khomeini: Life of the Ayatollah.* New York: Thomas Dunne Books, 2000.

Nabavi, Negin. *Intellectuals and the State in Iran: Politics, Discourse, and Dilemma of Authority.* Gainesville: University Press of Florida, 2003.

Khrushchev, Nikita (1894–1971) *general secretary of the Communist Party of the Soviet Union*

Nikita Sergeyevich Khrushchev was born in Kalinovka, Russia, on April 17, 1894, the son of an impoverished miner. In 1908 the family relocated to the Ukraine where he was employed as a factory worker. Deploring the conditions encountered there, Khrushchev became politically active and organized several strikes. Following VLADIMIR LENIN's seizure of power in 1917, he joined the Communist Party and fought in the Russian civil war as a political commissar. Afterward Khrushchev fulfilled various political assignments before passing through the Donets Industrial Institute in 1925 and the Industrial Academy in Moscow in 1929. With Moscow as his power base, he rose quickly through the party ranks and by 1933 was serving as secretary of the Moscow Regional Committee. There he came under the scrutiny of dictator JOSEPH STALIN, who recruited him into his faction. Khrushchev zealously supported Stalin, his forced collectivization of agriculture, his policy of mass deportations, and his bloody purge of enemies of the state. He thus became a trusted associate—and survived the reign of terror sweeping Russia. By 1938 he was part of the Politburo, the nation's highest decision-making body. The Great Patriotic War with Nazi Germany erupted in June 1941, and Khrushchev functioned as first secretary of the Ukraine. He also helped organize Red Army defenses as a political officer. After 1945 he remained in the devastated Ukraine to orchestrate relief efforts and rebuild the collapsed agricultural system. But Stalin summoned him back to Moscow in 1949, and he was installed as head of the Moscow city party.

Following Stalin's death in 1953 Khrushchev became part of an eight-man "collective leadership" that ran the country over the next few months. Here he cannily outmaneuvered several opponents and became general secretary of the Communist Party of the Soviet Union and de facto head of state. His first priority was a prompt de-Stalinization of the Soviet Union, which entailed ending totalitarianism, instituting curbs on secret police power, increasing freedom of academic and intellectual expression, and promoting a cultural thaw. These reforms crested in Khrushchev's "secret speech" to the combined party heads in 1956, in which he denounced Stalin's excesses. However, when this had the effect of generating political unrest in Hungary, he moved swiftly to crush a reform movement led by IMRE NAGY. Khrushchev was the first major Soviet leader to tout the notion of "peaceful coexistence" with the capitalist West. This became a byword of increased scientific competition with the United States, then viewed as the leading threat to the Soviet Union. Khrushchev also cut back on military expenditures—over the protests of his generals—and poured millions of rubles into scientific research, to overtake the Americans. The results were dramatically successful, and in 1957 Russia placed the first satellite, *Sputnik*, in orbit. Four years later Yuri Gagarin became the first man to orbit the Earth. For the Soviets, long viewed as technologically backward, these triumphs were a propaganda windfall and seemed to confirm Khrushchev's unshakable faith in the inevitable triumph of communism.

Internationally, Khrushchev pursued a dangerous game of brinkmanship to demonstrate Soviet resolve. In 1959 he visited the United States and conferred with President DWIGHT D. EISENHOWER, but the following year, after the downing of an American U-2 spy plane over Russia, he grew increasingly bellicose. He met with the new president, JOHN F. KENNEDY, at Vienna in April 1961, and threatened force against the American garrison in West Berlin. When this failed to intimidate Kennedy, he authorized WALTER ULBRICHT's East German regime to construct the infamous Berlin Wall and stop the flow of economic refugees. The pace of confrontation accelerated in October 1962, when the Russians secretly shipped nuclear-armed missiles to Fidel Castro's communist regime in Cuba. Kennedy reacted by imposing a naval blockade of the island until the missiles were removed. Several anxious days ensued until the military, realizing they would lose a nuclear war with America, prevailed upon Khrushchev to pull the missiles out. It was a humiliating setback for the formerly blustering leader, and his perceived weakness led to a breakdown in relations with Communist China's

MAO ZEDONG. The cold war was now being waged on two fronts, east and west.

By 1964 Khrushchev's vaunted agricultural reforms had failed to rectify critical food shortages, and the Soviet Union was forced to subsist on large purchases of Canadian wheat. This debacle, coupled with his mishandling of the Cuban missile crisis, unpopular defense cutbacks, and the alienation of conservative elements within the party, led to his dismissal from power on October 14, 1964. He was replaced by LEONID BREZHNEV and allowed to enter a quiet retirement outside of Moscow. Significantly, this was the first peaceful transfer of power in Soviet history. Khrushchev lived out the rest of his days as an official nonperson and died quietly on September 11, 1971. A complicated man, far more perceptive and wily than the bullying buffoon image he projected to the West, Khrushchev was a reformer who sincerely renounced the Stalinist past. His principal failing was in remaining firmly wedded to communism, a system beyond reform and then experiencing its initial stages of decay. He nonetheless remains the most influential Soviet reformer until MIKHAIL GORBACHEV.

Further Reading

Barber, John, and Mark Harrison. *The Soviet Defense Industry Complex from Stalin to Khrushchev.* Basingstoke, England: University of Birmingham Press, 2000.

Busky, Donald F. *Communism in History and Theory: From Utopian Socialism to the Fall of the Soviet Union.* Westport, Conn.: Praeger, 2002.

Khrushchev, Nikita. *Memoirs of Nikita Khruschev.* University Park: Pennsylvania State University Press, 2004.

Khrushchev, Sergei. *Nikita Khrushchev and the Creation of a Superpower.* University Park: Pennsylvania State University Press, 2000.

Nathan, James A. *Anatomy of the Cuban Missile Crisis.* Westport, Conn.: Greenwood Press, 2001.

Taubman, William. *Khrushchev: The Man and His Era.* New York: Norton, 2003.

Kiesinger, Kurt (1904–1988) *chancellor of Germany*

Kurt Georg Kiesinger was born in Ebingen, Germany, on April 6, 1904, the son of a bookkeeper. He studied law at Tübingen and Berlin Universities and commenced a successful legal practice. However, in 1933 he was persuaded by friends to join the Nazi Party and enhance his career prospects. Kiesinger, who evinced little interest in politics, complied but the decision would later haunt him. In 1938 he refused to join the National Socialist Lawyer's Guild after which he was closely watched by Nazi authorities. During World War II he was drafted into the foreign ministry and monitored radio broadcasts. Germany's defeat in 1945 resulted in Kiesinger's arrest and detention as a former Nazi, although he was subsequently cleared by a court and released 18 months later. Kiesinger resumed his legal career and in 1949 he was a leading founder of the new Christian Democratic Union (CDU). That year he gained a seat in the Bundestag (the legislature's lower house) and established himself as an authority on foreign affairs. He proved especially supportive of Chancellor KONRAD ADENAUER's efforts to establish closer ties to the United States and France, and served as the foreign committee chairman. But when Adenauer failed to appoint him foreign minister in 1957, Kiesinger left national politics to serve as minister president of Baden-Württemberg. Six years later he resumed his national career by winning a seat in the Bundesrat (upper house), where he served as president. In December 1966 the administration of Chancellor LUDWIG ERHARD was threatened when the Free Democratic Party pulled out of his coalition. Kiesinger was then tapped to succeed him and surprised the pundits by forming a "grand coalition" with the opposition Social Democratic Party, Sozialdemokratische Partei Deutschlands (SPD), under WILLY BRANDT, allowing Kiesinger to become chancellor, while Brandt served as vice chancellor and foreign minister.

In practice Kiesinger's government proved an awkward arrangement. The CDU had 10 seats in the ministry and the SDP nine, which constituted a wide spectrum of political viewpoints, right to left. Furthermore the chancellor had been publicly criticized for his allegedly Nazi past, which further strained relations with extreme elements within the SDP. But Kiesinger proved himself a skilled, determined leader and also rather independent-minded. Like his predecessors, he sought continuance of good relations with the United States and a rapprochement with France. But Kiesinger was also determined to focus greater attention upon Eastern Europe, a policy that Brandt later characterized as Ostpolitik. In 1967 diplomatic relations were established with Romania, and the following year an embassy was established in Yugoslavia. The German government also concluded a trade agreement with Czechoslovakia. Kiesinger concurrently took bold steps toward the Communist regime of East Germany for the first time. He established contacts with the government of WALTER ULBRICHT and discussed matters relating to trade and travel. The East Germans were cautiously receptive, but talks floundered on Ulbricht's insistence on complete diplomatic recognition—something the West Germans were not disposed to grant. Ultimately Kiesinger's attempts to normalize relations with the Warsaw Pact ended with the Soviet invasion of Czechoslovakia in August 1968. The chancellor vehemently denounced it as a violation of human rights, and he was especially angered by the participation of East German forces.

Kiesinger's government finally collapsed in October 1969, when new elections gave the SDP sufficient strength to enter coalition arrangements with the Free Democrats. Thus Kiesinger and his CDU entered the opposition for the first time in their history. He remained party leader until 1971 and finally retired from the legislature in 1976. To the end he was roundly critical of Brandt's headlong rush to improve relations with the East. Kiesinger died in Tübingen on March 9, 1988, the least known of Germany's postwar chancellors. His tenure in office remains significant for initiating the policies of Ostpolitik, thus paving the ground for Brandt's celebrated successes there.

Further Reading

Aspalter, Christian. *Importance of Christian and Social Democratic Movements in Welfare Politics.* New York: Nova Science Publishers, 2001.

Gray, William G. *Germany's Cold War: The Global Campaign to Isolate East Germany, 1949–1969.* Chapel Hill: University of North Carolina Press, 2003.

Kiesinger, Kurt. "A Swabian Childhood." *American-German Review* 34, no. 3 (1968): 8–15.

Muller, Jan-Werner. *German Ideologies since 1945: Studies in the Political Thought and Culture of the Bonn Republic.* New York: Palgrave, 2002.

Umbach, Maiken. *German Federalism: Past, Present, and Future.* Basingstoke, England: Palgrave, 2002.

Williamson D. G. *Germany from Defeat to Partition, 1945–1963.* New York: Longman, 2001.

King, William Lyon Mackenzie (1874–1950)
prime minister of Canada

William Lyon Mackenzie King was born in Kitchener, Ontario, on December 17, 1874, the son of a lawyer. He was also the grandson of William Lyon Mackenzie, the great rebel of 1837 who unsuccessfully tried to overthrow oligarchic rule in Canada. King passed through the University of Toronto in 1895 and subsequently obtained advanced degrees from the University of Chicago and Harvard. In 1900 he joined the administration of WIL-FRID LAURIER as deputy minister of labor, and eight years later, acquired a seat in Parliament as a Liberal Party candidate. At that time Laurier appointed him Canada's first minister of labor, and he gained a reputation for promoting reconciliation between management and unions. When he lost his seat in 1911, he worked for several years with the Rockefeller Foundation in New York, conducting labor research and publishing a book on the subject. He also helped in arbitrating a violent strike in one of Rockefeller's coal mines in Ludlow, Colorado. After Laurier died in 1919, the liberals elected King their party head and he spent the next two years in opposition. Two years later he became prime minister through a coalition with the Progressive Party. During his first term a constitutional crisis arose from Governor General Lord Julian Byng's refusal to dissolve Parliament for new elections, known as the "King-Byng" affair. This resulted in a short-lived administration under Conservative ARTHUR MEIGHEN, after which elections were finally scheduled and the Liberals returned to power with an increased majority. King also participated in the Imperial Conferences of 1923 and 1926, which laid the foundations of the British Commonwealth in 1931. King adroitly asserted Canada's autonomy in both gatherings and joined the new League of Nations only after pledging "no commitments," that is, military obligations abroad. King remained prime minister until defeated by the Conservatives under RICHARD BEDFORD BENNETT in 1930. Previously, he had made one of his few political mistakes by threatening, during an economic slump, to withhold unemployment assistance to any province with a Conservative governor. However, the ensuing Great Depression hurt the Conservatives badly, and in 1935 the Liberals were swept back into office. Over the next 13 years King waged a carefully honed campaign to introduce progressive reforms while maintaining economic growth. King generally succeeded at both, and in 1940 he introduced unemployment benefits for the first time.

Mackenzie King *(Library of Congress)*

The greatest challenge facing King in his second term in office was the onset of World War II. When Great Britain declared war on Germany in September 1939, Canada fulfilled its Commonwealth obligations by following suit. But King quickly assured Canadians that the war effort would be waged by volunteers only and not through a draft. The national polity was deeply riven by differing perceptions of military service in the English- and French-speaking communities. The English generally favored military conscription to assist England, but French-speaking Quebec did not. The nation had been bitterly divided over conscription during World War I, and King determined to keep it from becoming an issue. In 1942 a plebiscite on the draft was passed by most of Canada and rejected by Quebec, so the nation soldiered on without it. But by 1944 Canadian losses were so heavy that King was forced to introduce conscription for defense forces, pledging not to send them overseas. The war ended before the issue corroded national unity. Furthermore King promoted harmony between segments of Canadian society and managed to keep the diverse Liberal party from splintering apart.

During the war years King also displayed diplomatic ability in his dealings with American president FRANKLIN D. ROOSEVELT. Both leaders sought to coordinate their respective war efforts closely through the Ogdensburg Agreement of 1940 and the Hyde Park Agreement of 1941. Throughout the war years while confronted by a common enemy, relations between the two neighbors were never closer. In 1945 King signed the Washington declaration on atomic energy with President HARRY S. TRUMAN and British prime minister CLEMENT ATTLEE, further enhancing Canada's international stature. He relinquished power in 1948, in favor of LOUIS ST. LAURENT, and died in Kingsmere, Quebec, on July 22, 1950. A bland, uncharismatic figure, King served longer than any other prime minister in Canadian history. Moreover, his record 21 years in office exceeds that of any other chief executive in the history of the British Commonwealth. King's longevity reflects a keen sense for politics, a talent for promoting cooperation, and his ruthlessness in dealing with the opposition.

Further Reading

English, John, and Kenneth McLaughlin, eds. *Mackenzie King: Citizenship and Community: Essays Marking the 125th Anniversary of the Birth of William Lyon Mackenzie King.* Toronto: Robin Brass, 2002.

Esberey, Joy E. *Knight of the Holy Spirit: A Study of William Lyon Mackenzie King.* Buffalo, N.Y.: University of Toronto Press, 1980.

Gray, Charlotte. *Mrs King: The Life and Times of Isabel Mackenzie King.* Toronto: Viking, 1997.

King, William L. M. *Canada and the Fight for Freedom.* New York: Duell, Sloan, Pearce, 1944.

Nolan, Brian. *King's War: Mackenzie King and the Politics of War, 1932–1945.* Toronto: Random House, 1988.

Roazen, Paul. *Canada's King: An Essay in Political Psychology.* Buffalo, N.Y.: Mosaic Press, 1998.

Wardhaugh, Robert A. *Mackenzie King and the Prairie West.* Buffalo, N.Y.: University of Toronto Press, 2000.

Koivisto, Mauno (1923–   ) *president of Finland*
Mauno Henrik Koivisto was born in Turku, Finland, on November 25, 1923, the son of a carpenter. He fought in World War II and afterward served as a dockworker while attending night school. He obtained his doctorate from the University of Turku in 1956 and joined the left-leaning Social Democratic Party. Koivisto was interested in national finance and by 1968 he had become president of the Bank of Finland. This was a semiautonomous body, independent of the political structure, that maintained the well-being of Finland's economy. Koivisto performed well in his appointed tasks and consequently received appointments as Finland's representative to the International Bank for Regional Development and the International Monetary Fund (IMF). His political affiliations served him well, and in 1966 he was appointed minister of finance. In 1968 he advanced his political ambition by becoming prime minister for the first time, serving two years. By 1979 he again held the office, at a time when the health of the long-serving president URHO KEKKONEN was a doubt. Although socialist by inclination, Koivisto preferred to expand the welfare state, rather than adopt a regimented, socialist society. His internal policies proved therefore somewhat mild and bent upon pursuing growth through tightly controlled management and fiscal responsibility. Consequently, Finland enjoyed one of Europe's most robust economies, a fact enhancing Koivisto's national standing and ability to seek higher office.

By 1981 Kekkonen's health required him to step down, and Koivisto became acting president. The following year he actively campaigned for office and won, becoming Finland's first socialist executive. He achieved victory through a close and abiding relationship with the small but dedicated Communist Party of Finland. Like Kekkonen, he found them useful political allies and worked to integrate them closely into the government. Benefitting from his low-key persona, the new president was viewed as a welcome change after 25 years of Kekkonen's autocratic disposition. But like his predecessor, Koivisto remained unequivocally committed to friendly relations with Finland's giant neighbor, the Soviet Union. Since the end of World War II, a unique system of Finnish subservience to Moscow evolved, which cast Finland's neutrality in Russian terms. This process, derided as "Finlandization" in the West, guaranteed peaceful relations while protecting Finnish sovereignty. If anything, Koivisto carried the process a step further by binding the national economy closely to Russia's. Finland thus received the bulk of its oil imports from the Soviets, along with most of its trains and military aircraft. In return, Russia became the single biggest market for high-quality Finnish technology. It proved a profitable arrangement to both parties and underscored the need to harmonize their relations as neighbors. Finland was also free to pursue economic arrangements with Western Europe and, after the fall of the Soviet Union in 1991, Koivisto gently nudged his nation into a European orbit. In 1994, after intense national debate, he took the first steps toward entering the European Union (EU). He also offered his nation as a role model of prosperity and neutrality for the newly independent Baltic states bordering Russia. The Finnish people overwhelmingly approved of Koivisto's policies, and in 1988 he was reelected by an even wider margin.

Despite his socialist leanings Koivisto was never comfortable with strong, centralized political authority—a hallmark of the Finnish system. Therefore he spent the bulk of his second term attempting to redefine the relationship between his office and that of the Eduskunta (legislature). Specifically he tried enhancing the power of the legislature by dismantling what he viewed as the excessive power of the Finnish executive. Koivisto sought a better balance between the two branches of government, with a power distribution modeled more closely on other modern parliamentary systems. Koivisto left office in 1994 and returned to the financial sector where he remains today. He is best remembered for guiding Finland through a transitional period in its relations with Russia, while seeking a closer relationship with the rest of Europe.

Further Reading

Bergland, S. "The Finnish Presidential Election of 1988." *Electoral Studies* 7 (December 1988): 279–281.

Ekman, Rolf. "Mauno Koivisto: The Prime Minister of Finland." *American-Scandinavian Review* 58, no. 1 (1970): 5–9.

Kirby, David. "The Finnish Presidential Election, January 1982." *Western European Politics* 5 (October 1982): 137–140.

Koivisto, Mauno. *Witness to History: The Memoirs of Mauno Koivisto, President of Finland, 1982–1994.* Carbondale: Southern Illinois University Press, 1997.

Krosby, H. Peter. "Finland after Kekkonen." *Current History* 81, no. 478 (1982): 381–383, 394, 400.

Paastela, J. "The 1988 Presidential Election in Finland." *Scandinavian Political Studies* 11 (July 1988): 159–188.

Konoe Fumimaro (1891–1945) *prime minister of Japan*

Konoe Fumimaro was born in Tokyo, Japan, on October 12, 1891, a scion of the great Fujiwara family, which had influenced national affairs since the ninth century. His father, Konoe Atsumaro, was also a distinguished statesman. Konoe attended Kyoto Imperial University to study law, literature, and Western philosophy, and proved himself a bright, if undistinguished student. After graduating he inherited the title of prince and a seat in the Japanese Diet (legislature) previously filled by his father. In 1919 Konoe accompanied Prime Minister SAIONJI KIMMOCHI to the Paris Peace Conference, acquiring firsthand experience in the realm of international diplomacy. In 1932 he became vice president of the upper house of the Diet, and two years later served as its president. The 1920s had been a flourishing period for democracy, but after the Great Depression in 1929 Japan became increasingly nationalistic. Konoe, although rather liberal by nature, was clearly caught up in the tide of events, and in 1931 he supported the Japanese conquest of Manchuria. In time, however, he came to realize the extent of Japanese army interference in foreign affairs and called for political reforms. In 1936 Emperor HIROHITO asked him to form a cabinet as prime minister, but he declined. The following year he accepted the invitation to form a nonparty cabinet to solidify national support behind the government. Konoe realized that the excesses of the army faction had to be reined in, but in July 1937 full-scale war erupted between Japan and China. Again he lent lip service to the effort, by declaring creation of the "Greater East Asia Co-prosperity Sphere," a synonym for the Japanese empire. But when Konoe failed to find a diplomatic solution to the China war, he resigned from office in January 1939. He was especially disturbed by his inability to restrict the rising tide of irrational militarism.

As Japan drifted toward entry into World War II, Konoe headed the Privy Council. In June 1940 he planned to develop a mass national movement, the

Imperial Rule Assistance Association, which would supplant political parties to foster national unity. The following month he became prime minister for the second time, and took definite steps to shore up Japan's diplomatic position. In September 1940 he concluded the Tripartite Pact with Germany's ADOLF HITLER and Italy's BENITO MUSSOLINI, and also signed a nonaggression pact with JOSEPH STALIN of the Soviet Union. But the ongoing war in China undermined relations with the United States and Great Britain. Konoe, who opposed Western imperialism in Asia, genuinely sought to prevent the conflict from expanding into the Pacific. He tried to confer with President FRANKLIN D. ROOSEVELT, but the Americans declined. His failure to concoct a peaceful solution triggered his second resignation, but in July 1941 he managed to form a third cabinet. For the next four months Konoe devoted all his efforts to heading off a war with the United States. When it became apparent that the Japanese military was embarking on aggression anyway, Konoe resigned a third time in October 1941. He was replaced by the aggressive defense minister, TOJO HIDEKI.

The Japanese attack on the U.S. installation at Pearl Harbor, Hawaii, on December 7, 1941, accelerated the pace of Japanese expansion and aggression in Asia. Konoe, while not officially a part of the government, worked diligently behind the scenes to achieve a diplomatic solution, but without success. In 1944 he helped engineer the downfall of the Tojo government and, after Japan surrendered in September 1945, he served as deputy minister of national affairs in the Higashikuni government. Unfortunately, the Americans regarded his bellicose statements in the 1930s as endorsements of militarism, and he was ordered to stand trial as a war criminal. On December 16, 1945, the day before his trial, Konoe committed suicide. He was ineffective in his attempts to preserve peace but is still regarded as one of the most influential Japanese politicians of the interwar period.

Further Reading

Bergen, Gordon M. "Japan's Young Prince: Konoe Fumimaro's Early Political Career, 1916–1931." *Monumenta Nipponica* 29, no. 4 (1974): 451–476.
Brendan, Piers. *The Dark Valley: A Panorama of the 1930s.* New York: Knopf, 2000.
Hanneman, Mary. *Japan Faces the World, 1925–1952.* New York: Longman, 2001.

McNelly, Theodore. *The Origins of Japan's Democratic Constitution.* Lanham, Md.: University Press of America, 2000.
Nish, Ian H. *Japanese Foreign Policy in the Interwar Period.* Westport, Conn.: Praeger, 2002.
Oka, Yoshitake. *Konoe Fumimaro: A Political Biography.* Tokyo: University of Tokyo Press, 1983.
Tohmatsu, Haruo. *A Gathering Darkness: The Coming of War to the Far East and the Pacific, 1921–1942.* Wilmington, Del.: Scholarly Resources, 2004.

Kreisky, Bruno (1911 1990) *chancellor of Austria*

Bruno Kreisky was born in January 22, 1911, the son of Jewish industrialists. A nonpracticing Jew, he joined the Social Democratic Party as a teenager and participated in the socialist uprising against conservative chancellor ENGLEBERT DOLLFUSS in February 1934. Jailed and released intermittently, Kreisky fled Austria after its seizure by Nazi Germany in 1938, and immigrated to Sweden. He spent the next seven years working as an economic adviser in Stockholm, where he met and befriended WILLY BRANDT and OLAF PALME, two future socialist leaders. He was indelibly impressed by the Scandinavian brand of moderate socialism and the benefits of a comprehensive welfare state. Kreisky returned to Austria in 1946 and joined the diplomatic corps under President KARL RENNER. After repeated tours of various Scandinavian countries he returned in 1951, whereupon Chancellor JULIUS RAAB appointed him state secretary for the foreign office. In this capacity he had a prominent role in negotiating with the Soviet Union for Austrian neutrality and independence. After Austria was released from four-power military occupation in May 1955, Kreisky continued rising through the party hierarchy. In 1959 Raab made him foreign minister, a post he occupied for 15 years. That same year he championed Austrian entry into the European Free Trade association. Kreisky also demonstrated diplomatic skill by brokering a difficult summit between American president JOHN F. KENNEDY and Soviet premier NIKITA KHRUSHCHEV in April 1961. But in 1966 when the socialists lost power for the first time in two decades, Kreisky became chairman and set about modernizing the party. He did so by forcefully discarding traditional class-struggle rhetoric and thinking in favor of political pragmatism. Kreisky foisted these changes on the socialists in order to attract votes from the burgeoning middle class. In 1970 he campaigned on a platform of national modernization, won a minority government, and became chancellor. The following year Kreisky called for new elections and won an absolute majority in the legislature—the first single-party government to rule Austria since World War II.

True to his creed, Kreisky followed through on his reformist impulses with inclusive and democratizing policies. He expanded educational opportunities to poor children, gave small parties greater political protection, and modernized the defense forces to ensure Austria's "armed neutrality." He then granted legal equality to women, liberalized divorce laws in this very Catholic nation, and provided one of Europe's most comprehensive social welfare programs. This included blanket coverage of every citizen in a social, health, and pension insurance system, along with five weeks of paid vacation. In many respects the Austrian brand of state socialism equaled or exceeded its more famous Scandinavian counterparts. He also enjoyed considerable success expanding the private sector and promoting economic growth throughout the recession-prone 1970s. Austria now consistently enjoyed the lowest unemployment of any Western nation, even while shouldering higher public debts.

Kreisky availed himself of Austrian neutrality to exert influence upon international events. He strove to promote detente between East and West, but proved a strident critic of Soviet military intervention against Hungary in 1956 and Czechoslovakia in 1968. He also actively cultivated closer relationships with East European nations and neighbors. And, in his most controversial move, he became the first Western head of state to insist that any Middle Eastern peace must include the Palestine Liberation Organization (PLO). To that end he invited PLO chairman Yasser Arafat to Vienna in 1974 and spoke out against hard-line Israeli administrations. This gained him the enmity of Jews worldwide, who accused him of selling out his former religion. Kreisky nevertheless remained a vocal proponent of world peace and worker solidarity and served as president of the Socialist International between 1976 and 1989. After running Austrian affairs capably for 13 years, Kreisky stepped down in 1983 after election losses resulted in a coalition government. Thereafter he served as a respected elder statesman until his death in Vienna on July 27, 1990. Such was his longevity in office, the longest since the Hapsburg monarchy, that he

was jocularly known as "Kaiser Bruno." Kreisky remains celebrated for wielding the biggest influence on Austria's national and international standing since Count Metternich in the 19th century.

Further Reading

Bischof, Gunter, and Anton Pelinka, eds. *The Kreisky Era in Austria.* New Brunswick, N.J.: Transaction Publishers, 1994.

Bunzl, John. *Between Vienna and Jerusalem: Reflections and Polemics on Austria, Israel, and Palestine.* New York: Peter Lang, 1997.

Etzerdorfer, Irene. "From the Sphinx with—to the Sphinx without a Puzzle: A Subjective Leadership Perceptions Comparison between Bruno Kreisky and Franz Vranitzky." *Contemporary Austrian Politics* 7 (1999): 56–77.

Kreisky, Bruno, *The Struggle for a Democratic Austria.* New York: Berghan Books, 2000.

Secher, H. Pierre. "The 'Jewish' Kreisky: Perception or Reality?" *History of European Ideas* 20 (February 1995): 865–870.

———. *Bruno Kreisky.* Pittsburgh, Pa.: University of Pittsburgh Press, 1993.

Krenz, Egon (1937–) *general secretary of the Socialist Unity Party of East Germany*

Egon Krenz was born in Kolberg, Germany, on March 19, 1937, the illegitimate son of a tailor. After 1945 Germany was partitioned by the victorious Allied powers and the area known as East Germany fell under the Soviet Union's sphere of influence. In 1949 the communist-controlled German Democratic Republic was declared under WALTER ULBRICHT. Krenz had by then become active in communist youth activities and he eventually joined the Free German Youth, Freie Deutsche Jugend (FDJ), as a teenager. Two years later he was admitted into the Sozialistische Einheitspartei Deutschlands (SED), Socialist Unity (Communist) Party, while studying to be a teacher. Rather ambitious, Krenz forsook education to pursue a career in politics. After serving his compulsory two years of military service in 1959–61 he rejoined the FDJ as secretary of the Central Committee. He next studied at the prestigious Communist Party staff school in Moscow and obtained a social science degree by 1967. Hard work and unswerving dedication to party principles brought him a post on the SED Central Committee in 1973 and he caught the attention of General Secretary ERICH HONECKER, who adopted him as a protégé.

Krenz enjoyed a well-deserved reputation as a loyal apparatchik and continued his meteoric climb through the party hierarchy with Honecker's patronage. By 1983 he was a full voting member of the Politburo, East Germany's highest decision-making body, and assumed the portfolios of security, sports, and youth affairs. His appointment to security affairs proved ominous, for he was now responsible for running the notorious East German secret police (Stasi). In addition to repressing political dissent, the Stasi's duties included shooting all citizens attempting to flee for West Germany. In May 1989 Krenz was present in Beijing, China, in the aftermath of the massacre at Tiananmen Square, and he congratulated his hosts for restoring order. East Germany, however, was also undergoing a rising tide of popular resentment against communist tyranny and it became Krenz's responsibility to crack down. The tumult only increased after Soviet premier MIKHAIL GORBACHEV began promoting greater political freedom for all East European satellite states. Honecker, a hard-line communist, denounced such liberalization and refused to depart from the failed policies of the past. Krenz then unceremoniously ended his mentor's 18-year reign as head of East Germany by deposing Honecker in a party coup on October 18, 1989.

Krenz was now party general secretary and prime minister of East Germany. His political instincts gravitated toward reforming the ossified political system before an open revolt occurred. He traveled the country widely, listened to grievances, and promised immediate reform. "My motto remains work, work, work, and more work," he declared, "but work that should be pleasant and serve all the people." However, Krenz was so closely identified with the communist leadership that nobody believed him. Massive public demonstrations erupted throughout East Germany, demanding an end to communism and freedom to travel abroad. Under intense pressure and unwilling to have security forces fire upon the citizenry again, Krenz opened the borders to West Germany on November 9, 1989. When the infamous Berlin Wall was literally torn down by exasperated and joyous Germans from both sides of the border, East Germany—and Krenz—were doomed. On December 1, 1989, the SED People's Chamber stripped him of his rank and power, expelling him from the

party; he had been in power for only 46 days. East Germany did not long outlast him for it was voted out of existence and amalgamated into the German Federal Republic the following spring.

Krenz's problems did not end there. In August 1997 he was held responsible for the notorious "shoot to kill" policy at the Berlin Wall. Since 1961 more than 1,000 German citizens were slain while trying to escape in Berlin and elsewhere along the border. Krenz professed his innocence and insisted that the policy was more the responsibility of the Soviet Union than East Germany, but on August 25, 1997, he was convicted of manslaughter and sentenced to six and a half years in prison. "I am starting my sentence, not as a criminal, but as a victim of political persecution," he declared. Krenz was jailed in January 2000 and on March 22, 2001, the European Court of Human Rights upheld his conviction. He is slated to remain behind bars at Berlin's Hakenfelde prison until 2006, the last communist leader of the Democratic German Republic.

Further Reading

Childs, Timothy. *The Fall of the German Democratic Republic: Germany's Road to Unity.* New York: Longman, 2000.

Dennis, Mike. *The Rise and Fall of the German Democratic Republic, 1945–1990.* New York: Longman, 2000.

Grix, Jonathan. *The Role of the Masses in the Collapse of the German Democratic Republic.* New York: St. Martin's Press, 2000.

Hough, Dan. *The Rise and Fall of the PDS in Eastern Germany.* Birmingham, England: University of Birmingham Press, 2001.

Peterson, Edward N. *The Secret Police and the Revolution: The Fall of the German Democratic Republic.* Westport, Conn.: Praeger, 2002.

Ross, Corvey. *The East German Dictatorship: Problems and Perspectives in the Interpretation of the GDR.* New York: Oxford University Press, 2002.

Kubitschek, Juscelino (1902–1976) *president of Brazil*

Juscelino Kubitschek de Oliveira was born in Diamantina, Brazil, on September 12, 1902, a descendant of Czech immigrants. He was educated at a local seminary and decided to pursue medicine while working as a telephone operator. Kubitschek graduated from the University of Minas Gerais in 1927 and enhanced his proficiency by studying in France, Germany, and Austria. He returned home in 1932, just as a rebellion arose against President GETÚLIO VARGAS. Kubitschek was then conscripted into the military medical corps and came to the attention of governmental authorities. He was encouraged to enter politics, and two years later won a seat in the Chamber of Deputies. In 1937 Vargas dissolved Congress and instituted a fascist dictatorship. Kubitschek quit the government to resume his medical profession. However, his political fortunes improved in 1940 when he was appointed governor of Belo Horizonte, capital of Minas Gerais state. Here Kubitschek displayed remarkable talent as a modernizer, and overhauled the transportation network, constructed numerous medical clinics, and designed a model neighborhood. After the Vargas regime collapsed in 1945, Kubitschek was elected again to the Chamber of Deputies. He remained there until Vargas was reelected president in 1950 and the following year Kubitschek left to be elected governor of Minas Gerais. As before, he carried through a series of impressive programs to modernize the state infrastructure with new hydroelectric plants, highways, and assistance to new industries. Once Vargas was finally driven from office in 1955, Kubitschek was tapped to lead the Social Democratic Party. From there he ran for the presidency and conducted a clever campaign promising the Brazilian people "50 years of progress in five years." He also selected the progressive João Goulart as his running mate to acquire votes of the poor and downcast. Together they eked out a slight electoral victory and were sworn into office in January 1956.

Kubitschek assumed power with an ambitious national modernization campaign in mind. As before, he spent lavishly on public works projects, creating hydroelectric dams, highways, and new businesses. The government borrowed heavily and invested millions in new steel plants and a modern infrastructure upon which the country could grow. But Kubitschek's most ambitious project was in relocating the capital from Rio de Janeiro on the coast to Goias state, 600 miles within Brazil's interior. There he intended to design and build a new, ultra-modern capital called Brasilia, connected by lengthy highways, to stimulate development of this neglected region. Kubitschek then called upon local architects and engineers to design a steel and glass miracle in

the jungle to serve as a symbol of Brazil's confident future. This intricate task was exceedingly well planned, unfolded smoothly, and was completed within three years. It remains a lasting monument of one man's vision of his nation.

Unfortunately, Kubitschek's obsession with construction saddled the country with deep-rooted economic problems. Yearly growth rates of 7 percent were achieved but at the cost of borrowing millions of dollars and increasing the national debt. In time, inflationary pressures arose that cut into Brazil's economic vitality for the next several decades. But Kubitschek's dream would not be thwarted by mere economics, and in 1959, when the International Monetary Fund (IMF) insisted he scale back his plans and begin austerity measures, he dropped their assistance rather than slow down. By the time Kubitschek relinquished his office in 1961 in favor of JÂNIO QUADROS, the nation was booming and awash in a sense of greatness. He then parlayed his popularity back into politics by becoming a senator from Goias in 1962. Two years later the Social Democrats again nominated him as their presidential candidate, but in March 1964 the military toppled the government, stripped Kubitschek of his rights, and imposed a junta that lasted 15 years. Kubitschek entered voluntary exile in the United States for three years but returned in 1967 to serve as an investment banker. He died in a car accident on August 22, 1976. His public funeral occasioned such an outpouring of grief that the military declared a three-day mourning period in his honor. The far-sighted Kubitschek remains one of Brazil's most popular figures, an embodiment of postwar Brazilian confidence.

Further Reading

Alexander, Robert J. *Juscelino Kubitschek and the Development of Brazil.* Athens: Ohio University Press, 1991.

———. "Juscelino Kubitschek and the Politics of Exuberance, 1956–1961." *Luso-Brazilian Review* 27, no. 1 (1990): 31–45.

Conduru, Guilherme F. *The Robore Agreements (1958): A Case Study of Foreign Policy Decision Making in the Kubitschek Administration.* Oxford, England: Centre for Brazilian Studies, University of Oxford, 2001.

Eakin, Marshall C. *Tropical Capitalism: The Industrialization of Belo Horizonte.* New York: Palgrave, 2001.

Maram, Sheldon. "Juscelino Kubitschek and the 1960 Presidential Election." *Journal of Latin American Studies* 24 (February 1992): 123–145.

Pang, Eul-Soo. *The International Political Economy of Transformation in Argentina, Brazil, and Chile since 1960.* New York: Palgrave Macmillan, 2002.

Kuwatli, Shukri al- (1892–1967) *president of Syria*

Shukri al-Kuwatli was born at Damascus, Syria, in 1892, part of a wealthy landowning family. A subject of the Turkish-run Ottoman Empire, he attended college in Constantinople and struck up relations with clandestine Arab nationalists residing there. He consequently joined a secret organization, al-Fatah, to agitate for Arabic independence. However, Kuwatli was caught, imprisoned, and tortured by Ottoman authorities before being released during World War I. When the Arabs finally revolted against the Turks in 1916, Kuwatli joined the army of Faisal al Hussein and campaigned with distinction. Afterward he helped organize the Arab Independence Party to promote Syrian independence and nationhood. In 1920 his commander was enthroned as FAISAL I of Syria amid widespread public support. However, the French protested his coronation, because they had been promised Syria and Lebanon in the 1919 Treaty of Versailles. They quickly deposed Faisal while Kuwatli exiled himself to Egypt and was tried and condemned to death in absentia. Over the next decade, as France consolidated its rule over Syria, Kuwatli secretly channeled money and arms to resistance fighters there. It was not until 1930 that he returned under a general amnesty and two years later joined a new party, the National Bloc, to press for independence. The French resisted any such overtures but Kuwatli helped organize general strikes to gain leverage. That year he also won a seat in the legislature and, in light of his great popularity, gained appointments as minister of defense and finance. Two years later he resigned to protest Syria's limited resolve in pressuring France for greater concessions. After the fall of France in May 1940, he again demanded full independence. The Vichy regime in Paris finally complied on September 27, 1941, although the country remained garrisoned by French troops. This fact brought on an invasion by Free French and British forces, but Kuwatli cleverly played one side off against the other and nei-

ther achieved the upper hand. In August 1943 he was finally elected president of Syria by the National Bloc members of the legislature. In this capacity he turned a blind eye toward continuing strikes and riots, until France finally agreed to pull all its forces out of Syria in April 1946.

As the leader of a young nation, Kuwatli fully embraced the Pan-Arabism sweeping the Middle East after World War II and he orchestrated Syrian entrance into the Arab League in 1945. But his regime was beset by mounting political instability and economic recession. Attempts at agrarian reform failed, production stumbled as the French franc was devalued, and there were increasing charges of corruption and cronyism against the government. Kuwatli grew increasingly ambitious in office and in 1947 he effected constitutional changes so he could serve a second consecutive term. The turning point in his political fortunes occurred after the defeat of combined Syrian-Egyptian forces during the 1948 war in Palestine, from which emerged the Jewish state of Israel. This embarrassing reversal revealed astonishing degrees of incompetence and corruption within Kuwatli's administration and stimulated domestic unrest. On March 30, 1949, he was overthrown by a military coup and arrested. Kuwatli eventually settled in Egypt, where he remained five years. By this time he had acquired the nickname of "the camel" owing to his stubbornness and prickly temperament when angered.

A series of coups and countercoups kept the Syrian government in turmoil until civilian authority finally asserted itself in 1954. Kuwatli then returned as part of the new Nationalist Party, and in 1955 he was elected president a second time. This time, however, he ruled strictly as a figurehead, for most political power had been usurped by the military. Kuwatli enjoyed greater success in the diplomatic area and closely aligned himself with Egypt and Saudi Arabia to confront the growing strength of Israel. He was a vocal ally of Egypt through the 1956 Suez Canal Crisis and later agreed to President GAMAL ABDEL NASSER's proposed union of their two countries. In 1958 he retired from office while Nasser became leader of a new, combined Egyptian-Syrian entity, the United Arab Republic (UAR). Kuwatli, feeling that his political career was over, retired from public life with the honorary title "First Arab Citizen." He died in Beirut, Lebanon, on June 30, 1967, a key figure in the quest for Syrian independence but unable to grasp the reins of power and rule effectively.

Further Reading

Gaunson, A. B. *The Anglo-French Clash in Lebanon and Syria, 1940–45.* New York: St. Martin's Press, 1987.

Heydemann, Steven. *Authoritarianism in Syria: Institutions and Social Conflict, 1946–1970.* Ithaca, N.Y.: Cornell University Press, 1999.

Moubayed, Sami M. *Damascus between Democracy and Dictatorship.* Lanham, Md.: University Press of America, 2000.

Sadowski, Yahya M. "Political Power and Economic Organization in Syria: The Course of State Intervention, 1946–1958." Unpublished Ph.D. diss., University of California–Los Angeles, 1984.

Said, Jamal A. "The Emergence of Syria and Lebanon, 1920–1946." Unpublished Ph.D. diss., Johns Hopkins University, 1964.

Talhami, Ghada H. *Syria and the Palestinians: The Clash of Nationalisms.* Gainesville: University Press of Florida, 2001.

Kyprianou, Spyros (1932–2002) *president of Cyprus*

Spyros Kyprianou was born in Limassol, Cyprus, on October 28, 1932, the son of a successful businessman. As part of the island's elite, he was sent to study in England and graduated from the City of London College in 1951. Three years later, he was called before the bar and remained in England as a Cypriot spokesman. Cyprus had been an English colonial possession since 1878, and the Greek majority sought independence, to be followed by an immediate *enosis* (union) with mainland Greece. Such a move met strong opposition from the English, who maintained naval bases on the island, as well as the small but vocal Turkish minority, who feared a loss of civil rights. Kyprianou nonetheless presented his case in diplomatic circles as a personal representative of Archbishop MAKARIOS III. He also functioned as president of the National Union of Cypriot Students in England. Events quickened in 1955 when Greek guerrillas began a campaign of violence against the Turks, which prompted the deployment of British troops on Cyprus. Kyprianou was then deported from England

and resettled in the United States to plead his case for reunification before the United Nations. However, by 1957 he returned to London to take part in independence talks for Cyprus. A treaty was signed in 1959 giving the island its sovereignty, but only with extensive protection for Turks: they were allotted 30 percent of seats in the House of Representatives, the office of vice president was reserved for a Turk, and they could veto any legislation deemed threatening to their interests. It was a far from perfect solution for traditional ethnic enmities.

Back home Kyprianou helped found the National Democratic Front for Reconstruction, through which Makarios was elected president in August 1960. Kyprianou was then appointed minister of justice and finally foreign minister, an office he held for the next 12 years. In this capacity he conducted the island's affairs as a nonaligned nation and cultivated close ties with other emerging countries. He also secured membership in the new European Common Market, and in 1967 functioned as president of the Committee of Foreign Ministers of the Council of Europe. Unfortunately, fighting between Greeks and Turks erupted again in 1963, for which United Nations peacekeeping forces were deployed. Tensions further escalated in 1967 when both Greece and Turkey prepared to go to war to protect their respective communities. At this juncture both Makarios and Kyprianou began counseling caution and moderation in their dealing with the Turks, a stance resented by the military dictatorship running Greece. In 1972 they applied sufficient pressure to have Kyprianou removed as foreign minister, and he practiced law for four years. In July 1974 the junta also deposed Makarios by a coup, at which point the Turks invaded and seized the northern third of the island. War between the two nations seemed imminent, and Greek and Turkish Cypriots now conducted their affairs at gunpoint.

Kyprianou was active at the United Nations for several years and pressed for the removal of Turkish troops from Cyprus. He also founded the new Democratic Front, and in September 1976 was appointed president of the House of Representatives. After Makarios died in exile the following year, Kyprianou was elected president of the island's Greek half. He continually sought peaceful resolution and the island's reunification, eventually settling upon a federal scheme with two distinct governments under one administration, but the Turks were immovable. Kyprianou was nonetheless reelected by wide margins after 1978 before stumbling in 1993. He then resumed his post as House Speaker and in April 1999 acted as a special U.N. envoy to gain the release of three American servicemen captured by Serbia during a bombing campaign there. Kyprianou was sympathetic to the Serbs and personally conferred with President Slobodan Milosevic, but proved unable to secure their freedom. "I am not a military expert but I have seen things that shocked me," he confided. After failing in another presidential bid in 1998, he led the legislature until ill health forced his retirement. Kyprianou died in Nicosia on March 12, 2002, remembered as a tireless proponent of the Cypriot cause and a leading architect of the island's independence.

Further Reading

Borowiec, Andrew. *Cyprus: A Troubled Island.* Westport, Conn.: Praeger, 2000.

Dietz, Thomas, ed. *The European Union and the Cyprus Conflict: Modern Conflict, Postmodern Union.* New York: Manchester University Press, 2002.

Dodd, C. H. *Storm Clouds over Cyprus.* Huntingdon, England: Eothen, 2001.

James, Alan. *Keeping the Peace in the Cyprus Crisis of 1963–64.* New York: Palgrave, 2002.

Leventis, Yiorghos. *Cyprus: The Struggle for Self Determination in the 1940s: Prelude to Deeper Crises.* New York: Peter Lang, 2002.

Meinarous, R. "Developments in the Cyprus Question." *Orient* 78 (December 1987): 432–519.

L

Lange, David (1942–) *prime minister of New Zealand*

David Russell Lange was born in Otahuhu, Auckland, New Zealand, on August 4, 1942, the son of an activist doctor. From his father he absorbed a great deal of sympathy for disadvantaged people, which later propelled him to study law at the University of Auckland. After graduating and being called to the bar in 1966, he ventured to London, England, where he delivered low-cost legal aid to poor people. Two years later he returned home to serve as a tutor at Auckland University. Lange acquired his advanced law degree in 1970 and spent the next seven years as a defense lawyer for the poor. He there acquired a sterling reputation as a defense attorney. In 1976 Lange parlayed his sense of social justice into a political career by running for office as a Labor Party candidate. He failed to gain a seat on his first attempt but won a by-election in 1977. Lange shone as an aggressive debater in the House of Representatives, and by 1979 he had risen to deputy leader of the opposition. Four years later he supplanted Wallace Rowling, who had lost three consecutive national elections, as Labor leader. In July 1984 conservative prime minister ROBERT MULDOON called a snap election and was overwhelmingly defeated by Labor. Lange thus became New Zealand's youngest prime minister of the 20th century and also retained the offices of foreign minister and education minister.

Lange began his tenure in office on a controversial note by unilaterally banning all warships carrying nuclear weapons from New Zealand waters. Because vessels of the United States Navy neither confirm nor deny the existence of such devices on board, they were now forbidden from visiting New Zealand ports or conducting naval exercises within its territory. This ban was viewed as violating the 1951 ANZUS (Australia-New Zealand-United States) Treaty that allows for mutual defensive arrangements. President RONALD REAGAN was angered by Lange's recalcitrance and he canceled American participation in ANZUS activities, as did Australian prime minister ROBERT HAWKE. The United States further downgraded New Zealand's status from an allied nation to merely a "friendly" one. This contretemps may have compromised New Zealand's defenses but it enhanced Lange's public standing and a majority of citizens, when polled, supported their prime minister. New Zealand was also an outspoken critic of France's decision to resume nuclear testing in the southern Pacific. In 1986 French agents sank the environmentalist ship *Rainbow Warrior* in Auckland Harbor, killing a passenger. An angry Lange then confronted French president François Mitterand, demanding an apology and reparations, and obtaining both.

Domestically Lange pursued a surprisingly conservative economic agenda. He embraced the free market and restructured the national economy through liberalization. He was unyielding in his criticism of South Africa's apartheid regime and closed the New Zealand embassy in Pretoria. Because of his principled stance, Labor won an easy reelection in 1987 and increased its margin in Parliament. Lange then instituted major reforms of the national education system, especially with regard to women's rights and the Maori minority. But the stability of Lange's administration was threatened by his criticism of Roger Douglas, the conservative finance minister. Lange pressured him to resign from office in 1988, which prompted other conservatives in the Labor Party to complain. Lange himself resigned as prime minister in August 1989, ostensibly for health reasons. He continued on as attorney general under the administration of Geoffrey Palmer until Labor was tossed from power in 1990. Thereafter he served in Parliament until 1996, when he retired from public life. Lange remains one of New Zealand's most popular yet controversial political leaders.

Further Reading

Alves, Dora. "New Zealand and ANZUS: An American View." *Round Table* 302 (1987): 207–222.

Clements, Kevin P. *Breaking Nuclear Ties: The Case of New Zealand.* Boulder, Colo.: Westview Press, 1997.

Dilger, Patrick J. "ANZUS and New Zealand's Nuclear Ship Ban: New Zealand and American Perspectives." Unpublished master's thesis, University of North Carolina–Chapel Hill, 1987.

Holland, Martin. "New Zealand's Relations with Africa: The Changing Foreign Policy of a Small State." *Round Table* 303 (1987): 343–360.

Lange, David. *Nuclear Free: The New Zealand Way.* New York: Penguin Books, 1990.

McKinley, Michael. "Labour, Lange, and Logic: An Analysis of New Zealand's ANZUS Policy." *Australian Outlook* 39, no. 3 (1985): 133–138.

Wright, Vernon. *David Lange, Prime Minister.* Boston: Unwin Paperbacks with Port Nicholson Press, 1984.

Laurier, Sir Wilfrid (1841–1919) *prime minister of Canada*

Henri Charles Wilfrid Laurier was born in St. Lin, Quebec, Canada, on November 20, 1841, the son of a francophone, liberal-minded farmer. He inherited his father's outlook on politics and passed through McGill University in 1864 studying law. He opened a successful law practice in Montreal, but intermittent health problems induced him to undertake politics as a profession. Laurier was uniquely disposed in this regard, being fluently bilingual and steeped in the English Whig tradition of liberalism. After serving as a Liberal in the Quebec legislature, he was elected to Parliament in 1874 and spent the next 45 years in Ottawa, the national capital. A charismatic orator, Laurier soon emerged as a champion of English political philosophy and French language and religious rights. In 1877 he delivered his most important speech, a defense of English-style liberalism against its strident, anticlerical French equivalent. This act greatly bolstered his political fortunes in Quebec, and he emerged as the rising star of the Liberal Party. In 1887 he succeeded Edward Blake as party leader and sought to establish the Liberals as a national entity to bring Canadians together. But four years later Laurier lost a general election to conservatives under John A. Macdonald by advocating trade reciprocity with the United States. In 1895 Canada faced a new crisis over the issue of schools in Manitoba and whether public funds should be spent on Catholic education for French Canadians living there. Laurier, insisting on "sunny ways" to solve the problem, crafted a compromise allowing Catholics to receive religious instruction after normal class hours. This solution cemented Laurier's reputation as a compromiser and led to his election to prime minister in 1896. He was the first French Canadian to hold that office.

Laurier's tenure in office largely coincided with a booming Canadian economy and he determined to assist by authorizing construction of three transcontinental railways to link the vast nation together. These not only facilitated settlement and development of the new prairie provinces, they also lessened Canadian economic dependence on the United States. But in 1899 Laurier faced a potential crisis from overseas. The Boer War had commenced in South Africa and many English-speaking Canadians felt obliged to assist Great Britain in the fighting there. However, French-speaking Canadians resisted any move to fight and die on behalf of the British Empire. Ultimately Laurier was obliged to send Canadian troops abroad, where they fought with distinction, but the act signaled a growing rift between Quebec and the rest of Canada. Thereafter he repeatedly opposed any effort by the British Empire to impose unification over its dominions and argued for greater national autonomy. In 1910 foreign affairs again intruded into domestic affairs as Laurier, confronted with the naval might of Imperial Germany, felt obliged to assist Britain by constructing several warships. He was immediately attacked for caving in to English demands by the French, and accused of not doing enough for Britain by the English. Ultimately the Navy Bill failed in 1911 due to a direct assault by his fellow French Canadian, Henri Bourassa. That year Laurier made another ill-fated attempt at trade reciprocity with the United States, and the prospective loss of protective tariffs thoroughly alarmed Canadian manufacturers. General elections held that September turned the Liberals out of power in favor of Conservatives under ROBERT LAIRD BORDEN. Laurier spent the last eight years of his life leading the opposition in Parliament.

The onset of World War I in August 1914 further exacerbated Canada's sectional rivalries. The army initially relied upon volunteers to man the ranks, but heavy losses forced the Borden government to introduce conscription. Laurier dutifully supported Canadian participation in the war, exhorting his fellow French Canadians to join and serve, but he unalterably opposed a draft. Attitudes hardened along cultural lines, and in 1917 Borden formed a national government without any French Canadians in it. When Laurier refused to join the unity government, many English-speaking Liberals deserted him and joined the Conservatives. The general election was fraught with cries of disloyalty, and in 1917 the Liberals were eliminated as a political force, save in Quebec. This national schism was the very condition that Laurier had striven so long and hard to prevent. He died in Ottawa on February 17, 1919, a disillusioned man and the first national leader thwarted by Canada's English-French division. But for 15 years he dominated Canadian politics and led his nation into the 20th century with confidence, grace, and panache. Despite the increasing political shrillness, Laurier was one of few politicians who elicited admiration from both friends and opponents alike.

Further Reading

Clippingdale, Richard. *Laurier, His Life, and World.* New York: McGraw-Hill Ryerson, 1979.

Cook, Ramsay. "Dafoe, Laurier, and the Formation of Union Government." *Canadian Historical Review* 42, no. 3 (1961): 185–208.

La Pierre, Laurier C. *Sir Wilfrid Laurier and the Romance of Canada.* Toronto: Stoddart, 1996.

Miller, Carman. *Painting the Map Red: Canada and the South African War, 1899–1902.* Buffalo, N.Y.: Canadian War Museum and McGill-Queen's University Press, 1993.

Perin, Roberto. *Rome in Canada: The Vatican and Canadian Affairs in the Late Victorian Age.* Toronto: University of Toronto Press, 1990.

Schneider, Fred D. "Laurier and Canada's Two Nations." *South Atlantic Quarterly* 61, no. 3 (1962): 365–377.

Laval, Pierre (1883–1945) *prime minister of France*

Pierre Jean-Marie Laval was born in Chateldon, France, on June 28, 1883, the son of an innkeeper. An accomplished student, he attended law school while working as a tutor, and in 1909 he gained admittance to the Paris bar. Here Laval specialized as a defense attorney in trade unionist matters and also joined the Socialist Party. In 1914 he was elected to the Chamber of Deputies as a pacifist and spent the next four years promoting a negotiated end to World War I. In 1919 he voted against the Treaty of Versailles for being too harsh on Germany and lost his seat. But thereafter rapprochement with Germany became a recurrent theme in Laval's political philosophy, along with an increasing tendency toward opportunism. Laval spent the next five years in business, acquiring a small fortune in banking and radio concerns. He gained his seat back in 1924, although he had broken his connections to the Socialists by this time. Laval then held down a number of ministerial portfolios until the leftists were turned out of office in 1926. The following year he became a senator, having joined the right-wing National Republican Union. He served as foreign minister under André Tardieu until January 1931, when he himself became prime minister and foreign minister.

Laval's first term as chief executive lasted only a year but he pursued his vision of Franco-German reconciliation. He became the first French head of state to visit Berlin since the war, and he denounced the Polish Corridor separating the Free City of Danzig from the rest of Germany. In 1932 he was removed from power due to parliamentary bickering and resumed his senate seat. Three years later Laval returned to the inner circle as foreign minister in Gaston Doumergue's cabinet. He then negotiated with Italian dictator BENITO MUSSOLINI on trading minor colonial possessions in Africa. However, when the new German chancellor ADOLF HITLER formally renounced the Versailles Treaty in 1935 and began rearming, Laval sought to condemn the action by acquiring a three-power declaration. But parlement pressured him to seek a Franco-Soviet understanding for mutual assistance with JOSEPH STALIN. Laval, sternly anticommunist, reluctantly complied and then delayed having the treaty ratified. In June 1935, when the government collapsed from an ongoing financial crisis, he became prime minister once again.

As previously, Laval's second tenure in office was dominated by foreign considerations. He was acutely cognizant of France's military weakness and embraced appeasement of the fascist powers to avoid war. In December 1935 he secretly negotiated the Hoare-Laval Agreement among France, Italy, and Great Britain, which guaranteed Mussolini two-thirds of Ethiopia in exchange for a halt to aggression. But when word was leaked to the press, the British quickly backed out of the deal, and the ensuing uproar cost Laval his premiership. He resumed his seat in the senate and thereafter detested the English. Hitler was making strident demands for new territory, and Laval's only proposal was to form a "Latin bloc" (France, Italy, and Spain) to oppose possible aggression. He was clearly in the defeatist camp once World War II commenced and once again sought a negotiated end to hostilities. Following the German conquest of France in May 1940, Laval convinced the parlement to vote itself out of office and grant Marshal PHILIPPE PÉTAIN emergency powers. He was then again appointed prime minister under the new Vichy regime.

Back in power, Laval determined to seek closer relations with Germany if only to mitigate the hardships in Occupied France. He conferred with Hitler at Montoire in October 1940 and pledged French collaboration with the Nazi war effort. His willingness to appease Hitler led to his dismissal by Vichy in 1941, but he was reinstated the following year on German insistence. Laval then engaged in his most controversial acts. He actively cooperated in the rounding up of foreign Jews for shipment to German death camps and also instituted a policy of drafting French laborers for work in German factories. This practice swelled the ranks of the armed resistance, upon whom Laval ordered a harsh crackdown. Moreover, in June 1942 he openly wished for a German victory to prevent the rise of communism throughout

Europe. But by 1944 Hitler had clearly lost the war and Laval was taken hostage and transported to Germany. He made his way to Spain afterward but was arrested by General FRANCISCO FRANCO and returned to France. There Laval was put on trial for his life as the most identifiable symbol of the detested Vichy regime. He argued brilliantly in his own defense and insisted that he had acted only in France's best interests. The trial itself was badly handled, the defendant was openly mocked by the jury, and he received the death penalty for treason. Laval appealed his conviction on sound legal grounds, but head of state General CHARLES DE GAULLE refused him a new trial. Laval tried cheating his fate by taking poison on October 15, 1945, but he was revived by guards and led to the firing squad. He remains the most controversial French leader of World War II.

Further Reading

Brody, J. Kenneth. *The Avoidable War, vol. 2: Pierre Laval and the Politics of Reality, 1935–36.* New Brunswick, N.J.: Transaction Publications, 2000.

Cointet, Jean-Paul. *Pierre Laval.* Paris: Fayard, 1993.

Curtis, Michael. *The Verdict on Vichy.* New York: Arcade Pub., 2003.

Johnson, Douglas. "A Question of Guilt: Pierre Laval and the Vichy Regime." *History Today* 38 (January 1988): 11–17.

Laval, Pierre. *The Diary of Pierre Laval.* New York: Scribners, 1948.

Strang, G. B. "Imperial Dreams: The Mussolini-Laval Accords of January, 1935." *Historical Journal* 44 (September 2001): 799–809.

Law, Andrew Bonar (1858–1923) *prime minister of Great Britain*

Andrew Bonar Law was born in Kingston, New Brunswick, Canada, on September 16, 1858, the son of a Scottish immigrant Presbyterian minister. He was raised in Glasgow, Scotland, and entered the iron business in 1885. Law proved particularly adept at management, and in 1900 he was elected to Parliament as a Conservative from Glasgow. Given his business background, he strongly favored protective tariffs, and his numerous debates brought him appointment as secretary of the Board of Trade under Prime Minister ARTHUR BALFOUR. Law displayed a streak of political pragmatism in his ability to reach out to the opposition

Liberal Party. He advocated a broad-based referendum on tariff reform to secure as much support as possible. Coming from a middle-class background, he felt that revenues raised in this manner could best be spent assisting the struggling working class and thereby negate the onset of socialism. Law's command of economic subjects, fierce debating skills, and all-around excellence as a politician culminated in his being chosen to head the Conservative Party in November 1911 after Balfour's resignation. However, the issue that overwhelmingly defined his conservatism was home rule for Ireland. As the son of a Presbyterian minister, he vociferously opposed any moves by the British government to grant independence to Catholic Ireland—without first securing the rights and religious freedoms of Protestant Ulster. After 1911 he utilized every conceivable parliamentary tactic to delay Liberal introduction of home rule and openly endorsed the training of Protestant militias to underscore the threat of violence. He remained an outspoken proponent of the Unionist (anti-Catholic) wing of the Conservative Party until the summer of 1914, when both parties delayed further consideration of home rule until after World War I. But Law made it clear to colleagues that he would support no less than civil war in Ireland to protect the Protestant minority there.

When fighting commenced in Europe in August 1914, Law was drawn into a coalition government under HERBERT HENRY ASQUITH and served as secretary of the colonies. However, many Conservatives grew dissatisfied with Asquith's wartime leadership, and Law conspired with his long-time nemesis, DAVID LLOYD GEORGE of the Liberals, to replace him. Accordingly, when Lloyd George became prime minister in December 1916, Law acquired the portfolio of chancellor of the Exchequer. In this capacity, he capably floated numerous loans and bonds that helped finance the war. In the interest of national unity, he also supported Lloyd George's administration in the face of attacks by fellow Conservatives. Consequently, after hostilities concluded in 1918, Law was allowed to remain in the government. Declining health required him to accept the less strenuous posting of Lord Privy Seal within months. Furthermore, by 1920 he had reversed his opposition to Irish Home Rule once Lloyd George set aside the four Protestant counties known as Northern Ireland. Law surrendered his post as leader of the Conservative Party in 1921 on the grounds of poor health.

By October 1922 Conservative dissatisfaction with Lloyd George was rife. They left the coalition and held new elections, reinstating Law as party head and prime minister on October 23, 1922. However his tenure in office proved very brief, only six months, and he failed to accomplish any goals worthy of note. Law resigned after only 209 days in office in May 1923, fatally stricken by throat cancer. He died on October 30, 1923, eulogized as the "unknown prime minister." Throughout his life, Law acquired the reputation of a gaunt, grave, even melancholy figure, greatly afflicted by bouts of depression. Nonetheless, his tenure as head of the Conservative Party proved crucial, for he kept them from splintering into several bickering factions. In 1922 this fate befell the Liberal Party when it split into Liberal and Labour factions. Conservatives, largely because of this leftist schism, have managed to run Great Britain for most of the 20th century: it is Law's political legacy. He was also the first prime minister to have been born outside Great Britain.

Further Reading
Adams, R. J. Q. *Bonar Law.* Stanford, Calif.: Stanford University Press, 1999.
Blake, Robert. *An Incongruous Partnership: Lloyd George and Bonar Law.* Aberystwyth: National Library of Wales, 1992.
Goodland, Graham D. "The 'Crisis' of Edwardian Conservatism." *Modern History Review* 9, no. 4 (1998): 10–13.
Rose, Inbal A. *Conservatism Foreign Policy During the Lloyd George Coalition, 1918–1922.* Portland, Ore.: Frank Cass, 1999.
Smith, Jeremy. *The Tories and Ireland: Conservative Party Politics and the Home Rule Crisis, 1910–1914.* Portland, Ore.: Irish Academic Press, 2000.
Yearwood, Peter J., and Cameroon Hazlehurst. "'The Affairs of a Distant Dependancy': The Nigerian Debate and the Premiership of 1916." *Twentieth Century British History* 12, no. 4 (2000): 397–431.

Lee Kuan Yew (1923–) *prime minister of Singapore*
Lee Kuan Yew was born in Singapore on September 16, 1923, the son of an affluent Chinese lawyer. His native island, an enclave off the southern coast of Malaysia, was then a British Crown colony. Lee was educated at

English schools, performing exceptionally well. He endured the brutality of Japanese occupation during World War II and vowed that Singapore should not be subject to the whim of any colonial power. After World War II he ventured to England to attend the London School of Economics and Cambridge University, graduating with distinction. He returned home in 1950 and commenced a successful law practice. However, Lee had become politically active by helping to found the People's Action Party (PAP) in 1954. This was envisioned as a platform for anticolonial sentiments while staking out anticommunist positions as well. In light of Singapore's extreme vulnerability, Lee also wanted PAP to advocate a federal union with neighboring Malaysia for security reasons. Great Britain was then allowing its colonial possessions greater autonomy, and a national assembly was granted to Singapore. Lee proved particularly astute at garnering political support from the island's diverse ethnic population, and in 1959 PAP swept the first national elections. As general secretary of PAP, Lee thus became Singapore's first prime minister—a position he held for 31 years.

Lee quickly commenced intense negotiations with ABDUL RAHMAN, the head of Malaysia, about a political union. The talks proved successful, and in September 1963 the two entities were merged into the new Federation of Malaysia, along with British North Borneo. However, the union was undercut by simmering ethnic tension between Chinese and Malays, once Lee began expanding PAP's political influence beyond the island. To Rahman and other Malays, his headstrong approach struck them as a Chinese attempt to take control of the federation. Consequently, in August 1965 Singapore was summarily ejected from the federation and cast adrift on its own. Lee quickly realized that the island's only chance of survival in a hostile Third World region was to become a first-class economy. He then drew up a comprehensive plan to transform the poverty-stricken city-state into a self-sufficient nation. This proved an exceedingly tall order, as the majority of citizens were poor and uneducated, while Singapore itself possessed no natural resources. But Lee felt that Singapore's people were the only resource necessary for success and he went about reordering political and economic life on a heretofore unimaginable scale.

Lee began by surrounding himself with the best and brightest minds Singapore had to offer. Obedience and hard work became the national mantra and any official who failed to inculcate these dictates was summarily dismissed. Curiously, Lee chose Israel as his model for economic development, and openly invited foreign corporations to invest in Singapore with little governmental oversight. Freewheeling capitalism then became the norm, although subject to and guided by careful government planning. Lee's plan worked beyond all expectations for within a decade Singapore enjoyed a living standard and productivity rate second only to Japan's.

Lee's success, however, carried a price in terms of civil liberties. He was personally intolerant of dissent, political or otherwise, and protesters were routinely harassed by police, arrested, and jailed. The press and media were also closely scrutinized and subject to strict government guidelines. Virtually every aspect of public life, from a prohibition on chewing gum to the imposition of strict politeness, were carefully and meticulously enforced. "We were called a Nanny state," Lee recalled with pride. "But the result is that we are today better behaved and we live in a more agreeable place than 30 years ago." Nonetheless, Lee remained a popular prime minister, and he was repeatedly elected over the next three decades. He retired in 1990 only after choosing Goh Chok Tong his appointed successor. Nor has old age much diminished Lee's tremendous influence on island affairs. He has since assumed a behind-the-scenes role as senior minister and he keeps a worried eye trained on future considerations. Lee is especially keen at exhorting the younger generation to become risk takers "It's a time for a new burst of creativity in business," Lee insisted in July 2000. "We need many new tries, many start-ups." In view of Singapore's startling economic success, social harmony, and general affluence, Lee Kuan Yew is one of the most influential Asian national leaders of the 20th century. More than any other individual, he transformed Singapore from a rusting port into a world center for finance, high technology, and manufacturing.

Further Reading

Barr, Michael D. *Lee Kuan Yew: The Belief Behind the Man.* Washington, D.C.: Georgetown University Press, 2000.

Holden, Philip. "A Man on an Island: Gender and Nation in Lee Kuan Yew's The Singapore Story." *Biography* 24, no. 2 (2001): 401–424.

Juan, Chee Soon. "Pressing for Openness in Singapore." *Journal of Democracy* 12 (April 2001): 157–167.

Lam, Peng Er, and Kevin Tam. *Lee's Lieutenants: Singapore's Old Guard.* St. Leonards, New South Wales: Allen and Unwin, 1999.

Lee, Kuan Yew. *The Singapore Story: Memoir of Lee Kuan Yew.* London: Prentice Hall, 1998.

Trocki, Carl A. "Race and Politics in Singapore: Lee Kuan Yew's Dilemma." *Asian Ethnicity* 3 (March 2002): 103–108.

Lenin, Vladimir (1870–1924) *chairman of the Council of People's Commissars of the Soviet Union*

Vladimir Ilyich Ulyanov was born in Simbirsk, Russia, on April 22, 1870, the son of professional, affluent parents. In 1887 his elder brother was hung for attempting to assassinate Czar Alexander III, which induced the younger sibling to become a professional revolutionary. He studied law at the University of Kazan before being expelled for political activities. Thereafter he adopted the surname Lenin, one of several pseudonyms, while editing revolutionary newspapers. Lenin worked his way through a law degree by 1891 and briefly practiced law in St. Petersburg, but after 1893 he was increasingly absorbed by political theory. He was engrossed by the political concepts behind Karl Marx's landmark treatise *Das Kapital,* but realized Russia was far too primitive to conform to its industrial-based precepts. Lenin spent the next two decades in and out of exile, continually honing his revolutionary theories. He gained attention during the Third Party Congress of the Russian Social Democrats in 1905 (held in London), when the party split into two distinct factions: the Mensheviks ("Minority") under Leon Trotsky, who were doctrinaire Marxists, and the Bolsheviks ("Majority") under Lenin. The latter insisted that revolution could succeed in Russia only if guided by a small cadre of professional revolutionaries. And while conceding that party decisions should be vigorously debated, rank and file must unconditionally accept any decisions rendered: discipline was the key to survival. In continuing to revise Marx to suit his own circumstances, Lenin also stipulated that imperialism was the last stage of capitalistic development, before a proletarian (worker) mass uprising brought down the established order. And, unlike Marx, Lenin sought to involve the unskilled peasantry in party matters to create a mass movement. Not every Russian revolutionary accepted Lenin's doctrines at first, but they gradually crystallized Marxism into a new revolutionary creed—communism.

As Lenin bided his time in exile, imperial Russia was slowly unraveling under the weight of its own oppression, incompetence, and gross inequities. The failure of the Russo-Japanese War in 1904 triggered the failed revolution of 1905, which was brutally suppressed and further undermined support for the regime of Czar NICHOLAS II. Russia endured an even bigger disaster during World War I. Millions of conscripted peasants died in combat while millions more suffered from poor supplies, bad equipment, and shoddy leadership. Events crested early in 1917 when the February revolution led to Nicholas's abdication. Russian participation in the war was imperiled by mismanagement, and the German government, eager to further weaken their enemy, allowed Lenin to travel from Switzerland to St. Petersburg in a sealed car. Once in Russia he immediately agitated for an end to hostilities and the immediate redistribution of land to peasants. Bolshevik political

Vladimir Lenin *(Library of Congress)*

obstructionism in the Duma (parliament) negated and brought down the moderately socialist regimes of GEORGI LVOV and ALEKSANDR KERENSKY, and on November 6, 1917, communist revolutionaries captured the czar's Winter Palace in Petrograd, the former St. Petersburg. Competing leftist factions were harshly dealt with, confirming the seriousness of Lenin's insistence upon complete party discipline. The Russian revolution became the first communist insurgency in history, and its sheer ruthlessness underscored stark differences with socialism. Lenin was then installed as chairman of the Council of People's Commissars and ruled Russia as a virtual dictator.

Once in power Lenin faced two immediate challenges: concluding World War I and the onset of civil war. To address the former he advanced the notion of "peace at any price" and signed the humiliating Treaty of Brest-Litovsk with Germany in 1918. This knocked Russia out of the war at a tremendous cost in territory, but it preserved the Russian revolution. Lenin then conducted a bloody civil war pitting revolutionary Red armies against conservative White armies, aided and abetted by the hated West. Millions died, but the most visible victims were the czar and his family, murdered by the Bolsheviks to prevent their release. By 1920 the communists had finally triumphed and Lenin was free to embark on his Marxist-Leninist experiment. Industry was nationalized, farming and agriculture were collectivized, while private property and class distinctions were abolished. Worse, dissent was totally outlawed and political order strictly enforced by the dreaded Cheka, or secret police. This insidious force was empowered to summarily round up and execute all enemies of the state, real or imagined. "It is true that liberty is precious," Lenin once declared, "so precious that it must be rationed." The traditional authoritarian repression of the czars was now updated and modernized by the communists.

In 1918 Lenin barely survived an assassination attempt, and his health had declined ever since. A series of strokes gradually reduced his ability to govern and several contenders began positioning themselves to succeed him. Before he died Lenin had specifically warned the party leadership not to trust JOSEPH STALIN, but his memo was suppressed. Lenin passed away in Gorky on January 21, 1924, hailed by many Russians as the founder of the new Soviet Union. Against his wishes his body was embalmed and placed on permanent display in Red Square, Moscow. But as was predicted and

feared, command gradually passed into the hands of Stalin's heinous cohorts, whose ascent occasioned the rise of a terrible totalitarianism. Lenin nonetheless remains the single most important revolutionary of the 20th century and possibly of all time.

Further Reading

Busky, Donald F. *Communism in History and Theory: From Utopian Socialism to the Fall of the Soviet Union.* Westport, Conn.: Praeger, 2002.

Lenin, Vladimir I. *The Lenin Anthology.* New York: Norton, 1975.

Lee, Stephen J. *Lenin and the Bolsheviks, 1903–1924.* London: Routledge, 2002.

———. *Lenin and Revolutionary Russia.* New York: Routledge, 2003.

Ross, Stewart. *The Russian Revolution.* Austin, Tex.: Raintree-Steck-Vaughn, 2003.

Salomoni, Antonella. *Lenin and the Russian Revolution.* Northampton, Mass.: Interlink, 2002.

Service, Robert. *Lenin—a Biography.* Cambridge, Mass.: Harvard University Press, 2000.

White, James D. *Lenin: His Theory and Practice of Revolution.* New York: Palgrave, 2001.

Lie, Trygve (1896–1968) *secretary general of the United Nations*

Trygve Halvdan Lie was born in Oslo, Norway, on July 16, 1896, the son of a carpenter. He joined the Norwegian Labor Party at 16 and worked his way through the University of Oslo. In 1919 Lie obtained his law degree and served as a legal adviser with the Trade Union Federation. He joined the party's executive board in 1926 and 10 years later won a set in the legislature. Lie subsequently held several ministerial portfolios, including minister of justice and minister of trade. In the former capacity he granted Soviet activist Leon Trotsky asylum in Norway but subsequently expelled him after revelations that he used Norway as a base of operations against JOSEPH STALIN. By 1940 Lie had advanced to foreign minister, a post he held briefly before the German invasion of Norway forced him to flee the country. He then joined the government in exile in London as foreign minister and spent the war coordinating the efforts of Norwegian expatriates. Lie performed capably, and in December 1945 he ventured to San Francisco as head of the Norwegian delegation to the United Nations convention. The UN was envisioned as an international body that would serve as a deterrent to war and would also expedite numerous aid, scientific, and cultural functions. Lie was initially nominated to serve as president of the UN General Assembly, but he lost out to Belgium's Paul Henri Spaak in January 1946. The more important vacancy of secretary general then occurred, and Lie was nominated by Soviet ambassador Andrei A. Gromyko. In February 1946 he was overwhelmingly elected the UN's first secretary general, being endorsed by both the United States and the Soviet Union.

The United Nations, once formed, had yet to solidify its administrative structure and functions. Lie proved invaluable because he resolved that the secretary general's office must be positioned to profoundly affect the conduct of affairs. From his new office in New York City he laid the groundwork for such future agencies as the High Commissioner for Refugees, the International Court of Justice, the Food and Agricultural Organization, and the UN Educational, Scientific, and Cultural Organization (UNESCO). His prior skill as a labor organizer and arbitrator proved essential in establishing workable rules and organizational guidelines. In many respects Lie got the UN on its feet and prepared it for the role and challenges that lay ahead.

Lie assumed his role just as the cold war was entering its initial phases. Although the UN was dominated by Western countries, he trod carefully between Western and Eastern camps to promote objectivity. This became increasingly hard to do in the wake of Soviet misbehavior. Despite initial Soviet support, Lie was distrusted by Stalin who regarded him as little more than a puppet of the United States. Lie greatly resented the inference but he gradually came over into the Western camp after the Berlin Blockade of 1948, the communist coup in Czechoslovakia, the Soviet-inspired Greek civil war, and Soviet occupation of northern Iran. In every instance Lie used his usual tact and diplomacy to prod Russia into moderating its belligerence. He also worked against American resistance toward seating the People's Republic of China. However, the North Korean attack on South Korea in June 1950 was a decisive turning point in the history of the United Nations. Lie strongly condemned communist aggression and organized a speedy vote in the Security Council to authorize a military response to the invasion. Furthermore, he did so in the absence of the Soviet ambassador to the UN, for Russia—as one of five permanent members of the

Security Council—could have easily vetoed the measure. This maneuver greatly angered the Soviets and thereafter they worked diligently to undermine Lie's authority and legitimacy as general secretary.

When Lie's first five-year term expired in October 1950, the Soviets blocked any consideration of a second one. The United States then made it clear that they would accept no candidate other than Lie. The ensuing impasse paralyzed United Nations operations for several weeks until the General Assembly voted overwhelmingly to extend his term by three years. The Soviets then declared the vote illegal and vowed they—and the bloc of nations they controlled—would no longer recognize Lie as secretary general. Lie was then also assailed by U.S. senator Joseph McCarthy, who accused him of appointing disloyal Americans to UN positions. At this juncture, the secretary general threw up his hands and declared he would resign in the interest of promoting harmony. In April 1953 he was replaced by Sweden's DAG HAMMARSKJÖLD and returned to Norway. Lie resumed his political career with the Labor Party and held various ministerial portfolios including mayor of Oslo, minister of industries, and minister of commerce. He died in Geilo on December 30, 1968. Lie's tenure as the first UN secretary general was certainly capable and well-intentioned, but it foundered upon the rocks of cold war superpower rivalry.

Further Reading

Barros, James. *Trygve Lie and the Cold War: The U.N. Secretary General Pursues Peace, 1946–1953.* DeKalb: Northern Illinois University Press, 1989.

———. "Pearson and Lie: The Politics of the Secretary General's Selection, 1946." *Canadian Journal of Political Science* 10, no. 1 (1977): 65–92.

Gaglione, Anthony. *The United Nations under Lie Trygve, 1945–1953.* Lanham, Md.: Scarecrow Press, 2001.

Lie, Trygve. *In the Cause of Peace: Seven Years with the United Nations.* New York: Macmillan, 1954.

Young, Peter Y. S. "A Critical Study of Secretary General Trygve Lie's Crisis Management." Unpublished master's thesis, Occidental College, 1978.

Lini, Walter (1942–1999) *prime minister of Vanuatu*

Walter Lini was born in Agatoa, Pentecost Island, in 1942. His homeland formed part of the New

Hebrides, a chain of 83 islands in the Pacific that was jointly administered by Great Britain and France. Lini was educated locally at missionary schools before entering the ministry at St. Peter's College in the Solomon Islands in 1962. He subsequently passed through St. John's College in Auckland, New Zealand, in 1968, and came home. The following year Lini was ordained a deacon in the Anglican Church. However, the Melanesian population continually chafed under colonial administration and voices were elevated for independence. Lini himself, stung by the racial discrimination he encountered in the church, took up the cause and edited several militant newspapers. In 1973 the movement had gathered sufficient momentum for Lini to found the New Hebrides National Party (Vanua'aku Pati, or VP) and the following year he was elected its first president. He then obtained a leave of absence from church duties to devote all his time to the cause of national independence. His task was greatly complicated by continuing rivalry and obstructionism between native Melanesians, the British-speaking population, and their French-speaking counterparts. But public pressure eventually forced both colonial administrations to accede to legislative elections. In 1975 the VP won the contest resoundingly, yet a crisis ensued when the French refused to yield their appointed seats. Lini felt he had little recourse but to establish a parallel government and proceed. Further negotiations with England and France finally resulted in New Hebrides obtaining its political independence on July 29, 1980, with Lini as its first prime minister. The islands were renamed the Republic of Vanuatu, which means "Our Land Eternally" in the local dialect.

No sooner had Lini consolidated his control of power than a rival group under Jimmy Stephens Nagriamel attempted a secessionist movement on Espiritu Santo, the largest island in the chain. Lini was forced to solicit help from neighboring Papua New Guinea, which provided the troops that put down the rebellion and arrested Nagriamel. With that crisis diffused, the prime minister faced the daunting task of placating various native, French, and English factions among the population. This required tact and diplomacy of a very high order and Lini was initially careful not to offend France as he depended upon its financial assistance. But French intransigence proved insurmountable. Lini then enhanced his national standing among fellow islanders by disputing a French claim to Hunter and Matthew Islands, both uninhabited outcroppings but sources of national pride. Lini also vociferously opposed the French government's decision to resume nuclear testing in the South Pacific. But he enjoyed his biggest success on the domestic front by winning land claims against Europeans on behalf of fellow islanders.

Over the next 11 years, Lini established a popular administration and he was reelected prime minister twice. He also managed to defeat two "no confidence" votes against him in the 1980s, brought on by charges of influence peddling and he also clung to the party leadership. But by 1991 the tenor of Lini's administration became increasingly authoritarian and occasioned complaints from ministers within his own cabinet. When he dismissed the offending executives, Lini was expelled as party head and ousted as prime minister in September 1991. Undeterred, he next formed a new organization, the Vanuatu National Unity Party (VNUP), which split off from the existing VP. Lini mustered a coalition with other small parties until August 1993, when he withdrew from government. Three years later he returned to public life as minister for culture, justice, and women's affairs. Lini died on February 21, 1999, contentious but much respected as the architect of Vanuatu's independence.

Further Reading

Henningham, S. "Pluralism and Party Politics in a South Pacific State: Vanuatu's Ruling Vanua'aku and Its Rivals." *Conflict* 9, no. 2 (1989): 171–196.

Lini, Walter. *Beyond Pandemonium: From the New Hebrides to Vanuatu.* Wellington, New Zealand: Asia Pacific Books, 1980.

Premdas, Ralph R. *Politics and Government in Vanuatu: From Colonial Unity to Postcolonial Disunity.* Saskatoon: University of Saskatchewan, 1989.

———. "Vanuatu: The 1991 Elections and the Emergence of a New Order." *Round Table* no. 313 (January 1990): 43–64.

———. "Melanesian Socialism: Vanuatu's Quest for Self-definition and Problems of Implementation." *Pacific Studies* 11, no. 1 (1987): 107–129.

———, and Jeffrey S. Steeves. "Vanuatu: The Politics of Anglo-French Cooperation in the Post-Lini Era." *Journal of Commonwealth and Comparative Politics* 32 (March 1994): 68–86.

Liu Shaoqi (Liu Shao-ch'i) (1898–1969)

chairman of the People's Republic of China

Liu Shaoqi was born in Hunan Province, China, on November 24, 1898, the son of affluent peasants. He attended the same school as MAO ZEDONG in Chang-sha, and in 1920 he joined the Socialist Youth League. Intrigued by radical politics, Liu next ventured to Moscow to study at the University for the Toilers of the East, where he also joined the nascent Chinese Communist Party (CCP). He returned to China in 1922 and served as a political aide to Mao. He became closely involved with the labor movement and organized several successful strikes. Liu by this time had acquired a reputation as a taciturn, stoic, and highly efficient bureaucrat, completely devoted to the cause of Chinese communism. In 1927 he went underground to organize communist cells behind Nationalist Chinese lines. By 1932 he had rejoined Mao in Jiangxi (Kiangsi) Province and took part in the Long March (1934–35); four years later he became closely associated with the New Fourth Route Army. In this capacity he helped organize armed resistance to Japanese invaders and in 1939 he penned a landmark publication entitled *How to Be a Good Communist*. This pamphlet codified the duties and sacrifices expected of communist party cadres and established Liu as the party's leading theoretician. He thus performed incalculably good work as the organizer and ideologue of the CCP, bequeathing it both an intellectual and practical framework to build upon. Liu had also by this time become such a trusted figure that he served as acting chairman during Mao's absences. The People's Republic of China was proclaimed on October 1, 1949, and Liu, who had done more than any individual besides Mao to ensure a communist triumph, was installed as vice chairman.

Liu's prior experience with the Soviet Union made him an ideal liaison between the two governments, and he was dispatched to Moscow to confer with Premier JOSEPH STALIN. He was thereafter entrusted with running the Sino-Soviet Friendship Association and proved instrumental in securing Russian technical advice and assistance during the initial phases of industrialization. By 1954 he was elevated to chairman of the Standing Committee and tasked with purging uncooperative regional leaders. As early as 1956 the cool, efficient Liu had apparently been chosen by Mao as his heir apparent. But following the failure of Mao's costly Great Leap Forward of 1957–58, which nearly ruined Chinese agri-

culture, Liu authorized policies that relaxed collectivization and permitted private plots and financial incentives. The idealistic Mao, however, denounced such reforms as "capitalistic," and initiated a growing rift between the two leaders and their political vision of China. The trend accelerated after 1959 when Mao stepped down as chairman of the republic and was replaced by Liu. Thereafter a collision between pragmatic moderates under Liu and dogmatic radicals under Mao became inevitable.

As head of state Liu traveled extensively abroad to various communist and Third World countries and unsuccessfully tried to mend relations between China and the Soviet Union's NIKITA KHRUSHCHEV. He even managed to moderate Mao's radicalism with respect to mass industrialization and placed greater emphasis on a Soviet-style centralized state. Mao viewed both moves as a threat to his peasant-oriented ideology, and in 1965 organized and unleashed the youth-oriented Great Proletarian Cultural Revolution. Citizens and party members suspected of being "capitalist roaders" were summarily arrested in droves and sent into the countryside for "reeducation." Not surprisingly, Mao's preeminent target was Liu himself. Commencing in 1966, the chairman was roundly denounced as a "traitor" and a "scab," along with other reformers like Deng Xiaoping. In October 1968 he was stripped of his party credentials and condemned by radicals as the "Chinese Khrushchev." The ailing Liu was then arrested and imprisoned in an unused bank vault in Hunan Province for many months. Denied proper medical treatment, he died there on November 12, 1969, an official non-person. His family was not informed of his fate for years to come.

It was not until the Chinese radicals themselves were purged after the death of Mao in 1976 that Liu's fate became publicly known. In February 1980 Chairman HUA GUOFENG ordered him posthumously rehabilitated, and the forlorn chairman was reinstated as "a great Marxist and proletarian revolutionary." Liu remains the most prominent victim of the notorious Cultural Revolution, and his untimely demise underscores the essentially divisive and murderous nature of Chinese communist politics.

Further Reading

Dittmer, Lowell. "The Chinese Cultural Revolution Revisited: The Role of the Nemesis." *Journal of Contemporary China* 5 (November 1996): 255–268.

————. *Liu Shaoqi and the Chinese Cultural Revolution.* Armonk, N.Y.: M. E. Sharpe, 1998.

Law, Kam-yee, ed. *The Chinese Cultural Revolution Reconsidered.* New York: Palgrave Macmillan, 2003.

Liu Shaoqi. *Selected Works of Liu Shaoqi.* New York: Foreign Languages Press; Distributed by Pergamon Press, 1984.

Liu, Shin Il. "The Relationships among Ideology, Policy, and Economic Performance: Mao Tsetung, Liu Shacci, and the Economy in China." Unpublished Ph.D. diss., University of Nebraska, Lincoln, 1991.

Teiwes, Frederick C. *Politics at Mao's Court.* Armonk, N.Y.: M. E. Sharpe, 1989.

Lleras Camargo, Alberto (1906–1990) *president of Colombia*

Alberto Lleras Camargo was born in Bogotá, Colombia, on July 3, 1906, into a middle-class family with a long tradition of public service. He briefly attended the National University in Bogotá to study politics, but dropped out to pursue journalism. Lleras then commenced his long association with the Liberal Party by editing several of their newspapers. He also developed an interest in politics, and by 1931, he had gained election to the Chamber of Deputies as a Liberal. At that time the long political ascendancy of the rival Conservative Party was ending, and Alfonso López Pumarejo became the first Liberal president of the 20th century. Lleras joined the administration as his general secretary and in 1935 he became minister of government, the youngest such official in Colombian history. By 1938 Lleras had strayed back into journalism by founding *El Liberal,* the nation's second-largest newspaper, but he subsequently returned to the Chamber of Deputies. In 1943 he served briefly as ambassador to the United States but was soon recalled to serve as minister of government again. Two years later President López suddenly resigned from office, and Lleras succeeded him as an interim executive—he was then one of the world's youngest heads of state. In 1946 the Conservatives returned to power and Lleras resumed his journalistic endeavors.

In 1947 Lleras made history by becoming the first Latin American executive of the Pan American Union, a collective deliberative body of North and South American countries. A year later this was renamed the Organization of American States (OAS) with Lleras as its first secretary general. For the next six years he functioned efficiently and sought to impose unity and consensus among the squabbling members. His greatest single accomplishment was in positioning the OAS as an instrument for the peaceful settlement of disputes. But these efforts were ultimately thwarted by ongoing divisiveness, and he tendered his resignation in 1954. Lleras then returned to Colombia to serve as rector of the University of the Andes and to dabble once more in journalism. The nation was then controlled by an unpopular military dictatorship run by GUSTAVO ROJAS PINILLA, and in July 1956 Lleras ventured to Spain to confer with exiled Conservative president LAUREANO GÓMEZ CASTRO to discuss plans for overthrowing the regime. They settled upon establishment of the new National Front, under which control of the national government would alternate between Conservative and Liberal administrations on a regular basis. Rojas Pinilla was subsequently overthrown by a coup in July 1957 and the following year Lleras became the first president elected under the power-sharing scheme. Through this unique political expedient, which lasted 16 years, peace and political stability were finally restored to Colombia.

Over the next four years Lleras and his National Front administration set about restoring the nation's economic vitality. Since 1945 Colombia had been rocked by politically inspired violence between Conservative and Liberal Party adherents. This outbreak, known as La Violencia, had cost the lives of some 200,000 citizens and Lleras determined to end it. He therefore legalized freedom of speech and freedom of the press, and resurrected long-suppressed civil rights. The government also enacted austerity measures to bring down inflation, reduced overall imports, and expanded government services to the needy. By 1959 the levels of violence in the countryside had been greatly reduced, so he lifted the decade-old state of emergency. When Lleras finally left office in 1964, the country was on a much firmer and more peaceful footing. Part of his success lay with cultivating friendly ties to the United States, whereby he obtained generous technical assistance and financial aid. Lleras was stridently anticommunist and actively encouraged the OAS to politically quarantine Fidel Castro's Cuba. Out of office, he resumed his journalistic career by founding several influential magazines while also serving as a distinguished elder statesman. Lleras died in Bogotá on January 4, 1990, still regarded as one of Colombia's most successful politicians and a South American figure with international stature.

Further Reading

Kofas, Jon V. *The Sword of Damocles: U.S. Financial Hegemony in Colombia and Chile, 1950–1970.* Westport, Conn.: Praeger, 2002.

Lleras Camargo, Alberto. *The Inter-American Way of Life: Selections from the Recent Addresses and Writings of Alberto Lleras.* Washington, D.C.: Pan American Union, 1951.

———. *The Organization of American States: An Example for the World.* Lewisburg, Pa.: Bucknell University Press, 1954.

Lulow, Anne K. "Alberto Lleras Camargo, First Secretary General of the Organization of American States." Unpublished Ph.D. diss., American University, 1972.

Roldan, Mary. *Blood and Life: La Violencia in Antioquia, Colombia, 1946–1953.* Durham, N.C.: Duke University Press, 2002.

Stafford, Frank. *Colombia: Fragmented Land and Divided Society.* New York: Oxford University Press, 2002.

Lloyd George, David (first earl Lloyd-George of Dwyfar) (1863–1945) *prime minister of Great Britain*

David Lloyd George was born in Manchester, England, on January 17, 1863, the son of Welsh schoolteacher William George. His father died during his infancy, and he was raised in Wales by his uncle, Richard Lloyd. Thereafter he adopted both surnames. Lloyd George was indifferently educated, but he eventually joined a law firm as a clerk. Bright and expeditious, he studied law on his own and was finally called to the bar in 1884. After several years of successful practice, Lloyd George commenced his political career in 1890 with a seat in the House of Commons from Caernarvon—which he held for the next 55 years. Over the intervening decades, Lloyd George established himself as a rabble-rousing radical within the Liberal Party. In 1895 he successfully passed legislation that removed the Church of England as the official church of Wales, and Welsh citizens who were not Anglican no longer paid taxes to support it. In 1900 he made national headlines by stridently opposing the Boer War in South Africa. When the Liberals resumed power in 1905 under HENRY CAMPBELL-BANNERMAN, Lloyd George was appointed president of the board of trade and gained a reputation as a brilliant administrator. In 1908 a new Liberal prime minister, HERBERT HENRY ASQUITH, made him chancellor of the Exchequer. Again, Lloyd George garnered national prominence by pioneering radical social legislation, such as the Old Age Pensions Act and the National Insurance Act. In April 1909 he also promulgated the so-called People's Budget, which raised taxes on the rich to pay for old-age pensions and increase naval expenditures. When the House of Lords vetoed the bill, a constitutional crisis ensued, and Lloyd George had a prominent role in reducing the Lords' ability to impede budget legislation. Through these acts he became celebrated as "the people's champion."

Lloyd George initially opposed Britain's participation in World War I, but when German armies violated Belgian neutrality in August 1914, he gave the war effort wholehearted support. Asquith transferred him to the Ministry of Munitions, where he worked wonders in cutting through red tape, visiting factories to encourage production, and greatly enhancing procurement. In June 1916 Lloyd George became minister of war following the death of Lord Kitchener. Here he made positive contributions to the war by dismissing incompetent generals and arguing for campaigns against the Balkans and Middle East. However, Lloyd George and many Conservative politicians were disillusioned by Asquith's seemingly lackluster direction of the war. In December 1916 he resigned from the war ministry, an act that brought down the Asquith government, and he was subsequently appointed prime minister with the help of Conservative ANDREW BONAR LAW. The coup was well timed and adroitly handled, but it forever split the Liberal Party into two competing factions. Nonetheless the dynamic, energetic Lloyd George was finally in his prime. He proved instrumental in bolstering the British war effort, increasing wartime production, and better coordinating men and materiel on the Continent. In concert with French prime minister GEORGES CLEMENCEAU, the invigorated Allies forced Germany to sign an armistice in November 1918. Elections that fall went overwhelmingly to the Conservatives, although they opted to keep Liberal Lloyd George as prime minister through dint of sheer popularity. During the Paris peace talks of 1919, he moderated between the punitive measures of

Clemenceau and the unbridled idealism of American president WOODROW WILSON. Once the treaty was signed, Lloyd George was hailed at home as the "man who won the war."

The onset of peace ushered in a period of political instability in British politics. In 1921 Lloyd George finally granted Ireland home rule, although at the expense of Conservative support. His efforts at introducing new social legislation also came to naught. The breaking point occurred in 1922 over the prospect of war with Turkey, and the Conservatives under Arthur Baldwin withdrew from the coalition. Unfortunately for Lloyd George, the Liberals remained badly split over his handling of Asquith's dismissal, and they never again rose to power. He nonetheless became party head in 1926 and led them until 1931. He also argued over the next two decades for the implementation of far-reaching social reforms, especially after the Great Depression commenced in 1929. Lloyd George then turned his attention back to European affairs, and in 1935 expressed mistaken admiration for ADOLF HITLER's economic policies. Five years later he strongly criticized Prime Minister NEVILLE CHAMBERLAIN's policy of appeasing the Nazis and supported his replacement by WINSTON CHURCHILL. Churchill cordially invited the old war hero to serve in his cabinet, but he declined owing to poor health. Lloyd George spent his last years confined to home, where he was elevated to the peerage. He died in Ty Newydd, Wales, on March 26, 1945, one of England's greatest wartime leaders and one of the 20th century's most outspoken proponents of social reform. However, his very success spelled the demise of the Liberals as a force in national politics.

Further Reading

Grayson, Richard S. *Liberals, International Relations, and Appeasement: The Liberal Party, 1919–1939.* Portland, Ore.: Frank Cass, 2001.

Grigg, John. *Lloyd George: War Leader, 1916–1918.* New York: Penguin Putnam, 2002.

Johnson, Gaynor. "Curzon, Lloyd George, and the Control of British Foreign Policy, 1919–22: A Reassessment." *Diplomacy and Statecraft* 11 (November 2000): 49–71.

Lentin, Anthony. *Lloyd George and the Lost Peace: From Versailles to Hitler, 1919–1940.* London: Palgrave, 2001.

Lloyd George, David. *War Memoirs of David Lloyd George,* 6 vols. Boston: Little, Brown, and Company, 1933–37.

Packer, Ian L. G. *Lloyd George, Liberalism, and the Land: The Land Issue and Party Politics in England, 1906–1914.* Rochester, N.Y.: Boydell Press, 2001.

Veeder, V. V. "Lloyd George, Lenin, and Cannibals: The Harriman Arbitration." *Arbitration International* 16, no. 2 (2000): 39–115.

Winter, J. M. *The Great War and the British People.* New York: Palgrave, 2003.

Lon Nol (1913–1985) *president of Cambodia*

Lon Nol was born in Prey Veng Province, Cambodia, on November 13, 1913, the son of a civil servant. He received a French education locally and went on to attend the prestigious Lycée Chasseloup Laubat in Saigon. He returned home in 1937 and joined the colonial civil service as a magistrate. A simple man, Lon also expressed great devotion to the ruling crown prince, Norodom Sihanouk, who assisted in getting him a military commission. After Cambodia achieved independence from France in 1955, Lon was appointed as head of the Cambodian armed forces. He served his prince loyally, ruthlessly suppressing all forms of political dissent. He was particularly quick to direct his anger against ethnic Vietnamese living in Cambodia, whom he hated. Sihanouk nonetheless found him a pliant subordinate, and in 1966 he appointed Lon prime minister. By this time the war in neighboring South Vietnam was expanding, and the communist government in Hanoi began using Cambodian territory as a sanctuary against American bombing. This greatly angered the Cambodian military, who wished to drive the invaders out, but Sihanouk opted for a course of strict neutrality. As long as the Vietnamese communists did not interfere in Cambodian politics he turned a blind eye to their presence. But on March 18, 1970, Lon and Vice Premier Sirak Matak executed a bloodless coup that toppled the regime. Thereafter Cambodia was closely allied with the United States in the war against North Vietnam.

Once in command, Lon carried out an extensive purge of Vietnamese living in Cambodia, in which several thousand people died. He allowed the Americans to conduct intensive bombing operations against communist bases throughout the country. In retaliation, the Vietnamese began arming and training an indigenous communist force, the Khmer Rouge, under POL POT, who fought a guerrilla war against Lon and his American sponsors. Worse, in May 1970 American forces in South Vietnam invaded Cambodia in a futile attempt to shut down communist sanctuaries. The Vietnamese simply pulled farther into the interior, brushing aside inept Cambodian resistance, and assisting the Khmer Rouge to entrench themselves deeper in the countryside. The escalating cycle of violence destabilized the economy and, with it, Cambodia's ability to feed itself. Desperate peasants flocked to the Khmer Rouge for support in order to survive, swelling their ranks and expanding the insurgency.

To shore up their hard-pressed ally, the United States poured millions of dollars in financial and military aid into Cambodia. Lon, however, proved as corrupt as he was incompetent. His cronies routinely skimmed off money for themselves, while their soldiers, never paid or supplied, looted peasant villages and stole their food. Worst of all, Lon was a confirmed mystic: in virtually every matter of state, he consulted his astrologer, and acted accordingly. His ineptitude turned the majority of Cambodia's population against the central government, whose leadership had grown increasingly detached from reality. Lon began spouting grandiose, impractical schemes to solve the nation's problems, and exhorted his soldiers to cast magic spells on the enemy to defeat them. Such behavior, in concert with continuing corruption and repression, only exacerbated his lack of popular support. He retired from office briefly in 1972, then returned with a new constitution proclaiming the new Khmer Republic with himself as president. For three years he tried to control his rapidly deteriorating situation, while the United States stepped up its secret bombing and the Khmer Rouge kept increasing in strength. By 1973 communist forces controlled two-thirds of the countryside and were firmly ensconced on the outskirts of the capital of Phnom Penh. Two more years of bloody stalemate followed before Lon fled the country on April 1, 1975, just before the victorious Khmer Rouge took the city.

Lon fled to the United States and set up a luxurious residence in Hawaii. His countrymen, meanwhile, were rounded up by Pol Pot's henchmen and forced into death camps, where several million perished. Lon himself died in Fullerton, California, on November 17, 1985, having overseen one of the more quixotic interludes of the long and bloody Southeast Asian war.

Further Reading

Chandler, David P. *The Tragedy of Cambodian History: Politics, War, and Revolution since 1945.* New Haven, Conn.: Yale University Press, 1991.

Coleman, J. D. *Incursion: From America's Choke-hold on the NVA Lifelines to the Sacking of the Cambodian Sanctuaries.* New York: St. Martin's Press, 1991.

Corfield, Justin J. *Khmers Stand Up!: A History of the Cambodian Government, 1970–1975.* Clayton, Victoria: Centre of Southeast Asian Studies, Monash University, 1994.

Kamm, Henry. *Cambodia: Report from a Stricken Land.* New York: Arcade Pub., 1998.

Peac, Wilfred P. *Road to the Killing Fields: The Cambodian War of 1970–1975.* College Station: Texas A & M University Press, 1997.

Scott, Peter. *Lost Crusade: America's Secret Cambodian Mercenaries.* Annapolis, Md.: Naval Institute Press, 1998.

López Mateos, Adolfo (1910–1969) *president of Mexico*

Adolfo López Mateos was born in Atizapán de Zaragoza, Mexico State, Mexico, on May 26, 1910, the son of a dentist. His father died during his infancy and his mother relocated to Mexico City where he was educated. By 1934 he had passed through the National Autonomous University with a law degree and entered politics, becoming a regional secretary of the National Revolutionary Party (PNR), subsequently renamed the Institutional Revolutionary Party (PRI). López Mateos functioned capably, and in 1946 he gained appointment to the national Senate, where he sat six years. In 1952 he served as the campaign manager for PRI presidential aspirant ADOLFO RUIZ CORTINES. Following the election, López Mateos was appointed his minister of labor. Here he demonstrated considerable finesse in resolving several bitter disputes and ended up conducting over 10,000 arbitrations. His success, coupled with intelligence, drive, and good oratory skills, won him a nomination as Ruiz Cortines's successor in 1958. Because Mexico was a tightly controlled one-party state, any PRI nomination was virtually guaranteed to win, and López Mateos garnered 90 percent of votes cast. He also became the first Mexican executive to have originated from within the labor ministry.

López Mateos proved a distinct departure from previous PRI candidates, who were very conservative and favorably inclined toward business. In fact the new executive declared himself as "left within the constitution," and sought to embrace the egalitarian ideals of the Mexican Revolution. He quickly adopted new programs aimed at accelerating the pace of social reform. López Mateos's greatest success was in land redistribution to poor peasants: in six years he allocated no less than 30 million acres, an amount exceeded only by the other great reformer, LÁZARO CÁRDENAS. He next invoked an obscure article in the Mexican constitution that stipulated a profit-sharing agreement between industry and its workers. A government board drew up a complicated profit-sharing formula for various aspects of the economy, and by 1964 most Mexican wages increased by 5 to 10 percent. López Mateos was equally quick to implement changes to government-funded medical care and retirement pensions. Public health programs were also enlarged and expanded upon, with commensurate declines in serious maladies like polio, tuberculosis, and malaria.

Under López Mateos, Mexico's foreign policy also displayed a pronounced leftist bent, and he embraced deeply held beliefs of self-determination and nonintervention. He was openly sympathetic toward the Cuban revolution of Fidel Castro and opposed the Organization of American States (OAS) in its attempts to politically quarantine the island. He also spearheaded an effort to eliminate foreign control of the electrical industry through nationalization. However, López Mateos also cultivated friendly ties with American president JOHN F. KENNEDY. His cordial relations paid dividends in 1963, during settlement of a border dispute along the Rio Grande separating the two nations. When the river shifted northward it left barren a strip of land called El Chamizal on the Mexican side that both countries claimed. Astute negotiations convinced the Americans to transfer the territory to Mexico, signifying the first such peaceful acquisition of land since 1854.

For all his leftist credentials, López Mateos was no communist sympathizer. From the onset of his tenure in office, his administration was faced with a series of potentially crippling strikes, all of which he settled by force. He was particularly rough on a strike by railway workers and had their communist leadership arrested. The government borrowed heavily and spent lavishly on improving the national infrastructure, including new roads, dams, and low-cost public housing. Mexico consequently experienced six years of unprecedented growth and a booming economy. López Mateos then determined to tackle the problem of widespread illiteracy head-on through government publication of standardized school texts. This gave rise to criticism from the Catholic Church, whose schools were forced to use the books, but it spurred the growth of mass literacy. By the time López Mateos stepped down in 1964 and was succeeded by GUSTAVO DÍAZ ORDAZ, the nation was in excellent economic shape. In 1967 he was tapped to head the national committee that brought the XIX Olympics to Mexico City, but declining health forced him to relinquish his duties. López Mateos died in Mexico City on September 22, 1969, being one of the most successful and popular chief executives in Mexican political history.

Further Reading

Engel, James F. "Mexican Reaction to the United States Cuban Policy, 1959–1963." Unpublished Ph.D. diss., University of Virginia, 1964.

Middlebrook, Kevin J. *The Paradox of Revolution: Labor, the State, and Authoritarianism in Mexico.* Baltimore: Johns Hopkins University, 1995.

Preston, Julia. *Opening Mexico: A Country's Tumultuous Passage to Democracy.* New York: Farrar, Straus and Giroux, 2004.

Purcell, Susan K. "Decision Making in an Authoritarian Regime: Theoretical Implications for a Mexican Case Study." *World Politics* 26, no. 1 (1973): 28–54.

Smith, Arthur K. "Mexico and the Cuban Revolution: Foreign Policy Making in Mexico under President Adolfo López Mateos, 1958–1964." Unpublished Ph.D. diss., Cornell University, 1970.

Williams, Edward J. "Mexico's Central American Policy: Apologies, Motivations, and Principles." *Bulletin of Latin American Research* 2, no. 1 (1983): 21–41.

López Portillo, José (1920–2004) *president of Mexico*

José López Portillo was born in Mexico City, Mexico, on June 16, 1920, the son of an engineer. He was educated locally and attended both the University of Chile and the National Autonomous University in Mexico City. In 1947 he began teaching as a professor of law and political science. López Portillo did not formally commence his political career until 1958, aged 39 years, when he served as an adviser to president ADOLFO LÓPEZ MATEOS. He was then rewarded with a post within the Secretariat of National Patrimony, which controlled the nation's natural resources. For a decade López Portillo functioned capably, if quietly, and in 1973 his close friend President LUIS ECHEVERRÍA appointed him finance minister. He initiated several useful reforms of the tax code to improve collection and reduce cheating. In light of his excellent bureaucratic performance, Echeverría made him the presidential candidate of the Partido Revolucionario Institucional (PRI), Institutional Revolutionary Party, in 1976. Mexico then being a tightly controlled, one-party state, his victory was virtually assured. He nonetheless conducted an active campaign, promising to improve economic planning and streamline the bureaucracy. López Portillo was formally sworn into office on December 1, 1976—after all opposition parties boycotted the election.

The new executive was more conservatively oriented than his predecessors and sought to make amends with the estranged business community. He therefore deemphasized land redistribution while paying greater attention to industrial growth and development. López Portillo assumed office at a fortuitous time, for Mexico had recently discovered vast oil reserves, among the world's largest. The price of that commodity had never been higher, thanks to the Arab oil embargo of 1973, and López Portillo sought to underwrite modernization with petroleum revenues. Mexico, which enjoyed excellent credit ratings, then borrowed heavily on the world money market and invested funding in state-owned factories and other industries. Foremost among these was PEMEX, the national oil company, which would develop the nation's oil resources—Mexico soon became the world's fourth-largest oil exporter. López Portillo also took a crack at political reform by expanding the Chamber of Deputies to 400 seats, of which 100 were reserved for previously suppressed opposition parties. He also drastically streamlined the national bureaucracy in the hopes of improving efficiency and accountability.

Overseas López Portillo pursued an independent approach to foreign policy. He did not support U.S. president JIMMY CARTER's call for a boycott of the 1980 Moscow Olympics following the Soviet invasion of Afghanistan. Openly sympathetic to the communist-inspired Sandinista revolution in Nicaragua, he also expressed support for leftist rebel forces in El Salvador. This placed him on a collision course with the next U.S. president, RONALD REAGAN, who strove to isolate the movements politically. Relations between the two neighbors sank accordingly, and worsened when Reagan refused to lend the Mexican government additional money. However, following the death of Spanish dictator FRANCISCO FRANCO in 1975, López Portillo resumed diplomatic relations with Spain for the first time in four decades. But events took a dramatic turn for the worse in 1981 when the worldwide oil glut caused prices to plunge, greatly reducing Mexico's gross annual income. The country was then unable to make payments on its foreign debt, and capital began fleeing the country in search of safer markets. López Portillo responded in 1982 by nationalizing the banking industry, which convinced many observers that he had lost control of the situation. Mexico's economic instability ultimately triggered a debt crisis throughout Latin America that lasted well into the 1980s.

By the time López Portillo turned over the reins of power to MIGUEL DE LA MADRID on December 1, 1982, the Mexican economy was in a shambles. The national debt had mushroomed to $80 billion—four times what it had been in 1976—which accelerated inflationary pressures. Moreover the peso had to be devalued to the ratio of 100 per U.S. dollar, its lowest rate ever. But worst of all was the pervasive sense of corruption and nepotism that permeated all sectors of government and business. De la Madrid took legal action against several high-level officials, including the head of PEMEX, to account for billions of petro-dollars that had been either stolen or squandered. López Portillo for his part was never charged with corruption, but onlookers angrily noted that he left office a conspicuously wealthy man, far in excess of what a presidential salary would allow. He has since relocated to Europe and has steadfastly declined all invitations to be interviewed. López Portillo's tenure in office, which began with such high hopes, proved devastating to the Mexican economy and to the office of the presidency.

Further Reading

Castañeda, Jorge. *Perpetuating Power: How Mexican Presidents Were Chosen.* New York: New Press, 2000.

Eschbach, Cheryl L. "Dilemmas of Sovereignty: Mexican Policy toward Central America under Presidents López Portillo and De la Madrid." Unpublished Ph.D. diss., Princeton University, 1989.

Meacham, Tina L. "Mexican Foreign Policy under Jose López Portillo." Unpublished master's thesis, Texas Tech University, 1984.

Preston, Julia. *Opening Mexico: A Country's Tumultuous Passage to Democracy.* New York: Farrar, Straus and Giroux, 2004.

Richmond, Douglas. "Crisis in Mexico: Luis Echeverria and López Portillo, 1970–1982." *Journal of Third World Studies* 5, no. 1 (1986): 160–171.

Schmidt, Henry C. "The Mexican Foreign Debt and the Sexennial Transformation from López Portillo to De la Madrid." *Mexican Studies* 1, no. 2 (1985): 227–254.

Lumumba, Patrice (1925–1961) *prime minister of Congo*

Patrice Emergy Lumumba was born in Kasai Province, Belgian Congo, on July 2, 1925, a member of the small Batetela tribe. He was educated locally at Catholic and Protestant missionary schools, where he familiarized himself with the writings of Karl Marx. Lumumba was extremely intelligent, and by the time he reached adulthood he attained fluency in French and several local dialects. In 1954 he found employment with the colonial administration as a postal clerk in Statesville (Kisangani), where he worked his way up to the status of an *évolué*, a highly westernized African civil servant. Under Belgian colonial administration, that was the highest rank to which a black African could aspire. In this capacity Lumumba began testing the waters of national politics by writing articles on the subject of national independence. This activity brought him to the attention of Belgian authorities, and in 1956 Lumumba was arrested and charged with embezzling postal funds. He was released the following year and found employment with a brewery in Leopoldville, but the experience only hardened his attitude toward colonialism. In 1957 he helped found the Mouvement National Congolais (MNC), Congo National Movement, with fellow *évolués* and began agitating for complete independence from Belgium. The Congo had seen earlier party formations, but the MNC was distinct in being nationally, not ethnically, based. In 1958 Lumumba ventured to Accra, Ghana, to attend the All-African People's Conference, where he met and befriended such Pan-African nationalists as KWAME NKRUMAH. Thereafter he grew increasingly impatient with colonial rule and delivered fiery speeches on behalf of independence. Belgian authorities arrested him again in November 1959 for inciting violence, but Lumumba by now was the most popular national figure in the colony. In 1960 he was allowed to attend the Roundtable Conference in Brussels that established a timetable for granting independence. General elections were held in May 1960, and the MNC won the largest number of seats, although short of an absolute majority. A coalition deal was then struck whereby Lumumba became prime minister and JOSEPH KASAVUBU of the rival ABAKO party served as president.

From the onset the two willful leaders were at cross purposes with each other. Lumumba was a proponent of a unified state, governed by a strong central government. In contrast Kasavubu was a federalist who envisioned the Congo as a collection of semi-autonomous states. However, no sooner did they assume power than the national army rebelled in several locations. This act emboldened the governor of the copper-rich province of Katanga, MÖISE TSHOMBE, to secede from the Congo altogether. Shortly after, the region of Southern Kasai also rebelled. The internal tumult only heightened when Belgium rushed in troops to protect its citizens and their property. Lumumba was enraged and felt that Europeans were trying to reassert colonial control. He demanded that the United Nations act immediately to evict the foreigners and help restore order. The UN complied but made no move against the Belgians or the rebels. Feeling betrayed, Lumumba made overtures to the Soviet Union to send troops to quell the rebellions. Kasavubu, staunchly Western in outlook, was repelled by Lumumba's actions, and on September 5, 1960, he summarily dismissed him from office. Lumumba countered by declaring the move unconstitutional and declared Kasavubu ineligible for high office. The National Assembly, meanwhile, quickly reinstated both men until a faction of the army under Colonel Joseph Desire Mobutu deposed the government on September 14, 1960.

Within days Kasavubu was restored to the presidency and the United Nations quickly recognized him as the Congo's sole legitimate leader. Lumumba, under house arrest for several months, was championed by the

Patrice Lumumba *(Library of Congress)*

Soviet Bloc and China. What happened next is not entirely clear. Lumumba managed to slip past his captors and made for Stanleyville but was apparently captured by soldiers loyal to Tshombe. After detaining him for several days, his captors flew him to Elisabethville, where, on January 18, 1961, the former prime minister was murdered. Lumumba's death triggered a wave of resentment throughout Africa and the world. He was lionized by the Soviet Union, which named Patrice Lumumba University in Moscow in his honor. The slain prime minister had served his nation too briefly to make a positive impact, but he transcended death to become one of Africa's best known symbols of nationalism and anticolonialism.

Further Reading

DeWitt, Ludo. *The Assassination of Lumumba.* New York: Verso, 2001.

Edgerton, Robert B. *The Troubled Heart of Africa: A History of the Congo.* New York: St. Martin's Press, 2002.

Fetter, Bruce. "Who Murdered Lumumba?" *Journal of African History* 43, no. 2 (2002): 313–376.

Gondola, Didier. *The History of the Congo.* Westport, Conn.: Greenwood Press, 2003.

Kyle, Keith. "Lumumba." *International Affairs* 78, no. 3 (2002): 595–604.

Lumumba, Patrice. *Congo, My Country.* New York: Praeger, 1962.

———. *Lumumba Speaks: The Speeches and Writings of Patrice Lumumba, 1958–1961.* Boston: Little, Brown, 1972.

Lvov, Georgi (1861–1925) *prime minister of Russia*

Prince Georgi Yevgenyevich Lvov was born in Tula, Russia, on November 2, 1861, the son of an impoverished aristocrat. His family was among the country's most illustrious and traced its lineage back to the ninth century. Because of his poverty, Lvov was raised among the peasantry and closely identified with them and their plight—in contrast to his fellow aristocrats. He subsequently acquired a law degree from the University of Moscow, before joining the civil service in the ministry of internal affairs. Lvov became closely affiliated with the *zemstvo* (provincial council) movement then springing up around Russia, and in 1902 he became chairman of the Tula branch. He professed his belief that the aristocracy was obliged to help improve society by working on behalf of the people. His reputation soon spread among progressive political circles throughout Russia, and he organized *zemstvos* in other districts. Once the movement formed secret societies to discuss constitutional reforms, Czar NICHOLAS II dismissed radical members in 1899. Lvov then continued on as head of the Beseda, a secret discussion group propagating the need for constitutional reform. His reputation was further enhanced after the Russo-Japanese War erupted in 1904, when he ventured to Asia to organize medical relief efforts for wounded soldiers. His success made him a national hero in a conflict otherwise marred by disaster. In 1905 Lvov became vice chairman of the national *zemstvo*, Russia's first national assembly.

Mounting political unrest after 1905 forced the czar to allow formation of political parties, and Lvov joined the Constitutional Democrats or Kadets. His criticism of the government's slowness in implementing reform led to his dismissal from the Tula *zemstvo*, but the following year he was elected to represent the Kadets in the newly formed Duma, Russia's first legislature. This body convened in May 1906 but was dissolved by Nicholas II two months later because of its radical tenor. This dismissal only enhanced Lvov's national stature as a progressive reformer while underscoring his calls for dramatic political change. When World War I began in August 1914 Lvov gained successive appointments as head of the All Russian Union of Zemstvos and of the Zemgor (Union of Zemstvos and Towns). These were created to assist the military in dealing with issues of logistics, supplies, and mobilization. The Russian army administration proved sadly inept throughout the war, and the union, under Lvov's competent leadership, performed useful work. But by 1917 Russia was on the verge of military and political collapse. Lvov by then reluctantly supported the idea that a revolution was necessary to modernize and democratize the political establishment. This lukewarm endorsement further enhanced his popularity among the various factions vying for power behind the scenes. The February revolution of 1917 finally induced the czar to abdicate, and a new provisional government was installed in his place. Lvov, given his national reputation for competence and progressive reform, was the natural choice to lead Russia during its flirtation with democracy. He became Russia's first democratically elected prime minister on March 15, 1917.

Sadly, Lvov's administration lasted only four months. Intent on maintaining a moderate course, he was continually undermined by more radical Social Democrats and the small but vocal Bolsheviks of VLADIMIR LENIN. Moreover, he feared violence and was loath to impose order by military force. Chaos and paralysis ensued. When a popular uprising in Petrograd (St. Petersburg) had to be suppressed by force, Lvov gave up and turned the government over to the moderate socialist ALEKSANDR KERENSKY on July 21, 1917. When Kerensky subsequently failed to either improve the national condition or bring about political stability, he was overthrown in turn by the Bolsheviks that October. Lvov was arrested for several months, but was eventually released and relocated to the United States. When he failed to convince President WOODROW WILSON to recognize his deposed administration, he ventured to Paris for the same purpose. Lvov failed once again, but not until 1923 did he finally admit that Lenin's communist regime apparently enjoyed popular support. He died in Paris on March 7, 1925, a moderate, well-intentioned reformer swept away by the forces of revolution.

Further Reading

Holquist, Peter. *Making War, Forging Revolution: Russia's Continuum of Crisis, 1914–1921.* Cambridge, Mass.: Harvard University Press, 2002.

Lvov, Georgi. *Russian Union of Zemstvos: A Brief Report of the Union's Activities during the War.* London: P. S. King and Son, Ltd., 1917.

Porter, Thomas E. "Prince Georgii Evgenevich Lvov: A Russian Public Servant." *Canadian-American Slavic Studies* 31, no. 4 (1997): 375–396.

Raleigh, Donald J. *Experiencing Russia's Civil War: Politics, Society, and Revolutionary Culture in Saratov, 1917–22.* Princeton, N.J.: Princeton University Press, 2002.

Sanborn, Joshua A. *Drafting the Russian Nation: Military Conscription, Total War, and Mass Politics, 1905–1925.* DeKalb: Northern Illinois University Press, 2003.

Wood, Alan. *The Origins of the Russian Revolution, 1867–1917.* New York: Routledge, 2003.

M

Macapagal, Diosdado P. (1911–1997) *president of the Philippines*

Diosdado Macapagal was born in Lubao, the Philippines, on September 28, 1911, the son of poor peasant farmers. He overcame abject poverty to attend the University of Santo Tomas in Manila, obtaining a law degree in 1941. Throughout World War II he maintained his legal practice under Japanese occupation, allegedly to gather intelligence for the underground resistance. After the war he returned to school, received a doctorate in law, and served with the legal division of the Department of Foreign Affairs. By 1948 Macapagal was employed at the national embassy in Washington, D.C., and the following year he functioned as a counselor on legal affairs in the Foreign Relations Department. In 1949 he won a seat in the House of Representatives as part of the Liberal Party. In 1951 Macapagal gained international recognition as chairman of the Philippine UN delegation when he debated the Soviet foreign minister over the Korean War. By 1957 his national renown was such that he easily won his party's nomination as vice president and was elected along with CARLOS P. GARCIA of the National Party. Despite this success, Macapagal was treated as an outcast by Garcia and was deliberately excluded from cabinet meetings. He endured this abuse for four years before running against Garcia in the presidential contest

of 1961. Macapagal toured the country widely, proudly celebrating his peasant origins and declared "Let me reap for you the harvest of the poor. Let us break the chain of poverty." He stridently denounced Garcia for the graft permeating his administration and promised a crusade against corruption. In November 1961 Macapagal was elected the fifth president of the Philippine Republic by a wide margin.

Macapagal came to office determined to relieve the plight of the poor majority. In August 1963 he managed to pass the landmark Land Reform Code, which replaced the colonial tenancy tradition with a leasehold system that allowed peasants to own the land they worked. This was undertaken partly to diffuse longstanding communist-inspired unrest in central Luzon over the issue of land ownership. He also enacted a major public clearance program to create new farmland and enhance national food sufficiency. Moreover, to reduce unemployment rates, Macapagal allowed the national currency to float, removed foreign exchange controls, and eliminated tariffs on consumer goods. The Philippine economy was thus decentralized while foreign investment and economic diversification were encouraged.

Macapagal also made an impact on international affairs. Despite long ties to the United States he wished the Philippines to be more oriented toward neighboring

Asian countries. In July 1962 he promulgated his plan for a Pan-Asian Union among the Philippines, Indonesia, and Malaysia. On July 31, 1962, Macapagal signed the Manila Accord, which laid the groundwork for an agreement with Indonesia's SUKARNO and Malaya's ABDUL RAHMAN. However, the idea collapsed the following year after Great Britain sponsored its own scheme for a Federation of Malaysia. Macapagal was sternly anticommunist and vowed never to recognize the People's Republic of China. But he further distanced himself from the United States in 1961 by changing the date of Filipino independence from July 4 to June 12. This was the day in 1898 when General Emilio Aguinaldo first declared independence from Spain and better reflected Philippine priorities.

For all his good intentions Macapagal proved no more successful at rooting out corruption than his predecessor. He had previously dismissed dishonest officials and reiterated his commitment to help the nation's poor majority. But this did not prevent vested interests in congress and the private sector from accumulating vast amounts of wealth illegally. In 1962 Macapagal was confronted by the Stonehill scandal, which uncovered vast corruption at all levels of government. He himself was never implicated but the political damage had been done. In 1965 Macapagal lost the presidential contest to National Party leader FERDINAND MARCOS, who went on to rule the Philippines for 20 years. Macapagal left office, having failed to significantly improve the economy or the plight of the impoverished. Nonetheless, in 1979 he organized the National Union for Liberation to oppose the Marcos dictatorship. Macapagal died in Makati on April 21, 1997, but in 2001 his daughter, Gloria Macapagal-Arroyo, partly rehabilitated his political legacy by becoming president of the Philippine Republic.

Further Reading

Kang, David C. *Crony Capitalism: Corruption and Development in South Korea and the Philippines.* New York: Cambridge University Press, 2002.

Macapagal, Diosdado. *A Stone for the Edifice: Memoirs of a President.* Quezon, Philippines: Mac Pub. House, 1968.

———. *Democracy in the Philippines.* Downsville, Ont.: R. J. Cusipag, 1976.

McFerson, Hazel M., ed. *Mixed Blessing: The Impact of the American Colonial Experience on Politics and Society in the Philippines.* Westport, Conn.: Greenwood Press, 2002.

Reynolds, Quentin J. *Macapagal the Incorruptible.* New York: D. McKay Co., 1965.

Sussman, Gerald. "Macapagal: The Sabah Claim and Maphilindo: The Politics of Penetration." *Journal of Contemporary Asia* 13, no. 2 (1983): 210–228.

MacDonald, Ramsay (1866–1937) *prime minister of Great Britain*

James Ramsay MacDonald was born in Lossiemouth, Scotland, on October 12, 1866, the illegitimate son of a washerwoman. Educated at public schools he moved to Bristol, England, in 1885, to work the docks and was exposed to socialistic ideals. The following year he relocated to London to clerk in a warehouse and he also studied science and politics. By 1891 MacDonald was active in the Social Democratic Federation but, finding them too radical, he switched over to the nonrevolutionary Fabian Socialists. In 1894 he unsuccessfully stood for a seat in Parliament but two years later married Margaret Gladstone, a wealthy social worker, which gave MacDonald both social status and the ability to travel. In 1900 he gained appointment as secretary of the Labour Representation Committee in Parliament, the group that eventually gave rise to the Labour Party. Six years later he finally won a seat in the House of Commons as an Independent Labour member. He worked closely with the rival Liberal Party to contest the Conservatives, and by 1911 he was party chairman. But MacDonald's career hit an unexpected bump when he strongly opposed World War I and was publicly portrayed as a tool of German propagandists. In 1917 he made another mistake by strongly endorsing the socialist government of ALEKSANDR KERENSKY in Russia amid accusations of sympathy for Bolshevism. Consequently MacDonald lost his seat in 1918 and he spent the next four years convincing the Labour Party to formally renounce any ties to communism. He was reelected in 1922 and led the opposition. On January 17, 1924, the Conservative administration of STANLEY BALDWIN lost a vote of confidence, and MacDonald, assisted by HERBERT HENRY ASQUITH of the Liberals, was called upon to form the first Labour government.

MacDonald's first term as prime minister lasted only 10 months and he presided over a minority government with Liberal help. Nonetheless he worked with

French prime minister ÉDOUARD HERRIOT to have the Dawes Plan for reparations accepted by Germany and France. He also arranged British diplomatic recognition of the Soviet Union. His administration subsequently fell over a scandal concerning potential communist subversion but he had amply demonstrated Labour's capacity to govern. Between 1923 and 1929 MacDonald remained on as head of the opposition and honed his socialist beliefs through numerous publications. In 1929 Labour returned to power and MacDonald was reinstated as prime minister. As before he enjoyed his greatest success in foreign affairs, and in 1930 he became the first British prime minister to visit the United States. There he closely conferred with President HERBERT HOOVER over the upcoming London Five-Power Naval Conference for global disarmament. He also initiated the Round Table discussions to weigh the possibility of eventual Indian independence. However, domestically MacDonald was hamstrung by the onset of the Great Depression. In August 1931, when the Labour majority in Parliament refused to pass his austerity measures his government collapsed. However, King George V desired MacDonald to rule at the head of a national government, in concert with Conservatives and Liberals, and he quickly accepted. This single move outraged the Labourites, who now viewed MacDonald as a traitor to their cause. After he and several cabinet ministers were ejected from the party, new elections were scheduled, and Labour was easily defeated. MacDonald then took the reins of a government that was resoundingly conservative in tenor and outlook. Opponents, including many lifelong friends, now viewed him as more of a political opportunist than a bona fide socialist.

Over the next four years MacDonald wrestled with the hardships of high unemployment and low productivity. In 1932 he played a conspicuous role in the Geneva disarmament conference, which failed in its goal to reduce the international arms race. His discomfiture increased in 1933 when, following the election of ADOLF HITLER as chancellor of Germany, MacDonald had to press for national rearmament. Poor health prompted him to suddenly resign from office on June 7, 1935, and he was replaced again by Baldwin. He spent the next two years as lord president of the council, a largely ceremonial cabinet role, and was reelected to Parliament in 1936. MacDonald died at sea while vacationing on November 9, 1937. Like DAVID LLOYD GEORGE, he was a commoner bereft of college education, yet by dint of hard work and astute political instinct, occupied the highest office in the land. The Labour Party is certainly indebted to MacDonald for elevating it to the status of a national party, but he never overcame his stigma as a "traitor" for aligning with conservatives simply to retain power.

Further Reading
Ball, Stuart. "The Conservative Party and the Formation of the National Government: August 1931." *Historical Journal* 29 (March 1986): 159–182.

Barker, Bernard, ed. *Ramsay MacDonald's Political Writings*. London: Allen Lane, 1972.

Howell, David. *MacDonald's Party: Labour Identities and Crisis, 1922–1931*. New York: Oxford University Press, 2002.

Marguand, David. *Ramsay MacDonald*. London: Richard Cohen, 1997.

Riddell, Neil. *Labour in Crisis: The Second Labour Government, 1929–1931*. New York: Manchester University Press, 1999.

Walls, Duncan. *Ramsay MacDonald: A Labour Tragedy?* London: Hodder and Stoughton, 1998.

Machel, Samora (1933–1986) *president of Mozambique*

Samora Moisès Machel was born in Chilembene, Portuguese East Africa, on September 29, 1933, the son of a Protestant minister. He was educated at Catholic missionary schools and earned a degree in nursing at night. However, Machel deeply resented Portuguese colonial rule and the discrimination it represented for African citizens. In June 1962 a group of Mozambican expatriates under Eduardo Mondlane gathered in neighboring Tanzania to found the Frente de Libertação de Moçambique (Frelimo), Front for the Liberation of Mozambique, which was dedicated to overthrowing colonial rule. Machel readily subscribed to its cause, and that year he slipped away to Tanzania and joined. Accompanied by a handful of cadres, he next visited Algeria to receive guerrilla training before returning to Mozambique in 1964. Hostilities commenced in September of that year when Machel personally led an attack on a Portuguese outpost. Over the next nine years Machel distinguished himself as an insurgent leader and took responsibility for training new guerrillas. In 1969 Mondlane was killed, apparently in an intraparty squabble, and Machel was appointed the new head of Frelimo. He directed operations that drove the Portuguese out of the hinterlands, while he preached his own version of Marxism-Leninism to the peasants. Events crested in April 1974 when the Portuguese government was toppled by a military coup. Machel then negotiated for complete independence, which was granted on June 25, 1975. In light of his reputation as a dogged war hero, the Frelimo executive committee made Machel the nation's first African president.

Now in power, Machel faced the daunting task of rebuilding his wartorn country. He nationalized broad sectors of the economy, including law, medicine, and education. Building schools and hospitals was emphasized, and it became a national priority to afford basic services to the bulk of Mozambique's poverty-stricken masses. Authorities confiscated missionary schools, and by 1979 the number of students doubled. In 1977 Machel had determined to transform his nation into a doctrinaire Marxist-Leninist state, and he established abiding relations with the Soviet Union and other East Bloc nations. But the onset of independence did little to ameliorate Mozambique's security problems, as it became caught up in the war against the racist regimes of South Africa and Rhodesia. The national economy had been tottering, but when IAN SMITH declared independence from Great Britain in 1975, Machel promptly closed his border and with it all business transactions. This act further depressed Mozambique's economic outlook but also heightened Machel's standing as an African nationalist. Mozambique consequently experienced retaliatory military raids from Rhodesia, which also bankrolled the Mozambique National Resistance (MNR) against the socialist regime. Internecine fighting further devastated the countryside and increased the population's misery. In this weakened condition Machel felt he had no recourse but to sign the Nkomati Accord with South Africa; in it he pledged to stop harboring African National Congress (ANC) guerrillas while Pretoria stopped funding the MNR movement. This was not a popular decision among other frontline states in the war against apartheid, but it bought Mozambique a much needed respite.

For all the hardships that socialism and guerrilla war imposed on the people of Mozambique, Machel remained a popular national figure through his 11-year tenure as president. He was charismatic, an enthralling orator, and genuinely concerned with the wellbeing of his country. Machel was also ideologically pragmatic and by 1980 he dropped the more strident features of socialist economic planning in favor of a mixed economy. However, on October 19, 1986, his promising career was cut short when his Soviet-flown transport crashed into the Lebombo Mountains while returning from a conference in Zambia. His successor, Joaquim Chissano, formally accused South Africa of luring the plane into the mountains through a false navigation beacon, a charge it denied. Nonetheless, Machel's widow Graca, now married to former South African president Nelson Mandela, prevailed on the government to commence an investigation. In January 2003 the government announced that the Scorpions, a special investigation unit, would reopen the inquiry into Machel's untimely demise. He remains one of Africa's most revered anticolonial figures.

Further Reading

Alden, Chris. *Mozambique and the Construction of the New African State: from Negotiations to National Building.* New York: Palgrave, 2001

Bowen, Merle L. *The State against the Peasantry: Rural Struggles in Colonial and Postcolonial Mozambique.* Charlottesville: University Press of Virginia, 2000.

Cabrita, Joao M. *Mozambique: The Torturous Road to Democracy.* New York: St. Martin's Press, 2000.

Christie, Iain. *Samora Machel: A Biography.* Atlantic Highlands, N.J.: Panaf, 1989.

Manning, Carrie L. *The Politics of Peace in Mozambique.* Westport, Conn.: Praeger, 2002.

Pitcher, M. Anne. *Transforming Mozambique: The Business of Politics, 1975–2000.* New York: Cambridge University Press, 2002.

Macías Nguema, Francisco (1924–1979)
president of Equatorial Guinea

Francisco Masie Nguema was born in Nsegayong village, Río Muni, Spanish Guinea, on January 1, 1924, a member of the large Fang tribe. He was educated at Catholic missionary schools and, at an early age, displayed tendencies toward paranoia. He felt particularly inferior toward Europeans, and as a young man he changed his name to the more Spanish-sounding Macías. In 1944 he joined the colonial administration as a clerk, worked diligently, and earned the coveted status, "emancipated." This was the highest rank that a black

African could achieve under colonial rule. By turns he also served as a court interpreter and mayor of Mongomo. By 1963 Spain was willing to grant its colonies greater political autonomy and that year Macías joined the Idea Popular de Guinea Ecuatorial (IPGE), Popular Idea of Equatorial Guinea, to advocate independence. However, when the party split over the issue of unifying with Cameroon, Macías transferred his loyalties to the newly formed Movimiento de Unión Nacional de Guinea Ecuatorial (Munge), National Union Movement of Equatorial Guinea, another moderate group, headed by Ondo Edu. Macías soon grew more radical in his views and he switched alliances again by joining the more strident Movimiento Nacional de Liberación de Guinea Ecuatorial (Monalige), National Liberation Movement of Equatorial Guinea, which demanded immediate independence. He was then elected to the first national legislature. In 1968 he participated in a constitutional conference just prior to independence. Elections were held in September 1968 to pick a national leader, and Macías defeated Edu to become Equatorial Guinea's first president.

Macías soon proved himself to be one of Africa's most repressive and murderous dictators. Though dapper in appearance and manners, he was extremely paranoid and megalomaniac, and detested any opposition. When Ondo Edu fled to Gabon after the election, Macías offered him a safe return—then had him murdered. Thereafter he engaged in periodic purges of all enemies, real and imagined. His victims list includes Equatorial Guinea's UN ambassador, government officials, doctors, and other skilled people. In fact Macías was so self-conscious about his own lack of education that he officially forbade using the word *intellectual* in public. By 1969 he focused his animus upon Spain, which prompted that country to dispatch troops and evacuate 7,000 citizens. Thereafter, relations between Spain and its former colony were extremely tense. This move also eliminated Equatorial Guinea's trained business and professional classes, and the economy quickly unraveled. Macías responded by declaring a state of emergency and announcing that he had defeated a coup attempt against him. This gave the government additional pretext for rounding up numerous critics and executing them. By 1970 Macías had combined all existing parties into a single entity, the Partido Unido Nacional del Trabajador (PUNT), United National Worker Party. His grasp on power was absolute.

Macías's excesses had cost more than 600 lives by 1979 and resulted in the flight of 120,000 people to neighboring countries. His policy of conscripted farm labor also engendered discontent and contributed to the mass of refugees. He nonetheless continued reveling in his own omnipotence and constructed a heavily fortified palace estimated to have cost $12 million. In 1972 he also declared himself president for life and "The Unique Miracle of Equatorial Guinea." At length his delusions moved him to outlaw the Catholic Church, and in 1976 he gave his subjects six months to Africanize their European names under the penalty of severe fines. Macías's insecurity had grown so overwhelming that by 1979 he lived virtually alone and confided only in three close relatives. One of these, Teodoro Obiang Nguema Mbasogo, head of the armed forces, finally overthrew his deranged uncle on August 3, 1979. Macías was then put on trial for corruption, brutality, and other crimes of state. The erratic leader was executed, along with six cabinet members, on October 1, 1979, concluding one of the most bizarre and brutal chapters of West African political history. The anniversary of Macías's demise is still celebrated as national holiday.

Further Reading

Decalo, Samuel. *Psychoses of Power: African Personal Dictatorships.* Boulder, Colo.: Westview Press, 1989.

Fegley, Randall. *Equatorial Guinea: An African Tragedy.* New York: P. Lang, 1989.

Liniger-Goumaz, Max. *Historical Dictionary of Equatorial Guinea.* Lanham, Md.: Scarecrow Press, 2000.

———. *Small Is Not Always Beautiful: The Story of Equatorial Guinea.* Totowa, N.J.: Barnes and Noble Books, 1989.

Sundiata, Ibrahim K. *Equatorial Guinea: Colonialism, State Terror, and the Search for Stability.* Boulder, Colo.: Westview Press, 1990.

———. "The Roots of African Despotism: The Question of Political Culture." *African Studies Review* 31, no. 1 (1988): 9–31.

Macmillan, Harold (1894–1986) *prime minister of Great Britain*

Maurice Harold Macmillan was born in London, England, on February 10, 1894, the son of a noted publisher. He was well educated at Eton preparatory school and Balliol College, Oxford, before World War I interrupted his studies. Macmillan quit school and was commissioned in the Grenadier Guards, where he was thrice wounded. After the war he came home and accepted a post as secretary to the English-appointed governor general of Canada. There he met and married his daughter, Lady Dorothy Cavendish, joining one of the wealthiest and most conservative households in England. But for all his impeccable lineage Macmillan demonstrated genuine concern for the poor and underprivileged. In 1923 he unsuccessfully ran for a seat in Parliament as a Conservative, but the following year he was elected from the poor industrial city of Stockton. Macmillan quickly established himself as part of the party's progressive wing, and in 1938 he published a tract entitled *The Middle Way,* which justified limited state intervention in the economy. That year he also gained national recognition for vehemently denouncing Prime Minister NEVILLE CHAMBERLAIN's appeasement policy toward Nazi Germany. In May 1940 Macmillan was one of several Conservative Party members who forced Chamberlain to resign from office. That year he also came to the attention of the new prime minister, WINSTON CHURCHILL, who appointed him to successively more important offices throughout World War II. As minister resident in North Africa, Macmillan worked closely with generals DWIGHT D. EISENHOWER and CHARLES DE GAULLE to smooth over differences in allied strategy and policy. However, after the war the Conservatives were turned out of office by the Labourites, and Macmillan lost his seat. In 1947 he was reelected and established himself as a leading member of the opposition. He was also the major force behind the Conservative "industrial charter," which formally rationalized limited government control and nationalization of private industry.

In 1951 the Conservatives returned to power under Churchill, and Macmillan was appointed housing minister. He performed brilliantly in this capacity, constructing 300,000 housing units for Britain's burgeoning population. Following a brief stint as minister of defense he subsequently served as foreign secretary and chancellor of the Exchequer under ANTHONY EDEN. Eden's administration did not long survive the botched Suez Crisis of 1956, which underscored Great Britain's limitations in the postwar world, and on January 9, 1957, he was succeeded by Macmillan. The new prime minister moved quickly to shore up the pound by introducing government bonds and improving foreign trade. When several cabinet ministers resigned rather than go along with Macmillan's progressive policies, he publicly shrugged it off as a family squabble and appointed successors. By 1959 the economic outlook had grown so rosy that taxes were cut, and the Conservatives won a resounding victory at the polls that October. Thereafter the aristocratic Macmillan was dubbed "Supermac" by the press.

One of Macmillan's top priorities was mending fences with the United States, and he visited and discussed cold war polices with President Dwight D. Eisenhower. It became Macmillan's melancholy duty to recast Britain's world role in a much reduced format but, ever the realist, he went about the distasteful task forcefully. In 1960 he addressed the South African parliament and warned them that the "winds of change" were sweeping the continent and that an end to apartheid was inevitable. But in 1962 he shored up Great Britain's reputation as America's most reliable cold war ally by backing President JOHN F. KENNEDY during the Cuban missile crisis. When this near disaster was averted, he next helped to broker the Nuclear Test Ban Treaty with Soviet premier NIKITA KHRUSHCHEV. But Macmillan was still determined that Britain should maintain a nuclear deterrence of its own, and he prevailed upon Kennedy to provide the Royal Navy with Polaris submarine-launched missiles. Macmillan's major policy setback was the exclusion of Great Britain from the European Common Market in 1963—vetoed by French president de Gaulle. By this time the British economy had also soured and Macmillan's austerity measures caused public discontent. In 1962 his administration was rocked by the Profumo spy and sex scandals, which further eroded public confidence. On October 10, 1963, Macmillan stunned his party by announcing his resignation on the grounds of poor health, and he was replaced by ALEXANDER DOUGLAS-HOME.

Back in private life, Macmillan turned to publishing and churned out a great number of memoirs that were eloquent and engaging. In 1984 he was inducted into the peerage as the Earl of Stockton and seated in the House of Lords. One of his last political acts was to criticize MARGARET THATCHER's neo-liberal economic policies for the harm they caused the lower classes. Macmillan died in Birch Grove, Sussex, on December 29, 1986, one of the most influential Conservative statesmen of 20th-century Britain.

Further Reading

Ashton, Nigel. *Kennedy, Macmillan, and the Cold War: The Irony of Interdependence.* New York: Palgrave Macmillan, 2002.

Catterall, Peter. *The Macmillan Diaries: The Cabinet Years, 1950–1957.* London: Macmillan, 2003.

Gearson, John P. S. *Harold Macmillan and the Berlin Wall Crisis, 1958–62: The Limits of Interests and Force.* New York: St. Martin's Press, 1998.

Geelhoed, E. Bruce. *Eisenhower, Macmillan, and Allied Unity, 1957–1961.* New York: Palgrave Macmillan, 2002.

Macmillan, Harold. *At the End of the Day.* New York: Harper and Row, 1973.

Scott, L. V. *Macmillan, Kennedy, and the Cuban Missile Crisis: Political, Military, and Intelligence Aspects.* London: Macmillan, 1999.

Madero, Francisco (1873–1913) *president of Mexico*

Francisco Indalecio Madero was born in Parras, Coahuila state, Mexico, on October 30, 1873, into one of that country's most affluent families. A child of privilege, he was tutored locally and attended college in the United States and France. There he became steeped in the nuances of constitutional democracy and wished to transplant that system to his homeland. Mexico was under the control of dictator PORFIRIO DÍAZ, who had wielded power for 35 years. Madero admired the political stability and technological progress the regime imparted but resented the great concentration of wealth and the grinding poverty of the peasantry. He came home in 1893 to manage one of the family's estates and distinguished himself by providing social benefits to the peasants he employed. In 1904 Madero tested the political waters by running for local office and criticizing the Díaz government, and he lost. However, he ran again the following year and won, becoming the country's most vocal proponent of change. The turning point in Madero's political fortunes—and Mexico's—occurred in 1908 when President Díaz informed an American journalist that he would not seek reelection. This prompted Madero to write and publish his famous pamphlet, *The Presidential Succession of 1910*, which called for a return to democracy and the right of Mexicans to choose their leader. The tract was enthusiastically received, which prompted Madero to found the Anti-reelection Center in Mexico City as a locus of anti-Díaz activity. The pace of events quickened when Díaz suddenly retracted his earlier statement and promised to run for office again. This turnaround disillusioned many of the aging dictator's supporters and in 1910 Madero presented himself as a challenger for the presidency. Díaz responded by having him arrested in June 1910, but he escaped and settled in San Antonio, Texas.

Within months, Madero composed a second tract, the *Plan of San Luis Potosí,* which called for an armed uprising against the Díaz regime. By February 1911 sporadic fighting arose in various places across Mexico. Madero himself led an aborted effort to cross the border and was defeated, but in April 1911 General Emiliano Zapata led a large-scale uprising in the state of Morelos. This was followed by similar efforts in the north by Francisco "Pancho" Villa and Pascual Orozco. Díaz hastily mobilized the federal army to confront the rebels but his men were outnumbered and outgunned. On May 10, 1911, Madero, assisted by forces under Villa and Orozco, attacked and stormed the key border town of Ciudad Juárez. This defeat convinced Díaz that the war was lost and he fled Mexico City for Veracruz and the safety of Europe. The exhilarated rebels then took the capital, whereupon Madero declared himself provisional president. Mindful of his commitment to democracy, he also held the nation's first free elections in decades and won handily. Much was expected from the new government—and much was needed.

Madero had proved adept as an insurgent, and successfully harnessed the powers of revolution to overthrow the dictatorship. But he unfortunately possessed no practical experience or talent when it came to administering national affairs. Madero recognized the need for comprehensive social reforms, particularly the redistribution of land to the peasantry, but his efforts were thwarted by Díaz loyalists still controlling the congress. Zapata, the darling of the left, grew disenchanted with the pace of change and rose in rebellion a second time. Conservatives were also angered by Madero's moderation, and the generals Bernardo Reyes and Félix Díaz likewise revolted against the government. Madero, whose grip on national politics was slipping fast, then turned to another conservative leader, VICTORIANO HUERTA, to restore order. This was done at frightful cost to the Mexican citizenry and ultimately to Madero himself. On February 19, 1913, Huerta had Madero and Vice President José María Pino Suarez arrested. After several days of captivity both men were summarily shot in the back "while attempting to escape."

Madero's murder served as a catalyst for the next phase of the revolution, 1913–29. Disparate rebel forced united in their hatred of Huerta and drove him out of the country. The great social reforms that the slain president tried and failed to enact were then successfully implemented to the benefit of Mexico's poor majority. Madero's 15 months in office mark him as a less than successful political leader, but he is esteemed as a national martyr and father of the Mexican Revolution.

Further Reading

Boggs, Kevin W. "The Madero Revolution: Overcoming Obstacles on Both Sides of the Border." Unpublished master's thesis, Michigan State University, 1992.

Johnson, David N. *Madero in Texas.* San Antonio, Tex.: Corona Pub. Co., 2001.

La France, David G. *The Mexican Revolution in Puebla, 1908–1913: The Maderista Movement and the Failure of Liberal Reform.* Wilmington, Del.: Scholarly Resources, 1989.

Madero, Francisco I. *The Presidential Succession of 1910.* New York: P. Lang, 1990.

Myers, William K. *Forge of Progress, Crucible of Revolt: Origins of the Mexican Revolution in La Comarca Lagunera, 1880–1911.* Albuquerque: University of New Mexico Press, 1994.

Osorio, Ruben. "The Death of a President and the Reconstruction of the Mexican Federal Army." *Journal of Big Bend Studies* 12 (2000): 105–131.

Maga, Hubert (1916–2000) *president of Dahomey*
Coutoucou Hubert Maga was born in Parakou, Dahomey, on August 10, 1916, the son of Barina parents from Burkina Faso. He was fortunate enough to be educated at Catholic missionary schools and subsequently studied to be a teacher at the noted William Ponty School in Dakar, Senegal. Maga, born a Muslim, converted to Christianity and returned home to teach in 1935. Within a decade he was headmaster and also took an interest in national politics. In the wake of World War II France allowed its colonies greater autonomy and representation, so in 1945 Maga joined the Union progressiste dahoméenne (UPD), Progressive Dahomey Union, of SOUROU MIGAN APITHY and also served in the Dahomey General Council. In 1951 Maga left the UPD in favor of the northern-based Mouvement pour la démocratie et le développement (MDD), Democratic Dahomey Movement, and also won election to the French National Assembly. He served until 1958 and also worked for the French government as undersecretary of state for labor, 1957–58. Around this time the French were preparing Dahomey for independence so Maga returned home and founded his own party, the Rassemblement démocratique dahoméen (RDD), Dahomey Democratic Rally. Elections held in April 1959 gave the RDD 22 seats out of 70, and it merged with Apithy's new Republican Party of Dahomey to form a coalition government, squeezing out Justin Ahomadégbé's Union démocratique dahoméenne (UDD), Dahomey Democratic Union, from power. As prime minister, it fell upon Maga's shoulders to lead the country into political independence on August 1, 1960.

While in office Maga acquired a reputation as a spendthrift. He ignored limited resources and spent lavishly on his presidential palace, estimated to be worth $3 million. He conducted an ethnically based regime, relying on his northern political base to the exclusion of all other groups. Nonetheless, in December 1960 new elections were held and Maga was elected president with Apithy his vice president. Ahomadégbé was hounded out of politics and jailed, his party banned. And to eliminate any chance of Apithy's contesting his rule, Maga dispatched him to France as ambassador in 1963. Dahomey's economy continued sinking, however, and the president was forced to impose austerity measures, which provoked violent demonstrations by students and union members. Popular discontent mounted when Maga refused to dismiss a National Assembly member accused of murder. Events crested on October 23, 1965, when the army under General Christophe Soglo bloodlessly toppled the regime.

General Soglo tried to reinstate civilian authority in the form of a shared presidential triumvirate, but Maga, Apithy, and Ahomadégbé refused to cooperate. The three senior politicians were then arrested and Maga was exiled to Paris. He remained there until 1970, when a new military regime formally invited him back to Dahomey to serve in a new triumvirate with his old adversaries, Apithy and Ahomadégbé. However, when Colonel de Souza refused to allow Maga to occupy the presidency in April 1970, he retired to his northern homeland to stir up support. Maga organized the Assembly of Peoples of the North, which threatened to secede if he were not allowed to serve. The crisis was solved with creation of a presidential council whereby the three men served two-year rotating terms as chairman. Maga resumed his duties as president in May 1970.

As before, Maga displayed little restraint when lavishing public funds on himself. The overall fragility of Dahomey's economy only fueled resentment against the chief executive. In 1972 Maga weathered several coup attempts, though he refused to dismiss a minister charged with corruption. In May 1972 he peacefully transferred power to Ahomadégbé, who ruled until the military intervened again on October 26, 1972, putting all three executives under house arrest. Maga was detained until 1981 when Major Mathieu Kerekou released him after a new coup. A one-party state was established and Maga promptly withdrew from the political scene. Dahomey has since been renamed Benin, and in 1990 the military made allowances for multiparty democracy. Maga, eager as ever, reformed his old RDD party but it failed to register marked gains. He died on May 7, 2000.

Further Reading

Allen, Christopher. *Democratic Renewal in Africa: Two Essays on Benin.* Edinburgh: Centre of African Studies, University of Edinburgh, 1992.

Decalo, Samuel. *Historical Dictionary of Benin.* Metuchen, N.J.: Scarecrow Press, 1987.

Houngnikpo, Mathurin C. *Determinants of Democratization in Africa: A Comparative Study of Benin and Togo.* Lanham, Md.: University Press of Maryland, 2001.

Manning, Patrick. *Slavery, Colonialism, and Economic Growth in Dahomey, 1640–1960.* New York: Cambridge University Press, 1982.

Morton-Williams, Peter. *Benin Studies.* New York: International African Institute, Oxford University Press, 1973.

Ronen, Dov. *Dahomey: Between Tradition and Modernity.* Ithaca, N.Y.: Cornell University Press, 1975.

Magsaysay, Ramón (1907–1957) *president of the Philippines*

Ramón Magsaysay was born in Iba, Zambales, the Philippines, on August 31, 1907, the son of a blacksmith. He worked as a chauffeur while putting himself through Jose Rizal College where he obtained a commerce degree in 1928. Magsaysay was superintendent of a bus company when the Pacific war erupted in December 1941, and he fought as a guerrilla in the hills of western Luzon. His group of fighters performed useful and hazardous work preparing the islands for their eventual recapture by the United States. After the war, General Douglas MacArthur appointed him military governor of Zambales, and in April 1946 he was elected to the Philippine House of Representatives with the Liberal Party. He chaired committees on national defense, and in 1948 President MANUEL ROXAS allowed him to lead a Filipino deputation to Washington, D.C., to secure veteran's benefits. In 1950 Magsaysay was reelected to congress but he had grown disillusioned with the Liberals and castigated them for corruption and insensitivity to mounting social distress. In fact, conditions in the Philippines had degenerated to the point where a communist-inspired Hukbalahap (or simply Huk) rebellion raged with great fury. To counter this national peril President ELPIDIO QUIRINO appointed Magsaysay secretary of defense on September 1, 1950.

Magsaysay fulfilled his role brilliantly. He completely overhauled the Philippine military, ended corruption, and fired incompetent generals. Special anti-guerrilla units were created and unloosed against the insurgents. But the key to Magsaysay's success was his approach to public relations: he strictly enforced military discipline in relation to the peasants. The army constructed schools, hospitals, and farmhouses for the poorest. Magsaysay offered amnesty, medical treatment, and free land in the Mindanao jungle to any rebels who surrendered. As public opinion of the military rose, that of the Huks declined, and by 1952 most of the rebellion's leaders had been either captured or killed. All told Magsaysay orchestrated a tremendously successful campaign against the communists and other subversives. His success and reputation for honesty led to his nomination for president as a National Party leader. On November 10, 1953, he and vice presidential candidate CARLOS P. GARCIA decisively defeated Quirino by running as champions of the "common man." Magsaysay was the first Filipino president to originate from the lower middle classes and he never forsook his roots. And, to further emphasize his Malay origins, he took the oath of office wearing a *barong tagalog*, the common shirt of Filipino men. As chief executive Magsaysay cultivated extremely close ties to the United States in both economic and security matters. He was especially keen on cooperating with the Central Intelligence Agency to root out any remnants of communism in the islands. He also sought to shore up regional defenses by enlisting the Philippines in the newly organized Southeast Asia Treaty Organization (SEATO) in September 1954.

The Philippines were still riven by a maldistribution of wealth, and Magsaysay embarked on badly needed social legislation to address such disparities. He strove for comprehensive land reforms to assist the majority poor but his efforts were perpetually thwarted by conservative members in congress. Nonetheless he managed to acquire land settlements for homeless peasants, lowered the price of consumer goods, and broke up several of the large landed estates. Despite his lack of legislative success, Magsaysay remained extremely popular with the Philippine electorate and was seemingly destined to win a second term in office. However, he completed only two years in office before dying in an airplane crash on March 17, 1957. Magsaysay's political legacy remains mixed, for he proved unable to address deep-seated problems within Filipino society. Still, he is remembered as a staunch anticommunist, extremely pro-American, and a hero of the poor and lower classes.

Further Reading

Cullather, Nick. "America's Boy? Ramon Magsaysay and the Illusion of Influence." *Pacific Historical Review* 62 (August 1993): 305–338.

Doronila, Amando. *The State, Economic Transformation, and Political Change in the Philippines, 1946–1972.* New York: Oxford University, 1992.

Gray, Marvin. *Island Hero: The Story of Ramon Magsaysay.* New York: Hawthorne, 1965.

Hedman, Eva-Letta. "Late Imperial Romance: Magsaysay, Lansdale, and the Philippine-American 'Special Relationship.'" *Intelligence and National Security* 14 (winter 1999): 181–194.

Nixon, Richard M. *Leaders.* New York: Warner Books, 1982.

Warner, M. S. "Democracy's Hall of Fame: Anti-Communist Heroes of the Third World." *Policy Review* no. 30 (fall 1984): 48–53.

Makarios III (1913–1977) *president of Cyprus*

Mikhail Khristodolou Mouskos was born in Pano Panayia, Cyprus, on August 13, 1913, the son of a shepherd. Cyprus had been a British Crown colony since 1914 and was considered of strategic significance to the eastern Mediterranean. Mouskos entered a monastery at the age of 13 and subsequently studied religion at the University of Athens and Boston University. In 1946 he was ordained a priest in the Greek Orthodox Church and adopted the name Makarios ("Blessed"). Two years later he was installed as archbishop of Cyprus, the youngest such executive in the island's history. Cyprus was in political turmoil over the issue of enosis (union with the Greek mainland). The large Cypriot Greek community, including Makarios, passionately embraced the notion, but it ran afoul of British concerns for military basing and the fate of the sizable Turkish community on Cyprus. Makarios nonetheless served as an articulate spokesman for enosis, and in 1952 he appeared before the United Nations to plead his case. He also struck up a cordial relationship with Colonel George Grivas, head of Ethnike Organosic Kypriakou Agonos (EOKA), the National Organization of Cypriot Fighters, a terrorist group intending to push the issue of independence from Great Britain by force. This move was viewed as essential, as the Greeks and Turks were highly polarized and girding for civil war. In April 1955 EOKA began attacking army outposts and Turkish communities, but the British responded with overwhelming military force. The guerrillas were rounded up while Makarios was arrested and exiled to the Seychelles in the Indian Ocean. In 1958 he was allowed to return to the island for joint talks over possible independence—any federated status with Greece was ruled out. Makarios was compliant with British demands, although he refused to allow partitioning of Cyprus into separate Greek and Turkish regions, and in February 1959 he signed the agreement granting the island freedom. This act required extensive political protection for the Turkish minority, along with a Turkish vice president. But a deal had been struck, and the following December Makarios was overwhelmingly elected the republic's first president, head of both church and state.

From the onset the island's politics were dominated by friction between Greeks and Turks. Cyprus is 600 miles from the Greek mainland but only 40 miles from Turkey, and the Turkish government promised to intervene with force to protect its citizens. To forestall a clash, Makarios distanced himself from violence and enosis, a move that angered extremists in the Greek camp. In fact, Makarios was the target of no less than four assassination attempts because of his willingness to accommodate the Turks. In 1967 he demanded the resignation of Grivas, now head of the national guard, for his harsh actions toward Turkish Cypriots. That same year he was forced to accept a Turkish Cypriot provisional government that regulated minority affairs outside of the central government. The Turks, meanwhile, refused to recognize him as president and routinely ignored the legislature's actions. Nonetheless, in 1965 Makarios's term in office was extended by three years, and in 1968 and 1973 he was again reelected.

The impasse pleased no one, despite Makarios's moderation. In July 1974 the Greek military junta orchestrated a coup and forced the president to flee to Malta. The Turks interpreted this as a move toward enosis, and they invaded in great force, seizing 40 percent of the island. They then proclaimed their portion a separate state, the Turkish Republic of Northern Cyprus, although it received no international recognition. Makarios was allowed to return following the invasion, and unsuccessfully pressed for the withdrawal of Turkish troops and the return of captured land, refusing to recognize the island's de facto partitioning into Greek and Turkish parts. Makarios was still among Cyprus's most popular figures when he died in Nicosia on August 3, 1977. The island's division along ethnic lines continues to be a problem in Turkish-Greek relations to the present time.

Further Reading

Hatzivassiliou, Evanthis. "Blocking *Enosis:* Britain and the Cyprus Question, March–December 1956." *Journal of Imperial and Commonwealth History* 19, no. 2 (1991): 247–263.

Joseph, J. "The International Power Broker: A Critical View of the Foreign Policy of Archbishop Makarios." *Mediterranean Quarterly* 3 (spring 1992): 17–33.

Makarios III. *Crusade for Freedom.* New York: Cyprus Federation of America, 1958.

Mayes, Stanley. *Makarios: A Biography.* New York: St. Martin's Press, 1981.

Sant Cassia, Paul. "The Archbishop in a Beleaguered City: An Analysis of the Conflicting Roles and Political Role of Makarios." *Byzantine and Modern Greek Studies* 8, no. 8 (1982): 181–212.

Westen-Markides, Diana. "Britain's 'New Look' Policy for Cyprus and the Makarios-Harding Talks, January 1955–March 1956." *Journal of Imperial and Commonwealth History* 23, no. 3 (1995): 479–505.

Maktoum, Mohammed Rashid bin Said al-
(1912–1990) *prime minister of the United Arab Emirates*

Rashid bin Said al-Maktoum was born in Dubai in 1912, a son of the ruling sheik, Said bin Maktoum al-Maktoum. Devoid of formal education, he spent his early years in the Dubai customs house, acquiring a cunning sense for business and negotiating. Maktoum was a forceful personality in his own right, so that after 1939, when he became regent to assist his aging father, he was the actual power behind the throne. In this capacity he orchestrated a remarkable modernization of Dubai, long an impoverished desert enclave celebrated for smuggling and piracy. Beginning in the 1950s he opened up the city-state to Iranian and Indian merchants who provided a thriving business atmosphere. Maktoum then turned his attention to infrastructure by dredging the harbor and developing Dubai as a port. He also had the foresight to develop a large, modern airstrip outside the city, making it the aviation center of the southern Persian Gulf. Maktoum was made emir following the death of his father in 1958. The pace of construction and modernization quickened in 1965 following discovery of large oil deposits, and the revenue these generated was quickly plowed back into the economy. While nominally a Muslim country, Dubai under Maktoum retained a remarkable degree of tolerance. The foreign community was free to practice its faiths in public, without hindrance. "We have mosques for those who want to use them," Maktoum declared, "bars for those who want to drink and jails for those who drink too much." By shrewd business practices and enlightened tolerance, Dubai emerged as the wealthiest emirate in the Arabian peninsula—a Hong Kong of the Persian Gulf.

The turning point in Dubai's political fortunes occurred in 1968 when Great Britain, which had maintained troops in the region for a century, declared its intention to leave. This left Dubai and its seven neighboring emirates open to aggression from Saudi Arabia and Iran, both of which made claims on the region. To circumvent the loss of independence, Maktoum entered into negotiations with his arch enemy, Emir Zayed bin Sultan Al Nahyan of Abu Dhabi, over the possibility of a federal union. The ensuing talks proved difficult and intricate, for Maktoum was unwilling to surrender his sovereignty to Zayed. But by December 1971 most differences had been resolved, and five emirates (or Trucial states) of the lower Persian Gulf joined forces to form the new United Arab Emirates. This entity loosely bound its member states under a Supreme Federal Council drawn from the leaders of each emirate. In return, each emir retains his own military and internal organization, being bound only to contribute to a general pool of resources for the benefit of all. The UAE remains a weak structure with excessive rights and powers granted to its constituent member states. Because Maktoum was responsible for laying the groundwork he became its first vice president and was also allowed to position his sons within the federation government.

Maktoum served as the UAE's vice president for 19 years and in 1979 he also assumed the role of prime minister. These were tumultuous times in the Gulf region, as the Iranian revolution was bent on exporting radical Islam abroad and exerting influence over its neighbors. Consequently, when the Iran-Iraq war erupted in 1980, the UAE provided financial support to Iraq. This ran the considerable risk of alienating and inflaming the large community of Shia Muslims who were imported as laborers, but unrest was forcefully contained. The following year Maktoum lent his weight to creation of the Gulf Cooperation Council to further curtail Iranian influence. When the war ended in 1988, Maktoum turned his attention back to the practice that he so excelled at—business. He was also acutely concerned with the welfare of his subjects and spent lavishly on public housing, free education, and modern medical facilities. Consequently, the UAE enjoys one of the healthiest, best educated, and freest populations of the entire Muslim world. Dubai continued thriving within the UAE and by the time Maktoum died on October 7, 1990, the state he founded enjoyed degrees of prosperity, modernity, and political stability rarely found in the Middle East. He is considered one of the most astute Arab leaders of the 20th century.

Further Reading

Abdullah, Muhammed M. *The United Arab Emirates.* New York: Barnes and Noble, 1978.

Bhatia, Asha. *The UAE: The Formative Years, 1965–75: A Collection of Historical Photographs.* London: Motivate Pub., 1999.

Forman, Werner. *Phoenix Rising: The United Arab Emirates, Past, Present, and Future.* London: Harvill Press, 1996.

Herad-Bey, Frauke. *From Trucial States to United Arab Emirates: A Society in Transition.* New York: Longman, 1982.

Lienhardt, Peter. *Shaikhdoms of Eastern Arabia.* New York: Palgrave, 2001.

Wilson, Graeme. *Father of Dubai: Sheikh Rashid bin Saeed al-Maktoum.* Dubai: Media Prima, 1999.

Malloum, Félix (1932–) *president of Chad*

Félix Malloum N'Gakoutou Bey'ndi was born in Sarh, in the French Equatorial Federation (Chad), a member of the large Sara tribal grouping. He was educated locally at Bongor before receiving military training at the Ecole Général Leclerc in Brazzaville, Congo, as part of the French colonial army. Malloum proved himself a capable soldier, and in November 1952 he was promoted to sergeant and assigned to the Frejus military academy in France. The following year he saw active fighting throughout Indochina and was promoted to lieutenant in 1955. Malloum then returned to France for paratrooper training and served with French forces fighting in Algeria. By the time he returned home in August 1961, Chad was a newly independent nation. He rose rapidly through the ranks of the Chadian military, rising to deputy chief of staff by 1966. However, President FRANÇOIS TOMBALBAYE grew uneasy over his growing popularity and suspended him from office for three months. Malloum was eventually reinstated and then resumed his climb through the ranks. By 1968 he was colonel, defense minister, and de facto head of the military. He campaigned against rebellions in the Kaneum, Guera, and Chari-Baguirmi regions. In light of his excellent service Tombalbaye appointed him chairman of defense and veterans affairs, and by October 1972 he had received formal command of the military, with a rank of general.

Malloum's excellent service, however, did little to allay Tombalbaye's suspicions of him. These crested in June 1973 when the general was arrested and charged with invoking sorcery to bring down the government. He was sentenced to house arrest for two years, until a military coup killed Tombalbaye on April 13, 1975. Malloum was subsequently released, restored to rank, and reassigned as military commander. He assumed control of the Supreme Military Council, as well as Chad's presidency. The country was then experiencing a civil war drawn broadly across ethnic and religious lines. This conflict pitted the largely Christian and western-ized south (to which Malloum belonged) against the largely Muslim, pastoral north. Moreover the Muslims received arms and encouragement from Libya, which was the largest supporter of the Front de Libération Nationale du Tehad (Frolinat), Front for the National Liberation of Chad. One of Malloum's first acts in office was to grant a general amnesty and call upon the rebels and regional warlords to lay down their arms and work with the regime. Many Frolinat commanders from the eastern part of the country complied and were taken into the government. However, the northern factions remained militant and continued their struggle. In 1976 Malloum barely survived an assassination attempt on the anniversary of his military coup, and by March 1978 the government's position had deteriorated so much that the president was forced to request French inter-vention on his behalf.

Fighting continued non-stop until January 1978 when Malloum invited HISSÈNE HABRÉ, commander of the Forces armées du nord (FAN), Armed Forces of the North, to serve as prime minister in a government of national reconciliation. He did so more in an attempt to drive a wedge between northern opposition forces than to achieve political unity. But Habré, being extremely ambitious, chafed in his subordinate role under Malloum and by December fighting broke out between their respective soldiers. A bloody impasse then ensued until a Frolinat commander, Goukouni Oueddei, marched down from the north in strength and seized the capital of N'Djamena. Peace was restored only when Oueddei became president and Habré was installed as defense minister. Further negotiations between northern and southern factions determined that Malloum, Chad's most conspicuous southerner, had to leave office altogether. He did so willingly and went into exile in Nigeria and France, where he maintains a residence to this day. Malloum, who had failed to cultivate either a regional base or a personal army like his adversaries, has taken no further part in the affairs of his country.

Further Reading

Azevedo, Mario, ed. *Cameroon and Chad in Historical and Contemporary Perspectives.* Lewiston, N.Y.: E. Mellen Press, 1988.

Burr, Millard. *Africa's Thirty Years' War: Libya, Chad, and the Sudan, 1963–1993.* Boulder, Colo.: Westview Press, 1999.

Decalo, Samuel. *Historical Dictionary of Chad.* Lanham, Md.: Scarecrow Press, 1997.

Harris, Gordon. *Central and Equatorial Africa Area Bibliography.* Lanham, Md.: Scarecrow Press, 1999.

Mays, Terry M. *Africa's First Peace Keeping Operation: The OAU in Chad, 1981–1982.* Westport, Conn.: Praeger, 2002.

Nolutshungu, Sam C. *Limits of Anarchy: Intervention and State Formation in Chad.* Charlottesville: University Press of Virginia, 1996.

Mannerheim, Carl Gustav (1867–1951) *president of Finland*

Carl Gustav Emil Mannerheim was born in Turku, Finland, on June 4, 1867, the son of an impoverished nobleman. Because Finland was then part of the Russian Empire, he entered a military academy in St. Petersburg and was assigned to the czar's elite chevalier guards. Mannerheim proved himself an extremely competent officer and one of the few Russian officers to distinguish himself in the ill-fated Russo-Japanese War of 1904–05. He rose to lieutenant general and corps commander during World War I, reinforcing his reputation as an outstanding planner and leader. However, once the Bolsheviks under VLADIMIR LENIN toppled the provisional government of ALEKSANDR KERENSKY in October 1917, Finland moved quickly to declare its independence. Mannerheim, a conservative aristocrat and a devout monarchist, returned home and tendered his services to the new country just as an internecine civil war erupted. At length he assumed command of the White Guards, a special force entrust-ed with ridding Finland of Russian soldiers and their Bolshevik sympathizers. Severe fighting ensued but within four months the Finns were completely victori-ous. Mannerheim, however, was disturbed that Germany had dispatched troops to Finland at the gov-ernment's request, and he argued that their presence might jeopardize future relations with Sweden and other Baltic states. When his opinions were officially ignored, he resigned his command and returned to private life in June 1918.

Shortly after Mannerheim left the military, the Finnish government appointed him as an interim regent until national elections could be organized. Over the next seven months he eased German influence out of the country and obtained diplomatic recognition for Finland from the Western Allies. He then ran for president but lost to Kaarlo J. Stahlberg and returned once more to private life. For the next 15 years Mannerheim devoted his energies to traveling, hunting, and serving as chairman of the Finnish Red Cross. But in 1931 he was recalled to active duty as head of the National Defense Council, with responsibility for defending Finland's neutrality. Europe was then slowly lurching back toward war, and Mannerheim correctly predicted that the Soviet Union under JOSEPH STALIN posed the greatest threat to national security. He therefore instituted construction of an extensive chain of fortifications across the Karelian isthmus—the so-called Mannerheim Line. The correctness of his strategy was verified in November 1939, when Stalin launched an unprovoked invasion of Finland to seize strategic territory. The Finns resisted tenaciously for 105 days and inflicted thousands of casualties before finally succumbing to superior numbers and resources. But Stalin was forced to accept a negotiated settlement on March 13, 1940. Finland subsequently lost the Karelian region to Russia but otherwise survived intact. Mannerheim, then 72 years old, was hailed as a national hero.

In June 1941 Nazi forces under ADOLF HITLER attacked the Soviet Union, and Finland experienced increasing pressure to become Germany's ally in the north. Mannerheim, distrusting the Germans, did so only reluctantly but he availed himself of the opportunity to seize lands that had been lost in 1940. Thereafter Finnish forces played only a defensive role in the war and refused to cooperate with German attacks upon Leningrad. Mannerheim, who was promoted to marshal in June 1942, stridently opposed Hitler's racial policy of persecuting Jews. By 1944 it was clear that the Germans were losing the war on the eastern front. Mannerheim was appointed president by parliament and authorized to negotiate an armistice with the Russians. He agreed to lose additional territory to placate Stalin, and to place the leaders responsible for the war on trial, but once again he kept the country free from Soviet occupation. Mannerheim, citing ill health, resigned from office on March 4, 1946. He died in Lausanne, Switzerland, on January 27, 1951, the most influential Finnish soldier-statesman of the 20th century and the father of modern Finland.

Further Reading

Jagerskold, Stig. *Mannerheim, Marshal of Finland.* Minneapolis: University of Minnesota, 1987.

Mannerheim, Carl G. *Memoirs.* New York: Dutton, 1954.

Rvotsila, Markku. "The Churchill-Mannerheim Collaboration in the Russian Intervention, 1919–1920." *Slavonic and East European Review* 80, no. 1 (2002): 1–20.

Screen, J. E. O. *Mannerheim: The Finnish Years.* London: C. Hurst, 2000.

Van Dyke, Carl. *The Soviet Invasion of Finland, 1939–40.* Portland, Ore.: Frank Cass, 1997.

Vehvilainen, Olli. *Finland in the Second World War: Between Germany and Russia.* New York: Palgrave, 2002.

Mao Zedong (Mao Tse-tung) (1893–1976)
chairman of the Communist Party of China

Mao Zedong was born in Hunan Province, China, on December 26, 1893, the son of prosperous peasants. He was well educated and worked in the countryside, where he was struck by the misery and poverty of the peasant majority. After working several years as a teacher he attended college in Beijing and was exposed to Marxism. Mao quickly embraced the philosophy, and in 1921 he helped to found the Chinese Communist Party (CCP). At that time China was being united by Nationalist forces under President SUN YAT-SEN and CHIANG KAI-SHEK. The communists joined them in an unlikely coalition to fight various warlords, until 1927 when Nationalist forces under Chiang suddenly turned and attacked their allies. Mao and his cohorts fled into the interior, where they established the Kiangsi Soviet. Here Mao honed his revolutionary beliefs, which were very different from the industrial proletariat ideals espoused by VLADIMIR LENIN. Mao originated the idea of a revolutionary peasantry, based in the countryside and not in the city, which would spearhead and perpetuate a communist revolution. In 1934 Nationalist forces drove Mao's guerrillas from their mountain stronghold in Jiangxi (Kiangsi) Province into what became the epic 6,000-mile "Long March" to distant Shaanxi Province. They were spared annihilation when the Japanese attacked China in 1937. Over the next eight years Mao consolidated his stronghold and established friendly contacts with the peasantry, who provided the bulk of his support. And, by deliberately fighting the invaders instead of simply defending the interior like the Nationalists, the communists gained both military expertise and broad popular appeal. World War II ended in 1945, but the following year Mao precipitated the Chinese civil war against Chiang's Nationalists, which ended four years later in a communist victory. On October 1, 1949, Mao proclaimed creation of the People's Republic of China, with himself as chairman and ZHOU ENLAI as premier. Against great odds the theory of revolutionary peasantry had triumphed.

The communists had no sooner consolidated power than they were drawn into the Korean War, 1950–53, against American president HARRY S. TRUMAN. Chinese forces suffered terrible losses to the technologically superior Americans, yet fought them to a draw. Mao also established close diplomatic and economic ties with Soviet dictator JOSEPH STALIN, for whom he had

Mao Zedong *(Library of Congress)*

genuine admiration. In 1956 Mao attempted to address China's pressing economic problems by promulgating the so-called Great Leap Forward, which entailed the mass collectivization of agriculture. The result was a disastrous famine that killed 20 million people and set back the economy a decade. He also instigated the Sino-Soviet split after Premier NIKITA KHRUSHCHEV denounced Stalin's excesses. This led to the immediate loss of technical and economic assistance from Russia and a militarization of borders between the two communist giants. Consequently, Mao's heretofore sterling reputation was irreparably damaged, and he yielded the chairmanship to LIU SHAOQI in 1959. He nevertheless remained chairman of the powerful Communist Party.

By 1966 Mao disliked the Soviet-style paths of development that Liu and other reformers had adopted. Determined to reignite revolutionary fervor among China's youth, he sided with radical factions and unleashed the great cultural revolution of 1966–76. For 10 years bands of armed Red Guards harassed, arrested, and executed millions of perceived "capitalist roaders" within the Communist Party. Among its many victims were Chairman Liu, who died in prison, and Deng Xiaoping—a future premier—who was stripped of party rank and sent to a farm. Mao then reinstituted his official cult of personality through a compilation of his quotations, the *Little Red Book,* of which more than 350 million copies were printed. But these excesses only weakened China. In the face of a resurgent Soviet Union under Premier LEONID BREZHNEV, even Mao and his fellow hard-liners felt he had little recourse but to mend fences with the United States, their bitterest ideological enemy. In 1972 he invited President RICHARD M. NIXON to Beijing to reestablish friendly relations. Mao by then was old and infirm, so direction of the cultural revolution fell upon his wife, Jiang Qing, and her radical gang of four. The great chairman died in Beijing on September 9, 1976, and was replaced by HUA GUOFENG, his handpicked successor. Within a year his wife and the gang of four were arrested and tried, while Deng Xiaoping was rehabilitated. The revolutionary fervor of Maoism was then officially dropped in favor of more pragmatic approaches. But Mao nonetheless was widely mourned. More than any other individual, he brought China out of backwardness and onto the world stage. His revolutionary strategy ensured the perpetuation of communist rule, but at a tremendous cost in lives and personal freedom. Yet such was Mao's reputation that party members dared not criticize him until 1981, which resulted in the sacking of Hua and his replacement by Deng. For all his crassness and ideological zealotry—and the deaths of an estimated 50 million people—Mao's efficacy as the father of modern China and a leading international statesman of the 20th century remains unquestioned.

Further Reading

Chen, Jian. *Mao's China and the Cold War.* Chapel Hill: University of North Carolina Press, 2001.

Chevrier, Yves. *Mao and the Chinese Revolution.* New York: Interlink Books, 2003.

Feigon, Lee. *Mao: A Reinterpretation.* Chicago: Ivan R. Dee, 2002.

Lynch, Michael J. *Mao.* New York: Routledge, 2004.

Mao Zedong. *On Guerrilla Warfare.* Urbana: University of Illinois Press, 2000.

Law, Kam-yee, ed. *The Chinese Cultural Revolution Reconsidered.* New York: Palgrave Macmillan, 2003.

Short, Philip. *Mao: A Life.* New York: Henry Holt, 2000.

Weststad, Odd Arne. *Decisive Encounters: The Chinese Civil War, 1946–1950.* Stanford, Calif.: Stanford University Press, 2003.

Marcos, Ferdinand (1917–1989) *president of the Philippines*

Ferdinand Edralin Marcos was born in Sarrat, Ilocos Norte, the Philippines, on September 11, 1917, the son of a politician. While studying law at the University of the Philippines in 1935, he was indicted for the murder of his father's political opponent. Marcos completed his studies in jail, and passed his bar exam brilliantly. He was subsequently cross-examined by the Philippine Supreme Court and ultimately released. During World War II, Marcos claimed, he fought with anti-Japanese guerrillas, but his record in combat is poorly documented. Nonetheless after the war, he served as a legal aide to President MANUEL ROXAS. In 1949 Marcos was elected to the House of Representatives with the Liberal Party where he remained for a decade. Marcos further enhanced his political appeal in 1954 when he married wealthy Imelda Romualdez from the island of Leyte. In 1959 he successfully ran for a seat in the Senate, rising to Speaker by 1965. That year he fully expected to be nominated as the party's presidential candidate but lost out to DIOSDADO MACAPAGAL. Marcos then angrily joined the Nationalist Party as its nominee and won the

election by a wide margin. In 1969 he also gained distinction by becoming the first Filipino executive officer reelected for a second consecutive term in office.

Marcos had entered office on a pledge to build up national industry, fight corruption, and suppress various armed insurgencies. Throughout his first two terms he enacted the necessary measures, but ingrained social problems changed little. Consequently, the nation was beset by the Maoist-inspired New People's Army and the Muslim-oriented Moro National Liberation Front. Rising public discontent with the worsening economy also triggered widespread student and worker demonstrations. Problems were further exacerbated by a manifold increase in corruption and cronyism, much of which could be laid at the administration's doorstep. Marcos did little to prevent his friends and allies from helping themselves to the public largesse, while his wife Imelda flaunted her opulent lifestyle. By 1972 Marcos would clearly lose elections slated for that year. Determined to retain power, he apparently ordered supporters to stage several unexplained bombings that could be blamed on the communists. Marcos used the ensuing confusion as a pretext for declaring martial law on September 21, 1972, and tightening his grip on power with a new constitution.

Marcos spent the next 10 years ruling as a despot, using the notorious Philippine Constabulary to crack down on dissent and arrest political opponents. Foremost among these was Senator Benigno Aquino, who was imprisoned for several years without trial. However, because Marcos always couched his actions in stridently anticommunist rhetoric, he never antagonized his biggest supporter, the United States. The Philippine economy, meanwhile, continued sinking under the weight of corruption and mismanagement. By 1980 Marcos was in poor health, the communist and Muslim insurgencies ran amok in the countryside, and the nation seemed ripe for change. Martial law was lifted in 1981, but Marcos continued ruling by decree. Senator Aquino, who had been allowed to visit the United States for medical treatment, then returned to the Philippines intending to oust the dictator from power. However, he had no sooner stepped off the plane on August 21, 1983, than he was murdered by soldiers loyal to Marcos. Public indignation over the senator's death led to an outpouring of sympathy for his widow, CORAZON AQUINO, who protested Marcos's continuation in power. A decisive corner had been turned in Philippine history.

In the fall of 1985 Marcos announced snap elections before the political opposition could crystallize around Aquino. But he had totally underestimated the depth of public resentment against his regime and the determination of Corazon to avenge her husband's death. Not surprisingly, Marcos was declared the winner on February 7, 1986, but amid charges of wholesale fraud. As discontent spread to the middle classes, who joined ever-growing street protests, Marcos ordered the military into action. Many troops rebelled rather than fire into the crowds and, furthermore, a rebellious army base was cordoned off by a million protesters. Neither the defense secretary not other leading generals would encourage the troops to take action. Marcos then realized that the game was up and, urged by the United States, he and Imelda left for Hawaii on February 25, 1986, just as Corazon Aquino was sworn into office. Their estimated personal worth was then in excess of between $5 billion and $10 billion, looted from the national treasury. While in exile Marcos used his great wealth to fund several aborted uprisings against the Aquino administration, all of which failed. Marcos died in Hawaii on September 28, 1989, a hated symbol of authoritarian excess upended by an ebullient display of people power. His body was not allowed to return to the Philippines until 1993.

Further Reading

Celoza, Albert F. *Ferdinand Marcos and the Philippines: The Political Economy of Authoritarianism.* Westport, Conn.: Praeger, 1997.

Lande, Carl H. "The Return of 'People Power' in the Philippines." *Journal of Democracy* 12 (April 2001): 88–102.

Marcos, Ferdinand E. *The Democratic Revolution in the Philippines.* Englewood Cliffs, N.J.: Prentice-Hall, 1979.

Roach, Frank R. "Benevolent Meddling: The United States's Involvement in the 1986 Overthrow of Ferdinand Marcos." Unpublished master's thesis, California State University–Dominguez Hills, 2000.

Thompson, Mark R. *The Anti-Marcos Struggle: Personalistic Rule and Democratic Transition in the Philippines.* New Haven, Conn:. Yale University Press, 1995.

Margai, Albert (1910–1980) *prime minister of Sierra Leone*

Albert Michael Margai was born in Gbangbatok, Sierra Leone, the son of a Mende businessman. He was educated at Catholic missionary schools and served several years as a medical nurse before being licensed as a pharmacist. In 1944 Margai visited England for the purpose of studying law and three years later he was called to the bar. He returned to Sierra Leone the following year, becoming the colony's first trained attorney. In this capacity Margai established a successful practice in the Protectorate region, which was in the hinterland and away from the Creole-dominated capital of Freetown. He was also active as a solicitor and advocate in the Sierra Leone Supreme Court. By 1951 Margai had been elected to the Protectorate assembly and with his brother, MILTON MARGAI, he helped to found the Sierra Leone People's Party (SLPP). This was an organization dedicated to political independence from Great Britain, if by gradual means. Over the next five years Margai enjoyed repeated success in local elections, but he grew disillusioned with his elder brother's conservatism. In 1957 he successfully challenged Milton for leadership of the SLPP, but he was talked into relinquishing control. When his brother became Sierra Leone's first prime minister in 1959, Albert declined a cabinet post and instead founded his own organization, the People's National Party (PNP), in concert with Siaka Stevens. The rift between the brothers remained unhealed until 1960, when Margai allowed the PNP to join a united front government for the purpose of constitutional negotiations with Great Britain. Margai had a conspicuous role in these discussions and won appointment as minister of natural resources. Stevens, meanwhile, who was increasingly more radical, broke with the PNP and founded his own All People's Congress (APC). On April 27, 1961, Sierra Leone became an independent nation with Milton Margai as prime minister and brother Albert holding the portfolio of minister of finance.

The pace of Margai's political fortunes quickened following his brother's death on April 29, 1964, when he was appointed prime minister to succeed him. Many in the SLPP leadership protested the constitutionality of this move, and several cabinet ministers were dismissed in consequence. Nonetheless Margai was knighted by Queen Elizabeth II in 1965 and generally accepted as the legitimate head of state. He also maintained a high visibility in African nationalist politics, and in 1966 he openly criticized Great Britain for its Rhodesian policies. As leader, Margai pursued economic policies that favored the southern reaches of the country where his Mende people predominated. The government also turned a blind eye to corruption and a failing economy, which further alienated many citizens. Margai then expressed admiration for the centralized regimes of Ghana and Guinea, hinting strongly that Sierra Leone should scrap its parliamentary system of governance in favor of a republican one and be ruled as a one-party state. This brought on suspicions that he was about to install a dictatorship, which only swelled the ranks of Stevens's opposition APC. Margai did little to allay such fears when he announced that a military plot to overthrow the government had been quashed and declared a state of emergency. To the citizenry of Sierra Leone it appeared that Sir Albert was losing his grip on power while being determined to maintain it.

New national elections held in March 1967 resulted in an APC victory, and the British governor general, Sir Henry Lightfoot-Boston, declared Stevens the new prime minister. However, General David Lansana, a Margai supporter, declared martial law and arrested both men. He then installed a National Reformation Council that ruled for a year before being overthrown. In 1968 Siaka Stevens was installed as prime minister and subsequent investigations proved that Margai had rigged the recent electoral contest. At this point the former executive stepped down from politics and entered self-imposed exile in London. He died in Washington, D.C., on December 18, 1980. Ironically it fell upon his rival, Stevens, to adopt a republican constitution in 1971 and he served as president of a one-party state.

Further Reading

Cartwright, John R. *Political Leadership in Sierra Leone.* Buffalo, N.Y.: University of Toronto Press, 1978.

Copins, John. *Albert Margai of Sierra Leone.* London: Nelson, 1966.

Ferme, Mariane C. *The Underneath of Things: Violence, History, and Everyday Life in Sierra Leone.* Berkeley: University of California Press, 2001.

Forna, Aminatta. *The Devil That Danced on Water: A Daughter's Memoir.* London: HarperCollins, 2002.

Hinton, Samuel S. *University Student Protests and Political Change in Sierra Leone.* Lewiston, N.Y.: Edwin Mellen, 2002.

Hirsch, John L. *Sierra Leone: Diamonds and the Struggle for Democracy.* Boulder, Colo.: Lynne Rienner, 2001.

Margai, Milton (1895–1964) *prime minister of Sierra Leone*

Milton Augustus Margai was born in Gbangbatok, Sierra Leone, on December 7, 1895, into the large Mende ethnic group. His homeland was referred to as the Protectorate to differentiate it from the main colony of Freeport on the coast. He attended missionary schools locally before venturing to England in 1920 to study medicine at the University of Durham. In 1926 he became the first African from the Protectorate to receive a medical degree. Back home Margai enjoyed a wide-ranging career in the colony's backcountry, where he pioneered advanced midwifery techniques for the primitive tribesmen. During a career that spanned 22 years, Margai rose to become the colony's chief medical officer. He befriended innumerable traditional tribal chiefs, upon whose support he could build a political career. Margai began dabbling in politics in 1946 when he founded the Sierra Leone Organization Society and three years later edited the first Protectorate newspaper, the *Sierra Leone Observer.* In 1950 Margai resigned from medicine altogether to concentrate on politics. His goal was eventual independence from Great Britain, although he sought this in a cautious, gradual manner. In 1951 the British allowed the formation of political parties and Margai established the Sierra Leone People's Party (SLPP), of which he was the head. This was a unique organization by local standards, for it solicited members from both the Protectorate tribes of the interior and the Creoles (descendants of freed slaves) concentrated in Freeport.

The first national elections held in 1951 established the SLPP as the majority party, and Margai served as parliamentary leader. He also held down a number of ministerial positions, such as health, agriculture, and business. Between 1954 and 1958 Margai served as Sierra Leone's chief minister in its dealings with Great Britain. But by 1957 more radical elements under Margai's younger brother, ALBERT MARGAI, grew impatient with the slow pace of reform. That year Albert successfully challenged the elder Margai for party head by a single vote—but peer pressure made him relinquish the post. Milton then resumed his role as head of parliament and in 1959 he was appointed Sierra Leone's first prime minister. In 1960 he led a United National Front coalition government to London for constitutional talks. When national independence was acquired on April 27, 1961, Margai became the nation's first prime minister. The transfer of power, fraught with peril, had been remarkable peaceful.

As a politician Margai remained a strong proponent of democracy. He sought proper representation for all ethnic groups and insisted that opposition forces enjoy freedom of speech. His governmental policies were inclusive by nature and included no less than five Creole cabinet ministers. Curiously Margai himself was hardly the image of the dynamic leader or forceful orator usually associated with Pan-African movements. He was instead mild-mannered, soft-spoken, and extremely shrewd. In fact the SLPP owed its very success to his practice of melding the modern national elites with traditional centers of power. The party thus enjoyed great popularity among the majority of Sierra Leone's population and banished the Creole minority from political dominance. The country benefited from this inherent sense of political stability, and from Margai's insistence upon friendly relations with Great Britain. His pro-business, free-market approach to national economics gave the former colony considerable prosperity in the immediate post-independence period. He was knighted by Queen Elizabeth II in 1959 and died peacefully in Freetown on April 28, 1964. Margai was the architect of Africa's most peaceful and conservative transition from colonialism to viable independence. He was succeeded by his brother Albert.

Further Reading

Abraham, Arthur. *Mende Government and Politics under Colonial Rule: A Historical Study of Political Change in Sierra Leone, 1890–1937*. New York: Oxford University Press, 1979.

Ferme, Mariane C. *The Underneath of Things: Violence, History, and Everyday Life in Sierra Leone*. Berkeley: University of California Press, 2001.

Hirsch, John L. *Sierra Leone: Diamonds and the Struggle for Democracy*. Boulder, Colo.: Lynne Rienner, 2001.

Jackson, Michael. *In Sierra Leone*. Durham: Duke University Press, 2004.

Kandeh, Jimmy D. "Dynamics of State, Class, and Political Ethnicity: A Comparative Study of State-Society Relations in Colonial and Post-Colonial

Sierra Leone (1896–1986)." Unpublished Ph.D. diss., University of Wisconsin-Madison, 1987.

Wyse, Akintola J. G. *H. C. Bankole-Bright and Politics in Colonial Sierra Leone, 1919–1958*. New York: Cambridge University Press, 1991.

Marković, Ante (1924–) *prime minister of Yugoslavia*

Ante Marković was born in Konjic, Bosnia-Herzegovina, on November 25, 1924, and as a teen he developed an affinity for progressive politics by joining the Organization of the Communist Youth of Yugoslavia. After the nation had been invaded by German forces in 1941 he fought with the underground partisan movement of MARSHAL TITO and in 1943 was elected a member of the Yugoslav Communist Party. The war ended with a complete victory for Tito's forces, and in 1945 he established the People's Republic of Yugoslavia. This was a tightly controlled federation of six ethnic enclaves, or republics, all centralized under the control of the Community Party. Marković used his party credentials to attend college and in 1954 he graduated from the University of Zagreb with a degree in electrical engineering. He had settled in Croatia and began accepting various managerial assignments. Foremost among these was as director of Rade Koncar, one of the country's largest machine factories. Marković acquired a reputation as a political maverick for his liberal, pro-Western viewpoints. In 1982 he was chosen to serve as president of the Executive Council of Croatia, and in May 1986 he became president of Croatia.

Toward the end of the 1980s Yugoslavia was beset by recurring economic crises that threatened to unravel its cohesiveness. Through 1988 the sitting prime minister, Branko Mikulic, attempted to resolve the situation through extensive economic reforms, but he was stymied by an uncooperative legislature. Basically, delegates from the more advanced, Western-looking republics of Slovenia and Croatia could not agree with leaders of the less developed, more doctrinaire Serbia. That republic, which boasted the strongest communist party of the nation, was loath to undertake any reforms that might undercut its dominance in national affairs. When Mikulic failed to overcome the impasse, he tendered his resignation on December 30, 1988. Throughout January 1989 Serbian leader Slobodan Milosevic managed to obstruct the election of Stipe

Mesic as Yugoslavia's new prime minister. It was not until March 16, 1989, that Croats and Serbs could agree upon Marković as a compromise candidate and allow him to be sworn into office.

Marković faced the unenviable task of trying to revitalize the moribund, state-controlled economy while simultaneously holding the patchwork republic together. But he had long enjoyed the reputation of an unorthodox communist, who readily forsook ideology when pragmatism was needed. Therefore in January 1990 he stunned the political establishment by calling for the expected economic liberalization to coincide with the legalization of multiparty pluralism. He then advanced an ambitious blueprint to construct an entirely "new form of socialism" based upon technology and political freedom. He immediately applied "shock therapy" to the economy with wage freezes and spending cuts to rein in the 500 percent annual inflation rate. Within months the economy improved, along with Yugoslavia's standing among Western creditors. Marković sought no less than implementation of a free-market economy and closer integration with Western Europe. But the turning point in his political fortunes—and Yugoslavia's—happened in January 1990 when the League of Communists splintered and collapsed. A political free-for-all began in earnest.

Unfortunately for Marković—and Yugoslavia itself—the onset of political liberalization triggered a concomitant rise in nationalistic aspirations. "Our situation is very complex," he conceded. "We are one country with two alphabets, three religions, four languages, five nationalities, and twenty-three million incorrigible individualists." By 1990 five republics began questioning their continuing alliance to the Yugoslav federation, while Serbia turned belligerent, threatening to use the federal army (mostly Serbian) to enforce unity. Slovenia and Croatia disregarded the threat and began seceding from the union, so in July 1990 the Serbs launched full-scale invasions of both. Try as he might to placate the combatants, Marković was unable to restore order after six months of internecine fighting. Seeing the futility of his position and correctly sensing that the nation was doomed as a political entity, he resigned from office on December 20, 1991, the last prime minister of Yugoslavia. Marković has since returned to business in the new democratic nation of Croatia, which was built upon the ashes of the old communist-dominated republic.

Further Reading

Andrejevich, M. "What Future for the League of Communists?" *Report of Eastern Europe* 1 (March 2, 1990): 32–37.

Latey, M. "The General Crisis of Socialism." *World Today* 45 (August–September 1989): 131–134.

Malesevic, Sinisa. *Ideology, Legitimacy, and the New State: Yugoslavia, Serbia, and Croatia.* Portland, Ore.: Frank Cass, 2002.

Naimark, Norman M., and Holly Case. *Yugoslavia and Its Historians: Understanding the Balkan Wars of the 1990s.* Stanford, Calif.: Stanford University Press, 2003.

Ramet, Sabrina P. *Balkan Babel: The Disintegration of Yugoslavia from the Death of Tito to the Fall of Milosevic.* Boulder, Colo.: Westview Press, 2002.

Rogel, Carole. *The Breaking Up of Yugoslavia and Its Aftermath.* Westport, Conn.: Greenwood Press, 2004.

Thomas, Raju G. G. *Yugoslavia Unraveled: Sovereignty, Self Determination, Intervention.* Lanham, Md.: Lexington Books, 2003.

Martens, Wilfried (1936   ) *prime minister of Belgium*

Wilfried Martens was born in Sleidinge, Belgium, on April 19, 1936, the son of farmers. His father died while he was young, and he was raised by a stepfather. Martens was Flemish, that is, a Dutch-speaking Belgian citizen, and closely identified with his language and culture. This put him at odds with the French-speaking Walloon population, and tensions between the two groups have by and large dominated and defined Belgian national politics. In 1954 Martens enrolled in the Catholic University of Leuvens, where he obtained a doctorate in law four years later. He was also active in Flemish youth organizations, and during the 1958 World's Fair in Brussels, he was arrested for painting over French signs that did not contain Dutch. Martens initiated his political career in 1962 by joining the Flemish Social Christian Party, in which he held several posts and eventually rose to be chairman in 1972. He also demonstrated considerable skill as a negotiator, so commencing in 1965, he served as a cabinet-level adviser. Martens himself was finally elected to the legislature in 1974 as a Flemish activist. He continued enhancing his reputation for astute politics, and in April 1979, following the resignation of Prime Minister Paul van den Boeynants, he was authorized to form a government. The 42-year-old Martens's ascension surprised political pundits, for he was the first Belgian executive to hold office without first having served in a ministerial capacity.

Martens remained in office almost continuously for 13 years, a good indication of his ability to strike a bargain with competing interests. More often than not, his government consisted of weak coalitions between an assortment of Christian Democrats, Socialists, and Liberals. His tenure was marred by intensifying conflict between the nation's French- and Dutch-speaking communities. Martens had moderated his earlier inflexibility on linguistic and cultural matters and sought wide-scale accommodation. He cleverly accomplished this through major constitutional reforms that altered the fundamental nature of Belgium's government. Discarding the centralized, unitary state, Martens implemented a new federal republic that bequeathed to warring regions greater autonomy in matters of language, education, and finance. The changes did not defuse all tensions arising from ethnic rivalry but did grant Belgium a more harmonious polity and allowed the government to spend more time on equally pressing matters.

Belgium, as a member of NATO, was beholden to security arrangements agreed on by its ruling council. In March 1985 this entailed deployment of American-built cruise and Pershing II nuclear-tipped missiles to counteract a massive arms buildup by the Soviet Union. Martens agreed to accept the missiles but, as a sop to the nation's burgeoning antinuclear lobby, only after American-Soviet arms-reduction talks were concluded. When they failed to produce any new breakthroughs, Martens accepted the weapons as promised. Their arrival triggered a mass protest by peace activists, but Belgium had reconfirmed its determination to act as a responsible NATO member.

Martens had less luck invigorating the moribund Belgian economy. Businesses had long been held hostage to mandatory wage increases that sapped the vitality out of their growth. To counter such practices Martens instituted badly needed wage freezes and other austerity measures. By 1981 this caused the Socialists to bolt from the coalition, and Martens was replaced by Mark Eyskens that April. However, new elections were held and a surprising showing by Liberals and Christian Democrats enabled Martens to resume power by December. He was also actively promoting European

unity. In 1976 he helped found the European People's Party to serve in the new multinational legislature. When he was forced to resign as prime minister in the fall of 1991 in favor of Jean-Luc Dehaene, Martens had compiled the longest record of any 20th-century Belgian executive. All told he presided over 10 separate coalition governments. Having been elected president of the European People's Party in 1990, he headed the group in the legislature in 1994. Between 1993 and 1996 Martens also served as head of the European Union of Christian Democrats. The architect of Belgian federalism remains active in European legislative matters to the present time.

Further Reading

Fitzmaurice, John. *The Politics of Belgium: A Unique Federation.* Boulder, Colo.: Westview Press, 1996.

Hooghe, Liesbet. *A Leap in the Dark: Nationalist Conflict and Federal Reform in Belgium.* Ithaca, N.Y.: Cornell University Press, 1991.

Leonard, Dick. "The Belgian General Election of 13 December 1987." *Electoral Studies* 8, no. 2 (1989): 157–162.

Meerhaeghe, Marcel A. *Belgium and EC Membership Evaluated.* New York: St. Martin's Press, 1992.

Noppe, Jo. "The Parliamentary Activity of the Belgian and Dutch PMs: A Comparison between the Martens VIII, Dahaene I, and Lubbers III Administrations." *Res Publica* 42, no. 4 (2000): 521–545.

Timmermans, Arco. *High Politics in Low Countries: Functions and Effects of Coalition Agreements in Belgium and the Netherlands.* Burlington, Vt.: Ashgate, 2003.

Masaryk, Tomáš (1850–1937) *president of Czechoslovakia*

Tomáš Garrigue Masaryk was born in Hodonin, Moravia, on March 7, 1850, the son of a Slovak coachman father and a Czech servant mother, and a subject of the Austro-Hungarian Empire. Masaryk overcame poverty to attend the University of Vienna, where he obtained a doctorate in philosophy in 1876. He pursed advanced graduate work at the University of Leipzig, Germany, and met his American future wife, Charlotte Garrigue. Masaryk then ventured to the United States in 1878, where he married Garrigue and attached

Tomáš Masaryk *(Library of Congress)*

her maiden name to his own to demonstrate gender equality. Masaryk finished his education in 1882 and subsequently accepted a professorship in philosophy at the University of Prague. He soon established himself as a leading scholar of his time and wrote voluminously on a variety of topics. Masaryk also began dabbling in Czech nationalism and argued for a federal arrangement within the Austro-Hungarian Empire for greater political and cultural autonomy. In 1880 he set out to put his beliefs into practice by being elected to the national legislature as part of the Young Czech Party. For two years he championed minority rights, educational reform, and personal freedom, acquiring a reputation as a dangerous radical. In 1892 he resumed his academic career and also edited several Czech nationalist publications. In this capacity Masaryk distinguished himself for rejecting the Pan-Slavic notion of embracing Russia as a model, and instead endorsed the democratic institutions of Britain and France. By 1901 he had returned to politics as part of the Realist Party, where he agitated for Czech autonomy and also denounced the empire's acquisition of

Bosnia-Herzegovina. Up to this point Masaryk had been willing to reform the Austro-Hungarian Empire but after the commencement of World War I in August 1914, he felt that the only logical recourse was its abolishment.

In December 1914 Masaryk fled Vienna for Paris and began courting the Western Allies to support an independent Czech-Slovak state. He was accompanied in these efforts by EDVARD BENEŠ, his most accomplished student. Masaryk went on to London, while Beneš remained behind to staff the new Czechoslovak National Council, an unofficial government in exile. In 1917 Masaryk ventured to Bolshevik Russia to negotiate creation of a Czech Legion of captured soldiers and lead it out of Siberia. The legion was then reconstituted as an 80,000-strong military force on the western front, with Masaryk as commander in chief. Once back in the United States, he originated and concluded the so-called Pittsburgh Pact with Slovak leaders, which established a federal state of two autonomous regions. He subsequently conferred with American president WOODROW WILSON, his fellow philosopher, and convinced him to recognize the government in exile. Recognition was granted on October 28, 1918, and Masaryk returned in triumph to Prague as a liberator. The following December he was elected the first president of the new nation of Czechoslovakia.

Despite his origins and education, Masaryk was steeped in the traditions of Western-style democracy and he determined to make his country the only such system in central Europe. To that end a republican government and a constitution were adopted along French lines. Czechs and Slovaks were thus welded together into a single, federal state with each half enjoying complete autonomy in cultural and linguistic matters. As president, Masaryk assumed a post with only ceremonial powers—the prime minister actually ran the country—but he wielded tremendous moral authority in national affairs. The looming presence of nearby Germany convinced him to support the new League of Nations as a hedge against future aggression, and in 1924 he shored up national defenses by entering alliances with France, Yugoslavia, and Romania. Furthermore, Masaryk put himself in the forefront of civil liberties by cultivating respect for the national legislature and strongly endorsing protection for all ethnic minorities. He proved a popular executive and was reelected by wide margins in 1920, 1927, and 1934.

Masaryk's scholarly bent and democratic demeanor proved so endearing that the government granted him his own castle at Lany as a token of gratitude. Poor health forced the aging philosopher/president to conclude 17 years of sterling service by resigning from office in 1935 and he was succeeded by Beneš. He died at Lany on September 14, 1937, honored as both the liberator and father of his country.

Further Reading

Masaryk, Tomáš G. *President Mararyk Tells His Story.* New York: G. P. Putnam's Sons, 1935.

Ncudorf, Mariel. "T. G. Masaryk's Perception of Czech Nationalism before 1914." *History of European Ideas* 15 (August 1992): 571–576.

Orzoff, Andrea R. "Battle for the Castle: The Friday Men and the Czechoslovakia Republic, 1918–1938." Unpublished Ph.D. diss., Stanford University, 2001.

Skilling, H. Gordon. *T. G. Masaryk: Against the Current, 1882–1914.* University Park: Pennsylvania State University Press, 1994.

Winters, Stanley B., Robert B. Pynsent, and Harry Hanak, eds. *T. G. Masaryk (1850–1937),* 3 vols. London: Macmillan, 1990.

Zeman, Z. A. B. *The Mararyks: The Making of Czechoslovakia.* New York: I. B. Tauris, 1990.

Massamba-Débat, Alphonse (1921–1977)

president of Congo

Alphonse Massamba-Débat was born in Nkolo, French Equatorial Africa, in 1921, a member of the Lari tribe. He was educated locally at missionary schools, and in 1934 he served as a teacher in neighboring Chad. By 1940 the region was swept by mounting anticolonial fervor, and Massamba-Débat joined the Chadian Progressive Party. He subsequently enhanced his political skills by serving as general secretary of the Association for the Development of Chad in 1945. Massamba-Débat relocated to Brazzaville (in present-day Congo) in 1947 as a school headmaster and also joined the Progressive Party of Congo (PPC). By this time other progressive movements had taken root, most notably the Union démocratique pour la défense des intérêts africains (UDDIA), Democratic Union for the Defense of African Interests, under Abbe Fulbert Youlou, a Catholic priest. Massamba-Débat joined the new organization, and by 1957 he had abandoned

teaching to pursue politics full time. That year he received the portfolio of minister of education, and two years later he was elected to the legislative assembly. Massamba-Débat handled his affairs adroitly and in 1959 he rose to president of the assembly. Congo gained its independence from France in August 1960 and Youlou was elected the first president. Massamba-Débat was then successively appointed minister of state and of planning. But over the next three years many citizens resented what they perceived as a corrupt and inefficient administration, so protests mounted. Even Massamba-Débat criticized the regime for being excessively conservative in domestic affairs and overly reliant on France, so he resigned from office. Events crested in May 1963 when Youlou was forced from office and Massamba-Débat became the nation's second executive.

Massamba-Débat was sworn into office on December 19, 1963, and introduced a Marxist political agenda. Intent upon securing better control of political affairs, he introduced one-party rule under the new National Revolutionary Movement in July 1964. As secretary general of the party he tried to weld all disparate political factions under one roof in the pursuit of "scientific socialism." He also swung Congo sharply to the left by nationalizing broad sectors of the economy and establishing close diplomatic ties to the Soviet Union and Communist China. To cement his credentials as a Pan-African nationalist, Massamba-Débat also granted sanctuary to rebel fighters attempting to overthrow the colonial regime in neighboring Angola. He further radicalized national politics by nationalizing missionary schools, and instituted a people's militia to counteract the military's growing influence. In 1966 he attempted to meld the army and military under a single command, which prompted a mutiny by junior officers. Massamba-Débat relented but thereafter his relations with the military remained uneasy.

Throughout Massamba-Débat's tenure in office, Congo's economy quickly sank under the weight of centralized planning. The president felt it necessary to keep the national currency in the Franc zone and maintained it over cries of neocolonialism from more strident factions. At length, Massamba-Débat was caught between doctrinaire Marxists in his party and political interference from the army—both of which were beyond his control. On September 4, 1968, a sluggish economy and military dissatisfaction with political affairs prompted Major Marien Ngouabi to depose Massamba-Débat in a bloodless coup. The former executive was then placed under house arrest until Ngouabi was assassinated in 1977. Military officials suspected the former president was the guiding hand behind a political conspiracy, so they executed him without trial on March 25, 1977.

Further Reading

Amphas-Mampoua. *Political Transformations of the Congo.* Durham, N.C.: Pentland Press, 2000.

Decalo, Samuel, Virginia Thompson, and Richard Adloff. *Historical Dictionary of Congo.* Metuchen, N.J.: Scarecrow Press, 1996.

Beckett, Paul. "Revolutionary Systems: A Conceptual and Comparative Study of Four African Revolutionary Regimes," 2 vols. Unpublished Ph.D. diss., University of Wisconsin–Madison, 1970.

Gauze, Rene. *The Politics of Congo-Brazzaville.* Stanford, Calif.: Hoover Institution Press, 1973.

Hawn, James R. "Difficulties in Diplomacy: A Case Study of Relations between the United States and the Republic of Congo, 1960–1965." Unpublished master's thesis, Old Dominion University, 1998.

Tevoedjre, Eric. "The Limits and Uses of Deviance in Franco-African Relations: The Relations of Guinea (Conakry), Congo, and Benin with France, 1958–1981." Unpublished Ph.D. diss., Johns Hopkins University, 1990.

Massey, William (1856–1925) *prime minister of New Zealand*

William Ferguson Massey was born on March 26, 1856, in Londonderry, Ireland, the son of a farmer. He immigrated with his family to New Zealand in 1870 and eventually settled near Auckland. A farmer himself, he was attracted to agrarian politics and successfully ran for a seat in the House of Representatives in 1894—he held it for the next 31 years. New Zealand was then under the political sway of the Liberal Party led by Richard Seddon, and farmers feared he would nationalize their landholdings. Massey countered by demanding that farmers with leases be able to purchase and own the land they worked. His leadership resonated with agrarian interests, and soon various conservative political elements coalesced around him. Being an astute politician and an effective debater, Massey was elected opposition leader in Parliament in September 1903. He took the

process a step further in February 1909 by cobbling various conservative interests into a single entity, the Reform Party. Massey provided effective political opposition to the Liberals, whose power waned after the death of Seddon in 1906, and in July 1912 he formed a coalition government of his own. As prime minister, one of his first acts was to allow freeholders to buy land at its original value. He also acted decisively to crush two violent strikes by miners and dock workers in 1912 and 1913. The latter was terminated through use of mounted police forces raised in rural areas and derided as "Massey's Cossacks." His rough handling of the strikes also gave additional impetus to the rise of the new Labor Party in 1916. Nonetheless Massey's swift actions garnered public approval and he was to remain in office for the next 13 years—usually without a majority in Parliament.

Massey's tenure in office coincided with the onset of World War I. Despite their distance from the European theater, his fellow New Zealanders felt obliged to support Great Britain in its hour of need. In August 1915 the prime minister promoted a National Government in concert with Liberal Party leader Joseph Ward, who received the portfolio of finance minister. The two strong willed individuals did not mesh favorably with each other but their consistent support of the war effort rendered New Zealand a valuable Pacific ally. During the course of events Massey was twice summoned to London to participate in the Imperial War Cabinet, and in 1919 he was also present during the signing of the Treaty of Versailles. Under his tutelage New Zealand began asserting itself on the international scene for the first time and he vociferously supported creation of the new League of Nations. However, Massey was keen to recognize the British monarch as head of the empire, and he opposed granting any of its dominions greater autonomy. This stance was a reflection of his general conservative nature, which colored both his world view and reaction to domestic events.

Massey's good performance during the war years resulted in an impressive victory for the Reform Party in 1919 and he was able to drop his contentious coalition with the Liberals. But the onset of peace led to an economic downturn and, to shore up rural support, the government enacted export controls on meat and dairy products, the nation's primary exports. When the economy failed to revive by 1922, disenchanted voters favored the Labor Party in large numbers, and Massey was again forced to turn to the Liberals to remain in power. He still managed to effect a reduction in income taxes and a return to penny postage but his health began to fail him the following year. Massey died in office on May 10, 1925, enjoying the second-longest tenure in office of any New Zealand prime minister. Despite rather conservative tendencies he is regarded as a fine organizer and a talented administrator of indomitable will.

Further Reading

Gardner, W. J. "W. F. Massey in Power, 1912–1925." *Political Science* 13, no. 2 (1961): 3–30.

———. *William Massey.* Wellington, New Zealand: A. H. and A. W. Reed, 1969.

Hamer, D. A. *The New Zealand Liberals: The Years of Power, 1891–1912.* Auckland, New Zealand: Auckland University Press, 1988.

Massey, D. Christine. *The Life of Rt. Hon. W. F. Massey, P.C., L.L.D.* Auckland, New Zealand: D. C. Massey, 1999.

Moses, John A., and Christopher Pugsley. *The German Empire and Britain's Pacific Dominions, 1871–1919.* Claremont, Calif.: Regina Books, 2000.

O'Connor, P. S. "Some Political Preoccupations of Mr. Massey, 1918–20." *Political Science* 18, no. 2 (1966): 16–38.

Mazowiecki, Tadeusz (1927–) *prime minister of Poland*

Tadeusz Mazowiecki was born in Plonk, Poland, on April 18, 1927, into a family of Catholic intelligentsia. He studied law and journalism at the University of Warsaw and worked briefly as a publisher before communist authorities removed him for promoting Catholic viewpoints. He then joined the religious dissident group PAX and edited its weekly journal. However, when the strong-willed Mazowiecki clashed with his superiors, he was dismissed and joined another group, the Young Intelligentsia Club, where he edited a Catholic monthly. Mazoweicki was elected head of the small Catholic deputation to the Sejm, or parliament, and sought to reform the communist dictatorship from within. He also bravely disregarded official intolerance toward dissent and spoke out on behalf of religious and academic freedom. The decade of the 1970s witnessed an upsurge in illegal labor activities by Polish workers demanding higher standards of living. Around this time Mazowiecki sponsored intellectual dissident activities and cofounded an independent "Flying University" bereft of government control and censorship. But the turning point in his political career came during August 1980, when workers at the Lenin shipyard in Gdansk illegally went on strike. Mazowiecki arrived on the scene and gained employment as a chief legal adviser to dissident leader Lech Walesa. That same year the independent labor union Solidarity was formed with Mazowiecki as editor of the weekly newsletter. In this manner he strove to form a close alliance between Polish intellectuals and the worker's movement.

The rise of an independent labor union constituted a direct threat to the supremacy of the Communist Party, and the Polish government, under heavy pressure from the Soviet Union, was forced to crack down. Accordingly, in December 1991 General WOJCIECH JARUZELSKI imposed martial law and Mazowiecki, among others, was arrested. He spent nearly a year in jail before being released and resuming his union activities. But the winds of change were blowing throughout Eastern Europe, thanks to the new Soviet premier, MIKHAIL GORBACHEV, who actively promoted liberal reforms. By 1989 communist control of Poland was slipping, and Mazowiecki helped arrange the Roundtable discussions to promote multiparty pluralism. Elections held in June 1989 spelled the end of communist control in Poland, and the following month Walesa insisted that Jaruzelski appoint Mazowiecki as prime minister. He thus became Poland's first noncommunist head of state since the late 1940s.

No sooner did Mazowiecki assume office than he took active steps to dismantle the communist police state he inherited. Basic freedom of the press, speech, and religion were restored and the activities of the secret police curtailed. Moreover, he also began a crash program of economic restructuring to ditch the command economy in favor of a free market. In dealing with former communists Mazowiecki was entirely pragmatic and he retained the services of several experienced bureaucrats in his cabinet. This sparked a direct confrontation with Solidarity head Walesa, who demanded that communists be denied public office. Three ministers were subsequently dismissed but the episode engendered hard feelings between the two former allies. Additional criticism over the slow pace of reform finally induced Mazowiecki to break with Walesa altogether, and in December 1990 he ran for president at the head of his own Democratic Union (DU) party. However, because the economy had since soured, Mazowiecki finished a distant third behind Walesa, with a scant 18 percent of votes cast. One of his last acts in office was signing a treaty with German chancellor Helmut Kohl that confirmed the Oder-Neisse Rivers as the border between Poland and Germany. In April 1994 Mazowiecki united his DU with the Liberal-Democratic Congress party to form a new entity, the Freedom Union.

Mazowiecki has since paid increasing attention to international politics. In 1992 he gained appointment as a special United Nations envoy to Yugoslavia, charged with investigating war crimes. In July 1995 he issued a detailed report that found Serbian leader Slobodan Milosevic guilty of atrocities. Since then Mazowiecki has become closely involved in matters affecting the expansion of the European Union (EU). In January 2003 he represented Poland at talks in Copenhagen, Denmark, and successfully argued for a 1 billion euro loan to help Polish farmers adjust to the new single market. "It won't be an easy jump for our society," he insisted, "but now it is a moment to celebrate."

Further Reading

Castle, Marjorie. *Triggering Communism's Collapse: Perceptions and Power in Poland's Transition.* Lanham, Md.: Rowman and Littlefield, 2002.

Garton Ash, Timothy. *The Polish Revolution: Solidarity, 1980–89.* New Haven, Conn.: Yale University Press, 2002.

Sabbat-Swidlicka, A. "Mazowiecki's Year in Review." *Report on Eastern Europe* 2 (January 1991): 25–31.

Sanford, George. *Democratic Government in Poland: Constitutional Politics since 1989.* New York: Palgrave Macmillan, 2002.

Sharman, J. C. *Repression and Resistance in Communist Europe.* New York: RoutledgeCurzon, 2003.

Szulka, R. "The 1990 Presidential Election in Poland." *Scandinavian Political Studies* 16 (December 1993): 359–382.

M'Ba, Léon (1902–1967) *president of Gabon*

Léon M'Ba was born in Libreville, French Congo, in February 1902, the son of a Fang tribal chieftain. His elder brother was the first member of the tribe ordained a Roman Catholic priest. M'Ba himself was educated locally at missionary schools and subsequently held down menial jobs that Africans were restricted to. As he matured, M'Ba strongly resented French colonial oppression, and he strengthened his ties to various nationalist groups. By persistently presenting Fang grievances to the colonial administration he soon acquired the reputation of a troublemaker. After 1930 M'Ba became a leading exponent of Bwiti, the native Fang religion, which sometimes occasioned the use of human flesh for ceremonial purposes. At the urging of Christian missionaries, M'Ba was then arrested and spent three years in jail before being deported to Oubangui-Chari (modern Central African Republic). During this interval M'Ba studied hard and published numerous essays and booklets on Fang culture and religion, becoming a recognized authority on the subject. He was allowed back to the French Congo in 1946 to take part in radical, anticolonialist politics, and by 1952 he was secretary of the Bloc démocratique Gabonais (BDG), Gabon Democratic Bloc. M'Ba tried and repeatedly failed to win a seat in the territorial legislature, but in 1956 he gained election as mayor of Libreville. The following year the BDG won the majority of seats in popular elections and M'Ba became head of the new National Council. In this capacity he turned aside requests for the French Congo, a relatively affluent colony, to join a large federation of West African states for fear the Congo would be called upon to support poorer neighbors. In 1958 France allowed the colony to be self-governing and M'Ba was promoted to prime minister. In this capacity he led his country into independence as the new nation of Gabon on August 17, 1960.

From the onset M'Ba's tenure in office was marked by contentious controversy. He had previously accepted the legislature's decision to adopt a constitution designed with a weak executive office, but M'Ba sought revisions. A power scramble ensued between the prime minister, whom critics accused of being too pro-French, and the legislature, which wanted to maintain political control. M'Ba unhesitatingly arrested opponents and used intimidation to have the constitution modified in February 1961, which installed him as a strong executive. This was only a prelude to greater attempts at centralizing his control over the entire nation. In 1963 M'Ba sought to merge all opposing parties and factions into the BDG and, hence, under his control. This sparked an outburst of violence from the military, which briefly overthrew and imprisoned M'Ba in February 1964. However, because France regarded him as a valuable ally, its troops intervened and restored him to power. Thereafter M'Ba became solidly identified with French economic interests in Gabon. In fact, he sought to maintain close economic, political, and defense links with France for they buoyed the national economy and perpetuated his rule.

The tenor of M'Ba's administration grew increasingly authoritarian and repressive, to which the French government turned a blind eye. His determination to punish those whom he considered as political opponents basically ended the growth of democracy in Gabon. But by 1966 M'Ba's health had declined to the point where he was unable to run daily affairs of the nation, so he appointed his vice president, Albert Bernard Bongo, as his potential successor. M'Ba died in Paris while receiving medical treatment on November 27, 1967, and Bongo succeeded him. Though despotic and manipulative by nature M'Ba is still recognized as a driving force behind Gabonese independence.

Further Reading

Aicardi de Saint-Paul, Marc. *Gabon: The Development of a Nation.* New York: Routledge, 1989.

Barnes, James F. *Gabon: Beyond the Colonial Legacy.* Boulder, Colo.: Westview Press, 1992.

Darlington, Charles F. *African Betrayal.* New York: D. McKay Co., 1968.

Decalo, Samuel. *The Stable Minority: Civilian Rule in Africa, 1960–1990.* Gainesville, Fla.: FAP Books, 1998.

Gray, Christopher J. *Colonial Rule and Crisis in Equatorial Africa: Southern Gabon, 1850–1940.* Rochester, N.Y.: University of Rochester Press, 2002.

Weinstein, Brian. *Gabon: Nation-building on the Oggone.* Cambridge, Mass.: M.I.T. Press, 1966.

Meighen, Arthur (1874–1960) *prime minister of Canada*

Arthur Meighen was born in Anderson, Ontario, Canada, on June 16, 1874, the son of farmers. He passed through the University of Toronto in 1896 before proceeding west to Manitoba to teach. He also studied law and was called to the bar in 1902. Meighen concluded a successful law practice by being elected to the House of Commons in 1908 as a Conservative, and he quickly distinguished himself through vitriolic debating skills. When the Conservatives returned to power under ROBERT L. BORDEN, he appointed Meighen solicitor general in 1913. World War I erupted the following year, and in 1917 Borden formed a National Government in concert with the Liberals. Meighen then became secretary of state and figured prominently in the passage of several controversial pieces of wartime legislation, including nationalization of Canada's railway system to facilitate the war effort. Meighen also pushed through a highly contentious conscription bill, and he denounced the inhabitants of French-speaking Quebec as "backwards" for opposing it. Even more controversial was the Wartime Election Act that stripped voting rights from citizens of German or Austrian birth, while granting it to female members of military households. His rough handling of the Winnipeg general strike of 1919 also incurred the wrath of organized labor. But through it all Meighen maintained his reputation as a skilled parliamentarian and a sterling orator. When Borden resigned from office on July 10, 1920, he chose Meighen to succeed him as prime minister. Aged but 46 years he became Canada's youngest chief executive.

For all his skill in politics, Meighen's tenure as head of state was brief and stormy. His vitriol toward opponents and his overbearing personality won few friends within his own party and outright animosity from Liberals under WILLIAM LYON MACKENZIE KING. But in 1921 he proved the first Canadian executive officer to exert national priorities. During the Imperial Conference held in London that year, he opposed continuation of the Anglo-Japanese Alliance that had been in effect since 1901. Meighen argued persuasively that the treaty prevented Britain from criticizing Japan's ongoing expansion into China, and that the empire should instead cultivate close defensive ties with the United States. His presentation worked, and British prime minister DAVID LLOYD GEORGE declined to renew the treaty. But Meighen's efforts had little effect on the home front where the economy was in the doldrums. Worse, the conservative vote was split by the rise of the new, western-oriented Progressive Party and in December 1921, Meighen was turned out of office.

For the next five years Meighen functioned as head of the Conservative opposition in Parliament and he performed with his usual effectiveness. Elections held in 1925 made the Conservatives the largest single bloc in the House of Commons, but they failed to obtain a clear majority due to lingering resentment in Quebec over conscription. Mackenzie King was thus able to cobble together a coalition arrangement between Liberals and various small parties and remain in power. However, when the Progressives withdrew from the coalition Mackenzie King requested the British governor general of Canada, Lord Byng, to dissolve Parliament and schedule new elections. Byng not only refused the request, but also dismissed the sitting prime minister and asked Meighen to form a new government in June 1926. The Conservative did so obligingly but Mackenzie King persuasively argued that the entire process was unconstitutional. The Progressives then supported the Liberals in a vote of "no confidence" against Meighen and new elections were scheduled. That September Liberals won resoundingly and Meighen retired from politics to pursue business.

In 1932 Meighen resumed his political career when Prime Minister RICHARD B. BENNETT appointed him to the Senate, where he remained nine years. Meighen then resumed command of the Conservative Party until his bid to regain a seat in Parliament was defeated in 1942. He withdrew from politics a second time to work as an investment banker. Meighen died in Toronto on August 5, 1960, generally regarded as an effective politician but too strident and adversarial by nature to occupy high office.

Further Reading

English, John. *The Decline of Politics: The Conservatives and the Party System, 1901–20.* Buffalo, N.Y.: University of Toronto Press, 1993.

Graham, Roger. *Arthur Meighen: A Biography,* 3 vols. Toronto: Clarke, Irwin, 1960–65.

Graham, W. R. "Some Comments on a Credible Canadian." *Canadian Historical Review* 39, no. 4 (1958): 296–311.

Granatstein, J. L. *The Politics of Survival: The Conservative Party of Canada, 1939–1945.* Toronto: University of Toronto Press, 1967.

Meighen, Arthur. *Unrevised and Unrepented: Debating Speeches and Others.* Toronto: Clark, Irwin, 1949.

Meir, Golda (1898–1978) *prime minister of Israel*

Golda Mabovitch was born in Kiev, imperial Russia, on May 3, 1898, to Jewish peasant parents. As a child she witnessed many pogroms and other acts of violence by Cossacks against the Jewish community. To escape the persecution of czarist Russia, the family immigrated to Milwaukee, Wisconsin, in 1906 and she attended the Teacher's Training School. In 1917 Mabovitch married Morris Myerson and joined the Labor Zionist Party. In this capacity she became active in both socialist politics and efforts to resurrect the Jewish state of Israel. Consistent with her beliefs, in 1921 her family migrated to Palestine, then a League of Nations mandate under British supervision. Myerson subsequently lived on a kibbutz and became active in women's labor affairs. In 1929 she attended the World Zionist Organization as a delegate and also served on the executive board of the Jewish National Council. Soon Myerson was closely involved in organizing illegal Jewish emigration from

Golda Meir *(Library of Congress)*

Europe to Palestine. These activities brought her to the attention of British authorities who watched her closely. In June 1946, when the British arrested leaders of the Jewish Agency, Myerson was tapped to serve as acting director. On May 14, 1948, she was the only female signatory to the Israeli declaration of independence and performed useful work on a clandestine diplomatic mission to King Abdullah of Jordan. Within a year the state of Israel had survived a combined Arab onslaught and became a reality.

In 1948 Myerson briefly served as an ambassador to the Soviet Union before returning home to gain a seat in the Knesset (legislature) as a Mapai (Labor) member. She sufficiently impressed Prime Minister DAVID BEN-GURION to gain an appointment as minister of labor and insurance. Myerson provided two essential services to the struggling Jewish state. First, she oversaw the construction of 200,000 low-income housing units to accommodate the endless stream of Jewish migrants. Second, she shepherded through the National Insurance Act, which provided comprehensive medical and welfare coverage to all Israeli citizens. Ben-Gurion subsequently lauded her as the "Only man in the cabinet." In 1956 Myerson next gained appointment as foreign minister and also, upon Ben-Gurion's insistence, she hebraized her name to Golda Meir. She then became responsible for deliberately cultivating close ties with newly emerging African nations. Ill health finally forced Meir to step down in 1966, but she remained active in party affairs and successfully welded the Mapai to two other socialist parties to form the new Israeli Labor Party. Meir served as party secretary over the next two years.

After Prime Minister LEVI ESHKOL died in March 1969, Meir was tapped to succeed him, becoming Israel's first woman executive. Her popularity proved sufficient to carry the Labor Party through national elections that fall and she subsequently won a full four-year term in office. Meir moved easily onto the international stage and conferred with American president RICHARD M. NIXON about continuing aid to Israel. With American encouragement, Israel opened tentative peace talks with neighboring Arab countries. But she was a hard-liner in dealing with Palestinian militants and supported the settlement of lands captured in the 1967 Arab-Israeli War. Meanwhile, the Egyptians under President ANWAR AL-SADAT, seconded by Syria, were feverishly making preparations for war. The Israeli intelligence community argued that Israel must launch a pre-emptive strike in order to survive, but Meir felt that the country would suffer tremendous diplomatic damage and preferred absorbing the first blow. But when the combined Arab armies struck in October 1973, initiating the so-called Yom Kippur war, the Israelis were caught off-guard. Heavy fighting and losses ensued before the attackers were beaten back and anger over the perceived mishandling of events resulted in new elections. Meir and Labor took losses and managed to stay in power, but the coalition proved untenable. Meir finally resigned on December 8, 1974, and was succeed by Yitzhak Rabin. Out of office Meir continued on as a respected international figure and a beloved national matron. She died in Jerusalem on December 8, 1978, one of the most influential women leaders of the 20th century.

Further Reading

Amdur, Richard. *Golda Meir: A Leader in War and Peace.* New York: Fawcett Columbine, 1990.

Eban, Abba S. *The Political Legacy of Golda Meir.* Milwaukee: Golda Meir Library, University of Wisconsin–Milwaukee, 1995.

Kumaraswamy, R. R., ed. *Revisiting the Yom Kippur War.* Portland, Ore.: Frank Cass, 2000.

Martin, Ralph G. *Golda: Golda Meir, the Romantic Years.* New York: Scribner, 1988.

Medding, Peter V. *Mapai in Israel: Political Organization and Government in a New Society.* Cambridge, England: Cambridge University Press, 1972.

Meir, Golda. *My Life.* New York: Putnam, 1975.

Mengistu Haile Mariam (ca. 1937–) *president of Ethiopia*

Mengistu Haile Mariam was born in Oromo Province, Ethiopia, around 1937, the son of a soldier. He followed into his father's profession by enlisting immediately after high school and was allowed to attend the prestigious Holeta Military Academy. In the course of his early military career Mengistu ventured twice to the United States for advanced training. He remained a relatively anonymous low-ranking officer until 1974, when dissatisfaction over low wages and famine led to the Ethiopian revolution against Emperor HAILE SELASSIE. When the emperor was deposed in September 1974, he was replaced by the Provisional Military Administrative Council, or Dergue (shadow). Mengistu formed part of the council but was primarily a background player during its initial phases. However, he proved himself a ruthless manipulator and over the next two years he arranged for the execution of most of the Dergue members. By 1977 Mengistu's faction had all but shot its way into power and he was formally installed as head of the Dergue's executive committee. In this capacity he officially proclaimed Ethiopia a Marxist-Leninist state and determined to rid it of its feudal institutions and outlook. He therefore proclaimed widespread collectivization of agriculture, the nationalization of private companies, and implementation of health and literacy programs. Ethiopia had also become a people's republic.

Mengistu may have had earnest intentions, but he fulfilled them with murderous intent. Over the next 13 years opponents of his regime, both real and perceived, were simply dragged into the street and executed, with their bloody remains placed on public display. When the United States, aghast at this behavior, cut off all foreign aid, Mengistu unhesitatingly turned to the Soviet Union for support. He received a massive influx of modern weapons essential for containing the numerous rebellions and invasions then occurring. The most serious of these proved the 1977 invasion of the Ogaden region by Somalia. Newly equipped Ethiopian forces successfully drove back the invaders with Cuban military help. But the regime had less success containing outbreaks of tribal violence in the Eritrean and Tigray regions and continuous fighting sapped the country of resources and manpower. Meanwhile, Mengistu survived numerous assassination attempts and in 1977 he unleashed his "Red Terror Campaign" against students and other radicals. To further consolidate his rule, in 1984 he established the Worker's Party of Ethiopia, with himself as general secretary and president.

Mengistu clung tenaciously to power, although in 1984 the nation was beset by the worst droughts in recent history. The lack of water, coupled with the failure of collectivized agriculture, resulted in the deaths of an estimated 1 million people. When protests became public, the government cracked down with mass imprisonment, executions, and exile. But the rebellions on the periphery continued unchecked and began gathering strength. In an attempt to salvage his regime, Mengistu announced a relaxation of doctrinaire socialism in March 1990. A new organization, the Democratic Unity Party, was also instituted, along with greater economic freedom. But the demise of the Soviet Union spelled the end of his regime. Cut off from new weapons, his tattered forces could no longer withstand the advance of two rebel armies whose leaders, angered by government excesses, refused to negotiate. When the rebels successfully fought their way up to the capital of Addis Ababa in May 1991, Mengistu fled the country for Zimbabwe.

The new government of Meles Zenawi had no sooner taken control of Ethiopia than it demanded the extradition of Mengistu to face trial for genocide. However, the government of Zimbabwean president Robert Mugabe refused to hand him over, as an extradition treaty between the two nations did not exist. Mengistu was then tried in absentia and sentenced to death for mass human rights violations. In November 1995 he narrowly survived an assassination attempt. But the Mugabe government refused to hand the former dictator over and in March 2001 he was granted permanent residence in Harare, the capital. For more than a decade Mengistu has lived in luxurious exile, but vengeful Ethiopians are still making their presence felt. In April 2002 the Zimbabwe security forces relocated him to a farm in Mazowe after his mansion in Harare was declared a security risk. Mengistu's 17-year reign of terror establishes him as one of the cruelest and most oppressive African tyrants of the 20th century.

Further Reading

Harbeson, J. W. "The Future of Ethiopia under Mengistu." *Current History* 92 (May 1993): 208–212.

Iyob, Ruth. "The Ethiopian-Eritrean Conflict: Diasporic vs. Hegemonic States in the Horn of Africa, 1991–2000." *Journal of Modern African Studies* 38 (December 2000): 4–28.

James, Wendy. *Remapping Ethiopia: Socialism and After.* Oxford: James Currey, 2002.

Orizio, Riccardo. "Dispatches—the Lion Sleeps Tonight: What Happens to a Dictator Disposed?" *Transition* 11, no. 89 (2001): 20–44.

Tewoldermedhin, Beyene G. "Mengistu and Political Developments in Ethiopia, 1974–1991." Unpublished master's thesis, University of South Florida, 1995.

Yehwalasket, Girma. *The Rape of a Nation.* London: Minerva, 1996.

Menzies, Sir Robert Gordon (1894–1978)
prime minister of Australia

Robert Gordon Menzies was born in Jeparit, Victoria, Australia, on December 20, 1894, the scion of a politically active family. Both his father and uncle were prominent local politicians. He graduated from the University of Melbourne with honors in 1918 and commenced a brilliant legal career. Menzies was a charismatic figure with a large commanding presence, a rapier wit, and a sense of destiny. In 1928 he parlayed his legal success into politics by gaining a seat in the provincial legislature. Four years later, at the behest of Prime Minister Joseph Lyons, he successfully ran for a seat in the federal House of Representatives with the United Australia Party (UAP). He was almost immediately made attorney general and was hailed as one of the rising stars among conservative politicians. In 1939 Lyons appointed him treasurer but, following the death of the prime minister that April, Menzies became head of state. National politics was then dominated by the drift toward World War II and, to strengthen his hand politically, Menzies drew the equally conservative Country Party into a coalition. However, the prime minister was heavily criticized about the slow pace of wartime preparations, and by August 1941 his coalition deserted him. He was succeeded by JOHN CURTIN of the Labor Party and resumed working among the back benches of Parliament to replace the largely defunct UAP.

It proved difficult, if not impossible, for a man like Menzies to accept defeat placidly. He spent the next four years heading the opposition while also constructing a new and more unified organization, the Liberal Party. After 1949, when the cold war was in its infancy but picking up momentum, Menzies roundly criticized Labor for its "socialist" tendencies—a back-handed reference to communism. In December 1949, following the failure of JOSEPH CHIFLEY to nationalize the banking industry, the Liberals and the Country Party won a resounding electoral victory and Menzies returned as prime minister. He quickly distinguished his priorities from Labor's by drawing close to the United States—which he referred to as his "powerful friend"—and supported its regional defense initiatives. Although he loved the British monarchy dearly, he realized that global power had shifted decisively away from Great Britain and toward America. In recognition of this fact Australia became a signatory state to the ANZUS Treaty along with the United States and New Zealand, and also a member of the Southeast Asia Treaty Organization (SEATO). Back home, Menzies continually flogged Labor over its alleged sympathies for communism, and readily dispatched Australian forces to fight in the UN-sponsored Korean War, 1950–53. However, he failed twice, once in the Supreme Court and once through public referendum, to have the Australian Communist Party outlawed. It was one of his rare setbacks.

Over the next 16 years Menzies enjoyed the good luck of presiding over one of the most prosperous periods in Australian history, referred to as "the Menzies era." The economy boomed, the middle class swelled, and Menzies, as champion of the "forgotten people," readily recruited them into the Liberal Party ranks. Labor, by contrast, was divided by an internal schism that split it into two feuding factions. But Menzies also broke new ground for conservatives by backing a system of financial support for private schools to secure the large Catholic vote. In 1963 he went against public opinion by declaring his support for American intervention in Vietnam and two years later dispatched Australian combat troops. He also continually visited Great Britain in a slavish display of loyalty to the Crown, so in 1965 he received the Order of the Thistle from Queen Elizabeth II and also replaced WINSTON CHURCHILL as lord warden of the Cinque Ports. He retired from office at the age of 71, still at the height of his political powers, to serve as chancellor of Melbourne University. Menzies died in Melbourne on May 15, 1978, a larger-than-life character and a towering figure in national politics. As Australia's longest-serving prime minister he was much less an innovator or a reformer than a source of great stability during a turbulent period in international affairs.

Further Reading

Day, David. *Menzies and Churchill at War.* London: Simon and Schuster, 2001.

Goldsworthy, David. *Losing the Blanket: Australia and the End of Britain's Empire.* Carlton South, Victoria: Melbourne University Press, 2002.

Lowe, David. *Menzies and the 'Great World Struggle': Australia's Cold War, 1948–1954.* Sydney: University of New South Wales Press, 1999.

Martin, Allen W. *Robert Menzies: A Life,* 2 vols. Portland, Ore.: International Specialized Book Services, 1993–99.

Menzies, Robert G. *Afternoon Light: Some Memories of Men and Events.* New York: Coward-McCann, 1968.

Murphy, John. *Imagining the Fifties: Private Sentiment and Political Culture in Menzies' Australia.* Annadale, Australia: Pluto Press, 2000.

Waters, Chris. "Macmillan, Menzies, History and Empire." *Australian Historical Studies* 32 (April 2002): 93–108.

Michael I (Mihai) (1921–   ) *king of Romania*

Michael was born in Bucharest on October 25, 1921, the son of Crown Prince Carol of Romania. He was part of the Hohenzollern-Sigmaringen dynasty, which had ruled Romania since 1866. His father, who proved something of a rake, was forced to renounce his claim to the throne. Therefore, when Michael's grandfather, King Ferdinand, died in July 1927, he was enthroned at the age of five under a regency council. He ruled in this manner until June 1930 when Carol returned to Romania and usurped the throne. Thereafter Michael became crown prince in line of succession with the title Duke of Alba Iulia. The unpopular king Carol's rule proved inept and ridden by scandal. Worse, when World War II erupted in 1939, fringe areas of Romania were annexed by the Soviet Union, Hungary, and Bulgaria. In September 1940 Carol was forced to abdicate and his son enthroned as Michael I, although real power rested in the hands of the pro-fascist general, Ion Antonescu. In June 1941 Romania declared war on the Soviet Union and assisted the Nazi invasion. Young Michael remained a token political figure throughout the Antonescu regime until it became clear that Germany was losing the war. On August 23, 1944, the young monarch bravely led a coup against the dictator, arrested him, and renounced Romania's allegiance to Germany. He was then hailed as a new and valuable ally by the Western powers and Soviet premier JOSEPH STALIN awarded him the Order of Victory in 1945.

In the final months of the war, Romania was overrun by Soviet forces and Michael was forced to accept the communist Petru Groza, a Soviet puppet, as his premier. Nonetheless, he refused to cooperate with Soviet authorities and declined to sign any government legislation placed before him. The communists quickly tired of his obstructionism and in November 1947, when Michael was away in London attending the marriage of his cousin, Princess Elizabeth (now Queen Elizabeth II), the communists moved to depose him. In his absence Romania was declared a people's republic and King Michael, after he returned, was forced to abdicate on December 30, 1947. He was then stripped of his citizenship and forced to flee for Western Europe with the rest of the royal family. In 1948 he married Princess Anne of Denmark and produced five daughters, but no male heir. To the communist regime in Bucharest it appeared they had finally rid themselves of the ancient Romanian monarchy.

Michael and his family eventually settled in Versoix, Switzerland, where he engaged in numerous business ventures. "I never had my heart in it," he confided to reporters. "I could never reconcile the double life I was leading, one minute mixing with high society, the next acting on behalf of my oppressed countrymen." But after the Romanian revolution of December 1989, which overthrew communist dictator NICOLAE CEAUȘESCU, the former monarch entertained thoughts of concluding his 50-year exile. "At last our country is free," Michael proclaimed. Negotiations with the new government ensued and they agreed to permit Michael a two-day visit home to observe the Orthodox Easter celebrations. His motorcade was greeted with thunderous applause by the public, who fondly recalled his heroic role in World War II and conscientiousness as a leader. His popularity stunned government officials, mostly former communists, as did the prospect of a revived monarchy. President Ion Iliescu then forbade the ex-king from returning to Romania. Fortunately, elections held in November 1996 established a strong prodemocracy government under Emil Constantinescu and Michael was invited back to stay. In February 1999 a high court in Bucharest formally restored his citizenship and in April 2002 the government announced its decision to restore a castle in Transylvania and other property back to the former king. President Iliescu, since reelected, has also mended fences with Michael and no longer regards him as a threat to Romania's fledgling democracy. In May 2001, the aged ex-monarch visited Elisabeta Palace, the site of his abdication 54 years earlier. "Those who provoked this thing are all gone," he reasoned. "Ironically, I am the only one left. That's what ought to be said."

Further Reading

Lee, Arthur S. *Crown against Sickle, the Story of King Michael of Romania.* New York: Hutchinson, 1950.

Light, Duncan, and David Phinnemore. *Post-Communist Romania: Coming to Terms with Transition.* New York: Palgrave, 2001.

Nastase, Adrian. *Battle for the Future.* Boulder, Colo.: East European Monographs, 2001.

Quinland, Paul. "King Michael: The Unknown Monarch." *New England Journal of History* 50, no. 3 (1994): 26–36.

Shafir, M. "King Michael's Second Expulsion." *Report on Eastern Europe* 2 (18 January 1991): 21–25.

Webster, Alexander F. C. "Kingdom of God in the Balkans." *East European Quarterly* 27 (winter 1993): 437–452.

Michelsen, Christian (1857–1925) *prime minister of Norway*

Christian Michelsen was born in Bergen, Norway, on March 15, 1857, the son of a businessman and politician. He enrolled in the University of Oslo in 1875 to study law and also served as the editor of a student newspaper. After graduating Michelsen forsook legal practice to open up a steamship company. In 1890 he became the first president of the new Shipowner's Association. By this time Michelsen had developed a taste for politics, and in 1891 he was elected to the Storting (legislature) as part of the Conservative Party. Political discussion was then dominated by the union between Sweden and Norway, which had been in effect since 1814. Norwegians had grown restive under Swedish domination and there were calls to establish an independent consular service as a prelude to independence. Michelsen entered into the fray, emphasizing the need to display political unity in the face of anticipated Swedish resistance. To that end he founded the new Unity Party in 1903 as tensions between the two nations escalated. By 1905 both sides appeared ready to resort to war.

In 1903 Michelsen was appointed minister to Sweden by Prime Minister Francis Hagerup to take part in protracted negotiations with the Swedish government, at a time when many in the Storting called for unilateral action. Michelsen saw the futility of future discussions and, when Hagerup insisted that talks resume, he and several other ministers resigned from the administration, bringing down the government. Owing to his hard-line stance, Michelsen was appointed prime minister on March 11, 1905. In May of that year he presented Swedish king Oscar II with a bill mandating a separate Norwegian consular service—and threatened to resign if it were vetoed. The king did exactly that but refused to accept Michelsen's resignation for the time being, because he could not form a government on his own. On June 7, 1905, Michelsen demanded that the Storting begin negotiations with Denmark to put Prince Carl of Denmark on the throne. He argued that since the Swedish monarch had vetoed the consular law and could not form a new government, he had failed in his constitutional duties. Michelsen considered this failure a de facto abdication, and, because there could be no union without a king, the Storting considered the union with Sweden nullified. That the Swedes peacefully agreed to Michelsen's reasoning is a tribute to his pragmatic moderation over confrontation.

In August 1905 the inhabitants of Norway overwhelmingly ratified a plebiscite supporting the actions of the Storting and Michelsen returned to Stockholm with a delegation to discuss the final dissolution. On September 23, 1905, after some minor trade and border concessions, Norway was allowed to become an independent nation. However, Prince Carl insisted that his candidacy also be placed before the public and in November 1905 it too was overwhelmingly passed. Carl was then enthroned as King Haakon VII of Norway. Michelsen's careful deliberation had paid tremendous dividends for the Norwegian people even though, as a conservative, he preferred a constitutional monarchy under a prime minister to an outright republic. He had nonetheless successfully navigated the most precarious six months in Norwegian history and was toasted as a national hero and the father of his country. He continued on in office for another two years in declining health and finally quit politics altogether in 1907. Michelsen then resumed his shipping activities but in 1909 he helped organize a new party, the Liberal Left, but declined to serve as its leader. Following World War I he also established a world-recognized institute for scientific, historical, social, and political research. He died in Fjosanger on June 28, 1925, the most influential Norwegian prime minister of the 20th century. The system of government he installed remains intact to the present day.

Further Reading

Barton, H. Arnold. *Sweden and Visions of Norway: Politics and Culture, 1814–1905.* Carbondale: Southern Illinois University Press, 2003.

Bucken-Knapp, Gregg. *Elites, Language, and the Politics of Identity: The Norwegian Case in Comparative Perspective*. Albany: State University of New York Press, 2003.

Fedde, G. Bernhard. "The Norwegian-Swedish Crisis of 1905." Unpublished master's thesis, Oregon State University, 1964.

Greve, Tim, and T. K. Derry. *Haakon VII of Norway: The Man and the Monarch*. New York: Hippocrene Books, 1983.

Lejren, Terje I. "National Monarchy of Norway, 1895–1905: A Study in the Establishment of the Modern Norwegian Monarchy." Unpublished Ph.D. diss., North Texas State University, 1978.

Lindgren, Raymond E. *Norway-Sweden: Union, Disunion, and Scandinavian Integration*. Princeton, N.J.: Princeton University Press, 1959.

Micombero, Michel (1940–1983) *president of Burundi*

Michel Micombero was born in Musenga, Burundi, in 1940, a part of the Hima clan within the larger Tutsi tribal group. The Tutsi had traditionally dominated the political structure of Burundi, even though they constituted only 15 percent of the population. The remaining 85 percent were Hutu who, despite their majority status, were systematically discriminated against. Relations between the groups were usually tense and prone to periodic outbreaks of extreme violence. Micombero was educated locally through Catholic mission schools and attended college in nearby Bujumbura. He was allowed to join the army, and in April 1960 enrolled at the Military Academy in Brussels, Belgium. However, his studies were interrupted in 1962 when, in anticipation of national independence, he was called home to lead the military police, and to join l'Unité pour le progrès national (Uprona), United Progressive National Party, which worked closely with the sitting *mwami* (king), Mwambutsa IV. Despite his extreme youth, Micombero was successively promoted through the ranks of the government hierarchy, becoming secretary of state for defense in 1963 and minister of defense two years later. He acquired the latter post after suppressing a Hutu-backed uprising in Muramvya Province and killing thousands.

By 1966 Micombero had risen to chief of the secretaries of state within the government. However, like many military officers, he grew weary of Mwambutsa's corruption and favoritism, and began conspiring with the king's 19-year-old son, Crown Prince Charles Ndizeye. In July 1966, while the king was traveling abroad, Micombero enacted a bloodless coup that toppled the king and installed the crown prince as King Ntare V. Consequently, the national constitution was suspended and Micombero was appointed prime minister. This promotion only whetted his appetite for political power and in October 1966 he abolished the monarchy altogether while Ntare was out of the country. He then declared Burundi a republic with himself as president, assisted by the National Council of Revolution, comprised mostly of Tutsi military officers. Micombero was but 26 years old at the time.

Micombero initially sought the confidence of the Hutu people by releasing several prominent prisoners and stressing the need for national unity. He then enacted a wide-reaching socialist program and sought close relations with the Soviet Union and Communist China. Micombero was no ideologue, however, and he sought pragmatic dealings with Western nations to secure foreign aid. But try as he might, Micombero never surmounted the underlying mistrust between Tutsi and Hutu. Tensions exploded in March 1972 when the government lured Ntare V back to Burundi and arrested him as he came off the plane. The king was then charged with treason and executed on April 29, 1972, at which point the president dismissed all his cabinet members. All-out war between Tutsi and Hutu then erupted and had to be contained by force. Micombero subsequently orchestrated a deliberate campaign of reprisals against the Hutu in which 150,000 were killed and another 100,000 fled the country as refugees. The Tutsi had once again prevailed but inter-Tutsi rivalries for power began dividing the regime. In 1973 Micombero promoted himself to lieutenant general, passed a new constitution that enshrined one-party rule, and was "reelected" president in November 1974. But he increasingly relied upon a cordon of loyal soldiers to protect him from his own people, Hutu and Tutsi alike.

After a decade in power, Micombero's mishandling of national affairs led to deteriorating economic conditions and civil unrest. He also resorted more and more to heavy drinking, which further impaired his ability to lead. At length a group of dissatisfied soldiers under Lieutenant Colonel Jean Baptiste Bagaza overthrew the president on November 1, 1976, and temporarily detained him. Micombero was then allowed to be exiled in Somalia, where he attended college and received an economics degree. He died in Mogadishu on July 16, 1983, the latest in a long series of bloody despots to rule Burundi.

Further Reading

Chretien, Jean-Pierre. *The Great Lakes of Africa: Two Thousand Years of History.* New York: Zone Books, 2003.

Eggers, Ellen K., and Warren Weinstein. *Historical Dictionary of Burundi.* Lanham, Md.: Scarecrow Books, 1997.

Evans, Glynne. *Responding to the Crises in the African Great Lakes.* New York: Oxford University Press, 1997.

Forster, Peter G., Michael Hitchcock, and E. F. Lyimo. *Race and Ethnicity in East Africa.* New York: St. Martin's Press, 2000.

Lemarchand, Rene. *Burundi: Ethnocide as Discourse and Practice.* New York: Cambridge University Press, 1994.

Scherrer, Christian P. *Genocide and Crisis in Central Africa: Conflict Roots, Mass Violence, and Regional War.* Westport, Conn.: Praeger, 2002.

Mintoff, Dom (1916–   ) *prime minister of Malta*

Dominic Mintoff was born in Cospicua, Malta, on August 6, 1916, the son of a Royal Navy cook. This small Mediterranean island had been a British Crown colony since 1814 and housed bases for a large military and naval presence. Mintoff briefly attended a seminary before passing through the University of Malta to study engineering. He subsequently won a Rhodes scholarship and attended Oxford University in England. Mintoff enjoyed the high ideals he encountered on campus but greatly resented the condescending attitudes of British colonial administrators. He nonetheless served with the British War Office as a civil engineer during most of World War II, and in 1944 he went home to help rebuild his war-ravaged island. That year he joined the Maltese Labor Party and assisted in its reorganization. Mintoff was then elected to a series of bureaucratic posts within the colonial administration until 1949. His politics, which were sharply socialist, conflicted with the more moderate views of party leaders, and he resigned from office. A vigorous contest for control of the Malta Labor Party ensued, and Mintoff, a fiery, charismatic figure, was elected chairman in 1955. He was singularly determined to recast the colonial nature of Malta's relationship with Great Britain.

In 1955 Mintoff was elected prime minister, and over the next three years he championed Malta's complete integration into the United Kingdom. When this plan failed he resigned from office in April 1958 and began campaigning for complete independence. He also entered a protracted contretemps with the archbishop of this primarily Catholic nation over the future role of the church. Mintoff denounced the institution for its part in helping maintain the status quo and in 1962 he was barred from receiving the sacraments. That year a massive turnout by Catholic voters elected the conservative Nationalist Party into power, where it remained seven years. Malta finally gained its independence in 1964 and Mintoff, upset by what he considered a lingering British presence, boycotted the ceremony. But realizing he had made a serious tactical error, Mintoff then assiduously mended fences with church authorities to enhance his political prospects. After nine years in the opposition, Labor finally prevailed in the 1971 elections, and Mintoff became prime minister once again. He was finally positioned to effect radical change in island politics.

Malta had nominally been a member of the British Commonwealth since 1964, but Mintoff unilaterally declared the island a republic and booted out the English governor general. He then charted a nonaligned foreign policy by establishing friendly relations with the Soviet Union, China, and various Arab countries. Foremost among these was the radical regime of Muammar Gadhafi of Libya, only 200 miles distant, although relations chilled over the issue of oil drilling on the seafloor between them. In 1979 British military leases on the island expired and Mintoff set such egregious restrictions for their continuance that the Royal Navy pulled out after nearly two centuries. In 1981 the prime minister again confronted the church over the status of religious schools, and in elections that year the Nationalists won the popular vote. Labor, however, managed to retain a one-seat majority in the legislature so Mintoff remained in office. Faced with this reduction in power, intractable fights with conservatives, and declining poll numbers, he resigned as prime minister in December 1984. He then served as a special adviser to Labor prime minister Carmelo Mifsud Bonnici until the opposition regained power in May 1987.

Mintoff retained his seat in parliament and relished his new role as a political gadfly. Vociferous as ever, in December 1998 he opposed a measure by Labor prime minister Alfred Sant to lease land to an American consortium to build a yacht marina. The 82-year-old Mintoff cast the deciding vote that defeated the measure, and Sant called for new elections. Labor, which controlled parliament by a single vote, subsequently lost by wide margins to the Nationalists under Eddie Fenech Adami. Mintoff has since retired to private life, a contentious and controversial elder statesman.

Further Reading

Craig, G. "Malta: Mintoff's Election Victory." *Western European Politics* 5 (July 1982): 20–34.

Dobie, Eith. *Malta's Road to Independence.* Norman: University of Oklahoma Press, 1967.

Dowdall, John. "The Political Economy of Malta: The Economics of Mr. Mintoff's Independence." *Round Table* no. 248 (1972): 465–473.

———. "Mintoff's Malta: Problems of Independence." *World Today* 28, no. 5 (1972): 189–195.

Micallef, Joseph V. "Mediterranean Maverick: Malta's Uncertain Future." *Round Table* no. 279 (1975): 238–251.

Pirotta, Godfrey A. "Malta's Foreign Policy after Mintoff." *Political Quarterly* 56 (April–June 1985): 182–186.

Mohammad Reza Pahlavi (1919–1980) *shah of Iran*

Mohammad Reza Pahlavi was born in Tehran, Persia, on October 26, 1919, the son of General REZA SHAH PAHLAVI. When his father was crowned shah of Persia in 1925, he was elevated to crown prince in line of succession. Pahlavi was educated by tutors and subsequently attended college in Switzerland. He also graduated first in his class from the Iranian Military College while being groomed for the throne. In August 1941 a combined British-Russian force deposed his father and Pahlavi was installed as the new shah on September 16, 1941. At this time power was mostly held by the Majlis (legislature), then under the sway of the extreme nationalist, MOHAMMAD MOSSADEGH. As a legislator Mossadegh forced through laws nationalizing the oil industry at the expense of foreign owners, a move that made him extremely popular and forced the

shah to appoint him prime minister in 1951. When Great Britain retaliated by freezing Iranian assets, Pahlavi fired Mossadegh from office. This act engendered violent rioting and, as the country seemed on the verge of civil war, the shah fled for Rome. At this juncture the British Intelligence Service and the Central Intelligence Agency, fearing a Soviet takeover, cleverly engineered a counter-coup that deposed Mossadegh and reinstalled the shah within days. Thereafter Pahlavi resolved never to tolerate conditions that encouraged disorder and he ruled in an increasingly autocratic fashion.

Pahlavi, like his father, was suspicious of British intentions but he had no problem cultivating close ties to the United States. The Americans, in turn, sought a stable ally in the Middle East to counter both Soviet influence and mounting Arab nationalism. Therefore the shah was all too happy to denationalize the oil industry on America's behalf in exchange for receiving financial and military assistance. In 1958 Iran joined the Central Treaty Organization, along with Great Britain, Turkey, Iraq, and Pakistan as a mutual defense pact. Consistent with the shah's unfailingly pro-Western stance, the Iranian military received highly advanced technology that transformed it into a regional superpower. Iran thus became the guardian of the gulf region once Britain withdrew in 1971. Pahlavi also reigned secure in the knowledge that the United States would rush to defend Iran's huge oil reserves from Soviet attack. But he continued ruling as a despot and created an especially effective secret police, SAVAK, to crush, torture, or murder dissenters at will. Ultimately, it proved the source of his own undoing.

Like his father, Pahlavi fully embraced the notion of modernization and westernization and in 1963 he initiated his so-called White Revolution. This large-scale reform program entailed the redistribution of land to peasants, the curtailment of the Islamic clergy, and increased literacy campaigns. Moreover, the shah championed the emancipation of women by allowing them to vote in this deeply conservative Muslim country. Unfortunately, very few Iranians actually benefited from modernization, for corruption and patronage ran very deep at all levels of government. The resulting resentment dovetailed with a resurgence of Islamic fundamentalism spearheaded by a celebrated cleric, RUHOLLA KHOMEINI, whom the shah first arrested in 1963. The ensuing oil boom of the next decade led to explosive urban growth, but with it came large-scale social dislocation in the cities. When protests did emerge, they were invariably put down by the army and SAVAK with great brutality. Events crested in 1979 when Khomeini, fanning the flames of Islamic revolution from his exile in Paris, incited widespread social violence. His exhortations that modernization and westernization ran counter to the teachings of Islam took hold with a vengeance, and the country was rapidly destabilized. The shah's forces proved unable to contain the upheaval, and on January 16, 1979, Pahlavi fled Iran for the second and final time. Khomeini arrived in Tehran shortly after and proclaimed an Islamic republic.

Pahlavi lived in Panama for several months before visiting the United States for cancer treatment in October 1979. This visit sparked massive demonstrations by Islamic radicals, and they seized the American embassy in Tehran, taking 50 hostages. They were held for nearly a year and contributed greatly to the defeat of President JIMMY CARTER's re-election bid. The shah, increasingly friendless, was then invited by ANWAR AL-SADAT to reside in Egypt, where he died in Cairo on July 27, 1980. His 38-year reign constitutes a turning point in the history of Iran, marking the mass politicization of Islam and intense enmity for the United States that persists to the present time.

Further Reading

Amini, Parrie M. "A Single Party State in Iran, 1975–78: The Rabtakhiz Party—the Final Attempt by the Shah to Consolidate His Political Power." *Middle Eastern Studies* 38 (January 2002): 131–168.

Ansari, Ali M. "The Myth of the White Revolution: Mohammad Reza Shah, 'Modernization,' and the Consolidation of Power." *Middle Eastern Studies* 37 (July 2001): 1–24.

Hoveyda, Fereydon. *The Shah and the Ayatollah: Iranian Mythology and Islamic Revolution.* Westport, Conn.: Praeger, 2003.

Matin-Asgari, Afshin. *Iranian Student Opposition to the Shah.* Costa Mesa, Calif.: Mazda Publishers, 2002.

Nasr, Vali. "Politics with the Late-Pahlavi State: The Ministry of Economy and Industrial Policy, 1963–69." *International Journal of Middle East Studies* 32 (February 2000): 97–122.

Pahlavi, Mohammad Reza. *Answer to History.* New York: Stein and Day, 1980.

Mohammed V (1910–1961) *king of Morocco*

Sidi Mohammed was born in Fez, Morocco, in 1910, the third son of Prince Moulay Yusuf, a brother of the ruling sultan, Moulay Hafid. In 1912 France occupied Morocco and reduced it to a protectorate (colony). Eager to rule with a pliant monarch, the French deposed Hafid that same year and installed Moulay Yusuf as the new sultan. Mohammed, meanwhile, received a traditional Koranic education along with some elements of modern Western culture. When his father died in 1927, the French selected him to become sultan before two elder brothers, as he was seen as a passive, docile figure. The young monarch initially conformed to French expectations, and in 1930 he incurred the wrath of traditionalists by allowing the inland Berber tribes to ignore *sharia* (Islamic law). This French-inspired exemption spawned the rise of a nascent nationalist movement, Istiqlal (Independence), to convert Mohammed to its side. But when two leading nationalists were exiled by France in 1937, the sultan offered no resistance. It was not until World War II that Mohammed's national consciousness was aroused. In 1943 Morocco hosted the Casablanca conference of Allied leaders, and American president FRANKLIN D. ROOSEVELT hinted to the sultan that he might support independence in exchange for military cooperation. The French were never informed of this discussion, but it raised Mohammed's expectations for an end to colonialism. In 1945 he began openly sympathizing with Moroccan nationalism and publicly demanded an end to French rule.

In the immediate postwar period, Mohammed received the red-carpet treatment during an official visit to France, then stunned his hosts by demanding complete independence. When the French realized that Mohammed was no longer cooperative, they began stirring up traditional centers of power against him. In January 1951 colonial authorities demanded that he condemn the activities of the Istiqlal movement, and when he refused, his palace was surrounded by tanks and he was forced to sign the statement. However, outbreaks of violence and the onset of guerrilla war against French settlers only hardened Mohammed's position against France. In response, he was forcibly taken from his palace by French agents in 1953 and exiled to Madagascar. Moulay Arafa, a puppet ruler, was then installed in his place. But Mohammed's gradual resistance to France rendered him a hero and a martyr in the eyes of his countrymen. Fighting continued until 1956 when France finally agreed to allow Mohammed to reoccupy the throne. He was greeted on his return by cheering throngs. His seemingly passive resistance to overwhelming strength had apparently prevailed.

Morocco finally gained its independence from France on March 2, 1956, amid public rejoicing. Mohammed, intent upon modernizing the outlook of his people, then abandoned his medieval position as sultan and officially adopted the title of King Mohammed V, 16th sovereign of the Alawite dynasty. His son Hassan II was installed as head of the new national military. The king then initiated steps to provide Morocco with its first legislative council as a prelude to democratic reforms. Furthermore, he determined to retain friendly ties to France while simultaneously supporting independence movements in Algeria and elsewhere. This sudden assertion of royal prerogatives surprised many in the Istiqlal movement, who assumed that they had earned the right to rule. But Mohammed proved a clever monarch who cordially entertained opposition figures and, when not charming them into subservience, pitted them against other groups. In April 1958 he cleverly legalized the formation of political parties and the Istiqlal broke up into numerous and feuding factions. So in his quiet manner, Mohammed evolved from a token figurehead to a sovereign of real ability. Moreover, he converted the throne from an anachronism to a symbol of national unity for all Moroccans to rally behind. By 1960 he outmaneuvered several of his cabinet members to assume a role as his own prime minister. By the time Mohammed died in Rabat on February 26, 1961, Morocco was a thriving, unified kingdom, and a far cry from the primitive protectorate he inherited. His skill, patience, and determination to outlast an infinitely superior foe was sagacious and marks him as one of the leading Arabic statesmen of his day.

Further Reading

Bourqia, Rahma, and Susan G. Miller. *In the Shadow of the Sultan: Culture, Power, and Politics in Morocco.* Cambridge, Mass.: Harvard University Press, 1999.

Gershovich, Moshe. *French Military Rule in Morocco: Colonialism and Its Consequences.* Portland, Ore.: Frank Cass, 2000.

Gould, St. John. *Morocco: Transformation and Continuity.* London: Routledge, 2002.

Landau, Rom. *The Sultan of Morocco.* London: R. Hale, 1951.

Pennell, C. R. *Morocco since 1830: A History.* New York: New York University, 2000.

Sangmuah, Egya N. "Sultan Mohammed ben Yousef's American Strategy and the Diplomacy of North African Liberation, 1943–1961." *Journal of Contemporary History* 27 (January 1992): 129–148.

Morales Bermúdez, Francisco (1921–)
president of Peru

Francisco Morales Bermúdez Cerruti was born in Lima, Peru, on October 4, 1921, the son of a military officer and the grandson of a Peruvian president. He graduated from the Chorrillos Military Academy in 1943 as a lieutenant of engineers, and compiled a distinguished military record. During the short-lived military coup of 1962–63 he prepared the nation for new elections. Later he attended several advanced military schools, foremost among them the Center for High Military Studies, which stressed sociology, economics, and national development to prepare the armed forces as an agent of modernization. Morales Bermúdez was promoted to general in 1968 and then served as minister of finance and commerce under President FERNANDO BELAÚNDE TERRY. When this regime floundered under the weight of poor economic direction, Morales Bermúdez helped depose the president in October 1968, when he was installed as minister of economy and finances in the Revolutionary Government of the Armed Forces under General JUAN VELASCO ALVARADO. He was entrusted with sweeping reforms of the national economy, including refinancing the national debt, overhauling the prevailing tax structure, and stabilizing the currency. He also directed the nationalization of vital sectors of the economy and promulgated the Industrial Reform Law, which gave Peruvian workers partial ownership of their companies. In 1975 Morales Bermúdez became prime minister and minister of war, and that August he orchestrated a coup against General Velasco for failing to significantly improve the economy. He himself was then sworn in as president of Peru and undertook the "Second Phase" of the so-called military revolution.

As chief executive, Morales Bermúdez faced two exceedingly tall challenges: rebuilding the national economy and restoring Peruvian democracy. But facing inflation rates of 75 percent and a burgeoning national debt he had no recourse but to adopt austerity measures dictated by the International Monetary Fund (IMF), including scaling back the Industrial Reform Law, which until then was one of Latin America's most progressive social programs. Moreover he divested the state of various unproductive industries and generally slowed the pace of reform to a crawl. Such changes entailed a great deal of unemployment, but at length inflation was brought down and the economy stabilized. Overall, he failed to manifestly improve Peru's economic outlook, which was further battered by droughts and floods.

As a military populist Morales Bermúdez enjoyed better luck in the political sphere. He gradually relaxed the state of emergency that had been in place since 1977 and eased press and publishing restrictions. In 1978 the government allowed for the election of a constituent assembly to draw up a new constitution. This document mandated a single, five-year, nonrenewable term for all future presidents along with universal suffrage. By 1980 Morales Bermúdez judged Peru ripe for national elections and the contest was won by Belaúnde Terry, who had been removed from office 12 years earlier. On July 28, 1980, the former general officially surrendered the presidency to his duly elected successor, concluding Peru's longest period of 20th-century military rule. While repressive by nature, the army accomplished much-needed political and economic reforms that would have been otherwise impossible to implement.

Back in civilian life Morales Bermúdez wrote books, lectured extensively, and attempted to enter the political arena on his own. In 1985 he founded a new party, the Democratic Front of the National Union, and ran for the presidency. He finished a poor fifth and subsequently withdrew from public life. Morales Bermúdez emerged briefly in April 2000 to lambaste the rigged victory of Alberto Fujimori over Alejandro Toledo. "It was the most fraudulent and aberrant process in national history," he declared.

Further Reading

Cameron, Maxwell A., and Philip Mauceri. *The Peruvian Labyrinth: Polity, Society, Economy.* University Park, Pa.: Pennsylvania State University Press, 1997.

Costentino, Christine M. "The Progressive Military in Peru, 1968–1980." Unpublished master's thesis, University of Virginia, 1980.

Klaren, Peter R. *Peru: Society and Nationhood in the Andes.* New York: Oxford University Press, 2000.

McClintock, Cynthia, and Abraham F. Lowenthal, eds. *The Peruvian Experiment Reconsidered.* Princeton, N.J.: Princeton University Press, 1983.

Pion-Berlin, D. *The Ideology of State Terror: Economic Doctrine and Military Repression in Argentina and Peru.* Boulder, Colo.: Lynne Rienner Pubs., 1989.

Thomson, Sinclair. *We Alone Will Rule: Native Andean Politics in the Age of Insurgency.* Madison: University of Wisconsin Press, 2002.

Mossadegh, Mohammed (1880–1967) *prime minister of Iran*

Mohammed Mossadegh was born in Tehran, Persia, in 1880, the son of a ranking public official who was related by marriage to the ruling Qajar dynasty. In 1909 he left for Paris to attend college and in 1914 he completed his doctorate in Islamic studies at the University of Lausanne, Switzerland. He then taught political science for many years before gaining appointment as undersecretary in Persia's ministry of finance. In 1924 Mossadegh was elected to the Majlis (legislature), where he proved an outspoken proponent of democratic constitutionalism and national sovereignty. The following year he opposed legislation that formalized REZA SHAH PAHLAVI's usurpation of the throne and installation of the Pahlavi dynasty. He proved such an irritant to the monarchy that the shah excluded him from politics altogether. As of 1936 Mossadegh was exiled to his home in Ahmadabad and four years later he was imprisoned. After two failed attempts at suicide he was finally released by the shah's son, Crown Prince MOHAMMAD REZA PAHLAVI. He resumed his political career in 1944 by returning to the Majlis, where he bitterly opposed granting any oil concessions to the Soviet Union. Furthermore, he began a concerted campaign to denounce the Anglo-Persian Treaty of 1919, which gave Great Britain controlling interest in Iran's oil industry, and stridently called for nationalization. In 1949 he also founded the National Front to agitate for honest elections, freedom of the press, and an end to martial law. Such militancy greatly enhanced Mossadegh's popularity and in 1950 he returned to the Majlis with even larger margins. He was Iran's most popular politician.

Ongoing negotiations with the British over their control of the oil assets availed the Iranian government nothing, so in May 1951 Mossadegh passed legislation to nationalize the industry. Given his immense popularity and national standing, the shah was compelled to appoint him prime minister. But Mossadegh's actions triggered a sharp response from the British government, for they boycotted Iranian oil and sent warships to maneuver in the Persian Gulf. Mossadegh tried resuming negotiations to avert an international incident but only with the understanding that nationalization was irrevocable. The impasse continued until Mossadegh, having failed to obtain control of the War Ministry, suddenly resigned from office in July 1952. His departure sparked public outrage, and mass demonstrations obliged the shah to reappoint him as prime minister. At length the United States was contacted in an attempt to secure financial assistance to stabilize the Iranian economy. While the administration of President HARRY S. TRUMAN proved sympathetic and he discouraged the British from making overt moves to recover the oil fields, he refused to subsidize Mossadegh's nationalization policy. The prime minister, feeling that he had no choice, finally turned to the Soviet Union for financial assistance.

Mossadegh's overtures to Moscow and a resurgence of the outlawed Tudeh (communist) Party, convinced officials in Washington and London that a Soviet-inspired coup was imminent. If accomplished, it would place Soviet influence, backed by armed force, astride the West's strategic oil lifeline. President DWIGHT D. EISENHOWER had none of his predecessor's hesitancy to interfere in Iranian affairs and he directed the Central Intelligence Agency to work with the British Secret Service to overthrow Mossadegh. By August 1953 they had stirred up sufficient unrest against the prime minister that the shah attempted to remove him from office. The result was an explosion of public indignation and the shah temporarily fled the country. However, the Americans and British then staged a coup of their own that toppled the regime, allowing the shah to return and arrest Mossadegh. The shah then renounced the bulk of oil nationalization on behalf of the British and Americans and thereafter he remained firmly committed to the West. Mossadegh was subsequently tried for treason and sentenced to three years' imprisonment. Afterward he remained under house arrest until his death in Ahmadabad on March 5, 1967. Mossadegh is remembered as an early symbol of Iranian nationalism and resistance to royal autocracy.

Further Reading

Abrahamian, Ervard. "The 1953 Coup in Iran." *Science and Society* 65, no. 2 (2001): 182–215.

Behruoz, Mazziar. *Rebel with a Clause: The Failure of the Left in Iran.* New York: I. B. Tauris, 2000.

Diba, Frahad. *Mohammed Mossadegh: Political Biography.* Dover, N.H.: Croom Helm, 1986.

Gavin, Francis. "Politics, Power, and U.S. Policy in Iran, 1950–53." *Journal of Contemporary World Studies* 1, no. 1 (1999): 56–89.

Goode, James F. *The United States and Iran: In the Shadow of Musaddiq.* Basingstoke: Macmillan, 1997.

Halliday, Fred. "The Limits of Misperception: Re-examining Iranian-U.S. Relations." *Diplomatic History* 24, no. 2 (2000): 361–364.

Katouzian, Homa. *Musaddiq and the Struggle for Power in Iran.* New York: I. B. Tauris, 1999.

Marsh, Steve. *Anglo-American Relations and Cold War Oil: Crisis in Iran.* New York: Palgrave Macmillan, 2003.

Musaddiq, Mohammed. *Musaddiq's Memoirs.* London: JEBHE, National Movement of Iran, 1988.

Muhammed, Murtala Ramat (1938–1976)
president of Nigeria

Murtala Ramat Muhammed was born in Kano, Nigeria, on November 8, 1938, into a devout Muslim family. After attending primary school and passing through the Government College in Zaria, he joined the Nigerian army in 1957 and was sent off to the Royal Military Academy, Sandhurst, in Great Britain. Muhammed was subsequently commissioned a lieutenant in 1961 and assigned to work with United Nations peacekeeping forces in the Congo. He proved himself an attentive soldier, gained promotion to major in 1965, and served as acting signals chief officer for the military. However, the Nigerian military, like Nigeria itself, was riven by ethnic and religious differences. In early 1966 several high-ranking Ibo officers from the south overthrew the civilian regime and made General Johnson Aguiyi-Ironsi head of state. However, in July 1966 many northerners, including Muhammed, responded with a coup of their own that toppled Aguiyi-Ironsi and installed YAKUBU GOWON as president. The following year the Biafran war of secession broke out, and Muhammed took command of the newly raised Second Division. He distinguished himself by hard fighting and gradually recaptured the cities of

Benin and Onitsha. By the time the war ended in 1970, Muhammed was a national war hero, promoted to brigadier general in 1971.

The onset of peace did little to ameliorate Nigeria's economic woes, and on July 29, 1975, Muhammed ousted Gowon from power and assumed the roles of head of state and commander in chief. He strongly felt that the nation had been plunging headlong into chaos and violence and that the Gowon regime was too indecisive and undisciplined to provide leadership. But once in charge, Muhammed quickly took remedial steps. He trimmed the government payroll of 10,000 superfluous public officials to reduce government spending. The general then outlined a program to restore Nigeria to democracy by 1979, and further rectified the political situation by increasing the number of states from 12 to 19 in February 1976. A new federal constitution and wide-ranging local reform also facilitated the growth of democracy. In a final symbolic gesture, Muhammed also relocated the national capital from Lagos on the coast to Abuja in the center of the nation. It was through all these expedients, he hoped, that the military could buttress the machinery of political administration, while at the same time promoting a return to normalcy.

Muhammed, all the while, remained a modest, simple individual, not given to ostentatious display. He was also highly popular as a reformer and widely respected in both the Christian and Muslim communities. However, even he failed to uproot the deep-seated ethnic animosities still prevalent in the Nigerian officer corps. Because Muhammed was intent on living his austere lifestyle and refused to accept a bodyguard, he remained vulnerable to the machinations of subordinates. On February 13, 1976, Lieutenant Colonel Dimka, a former Gowon associate, assassinated the well-intentioned general. After much infighting Muhammed was finally succeeded by General Olusegun Obasanjo. The lamented leader has since been saluted as a symbol of national unity, while his portrait adorns various currency pieces. Muhammed ruled briefly, yet is recognized for having imparted lasting and positive change to the government of Nigeria.

Further Reading

Abegunrin, Olayiwola. *Nigerian Foreign Policy under Military Rule, 1966–1999.* Westport, Conn.: Praeger Publications, 2003.

Adekson, J. Bayo. *Nigeria in Search of a Stable Civil-military System.* Boulder, Colo.: Westview Press, 1981.

Falola, Toyia. *The Military Factor in Nigeria, 1966–1985.* Lewiston, N.Y.: Edwin Mellen Press, 1994.

Ogbondah, Chris W. *Military Regimes and the Press in Nigeria: Human Rights and National Development.* Lanham, Md.: University Press of America, 1994.

Oyediran, Oyeleye, ed. *Nigerian Government and Politics under Military Rule, 1966–1979.* New York: St. Martin's Press, 1979.

Peters, Jim. *The Nigerian Military and the State.* New York: Tauris Academic Studies, 1997.

Wright, Stephen. *Nigeria: A Struggle for Stability and Status.* Boulder, Colo.: Westview Press, 1998.

Muldoon, Robert (1921–1992) *prime minister of New Zealand*

Robert David Muldoon was born in Auckland, New Zealand, on September 21, 1921, into modest circumstances. He lost his father at an early age and was supported solely by his mother. During World War II Muldoon joined the infantry and served with distinction. He studied accounting while stationed in England and came home to establish a successful business practice. In 1947 he joined the conservative National Party and made two failed attempts, in 1954 and 1957, to gain election to Parliament. However, he successfully ran for a seat in 1960 from the Tamaki district and held it for the next 31 years. Muldoon, a brusque, no-nonsense individual, quickly established himself as a force within the National Party. Over the next decade he held a succession of important ministerial posts, including minister of finance, minister of tourism, and deputy prime minister under KEITH HOLYOAKE. After the Nationals were turned out of power by Labor in 1974, a struggle for control of the party ensued, and Muldoon, by sheer dint of personality, overcame several challengers. He proved himself a formidable head of the opposition in Parliament through his fierce demeanor and scathing invective. Muldoon seemed just what New Zealand was looking for in November 1975 and that year he handily defeated Labor prime minister Wallace Rowling. In addition to becoming prime minister, Muldoon also held the essential portfolio as minister of finance. His political philosophy, bluntly— and typically—put, was "to leave New Zealand no worse than I found it."

Never shy about expressing his opinions, Muldoon proved himself to be one of the nation's most forceful politicians. He was renowned for his fiscal expertise and, as finance minister, set the spending limits of all other cabinets as he saw fit. Ministers who protested this usurpation of responsibility were bluntly told to fall in line—or quit. Curiously, Muldoon's economic practices were much closer to Labor's. He strongly embraced government intervention in the economy to ensure the well-being of the citizenry. To this end he helped pass the superannuating act that ensured all citizens over 60 were guaranteed a modest stipend regardless of their economic status. Muldoon also reversed the anti-inflationary measures of the previous administration to keep money in people's pockets and thus perpetuate a sense of well-being. However, a major drawback to this generosity was rising inflation, high unemployment, and low productivity. And, upon Muldoon's insistence, the economy was heavily skewed to favor business and agrarian interests at the expense of other sectors.

Muldoon's foreign policy was marked by a vigorous anticommunism that established him as one of the most stalwart Western allies during the cold war. In 1979 he bitterly denounced the Soviet Union's invasion of Afghanistan and persistently warned about the communist threat to the Pacific. For that reason he constantly touted New Zealand's support for the ANZUS Treaty with the United States and Australia. However, he was less strident toward South Africa's apartheid system, and when he allowed their racially segregated rugby team to tour New Zealand in 1981, riots ensued. The following year he also strongly supported British prime minister MARGARET THATCHER during the 1982 Falklands War. Muldoon proved so beholden to his own perspective of world and domestic events that he failed to detect shifting attitudes in the New Zealand public. Feminists, the anti-nuclear lobby, and the indigenous Maori people were all falling into a pro-Labor orientation—while he did nothing but scoff. At length dissenters within the National Party sought to remove him as party leader in 1984 but failed. To redeem himself, Muldoon then scheduled snap elections and lost overwhelmingly to Labor under DAVID LANGE.

For the next nine years Muldoon functioned as the acerbic head of opposition in Parliament. In 1986 he received appointment as shadow prime minister, which he retained until his retirement in 1991. Muldoon died in Wellington, New Zealand, on August 5, 1992, and his passing marked the end of an era. Thereafter both the National and Labor parties adopted the free market economics he loathed and abandoned the conservative foreign policies he cherished.

Further Reading

Gustavson, Barry. *His Way: A Biography of Robert Muldoon.* Auckland: Auckland University Press, 2001.

McCraw, David. "From Kirk to Muldoon: Change and Continuity in New Zealand's Foreign Policy Priorities." *Pacific Affairs* 55, no. 4 (1982): 640–659.

Martin, Ged. "From Muldoon to Lange: New Zealand Votes in 1984." *Round Table* no. 292 (1984): 392–402.

Moon, Paul. *Muldoon: A Study in Political Leadership.* Wellington, New Zealand: Pacific Press, 1999.

Muldoon, Robert. *My Way.* Wellington, New Zealand: Reed, 1981.

Pugh, M. "New Zealand: The Battle for the Middle Ground." *The World Today* 40 (July 1984): 308–314.

Templeton, Hugh. *All Honourable Men: Inside the Muldoon Cabinet, 1975–1984.* Auckland: Auckland University Press, 1995.

Mussolini, Benito (1883–1945) *dictator of Italy*

Benito Amilcare Andrea Mussolini was born in Dovia di Predappio, Italy, on July 29, 1883, the son of a blacksmith. From his father, an ardent socialist, he inherited a passion for extremist politics. Mussolini himself was highly intelligent but rather headstrong, and was expelled repeatedly from school for assaulting other students. After working for some time as a schoolteacher, he fled to Switzerland in 1902 to escape compulsory military service. There he immersed himself in radical literature, including Karl Marx, and returned to Italy three years later a committed socialist. By 1912 he was editing the party newspaper and organizing labor strikes. However, he parted company with the socialists over Italian entry into World War I; he supported it, while party leaders did not. Expelled by the socialists, Mussolini then joined the army, was wounded, and began formulating a new, far-right ideology—fascism. This was his own blend of several disparate trains of thought, including nationalism, imperialism, and corporatism. The resulting corporate state was a carefully balanced alliance between government and large business interests. In March 1919 he officially founded the National Fascist Party and began his political conquest of Italy. To that end Mussolini theatrically cast himself as a "man of destiny" proclaiming fascism as the ideology of the future.

The political climate was ripe for Mussolini's bombastic exhortations: the economy was severely depressed, military veterans were disillusioned, and the nation was saddled with a corrupt and unresponsive parliamentary system. Through radical oratory and orchestrated street violence, the Fascists gained considerable popularity, and in 1922 King Victor Emanuel III appointed Mussolini the nation's youngest prime minister. Backed by his paramilitary thugs, the Blackshirts, Mussolini staged an elaborate march on Rome and began stripping away the rule of law. Within a year the Fascists acquired a parliamentary majority, and a military dictatorship arose with Mussolini holding uncontested power. He cracked down ruthlessly on political dissent and laid the foundations for a modern totalitarian state. In 1924, when the outspoken socialist deputy Giacomo Matteotti attacked the regime, he was brutally murdered. On a positive note, if one can be found, Mussolini ended church-state conflicts by concluding the Lateran Pact with the Catholic Church in October 1929; this stipulated the loss of the Papal States to Italy in exchange for creation of a new sovereign state, Vatican City. Mussolini then placed the national economy on a wartime footing to ease unemployment, and began ill-advised military adventurism abroad. In 1936 Italian forces conquered Ethiopia and drove Emperor HAILE SELASSIE into exile. In 1936 Mussolini lent extensive military assistance to General FRANCISCO FRANCO during the Spanish civil war, and found himself cooperating closely with Nazi dictator ADOLF HITLER of Germany. In 1937 the German and Italian leaders aligned themselves against the Western democracies by signing the Rome-Berlin Axis Pact. To further placate Hitler, Mussolini then embarked on his own anti-Semitic campaign, although it found little domestic support. Nonetheless he anticipated that the eventual onset of hostilities would allow Italy to resurrect the Roman Empire with himself as supreme leader.

Mussolini got the war he wanted in 1939, and it proved his downfall. The Italians had no problem overrunning primitive Albania but were unable to join in the defeat of France the following year. Italian forces were then dogged by failure during an attack on Greece in 1941 and had to be bailed out by Germany. In truth Mussolini's military establishment, badly trained and poorly equipped, was tottering even before hostilities commenced. Throughout 1941 Italian forces in North Africa also fared poorly, and by July 1943 the Allies had counterattacked and taken Sicily. This act forced the Fascist Grand Council to vote "Il Duce" (the leader) out of power, and King Victor Emanuel had him arrested. Mussolini was detained until September 1943 when he was freed by a German commando mission. Hitler then appointed him the puppet leader of a small fascist regime in northeastern Italy, where he spent the last days of World War II. As Germany collapsed in April 1945 Mussolini and his mistress tried to slip across the border into neutral Switzerland, but they were apprehended by Communist partisans. The ill-fated dictator was then

Benito Mussolini *(Library of Congress)*

executed and his body publicly displayed on April 28, 1945. In view of all the misery he had heaped on his compatriots during 19 years of iron-fisted rule, Il Duce's passing was scarcely noticed.

Further Reading

Adamson, Walter. "Avante-garde Modernism and Italian Fascism: Cultural Politics in the Era of Mussolini." *Journal of Modern Italian Studies* 6, no. 2 (2001): 230–248.

Bosworth, R. J. B. *Mussolini*. London: Arnold, 2002.

Corner, Paul. "Italian Fascism: Whatever Happened to Dictatorship?" *Journal of Modern History* 74 (June 2002): 325–351.

Knight, Patricia. *Mussolini and Fascism*. New York: Routledge, 2003.

Mallet, Robert. *Mussolini and the Origins of the Second World War, 1933–1940*. New York: Palgrave Macmillan, 2003.

Morgan, Philip. *Italian Fascism, 1919–1945*. New York: Palgrave Macmillan, 2004.

Mussolini, Benito. *My Rise and Fall*. New York: Da Capo Press, 1998.

Pauley, Bruce F. *Hitler, Stalin, and Mussolini: Totalitarianism in the 20th Century*. Wheeling, Ill.: Harland Davidson, 2003.

Strang, G. Bruce. *On the Fiery March: Mussolini Prepares for War*. Westport, Conn.: Praeger, 2003.

N

Nagy, Imre (1896–1958) *prime minister of Hungary*

Imre Nagy was born in Kaposvár, Austria-Hungary, on July 6, 1896, the son of a poor peasant family. Trained as an engineer, he was drafted into the army to fight in World War I and was captured by the Russians. There he witnessed the Russian revolution, enlisted in the Red Army, and fought for the Bolsheviks. Nagy eventually returned home to newly independent Hungary in 1920, where he joined the Social Democrats. When that party eventually split into two factions, he gravitated toward the newly constituted Communist Party as an agrarian specialist. The government subsequently outlawed the communists, and Nagy went underground before fleeing to Austria in 1928. He soon made his way back to the Soviet Union and was assigned to the International Agronomy Institute in Moscow. Nagy was fortunate to survive the bloody communist purges orchestrated by dictator JOSEPH STALIN, and he witnessed firsthand the failures of Soviet-style collectivism. He nonetheless remained loyal to his creed, and during World War II he served as a Hungarian-language broadcaster for Radio Kossuth. After Hungary was occupied by the Red Army, he was entrusted with drawing up plans for extensive agrarian reform. Nagy finally came home in the spring of 1945 and assumed a number of agrarian-related posts in the new communist government.

Nagy initially served as minister of the interior, but he also gained appointment as president of the legislature. Despite sterling communist credentials he took the courageous step of opposing Soviet-style collectivization of agriculture. He also questioned the overwhelming emphasis on heavy industrialization at the expense of other sectors of the national economy. In 1949 Hungarian leader MÁTYÁS RÁKOSI, on Stalin's insistence, dismissed Nagy from the Politburo, and he took up a teaching position with the University of Agronomy. However, in 1951 he was allowed to rejoin the Politburo and eventually climbed the hierarchy to become second deputy of the national council. The turning point in his career occurred in February 1953 after Stalin's death. A deliberate scheme of political liberalization was imposed upon Hungary by the new Soviet leadership, and Rákosi was dismissed from power. Nagy became prime minister in his place and enacted far-reaching political and economic reforms. When the hard-line Rákosi denounced his efforts as a threat to communist supremacy, superiors in Moscow agreed and Nagy was obliged to step down. By December 1955 he was formally expelled from the Communist Party and became an official nonentity.

Unknown to Soviet leaders, their initial efforts at liberalization touched off a national fervor to mitigate the effects of communist rule. Strikes and demonstrations

Imre Nagy *(Library of Congress)*

brutally crushed four days later. More than 200,000 Hungarians fled to Western Europe as refugees, while Nagy himself sought refuge in the Yugoslav embassy. A new communist hard-line regime under JÁNOS KÁDÁR was installed with Soviet blessings.

Nagy remained holed up at the embassy until November 22, 1957, when Kádár granted him a pass to leave the country. But he was suddenly arrested in Romania, sent to Budapest, and tried for treason. Nagy faced the hangman's noose on June 16, 1958, one of the last victims of the ill-fated Hungarian revolution. He was buried in an unmarked grave until 1989, when communism collapsed in Hungary. The martyred prime minister was then posthumously rehabilitated by the Hungarian Supreme Court. Nagy's remains were exhumed and interred with all the solemnities befitting a national hero.

Further Reading

Bekes, Csaba, Malcolm Byrne, and Janos Ranier, eds. *The 1956 Hungarian Revolution: A History in Documents.* New York: Central European University Press, 2002.

Benziger, Karl P. "The Funeral of Imre Nagy: Contested History and the Power of Memory Culture." *History and Memory* 12 (fall-winter 2000): 142–164.

———. "Imre Nagy, Martyr of the Nation: Contested Memory and Social Cohesion." *East European Quarterly* 36 (summer 2002): 171–191.

Dornbach, Alajos, ed. *The Secret Trial of Imre Nagy.* Westport, Conn.: Praeger, 1994.

Rainer, Janos M. "The Development of Imre Nagy as a Politician and a Thinker." *Contemporary European History* 6, no. 3 (1997): 263–277.

———. "The Life Course of Imre Nagy." *Journal of Communist Studies and Transition Politics* 13 (June 1997): 141–151.

Nakasone Yasuhiro (1918–   ) *prime minister of Japan*

Nakasone Yasuhiro was born in Takasaki, Gumma Prefecture, Japan, on May 27, 1918, the scion of a rich lumber merchant. He passed through Tokyo Imperial University with a law degree in 1941 and took up a position with the ministry of the interior. Soon after he was called away for military service and ended World War II as a lieutenant commander in the Imperial Japanese Navy. Unlike many contemporaries

forced Rákosi to resign as prime minister a second time in October 1956, and Nagy was recalled by popular demand to succeed him. At no time did Nagy call for an end to communist-style socialism; instead he simply wanted to adapt it to local circumstances. He subsequently took to the airwaves and called for calm even as communist control of the government crumbled around him. However, Hungary was swept by anti-Soviet violence, and street fighting erupted. Russians and communist loyalists beat a hasty retreat, while Nagy assured Soviet premier NIKITA KHRUSHCHEV of the nation's loyalty to Moscow. But when a new government was formed, Nagy declared the onset of multiparty democracy and withdrew from the Soviet-sponsored Warsaw Pact. Khrushchev responded by pledging nonintervention in Hungarian affairs—while massing troops on the border. They rolled into Hungary on November 1, 1956, and the uprising was in postwar Japan, young Nakasone remained stridently nationalistic and criticized the nation's new role as a passive American client state. In 1947 he joined the conservative Japan Democratic Party (JDP) and earned a controversial reputation by campaigning for office while displaying the Japanese national flag—then banned by U.S. occupation authorities. Nakasone was resoundingly elected to the national Diet (legislature) where he remained for over four decades. In 1955 the JDP merged with the Japan Liberal Party to form a new entity, the Liberal Democratic Party (LDP), which ultimately dominated national politics. Nakasone, a blunt, outspoken, charismatic personality, quickly established himself as a rising force in party politics. And due to his willingness to switch sides on political issues to advance his personal agenda, he was also sometimes derided as "Mr. Weathervane." In 1967 Prime Minister SATO EISAKU appointed him minister of transport, and in 1972 he became head of the self-defense agency and the Ministry of International Trade and Industry (MITI) under TANAKA KAKUEI. By 1982 Nakasone had established himself as a key figure within the LDP senior leadership, and that year he was elected party head. Because the LDP had the greatest number of seats in the Diet, Nakasone became prime minister.

Nakasone occupied high office at an opportune time, for the economy was booming and the balance of trade with the United States and other nations had never been more lopsided in Japan's favor. However, this very success was a source of friction with Japan's trading partners and he resolved to improve relations by reducing the nation's labyrinthine trade barriers. He lowered tariffs, decreased trade regulations, and made it easier for foreign products to compete in the Japanese marketplace. An aggressive populist by nature, Nakasone also took the unprecedented step of insisting that education should stress national pride and Japan's place in the world. This struck many as a throwback to the 1930s when acute nationalism led directly to war, but the prime minister strongly felt that all Japanese should be proud of their nation and its postwar accomplishments. To underscore his determination to confront the past, Nakasone became the first postwar national leader to pay homage at the Yasukuni war shrine commemorating Japan's war dead. He also tried changing the constitution to allow Japanese prime ministers to be elected by a direct popular vote, but the legislation was thwarted by entrenched interests in the Diet.

Nakasone made his greatest impact on foreign affairs. Staunchly anticommunist, he openly courted closer defense relationships with the United States and was repeatedly hosted by American president RONALD REAGAN. Their many well-publicized encounters were parodied in some quarters as the "Ron and Yasu Show," but Nakasone insisted that Japan be treated like an equal and shoulder its responsibilities for national defense. He then made history by raising defense expenditures past the psychological limit of 1 percent of gross national product, and touted Japan as an "unsinkable aircraft carrier" for the defense of Asia. Such talk alarmed leftist segments of Japanese society, but the public embraced rearmament, and in 1984 the LDP swept national elections by its biggest margins to date. He thus held onto high office for five years, making him one of the longest-serving Japanese heads of state in the 20th century. However, party rules forbade any individual from seeking a third term, so Nakasone stepped down in 1987. At that time Japan enjoyed one of its longest periods of sustained economic growth and was asserting national priorities throughout the Pacific for the first time since World War II. Nakasone was the only postwar prime minister to appoint his own successor, TAKESHITA NOBORU.

Out of office, Nakasone continued on as party head and an influential elder statesman within the LDP hierarchy. However, he resigned his post after being implicated in an insider trading scheme and did not resume his political activities with the LDP until April 1991. He remains a major force in national politics to the present time and will be remembered as the prime minister who decisively recast Japan's international role in the cold war era.

Further Reading

Angel, Robert C. "Prime Ministerial Leadership in Japan: Recent Change in Personal Style and Administrative Organization." *Pacific Affairs* 61, no. 4 (1989): 583–602.

Dei, Sharon. "Rhetorical Strategies to Bridge the Cross-cultural Gap: Nakasone at the Sorbonne." *Asian Thought and Society* 15, no. 45 (1990): 255–267.

Hayo, Kenji. *The Japanese Prime Minister and Public Policy.* Pittsburgh: University of Pittsburgh Press, 1993.

Hood, Christopher P. *Japanese Education: Nakasone's Legacy.* New York: Routledge, 2001.

Muramatsu, Michiro. "In Search of National Identity: The Politics and Policies of the Nakasone Administration." *Journal of Japanese Studies* 12, no. 2 (1987): 307–342.

Nakasone, Yasuhiro. *Japan: A State Strategy for the Twenty-First Century.* New York: RoutledgeCurzon, 2002.

Takeshige, K. "A Bitter Election Pill for Nakasone." *Japan Quarterly* 34 (July–September 1987): 259–262.

Nasser, Gamal Abdel (1918–1970) *president of Egypt*

Gamal Abdel Nasser was born in Bani Mor, Egypt, on January 15, 1918, the son of a postmaster. As a youth he exhibited profound dislike for British colonialism and was arrested several times for leading protests. Nasser passed through the Royal Military Academy in 1938 and served as an infantry lieutenant. While stationed in the Sudan he met and befriended several other reform-minded officers, like ANWAR AL-SADAT, who were determined to end British rule of Egypt and oust the royal family. Nasser fought with distinction during the 1948 Arab-Israeli war. Dissatisfaction with the extent of corruption and incompetence permeating the Egyptian government, culminated in formation of a secret revolutionary organization, the Free Officers, with Nasser as its leader. On July 23, 1952, the Free Officers deposed King FAROUK, and a Revolutionary Command Council was installed led by General Mohammad Naguib. However, Naguib wished to return to parliamentary rule as soon as possible, while Nasser felt that a military junta was the best solution for instituting badly needed reforms. In 1954 Nasser overthrew Naguib and proclaimed himself prime minister. By 1956 he had promulgated a new constitution that declared Egypt a socialist Arab state governed by a one-party system. That year Nasser ran unopposed for the presidency and was elected with 99 percent of votes cast.

Nasser assumed power intending to effect radical change to improve the plight of Egypt's poor majority through "Arab socialism." He passed land-reform legislation that broke up the landed estates owned by foreigners and forbade any citizen from owning more than 100 acres. The government then nationalized the banks and various sectors of the economy, which now placed increasing emphasis on heavy industry. Nasser also recognized the centrality of religion to the Egyptian people, although he determined that it should not be a hindrance to modernization. Egyptian women thus received more political freedom than they had heretofore known. And, with Soviet help, Nasser embarked on the ambitious Aswan High Dam project to electrify the countryside. Egypt had also received pledges of financial support from Great Britain and the United States, but this was revoked when Nasser signed an extensive arms deal with Communist Czechoslovakia. Unperturbed, the president summarily nationalized the British-owned Suez Canal and sought to use the tolls collected to finance the dam. This move prompted a combined British-French-Israeli invasion of the Sinai and canal region in October 1956. The Egyptians were decisively defeated but the invaders withdrew, under heavy pressure from the United Nations, the United States, and the Soviet Union. In light of his success in nationalizing the canal and standing up to the West, Nasser became the darling of Arab nationalists around the globe.

Gamal Abdel Nasser *(Library of Congress)*

Despite his growing reliance upon the Soviet Union and its allies for money and arms, Nasser became an outspoken proponent of the Third World non-aligned movement, which sought to distance itself from cold war global politics. In concert with MARSHAL TITO of Yugoslavia and JAWAHARLAL NEHRU of India, the Egyptian gained international stature as a spokesman for developing regions of the world. Nasser also boldly dreamt of unifying the entire Muslim world of 450 million under his leadership. In 1958 he took the important step of bringing his nation and Syria into a political union called the United Arab Republic (UAR), although the arrangement dissolved after 1961. The following year Nasser supported a revolution in North Yemen with troops to counter Saudi Arabian influence in the peninsula region. He also lent money and material assistance to revolutionary guerrilla movements in Palestine and Algeria. However, Nasser's ambitions were dashed in June 1967 after Egypt demanded the removal of UN peacekeeping forces from the Sinai and Gaza regions, and also blockaded Israeli access to the Red Sea. This brought a sharp and humiliating military response from Israel in the form of the Six Day War, whereby Egyptian and Syrian armies were routed and the West Bank annexed. Nasser's humiliation was so profound that he resigned as president, but massive street demonstrations convinced him to remain in office. Nasser spent the next three years trying to regain his former prestige among Arabs, although he accepted a U.S.-sponsored plan for peace negotiations with the Israelis. He died in Cairo on September 28, 1970, before his dream of Arab unity could be realized. Nevertheless, his state funeral was attended by an estimated 4 million Egyptians.

Nasser remains one of the most significant Arab nationalists of the 20th century. He ruled over a virtual police state and severely punished political opponents of his regime, secular and religious alike, but to the very end this intelligent, charismatic reformer commanded the loyalty and affection of Arab people around the world.

Further Reading

Aburish, Said K. *Nasser: The Last Arab.* New York: St. Martin's Press/Thomas Dunne Books, 2004.

Jankowski, James. *Nasser's Egypt, Arab Nationalism, and the United Arab Republic.* Boulder, Colo.: Lynne Rienner, 2002.

Kear, Simon. "Diplomatic Innovation: Nasser and the Origins of the Interests Section." *Diplomacy and Statecraft* 12 (September 2001): 65–86.

McNamara, Robert. *Britain, Nasser, and the Balance of Power in the Middle East, 1952–1967.* Portland, Ore.: Frank Cass, 2003.

Nasser, Gamal A. *The Philosophy of Revolution.* Washington, D.C.: Public Affairs Press, 1955.

Petersen, Tore T. *The Middle East between the Great Powers: Anglo-American Conflict and Cooperation, 1952–7.* New York: St. Martin's Press, 2000.

Takeyh, Ray. *The Origins of the Eisenhower Doctrine: The U.S., Britain, and Nasser's Egypt, 1953–57.* New York: St. Martin's Press, 2000.

Nehru, Jawaharlal (1889–1964) *prime minister of India*

Jawaharlal Nehru was born in Allahabad, India, on November 14, 1889, into an upper-class Brahmin family. His father was a wealthy lawyer and, India being then a British possession, he provided his son with a thorough English education. In 1905 young Nehru was sent to England where he attended Harrow, an elite preparatory school. Two years later he studied science at Trinity College, Cambridge University, and by 1910 he had been admitted to the English bar. Back in India, he started a successful law practice but was gradually drawn into nationalist politics after encountering the Hindu traditionalist Mahatma Gandhi in 1916. His consciousness was further raised following a 1919 massacre of peaceful protesters by British troops. As part of the high-brow upper caste, Nehru had virtually no contact with the poor majority of India, and when he first encountered the poverty and despair of the countryside, he was shocked and ashamed. Thereafter he became a devotee of the Indian Congress Party, which agitated for independence from Great Britain, and also dabbled in socialist politics. Nehru's flamboyant style and willingness to engage in confrontational politics were a marked contrast to Gandhi, an avowed pacifist, but the two men maintained a ready alliance. Commencing in 1928 Nehru began relentlessly pushing for independence. He was arrested nine times, and spent a total of nine years behind bars. But through this sacrifice Nehru gained recognition as a national leader and a potential successor to Gandhi. By 1930 he was president of the National Congress Party and accelerated the drive against imperi-

Jawaharlal Nehru *(Library of Congress)*

to feed one of the world's most populous nations. Progress was eventually made, but national harmony was perpetually beset by continuing sectarian violence between Hindu and Muslim communities. Nehru himself suffered a tremendous personal loss when his friend and mentor, Gandhi, was assassinated by a Hindu fanatic in January 1948. "The light has gone out of our lives," he declared, "and there is darkness everywhere." Overall his efforts to modernize the Indian economy enjoyed mixed results; India finally acquired an industrial base, but gains were offset by the nation's burgeoning population.

Nehru enjoyed somewhat better luck in the realm of foreign policy. Though a socialist, he viewed communism as a virulent form of Western imperialism and distanced himself from the Soviet Union. He also endeavored not to draw too close to the United States and thus avoid participation in the cold war. Nehru gained global stature as an advocate for the impoverished developing countries, and for his policy of strict neutrality, or non-alignment, in world affairs. To that end he declined all invitations to join military alliances and also sought a ban on all nuclear weapons testing. But Nehru himself was not above using force when it suited national interests; in 1961 he deployed troops to wrest the colony of Goa from Portugal and Indian forces sporadically engaged Pakistani troops over disputed Kashmir province. However, his biggest setback occurred during a border dispute with China in 1962. The Chinese launched a well-coordinated attack that drove Indian forces from a disputed region of the Himalayas. Thereafter Nehru reconsidered his prior emphasis on non-alignment status and sought Western assistance to defend his borders.

Nehru died in New Delhi on May 27, 1964, and was mourned as one of the chief architects of Indian independence. He had also bequeathed to his nation the basic machinery for self-governance and the political dominance of the Indian Congress Party. Indirectly, he further established India's first political dynasty, as both his daughter, INDIRA GANDHI, and his grandson, RAJIV GANDHI, became prime ministers of the world's most populous democracy.

alism. In 1939 Nehru strongly opposed India's participation in World War II unless the country was immediately set free, and he was arrested for the last time. He was finally freed in 1945 just as a new Labour government in England prepared to grant self-rule to the subcontinent. Nehru subsequently emerged as India's first prime minister on August 17, 1947, a position he held for the next 17 years.

Prior to independence, both Nehru and Gandhi negotiated with Muslim leader MOHAMMED ALI JINNAH over the possibility of keeping Pakistan as part of India, but discussions failed and partition became a reality. Now in charge, Nehru faced enormous problems of promoting democracy in a nation once consisting of 500 princely kingdoms. He nonetheless tackled his responsibilities energetically and made plans to blend socialist economic planning with liberal democracy. Nehru sought to nationalize wide sectors of the economy and took positive steps to end tenancy and promote land ownership for the poor majority. He also struggled with increasing agricultural production

Further Reading

Baxter, Craig, et. al. *Government and Politics in South Asia.* Boulder, Colo.: Westview Press, 2002.

Brown, Judith M. *Nehru.* New York: Longman, 2000.

Guha, Ramachandra. "Democracy's Biggest Gamble: India's First Free Elections in 1952." *World Policy Journal* 19 (spring 2002): 95–103.

Mitra, S. K. "Nehru's Policy Towards Kashmir: Bring Politics Back in Again." *Journal of Commonwealth and Comparative Politics* 35 (July 1997): 55–74.

Nehru, Jawaharlal. *Glimpses of World History: Being Further Letters to His Daughter, Written in Prison.* New York: Oxford University Press, 1989.

Wolpert, Stanley A. *Nehru: A Tryst with Destiny.* Bridgewater, N.J.: Replica Press, 2000.

Zachariah, Benjamin. *Nehru.* New York: Routledge, 2004.

Neto, Antonio (1922–1979) *president of Angola*

Antonio Agostinho Neto was born in Icolo e Bengo, Angola, on September 17, 1922, the son of a Methodist preacher from the Mbundu ethnic group. He was fortunate enough to secure a sound education before joining the Portuguese colonial medical service as a nurse. The gross disparities in pay and working conditions greatly angered Neto, who showed a flair for poetry and published several acclaimed volumes in protest. This put him at the forefront of an Angolan cultural revival movement that was banned by colonial authorities. In 1948 Neto nevertheless received a scholarship to study medicine at the University of Lisbon and concurrently expanded his revolutionary activities. He struck up a close relationship with fellow student AMILCAR CABRAL of Cape Verde, and for protesting the fascist dictatorship of ANTÓNIO SALAZAR he was repeatedly arrested and jailed. After graduating in 1959, Neto returned home to work as one of the few African medical doctors in Angola. He also participated in anticolonial demonstrations, and on June 8, 1960, Neto was arrested at his hospital and exiled to Cape Verde and Portugal. His apprehension stirred considerable unrest, and Portuguese soldiers killed 30 demonstrators in Catete. However, Neto managed to escape his captors in 1962 and made for Leopoldville, Congo, headquarters of the Movimento Popular de Libertação de Angola (MPLA), Popular Movement for the Liberation of Angola. An intelligent, highly cultured individual, he was soon after elected president of the movement, which was pledged to end Portuguese colonial rule at any cost.

For nearly a decade the MPLA conducted low-level guerrilla warfare against the colonial establishment.

Neto, meanwhile, traveled extensively throughout Europe and the Soviet bloc, soliciting arms and support. After 1965 he managed to secure the backing of sympathetic regimes in Zambia and Tanzania. But the move toward independence was hampered from the onset by the rise of competing guerrilla factions. Foremost among these was the Frente Nacional de Libertação de Angola (FNLA), National Front for the Liberation of Angola, under Holden Roberto, a former MPLA member, and the União Nacional para a Independência Total de Angola (UNITA), National Union for the Total Independence of Angola, under Jonas Savimbi. Neto, as a practicing Marxist, ensured that the MPLA maintained its revolutionary slant. Moreover, it actively cultivated peasant support in the countryside by establishing schools and hospitals for the local population. Consequently, and thanks to Neto's ideology, MPLA remained the largest guerrilla group and controlled the largest stretches of land. The turning point in the war occurred in April 1974, when Portugal's government was overturned by a left-wing junta that declared its support for African independence. After 20 years of exile, Neto finally returned home.

The Portuguese abandoned Angola without choosing a successor regime from the three competing factions. Roberto, Neto, and Savimbi all agreed to a tentative cease-fire to arrange a coalition government, but it quickly dissolved and the victors began fighting among themselves. On November 11, 1975, Neto, whose MPLA controlled the capital of Luanda, was declared president. The pace of events quickened when the Soviet Union airlifted some 18,000 Cuban soldiers into Angola to combat the FNLA and UNITA. This sudden influx of modern firepower sent the guerrilla factions scampering back into the bush, and Neto strengthened his grip on power by establishing a Marxist-Leninist police state. True to his creed, he nationalized what little industry remained in Angola and monopolized political power through creation of the MPLA Party of Workers. Such slavish devotion to communism set off alarms in the United States and South Africa, which sought to curtail Soviet influence on the continent. The Americans then began supplying the FNLA and UNITA with weapons of their own, while South Africa launched several punitive campaigns against the Cuban occupiers.

For the next four years the Angolan civil war raged, taking a terrible toll on the civilian population and the economy. The MPLA, enjoying every military advantage, proved unable to suppress the wily Western-supplied guerrillas. Conditions deteriorated to the point where Neto endured a coup attempt against him in May 1977. Thereafter he purged the party of malcontents, abolished the prime minister's office, but also abandoned his hard-line Marxist stance by soliciting Western investment. Neto's effort to turn Angola into a socialist state finally ended on September 10, 1979, when he died in Moscow while receiving medical treatment. His successor, Jose Eduardo dos Santos, eventually reached an accord with the rebels in 2002 following the death of Savimbi. The Angolan civil war, precipitated by Neto's policies, proved to be among Africa's costliest and most prolonged conflicts.

Further Reading

Birmingham, David. *Portugal and Africa*. New York: St. Martin's Press, 1999.

Duarte, Malfada. *Aid Policy in War-torn Countries: Promoting Development in Conflict Situations: The Case of Angola*. Lanham, Md.: University Press of America, 2002.

Guimaraes, Fernando A. *The Origins of the Angolan Civil War: Foreign Intervention and Domestic Political Conflict*. Basingstoke, England: Macmillan, 2001.

Heywood, Linda M. *Contested Power in Angola: 1840s to the Present*. Rochester, N.Y.: University of Rochester Press, 2000.

Hodges, Tony. *Angola: From Afro-Stalinism to Petro-diamond Capitalism*. Bloomington, Ind.: Indiana University Press, 2001.

Keller, Alene. "The U.S. Policy of 'Containment' and U.S. Intervention in Angola's Civil War: A Case Study." Unpublished master's thesis, University of South Florida, 2001.

Ne Win (1911–2002) *president of Burma*

Shu Maung was born in Prome, Burma, on May 24, 1911. He briefly attended the University of Rangoon in 1930 but dropped out to participate in the anti-British nationalist movement Dobama Asiayone. He struck up cordial relations with nationalist leader Aung San and in 1941 accompanied 28 other Burmese recruits to Japan for military training. At that time he changed his name to Ne Win (Bright Sun) and returned home in 1942 after the Japanese had ousted the British from Burma. Ne Win was subsequently appointed commander of the Burma Defense Army while Aung San served as war minister. However, both men despised Japanese colonialism as much as the British variety and they began plotting against their erstwhile benefactors. In 1944 the Burmese staged an armed uprising against the retiring Japanese and Ne Win distinguished himself as a military commander.

After the war Ne Win continued on in the regular army, while Aung San agitated for national independence until his assassination in July 1947. Burma regained its sovereignty in January 1948, and the following year Ne Win was promoted to commander in chief of the armed forces. In this capacity he put down numerous rebellions by tribal minorities and bands of communists. His excellent service to the state came to the attention of Prime Minister U NU, who appointed him minister for defense. Ne Win continued serving capably and loyally until 1958, when a split developed within U Nu's government over the issue of insurgencies. At that point Ne Win intervened, toppled the government in a bloodless coup, and appointed himself prime minister. Over the next two years he worked hard at restoring national order, and in February 1960 new elections were held. U Nu was then returned to office until March 2, 1962, when Ne Win deposed him for good. Intent upon retaining power, the general also suspended the constitution, dissolved the legislature, and jailed most leading politicians. Power was now wielded by the Revolutionary Council of the Union of Burma, which consisted primarily of military officers. Ne Win then embarked on what he called the "Burmese Way to Socialism," by nationalizing various segments of the economy and clamping down on all forms of political dissent. His goal was to seek economic autarky, or self-sufficiency, and he pursued a deliberate policy of global isolationism. In 1971 Ne Win consolidated his grip on power by instituting a one-party police state in which his Burma Socialist Program Party (BSPP) became the only legal outlet for political activity. In 1974 Ne Win promulgated a new constitution and assumed the role of president. The administration itself was reviled for being ruthless and corrupt in equal measure.

Ne Win ruled Burma with an iron hand for nearly 25 years before publicly "retiring" from office in 1981. His maniacal pursuit of socialist economics bankrupted the nation and left his previously wealthy country virtually destitute. His mismanagement was so profound that Burma, once a major rice exporter, was forced to ration that staple crop to curtail famine. He stepped down from power officially in July 1988 but still remained head of the BSPP and, hence, continued to function as the power behind the throne. His retirement triggered mass protests by prodemocracy students that were brutally crushed with great loss of life. In September 1988 General Saw Maung sponsored a coup that formally returned the military to power, apparently with Ne Win's blessing. Thereafter national rule devolved upon the State Law and Order Restoration Council, which continued the old socialist economic line. The nation, now called Myanmar, remained one of the poorest in Asia, and in 1987 was classified as among the least developed by the United Nations.

Ne Win died on December 5, 2002, scarcely lamented. He was a quixotic dictator, much given to numerology and mysticism. The reason for his retirement on August 8, 1988, was that 8.8.88 was viewed as a lucky number. He also dictated that the national currency, the *kyat,* be issued only in denominations of 45 and 90 because each was divisible by nine. But since his passing, the country has witnessed the rise of a prodemocracy movement orchestrated by Aung San Suu Kyi, daughter of his old compatriot, Aung San. In the spring of 2002, members of Ne Win's own family were arrested and sentenced to death for plotting a coup against the military government.

Further Reading

Alamgir, Jalat. "Against the Current: The Survival of Authoritarianism in Burma." *Pacific Affairs* 16, no. 1 (1992): 81–97.

Haseman, J. B. "Destruction of Democracy: The Tragic Case of Burma." *Asian Affairs* 20 (spring 1993): 17–27.

Johnson, R. L. "The Burmese People's Struggle." *Peace Review* 10 (June 1998): 215–220.

Maung Maung, U. *Burma and General Ne Win.* New York: Asia Pub. House, 1969.

Mawdsley, James. *The Iron Road: A Stand for Truth and Democracy in Burma.* New York: North Point Press, 2002.

Steinberg, David. *Burma's Role Toward Development: Growth and Ideology under Military Rule.* Boulder, Colo.: Westview Press, 1981.

Taylor, R. H. "The Enduring Military Role in Burma." *Current History* 89 (March 1990): 105–108, 134–135.

Ngo Dinh Diem (1901–1963) *president of South Vietnam*

Ngo Dinh Diem was born in Quang Binh Province on January 3, 1901, the son of a government official with close ties to the imperial court. Diem's family was unique in this predominantly Buddhist nation for having embraced Catholicism in the 17th century. He received a strict religious upbringing and the classical Chinese-style education consistent with his class. Diem initially toyed with joining the clergy but opted instead to study politics and law at the University of Hanoi. He graduated in 1921 and proved himself a highly intelligent and capable bureaucrat. By 1929 he was serving as governor of Phan-Thiet Province, and two years later Emperor Bao Dai appointed him minister of the interior. But because Vietnam was a French colonial possession, the indigenous government retained little leeway in administrative affairs, and in 1933 Diem resigned in protest. He spent the next 12 years in self-imposed exile, although he flirted with nationalist organizations and roundly condemned French colonialism. When the Japanese acquired Vietnam in 1941 they approached Diem to serve as prime minister under their control, but he refused to serve colonial powers of any stripe. After 1945 Vietnam was supposed to be returned to French colonial control but a communist insurgency under HO CHI MINH declared an independent republic. Diem was kidnapped from his home by communist agents attempting to entice him to join a coalition government with them, but he refused all overtures. The sternly religious mandarin despised communism as much as colonialism, and in 1950 he fled to the United States to seek American assistance. There he conferred with Senator JOHN F. KENNEDY, a fellow Catholic, and also reestablished his former ties with Bao Dai.

After Ho Chi Minh's triumph over France in the First Indochina War in 1954, the Geneva Accords divided Vietnam into a communist-controlled north and a democratic south. The issue of reunifying both halves was subject to a public referendum in the future. Ho was the most popular political figure in the entire country and would have easily carried the day. However, U.S. president DWIGHT D. EISENHOWER, fearing communist expansion into Southeast Asia, prevailed upon Diem to return home and serve as prime minister under Bao Dai. He agreed and began developing his power base among Vietnam's small but influential Catholic minority. Cognizant that the communists would win any elections, he summarily suspended the Geneva Accords and instead formulated a referendum to depose the emperor and install himself as chief executive. The ensuing "election" was egregiously rigged but on October 26, 1955, Diem became the first president of the newly proclaimed Republic of Vietnam, better known as South Vietnam.

Diem was well-intentioned and fiercely anticommunist, but he proved temperamentally unsuited to lead the country. He took an authoritarian hard line against all perceived opponents of his regime and actively quashed communist cells, criminal organizations, and Buddhist militants with equal abandon. After 1961 North Vietnam responded by infiltrating regular army troops to assist the South Vietnamese communist movement, or Viet Cong. Diem, lacking popular support and reneging on pledges to promote

land reform, proved unable to stop the popular growth of communism. He resorted to harsher repression and greater reliance on the United States for financial and military assistance. Despite such aid, he summarily refused American requests for reform and moderation toward opponents. Diem also remained adamantly opposed to the introduction of U.S. combat troops, a reflection of his staunch anti-colonialism. The turning point occurred in the summer of 1963, when several Buddhist monks, enraged over what they deemed favoritism toward the Catholic minority, immolated themselves in public. This convinced the South Vietnamese military and their American backers that Diem was immovable politically. Worse, his recalcitrant attitude, coupled with nepotism and corruption, was actually aiding the swelling communist insurgency. On November 1, 1963, the generals overthrew the Diem regime in Saigon, murdering the president and several family members on the following day. A military junta under General Duong Van Minh then assumed control of the government. The exact role of President Kennedy's administration in this matter has never been established, but the Americans certainly welcomed the change. The stage was now set for growing American involvement in the Vietnamese civil war under President LYNDON B. JOHNSON.

Further Reading

Adamson, Michael R. "Ambassadorial Roles and Foreign Policy: Elbridge Durbrow, Frederich Nolting, and U.S. Commitment to Diem's Vietnam, 1956–61." *Presidential Studies Quarterly* 32 (June 2002): 229–255.

Catton, Philip E. *Diem's Final Failure: Prelude to America's War in Vietnam.* Lawrence: University Press of Kansas, 2003.

Jones, Howard. *Death of a Generation: How the Assassinations of Diem and JFK Prolonged the Vietnam War.* New York: Oxford University Press, 2002.

O'Leary, Bradley S., and Edward Lee. *The Death of the Cold War Kings: The Assassinations of Diem and JFK.* Baltimore: Cemetery Dance Publications, 2000.

Topmiller, Robert J. *The Lotus Unleashed: The Buddhist Peace Movement in South Vietnam.* Lexington: University Press of Kentucky, 2002.

Winter, Francis X. *The Year of the Hare: America in Vietnam, January 25, 1963–February 15, 1964.* Athens: University of Georgia Press, 1997.

Ngo Dinh Diem *(Library of Congress)*

Nguyen Cao Ky (1930–   ) *vice president of South Vietnam*

Nguyen Cao Ky was born in Son Tay Province, Vietnam, on September 8, 1930, the son of a schoolteacher. He was raised a devout Buddhist, and was about to enroll at college when he was drafted into the French-controlled Vietnamese army to fight a communist-inspired insurgency. Ky served with distinction as an infantry officer, and in 1951 he ventured to France to undergo pilot training. He returned home in 1954 and flew transport planes for several years. That same year the First Indochina War concluded with a decisive French defeat and Vietnam was partitioned into a communist north and a democratic south. After the rise of NGO DINH DIEM in 1955, United States military advisers and assistance were increasingly drawn into the ongoing guerrilla war waged by South Vietnamese communists (Viet Cong). Ky showed himself to be a competent leader, and after 1960 he flew clandestine missions into North Vietnam for the Central Intelligence Agency. In November 1963 he also figured prominently in the coup that toppled the Diem regime and he was promoted to brigadier general and head of the fledgling South Vietnamese Air Force. The dashing Ky was also a rigorous disciplinarian, and he quickly rendered his air force an effective military arm in the war against communism. However, he continually took part in numerous plots and counterplots against the government. In June 1965 Ky joined generals NGUYEN VAN THIEU and Duong Van Minh in a coup that ousted Premier Phan Huy Quat, whom they deemed too accommodating toward communism. Ky's influence was great enough that he had to be included in the new triumvirate of generals who assumed control. In this capacity he began an ongoing power struggle with Thieu as both battled the rising tide of communist insurgency.

As a leader Ky proved effective in the field but he was ruthless against his political opponents, especially the Buddhists. However, his national visibility was greatly heightened when he conferred with American president LYNDON B. JOHNSON in Hawaii in February 1966. This meeting set in motion a quest for greater political legitimacy, and in March 1967 Ky was elected the nation's youngest prime minister, while Thieu served as president. Again, competition between the two strong-willed individuals proved incessant and weakened the overall war effort. But Ky responded to American pressure for change, and he helped sponsor modest land reforms, school construction, and other useful measures. New elections were held the following September, whereupon Thieu and Ky served as president and vice president, respectively, on a unified ticket. "Our only object is to restore peace and return prosperity to the country after defeating the communists," Ky declared to the press. But for the rest of the republic's short life, the government remained far from unified.

No amount of internal wrangling could overcome the single-minded determination of North Vietnam to conquer and unify with the south. Over the next eight years the United States and its Vietnamese allies waged a gallant struggle against the communist forces but proved unable to stem the tide of guerrilla infiltration. Thieu remained contemptuous of his subordinate and in the 1971 elections he managed to have him legally removed as a political opponent. Ky then abandoned politics altogether and concentrated on leading the air force. American troops were completely withdrawn by 1975, and the communists launched an all-out offensive to win the war. South Vietnamese defenses crumbled under the onslaught, and in April 1975 Ky led a highly publicized demonstration in front of the U.S. embassy, declaring an intention to fight to the end. A few days later the former vice president apparently had second thoughts, for on April 29, 1975, he was evacuated to an American ship offshore. The capital of Saigon fell to communist forces soon after and the costly second Indochinese war came to an end.

Ky subsequently relocated to Los Angeles where he opened a liquor store. He also toured, lectured, and published widely on the war and ascribed its loss directly to the muddled leadership of Thieu, "who wanted power and glory but he did not want to do the dirty work." He also feels vindicated that the communists in Vietnam are finally beginning to dabble in free-market economics.

Further Reading

Daum, Andreas W., Lloyd C. Gardner, and Wilfried Mausbach, eds. *America, the Vietnam War and the World.* New York: Cambridge University Press, 2003.

Neale, Jonathan. *A People's History of the Vietnam War.* New York: New Press, 2003.

Ninh, Kim Ngoc Bao. *A World Transformed: The Politics of Culture in Revolutionary Vietnam, 1945–1965.* Ann Arbor: University of Michigan Press, 2002.

Nguyen Cao Ky. *Buddha's Child: My Fight to Save Vietnam.* New York: St. Martin's Press, 2002.

———. *How We Lost the Vietnam War.* New York: Cooper Square Press, 2002.

———. *Twenty Years and Twenty Days.* New York: Stein and Day, 1976.

Nguyen Van Thieu (1923–2001) *president of South Vietnam*

Nguyen Van Thieu was born in Ninh Thuan, Vietnam, on April 5, 1923, the son of a small landowner. As a youth he flirted briefly with communism by joining HO CHI MINH's Viet Minh, but recoiled at their barbarity toward civilians. Thieu then joined the French-controlled Vietnamese National Army in 1949 to take part in the ongoing war against communism. He proved an adept soldier and, following the election of NGO DINH DIEM as president in 1955, he was sent to the United States to further his military training. He also converted from Buddhism to Catholicism, as the Diem regime favored officers of that creed. Vietnam at this time had been divided into two regions by the 1954 Geneva Accords. The north was controlled by the communists under Ho, while the south remained under the authoritarian regime of Diem. After 1961 the communists began a determined campaign of guerrilla infiltration that lasted 14 years. Thieu, meanwhile, returned home and began steadily climbing through the military hierarchy. In November 1963 he was in the military coup that toppled Diem, and thereafter he struck an uneasy alliance with NGUYEN CAO KY, his principal competitor for political laurels. By 1965 the two had outmaneuvered several leading contestants and seized control of the government. Ky was then installed as prime minister while Thieu had to settle for the titles of head of state and commander in chief. In this capacity both men bartered with American president LYNDON B. JOHNSON for military assistance and direct United States intervention. Johnson agreed and ultimately committed over 500,000 troops but he also insisted on a more democratic means of holding power. New elections were scheduled for 1967, when Thieu suddenly announced that he was running for president against Ky. Such a move threatened to split military support for either candidate, so a compromise was effected: henceforth Thieu was to run for president while Ky accepted a subordinate position as vice president. During elections that year their joint ticket accrued only 35 percent of votes cast, but the tally was far larger than that of any other competitors. The Americans hoped Thieu's ascension would promote political stability at home and allow the government to concentrate on fighting the communists.

In reality, Thieu's regime enjoyed little public sympathy because of its inability to promulgate badly needed agrarian and social reforms. It existed solely because of overwhelming support from a corrupt clique of military leaders. The Vietnam war raged with escalating fury until the surprise 1968 Tet offensive, which convinced the United States that the war could not be won. Therefore a new U.S. president, RICHARD M. NIXON, began a process known as Vietnamization. Here American ground forces were slowly withdrawn from the theater of operations as the South Vietnamese army, backed by American air power, took over the fighting. Thieu, meanwhile, dropped all pretense of democratic elections by maneuvering Ky out of the 1971 presidential contest so that he could run unopposed. Nixon entered into direct peace negotiations with Hanoi in Paris, an act that Thieu publicly regarded as a sellout. Nonetheless, in the spring of 1973 he was forced to sign the Paris Peace Accords to stop the fighting, and a temporary impasse ensued.

With the American forces gone, the soldiers of both Vietnams braced themselves for renewed fighting. The communists then broke the cease-fire in January 1974, and the battle was joined. However, the South Vietnamese fared poorly without American air power while the communists received a continuous flow of arms from China and the Soviet Union. South Vietnamese forces resisted pluckily but by March 1975 they were on the verge of losing the northern half of the country. At that decisive moment Thieu ordered troops withdrawn from the northern provinces to reinforce the south. The retreat was carelessly handled, and a large-scale rout ensued. By April 1975 communist forces were at the very gates of Saigon and Thieu went on the air castigating the new American president, GERALD R. FORD, for not honoring prior treaty commitments to assist his regime. "You ran away and left us with the job that you could not do," he angrily declared. Thieu then fled the country for Taiwan shortly before communist tanks crashed through the presidential palace gates. Their victory concluded an unsuccessful 25-year effort by the United States to build popular support for a democratic government in the south. Thieu resided temporarily in Great Britain before finally relocating to a new home in Boston, Massachusetts. There he lived quietly, apparently off the great wealth he had accumulated while in office. He died there on September 30, 2001. His eight-year tenure as head of South Vietnam coincided with one of the bloodiest and most divisive wars of recent history.

Further Reading

Asselin, Pierre. *A Bitter Peace: Washington, Hanoi, and the Making of the Paris Agreement.* Chapel Hill: University of North Carolina Press, 2002.

Joes, Anthony J. *The War for South Viet Nam.* Westport, Conn.: Praeger, 2001.

Lamb, David. *Vietnam Now: A Reporter Returns.* New York: Public Affairs, 2002.

Moss, George. *Vietnam, an American Ordeal.* Upper Saddle River, N.J.: Prentice Hall, 2002.

Nguyen, Gregory, Tien Hung, and Jerrold L. Schecter. *The Palace File.* New York: Harper and Row, 1987.

Toczek, David M. *The Battle of Ap Bac, Vietnam: They Did Everything But Learn from It.* Westport, Conn: Greenwood Press, 2001.

Nicholas II (1868–1918) *czar of Russia*

Nicholay Aleksandrovich Romanov was born in Tsarskoye Selo, Russia, on May 6, 1868, a son of Crown Prince Alexsandr Aleksandrovich, the future Czar Alexander III. The Romanov family was one of Europe's most illustrious dynasties and had governed Russia since 1613. Nicholay himself was well-educated by private tutors and showed great linguistic abilities. But he also led a sheltered existence as a child, and he grew up to be somewhat shy and awkward in public. He nonetheless fulfilled his princely duties in state and court functions for many years until his father suddenly died on November 1, 1894. Nicholay then took the throne as Nicholas II and shortly afterward married Princess Alix of Hesse. As empress she converted to the Eastern Orthodox faith and Russianized her name to Alexandra, but her distant, aloof nature failed to win the affection of the Russian people. As a couple Nicholas and Alexandra were completely devoted to each other and their five children but they proved totally incapable of ruling Russia during a turbulent, transitional period in its long history. This ineptitude can be partially traced to Nicholas's belief that he was mandated by God to preserve the Russian tradition of autocracy in the face of rising demands for greater democracy. His prevailing sense of self-doubt, his limited academic abilities, and his willful inflexibility in accommodating change sowed the seeds for the monarchy's ultimate destruction.

Nicholas's ascension to the throne coincided with Russia's painful transition from an agrarian society to a modern industrial one. The displacement of millions of landless former serfs from the countryside to the inner cities created great poverty, unrest, and the rise of revolutionary secret societies. Unfortunately, the czar's response to frequently legitimate grievances was to crack down harshly with military force and intimidate dissenters through the secret police. Moreover, he continued his father's policy of oppressing Jews and minority Christian sects while also accelerating the Russianization of holdings in Eastern Europe and Central Asia. Furthermore the czar proved hostile to notions of democracy and openly scoffed at allowing the *zemstva* (local assemblies) to play more prominent roles in daily life. As early as 1905 Russia was a tinderbox awaiting a match to ignite it. The spark arrived in the form of the 1904–05 Russo-Japanese War, in which the Russians were completely humiliated. Resentment from the defeat culminated in large demonstrations at St. Petersburg, which were fired upon by the military. To avoid full-scale revolution, Count SERGEI WITTE, minister of finance, prevailed upon Nicholas to allow creation of a duma (legislature) and a constitutional monarchy in October 1905. However, the czar had little respect for legislative assemblies and he dissolved the Duma in 1906. Witte himself was forced to resign soon after, and he was replaced by the hard-line authoritarian PYOTR STOLYPIN. The stage was being set for an even more violent confrontation between the ruler and the ruled.

The final blow to Romanov rule was the cataclysm of World War I. The nation was militarily and economically weak but when Austria threatened Serbia in 1914 Nicholas felt obliged to mobilize the army on behalf of his fellow Slavs. This act incurred the wrath of Kaiser WILHELM II, and fighting broke out that August.

Russian troops fought bravely but ineptly over the next three years, taking horrendous casualties and suffering from acute shortages of food, clothing, and weapons. Worse, when Nicholas felt compelled to leave St. Petersburg (renamed Petrograd) and assume command at the front in 1915, he left affairs of state in the hands of Alexandra and her devious mystical adviser, Rasputin. Rasputin's influence was viewed as such a menace by the imperial circle that he was assassinated in 1916, an act fueling further resentment against the Romanovs. The end came in the revolution of February 1917 when the czar, faced with riots and revolutionaries in the streets, abdicated the throne in favor of a new provisional government under GEORGI LVOV. Nicholas and his family were placed under house arrest, and in early 1918 they were forcibly relocated to Yekaterinburg in the Ural Mountains. By that time the Bolsheviks under VLADIMIR LENIN had seized power. When it appeared that anticommunist forces were preparing to rescue the imprisoned czar, Lenin ordered him, his wife, four daughters and one son brutally executed on July 17, 1918. The Romanov dynasty had reached its ignominious and tragic end.

In 1991 the remains of Nicholas II and his family were uncovered and positively identified through DNA testing. The last Russian czar finally received a state burial in 2000 and was formally canonized by the Russian Orthodox Church. But the brutality of Nicholas's demise cannot erase the legacy of ineptitude and resistance to change that characterized his reign and accelerated the communist revolution that cost Russia so dearly in decades to come.

Further Reading

Holquist, Peter. *Making War, Forging Revolution: Russia's Continuum of Crisis, 1914–1921.* Cambridge, Mass.: Harvard University Press, 2002.

King, Greg. *The Fate of the Romanovs.* Hoboken, N.J.: John Wiley and Sons, 2003.

McNeal, Shay. *The Plots to Rescue the Czar.* London: Arrow, 2002.

Pares, Bernard. *The Fall of the Russian Monarchy.* London: Phoenix, 2001.

Tomaszewski, Fiona K. *A Great Russia: Russia and the Triple Entente, 1905–1914.* Westport, Conn.: Praeger, 2002.

Wood, Alan. *The Origins of the Russian Revolution, 1861–1917.* New York: Routledge, 2003.

Nimeiri, Gaafar (1930–) *president of Sudan*

Gaafar Muhammed al-Nimeiri was born in Omdurman, Sudan, on January 1, 1930, the son of a postman. Sudan, Africa's largest nation, was sharply divided between a Muslim north and a predominantly Christian south, jointly administered by a British-Egyptian condominium government. Nimeiri obtained a Koranic education and passed through the Sudanese Military College in 1952. He then underwent further training in Egypt where he came under the influence of GAMAL ABDEL NASSER, the great Arab nationalist. Spurred on by his anticolonial success, Nimeiri and other young officers sought to consciously imitate their Egyptian counterparts by founding the Free Officer's Association—dedicated to the end of colonial rule in Sudan. When his country became independent from Britain in 1956, Nimeiri was arrested by the ruling Umma Party and dismissed from the military. Soon after, the army overthrew the civilian regime and a new leader, General Ibrahim Abboud, reinstated Nimeiri and posted him in the south. There he experienced firsthand the intense regional resentment of Christians and animists toward the government for attempts to forcibly convert them to Islam. Nimeiri was sent abroad to Europe and the United States to continue his education. After coming home in 1964 he was arrested and accused of plotting against the government, but ultimately released. Nimeiri then fulfilled a number of important military positions over the next five years, apparently biding his time. On October 28, 1969, he led a bloodless coup that toppled the government of President SAYYID AL-AZHARI, and he was installed as prime minister under a new Revolutionary Command Council.

No sooner had Nimeiri consolidated control than he was confronted by revolts from the extreme right and left. In 1970 his biggest challenge came from the militant Islamic Ansar sect, which mustered 30,000 warriors to oppose him. Nimeiri, in a singular display of force, dispatched heavily armed troops against the insurgents, killing thousands. Then, having incorporated the small but influential Sudanese Communist Party into government, he was briefly overthrown by them on July 19, 1971, before loyalist troops restored him to power. Thereafter Nimeiri went after the leftists with a vengeance, and also disbanded the council. By October 1971 he was positioned to introduce a new constitution and ran unopposed for the presidency, receiving 98 percent of votes cast. Thereafter the nation was ruled as a one-party state under the aegis of the Sudanese Socialist Union (SSU) of which he was also head.

Now firmly entrenched in power, Nimeiri sought to address the longstanding civil war in the south by negotiating with the rebels. At length the government halted forced religious conversions and allowed greater regional autonomy in exchange for a halt to secessionism. The ploy worked, and in 1972 a peace treaty was concluded. Nimeiri was next forced to confront the Sudan's rapidly sinking economy. But all attempts at centralized state control had failed miserably and plunged the nation into poverty and hunger. Nimeiri then embraced free-market economics in an attempt to turn the Sudan into a self-sufficient, food-exporting center, but the effort failed because of corruption and mismanagement. Nimeiri also weathered several attempted coups by disaffected parts of the military and a rising tide of Muslim fundamentalism. On the international scene Nimeiri was prominent as head of the Organization of African Unity (OAU) and in 1978 he was also the first Muslim leader to back Egyptian president ANWAR AL-SADAT's peace talks with Israel. In exchange for a promise of American aid, Nimeiri cooperated in efforts to relocate Ethiopian Jews by letting them gather in the Sudan. He also argued that the continent should steer clear of cold war entanglements and maintain a non-aligned stance. However, by 1983 he was forced to shore up political support from the extremist Muslim community by imposing the rigid *sharia* or Islamic law, upon Sudan in September 1983. This caused an immediate renewal of fighting in the Christian and animist south, which further exacerbated the country's weakened economic performance. Disenchantment crested on April 6, 1985, when Nimeiri was overthrown during a visit to the United States. His 14 years of leadership had failed to address the pressing problems of stagnation, sectarian violence, and political disunion.

Nimeiri remained exiled in Egypt until May 1999, when he was cordially invited home to observe the 30th anniversary of the coup that brought him to power. Shortly after arriving he was granted permanent residency and allowed to run in the 2000 national elections. These were handily won by the current strongman, President Omar Hassan al-Bashir, and Nimeiri has since slipped back into political anonymity.

Further Reading

Idris, Amir H. *Sudan's Civil War: Slavery, Race, and Formational Identities*. Lewiston, N.Y.: Edwin Mellen Press, 2001.

Jendia, Catherine. *The Sudanese Civil Conflict, 1969–1985*. New York: Peter Lang, 2002.

O'Ballance, Edgar. *Sudan, Civil War, and Terrorism, 1956–99*. New York: St. Martin's Press, 2000.

Layish, Aharon. *The Reinstatement of Islam under Numayri*. Boston: Brill, 2002.

Salam, A. H. Abdel, and Alexander De Wall. *The Phoenix State: Civil Society and the Future of Sudan*. Trenton, N.J.: Red Sea Press, 2001.

Woodward, Peter, ed. *Sudan after Nimeiri*. New York: Routledge, 1991.

Nixon, Richard M. (1913–1994) *president of the United States*

Richard Milhous Nixon was born in Yorba Linda, California, on January 9, 1913, the son of a small businessman. Raised in the Quaker faith, he attended Whittier College before passing through the Duke University Law School in 1937. Nixon established a successful practice in California before relocating to Washington, D.C., to serve with the Office of Price Administration. During World War II he joined the navy and eventually made the grade of lieutenant commander. Nixon commenced his political activities in 1946 by running for a seat in the House of Representatives as a Republican. His successful campaign was marked by pronounced anticommunism, a theme that served him well throughout the remainder of his long career. In 1950 he won a hard-fought campaign for a Senate seat against a popular Democrat, Helen Gahagan Douglas, once more invoking the charge that she was "soft on communism." Now a senator, Nixon gained national prominence by promoting a perjury case against Alger Hiss, a leading State Department official who had lied about his prior membership in the Communist Party. Nixon's high standing in the Republican Party induced DWIGHT D. EISENHOWER to select him as his vice presidential running mate for 1952. At that time it was alleged that Nixon had accepted gifts as a public figure, an illegal act. However, Nixon appeared on television in a surprisingly emotional performance, denied the charges, and maintained that the only gift he received—and would not return—was his dog Checkers. His reputation was rehabilitated overnight, and Nixon campaigned vigorously for Eisenhower that fall. The ticket was victorious and, as vice president, Nixon traveled around the world promoting American policy. During a 1959 visit to Moscow, he engaged in the famous "kitchen debate" with Soviet premier NIKITA KHRUSHCHEV. The next year he won the nomination to serve as the Republican candidate for president.

Nixon by this time had gained a formidable reputation politically but he had a difficult relationship with the press and never mastered the art of having people like him. Worse, his opponent in 1960 was JOHN F. KENNEDY, a young and boyishly handsome Democrat. In their celebrated televised debate Nixon came off as nervous while the photogenic Kennedy appeared charismatic and was considered the winner. Curiously, those who listened to the debate on the radio felt that Nixon had prevailed. Nevertheless, the ensuing election was extremely close and Kennedy won by an extremely narrow margin of 100,000 votes out of nearly 70 million cast. Nixon then retired to his estate in California, where he tried and failed to win the governorship in 1962. Admonishing the press that "You won't have Richard Nixon to kick around anymore," the former vice president quit politics altogether and resumed his law practice in New York City. But by 1968 the national mood had been badly jarred by President LYNDON B. JOHNSON's mishandling of the war in Vietnam. Nixon, gauging the time right, staged a remarkable comeback and won the party nomination. In November 1968 he beat both the Democratic nominee, Vice President Hubert Humphrey, and independent candidate George Wallace to finally win the White House.

Nixon had campaigned on a pledge to end the war in Southeast Asia and in 1969 he informed President NGUYEN VAN THIEU of South Vietnam of the process of "Vietnamization," whereby American forces would be slowly withdrawn and replaced by Vietnamese forces. He also entered into difficult negotiations with the Communist regime of North Vietnam, which consented to cease-fire arrangements only after an intense bombardment campaign. However, Nixon also allowed limited forays against communist sanctuaries in Laos and Cambodia, which stirred up fierce U.S. student protests against the war. By 1972 the pacifist tenor of the Democratic Party resulted in the nomination of George McGovern while Nixon campaigned on trusted

Richard M. Nixon *(Library of Congress)*

themes of anticommunism, law and order, and patriotism. And even while the war in Vietnam raged, Nixon made history by eschewing his trademark anticommunist foreign policy in favor of a more pragmatic approach. In 1972 he visited Moscow again and concluded the Strategic Arms Limitation Treaty (SALT I) with Soviet premier LEONID BREZHNEV, which placed a ceiling on nuclear weapons. But an even bigger coup occurred that same year when Nixon went to China to confer with MAO ZEDONG and ZHOU ENLAI in Beijing. This constituted the first direct contact between the United States and the People's Republic of China since 1949. This unprecedented and magnificently handled performance all but sealed McGovern's fate the following November. The ensuing election was a debacle for the Democrats, who carried only one state and 17 electoral votes. It appeared that Nixon had finally acquired the respect and vindication he sought for so long.

Unfortunately, Nixon's legacy was to prove neither happy nor efficacious. Apparently he had authorized a burglary of Democratic National Party headquarters in Washington, D.C., for the purpose of tapping phones. On June 17, 1972, the burglars were caught in the Watergate Hotel, and subsequent investigations increasingly pointed to an official coverup. Nixon resorted to every legal ploy available to him to sideline and stonewall the investigation, but in August 1974 the Supreme Court ruled that he had to turn over taped conversations that demonstrated, beyond a doubt, his culpability. By that time the Democrat-controlled House of Representatives had passed four articles of impeachment against the president for perjury and obstruction of justice. Once it became clear that the Congress might have the votes to remove him from office, he resigned as president on August 9, 1974. Criminal proceedings were then in play against him but his successor, GERALD R. FORD, issued a presidential pardon to close the affair. The entire episode fueled a cynicism and distrust of government that lingers to the present day.

Over the next two decades Nixon refrained from politics and sought vindication by publishing memoirs and granting interviews. In the end he slowly emerged as a respected elder statesman whose wisdom in foreign affairs laid the foundations of the post–cold war world. However, he remained stigmatized by Watergate to the very end of his life, which concluded in New York on April 22, 1994. Historical assessments of Nixon remain polarized and objective soundings elude most scholars. He was clearly a gifted individual and an astute politician, but intrinsically insecure. Above all, he was an unlikable tragic figure. Unquestionably Nixon did incalculable work in foreign affairs by ending the Vietnam War, initiating meaningful arms control, and opening the doors to China. But the ultimate irony is that in the end he became his own worst enemy—literally—and set in motion his own downfall. Nixon remains the only sitting president to have resigned from office.

Further Reading

Berman, Larry. *No Peace, No Honor: Nixon, Kissinger, and the Betrayal in Vietnam.* New York: Free Press, 2001.

Ito, Go. *Alliance in Anxiety: Detente and the Sino-American-Japanese Triangle.* New York: Routledge, 2003.

Liebovich, Louis. *Richard Nixon, Watergate, and the Press: A Historical Retrospective.* Westport, Conn.: Praeger, 2003.

Matheson, Sean. "Partial Justice: Congressional Argumentation and Presidential Impeachment." Unpublished Ph.D. diss., University of Illinois, Urbana-Champaign, 2002.

Morgan, Iwan N. *Nixon.* New York: Oxford University Press, 2002.

Nixon, Richard M. *Into the Arena: A Memory of Victory, Defeat, and Renewal.* New York: Simon and Schuster, 1990.

———. *RN: The Memoirs of Richard Nixon.* New York: Simon and Schuster, 1990.

Reeves, Richard. *President Nixon: Alone in the White House.* New York: Simon and Schuster, 2001.

Strober, Deborah H. *The Nixon Presidency: An Oral History of the Era.* Washington, D.C.: Brassey's, 2003.

Thornton, Richard C. *The Nixon-Kissinger Years: Reshaping America's Foreign Policy.* St. Paul, Minn.: Paragon House, 2001.

Nkrumah, Kwame (1909–1972) *president of Ghana*

Kwame Nkrumah was born in Nkroful, Gold Coast, on September 21, 1909, the son of a goldsmith. He was educated locally at missionary schools and graduated from Achimota College in 1931 as a teacher. He taught several years at Catholic schools and seminaries, but in 1934 his Nigerian friend NNAMDI AZIKIWE convinced him to further his education in the United States. Accordingly Nkrumah received degrees from Lincoln University in Pennsylvania, and the University of Pennsylvania, where he immersed himself in the revolutionary writings of Karl Marx, Gandhi, and others. However, he was most impressed by the Pan-African writings of Marcus Garvey who espoused a "Back to Africa" movement. After teaching several years in the United States, Nkrumah ventured to England to study law at the London School of Economics in 1945. There he participated in numerous Pan-African activities, by editing a student journal and helping to organize the Fifth Pan-African Conference in Manchester. He returned home in 1947 brimming with revolutionary fervor and joined the United Gold Coast Convention (UGCC) to agitate against colonial rule. Nkrumah was jailed repeatedly for civil disobedience, and in 1949 he broke with the UGCC to found his own radical organization, the Convention's People's Party (CPP).

"We prefer self-government in danger to servitude in tranquility," he declared. Nkrumah again took to the streets demanding immediate independence from Great Britain and was summarily detained by colonial authorities. However, when elections in 1951 resulted in a complete victory of the CPP, he was released and allowed to become the Gold Coast's first prime minister the following year. Five more years of tenuous self-rule and delicate negotiations followed before independence finally arrived in March 1957. This former colony, the first in Africa to shed its colonial chains, adopted the new name of Ghana and Nkrumah became Africa's first head of state in the new postcolonial era.

The prime minister entertained lofty aspirations for both his nation and the entire African continent. Nkrumah published widely on the subject of African unity and became a leading spokesman for the cause, a role model and a hero to other political aspirants on the continent. He also proved himself a driving force behind creation of the All-Africa People's Congress in 1958 and the Organization of African Unity (OAU) in 1963. His popularity was further enhanced through the construction of schools, roads, and hospitals, now built and used by native Ghanaians instead of white colonialists. Within three years Nkrumah also effected constitutional changes and Ghana was transformed into a republic, of which he was president. He intended that his country serve as a model for African development everywhere.

For all his good intentions internationally, Nkrumah remained a doctrinaire socialist economically and he imposed a centrally planned economy on the formerly prosperous colony. Within a few years Ghana stagnated economically and public discontent rose. Unfortunately, Nkrumah displayed very authoritarian tendencies from the onset and proved intolerant of dissent. As early as 1958 he enacted the Preventive Detention Act, which enabled him to jail opponents without trial. Tensions increased to the point where he narrowly survived an assassination attempt in 1962, which, in turn, only fueled his repressive tendencies. Furthermore, as Western powers grew disillusioned by his police state and socialist policies, they began withholding valuable foreign aid and assistance. Nkrumah countered by gradually entering into a communist orbit, striking up cordial relations with the Soviet Union and China. In 1964 he declared Ghana a one-party state with himself as "president for life." Several more assassi-

nation attempts made the chief executive even more reclusive and less accessible, and he started a "cult of personality" to perpetuate his domestic image. Nkrumah's name and portrait began appearing everywhere and he began touting himself as the "Redeemer," while the national economy continued sliding into paralysis. Many African leaders ridiculed their former hero in private and JULIUS NYERERE of Tanzania publicly denounced Nkrumah for his repression.

The break occurred in February 1966 when Nkrumah was visiting China: the army toppled his administration in a bloodless coup. The sense of public relief was immediate, and throngs of people began smashing his statues and erasing his name from public places. Nkrumah subsequently sought refuge in neighboring Guinea where his friend, President AHMED SÉKOU TOURÉ, appointed him "co-ruler." The former revolutionary turned head of state languished in exile until his death in Bucharest, Romania, on April 27, 1972, while receiving medical treatment. He continued writing and expounding Pan-African platitudes until the very end, despite their irrelevance to the new generation of national leaders. But he remains the most significant African nationalist of his generation and an inspiration to the anti-colonial movements of his day.

Further Reading

Boateng, Charles A. *The Political Legacy of Kwame Nkrumah of Ghana.* Lewiston, N.Y.: Edwin Mellen Press, 2003.

Botwe-Asamoah, Kwame. *Kwame Nkrumah's Politico-Cultural Thought and Policies: An African-Centered Paradigm for the Second Phase of the African Revolution.* New York: Routledge, 2004.

Nkrumah, Kwame. *The Autobiography of Kwame Nkrumah.* London: Panaf, 1973.

———. *Kwame Nkrumah: The Conakry Years, His Life and Letters.* Atlantic Highlands, N.J.: Panaf, 1990.

Nwaubani, Ebere. "Eisenhower, Nkrumah, and the Congo Crisis." *Journal of Contemporary History* 36 (October 2001): 599–622.

Pobee, J. S. *Kwame Nkrumah and the Church in Ghana: 1949–1966.* Denver, Colo.: iAcademic Books, 2000.

Rathbone, Richard. *Nkrumah and the Chiefs: The Politics of Chieftaincy in Ghana, 1951–1960.* Athens: Ohio University Press, 2000.

Noriega, Manuel (1938–) *dictator of Panama*

Manuel Noriega was born in Panama City, Panama, on February 11, 1938, into a life of poverty. He was orphaned at an early age and raised by his aunt. Noriega weathered his hardscrabble existence and performed well in high school, although he lacked the finances to study medicine in college. He therefore opted for a military career and passed through the Chorrillos Military Academy in Lima, Peru. Noriega subsequently joined the Panama National Guard in 1962 where he struck up a close relationship with his superior, Colonel OMAR TORRIJOS. In October 1968 Noriega assisted Torrijos in the coup that toppled President Arnulfo Arias from power. In December 1969 he helped shield his superior from an attempted coup against him and was promoted to lieutenant colonel of military intelligence. In this capacity Noriega also forged links to the American Central Intelligence Agency (CIA) for information about communist activities throughout Central America. But more than anything, Noriega became an instrument of political repression, intimidating Torrijos's opponents, suppressing, and in some instances murdering them. He also became a leading player in the rapidly expanding Colombian drug trade and was well placed to expedite shipments of cocaine to the United States and help launder the proceeds. Noriega became such a visible adjunct to the drug cartels that at one point U.S. president RICHARD M. NIXON contemplated his assassination.

In 1981 Torrijos died in an unexplained helicopter crash, possibly engineered by Noriega himself, and a succession crisis arose in the Panamanian military. By 1983 he had emerged as the victor and promoted himself to the rank of general of the newly redesignated Panamanian Defense Force (PDF). By this time he had also become the de facto ruler of Panama. He controlled the legislature through intimidation and violence, and ordered the killing of several high-profile opponents. However, Noriega's despotism did little to diminish his importance to the United States as an intelligence asset. The CIA paid him millions of dollars to funnel arms and assistance to freedom fighters opposing the communist Sandinista regime in Nicaragua. Concurrently, Noriega also functioned as a double agent by providing the same services to left-wing insurgents in El Salvador and establishing ties with Cuban dictator Fidel Castro. He also expanded his control of the drug trade passing through Panama en route to America, amassing millions of dollars in kickbacks and payoffs from the cartels.

At length Noriega's excesses became too much for an embarrassed United States to tolerate further, and beginning in 1986 the government of President RONALD REAGAN began reducing financial and military aid to Panama. Noriega countered by increasing political repression to the point where he weathered several unsuccessful coups against him. When political unrest and demonstrations against his dictatorship spilled onto the streets, he brutally repressed them with specially trained riot police known as the "Dobermans." In 1988 he deposed constitutionally elected president Eric Arturo Delvalle and appointed a political stooge in his place. That same year Noriega was indicted by a U.S. federal grand jury for drug smuggling and racketeering. By this time President GEORGE BUSH decided that it was imperative to remove Noriega by force to prevent him from seizing control of the Panama Canal. An important catalyst for events that followed was the shooting death of a U.S. Marine by the PDF on December 16, 1989, and the physical abuse of a navy officer and his wife. After several days of careful preparation the Americans unleashed 24,000 men in "Operation Just Cause" and overwhelmed the PDF. Noriega was forced to seek refuge in the Vatican embassy, which was quickly surrounded by troops. After several days of negotiations, the former dictator, sensing that the game was up, surrendered to the Americans on January 20, 1990, and was flown to Miami for trial. He was succeeded by Guillermo Endara once United States troops restored democracy to Panama.

In April 1992 Noriega was tried and convicted of drug trafficking, racketeering, and money laundering, and received a 40-year sentence. This was subsequently reduced to 30 years although in March 2000 prison authorities refused his request for an early parole. He will continue serving his sentence until his next parole date in 2007. Noriega remains the only head of state prosecuted and imprisoned by the United States as a criminal.

Further Reading

Albert, Steve. *The Case against the General: Manuel Noriega and the Politics of American Justice.* New York: Maxwell Macmillan International, 1993.

Flanagan, E. M. *Battle for Panama: Inside Operation Just Cause*. Washington, D.C.: Brassey's, 1993.

Harris, David. *Shooting the Moon: The True Story of an American Manhunt unlike Any Other*. Boston.: Little, Brown, 2001.

Margolis, Darren. "The Invasion of Panama: An Analysis of Operation Just Cause under International Law." *Towson State Journal of International Affairs* 30, no. 1 (1994): 27–40.

Noriega, Manuel. *America's Prisoner: The Memoirs of Manuel Noriega*. New York: Random House, 1997.

Sosa, Juan B. *In Defiance: The Battle against General Noriega Fought from Panama's Embassy in Washington*. Washington, D.C.: Francis Press, 1999.

Nu, U   See U NU.

Nyerere, Julius   (1922–1999) *president of Tanzania*

Kambarage Nyerere was born in Butiama, Tanganyika, on April 13, 1922, the son of a minor chief within the small Zanaki tribe. Tanganyika had been ruled by Great Britain as a League of Nations trust since 1918 and Nyerere was educated at English missionary schools. He was a perceptive student and won a scholarship to attend the Makerere College in Kampala, Uganda, in 1943. After teaching several years Nyerere was baptized with the Christian name Julius and in 1949 he gained entry into the University of Edinburgh, Scotland. Two years later he obtained a master's degree in history, becoming the first resident of Tanganyika to receive a college degree. In this capacity he became familiar with Fabianism, a non-Marxist form of socialism, and he readily inculcated its tenets. Nyerere came home in 1953 to resume teaching, but he also became politically active by joining the Tanganyika African Association, which served as a discussion group. However, under his inspired leadership it was readily expanded and transformed into the Tanganyikan African National Union (TANU) for the sole purpose of ending British colonialism and securing national independence. Over the next seven years Nyerere and TANU waged a relentless but peaceful campaign to oust the British, buoyed by the party's insistence on nonracial politics and nonviolence. In August 1960 TANU easily swept the first national elections and Nyerere became Tanganyika's first prime minister. After independence was achieved in December 1961, he stepped down from office to concentrate on strengthening his party, and in December 1962 he was formally elected the nation's first president.

Nyerere quickly established himself as one of Africa's most outstanding heads of state. His earliest challenge occurred in 1964 when a rebellion in nearby Zanzibar spilled over to the mainland, and the government was nearly toppled by the military. British troops soon restored order and Nyerere invited the Zanzibar leadership to join Tanganyika in a federation arrangement. In April 1964 the union was effected and a new country, the Republic of Tanzania, was peacefully proclaimed. After 1977 the ruling parties of both regions were combined into a new entity, the Revolutionary Party of Tanzania (Chama Cha Mapinduzi, or CCM). True to his socialist leanings Nyerere had imposed one-party rule over the country, although his motives were entirely altruistic. He firmly believed that Tanzania, divided up into 112 distinct ethnic groups, was not ready for multiparty democracy and feared that the country would descend into tribal infighting.

Nyerere ended up ruling Tanzania for 23 years without interruption. His tenure is even more remarkable considering that he was repeatedly reelected president by wide margins in free and open elections. As a leader, he tried to position himself as a moral force within Tanzania and also beyond its borders. At a time when most African rulers were enriching themselves at public expense, Nyerere maintained an austere lifestyle and took active measures to crack down on corruption. He was also one of the first African leaders to condemn the continuation of European colonialism and apartheid rule in South Africa. He lent his national resources to independence movements across the continent. He openly supported the FRELIMO guerrilla movement in Mozambique until his friend SAMORA MACHEL came to power. But Nyerere proved equally harsh with African dictators, and he roundly condemned the brutal excesses of General IDI AMIN in Uganda. In 1979 Nyerere ordered his army into Uganda and restored refugee president MILTON OBOTE to power. However, he differed with the capitalistic mores of Kenya's JOMO KENYATTA and, following the collapse of the East African Community, he closed down border trade for six years.

Nyerere's greatest failing was his fragile grasp of economics. Determined to graft an Africanized form of socialism onto Tanzania, he originated the scheme of *ujamma,* or sharing, to collectivize national agriculture and render the nation self-sufficient. The result was a near disaster, and for many years Tanzania remained one of the poorest nations in Africa. But dramatic improvements were made in the fields of public health, education, and adult literacy, and the nation was held as a model for African development. Having accomplished much to promote political stability and racial harmony at home, Nyerere further enhanced his reputation by voluntarily resigning the presidency on November 5, 1985, and he was succeeded by Ali Hassan Mwinyi. He remained active in politics as head of the CCM until 1990 and openly criticized his successor's attempts to institute free-market economics. He also wrote voluminously on the topic of politics and African unity. Nyerere died in London, England, on October 14, 1999, the father of his country and one of Africa's most respected statesmen. That Tanzania continues on as a model of tolerance and stability is his greatest legacy, and he is universally lauded as *mwalimu* (teacher).

Further Reading

Assensoh, A. B. *African Political Leadership: Jomo Kenyatta, Kwame Nkrumah, and Julius K. Nyerere.* Malabar, Fla.: Krieger Pub. Co., 1998.

Johnson, R. W. "Nyerere: A Flawed Hero." *National Interest* 60 (2000): 66–75.

Macdonald, David A., and Eunice Njeri Sahle, eds. *The Legacies of Julius Nyerere: Influences on Development Discourse and Practice in* Africa. Trenton, N.J.: Africa World Press, 2002.

Mulenga, Derek. "Mwalimu Julius Nyerere: A Critical View of his Contributions to Adult Education and Postcolonialism." *International Journal of Lifelong Education* 20, no. 6 (2001): 446–470.

Nyerere, Julius K. *Crusade for Liberation.* New York: Oxford University Press, 1978.

Pratt, Cranford. "Julius Nyerere: The Ethical Foundation of His Legacy." *Round Table* no. 356 (2000): 365–375.

Thomas, Darryl C. *The Theory and Practice of Third World Solidarity.* Westport, Conn.: Praeger, 2001.

O

Obote, Milton (1924–) *president of Uganda*

Apollo Milton Obote was born in Akoroko, Uganda, on December 28, 1924, the son of a minor chief of the Lango tribe. He was educated at missionary schools and briefly attended Makerere College before British colonial authorities expelled him for political activism. Obote next moved to Kenya to work, where he was caught up in the nationalist activities orchestrated by JOMO KENYATTA. By the time he returned to Uganda in 1957, Britain had allowed for popular sovereignty through a national legislature. Obote won a seat representing the Uganda National Congress Party (UNCP) where he was outspoken in his criticism of colonialism. Finding the UNCP too conservative for his socialist inclinations, Obote broke with them in 1960 and founded a new organization, the Uganda People's Congress (UPC). As UPC leader he began complex negotiations with the archconservative Kabaka Yekka (King Alone) Party of Buganda to establish a ruling coalition after independence. This proved a tricky proposition at best, for the nation consisted of several traditional tribal kingdoms, of which Buganda was the largest and most powerful. Obote next lent his expertise to devising a constitution that encompassed Uganda's four distinct kingdoms in a federal framework. When the nation finally broke with Great Britain on October

8, 1962, King Mutesa II of Buganda became president while Obote served as prime minister.

At length Mutesa's conservatism and Obote's desire for a socialist one-party state collided over the issue of corruption. In February 1966, both the prime minister and his leading general, IDI AMIN, were accused by the legislature of misappropriating war booty taken in the Congo. Obote countered by suddenly arresting numerous ministers, suspending the constitution, and expanding the central government's powers. When Mutesa protested this usurpation of power, Obote directed Amin to attack the king's palace, and Mutesa fled to exile in Great Britain. The prime minister was now well-positioned to attain the kind of centralized authority he always coveted. In September 1967 he authorized passage of a new constitution that eliminated the federal arrangement, abolished the kingdoms, and established a unitary state with himself as president. His control of affairs was further abetted once the UPC became the nation's sole legitimate party.

Once in power, Obote initiated a dramatic move to the left through adoption of his "Common Man Charter." Banks and many industries were nationalized, and he passed new laws that made the president of the UPC also the chief executive of the nation. However, this one-party rule engendered considerable disunity in Uganda, which was deeply cleft between tribal rivalries and religious differences. As protests mounted against the regime, Obote was forced to rely more and more on the military to enforce order, and thousands were killed. At length he began distrusting Amin, his leading general, and promoted him to a new position of very little responsibility. His distrust was well-founded, for while Obote was visiting Singapore in January 1971, Amin staged a bloodless coup and deposed him. A reign of terror and brutality ensued in Uganda over the next eight years while Obote sought refuge in Tanzania. The former president eventually prevailed upon President JULIUS NYERERE to invade Uganda in 1979 and eliminate Amin. Obote then returned home to schedule new elections on December 9, 1980—the first in over 18 years. Voting fraud was rife and, not surprisingly, he was reelected to another term in office.

Unfortunately Obote's second tenure proved an even bigger disaster than the first. He inherited a nation with a ruined economy and a large, displaced population. Worse, guerrilla factions sprang up around Uganda and the president resorted to military force to retain order. This time, however, he was utterly ruthless toward dissenting elements, and an estimated 100,000 people died. Public resentment toward Obote crested in July 1985 when he was overthrown by the military, and within months a new regime under Yoweri Museveni's National Resistance Army came to power. Obote remained in exile in Zambia until April 1999, when Museveni formally invited him home under a full pardon. Between Obote and Amin, Uganda had endured two of Africa's most oppressive regimes of the 20th century.

Further Reading

Bwengye, Francis A. W. *The Agony of Uganda: From Idi Amin to Obote: Repressive Rule and Bloodshed.* New York: Regency Press, 1985.

Clentworth, Garth, and Jan Hancock. "Obote and Amin: Change and Continuity in Modern Uganda Politics." *African Affairs* 72 (July 1973): 237–255.

Dinwiddy, Hugh. "The Ugandan Army and Makerere under Obote, 1962–71." *African Affairs* 82 (January 1983): 43–59.

Gingyera-Pinycwa, A. G. G. *Apollo Milton Obote and His Times.* New York: NOK Publishers, 1978.

Ingham, Kenneth. *Obote: A Political Biography.* New York: Routledge, 1994.

Mittleman, J. H. *Ideology and Politics in Uganda: from Obote to Amin.* Ithaca. N.Y.: Cornell University Press, 1975.

Obregón, Álvaro (1880–1928) *president of Mexico*

Álvaro Obregón was born in Alamos, Sonora, Mexico, on February 19, 1880, the son of a poor farmer. He was indifferently educated yet worked hard to establish himself as a respectable businessman, and in 1911 he gained appointment as mayor of Huatabampo. The Mexican Revolution began in 1910 when FRANCISCO MADERO overthrew President PORFIRIO DÍAZ, but Obregón stood aloof. He did not become an active player until Madero's murder at the hands of General VICTORIANO HUERTA in 1913. Obregón quickly raised a small army of Maya Indians and allied himself with the Constitutionalists under VENUSTIANO CARRANZA. Huerta was driven out of the country in 1914, and Obregón captured Mexico City for the Constitutionalists in August of that year. However, the victors soon began squabbling among themselves, and Obregón, who displayed real military talent, was assigned to stop the famous insurgent, Francisco "Pancho" Villa. He defeated Villa in a number of major engagements, losing his right arm to a cannon shell in 1915. While recovering, Obregón wielded considerable influence at the Constituent Assembly in 1917 and helped the radical platforms to pass. Once Carranza became president in 1917, Obregón retired from politics to resume farming. He gained a measure of fame for designing a mechanical chick pea (garbanzo) seeder, but foremost Obregón is considered the finest military leader of the revolution.

In 1919 Obregón announced his intention to run for the presidency. He first had to deal with his former superior Carranza, who intended to handpick his own successor. Obregón took up arms over the issue, and he was quickly joined by PLUTARCO ELÍAS CALLES. Together they revolted against the government under the Plan of Agua Prieta and drove Carranza out of office. Before Carranza was assassinated by malcontents he was briefly succeeded by Adolfo de la Huerta, but on December 1, 1920, Obregón was formally elected to the office. His success marked a turning point in the Mexican Revolution, for it signaled a lengthy period of reconstruction, reformation, and political consolidation.

Álvaro Obregón *(Library of Congress)*

that was contained and crushed. Once Obregón's constitutionally mandated one term in office expired, he next prevailed upon Calles to alter the constitution and allow him to run for a second, nonconsecutive term. He then retired back to his farm in 1924 and returned four years later to run for the presidency. Obregón was easily reelected president, but before taking office he was assassinated in Mexico City on July 17, 1928, by a religious fanatic who blamed him for oppressing the Catholic Church. Despite his untimely demise, Obregón is credited for holding the country together during a difficult transition and laying the foundation for successive civilian administrations.

Further Reading

Gonzales, Michael J. *The Mexican Revolution, 1910–1940.* Albuquerque: University of New Mexico Press, 2002.

Hall, Linda B. *Álvaro Obregón: Power and Revolution in Mexico, 1911–1920.* College Station: Texas A & M University Press, 1981.

Hansis, Randall. "The Political Strategy of Military Reforms: Álvaro Obregón and Revolutionary Mexico." *Americas* 36, no. 2 (1979): 199–233.

Heilman, Jaymie. "The Demon Inside: Madre Conchita, Gender, and the Assassination of Obregón." *Mexican Studies* 18, no. 1 (1992): 23–60.

Hindman, Ewell J. "The United States and Álvaro Obregón." Unpublished Ph.D. diss., Texas Tech University, 1972.

Randall, George H. "Álvaro Obregón, the Mexican Revolution, and the Politics of Consolidation, 1920–1924." Unpublished Ph.D. diss., University of New Mexico, 1971.

Once in power, he initiated a radical program of land reform that had been shelved by his predecessor, in which more than 10 million acres were distributed to landless peasants. He also sponsored wide-ranging educational and cultural reforms by Jose Vasconcelos, who intended to improve the lot of Mexico's poor majority. But most important, Obregón finally secured diplomatic recognition from the United States in 1923, following a pledge not to nationalize American assets in the oil industry.

One major facet of the revolution that Obregón conspicuously failed to enforce was the constitution's stringent anticlerical measures against the Catholic Church. These strictly forbade clergymen from appearing in public in clerical garb, but the president strove for a moderate accommodation between church and state. He was also favorably disposed toward labor unions, and generally protected working rights. In 1923 Obregón emulated Carranza by handpicking Calles as his successor, which resulted in a brief rebellion by de la Huerta

Odría, Manuel (1897–1974) *president of Peru*

Manuel Apolinario Odría Amoretti was born in Tarma, Peru, on November 26, 1897, into a middle-class family. In 1919 he graduated from the Chorillos Military Academy at the head of his class and commenced a distinguished army career. Over the next two decades he held a succession of important command positions, and in 1941 he distinguished himself by winning the battle of Zarumilla against Ecuadorian forces. Odría was promoted to colonel, sent to the United States for advanced training, and returned as head of the army war college. He rose to chief of staff in 1946 but Odría, who up until then studiously avoided politics, was tapped by President José Luis Bustamante to serve as interior minister. At this time Peru was racked by political unrest instigated by the left-leaning American Popular Revolutionary Alliance (APRA) under Víctor Paúl de la Torre. Once President Bustamante failed to take strong action against the rioters in 1947, Odría resigned from his position in the cabinet. A radical faction within APRA then tried to rebel against the government in October 1948 and, when Bustamante again failed to take strong action and restore order, the generals began calling for his replacement. On October 27, 1948, Odría staged a bloodless coup and declared himself head of the government. He then dissolved congress and ruled by decree until June 1950, when new elections were held. However, because Odría's name was the only one printed on the ballots, he failed to establish his political legitimacy.

The ensuing eight years have gone down in Peruvian history as the "Ochenio." Odría went to great lengths to restore law and order to the nation and readily suspended civil rights whenever necessary. He cracked down on APRA and its adherents, instituting new security laws to stifle dissent. Taking a leaf from his idol JUAN PERÓN of Argentina, he shored up political support from the nation's poor majority by enacting social and economic reforms, including wage hikes and creation of squatter camps in and around the capital of Lima. To improve Peru's foreign image, he also began payments on its foreign debt for the first time since 1931. Odría then embraced a free-wheeling approach to market economics that liberalized the economy to bring in foreign investment, especially for Peru's critical oil and copper mining industries. Fortunately the onset of the Korean War in 1950 led to sharp increases in export prices for most commodities, and Peru experienced a period of economic prosperity. A far-ranging program of public works constructed no less than 1,500 schools. Conditions worsened by 1953, however, and Peru's economic gains slowly unraveled. Over the next three years Odría did little else but respond to public unrest with increasingly harsh repression. He gained further public enmity by flaunting his luxurious lifestyle and tolerating unprecedented levels of official corruption.

By 1956 Odría's presidency had all but run its course and he was convinced by the military and oth-ers to stand down and permit free elections. These were won by Manuel Prado, a leading opposition fig-ure. The general entered a self-imposed exile in the United States, where he remained five years. In 1961 he returned to Peru to found his own party, the Unión Nacional Odriísta (UNO), National Odriist Union, from former supporters and the rural poor who recalled his reform programs. National elections held in 1963 quickly dampened his prospects for high office when he finished behind de la Torre and the winner, FERNANDO BELAÚNDE TERRY. Determined to make his presence felt, Odría then struck up an unholy alliance with his old nemesis APRA, and their coalition managed to thwart Belaúnde's political agen-da over the next five years. When the military under General JUAN VELASCO overthrew the civilian regime in 1968, they also distanced themselves from Odría, whom they regarded as a pariah. He subsequently died in Lima on February 18, 1974, a former and largely forgotten dictator.

Further Reading

Atwood, Roger. "Democratic Dictators: Authoritarian Politics in Peru from Leguia to Fujimori." *SAIS Review* 21 (summer-fall 2001): 155–176.

Masterson, Daniel M. "Caudillismo and Institutional Change: Manuel Odría and the Peruvian Armed Forces, 1940–1956." *Americas* 40, no. 4 (1984): 479–484.

———. *Militarism and Politics in Latin America: Peru from Sanchez Cerro to Sendero Luminoso.* New York: Greenwood Press, 1991.

Szulc, Tad. *Twilight of the Tyrants.* New York: Holt, 1959.

Zook, David H. *Zarumilla-Maranon: The Ecuador-Peru Dispute.* New York: Bookman Associates, 1964.

Ojukwu, Chukwuemeka (1933–) *president of Biafra*

Chukwuemeka Odumegwu Ojukwu was born in Zungeru, Nigeria, on November 4, 1933, the son of a wealthy transportation magnate. He was also an Ibo, a largely Christian tribal grouping that dominates the eastern half of the country. Ojukwu received a splendid private education in the capital of Lagos, and in 1952 he entered Oxford University. He graduated with honors in 1956 and returned home to briefly join the Nigerian civil service, but that year he also enlisted in the colonial army. Ojukwu was the first Nigerian to pass through Eaton Hall in England for officer training, and he returned home as a military instructor. Nigeria became independent from Great Britain in 1960, and Ojukwu accompanied the army during United Nations peacekeeping operations in Congo the following year. After completing additional training in England, he advanced to battalion commander in the Kano region. And, although an Ibo, he apparently did not support the January 1966 coup by eastern officers that toppled the civilian administration. Regardless, he soon was promoted to military governor of the eastern region. However, in July 1966 military officers from the predominantly northern and western reaches of the country staged another coup that killed Ibo general Aguiyi-Ironsi and installed Colonel YAKUBU GOWON as head of state. Ojukwu cooperated with the new regime until September 1966, when there was a general massacre of easterners living in the north. The ensuing mass of refugees crowded into the eastern region, severely taxing Ojukwu's ability to feed and house them. Great resentment then arose against the federal government for allowing the massacre to take place, and calls for secession arose. Ojukwu and Gowon met briefly at Aburi, Ghana, in January 1967, to forestall the onset of violence, but the impasse remained. Feeling a threat of genocide against his people, Ojukwu reluctantly agreed that secession was all but inevitable and on May 27, 1967, he proclaimed the independence of the new Republic of Biafara.

Ojukwu's decision sparked a swift reaction from the federal government under Gowon, who massed his forces and invaded the eastern region in force. The rebels fought bravely, and at one point had advanced their columns to within 60 miles of Lagos before being halted. For the next two and a half years the Biafran war ground on as federal forces bit off increasingly larger chunks of rebel territory. They also imposed a complete land, air, and naval blockade of Biafra, which resulted in widespread starvation. By 1970 the death rates were soaring to 8,000 per day, but Ojukwu refused to seek a negotiated settlement. The rebels thus clung to an ever-shrinking area of land while the Western news media closely covered the sufferings of civilians. Ojukwu himself addressed the Organization of African Unity to solicit support for his faltering rebellion, but to no avail. In January 1970 federal forces captured the rebel capital of Enugu, and Ojukwu fled for voluntary exile to Cote d'Ivoire. Deaths in the Biafran secession have been variously estimated at between 1 million and 8 million people. Fortunately, Gowon proved magnanimous and allowed the former rebels to be repatriated into society.

Ojukwu pursued business ventures in Cote d'Ivoire until 1982, when the civilian regime of Shehu Shagari invited him back under a general amnesty. He returned to his native eastern region to thunderous applause and sought to parlay his popularity into a viable political career. He joined the National Party of Nigeria (NP) in 1983 but lost his bid for the senate. When the civilian government was overthrown by the military in December 1983, Ojukwu was arrested and detained for almost a year. Thereafter he resumed his political activities, and in August 1998, founded his own party, the People's Democratic Congress. He continues on as a significant regional figure. But Ojukwu has no reservations or regrets about initiating steps that led to civil war three decades earlier. "My people—the Ibo—were faced with genocide," he maintains. "We had no choice."

Further Reading

Forsyth, Frederick. *The Biafra Story: The Making of an African Legend.* London: Leo Cooper, 2001.

Jacobs, Daniel. *The Brutality of Nations.* New York: A. A. Knopf, 1987.

Nwaozuzu, Hillary A. "Emeka Ojukwu's Rhetoric of Secessionism and Yakubu Gowon's Anti-secessionist Rhetoric: A Critical and Historical Analysis." Unpublished Ph.D. diss., State University of New York, Buffalo, 1985.

Ojukwu, Chukuemeka O. *Biafra: Selected Speeches and Random Thoughts of C. Odumegwu Ojukwu.* New York: Harper and Row, 1969.

Thompson, Joseph E. *American Policy and African Famine: The Nigeria-Biafra War, 1966–1970.* Westport, Conn.: Greenwood Press, 1990.

Olympio, Sylvanus (1902–1963) *president of Togo*

Sylvanus Épiphanio Olympio was born in Lome, Togoland, on September 6, 1902, the son of wealthy Brazilian émigrés. Because his country was then a German colony he received a good primary education and was able to attend both the University of Vienna and the London School of Economics. After World War I Togoland was divided between Great Britain and France, and in 1926 Olympio settled in the francophone section. There he worked for the United Africa Company and within a decade had risen to general manager—the highest position allowed to native Africans. During World War II Olympio sympathized with the government in exile of General CHARLES DE GAULLE, and was arrested and detained by Vichy colonial authorities. After the war he was released and in 1946 he won a seat in the new territorial legislature as part of the Comité del'Unité Togolais (CUT), Togolese Unity Committee, which he had founded five years earlier. Its goal was to unite the Ewe people presently dispersed over French Togoland, British Togoland, and the nearby British Gold Coast. In time Olympio emerged as the most articulate spokesman for Ewe unification and was allowed to address the United Nations for recognition of their efforts. However, his militancy caused French colonial authorities to ban him from office, and he remained sidelined from 1952 to 1958 as the movement for national independence gathered force. The notion of Ewe unity was ultimately dashed in 1956 once the United Nations authorized a plebiscite on the subject–and British Togoland opted to merge with Gold Coast to form the new nation of Ghana. That same year French Togoland became a semiautonomous entity under Prime Minister Nicolas Grunitzky of the pro-French Togolese Progress Party. But within two years Olympio staged an impressive comeback when CUT dominated the next round of elections and he became prime minister. In this capacity he guided his country to independence from France on April 27, 1960. The previous year he had won election as mayor of Lome, the nation's capital.

Olympio spent most of his first year in office pressing for constitutional reforms, and in 1961 Togo became a republic with him as president. Trained as an economist, the new executive set an austere budgetary program for the new nation to win foreign monetary approval. He also actively sought foreign investment in various sectors of the economy and was generally friendly to France. However, when he refused all overtures by President KWAME NKRUMAH of Ghana to enter into a federation arrangement, the latter summarily closed the border and ended all trade. This had the effect of depressing the small national economy further,

which resulted in additional austerity measures. Olympio had also taken steps to rule Togo as a one-party state under CUT, and the authoritarian tone of his administration discouraged all political opposition. At length his policies alienated three important segments of society: the Western-educated elites who sought greater democracy, the northern Ewe who felt neglected by their southern counterparts, and the military. To save money Olympio had reduced Togo's army to a mere 250 men and, furthermore, he refused to absorb African French army veterans recently discharged. He even managed to alienate the youth wing of CUT, known as JUVENTO, for pursuing policies they viewed as too accommodating toward France. At length he exiled several youthful party leaders from the nation underscoring his diminishing control of political affairs.

Events crested in the spring of 1963 when disgruntled military personnel launched a spontaneous attack upon the presidential palace. Olympio fled the residence for his life and tried to escape by scaling the walls to the U.S. embassy. Unfortunately, he was spotted by renegade soldiers and shot to death on January 13, 1963. His killer turned out to be Gnassingbe Eyadema, a future Togolese president. Olympio thus enjoys the dubious distinction of being the father of Togo's independence and the first postcolonial African head of state to be overthrown by a coup. His violent passing also marked the beginning of an age of political disillusionment throughout the African continent.

Further Reading

Aligwekwe, Iwuoha E. "The Ewe and Togoland Problem: A Case Study in the Paradoxes and Problems of Political Transition in West Africa." Unpublished Ph.D. diss., Ohio State University, 1962.

Ate, B. E. *Regional Policy Relationship: The Necessity for Moderation and Cooperation.* Boulder, Colo.: Westview Press, 1987.

Houngnikpo, Mathurin C. *Determinants of Democratization in Africa: A Comparative Study of Benin and Togo.* Lanham, Md.: University Press of Maryland, 2001.

Nugent, Paul. *Smugglers, Secessionists & Loyal Citizens on the Ghana-Togo Frontier: The Life of the Borderlands since 1914.* Athens: Ohio University Press, 2002.

Seely, Jennifer C. "Transitions to Democracy in Comparative Perspective: The National Conferences in Benin and Togo." Unpublished Ph.D. diss., Washington University, 2001.

O'Neill, Terence (1914–1990) *prime minister of Northern Ireland*

Terence Marne O'Neill was born in County Antrim, Northern Ireland, on September 10, 1914, scion of an impeccably aristocratic Anglo-Irish family that traced its ancestry back to Irish kings of the O'Neill dynasty. His homeland, Northern Ireland, consists of six Protestant-dominated northern counties that seceded from the Catholic Republic of Ireland in 1921. After being educated at Eton, O'Neill followed family precedent by serving as an officer in the Irish Guards during World War II—the same regiment in which his father was killed during World War I. Afterward he opted for a career in politics and was elected to the Northern Ireland Parliament in 1946 as a Unionist. This party stands for both permanent separation from Catholic Ireland and the preservation of Protestant supremacy. O'Neill functioned well in a variety of capacities, successively serving as minister of health, deputy speaker of the house, and minister of home affairs. However, his political profile was immeasurably raised in 1956 when he gained appointment as finance minister. In this capacity O'Neill broke new ground economically by attracting new industries to the region, along with a dramatic growth in tourism. The result was a slow but steady increase in the standard of living for Northern Ireland. In 1963 O'Neill's success was acknowledged in his rise as head of the Unionist Party and his appointment as prime minister.

Unlike many contemporaries in the fiercely Protestant Unionist Party, O'Neill was decidedly liberal and tolerant toward the Catholic minority. In fact he viewed their social emancipation as necessary to the continuing economic growth of Northern Ireland itself. He therefore dedicated himself to the touchy but essential task of ending discrimination against Catholics in all its forms. Such reforms brought howls of protest from the more militant Unionist faction under the Reverend Ian Paisley, but O'Neill determined to press ahead. In 1965 he invited his Irish counterpart, Taoiseach (prime minister) Sean Lemass, to Northern Ireland, the first face-to-face meeting between the two governments since 1921. The following year O'Neill was cordially invited south, albeit under tight security. He also sponsored contentious legislation protecting the Catholic minority against discrimination in jobs and housing, along with greater outlets for political expression. In October 1968 these newfound freedoms culminated in bloody clashes between Catholic and Protestant street marchers. Ultimately the British army had to be sent in by British prime minister HAROLD WILSON to maintain peace. O'Neill's well-intended reforms met with entrenched resistance from militant Unionists and the Order of Orange, which only spurred on terrorist attacks by the outlawed Irish Republican Army (IRA). In fact, 1968 marked a turning point in relations between the two religious communities, which has been marked by ongoing violence and vitriol for the past three decades.

At best, O'Neill's efforts represented only token civil rights reform, but Paisley and others denounced them as a sellout to the Catholic south. Throughout his tenure in office the prime minister survived no less than five "no confidence" votes—sponsored mainly by his own party. The Unionists thus remained sharply divided between pro- and anti-O'Neill factions, and to clarify the issue the prime minister called for a snap election in February 1969. While he hoped for a clean sweep, the results were less than gratifying, and an intra-party impasse ensued. Rather than struggle further, O'Neill simply resigned as prime minister on April 28, 1969. One of his last acts was having the national polity adopt the same "one man, one vote" philosophy as the rest of the United Kingdom. In 1970 he was elevated to the peerage as Baron O'Neill of the Maine and was seated in the British House of Lords. There he occasionally addressed issues pertaining to Northern Ireland, although he remained disillusioned by the diehard recalcitrance and animosity characterizing its politics. He died in Lymington, Hampshire, England, on June 12, 1990, an earnest reformer but unable to fathom the depth of sectarian hatred confronting his efforts. Ironically his former seat in Parliament was subsequently won by Ian Paisley, his great nemesis.

Further Reading

Clifford, Brendan. *Road to Nowhere: A Review of Unionist Politics from O'Neill to Molyneaux and Powell.* Belfast: Athol, 1987.

Gordon, David. *The O'Neill Years: Unionist Politics, 1963–1969.* Belfast: Athol Books, 1989.

Mulholland, Marc. "Assimilation versus Segregation: Unionist Strategy in the 1960s." *Twentieth Century British History* 11, no. 3 (2000): 284–307.

———. *Northern Ireland at the Crossroads: Ulster Unionism in the O'Neill Years, 1960–9.* New York: St. Martin's Press, 2000.

Nic Craith, Mairead. *Culture and Identity Politics in Northern Ireland.* New York: Palgrave Macmillan, 2003.

O'Neill, Terence. *The Autobiography of Terence O'Neill.* London: Hart-Davis, 1972.

Ortega, Daniel (1945–) *president of Nicaragua*

Daniel Ortega Saavedra was born in La Libertad, Nicaragua, on November 11, 1945, the son of an accountant. His family was deeply enmeshed in the struggle against the dictatorship of the Somoza family, which had dominated national affairs since 1936, and several members of his immediate family were either arrested or murdered by ANASTASIO SOMOZA GARCÍA. Ortega received a Catholic education, yet even at an early age he demonstrated an interest in revolutionary activities. While a student he was arrested numerous times for antigovernment agitation and repeatedly expelled. Ortega then enrolled at the Central American University to study law, but he ultimately quit to take up revolutionary politics. By 1963 he had joined the Frente Sandinista de Liberación Nacional (FSLN), Sandinista National Liberation Front, a clique of Marxist revolutionaries bent on overthrowing the Somoza regime. Ortega threw himself wholeheartedly behind the effort, and in 1967 he was captured and charged with bank robbery. He remained imprisoned until the Sandinistas took several ranking Somoza hostages, and he was exchanged in 1974. Ortega then relocated to Cuba to receive military training from communist leader Fidel Castro. More important, he shifted his tactics dramatically. Until then the FSLN had been dogmatically waging war in isolation from various non-Marxist revolutionaries, so he formed a new faction, the Terceristas, which was more pragmatic in outlook and preached a "broad front" against Somoza. Thereafter the Nicaraguan revolution slowly gathered steam in the face of government oppression and a poor economy. By July 1979 the position of President ANASTASIO SOMOZA DEBAYLE was untenable, and he fled Nicaragua. The victorious FSLN then assumed control, with Ortega serving as head of the nine-man National Directorate.

From the onset, Ortega and his fellow revolutionaries undertook a gradual transformation of Nicaragua into a Marxist dictatorship. Civil rights were curbed, press freedoms revoked, and large segments of the national economy nationalized. Worse, the rebels sought to bolster their control by importing large numbers of weapons from the Soviet Union and military advisers from Cuba. In this manner Ortega positioned Nicaragua as the willing agent of Soviet and Cuban military adventurism throughout Central America. At length many former FSLN supporters, including Violeta Chamorro, widow of a slain journalist, and the Catholic Church, questioned Ortega's motives and broke with the FSLN. The United States government under President JIMMY CARTER had been cautiously hesitant in its dealing with the Sandinistas until Ortega began a concerted campaign to arm Marxist rebels fighting the democratically elected government of neighboring El Salvador. After 1981 the new administration under RONALD REAGAN seized upon growing discontent with Sandinista oppression to arm and supply a popular counterrevolutionary movement, the Fuerza Democrática Nicaragua (FDN), the Nicaraguan Democratic Force, better known as the contras. He also instituted an economic embargo to destabilize the economy and oblige the FSLN to spend a disproportionate percentage of the shrinking national income upon military expenditures.

By 1984 Ortega wished to demonstrate that the revolution enjoyed a popular mandate and he was elected president of Nicaragua by large margins. However, the economy began sliding into disarray, with inflation and unemployment rising dramatically. Nor could he forcibly defeat the contras, who were supported by the Central Intelligence Agency in Honduras and enjoyed a great deal of popular support in the countryside. To buy time Ortega signed onto the peace initiative originated by OSCAR ARIAS of Costa Rica, although he continued assisting rebel forces in El Salvador. By 1990 Nicaragua's economy was in ruins and the ongoing civil war forced him to introduce conscription to oppose the contras. He also ran for reelection that year but was soundly defeated by Chamorro's Unión Nacional Opositora (UNO), National Opposition Union, and she became Nicaragua's first female head of state. Despite this, Ortega was quickly affirmed as head of the Sandinista Party in Congress, and in 1996 he lost another presidential bid to conservative candidate Arnoldo Alemán. Ortega was charged by his stepdaughter with sexual misconduct and placed under investigation. He ran again for the presidency in 2001 and lost heavily to another conservative, Enrique Bolaños. This string of defeats apparently sealed the fate of the Sandinistas as a political force in Nicaragua, and many younger members began crying out for new leadership. However, in December 2002 the high court cleared Ortega of rape charges because the statute of limitations had passed for the crime. On March 19, 2002, he was reelected head of the FSLN and continues on as leader of the opposition in Congress.

Further Reading

Booth, J. J., and P. A. Richard. "The Nicaraguan Elections of October 1996." *Electoral Studies* 16 (September 1997): 386–393.

Brown, Timothy C. *The Real Contra War: Highlander Peasant Resistance in Nicaragua.* Norman: University of Oklahoma Press, 2001.

Horton, Lynn. *Peasants in Arms: War and Peace in the Mountains of Nicaragua, 1979–1994.* Athens: Ohio University Center for International Studies, 1998.

Isbester, Katherine. "Nicaragua, 1996–2001: Sex, Corruption, and Other National Disasters." *International Journal* 56 (autumn 2001): 632–648.

Pastor, Robert A. *Not Condemned to Repetition: The United States and Nicaragua.* Boulder, Colo.: Westview Press, 2002.

Vander, H. E. and G. Prevost, eds. *The Undermining of the Sandinista Revolution.* New York: St. Martin's Press, 1997.

P

Palme, Olof (1927–1986) *prime minister of Sweden*

Sven Olof Joachim Palme was born in Stockholm, Sweden, on January 30, 1927, the son of a wealthy insurance company director. Raised in affluence, he attended private academies before traveling to the United States to study at Kenyon College, Ohio. After graduating in 1948 he hitchhiked across the country for several months and was visibly moved by the pockets of poverty he encountered. He then came home to study law at the University of Stockholm and also served as chairman of the Swedish National Union of Students. By then Palme was a committed socialist, and after graduating in 1951, he formally joined the left-leaning Sveriges Socialdemokratiska Arbetarepartiet (SAP), Swedish Social Democratic Worker's Party. In 1953 he had a chance encounter with Prime Minister TAGE ERLANDER, the architect of the Swedish welfare state, who was impressed by the youthful Palme's drive and intelligence. Accordingly he appointed Palme his secretary and speech writer. Two years later he was entrusted to head the Social Democratic Youth league and in 1958 Palme commenced his political career by winning a seat in the Rikstag (legislature). Over the next 10 years his career became closely intertwined with that of Erlander, who granted him a succession of important governmental posts. Most strikingly, as minister of transportation he initiated the change in Sweden's traffic flow from the left to the right lanes. But in 1968 he incurred considerable international controversy by denouncing the United States role in the Vietnam War and even participated in an antiwar march with the North Vietnamese ambassador. He also advocated stronger ties to the developing world and on behalf of international peace movements. When Erlander stepped down from office in September 1969, Palme was chosen by a unanimous vote to succeed him. At that time he was Europe's youngest head of state.

Palme rose to high office at a fortuitous period in Swedish history: the nation was prosperous and enjoyed one of the world's highest standards of living. Still, he was intent upon instilling Swedish society with an even greater sense of egalitarianism by increasing the coverage of the welfare state, even if this meant raising already high tax rates. He thus engendered the notion of "industrial democracy" whereby workers enjoyed increasing participation in overall management, along with greater emphasis on helping the poor, women, and the disadvantaged. Hereafter the government was entrusted with playing an ever-increasing role in all aspects of the political, economic, and social life of the individual. In 1972 he further estranged his government from the United States by criticizing the war effort in Vietnam, causing President RICHARD M. NIXON to refuse to accept a Swedish ambassador for nearly two years. Conservatives also railed that Palme was leading the nation down the road to totalitarianism and, as the usually robust Swedish economy began faltering, the Social Democrats experienced declines in public support for their programs. In 1976 SAP was turned out of power for the first time in 44 years and replaced by a conservative coalition government.

Over the next six years Palme headed the opposition in the legislature, although he managed to find time to serve as a roving ambassador for peace. In 1979 he visited Iran to help secure the release of American hostages, and the following year he became a UN special envoy to mediate the vicious Iran-Iraq war. By 1979 the conservative administration had lost its steam and Palme was returned to the prime minister's office. His next seven years in office were marked by renewed emphasis on expanding social welfare benefits, even as this trend was being reversed in Europe and elsewhere. He was also repeatedly embarrassed by the incursion of Soviet submarines into Swedish territorial waters, and roundly criticized by Swedish naval officers for not taking a harder stance. On February 28, 1986, Palme was assassinated while returning from the theater with his wife. No motives or suspects were ever established for his murder, the first killing of a Swedish ruler in 200 years. Alive or dead, Palme remains the most controversial Swedish leader of the 20th century.

Further Reading

Cooper, H. H. A. *The Murder of Olof Palme: A Tale of Assassination, Deception, and Intrigue.* Lewiston, N.Y.: Edwin Mellen Press, 2004.

Esaiasson, Peter, and Donald Granberg. "Attitudes toward a Fallen Leader: Evaluations of Olof Palme before and after the Assassination." *British Journal of Political Science* 26 (July 1996): 429–439.

Freeman, Ruth. *Death of a Statesman: The Solution to the Murder of Olof Palme.* London: R. Hale, 1989.

Johansson, O. "Swedish Reaction to the Assassination of Swedish Prime Minister Olof Palme." *Scandinavian Political Studies* 18 (December 1995): 265–283.

Mosey, Chris. *Cruel Awakening: Sweden and the Killing of Olof Palme.* New York: St. Martin's Press, 1991.

Palme, Olof. *Socialism, Peace, and Solidarity: Selected Speeches of Olof Palme.* New York: Advent Books, 1990.

Ruin, Olof. "Three Swedish Prime Ministers: Tage Erlander, Olaf Palme, and Ingvar Carlsson." *West European Politics* 14 (July 1991): 58–82.

Papandreou, George (1888–1968) *prime minister of Greece*

George Papandreou was born in Kalentzi, Greece, on February 13, 1888, and he graduated from the University of Athens in 1911. After completing graduate work at the University of Berlin in 1915 he returned home to accept a post as governor of the island of Lesbos. Papandreou also started a close association with ELEUTHÉRIOS VENIZÉLOS of the Liberal Party, who continually advanced his career. He was elected to the legislature in 1923 as a Liberal, and in 1930, when Venizelos became prime minister, Papandreou served as minister of education. In this capacity he initiated extensive building programs to increase the number of schools, but he grew disillusioned with party leaders over unconstitutional methods for enacting policy. Papandreou then founded the Democratic Socialist Party and resumed his career in the legislature. In 1936 General Ioannis Metaxis came to power in Greece, and he had Papandreou jailed and placed in internal exile. He was released following the German occupation of Greece in 1941, and took an active role with the armed resistance. Papandreou was jailed again by the Germans, but he escaped and made his way to Cairo to link up with numerous Greek expatriates. There they formed a government in exile with Papandreou acting as prime minister. After Greece was liberated by Allied forces in 1944, he was installed as the head of government, only to face a new communist insurgency. A bitter civil war broke out and Papandreou resigned from office, taking numerous ministerial positions in a succession of governments.

Over the next 15 years Papandreou continued on as a high-level government official and a champion of democracy. Throughout that period he reconciled ideological differences between the Liberals and his own Democratic Socialist Party, and in 1961 the Center Union coalition emerged. This was a center-left organization and by no means sympathetic to communism. Elections that year indicated a coalition victory, but the results were annulled by the conservative government, and Papandreou cried foul. He spoke out stridently and effectively for responsible democracy, and in 1963 the Center Union scored another narrow victory over the military-backed National Radical Union Party under Constantine Karamanlis. Papandreou then became prime minister for the second time, but he resigned from office soon after to secure a stronger mandate for his coalition. In 1964 new elections finally brought the Center Union to power with a respectable majority in the legislature and Papandreou set about restoring a sense of normalcy to the usually fractious Greek polity.

As prime minister, Papandreou sought to completely overhaul Greek education and allocated greater funding for that goal. He was also critical of what he deemed a subservient position to the United States in foreign affairs and pursued a more independent course. Around this time relations between Greeks and Turks on the disputed island of Cyprus had reached crisis proportions, which led to a degeneration of diplomatic relations with neighboring Turkey. Papandreou's ability to lead was also severely compromised in a long-running feud with King Constantine II and conservative opposition to the appointment of his son, Andreas Papandreou, as defense minister. Events crested in July 1965 when the king dismissed Papandreou as prime minister. Over the next two years he functioned as head of the opposition in the legislature, and in May 1967 new elections were finally called for. However, when it appeared that the Center Coalition was poised to win a majority of seats, the army stepped in on April 21, 1967. The constitution was then suspended and thereafter Greece was run by a clique of conservative-minded colonels. Papandreou, being the most visible target of the coup, was summarily arrested, charged with harboring communist sympathies, and kept under house arrest. He died at his home on November 1, 1968, still the most influential Greek politician of the postwar period. His popularity can be gauged by the fact that nearly one-fifth of the Athens population turned out for his funeral.

Further Reading

Close, David. *Greece since 1945: Politics, Economy, and Society.* New York: Longman, 2002.

Couloumbis, Theodore A., Theodore Kariotis, and Fotini Bellou, eds. *Greece in the Twentieth Century.* Portland, Ore.: Frank Cass, 2003.

Featherstone, Kevin, ed. *Political Change in Greece: before and after the Colonels.* Kent, England: Croom Helm, 1988.

Kourvetaris, George A. *Studies on Modern Greek Society and Politics.* Boulder, Colo.: East European Monographs, 1999.

Kouyoumdjian, Natalia. "George Papandreou and Greece's Turbulent Years." Unpublished master's thesis, California State University–Sacramento, 1971.

Papen, Franz von (1879–1969) *chancellor of Germany*

Franz von Papen was born in Werl, Westphalia, Germany, on October 29, 1879, a part of the traditional land-owning gentry. Like many of his caste he pursued a military career and was commissioned as a cavalry officer. During World War I he was initially stationed in Mexico and the United States as a military attaché, but in 1916 he was expelled from America for espionage activities. Thereafter he transferred to the Turkish army as an adviser and staff officer. An arch-monarchist, he came home in 1919 totally dissatisfied with the democratic Weimar Republic and joined the reactionary wing of the Catholic Center Party. In 1920 Papen was elected to a seat in the Prussian legislature, where he remained for the next 12 years. He sought to extend his influence by serving on the editorial board of a conservative Catholic newspaper and by marrying into the family of a wealthy industrialist. Papen then founded the *Herrenklub,* an association of wealthy conservatives and military reactionaries bent on overthrowing the republic and restoring the monarchy under WILHELM II. But in 1925 Papen broke with Center Party leadership by backing the conservative PAUL VON HINDENBURG for president instead of the party's candidate. He continued to associate and ingratiate himself with conservative interests until defense minister Kurt von Schleicher prevailed upon the tottering Hindenburg to dismiss HEINRICH BRÜNING as chancellor and appoint Papen in his place on June 1, 1932. Considering his unknown status and relative inexperience, Papen's rise came as a shock to most political observers—and would bear the most unsavory consequences.

As chancellor, Papen made no effort to disguise his contempt for Weimar's shaky democratic institutions. He firmly believed, like many wealthy conservatives, that only the restoration of authoritarian rule could save Germany from its economic doldrums and social instability. He inherited a cabinet that was staffed by so many conservative aristocrats—handpicked by Schleicher—that it was publicly derided as the "Cabinet of Barons." Papen was determined to rescue the country from a communist takeover by appealing to extreme right-wing elements. Foremost among these were the National Socialists (Nazis) under ADOLF HITLER, a previously obscure firebrand with a devoted following. The government therefore lifted its prohibitions against the Nazi Sturmabteilung (SA) militia, while Papen also suspended the constitution in Prussia to remove its socialist governor, Otto Braun, from power. Papen then usurped direct rule of the state as a reich commissioner. However, the onset of reactionary rule did not translate into a public mandate for Papen, for in elections held that summer and fall, only the extreme right and left benefited. But he continued appointing right-wing nationalists to various positions within the government, thereby cementing antidemocratic trends at the highest levels of leadership. When the reichstag (legislature) passed a motion of "no confidence" against Papen that September, he summarily dissolved it, knocking the final democratic prop out from beneath the Weimar republic.

During his six-month tenure as chancellor Papen could claim only one minor success: the cancellation of Germany's wartime reparations at the Lausanne Conference in Switzerland. But at length, his reactionary tendencies proved too much for Schleicher, who coveted the office of chancellor himself, and he induced Hindenburg to dismiss Papen from office in December 1932. Papen angrily retaliated against Schleicher by entering into negotiations with Hitler in January 1933—the same month he convinced Hindenburg to appoint the Nazi neophyte as chancellor. Papen had also made arrangements to serve as vice chancellor, being fully convinced he could manipulate Hitler to his own ends. This proved a grave miscalculation. Within weeks it became apparent that Hitler could not be controlled and when Papen publicly railed about Nazi excesses, he was marked for death. He only narrowly escaped being killed in the Rohm purge on June 30, 1933 and, taking the hint, Papen resigned as vice chancellor. He subsequently accepted the post of ambassador to Austria and, in the wake of Chancellor ENGLEBERT DOLLFUSS's murder by Nazis, he prevailed upon the government there to accept unification with Germany in March 1938. From 1939 to 1944 Papen also served as ambassador to Turkey, and he served Germany well by keeping that country neutral during World War II as long as possible.

After the war ended Papen returned to Germany where he was arrested by Allied authorities and charged as a war criminal. He was acquitted by the Nuremberg Military Tribunal, but a German court sentenced him to eight years for being a Nazi accomplice. Papen served only a few months before being released, and he lived the rest of his life in pampered obscurity. He died at Obersasbach, Germany, on May 2, 1969, a political nonentity save for his role in facilitating the rise of Hitler and the Nazi dictatorship.

Further Reading

Adams, Henry M., and Robin K. Adams. *Rebel Patriot: A Biography of Franz von Papen.* Santa Barbara, Calif.: McNally and Loftin, 1987.

Balderston, Theo. *Economics and Politics in the Weimar Republic.* New York: Cambridge University Press, 2002.

Evans, Richard J. *The Coming of the Third Reich: A History.* New York: Penguin Press, 2004.

Fischer, Conan. *The Rise of the Nazis.* New York: Manchester University Press, 2002.

Papen, Franz von. *Memoirs.* New York: Dutton, 1953.

Rolfs, Richard W. *The Sorcerer's Apprentice: The Life of Franz von Papen.* Lanham, Md.: University Press of America, 1996.

Park Chung Hee (1917–1979) *president of South Korea*

Park Chung Hee was born in Kumi, Korea, on September 30, 1917, the son of a poor farmer. He matured into a reticent, aloof young man but with an excellent academic record. Korea at that time was part of the Japanese Empire and the only avenue for social advance was through military service. After passing through the Manchukuo Military Academy with distinction, he was allowed to attend the Imperial Military Academy in Tokyo. Park was then commissioned a lieutenant in the Japanese army and he served in Manchuria until the end of World War II. Once demobilized and back home, he applied for work in the newly independent South Korean constabulary. However, he was soon connected with communist-inspired unrest at Yosu in 1947 and was forced to resign. He was not called back to the colors until June

1950, in the wake of North Korea's attack upon the South. Park served with distinction as a military officer and ended the war as the army's youngest brigadier general. His reputation for loyalty and bravery seemingly erased his earlier flirtation with communism, and he was allowed to receive advanced training in the United States. In time many within the Korean military were increasingly dissatisfied with the corrupt administration of President RHEE SYNGMAN. Park and other senior leaders were plotting a coup against him. However, they shelved their idea after student protests brought Rhee down and ended the First Republic. A short-lived Second Republic under Chang Myuon came to the fore but it proved incapable of restoring order or ending pervasive political corruption. On May 16, 1961, Park and his military coterie toppled the government in a bloodless coup and established the Supreme Council for National Reconstruction. Park was installed as nominal head of the junta, but pressure from American president JOHN F. KENNEDY persuaded him to resign from the army and run for the presidency as a civilian. On October 15, 1963, Park obliged his greatest benefactor and easily defeated Yun Po-sn for high office. The Third Republic of Korea was then initiated.

Since its independence in 1945, South Korea had been one of the world's poorest nations and remained almost completely dependent on assistance from the United States to survive. Park, a strident nationalist, was determined to improve his country's lot. Through a series of highly detailed five-year plans he sought to enhance industrialization, urbanization, and national infrastructure. Soon South Korea was experiencing annual growth rates of 10 percent a year and by 1972 no longer required foreign assistance of any kind. In fact, the Korean export market was booming and seriously threatening Japanese trade supremacy. Through discipline, sacrifice, and foresight, Park had ushered in the age of the "Korean miracle" and turned his country, along with Singapore, Taiwan, and Malaysia, into one of the four "Asian tigers." In terms of foreign affairs, normalized relations with Japan were established—no mean feat considering their mutual antipathy—which led to increased trade and access to foreign markets. Park also sought to maintain close ties to the United States and in 1965 he agreed to commit South Korean combat troops to the American-led war in Vietnam. He was rewarded for his loyalty by a lack of criticism for his generally authoritarian regime.

Park Chung Hee *(Library of Congress)*

Since coming to power Park remained generally disdainful of civil rights, and he imposed strict controls over freedom of speech, the press, and the media. He justified his excesses on the basis that communist North Korea was a direct threat to the nation and that dissent was intolerable under such conditions. Park had been reelected to the presidency in 1967 but had been constitutionally banned from running a third time. In a show of force, he threatened to resign from office in 1969 unless the constitution was altered to allow him a third term. Park's demands were sullenly met, and he won another four-year term in 1971. However, the following year he promulgated a new constitution that granted him dictatorial powers and extended his stay in office indefinitely. It also allowed him to legally outlaw all criticism of the government. Park then responded to mounting student unrest with brutal force and growing despotism. His tenure in office came to a sudden end on October 26, 1979, in Seoul, when he was assassinated by the head of the Korean Central Intelligence Agency (KCIA). Park's 18-year legacy is a mixed one: he placed Korea irrevocably on the path to modernity and provided impetus for spectacular economic growth and high standards of living. But he also established a precedent for military intervention in politics that held sway over the next 30 years. Not surprisingly, his successor was another former general, CHUN DOO HWAN.

Further Reading

Hurst, Cameron G. *The Park Chung Hee Presidency in Historical Perspective.* Hanover, N.H.: American Universities Field Staff, 1980.

Kim, Hyung-A. *Korea's Development under Park Chung Hee: Rapid Industrialization, 1961–1979.* New York: Routledge/Curzon, 2004.

Lee, Eva Hu. "The Military and Politics in South Korea: The Performance of the Park Chung Hee Government, 1961–1979." *Asian Thought and Society* 6, nos. 17–18 (1981): 193–206.

Lee, Jae II. "An Analysis of the Relationship between Korean Mass Media and Politics under Presidents Park and Chun." Unpublished master's thesis, Western Illinois University, 1995.

Lee, Jung Nam. "Comparative Political Leadership: A Study of Lyndon B. Johnson and Park Chung Hee." Unpublished Ph.D. diss., Northern Arizona University, 1991.

Olsen, Edward A. "Korea, Inc.: The Political Impact of Park Chung Hee's Economic 'Miracle.'" *Orbis* 24, no. 1 (1980): 69–84.

Park Chung Hee. *Korea Reborn: A Model for Development.* Englewood Cliffs, N.J.: Prentice Hall, 1979.

Pašić, Nikola (1845–1926) *prime minister of Serbia*

Nikola Pašić was born in Zaječar, Serbia, on December 18, 1845, and studied as an engineer in Belgrade and in Zurich, Switzerland. While abroad he immersed himself in socialist thinking and returned home determined to agitate for parliamentary rule. This placed him in opposition to King Milan of the Obrenovíc dynasty, who viewed Pašić and his ilk as dangerous radicals. Nonetheless, in 1878 Pašić was elected to the National Assembly as part of the newly created Radical Party. However, far from socialistic, he presented himself as an agent of nationalism and monarchy to win a broad spectrum of support from Serbia's peasantry. By 1883 Pašić's quarrels with the king forced him into exile, but he returned six years later to serve as prime minister. He was to hold that office no less than 22 times over the next five decades.

Once in power Pašić continued his running feud with the Crown, primarily over its favorable attitudes toward the Austro-Hungarian Empire. Pašić, a Pan-Slavic nationalist, sought to reorient Serbia's national policies in favor of the Russian Empire. He was consequently arrested twice, in 1897–99, and his career effectively ended until a military coup ousted the Obrenović dynasty in 1904. The new leader, Peter Karadjordjević, reinstated Pašić as prime minister and he resumed his pro-Russian policies. In 1912–13, he helped organize a modern Serbian army that threw Ottoman forces out of most of the Balkans and doubled the size of Serbian territory. The notion began taking root of a "greater Serbia" with hegemony over other regional Slavs.

By 1914 the Balkan region was a tinderbox of nationalist unrest, with continuing Austrian domination. When Archduke Francis Ferdinand was assassinated in Belgrade that June, Emperor FRANZ JOSEPH I summarily blamed Serbia's government for the murder and demanded that they surrender the terrorists. Pašić responded personally to the ultimatum in a conciliatory fashion but otherwise refused to capitulate, thanks to a promise of Russian support from Czar NICHOLAS II. Military mobilization across the length and breadth of Europe that August culminated in World War I and Pašić was forced to fend off an Austrian invasion from the north. Furthermore, because Russia could not mobilize its forces quickly enough, Serbia was completely overrun in 1915 and the leadership forced to flee to Corfu. A government in exile was subsequently established as Pašić began drawing up postwar plans for a unified ethnic state.

Although Pašić agreed in principle to a new Slavic kingdom, he insisted that the Serbians enjoy a monopoly of power over an assortment of Albanians, Croats, Slovenes, and Macedonians. In 1917 he signed onto the Corfu Declaration with other Slavic leaders regarding a dominion for their people—but held out for Serbian domination. After Austria-Hungary was dissolved in 1919 by the Paris Peace Conference, Serbian affairs fell increasingly upon Crown Prince Alexander, who regarded Pašić as old and irrelevant. When the new kingdom of Serbs, Croats, and Slovenes was established in 1919, Pašić was summarily dropped as prime minister and forced into retirement. However, he was arguably the most popular Serbian national figure of the day and in 1921 he returned to high office. Pašić then set about instituting reforms that made Serbia first among equals in the new Yugoslavian Federation. This was accomplished only over the objections of other groups, notably the Croats under Stjepan Radić. The new Vidovdan Constitution was then adopted that conferred a centralized administration scheme favoring the Serbs and also abolished all autonomous regions. Such changes stimulated tremendous unrest through the six major nationalities comprising Yugoslavia but Pašić's view prevailed. By the time he retired from office for the last time in March 1926, the new nation was fatally flawed by ethnic divisions that would prove its undoing by the end of the century. Pašić died in Belgrade on December 10, 1926, having dominated Serbia's political landscape for nearly 50 years. Historians still remain divided as to his culpability in the assassination of Archduke Ferdinand in 1914 and the conflagration it engendered.

Further Reading

Cox, John K. *The History of Serbia.* Westport, Conn.: Greenwood Press, 2002.

Dragnich, Alex N. *Serbia, Nikola Pašić, and Yugoslavia.* New Brunswick, N.J.: Rutgers University Press, 1974.

Fryer, Charles. *The Destruction of Serbia in 1915.* Boulder, Colo.: East European Monographs, 1997.

Lyon, James B. "Serbia and the Balkan Front, 1914." Unpublished Ph.D. diss., University of California–Los Angeles, 1995.

Matic, Natasa M. "Nikola Pašić and the Radical Party, 1845–1941." Unpublished Ph.D. diss., Boston University, 2000.

Pavlowitch, Stevan K. *Serbia: The History behind the Name.* London: Hurst and Co., 2002.

Skoric, Sofija. "The Populism of Nikola Pašić: The Zurich Period." *East European Quarterly* 14, no. 4 (1980): 469–485.

Paul VI (Giovanni Battista Montini) (1897–1978)
pope of Catholic Church

Giovanni Battista Montini was born in Concesio, Lombardy, Italy, on September 26, 1897, into a highly religious, aristocratic family. His parents were politically active Catholics and impressed upon the young man the need for piety and devotion to the poor. Montini studied at local Jesuit schools and he attended a seminary in 1920. He was ordained four years later and subsequently studied canon law at Gregorian University in Rome before being assigned to the Vatican secretary of state. In this capacity he came to the attention of Cardinal Eugenio Pacelli, the future POPE PIUS XII, who appointed him to his personal staff in 1930. Montini also spent nearly a decade working with various Catholic university student organizations to combat the rise of Italian fascism. During World War II he was entrusted to various relief agencies and also tended to the diplomats isolated in Vatican City. Afterward Pius XII offered to elevate Montini to the rank of cardinal, but he declined in favor of becoming archbishop of Milan. Here he gained considerable renown as a man of the people, constantly visiting churches and workers to instill and enrich their faith. Because Milan was also a center of Italian communism, he was frequently abused by activists, but though such efforts Montini acquired a reputation as "archbishop of the workers." In 1958 Pope JOHN XXIII elevated Montini to cardinal, the same year that he summoned the famous Vatican II Council to modernize church doctrine. Montini enthusiastically welcomed the change and served as an adviser to the pope during the initial sessions of 1962. When John XXIII died in June 1963 Montini was elected by the college of cardinals to serve as the new pope under the name Paul VI.

Paul VI assumed power at a critical juncture in church history. He immediately announced that the work of his predecessor would continue during the remainder of Vatican II. This proved a monumental event in church history, for it totally revamped existing approaches to ecumenical practice. Henceforth Latin masses were dropped in favor of local languages, and the laity was invited to participate in local church affairs. But Paul VI also reaffirmed longstanding tenets of church doctrine, especially in regard to birth control and clerical celibacy. His encyclical entitled *Humanae Vitae* was a strongly worded document demanding that Catholics refrain from using artificial contraception out of respect for the dignity of human life. In many respects his unwillingness to modify his stance disappointed more liberal members of the church but it underscored Paul VI's basic conservatism. The means of imparting church doctrine could be modernized but the message it imparted remained the same. This determination to preserve basic elements of church belief later served as a source of tension between conservative and reform elements. In 1965 he successfully concluded the

Second Vatican Council and set about implementing its changes.

Over the next 14 years Paul VI established himself as one of the most important church leaders of the 20th century. He lifted the veil of secrecy behind most church administration and invited the public to observe some processes. He was also the first pontiff to employ the medium of television on a regular basis. But above all Paul VI was a diplomat of the first order. He constantly traveled the globe to meet with religious leaders, Christian and non-Christian alike, and spoke unceasingly about the need for world peace. To that end he had personal conferences with American president LYNDON B. JOHNSON and United Nations secretary general U THANT to find a peaceful solution to the Vietnam War. In due course he also visited Latin America, India, and the Middle East, and even addressed the United Nations. In 1964 he convened with the patriarch of the Greek Orthodox Church, the first meeting between the Eastern and Western churches since 1054. Moreover, Paul VI was a staunch defender of developing nations and called for a redistribution of wealth to assist the poor. By the time Paul VI died in Rome on August 6, 1978, he had accomplished much useful work in bringing the Catholic Church in line with the realities of 20th-century life. Hereafter the church labored as a full partner in the crusade for human rights, social justice, and world peace. For this reason he is highly regarded as one of the most influential pontiffs of modern times.

Further Reading

Chadwick, Henry. "Paul VI and Vatican II." *Journal of Ecclesiastical History* 41 (July 1990): 463–469.

Coppa, Frank J. *The Great Popes through History,* 2 vols. Westport, Conn.: Greenwood Press, 2002.

Guitton, Jean. *The Pope Speaks: Dialogues of Paul VI with Jean Guitton.* London: Weidenfeld and Nicolson, 1968.

Hibblethwaite, Peter. *Paul VI: The First Modern Pope.* New York: Paulist Press, 1993.

Higginson, Paul. "The Vatican and Communism from 'Divini Redemptoris' to Paul VI." *New Blackfriars* 61 (April 1980): 158–171.

Kirby, Dianne, ed. *Religion and the Cold War.* New York: Palgrave, 2002.

Von Hildebrand, Dietrich. *Love, Marriage, and the Catholic Conscience: Understanding the Church's Teaching on Birth Control.* Manchester, N.H.: Sophia Institute Press, 1998.

Paz Estenssoro, Víctor (1907–2001) *president of Bolivia*

Víctor Paz Estenssoro was born in Tarija, Bolivia, on October 2, 1907, into an affluent family of mixed Spanish-Indian heritage. He studied law at the Universidad Mayor de San Andrés in La Paz and subsequently served as a government finance official. Paz Estenssoro was drafted into the military during the disastrous Chaco War of 1932 against Paraguay and the ensuing defeat disillusioned him toward the existing political system. After teaching economic history at La Paz he was elected to the chamber of deputies in 1940. There he commiserated with other reformist political and military figures, distraught over Bolivia's continuing corruption, nepotism, and political repression. In 1941 Paz Estenssoro helped found the Movimiento Nacionalista Revolucionario (MNR), National Revolutionary Movement, to counter these entrenched social ills. The following year the MNR, assisted by the military, deposed President Enrique Peñaranda and installed the reformist, Major Gualberto Villaroel, as president. For his efforts Paz Estenssoro served as minister of finance, although in 1946 he fled to Argentina just prior to a counterrevolution that toppled Villaroel. There he became a protégé of President JUAN PERÓN, and absorbed his techniques for rallying support from the lower classes. While abroad, Paz Estenssoro also kept in touch with MNR leaders back home and began plotting his comeback. In 1951 he ran for the presidency as a write-in candidate and defeated his conservative opponent. However, when the military refused to allow him to take office, a spontaneous revolution of students, miners, and urban workers erupted and drove them from power. Paz Estenssoro then returned to Bolivia in May 1952 and took the oath of office along with his vice president, HERNÁN SILES ZUAZO.

Paz Estenssoro had long urged dramatic reforms to correct the nation's glaring social and economic inequities, and he implemented a bold reform agenda. Most important, he expanded the voting franchise from 2 percent to 100 percent of adults, a move calculated to win support from the non-Spanish Indian majority. Next he moved to nationalize the important tin industry, which had been traditionally controlled by three families. Finally, the government initiated sweeping land redistribution for landless Indian peasants and allowed many to return to their ancestral homelands. The United States, which had withheld diplomatic recognition in 1943, now viewed Paz Estenssoro's reforms as an attractive alternative to communism and supplied ample financial assistance. By the time he stepped down from office in 1956 to become Bolivian ambassador to England, his nation had been irrevocably transformed.

In 1960 Paz Estenssoro was again eager for high office, and he returned home to announce his candidacy for the presidency. He did this over the objection of the MNR, which fielded a candidate of its own, but he easily was reelected. His next four years were less productive than his first term in office, owing to the depressed nature of the economy. He did manage to have constitutional reforms passed that allowed him to run again for consecutive terms in office. By 1964 the economic situation was such that, to placate the military, Paz Estenssoro was forced to accept General RENÉ BARRIENTOS ORTUÑO as his running mate. The ticket was victorious in the general election but on November 4, 1964, Barrientos overthrew the government and Paz Estenssoro fled to exile in Peru. He taught economics in Lima for many years before returning to Bolivia and reentering national politics. Paz Estenssoro retained a great national popularity, and in 1985 he won an unprecedented fourth term as president against incumbent Hugo Bánzer Suárez. He then imposed his "New Economic Policy" on the country to combat astronomical inflation rates of 22,000 percent, which marked his final transformation from a revolutionary to a conservative. The measures adopted were extremely austere, and the hardships they caused precipitated considerable social unrest. But when Paz Estenssoro left office for the fourth and final time in 1989 the economy had completely rebounded. Moreover the "shock therapy" approach he so dramatically instituted served as a model for many developing nations in Eastern Europe, with similar results. Paz Estenssoro died in La Paz on June 7, 2001, easily the most influential Bolivian politician of the 20th century. His widespread social reforms both revolutionized society and placed it on the path of modernity and democracy.

Further Reading

Brill, William H. *Military Intervention in Bolivia: The Overthrow of Paz Estenssoro and the MNR.* Washington, D.C.: Institute for the Comparative Study of Political Systems, 1967.

Claros-Rosales, Rosa V. "The Political Thought of Victor Paz Estenssoro." Unpublished master's thesis, University of Texas–El Paso, 1975.

Grindle, Merilee, and Pilar Domingo, eds. *Proclaiming Revolution: Bolivia in Comparative Perspective.* Cambridge, Mass.: David Rockefeller Center for Latin American Studies, Harvard University, 2003.

Kofas, J. V. "The Politics of Austerity: The IMF and U.S. Foreign Policy in Bolivia, 1956–1964." *Journal of Developing Areas* 29 (January 1995): 213–236.

Lehman, Kenneth D. *Bolivia and the United States: A Limited Partnership.* Athens: University of Georgia Press, 1999.

Malloy, James M. "Democracy, Economic Crisis, and the Problem of Governance: The Case of Bolivia." *Studies in Comparative International Development* 26 (summer 1991): 37–58.

Pearson, Lester (1897–1972) *prime minister of Canada*

Lester Bowles Pearson was born in Newtonbrook, Ontario, Canada, on April 23, 1897, the son of a Methodist minister. He entered the University of Toronto in 1913 but quit the following year to participate in World War I. Injured in a bus accident, he returned home to serve as a flying instructor and in 1922 he accepted a fellowship to study at Oxford University. Pearson graduated in 1925 and spent several years teaching history at the University of Toronto. However, in 1928 he took the civil service exam and became a secretary in the Department of External Affairs. By 1935 the affable, intelligent Pearson was serving in London with the Canadian High Commission, where he observed Europe's gradual slide toward World War II. This indelibly impressed upon him the need for collective security arrangements to deter future aggression. He came home in 1942 and served with the Canadian Legation in Washington, D.C., and in 1945 was named ambassador to the United States. A man of great charm, totally at ease with the press, he quickly became a favorite in diplomatic circles and represented Canada during the founding conference of the United Nations. In September 1946 Prime Minister WILLIAM LYON MACKENZIE KING summoned Pearson home to serve as deputy minister of external affairs and guide Canadian participation in the North Atlantic Treaty Organization (NATO) as a hedge against Soviet expansionism. In 1948 he was promoted to minister of external affairs and also began his political career by winning a seat in the House of Commons with the Liberal Party. There he performed valuable work directing Canada's military commitment to the Korean War, 1950–53, while also seeking a mediated solution at the UN. He was instrumental in drawing up the partition plan that led to the creation of Israel and Palestine in 1947. However, Pearson gained international recognition during the ill-fated Suez Canal Crisis of 1956 when Great Britain, France, and Israel attacked Egypt. Though nominally allied to England, Pearson condemned the action and instituted the plan that brought UN peacekeeping forces into the region. For his actions he became the first Canadian to receive the Nobel Peace Price in 1957.

By 1958 Pearson had resigned from diplomacy to concentrate on politics. The previous year the Liberal administration of LOUIS ST. LAURENT had been turned out of power, largely over the Suez affair, and Pearson was nominated party head to succeed him. Pearson, ever the consummate diplomat, spent several years rebuilding the ideological base of his splintered party until 1963, when the administration of JOHN DIEFENBAKER collapsed over his refusal to deploy nuclear weapons. Pearson argued that the nation was bound to observe treaty commitments, and elections held that year enabled the Liberals to form a minority coalition government on April 22, 1963.

Because Pearson depended on the goodwill of several small parties to retain power, he never was able to craft and implement a clearly Liberal agenda for the nation. In 1965 his weakness was underscored when he called new elections, yet failed again to win a parliamentary majority. Nonetheless, Pearson enjoyed considerable success in giving Canada its first national health and pension plans, universal medicare, and a unified armed forces. He also resolved to remove the final vestiges of British colonial rule by designing a new national flag, red and white with a centered maple leaf, which first flew in 1965. But Pearson's biggest problem remained the French-speaking province of Quebec where separatist agitation and terrorism were on the rise. Tensions were greatly exacerbated during a trip there by French president CHARLES DE GAULLE in 1968, when he publicly lauded the notion of an independent Quebec.

Pearson promptly fired off an angry missive to the former general and he departed Canada in a huff. But rather than worry about Canada's bicultural split, Pearson chose to celebrate it as an integral part of the nation's distinctiveness. He also established the Royal Commission on Bilingualism and Biculturalism to encourage greater harmony between the two feuding communities. Pearson declared his determination to remain party head until April 1968, when the up-and-coming PIERRE TRUDEAU, who had served in his cabinet, replaced him. Pearson resumed a teaching career at Carleton University for many years and served on a commission with the World Bank before dying in Ottawa on December 27, 1972. His legislative success in office is regarded as the high point of the Canadian welfare state.

Further Reading

Egerton, Lester B. "Lester B. Pearson and the Korean War: Dilemmas of Collective Security and International Enforcement in Canadian Foreign Policy, 1950–1953." *International Peacekeeping* 4 (spring 1997): 51–74.

English, John. *The Worldly Years: The Life of Lester Pearson.* New York: A. A. Knopf Canada, 1992.

Glazov, Jamie. *Canadian Policy toward Khrushchev's Soviet Union.* Montreal: McGill-Queen's University Press, 2002.

Hilmer, Norman. *Pearson: The Unlikely Gladiator.* Ithaca, N.Y.: McGill-Queen's University Press, 1999.

Pearson, Lester B. *Mike; the Memoirs of the Right Honorable Lester B. Pearson,* 3 vols. New York: Quadrangle, 1972.

Simpson, Erika. *NATO and the Bomb: Canadian Defenders Confront Critics.* Ithaca, N.Y.: McGill-Queen's University Press, 2001.

Tauber, Eliezer. *Personal Policy Making: Canada's Role in the Adoption of the Palestine Partition Resolution.* Westport, Conn.: Greenwood Press, 2002.

Pereira, Aristides (1923–) *president of Cape Verde*

Aristides Maria Pereira was born on Boa Vista, Cape Verde Islands, on November 17, 1923. His homeland had been a Portuguese colony for many centuries and black-skinned Africans residing there had been largely acculturated. Cape Verde was also closely administered as a part of neighboring Guinea-Bissau, despite profound ethnic differences. Pereira had been educated locally and sent to Portugal to train as a radio-telegraph technician. However, like many Cape Verdeans, he resented Portuguese colonial rule, and in 1956 he was a founding member of the Partido Africano da Independência de Guinée Cabo Verde (PAIGC), African Party for the Independence of Guinea and Cape Verde, under AMÍLCAR CABRAL. In 1959 he was working in Guinea-Bissau and helped organize a strike by dockworkers. However, when the Portuguese army intervened and killed 50 peaceful demonstrators, PAIGC renounced pacifist tactics and commenced an armed struggle. In time Pereira rose to be secretary general of the movement and also part of its war council. His career also became closely intertwined with that of Cabral and his brother, Luis Cabral, and they agreed that both Cape Verde and Guinea-Bissau should be liberated in unison. When Cabral was assassinated by Portuguese agents in January 1973, Pereira was tapped to succeed him and continue the struggle. Within a year the government of Portugal was overthrown by a left-wing coup, resulting in freedom for all its African possessions. Curiously, while Cape Verde and Guinea-Bissau both achieved independence, they were to be jointly ruled by PAIGC. On July 5, 1975, the newly constituted national assembly on Cape Verde elected Pereira the nation's first president.

The political union between Cape Verde and Guinea-Bissau proved transitional because of deep-rooted resentments of the latter toward the former. Cape Verde was more closely assimilated to Portugal than the mainland and hence always enjoyed a privileged position within the colonial regime. In November 1980 a coup in Guinea-Bissau overthrew Luis Cabral, and Pereira decided to terminate his relationship with PAIGC altogether. In January 1981 he founded the new Partido Africano de Independência de Cabo Verde (PAICV), African Party for the Independence of Cape Verde, and took the country down its own path. For Pereira, this meant embarking on socialist economics and establishing diplomatic relations with the Soviet Union and other Eastern Bloc nations. However, due to the sheer poverty of Cape Verde and its overwhelming dependence on food imports to survive, he was pragmatic in his dealings with Western nations and solicited friendly relations. Pereira continued ruling Cape Verde as a one-party

state through PAICV, and with such radical reforms as land redistribution, he acquired genuine public support. In 1981 and 1986 he was easily reelected president by the assembly and continued toeing a Pan-Africanist line. He criticized the apartheid regime of South Africa, but refused to sever economic or diplomatic ties due to the island's extreme poverty. Even the radical African National Congress (ANC) appreciated Cape Verde's predicament, and Pereira was never sanctioned for his South African relationship.

By 1990, the end of the cold war had placed one-party states like Cape Verde under intense pressure to adopt multiparty democracy. At length political opposition coalesced around the Catholic Church and some wealthy expatriates, who organized the Movimento para a Democracia (MPD), Movement for Democracy, in June 1990. The government entered into a dialogue with them and at length decided to repeal the one-party section of the national constitution. In two rounds of national elections held in January and February 1991, Pereira and PAICV lost decisively to Antonio Mascarenhas Monteiro of the MPD. Pereira thus became the first postcolonial African leader to lose office through peaceful means. Fortunately he accepted the verdict of the people and turned over power graciously after 16 years. Pereira has since served as a private citizen, although he occasionally resurfaces to comment on national affairs.

Further Reading

Carreira, Antonio. *The People of the Cape Verde Islands: Exploitation and Emigration.* Hamden, Conn.: Archon Books, 1982.

Davidson, Basil. *The Fortunate Isles: A Study in African Transformation.* Trenton, N.J.: Africa World Press, 1989.

———. *No Fist Is Big Enough to Hide the Sky: The Liberation of Guinea and Cape Verde.* London: Zed, 1981.

Foy, Colm. *Cape Verde: Politics, Economics and Society.* New York: Pinter Publishers, 1988.

Lobban, Richard. *Cape Verde: Crioulo Colony to Independent Nation.* Boulder, Colo.: Westview, 1995.

Meintel, Deirdre. *Race, Culture and Portuguese Colonialism in Cabo Verde.* Syracuse, N.Y.: Maxwell School of Citizenship and Public Affairs, Syracuse University, 1984.

Rego, Marcia S. "Echoes from an Empire, Voices of the Nation: Hierarchy, Disorder, Speech and Textuality in Cape Verde." Unpublished Ph.D. diss., University of California–San Diego, 2001.

Pérez de Cuéllar, Javier (1920–   ) *secretary general of the United Nations*

Javier Pérez de Cuéllar was born in Lima, Peru, on January 19, 1920, into an affluent business family. He attended Lima's Catholic University, studying law and gaining fluency in English and French. Pérez de Cuéllar also supported himself by working as a clerk in the Ministry of Foreign Affairs and developed an affinity for diplomacy. In 1944 he joined the Peruvian diplomatic corps as a third secretary and was initially posted to Paris, France. This was the start of a long and distinguished career on the international scene, for the young man demonstrated the high degrees of intelligence, charm, and tact essential for this line of work. In 1946 he represented Peru during the charting session of the new United Nations in San Francisco. He then moved up to first secretary while holding diplomatic posts in London, La Paz, and Rio de Janeiro. In 1967 Pérez de Cuéllar gained his first ambassadorial assignment in Switzerland, and two years later he became Peru's first ambassador to the Soviet Union. Good work here resulted in his reassignment to Peru's permanent delegation to the United Nations in 1971, where he remained three years. In 1975 Secretary General KURT WALDHEIM dispatched him on an important peacemaking mission to the troubled island of Cyprus, and while the ongoing crisis between Greeks and Turks was not resolved, he managed to initiate negotiations between them. Over the next six years he alternated between diplomatic assignments in Brazil and Venezuela, while also helping to quell a potential conflict between Pakistan and Afghanistan. Pérez de Cuéllar served capably in all these capacities and in the fall of 1981 he was tapped to succeed Waldheim as general secretary of the United Nations. As the first Latin American to hold that post, he began his first five-year term on January 1, 1982, fully cognizant that the body he led suffered from numerous shortcomings. Nonetheless his quiet, self-effacing nature was also a distinct and welcome departure from his flamboyant and controversial predecessor.

From the onset Pérez de Cuéllar inherited a world full of mounting crises. In 1983 he tried unsuccessfully to resolve the Falkland Islands War between Great Britain and Argentina. UN attempts at mediation also conspicuously failed to produce results in Lebanon and in the Persian Gulf War between Iran and Iraq. However, none of these setbacks reflected badly upon Pérez de Cuéllar, who enjoyed continuing respect in diplomatic circles. He fully intended to resign when his first term expired in December 1986, but then stayed on for a second term when five permanent members of the security council asked him to do so.

His later tenure in office was as fraught with peril as the first. Pérez de Cuéllar was consistently and actively employed in efforts to ameliorate the 1990 Iraqi invasion of Kuwait by Saddam Hussein. He saw war as only a last resort, but steadfastly supported the UN military effort, spearheaded by United States president GEORGE H. W. BUSH, to evict Iraq from their conquered land. Fortunately, he enjoyed much better success elsewhere and in 1989 he helped conclude two disastrous military episodes: the Soviet invasion of Afghanistan and the Iran-Iraq conflict. The pinnacle of his personal brand of diplomacy occurred literally during the last hours of his term as secretary general when he went to Mexico to oversee the treaty that ended El Salvador's 11-year civil war. In January 1992 the genial Peruvian was replaced by the Egyptian, Boutros Boutros Ghali, and could look back with satisfaction on a decade of conscientious work.

After leaving the United Nations, Pérez de Cuéllar settled in Paris before returning to Peru in 1995. Once home he established the Union for Peru Party in an unsuccessful bid to become president, but he lost heavily to Alberto Fujimori. Pérez de Cuéllar then returned to Paris until November 2000, when President Valentín Paniagua invited him back to serve as prime minister during an interim administration that succeeded the disgraced Fujimori. When new elections were won by Alejandro Toledo in April 2000, Pérez de Cuéllar relinquished his office and returned to Paris. On August 9, 2001, the 81-year-old consummate diplomat was appointed ambassador to France at the behest of Peruvian foreign secretary Diego Garcia. His mission, specifically, is to solicit European aid for Peru's economic recovery under the Social Emergency Program. Age has proved no stumbling block to Pérez de Cuéllar and he relishes the chance to be back in the diplomatic limelight. He remains a highly respected elder statesman and quite possibly the most distinguished Peruvian of his generation.

Further Reading

Alleyne, Mark D. *Global Lies? Propaganda, the UN, and World Order.* New York: Palgrave Macmillan, 2003.

Kraasno, Jean E. *The United Nations and Iraq: Defanging the Viper.* Westport, Conn.: Praeger, 2002.

Lankevich, George J. *The United Nations under Javier Pérez de Cuéllar, 1981–1991.* Lanham, Md.: Scarecrow Press, 2001.

Loescher, Gil. *The UNHCR and World Politics: A Perilous Path.* New York: Oxford University Press, 2001.

Pérez de Cuéllar, Javier. *Pilgrim for Peace: A Secretary General's Memoirs.* New York: St. Martin's Press, 1997.

Pérez Jiménez, Marcos (1914–2001) *president of Venezuela*

Marcos Pérez Jiménez was born in Michelena, Venezuela, on April 25, 1914, the son of a farmer. In 1930 he enrolled at the Military Academy of Venezuela and graduated four years later at the top of his class. Pérez Jiménez subsequently received additional training in Peru and became convinced that the military was uniquely positioned to bring modernization to society. However, he had grown disillusioned by the dictatorship of General Isaias Medina Angarita, and in 1944 he organized the Patriotic Military Union, a secret revolutionary clique. In concert with the group Acción Democrática (AD), Democratic Action, they conspired to overthrow the government on October 18, 1945, and restore civilian rule to Venezuela. But the president, RÓMULO BETANCOURT, did not trust Pérez Jiménez and declined to make him part of the new regime. Worse, he dispatched the young officer on a lengthy diplomatic tour to keep him out of the country for as long as possible. Pérez Jiménez resented the slight and began drawing up plans against the democratically elected administration of Rómulo Gallegos, who followed Betancourt. On November 24, 1948, the military disposed of Gallegos, and Pérez Jiménez became part of a military junta under Carlos Delgado Chalbaud, the former defense secretary. However, when Delgado was mysteriously assassinated in 1950, Pérez Jiménez moved quickly to consolidate control of the government through his Independent Electoral Front (Frente Electoral Independiente, FEI). He scheduled new elections in April 1953, but when the Democratic Republic Union appeared to win control of the assembly, he stopped the vote count and declared himself president.

Over the next six years Pérez Jiménez established one of the most repressive dictatorships in Latin America. Virulently anticommunist, he suppressed all forms of political dissent from intellectuals, students, or labor unions, and even closed the national university. He created a far-reaching secret police to enforce his will and arrest, torture, and murder any known malcontents. Political parties like Democratic Action were also outlawed, and all the land reforms they enacted were reversed. But Pérez Jiménez, true to his indoctrination, remained acutely interested in promoting modernization. Buoyed by oil revenues, he embarked on a lavish program of public works to keep the poor employed and win their support. Skyscrapers, hotels, resorts, and South America's best highway system were all launched and completed under his aegis. Caracas, the formerly sleepy national capital, soon emerged as a shiny, modern urban center. All told Pérez Jiménez had radically transformed the outlook of Venezuela, at least on the surface, and for being such a stalwart ally in the war against communism American president DWIGHT D. EISENHOWER presented him with the Congressional Legion of Merit, the highest award available to a foreigner.

This extravagant facade could not disguise the fact that Pérez Jiménez tolerated corruption on a vast scale. Military and political figures associated with his regime routinely skimmed millions of dollars from building projects and pocketed the profits. Meanwhile, expenditures for schools, hospitals, and other necessities were all sacrificed under his New National Ideal plan. Pérez Jiménez amassed a personal fortune estimated at $250 million before he alienated key sectors of the political and military establishment through corruption and oppression. In January 1958 he was toppled by a mass uprising and fled to the United States. That same year Betancourt, who was returned to power through elections, charged the former dictator with embezzlement and demanded his return. In 1963 Pérez Jiménez was arrested in Miami and forcibly returned to Venezuela to face trial; he was the first foreign national ever extradited by the United States. His trial lasted five years and in 1968 he was sentenced to the four years in jail he had already served and was exiled to Spain. That year he organized the Nationalistic Civic Crusade from abroad to support his candidacy for the senate, and he won in absentia. His victory was overturned on a technicality but in 1972 he again briefly returned home to run for the presidency. He was thwarted by a constitutional amendment that forbade convicted felons from holding high office. Pérez Jiménez returned to Spain, where he died in Madrid on September 20, 2001, last of the old-style Latin American military dictators.

Further Reading

Burggraaff, Winfield J. *The Venezuelan Armed Forces in Politics, 1935–1959.* Columbia: University of Missouri Press, 1972.

Derham, M. "Undemocratic Democracy: Venezuela and the Distortion of History." *Bulletin of Latin American Research* 21 (April 2002): 270–289.

Ellner, Steve. "Venezuelan Revisionist Political History, 1908–1958: New Motives and Criteria for Analyzing the Past." *Latin American Research Review* 30, no. 2 (1995): 91–121.

Ewell, Judith. *The Indictment of a Dictator: The Extradition and Trial of Marcos Pérez Jiménez.* College Station: Texas A & M University Press, 1981.

Krehm, William. *Democracies and Tyrannies of the Caribbean in the 1940s.* Toronto: Lugus, 1999.

Salazar-Carrillo, Jorge. *Oil and Development in Venezuela during the 20th Century.* Westport, Conn.: Praeger, 2004.

Taylor, Philip B. *The Venezuelan Golpe de Estado of 1958: The Fall of Marcos Pérez Jiménez.* Washington, D.C.: Institute for the Comparative Study of Political Systems, 1968.

Perón, Juan (1895–1974) *president of Argentina*

Juan Domingo Perón was born in Lobo, Argentina, on October 8, 1895, the son of a middle-class rancher. While growing up he was indelibly impressed by the conditions of the working poor on his ranch and thereafter sought to redress such glaring social inequities. Perón eschewed college education in favor of a military career, and in 1911 he enrolled in the national military academy. He graduated in 1913 and proved a competent soldier with easy-going manners. Perón held down successively important military assignments and in 1929 he was promoted to the army general staff. The following year he experienced his first taste of politics by participating in a military coup that deposed President HIPÓLITO YRIGOYEN in 1930. He was billeted with the Superior War School as a reward, and in 1936 became the Argentine military attache in Rome. There Perón observed and was impressed by the fascist regime of dictator BENITO MUSSOLINI and throughout World War II he sided with a faction of Argentine military officers that supported the Axis powers. On June 4, 1943, Perón helped orchestrate another military coup that toppled civilian president Ramón Castillo, and he was installed as secretary of labor. In this capacity he deliberately began building a political base among Argentina's working poor by raising wages, strengthening unions, and supporting welfare legislation. In October 1945 another coup restored civilian authority and Perón was arrested, but a massive turnout by organized labor forced his release within days. He then addressed a crowd of 300,000 followers and declared his candidacy for president. Perón went on to found his own Justicialist (or Peronist) Party, dedicated to the principles of social justice, nationalism, and strong leadership. The new party exhibited decidedly fascist overtones but in February 1946 he was elected president by 54 percent of votes cast. Shortly after he married the noted actress turned social activist Eva Duarte—popularly known as Evita—who soon became his most trusted political adviser.

Tall, ruggedly built, and handsome, Perón cut an imposing, charismatic figure, and he knew how to articulate a populist agenda. Once in power he made sweeping changes to Argentina's economy to champion the lower classes. Committed to government intervention in the economy, he nationalized the railroads, poured government money into industrialization projects, promoted full employment, and raised salaries. In fact, his goal was to find a third way of governance between capitalism and communism. The working poor were the country's biggest beneficiaries, and they flocked to the Peronist Party in huge numbers. But from the onset Perón's administration exhibited authoritarian tendencies: the press was muzzled, critics were jailed, and education closely monitored. Worse, the government's overemphasis on industry seriously dislocated the national economy, heretofore dependent upon agriculture, and export prices declined steeply while inflation rose. Perón was reelected by a smaller margin in 1951, a sign of growing disillusionment with his handling of the economy and incessant oppression. When Evita died in 1952 Perón lost his most astute supporter and valuable symbol of union support. In 1954 he tried reducing the power of the Catholic Church but was excommunicated, while his coalition of trade unionists, clergy, and military leaders continued eroding. In September 1955 Perón was overthrown by the military and allowed to immigrate to Spain. But the Peronismo movement he left behind continued exerting a powerful influence in his absence.

Over the next two decades Perón managed to keep tight control over his party, which was riven by competing right- and left-wing factions, and prevented a successor from taking his place. By 1973 Argentina was seriously disrupted by economic distress and guerrilla movements, so a military regime allowed him to return and run for office. Perón's reappearance was greeted by wild applause, and in 1973 he and his new wife Isabel were elected president and vice president respectively, with 62 percent of the vote. But the country was still polarized by right- and left-wing militants and remained ungovernable. Perón failed to restore the country's economic vitality before he died in Buenos Aires on July 1, 1974. He was succeeded by his wife, Isabel. When she was deposed by the military two years later, it appeared that Peronism was politically bankrupt and had finally run its course. However, after a succession of military juntas, democratic rule was finally restored in 1989, and the presidency was won by Peronist Carlos Saúl Menem. Perón remains the most important political icon of 20th-century Argentina.

Further Reading

Allison, Victoria C. "The Bitch Goddess and the Nazi Elvis: Peronist Argentina in the U.S. Popular Imagination." Unpublished Ph.D. diss., State University of New York–Stony Brook, 2001.

Di Tella, Torcuato S. *Perón and the Unions: The Early Years*. London: University of London, Institute of Latin American Studies, 2002.

Dorn, Glenn J. "Perón's Gambit: The United States and the Argentine Challenge to the Inter-American Order, 1946–1948." *Diplomatic History* 26 (winter 2002): 1–20.

Foss, Clive. "Selling a Dictatorship: Propaganda and the Peróns." *History Today* 50 (March 2000): 8–14.

Perón, Juan D. *Perón Expounds his Doctrine*. New York: AMS Press, 1973.

Plotkin, Mariano B. *Mañana es San Perón: A Cultural History of Perón's Argentina*. Wilmington, Del.: Scholarly Resources, 2002.

Rein, Raanan. *Argentina, Israel, and the Jews: Perón, the Eichmann Capture, and After*. Potomac, Md.: University Press of Maryland, 2002.

Pétain, Philippe (1856–1951) *French head of state*

Henri Philippe Pétain was born in Cauchy-à-la-Tour, France, on April 24, 1856, into a peasant family. He overcame poverty and attended the prestigious French military academy at St. Cyr in 1876. Commissioned two years later, Pétain gained high marks as a professional soldier, but his career was hampered by an unorthodox belief in defensive tactics at a time when the offense was viewed as paramount. He rose slowly and unspectacularly to colonel and was on the verge of retirement when World War I erupted in 1914. He quickly distinguished himself at the decisive Battle of the Marne that fall, and in 1916 was appointed commander of the vital Verdun front. Declaring "they shall not pass," Pétain bested superior German forces in a bloody battle of attrition that made him a national hero. In 1917 he rose to commander in chief in the wake of a serious mutiny and quickly restored the army's morale and efficiency. By the time the war ended in 1918 he was one of only three French leaders elevated to the coveted rank of marshal. Pétain continued serving with distinction in the postwar period and imposed his defensive-minded approach to war on current military strategy. Hence, offensive tactics gave way to static defense, best exemplified by the extensive Maginot Line, which was designed to blunt a future German attack. In 1934 he briefly served as minister of war, and disparaged republican government and its toleration of communists and other "undesirable" elements. In 1939 the government appointed him ambassador to Spain and he was favorably received by dictator FRANCISCO FRANCO, a former subordinate of his from the Rif wars in Morocco.

World War II commenced in 1939, and the following spring tank-led German forces launched a devastating assault around the Maginot Line that crumpled French defenses. On June 16, 1940, Pétain was summoned home by President Albert Lebrun and made prime minister. In this capacity the former war hero arranged a hasty armistice with the Nazis, who were then permitted to occupy the northern two-thirds of the country. Pétain painfully realized that France's defeat was total and national survival now was predicated on collaboration with Germany. Therefore, on July 10, 1940, he insisted that the French parlement, holed up in the resort town of Vichy, vote itself out of existence and grant him dictatorial powers as head of state. Only a figure of Pétain's standing would have dared make such a request. The parlement agreed, and out of the ashes of the Third Republic Vichy France was born. In concert with Vice Premier PIERRE LAVAL, Pétain next implemented an authoritarian form of government that closely approximated the German dictatorship. Henceforth the revolutionary principles of "Liberty, equality, fraternity" were replaced by the more ominous slogan of "Work, family, fatherland." Pétain firmly believed that by cooperating with Hitler, France would not suffer harshly under military occupation, but he found Laval such a Nazi sycophant that he dismissed him in December 1940. However, German pressure resulted in Laval's reinstatement the following April, and the Nazis made increasing demands upon France for food and machinery to fuel their war machine. Most horridly, Pétain also authorized the removal of 80,000 French Jews and communists to the Nazi death camps. Vichy France was by this juncture little more than a German puppet state, but the 84-year-old veteran sincerely believed he was acting in the best interests of his countrymen.

The Vichy regime was basically irrelevant following Allied landings in North Africa during the fall of 1942, for then the Germans occupied all of France by force. Pétain had secretly ordered French forces stationed in Africa to join the invaders but he refused to flee and was typically determined to endure the fate of his countrymen. But he also failed to curb his relentless war against French resistance fighters, many of whom were caught and executed. Once the Allies landed in France in June 1944, he was forcibly taken to Germany and detained there until war's end. Pétain was released in neutral Switzerland and could have remained there, but he insisted upon returning to his homeland. The former war hero was immediately arrested and tried for treason. Found guilty, he was ordered to face a firing squad but his sentence was commuted to life imprisonment by General CHARLES DE GAULLE. The former hero of Verdun languished in prison on the island of Yeu until he died on July 23, 1951, one of the most divisive figures of French history.

Further Reading

Atkin, Nicholas. *Pétain.* New York: Longman, 1998.

Curtis, Michael. *Verdict on Vichy.* New York: Arcade Pub., 2003.

Jennings, Eric T. *Vichy in the Tropics: Petain's National Revolution in Madagascar, Guadeloupe, and Indochina, 1940–1944.* Stanford, Calif.: Stanford University Press, 2001.

Peschanski, Denis. *Collaboration and Resistance: Images of Life in Vichy France, 1940–44.* New York: Harry N. Abrams, 2000.

Petain, Philippe. *Verdun.* New York: L. MacVeagh, 1930.

Szaluta, Jacques. "Marshal Pétain and French Nationalism: The Interwar Years and Vichy." *History of European Ideas* 15 (August 1992): 113–118.

Philippe Pétain *(Library of Congress)*

Webster, Paul. *Pétain's Crime: The Full Story of French Collaboration in the Holocaust.* Chicago: I. R. Dee, 1991.

Piłsudski, Józef (1867–1935) *Polish head of state*

Józef Klimens Piłsudski was born in Zulow, Russian Poland, on December 5, 1867, into an impoverished noble family. Poland, one of the great states of medieval Europe, had been constantly partitioned by neighboring Prussia, Austria, and Russia, and finally disappeared in the late 18th century. When he was young, Piłsudski's family had relocated to Lithuania where he acquired a profound hatred of everything Russian and determined to one day free his country from foreign domination. In 1886 he was ejected from Kharkov medical school for political activities, and the following year he was accused of plotting to assassinate Czar Alexander III. He was exiled to Siberia for five years where he encountered many Polish expatriates whose suffering deepened his convictions. Once home in 1892 Piłsudski joined the outlawed Polish Socialist Party and within two years had risen to be both its leader and its newspaper editor. But unlike other revolutionaries, Piłsudski advocated Polish independence as a major feature of revolution. He was arrested again in 1901, but escaped and made his way across Europe. During the 1904–05 Russo-Japanese War he ventured to Tokyo in an unsuccessful bid to raise money for Polish revolutionaries. Though thwarted, he returned home and began raising a private army with clandestine Austrian assistance. When World War I erupted in August 1914, he raised a 3,000-man Polish Legion—reminiscent of the forces who fought for Napoleon—and joined the Austrian army. He performed well and in 1916 became overall leader of Polish mercenaries. However, when he refused to take an oath of allegiance to the Central Powers and demanded that his legion provide the core of a new Polish state, he was arrested. Piłsudski was freed after the war ended in 1918 and returned home to the newly reconstituted Poland as a national hero.

As a new nation, Poland lacked strong national leadership, and Piłsudski was appointed head of state by the legislature (Sejm). The country was weak and surrounded by much larger neighbors, so his first priority was establishing a viable military. With his expert advice this was accomplished in months and, perceiving that Russia was still weak from its Bolshevik revolution, he attacked eastward to claim land that historically had belonged to Poland. However, the Russian resistance proved stronger than anticipated and by March 1919 they had driven to within a few miles of Warsaw, the capital. It was here that Piłsudski staged a major offensive that crippled the Soviet forces and drove them out of Poland entirely. The Treaty of Riga was signed in 1921 that formally recognized Poland's new boundaries, and Piłsudski returned home, hailed now as a national savior.

In 1921 Poland adopted a new constitution based on French parliamentary rule that featured a relatively weak president. This enraged Piłsudski, who felt that the country needed a republican form of government with a strong executive to survive. He grew rapidly disillusioned by the onset of squabbling factionalism—the bane of Polish governance since the 17th century—and he retired from office and the military in 1923. He then watched helplessly as the new nation was consumed by vicious infighting, and economic paralysis set in. Mindful of the resurgent Soviet Union under JOSEPH STALIN directly across the eastern boundary, Piłsudski collected a motley assortment of loyal troops, marched on Warsaw, and toppled the government on May 12, 1926. This initiated his Sanacja (Moral Reform) program. Piłsudski, disgusted by politics, declined the title of president and preferred to serve as minister of defense and, occasionally, prime minister. He then ruled through a puppet president and erected an effective secret police to harass and arrest parliamentary adversaries. Piłsudski unhesitatingly considered it expedient to sacrifice political freedom in the interest of national survival. But while his dictatorship restored centralized government to Poland, it could do little to improve its strategic situation, and after 1933 he confronted the specter of a rearmed Germany under ADOLF HITLER. Piłsudski failed to convince France to launch a preemptive strike against the Nazis so he was forced to conclude 10-year nonaggression pacts with Stalin in 1932 and Hitler in 1934. Neither treaty was observed.

When Piłsudski died on May 12, 1935, he was interred at Wawel Cathedral with all the solemnities befitting the father of modern Poland. His legacy was mixed: Poland had emerged as a viable independent state for the first time in centuries, but it remained politically divided and economically weak. Worst of all, Piłsudski's efforts could not prevent the conquest of

Poland in 1939 and its fourth partition between Germany and Russia. The country ultimately remained under Soviet domination until 1989.

Further Reading

Bernhard, Michael. "Institutional Choice and the Failure of Democracy: The Case of Interwar Poland." *East European Politics and Societies* 13, no. 1 (1999): 34–70.

Garlicki, Andrzej, and John Coutouvidis. *Jozef Piłsudski: 1867–1935.* Brookfield, Vt.: Ashgate Publishing, 1995.

Gasiorowski, Zygmunt J. "Jozef Piłsudski in the Light of British Reports." *Slavonic and East European Review* 50 (October 1972): 558–569.

Jnedrzejewicz, Waclaw. *Piłsudski: A Life for Poland.* New York: Hippocrene Books, 1982.

Piłsudski, Jozef. *The Memories of a Polish Revolutionary and Soldier.* London: Faber and Faber, 1931.

Wandy, P. S. "Poland's Place in Europe in the Concepts of Piłsudski and Dmowski." *Eastern European Politics and Society* 4 (fall 1990): 451–460.

Watt, Richard M. *Bitter Glory: Poland and Its Fate, 1918–1939.* New York: Barnes and Noble, 1998.

Pinochet, Augusto (1915–) *president of Chile*

Augusto Pinochet Ugarte was born in Valparaíso, Chile, on November 25, 1915, the son of a customs official. After several attempts he finally gained admittance to the National Military Academy in 1932 and graduated four years later. As a professional career military officer he held down a succession of important assignments, including as an instructor at War Academy, and he wrote a number of respected books on military geography. And, while nominally aloof from national politics, Pinochet demonstrated a pronounced dislike of communism and socialism. In 1969 President EDUARDO FREI promoted him to brigadier general, although Pinochet disagreed with his attempts to politicize the lower classes. By 1970 a new organization, the Popular Unity Party, had formed that served as an umbrella organization for various leftist groups. That year their candidate, SALVADOR ALLENDE, who won the Chilean presidential election by the narrowest of margins, implemented a drastic left-wing program to nationalize banks, factories, and international corporations. His efforts were met with extreme resistance by middle and upper classes, who stood to lose the most, and a period of economic destabilization set in. The chaos was further abetted by the American Central Intelligence Agency (CIA), which provided funding for anti-Allende groups. At length Allende appointed Pinochet the commander in chief of the armed forces and therefore tasked with the defense of the nation. Faced with a rising spiral of chaos and violence that threatened to tear the country apart, Pinochet suddenly toppled Allende in a bloody coup on September 11, 1973. This terminated Chile's flirtation with communist dictatorship and a junta, headed by Pinochet, came to the fore. Many right-wing sympathizers and Christian Democrats initially assumed that the military would surrender power once order had been restored, but in 1974 Pinochet had himself declared president, suspended the constitution, dissolved congress, and outlawed all political parties. The general would rule Chile with an iron fist for the next 16 years.

From the onset the Pinochet regime engaged in gross human rights violations under the Doctrine of National Security. An estimated 130,000 suspected leftists were rounded up and tortured under questioning in a determined effort to quash all communist resistance. An estimated 3,000 suspects disappeared without a trace and are assumed to have been murdered by the military. Nor were political assassinations confined to Chile; in 1976 Pinochet's intelligence operatives killed opposition leader Orlando Letelier in Washington, D.C. But the junta was also quick to institute free-market economic reforms to jump-start the failing economy. Taxes were cut, foreign investors were called in, and government industries privatized. In a few years Chile rebounded completely and boasted the fastest-growing economy in the region. Inflation and unemployment also dropped to acceptable levels, which gave the regime a degree of public popularity. In 1980 a referendum was passed on a new constitution that enabled Pinochet to remain president for another eight years, at which point his candidacy would be put to the vote. By 1989 Chile was once again a stable, prosperous nation, but voters summarily defeated Pinochet's attempt at reelection. The 1990 elections were overwhelmingly won by Christian Democrat Patricio Aylwin Azócar and Pinochet resigned from office. However, previous constitutional arrangements allowed him to remain on as commander in chief of the military for the next eight years—as a political watchdog.

In 1998 Pinochet finally resigned from the military and was appointed senator for life, which granted him immunity from prosecution. But that same year, while visiting Great Britain for medical treatment, he was arrested on a warrant issued by Spain for the disappearance of several Spanish citizens. An international imbroglio unfolded as the Chilean government protested the detention of one of its citizens and a member of its government. But in January 2000 the British high court found the former dictator in poor health and unable to withstand the rigors of a trial, so he was released. Once home Pinochet slipped into obscurity although the leftist opposition agitated to have him tried. But on July 1, 2002, the Chilean Supreme Court formally dropped all charges against him, again on the basis of declining health and mental faculties. Pinochet, lacking any further need for immunity from prosecution, then resigned from the senate and retired from public life. His acquittal greatly angered the families of victims of torture, but the nation gave a collective sign of relief. "Today we close a chapter in history," President Ricardo Lagos declared. "We hope that this brings a little more tranquility to all sectors." Pinochet thus leaves behind a mixed and controversial legacy: revered by some for having restored stability and prosperity, yet reviled by others for his willingness to violate human rights in the pursuit of order.

Further Reading

Barros, Robert. "Personification and Institutional Constraints: Pinochet, the Military Junta, and the 1980 Constitution." *Latin American Politics and Society* 43, no. 1 (2001): 5–28.

Beckett, Andy. *Pinochet in Piccadilly: Britain and Chile's Secret History.* London: Faber and Faber, 2002.

Dorfman, Ariel. *Exorcizing Terror: The Incredible Unending Trial of General Augusto Pinochet.* London: Pluto, 2003.

Ensalaco, Mark. *Chile under Pinochet: Recovering the Truth.* Philadelphia: University of Pennsylvania Press, 2000.

O'Shaughnessy, Hugh. *Pinochet: The Politics of Torture.* New York: New York University Press, 2000.

Sugarman, D. "The Pinochet Case: International Criminal Justice in Gothic Style?" *Modern Law Review* 64 (November 2001): 933–944.

Weeks, Gregory B. *The Military and Politics in Post-Authoritarian Chile.* Tuscaloosa: University of Alabama Press, 2003.

Pinto da Costa, Manuel (1937–) *president of São Tomé and Príncipe*

Manuel Pinto da Costa was born in Agua Grande, São Tomé and Príncipe, on August 5, 1937, the son of a plantation worker. His nation, which consists of two small islands 400 miles off the West African coast, had been a heavily exploited Portuguese colony for several centuries. Pinto da Costa was educated locally and went on to pursue economics at the University of London. He subsequently visited Cuba and received his doctorate in economics during a prolonged visit to East Germany. Pinto da Costa came home in 1960 and began fomenting anticolonial sentiment by founding the Committee for the Liberation of São Tomé and Principe (CLSTP). Because it called for agrarian reform and distribution of land to peasants, colonial authorities regarded CLSTP as subversive and drove it underground. After several years of political infighting, Pinto da Costa reorganized his group as the Movement of Liberation of São Tomé and Príncipe (MLSTP) in 1972. To avoid Portuguese harassment the new organization was based in neighboring Guinea, and Pinto da Costa was appointed its general secretary. However revolutionary in outlook, the MLSTP did not possess an armed wing and it did not instigate violence. Following the April 1974 coup in Portugal that deposed dictator ÁNTONIO SALAZAR, expectations for independence rose on São Tomé and Príncipe. Pinto da Costa, assisted by his friend and confidant Miguel Trovoada, entered into negotiations with the new military regime for independence, which was granted on July 12, 1975. A new constituent assembly was then founded that elected Pinto da Costa the new nation's first president and Trovoada its first prime minister.

A Marxist by inclination and training, Pinto da Costa established one-party rule through the MLSTP, of which he remained secretary. He also instituted a secret police and forbade opposition political groups and criticism of the government. In practice he also accumulated considerable power by controlling such important ministries as defense and foreign relations. Pinto da Costa then established close relationships with China, the Soviet Union, and other Eastern Bloc nations. He also convened a conference of the former Portuguese colonies of Cape Verde, Angola, Guinea-Bissau, and Mozambique in a display of revolutionary solidarity. But despite the trappings of dictatorship, the new regime carried through on promises of land reform, carved up large colonial plantations, and gave the land to the peasantry. Pinto da Costa consequently enjoyed genuine popular support, and he was reelected president in 1980 and 1985 against token opposition.

Unfortunately for Pinto da Costa, São Tomé and Príncipe remained among the poorest nations on Earth. Overpopulated, lacking an industrial base, and almost completely dependent upon cocoa exports for income, he had to be ideologically flexible to secure desperately needed foreign aid. The government therefore maintained close and friendly ties to Portugal and also extended a friendly hand to the United States and other Western nations. Toward the end of his third term, he also moderated some of his strident socialist policies and allowed state-run plantations to be run along capitalist lines. However, the government still came under increasing domestic and international pressure to allow political plurality through creation of new parties. In March 1990 a new constitution was promulgated to accommodate these demands, and new elections were slated for January 1991. After 16 years as a Marxist ruler, Pinto da Costa was badly defeated by the Party of Democratic Convergence led by his former associate Trovoada, whom he had at one point jailed for two years. Pinto da Costa then surrendered power, one of the first African leaders to lose power through democratic means. He continued on as head of the MLSTP and in July 1996 lost to Trovoada a second time. On August 1, 2001, Pinto da Costa tried again to win the presidency, but lost again, to businessman Fradique de Menezes of the Independent Democratic Alliance by 56 percent to 38 percent. This last defeat probably spells the end of Pinto da Costa's political career, but he made history as the prime mover behind national independence and—by losing gracefully—a contributor to the growth of democracy.

Further Reading

Carreira, Antonio. *The People of the Cape Verde Islands: Exploitation and Emigration.* Hamden, Conn.: Archon Books, 1982.

Eyzaguirre, Pablo B. "Small Farmers and Estates in São Tomé, West Africa." Unpublished Ph.D. diss., Yale University, 1996.

Gerhard, Seibert, *Comrades, Clients, and Cousins: Colonialism, Socialism, and Democratization in São Tomé and Principe.* Leiden, Netherlands: Leiden University, 1999.

Hodges, Tony, and Malyn D. D. Newitt. *São Tomé and Príncipe: From Plantation to Microstate.* Boulder, Colo.: Westview Press, 1988.

Lorenzino, Geraldo. "The Angolar Creole Portuguese of São Tomé: Its Grammar and Sociolinguistic History." Unpublished Ph.D. diss., City University of New York, 1998.

Shaw, Caroline, S. *São Tomé and Principe.* Santa Barbara, Calif.: ABC-Clio Press, 1994.

Pius XII (Eugenio Maria Giuseppe Giovanni Pacelli) (1876–1958) *pope of the Catholic Church*

Eugenio Maria Giuseppe Giovanni Pacelli was born in Rome, Italy, on March 2, 1876, the son of a lawyer. His family had supplied the Vatican with attorneys since 1816 and, because of poor health, he studied for the priesthood at home. Pacelli was ordained in 1899 and studied canon law while working with the Vatican secretariat of state. In 1912 he was appointed papal nuncio (ambassador) to Bavaria, where he remained the next 15 years. Pacelli came to love Germany's language and culture and he was perturbed by the rise of fascism and communism there. In 1929 he returned home as a cardinal and served as secretary of state under Pope Pius XI. Pacelli returned to Germany in 1933 and concluded a concordat with German vice chancellor FRANZ VON PAPEN to protect the status of the church and its property. In 1937 he helped draft a papal encyclical condemning Nazism and two years later, following the death of Pius XI, he became pope on March 2, 1939. Assuming the name Pius XII he was also the first Roman-born pope since 1721.

No sooner had Pius XII assumed office than World War II erupted when ADOLF HITLER invaded Poland on September 1, 1939. Therefore his first papal encyclical condemned the onset of hostilities and openly denounced totalitarian ideologies such as Nazism and communism as anti-Christian. Pius XII was extremely saddened by his inability to dissuade Italian dictator BENITO MUSSOLINI from entering the fray in 1940 on behalf of the Axis. Because Italy itself was a fascist power and soon to be occupied by German troops, the Catholic Church faced a potentially disastrous dilemma. Pius XII was personally committed to a peaceful resolution of the conflict; therefore it was incumbent upon him to retain diplomatic ties with belligerents on both sides. He opted to pursue a policy of quiet diplomacy and constructive engagement to save as many lives as possible. The wisdom of this choice was underscored by events in Holland, where the bishops openly condemned the Nazi policy of persecuting Jews. The Gestapo responded by rounding up Catholics who were Jewish converts—including nuns and clergy—and shipping them off to extermination camps. There was also the very real danger that fascist and Nazi elements in Rome might storm the Vatican. Pius thus came to the calculated and realistic determination that more Jewish lives could be saved—and the church's own survival ensured—through the clandestine smuggling and sheltering of religious refugees. When urged by the Western powers to publicly condemn Hitler's genocidal policies, he refused—unless he could also make similar statements against the Soviet Union's JOSEPH STALIN, then a Western ally. By war's end the Vatican had expended more than $4 million in rescuing Jews and other dissidents from the gas chamber. It had been a heroic if unheralded performance.

After the war Italy was confronted with the specter of rising communism among its sizable working classes. Pius XII, who had witnessed Bolshevik riots in Germany in the 1920s, proved implacably hostile to the creed and determined to keep his homeland free. Using all the diplomatic resources at his disposal, he worked closely with the governments of the United States and Great Britain to funnel money to Western-oriented parties like the Christian Democrats. Furthermore, he forbade Catholic voters from electing communists and formally excommunicated any Catholic who joined their party. Pius took similar measures against Catholic heads of state in eastern Europe and spent lavishly on the resettlement of political refugees from that quarter. Theologically speaking, Pius XII was extremely conservative in outlook but he did embrace the use of modern research techniques for biblical scholarship. He also pioneered the practice of appointing bishops from native areas around the world instead of choosing them from Rome. Pius XII died in Rome on October 9, 1958, after reigning 19 years—a tally exceeded only by Pope John Paul II. His replacement was JOHN XXIII, who introduced revolutionary practices that his conservative forebear was either unable or unwilling to do.

Pius XII's handling of church affairs during World War II continues to attract much controversy. Criticism from Jewish scholars prompted the Vatican to open up part of its secret archives to the public in February 2002.

In this manner it is hoped that posterity, Jewish and Christian alike, may appreciate the delicate balancing act that Pius XII performed during a very dark period of human history. In the words of Reverend Peter Gumpel, the German investigator promoting the former pope to sainthood, "No one did as much to help the Jews as did Pius XII."

Further Reading

Friedlander, Albert H. "Pius XII and the Jews: The Clash between History and Theology." *European Judaism* 35 (autumn 2002): 1131–1146.

Kent, Peter C. *The Lonely Cold War of Pope Pius XII: The Roman Catholic Church and the Division of Europe, 1943–1950*. Ithaca, N.Y.: McGill-Queen's University Press, 2002.

Phayer, Michael. *The Catholic Church and the Holocaust, 1930–1965*. Bloomington: Indiana University Press, 2000.

Ritter, Carol Ann, and John K. Roth. *Pope Pius XII and the Holocaust*. New York: Leicester University Press, 2002.

Sanchez, Jose M. *Pius XII and the Holocaust: Understanding the Controversy*. Washington, D.C.: Catholic University of America Press, 2001.

Tittmann, Harold H. *Inside the Vatican of Pius XII: Memoirs of Harold H. Tittmann, Jr. during World War II*. New York: Doubleday, 2004.

Zuccotti, Susan. *Under His Very Windows: The Vatican and the Holocaust in Italy*. New Haven, Conn.: Yale University Press, 2001.

Plaza Lasso, Galo (1906–1987) *president of Ecuador*

Galo Plaza Lasso was born in New York City on February 17, 1906, the son of diplomat and former two-term Ecuadorian president Leonidas Plaza Gutiérrez. He was educated in Quito and subsequently attended universities in California, Maryland, and Washington, D.C. Plaza Lasso was an authority on agrarian mechanization, and he introduced modern methods of administration and production on his family farm. Like his father, he joined the Liberal-Radical Party, and in 1938 he was elected mayor of Quito. The following year he became minister of defense and in 1946 President JOSÉ VELASCO appointed him ambassador to the United States. In this capacity he attended the charting session of the United Nations at San Francisco in 1945. Plaza Lasso returned home in 1946 and resumed his political career by winning election to the national senate with the National Democratic Civic Movement (MCDN). Capitalizing on the memory of his father's presidency, he ran for that office and was elected in 1948. Plaza Lasso assumed power at a fortuitous interval in Ecuadorian history as the country was undergoing a rare interlude of domestic tranquility and prosperity. In office he promoted the growth of civil liberties and modern industrialization. As an agricultural specialist, he was keen on developing Ecuador's export crops, including bananas, cacao, and coffee, with impressive results. Careful economic planning received a high priority and, consequently, the nation enjoyed considerable abundance. More important, democracy flourished without interruption by the military. He left office in 1952 and was succeeded by Velasco Ibarra, the first time in 28 years that an Ecuadoran executive completed his full term in office—and then peacefully transferred power.

A charismatic individual with a pleasant demeanor, Plaza Lasso next ventured into the realm of international diplomacy as a mediator. In 1958 he headed the Special Committee of the Economic Commission for Latin America, a precursor of the Latin American Free Trade Area (common market). That same year he also served as United Nations observer during the civil war in Lebanon. In 1960 Plaza Lasso was tapped by the UN to oversee the evacuation of Belgian military forces from the Democratic Republic of Congo. He then came home and made an unsuccessful attempt to serve again as president but was defeated by Velasco Ibarra. A major reason for his loss was a rising tide of anti-Americanism in Latin America, and Plaza Lasso, who was closely identified with the United States, lost decisively. He then returned to diplomacy and in 1965 served as the UN secretary general's personal representative to Cyprus. His efforts proved instrumental in restoring a semblance of order and stability to that crisis-racked island. He performed a similar task at home in 1966 by serving as provisional president following the collapse of the latest military junta.

In February 1968 Plaza Lasso accepted his final and most rewarding assignment, that of secretary of the Organization of American States (OAS). However, he was chosen only after the sixth ballot because of concerns about his relationship to the United States. Once elected, Plaza Lasso embarked on making lasting improvements and reorganized the secretariat to make it a more forceful, effective office. Over the next seven years he also articulated a clear vision and decisive leadership that had been heretofore lacking at OAS. In 1969 he oversaw the mediation of the 1969 El Salvador-Honduras War and in 1973 visited Chile in the wake of SALVADOR ALLENDE's overthrow to secure the release of political prisoners. His only conspicuous failure was in trying to arrange a diplomatic rapprochement between Communist Cuba and the United States. Plaza Lasso finally retired in 1975 as a respected elder statesman. His final task was serving with the Inter-American Dialogue, before his death in Quito on January 28, 1987. He was one of the most successful presidents in Ecuador's generally tortured democratic experience and acknowledged as a first-rate diplomat.

Further Reading
Hurtado, Osvaldo. *Political Power in Ecuador.* Boulder, Colo.: Westview Press, 1985.

Martz, John D. *Politics and Petroleum in Ecuador.* New Brunswick, N.J.: Transaction Books, 1987.

Plaza Lasso, Galo. *Latin America Today and Tomorrow.* Washington, D.C.: Acropolis Books, 1971.

———. *Problems of Democracy in Latin America.* Chapel Hill: University of North Carolina Press, 1955.

———. *Seven Years of Change.* Washington, D.C.: Organization of American States, 1975.

Selcher, Wayne A. "The Administration of Galo Plaza in Ecuador, 1948–1952: A Step Towards Stability." Unpublished master's thesis, University of Florida, 1965.

Striffler, Steve. *In the Shadows of State and Capital: The United Fruit Company, Popular Struggle, and Agrarian Restructuring in Ecuador, 1900–1995.* Durham, N.C.: Duke University Press, 2002.

Poincaré, Raymond (1860–1934) *president and prime minister of France*

Raymond Poincaré was born in Bar-le-Duc, France, on August 20, 1860, the son of a civil engineer. His childhood was largely shaped by his tolerant, middle-class upbringing and the hardships of German military occupation following the Franco-Prussian War of 1870. Thereafter Poincaré was always moderately conservative, politically speaking, and an ardent nationalist. A brilliant student, he studied law at the Sorbonne and in 1880 became one of France's youngest attorneys. He was elected to the Chamber of Deputies in 1887, displaying considerable grasp of economic and budgetary matters. In 1893 he joined the government as minister of education and three years later accepted the portfolio of minister of finance. By this time Poincaré had acquired the reputation of a thoroughly honest politician beset by a cold and aloof personality. In 1903 he successfully ran for a seat in the senate and became de facto leader of the *bloc national,* a coalition of conservative interests. His reputation for efficiency and reliability resulted in his appointment as prime minister in 1912. In this capacity he flaunted his nationalist credentials by shoring up France's defenses through multilateral treaties with Russia and Great Britain, the famous Triple Entente. He also lent his weight to passage of an important military bill that increased military service from two years to three. In January 1913 Poincaré confounded political observers by giving up his premiership to run for the presidency, an office of largely ceremonial functions. Poincaré, as usual, had other ideas, and he was intent upon strengthening his office to better influence foreign policy and the selection of new prime ministers.

Poincaré was successfully elected president and, following the outbreak of World War I in August 1914, he used it as a symbol of national unity. He promulgated plans for formation of a *union sacrée* (sacred union), which encompassed political factions from the left, right, and center. In addition to his political responsibilities, Poincaré tirelessly promoted morale among the troops and visited them in the field, the camps, and the trenches. The war effort badly stumbled in 1917 when nearly half the army mutinied and Poincaré displayed genuine statesmanship by appointing his hated arch-adversary GEORGES CLEMENCEAU as prime minister. Together they restored military morale and steeled the nation for further sacrifices that led to victory in November 1918. Thereafter Poincaré vociferously supported a hard line toward a defeated Germany, demanding reparations and seeking to detach the Rhineland as an autonomous state. In this he was thwarted by Clemenceau and the British, who proved far less vindictive toward the vanquished. When Poincaré's term expired in January 1920 he returned to the senate. He was the only senior government official to continuously hold office throughout the war years.

Postwar economic difficulties resulted in Poincaré replacing ARISTIDE BRIAND as prime minister in January 1922 and also serving as minister of foreign affairs. Germany's economy was also experiencing difficulties and it failed to make reparation payments as scheduled. An angry Poincaré conferred with British and German dignitaries in London and Paris, but they reached an impasse. Determined to achieve satisfaction, he then unilaterally ordered French troops to occupy the industrialized Ruhr River valley until payments resumed. The cash-strapped Germans simply resorted to passive resistance while the mounting costs of occupation also strained the French economy. But by 1924, the British and American governments hammered out the Dawes Plan, signed by Poincaré and German chancellor GUSTAV STRESEMANN, which reduced reparations to more realistic levels. However, when Poincaré imposed new and unpopular taxes to help subsidize the occupation, the Radical and Socialist Cartel of the Left defeated the conservatives, and Poincaré resigned.

By 1926 France was headed for an economic crisis and Poincaré was recalled as prime minister to head a National Union government. He levied new taxes, sponsored a constitutional amendment to fund bond payments, balanced the budget, and returned France to the international gold standard. This caused the declining French franc to stabilize and, against all expectations, the economy rebounded and enjoyed a period of prosperity over the next two years. When the Radicals and Socialists withdrew their support from the government in November 1928, Poincaré cobbled together a new coalition and remained in office. Bad health finally required him to withdraw in July 1929, and he turned to writing his voluminous memoirs. Poincaré died in Paris on October 15, 1934, a towering figure of the French Third Republic (1870–1940) and its most influential president. And, in a period dominated by leftists, he was France's most conspicuous and successful conservative politician.

Further Reading

Dutton, Paul V. *Origins of the French Welfare State, 1914–1947.* New York: Cambridge University Press, 2002.

Fortescue, William. *The Third Republic in France, 1870–1940.* New York: Routledge, 2000.

Keiger, J. F. V. *Raymond Poincaré.* New York: Cambridge University Press, 1997.

Martin, Benjamin F. *France and the Apres Guerre, 1918–1924: Illusions and Disillusionment.* Baton Rouge: Louisiana State University Press, 1999.

Moure, Kenneth. *The Gold Standard Illusion: France, the Bank of France, and the International Gold Standard, 1914–1939.* New York: Oxford University Press, 2002.

Poincaré, Raymond. *The Memoirs of Raymond Poincaré,* 4 vols. Garden City, N.Y.: Doubleday Page, 1926–31.

Sowerine, Charles. *France since 1870: Culture, Politics, and Society.* New York: St. Martin's Press, 2000.

Pol Pot (1925–1998) *prime minister of Cambodia*

Saloth Sar was born in Kompong, Thom Province, Cambodia, on May 19, 1925, the son of a prosperous landowner. He was educated locally at a Buddhist monastery and Catholic schools before being sent to France to study electronics. Sometime beforehand it is suspected that Saloth Sar was influenced by the anticolonial activities of HO CHI MINH and took an interest in revolutionary affairs. While in Paris he became affiliated with the French Communist Party and returned home in 1953 to teach. Saloth Sar also joined the Khmer People's Revolutionary Party (KPRP) around that time to foment rebellion against French colonialism and the Royal House of King Norodom Sihanouk. His movement was popularly known as the Khmer Rouge, or Red Cambodians. Saloth Sar worked as a teacher for many years, closely watched by the police, but he continued developing an ideological following. In September 1960 he founded the new and more radical Worker's Party of Kampuchea (WPK) and clandestinely ventured to Hanoi and Beijing to secure funding and military assistance. He also changed his name to Pol Pot, which bears no special meaning. His initiation of guerrilla warfare against Sihanouk coincided with the larger Vietnamese war against the United States, 1964–75. The conflict spilled over into Cambodia and Sihanouk was eventually ousted by an American puppet, LON NOL. But Pol Pot's forces, renamed the Communist Party of Kampuchea (CPK), proved elusive and an important adjunct to the North Vietnamese war effort. At length the Americans began an intense, secret bombing campaign against Cambodian guerrillas to prop up Lon Nol's regime. However, once the Americans withdrew from the region, Pol Pot emerged from the jungle, top-

pled the government on April 17, 1975, and declared the creation of the Democratic Republic of Kampuchea with himself as premier.

No one, even after two decades of incessant fighting, could have anticipated what would follow. Pol Pot espoused an extreme version of Maoism and Stalinism that was bent upon transforming Cambodia into an agrarian-based Marxist utopia. But to accomplish this, many undesirable elements of society had to be rounded up and reeducated. This entailed evacuating entire cities and villages and resettling the population in the countryside. Those individuals not willing to participate, or those viewed as tainted with Western education and values, were summarily executed in gruesome fashion. Pol Pot also determined to uproot every last vestige of colonial culture; banks were closed, money outlawed, and religion banned. People began dying from exposure and malnutrition by the thousands but the Khmer Rouge diligently enforced Pol Pot's dictates and an estimated 2 million people—one-fifth of the population—were systematically exterminated. The nation in that period has been called the killing fields. Pol Pot's bloodthirsty regime lasted only four years but proved one of the most brutal, repressive states in history while it lasted.

Pol Pot finally overreached in 1978 when he began guerrilla attacks on Vietnam—a fellow communist state—in an attempt to win back lost territory. This brought on a sharp response from Hanoi, which launched a massive invasion of Cambodia and drove the Khmer Rouge deep into the jungle by January 1979. Pol Pot responded by conducting an internecine guerrilla struggle against the invaders, usually alongside noncommunist factions loyal to Sihanouk. Even after the Vietnamese withdrew and Sihanouk was reinstalled as king in 1992, Pol Pot continued fighting. By this time many of the younger cadres had grown disillusioned with his leadership, and he was stripped of his official party positions. Pol Pot was by then an international fugitive wanted for massive human rights violations and charged with genocide. He continued to evade capture until April 1998 when he was apparently arrested by a faction within the Khmer Rouge. Tried and placed under house arrest by his erstwhile allies, Pol Pot died of natural causes near Anlong Veng, Cambodia, on April 15, 1998. He left behind a ghastly legacy that rivals ADOLF HITLER's in its savagery and barbarity.

Further Reading

Bizot, François. *The Gate.* New York: Knopf, 2003.

Chandler, David. *Brother Number One: A Political Biography of Pol Pot.* Boulder, Colo.: Westview Press, 1999.

Gottesman, Evan R. *Cambodia after the Khmer Rouge: Inside the Politics of Nation Building.* New Haven, Conn.: Yale University Press, 2002.

Morris, Stephen J. *Why Vietnam Invaded Cambodia: Political Culture and the Cause of War.* Stanford, Calif.: Stanford University Press, 1999.

Pol Pot. *Genocide in Cambodia: Documents from the Trial of Pol Pot and Leng Sang.* Philadelphia: University of Pennsylvania Press, 2000.

Ung, Loung. *First They Killed My Father: A Daughter of Cambodia Remembers.* New York: HarperCollins, 2000.

Pompidou, Georges (1911–1974) *prime minister and president of France*

Georges Pompidou was born in Montboudif, France, on July 5, 1911, the son of schoolteachers. He followed into his parents' profession by attending the Ecole Normale Superieure and subsequently passed through the Ecole des Sciences Politiques. Pompidou began teaching in 1934 but his career was interrupted by military service in World War II. Although never active in the underground resistance, he struck up cordial relations with General CHARLES DE GAULLE after France's liberation and became his personal secretary during the provisional government, 1944–46. After de Gaulle abruptly resigned from the government, Pompidou returned to the civilian sector, joined the Rothschild bank, and worked his way up to director by 1958. When de Gaulle finally returned to power in 1959 under a new constitution, he made Pompidou an unofficial adviser and personal representative. In this capacity he arrived in Algiers to conduct secret negotiations with rebel leaders and made arrangements for an honorable French withdrawal. He also outlined a new economic recovery plan. De Gaulle rewarded his competence and loyalty by appointing him prime minister of the Fifth Republic in 1962.

Pompidou's ascension to the premiership of France stunned political pundits because he was unknown to the public at large and, in fact, had never been elected to office. The National Assembly, jealous over its preroga-

tives in choosing prime ministers, also considered Pompidou's appointment a snub from the general and passed a vote of "no confidence." De Gaulle angrily responded by dissolving parlement and calling for new elections that his party, the Gaullists, won handily. Pompidou thus remained in power and now enjoyed a working majority. For six years he capably handled affairs of state under de Gaulle's looming shadow and worked to establish a permanent political base for the party. He continued modernizing the outdated French economy to the point where it actually outperformed West Germany's. But his greatest contribution to the Fifth Republic came in the wake of the violent student-worker riots of May 1968. A negotiator and conciliator by nature, Pompidou met with strikers and calmly negotiated an end to civil strife. When de Gaulle again dissolved the parlement for new elections, Pompidou became point man for the Gaullist cause, and they swept the election by their largest margin ever. Sensing that he had created a potential rival, de Gaulle suddenly dismissed Pompidou from office and appointed a loyal sycophant. By that time Pompidou had served longer as prime minister than any individual since the mid-19th century.

Pompidou returned to the Chamber of Deputies and bided his time. When de Gaulle angrily resigned over a failed referendum in April 1969, he ran for the presidency and easily triumphed the following July. And while Pompidou's administration shared distinct continuities with his haughty predecessor, his approach to national leadership proved far less strident and imperious. Pompidou reached across the aisles and brought in numerous technocrats from the center and left to better promote harmony and expertise. Unlike de Gaulle, Pompidou was reluctant to allow government intervention in the private sector and wanted French industry to be competitive and stand on its own. Hence corporate welfare was slashed while social benefits for individuals were expanded. In foreign policy, Pompidou made conscious efforts to mend relations with the United States—severely strained under de Gaulle—and formally dropped French opposition to England's entry into the European Common Market. France basically prospered throughout his tenure until the 1971 Arab oil embargo engendered fuel shortages and rising inflation. He raised some controversy by constructing a center of modern technology in the heart of downtown Paris: purists insisted it ruined the city's traditional skyline.

Pompidou was ill toward the end of his time in office and died of cancer in Paris on April 2, 1974. He was succeeded by yet another pragmatic Gaullist, VALÉRY GISCARD D'ESTAING. Pompidou, while less dramatic than de Gaulle, performed far more useful service to the Fifth Republic by establishing political mechanisms necessary for its ultimate survival. In sum, he demonstrated that the Gaullist Party—and the principles it stood for— could flourish without its illustrious founder.

Further Reading

Bernstein, Serge, and Jean-Pierre Rioux. *The Pompidou Years, 1969–1974.* New York: Cambridge University Press, 2000.
Knapp, Andrew. "Perspectives on Pompidou." *Modern and Contemporary France* 3, no. 1 (1995): 68–71.
Ross, Kristin. *May '68 and Its Afterlives.* Chicago: University of Chicago Press, 2002.
Rynning, Sten. *Changing Military Doctrine: Presidents and Military Power in Fifth Republic France, 1958–2000.* Westport, Conn.: Praeger, 2001.
Volkmar, Lauber. *The Political Economy of France: from Pompidou to Mitterrand.* New York: Praeger, 1983.
Wilson, Frank L. "Gaullism without De Gaulle." *Western Political Quarterly* 26, no. 3 (1973): 485–506.

Prasad, Rajendra (1884–1963) *president of India*
Rajendra Prasad was born in Saran District, Bihar State, India, on December 3, 1884, the son of an affluent landowner. He received a classical Hindu upbringing and subsequently attended Presidency College, Calcutta, to study law. Prasad proved adept as an attorney and established successful practices in Calcutta and Patna. However, the turning point in his life occurred in 1917 when the Indian cultural nationalist Mahatma Gandhi arrived in Bihar to promote his policy of noncooperation against the British. Prasad quickly became his disciple and joined the nationalist Indian National Congress Party to agitate for independence. He quit law, served as principal of National College in Bihar, and edited several nationalist newspapers in Hindi and English. Throughout the 1920s he proved Gandhi's staunchest ally in his numerous constructive programs, including the native production of homespun cloth. Prasad was also an astute political operator and by 1934 he had risen to president of the Congress Party. Serious internal struggles

ensued over the next decade as to how best to confront English colonialism, and the Gandhi faction prevailed, largely through Prasad's influence; in 1939 he again served as president. When World War II commenced, he opposed Indian participation and spent the next several years in jail.

By 1946 England was making preparations to free the subcontinent and Prasad was tapped to serve as minister of food and agriculture in the provisional government. In this capacity his slogan of "Grow more food" became a national mantra. After independence arrived in 1947 he assumed the presidency of the constituent assembly and helped draft the new national constitution. The Republic of India was finally founded in 1949 and Prasad became its first president. The Indian presidency is a largely ceremonial post below the prime minister's office, but it is rich in the symbolism of national unity. Prasad drew upon his reputation as an acknowledged Hindu scholar protégé of Gandhi to lend harmony and purpose to proceedings in the otherwise raucous National Assembly. A quiet, self-effacing, and modest individual, he worked closely with the dynamic JAWAHARLAL NEHRU to smooth out the difficulties of the postcolonial period. "Ambitions I have none," he once confided to friends, "except to be of some service to the Motherland." The Indian polity proved fractious and difficult to handle but such was Prasad's reputation that he easily won reelection in 1952 and 1957. He used his office to champion the use of Hindi as a national language and praised the ancient cultural treasures of the vast and diverse Indian people. He was particularly effective as a spokesman for Gandhi's scheme for basic, universal education for all Indians. However, Prasad's underlying conservatism made him somewhat uneasy with the drive toward modernization, and he invariably acted as a moderating influence on most policies.

Having led the assembly for 12 years, Prasad retired in 1962. The unexpected death of his wife and a serious military defeat by Chinese forces in a border confrontation that year severely compromised his physical well-being. Prasad died in Patna on February 28, 1963, a beloved national leader and the embodiment of Gandhian principles. In light of his scholarly achievements and impeccable personal honesty, Nehru eulogized him as having "truth looking at you through his eyes."

Further Reading

Cavaliero, Roderick. *Strangers in the Land: The Rise and Decline of the British Indian Empire.* London: I. B. Tauris, 2002.

Chakrabarti, Anjan. *Transition and Development in India.* New York: Routledge, 2003.

Copeland, Ian. *The Princes of India in the Endgame of Empire, 1917–1947.* Cambridge: Cambridge University Press, 2002.

Mcleod, John. *The History of India.* Westport, Conn.: Greenwood Press, 2002.

Nanda B. R. *Pan-Islamism, Imperialism and Nationalism in India.* Oxford: Oxford University Press, 2002.

Panjab, Kewalram L. *Rajendra Prasad, First President of India.* New York: St. Martin's Press, 1960.

Prasad, Rajendra. *At the Feet of Mahatma Gandhi.* New York: Asia Pub. House, 1961.

Price, George (1919–) *prime minister of Belize*

George Cadle Price was born in Belize City, British Honduras, on January 15, 1919, the son of an auctioneer. Of half-Mayan, half-Scottish descent, he attended Catholic schools and was admitted to St. Augustine's College, Mississippi, in 1936 to study for the priesthood. After a brief stint at the Guatemalan National Seminary in 1941, he returned home to attend to his sick father. Price then left the clergy to serve as a secretary to a Creole millionaire and acquired a taste for politics. He failed in his first bid for a seat on the Belize Town Board in 1943 but subsequently won it two years later. Price expressed little interest in colonial affairs until 1950, when the British arbitrarily devalued the national currency in a move that distressed consumers and workers. He then founded the People's United Party (PUP) that year and began agitating for independence. Over the next few years he successively served as general secretary and party leader while the PUP swept the colonial legislature. In 1956 Price ventured to London for discussions about British Honduras, but when it was learned he had consulted with representatives of the Guatemalan government, he was arrested and charged with sedition. Price was subsequently acquitted, and the English authorized a new constitution allowing for greater self-governance in 1961. When PUP again swept the elections, Price returned to London for further discussions and was allowed to become the colony's first prime minister on

January 1, 1964. He remained determined to pursue independence, but for the time being the colony was preoccupied with a sagging economy and military threats from Guatemala. That nation had always considered the region part of its own territory and illegally expropriated by the British. Years of negotiations followed without a resolution and tensions increased when Britain announced that it would withdraw all military forces following independence. Events unfolded slowly and it was not until 1973 that the colony formally adopted the new name Belize, a word of Mayan extraction. Despite continuing tensions with Guatemala, Belize became a country within the framework of the British Commonwealth on September 21, 1981.

With independence won, Price continued on as prime minister. His PUP now faced stiff opposition from the more conservative United Democratic Party (UDP), which represented business interests. Over the next three years the government weathered internal party dissent over leftist policies and a general economic downturn. By 1984 voters deemed the time right for a change and they defeated the PUP so thoroughly that even Price lost his seat in Parliament—his first election loss in 37 years. The UDP's Manuel Esquivel then occupied the premiership while Price, reduced to party head, gradually rebuilt his base over the next five years. When the UDP failed to demonstrably improve the national economy by 1989, the PUP was restored to power by a two-seat majority and Price resumed high office again. By this time the PUP had moderated its socialist economic policies and was more attuned to free trade. An important exception was foreign investment, which Price curtailed in favor of smaller-scale investment by native Belizeans.

Price enjoyed considerable success for the ensuing four years and in the spring of 1993 he capped his good fortune by winning two landslide victories in local and national elections. He tried to further consolidate his power by calling a third snap election in July, just as international events intervened. That May a military coup in Guatemala elevated fears of possible armed intervention again and Britain finalized its decision to withdraw for good. The UDP then campaigned on a promise to suspend the Maritimes Areas Act, which granted Guatemala use of Belizean territory, and it defeated the PUP again on June 30, 1994. Price was reduced to head of the opposition in Parliament, and in

October 1996 he surrendered control of the party to the much younger Said Musa. He has since retired to private life, having dominated national politics for four decades. Price is still regarded as the driving force behind Belizean nationhood.

Further Reading

Benske, John L. "George Price and Belize: The Creation of a Nation." Unpublished master's thesis, University of Florida, 1990.

Bolland, O. Nigel. *Belize: A New Nation in Central America.* Boulder, Colo.: Westview Press, 1986.

Fernandez, Julio A. *Belize: Case Study for Democracy in Central America.* Brookfield, Vt.: Avebury, 1989.

Payne, A. "The Belize Triangle: Relations with Britain, Guatemala, and the United States." *Journal of Interamerican Studies and World Affairs* 32 (spring 1990): 119–136.

Philip, G. "Belize: The Troubled Regional Context." *The World Today* 40 (August 1984): 370–376.

Young, Alma H., and Dennis H. Young. "The Impact of the Anglo-Guatemalan Dispute on the Internal Politics of Belize." *Belizean Studies* 18, no. 1 (1990): 11–35.

Qassem, Abdul Karim (1914–1963) *prime minister of Iraq*

Abdul Karim Qassem (or Kassem) was born in Baghdad, Iraq, on November 21, 1914, the son of a poor carpenter. He was educated locally before passing through the Iraqi Military College in 1932. Qassem proved himself a competent soldier, although, like many young officers, he resented the pro-Western bias of the Iraqi royal family and the pervasive British influence they tolerated. He nonetheless served the monarchy well by fighting numerous Kurdish insurrections throughout the 1940s and in 1948 he distinguished himself as a battalion commander in the Arab-Israeli War. Defeat further alienated him from the ruling regime, which he viewed as corrupt and inept. After commanding Iraqi troops in Jordan throughout the 1956 Suez Canal Crisis, he began actively plotting to overthrow the government through a clandestine "Free Officers" movement. His chance arrived in 1958 when anti-Western rioting erupted in Lebanon. Qassem was ordered to take his brigade through Baghdad en route to Jordan, but he suddenly stormed the royal palace, killing King Faisal II and his entire family on July 14, 1958. Qassem then proclaimed the Republic of Iraq with himself holding the portfolios of prime minister and defense minister. He was seconded by his friend

and long-time associate Abdul Salim Arif, who became vice premier.

Coming from a background of poverty, Qassem was acutely concerned about the country's poor and took deliberate steps to ameliorate their suffering. He limited the size of landholdings and encouraged distribution to the landless. Women's rights were expanded in matters pertaining to divorce and inheritance. But his biggest accomplishment was seizing the lands operated by the foreign-dominated Iraq Petroleum Company to further reduce British influence. Such moves naturally made Qassem a national hero to the poorer segments of society. However, he enjoyed less success consolidating his own political base. The Middle East was awash in Pan-Arabic nationalism, best exemplified by the creation of the United Arab Republic (UAR) through the merger of Egypt and Syria under Egyptian president GAMAL ABDEL NASSER. Qassem was under tremendous local pressure to join the UAR but he remained aloof, distrusting Nasser. This earned him the wrath of other Pan-Arabists, and in 1958 he had his deputy leader Arif imprisoned. Qassem's hold on power proved so tenuous that his only political ally proved the small but vocal Communist Party. When a Pan-Arabic revolt erupted in Mosul in 1959, Qassem relied on communist support to help quell it. Once this was accomplished, however, the communists demanded a greater role in government and the formulation of government policy. Qassem refused to share power and ended up outlawing them as well. He was nearly assassinated that same year by the left-wing Ba'ath Socialist Party, which was then persecuted out of the country. Qassem had managed to retain power, but his only base of support was the military. His enemies were further abetted by Nasser, who channeled and supplied arms and money to undermine the government.

Qassem's regime began spiraling downward in the wake of a large Kurdish revolt in 1960. The military proved unable to crush the rebellion, and he sacked many unreliable officers in consequence. He also alienated his regime from other Arab states following the emergence of newly independent Kuwait in 1961. Qassem declared that Kuwait was part of Iraq and threatened to take it by force—which triggered the arrival of British and Arab forces to defend it—and he was forced to back down. By 1962 Qassem was at odds with nearly the entire Iraqi political spectrum including nationalists, communists, and Islamic fundamentalists, who viewed him as insufficiently religious. Even the military, his own source of real power, chafed under his increasing erratic leadership. On February 9, 1963, a coalition of Ba'ath Party members, backed by army units, stormed Baghdad, captured Qassem, and executed him. Though his five-year regime was considered a failure, it expunged the last vestiges of Western influence from Iraq.

Further Reading

Dann, Uriel. *Iraq under Qassem: A Political History, 1958–1963.* New York: Praeger, 1969.

Davis, Eric. *Memoirs of State: Politics, History, and Collective Identity in Modern Iraq.* Berkeley: University of California Press, 2004.

Elliot, Matthew. *'Independent Iraq': The Monarchy and British Influence, 1941–1958.* New York: Tauris Academic Studies, 1996.

Farouk-Sluglett, Marion, and Peter Sluglett. *Iraq since 1958: From Revolution to Dictatorship.* New York: I. B. Tauris, 2001.

Haj, Samira. *The Making of Iraq, 1900–1963: Capital, Power, and Ideology.* Albany, N.Y.: State University of New York Press, 1997.

Yousif, Bassam Y. "Development and Political Violence in Iraq, 1950–1990." Unpublished Ph.D. diss., University of California–Riverside, 2001.

Quadros, Jânio (1917–1992) *president of Brazil*

Jânio da Silva Quadros was born in Campo Grande, Mato Grosso, Brazil, on January 25, 1917, the son of a doctor. His family relocated to São Paulo when he was an infant, and he attended local schools. Quadros graduated from the University of São Paulo in 1939 with a degree in law, and he subsequently joined the small Christian Democratic Party. He commenced his political career by being elected to the city council of São Paulo in 1948 and rose successively to the major's office by 1953. Quadros, a rather quixotic, unpredictable individual, made clear his intention to promote honest, efficient government, and followed through on his promises. In 1954 he crowned his local success by becoming governor of São Paulo state. Again, he assured the electorate of responsible government and fulfilled his pledge by streamlining the bureaucracy, cutting expenditures, and assisting the poor majority. Like many populists, he sought a redistribution of national wealth but differed from leftists by shying away from radical politics. Instead he sought to enrich the electorate through hard work, intelligent planning, and equal opportunity. In time he acquired a reputation as one of Brazil's most accomplished political figures and in 1959 he announced his candidacy for the national congress. Quadros was elected there by a landslide, and within a year, his popularity induced him to run for president under the União Democrática Nacional (UPD), Democratic National Union, banner. He toured and campaigned throughout the country carrying a broom, symbolizing his determination to "sweep clean" national politics. His message resonated strongly with the electorate, and in 1960 he was elected president by 48 percent of votes cast—the largest tally ever garnered by a Brazilian presidential candidate. He was also the nation's youngest executive and the first to be sworn into office in the glittering new capital of Brasília.

The Brazilian electorate had high expectations for Quadros and his administration. His predecessor, JUSCELINO KUBITSCHEK, had embarked on a national spending spree to upgrade the country's infrastructure, which expanded the national debt and brought inflation rates of 500 percent. Quadros responded in his usual, no-nonsense manner by cutting expenditures, reducing the bloated bureaucracy, and imposing extreme fiscal austerity on Brazil. He also embarked on an independent-minded foreign policy to lessen what he called Brazil's overwhelming dependency on the United States. Consequently, he drew closer to developing countries while establishing relations with the Soviet Union and China. He further alienated conservative interests at home by voicing support for Fidel Castro's Communist Cuba and by awarding Cuban finance minister Che Guevara, the future Marxist guerrilla, with a medal. He also banned bikini contests and outlawed cockfighting and advertising in movie theaters. Other dramatic moves were pending, but Quadros quickly ran afoul of entrenched interests in congress that managed to block his initiatives. Not to be upstaged, he suddenly and unexpectedly announced his resignation on August 24, 1961, after only seven months in office. Quadros apparently viewed himself as the indispensable man and waited for congress to call him back, but it did not happen. Instead he was succeeded by his vice president, leftist João Goulart, who led the country on an unprecedented flirtation with socialism. By 1964 the country and the economy were in chaos, and the military tossed out the civilian regime. Quadros then found himself deprived of civil rights and sent off into exile. Political pundits remain at a loss to fathom exactly why he left office when he did, but they also concur it set the stage for more than two decades of military rule. Quadros remained abroad until 1980, when he was recalled under a general amnesty. Once back he ran for the governorship of São Paulo and lost. He enjoyed better luck in being elected mayor of São Paulo in 1985. He died there on January 16, 1992, a quirky, if well-intentioned, populist and one of the more indecipherable figures of modern Brazilian politics.

Further Reading

Cohen, Youssef. *Radicals, Reformers, and Reactionaries: The Prisoner's Dilemma and the Collapse of Democracy in Latin America.* Chicago: University of Chicago Press, 1994.

Dulles, John W. F. *Unrest in Brazil: Political-Military Crises 1955–1964.* Austin: University of Texas Press, 1970.

Johnson, Ollie A. *Brazilian Party Politics and the Coup of 1964.* Gainesville: University Press of Florida, 2001.

Prado, Ney. "The Effects on the Brazilian Political System of the Resignation of President Jânio Quadros in 1961." Unpublished master's thesis, Marquette University, 1971.

Parker, Phyllis R. *Brazil and the Quiet Intervention, 1964.* Austin: University of Texas Press, 1979.

Sikkink, Kathryn. *Ideas and Institutions: Developmentalism in Brazil and Argentina.* Ithaca, N.Y.: Cornell University Press, 1991.

Quezon, Manuel (1878–1944) *president of the Philippines*

Manuel Luis Quezon was born in Baler, Tayabas Province, Philippines, on August 19, 1878, the son of schoolteachers. He was studying law at the University of Santo Tomas in 1898 when the Spanish-American War resulted in a complete victory for the United States and acquisition of the Philippines. However, the following year he joined rebel forces under Emilio Aguinaldo to resist American occupation and was forced to surrender in 1902. After six months' imprisonment, Quezon resumed his legal studies and graduated with honors in 1903. Quezon had the makings of a talented politician, and he was determined to rid his country of foreign interference. But because he realized that more ground could be covered by cooperating with the United States than opposing it, he sought to master the nuances of colonial politics. After being elected governor of Tayabas in 1905 he successfully stood for a seat in the newly constituted Philippine Assembly. In 1907 he joined political adversary Sergio Osmena in founding the Nationalist Party, which dominated Filipino politics for decades to come. Two years later Quezon ventured to Washington, D.C., as a nonvoting member of the U.S. House of Representatives, where he stridently advocated Philippine independence. He proved instrumental in passage of the 1916 Jones Act, whereby the Philippines acquired a bicameral legislature, greater autonomy, and a promise of eventual freedom. The following year Quezon returned home a national hero and was overwhelmingly elected to the new senate. Within months he was president of the senate, the highest office to which native-born Filipinos could aspire.

Over the next 15 years Quezon used his influence to accelerate the drive for independence. Furthermore he resented the patronizing attitude of the United States toward "their little brown brothers" and once declared he preferred "a government run like Hell by Filipinos to one run like heaven by Americans." By 1934 his machinations resulted in passage of the Tydings-McDuffie Act, which established a definitive timetable for self-governance within 10 years. The new bill also established the Commonwealth of the Philippines and on September 17, 1935, Quezon was formally elected the first president. In this capacity he took active measures to promote land reform for the nation's poor majority and improved the legal status of women. He also waged a long battle against governmental corruption and encouraged settlement of the largely unoccupied southern island of Mindanao. Unfortunately, because this province was predominantly Muslim and the new arrivals largely Christian, his policy planted the seeds of a Muslim separatist movement that persists to the present. Quezon was also acutely aware of the rising tide of Japanese militarism in the Pacific and their designs on the Philippine homeland. He therefore solicited the support of American general Douglas MacArthur as commander in chief of the new national military and assigned him to prepare the island's defenses. To further shore up his own position, he also passed measures that greatly strengthened the office of the presidency at the expense of an already rubber-stamp legislature. The Emergency Powers Bill passed in August 1940 granted him near dictatorial powers with the power to outlaw strikes, commandeer vehicles, and conscript civilians into government service. Quezon's presidency, while not quite a dictatorship, was perilously close to one and established precedents for strong, centralized authority.

When the Japanese attacked the Philippines in December 1941, Quezon rallied behind the Americans and urged his countrymen to resist. He stayed in the islands as long as he could, and left his homeland only after an appeal by American president FRANKLIN D. ROOSEVELT. Quezon then led a government in exile until he died of tuberculosis at Saranac Lake, New York, on August 1, 1944. He thus failed to see his labors come to fruition in 1946 when the Philippines finally became independent from the United States. Quezon is still heralded as the father of his country and a master at dealing from a position of weakness.

Further Reading

Goettel, Elinor. *Eagle of the Philippines.* New York: J. Messner, 1970.

Meixsel, Richard B. "Manuel L. Quezon, Douglas MacArthur, and the Significance of the Military Mission to the Philippine Commonwealth." *Pacific Historical Review* 70, no. 2 (2001): 255–292.

Petillo, Carol. "Douglas MacArthur and Manuel Quezon: A Note on the Imperial Bond." *Pacific Historical Review* 48, no. 1 (1979): 407–417.

Quezon, Manuel L. *The Good Fight.* New York: Appleton-Century, 1946.

Tarling, Nicholas. "Quezon and the British Commonwealth." *Australian Journal of Politics and History* 23 (August 1977): 182–206.

Quirino, Elpidio (1890–1956) *president of the Philippines*

Elpidio Quirino was born in Vigan, Ilocos Sur Province, the Philippines, on November 16, 1890, the son of a jail warden and former Spanish soldier. He graduated from the University of the Philippines with a law degree in 1915 and served in the newly constituted Senate as secretary to MANUEL QUEZON. Quirino commenced his own political career in 1919 by winning a seat in the House of Representatives, and four years later joined Quezon in the Senate. He chaired several important committees, gained reelection in 1931, and became closely identified as an ally of the Quezon faction within the Nationalist Party. In 1934 Quirino accompanied Quezon to Washington, D.C., and helped hammer out details of the Tydings-McDuffie Act, which guaranteed Filipino independence in 1946. Thereafter Quirino functioned as secretary of finance and also helped draft the new constitution in anticipation of independence from the United States. Once the Philippine Commonwealth was realized in November 1935, he served consecutively as minister of finance and of the interior. However, when the Pacific War broke out and Japan conquered the Philippines in 1942, he quit politics to serve with the underground resistance. Quirino was captured and brutally interned, while his wife and three children were executed by the enemy. After the war concluded in 1945 Quirino resumed his Senate seat, serving now as president pro tempore. The newly independent Philippine Republic emerged the following year, and he became vice president under President MANUEL ROXAS of the Liberal Party.

For two years into the Roxas administration Quirino also fulfilled duties as secretary of foreign affairs. Here he became a vocal proponent of close relations with the United States and was the recipient of loans, low tariffs, and other useful amenities. When Roxas died in office on April 15, 1948, Quirino succeeded him constitutionally and the following year was elected executive officer—becoming the second president of the independent Philippines. Many questions were raised, however, as to the honesty of the actual election. But once in power Quirino pursued policies that rendered him the father of national industrialization. He succeeded in establishing many factories that boosted employment levels and gave the country its first industrial infrastructure. Through tight, cost-cutting measures he also managed to stabilize the peso and balance the budget. Unfortunately, Quirino proved less adept at addressing deep-seated inequities in land distribution and wealth, especially in remote rural areas. This gross disparity, mostly in the south, was a leading factor in the outbreak of the so-called Hukbalahap (or "Huk") rebellion, a communist-inspired insurgency. The fighting was accompanied by the rise of terrorism, demoralization, and economic paralysis. To buy time for his administration and promote peace, he authorized a blanket amnesty toward the rebels in June 1948, but fighting resumed with renewed intensity. To prevent the crisis from spreading, Quirino appointed RAMON MAGSAYSAY defense secretary to quell the uprising. This was accomplished after much violence and the lure of agrarian reform. But Quirino ignored the incipient corruption present in Filipino society, and he initiated no moves against vested interests. This ethical lapse greatly angered Magsaysay, who broke from the Liberals to run against Quirino in 1953. Quirino was roundly defeated and retired to private life. He died at Novaliches on February 28, 1956, having overseen an important period of postwar reconstruction and economic prosperity. He was an early proponent of national independence but unable to surmount the entrenched corruption accompanying it.

Further Reading

Gleeck, Lewis R. *Dissolving the Colonial Bond: American Ambassadors to the Philippines, 1946–1984.* Denver, Colo.: iAcademic Books, 2001.

Goldman, R. M., and H. Pasqual. "NAMFREL: Spotlight for Democracy." *World Affairs* 150 (spring 1988): 223–232.

Kerkviet, Benedict J. *The Huk Rebellion: A Study of Peasant Revolt in the Philippines.* Berkeley: University of California Press, 1977.

Kesavan, K. V. "The Attitude of the Philippines towards the Japanese Peace Treaty." *International Studies* 12, no. 2 (1973): 222–250.

McFerson, Hazel M., ed. *Mixed Blessing: The Impact of the American Colonial Experience on Politics and Society in the Philippines.* Westport, Conn.: Greenwood Press, 2002.

Quirino, Isabel P. "A Political Biography of Elpidio Quirino: Second President of the Republic of the Philippines, 1948–1953." Unpublished master's thesis, University of Cincinnati, 1968.

Elpidio Quirino *(Library of Congress)*

Quisling, Vidkun (1887–1945) *prime minister of Norway*

Vidkun Abraham Lauritz Jonsson Quisling was born in Fryesdal, Norway, on July 18, 1887, the son of a Lutheran minister. He was an exceptionally bright student and graduated with such high grades from the Norwegian Military Academy that he received an audience with the king. Once commissioned in the artillery, Quisling commenced his career as military attaché in Petrograd after the Russian revolution. He was initially very sympathetic to communism, although his views evolved over time. Quisling was actively involved in relief efforts through the League of Nations and also performed similar work in Finland. For his efforts in facilitating British-Soviet detente he received a medal from the British government. But by the time he left the Soviet Union in 1928, Quisling was especially suspicious of communists and labor activists in general. He returned home as part of the mainstream Agrarian Party and in 1931 he gained appointment as minister of defense. In this capacity he railed against communists and labor unionists, using troops to break up a strike by hydroelectric workers. Quisling also experienced difficulty getting along with fellow ministers, so he was dismissed from office in 1933 by his own prime minister. Shortly thereafter he founded his own political movement, the Nasjonal Samling (NS), National Union Party, patterned closely after ADOLF HITLER's National Socialist (Nazi) Party. Not surprisingly this was a fanatically right-wing organization extolling the virtues of nation, family, and Nordic heritage—and quite outside the mainstream of Norwegian politics. Consequently, the NS performed poorly at the polls, never acquiring more than 2 percent of the national vote. Quisling's effort would have faded altogether had it not received timely subsidies from the Germans. Nonetheless, he met with Hitler in December 1939 and did everything in his power to convince him of his ability to lead Norway. He also welcomed direct Nazi intervention.

On April 9, 1940, German forces violated Norwegian neutrality and attacked, conquering the country. National defenses were quickly overrun based upon information received beforehand, but the degree of Quisling's complicity has never been established. Nonetheless the government fled and Quisling took to the airwaves to encourage capitulation. He also declared himself the new national leader, despite the fact he had never held elected office. But when the Germans failed to cater to his fantasies he was dismissed from power within a week. Quisling continued portraying himself as a legitimate head of state, and eventually Hitler realized that he might prove himself a useful tool, if closely watched. Therefore, in September 1940 Quisling was installed as "head of state" under Nazi reichskommissar Josef Terboven. In April 1942 he was elevated to the post of prime minister while the NS became the only legitimate party. If through these expedients the Germans hoped to rally the Norwegian people behind the Nazi war effort they sadly miscalculated, for Quisling became a hated symbol of treason and collaboration, and the butt of public humor—his presence hindered German efforts far more than it helped.

True to his extreme racial beliefs, Quisling was a rabid anti-Semite, and he determined to eliminate Norway's small community of Jews. He assisted the Germans in rounding up and deporting nearly 1,000 Jewish Norwegians and suspected communist sympathizers to the death camps. He also turned a blind eye to the barbarities of Nazi occupation toward civilians. By the time Germany had lost the war in May 1945, Quisling was a marked man. He was arrested by the resistance and interned at Akershus Fortress in Oslo. Quisling was then summarily tried for treason and murder, condemned to death, and executed by firing squad on October 24, 1945. His name has since passed into the political lexicon as synonymous with the word traitor.

Further Reading

Dahl, Hans F. *Quisling: A Study in Treachery.* New York: Cambridge University Press, 1999.

Hoidal, Oddvar K. *Quisling: A Study in Treason.* Oslo: Norwegian University Press, 1989.

Olson, Jeffery T. "Fascism in Norway: 1919–1937." Unpublished master's thesis, University of Idaho, 1999.

Quisling, Vidkun. *Russia and Ourselves.* London: Hodder and Stoughton, 1931.

Theien, Iselin. "Norwegian Fascism, 1933–40: The Position of the Nasjonal Samling in Norwegian Politics." Unpublished Ph.D. diss., University of Oxford, 2000.

R

Raab, Julius (1891–1964) *chancellor of Austria*
Julius Raab was born in St. Pölten, Austria-Hungary, on November 29, 1891, the son of a prosperous craftsman. He received a strict Catholic upbringing and attended the Technical University in Vienna until his studies were interrupted by World War I. Raab successfully completed his tour of military service before returning to a greatly reduced Austrian republic. He finished his studies and became politically active within the conservative Christian Social Party. In 1927 he was elected to the Nationalrat (legislature) and also commanded right-wing paramilitary units (Heimwehr) associated with his party. After 1933 Raab supported the Fatherland Front of ENGLEBERT DOLLFUSS, which banned all political parties in an attempt to curb Nazi influence in Austria. Raab served the government well and in 1938 he was promoted to minister of commerce. That same year German chancellor ADOLF HITLER annexed Austria in the *Anschluss,* and Raab, correctly fearing the worst, abandoned politics in favor of the construction industry. Consequently, by the end of World War II he was untainted by any prior association with Nazism and in 1945 was allowed to join the postwar reconstruction government under KARL RENNER. In this capacity he helped to found a new conservative organization, the Österreichische Volkspartei (OVP), Austrian People's Party. The following year he was appointed president of the new federal Chamber of Commerce and pioneered the notion of "social partnership" between business and employees.

Raab's good overall performance did not escape the attention of party elders and in 1951 he was elected chairman of the OVP. Two years later he became chancellor of Austria under a coalition government with the leftist Sozialdemokratische Partei Österreichs (SPO), Social Democratic Party. This marked a distinct departure from traditional Austrian politics, for the two parties had been implacable enemies and even resorted to civil war in 1933. Raab, as Austria's greatest exponent of compromise and reconciliation, managed to cobble together progressive alliances based on consensus. Both parties now pursued such diverse policies as full employment, generous welfare benefits, and currency stabilization. The result was a decade of political harmony and economic growth essential for Austria's postwar recovery. Despite his conservative leanings, Raab was able to strike up formal relations with the Soviet Union. This was essential, for Austria had been divided up and occupied by Russia and the three Western allies since 1945. Raab entered into intense negotiations with Soviet premier NIKITA KHRUSHCHEV to regain Austrian sovereignty. In May 1955 he signed the famous State Treaty whereby the four powers departed Austria in exchange for a pledge of neutrality. This event marked a considerable diffusion of cold war tensions and culminated in the Vienna Summit of July 1956. Raab's consummate diplomacy also made him a national hero. The OVP consequently swept national elections held in 1956.

Despite his victory, Raab hewed close to his course of cooperation with the rival SPO to promote political stability and national reconciliation. However, his health and political fortunes declined rapidly following a heart attack in 1959. Another major failing was his inability to adjust to the new medium of television, where his autocratic demeanor came across as old-fashioned. But it was his intractable stubbornness that did him in. When he insisted on maintaining his "grand coalition" in the face of mounting party criticism, he was removed as party leader in 1961 and replaced as chancellor the following year. He then resumed leadership of the federal Chamber of Commerce but lost a bid to win the largely ceremonial office of president in 1963. Raab died on January 8, 1964, the architect of Austria's impressive postwar recovery and its reentry into the community of sovereign nations. He remains one of the most prominent—and pragmatic—leaders of the cold war period.

Further Reading

Bischof, Gunter. *Austria in the First Cold War, 1945–55: The Leverage of the Weak.* New York: St. Martin's Press, 1999.

Bischof, Gunter and Anton Pelinka, eds. *Austria in the Nineteen Fifties.* New Brunswick, N.J.: Transaction Publishers, 1995.

Bischof, Gunter, and Sakai Dockrill, eds. *Cold War Respite: The Geneva Summit, July 1955.* Baton Rouge: Louisiana State University Press, 1998.

Bruckmuller, Ernst. *The Austrian Nation: Cultural Consciousness and Socio-Political Processes.* Riverside, Calif.: Ariade Press, 2002.

Carafano, James Joy. *Waltzing into the Cold War: The Struggle for Occupied Austria.* College Station: Texas A & M University Press, 2002.

Utgaard, Peter. *Remembering and Forgetting Nazism: Education, National Identity, and the Victim Myth in Postwar Austria.* New York: Berghahn Books, 2002.

Rahman, Abdul (1903–1990) *prime minister of Malaysia*

Tunku (Prince) Abdul Rahman was born in Alor Setar, Kedah, Malaya, on February 3, 1903, one of 47 children born to the sultan of Setar. His country was then a British colony. Rahman was educated locally before attending Cambridge University in England, where he acquired the reputation of a sports-minded socializer. He came home in 1949 to work in the Setar civil service. He briefly returned to England in 1949 and was called to the bar, then settled in as a deputy public prosecutor with the Malay Federal Legal Department. Rahman commenced his political career in 1951 by being elected head of the United Malay National Organization (UMNO), an ethnically oriented organization designed to advance political interests of the Malay majority. This was viewed as essential, for British colonial administrators had brought in large numbers of Chinese and Indian laborers and frequently favored them with political appointments. However, Rahman, given his eclectic upbringing, was much more given to racial toleration and compromise. As the movement for independence from Great Britain gathered momentum, he forged a communal alliance between various Chinese and Indian parties to present a united front against colonialism. Consequently, in 1955 his new Alliance Party swept the national elections and Britain announced its decision to withdraw from the region. When Malaya gained its independence on August 31, 1957, Rahman—more popularly known as the Tunku—became the nation's first prime minister.

Rahman's first priority as leader was continuation of a communist-based insurgency, which was finally suppressed with the aid of British and Australian forces in 1960. Thereafter, he sought to promote greater regional stability by proposing a new political federation between Malaya, Singapore, North Borneo, and Sarawak. Consequently, the new nation of Malaysia emerged on September 16, 1963, with Rahman as prime minister. But despite his best efforts ethnic tensions continued, especially on the Chinese-dominated island of Singapore under LEE KUAN YEW. After a tense, two-year standoff, Rahman formally evicted Singapore from the federation. In the process of political consolidation, he also had to weather a political confrontation with SUKARNO's Indonesia, which also opposed the union, but the impasse concluded peacefully. For many years thereafter, Rahman openly described himself as the "world's happiest prime minister."

Malaysia was, on the surface, an industrious and prosperous amalgamation of many ethnic and religious groupings, but in May 1969 continuing friction between Malays and Chinese exploded into street violence. The ensuing riots took some lives and caused great damage before Rahman declared a state of emergency and suspended the constitution. Once peace was restored he was accused by fellow Malays of playing to the Chinese at Malay expense and he concluded 13 years of national leadership by resigning in September 1970. Thereafter Rahman served as a respected elder statesman and wrote a weekly column for the newspapers. In 1987, despite poor health that necessitated the use of a wheelchair, the former prime minister took to the streets to protest the growing authoritarianism of Malaysia's new leader, Datuk Seri Mahathir bin Mohamad. He continued writing columns until his death in Kuala Lumpur on December 6, 1990. The Tunku is still fondly remembered as the father of his country and an agent of ethnic and religious tolerance.

Further Reading

Case, William. "Comparing Malaysian Leadership: Tunku Abdul Rahman and Mahathir Mohammad." *Asian Survey* 31 (May 1991): 456–473.

Easter, David. "British and Malaysian Covert Support for Rebel Movements in Indonesia during the 'Confederation', 1963–66." *Intelligence and National Security* 14, no. 4 (1999): 195–208.

Healy, Allan M. *Tunku Abdul Rahman.* New York: University of Queensland Press, 1982.

Lim, Joan A. "A Study of Lee Kuan Yew, Prime Minister of Singapore, and Tengu Abdul Rahman, Former Prime Minister of Malaysia, Utilizing a Personality Theory Approach." Unpublished master's thesis, Western Michigan University, 1982.

Shome, Anthony S. K. *Malay Political Leadership.* New York: Routledge, 2002.

Stubbs, Richard. *Hearts and Minds in Guerrilla Warfare: The Malayan Emergency, 1948–1960.* New York: Oxford University Press, 1989.

Zukifi, Abdul-Hamid. "A Rhetorical Analysis of the Selected Speeches of Tunku Abdul Rahman Putra on the Issues of Independence for Malaysia, 1951–1957." Unpublished Ph.D. diss., Ohio University, 1986.

Rahman, Mujibur (1920–1975) *prime minister of Bangladesh*

Sheikh Mujibur Rahman was born on March 17, 1920, in Tungipara, India, the son of a small landowner. Though a Muslim, he attended Christian missionary schools and ultimately attended Islamia College in Calcutta and the University of Dacca in Bengal. However, Rahman gained renown as a youthful political activist and was arrested repeatedly for anti-British agitation. He was initially a supporter of MOHAMMED ALI JINNAH, who sought to maintain Hindu-Muslim solidarity while opposing colonialism. In 1947 the subcontinent was finally partitioned into Hindu-dominated India and Muslim-dominated Pakistan, which consisted of two distinct entities, East and West Pakistan. These were separated by 1,000 miles of Indian territory and each region possessed distinct cultural and linguistic differences. Basically, the West was controlled by Urdu-speaking Punjabis while the East had a majority Bengali population. However, when it became evident that the Punjabis were determined to dominate both halves of the nation, Rahman helped found the Awami League in 1949, the nation's first opposition party, to seek greater rights for Bengalis. In 1954 he was elected to the East Pakistan legislature where his strident insistence on autonomy landed him in jail. The following year he entered the national Pakistani legislature and continued his protests. When General MOHAMMAD AYUB KHAN toppled the civilian regime in 1958, he had Rahman arrested as a threat to national stability. But immediately after his release the following year he resumed his campaign for East Pakistan's autonomy.

The notion of East Pakistani independence first emerged in the wake of the 1965 war with India, when West Pakistan failed to adequately protect it. The following year Rahman unveiled a six-point plan to place Pakistan under a federal arrangement whereby the Bengalis would have a free hand at maintaining their own interests. Ayub Khan responded by arresting him again. The turning point in Punjabi-Bengali relations occurred in the fall of 1970 when a tremendous cyclone ravaged East Pakistan, killing nearly 1 million people. The Pakistani government failed to mount adequate relief efforts and Rahman and others demanded a new round of regional elections. These were completely swept by the Awami League and its allies, granting them a majority in the national legislature. But the central government, under General Yahya Khan and ZULFIKAR ALI BHUTTO, refused to seat the legislature and allow Rahman to form a government. Rahman then angrily proclaimed a declaration of independence on March 23, 1971, and he was arrested again. This act triggered open warfare and millions of Bengali refugees consequently fled to India. On December 3, 1971, the Indian government under INDIRA GANDHI declared war on Pakistan, and 10 days later the war ended in a complete defeat for Pakistan. The new state of Bangladesh then emerged, and Rahman was released from prison to lead it in January 1972.

Rahman quickly prevailed upon his countrymen to adopt a parliamentary system with himself as prime minister. In this capacity he embarked on a socialist style of leadership, nationalizing large segments of the economy. But as Bangladesh was one of the world's poorest nations, he was dependent upon food from outside sources like the United States. Over the next four years little progress was made to alleviate national misery, and Rahman decided he needed a strong form of government to enact policies. In January 1975 he ignored mounting protests and had parliament adopt constitutional changes that made him president with dictatorial powers. When famine and poverty continued to increase, so too did opposition to the government. Rahman and his family were subsequently killed in a coup staged by disgruntled army officers on August 15, 1975. He had failed to alleviate Bangladesh's overwhelming social problems, but he is still considered the architect of national independence. In 1996 his daughter, Hasina Wazed, led the Awami party to victory and became the nation's first female prime minister.

Further Reading

Ahamed, Emajuddin. "The Coup of 1975 against Sheikh Mujib of Bangladesh." *Journal of South Asian and Middle Eastern Studies* 13, no. 3 (1990): 63–80.

Ahmed, Rafiuddin. *Religion, Identity & Politics: Essays on Bangladesh.* Colorado Springs, Colo.: International Academic Publishers, 2001.

Dhan, Z. R. "Leadership Parties and Politics in Bangladesh." *Western Political Quarterly* 29 (March 1976): 102–125.

Kabir, Bhuian. *Politics of Military Rule and the Dilemma of Democratization in Bangladesh.* Denver, Colo.: iAcademic Books, 2000.

Kabir, Muhammad G. *Changing Face of Nationalism: The Case of Bangladesh.* Denver, Colo.: iAcademic Books, 2001.

Ziring, Lawrence. *Bangladesh: From Mujib to Ershad: An Interpretive Study.* New York: Oxford University Press, 1993.

Rahman, Ziaur (1936–1981) *prime minister of Bangladesh*

Ziaur Rahman was born in Bogra, East Bengal, India, on January 19, 1936, the son of an Indian Muslim chemist. In 1947 the British partitioned the subcontinent into Hindu India and Muslim East and West Pakistan. Rahman was well educated by local standards and subsequently passed through the Pakistan Military Academy in 1955. He served throughout the presidency of MOHAMMED AYUB KHAN and in 1965 won plaudits commanding units during the First Indo-Pakistani War. Rahman later headed the Pakistan Military Academy and proved instrumental in raising several Bengali formations for the army. However, like many Bengalis, he was distressed by the favoritism shown to West Pakistani officers and the contempt displayed toward East Pakistan in general. On March 24, 1971, Rahman was alerted of a West Pakistani plot to disarm and arrest his fellow Bengali officers so, to preempt them, he seized Chittagong and declared independence for the new nation of Bangladesh. After several months of fighting and military assistance from Indian prime minister INDIRA GANDHI, Bangladesh won its freedom on December 16, 1971. Sheik MUJIBUR RAHMAN was then installed as the first president while Ziaur Rahman became deputy chief of staff of the military with a rank of major general. He functioned in this capacity until his superior was assassinated in August 1975 and Khandakar Mushtaq Ahmed became president. Rahman was then named full chief of staff but he was imprisoned in a countercoup in November 1975. After a few days he was freed and placed in command of a committee that ruled Bangladesh under martial law. Rahman then ran for the presidency in a popular referendum in April 1977, and the following June was formally made chief executive through free elections. In September 1977 Rahman also founded the Bangladesh National Party (BNP) to counter the influence of Mujibur Rahman's Awami League. However, in November 1977 there was a coup attempt against him, and Rahman turned his back on promised democratic reforms. Upward of 15,000 political prisoners were incarcerated. In 1979 Rahman finally resigned from the military to better emphasize the civilian nature of his regime.

Rahman inherited a nation beset by terrible social and economic problems. Bangladesh is the world's most densely populated region and among its poorest. Famine and disease were usually rampant, and economic growth was undermined by a small industrial base. To initiate change Rahman conceived two modernization campaigns for family planning and agricultural development. He had hoped to achieve zero population growth and self-sufficiency in food within a few years, unrealistic given the extent of national malaise. Similar efforts were made in rural development and creation of a South Asia Regional Cooperation organization. Rahman next sought to extend his contacts through the Muslim world by involving himself in several Islamic organizations and attempting to mediate the war between Iran and Iraq. His efforts were rewarded by 1977 when relations with Pakistan improved and Bangladesh was admitted to the United Nations. But despite his sometimes arbitrary rule, Rahman proved himself a charismatic leader and he enjoyed a good deal of political support, particularly from the countryside. Opponents in the Awami League, unfortunately, continued charging him with flouting constitutional rule and tolerating corruption among his supporters. In concert with high-ranking military officer, they began drawing their plans against him.

On may 31, 1981, a group of officers under General Muhammed Abul Manzoor assassinated Rahman in Chittagong. After several months of turmoil and infighting, order was restored by General HUSSEIN MOHAMMAD ERSHAD. Rahman, meanwhile, received a state funeral in Dacca in testimony to his brief but formative role in the history of the nation. His popularity with average Bangladeshis was demonstrated by the hundreds of thousands of mourners that accompanied his funeral procession.

Further Reading

Ahmed, Rafiuddin. *Religion, Identity and Politics: Essays on Bangladesh.* Colorado Springs, Colo.: International Academic Publishers, 2001.

Franda, Marcus F. *Bangladesh Nationalism and Ziaur Rahman's Presidency,* 2 vols. Hanover, N.H.: American Universities Field Staff, 1981.

Islam, Syed Serajul. "The State in Bangladesh under Zia (1975–1981)." *Asian Survey* 24, no. 5 (1984): 556–573.

Seabrook, Jeremy. *Freedom Unfinished: Fundamentalism and Popular Resistance.* New York: Zed Books in association with Dhaka Proshika, 2002.

Zafarullah, Habib M. *The Zia Episode in Bangladesh Politics.* Denver, Colo.: iAcademic Books, 2000.

Zaman, M. Q. "Ziaur Rahman: Leadership Styles and Mobilization Policies." *Indian Political Science Review* 18 (July 1984): 194–203.

Ziring, Lawrence. *Bangladesh: From Mujib to Ershad: An Interpretive Study.* New York: Oxford University Press, 1993.

Rákosi, Mátyás (1892–1971) *prime minister of Hungary*

Mátyás Rákosi was born in Ada, Serbia, on March 14, 1892, into a middle-class Jewish family. He was raised in Hungary and conscripted into the Austro-Hungarian army to fight in World War I. Rákosi was captured on the Russian front and, after witnessing the Bolshevik revolution in 1917, he became a committed communist. He came home in 1918 and joined the ill-fated Hungarian Soviet under Bela Kun that was crushed by conservative forces under MIKLOS HÓRTHY. Thereafter he fled back to the new Soviet Union to receive additional political training. Rákosi returned to Hungary in 1924 to clandestinely organize the outlawed Hungarian Communist Party (HCP). He was immediately arrested and sentenced to eight years in prison. Arrested again in 1935, Rákosi received a life sentence but was released and sent back to the Soviet Union in 1940. As head of the "Muscovite" faction of the HCP, Rákosi served JOSEPH STALIN well during World War II and was promoted to general secretary by March 1942. In this capacity he accompanied Soviet forces during their conquest of Hungary in 1944, when he helped arrange a provisional government that included communists.

Back home Rákosi used his "salami tactics," slicing up political adversaries one by one by taking control of the military and security forces. With Russian backing he arrested, tried, and executed opponents of the regime. The communists lost repeatedly at the ballot box but Rákosi, undeterred and with Stalin's backing, still managed to subvert Hungary's political system. In 1946 a "people's republic" was established, which signaled the onset of full-scale Stalinization, the nationalization of all industry, and collectivization of agriculture. Noncommunist politicians were then summarily rounded up and executed while the leftist Social Democrats were forcibly melded into the new Hungarian Worker's Party. No individual, no matter how highly placed, was safe. In 1949 Rákosi arrested Interior Minister Lázlo Rajik for suspected sympathies for Yugoslavia's MARSHAL TITO. He then instructed party leader JÁNOS KÁDÁR to coax a false confession out of him on the promise of parole. When the confession was signed, Rajik was immediately hanged. In time Rákosi gained renown—and infamy—throughout the communist world as a slavish devotee of Stalin and his methods.

Rákosi reigned as party chief until 1952, when he was promoted to prime minister. His rule was characterized by the worst sort of police terror, torture, and murder. However, after Stalin's death in 1953, his position was steadily undermined by Russian reformists under NIKITA KHRUSHCHEV and others. He was forced to concede the premiership to reformist IMRE NAGY in July 1953, although he retained the post of general secretary. A bare-knuckled power struggle ensued over the next two years, and in February 1955 Rákosi managed to have Nagy deposed. Hungary by this time was enjoying its first taste of political liberalization in a decade, and the country resisted the reimposition of Stalinization. Moreover, the Russians under Khrushchev feared the kind of mounting dissent that had developed in Poland, so in July 1956 they replaced Rákosi with reformist Ernö Gerö. But Hungary was too far gone to submit to communist rule any longer, and in October 1956 a full-scale rebellion swept the country. Rákosi fled back to Moscow just as Russian tanks rolled in to restore communist rule.

Rákosi, an ardent Stalinist, remained in Russia for the remainder of his life. The excesses of his rule were a direct cause for the outbreak of violence in 1956 and, to maintain the peace, he was never allowed back into Hungary. In 1962 Prime Minister Kádár underscored this determination by revoking his party membership. He reputedly ran a paper factory in Gorki until his death there on February 5, 1971. Rákosi remains a despised political figure to the present day.

Further Reading

Gollner, Andreas. "Foundations of Soviet Domination and Communist Political Power in Hungary: 1945–1956." *Canadian-American Review of Hungarian Studies* 3, no. 2 (1976): 73–105.

Granville, Johanna. "The Soviet-Yugoslav Detente, Belgrade-Budapest Relations, and the Hungarian Revolution (1955–1956)." *Hungarian Studies Review* 24, nos. 1–2 (1997): 15–63.

Haraszti-Taylor, Eva. *Britain and Hungary in the Post-war Years, 1945–51: A Parallel History in Narrative and Documents,* 2 vols. Nottingham, England: Astra Press, 2000.

Molnar, Miklos. *From Bela Kun to János Kádár: Seventy Years of Hungarian Communism.* New York: Berg, 1990.

Rákosi, Mátyás. *The Imprisonment and Defense of Mátyás Rákosi.* London: Lawrence and Wishart, 1959.

Werling, Dennis H. "Why Hungary Turned Soviet and Finland Did Not." Unpublished master's thesis, Western Illinois University, 2001.

Rakowski, Mieczysław (1926–) *prime minister of Poland*

Mieczysław Franciszek Rakowski was born in Kowalewko, Poland, on December 1, 1926, the son of peasants. His father was executed by Germans in World War II and in 1945 he joined the communist-controlled Polish army. After three years of service Rakowski also joined the Polska Partia Robotnicza, Polish (communist) Workers Party (PWP), as a propaganda officer. In this capacity he gravitated toward a career in journalism, and in 1956 he received a doctorate from the Warsaw Institute of Social Sciences. Rakowski went on to found and edit the respected paper *Polityka* in 1957, and contributed weekly columns. In an age of press control and journalistic sycophants, he demonstrated a remarkable degree of honesty and independence from the party line. Within a year he became chairman of the Association of Polish Journalists and trumpeted the reform efforts of WŁADYSŁAW GOMUŁKA. But Rakowski never forsook his Communist Party membership and in 1964 he was made a deputy member of the full committee. After 1970 he also championed the reform efforts attempted by the new party boss EDWARD GIEREK, which came to ruin in the wake of bloody food riots. Rakowski nevertheless touted his reformist line in a clever, nonthreatening manner and developed a national following. The party also continued trusting his loyalty and judgment, for in 1972 he joined the Sejm (legislature) as a deputy and three years later he rose to become a full member of the Central Committee. But it was not until he came to the attention of General WOJCIECH JARUZELSKI that Rakowski's political career flourished.

The year 1980 occasioned the rise of the independent trade union Solidarity under Lech Walesa, an electrician in the Lenin shipyard at Gdańsk. To counter the growing influence of this noncommunist movement, Jaruzelski appointed Rakowski deputy premier and authorized him to negotiate with Walesa to avoid potential problems. He subsequently backed off from his liberal reputation and took a hard-line communist stance about concessions and the rise of democracy. Talks with Solidarity leaders failed, and a spate of worker unrest ensued. Jaruzelski, wishing to forestall a Soviet invasion to restore order, declared martial law in December 1981. Walesa was arrested, while Rakowski was demoted to speaker of the Sejm, a near powerless position. In 1988 he was dispatched to London as ambassador to better explain the machinations of the rapidly disintegrating communist government. Rakowski returned to Poland in September 1988 during a new round of strikes by Solidarity, and he was made prime minister and first secretary of the PZPR in a last-ditch attempt to save communist control. "The new government will deem winning the trust of a significant part of society its primary task," he announced. "I am aware that this can be done not through words, but deeds."

From the onset, Rakowski's mission proved impossible. The forces of freedom unleashed by Soviet premier MIKHAIL GORBACHEV's liberalization of Eastern Europe could not be contained any longer. Nonetheless Rakowski embarked on a crusade to introduce "capitalist" innovations such as privatization to invigorate the moribund economy. He also gave grudging acceptance to the Round Table Negotiations held in the spring of 1991 whereby noncommunist parties were legalized for upcoming elections. Through such expedients Rakowski hoped to introduce limited democracy to Poland while still preserving communist supremacy. But elections held that August proved a rout and Solidarity candidate TADEUSZ MAZOWIECKI became Poland's first noncommunist prime minister in 40 years. Rakowski resigned after failing to win a seat in the Sejm and was reduced to party head. In January 1990 he presided over the last congress of the Polish Worker's Party, soon to be renamed the Social Democrats. Even then he was passed over for party leadership by the younger Aleksandr Kwasniewski.

Rakowski has since returned to journalism and edits several journals and newspapers. He was Poland's last communist leader.

Further Reading

Castle, Marjorie. *Triggering Communism's Collapse: Perceptions and Power in Poland's Transition.* Lanham, Md.: Rowman and Littlefield, 2002.

Castle, Marjorie, and Ray Taras. *Democracy in Poland.* Boulder, Colo.: Westview Press, 2002.

MacEachin, Douglas. *U.S. Intelligence and the Confrontation in Poland, 1980–81.* University Park: Pennsylvania State University Press, 2002.

Osa, Maryjane. *Solidarity and Contention: Networks of Polish Opposition.* Minneapolis: University of Minnesota Press, 2003.

Rakowski, Mieczyslaw. *Efficiency and Investment in a Socialist Economy.* New York: Pergamon Press, 1966.

Sharman, J. C. *Repression and Resistance in Communist Europe.* New York: RoutledgeCurzon, 2003.

Ramgoolam, Seewoosagur (1900–1985) *prime minister of Mauritius*

Seewoosagur Ramgoolam was born in Belle Rive, Mauritius, on September 18, 1900, the son of West Indian immigrants. His homeland, then a British colony, was originally occupied by Africans and had since experienced an influx of English aristocrats and Indian plantation workers. Ramgoolam was raised a Hindu but he was educated at Christian missionary schools and became indelibly Anglicized by choice. He was also an excellent student and easily passed through the prestigious Royal College of Medicine in Curepipe before venturing to England to study at the University of London Medical School. While there Ramgoolam encountered the Indian nationalist Mohandas K. Gandhi and also joined the socialist (non-Marxist) Fabian society. He returned home to practice medicine in 1935 and remained determined to improve the lot of plantation workers. The poverty he encountered prompted him to enter politics in 1940 through election to the Port-Louis municipal council. Thereafter he rose steadily through the local colonial administration and in 1951 he joined the Mauritius Labour Party (MLP). In this capacity Ramgoolam joined the island-wide movement promoting universal suffrage and in 1958 he rose to party head. The following year Ramgoolam led the

MLP to a sweeping victory in national elections and commenced negotiations with Great Britain for eventual independence. Given the island's strategic location in the middle of the Indian Ocean, the English proved hesitant to relinquish control but Ramgoolam, a pro-Western, pro-British figure, assuaged their fears. By 1961 he was functioning as the island's chief minister and in 1965, once independence was granted, he became Mauritius's first prime minister.

Ramgoolam's domain was not only small, but also poor and ethnically diverse. Still he determined to enact widespread social reform without alienating the former colonial elites. He thus embraced free market economics while laying the foundations for an extensive welfare state. Henceforth all citizens received free education, free medicine, social security, and old age pensions. His deft politics also diffused a potentially explosive situation by calling on all Mauritanians to celebrate their common heritage. He also enacted a nonaligned foreign policy, which balanced Third World nationalism and friendly relations with the West. Ramgoolam's success in protecting human rights on his island resulted in a 1973 United Nations Prize. In 1976 he was also called upon to serve as chairman of the Organization of African Unity, again with considerable success. All told, Ramgoolam's political style embraced moderation, toleration, and consensus, and helped steer Mauritius on a relatively peaceful transition from colony to nation.

Ramgoolam's principal failing as a politician was his inability to greatly improve the national economy, which was almost totally dependent upon sugar exports. Whenever the price of that commodity fell, exports declined and unemployment rose precipitously. Ramgoolam therefore sought to initiate economic diversification of Mauritius by establishing the Industrial Export Processing Zone to attract foreign investment. Results proved mixed at best and he faced a rising tide of criticism from the more radical Mauritius Militant Movement (MMM). In 1972 the outbreak of violent strikes induced the prime minister to declare a state of emergency, and he jailed MMM leaders without charges, outlawed labor activity, censored the press, and banned all political opposition. Life on the island did not return to normal until 1976, but Ramgoolam won the ensuing election. But in 1982, still faced with a balky economy and disenchantment over his intention to lease the island of Diego Garcia to the United States,

Ramgoolam was swept from power. By that time he had been the undisputed dominant figure of national politics for 40 years. He was also the first leader of an African nation to be replaced by free elections. Defeat finally closed his career, but Ramgoolam remained on the sidelines as a respected elder statesman. In 1983 the new government of Anerood Jugnauth further honored him with an appointment to the ceremonial post of governor general. Ramgoolam died while holding office on December 15, 1985, celebrated as the founding father of his country and a symbol of racial and national harmony. For this reason he is fondly recalled as *chacha* (uncle).

Further Reading

Alladin, Ibrahim M. *Education and Neocolonialism: A Study of Educational Development in Mauritius.* New York: P. Lang, 1996.

Dabee, Rajen, and David Greenaway. *The Mauritian Economy: A Reader.* New York: Palgrave, 2000.

Dommen, Edward, and Bridget Dommen. *Mauritius: An Island of Success: A Retrospective Study, 1960–1993.* Oxford, England: James Currey, 1999.

Eriksen, Thomas H. *Common Denominators: Ethnicity, Nation-building, and Compromise in Mauritius.* New York: Berg, 1998.

Jackson, Ashley. *War and Empire in Mauritius and the Indian Ocean.* New York: Palgrave, 2001.

Ramgoolam, Seewoosagur. *Selected Speeches of Sir Seewoosagur Ramgoolam.* London: Macmillan, 1979.

Reagan, Ronald (1911–) *president of the United States*

Ronald Wilson Reagan was born in Tampico, Illinois, on February 6, 1911, the son of a shoe salesman. Never intellectually inclined, he passed through Eureka College in 1932 and found work as a radio broadcaster. Soon after, he was discovered by a Hollywood agent and commenced a movie career that covered 50 films. During World War II Reagan served in the army and made training films. He was also a Democrat in the mold of FRANKLIN D. ROOSEVELT and a five-time president of the Screen Actors Guild. However, his encounters with communists and other radicals in Hollywood gradually converted him to conservative causes. During the late 1940s he openly cooperated with the House Un-American Activities Committee over supposed communist infiltration of the film industry. His film career had all but faded by the 1950s, so Reagan made an easy transition to the new medium of television. In 1962 he also made a political conversion by joining the Republican Party as a conservative. He supported the ill-fated 1964 presidential campaign of Barry Goldwater and two years later defeated an incumbent Democrat in the governor's race for California. In office Reagan pursued a basically conservative agenda of cutting taxes, reducing expenditures, and balancing the budget, but he also displayed a pragmatic streak when dealing with opposition Democrats. Consequently he was reelected by a landslide in 1970.

By 1976 Reagan felt successful enough to challenge GERALD R. FORD for the Republican presidential nomination. He narrowly lost and tried again in 1980, winning the party primary election over GEORGE H. W. BUSH, his subsequent vice presidential candidate. Together they went on to score a resounding win over incumbent Democrat JIMMY CARTER, whose handling of the economy and international affairs suggested ineptitude. Reagan, by contrast, exuded a confidence, charisma, and optimism that resonated strongly with the American electorate. "Ask yourself," he chided the voters, "are you better off than you were four years ago?" He also promised a rebirth of American global predominance in the war against communism and a halt to the taxes, bureaucracy, and welfare state at home. In November 1980 the Republicans resoundingly captured both the White House and control of the Senate for the first time in a generation. In March 1981 he survived an assassination attempt and commenced implementing his conservative agenda of tax cuts, domestic spending cuts, and dramatic military expansion. Part of Reagan's appeal as a politician was his ability to view the world in black and white terms, such as freedom versus communism and, as the "great communicator," impart his vision to the electorate. The economy suffered a recession in 1982 but quickly rebounded the following year and initiated the longest spell of economic growth in American history. He confronted Soviet leaders over their clandestine efforts to introduce medium-range nuclear weapons in Europe and countered with missiles of his own. This brought on a loud protest from the communist-orchestrated peace movement in Europe, but the missiles were deployed nonetheless. In October 1983 Reagan authorized an American invasion of the island of Grenada to free American student hostages

taken in a failed communist coup. He also established the policy of arming and supplying anticommunist guerrillas to oppose the Soviet regime in Afghanistan and DANIEL ORTEGA's Sandinista dictatorship in Nicaragua. He then commenced the Strategic Defense Initiative ("Star Wars"), a space-based defense system intent upon defeating Soviet strategic missiles in the event of war. The Soviet Union, saddled by an economy one-third the size of America's, could not realistically compete with Reagan's concerted buildup. By attempting to do so, the "evil empire," as Reagan castigated it, laid the seeds of its own destruction.

Domestically Reagan's presidency signaled the end of the welfare state that had been in effect since the Great Depression. The welfare rolls were purged, requirements tightened, and people obliged to look for work in an age of expanding economic opportunity. As a campaigner, Reagan also promised to appoint the first woman to the Supreme Court and he selected Sandra Day O'Connor. But above all the president mandated that Americans roll up their sleeves, believe in

Ronald Reagan *(Library of Congress)*

themselves, and set about finishing the tasks at hand. After four years of national malaise under Carter and the Democrats, Reagan's ebullience proved a catalyst for spiritual renewal. The nation's economy and morale registered impressive improvements immediately thereafter as the United States reasserted itself on a global scale. On the downside, the tremendous military buildup led to increased deficit spending, which tripled the national debt to $3 trillion. Ironically it fell upon the Democratic administration of Bill Clinton (1993–2001) to finally address this glaring problem.

Reagan's immense popularity carried over into the 1984 election cycle, when he routed the Democrats under Walter Mondale. But shortly after, his administration was clouded over allegations that he traded arms to Iran for the release of American hostages in Lebanon. Moreover, a percentage of the funds allocated illegally went to supply the Nicaragua freedom fighters in contravention of the so-called Boland Amendment outlawing such practices. A lengthy congressional investigation ensued and some convictions resulted, but Reagan, who professed innocence, remained unscathed. The president also broke new ground by entering into significant arms reduction talks with the new Soviet premier, MIKHAIL GORBACHEV, at Geneva and Reykjavik, which signaled the relaxation of tensions between the superpowers.

By the time Reagan left office in January 1989 he was among the most popular presidents in American history. A mere two years later, the Soviet Union, Reagan's ideological adversary, collapsed under the weight of its own incompetence and tyranny. Unfortunately, in 1997 the former executive publicly declared that he was suffering from Alzheimer's disease, a degenerative brain disease, and withdrew from the public arena he relished. Reagan, a cold war icon and a symbol of American spiritual renewal, now lives at his home in California. His eight-year tenure was rich in symbolism, long on achievements, and a decisive turning point in 20th-century history.

Further Reading

Conley, Richard S. *Reassessing the Reagan Presidency.* Lanham, Md.: University Press of America, 2003.

Franham, Barbara. "Reagan and the Gorbachev Revolution: Perceiving the End of the Threat." *Political Science Quarterly* 116 (summer 2001): 225–252.

Noonan, Peggy. *When Character was King: A Story of Ronald Reagan.* New York: Viking, 2001.

Reagan, Ronald. *An American Life.* New York: Simon and Schuster, 1990.

Rowland, Robert C., and John M. Jones. "Until Next Week: The Saturday Radio Address of Ronald Reagan." *Presidential Studies Quarterly* 32 (March 2002): 84–110.

Schlesinger, Arthur M., ed. *The Election of 1980 and the Administration of Ronald Reagan.* Philadelphia: Mason Crest Publishers, 2002.

Strober, Deborah H., and Gerald S. Strober. *The Reagan Presidency: An Oral History of the Era.* Washington, D.C.: Brassey's, 2003.

Wallison, Peter J. *Ronald Reagan: The Power of Conviction and the Success of his Presidency.* Boulder, Colo.: Westview Press, 2003.

Renner, Karl (1870–1950) *chancellor and president of Austria*

Karl Renner was born in Unter-Tanowitz, Moravia, Austro-Hungarian Empire, on December 14, 1870, the son of a peasant family. The hardship and deprivations he endured throughout childhood indelibly molded his political perceptions of social justice and democracy. After passing through the University of Vienna for a law degree in 1896, Renner joined the left-leaning Social Democrat Party. Officially, he was a Marxist from the non-violent wing of the spectrum but also a German nationalist. In 1907 he successfully ran for a seat in the Reichsrat where he railed against the authoritarianism of the Hapsburg monarchy. In fact, Renner had hoped to preserve the empire by adopting a federal, democratic structure to accommodate its various ethnic nationalities. He had supported Austrian participation in World War I, reasoning that defeat would impose the dramatic changes necessary for reform. Austria was defeated in 1918 and, following the Emperor Charles's abdication, the National Council declared a new republic with Renner as chancellor. In this capacity he ventured to the Paris Peace Conference of 1919 but could not curtail extensive territorial losses to the new states of Yugoslavia, Czechoslovakia, and Poland. On September 10, 1919, he was forced to sign the Treaty of St. Germain, which formalized these losses. Renner was now convinced that the only way the small Austrian republic could survive was through *Anschluss* (union) with Germany. He was reelected chancellor of the new First Republic and led several coalition governments until the conservatives swept the elections of 1920. In his brief tenure Renner distinguished himself by joining the new League of Nations and endorsing a strictly neutral foreign policy.

Renner resumed his seat in the Reichsrat, and in 1930 he became Speaker of the House. Austria was then embroiled in the Great Depression and the rise of Nazism in neighboring Germany, a fact prompting Chancellor ENGELBERT DOLLFUSS to outlaw political parties in 1934. Renner was briefly arrested and detained. Once released he remained on the political sidelines for several years, although he again supported *Anschluss* with ADOLF HITLER's Germany in 1938. He then resigned from the Reichsrat when this was accomplished and resumed his writing career. At heart, Renner was an evolutionary Marxist who supported both a peaceful transition from capitalism and the growth of democracy. This made him appear heretical to orthodox Marxist-Leninists in the Soviet Union, but Renner was by then an international figure of some repute and a leading exponent of the Austro-Marxist school of thought.

Renner remained detached from politics throughout World War II and by war's end he was untainted by the specter of Nazism. Once Austria was occupied by Soviet troops in 1945, he appeared at their headquarters and offered his services as head of state. Soviet dictator JOSEPH STALIN, who was familiar with his writings, allowed Renner's appointment, and on April 27, 1945, Austria was again declared "sovereign under the Second Republic. The elderly Renner served briefly as chancellor and minister of foreign affairs until November 1945 when the Social Democratic-Communist coalition was upended by the conservative Austrian Peoples Party (OVP). On December 20, 1945, the Reichsrat unanimously elected Renner as president, a largely ceremonial role but a useful symbol of national unity. His task was greatly complicated by the fact that after the war Austria was divided into American, British, French, and Soviet spheres of influence. He nonetheless worked assiduously to preempt any expansion of Soviet-style communism into Austria, and hence into the heart of Central Europe. He died in office on December 31, 1950, having twice resurrected the Austrian republic from the ashes of war and ruin.

Further Reading

Blum, Mark E. *The Austro-Marxist, 1890–1918: A Psychological Study.* Lexington: University Press of Kentucky, 1985.

Carafano, James J. *Waltzing into the Cold War: The Struggle for Occupied Austria.* College Station: Texas A & M University Press, 2002.

Lowenberg, Peter. "Karl Renner and the Politics of Accommodation: Modernization Versus Revenge." *Austrian History Yearbook* 22 (1991): 35–56.

Middleworth, David. "The Democratic Influence of Karl Renner in Austria." Unpublished master's thesis, Ohio State University, 1973.

Pelinka, Anton. "Karl Renner—a Man for All Seasons." *Austrian History Yearbook* 23 (1992): 111–119.

Piotrowski, Harry. "The Soviet Union and the Renner Government of Austria, April–November, 1945." *Central European History* 20, nos. 3–4 (1987): 246–279.

Renner, Karl. *The Institutions of Private Law and Their Social Functions.* London: Routledge and Kegan Paul, 1971.

Reza Shah Pahlavi (Reza Khan) (1878–1944)
shah of Iran

Reza Pahlavi was born in Alasht, Persia (now Iran), on March 16, 1878, the son of an army officer. Orphaned at an early age, he was raised in Tehran by an uncle, another military officer, and adopted his name of Khan. The young man joined the Persian Cossack brigade at the age of 14 and proved himself an intelligent and capable soldier. The Persian army at that time was largely staffed by Russian and other foreign officers, and Reza Khan determined one day to rid the nation of foreigners. In the wake of the Russian revolution of 1917 many officers returned home and Persian military leaders began asserting themselves. Many young officers like Reza Khan were disillusioned by the corrupt and ineffective rule of the Qajar dynasty and on February 21, 1921, they orchestrated a coup that toppled the government. Thereafter noted journalist Sayyid Zia od-Din became prime minister, while Reza Khan functioned as commander in chief. However, when the two men quarreled over what direction to take the country, Reza Khan prevailed, and Sayyid Zia departed. A more pliable prime minister was appointed, and over the next four years the ambitious general enlarged the military and subdued various warring tribes in the interior. This gave Persia a state of internal peace it had not known for many years, and the populace looked upon Reza Khan as a savior. But his growing strength convinced Ahmad Shah, the last Qajar king, to take an indefinite leave of absence and visit Europe. The new leader initially wanted to have a republic declared, but the public were loath to abandon their long monarchical traditions, so on October 21, 1925, the Majlís (legislature) acclaimed Reza Khan the new shah. After many decades of national weakness Persia had finally found a strong leader and the Pahlavi dynasty was born.

Enthroned now as Reza Shah, the new monarch determined to enact a sweeping reform agenda. He looked to his Turkish contemporary, KEMAL ATATÜRK, to provide impetus for modernization. He sought to vanquish the old order of governance and institute a more effective, Western-style leadership. The first object of Reza Shah's wrath was rooting out the entrenched Islamic clergy: hereafter their powers were curtailed, Islamic instruction banned from public schools, and religious processions outlawed. Moreover he ordered that Iranian males adopt Western-style dress while women were emancipated and abandoned Islamic-inspired veils and shawls. All this had the effect of endearing him with commoners for their new freedoms and he also won the support of the educated elites for the reforms and modernization engendered. Reza Khan enjoyed even more spectacular success in his dealings with foreigners. Persia had long been treated as a colony by business interests in England and Russia and he outlawed unfair business practices. The customs service was strengthened, foreigners were forbidden to issue currency notes, and in 1931 he forced the British to sign the Anglo-Persian Oil Treaty, which granted the nation greater revenues from petroleum profits. The dynamic monarch then set his sights on constructing the first national wire service and also built the impressive Trans-Persian Railway, stretching from the Persian Gulf to the Caspian Sea, without a loan or assistance from foreigners. But more than anything else, he effectively terminated all special foreign privileges and placed Iran on a more equal footing with its neighbors.

Reza Khan ruled Iran with an iron fist for many years, intolerant of dissent while promoting modernity. He became especially adept at playing Russian and British interests off against each other. However, during World War II Great Britain and the Soviet Union found themselves allied against Nazi Germany and it became imperative to establish a land corridor to support the Russian war machine. But the king, wary as ever of foreign influence, refused to cooperate, and the Allies invaded Iran in August 1941. Reza Khan decided to save his dynasty by abdicating in favor of his son, MOHAMMAD REZA PAHLAVI. The British exiled him to South Africa for the duration of the war. He died in Johannesburg on July 26, 1944, the architect of modern Iran. Considering his near-total lack of formal education, Reza Khan was an astonishingly effective agent for change in an otherwise medieval society.

Further Reading

Atabaki, Touraj, and Erik Jan Zurcher. *Men of Order: Authoritarian Modernization under Atatürk and Reza Shah.* London: I. B. Tauris, 2002.

Cronin, Stephanie. *The Army and the Creation of the Pahlavi State in Iran, 1910–1926.* New York: Tauris Academic Studies, 1997.

———, ed. *The Making of Modern Iran: State and Society under Riza Shah, 1921–1941.* New York: RoutledgeCurzon, 2003.

Ghani, Cyrus. *Iran and the Rise of Reza Shah: from Qajar Collapse to Pahlavi Power.* New York: St. Martin's Press, 1999.

Katouzian, Homa. *State and Society in Iran: The Eclipse of the Qajars and the Emergence of the Pahlavis.* London: I. B. Tauris, 2000.

Majd, Mohammed Gholi. *Great Britain and Reza Shah: The Plunder of Iran, 1921–1941.* Gainesville: University Press of Florida, 2001.

Rhee, Syngman (1875–1965) *president of South Korea*

Syngman Rhee was born in Pyongsan, Korea, on March 26, 1875, the scion of an aristocratic family that traced its lineage back 17 generations. He received a classical Confucian education but subsequently studied at Methodist missionary schools. Even as a young man Rhee was an ardent political activist and he founded a clandestine reformist group called the Independence Club in 1896. He was arrested and tortured for his beliefs by the Choson dynasty, and while imprisoned he wrote a significant political polemic, the *Spirit of Independence,* in 1906. This tract, which advocated democracy and modernization, was widely read by the Korean community at large. Following his release, Rhee visited the United States to attend George Washington University, Harvard, and finally Princeton, where he became the first Korean to receive a Ph.D. But by the time he came home in 1910 Korea had been annexed to the Japanese Empire and most cruelly administered. Rhee then commenced his lifelong quest for Korean unification and independence, and in 1912 he was exiled to Hawaii as head of an expatriate community. There he lent his expertise and reputation to a new organization, the Korean Commission, which functioned as a government in exile. In 1919 Rhee was appointed president and he lobbied the United States government ceaselessly to promote independence from Japan, but to no avail. He alternated his residence between Hawaii and Washington, D.C., over the next two decades, becoming the only well-known Korean nationalist leader. But the tempo of events accelerated following America's entry into World War II in December 1941, and four years later the Japanese Empire was defeated. The Korean peninsula was then jointly occupied by Soviet and American forces while both sides looked for indigenous leaders to support them in the new cold war.

Rhee came home in 1948 with his 30-year goal of independence and national unity seemingly steps away. He badgered the American military government into letting him run for president in 1948, which was successfully accomplished under United Nations–sponsored elections. Rhee's main claim to office was his international stature and sterling anticommunist credentials. Meanwhile, the Soviets, who controlled Korea north of the 38th parallel, installed a puppet figure of their own, Kim Il Sung. The leaders of both North and South Korea were implacably hostile toward each other, yet grimly determined to unite the peninsula by force. In June 1950, North Korean forces suddenly burst over the border, initiating the first armed conflict of the cold war. After three years of savage fighting United Nations forces under the United States had fought the combined might of the Communist world, including China and the Soviet Union, to a draw, and cease-fire negotiations ensued. Rhee, angered that the Americans were not going to reunite the two Koreas, did everything in his power to sabotage the peace talks, including his June 1953 release of 28,000 prisoners of war slated for repatriation. A truce was concluded on July 27, 1953, over his strident objections.

Unification proved beyond Rhee's capacity to achieve, so he settled into the role of an authoritarian leader. Nominally an elected figure, he ruled the country with near dictatorial powers. The press was censored, political opposition outlawed, and several opposition leaders murdered. The regime was notoriously corrupt, while the aging Rhee grew more and more detached from political realities. Anxious to retain power, he had the constitution amended in 1956 so that he could run for a third consecutive term. In 1960 he was reelected a fourth time by 90 percent of votes cast in rigged elections. His longevity spurred on such massive student demonstrations and civil disorder that the stability of the nation was threatened. Upon American urging, he finally stepped down from office in April 1960 and entered voluntary exile in Hawaii. He died there on July 19, 1965, a strident champion of Korean independence but also the first in a long line of dictators.

Further Reading

Chay, Jongsuk, *Unequal Partners in Peace and War: The Republic of Korea and the United States, 1948–1953.* Westport, Conn.: Praeger, 2002.

Foley, James A. *Korea's Divided Families: Fifty Years of Separation.* New York: Routledge, 2003.

Hong, Yong-pyo. *State Security and Regime Security: President Syngman Rhee and the Insecurity Dilemma in South Korea, 1953–60.* New York: St. Martin's Press, 1999.

Kim, Quee-Young. "From Protest to Change of Regime: The 4-19 Revolt and the Fall of the Rhee Regime in South Korea." *Social Forces* 74, no. 4 (1996): 1179–1208.

Kim, Stephen. "The Carrot and the Leash: Eisenhower, Syngman Rhee, and the Dual Containment of Korea." Unpublished Ph.D. diss., Yale University, 1999.

Oh, Bonnie B. C., ed. *Korea under the American Military Government, 1945–1948.* Westport, Conn.: Praeger, 2002.

Rhee, Syngman. *The Spirit of Independence: A Primer of Korean Modernization and Reform.* Honolulu: University of Hawaii Press, 2001.

Ríos Montt, Efraín (1926–) *president of Guatemala*

José Efraín Ríos Montt was born in Huehuetenango, Guatemala, on June 16, 1926, into a peasant family. Like the majority of Guatemalans he was a Ladino of mixed Indian and Spanish background. Ríos Montt joined the army at an early age and proved himself a capable soldier. In 1950 he received advanced military training in the United States and by 1970 he had risen to general. That year Ríos Montt was appointed army chief of staff under President Carlos Arana Osorio. Despite his military background, Ríos Montt was something of a liberal by Guatemalan standards, and he joined the small Christian Democratic Party. In 1974 he resigned his commission and ran for the presidency under the center-left National Opposition Front but lost to General Kjell Laugerud in a blatantly rigged election. Ríos Montt then rejoined the army and was effectively exiled from the country by being appointed military attaché to Madrid, Spain, until 1978. Around that time he also encountered missionaries from the Protestant Evangelical Church of the Complete Word, and he underwent religious conversion. This put him completely at odds with the rest of Guatemalan society, which is predominantly Roman Catholic. Ríos Montt then resigned from the military again to become a lay Protestant preacher for several years.

Throughout the late 1970s and into the 1980s, Guatemala was a nation besieged by a poor economy, gross disparities in wealth, and an armed leftist insurgency, primarily among western highland Indians. A series of military dictators failed to sufficiently address the problem, so on March 23, 1982, President Fernando Romero Lucas García was overthrown by disgruntled military officers. A three-man junta was then installed, which included Ríos Montt, serving as minister of defense. By June 1982 he had consolidated his position better than other contenders and became president. His first priority was restoration of stability by ending civil strife. Therefore, he offered the guerrillas amnesty for a brief period before declaring, "It is time to do God's work." Ríos Montt then declared a state of siege and ordered a campaign of extermination against all leftists. He promulgated a unique strategy called "beans and guns" whereby cooperative villagers were forcibly relocated to population centers. However, those refusing to cooperate were assumed to be in league with the insurgents and massacred. This stark choice produced 100,000 refugees in short order and led to the deaths of thousands of Indians, but the insurgency was finally crushed. "The guerrilla in the civil population is like a fish in water," Ríos Montt declared philosophically. "You take the water from the fish and the fish dies." Peace in the countryside was once more restored, but at a frightful toll in abuse and human rights violations.

Even apart from his success at battling guerrillas, Ríos Montt's administration proved extremely authoritarian by nature. Union and political activity were outlawed, the press was heavily censored, and civil rights were suspended. Moreover, special tribunals were established that guaranteed guerrillas and other troublemakers a quick trial—then a firing squad. He also replaced town rulers with his own followers. But Ríos Montt finally alienated his major source of power, the military, through an overreliance upon his Protestant religious advisers. The majority of Catholic officers resented the religious bent of his political conduct, and on August 8, 1983, Ríos Montt was overthrown by Defense Minister Oscar Humberto Mejía Victores after 17 months of bloody rule. In 1991 Ríos Montt formed the Frente Republicana Guatemalteco (FRG), Guatemalan Republican Front, to run for the presidency but was forbidden from winning by constitutional provisions excluding former coup leaders. He then endorsed his protégé, Jorge Serrano Elías, who went on to win. In 1994 Ríos Montt won a seat in the legislature as an FRG representative, eventually rising to president of congress. He was still serving in that capacity in 2000 when the Spanish National Court announced genocidal charges against him for a suspicious fire in the Spanish embassy in 1982.

Further Reading

Anfuso, Joseph. *Efrain Ríos Montt, Servant or Dictator? The Real Story of Guatemala's Born-Again President.* Ventura, Calif.: Vision House, 1984.

Armendariz, Anthony C. "The Regime of Religious Dictator José Efrain Ríos Montt, 1982–1983: A Phenomenon of Expediency." *UCLA History Journal* 7 (1986): 28–59.

Falla, Ricardo. *Massacres in the Jungle: Ixcan, Guatemala, 1975–1982.* Boulder, Colo.: Westview Press, 1994.

Holiday, David. "Guatemala: Precarious Peace." *Current History* 99, no. 634 (2000): 78–85.

Wadge, Gyl C. "The Rios Montt Regime: Change and Continuity in Guatemalan Politics." Unpublished bachelor's thesis, Tulane University, 1987.

Wilkinson, Daniel. *Silence on the Mountain: Stories of Terror, Betrayal and Forgetting in Guatemala.* Boston: Houghton Mifflin, 2002.

Rojas Pinilla, Gustavo (1900–1975) *president of Colombia*

Gustavo Rojas Pinilla was born in Tunja, Colombia, on March 12, 1900, and he was educated at the local Normal School. He then enrolled at the Colombian Military Academy in 1917 and was commissioned three years later in the engineers. In 1927 he attended Tri-State College, Indiana, in the United States, for advanced engineering studies and returned as an authority on civil aeronautics. As a military officer he first gained national attention in his brutal suppression of riots in Bogotá following the assassination of Jorge Eliécer Gaitán in April 1948. He was then promoted to commander in chief by Conservative president LAUREANO GÓMEZ CASTRO in 1950, and two years later he arrived in Korea to inspect the Colombian detachment fighting there. Colombia at that time was in the grip of a violent civil war, called La Violencia, between supporters of the Liberal and Conservative Parties. When Gómez proved unable or unwilling to restore order, Rojas led a bloodless coup against him in June 1953. The change of government sparked immediate relief throughout the nation, for Rojas, now president, promised to restore Colombia to peace and prosperity.

In practice, Rojas proved no better at promoting democracy and economic growth than his predecessor and in many respects was even worse. He moved quickly to offer an amnesty to communist and liberal insurgents, but otherwise squandered his reservoir of goodwill by his repressive rule. All political activity was halted, union activity banned, and the press heavily censored. The government itself, besides being inept, was also incipiently corrupt and run by cronies for their own enrichment. Rojas also further escalated violence in the countryside by forcibly rounding up peasants—suspected leftists—and relocating them to the cities. Those who resisted were executed in large numbers, so that by 1957 an estimated 300,000 people had died. Rojas's misrule proved so pervasive that it actually forced Liberal and Conservative leaders in exile to create a National Front to depose him. His final mistake was in altering the constitution to enable him to run for a second consecutive term—then suspending the election process. On May 9, 1957, the military overturned Rojas in a bloodless coup and he exiled himself to the United States. Thereafter Liberals and Conservatives agreed under the National Front to alternate rule every four years and thus preserve national harmony.

Rojas remained abroad until October 1958 when he returned, was impeached by the senate, and stripped of all civil rights. He nonetheless reentered politics by creating the Alianza Nacional Popular (ANAPO), National Popular Alliance, which—taking a leaf from Argentine dictator JUAN PERÓN—catered to the lower classes. Rojas then ran for president in 1962, receiving only 2.5 percent of the vote. However, by 1967 the courts ruled that the former executive could not be denied his civil rights and they were restored. Rojas cleverly used the next few years to build up his popular base with a far-ranging party apparatus that reached into virtually every district in the nation. He then campaigned for the presidency again with a renewed sense of legitimacy in April 1970. That year he came within 60,000 vote of winning, but lost to Conservative candidate Misael Pastrana Borrero. Rojas claimed fraud and his supporters rioted, but martial law was declared and the verdict was allowed to stand. In 1974 his daughter, Senator María Eugenia Rojas de Moreno, also ran for the presidency and lost badly. Rojas himself died in Bogotá on January 17, 1975, one of the most repressive and ineffectual dictators of Colombian history. His once influential ANAPO has also declined into insignificance.

Further Reading

Dix, Robert H. "The Varieties of Populism: The Case of Colombia." *Western Political Quarterly* 31, no. 3 (1978): 334–351.

Hartlyn, J. "Military Governments and the Transition to Civilian Rule: The Colombian Experience of 1957–58." *Journal of International American Studies* 26 (March 1984): 245–281.

Roldan, Mary. *Blood and Fire: La Violencia in Antioquia, Colombia, 1946–1953.* Durham, N.C.: Duke University Press, 2002.

Safford, Frank. *Colombia: Fragmented Land, Divided Society.* New York: Oxford University Press, 2002.

Torres, Javier A. "Military Government, Political Crisis, and Exceptional State: The Armed Forces in Colombia and the National Front, 1954–1974." Unpublished Ph.D. diss., State University of New York–Buffalo, 1986.

Roosevelt, Franklin D. (1882–1945) *president of the United States*

Franklin Delano Roosevelt was born in Hyde Park, New York, on January 30, 1882, the son of wealthy, upper-class parents. His patrician origins afforded him an excellent education, and he graduated from both Harvard and Columbia University Law School. However, he had his heart set upon pursuing politics and in 1911 he successfully ran as a Democrat for a state senate seat. In this capacity Roosevelt gained renown for his willingness to fight corruption and the Tammany political machine that had dominated state politics for a generation. In 1912 he campaigned for the presidency of WOODROW WILSON and was rewarded with an appointment as assistant secretary of the navy. Roosevelt threw himself into his work with characteristic energy and helped prepare the navy for its successful role in World War I. Now a national figure, Roosevelt ran for the vice presidency with Democratic candidate James M. Cox in 1920, but was defeated by Republican WARREN G. HARDING. Worse, in 1921 he contracted polio, which deprived him of the use of his legs for the remainder of his life. Fortunately, in 1905 Roosevelt

Franklin D. Roosevelt *(Library of Congress)*

had married a remarkable woman, Eleanor Roosevelt, a distant cousin and niece of former president THEODORE ROOSEVELT. She proved herself every bit as astute politically as her husband, supported him fitfully through his long rehabilitation, and became an important conduit for his liberal brand of politics.

After an eight-year hiatus, Roosevelt resumed his political career in 1928 by capturing the New York governor's mansion. However, the following year witnessed the onset of the Great Depression and a dramatic increase in unemployment, an economic downturn, and personal hardships. Roosevelt, despite his aristocratic upbringing—or perhaps because of it— was always beholden to *noblesse oblige,* a sense of commitment to those less fortunate than himself. He therefore enacted sweeping state programs to help alleviate unemployment, put people back to work, and give them hope. His programs served as a blueprint for what would follow at the federal level, and in 1930 he was reelected by wide margins. Roosevelt's success in New York, combined with his personal warmth and charisma, made him an attractive candidate for the presidency in 1932. The extent of social dislocation at the time, and the perception that Republican president HERBERT HOOVER was doing little about it, led to Roosevelt's landslide election. More than a political victory, it proved a turning point in the way that most Americans perceived the role of government.

Now in control, Roosevelt attacked the problem with resolve and energy. He was never a profound thinker or a committed ideologue, but his overwhelming motivation was to do something to help the public. He therefore summoned a special session of Congress and passed landmark legislation promoting government intervention in economic matters. New banking and monetary agencies arose, as did numerous "make work" projects to put federal money into people's pockets. In fact this congressional session, called the "Hundred Days," passed legislation that laid the groundwork for the "New Deal," an American welfare state. Foremost among these was the Social Security Act, which guaranteed elderly citizens an income regardless of their circumstances. The effect of Roosevelt's New Deal legislation was mixed overall, but it gave people a sense that the government was taking an active role in their lives. Furthermore, Roosevelt was the first president to take to the airwaves on a regular basis, and offered the public confidence and assurances through his famous "fireside chats." Consequently, Roosevelt was reelected by another landslide in 1936. However, some of his efforts were strongly rebuffed by the Supreme Court as unconstitutional. In 1937 the president countered by proffering an ill-conceived plan to "pack" the Supreme Court with seven new justices more favorably disposed toward his programs. The public reacted strongly against the move and Republican gains in Congress effectively throttled future New Deal legislation. But Roosevelt had irrevocably altered the American political landscape and rendered government a powerful influence in individual lives. In 1940 he also became the first American executive elected to three terms.

The bulk of Roosevelt's third term in office was dominated by foreign affairs. The rise of fascist governments in Germany under ADOLF HITLER, Italy under BENITO MUSSOLINI, and Japan under TOJO HIDEKI placed the world on an irrevocable slide toward war. The president confronted rising isolationist sentiment at home and the challenge to ship arms abroad to struggling allies. In 1940 his efforts to reactivate the military draft succeeded by a single vote, but America finally began rearming. He subsequently formed a close and abiding relationship with English prime minister WINSTON CHURCHILL, then fighting Nazi Germany alone, and provided him with ships and aircraft under the new Lend-Lease Program. After the United States was attacked by Japanese forces at Pearl Harbor on December 7, 1941, Roosevelt assumed his most challenging role: commander in chief. He surrounded himself with the nation's best and brightest minds from the military and business communities, and converted America into the "arsenal of democracy." And, having tendered the Soviet Union diplomatic recognition in 1933, Roosevelt also sought close relations with dictator JOSEPH STALIN. Over the course of the war, Roosevelt, Stalin, and Churchill met repeatedly at various locations to hammer out the details of a concerted, war-winning strategy. He was reelected to an unprecedented fourth term in 1944. But by then his health was failing and may have seriously impaired his judgment. Roosevelt has since been criticized for allowing Stalin to control Eastern Europe after 1945, but defenders maintain that since the Red Army was already there in force there was little either he or Churchill could do about it. For all his contributions to handling the war effort, Roosevelt did not live to see its successful conclusion. He died while on vacation at Warm Springs, Georgia,

on April 11, 1945, and was succeeded by HARRY S. TRUMAN. Roosevelt bequeathed a legacy of decisive leadership that helped America weather its two most traumatic interludes of the 20th century: the Great Depression and World War II. His inspirational success renders him one of the most effective and beloved presidents of all time. Ironically his greatest legacy, the American welfare state, endured a half-century before being dismantled by another Democratic executive, Bill Clinton, in 1996.

Further Reading

Asbell, Bernard. *The F. D. R. Memoirs.* Garden City, N.Y.: Doubleday, 1973.

Axelrod, Alan. *Nothing to Fear: Lessons in Leadership from FDR, President of the Greatest Generation.* New York: Portfolio, 2003.

Beschloss, Michael. *The Conquerors: Roosevelt, Truman, and the Destruction of Nazi Germany.* New York: Simon and Schuster, 2003.

Casey, Steven. *Cautious Crusade: Franklin D. Roosevelt, American Public Opinion, and the War against Nazi Germany.* New York: Oxford University Press, 2001.

Howard, Thomas C., and William D. Pederson. *Franklin D. Roosevelt and the Formation of the Modern World.* Armonk, N.Y.: M. E. Sharpe, 2003.

Larrabee, Eric. *Commander in Chief: Franklin Delano Roosevelt, His Lieutenants, and Their War.* Annapolis, Md.: Naval Institute Press, 2004.

Meacham, John. *Franklin & Winston: An Intimate Portrait of an Epic Friendship.* New York: Random House, 2003.

Persico, Joseph E. *Roosevelt's Secret War: FDR and World War II Espionage.* New York: Random House International, 2003.

Robinson, Greg. *By Order of the President: FDR and the Internment of Japanese Americans.* Cambridge, Mass.: Harvard University Press, 2001.

Roosevelt, Theodore (1858–1919) *president of the United States*

Theodore Roosevelt was born in New York City, New York, on October 27, 1858, into a wealthy, aristocratic family. Sickly as a child he subjected himself to a rigorous routine of exercise and developed a passion for outdoor living. He graduated from Harvard University in 1880 and also penned *The Naval War of 1812,* the first of 30 historical tomes. Roosevelt subsequently obtained a law degree from Columbia University but forsook legal practice in favor of politics. He was elected to the state legislature as a Republican in 1881, becoming closely identified with the "progressive" or reform element. When his wife died in 1884, Roosevelt temporarily relocated to his ranch in North Dakota to continue writing. He returned to New York in 1884 and five years later joined the Civil Service Commission to end corruption and fraud. In 1895 Roosevelt capitalized on his success by becoming police commissioner of New York City and his reforms antagonized vested interests in Democratic and Republican Parties alike. But Roosevelt first captured national attention in 1897 when President William McKinley made him assistant secretary of the navy. In this capacity he worked diligently preparing the navy for war with Spain in 1898 and then quit his post to command a volunteer cavalry regiment in Cuba. Roosevelt won fame while leading his "Rough Riders" in the Battle of San Juan Hill, and he returned home a national hero. Consequently, in November 1898 he was elected governor of New York and embarked on his usual reform efforts. When vested interests in the business community complained, the Republican leadership sought to remove Roosevelt from power by making him the vice presidential nominee to run with McKinley in 1900. The ticket won easily, but when McKinley was assassinated in September 1901, Roosevelt became the youngest president of the United States.

As an individual, Roosevelt combined an exuberance for living with a hands-on, no-nonsense approach to governance. Despite his affluence, he was determined to strike a "Square Deal" for the average American and would not hesitate to antagonize wealthy business interests. He was not necessarily anti-business but, as an upright moralist, Roosevelt determined to control what he deemed the unprincipled greed of the "robber barons." In 1902 he successfully sued the Northern Securities Company for violating the Sherman Antitrust Act, dissolved this large railroad conglomerate, and gained a reputation as a "trust buster." He then oversaw creation of the Bureau of Corporation to oversee and investigate fraudulent business practices. Again, Roosevelt insisted on honesty and accountability from the wealthy. In another major departure from previous administrations, Roosevelt was decidedly friendly toward legitimate union activity. When a major strike

closed the coal mines, he refused to send troops in, and instead served as a personal mediator and resolved the dispute peacefully. This represented the first time that the federal government involved itself in labor issues. Roosevelt also distinguished himself in the field of nature conservation. A devotee of outdoor living, he determined to preserve the pristine American wilderness for future generations and he established many bird sanctuaries and national parks. Today he would be considered an environmental activist. For his forceful prudence and foresight—all with the public's wellbeing in mind—Roosevelt was elected by a landslide in 1904.

On the world stage, TR, as he came to be known, worked actively to promote America's image as a world power. In 1903, when the region of Panama revolted against Colombia, he extended immediate diplomatic recognition—and negotiated construction of the strategic Panama Canal. The president then enunciated the Roosevelt Corollary to the now famous Monroe Doctrine, which stipulated that the United States dominated the Western Hemisphere and European interference would not be tolerated. In 1906 he took his mediation skills to a new level by negotiating a peace treaty between Russia and Japan, thereby ending the Russo-Japanese War in Asia. For this he became the first United States executive to receive the Nobel Peace Prize. Finally and most symbolically, in 1907 he dispatched a squadron of warships, the "Great White Fleet," on a global diplomatic mission to underscore America's arrival as a world power.

In 1909 Roosevelt stepped down from power in favor of his successor, WILLIAM HOWARD TAFT. He then embarked on a famous series of safaris and exploring expeditions in Africa and South America. However, by 1912 he had grown dissatisfied with the resurgence of conservatism in the Republican Party under Taft, so he formed his own Bull Moose Party from disaffected progressives like himself. Presidential elections that year were won by Democrat WOODROW WILSON, but Roosevelt's party finished second, garnering more votes than any third party in American history. Over the next few years he vigorously championed American entry into World War I and castigated Wilson's reluctance to commit forces. When war was finally declared in 1917, Roosevelt pleaded to be made a commander, but Wilson, smarting from his earlier remarks, refused. Roosevelt was preparing to run again for the presidency when he died at Oyster Bay, New York, on January 6,

1919. The cause of death was malaria contracted from one of his forays into the Brazilian jungles. But more than any individual, TR modernized the American presidency and prepared the nation for the global roles it would assume for the remainder of the 20th century. Roosevelt is also immortalized by the "Teddy Bear," so christened after he refused to shoot a bear cub while on a hunting trip.

Further Reading

Corry, John A. *A Rough Ride to Albany: Teddy Runs for Governor.* New York: J. A. Corry, 2000.

Dalton, Kathleen. *Theodore Roosevelt: A Strenuous Life.* New York: Alfred A. Knopf, 2002.

Kingseed, Wyatt. "Teddy Roosevelt's Frontier Justice." *American History* 36, no. 6 (2002): 22–28.

Morris, Edmund. *Theodore Rex.* New York: Random House, 2001.

Rauchway, Eric. *Murdering McKinley: The Making of Theodore Roosevelt's America.* New York: Hill and Wang, 2003.

Roosevelt, Theodore. *The Man in the Arena: The Selected Writings of Theodore Roosevelt.* New York: Forge, 2003.

Watts, Sarah L. *Rough Rider in the White House: Theodore Roosevelt and the Politics of Desire.* Chicago: University of Chicago Press, 2003.

Zimmerman, Warren. *First Great Triumph: How Five Americans Made Their Country a World Power.* New York: Farrar, Straus, and Giroux, 2002.

Roxas, Manuel (1892–1948) *president of the Philippines*

Manuel Roxas y Acuña was born in Capiz, Panay, the Philippines, on January 1, 1892, and in 1911 he graduated from the University of the Philippines with a law degree. After serving as a law professor in Hong Kong, he came home and was elected governor of his native province of Capiz in 1919. Two years later he successfully ran for a seat in the House of Representatives as a member of the Nationalist Party. There he struck up cordial relations with MANUEL QUEZON, president of the Senate, who assisted him in his efforts to become house speaker. Politics were then dominated by the issue of obtaining independence from the United States. Roxas attended several conferences in Washington, D.C., to facilitate this goal, but he clashed with Quezon over the exact treaty provisions. By 1934 both governments agreed to the establishment of a Filipino commonwealth to be followed by independence in 1946. Roxas then attended the constitutional conventional to draft a governing document and again differed with Quezon over details. However, when Quezon was elected the first president of the commonwealth in 1936, the two men apparently settled their differences and Roxas was appointed to the National Economic Council. In 1938 he joined the president's cabinet as secretary of finance.

Roxas was elected to the Senate just as World War II erupted in the Pacific in December 1941. He promptly resigned from office, took up arms, and fought in the Philippine Army Reserve as an aide to American general Douglas MacArthur. Unlike Quezon, Roxas stayed behind during the Japanese occupation and fought as a guerrilla. Captured in 1942, he was coerced into serving under a puppet government as chairman of the Economic Planning Board. This led to charges of collaboration with the enemy, but in reality Roxas was a high-ranking Allied spy. Following Japan's defeat in 1945, he was arrested as a traitor but subsequently released on the orders of the newly returned general MacArthur.

Having cleared his reputation, Roxas next served as president of the Senate. He then announced his candidacy for the national presidency and established the new Liberal Party. Roxas defeated Sergio Osmena of the Nationalist Party, who succeeded to high office following the death of President Quezon in 1944. Roxas assumed office in April 1946, becoming the last president of the Philippine commonwealth. Following the full transfer of sovereignty the following July, he became the first president of the Philippine republic. Roxas faced the unenviable task of running a nation and an economy ruined by war. Worse, a group of communist guerrillas, the Hukbalahap, having fought the Japanese, now refused to lay down their arms and resisted the new government. There was little Roxas could do in either instance but accept large amounts of aid in exchange for political compliance with the Americans. In fact, his government was basically an extension of General MacArthur's headquarters, and he proved slavishly obedient to the latter's dictates. Through his cooperation, the United States acquired 99-year leases on 23 sites, including Subic Naval Base and Clark Air Force Base. He also generally sided with the landed elite against the wishes and interests of the majority poor. Roxas continued working closely with the Americans until his sudden death at Clark Air Force Base on April 14, 1948, while delivering a speech. His successor was ELPIDIO QUIRINO.

Further Reading

Gleeck, Lewis E. *Dissolving the Colonial Bond: American Ambassadors to the Philippines, 1946–1984.* Denver, Colo.: iAcademic Books, 2001.

Go, Julian, and Anne L. Foster. *The American Colonial State in the Philippines: Global Perspectives.* Durham, N.C.: Duke University Press, 2003.

Martinez, Carlos M. "Filipino Collaboration and Resistance Movement Against the Japanese during World War II." Unpublished master's thesis, San Diego State University, 2001.

McFerson, Hazel M., ed. *Mixed Blessing: The Impact of the American Colonial Experience on Politics and Society in the Philippines.* Westport, Conn.: Greenwood Press, 2002.

Roxas, Manuel. *The Philippines.* New York: Foreign Policy Association, 1930.

Salamanca, Bonafacio S. "Quezon, Osmena, Roxas, and the American Military Presence in the Philippines." *Philippines Studies* 37, no. 3 (1989): 301–316.

Ruiz Cortines, Adolfo (1891–1973) *president of Mexico*

Adolfo Ruiz Cortines was born in Veracruz, Mexico, on December 30, 1891, the son of a poor civil servant. His father died while he was still young and he quit school support his family. When the Mexican Revolution recommenced in 1914, Ruiz Cortines joined the army under VENUSTIANO CARRANZA in the fight against VICTORIANO HUERTA. He subsequently served as an aide to Alfredo Robles Domínguez, governor of the Federal District (Mexico City). Despite his lack of formal education, Ruiz Cortines was an accomplished administrator known for his honesty. By 1937 he was serving in the administration of MANUEL ÁVILA CAMACHO within the government secretariat and in 1944 he won election as governor of Veracruz. In 1948 he resumed working for the secretariat, only this time under President MIGUEL ALEMÁN VALDÉS, a friend and mentor. After serving capably for three years, Alemán nominated Ruiz Cortines as the presidential candidate for the Partido Revolucionario Institucional (PRI), Institutional Revolutionary Party. Mexico being a one-party state, this nomination virtually ensured election, and in December 1952 Ruiz Cortines became president with 74 percent of votes cast. He was the last man of the revolutionary generation to hold high office in Mexico.

Ruiz Cortines inherited from his predecessor a demoralized government rife with corruption and nearly bankrupt from extravagant expenditures. Therefore he quickly embarked on a course to combat institutionalized corruption and implemented a program of national austerity. Ruiz Cortines pursued basic conservative economic and social policies, but he continued emphasizing Alemán's plans for the infrastructure, including greater efforts to modernize the railways, enlarge the electrical industry, and accelerate oil exploration. Furthermore, he increased the amount of acreage under cultivation and spurred on efforts to improve irrigation. That he was able to accomplish all these measures in an atmosphere of fiscal retrenchment is stirring tribute to his skills as an administrator. The government was thus able to reduce corruption and balance the budget. Economic growth, while slower than previously, remained constant throughout his presidency. On the downside, Ruiz Cortines was forced to devalue the peso twice to curb inflation, engendering labor unrest because it reduced spending power. All told, his administration exerted a moderating effect on the usually unpredictable Mexican economy and ushered in a badly needed period of stability.

In addition to his fine handling of the economy, Ruiz Cortines scored positive progress in social matters as well. He insisted that women be enfranchised in 1953 and he also sought to enlarge the Mexican social security agency. This entailed extending the program to workers in the countryside for the first time, as well as hikes in the rates for those living in and around Mexico City. On the international scene, his administration maintained cordial relations with American president DWIGHT D. EISENHOWER, and the two men met to inaugurate the newly constructed Falcon Dam on the border. To display a measure of political independence from the United States, Ruiz Cortines also allowed Guatemalan president JACOBO ARBENZ GUZMÁN and Cuban revolutionary lawyer Fidel Castro political asylum in Mexico. By the time he turned the government over to ADOLFO LÓPEZ MATEOS in December 1958, the Mexican economy was sound and the society tranquil.

As the country's leader, Ruiz Cortines was noted for his extreme humility and personal honesty. He sought to impose his high moral standards on government officials by requiring them annually to publish their monetary assets. Moreover, throughout six years in office he declined the government limousine and drove himself to work. Ruiz Cortines continued living modestly until his death in Veracruz on December 3, 1973. He remains highly regarded as a leader of personal integrity.

Further Reading

Glade, William P. *Politics, Policies, and Economic Development in Latin America.* Stanford, Calif.: Hoover Institution Press, 1984.

Memmott, Kip R. "Enduring Friendship: An Analysis of United States-Mexican Foreign Relations, 1950–1970." Unpublished master's thesis, Arizona State University, 1995.

Moreno, Julio. *Yankee Don't Go Home!: Mexican Nationalism, American Business Culture, and the Shaping of Modern Mexico.* Chapel Hill: University of North Carolina Press, 2003.

Parsons, Patricia. "The First Two Years of the Ruiz Cortines Administration." Unpublished master's thesis, Stanford University, 1955.

Preston, Julia. *Opening Mexico: A Country's Tumultuous Passage to Democracy.* New York: Farrar, Straus and Giroux, 2004.

Rwagasore, Louis (1932–1961) *prime minister of Burundi*

Prince Louis Rwagasore was born in Gitega, Burundi, a son of Mwami (king) Mwambutsa. His homeland had been ruled by Belgium as a League of Nations mandate since 1916. It was beset by intense ethnic rivalries between competing clans of Tutsis and Hutus, which occasionally flared up into massacres of genocidal proportions. Rwagasore passed through Catholic missionary schools before attending the Groupe Scolaire D'Astrida, a school for tribal elites, in 1945. He subsequently ventured to Antwerp, Belgium, for additional training at college, but performed poorly. Rwagasore came home in 1956 determined to challenge Belgian authority. He entered politics by organizing farming cooperatives without European interference—

or permission—which colonial authorities declared illegal. The following year Rwagasore took measures a step further by founding the Union pour le Progrès National (UPRONA), Union for National Progress, as an agent for political change. At the onset he supported the continuation of Burundi's traditional kingship within the framework of greater colonial autonomy. However, he failed to mesh his progressive viewpoints with his father's inherent conservatism and began questioning the throne's relevance to national politics. And, despite his affiliation with the Crown, colonial authorities had branded him a communist for his political agitation. "The Belgians accuse us of being communists," he later quipped. "At the same time they accuse us of being monarchists and feudal. They must make up their minds what we really are."

By 1960 the pace of decolonizing quickened when Belgium announced that the neighboring Congo was about to receive its independence. This caused political ripples throughout Burundi and renewed calls for nationhood. Ironically, Rwagasore's biggest opponent was his father, the king, who feared a loss of traditional power and began siding with the Belgians. He also met opposition at the hands of the Parti Démocrate Chrétien (PDC), Christian Democratic Party, which sought to maintain the political status quo. When legislative elections were finally granted in 1960, UPRONA, formally opposed by Mwambutsa and the Europeans, "lost" handily. But Rwagasore, angered by rigged elections, went before the United Nations to declare that Belgium mishandled its civic responsibilities toward the mandate and demanded new elections. He was supported by his friend and ally JULIUS NYERERE of Tanganyika, and the UN agreed to sponsor a new round of elections. These took place in September 1961, and UPRONA was completely victorious. Rwagasore then became Burundi's first prime minister.

The movement toward eventual independence was still perilous owing to uneasy relationships between the Tutsi minority and the Hutu majority. Therefore, when assembling his cabinet, Rwagasore was careful to balance off four Hutus against four Tutsis. He also pledged that members of opposition parties would eventually be merged into the government. Furthermore, in light of Burundi's small size, extreme poverty, and total dependence upon Belgium for financial and technical assistance, Rwagasore favored entering a federation arrangement with neighboring Tanganyika and Rwanda. However, on October 13, 1961, the youthful 29-year-old prime minister was assassinated at a restaurant by a hired gunman. Subsequent investigations pointed to Belgian complicity, although several leaders of the PDC were eventually arrested and executed. Burundi went on to acquire its independence on July 1, 1962. Rwagasore has since been mourned as the father of his country and a voice of moderation and restraint. With his passing came the introduction of radicalized politics, the abolishment of the kingship, and years of bloody repression under the genocidal dictator MICHEL MICOMBERO. Most political observers feel that Burundi might have evolved more peacefully had Rwagasore lived.

Further Reading

Chretien, Jean-Pierre. *The Great Lakes of Africa: Two Thousand Years of History.* New York: Zone Books, 2003.

———. "Burundi: The Obsession with Genocide." *Current History* 95 (May 1996): 206–211.

Forster, Peter G. *Race and Ethnicity in East Africa.* New York: St. Martin's Press, 2000.

Scherrer, Christian P. *Genocide and Crisis in Central Africa: Conflict Roots, Mass Violence, and Regional War.* Westport, Conn.: Praeger, 2002.

Weinstein, Warren. "A Sea of Troubles: Decolonization in Burundi, 1958–1962." Unpublished master's thesis, Columbia University, 1973.

S

Sadat, Anwar al- (1918–1981) *president of Egypt*
Muhammad Anwar al-Sadat was born in Mit Abdul-Kum, Egypt, on December 25, 1918, the son of a lower-middle-class civil servant. He matured at a time when the country was under British domination, which stirred his sense of Arab nationalism. In 1936 Sadat became one of the first persons of modest background to attend the Royal Military Academy, where he met and befriended another nationalist, GAMAL ABDEL NASSER. After graduating in 1938 he and Nasser founded the Free Officers Organization, a secret revolutionary society intent upon expelling the British and overthrowing the Egyptian royal family. During World War II he was implicated in several attempts to aid Nazi intelligence, was imprisoned, and escaped. After the war Sadat continued with his revolutionary activities and bore a direct role in the assassination of Egypt's pro-British finance minister. Egypt's economy began deteriorating through the corrupt misrule of King FAROUK, so in July 1952 the Free Officers ousted him in a bloodless coup. A republic was declared with Nasser as president, while Sadat became vice president in 1964. He served his cause loyally, if in a low-keyed manner, and when Nasser died suddenly in September 28, 1970, Sadat succeeded him as interim president. The following month he was formally elected to office.

Sadat's ascension marked a sea change in the political landscape of the Middle East. Since losing the Arab-Israeli War in 1967, he wanted to fight again to improve Egypt's bargaining position. Nasser had previously established close relations with the Soviet Union, which provided arms and military advisers but also an unwelcome political presence. On May 27, 1971, Sadat also willingly signed a 15-year treaty of friendship with the Soviets to acquire aid and modern arms. But, intent upon demonstrating his independence, he suddenly and unceremoniously expelled the Russians from Egypt in 1972. He then made the first friendly overtures to the United States in 20 years, with set Egypt on a pro-Western course. But the turning point in Sadat's career occurred in October 1973, when Egyptian and Syrian forces launched the surprise Yom Kippur War against the Jewish state. Israeli forces, heretofore considered invincible, were caught flat-footed and driven far into the Sinai Peninsula. Both sides suffered heavy losses before a truce was arranged, but Sadat had proved his point: henceforth it would be better to bargain than fight. At that juncture he began secret negotiations with the United States and Israel for possible peace talks—an unthinkable prospect only months before. On November 20, 1977, Sadat made a bold and triumphal appearance in the Israeli Knesset (parliament) to plead for peace and normalized diplomatic relations—the first-ever appearance by an Arab head of state. Two years of fruitless and highly charged talks ensued before American president JIMMY CARTER invited Sadat and Israeli prime minister MENACHEM BEGIN to Camp David, Maryland. After fits and starts, a peace accord was signed on March 29, 1979, through which Israel abandoned captured land in the Sinai Peninsula while Egypt established diplomatic relations with Israel. This was the first formal recognition of the Jewish state by an Arab power and Sadat and Begin received the Nobel Peace Prize for their heroic breakthrough efforts.

Sadat was hailed in the West for his personal courage, but utterly castigated at home and throughout the Arab world as a pariah. Egypt was summarily kicked out of the Arab League, while Muslim fundamentalists at home called for his assassination. Despite Western aid, Egypt's burgeoning population prevented economic growth, and resistance to Sadat's rule increased. He responded with escalating repression, and at one point even exiled the Coptic Christian pope to the desert. Sadat and his free-wheeling, half-British wife Jihan also lived a life of conspicuous wealth, which further alienated people in this conservative Muslim society. On October 6, 1981, Sadat was assassinated by religious zealots while reviewing a military parade. His state funeral was attended by many Western dignitaries, including three former American presidents—but only one Arabic head of state. Sadat's successor, Hosni Mubarak, has continued his pro-Western policies and diplomacy.

Further Reading

Ayubi, Shaheen. *Nasser and Sadat: Decision Making and Foreign Policy (1970–1972)*. Lanham, Md.: University Press of America, 1994.

Beattie, Kirk J. *Egypt during the Sadat Years.* New York: St. Martin's Press, 2001.

Israeli, Raphael. "Egypt's Nationalism under Sadat." *Journal of South Asian and Middle Eastern Studies* 21, no. 4 (1998): 1–23.

Ronen, Y. "Personalized Politics: Qadhafi, Nasser, Sadat, and Mubarak." *North African Studies* 6 (autumn 2001): 1–10.

Sadat, Anwar. *Those I Have Known.* New York: Continuum, 1984.

Stein, Kenneth W. *Heroic Diplomacy: Sadat, Kissinger, Carter, Begin, and the Quest for Arab-Israeli Peace.* New York: Routledge, 1999.

St. Laurent, Louis (1882–1973) *prime minister of Canada*

Louis Stephen St. Laurent was born in Compton, Quebec, Canada, on February 1, 1882, the son of a small store owner. His father and mother being French and Irish respectively, he was raised in a bilingual environment and gained fluency in both languages. St. Laurent passed through Laval University Law School in 1905 and established a brilliant legal career. He taught as a law professor at Laval, served as head of the Quebec Bar Association, and then president of the Canadian Bar Association. In 1937 St. Laurent was appointed to the Royal Commission on Dominion-Provincial Relations, where he remained until 1940. That year Prime Minister WILLIAM LYON MACKENZIE KING tapped him to serve as Canada's new minister of justice. St. Laurent, who had taken no interest in politics and lacked any party affiliation, hesitated initially but finally accepted out of a sense of duty. Throughout World War II he effectively represented French Canadian interests in the cabinet. This proved a delicate proposition, for heavy manpower losses required Mackenzie King to impose conscription on all of Canada—including Quebec—to maintain the war effort. The French-speaking community was traditionally averse to a draft, and unwilling to shed blood for the British Empire, and when it came in 1944, St. Laurent promoted national unity among his fellow Quebecers. In 1945 he was persuaded to remain in office another term. He then assumed the portfolio of external affairs minister and represented Canada during the drafting conference of the United Nations in San Francisco. To further raise Canada's international profile, he also advocated membership in the new North Atlantic Treaty Organization (NATO) to contain Soviet communism in Europe. In November 1948, following Mackenzie King's retirement, St. Laurent was persuaded to succeed him in office. More out of a sense of duty than desire, he became head of the Liberal Party and prime minister of Canada. He was only the second French Canadian head of state since WILFRID LAURIER.

St. Laurent's period in office happily coincided with a booming national economy and full governmental coffers. St. Laurent set about spending the money wisely and invested in the country's infrastructure. Among his most significant accomplishments were construction of the Trans-Canada national highway, commencement of the St. Lawrence Seaway with the United States, and the admission of Newfoundland into the dominion as a province. He also tackled the touchy issue of equalization payments whereby wealthy provinces like Ontario contributed money to assist poorer regions so that all offered the same quality of social programs. St. Laurent also oversaw enlargement of the welfare state with enhanced benefits. Under his persuasive leadership, the Liberals easily won elections in 1949 and 1953. Considering his reluctance to lead, his time in office was highly productive.

On the diplomatic front, St. Laurent took deliberate measures to ensure Canada's standing as an international player. The Korean War commenced in June 1950, and he authorized the deployment of Canadian forces under United Nations supervision for the next three years. Stridently anticommunist, St. Laurent closely coordinated his defense and diplomatic efforts with American president DWIGHT D. EISENHOWER in confronting Soviet threats to peace. But after a round-the-world trip in 1956, the prime minister seemed tired and disinterested in politics. His sharp criticism of Great Britain's handling of the Suez Crisis alienated segments of the English-speaking community, who were quick to rally to Britain's side. Ironically, St. Laurent's downfall came through one of his pet projects: the Trans-Canada Pipeline. When it became known that this ambitious project was to be constructed by an American company, the opposition threw Parliament in turmoil and the Liberals deliberately closed down debate. This angered the public at large, and in 1957 the Conservatives under JOHN G. DIEFENBAKER were swept back into office after 22 years in the opposition. St. Laurent remained as head of the Liberals for another year, but subsequently stepped down in favor of LESTER B. PEARSON in 1958. He died in Quebec City on July 25, 1973. He had been regarded from the onset as a colorless technocrat, but his grandfatherly demeanor earned him the sobriquet Uncle Louis.

Further Reading

Bercuson, David J. *Blood on the Hills: The Canadian Army in the Korean War.* Buffalo, N.Y.: University of Toronto Press, 1999.

Glazov, Jamie. *Canadian Policy toward Khrushchev's Soviet Union.* Montreal: McGill-Queen's University Press, 2002.

Pickersgill, J. W. *My Years with Louis St. Laurent: A Political Memoir.* Buffalo, N.Y.: University of Toronto Press, 1975.

St. Laurent, Louis. *The Foundations of Canadian Policy in World Affairs.* Toronto: University of Toronto Press, 1947.

Thomson, Dale C. *Louis St. Laurent, Canadian.* New York: St. Martin's Press, 1968.

Whitaker, Reginald. *Cold War Canada: The Making of a National Insecurity State, 1945–1957.* Buffalo, N.Y.: University of Toronto Press, 1994.

Saionji Kimmochi (1849–1940) *prime minister of Japan*

Saionji Kimmochi was born in Kyoto, Japan, on December 7, 1849, into a prestigious aristocratic family with close links to the emperor. At the age of three he was adopted by a higher-ranking family, which brought him closer to the center of national power. Saionji matured during a time of great national ferment, when the Tokugawa shogunate, or military regimen, was about to be overthrown by the imperial household. This event, known as the Meiji restoration of 1868, concluded nearly three centuries of isolation and reintroduced Japan to world politics. Saionji was a promising scholar, and in 1871 he ventured to France and enrolled at the Sorbonne. He remained in France for a decade, studying Western philosophy and democracy before returning home in 1880. At that time he established a law school and also initiated a radical newspaper, the *East Asian Free Press,* which advocated both democracy and modernization. He refused strong pressure to resign, until personally ordered by the emperor to relent. In 1882 he returned to Europe for additional study and served as minister to Austria and Germany. Saionji then came home to serve as minister of education, acting prime minister in 1900, and founder of the Rikken Seiyukai (Friends of Constitutional Government) Party. In all these capacities Saionji wielded great influence on the course of political affairs in Japan and in 1903 he was elected party head. The nation at that time was still attempting to adjust to the nuances of democracy and in 1906 he was elevated to prime minister.

Saionji served in high office until 1908 and his most notable accomplishment was nationalizing the railway system. After more internal wrangling, he again assumed high office in 1911 but resigned the following year after refusing to expand the army. At that time the Taisho emperor elevated him to the position of genro,

Kimmochi Saionji *(Library of Congress)*

power was the only method of securing Japan's future. For nearly a decade Saionji waged a lonely and futile battle to keep the army and navy in check. In May 1932 militarists assassinated the civilian prime minister, at which point party cabinets ceased to be formed. Thereafter Saionji recommended the selection of military figures for high office, as they were less likely to be marked for assassination. As the decade of the 1930s unfolded, the Japanese military embarked on several episodes of imperialistic aggression against China, which Saionji and other civilians proved powerless to stop. "Military men advocate national unity, but their national unity is no unity at all," he warned, "it just means submission to them." Still, he sought peaceful relations with Great Britain and the United States to avert what he viewed as a potentially disastrous war. In February 1936 he narrowly survived an assassination attempt caused by his peaceful inclination. Just before resigning in 1937 Saionji selected Prince FUMIMARO KONOE to serve as prime minister in the mistaken belief that he could curtail the military. He died in Tokyo on November 24, 1940, the longest living survivor of Meiji generation leadership, whose career spanned seven decades.

Further Reading

Banno, Junji. *Democracy in Pre-war Japan: Concepts of Government, 1871–1937: Collected Essays.* New York: Routledge, 2000.

Connors, Lesley. *The Emperor's Advisor: Saionji Kimmochi and Pre-war Japanese Politics.* London: Croom Helm, 1987.

Harada, Kumao. *Fragile Victory: Prince Saionji and the 1930 London Treaty Issue.* Detroit: Wayne State University Press, 1968.

Jansen, Marius B. *The Making of Modern Japan.* Cambridge, Mass.: Belknap Press of Harvard University Press, 2000.

Nish, Ian H. *Japanese Foreign Policy in the Interwar Period.* Westport, Conn.: Praeger Publishers, 2002.

Ohara, Masayo. *Democratization and Expansionism: Historical Lessons, Contemporary Challenges.* Westport, Conn.: Praeger, 2001.

Oka, Yoshitake. *Five Political Leaders of Modern Japan.* Tokyo: University of Tokyo Press, 1986.

Saionji, Kimmochi. *The Saionji-Harada Memoirs.* Washington, D.C.: University Publications of America, 1978.

or elder statesman, which marks the most important phase of his long political career. Several other former samurai of his generation had also been accorded that rank, but Saionji became the only court aristocrat so honored. In this capacity he represented Japan during the 1919 Paris Peace Conference and presided over Japan's entry into the League of Nations. Thereafter he served as a senior political adviser to the new emperor HIROHITO, working behind the scenes and dispensing useful advice, concerning, among other affairs of government, the selection of prime ministers. His power was greatly consolidated after 1924 when he became the last surviving genro and a persuasive force in governmental affairs.

Unfortunately for Japan, its tenuous experiment with democracy began fading in the wake of the Great Depression of 1929. The hardships encountered convinced militarists and nationalists that overt military

Salazar, António (1889–1970) *prime minister of Portugal*

António de Oliveira Salazar was born in Vimiero, Portugal, on April 28, 1889, the son of poor shopkeepers. Studious and pious as a youth, he studied several years at a seminary before leaving the clergy to study economics at Coimbra University. After receiving his doctorate in 1918 he taught several years and became politically active in 1921 when he was elected to the Cortes (legislature) with the Catholic Center Party. However, Salazar served only for a day before concluding that the legislature was useless and he resumed teaching. He also resented the First Republic for its leftist tendencies and pronounced anticlericalism. When a military junta overthrew the republic in 1926, he was cordially invited to serve as minister of finance but declined because of his inability to control the economy. Two years later the government agreed to his terms, and he assumed public office for the first time. Salazar, a fiscal conservative, adopted tight-fisted spending cuts and high-tax policies to balance the budget and end deficit spending. The economy rebounded remarkably within two years and Salazar was rewarded with the portfolio of minister of colonies in 1931. When the military finally authorized civilian rule in July 1932, Salazar became prime minister with near dictatorial powers. He would remain head of state for the next 32 years.

In office Salazar adopted what can best be described as a quasi-fascist, authoritarian style of governance, the so-called New State. This was a corporate, conservative regime with striking similarities to BENITO MUSSOLINI's Italy. Unions and political parties were outlawed, strikes forbidden, and order enforced by secret police. The nation was divided up into white- and blue-collar blocs, with the government acting as intermediary between them. The Catholic Church was given free rein to operate schools and run charities as an adjunct of the state and, consequently, became a pillar of Salazar's support. Henceforth, "Nothing against the nation, everything for the nation" became the political mantra. For over a decade the government enjoyed considerable popularity and contributed much to the economic well-being of the nation, which Salazar considered far more important than individual liberties. A plethora of important social reforms, including social security, workmen's compensation, and public works, were enacted with impressive results.

After 1936 Salazar proved himself a stalwart ally of Spanish dictator FRANCISCO FRANCO and dispatched men and supplies to him throughout the Spanish civil war. After 1939 the Iberian peninsula could tout two right-wing authoritarian regimes with sterling anticommunist credentials. In terms of foreign policy, Salazar adhered to a closely regulated policy of neutrality. Despite his admiration for ADOLF HITLER's Nazi Germany, he declined to become an ally. He judged the war lost by 1944 and secretly allowed the Allies basing rights in the Azores off the Portuguese coast, to combat the U-boat menace. Given Portugal's strategic position in the cold war, Salazar's government was openly courted by the United States and Great Britain, and in 1948 he was coaxed out of neutrality to join the North Atlantic Treaty Organization (NATO). By this time, however, Salazar had begun assuming more and more power for himself and ruling in a dictatorial fashion. His mounting repression led to a steady exodus of middle-class bureaucrats with detrimental effects upon the economy. He refused to acknowledge the trend toward decolonization around the world and tenaciously maintained the facade of empire. In 1961 he lost the Portuguese colony at Goa to an Indian invasion, while the Soviet Union began arming liberation movements in Angola and Mozambique. With ever-shrinking resources, Salazar committed heavily to the defense of African possessions. The declining economy and mass immigration contributed to growing discontent and cries for increased democracy. Salazar remained oblivious to change, but in 1968 he had a stroke that effectively removed him from power. He died in Lisbon on July 27, 1970, one of the longest-serving heads of state in the 20th century. Unfortunately, his legacy was largely one of oppression.

Further Reading

Costa Pinto, Antonio. *The Blue Shirts: Portuguese Fascists and the New State.* Boulder, Colo.: Social Science Monographs; New York: dist. by Columbia University Press, 2000.

———. *Salazar's Dictatorship and European Fascism: Problems of Interpretation.* Boulder, Colo.: Social Science Monographs, 1995.

Lewis, Paul H. *Latin Fascist Regimes: The Mussolini, Franco, and Salazar Regimes.* Westport, Conn.: Praeger, 2002.

Machado, Diamantino P. *The Structure of Portuguese Society: The Failure of Fascism.* New York: Praeger, 1991.

Raby, Dawn L. *Fascism and Resistance in Portugal: Communists, Liberals, and Military Dissidents in the Opposition to Salazar, 1941–1974.* New York: Manchester University Press, 1988.

Salazar, António. *Doctrine and Action: Internal and Foreign Policy of the New Portugal, 1928–1939.* London: Faber and Faber, 1939.

Sarkis, Elias (1924–1985) *president of Lebanon*

Elias Sarkis was born in Shibaniyah, Lebanon, on July 20, 1924, the son of a small shopkeeper and a Maronite Christian. Despite humble origins he proved adept as a student and passed through St. Joseph University with a law degree. In 1953 he came to the attention of President CAMILLE CHAMOUN, who appointed him a judge with the Court of Audits. In this capacity he demonstrated ability and integrity, so in 1958 he transferred to the administration of President Fuad Chehab as a legal adviser. There he figured prominently in strengthening the powers of the presidency and subsequently rose to chief of staff. Sarkis then organized the Deuxième Bureau, a clandestine security agency aimed at keeping various armed factions under control. When President Charles Helou took office, he successively appointed Sarkis chairman of the Banking Control Commission in 1963 and governor of the Central Bank in 1968. Sarkis, who had no interest in politics, was encouraged by friends to run for the presidency in 1970. Through a unique power-sharing arrangement, the Lebanese presidency was reserved for a Christian, the prime minister's office for a Sunni Muslim, and the Speaker of the House a Shiite Muslim. Tight-lipped and reticent, Sarkis was known jocularly as "The Sphinx" and respected for his honesty, but he lost to Suleiman Franjiyeh by a single vote. However, the fractious Lebanese polity grew increasingly tense in the face of religious fundamentalism, and in 1975 a three-way civil war erupted among Christians, Sunnis, and Shiites. Complicating this picture was the presence of thousands of armed refugees under the Palestine Liberation Organization (PLO), and a looming Syrian military presence. Heavy fighting ensued before peace could be restored and new elections held.

It now fell upon Syrian president Hafiz al-Assad to play kingmaker in Lebanon. Finding he could not manipulate the PLO or the Muslim militias to his liking, he next courted the Maronites under Sarkis, who appeared more pliable. Syrian pressure was applied accordingly, and in May 1976 Sarkis was elected president by the national assembly. He was the first person of common background to hold high office, but he inherited a rapidly deteriorating situation. The various armed militias began fighting among themselves, while the PLO launched guerrilla attacks into northern Israel. This prompted sharp military responses from the Jewish state, and in 1978 Israel briefly occupied southern Lebanon to establish a buffer zone defended by Christian militia. By that time the country was a battleground of bickering factions and rapidly changing alliances. Sarkis initially looked to his Syrian sponsors for help in disarming the PLO fighters by force. But because Israel would not allow the Syrians into southern Lebanon, Assad declined to risk a military confrontation, and the Palestinians remained a force to reckon with. In time the Maronites and Syrians also turned against one another, forcing Sarkis to rely on Israel for support. In June 1982 Israel launched a full-scale invasion of Lebanon and occupied Beirut, further destabilizing the situation. Sarkis did everything in his limited powers to reconcile the warring factions and hold the nation together, but he proved powerless to influence events.

On August 23, 1982, the new president-elect, Maronite Bashir Gemayel, was assassinated days before taking office. Previously Sarkis had tried moving him away from dependence upon Israel and closer to the United States. Bashir Gemayel was succeeded by his younger brother AMIN GEMAYEL, and Sarkis resigned. The former Lebanese president was completely disillusioned by his lack of control over events in Lebanon, and he withdrew from public life. The fighting between factions increased over time, prompting him to leave the country and settle in Paris. He died there on June 27, 1985, a capable man in an impossible position.

Further Reading

Baqraduni, Karim. *Stillborn Peace: The Mandate of Elias Sarkis, 1976–1982.* Beirut, Lebanon: Editions FMA, 1985.

Deeb, Marius. *Syria's Terrorist War on Lebanon and the Peace Process.* New York: Palgrave, 2003.

Fisk, Robert. *Pity the Nation: The Abduction of Lebanon.* New York: Oxford University Press, 2001.

Khalaf, Samir. *Cultural Resistance: Global and Local Encounters in the Middle East.* London: Saqi, 2001.

Phares, Walid. *Lebanese Christian Nationalism: The Rise and Fall of an Ethnic Resistance.* Boulder, Colo.: Lynne Rienner Publishers, 1995.

Rabil, Robert G. *Embattled Neighbors: Syria, Israel, Lebanon.* Boulder, Colo.: Lynne Rienner Publishers, 2003.

Sarney, José (1930–) *president of Brazil*

José Ribamar Ferreira Araujo was born in Pinheiro, Maranhão, Brazil, on April 24, 1930, one of 14 children from a poor peasant family. In 1968 he legally adopted his childhood nickname of José Sarney. He studied law in nearby São Luis, worked briefly as a journalist, and wound up on the governor's staff in Maranhão state by 1950. In 1954 Sarney won a seat in the federal legislature as a member of the National Democratic Union and was twice reelected in 1958 and 1962. He lost his seat after the 1964 military coup that outlawed political activity, but the following year was elected governor of Maranhão under the Alliança per la Renovaçõ Nacional (ARENA), Alliance for National Renewal. In this capacity he subsequently founded the Partido Democrata Social (PDS), Social Democratic Party, and twice served as president. Following the gradual relaxation of military rule and a resumption of the political process, Sarney captured a senate seat in 1970 and won it again six years later. By this time he was clearly identified with conservative interests but, when asked by the government to support the hard-line conservative candidacy of Paulo Maluf, he refused and denounced the party apparatus. After the first free elections were scheduled for 1985, Sarney switched alliances by joining the leftist Democratic Alliance ticket under presidential candidate Tancredo de Almeida Neves. That year the two men were successfully elected to high office, but Neves was taken ill before he could be sworn in, and Sarney functioned as interim president. When the president-elect died soon after, Sarney was sworn in as Brazil's first civilian executive in 21 years in March 1985. Outgoing conservative president JOÃO BAPTISTA FIGUEIREDO was so outraged by his defection to the left that he boycotted the swearing-in ceremony.

Sarney inherited a nation verging on economic collapse. Previous administrations had saddled Brazil with the largest national debt of any developing country, and inflation rates approaching 1,700 percent a year. Unemployment was also high and hunger was growing. The picture was further complicated by the notion that Sarney, a likable but noncharismatic pragmatist, lacked the skills and drive to lead the country back to solvency. Fortunately he was determined to surprise his critics. "I had to rise to the occasion and try to be larger than I am," he confided. He then unveiled his Crusader plan, which entailed tax increases, a temporary moratorium on income tax, and high interest rates. But despite his best efforts the Brazilian economy continued faltering, and by 1990 the national debt ballooned to $115 billion. Sarney was then forced to suspend interest payments on the debt and invoke other austerity measures to keep the economy moving. However, he ignored calls for greater cuts in social spending. "With this I cannot agree because I am responsible for the welfare of human beings and not for abstract numbers," Sarney insisted. Faced with mounting labor unrest, the president also faced down charges that his government tolerated corruption. His only positive contribution was the new 1988 constitution that weakened the powers of the executive while commensurately strengthening those of the legislature and judiciary.

By the time Sarney stepped down on March 15, 1990, and was succeeded by Fernando Collor de Mello, Brazil's economy was still in flux but national democracy had been strengthened decisively. He then founded the new Partido de Movimento Democratico Brasileiro (PMDB), Brazilian Democratic Movement Party, and returned to the senate under its banner. In 1994 he failed to gain the party's presidential nomination, but his daughter was elected to the senate. Sarney remains a force in national politics and has gained considerable renown as a writer and a poet.

Further Reading

Ames, Barry. *The Deadlock of Democracy in Brazil.* Ann Arbor: University of Michigan Press, 2002.

Cleary, David. *Local Boy Makes Good: José Sarney, Maranhão, and the Presidency of Brazil.* Glasgow, Scotland: University of Glasgow, 1987.

Flynn, Peter. "Brazil: The Politics of the Cruzado Plan." *Third World Quarterly* 8 (October 1986): 1151–94.

Pang, Eul-Soo. "The Darker Side of Brazilian Democracy." *Current History* 87 (January 1988): 21–24, 40–41.

Sarney, José. "Brazil: A President's Story." *Foreign Affairs* 65, no. 1 (1986): 101–117.

Valencia, M. M. "The Closure of the Brazilian Housing Bank and Beyond." *Urban Studies* 36 (September 1999): 1747–68.

Sato Eisaku (1901–1975) *prime minister of Japan*

Sato Eisaku was born in Tabuse, Japan, on March 27, 1901, the son of a prosperous brewer. His parents impressed on him a sense of duty to the nation, and in 1924 he graduated from Tokyo Imperial University with a law degree. Having entered the Ministry of Railways, Sato ventured abroad to the United States and Europe, and during World War II he served as the railways' chief of the bureau of control. He was not tainted as a militarist during the U.S. occupation of Japan and in 1948 was allowed to become vice minister of transportation. In this capacity Sato drew nearer to Prime Minister YOSHIDA SHIGERU, who made him chief cabinet secretary. Shortly after, he abandoned the bureaucracy altogether for politics and won a seat in the Diet (legislature). As Sato's protégé he held down a number of important government assignments, and in 1954 Yoshida used his influence to save Sato from accusations of bribery and corruption. Once the Liberal Democratic Party was formed, Sato threw his weight behind his brother, Nobusuke Kiski, to become prime minister in 1957, and functioned as his finance minister. He gained valuable experience as minister of international trade and industry and also coordinated the 1964 Olympics in Tokyo. That year Sato challenged IKEDA HAYATO to be party head but lost. However, when illness forced Ikeda out shortly after, Sato succeeded him as prime minister.

Sato assumed power at a significant crossroads in Japanese history. The economy was booming, and the nation was ripe for asserting its strategic and economic priorities in the Pacific. In 1965 he negotiated a treaty with South Korea that finally normalized diplomatic relations between the old adversaries. Sato then tackled the touchy issue of American military occupation of Okinawa, the largest of the Ryukyu Islands south of Japan. The United States military had maintained a visible military presence there since 1945, but residents chafed under its governance. In 1969 Sato ventured to

Washington, D.C., conferred with President RICHARD M. NIXON, and signed a new treaty that peacefully returned the Ryukyu and Bonin Islands to Japan. In exchange, Sato voiced his support for the American war in Vietnam and also pledged continuing close relations with the Nationalist regime on Taiwan under CHIANG KAI-SHEK. He also confronted serious domestic disturbances at home. Japan's college campuses, like those around the world, were beset by political and social unrest, but Sato quickly cracked down and reimposed order. His firmness and success at dealing with the Americans made him extremely popular, and he easily won reelection by wide margins in December 1969.

Sato enjoyed great success at expanding Japan's technological base, making it the world's second-largest economy after America. Throughout his tenure Japanese consumer and electronic products flourished around the globe and contributed to an embarrassing trade imbalance with the United States and other nations. However, like many Japanese politicians, he was shocked by President Nixon's surprise decision to visit China in 1972, and his government quickly initiated moves to normalize relations with its former adversary. In 1971 Sato managed to revise the existing Okinawa treaty with the United States, which allowed the Americans to maintain bases on the island under a pledge never to introduce nuclear weapons either there or on the mainland. His decision to allow the Americans to remain incurred political difficulties at home, as did his decision to pursue relations with China while still supporting Taiwan. In the face of interparty squabbling he resigned as prime minister in July 1972 and was replaced by TANAKA KAKUEI. Sato had led Japan for eight years, becoming the longest-serving Japanese prime minister of the 20th century. He died in Tokyo on June 2, 1975, one year after receiving the 1974 Nobel Peace Prize for his work in nuclear disarmament. His tenure in office also coincided with Japan's reemergence as a major international player.

Further Reading

Dixon, Carl V. "A Transitional Analysis of Political Leadership and Policies in Japan, 1970 to 1973, and Their Effect on the Political Future of Japan." Unpublished master's thesis, University of Texas–Arlington, 1978.

Ijiri, Hidenori. "The Politics of Japan's Decision to Normalize Relations with China, 1969–72."

Unpublished Ph.D. diss., University of California–Berkeley, 1988.

Ikeo, Aiko, ed. *Japanese Economics and Economists since 1945.* New York: Routledge, 2000.

Ito, Go. *Alliance in Anxiety: Detente and the Sino-American-Japanese Triangle.* New York: Routledge, 2003.

Luther, Catherine A. *Press Images, National Identity, and Foreign Relations: A Case Study of U.S.-Japan Relations from 1955–1995.* New York: Routledge, 2001.

Saud, Abd al-Aziz ibn (ca. 1881–1953) *king of Saudi Arabia*

Abd al-Aziz Ibn Saud was born in Riyadh around 1881, the son of an influential religious figure, Abd al-Rahman. The house of Saud had dominated the Arabian peninsula since the 1750s but their control fluctuated and proved tenuous. Intermittent difficulties with the rival house of Rashid resulted in exile to Kuwait in 1891, where Saud was raised in a conservative religious atmosphere. His sect in particular, Wahhabism, stressed purity of Islam and frowned upon corrupting outside influences. Saud matured into an intelligent and courageous young warrior, steeped in the nuances of Arabian tribal politics. Judging the moment right, he raised a small army in 1902, captured Riyadh from the Turks, and extended his control throughout the Qasim region. By 1913 he had captured al-Hasa on the Persian Gulf, which brought him into direct contact with British influence. Two years later Saud signed his first treaty with Great Britain, which promised not to interfere in tribal affairs provided he did not attack British interests. Saud also steered a neutral course during World War I out of his antipathy for the rival Hashemite leaders ABDULLAH IBN HUSSEIN and FAISAL I, but he was nonetheless rewarded by the British with money and weapons. Thus armed, he renewed his conquest of the peninsula, capturing the holy cities of Mecca and Medina in 1925. Further annexations followed, and in September 1932, Saud declared himself king of Saudi Arabia. He rejected modernism in favor of traditionalism and ruled as a desert sheik with several wives and 43 children. Furthermore he forbade modern representative political institutions and based his rule on strict accordance with traditional Islamic law. However, Saud recognized the use of modern technology, and he tempered his religious zeal to allow the importation and use of telephones, telegraphs, and highways.

Arabia had been a poverty-stricken region dominated by warring clans and religious feuds. Saud imposed order and discipline on his subjects through threats, entreaties, and intermarriage. He also eliminated brigandage by force and ensured that pilgrims could complete their annual trek to Mecca without interference. But the turning point in the history of the peninsula followed the discovery of vast reserves of oil in 1938. He immediately contracted with American companies to form the Arabian American Oil Company and received a steady influx of money from the profits. By 1953 these revenues tallied $2.5 million per week. Within a decade the house of Saud was among the richest families in the world. Cautious and conservative, Saud remained neutral throughout World War II, while still favoring Britain and the United States. In 1945 he gained international stature as a world leader for meeting with President FRANKLIN D. ROOSEVELT. That same

Abd al-Aziz ibn Saud *(Library of Congress)*

year, in light of the coming postcolonial era, he helped to found the Arab League to promote unity among the otherwise fractious Arab polity. Saud reaffirmed his position as a staunch American ally throughout the cold war and received their military protection in return.

By the time Saud died on November 9, 1953, Saudi Arabia had been transformed into a region of global and strategic significance. His judicious rule upheld traditional Islamic values and forestalled the onset of political corruption brought about by incredible wealth. He was succeeded by his sons Saud bin Abdul Aziz and, after 1964, FAISAL bin Abd al-Aziz. Still another son, Fahd ibn Abdul Aziz, continues to occupy the throne to the present time.

Further Reading

Armstrong, Harold C. *Lords of Arabia: Ibn Saud.* New York: Kegan Paul International, 1998.

McLoughlin, Leslie. *Ibn Saud: Founder of a Kingdom.* New York: St. Martin's Press, 1993.

Peterson, John. *Historical Dictionary of Saudi Arabia.* Lanham, Md.: Scarecrow Press, 2003.

Rasheed, Madawi al-. *A History of Saudi Arabia.* New York: Cambridge University Press, 2002.

Sander, Nestor. *Ibn Saud: King by Conquest.* Tucson, Ariz.: Hats Off Press, 2001.

Schwartz, Stephen. *The Two Faces of Islam: The House of Sa'ud from Tradition to Terror.* New York: Doubleday, 2002.

Teitelbaum, Joshua. *The Rise and Fall of the Hashemite Kingdom of Arabia.* New York: New York University Press, 2001.

Schmidt, Helmut (1918–) *chancellor of Germany*

Helmut Schmidt was born in Hamburg, Germany, on December 23, 1918, the son of schoolteachers. He was drafted into the German army in 1937 and was highly decorated during World War II. During his captivity with Allied forces he became politically active by joining the Sozialdemokratische Partei Deutschlands (SPD), Social Democratic Party. Once out of detention Schmidt passed through the University of Hamburg with an economics degree and held various positions within the town government. He was elected to the Bundestag (legislature) as an SPD member in 1953 and quickly gained notice for his effective speaking style.

Schmidt proved himself an outspoken critic of just about everything—including his own party. In 1959 he helped to draft the Godesberg Program, which forced the party to abandon its traditional far-left positions and move to more mainstream approaches. Schmidt himself published and lectured widely on the subject of national defense, becoming a noted authority—much to the annoyance of SPD radicals. Disillusioned by his opposition role, he left the federal government in 1961 and returned to city politics back in Hamburg. He particularly distinguished himself for organizational skills during the great flood of February 1962 and resumed a career in national politics three years later. Again, Schmidt proved pivotal in helping to arrange a grand coalition between the nominally hostile SPD and the Christian Democrats. In 1969 new elections allowed the SPD to form a coalition government with the liberal Free Democratic Party under WILLY BRANDT, the first Social Democratic government since the 1920s. Schmidt was successively awarded the portfolios of defense and finance, distinguishing himself in both capacities. When Brandt resigned on account of a spy scandal in May 1974, Schmidt was the overwhelming choice to succeed him as chancellor.

Unlike the visionary Brandt, Schmidt was a pragmatic centrist in both economics and foreign affairs. He determined to continue his predecessor's policy of pursuing Ostpolitik with ERICH HONECKER's East Germany, and he became the first West German chancellor to visit. Schmidt also sought diffusion of cold war tensions through good relations with Poland and the Soviet Union. But he was also fully committed to the North Atlantic Treaty Organization (NATO) as a bulwark against communist aggression, and he strongly supported the Western alliance. Given the traditional animosity between France and Germany in the 20th century, he sought out especially close ties with French prime minister VALÉRY GISCARD D'ESTAING for coordinating economic policies. Their talks culminated in preliminary steps toward establishing the European monetary union, whose common currency is known today as the euro. Schmidt's clear-eyed policies clearly resonated with the German electorate, and they reelected him twice in 1976 and 1980.

Despite Schmidt's reputation as a consensus builder, relations with his own party were buffeted by a return to cold war tensions following the 1979 Soviet invasion of Afghanistan. He worked closely with American president

JIMMY CARTER to promulgate a "dual track" policy of negotiating arms reductions with the Soviet Union—but threatening to upgrade NATO defenses if reductions were not achieved. When progress proved fleeting, he ignored protests from dissenting elements of the SPD and authorized deployment of new Pershing II and cruise missiles. In 1977 Germany was besieged by a wave of terrorism aimed at destabilizing the government, including kidnappings and airplane hijackings; Schmidt also authorized the first use of military force outside Germany since 1945. His willingness to use force and allow new missiles on German soil severely tested his relations with more leftist members of the SPD, but he otherwise remained true to traditional socialist values. In October 1982, when Schmidt refused to scale back the benefits of the generous welfare state to balance the budget, the Free Democrats bolted from the coalition and he lost a vote of confidence. New elections then placed Helmut Kohl in the chancellor's office and a new era of conservative dominance commenced. Schmidt retained his seat in the Bundestag until 1987, then retired to become editor of the noted German periodical *Die Zeit.* Even in retirement, Schmidt remains as outspoken on controversial issues as ever. In March 2002 he took part in the highly emotional national debate over increasing immigration into the country. Again, taking issue with his own party, he insisted that, "Due to idealistic convictions which were formed on the experiences of the Third Reich, we allowed in far too many foreigners. That was something we did not have to do." Schmidt also contends that Germans are too xenophobic by nature to assimilate the new arrivals.

Further Reading

Berry, P. "The Organization and Influence of the Chancellory during the Schmidt and Kohl Chancellorships." *Governance* 2 (July 1989): 339–355.

Bluth, Christopher. *The Two Germanies and Military Security in Europe.* New York: Palgrave Macmillan, 2002.

Carr, Jonathan. *Helmut Schmidt: Helmsman of Germany.* New York: St. Martin's Press, 1985.

Dyson, Kenneth. "The German Model Revisited: From Schmidt to Schroeder." *German Politics* 10 (August 2001): 135–154.

Miller, Leroy. "Schmidt, Carter, Reagan, and Double Dependency." *War and Society* 5, no. 2 (1987): 89–105.

Muller, Stefanie E. "Helmut Schmidt and the NATO Double Track Decision." Unpublished master's thesis, Arizona State University, 1994.

Schmidt, Helmut. *Men and Powers: A Political Memoir.* New York: Random House, 1990.

Scullin, James Henry (1876–1953) *prime minister of Australia*

James Henry Scullin was born on September 18, 1876, in Trawalla, Australia, the son of Irish immigrants. He attended only primary school and completed his education through correspondence. Scullin joined the Labor Party in 1903 and three years later unsuccessfully contested Prime Minister ALFRED DEAKIN for his seat in Parliament. He was finally elected in 1910 and gained a reputation as a skilled debater. Defeated in 1913, he edited a labor newspaper for many years and garnered further national attention for himself. In 1916 he represented Victoria state in a federal convention summoned to discuss the volatile issue of conscription. Like many Laborites, Scullin strongly opposed the notion of forced service during World War I. He was also a staunch Irish nationalist who opposed England's policies in Ireland and embraced what was then a radical socialist agenda. He concluded his eight-year hiatus from office by regaining his seat in the House of Representatives in 1922 and slowly moderated his political views. In 1928 Scullin was elected leader of the Labor Party largely on the basis of his renowned speaking ability and impressive familiarity with finance and tax issues. In October 1929 he defeated STANLEY BRUCE and became the new prime minister of Australia. Labor also won its largest majority in the House since 1901 but the Senate, still in conservative hands, proved intractable and uncooperative. Another contentious point was the fact that Scullin's cabinet, when it was appointed, contained only two members with any appreciable experience in office.

No sooner had Scullin assumed power that he was confronted by the onset of the Great Depression, an event that subsequently shaped and defined his administration. The economy withered, unemployment rose alarmingly, and as loans failed the government was faced with responsibilities toward foreign bond owners. Worse, the conservative Senate refused to pass most of his reform packages, while he faced additional resistance from the Commonwealth Bank of Australia.

Scullin quickly adopted a draconian program to fight the depression: wage decreases, rationing, balancing the budget, and fiscal austerity in general. He sought economic recovery, but in such a manner as to promote, in his own words, "equality of sacrifice." Initially Scullin was assisted by Secretary of the Treasury Edward Granville Theodore, but Theodore subsequently resigned from office on account of a mining scandal in 1930. This threw administration economic policy into disarray because cabinet members split off into three different factions—a reflection of Labor's larger malaise. To combat political fallout Scullin convinced Theodore to rejoin the cabinet and assist in drafting a credit expansion plan. But this moderate stance only further divided the already fractious Labor Party and in December 1931 elections Scullin went down to defeat.

Scullin remained as head of the party and the opposition in Parliament until 1935 when he was replaced by JOHN CURTIN. Curtin graciously offered him numerous government posts during World War II, but he declined to accept. He remained an influential force within Parliament until his resignation in 1949. Scullin died in Melbourne on January 28, 1953. He was regarded as an upright and scrupulously honest public figure, but overwhelmed by events he could not control—and a party divided against itself.

Further Reading

Colegrove, John W. "J. H. Scullin, Prime Minister in Adversity." Unpublished bachelor's thesis, University of Queensland, 1968.

Crisp, L. F., and B. C. Atkinson. "Ramsay Macdonald, James Scullin, and Alfred Deakin at Ballart Imperials Standards, 1906." *Australian Journal of Politics and History* 17 (April 1971): 73–81.

Denning, Warren, and Frank Moorehouse. *James Scullin.* Melbourne, Victoria: Black, Inc., 2001.

Gregory, R. G., and N. G. Butlin, eds. *Recovery from the Depression: Australia and the World Economy in the 1930s.* New York: Cambridge University Press, 1988.

Robertson, John. *J. H. Scullin: A Political Biography.* Nedlands: University of Western Australia Press, 1974.

Spenceley, Geoffrey F. R. *A Bad Smash: Australia in the Depression of the 1930s.* New York: McPhee Gribble, 1990.

Senghor, Léopold Sédar (1906–2002) *prime minister of Senegal*

Léopold Sédar Senghor was born in Joal, French West Africa, on October 9, 1906, the son of a wealthy merchant. In addition to belonging to the minority Serer tribe, he was also raised Catholic in a predominantly Muslim land. Senghor attended local missionary schools, where his brilliance earned him a scholarship to study in France. He subsequently passed through the Sorbonne, majoring in the French language, and proved so adept that in 1935 he became the first African to earn a teaching certificate. One of his closest friends was future French president GEORGES POMPIDOU and they maintained a lifelong relationship. While in Paris Senghor also sought out various black intellectuals, and together they helped establish a literary and cultural movement called Negritude, a celebration of "Africanness" in all its forms. And, in spite of his profound attachment to everything French, he sought to liberate native cultures from colonial domination. In time he became the leading exponent and poet of the Negritude movement. Senghor taught in France until World War II, when he was drafted and captured by the Germans. Released in 1942, he joined the French underground resistance until war's end. After 1946 France began granting its African colonies greater internal autonomy, and that year Senghor was elected to the French National Assembly with the African Bloc, a party affiliated with the Socialists. In this capacity he advocated independence for Africa, but only in the guise of a large French-speaking federation. To do otherwise, Senghor felt, was to promulgate a series of small, politically unstable states. In 1958 President CHARLES DE GAULLE offered the colonies independence at the risk of losing all French financial and technical support. This was the scenario Senghor feared most and in 1959 he spent several months crafting a federation between French West Africa, Dahomey, Upper Volta, and French Sudan as the new Mali Federation. When this entity finally collapsed a year later, the new nation of Senegal arose on August 20, 1960, with Senghor as president. He was also head of the Union de Progressif de Senegalese (UPS), Senegalese Progressive Union, the nation's only legal party.

Senghor may have possessed the appearance of a mild-mannered intellectual and poet, but he proved himself to be an astute politician. Officially, he embraced a moderate form of socialism within the confines of a one-party state. He also made deliberate efforts to mitigate the effects of independence by maintaining close political and economic ties to France. However, in December 1962 his prime minister, Mamadou Dia, who wanted to organize Senegal along strict socialist lines, attempted an unsuccessful coup against him. Senghor countered by formalizing UPS rule under a new constitution in February 1963 that granted him greater powers. Otherwise he proved himself a wise and benevolent leader, and highly successful in spite of the fact he was a Christian leading an Islamic nation. To that end he struck close alliances with traditional Muslim leaders in the countryside and also founded economic cooperatives dependent upon his regime. By 1976 Senghor felt his nation was ready for pluralistic politics, and he authorized the legalization of four dissident parties. On December 31, 1980, he suddenly resigned from office midway through his fifth term in favor of Prime Minister Abdou Diouf. His two decades of power marked the rise of Senegal as one of Africa's freest and most stable nations. Senghor was also the first African head of state to voluntarily relinquish power.

In addition to politics, Senghor gained international renown as one of the foremost African poets and essayists of his day. He published several books on prose and poetry that were translated into many languages and sold around the world. In 1984 the prestigious French Academy recognized his efforts by making him their first African member. Senghor died in Dakar on December 20, 2002, a capable leader and a talented writer. He remains highly admired as the father of Senegal's independence and the architect of its present stability and prosperity.

Further Reading

Coats, Geoffrey C. "Pre-independence Conceptions of the State in French West Africa: The Political Philosophy of Ahmed Sékou Touré and Léopold Sédar Senghor." Unpublished master's thesis, James Madison University, 1994.

Johnson, Nancy K. "Senegalese 'into Frenchmen'?: The Politics of Language, Culture, and Assimilation (1891–1960)." Unpublished Ph.D. diss., Cornell University, 2001.

Kluback, William. *Léopold Sédar Senghor: From Politics to Poetry.* New York: P. Lang, 1997.

Senghor, Léopold S. *On African Socialism.* New York: Praeger, 1964.

Léopold Sédar Senghor *(Library of Congress)*

Spleth, Janice S., ed. *Critical Perspectives on Léopold Sédar Senghor.* Colorado Springs, Colo.: Three Continents Press, 1993.

Vaillant, Janet G. "Homage to Léopold Sédar Senghor, 1906–2001." *Research in African Literatures* 33, no. 4 (2002): 17–24.

———. *Black, French, and African: A Life of Léopold Sédar Senghor.* Cambridge, Mass.: Harvard University Press, 1990.

Siad Barre, Mohamed (1919–1995) *president of Somalia*

Mohamed Siad Barre was born in Shiilaabo, Italian Somaliland, in 1919, the son of a traditional Marehan shepherd. Orphaned at the age of 10, he showed great initiative in improving himself and joined the local police while the region was occupied by the British in World War II. Once the Italians returned to the region Siad Barre was selected to receive military training in Italy, and he subsequently transferred to the nascent Somalian army after independence in 1960. He was successively promoted and by July 1965 was functioning as commander of the armed forces. Like many young officers, Siad Barre had grown disillusioned by the corruption associated with civilian rule and, after the assassination of President Abdirashid Ali Shermarke in October 1969, he resolved to strike quickly. Siad Barre and a small clique of officers assumed control of the government, dissolved the national assembly, and established a Supreme Revolutionary Council (SRC) to run the country. The new regime subsequently embarked on a broad implementation of Marxist-Leninist policies designed to eliminate "tribalism, corruption, nepotism, and misrule," in their own words. Ironically, while a staunch communist, Siad Barre was also a practicing Muslim and had no difficulty mixing "scientific socialism" with elements of traditional Islam. He also struck up a close and abiding relationship with the Soviet Union in exchange for an influx of modern weapons and thousands of technical advisers.

Somalia, one of the world's poorest countries, was further hindered developmentally by the lack of a written national language. In virtually his only positive contribution to the nation, Siad Barre oversaw adoption of written Somali using a modified Roman alphabet. Great emphasis was also placed on improving literacy and health services for his impoverished countrymen. But as time passed Siad Barre revealed an authoritarian streak in his governance. By 1976 he had adopted a new constitution that made the Somali Revolutionary Socialist Party (SRSP) the nation's only legal political entity. Siad Barre himself ruled by decree through a rubber-stamp national assembly that he closely controlled. All executive functions, including defense and foreign affairs, were likewise concentrated in his hands. To further grant a facade of legitimacy, the assembly "reelected" him president by unanimous votes in 1980 and 1986. Siad Barre's only major foreign policy accomplishment was in joining the Arab League in 1974—and soliciting funds from rich Arab states.

Siad Barre initially toed the Soviet line in foreign policy and seriously considered their suggestion for entering a confederation with communist-controlled Ethiopia. However, in 1974 the Somali-dominated Ogaden region of neighboring Ethiopia rose in revolt against President MENGISTU HAILE MARIAM. Intent upon helping his kinsmen, Siad Barre then launched a full-scale invasion of the barren Ogaden desert, intent upon annexing it to Somalia proper. The Soviets, unable to control their ally, summarily cut off arms shipments and withdrew their advisers to Ethiopia. They inserted large numbers of Cuban mercenaries into the region, who slowly drove the attackers back. Eventually Siad Barre patched up his differences with Ethiopia in 1977 and concentrated instead on squelching the Somali National Movement, a guerrilla group based in the borderlands. After protracted fighting and great cruelty toward suspected sympathizers, the government failed to crush the insurrection and it grew. Worse yet, a new faction, the United Somali Congress, also began concerted guerrilla activity in the south. Over the next three years Siad Barre waged a fierce but losing battle to retain control of the countryside, as popular support for his regime ebbed. When the victorious rebels began a concerted advance on the capital of Mogadishu in January 1991, Siad Barre finally fled the country and was replaced by the warlord Mohammed Farah Aidid. He initially found refuge in nearby Kenya but the government of President Daniel arap Moi found his presence in the country embarrassing and ordered him out. He subsequently resettled in Lagos, Nigeria, and died there on January 2, 1995. Siad Barre's regime had been among the most brutal and corrupt in all of Africa. In consequence of his 22 years of misrule, Somalia lapsed into a bitter civil war that flares up occasionally to the present day.

Further Reading

Fitzgerald, Nina J. *Somalia: Issues, History, and Bibliography.* Huntington, N.Y.: Nova Science Publishers, 2002.

Gebru, Tareke. "The Ethiopia-Somalia War of 1977 Revisited." *International Journal of African Historical Studies* 33, no. 3 (2000): 635–667.

Lewis, Ioan M. *A Modern History of the Somali: Nation and State in the Horn of Africa.* Oxford: James Currey, 2002.

Little, Peter D. *Economy without State: Accumulation and Survival in Somalia.* Oxford: James Currey, 2003.

Samaatar, Ahmed I. *Socialist Somalia: Rhetoric and Reality.* Highlands, N.J.: Zed Books, 1988.

Schraeder, Peter J., and Jerel A. Rosati. "Policy Dilemmas in the Horn of Africa: Contradictions in the U.S.-Somalia Relationship." *North East African Studies* 9, no. 3 (1987): 19–42.

Siles Zuazo, Hernán (1914–1996) *president of Bolivia*

Hernán Siles Zuazo was born in La Paz, Bolivia, on March 21, 1914, a son of Hernando Siles Reyes, a former president of that country. After performing military service in the Chaco War with Paraguay in 1932, he passed through the America Institute and San Andres University and obtained a law degree. Siles Zuazo practiced law briefly before being caught up in tumultuous national politics. In 1941 he assisted VÍCTOR PAZ ESTENSSORO in the founding of the Movimiento Nacionalista Revolucionario (MNR), National Revolutionary Movement, an eclectic blend of nationalism, Marxism, and fascism. In 1943 the movement toppled an unpopular dictator and seized power. A countercoup was launched in 1946 and Siles Zuazo was forced to flee the country. The military again intervened in 1951, and the following year a full-scale popular revolution broke out that expelled the army and allowed Paz Estenssoro to resume the presidency. Siles Zuazo served as vice president and four years later he was formally elected chief executive himself. Bolivia was then experiencing acute economic distress owing to high inflation and Siles Zuazo had little recourse but to adopt strict austerity measures imposed by the International Monetary Fund (IMF). The new program caused considerable distress among the lower classes and drove union support away from the MNR, but the economy finally stabilized. Siles Zuazo completed the remainder of his term uneventfully and stepped down from power in 1960 to serve as ambassador to Uruguay.

In 1964 the military under General RENÉ BARRIENTOS ORTUÑO again intervened and deposed both Paz Estenssoro and the MNR. Siles Zuazo then returned as an opposition member and sought the immediate restoration of democracy to Bolivia. His greatest political weakness was in failing to ally himself to sympathetic factions within the military and, consequently, he lacked support. Siles Zuazo was arrested and deported to Uruguay several times. In 1972 he founded his own MNR de Izquierda (MNRI), a more radical offshoot of his old party and led it into a broad-based political coalition called the Unidad Democrática y Popular (UDP), Popular and Democratic Union. He then served as the UDP presidential candidate in 1978, 1979, and 1980, received a majority of votes but was forbidden by the military to hold office. Alternately elected and exiled, he finally prevailed in October 1982 and was made president by congress. He was the first civilian leader elected after 18 years of military rule.

Siles Zuazo's second term was characterized by even more extreme hardships than his first. Like all Latin America, Bolivia was awash in national debt and facing the worst economic crisis in its history. Furthermore, both agriculture and the political infrastructure were slowly being eroded by a thriving cocaine industry that had enormous corrupting influences. The nation's distress was so pervasive that Siles Zuazo suspended payments on the national debt until more realistic terms were granted by the IMF. He was the first Latin American leader to do so and his stance so angered conservative elements that the president was briefly kidnapped and held hostage. When strict austerity measures were finally imposed to tackle surreal inflation rates of 26,000 percent, the economy shrank even further, triggering another round of labor strikes and protests. A broad spectrum of interest groups then began calling for his immediate resignation. At one point even Roberto Suarez Gómez, a major drug lord, offered to help pay off the national debt. With the authority of his presidency crumbling around him, Siles Zuazo called for national elections a year ahead of time, and he stepped aside in July 1985. He then quit politics altogether and relocated to Uruguay. Siles Zuazo died there in Montevideo on August 7, 1996. It was his misfortune to preside over what possibly was the most difficult period in all of Bolivia's history. But, despite his economic failures, he is regarded as the moving force behind Bolivia's belated resumption of democracy in the 1980s.

Further Reading

Alexander, Robert. "Bolivia's Democratic Experiment." *Current History* 84 (February 1985): 73–76, 86–87.

Cammack, P. "The Worker's Movement and the Bolivian Revolution Reconsidered." *Politics and Society* 11, no. 2 (1982): 211–222.

Kofas, J. V. "The Politics of Adversity: The IMF and U.S. Foreign Policy in Bolivia, 1956–1964." *Journal of Developing Areas* 29 (January 1995): 213–236.

Malloy, James M. *Revolution and Reaction: Bolivia, 1964–1985.* New Brunswick, N.J.: Transaction Books, 1988.

Mitchell, Christopher. *The Legacy of Populism in Bolivia: From the MNR to Military Rule.* New York: Praeger, 1977.

Padilla, John C. "Revolución aceptada: U.S. Relations with Bolivian Revolutionaries during the Eisenhower Era." Unpublished master's thesis, New Mexico State University 2002.

Smith, Ian (1919–) *prime minister of Rhodesia*

Ian Douglas Smith was born in Selukwe, Southern Rhodesia, on April 18, 1919, a son of Scottish settlers. This was a British colony and administered on a racial basis, in which 240,000 whites ruled over 4.5 million blacks. Smith was attending Rhodes University in South Africa when World War II began, so he joined the Royal Air Force as a fighter pilot. He served with distinction but facial injuries left him with a grim, unsmiling demeanor. In 1945 Smith resumed his studies and received a degree in economics. Three years later he was elected to the all-white Legislative Assembly as part of the conservative Liberal Party. When Southern Rhodesia was united with Nyasaland in 1953 to form a federation, Smith joined the new federal parliament with the United Front Party. He proved himself adept at backbench politics, and in November 1956 Prime Minister ROY WELENSKY appointed him the government whip. The federation was then exerting pressure upon Great Britain for independence, and in 1961 they adopted a new constitution allowing limited black representation, 15 seats out of 65. Smith, an ardent racist, felt the concession unwarranted and he quit the party to form a new and more militant organization, the Rhodesian Front (RF). This group utterly opposed concessions toward the black majority under any circumstances. Most white voters apparently agreed with their hard-line stance, and in 1962 the RF captured control of parliament. Smith served as treasury minister and in 1963 the federation was dissolved. On April 13, 1964, he became prime minister of Southern Rhodesia and defiantly exclaimed "I do not expect to see Africans ruling Rhodesia in my lifetime."

While continuing to press for independence, Smith dismissed British demands that he make provision for eventual African majority rule. In fact one of his first acts as prime minister was to imprison several leading African nationalists. Extensive talks with British prime minister HAROLD WILSON produced nothing, and on November 11, 1965, Smith unilaterally declared Rhodesia's independence from the Commonwealth. This was the first such incident since the American Revolution of 1776 and the British were powerless to intervene. When Wilson prodded the United Nations to employ economic sanctions against the rogue colony, the resilient Rhodesians found handy allies in neighboring South Africa and Portuguese-controlled Mozambique. In March 1970 Smith further thumbed his nose at the British by declaring Rhodesia a republic and severing all ties with the Commonwealth. But black resentment over white supremacy occasioned the rise of guerrilla movements under Joshua Nkomo and Robert Mugabe, and a costly and protracted bush war of liberation ensued. The small Rhodesian army and air force, splendidly trained and led, inflicted punishing blows upon the insurgents but ultimately failed to defeat them. The white community also displayed remarkable resilience in what was essentially a doomed effort, and in 1970 and 1974 they overwhelmingly reelected Smith to office. By 1975 even the recalcitrant Smith was willing to enact cosmetic changes to allow black suffrage. That year, when Mozambique was freed from Portuguese rule, a new guerrilla front opened up, and the whites were increasingly hemmed in on both sides. Smith then held talks with rebel leaders with the assistance of Prime Minister BALTHAZAR VORSTER of South Africa and President KENNETH KAUNDA of Zambia, but he stubbornly refused to compromise. By 1979 the white regime was on its last legs, and talks at Lancaster House in London finally drafted a new constitution guaranteeing black majority rule. The transition to majority rule went smoothly and national elections in February 1980 made Robert Mugabe the new prime minister. Smith continued on in government as minister without portfolio for several months while the country was renamed Zimbabwe.

Smith continued serving in parliament until 1987, and he proved one of the government's most strident critics. He has since retired to his farm in Chiruguri and continues speaking out against the growing tyranny of the Mugabe regime. In August 2001 Smith protested the government's policy of seizing white-owned farms to give to black guerrilla veterans, and urged the multiracial government of South Africa to apply pressure. "What we've got to do is get all the powers working together," he declared defiantly, "and I think there is hope."

Further Reading

Coggins, Richard T., and Nicholas Owen. "Rhodesian UDI and the Search for a Settlement, 1964–68." Unpublished Ph.D. diss., University of Oxford, 2002.

Home, Gerald. *From the Barrel of a Gun: The United States and the War against Zimbabwe, 1965–1980.* Chapel Hill: University of North Carolina Press, 2001.

King, Anthony, "Identity and Decolonization: The Policy of Partnership in Southern Rhodesia, 1945–62." Unpublished Ph.D. diss., University of Oxford, 2001.

Mungazi, Dickson A. *The Last Defenders of the Laager: Ian D. Smith and F. W. de Klerk.* Westport, Conn.: Praeger, 1998.

Nhema, Alfred G. *Democracy in Zimbabwe: From Liberation to Liberalization.* Oxford, England: African Books Collective, 2002.

Rowe, David M. *Manipulating the Market: Understanding Economic Sanctions, Institutional Change, and the Political Unity of White Rhodesia.* Ann Arbor: University of Michigan Press, 2001.

Smith, Ian D. *Bitter Harvest.* London: Blake, 2001.

Smuts, Jan (1870–1950) *prime minister of South Africa*

Jan Christian Smuts was born on May 24, 1870, in Ribeek West, Malmesbury district of Cape Province, South Africa, the son of a prosperous Boer (Dutch) farmer. A brilliant student, he graduated from Victoria College at Stellenbosch and subsequently studied law at Cambridge University, England, on a scholarship. Smuts again distinguished himself academically and was called to the bar in 1895, but he returned home to open a practice. Three years later he won appointment as state attorney of Transvaal at the age of 28. However, that same year the Boer War against Great Britain erupted and Smuts won renown as a guerrilla fighter. When the war was lost in 1902, he participated in peace negotiations with the British, further enhancing

his standing among fellow Boers. Smuts then resumed his legal practice, and in 1904 he joined forces with war hero LOUIS BOTHA to found the Het Volk (The People), a political party aimed at securing self-rule. In 1905 Smuts arrived back in England to confer with Prime Minister HENRY CAMPBELL-BANNERMAN, and self-government was granted. Smuts then worked with Botha to effect a political union among the four disparate colonies, and in 1910 the new Union of South Africa was born. Botha became prime minister, while Smuts accepted various portfolios as minister of mines, defense, and the interior. The Het Volk also merged with smaller parties to become the new South African Party (SAP).

A political crisis ensued following the outbreak of World War I when Botha, at Smuts's urging, declined neutrality and aligned the country with Great Britain. This caused a round of civil unrest from the conservative, anti-British Boers, and Smuts was dispatched to

Jan Smuts *(Library of Congress)*

restore order. He was then entrusted with the task of driving German forces out of Southwest Africa and Tanganyika, which was accomplished brilliantly. Consequently Smuts represented South Africa at the 1917 Imperial War Conference and was an architect of the Balfour Declaration granting Jews a national home in Palestine. He also proved instrumental in helping establish the Royal Air Force. In 1919 Smuts attended the Paris Peace Conference and called for lenient treatment for Germany and Austria but was overruled. However, he did make a lasting impression by calling for creation of the League of Nations, which materialized the following year. When Botha died in 1919, Smuts became prime minister to succeed him and led the nation through the difficult postwar era. Economic hardships induced a bitter strike by gold miners, and Smuts reluctantly but firmly dispatched troops to quell the disturbance. However, when the economy refused to improve he was defeated in 1924. The victors, the Boer-based National Party, began calling for severing all ties to England and promoting Afrikaner nationalism through strict racial separation (apartheid). The more moderately disposed Smuts then settled in as head of the opposition for a decade.

In addition to politics, Smuts published several philosophical tracts that were well received at home and abroad. In 1933 he joined Prime Minister James Hertzog in a fusion government under the United South African National Party banner to promote unity during the Great Depression. Smuts then served as minister of justice until World War II broke out in 1939 and he once again advocated a close alliance with Great Britain. When Hertzog insisted on neutrality he was turned out of office and Smuts became prime minister a second time. In this capacity he provided South African forces for the campaign in North Africa and Great Britain rewarded him with the rank of field marshal. When the war ended in 1945 Smuts attended the first assembly for the new United Nations in San Francisco and helped draft its charter. He returned home a hero but still had to confront a rising tide of Boer nationalism and demands for complete racial separation between black and white South Africans. Smuts, who was something of a liberal in racial matters, urged a gradual adoption of universal suffrage once blacks became "civilized" but he underestimated the appeal of the National Party. In 1948 they completely dominated national elections and Smuts stepped down

from office a second time. He served briefly as head of the opposition until his death at home on September 11, 1950. Although Smuts has been roundly criticized for failing to head off the apartheid politics that dominated South Africa for the next four decades, he wins universal acclaim as the nation's most prominent statesman of the 20th century.

Further Reading
Crowder, Michael. "Tshekedi Khama, Smuts, and South West Africa." *Journal of Modern African Studies* 25 (March 1987): 25–42.

Geyser, Alfred. "Jan Smuts and Alfred Milner." *Round Table* no. 360 (July 2001): 415–432.

———. *Jan Smuts and His International Contemporaries.* London: Covos-Day, 2002.

Harvey, Robert. *The Fall of Apartheid: The Inside Story from Smuts to Mbeki.* New York: Palgrave, 2001.

Hyam, Ronald. *The Lion and the Springbok: Britain and South Africa since the Boer War.* New York: Cambridge University Press, 2003.

Schlanger, Nathan. "Making the Past for South Africa's Future: The Prehistory of Field Marshal Smuts." *Antiquity* 76 (March 2002): 200–209.

Smuts, Jan C. *Toward a Better World.* New York: World Book Co., 1944.

Sobhuza II (1899–1982) *king of Swaziland*

Nkhotfotjeni was born in Zombodze, Swaziland, on July 22, 1899, a son of King Ngwane V. His father died months later and he was raised under a regency headed by his grandmother, Queen Labotsibeni. As crown prince he was educated locally before attending the Lovedale Institute in Cape Province, South Africa. Nkhotfotjeni came home in 1918 and was groomed for his succession to the throne. On December 6, 1921, he was crowned Sobhuza II at the age of 22. Among his many other formal titles was that of Ngwenyama (Lion of Swazi). Swaziland at that time had been a British protectorate since 1903 and subject to colonization and exploitation from white settlers in nearby South Africa. It was a poor, underdeveloped region, landlocked and surrounded by stronger tribes. Worse, it had recently lost two-thirds of its lands to Europeans. However, Sobhuza proved himself to be no ordinary monarch and determined to regain his territories. In 1922 he visited London with his royal entourage and pleaded his case before King George V. When his request was denied, he made a later appeal to the Privy Council in 1926, which was also turned down. Sobhuza spent the next 15 years exhausting all the legal appeals available to him, and in 1941 he petitioned the new monarch, King George VI. By this time England was at war with Germany and requested military assistance from Swaziland. Sobhuza played coy until the British agreed to demands that his former lands be purchased back from settlers and given to Swazis. In this fashion the wily monarch came to possess two-thirds of the land formerly constituting his domain. It was a rare African victory against England's colonial administration.

In addition to reacquiring land, Sobhuza also determined to end Swaziland's dependence on the outside world for goods and cultivated economic independence. He helped to found and manage large agricultural projects like the Usutu pine forests, the largest man-made reserves in Africa. He also pioneered new farming techniques and encouraged development of the iron ore industry. With considerable business savvy and insight, Sobhuza presided over the transformation of Swaziland from an impoverished backwater to a thriving economic state. Because he was landlocked between the apartheid regime in South Africa and the Marxist-run government of Mozambique, Sobhuza also proved himself diplomatically astute. He performed a delicate balancing act between the feuding nations, being dependent upon their transportation net to get Swaziland exports to market.

Sobhuza may have been a modernizer politically, but he was strictly a traditionalist in governance. Before granting Swaziland independence in September 1968, Britain made the king agree to reign as a constitutional monarch with limited powers and beholden to a parliamentary legislature. Sobhuza agreed in principle to the changes but he found the concept of democracy alien to traditional practices and therefore "un-Swazi." As king, he made it a point to dress in his royal regalia of feathers and hides and impressed upon his 600,000 subjects the necessity of preserving their identity through tradition. To facilitate this, he coopted the British by founding his own Imbokodvo (royal) Party in 1964, which was completely loyal to the Crown and controlled the legislature following independence. He toyed with democracy as long as it proved expedient, but by April 1973 the king had had enough. That month he unilaterally suspended the constitution, abolished parliament

and political parties, and substituted a more traditional council of appointed nominees. Henceforth he ruled as an absolute monarch by decree, while still evoking tremendous affection and respect from his people. Sobhuza further enhanced his power through an intricate system of intermarriage that bound up tribal loyalties to his own Dlamini clan. Ultimately he acquired 100 wives and sired upward of 600 children.

By the time Sobhuza died in Mbabane on August 21, 1982, he was the world's longest-serving monarch. His 61 years on the throne were marked by peace, prosperity, and independence, an achievement that made him one of the most successful African leaders of modern times.

Further Reading

Cocks, Paul. "The King and I: Bronislaw, King Sobhuza II of Swaziland, and the Vision of Cultural Change in Africa." *History of Human Sciences* 13 (November 2000): 25–47.

Gillis, D. Hugh. *The Kingdom of Swaziland: Studies in Political History.* Westport, Conn.: Greenwood Press, 1999.

Kunene, Gerard S. "British Colonial Policy in Swaziland, 1920–1960." Unpublished Ph.D. diss., York University, 1992.

Kuper, Hilda. *Sobhuza II, Ngwenyama and King of Swaziland: The Story of a Hereditary Leader and His Country.* New York: Africana, 1978.

Lowe, Christopher C. "Swaziland's Colonial Politics: Decline of Progressivist South African Nationalism and the Emergence of Swazi Political Traditionalism, 1910–1939." Unpublished Ph.D. diss., Yale University, 1999.

Simelane, Hamilton S. "War, Economy, and Society in Colonial Swaziland, 1939–1945." Unpublished Ph.D. diss., University of Toronto, 1991.

Somare, Michael (1936–) *prime minister of Papua New Guinea*

Michael Somare was born on Karau, New Guinea, on April 9, 1936, the son of a policeman. The eastern half of the island was then administered by Australia as a League of Nations mandate. He was educated at local missionary schools and completed teacher training at the Sogeri Secondary School in 1956. Somare then taught for a decade until 1965, when he enrolled at the

Administrative College in Port Moresby. His experience there with other native students radicalized his politics, and in 1967 he helped to found Panhu Pati (PP), a party dedicated to independence and self-governance. The following year he successfully ran for a seat in the House of Assembly and began promoting his cause. This proved no mean feat, for Papua New Guinea is home to 1,000 diverse tribes speaking over 500 languages. Moreover, separatist movements were already at play in the highlands and on the important island of Bougainville. Residents also feared a loss of Australian financial and technical aid should independence came. Nonetheless, Somare, a large, impressive man, continued rising politically by dint of his personality, and in 1972 he formed a coalition government with the rival United Party (UP) to become chief minister. This constituted Papua New Guinea's first indigenous administration and Somare wasted no time venturing into the highlands to cement political alliances there. Australia, meanwhile, sensed what was coming and generally supported the drive toward independence in an orderly, peaceful manner. Internal autonomy was granted in 1973 and that year Somare promulgated an Eight Point Plan containing his proposed social and economic policy. In September 1975 Papua New Guinea became a new nation and Somare continued on as its first prime minister.

Once in power, Somare had his hands full addressing economic issues, as well as a militant separatist movement on Bougainville. In 1976 the secessionists openly rebelled against the government, and many encouraged Somare to stamp out the rebellion by force. However, the prime minister arrived on the island to conduct talks with rebel leadership in person, and they reached a peaceful solution after agreeing to tax concessions. For his decisive performance, Somare was easily reelected in 1977 just as trouble in the highlands broke out. Crime and resentment against central authority proved endemic, and this time he was unable to address problems quickly. In March 1980 a new coalition was formed under Julius Chan, and Somare stepped down from office. Two years later the PP scored a complete election victory and Somare was reinstated as prime minister. He remained in power three more years before losing a vote of confidence over budgetary matters in November 1985 to Paias Wingti. When the PP returned to power three years later, Somare was made foreign minister and in 1990 he was knighted by Queen Elizabeth II. He was then forced to address another violent rebellion on Bougainville by separatist guerrillas. Somare, assisted by diplomats from New Zealand, finally managed to contain the movement peacefully in January 1991. Nevertheless Somare was ousted from office the following year when the PP lost a new round of elections. In 1993 he quit the PP leadership altogether and formed a new party, the National Alliance.

In July 1997 Somare attempted to regain the premiership but lost heavily, and the magnitude of the defeat seemed to spell the end of his career in politics. But on August 5, 2002, he was again elevated to prime minister by assembling a coalition government and ousting Sir Mekere Morauta's People's Democratic Movement from power. Curiously, and perhaps reflecting the fractious nature of Papua New Guinea politics, Somare's National Alliance holds only 19 seats of 109 in parliament, and is part of a seven-party coalition. In recognition of his skill as a negotiator and a consensus builder, Somare continues to be informally known as "the chief."

Further Reading

Hegarty, D., and P. King. "Papua New Guinea in 1982: The Election Brings Change." *Asian Survey* 23 (February 1983): 212–226.

King, Peter. "Papua New Guinea in 1983: Pangu Consolidates." *Asian Survey* 24, no. 2 (1984): 159–166.

Lenon, M. "Papua New Guinea: Remaking Alliances." *Arena* 80 (December 1987): 42–46.

O'Callaghan, Mary L. *Enemies Within: Papua New Guinea, Australia, and the Sandline Crisis: The Inside Story.* New York: Doubleday, 1999.

Saffu, Y. "Papua New Guinea in 1987: Wingati's Coalition in a Disabled System." *Asian Survey* 28 (February 1988): 242–251.

Siaguru, Anthony. *In-house in Papua New Guinea.* Canberra: Asia Pacific Press, 2001.

Somare, Michael T. *Sana: An Autobiography.* Port Moresby: Niugini, 1975.

Somoza Debayle, Anastasio (1925–1980)

president of Nicaragua

Luis Anastasio Somoza Debayle was born in León, Nicaragua, on December 5, 1925, a son of Nicaraguan president ANASTASIO SOMOZA GARCÍA. He was educated locally before being sent to the United States to attend a private military school. Somoza graduated from the U.S. Military Academy at West Point in 1946 and returned. He then became part of the feared Nicaraguan National Guard, which very much constituted the basis of the Somoza family's power. He would wield it as a private army. In 1956 Somoza became commander of the guard shortly before his father was assassinated. His brother Luis then assumed the presidency, while he undertook a brutal interrogation of suspects. In 1963 Luis Somoza stepped down from office in favor of René Shick, while Somoza used the National Guard to clamp down on political opposition. In 1967 he promoted himself to major general before resigning and declaring his candidacy as president. The ensuing process was marred by the usual violence and fraud, and he was "elected" to office, the third and final member of the Somoza family dynasty. Like his father, Somoza used his office for the sole purpose of self-enrichment and political repression. His tenure in office was marked by corruption and brutality toward all those who opposed him. Somoza proved eager to placate conservative critics and monied interests by guaranteeing them 40 percent of seats in the national legislature. Thus in 1971 they arranged for Somoza to succeed himself in office through constitutional amendment. But his excesses coincided with the rise of a Marxist resistance movement under DANIEL ORTEGA, the Sandinista National Liberation Front (FSLN), more commonly known as the Sandinistas. A vicious cycle of guerrilla warfare, interspersed with harsh crackdowns, then ensued for many years.

The turning point in Somoza's regime occurred in the wake of a deadly earthquake that struck Managua in December 1972. He used it as a pretext for declaring a state of siege and ruling by decree. Thousands of people were either killed or left homeless, but Somoza began a bidding war to start buying up victims' property. He also managed to abscond with significant portions of relief money sent to assist survivors. His behavior managed to unite a vast coalition of interests against him, ranging from extreme left to conservative right. Even the Catholic Church, a nominal Somoza ally, came down against him. But protests, when they emerged, were swiftly and harshly suppressed by force. Rigged elections in 1974 gave Somoza another six years in office while the ongoing Sandinista conflict resulted in human rights violations on both sides. In 1977 a new American

president, JIMMY CARTER, began reducing military assistance just as Cuba and the Soviet Union increased theirs to rebel forces. Curiously, during this same interval, Somoza expanded family holdings to virtually every aspect of Nicaraguan business, including real estate, banking, gambling, prostitution, and the drug trade. Before he died he was estimated to have amassed a personal fortune in excess of $900 million.

In January 1978 the regime overstepped its bounds by assassinating opposition newspaper editor Pedro Joaquín Chamorro. The result was a spontaneous outbreak of marches and demonstrations demanding Somoza's ouster. When the National Guard responded with its usual brutality, this time the ranks of the Sandinista guerrillas began to swell. A series of well-orchestrated offensives delivered larger and larger amounts of the countryside into their hands and they began attacking Managua with impunity. Somoza consented to an American mediation effort between his government and the guerrillas, but he refused all proposals to hold a national referendum on the future of his regime. Mounting internal opposition, coupled with a declaration from the Organization of American States in June 1979, finally induced Somoza to resign. On July 17, 1979 he turned affairs of state over to Vice President Francisco Urcuyo and left for Miami. His 13 years of misrule allowed the communists finally to establish a beachhead in Central America.

Somoza subsequently settled in Paraguay at the invitation of President ALFREDO STROESSNER. He was assassinated in Asunción by Argentine guerrillas on September 17, 1980. With his passing the bloody 43-year reign of the Somoza dynasty reached its ignominious ending.

Further Reading

Alegria, Claribel. *Death of Somoza.* Willimantic, Conn.: Curbstone Press, 1996.

Cruz, A. "After Somoza, the Flood." *North-South* 3 (August–September 1993): 18–23.

Gambone, Michael D. *Capturing the Revolution: The United States, Central America, and Nicaragua, 1961–1972.* Westport, Conn: Praeger, 2001.

Morely, Morris H. *Washington, Somoza, and the Sandinistas, 1969–1981.* New York: Cambridge University Press, 1994.

Pezzullo, Lawrence. *At the Fall of Somoza.* Pittsburgh: University of Pittsburgh Press, 1993.

Ryan, Phil. "Structure, Agency, and the Nicaraguan Revolution." *Theory and Society* 29 (April 2000): 187–213.

Somoza, Anastasio. *Nicaragua Betrayed.* Boston: Western Islands, 1988.

Somoza García, Anastasio (1896–1956)
president of Nicaragua

Anastasio Somoza García was born in San Marcos, Nicaragua, on February 1, 1896, the son of an affluent landowner. He was educated locally and subsequently attended the Pierce School of Business in Philadelphia, where he perfected his English language skills. Back home he enhanced his social standing by marrying into the wealthy Debayle family and becoming active in Liberal Party politics. Throughout the 1920s Nicaragua verged on civil war between competing factions, and United States Marines were dispatched to maintain order. Renewed fighting brought them back in the early 1930s and Somoza, given his language proficiency and familiarity with American culture, offered his services as a translator. In 1932 his wife's uncle, Juan Bautista Sacasa, was elected to the presidency and—with American blessing—Somoza was appointed commander of the new National Guard. Once the marines were withdrawn that year, he moved swiftly to consolidate his position within the military to provide a base of support. In 1934 Somoza orchestrated the assassination of rebel leader Augusto Cesar Sandino, who had gained renown by resisting American intervention, thereby cementing his allegiance with the business classes. Success emboldened Somoza to overthrow Sacasa in 1936, and he seized control of the government altogether. In January 1937 he became president through fraudulent elections but, with the National Guard looming in the background, criticism remained muted.

For the next two decades Somoza ran Nicaragua like a personal fiefdom, using every conceivable opportunity to line his pockets with the national treasure. He bought out the leadership of the Liberal Party and made it an official adjunct of his money-raising organizations. Furthermore, he headed off conservative opposition through bribery and accorded them 40 percent of seats in the national legislature. Those individuals failing to cooperate were persuaded by the National Guard to do so. In this manner Somoza became the biggest landowner in the country with assets totaling $150 million. He strove to project an air of modernity, and in 1939 American president FRANKLIN D. ROOSEVELT received him with great fanfare. Mindful that he could not rule forever by force alone, Somoza authorized certain reforms such as a labor code in 1944, an income tax in 1952, and a National Development Institute in 1953. He also implemented market changes to lessen the country's dependency on banana exports and marginally improved the working conditions of most peasants. These cosmetic changes notwithstanding, his grip on power remained absolute. In 1947, after prodding by the United States, Somoza briefly stepped down and allowed a succession of puppet presidents to run the nation. In 1950 Somoza arranged for his own reelection to high office where he remained another six years.

American criticism of Somoza's regime tapered off at the onset of the cold war, thanks to his peerless credentials as an anticommunist. He was more than willing to act as an American watchdog for Central America—since it coincided with his own best interests. In 1951 Somoza allowed CIA operatives to use Nicaraguan airfields in their coup against JACOBO ARBENZ GUZMÁN in Guatemala and he also allowed antigovernment guerrillas to stage attacks against Costa Rican president JOSÉ FIGUERES FERRER. But despite his impressive record of promoting economic growth, Somoza perpetually enriched himself while the majority of the population saw little benefit. The unbelievable disparity of wealth between the president and his cronies on one hand and ordinary citizens on the other incited resistance to his continuation in power. On September 21, 1956, Somoza was shot by a gunman shortly after being nominated for a fifth term in office. He died on September 30 at a U.S. Army hospital in Panama and was succeeded by his sons Luis Somoza Debayle (1956–63) and ANASTASIO SOMOZA DEBAYLE (1967–79), who continued the family's tradition of corruption and oppression.

Further Reading

Clark, Paul C. *The United States and Somoza, 1933–1956: A Revisionist Look.* Westport, Conn.: Praeger, 1992.

Gambone, Michael D. *Eisenhower, Somoza, and the Cold War in Nicaragua, 1953–1961.* Westport, Conn.: Praeger, 1997.

Gould, Jeffrey. "For an Organized Nicaragua: Somoza and the Labor Movement, 1944–1948." *Journal of*

Latin American Studies 19 (November 1987): 353–387.

Krenn, Michael L. "Life with Somoza: The United States and Dictatorship in Nicaragua, 1945–1954." *Secolas Annals* 26 (1995): 48–56.

Walter, Knut. *The Regime of Anastasio Somoza, 1936–1956.* Chapel Hill: University of North Carolina Press, 1993.

Souphanouvong (1909–1995) *president of Laos*

Souphanouvong was born at Luang Prabang, Laos, on July 13, 1909, a son of Viceroy Boun Khong. As a member of the royal Laotian family he was well educated in Hanoi before studying civil engineering in Paris, France. He became politically active while abroad and was attracted to the French Communist Party. Souphanouvong came home to construct bridges throughout Indochina, all the while resenting the second-class status accorded himself and fellow Asians by the French. After the Japanese withdrew from Vietnam in August 1945, he ventured to Hanoi to establish contacts with Vietnamese nationalist and communist HO CHI MINH, who provided him with arms and a military escort back to the Laotian capital of Vientiane. There he became minister of defense until 1946, when the French returned in force and chased the nationalists to Thailand. Thereafter Souphanouvong became so closely allied to the Vietnamese communists that he gained the sobriquet of Red Prince. From exile he founded a Laotian communist movement in 1950, the Pathet Lao (Lao Nation), and commenced a guerrilla war against the Westerners. In 1953 the French formally relinquished control of Indochina, and the following year Souphanouvong conferred in Geneva with his half brother, SOUVANNA PHOUMA, about forming a coalition government. He subsequently received the portfolio of minister of planning and economic development, while an uneasy truce prevailed between communist and royalist interests.

In office Souphanouvong proved himself a vigorous official, and he was elected deputy from Vientiane by a large majority. He had originally hoped to integrate the Pathet Lao into the fabric of society but his close liaison with Vietnam—a traditional Laotian enemy—sparked a confrontation with conservative military elements. In July 1959 open hostility broke out between the opposing camps and Souphanouvong

was arrested and imprisoned. He escaped the following year and remained in the jungles until 1961, when he served as the Pathet Lao delegate to another Geneva conference on Laos. Souvanna Phouma then entreated him to join a new coalition government. This endeavor proved no more successful than the first, and it collapsed in 1963. Souphanouvong then made his way back to Hanoi to formally ally himself with the Vietnamese communists in a war of national liberation. By this time Southeast Asia was embroiled in the second Indochina war, this time against the United States, which clandestinely bombed Pathet Lao positions throughout Laos. Nonetheless, Laotian communists conducted a stubborn guerrilla war against the royalists and, after the Americans withdrew from the region in 1973, they quickly overran most of the countryside. That February Souvanna Phouma agreed to an armistice with the communists, and by April 1974 another shaky coalition government had been hammered out. However, with the final communist victory over South Vietnam in April 1975, Souphanouvong formally assumed control in Laos and installed a communist government.

In December 1975 the People's Democratic Republic of Laos came into being with Souphanouvong acting in the ceremonial role as president. This was more out of respect for his lifelong devotion to the party than for any innate political skills on his part. The Pathet Lao he founded was also disbanded and replaced by the Lao People's Revolutionary Party (LPRP) under Kaysone Phomvihane. Souphanouvong continued serving as president until poor health prompted his resignation in 1986. He nonetheless clung to a seat with the party Politburo until March 1991. The Red Prince died in Vientiane on January 9, 1995, a pivotal figure in the rise and ultimate triumph of Laotian communism.

Further Reading

Castle, Timothy N. *At War in the Shadow of Vietnam: U.S. Military Aid to the Royal Lao Government, 1955–1975.* New York: Columbia University Press, 1993.

Gunn, Geoffrey C. "Prince Souphanouvong: Revolutionary and Intellectual." *Journal of Contemporary Asia* 22, no. 1 (1992): 94–103.

Joiner, Charles A. "Laos in 1986: Administrative and Internationally Partially Adaptive Communism." *Asian Survey* 21, no. 1 (1987): 104–114.

Shaw, Geoffrey D. T. "Laotian 'Neutrality': A Fresh Look at a Key Vietnam War Blunder." *Small Wars and Insurgencies* 31, no. 1 (2002): 25–56.

Simms, Peter, and Sanda Simms. *The Kingdom of Laos: Six Hundred Years of History.* Richmond, Surrey: Curzon, 2001.

Souphanouvong, Prince. *Autobiography of Prince Souphanouvong.* Kuala Lumpur: Malaysia Mining Corporation Berhad, 1989.

Souvanna Phouma (1901–1984) *prime minister of Laos*

Souvanna Phouma was born in Luang Prabang, Laos, on October 7, 1901, a son of Viceroy Boun Khong. He attended private academies in Hanoi before enrolling in the Universities of Paris and Grenoble to study engineering. In 1931 Souvanna Phouma joined the Public Works Service, rising quickly to director by 1945. That year the Japanese occupying army urged Laos to declare its independence from France, and Souvanna Phouma joined the free national government. However, when the French reasserted control in 1946, both he and his half brother, Prince SOUPHANOU-VONG, fled to Thailand and safety. Souvanna Phouma remained there until 1949, when France finally allowed Laos to seek independence from colonial rule. He thereupon returned to occupy various government ministries and in November 1951 Souvanna Phouma was elected prime minister. However, the onset of independence did little to ameliorate the fractious nature of Laotian politics. While Souvanna Phouma worked for the royal government, his half brother solicited aid from HO CHI MINH's Vietnamese communists to overthrow it. Six years of low-level guerrilla warfare continued until November 1957 when Souvanna Phouma, striving to maintain Laotian neutrality, allowed the communist Pathet Lao into a coalition government. The arrangement lasted one year before conservative elements in the military, backed by the United States, kicked the communists out, and the insurgency resumed. Souvanna Phouma subsequently resigned from high office and submitted to political exile as ambassador to France.

After severe fighting in a three-way split between royalists, neutrals, and communists, the competing factions agreed to a Geneva conference in 1962 and another coalition was formed. This was done at the behest of the Soviet Union and the United States, who sought to preserve Laotian neutrality for their own ends. Souvanna Phouma was thus reinstated as prime minister and he resumed steering Laos down its perilous course between armed camps. Unfortunately, all of Southeast Asia was by then embroiled in the greater conflict between the United States and North Vietnam. The Americans, fearing that the Pathet Lao would overthrow the government, applied economic pressure on Souvanna Phouma to eject them from the coalition. He did so in 1963 and the civil war recommenced, only this time underscored by American air power, Thai and Hmong mercenaries, and increasing North Vietnamese aid and advisers. For a decade Souvanna Phouma sought reconciliation with the communists to bring them back into the fold, but they were too indebted to Hanoi to compromise. Likewise the United States would not tolerate any government with communists in it for fear they would covertly assist the North Vietnamese. Thus a secret and ancillary campaign evolved whereby the communists infiltrated large numbers of troops and supplies down the Ho Chi Minh trail through Laos while the Americans used air power and other means to interdict them. They also bombed Pathet Lao forces in the field whenever possible. Laos had unwillingly become a battleground between competing domestic factions, who were themselves pawns in a much larger game.

After 1973 the United States began withdrawing its forces from the region and Souvanna Phouma moved quickly to establish a cease-fire and a new coalition government with Souphanouvong. But following North Vietnam's conquest of South Vietnam in April 1975, the Pathet Lao insisted on complete dominance. The People's Democratic Republic of Laos was then established and Souvanna Phouma stepped down as prime minister for the last time. In recognition of his sincere efforts to secure Laotian neutrality during very tumultuous times, he was not punished and, in fact, remained on as a governmental adviser. He died in Vientiane on January 11, 1984, the most influential Laotian politician of the revolutionary generation.

Further Reading

Dickey, Angela. "Reporting Laos: U.S. Media and the 'Secret' War in Laos, 1955–1975." Unpublished master's thesis, University of Maryland–College Park, 2001.

Grant, Evens. *A Short History of Laos: The Land in Between.* Crowns Nest, New South Wales: Allen and Unwin, 2002.

Homsany, John-Thomas A. "John F. Kennedy, the Soviet Union, and the Laos Crisis, 1961–1962." Unpublished master's thesis, California State University–Fullerton, 2000.

Koprowski, Daniel C. "John F. Kennedy, the Development of Counterinsurgency Doctrine and American Intervention in Laos, 1961–1963." Unpublished master's thesis, University of Massachusetts–Amherst, 2000.

Quincy, Keith. *Harvesting Pa Chay's Wheat: The Hmong and America's Secret War in Laos.* Spokane, Wash.: Eastern Washington University Press, 2000.

Stuart-Fox, Martin. *Historical Dictionary of Laos.* Lanham, Md.: Scarecrow Press, 2001.

Verrone, Richard B. "Behind the Wall of Geneva: Lao Politics, American Counterinsurgency, and Why the U.S. Lost in Laos, 1961–1965." Unpublished Ph.D. diss., Texas Tech University, 2001.

Spínola, António de (1910–1996) *president of Portugal*

António Sebastião Ribeiro de Spínola was born in Estremoz, Portugal, on April 11, 1910, part of an established aristocratic family. He attended the Escola Militar and graduated in 1933 as a cavalry officer. That same year ANTÓNIO DE OLIVEIRA SALAZAR overthrew the republican government and established a right-wing dictatorship that lasted 40 years. Against this background Spínola fulfilled his military obligations to the country, first in assisting the regime of FRANCISCO FRANCO during the Spanish civil war and then as an observer of German forces during World War II. A competent professional soldier, he continued rising through the ranks on merit, and by 1961 he was a lieutenant colonel. At that time Portuguese African colonies were beset by communist-inspired wars of liberation, and Spínola was dispatched there to suppress them. An internecine bush war unfolded and Spínola acquired a national reputation for dash and heroism under trying circumstances. In 1964 he was recalled to head the National Republican Guard and two years later advanced in rank to brigadier general. However, the deteriorating situation in Africa demanded his return, so in 1968 he was appointed military governor of Portuguese Guinea (Guinea-Bissau). In a campaign for "hearts and minds," Spínola sought to win over the populace not simply through intimidation, but by building roads, hospitals, and schools. However, under the enlightened leadership of AMILCAR CABRAL, the rebel movement kept gaining popular support. Spínola had failed to crush the insurrection, but in 1973 he nonetheless returned home a national hero once more, was highly decorated, and promoted to deputy chairman of the Joint Chiefs of Staff.

To Spínola, Portugal's inability to retain its colonies—and the national obsession for doing so—spoke to a greater malaise in national society. In 1974 he addressed these problems in a book entitled *Portugal and the Future,* which shook the existing political order to its foundations. Here Spínola declared the colonial wars unwinnable and, while not advocating independence, suggested that the colonies should be allowed into a federal arrangement with the homeland and entitled to complete political rights. He further hinted that the nation itself should embrace democratic reforms and liberalization of the economy. His argument struck a responsive chord with the populace, who were weary of losing money and lives in a quixotic imperial strategy. Such honesty, long overdue in Portuguese political dialogue, further elevated his status as a national hero and spokesman, but the government responded by dismissing him from office.

It fell upon disenchanted elements within the army officer corps to effect immediate change by forming the Armed Forces Movement. On April 25, 1974, they staged a bloodless coup that toppled the dictatorship of Marcelo Caetano. Spínola's participation in the affair has never been documented, but he publicly lauded the rebels. As Portugal's greatest living military hero, he could confer both leadership and legitimacy on the young officers, so he became head of the Junta of National Salvation to initiate democratic change. In short order he authorized freedom of speech, of the press, and of political parties for the first time since 1933. The return of exiles, the release of political prisoners, and the disbanding of the secret police shortly followed. On May 15, 1974, Spínola was also appointed president of Portugal until national elections could be orchestrated. However, en route the national revolution was hijacked by communists and other radicals who sought to impose a left-wing dictatorship in place of the old, conservative one. Sympathetic military officers then seized the initiative by granting immediate independence to all African colonies. Spínola watched silently as events bore out, but he finally protested when the radicals began nationalizing industries. His more moderate approach brought him the wrath of the radical left, who branded him a traitor. With anarchy breaking out around him, Spínola attempted to seize complete power in March 1975 but was ousted in a coup. He then fled the country for Brazil but returned the following year as pent-up revolutionary zeal finally exhausted itself. The former general thereafter took no further role in national politics. He died in Lisbon on August 13, 1996. Spínola's tenure in office lasted less than a year, but his measures placed Portugal irrevocably down the road toward democracy after four decades of dictatorship.

Further Reading

Cabral, Adalino. "Voices from Portugal's Colonial War in Africa." Unpublished master's thesis, California State University–Dominguez Hills, 2001.

Cann, John P. *Counterinsurgency in Africa: The Portuguese Way of War, 1961–1974.* Westport, Conn.: Greenwood Press, 1997.

MacQueen, Norrie. "António de Spínola and the Decolonization of Portuguese Africa." *Diplomacy and Statecraft* 7, no. 2 (1996): 436–465.

Manuel, Paul C. *Uncertain Outcome: The Politics of the Portuguese Transition to Democracy.* Lanham, Md.: University Press of America, 1994.

Raby, Dawn L. *Fascism and Resistance in Portugal: Communists, Liberals, and Military Dissidents in the Opposition to Salazar, 1941–1974.* New York: St. Martin's Press, 1988.

Spínola, Manuel. *Portugal and the Future.* Johannesburg: Perskor Publishers, 1974.

Stalin, Joseph (Iosif Vissarionovich Dzhugashvili) (1879–1953) *secretary of the Communist Party of the Soviet Union*

Iosif Vissarionovich Dzhugashvili was born in Gori, Georgia (Russian empire), on December 21, 1879, into a poor peasant household. Highly intelligent, he won a scholarship to attend the Tiflis Orthodox Theological Seminary in 1893 and performed well. However, here he was first exposed to the radical ideas of Karl Marx and was subsequently expelled for revolutionary activities in 1898. Within two years

Dzhugashvili had become deeply involved in Marxist agitation throughout Georgia, was arrested, and exiled to Siberia. He escaped soon after and, secretly locating to Moscow, joined the Social Democratic Party. Around this time Dzhugashvili also adopted the pseudonym Stalin ("steel") as his last name. When the Social Democrats split into Menshevik and Bolshevik factions, he joined the latter under the auspices of professional revolutionary VLADIMIR LENIN. Stalin quickly established a reputation for craftiness and ruthlessness—even by Russian standards—so in 1912 he was allowed to join the party's Central Committee. In this capacity he helped orchestrate the clandestine campaign to overthrow the Russian monarchy and displayed genuine talent as a propagandist. After the revolution of October 1917 the Bolsheviks seized control of the country and eventually prevailed in a bloody civil war with conservative forces. Stalin, operating largely in the background of events, made his presence felt throughout the party even though Lenin and other revolutionaries, like Leon Trotsky, distrusted him

Joseph Stalin *(Library of Congress)*

intensely. Both underestimated the diminutive Georgian's guile, and on April 4, 1922, Stalin was appointed secretary of the Communist Party of the Soviet Union.

Before Lenin died in January 1924, he began warning his compatriots that Stalin could not be trusted and declared that in a memorandum. However, since Stalin controlled the party information apparatus, the memo was suppressed. Over the next four years he continually purged the party of his leading opponents, including Trotsky, and consolidated his grip on power. By 1929 he was free to implement his vision of a highly centralized, industrial state and issued the first of several five-year plans. The first entailed widespread collectivization of agriculture, namely, the forced concentration of farmers and equipment on state-owned farms. This was in essence a crash program designed to bring Russia out of the agrarian age and into the 20th century. Impressive progress was made in production, but collectivization met fierce resistance from the peasant classes. Stalin responded with wholesale repression and terror. He greatly expanded the NKVD, the dreaded secret police, who arrested, detained, and executed millions of people with abandon. The government also engineered an artificial famine in the Ukraine to wipe out the kulaks (wealthy peasants) as a class. By the 1930s the Soviet Union boasted an impressive industrial base and the world's largest military. But Stalin, a paranoid personality, continued seeing potential enemies everywhere around him. In 1934 he began purging the Communist Party of suspected malcontents, placing the accused in public "show trials" and executing them in droves. The event, known as the Great Terror, also extended to members of the military, and Stalin ordered the deaths of many leading generals. Concurrently, he began developing a national cult of personality around himself in which poets, painters, and songwriters commemorated him. If anything, Stalin raised totalitarianism to a fine art.

In June 1941 German dictator ADOLF HITLER commenced a massive invasion of the Soviet Union to destroy communism and acquire land. The massive Red Army, thanks to Stalin's interference, was routed in the early stages of the war and suffered astronomical casualties. Fortunately for Russia, the front stabilized, and Stalin began receiving military supplies and equipment from British prime minister WINSTON CHURCHILL and American president FRANKLIN D. ROOSEVELT, with

whom he also conferred on several occasions. After the deaths of nearly 20 million people, the Red Army, in concert with the forces of the Western Allies, finally defeated Nazi Germany in May 1945. Stalin, an able negotiator, had since secured from Churchill and Roosevelt pledges of noninterference while he acquired Eastern Europe as a buffer zone against future aggression. The Soviet Union by this time possessed one of the largest military establishments in history, but Stalin, paranoid as ever, refused to trust his erstwhile allies. He then sealed off Eastern Europe from their influences, an act prompting Churchill to declare that "an iron curtain" had fallen across the region. Stalin's aggressive posturing against his erstwhile allies commenced a new phase of global confrontation known as the cold war, which pitted the communist East against the capitalist West. In 1948 he orchestrated a land blockade of West Berlin in a failed attempt to evict the Allies from East Germany. He was thwarted by the Berlin airlift, the largest such supply effort in history. But Stalin's most direct action was in supplying arms and advisers to North Korea, which attacked neighboring South Korea, an American ally, in June 1950. The fighting escalated until American forces were committed by U.S. president HARRY S. TRUMAN. This, in turn, triggered Communist Chinese intervention under MAO ZEDONG. The bloody impasse continued up through June 1953, when an armistice was signed and both East and West girded themselves for future confrontations.

Through the early 1950s Stalin's health had seriously declined, and he was about to order another wholesale purge of the Communist Party when he suddenly died on March 5, 1953. A scramble for power in the Kremlin ensued, and a group of moderates under NIKITA S. KHRUSHCHEV finally prevailed. Many of Stalin's most loyal and notorious supporters were themselves rounded up and executed, suffering the same fate they had inflicted on untold millions. In 1956 Khrushchev took the unprecedented step of denouncing Stalin's crimes and atrocities before the assembled party leadership in Moscow. Without any exaggeration, Stalin was one of the most heinous dictators of all time and a black mark on Russian history. However, he also left a powerful legacy in transforming his nation from semifeudal status into a superpower capable of challenging the United States with nuclear weapons. Given the chaotic state of Russian affairs today, many former communists continue paying homage to the deceased tyrant.

In March 2003, the 50th anniversary of Stalin's death, over 3,000 communists and nationalists led a solemn procession past Stalin's grave on Red Square. Despite the deaths of over 20 million citizens by firing squads and starvation, and in the notorious Siberian gulags (labor camps), many Russians look favorably upon the discipline and vitality of the former Soviet Union with pride and laud him as a model leader. "Stalin was a great statesman who had a strong fighting character and a strong will," declared Communist leader Gennady Zyuganov. He is likely both to be reviled as a tyrant and hailed as a hero for many years to come.

Further Reading

Brackman, Roman. *The Secret File of Joseph Stalin: A Hidden Life*. Portland, Ore.: Frank Cass, 2002.

Brent, Jonathan. *Stalin's Last Crime: The Plot against the Jewish Doctors, 1948–1953*. New York: HarperCollins, 2003.

Filtzer, Donald A. *Soviet Workers and Late Stalinism: Labour and the Restoration of the Stalinist System after World War II*. New York: Cambridge University Press, 2002.

Hoyt, Edwin P. *Stalin's War: Tragedy and Triumph, 1941–1945*. New York: Cooper Square Press, 2002.

Mawdsley, Evan. *The Stalin Years: The Soviet Union, 1929–1953*. New York: Manchester University Press, 2003.

McLoughlin, Barry, and Kevin McDermott, eds. *Stalin's Terror: High Politics and Mass Repression in the Soviet Union*. New York: Palgrave Macmillan, 2002.

Miner, Steven M. *Stalin's Holy War: Religion, Nationalism, and Alliance Politics, 1941–1945*. Chapel Hill: University of North Carolina Press, 2003.

Stalin, Joseph. *The Stalin-Kaganovich Correspondence, 1931–1936*. New Haven, Conn.: Yale University Press, 2003.

Tread, Christopher. *The Stalin Years: A Reader*. New York: Palgrave Macmillan, 2002.

Van Ree, Erik. *The Political Thought of Joseph Stalin: A Study in Twentieth-Century Revolutionary Patriotism*. London: RoutledgeCurzon, 2002.

Stolypin, Pyotr (1862–1911) *prime minister of Russia*

Pyotr Arkadyevich Stolypin was born in Dresden, Saxony, on April 14, 1862, into a noble Russian family. He graduated from St. Petersburg University in 1885 and found work within the Ministry of State Domains. Hard-working and energetic, he rose quickly through the bureaucratic ranks, and in 1889 he was appointed district marshal of Kovno Province, Russian Poland. There he familiarized himself with the misery and drudgery afflicting the peasant classes, and it conditioned him for what followed. By 1903 he was serving as governor of Saratov Province on the Volga, then a notorious hotbed of revolutionary activity. Stolypin, a no-nonsense disciplinarian, quickly imposed draconian order on the unruly populace. Success there brought him to the attention of Czar NICHOLAS II, and in 1906 Stolypin became minister of the interior and president of the Council of Ministers (prime minister). He now confronted the entire spectrum of economic and social malaise afflicting imperial Russia, then in the final stages of decay. When serfdom had been abolished in 1861, the peasantry could be legally removed from the land, and most were so poverty-stricken that they could not afford to purchase their own. The year prior to Stolypin's appointment witnessed the bloody and violent revolution of 1905, which resulted in creation of the Duma, Russia's first elected body. Stolypin earnestly sought major reforms to improve the lot of the poor majority but, as an aristocrat and devoted monarchist, he disdained constitutional government. Furthermore, the agenda he promulgated consisted of social and agricultural reform coupled with severe political repression.

Stolypin sought to quickly implement widespread land reforms but he was stymied by the Duma, which demanded a hand in the process. He therefore dissolved it and circumvented the constitutional process by issuing executive decrees. These included extending voting rights to peasants for choosing local government representatives. Furthermore peasants were also encouraged, with government assistance, to buy land. Through such expedients Stolypin hoped to create a stable class of conservative landowners that would be loyal to the throne and oppose revolutionary overtures. However, Russia's deep-seated inequities were giving rise to a professional class of revolutionaries, and Stolypin typically responded with force. The secret police and military rounded up thousands of suspects who were then hung with such alarming regularity that the hangman's noose was called "Stolypin's necktie."

For all his good intentions, Stolypin's efforts alienated vast tracts of the Russian polity. Conservative landowners railed against his efforts to acquire their land and sell it to the peasantry, while the left and center assailed his willingness to dispense with constitutional procedures. In the end he was simultaneously accused of being both a revolutionary and a reactionary. Stolypin simply brushed off such criticism and instituted reforms by fiat—again symptomatic of his contempt for constitutional law. In 1907 he again dismissed the Duma for noncooperation, further impeding the growth of democracy and hardening attitudes toward the government. He also reimposed a strict Russification program upon Finland, creating an upsurge in nationalistic resentments. By 1911 his widely publicized land reforms had yet to produce the stable landowning class he sought. The czar was probably contemplating Stolypin's dismissal at this juncture but events intervened. On September 14, 1911, while attending the opera in Kiev, Stolypin was shot by a revolutionary with shadowy police connections. The prime minister lingered four days before dying on September 19, 1911, and his much-vaunted reform program died with him. Stolypin was certainly a gifted statesman, among the czar's most capable, but his willingness to discard constitutional processes undermined the very system he strove so hard to preserve.

Further Reading

Ascher, Abraham. *P. A. Stolypin: The Search for Stability in Late Imperial Russia.* Stanford, Calif.: Stanford University Press, 2001.

Cawood, I., D. Bell, and A. Hannah. "Tsarism, 1881–1905: A 'Superannuated' Form of Government?" "Petr Stolpyn: The Czar's Last Hope?" *Modern History Review* 10 (September 1998): 28–33.

Korros, Alexandra S. *A Reluctant Parliament: Stolypin, Nationalism, and the Politics of the Russian Imperial State Council, 1906–1911.* Lanham, Md.: Rowman and Littlefield, 2002.

Pisiotis, Argyrios K. "Orthodoxy versus Autocracy: The Orthodox Church and Clerical Political Dissent in Late Imperial Russia, 1905–1914." 2 vols. Unpublished Ph.D. diss., Georgetown University, 2000.

Waldron, Peter. *Between Two Revolutions: Stolypin and the Politics of Renewal in Russia.* Dekalb: Northern Illinois University Press, 1998.

Wartenweiler, David. *Civil Society and Academic Debate in Russia, 1905–1914.* New York: Oxford University Press, 1999.

Stresemann, Gustav (1878–1929) *chancellor of Germany*

Gustav Stresemann was born in Berlin, Germany, on May 10, 1878, the son of an innkeeper. He pursued economics at the Universities of Berlin and Leipzig, became a successful businessman, and married into a wealthy family by 1903. In 1907 he parlayed his success into a political career, being elected to the Reichstag with the National Liberal Party and becoming that body's youngest member. Stresemann proved himself a brilliant parliamentarian, and by 1917 he was party leader. He strongly supported Germany's expansionist policies during World War I and, in concert with General Erich Ludendorff, he helped orchestrate the removal of THEOBALD VON BETHMANN HOLLWEG as chancellor. In 1918 he opposed Germany's surrender and the following year voted against ratification of the Treaty of Versailles, which imposed heavy reparations. Following the abdication of Kaiser WILHELM II, the democratic Weimar Republic came into existence. Stresemann, an avowed monarchist, initially despised the new government and founded a conservative organization, the German People's Party, to oppose it. But by 1922 he resigned himself to constitutional governance and used his considerable skills on behalf of the nation. Consequently, in August 1923, Stresemann became chancellor at the head of a broad coalition of liberals and socialists.

Stresemann inherited a nation on the brink of chaos. The economy was in ruins, inflation was rampant, and Germany rocked by leftist and reactionary street gangs fighting to overturn the government. For that reason his administration was equally unstable and lasted only 100 days. But during that interval Stresemann achieved several important accomplishments, beginning with the stabilization of the currency. Next he sought to impose law and order by disbanding left-wing governments in Thuringia and Saxony. He also managed to have police forces squelch the aborted putsch of Nazi agitator ADOLF HITLER in Bavaria. Unfortunately, neither Stresemann nor the government could keep up with scheduled reparations payments to France, and in 1923 France forcibly occupied the industrialized Ruhr River valley. This caused the Social Democrats to bolt his coalition in November 1923, and he resigned, although retaining the portfolio of foreign minister.

As foreign minister, Stresemann indelibly imprinted the course of Weimar diplomacy with astonishing success. While dealing from a position of weakness, he determined to resurrect Germany's reputation and restore it to the world community as a trusted partner for peace. With consummate skill Stresemann convinced European leaders of Germany's intention to resolve international disputes through negotiation and reconciliation. In 1925 he persuaded France and Great Britain to adopt the American-sponsored Dawes Plan to ease the burden of reparation payments. The following year he signed the Locarno Treaty with French foreign minister ARISTIDE BRIAND, whereby his nation formally acknowledged the transfer of Alsace and Lorraine to France. This stance enabled Germany to join the League of Nations, and Stresemann and Briand consequently received the Nobel Peace Prize. Turning eastward, he next strove for rapprochement with the Soviet Union by concluding the Rapallo Agreement, whereby both countries would not intervene militarily in conflicts involving third parties. In 1928 he was a signatory to the Kellogg-Briand Pact, which outlawed war as a means of national advancement. The next year Stresemann topped his litany of achievement by supervising adoption of the Young Plan, which further reduced reparations and ended French military occupation of the Rhineland five years ahead of schedule. Stresemann's efforts thus allowed Germany to begin rehabilitating its reputation as a great power.

Unfortunately for the Weimar Republic, Stresemann died of complications arising from overwork on October 3, 1929. He was by far the most accomplished German diplomat of Weimar and the period 1923–29 is commonly regarded as the Stresemann era. He was spared seeing his life work demolished by the Great Depression—and the rise of Hitler's Nazis.

Further Reading

Eley, Geoff, and James Retallack, eds. *Wilhelmism and Its Legacies: German Modernities, Imperialism, and the Meanings of Reform, 1890–1930.* New York: Berghahn Books, 2003.

Grathwol, Robert P. *Stresemann and the DNVP: Reconciliation or Revenge in German Foreign Policy, 1924–1928.* Lawrence: Regents Press of Kansas, 1980.

Lee, Stephen J. *The Weimar Republic.* New York: Routledge, 1998.

McNeil, William C. *American Money and the Weimar Republic: Economics and Politics on the Eve of the Great Depression.* New York: Columbia University Press, 1986.

O'Riordan, Elspeth Y. *Britain and the Ruhr Crisis.* New York: Palgrave in association with King's College, London, 2001.

Stresemann, Gustav. *Gustav Stresemann: His Diaries, Letters, and Papers.* London: Macmillan, 1945–50.

Wright, Jonathan R. C. *Gustav Stresemann: Weimar's Greatest Statesman.* New York: Oxford University Press, 2002.

Stroessner, Alfredo (1912–) *president of Paraguay*

Alfredo Stroessner was born in Encarnación, Paraguay, on November 3, 1912, the son of a German immigrant father and a Paraguayan mother. In 1929 he entered the National Military Academy at Asunción and he served with distinction during the Chaco War of 1932 before his studies were completed. For bravery in combat he received a battlefield commission and continued rising through the ranks. In 1940 he was selected for advanced military training in Brazil and three years later remained loyal to the president, Higinio Moringo, during an abortive coup. He performed similar useful service during the civil war of 1947 when the country was dominated by the conservative Colorado Party. A succession of coups and countercoups ensued over the next five years, and at one point Stroessner was forced to flee the country. However, when his faction finally assumed power under President Federico Chaves, Stroessner returned and received an appointment as head of the armed forces. In this capacity he unceremoniously toppled Chaves in May 1954 and installed himself as president.

Stroessner remained in office for the next 34 years, longer than any other South American head of state. His longevity in power is attributable to several reasons. Unlike most Latin dictators, he was far from charismatic but enjoyed the advantages of being intelligent and hard-working. He depended on the army and the Colorado Party as the twin pillars of state, and erected a comprehensive system of patronage and punishment to enforce his will. He also encouraged the growth of factions within the party, which, while under his tight control, militated against the rise of a possible competitor. Over time he created a system of pervasive control that permeated virtually every aspect of Paraguayan life. All members of the civil service were required to have Colorado Party membership to join the bureaucracy, and loyalty was both expected and enforced. Stroessner also skillfully manipulated a mass following through patronage and membership in ancillary party organizations, which existed down to the city block and village level. Surprisingly, as long as the economy prospered, the regime enjoyed a good deal of popularity despite authoritarian overtones and intolerance for political opposition. The government also turned a blind eye to large-scale smuggling, a traditional Paraguayan source of wealth, which further cemented vested interests to the government.

Consistent with his extremely conservative views, Stroessner was adamantly anticommunist and sought friendly relations with the United States. He also participated in Operation Condor, a clandestine program undertaken to identify and eliminate all suspected communist operatives. Furthermore, the government unhesitatingly granted asylum to fellow conservatives such as JUAN PERÓN, ANASTASIO SOMOZA DEBAYLE, and scores of Nazi fugitives including the notorious Josef Mengele. In economic terms, Stroessner attracted foreign investors and spent heavily constructing the Itaipu Dam on the Paraná River between Paraguay and Brazil; it remains the world's largest hydroelectric facility. This project not only met the nation's electrical needs but it also provided surplus energy for sale to the rest of Latin America. Stroessner's rule remained uncontested until a worldwide recession plunged Paraguay into chaos during the 1980s. This sparked rising inflation, unemployment, and national debt. Discontent arose from the country's new and heretofore thriving middle class, which had depended upon the general's patronage. The nominally pliable Colorado Party also underwent a fractious period, with some leaders demanding Stroessner's resignation. On February 2, 1989, troops under General Andres Rodriguez deposed the aging tyrant in a bloodless coup and he was allowed to seek asylum in Brazil.

Stroessner lived in obscurity and anonymity until June 2001, when a Paraguayan judge issued a request to the Brazilian government for his extradition. He is charged with authorizing the kidnapping and murder of several political opponents. However, since the Brazilian government has declined to honor similar requests in the past, Stroessner is likely to finish his final days in peace.

Further Reading

Abente Brun, Diego. *Stronismo, Post-stronismo, and the Prospects for Democratization in Paraguay.* Notre Dame, Ind.: Helen Kellogg Institute for International Studies, University of Notre Dame, 1989.

Carter, Paul C. "The Role of the Paraguayan Catholic Church in the Downfall of the Stroessner Regime." *Journal of Latin American Studies* 23 (October 1991): 599–621.

Chambers, Kevin C. "Rural Transformation of Paraguay under General Alfredo Stroessner, 1954–1989." Unpublished Ph.D. diss., University of California–Santa Barbara, 2001.

Lambert, P. "A Decade of Electoral Democracy: Continuity, Change and Crisis in Paraguay." *Bulletin of Latin American Research* 19 (July 2000): 379–396.

Miranda, Carlos R. *The Stroessner Era: Authoritarian Rule in Paraguay.* Boulder, Colo.: Westview Press, 1990.

Sondrol, Paul C. *Power Play in Paraguay: The Rise and Fall of General Stroessner.* Washington, D.C.: Institute for the Study of Diplomacy, School of Foreign Service, Georgetown University, 1996.

Suazo Córdova, Roberto (1927–) *president of Honduras*

Roberto Suazo Córdova was born in La Paz, Honduras, on March 17, 1927, and he studied medicine at the University of San Carlos in Guatemala. He practiced country medicine for 25 years before joining the Liberal Party in 1957 and serving as a delegate in various constitutional conventions. He gained national recognition by becoming head of the Liberals in July 1979, and was closely associated with the Rodista, or conservative, wing. He sought a working relationship with General Gustavo Alvarez Martínez, the national security chief, in an attempt to return the country to democracy. In 1980 the junta decided to restore civilian governance under the aegis of a new constitution granting the armed forces veto power over cabinet appointments and total control over matters pertaining to national security. New elections were held in November 1981 and Suazo Córdova, as the Liberal nominee, easily defeated National Party candidate Ricardo Zúñiga Agustinus. He was the first elected official in nearly 20 years.

Once in office, Suazo Córdova faced several seemingly intractable problems. The first was the overall situation in Central America, dominated by the ongoing Nicaraguan civil war between the communist regime of DANIEL ORTEGA and American-backed guerrillas, the contras. As the insurgency gathered force, the United States desired a larger military presence in Honduras to check communist aggression throughout the region. Suazo Córdova, an ardent anticommunist, proved compliant and he allowed both American troops and contra fighters to be stationed on Honduran soil. He also joined the Central American Democratic Community with El Salvador and Costa Rica as an additional bulwark against Nicaragua. In exchange he was visited by President RONALD REAGAN, who promised greater financial aid to sustain the numerous refugee camps that arose from the fighting. Mindful of communist subversion on the home front, Suazo Córdova did not object to oppressive measures employed by security services to stifle dissent. Consequently Honduras acquired a dismal human rights record throughout his tenure in office. Another problem spot was the economy, which was in deep recession. Suazo Córdova initially backed a plan of moderate agrarian reform, but it proved unequal to the task of easing economic distress. Recovery efforts were further beset by rising military expenditures, which increased the national debt and fueled inflation. By the time he left office, Suazo Córdova had accomplished little to promote growth.

The president enjoyed greater success promoting Honduran democracy. He came to office with the military establishment looming in the background and in 1983 he supported constitutional reforms that transferred his responsibilities as commander in chief to General Alvarez. Suazo Córdova was temporarily incapacitated by a heart attack in 1983, which made Alvarez appear politically stronger and fueled rumors of an impending coup. Surprisingly, in March 1984 Suazo Córdova dismissed Alvarez from office and appointed

his successor. In return, the general began hatching an assassination plot against the president and was arrested by FBI agents in November 1984. Civilian authority over the military had finally been reaffirmed. When Suazo Córdova left office in 1985 Honduras was still embroiled in regional conflict and experiencing economic dislocation. Public discontent with both his performance in office and the strong American military profile he solicited manifested in his inability to enforce his choice of a successor. Suazo Córdova wanted the Liberal Party to nominate Carlos Flores Faccuse, but instead the vote went to JOSÉ AZCONA HOYO, who went on to win the election. Suazo Córdova has since retired from public life although he remains a force in Liberal Party politics.

Further Reading
Bailey, J. M., and J. H. Sood. "The Honduran Agrarian Reform under Suazo Córdova, 1982–1985: An Assessment." *Inter-American Economic Affairs* 39 (fall 1985): 45–62.

Booth, J., M. Rosenberg, and M. Seligson. *Elections and Democracy in Central America.* Chapel Hill: University of North Carolina Press, 1989.

Coats, John D. "Parallel Interests: United States-Honduran Relations, 1981–1987." Unpublished master's thesis, Texas A & M University, 1991.

Schultz, Donald E., and Deborah S. Schultz. *The United States, Honduras, and the Crisis in Central America.* Boulder, Colo.: Westview Press, 1994.

Shepherd, Frederick M. "State, Countryside, and External Forces in Honduras and Nicaragua." Unpublished Ph.D. diss., Georgetown University, 1991.

Tervo, Kathryn H. "Honduras and the Contras: Effects of the 1980s U.S.-Sponsored Contra War on the Central American Republic of Honduras." Unpublished master's thesis, Central Connecticut State University, 1998.

Sukarno (1901–1970) *president of Indonesia*
Sukarno was born in Surabaya, Dutch East Indies, on June 6, 1901, the son of a Javanese father and a Balinese mother. He performed well in Dutch missionary schools and ultimately graduated from the Bandung Institute of Technology in 1926. However, Sukarno proved himself a peerless patriot and commenced his

anticolonial agitations by founding the Partai Nasional Indonesia (PNI), Indonesian National Party, that same year. He was a brilliant inflammatory speaker, so much so that Dutch authorities arrested him and outlawed the PNI in 1929. After his release in 1932, Sukarno served as chairman of the new Partai Indonesia (PI), Indonesian Party, until his arrest the following year. This time Sukarno remained incarcerated until 1942, when he was freed by Japanese occupiers. They prevailed on him to cooperate with the military government and he obliged, but only to eventually declare national independence. In June 1945 he issued the Panjat Sila—the five principles of Indonesian sovereignty: unity, respect for humanity, consensus, social justice, and faith in one God. These tenets served as the backbone of the forthcoming Indonesian state. Once the Japanese surrendered in August 1945, Sukarno, backed by MOHAMMAD HATTA, unilaterally declared Indonesia's independence, and the two men served as president and vice president, respectively. However, the Netherlands was determined to retain the islands as a colony, and over the next four years a guerrilla war ensued. The Dutch finally abandoned their quest in December 1949, and the new Republic of Indonesia emerged and was allowed into the equally new United Nations.

In practice, Sukarno proved more capable as a revolutionary than as the head of a new government. He subscribed to a unique blend of socialism and Islam that proved unworkable and also failed to establish a coherent, long-term agenda for development. Consequently the economy faltered and instability ensued. Sukarno also revealed a strong authoritarian streak in slowly undoing the 1946 constitution and its parliamentary democracy in favor of what he called "guided democracy," under his dictatorial rule. Here the progress of the state was of far more importance than individual liberties. The ensuing crackdown on dissent led to several outright rebellions on Sumatra and Sulawesi in 1958. Sukarno also had designs on the remaining European colonies in his region, and in 1961 he took military action to seize the western half of New Guinea from the Dutch.

In foreign policy, Sukarno alternated between conciliatory and hostile. In 1955 he summoned newly emerging states from Africa and Asia to a conference to endorse a nonaligned status independent of both the United States and the Soviet Union. In 1963 he strongly opposed the transformation of Malaya into Malaysia owing to territorial claims there, and embarked on a "confrontation" with the new government. He was so angered by the latter's admission into the United Nations that he withdrew Indonesia from that body in 1965. As a developing nation, Sukarno was eager to solicit assistance from the United States and the USSR, but when either side balked, he turned increasingly to Communist China for help. At home Sukarno fell under increasing criticism for his alleged friendly ties to the Partai Komunis Indonesia (PKI), Indonesia Communist Party, a stance he denied. But by 1962 he had appointed several of its members to high ministerial positions, and they generally lent him political support. However, on September 30, 1965, the communists launched a mass uprising while attempting to topple Sukarno's regime. They were easily defeated by army general Suharto, hunted down, and slaughtered. But like most military figures, Suharto held the president responsible for the disturbance, owing to his cozy relations with the communists. Therefore throughout the fall of 1965, Sukarno was forced to gradually surrender power to the military, and in March 1966 he was forced out of office and placed under house arrest. He nevertheless retained the honorary title of "lifetime president." Sukarno died in Jakarta, Indonesia, on June 21, 1970, a driving force behind Indonesian nationalism whose erratic 21 years in office imbued his country with unnecessary conflict. Nonetheless his funeral was attended by half a million mourners.

Further Reading

Easter, David. "British Intelligence and Propaganda during the 'Confrontation', 1963–1966." *Intelligence and National Security* 10, no. 2 (2001): 83–102.

Guan Ang, Cheng. "The Johnson Administration and 'Confrontation'." *Cold War History* 2 (April 2002): 111–128.

Kingsbury, Damien. *The Politics of Indonesia.* New York: Oxford University Press, 2002.

Saltford, John. *The United Nations and the Indonesian Takeover of West Papua, 1962–1969: The Anatomy of Betrayal.* New York: Routledge Curzon, 2002.

Subritzky, John. *Confronting Sukarno: British, American, Australian, and New Zealand Diplomacy in the Malaysian-Indonesian Confrontation, 1961–65.* New York: St. Martin's Press, 1999.

Taylor, Jean G. *Indonesia: Peoples and Histories.* New Haven, Conn.: Yale University Press, 2003.

Sun Yat-sen (Sun Yixian) (1866–1925) *president of China*

Sun Yat-sen was born in Guangdong Province, China, on November 12, 1866, the son of a small farmer. Sun received a classical Chinese education but relocated to Hawaii while a teenager and attended missionary school. In this manner Sun became both a Christian and fluent in English. He subsequently studied medicine in Hong Kong and graduated in 1892. By then Sun, like many Chinese of his generation, was disillusioned by Europe's interference in China, which was largely brought on by the corruption and weakness of the Manchu dynasty. These were descendants of Manchurians who had conquered China in 1644 and were still regarded as outsiders. In 1894 Sun submitted a detailed list of reformations to the government but was

Sun Yat-sen *(Library of Congress)*

officially rebuffed. He then became a revolutionary bent on overthrowing the Manchu dynasty and establishing a Chinese republic. Later that year he returned to Hawaii, founded the Society to Revive China, and began organizing for revolution. Sun directed a failed rebellion in Canton the following year and had to flee the country. He then set up residence in London where he was kidnapped by Chinese agents and freed only upon the insistence of the British government. Sun also immersed himself in Western political philosophy, especially Karl Marx, and he opted for a mixed national economy containing elements of both capitalism and socialism. He then relocated to Japan, where large numbers of Chinese students were studying, and organized a revolutionary group, the United League, in 1905. Around this time he began espousing his Three People's Principles for the governance of China; nationalism, democracy, and the people's livelihood. Sun, like many other young bureaucrats, railed against the Manchu dynasty's refusal to modernize the country, leaving it weak in the face of Western and Japanese expansionism.

Several more failed uprisings ensued, but in October 1911 a force of rebels and army units finally toppled the Manchus from power. Sun, who was overseas at the time, immediately rushed home and, for his earlier efforts, he became the first president of the new Republic of China on December 29, 1911. But independence alone could not solve China's political instability. No sooner had Sun become president than his authority was challenged by YUAN SHIKAI, a powerful northern warlord who was prime minister. To promote national unity, Sun voluntarily stepped down from office in February 1912 after serving a few months. He then spent most of his energies transforming the United League into China's first political party, the Kuomintang (KMT), a nationalist organization. Yuan, however, was determined to install himself as emperor of China and begin a new dynasty. When the KMT parliamentary representatives were attacked and dispersed by forces loyal to Yuan, Sun was forced to flee China a second time, in August 1913. Worse, when Yuan died suddenly in June 1916, his various military commanders established themselves as regional warlords and the country descended into chaos. Sun then returned home once again and labored to reestablish constitutional governance in China.

From his southern base in Guangdong Province, where he served as provisional president, Sun began marshaling military assets of his own under his military adviser CHIANG KAI-SHEK. He concurrently solicited the Western powers to invest heavily in China's new but mildly socialist economy. When aid was not forthcoming, the KMT turned to the Soviet Union for help and it was instrumental in establishing the famous Wampoa Military Academy in Canton. China was still riven by dissent and feuding between warlords, so in November 1924 Sun ventured to Beijing and made a plea for national unity. Failing this he intended to unleash the KMT in a northern expedition to unify the country by force. Unfortunately Sun died of cancer on March 12, 1925, and never saw the dream of a unified, modernized China realized. He was also regarded as something of a reckless revolutionary lacking a firm grasp of political realities and organization. However, Sun was the driving spirit behind China's unification and his three principles for governance are jointly claimed as their inspiration by the KMT party on Taiwan and the Communist Party of mainland China. He thus remains a cherished symbol of China's determination to modernize and rid itself of foreign influence.

Further Reading

Bergere, Marie Claire. *Sun Yat Sen*. Stanford, Calif.: Stanford University Press, 1998.

Harrison, Henrietta. *The Making of the Republican Citizen: Political Ceremonies and Symbols in China, 1911–1929*. New York: Oxford University Press, 2000.

Kriukov, Vassily. "Sun Yatsen and the 'Third Revolution': The Shandong Version." *Far Eastern Affairs* 1 (November–December 2001): 64–80.

Lum, Yansheng Ma. *Sun Yat Sen in Hawaii: Activities and Supporters*. Honolulu: Hawaii Chinese History Center, 1999.

Sun Yat Sen. *Memoirs of a Chinese Revolutionary*. New York: AMS Press, 1970.

Wells, Audrey. *The Political Thought of Sun Yat-sen: Development and Impact*. New York: Palgrave, 2001.

T

Taft, William H. (1857–1930) *president of the United States*

William Howard Taft was born in Cincinnati, Ohio, on September 15, 1857, into a prominent political family. He graduated from Yale with honors in 1878 and subsequently earned a law degree from the Cincinnati Law School. Taft then became active in Republican political circles and in 1882 President Chester A. Arthur appointed him district collector of internal revenue. Five years later he served as a judge on the state superior court. In 1890 President Benjamin Harrison made Taft the solicitor general before the federal Supreme Court and the following year he obtained a federal judgeship, in becoming the first federal jurist to declare that workers have the right to strike. Taft's tenure with the Court was extremely productive and he made clear his desire to become a Supreme Court justice, but in 1901 President William McKinley asked him to serve as the first civilian governor of the newly annexed Philippine Islands. Taft, never a confident man, agreed only after much hesitation, but his handling of such complicated matters proved adroit and confirmed his expertise as a legal authority. He enjoyed his overseas work to such an extent that he declined two invitations from President THEODORE ROOSEVELT to become a Supreme Court justice. However, he did return home in 1904 to become Roosevelt's secretary of war, and even-

tually, one of his most trusted political advisers. Roosevelt was so impressed by Taft's administrative abilities that in 1908 he arranged for him to secure the Republican presidential nomination. That fall Taft handily defeated Democrat William Jennings Bryan and gained the White House.

In contrast with the high-powered and overtly confident Roosevelt, Taft proved something of a shrinking violet. Whereas the former relished political infighting, the latter shunned confrontation in favor of consensus and never fully engaged himself in the politics of policy making. He was also hindered by a close association with Speaker of the House Joseph Cannon, a tyrannical conservative figure. In this manner Taft managed to alienate the progressive wing of the Republican Party—Roosevelt's base of popularity. Nonetheless, his administration accomplished much in the way of useful legislation. Among other feats, he signed laws calling for the direct election of U.S. senators and the first implementation of income taxes, overhauled the postal system, and attempt to break up the large steel monopolies. But his party split over the issue of tariffs: the eastern establishment sought high tariffs to protect American industries, but western, progressive interests wanted them lowered to reduce the costs of living. The result was a badly splintered party, whose unity was further eroded by Roosevelt's mounting antipathy for his former friend.

Believing that Taft had sold out to the conservatives, Roosevelt decided to challenge him for the Republican Party nomination in 1912. When he failed to unseat Taft, Roosevelt went on to establish his own progressive Bull Moose Party as an alternative. The national vote was thus split three ways during the election, with Democrat WOODROW WILSON coming first, Roosevelt second, and Taft a distant third. Curiously, Taft had no regrets over handing the White House over to Democrats, as he believed that Roosevelt was planning a constitutional coup against the government.

Out of Washington, Taft taught law for several years at Yale University and was also voted president of the American Bar Association. In 1921 he fulfilled a life-long ambition when President WARREN G. HARDING appointed him chief justice of the Supreme Court. He again displayed considerable flair and his Judiciary Act of 1925 proved instrumental in allowing the Court to refuse cases, thereby reducing its overwhelming work load. This was undoubtedly the happiest period in Taft's public career and he looked back upon his years in the White House as an unhappy aberration. "The truth is," he confided, "that in my present life I don't remember that I ever was president." He died in Washington, D.C., on March 8, 1930, a highly respected, congenial figure on the national landscape but unable to unite party factions behind strong, decisive leadership. A towering figure weighing over 300 pounds, Taft was the largest man to occupy the White House, and his sheer girth became the butt of public humor. But his political and judicial achievements, where he was able to achieve them, proved significant.

Further Reading

Anderson, D. F. "The Legacy of William Howard Taft." *Presidential Studies Quarterly* 12 (winter 1982): 54–65.

Burton, David H. *Taft, Holmes, and the 1920s Court: An Appraisal.* Madison, N.J.: Fairleigh Dickinson University Press, 1998.

———. *Taft, Wilson, and World Order.* Madison, N.J.: Fairleigh Dickinson University Press, 2003.

Renstrom, Peter G. *The Taft Court: Justices, Rulings, and Legacy.* Oxford: ABC-Clio, 2003.

Romero, Francie S. *Presidents from Theodore Roosevelt through Coolidge, 1902–1929: Debating the Issues in Pro and Con Primary Documents.* Westport, Conn.: Greenwood Press, 2002.

Taft, William H. *The Collected Works of William Howard Taft.* Athens: Ohio University Press, 2001.

Takeshita Noboru (1924–2000) *prime minister of Japan*

Takeshita Noboru was born in Kakeya, Shimane Province, Japan, on February 26, 1924, the son of a sake brewer and local politician. He enrolled at Waseda University in 1942 and two years later was drafted into the military before graduating. Takeshita resumed his studies after the war and taught English for several years. In 1952 he commenced his political career by being elected to a local assembly and four years later joined the lower house of the legislature (Diet) as part of the Liberal Democratic Party (LDP). This was the nation's largest political organization and would rule Japan for the next four decades. He was reelected from the same district 11 consecutive times. Despite his relative youth and inexperience, Takeshita proved himself adept at behind-the-scenes machinations and in 1964 Prime Minister SATO EISAKU appointed him deputy cabinet secretary. Almost a decade later he occupied the post of cabinet secretary under TANAKA KAKUEI. In short order the two leaders became identified with a drive toward greater consensus and coalition building at the expense of new or innovative policies. In fact, the entire government was beholden to the politics of rapid economic growth. Despite this overwhelming emphasis, both leaders were quick to ensure that the rice farmers—the LDP's most important voting constituency—received subsidies. When Tanaka resigned in 1976 over a bribery scandal, Takeshita transferred over as minister of construction under Takeo Miki, and in 1982 NAKASONE YASUHIRO made him finance minister. His most significant work was signing the Plaza Accord, which allowed the yen to float against the dollar and sent the economy on such a robust ride that the period was known as the "bubble years." It also precipitated one of Japan's worst recessions.

Takeshita became head of the LDP in 1987 and, hence, prime minister. His superlative back-benching abilities were now exposed to the full glare of public exposure, and he did not fare as well. In fact, the shy, somewhat retiring prime minister failed to enunciate a distinct philosophy for either economics or governance, choosing instead to allow others to speak for him. The most constructive event of his 18 months in office was imposition of a 3 percent sales tax that proved widely unpopular. In April 1987 Takeshita was embroiled in a bribery scandal of his own involving the Recruit company's attempt to buy influence. Having admitted to taking stock and cash donations, Takeshita publicly apologized for his indiscretion and resigned from office.

Out of the spotlight, where he felt infinitely more comfortable, Takeshita wielded enormous influence over the selection of future LDP prime ministers like Obuchi Keizo. In fact he was commonly referred to as the "puppet master" for his uncanny ability to manipulate votes and politics to his liking. In 1992 allegations of another scandal involving organized crime and far-right smear groups emerged, but he was never charged with a crime. Takeshita finally retired from politics in April 2000 and he died in Tokyo on June 19, 2000. He was the first Japanese prime minister to be born of humble origins and perhaps best exemplified the old-style machine politics of his generation.

Further Reading

Fukui, Haruhiro. "Japan in 1988: At the End of an Era." *Asian Survey* 29 (January 1989): 1–11.

———. "Japan's Takeshita at the Helm." *Current History* 87, no. 528 (1988): 173–175.

Hoshi, Iwao. *Japan's Pseudo-Democracy.* New York: New York University Press, 1993.

Imai, Masatoshi. "Support for the Cabinet." *Japan Quarterly* 35, no. 4 (1988): 377–382.

Kenzo, Uchida. "Slow and Steady: The Takeshita Administration's First Year." *Japan Quarterly* 35 (October–December 1988): 371–376.

Woodall, Brian. *Japan Under Construction: Corruption, Politics, and Public Works.* Berkeley: University of California Press, 1996.

Tanaka Kakuei (1918–1993) *prime minister of Japan*

Tanaka Kakuei was born in Futada, Niigata Province, Japan, on May 4, 1918, the son of a cattle dealer. He obtained only a secondary education before being drafted into the army during World War II and receiving a medical discharge. Tanaka then returned home and entered the construction industry, accruing a minor fortune before the war ended. In 1947 he was elected to the lower house of the legislature (Diet) and the following year was appointed vice minister of the justice ministry under Prime Minister YOSHIDA SHIGERU. Tanaka quickly demonstrated his mastery of the deal making and consensus building essential to Japanese politics and he fulfilled a succession of important ministerial posts under IKEDA HAYATO. But his most significant assignment was as head of the vital Ministry for International Trade and Industry (MITI) under SATO EISAKU, where he showed great foresight appreciating the value of communication and information technology. He also determined to interject economic vitality into the western reaches of the nation, traditionally poverty stricken, and likewise address urban decay in older cities. Beginning in 1955, when the Liberal Democratic Party (LDP) was first formed, Tanaka also seized the opportunity to command one of the largest factions within the party and, with it, the ability to influence overall policy. Furthermore, as party secretary, he proved effective at quelling intraparty rebellions against sitting prime ministers, and his influence and control allowed Sato to remain in office eight years—longer than any other incumbent. In 1972 Tanaka was elected head of the LDP and with it gained the office of prime minister, becoming the youngest in Japanese history, in an unexpected upset over Sato's hand-picked successor. A colorful, dynamic figure and quite different from the usual nondescript variety of Japanese leaders, Tanaka initially enjoyed a surge in public opinion polls and much was expected of him.

Tanaka's most important act came in 1974 when he visited Beijing and established diplomatic relations with the People's Republic of China. However, his political legitimacy was undercut by revelations of political corruption. Tanaka had apparently accepted bribes from the America's Lockheed Corporation to secure Japanese purchases of their transport aircraft. As his once-soaring popularity figures dropped, he was forced to resign in December 1974 and was replaced by TAKESHITA NOBORU. Two years later he was arrested and charged with accepting $2 million from Lockheed, and his trial lasted seven years. Found guilty, he was heavily fined and received a four-year suspended sentence. He was also forced out of the LDP.

As embarrassing as Tanaka's predicament was, it did little to diminish his popularity with the voters in Niigata. He expended considerable effort revitalizing the poorer half of the country and he was reelected to the Diet as an independent. In this capacity he continued to wield tremendous influence over the largest faction within the LDP and played a king-making role in selection of the next three prime ministers. Tanaka suffered a stroke in 1985, and afterward his ability to control events diminished. He died in Tokyo on December 16, 1993, and, though largely remembered for the scandal that brought him down, he was possibly the most influential Japanese politician of his generation. Tanaka was also the only post–World War II prime minister to lack a college education.

Further Reading

Babb, James. *Tanaka and the Making of Postwar Japan.* White Plains, N.Y.: Longman, 2000.

Hunziker, Steven, and Ikuro Kamimura. *Kakuei Tanaka: A Political Biography of Modern Japan.* Los Gatos, Calif.: Daruma International, 1995.

Hurst, Cameron G. *Tanaka Kakuei and Postwar Japanese Politics.* Hanover, N.H.: Universities Field Staff International, Inc., 1983.

———. *The Tanaka Decision: Tanaka Kakuei and the Lockheed Scandal.* Hanover, N.H.: Universities Field Staff International, Inc., 1983.

Ito, Go. *Alliance in Anxiety: Detente and the Sino-American-Japanese Triangle.* New York: Routledge, 2003.

Johnson, Chalmers. "Tanaka Kakuei: Structural Corruption and the Advent of Machine Politics in Japan." *Journal of Japanese Studies* 12, no. 1 (1986): 1–28.

Toyozo, T. "Breakup of the Tanaka Faction: End of an Era." *Japan Quarterly* 34 (October–December 1987): 371–376.

Thant, U See U THANT.

Thatcher, Margaret (baroness Thatcher of Kesteven) (1925–) *prime minister of Great Britain*

Margaret Hilda Roberts was born in Grantham, England, on October 13, 1925, the daughter of a prosperous grocer. She endured a strict Methodist upbringing before attending Oxford University to study chemistry. Despite her middle-class background, she became politically active by joining campus conservative organizations. In 1951 she married Dennis Thatcher, a wealthy businessman, who enabled her to pursue a law degree and ultimately politics. She ran twice unsuccessfully for office but succeeded on the third attempt in 1959. Despite the fact there were very few women in British politics—and even fewer operating in conservative circles—Thatcher displayed a resolve to succeed that belied her gender. Throughout the 1960s, when the party was in opposition, she fulfilled several positions in the "shadow cabinet" of EDWARD HEATH, whom Thatcher respected but never really liked. Nonetheless, when Heath was elected prime minister in 1970, he appointed her to serve as secretary of state for education and science. Thatcher thrived in the role, despite her growing reputation for a personal stridency bordering on imperiousness. When Heath was defeated in 1975, she was among the first Conservative Party leaders to challenge him for the leadership. Surprisingly, she easily defeated Heath on the first ballot—sowing enmity between them—but catapulting herself into the national limelight. Over the next four years Thatcher gained renown as a fierce, well-informed parliamentary debater with a commanding physical and media presence. When the conservatives were finally returned to power in 1979, Thatcher became Great Britain's first-ever woman prime minister.

Early on Thatcher determined to leave her mark on the political landscape by disparaging and dismantling the "welfare state" that had been in effect since 1945. Because she ascribed the country's decline as a world power to the cult of government dependency, numerous state programs were targeted for elimination. In their stead Thatcher proposed a return to free-market principles and greater self-reliance. The prime minister was especially eager to reduce the size of government, privatize government holdings, cut back on government bureaucracy, and roll back the power of unions. She also sought to tackle the problem of spiraling inflation by adopting strict monetary measures and fiscal austerity, which caused unemployment to rise but restored economic growth. Furthermore, she received an additional boost in public ratings through her firm handling of the 1982 Falkland Islands war, initiated when Argentine president LEOPOLDO GALTIERI seized the colony by force. A complete British victory and a badly split Labour Party resulted in her stunning reelection in 1983.

Aside from her domestic agenda, Thatcher was also a cold war warrior of the first rank. She abhorred communism and greatly increased military spending. Together with her friend and ally President RONALD REAGAN, they presented a solid front against Soviet expansionism in Afghanistan and elsewhere. She also allowed the

Americans to base cruise missiles in England and use local airbases to bomb Libya in 1986. Such was her resolve to confront communism that Kremlin leaders bestowed on her the none too flattering sobriquet of The Iron Lady, an accurate reflection of her persona. Back at home, Thatcher's second term in office was characterized by a determined campaign to end the coal miners' strike by force, and break their stranglehold on the labor market. Thatcher also proved herself a staunch British nationalist whose distrust of Europe bordered on outright dislike. For this reason, while she supported a common market, she railed against the adoption of a unified currency as an assault upon national sovereignty. Thatcher's stridency over the issue occasioned several high-ranking resignations, along with poor-natured sniping from fellow conservative Heath, who openly detested her policies. But in 1987 Thatcher made history by winning her third general election, if by reduced margins. She now gained the ire of the middle class she once championed by imposing a hated "poll tax" upon all residents to help pay for public services. Her increasing unpopularity cause a revolt among large segments of the Conservative Party and in 1990 they prevailed upon her to resign from power. Thatcher did so obligingly out of concern for her party and endorsed the candidacy of John Major, who went on to secure the Conservatives' fourth straight election victory.

Shortly before her resignation, Thatcher was elevated to the House of Lords as baroness of Kesteven. She continues on as a respected elder stateswoman and continues drawing crowds for speaking and book-signing engagements. Her 11-year term in office is the longest continuous tenure as prime minister since William Pitt in the 1790s. It marked Great Britain's resurgence as a world power and led to a permanent diminution of the welfare state that had dominated national politics for most of the 20th century. Thatcher also forced the Labour Party opposition to moderate its position on many controversial issues. Not surprisingly, the conservative philosophy she espoused has passed into history as "Thatcherism."

Further Reading

Campbell, John. *Margaret Thatcher*. London: Jonathan Cape, 2000.

Dorman, Andrew M. *Defense under Thatcher*. New York: Palgrave, 2002.

Evans, Eric J. *Thatcher and Thatcherism*. New York: Routledge, 2004.

Hoskyns, John. *Just in Time: Inside the Thatcher Revolution*. London: Aurum, 2000.

Maddox, Brenda. *Maggie: The Personal Story of a Public Life*. London: Hodder and Stoughton, 2003.

Parker, Mike. *Thatcherism and the Fall of Coal*. New York: Oxford University Press, 2000.

Reitan, E. A. *The Thatcher Revolution: Margaret Thatcher, John Major, and Tony Blair, 1979–2001*. Lanham, Md.: Rowman and Littlefield, 2003.

Thackery, Frank W., and John E. Findling, eds. *Events That Changed Great Britain since 1689*. Westport, Conn.: Greenwood Press, 2002.

Thatcher, Margaret. *The Path to Power*. New York: HarperCollins, 1995.

———. *Statecraft: Strategies for a Changing World*. New York: HarperCollins, 2002.

Tisza, István (1861–1918) *prime minister of Austria-Hungary*

István Tisza was born in Budapest, Hungary, on April 22, 1861, the son of Kalman Tisza, an aristocrat and influential politician. Hungary was then part of the Austro-Hungarian Empire, which since the 1867 *Ausgleich* (compromise) had been ruled by a dual crown. This entailed the Austrian emperor also serving as the king of Hungary. The elder Tisza felt strongly that a close working relationship with German-speaking Austria was essential if Hungary's distinct culture was to survive while surrounded by a host of Slavic nationalities. The younger Tisza was educated in Berlin and Heidelberg and, like his father, he joined the conservative-leaning Liberal Party, which represented large, landholding interests. He too saw the need of maintaining the Dual Crown at any cost to preserve Hungary's sovereignty and gained election to the legislature on that platform in 1886. From the onset his stance put him at odds with Magyar nationalists who wanted less Austrian influence and liberals who sought greater rights for Hungary's sizable minority population. By the turn of the century Hungary's politics were also roiled over attempts to enlarge the Hungarian contingent of the polyglot, multinational army. Nationalists demanded a separate Hungarian force within a federal structure while Tisza sought to maintain a unitary force under one command to preserve the Hapsburg monarchy. When Tisza became prime minister of Hungary in October 1903 he vigorously pursued an army bill intent upon strengthening the size and control of that force. However, public resentment proved so overwhelming against the measure that in January 1905 the Liberal Party was completely defeated and he resigned from office.

Back in the legislature, Tisza set about reorganizing the Liberals into a new organization, the National Party of Work. He was also a skilled politician who gradually wrested control away from the nationalists by taking a majority of seats in the 1910 elections. Tisza continued exerting control as president of the Chamber of Deputies, pushing through additional army bills and rules for limiting the practice of filibustering legislation. In June 1913 Tisza again occupied the prime minister's office while all of Europe anxiously awaited the outbreak of war. The spark that lit the fuse happened in Sarajevo on June 28, 1914, when Serbian nationalists assassinated Archduke Francis Ferdinand. Tisza then attended an emergency summit of the Crown Council on July 14, 1914, to consider a declaration of war against Serbia. The Hungarian prime minister strongly opposed the move, for it might entail the annexation of Serbia to the empire. Tisza considered any increase of the empire's Slavic population to be detrimental to national security and, hence, to the dual crown. However, Emperor FRANZ JOSEPH opted for hostilities, and Tisza fell into line behind his sovereign.

Over the next three years Tisza served as a capable and forceful exponent of victory and urged strong cooperation with Germany's Kaiser WILHELM II. It was hoped that victory in the east would prevent any attempt by the Russian Empire to unify the Slavs into a threat against Hungary. Moreover, Tisza ruled in a dictatorial fashion that trampled countering opinions and created great antipathy toward the monarchy and the war effort. He singularly refused to grant Italy and Romania minor territorial concessions that might have kept them neutral and considered such talk a sign of weakness. Tizsa also refused to enlarge and expand the voting franchise in Hungary, leaving only 10 percent of the population eligible to participate. In 1916 Franz Joseph died and was replaced by a new emperor, Charles I (King Charles IV of Hungary), a committed reformer. The new king determined to liberalize and modernize the Hungarian political system and clashed repeatedly with Tisza, who finally resigned from office on May 22, 1917. But because his National Party of Work continued controlling the legislature, he still managed to stymie all attempts at constitutional or social reform.

For the rest of World War I Tisza served as an infantry officer on the Italian front. Unfortunately few of his fellow Hungarians were aware of his efforts to prevent the outbreak of hostilities and many blamed him for the hardships they endured. On October 31, 1918, he was murdered by a group of resentful soldiers. Tizsa was an outstanding political operator but fatally beholden to the old political order.

Further Reading

Cornwall, Mark. *The Last Years of Austria-Hungary: A Multi-national Experiment in Early Twentieth-Century Europe.* Exeter: University of Exeter Press, 2002.

———. *The Undermining of Austria-Hungary: The Battle for Hearts and Minds.* New York: St. Martin's Press, 2000.

Healy, Maureen. *Vienna and the Fall of the Hapsburg Empire: Total War and Everyday Life in World War I.* New York: Cambridge University Press, 2004.

Jeszenszky, Geza. "István Tisza: Villain or Tragic Hero? Reassessments in Hungary—Verdict in the U.S." *Hungarian Studies Review* 14, no. 2 (1987): 45–57.

Tisza, István. *Count Stephen Tisza, Prime Minister of Hungary: Letters (1914–1916).* New York: P. Lang, 1991.

Vermes, Gabor. *István Tisza: The Liberal Vision and Conservative Statecraft of a Magyar Nationalist.* New York: Columbia University Press, 1986.

Tito, Marshal (Josip Broz) (1892–1980) *president of Yugoslavia*

Josip Broz was born in Kumrovec, Croatia, on May 25, 1892, into a large peasant family. Croatia was then part of the Austro-Hungarian Empire and, after being trained as a locksmith, Broz was drafted into the army to fight in World War I. He was captured by the Russians in 1917 and witnessed the Bolshevik revolution that fall. Having volunteered to fight in the Red Army, he returned home in 1920 as a communist agent. His homeland had since been freed of Austrian domination and renamed the Kingdom of Serbs, Croats, and Slovenes, or Yugoslavia. Broz continued his subversive activities until he was caught and imprisoned. In 1925 he was released and ventured back to Moscow for further political training. Broz sufficiently impressed Soviet dictator JOSEPH STALIN with his trustworthiness and in 1937 he was sent home as secretary general of the Yugoslav Communist Party. He also referred to himself as Tito, after a pen name. When German forces under ADOLF HITLER attacked and conquered Yugoslavia in April 1941, Tito followed Stalin's strict orders to remain neutral in accordance with the recent non-aggression pact. But, when Hitler invaded the Soviet Union two months later, Tito began raising partisan forces to resist. The next four years established Tito as one of history's most brilliant guerrilla fighters for, always outnumbered and outgunned, he defied all attempts to eradicate his little band. When he was not fighting Germans, his communists found time to resist Serbian royalists under General Draja Mikhailovich—in effect a civil war within a war. Tito's success enabled the Allies to supply him with arms after 1943, and he succeeded in pushing the Germans out of Yugoslavia completely the following year—the only guerrilla leader in World War II to do so. In 1945 he proclaimed creation of the People's Republic of Yugoslavia with himself as prime minister.

Tito was at heart a doctrinaire communist and he imposed a Stalinist one-party dictatorship on the country, replete with a large and effective secret police. He also nationalized the economy and made the six different nationalities comprising Yugoslavia pledge loyalty to the concept of "brotherhood and unity." But, because Yugoslavia was neither liberated by Soviet troops nor occupied by them, he felt less inclined to follow the Stalinist line and render his country a Soviet puppet state. He also refused to erect an extremely centralized regime along Soviet lines, preferring instead a federal model with plenty of autonomy for the six different regions. These heretical stances brought him the ire of Stalin, who in 1949 expelled Yugoslavia from the Cominform, a communist trade organization. Tito countered by seeking aid from the capitalist West to buoy up his economy and supply him with weapons. And, while solidly in the communist camp philosophically, he gained international renown as a maverick communist seeking his own path to socialism. To that end he ruled over the most liberal communist regime of Eastern Europe where some minor dissent was eventually allowed.

In 1953 Tito promulgated a new constitution that made him president of the republic. He was theoretically elected to high office every five years but, as the indis-

Marshal Tito (Library of Congress)

pensable man, he never faced serious opposition. After Stalin's death he was wooed by new premier NIKITA KHRUSHCHEV to return to the fold but Tito refused. Instead, in 1956 he helped to establish the Nonaligned Movement of developing nations in concert with Egypt's GAMAL ABDEL NASSER and India's JAWAHARLAL NEHRU. Soviet misbehavior allowed him to enlarge his role as a socialist maverick by roundly condemning the 1956 invasion of Hungary and the 1968 invasion of Czechoslovakia. He remained on especially good terms with another East Bloc rebel, NICOLAE CEAUŞESCU of Romania. Tito ruled Yugoslavia oppressively but, ironically for a communist leader, he unabashedly acquired a reputation for fine cars and luxurious living. He died in Ljubljana on May 4, 1981, greatly mourned. For 30 years he presided over an ethnic and religious tinderbox and, on the surface at least, made it work. But his successors lacked the charisma and vision for success, and the system he founded barely survived him by a decade. In 1990 Yugoslavia disintegrated in a deluge of warring factions and was disbanded. Tito is nonetheless one of the most important cold war figures for his brilliance as a guerrilla and his unbridled defiance of the Soviet Union.

Further Reading

Benson, Leslie. *Yugoslavia: A Concise History.* New York: Palgrave Macmillan, 2003.

Djokiac, Dejan, ed. *Yugoslavism: Histories of a Failed Idea, 1918–1992.* Madison: University of Wisconsin Press, 2003.

Granville, Johanna. "Hungary 1956: The Yugoslav Connection." *Europe-Asia Studies* 50, no. 3 (1998): 493–517.

Hudson, Kate. *Breaking the South Slav Dream: The Rise and Fall of Yugoslavia.* Sterling, Va.: Pluto Press, 2003.

Lees, Lorraine M. *Keeping Tito Afloat: The United States, Yugoslavia, and the Cold War, 1945–1960.* University Park: Pennsylvania State University Press, 1997.

Lensink, Paul D. "Building Tito's Separate Road: Yugoslavia and the United States, 1949–1957." Unpublished Ph.D. diss., Indiana University, 1995.

West, Richard. *Tito and the Rise and Fall of Yugoslavia.* New York: Carroll and Graf, 1995.

Tojo Hideki (1884–1948) *prime minister of Japan*

Tojo Hideki was born in Tokyo, Japan, on December 30, 1884, into an old military family. He graduated from a military academy in 1899 and saw service in the Russo-Japanese War, 1904–05. After passing through the army war college in 1915 Tojo was sent to Europe for additional studies in Switzerland and Germany. He came home in 1922 and commenced a rapid rise through the military hierarchy, proving himself both capable and ruthless. He was promoted to lieutenant general in 1936, just as Japan was swept by a tide of aggressive ultranationalism. Tojo was active during the initial phases of the renewed Sino-Japanese conflict in 1937 and helped subdue Inner Mongolia. The following year he was recalled to Japan to serve as vice minister of war and argued stridently for expanding the conflict to include the Soviet Union. In 1940 Tojo gained appointment as war minister under Prime Minister KONOE FUMIMARO and was a driving force behind the Tripartite Pact with ADOLF HITLER and BENITO MUSSOLINI. Following the German

conquest of France in May 1940, Japan was allowed to obtain French colonial possessions in Indochina. However, this expansion drew a sharp response from American president FRANKLIN D. ROOSEVELT, who placed an oil embargo on Japan until it withdrew its forces from the Asian mainland. To Tojo and his fellow militarists, only a victorious war with the United States, Great Britain, and the Netherlands would grant Japan access to the raw materials it so desperately needed. They equated conflict with nothing less than national survival.

When Konoe tried and failed to reach a negotiated settlement with the Americans over China, he resigned as prime minister in October 1941 and was replaced by Tojo. Previously, Tojo decided against attacking the Soviet Union despite the fact that it was being pummeled by German forces. This proved one of the biggest strategic missteps of military history for if Japan had attacked Russia the battered forces of Soviet dictator JOSEPH STALIN could not have decisively reinforced their western front. Tojo then badgered army and navy leaders into attacking Western colonial possessions throughout the Pacific to establish a "Greater East Asia Co-prosperity Sphere"—an enlarged Japanese Empire. After the failure of last-minute negotiations in Washington, D.C., Japanese naval forces attacked the American naval installation at Pearl Harbor, Hawaii, on December 7, 1941. This single act precipitated World War II in the Pacific.

In addition to prime minister, Tojo also held the portfolios of war minister and home minister. Over the next three years he directed the Japanese military onslaught, which, while spectacularly successful at first, gradually slowed and stopped after stiffened Allied resistance. By 1944 the tide of war had turned inexorably against Japan despite fanatical sacrifices by Japanese soldiers, sailors, and airmen. Through it all Tojo put on the best face possible and promised his countrymen ultimate victory if they would only persevere. However, the American conquest of Saipan in July 1944 put the Japanese homeland within reach of American bombers, and Tojo was forced to resign from office. For almost a year he watched the American military juggernaut gather steam and grind down Japanese defenses. After the atomic bombings of Hiroshima and Nagasaki in August 1945, Emperor HIROHITO acted decisively and ordered his generals to surrender. Japan was soon after occupied by American forces under General Douglas MacArthur, who arrested Tojo as a war criminal. The former prime minister failed at a suicide attempt in September 1945 and was put on trial, charged with plotting aggression and condoning atrocities committed by Japanese forces. Tojo was found guilty and hanged as a "Class A" war criminal on December 23, 1948, having guided Japan into its most destructive conflict. His entire career closely mirrored the rise of militarism in Japan, its triumphant dominance of national politics, and its spectacular demise.

Further Reading

Hoyt, Edwin P. *Warlord: Tojo Against the World.* New York: Cooper Square Press, 2001.

Li, Peter, ed. *Japanese War Crimes.* New Brunswick, N.J.: Transaction Publishers, 2002.

Rees, Laurence. *Horror in the East: Japan and Atrocities of World War II.* Cambridge, Mass.: Da Capo Press, 2002.

Slavinsky, Boris N. *The Japanese-Soviet Neutrality Pact: A Diplomatic History, 1941–45.* New York: RoutledgeCurzon, 2003.

Tanaka, Toshiyuki. *Japan's Comfort Women: Sexual Slavery and Prostitution during World War II and the U.S. Occupation.* New York: Routledge, 2001.

Yamazaki, Jane W. "A Nation Apologizes: Japanese Apologies for World War II." Unpublished Ph.D. diss., Wayne State University, 2002.

Zeiler, Thomas W. *Unconditional Defeat: Japan, America, and the End of World War II.* Wilmington, Del.: Scholarly Resources, 2003.

Tombalbaye, François (1918–1975) *president of Chad*

François Tombalbaye was born in Bessada, Chad, on June 15, 1918, the son of a Protestant Sara trader. His religion and background made him something of an anomaly in this predominantly Catholic and Muslim French colony. Having passed through missionary schools, Tombalbaye took up teaching for several years and also became active in union activities. In 1950 he helped to found the Parti Progressiste Tchadien (PPT), Chadian Progressive Party, to agitate against continuance of French rule. His defiance angered colonial administrators, and he was stripped of his teaching license and forced to fend for himself as a brick maker.

However, after France began relaxing its grip on African colonies in 1956 and permitted greater regional autonomy, Tombalbaye was elected to the territorial legislature as a PPT delegate. The following year he replaced the Marxist-oriented Gabriel Lisette as head of the party and in 1959, when the PPT swept national elections, Tombalbaye was installed as prime minister. Chad was finally granted independence on August 11, 1960, and Tombalbaye became the nation's first president.

Tombalbaye inherited an impoverished desert nation, deeply split between a largely Muslim, Arabic north and a Christian, African south. Therefore, to enforce order and ensure his rule, he established a one-party dictatorship from the onset and abolished all opposition parties in 1962. He also founded a far-ranging criminal court system to arrest and eliminate his enemies from power. After 1964 Tombalbaye also initiated a policy of deliberate Africanization to expunge all French influence. The number of trained French bureaucrats was drastically reduced and replaced by inexperienced native labor. Consistent with this policy, he also changed his given name to Ngartha. And, as a Christian African, Tombalbaye proved less than diplomatic in his favoritism toward members of his own region, which further alienated the Muslim north. When he cracked down on numerous hard-line clerics who opposed his rule in 1965, an internecine civil war erupted along racial and religious lines. The strength of rebel groups was greatly abetted by aid and advisers from neighboring Libya and Sudan, and Tombalbaye turned to France for help. In exchange he was forced to liberalize his regime, release political prisoners, and bring more northerners into the government by 1971. However, after a failed coup attempt against him the following year, Tombalbaye clamped down on dissent, crushed student strikes, and resumed his dictatorial rule.

After a decade of civil strife it was clear to Tombalbaye that he would have to accommodate his Muslim neighbors in order to survive. Accordingly, he reestablished closer ties with Libyan strongman Muammar Gadhafi in December 1972, quietly granted him access to the coveted Aouzou strip in the north, and broke off diplomatic relations with Israel to appease other Arab states. Consequently, Arab support for the northern rebel groups waned. The following year he attempted to consolidate his own power base by reintroducing widespread Africanization to such an extent that even foreign-sounding street names were ordered changed. Worse, he also made his Sara tribe practice of yondo, a painful initiation rite involving facial scars, mandatory for employment in the civil service. This move only alienated fellow southerners who did not share the same tribal customs. By 1974 Tombalbaye's regime was further battered by a prolonged drought and a mishandling of relief aid. At this juncture many military officers began drawing up plans against him. Tombalbaye was apparently alert for such dissension, for in March 1975 he ordered the arrest of several ranking officers whom he viewed as hostile. On April 13, 1975, he was suddenly killed in a coup. Unfortunately, the dissension he had sown between northerners and southerners kept Chad in turmoil up through the 1990s. Tombalbaye himself was buried in an unmarked grave for 19 years and not reinterred in his home village of Bessada until April 13, 1994.

Further Reading

Azevedo, Mario J. *Chad: A Nation in Search of Its Future.* Boulder, Colo.: Westview Press, 1998.

Burr, Millard. *Africa's Thirty Years' War: Libya, Chad, and the Sudan, 1963–1993.* Boulder, Colo.: Westview Press, 1999.

Decalo, Samuel. *Historical Dictionary of Chad.* Metuchen, N.J.: Scarecrow Press, 1997.

Nolutshungu, Sam C. *Limits of Anarchy: Intervention and State Formation in Chad.* Charlottesville: University Press of Virginia, 1996.

Talbot, George T. "Origins, Causes, and Effects of the Tchadian Civil War and the French Interventions, 1968–1971." Unpublished Ph.D. diss., University of Notre Dame, 1974.

Wright, John L. *Libya, Chad, and the Central Sahara.* Totowa, N.J.: Barnes and Noble Books, 1989.

Torrijos, Omar (1929–1981) *president of Panama*

Omar Torrijos Herrera was born in Santiago, Panama, on February 13, 1929, the son of schoolteachers. He opted for a military career and received military training in El Salvador and the United States before becoming an officer in the Panamanian National Guard in 1952. Panama, traditionally ruled by a handful of white European families, was experiencing political pressure to allow the newly rising middle class to share power. In May 1968 Arnulfo Arias Madrid was elected to the presidency on a platform of radical reforms to enhance the poor and middle classes. However, he was quickly overthrown by a coterie of National Guard officers, including Torrijos, who eventually emerged as the new strongman by January 1969. He then assumed the title, Chief of Government and Supreme Leader of the Panamanian Revolution. In this capacity the head of state purged radical students from the universities, shut down opposition presses, and arrested political dissidents. Torrijos then broke with the established pattern of military rule by appointing several well-known leftists to places of prominence within the government. In December 1969 disgruntled officers launched a coup against him while he was outside the country, but Torrijos acted energetically, returned home, and defeated the insurgents. His capacity for decisive action and determination to succeed favorably impressed his fellow citizens. In 1972 he was granted full civil and military authority by the national assembly and ruled by decree.

The rise of military leaders was nothing new in Latin America, but Torrijos, a staunch nationalist and a populist, determined to forever alter the political landscape of Panama. More than anything he wished to break the monopoly of power held by the traditional elites. Torrijos toured the country in uniform, deliberately talking to peasants and workers to hear their grievances—an unprecedented act in Panama. He then instituted a far-reaching system of land reform for thousands of poor and needy families. The government also expanded educational and technical training opportunities for those traditionally excluded from the system, and established new schools throughout the countryside. Moreover, Torrijos made concerted efforts to improve and expand health care for the masses, construct new hospitals in the hinterland, and improve national infrastructure with new bridges and roads. On the labor front, he supported union activities and ordered that collective bargaining be mandatory. But for all his good intentions, Torrijos was no democrat and continued to rule with tight control. Political parties were outlawed save for his own Partido Revolucionario Democrático (PRD), Democratic Revolutionary Party, which he intended as the first step towards one-party rule.

As a nationalist, Torrijos centered his policy on reclaiming the Panama Canal from the United States, which had constructed and operated that famous facility since the early 20th century. Torrijos began insisting on talks to turn over the canal in 1971 but, despite threats and entreaties, he made no progress for eight years. Ownership of the canal was a highly emotional issue in both countries, but it was not until the election of American president JIMMY CARTER that real negotiations got under way. A treaty was then signed in September 1977, whereby the Americans eliminated the canal zone immediately, while sovereignty of the canal itself would transfer slowly and be surrendered on January 1, 2000. However, the United States insisted upon, and Torrijos was forced to agree to, clauses that gave the Americans the right to intervene militarily to keep the canal open. The entire affair marked a turning point in United States relations with Central America and rendered Torrijos a hero throughout the region.

In international relations, Torrijos was no Marxist but he was certainly his own man. He reestablished diplomatic relations with Cuba for the first time since 1959, and struck up cordial relations with dictator Fidel Castro. He also expressed sympathy for the ongoing Nicaraguan revolution and allowed rebels to use Panama as a transit point for weapons shipments. But in 1979 he honored an American request to allow the deposed shah of Iran to seek refuge in the country. By 1980 the Panamanian economy was slipping under the weight of Torrijos's excessive borrowing, and he resigned as head of the government in favor of a civilian puppet. However, as chief of the National Guard, he remained the real power behind the throne—and a popular national leader. Torrijos died suddenly in a helicopter crash on August 1, 1981, and he was replaced by his henchman, MANUEL NORIEGA. His death has never been explained and has been variously ascribed to both the American CIA and the ambitious Noriega himself.

Further Reading

Conniff, Michael L. *Panama and the United States: The Forced Alliance.* Athens: University of Georgia Press, 2001.

Guevara Mann, Carlos. *Panamanian Militarism: A Historical Interpretation.* Athens: Ohio University Center for International Studies, 1996.

Harding, Robert C. *Military Foundations of Panamanian Politics.* New Brunswick, N.J.: Transaction Publishers, 2001.

Koster, R. M., and Guillermo Sanchez Borbon. *In the Time of Tyrants: Panama, 1968–1989.* New York: W. W. Norton, 1990.

Major, John. *Prize Possession: The United States Government and the Panama Canal, 1903–1979.* Cambridge, England: Cambridge University Press, 2002.

Priestly, George. *Military Government and Popular Participation in Panama: The Torrijos Regime, 1968–75.* Boulder, Colo.: Westview Press, 1986.

Touré, Ahmed Sékou (1922–1984) *president of Guinea*

Ahmed Sékou Touré was born in Faranah, French Guinea, on January 9, 1922, a Muslim of mixed Soussou and Malinke parentage. After receiving a Koranic education, he was admitted to the prestigious Georges Poiret technical school in Conakry but was expelled for organizing students. He subsequently finished his education through correspondence courses and also became enamored of the teachings of Karl Marx. By 1940 Touré was working within the colonial post and telecommunications department and five years later became head of the local union. In 1946 he was a founding member of the Rassemblement Democratique Africain (RDA), an intercolonial political party demanding independence from France. Touré, a noted activist and an accomplished speaker, was French Guinea's best-known politician by 1952 and he was appointed secretary of the Parti Démocratique de Guinée (PDG), Democratic Party of Guinea, a regional wing of the RDA. In this capacity he led a successful two-month strike in 1953 and was elected to the Territorial Assembly. Touré, whose politics were increasingly radicalized, was disenchanted by the conciliatory policies of the RDA and demanded direct confrontation with colonial authorities. His stance enabled him to be twice elected to the French National Assembly, but he was as often denied a seat. Such controversy only heightened his visibility and popularity and in 1956, after France allowed its colonies greater internal autonomy, he was elected vice president. Two years later French president CHARLES DE GAULLE offered all colonies independence or membership in an "international community." Touré, stridently anticolonial in outlook, opposed any further association with France, insisting, "We prefer poverty in freedom to opulence in slavery." Accordingly, when given the choice in a public plebiscite, the voters of Guinea decisively voted for independence, becoming the first French African colony to do so. At that point an angry de Gaulle withdrew all technical and financial support from France's former colony—further impoverishing it. Nonetheless, Touré basked in his role as a leading national figure, and he became the first president of Guinea in October 1958.

Bereft of outside support, Touré turned to neighboring KWAME NKRUMAH of Ghana for a loan to stabilize the sinking Guinean economy. Thereafter the two Pan-Africanist leaders coordinated their foreign policies closely to develop a multinational union between Guinea, Ghana, and Mali. The effort collapsed over irreconcilable differences by 1961, but Touré continued on his radical course. He initially sought a close relationship with the Soviet Union but grew dissatisfied with their political interference and expelled their ambassador in 1962. Thereafter he placed greater emphasis on friendly relations with the West for money and technical assistance, all the while imposing a radical socialist regimen upon the nation. He cemented his credentials as a radical in 1966 by allowing the deposed Nkrumah to reside in Guinea and appointing him co-president.

Touré ruled Guinea dictatorially for 26 years. He enjoyed considerable prestige throughout Africa as a nationalist but at home he functioned as a tyrannical despot. The PDG became the nation's sole legal organization, dissenters were arrested or murdered, and extreme limits on press freedom and civil rights enacted. At length over 1 million Guineans fled to neighboring countries rather than submit to Touré's increasingly paranoid regime. Political opponents were routinely arrested, tried, and publicly executed. In 1971, suspecting a coup against him, Touré ordered a widespread crackdown against all enemies of the state—real or imagined—while he continued running for the presidency unopposed. But as Guinea's socialist command economy became hopelessly mired, he was forced to seek closer relations with his old adversary France by 1978. The West provided aid but also applied political pressure to promote liberalization efforts, which Touré steadfastly resisted. He finally died in Cleveland, Ohio, on March 26, 1984, while receiving medical treatment in the United States, and the military overthrew his government a few days later. While acknowledged as a leading architect of independence in French West Africa, Touré's legacy was built on and sustained by oppression and murder.

Further Reading

Camara, Mohammed S. "From Military Politicization to Militarization of Power in Guinea-Conakry." *Journal of Politics and Sociology* 28 (winter 2000): 311–326.

Coats, Geoffrey C. "French West Africa: The Political Philosophy of Ahmed Sékou Touré and Leopold Sedar Senghor." Unpublished master's thesis, James Madison University, 1994.

Cort, Leon L. "The Quest for Socio-economic and Political Change in Guinea: Aspects of the Political Ideology of Ahmed Sékou Touré." Unpublished Ph.D. diss., Boston University, 1982.

Diallo, Geraldyne P. "The Philosophy of Ahmed Sékou Touré and Its Impact on the Development of the Republic of Guinea, 1958–1971." Unpublished Ph.D. diss., 1990.

Ingham, K. *Guinea United against the World: Politics in Modern Africa.* London: Routledge, 1990.

Touré, Ahmed Sékou. *Africa on the Move.* London: Panaf Books, 1979.

Trudeau, Pierre (1919–2000) *prime minister of Canada*

Pierre Elliott Trudeau was born in Montreal, Quebec, on October 18, 1919, into an affluent business family. He was well educated at the University of Montreal, Harvard University, and the London School of Economics before embarking on a round-the-world tour in 1948. The inequities and hardships he encountered on this trip indelibly altered Trudeau's world view, and thereafter he became a staunch member of the Liberal Party. Back home he served as a lawyer specializing in labor issues and also edited a progressive monthly magazine. But unlike many contemporaries in his native Quebec, Trudeau treated the issue of French Canadian nationalism with disdain and considered it harmful to Canada. He boldly attacked its proponents for promoting cultural intolerance and contributing to the province's political backwardness. By 1960 Trudeau was teaching law at the University of Montreal where he argued that Quebec's interests were better served by remaining a part of Canada than seceding from it. His outspokenness brought him to the attention of Prime Minister LESTER B. PEARSON, who encouraged him to run for office in 1965. He succeeded and was next appointed Pearson's parliamentary secretary. Trudeau, a natural-born politician with a flair for media, excelled as a political lightning rod and he subsequently received the high-visibility portfolio of minister of justice. In this capacity he embarked on a crusade to liberalize Canadian society and relaxed long-standing strictures against homosexuality, abortion, and divorce. These were all controversial issues and never universally applauded, but also indicative of his daring brand of politics. In 1968 Pearson decided to resign from office and Trudeau, among others, stepped forward to succeed him. His flashy flamboyance certainly separated him from the traditional stodgy image of Canadian heads of state and he easily won leadership of the Liberal Party and the prime minister's office. In fact, the country and media were so enthralled by his refreshing panache that the expression Trudeaumania was coined. His popularity was confirmed when the Liberals swept national elections later that year and a new era in Canadian politics emerged.

For most of his term in office, Trudeau was overtly concerned by events in his home province of Quebec. It had long been his contention that, as a federal arrangement, Canada could easily accommodate French and English language and cultures on an equal footing. To placate the rising sense of French cultural nationalism—with its attendant calls for secessionism—Trudeau introduced official bilingualism throughout the civil service in 1969. For the first time in three centuries, French was finally given parity with English in matters of governance. However, this concession did little to dampen the growth of secessionist sentiment. In 1970 militants from the Front de Liberation du Quebec kidnapped the British high commissioner to Canada and murdered a Quebec cabinet minister. Trudeau countered with the imposition of the War Measures Act, which suspended civil rights in the province and led to hundreds of arrests. Through such heavy-handed tactics the radical secessionists were effectively squelched. Most Canadians applauded his handling of the crisis, but Trudeau was less successful at improving the national economy. After 1972 the Liberals could retain power only by forming a coalition with the small Free Democratic Party.

Over the next seven years Trudeau's administration remained transfixed by events in Quebec and a sagging economy. Moreover, the western provinces, angered by what they considered Trudeau's kowtowing toward Quebec, increasingly swerved toward the Conservatives. Events crested in 1979 when the Liberals were narrowly defeated and Trudeau was briefly replaced by JOE CLARK.

But within months the Liberals eked out a victory and Trudeau returned to power for another four years. His second term in office was consumed by a drive to update the Canadian constitution with a written bill of rights (the Charter of Rights and Freedoms) and to formally sever its ties to the British Parliament. This was accomplished in 1982 amid great pomp and ceremony, with Queen Elizabeth II in attendance. When the specter of French secessionism again arose in 1980, he led an intense effort to defeat a public referendum that would have granted Quebec sovereignty. He also displayed his independence from the United States—always a touchy issue in Canada—by recognizing Communist China in 1970, visiting Fidel Castro's Cuba, and touring the Soviet Bloc promoting nuclear disarmament. But for all his energy and drive, Trudeau was singularly unable to improve Canada's economic lot, which was burdened by rising deficits and unemployment. He was further beset by his controversial marriage to jet-setter Margaret Sinclair, with whom he endured a high-profile divorce. Trudeau, worn out and disappointed, announced his resignation in February 1984, and he was replaced by JOHN TURNER. His 16 years in office establish him as the second-longest-serving Canadian prime minister after WILLIAM LYON MACKENZIE KING and among the most influential. Trudeau died in Montreal on September 28, 2000, a Canadian statesman of the first order and a French Canadian original.

Further Reading

Axworthy, Tom. *Towards a Just Society: The Trudeau Years.* Toronto: Penguin Books, 2000.

Bowering, George. *Egotists and Autocrats: The Prime Ministers of Canada.* Toronto: Penguin, 2000.

Carment, David, John F. Stack, and Frank P. Harvey. *The International Politics of Quebec Secession: State Making and State Breaking in North America.* Westport, Conn.: Praeger, 2001.

Chennells, David. *The Politics of Nationalism in Canada: Cultural Conflict since 1760.* Toronto: University of Toronto Press, 2001.

Coleman, Ron. *Just Watch Me! Trudeau's Tragic Legacy.* Victoria, B.C.: Trafford, 2003.

Kinsman, Jeremy. "Who Is My Neighbor? Trudeau and Foreign Policy." *International Journal* 51 (winter 2001–2002): 57–77.

Sanger, Clyde. "Trudeau and the Commonwealth." *Round Table* no. 358 (January 2001): 95–201.

Trudeau, Pierre E. *Memoirs*. Toronto: McClelland and Stewart, 1993.

Trujillo, Rafael (1891–1961) *president of the Dominican Republic*

Rafael Leónidas Trujillo Molina was born in San Cristóbal, the Dominican Republic, on October 24, 1891, the son of a small businessman. As part of the lower-middle class his economic prospects were limited on an island dominated by the landed elite, and for many years he held down numerous odd jobs. However, in 1915 the Dominican Republic was occupied by U.S. Marines in an attempt to restore order. Part of this process entailed establishment of the Dominican National Guard in 1918, which for Trujillo became a vehicle of social and economic mobility. He proved himself an excellent and attentive soldier and, once the marines were withdrawn from the island in 1924, he rose steadily through the ranks. Within four years Trujillo had become head of the National Guard and he began undermining civilian authority with staged civil disturbances. Having intimidated the political opposition, Trujillo ran for the presidency in May 1930 representing the Confederation of Parties. He went on to win a fraudulent election and subsequently chased a supreme court justice out of the country for challenging the results. Trujillo was to remain in power over the next 31 years. In 1938 he "stepped down" from office and was replaced by a puppet president while still controlling events from behind the scenes. As an American sycophant, he was warmly received by President FRANKLIN D. ROOSEVELT in 1939, and the following year they concluded the Trujillo-Hull Treaty that ended custom duties of Dominican imports. Trujillo was the first Latin American leader to declare war on the Axis during World War II and his administration was bolstered by a massive influx of American military and financial assistance. He resumed office in 1942 and during the cold war years he further cemented relations to Washington, D.C., by expressing virulent anticommunism and providing intelligence from throughout the Caribbean.

In time Trujillo erected one of the most thorough and efficient dictatorships in Latin American history. He ruled brutally through violence and intimidation, unhesitatingly arresting, torturing, or executing all perceived enemies. Furthermore, all political parties, freedom of the press, and union activities were expressly forbidden. Trujillo's most visible symbol of authority, the National Guard, was his bodyguard, utterly ruthless and the instrument of his political will. In October 1937, in an attempt to "whiten" the Dominican half of the island of Hispaniola, Trujillo ordered the murder of nearly 20,000 Haitian squatters. It was one of the biggest massacres in the Western Hemisphere but went largely unnoticed in the United States because of Trujillo's determination to maintain excellent economic relations, especially respecting the sale of sugar. To that end he also controlled virtually every aspect of the national economy, with the state treasury receiving a flat 10 percent donation from all workers. The entire island thus toiled to enrich Trujillo and the members of his immediate family. It is estimated that he amassed a fortune in excess of $800 million at a time when most of his fellow citizens were malnourished and impoverished.

In 1930 the Dominican Republic was a backward island community overwhelmingly dependent on the sugar trade. Trujillo may have been a tyrant, but he also served as a badly needed agent for modernization. Under his aegis roads were built, harbors enlarged, and factories constructed. Through his efforts the Dominican Republic enjoyed a thriving economy, even if most of the fruits were for Trujillo alone. However, by the 1950s his control of the economy had stymied the rising expectations of the flourishing middle class and civil unrest mounted. In 1959 Cuban dictator Fidel Castro and Venezuelan president RÓMULO BETANCOURT tried and failed to overthrow Trujillo by arming numerous refugees. Trujillo countered with an assassination attempt that nearly killed Betancourt and led to an embargo by the Organization of American States (OAS). By this time the Americans had concluded that they could no longer afford the embarrassment of close relations with the aging despot. On May 31, 1961, four assassins, armed and trained by the Central Intelligence Agency, killed Trujillo in his car. Members of his family attempted to maintain themselves in power but they were ousted by the end of the year. Ironically, among the older generation of Dominicans, Trujillo is remembered not such much for his oppression as for the discipline and prosperity he brought to that troubled island.

Further Reading

Calzler, B. J. *The Impact of Intervention: The Dominican Republic during the U.S. Occupation of 1916–1924*. Chicago: University of Illinois Press, 1984.

Chester, Eric T. *Rag-tags, Scum, Riff-raff, and Commies: The U.S. Intervention in the Dominican Republic, 1965–1966.* New York: Monthly Review, 2001.

Diederich, Bernard. *Trujillo: The Death of the Dictator.* Princeton, N.J.: Markus Wiener, 2000.

Hall, Michael R. *Sugar and Power in the Dominican Republic: Eisenhower, Kennedy, and the Trujillos.* Westport, Conn.: Greenwood Press, 2000.

Roorda, Eric P. *The Dictator Next Door: The Good Neighbor Policy and the Trujillo Regime in the Dominican Republic, 1930–1945.* Durham, N.C.: Duke University Press, 1998.

Turits, Richard L. *Foundations of Despotism: Peasants, the Trujillo Regime, and Modernity in Dominican History.* Stanford, Calif.: Stanford University Press, 2003.

Truman, Harry S. (1884–1972) *president of the United States*

Harry S. Truman was born in Lamar, Missouri, on May 8, 1884, the son of a farmer. After completing high school—his only education—he worked on the family farm for several years before serving in the army during World War I. He returned home to work in a haberdashery store and when it failed he turned to politics as a Democrat. As part of the political machine operated by Thomas J. Pendergast, Truman was successively elected county judge and presiding judge in Jackson County, Missouri. When the Great Depression swept the country in 1929, he distinguished himself by devising civic work projects, and in 1934 Truman was elected to the U.S. Senate. In this capacity he strongly supported the New Deal legislation of President FRANKLIN D. ROOSEVELT, although the latter, while cordial, considered him simply a machine politician. But Truman was reelected in 1940 on the basis of his no-nonsense performance and during World War II he chaired the influential Senate committee investigating government expenditures and contracts. His thorough inquiries exposed shocking degrees of waste, inefficiency, and corruption, and the changes he instituted saved the taxpayers millions of dollars. Truman was by now a respectable figure within the Democratic Party—if little known nationally—and in 1944 Roosevelt tapped him to serve as his vice presidential candidate. Truman complied more out of a sense of duty than desire, yet he campaigned vigorously for the ticket and won. The two leaders virtually never communicated during his vice presidency—Roosevelt's behavior toward him remained cool but correct. But after Roosevelt's death on April 12, 1945, Truman constitutionally succeeded him and assumed power at a critical juncture in American history. He was still relatively unknown to the public and, compared to his aristocratic predecessor, exuded a decidedly simplistic and homespun air.

World War II had nearly ended in Europe but fighting in the Pacific raged with great fury. It fell upon Truman to execute a momentous decision in human history by authorizing the use of atomic bombs against the Japanese cities of Hiroshima and Nagasaki in August 1945, rather than attempt a costly invasion of the islands. The bombs staggered the Japanese government, and Emperor HIROHITO ordered his nation to lay down its arms, thereby sparing millions of lives on both sides. The episode is indicative of Truman's penchant for decisive action and his unflinching determination to accept responsibility, no matter how grave, for his actions.

The postwar era posed difficulties of a different nature when, faced with inflation and rapid demobilization of the military, Truman attempted to continue the New Deal policies of his predecessor. He dealt with an uncooperative Republican Congress that stymied legislation on full employment, but he managed to secure laws promoting housing and unemployment benefits. In 1948 Truman also scored a major triumph for civil rights by ordering the armed forced desegregated. Shortly thereafter, foreign affairs intruded on his domestic agenda and dominated his activities for the rest of his presidency. Aggressive actions by Soviet dictator JOSEPH STALIN in Eastern Europe signaled the start of the cold war, and in 1947, the president promulgated his famous Truman Doctrine. Henceforth the United States would provide millions of dollars in aid to Greece and Turkey to prevent a communist takeover, which would be followed by billions of dollars in aid for Europe through the Marshall Plan. Thus was born the global strategy of "containment." Truman was also the driving force behind creation of the North Atlantic Treaty Organization (NATO) in 1949, which was created as a bulwark against communist aggression. In 1948, when Stalin ordered a land blockade of Berlin to starve the Allies out, Truman ordered a massive airlift that kept the populace fed through the winter and forced the Russians to relent. For all his decisiveness, Truman faced a close election in 1948 against Republican candidate Thomas

Harry S. Truman *(Library of Congress)*

Korean War (1950–53). Truman reacted with typical decisiveness and dispatched American forces to the peninsula while courting United Nations assistance. As the war ground on, he dismissed popular war hero General Douglas MacArthur for insubordination when—in defiance of orders—he tried extending the war into Manchuria. The result was a bloody three-year stalemate that saw Truman's popularity plummet. Rather than run for a third term, he announced his resignation in 1952 and the Republicans returned to power under the aegis of DWIGHT D. EISENHOWER. Truman left the White House an embittered man, convinced that he was a failure.

Out of office, the plain-talking Truman lived on his farm in Independence, Missouri, where he wrote his typically candid memoirs. He occasionally campaigned for Democratic candidates around the country before dying at home on December 26, 1972. Truman has since passed into history as one of America's most effective and popular executives. Thanks to his determined leadership the United States remained engaged as a world player after 1945 and did not sink back into its traditional isolationism. Whatever he lacked in education or personal finesse was amply compensated by his bluntness, unimpeachable honesty, and an attitude of governance encapsulated in his personal dictum that "The buck stops here."

E. Dewey. The night of the election several newspapers predicted the outcome with headlines declaring "Dewey defeats Truman" only to discover the next morning that Truman won by a close margin of 2 million votes. This come-from-behind victory astonished the pundits and became the stuff of political legend.

Truman's second administration continued to be battered by foreign affairs and domestic fears of communist subversion, and in 1947 he enacted a loyalty oath for prospective civil servants but the Democrats fell under increasing attack by Republican senator Joseph McCarthy for being "soft" on communism. When the Chinese regime of CHIANG KAI-SHEK was driven from the mainland to Taiwan by MAO ZEDONG's communists, Truman was accused of having "lost" China for lack of proper support. But the biggest jolt occurred in June 1950 when the army of North Korean dictator Kim Il Sung suddenly attacked the South Korean regime of SYNGMAN RHEE, precipitating the

Further Reading

Axelrod, Alan. *When the Buck Stops with You: Harry S. Truman on Leadership.* New York: Portfolio, 2004.

Beschloss, Michael R. *The Conquerors: Roosevelt, Truman, and the Destruction of Hitler's Germany, 1941–1945.* Waterville, Me.: Thorndike Press, 2002.

Byrnes, Mark S. *The Truman Years, 1945–1953.* New York: Longman, 2000.

Hess, Gary R. *Presidential Decisions for War: Korea, Vietnam, and the Persian Gulf.* Baltimore: Johns Hopkins University, 2001.

Karabell, Zachary. *The Last Campaign: How Harry Truman Won the 1948 Election.* New York: Knopf, 2000.

Parry-Giles, Shawn J. *The Rhetorical Presidency, Propaganda, and the Cold War, 1945–1955.* Westport, Conn.: Praeger, 2002.

Pierce, Ann R. *Woodrow Wilson and Harry Truman: Mission and Power in American Foreign Policy.* Westport, Conn.: Praeger, 2003.

Truman, Harry S. *The Autobiography of Harry S. Truman.* Columbia: University of Missouri Press, 2002.

———. *Memoirs of Harry S. Truman,* 2 vols. New York: Da Capo Press, 1986–87.

Tshombe, Moïse (1919–1969) *prime minister of the Democratic Republic of the Congo*

Moïse Kapenda Tshombe was born in Katanga Province, Belgian Congo, on November 10, 1919, the son of an affluent businessman. He was also part of the large and influential Lunda tribe, the majority within the mineral-rich Katanga region. Tshombe was educated at local missionary schools and followed his father into business, where he displayed no aptitude. After nearly driving the family into bankruptcy, Tshombe next pursued politics as an *evolue,* one of Congo's westernized elites. In 1956 he founded the Confederation of Tribal Associations, or Conaket, to advance Lunda interests. For Tshombe, this meant striking up cordial relations with Belgian economic and mining interests in Katanga just as the region girded itself for independence. In 1960 Tshombe attended round table discussions in Brussels to determine the future of Congo. He specifically favored a federal arrangement whereby the regions—especially Katanga—would enjoy broad swathes of autonomy. This view contrasted sharply with that of the radical PATRICE LUMUMBA, who argued for a strict unitary state under a highly centralized government. In the end Lumumba's argument won out. In May 1960 elections granted Conaket only eight seats out of 137 in the new national legislature, which further underscored Tshombe's minority status. When the Democratic Republic of the Congo was declared on June 30, 1960, Lumumba was installed as prime minister while JOSEPH KASAVUBU served as president.

Unfortunately for all involved, independence only accelerated the trend toward sectionalism and tribal violence. Within 10 days the army mutinied against the government and Tshombe, sensing an opportunity, declared Katanga's independence from the Congo. On August 8, 1960, the provincial legislature voted him president and he backed up his claim with white mercenaries and financial support from business contacts in Belgium. Lumumba decried the move as treason, but he had his hands full dealing with other machinations instigated by Kasavubu. When Lumumba was finally deposed that September he was arrested, flown to Katanga, and murdered by troops loyal to Tshombe. Events were further complicated when United Nations general secretary DAG HAMMARSKJÖLD flew out to help settle the dispute and died in a mysterious plane crash. Kasavubu subsequently tried negotiating a settlement to the Katanga secession, but Tshombe refused all overtures until he was suddenly arrested and forced to sign a written agreement. He immediately recanted the deal after his release; United Nations forces were introduced to end the rebellion by the summer of 1961. Two years later, with his forces defeated and his regime crumbling, Tshombe fled the province for exile in Spain.

Tshombe's exile proved relatively short-lived for in 1964 Kasavubu suddenly summoned him back and appointed him prime minister. In this capacity he was made responsible for putting down a tribal rebellion in the eastern Congo. Again, Tshombe relied heavily on his Western contacts, assembled a force of European mercenaries, and crushed the rebellion by force. His harshness in dealing with the rebels and his willingness to hire foreigners only contributed to his national unpopularity. Worse, after a new constitution had been adopted that year which granted the prime minister expanded powers, Tshombe's party scored exceptionally well and he was apparently preparing to depose Kasavubu. The president preempted him with a dismissal on October 13, 1965, and a military impasse ensued for several weeks. The stalemate finally ended on November 24, 1964, when General Joseph Mobutu overturned both Tshombe and Kasavubu. Tshombe fled once again to the safety of Spain and was condemned to death in absentia.

Tshombe remained abroad for several years and was apparently planning a return to power. However, on June 30, 1967, the passenger liner he flew in was hijacked over the Mediterranean and he was conveyed to Algeria and arrested. The government of HOUARI BOUMÉDIENNE refused all demands for extradition and Tshombe remained under house arrest until his death there on June 29, 1969. His tenure as a Congolese national figure remains controversial and contentious, and partially laid the groundwork for Mobutu's corrupt and brutal dictatorship. Tshombe is also held largely responsible for ordering Lumumba's death and for the instability it engendered.

Further Reading

Bouscaren, Anthony T. *Tshombe.* New York: Twin Circle Pub. Co., 1967.

Colvin, Ian G. *The Rise and Fall of Moïse Tshombe: A Biography.* London: Frewin, 1968.

Linavo, J. V. "The Causes of the Shaba I and Shaba II Rebellions in Zaire during the Second Republic." Unpublished Ph.D. diss., University of Denver, 1984.

Lumumba-Kasongo, Tukumbi. "Katanga Secession: Creation of the West or Manifestation of the Congolese Internal Power Struggle? *Journal of African Studies* 15, nos. 3–4 (1988): 101–109.

Nzongaola-Ntalaja, Georges. *Resistance and Repression in the Congo: Strengths and Weaknesses of the Democracy Movement, 1956–2000.* New York: Zed Books, 2001.

Tshombe, Moïse. *My Fifteen Months in Government.* Plano, Tex.: University of Plano, 1967.

Tsiranana, Philibert (1912–1978) *president of Madagascar*

Philibert Tsiranana was born in Majunga, Madagascar, on October 18, 1912, into a Tsimihety peasant family. His homeland was then a French colony and beset by traditional tensions between his tribe, which inhabited the coastline, and the Merinas, who dominated the island's interior. Poverty forced him to tend his father's flock and he did not attend school until the age of 12. Eventually Tsiranana proved himself adept academically and he ultimately passed through the University of Montpelier, France, for a teaching credential. Meanwhile, resentment against colonialism culminated in a bloody rebellion in 1947 after which the French began modifying their rule. Tsiranana returned home in 1950 to work as a teacher and two years later commenced his political career by winning a seat in the territorial legislature. Madagascar remained chafing under the continuance of French control, but Tsiranana, like most coastal dwellers, did not want to see a resurgence of Merina rule. Therefore he argued for a gradual relaxation of colonial rule to forestall either the rise of communism or Merina domination. In 1956 France granted its colonies direct representation in its National Assembly and Tsiranana was elected. While attending he also joined the French Socialist Party. The following year he was appointed head of the Council of Government back in Madagascar as the French allowed a proliferation of political parties to form. Tsiranana then founded the Parti Social Democratique du Madagascar (PSD),

Social Democratic Party, which, despite socialist overtones, sought to maintain a French presence on the island. Continuing political maneuvers on his part allowed Madagascar to seek independence while remaining part of the French international community. In June 1960 the Malagasy Republic was proclaimed, and Tsiranana was appointed its first president.

In power Tsiranana espoused his own peculiar brand of socialism that was hostile to communism, opposed the nationalizing of industry, and accepted the status quo in terms of landowning. He basically limited government intervention to supervising private investments and promoting mixed public/private companies. The nation was committed to free-market economics and welcomed foreign investment. Moreover, Tsiranana was extremely pro-Western in outlook for a former colonial head of state and rejected all overtures of friendship from the Soviet Union and Eastern Bloc. In fact, Tsiranana went on record as stridently opposing Communist China's admission to the United Nations in 1966. He also pursued a pragmatic, independent foreign policy that included diplomatic and trade relations with the apartheid regime in South Africa. This caused resentment among Pan-Africanist leaders, but did not prevent Tsiranana from serving as spokesman for the 12-nation association of former francophone colonies.

As long as the economy flourished, Tsiranana enjoyed political popularity and he was easily reelected in 1965. However, the onset of inflation and a global recession soured his political prospects and he called for snap elections in January 1972 to bolster his standing. Unfortunately, the process proved a sham whereby he received 99.9 percent of votes cast. This ploy quickly undermined his legitimacy and occasioned mass demonstrations by students and workers angered by continuing reliance upon France and close relations with South Africa. The Merinas of the interior were also agitating for a greater role in governance, while the declining economy sparked a round of violent labor unrest. Within months Tsiranana's position had become untenable and he resigned from office on October 11, 1972. Power was assumed by General Gabriel Ramanantsoa for the time being. Tsiranana remained active in party politics, with declining influence, until his death in Tananarive on April 16, 1978. His 12 years of power were instrumental in helping Madagascar make the transition to independence and democratic practices, but failed to address deep-seated fissures between coastal dwellers and highland inhabitants. The problems remain unresolved to the present time.

Further Reading

Allen, Philip M. *Madagascar: Conflicts of Authority in the Great Island.* Boulder, Colo.: Westview Press, 1995.

Brown, Mervyn. *A History of Madagascar.* Princeton, N.J.: Markus Wiener Publishers, 2001.

Cole, Jennifer. *Forget Colonialism?: Sacrifice and the Art of Memory in Madagascar.* Berkeley: University of California Press, 2001.

Kottak, Conrad P., ed. *Madagascar: Society and History.* Durham, N.C.: Carolina Academic Press, 1986.

Middleton, Karen, ed. *Ancestors, Power, and History in Madagascar.* Boston: Brill, 1999.

Sharp, Leslie A. *The Sacrificed Generation: Youth, History, and the Colonized Mind in Madagascar.* Berkeley: University of California Press, 2002.

Tubman, William (1895–1971) *president of Liberia*

William Vacanarat Shadrack Tubman was born in Cape Palmas, Liberia, on November 29, 1895, the son of a Methodist preacher. Liberia, Africa's first republic, had been established in 1847 as a haven for freed American slaves and largely administered by their descendants. Tubman, whose ancestors emigrated from Georgia, was thus part of the national elite. He attended local missionary schools and worked as a teacher for many years before studying law and being called to the bar in 1917. Tubman gained renown as a "poor man's lawyer" for outstanding help toward the poor, and in 1923 he gained election to the senate as a True Whig representative. This was the only legal party in Liberia at the time and likewise dominated by Americo-Liberians. Tubman served intermittently over the next decade and established himself as a leading national figure. In 1937 his career took an unexpected turn when he became an associate justice on the Supreme Court of Liberia, remaining until 1943. That year Tubman was tapped as the True Whig presidential candidate to replace President Edwin Barclay. In this tightly controlled one-party state, nomination alone was sufficient to ensure victory, and Tubman was sworn into office on January 3, 1944.

As a candidate Tubman pledged himself to enlarging the Liberian electorate by extending suffrage to include not only women, but also inhabitants of the interior traditionally excluded from power. He also sought to give tribesmen legal parity with the elites and bring them into the government. This reform was accomplished by a constitutional amendment, and Tubman further distinguished himself by erecting numerous schools, hospitals, and roads throughout the hinterland. Similar efforts were also expended upon communications, infrastructure, and education. Economically, Tubman sought to break the national dependency upon rubber exports and invited foreign investors to develop Liberia's natural resources, particularly the iron ore industry. Within a decade Liberia's gross national product thus soared from $1 million annually to over $30 million. More than any other individual in Liberia's history, Tubman did the most to finally bridge the deep-seated animosity between indigenous peoples and the traditional Americo-Liberian elites. His efforts at promoting harmony and economic growth were completely successful and resulted in reelection in 1950. However, to accomplish this, Tubman urged revising the constitution to allow him to serve consecutive terms. He was ultimately reelected six times.

Tubman matched his domestic endeavors with success in international affairs. In 1944 he visited Washington, D.C., to confer with American president FRANKLIN D. ROOSEVELT, becoming the first African head of state to ever sleep over in the White House. That year he also declared war on Germany and Japan, receiving an influx of military and financial aid in return. But for all his accommodation toward the West, Tubman was a Pan-Africanist dedicated to the end of white rule in Africa. He criticized the apartheid regime of South Africa, and in 1958 he joined KWAME NKRUMAH of Ghana and AHMED SÉKOU TOURÉ of Guinea in organizing the Accra Conference of Independent African States. However, Tubman rejected the notion of political integration in favor of promoting common interests and economic cooperation. In 1963 he was a cofounder of the new Organization of African Unity (OAU).

Tubman remained in office for 31 years, making him one of Africa's most successful statesmen. He was consistently reelected by wide margins even though various parties and candidates were tolerated. But his governance through patronage and discouragement of a genuine opposition alienated radical elements and resulted in several assassination attempts. By the time he died in London on July 23, 1971, Tubman enjoyed the enviable reputation as one of the continent's most visible and respected elder statesmen. At home he is best remembered for having modernized Liberia and bringing it into the 20th century. His administration remains the longest-serving in the history of that nation.

Further Reading

Boley, G. Saigbe. *Liberia: The Rise and Fall of the First Republic.* New York: St. Martin's Press, 1984.

Dunn, D. Elwood. *The Foreign Policy of Liberia during the Tubman Era, 1944–1971.* London: Hutchinson Benham, 1979.

Fahnbulleh, Henry B. *The Diplomacy of Prejudice: Liberia in International Politics, 1945–1970.* New York: Vantage Press, 1985.

Greenwood, Ralph. "The Presidency of William V. S. Tubman of Liberia, 1944–1971." Unpublished Ph.D. diss., Northern Arizona University, 1993.

Liebenow, J. Gus. *Liberia: The Quest for Democracy.* Bloomington: Indiana University Press, 1987.

Tubman, William V. S. *The Official Papers of William V. S. Tubman, President of Liberia.* London: Longmans, 1968.

Turner, John (1929–   ) *prime minister of Canada*
John Napier Turner was born in Richmond, England, on June 7, 1929, to an English father and a Canadian mother. His father died when he was three and his mother relocated and raised him in Rossland, British Columbia. Turner studied at the University of British Columbia and won a prestigious Rhodes Scholarship to Oxford University in 1949. By 1953 he had obtained his doctorate in law from the University of Paris and he settled in Montreal to establish a practice specializing in corporate law. In 1962 Turner commenced his political career by winning a seat in the House of Commons as a Liberal. Here he joined a vocal group of young politicians advocating party reform, who were eventually labeled the "Young Turks." Prime Minister LESTER B. PEARSON was sufficiently impressed by Turner's youth and drive to appoint him minister without portfolio in 1965, and two years later he served as minister of consumer and corporate affairs. By 1968 Turner felt emboldened to become the Liberal Party leader but he lost to an equally flashy newcomer, PIERRE ELLIOTT TRUDEAU. Trudeau then named him minister of justice, where he served four years and implemented numerous reforms. In 1972 Turner was chosen to serve as minister

of finance where he had to concoct and pass coalition budgets in concert with the New Democratic Party. The process generally discouraged him, so in 1975 he resigned from office and resumed his legal practice. However, he was careful to remain in touch with party leaders and keep abreast of political developments. Turner waited four years for Trudeau to finally retire in 1984 before returning to the fold and running for party head. In June 1985 Turner defeated Jean Chretien on the second ballot, becoming both party head and Canada's newest prime minister.

Turner's tenure in office lasted only 80 days. He had inherited from Trudeau a party that was totally dispirited and disorganized after 21 years in power. Furthermore, he, like the Liberal leadership in general, failed to acknowledge that the public was ready for a change in national direction. Nonetheless, he called for early elections, betting that a fresh new face would invigorate the Liberals' fortunes. Turner was sadly mistaken, for he and his party were crushed by the Progressive Conservatives under Brian Mulroney. Turner was lucky enough to hold onto his seat while Liberal representation was reduced to 40 members. He resigned on September 17, 1984, after one of the shortest and most humiliating tenures in Canadian history.

Over the next six years Turner functioned as head of the opposition in Parliament. Here he commenced the long and difficult process of rebuilding his party and was generally helped by a spate of scandals that embarrassed the Conservatives. In 1988 Mulroney was poised to offer the North American Free Trade Act (NAFTA) to the public as a referendum, an act that would eliminate trade barriers between Canada, the United States, and Mexico, thereby increasing competition and lowering prices. Turner, however, railed against the measure, viewing it as a threat to national sovereignty. He ran again for prime minister in 1988 on the basis of opposition to NAFTA and nearly won, but in the end the Conservatives prevailed and the agreement was signed. Turner remained on as party head until 1990—losing two more elections in the process—before finally resigning as party head. He has since abandoned politics and resumed his legal activities as a private lawyer.

Further Reading

Cahill, Jack. *John Turner: The Long Run.* Toronto: McClelland and Stewart, 1984.

Clarke, Harold D., Allan Kornberg, and Peter Wearing. *A Polity on the Edge: Canada and the Politics of Fragmentation.* Orchard Park, N.Y.: Broadview Press, 2000.

Huyer, Sophia. "What Constitutes a Social Movement? The Action Canada Network and Free Trade Opposition in Canada, 1983–1993." Unpublished Ph.D. diss., York University, 2000.

Lynch, Charles. *Race for the Rose: Election 1984.* New York: Methuen, 1984.

McCall, Christina. *Grits: An Intimate Portrait of the Liberal Party.* Toronto: Macmillan of Canada, 1982.

Simpson, Jeffrey. *The Friendly Dictatorship.* Toronto: McClelland and Stewart, 2001.

Turner, John N. *The Politics of Purpose.* Toronto: McClelland, 1968.

Weston, Greg. *Reign of Error: The Inside Story of John Turner's Troubled Leadership.* Toronto: McGraw-Hill Ryerson, 1988.

U

Ubico, Jorge (1878–1946) *president of Guatemala*

Jorge Ubico y Castañeda was born in Guatemala City, Guatemala, on November 10, 1878, the son of a prominent politician. He was partially educated in the United States before coming home to attend the Escuela Politecnica and being commissioned a lieutenant in the army. Ubico enjoyed a distinguished military career and reached the rank of colonel by the time he was 28 years old. He fought well in the 1906 border war with El Salvador and directed the National Sanitation Commission in its drive to eradicate yellow fever. In 1921 President José María Orellana appointed the young, hard-charging officer as his minister of war, and the following year Ubico was promoted to full general. However, by 1930 Guatemala was experiencing political chaos brought on by the Great Depression and, by dint of political maneuvering, he emerged as the sole candidate for presidential elections that year. Ubico enjoyed a reputation for decisive leadership and honesty, so much was expected from his administration.

Ubico's first priority was stabilizing the national economy, which had been nearly gutted by the falling price of coffee. He implemented acute cost-cutting measures and a severe austerity budget to bring inflation under control and also offered favorable conditions to attract foreign investment. Consequently, the national treasury, which contained only $27.00 when Ubico assumed power, was slowly and steadily built up along with Guatemala's international credit. However, the government outlawed union activities, and working conditions for the average Guatemalan deteriorated. Moreover, he abolished the centuries-old practice of holding Native Indians in servitude for debt and determined to bring them directly into the economy. This entailed a new law in 1933 that required all Indian males to work 150 days a year at minimum wage—and also two weeks a year without pay unless they paid a tax. Through this expedient Ubico broke the landlords' control over Indian lives and made them dependent upon the government. As the economy improved and money flowed into the coffers, Ubico next set about modernizing the primitive Guatemalan infrastructure. He began a crash construction program to build highways and roads connecting the distant interior to the capital for the first time. Over 6,000 miles of new roads were eventually added. Major public works, including buildings, hospitals, and schools, sprang up around the country while fresh water and electrification were made available in the countryside for the first time. The resulting economic boom led to the growth of Guatemala's tiny middle class, although the overwhelming majority of benefits were enjoyed by the wealthy landowners. Nonetheless, Guatemala acquired a modern infrastruc-

462

ture that served as the basis of its national economy for most of the 20th century.

For all Ubico's positive contributions to Guatemala, he also ran one of the most ruthless and efficient dictatorships in all Central America. His Liberal Progressive Party became the only legal outlet for political expression of participation. He also organized a well-funded and ruthless security apparatus that spied on citizens, arrested some, and executed others. Ubico was virulently anticommunist, and he ruthlessly suppressed Guatemalan leftists, union activists, and other undesirables. The country's thriving cultural life also suffered, for Ubico forbade any artistic expression that might be construed as criticism. Nor did he choose to respect constitutional law forbidding consecutive terms by executive officers. In 1936 and 1942 Ubico arranged to have the constitution amended to allow him to hold office indefinitely. But throughout the 1940s the regime began experiencing domestic and external pressures for change. During most of World War II he supported the Axis powers, but he finally cemented a relationship to the Allies and expropriated German-owned property on American insistence. The biggest movement for change, however, came from the very middle class that he had so painstakingly created. Shut off from opportunity by oligarchic control and desiring a greater say in governance, students, professional classes, and even young army officers began organizing marches against the government. In July 1944 dissidents staged a successful revolution that finally toppled Ubico, and he fled into exile. He left behind a 13-year record of impressive national growth underscored by a legacy of tyranny and oppression. Ubico died in New Orleans, Louisiana, on June 14, 1946, and his remains could not be peacefully returned to Guatemala until 1963.

Further Reading

Ciria, Alberto. "The Individual in History: Five Latin American Biographies." *Latin American Research Review* 20, no. 3 (1985): 247–267.

Dosal, Paul J. *Doing Business with the Dictators: A Political History of the United Fruit Company in Guatemala, 1899–1944.* Wilmington, Del.: SR Books, 1993.

Grieb, Kenneth J. *Guatemalan Caudillo: The Regime of Jorge Ubico: Guatemala, 1931–1944.* Athens: University of Ohio Press, 1979.

Pitti, Joseph A. *Jorge Ubico and Guatemala Politics in the 1920s.* Albuquerque: University of New Mexico Press, 1975.

Randolph, David E. "The Diplomatic History of Guatemala during the Administration of President Jorge Ubico, 1931–1944." Unpublished master's thesis, Arizona State University, 1980.

Sieder, R. "'Paz, Progresso, Justica y Honradez': Law and Citizenship in Alta Verapaz during the Regime of Jorge Ubico." *Latin American Research* 19 (July 2000): 283–302.

Ulbricht, Walter (1893–1973) *general secretary of the Socialist Unity Party of East Germany*

Walter Ulbricht was born in Leipzig, Germany on June 30, 1893, the son of a carpenter. He apprenticed as a cabinetmaker and joined the left-leaning Social Democratic Party (SDP) in 1912. After serving in World War I Ulbricht gravitated toward more radical politics, and in December 1918 he was a founder of the Kommunistische Partei Deutschlands (KPD), German Communist Party. He displayed real talent as a bureaucrat and an organizer so in 1923 he was elected to the party's central committee. Moreover, following the rise of JOSEPH STALIN in the Soviet Union, Ulbricht became irrevocably committed to the Stalinization of the KDP and to organizing it along a strict, centrally controlled basis. In 1928 he was also elected to the Reichstag (legislature). At that time the KDP was formally committed to overthrowing the democratic Weimar Republic and foolishly cooperated with the National Socialist Party (the Nazis) of ADOLF HITLER. But no sooner did Hitler assume power in January 1933 than he commenced a terror campaign against the communists and Ulbricht fled to Paris. There he functioned as an agent of Moscow and also served in the Spanish civil war with Republican forces. There Ulbricht successfully prosecuted Trotskyites to enhance Soviet control of Spanish communists, and by 1939 he was summoned back to Moscow. He became one of few foreigners to survive Stalin's bloody purge of the Communist Party. During World War II Ulbricht led the propaganda effort against German prisoners and became thoroughly trusted by Stalin. When the Red Army rolled through a defeated Germany in 1945 he accompanied them, now tasked with organizing and administering the new Soviet-occupied zone.

Though not initially in charge, Ulbricht performed several useful tasks to cement Russian control over its new possession. He proved instrumental in forcing a merger between the SDP and the KDP, which resulted in formation of the new Sozialistische Einheitspartei Deutschlands (SED), Socialist Unity Party, in April 1946. Three years later, when the German Democratic Republic was formed, Ulbricht was installed as deputy prime minister and general secretary of the SED. In this capacity he wielded real power over domestic affairs and was determined to apply the Stalinist political model to his situation. Ulbricht's doctrinaire and inflexible approach to governance resulted in a violent workers' rebellion in 1953, which had to be crushed by Russian tanks. He was lucky to have been retained by Soviet leaders, especially after the death of Stalin that year. The new Soviet premier NIKITA KHRUSHCHEV tried to effect liberalizing reforms throughout Eastern Europe in a program of de-Stalinization, but Ulbricht boldly refused to change. After the failed 1956 Hungarian revolution he purged the SED of its remaining moderates and ruled over the last Stalinist party in Europe. Following the death of President Wilhelm Pieck in 1960, Ulbricht unilaterally abolished that office and substituted a council of state with himself as chairman. He was now in complete control of East Germany's political apparatus. His authoritarian measures to increase industrial output at workers' expense led to a mass exodus toward West Germany and freedom. To counter this potentially fatal hemorrhage of skilled workers, in August 1961 Ulbricht authorized construction of the infamous Berlin Wall. This proved a propaganda embarrassment to the communist bloc as a whole, but did stabilize East Germany's economy for the time being. With time the Berlin Wall served as a hated symbol of communist oppression and tyranny.

Over the next decade Ulbricht remained true to his inflexible Stalinist creed. In 1968 he provided troops that invaded and crushed the Czechoslovakian Spring under ALEXANDER DUBČEK. In 1971 the East Germans proved somewhat receptive toward West German chancellor WILLY BRANDT's Ostpolitik but Ulbricht adamantly demanded recognition of the GDR as a precondition for better relations. His intransigence toward detente greatly angered Soviet premier LEONID BREZHNEV, who sought a lessening of tensions between the East and West blocs. In 1971 the Soviets helped orchestrate a minor coup that removed Ulbricht as general secretary in favor of the more flexible ERICH HONECKER. Ulbricht retained the honorary title as chairman of the state council, where he performed ceremonial functions until

his death in East Berlin on August 1, 1973. Dogmatic and stubborn, Ulbricht's 21-year reign established him as the dominant political figure of the GDR throughout its formative period.

Further Reading

Anderson, Sheldon R. *A Cold War in the Soviet Bloc: Polish-East German Relations: 1945–1962.* Boulder, Colo.: Westview Press, 2001.

Byrne, Malcolm, ed. *Uprising in East Germany, 1953: The Cold War, the German Question, and the First Major Upheaval behind the Iron Curtain.* New York: Central European University Press, 2001.

Gearson, John P. S., and Kori Schake, eds. *The Berlin Wall Crisis: Perspectives on Cold War Alliances.* New York: Palgrave Macmillan, 2002.

Gray, William G. *Germany's Cold War: The Global Campaign to Isolate East Germany, 1949–1969.* Chapel Hill: University of North Carolina Press, 2003.

Harrison, Hope M. *Driving the Soviets up the Wall: Soviet-East German relations, 1953–1961.* Princeton, N.J.: Princeton University Press, 2003.

Loth, Wilfried. *Stalin's Unwanted Child: The Soviet Union, the German Question, and the Founding of the GDR.* New York: St. Martin's Press, 1998.

Major, Patrick, and Jonathan Osmond, eds. *The Workers' and Peasants' State: Communism and Society in East Germany under Ulbricht, 1945–71.* New York: Manchester University Press, 2002.

U Nu (1907–1995) *prime minister of Burma*

U Nu was born in Walema, Burma, on May 25, 1907, the son of a small shopkeeper. Dissolute as a young man, U Nu rediscovered Buddhism, cured himself of alcoholism, and enrolled at the University of Rangoon to study law. There he became embroiled in anti-British agitation and served as head of the student union. U Nu subsequently taught for several years before joining a nationalist group, the Dobams Asiayone (We Burmans), to end colonial rule. In 1936 he led the first-ever student strike against the British, was arrested, and struck up cordial relations with his fellow revolutionary Aung San. U Nu continued his anticolonial actions and writings, and in 1940 he was arrested and jailed for sedition. He was not released until 1942 when the Japanese invaded Burma, forced the British out, and enticed him to serve in a puppet regime headed by Ba Maw. U Nu did as he was told, while secretly opposing Japanese rule, and he was relieved when the British returned in 1945. He next headed up the colony's most prominent political organization, the Anti-Fascist People's Freedom League (AFPFL), with a view toward pursuing independence. Two years of intense negotiations ensued before Great Britain finally allowed Burma its freedom. Aung San was slated to serve as the first interim executive, but he was assassinated by a political rival on July 19, 1947. Because U Nu was the only other Burmese politician of national stature, he was asked to serve as the nation's first prime minister as of January 1948. At that time Burma was invited to remain within the British Commonwealth but he chose instead to abandon it altogether.

U Nu inherited a country ruined by war and suffering from widespread poverty. Burma was also riven by an active communist insurgency and ethnic infighting throughout the countryside. But, as a celebrated Buddhist scholar, he was calm and resolute in the midst of seemingly insurmountable problems. U Nu subscribed to a relatively mild form of socialism and he enacted legislation to reduce the power of wealthy landlords. He was also an intensely religious figure and helped spark a national Buddhist revival through his publications and synods. Eager to sidestep the mounting tensions of the cold war, U Nu also helped champion the Nonaligned Movement among developing nations. He continued on with moderate success for a decade until 1958, when the military under General NE WIN temporarily deposed U Nu in a bloodless coup. He typically retired to a monastery to help reorganize his party apparatus and by 1960 the military was ready to allow a return to democracy. U Nu was easily reelected prime minister and resumed his course of trying to rule a divided, poor nation. In 1962 Ne Win again intervened and overthrew the government a second time, which spelled the end of democracy in Burma for the next 30 years. U Nu was summarily imprisoned until 1966.

Following his release U Nu was invited to join Ne Win's National Unity Advisory Board, where he demanded a return to parliamentary democracy. Rather than face possible arrest again, he left Burma for Thailand, ostensibly to study Buddhism but, in reality, to help organize a resistance movement. When this endeavor failed he subsequently relocated to India until

1980 when Ne Win summoned him home under a general amnesty. At this juncture U Nu became a Buddhist monk—but in 1988, following the overthrow of Ne Win, he declared himself head of a provisional government under his new National League for Democracy. Burma was then engulfed in mass prodemocracy movements, and the government felt sufficiently threatened to arrest U Nu again in 1989. He remained imprisoned until April 1992 and continued with prodemocracy agitation until his death in Rangoon on February 14, 1995. U Nu remains a venerated national figure and a driving force behind independence, but was also too infatuated with Buddhism to be an effective leader.

Further Reading

Butwell, Richard A. *U Nu of Burma*. Stanford, Calif.: Stanford University Press, 1969.

Callahan, Mary P. *Making Enemies: War and State Building in Burma*. Ithaca, N.Y.: Cornell University Press, 2003.

Fink, Christina. *Living Silence: Burma under Military Rule*. New York: Zed Books, 2001.

Thant Myint-U. *The Making of Modern Burma*. New York: Cambridge University Press, 2001.

Tucker, Shelby. *Burma: The Curse of Independence*. Sterling, Va.: Pluto Press, 2001.

U Nu. *U Nu, Saturday's Son*. New Haven, Conn.: Yale University Press, 1975.

U Thant (1909–1974) *secretary general of the United Nations*

U Thant was born in Pantanaw, Burma, on January 22, 1909, and he was educated at the National High School. He subsequently studied at University College, Rangoon, and befriended U NU, a future Burmese prime minister. After graduating in 1929 U Thant taught English and history in Pantanaw for many years before rising to headmaster. Following the Japanese conquest of Burma in 1942 he served as secretary of the Education Reorganization Committee but later quit to resume teaching. In 1945 the British returned to Burma and tried reimposing colonial rule, so U Thant joined U Nu's Anti-Fascist People's Freedom League (AFPFL) as head of the Information Department. After Burma obtained its independence in January 1948, he was invited to join the government as secretary of the Ministry of Information. U Thant excelled as an administrator and quickly became recognized as one of U Nu's most trusted advisers. In 1957 he was selected to represent Burma as one of its permanent representatives at the United Nations, and within a year the smooth-talking intellectual was elected vice president of that body. He continued functioning well in that capacity until Secretary General DAG HAMMARSKJÖLD died in a mysterious plane crash on November 3, 1961. Because the United States and the Soviet Union could not agree on a successor, U Thant's name was put forward as a compromise candidate, and he was immediately accepted. Having successfully fulfilled the balance of Hammarskjöld's term, U Thant was formally elected to his own five-year term as secretary general on December 2, 1962.

U Thant's acceptance of the UN mantle coincided with some of the most tumultuous years of the 20th century. His immediate concern was staving off an armed confrontation between American president JOHN F. KENNEDY and Soviet premier NIKITA KHRUSHCHEV over the deployment of nuclear missiles in Cuba. Acting as an intermediary, U Thant managed to facilitate removal of the Russian missiles without provoking an American invasion of Cuba. That year also witnessed the gradual absorption of Irian Jaya (western New Guinea) by Indonesia dictator SUKARNO, and large-scale peacekeeping operations in the former Belgian colony of Congo. In 1963 the island of Cyprus was racked by ethnic fighting between Greeks and Turks, which threatened to involve Greece and Turkey. U Thant managed to have UN peacekeeping forces deployed between the combatants and initiated talks to resolve the conflict peacefully. In 1967, the opposite occurred: Egyptian president GAMAL ABDEL NASSER demanded that the UN withdraw its forces separating Egypt from Israel, in anticipation of war, and U Thant reluctantly complied. He was later criticized for the move despite his insistence that the UN lacked any legal right to refuse Egypt's request. Nonetheless, in December 1966 U Thant was unanimously reelected to a second five-year term.

U Thant's most conspicuous failure as secretary general involved the unfolding Second Indochina War between North Vietnam and the United States. After the 1964 Tonkin Gulf incidents, which precipitated direct American air raids on Hanoi, the secretary general attempted to mediate indirectly between President LYNDON B. JOHNSON and HO CHI MINH. Johnson was not officially interested in peace talks at that stage, but he handed the issue off to his UN ambassador Adlai Stevenson for further discussion. Talks were fruitful, but Johnson rejected the "Rangoon initiative" along with a new Geneva peace conference. In a rare moment of anger, U Thant denounced the American administration for obstructionism, at which point Johnson denied that such talks had been undertaken in the first place. By 1968 public opinion in America was turning against the war, and U Thant arranged for Johnson to allow a partial bombing halt along with peace talks in Paris. Throughout the rest of his second term, the UN remained stretched thin over continuing crises in the Middle East and between India and Pakistan. Given the failure of peacekeeping efforts abroad, U Thant began placing greater emphasis on funding social and economic development programs, but he remained hard-pressed to come up with the financing. By 1972 U Thant had had enough, and he declined to run for a third consecutive term. That December he was replaced by KURT WALDHEIM of Austria and he retired to a home in upstate New York to compose his memoirs. U Thant died of cancer in New York City on November 25, 1974. He was the first non-European secretary general of the UN and among its most successful. Ironically, when his body was shipped back to Burma student riots erupted over the military government's refusal to bury it on the grounds of the university he had attended.

Further Reading

Firestone, Bernard J. *The United Nations under U Thant, 1961–1971.* Lanham, Md.: Scarecrow Press, 2001.

Gorman, Robert F. *Great Debates at the United Nations: An Encyclopedia of Fifty Key Issues, 1945–2000.* Westport, Conn.: Greenwood Press, 2001.

James, Alan. *Keeping the Peace in the Cyprus Crisis of 1963–64.* New York: Palgrave, 2002.

Nassif, Ramses. *U Thant in New York, 1961–1971: A Portrait of the Third United Nations Secretary General.* New York: St. Martin's Press, 1988.

Saltford, John. *The United Nations and the Indonesian Takeover of West Papua, 1962–1969: The Anatomy of Betrayal.* New York: Routledge Curzon, 2002.

U Thant. *View from the UN.* Garden City, N.Y.: Doubleday, 1978.

V

Vargas, Getúlio (1883–1954) *president of Brazil*

Getúlio Dorneles Vargas was born in São Borja, Rio Grande do Sul state, Brazil, on April 19, 1883, into a prominent political family. He briefly entertained a military career but quit and studied law to enter politics in 1908. In 1922 Vargas was elected to the national Chamber of Deputies and served four years. In 1926 President Luis Pereira de Souza appointed him minister of finance. However, Vargas left office two years later to successfully run for the governorship of his home state. His tenure there was characterized by effective leadership under centralized authority so in 1930 he announced his candidacy for the presidency of Brazil with the Liberal Alliance Party. Vargas was narrowly defeated but, rather then claim fraud, he temporarily accepted the outcome until a popular revolution tossed out the incumbent in October 1930. For the next two years Vargas was installed as provisional president with a mandate for change. Vargas was determined to change the basic nature of Brazilian governance by placing greater emphasis on social control and centralized authority. Brazil heretofore consisted of a loose confederation of semiautonomous states dominated by rural landowners and financed by agricultural exports. But Vargas changed the tax structure of the system to make the states dependent upon the government for funding and,

hence, more subservient to control. Next he greatly expanded the voting franchise by allowing women the right to vote and employing the secret ballot. Vargas was extremely concerned about the welfare of the working classes so he enacted sweeping educational reforms and introduced social security measures. Labor unions were organized—and controlled by the government—and a minimum wage adopted.

In economic terms Vargas also sought to revolutionize Brazil by de-emphasizing the traditional reliance upon coffee exports and stimulating the rise of a nascent industrial base. Factories were encouraged along with foreign investment, infrastructure, roads, and all the facets of a modern society. All these changes irrevocably altered Brazil's political landscape and placed it on the path to modernity. Because of his determination to break the power of big business and the landowners, he was hailed as the "father of the poor." However, Vargas extracted a steep political toll for his reforms. Having been formally elected president in 1932, he ruled as a despot. Congress was abolished, labor activity banned, and political parties outlawed. Police powers were also greatly expanded after a failed communist rebellion in 1935, and civil rights were suspended. In 1937 Vargas promulgated the New State (Estado Novo), a corporate authoritarian entity based on the fascist regimes of ANTÓNIO SALAZAR's Portugal, FRANCISCO FRANCO's

Spain, and BENITO MUSSOLINI's Italy. Here the rights of the individual were sacrificed for the benefit of the group, and were both aided and carefully monitored by the government.

Despite his sympathy for Nazi Germany, Vargas entered World War II on the side of the Allies—more to receive American financial aid than from any sense of altruism. However, the specter of Brazilian forces fighting for democracy in Europe undermined his own authority at home. On October 29, 1945, Vargas was bloodlessly deposed by the military after 15 years of uninterrupted rule. He was nonetheless extremely popular in his home state and was elected to the senate that fall. Vargas remained on the political sidelines for five years while Brazil experienced a period of economic stagnation. In 1950 he ran for the presidency a second time and was elected on a platform of labor reform and unbridled nationalism. To that end he nationalized the oil industry and granted wage increases, but was unable to cope with dramatic inflation. In August 1953 Vargas narrowly survived an assassination attempt, and the military withdrew its support from the government. They then demanded his resignation, but Vargas refused and, to underscore his indignation, he committed suicide on August 24, 1954. In a note left behind, the former executive dedicated his demise to the Brazilian people, for whom he claimed slavish devotion. Vargas was easily the most influential Brazilian politician of the 20th century and his legacy of centralized authority, nationalism, and populism remains a potent factor in national politics to present times.

Further Reading

Beattie, Peter M. *The Tribute of Blood: Army, Honor, Race, and Nation in Brazil, 1864–1945.* Durham, N.C.: Duke University Press, 2001.

Cardoso-Silva, V. A. *Foreign Policy and National Development: The Brazilian Experiment under Vargas, 1951–1954.* Urbana-Champaign: University of Illinois Press, 1985.

Dulles, John W. F. *Sobral Pinto, "the Conscience of Brazil": Leading the Attack against Vargas (1930–1945).* Austin: University of Texas Press, 2002.

Levine, Robert M. *Father of the Poor? Vargas and His Era.* New York: Cambridge University Press, 1998.

McCann, Frank D. *Soldiers of the Patria: A History of the Brazilian Army, 1889–1937.* Stanford, Calif.: Stanford University Press, 2004.

Rose, R. S. *One of the Forgotten Things: Getúlio Vargas and Brazilian Social Control, 1930–1954.* Westport, Conn.: Greenwood Press, 2000.

Steiger, William R. "What Once Was Desert Shall Be a World: Getúlio Vargas and Westward Expansion in Brazil, 1930–1945." Unpublished Ph.D. diss., University of California–Los Angeles, 1995.

Williams, Daryle. *Culture Wars in Brazil: The First Vargas Regime, 1930–1945.* Durham, N.C.: Duke University Press, 2001.

Velasco, Juan (1910–1977) *president of Peru*

Juan Velasco Alvarado was born in Piura, Peru, on June 16, 1910, the son of a civil servant. He left home to join the army in 1929 and, as an outstanding common soldier, was selected to attend the national military academy. Velasco graduated with distinction in 1934 and compiled a distinguished military career with diplomatic assignments in Paris and Washington, D.C. He was promoted to full general and head of the military in 1964 by President FERNANDO BELAÚNDE TERRY. As a soldier and a nationalist, Velasco believed that Peru was in dire need of social and economic reforms to circumvent a Marxist revolution similar to Communist Cuba's. His concerns were shared by President Belaúnde who tried implementing a package of modest reforms in 1968 but was thwarted by vested interests in congress. The president also experienced domestic pressure to nationalize the assets of the International Petroleum Company (IPC), an American firm with abiding control of Peru's oil industry. However, when Belaúnde inadvertently signed a controversial agreement favorable to the company it spurred great national resentment. On October 3, 1968, Velasco headed a bloodless coup that toppled Belaúnde and instituted the Revolutionary Government of the Armed Forces. He and his coterie of officers then determined that if politicians could not implement needed change, the military would. A top priority would be reducing Peru's overall economic dependence upon the United States.

Velasco conceived and implemented a series of sweeping reforms known collectively as Plan Inca. He capitalized on nationalistic fervor by nationalizing the property of IPC and other American-owned companies in the copper and iron industries. No compensation was offered and when the United States refused to grant

Peru further developmental loans, Velasco opened diplomatic relations with the Soviet Union to obtain funding there. He also instituted a 200-mile fishing limit off Peru's Pacific coast and impounded several American vessels for trespassing. The military next tackled the pressing problem of agrarian reform. Peru had long been dominated by large estates worked by landless Indian peasants for scant compensation. In 1969 Velasco announced sweeping changes that broke up the estates and distributed land to farmers, cooperatives, and landless peasants. The junta then oversaw the nationalization of the banking industry, railroads, and public utilities. State control was subsequently extended over international trade and also served as a source of revenue for new businesses.

In sum, Velasco concocted one of the most thorough economic programs in Latin American history, being both populist and reformist in tenor. He then set his sights on equally pressing social matters by enlarging the national pension program, providing medical service to the poor, and introducing clean water and ready supplies of electricity into the countryside. Furthermore, the government declared complete equality for women and granted Quechua—the Indian dialect of the Andes—parity with Spanish. To lay the groundwork for the eventual return to democracy, Velasco also sponsored the Sistema Nacional de Apoyo a la Mobilización Social (SINAMOS), Social Mobilization Support System, to integrate peasants and workers into a coherent voting bloc. On the downside, Velasco's regime, if not an outright dictatorship, was authoritarian by nature and brooked little dissent. The military initially enjoyed great public support and respected individual rights provided the economy was good. However, by 1973 Peru was experiencing a severe economic downturn, which led to labor unrest, strikes, and riots. Velasco responded with a harsh crackdown and also nationalized the country's newspapers to silence criticism. The general himself was increasingly sidelined with poor health that impaired his political judgment and led to increasingly erratic behavior. On August 29, 1975, Velasco was bloodlessly overthrown by General FRANCISCO MORALES BERMÚDEZ, who scaled back many of the state-owned enterprises in favor of free-market practices. Velasco lingered on for two years before dying in Lima on December 24, 1977. As a testimony to his enduring popularity with the largely poor Indian

population, his funeral procession was accompanied by 200,000 mourners. He remains the most popular and respected Peruvian executive of recent memory.

Further Reading

Atwood, Roger. "Democratic Dictators: Authoritarian Politics in Peru from Leguia to Fujimori." *SAIS Review* 21 (summer–fall 2001): 155–176.

Bamat, Thomas. "Peru's Velasco Regime and Class Domination after 1968." *Latin American Perspectives* 10 (spring 1983): 128–150.

Harik, Judith P. "'Nasserism' in the Andes? An Analysis of the Government of Peruvian General Juan Velasco Alvarado." Unpublished Ph.D. diss., University of Iowa, 1981.

Klaren, Peter F. *Peru: Society and Nationhood in the Andes.* New York: Oxford University Press, 2000.

Kruijt, Dirk. *Revolution by Decree: Peru, 1968–1975.* Amsterdam: Thela Publishers, 1994.

Valdes, Benjamin E. "The Development of Peruvian Indigenismo and Its Influence on the Regime of General Juan Velasco Alvarado." Unpublished master's thesis, Vanderbilt University, 1983.

Velasco Ibarra, José (1893–1979) *president of Ecuador*

José Velasco Ibarra was born in Quito, Ecuador, on March 19, 1893, the son of an engineer. He completed his doctoral thesis at the Sorbonne in Paris before coming home to work as a journalist. In 1932 Velasco was elected to the congress as a Liberal but he showed no real affinity for party politics. In fact, he presented himself as a supreme opportunist who struck alliances with any interest group that suited his purposes. But Velasco enhanced his appeal by being a skilled political operator and a charismatic orator. By 1933 he functioned as Speaker of the House, and in this capacity he led the fight against President Juan de Dios Martínez Mera, then accused of electoral fraud. When congress moved to declare the presidency vacant, Velasco stepped forward as a candidate and was elected with the backing of both Liberals and Conservatives. In power he proved himself a populist and a reformer but was also perpetually thwarted by oligarchic interests in congress. To break the legislative logjam Velasco unsuccessfully tried imposing a dictatorship and was exiled to Colombia in August 1935. This set the pattern for his remaining four terms in office. In light of his repeated exile he became popularly known as "The Great Absentee."

Velasco remained abroad until 1940 when he returned to Ecuador to run again for president. He lost to Liberal candidate Carlos Alberto Arroyo del Río that year and resumed his exile in Argentina. However, when Arroyo was overthrown by a coup in May 1944, Velasco came home again and was proclaimed head of state by the Constituent Assembly for a second term. His new administration was backed by a crazy quilt of parties spanning the ideological spectrum, and with their help he implemented a new constitution in 1946. However, Velasco was overthrown again by his own defense minister on August 23, 1947, and again returned to exile in Argentina. The following year free elections were won by GALO PLAZA LASSO, who completed a full term in office and retired in 1952. That year Velasco came home and successfully ran for office a third time. He was allowed to serve out a complete four-year term and accomplished several useful reforms in an unusually healthy economic climate. In 1956 he stepped down in favor of the Conservative Camilo Ponce. Four years later Velasco ran again against Plaza Lasso and a government candidate, handily defeating both with sizable left-wing support. But Velasco, at heart a conservative, proved hostile to Fidel Castro's Communist Cuba and also tried to increase taxes to fund new projects. His brusqueness so alienated the opposition that conservatives, liberals, and communists all formed an alliance to oppose him. The military, fearing the outbreak of civil war, then ousted Velasco for the third time on November 7, 1961. A series of provisional presidents and military juntas ensued until democratic rule was finally restored in March 1966.

In 1968 Velasco came home and successfully ran for the presidency for an unprecedented fifth term. As before he inherited a congress hostile to his reform agenda and he threatened to resign. This time the military entreated him to stay on in the interest of national stability, and in June 1970 he disbanded congress and declared a dictatorship. The following year a revolt among military officers forced Velasco to become a pawn of the military to remain in power. Velasco intended to retire at the end of his term, but the military asked him to extend his stay. He refused, and when new elections were held in 1972 and about to be won by the radical Assad Bucaram, the army intervened once more and installed a new junta.

Velasco went to Argentina for the next seven years but returned to his home town of Quito to die there on March 30, 1979. He enjoyed one of the longest political careers in Ecuadoran political history, principally for his ability to effortlessly shift alliances to gain an advantage. Velasco remains the most durable national figure of the 20th century but, given his lack of identifiable political values, he bequeathed no lasting legacy to the process.

Further Reading
Cueva Davila, Agustin. *The Process of Political Domination in Ecuador.* New Brunswick, N.J.: Transaction Books, 1982.
De la Torre, Carlos. *Populist Seduction in Latin America: The Ecuadorian Experience.* Athens: Ohio University Center for International Studies, 2000.
———. "Velasco Ibarra and 'La Revolucion Gloriosa': The Social Production of a Populist Leader in Ecuador in the 1940s." *Journal of Latin American Studies* 26 (October 1994): 683–711.
Isaacs, Anita. *Military Rule and Transition in Ecuador, 1972–92.* Pittsburgh: University of Pittsburgh Press, 1993.
Maier, Georg. "The Impact of Velasquismo on the Ecuadorian Political System." Unpublished master's thesis, Southern Illinois University, 1965.
Martz, John D. *The Military in Ecuador: Policies and Politics of Authoritarian Rule.* Albuquerque, N.M.: Latin American Institute, University of New Mexico, 1988.

Venizélos, Eleuthérios (1864–1936) *prime minister of Greece*

Eleuthérios Kyriakos Venizélos was born in Mounriés, Crete, on August 23, 1864, the son of a prominent Cretan revolutionary who fought against the Ottoman Empire. He followed his family into exile on the island of Siros and subsequently attended the law school at the University of Athens. After graduating in 1877 Venizélos came home to work as a journalist but became caught up in the island's revolutionary politics. He was elected to the national assembly as part of the Liberal Party and in 1897 helped lead an unsuccessful insurrection to unite Crete with Greece. With European help the Cretans received autonomy from the Ottomans, and Prince George, son of King George I of Greece, arrived as high commissioner. Venizélos, now serving as minister of justice, clashed repeatedly with the prince, and in 1906 led an insurrection that drove him back to the mainland. By that time Greece had fallen under the sway of a political clique known as the Military League and in August 1910 they encouraged Venizélos to run as a deputy from Athens. He was successful and subsequently gained appointment as prime minister.

Venizélos, a devout monarchist, amended the 1864 constitution to allow a prominent role to be played by the royal household in governance. He also enacted sweeping reform programs to modernize the military and initiate war against the Ottoman Empire. During the Balkan War of 1912–13, Greece, in concert with Bulgaria, successfully drove the Turks out of the region. Venizélos thus doubled the size of his nation by seizing Macedonia, Crete, and the Aegean islands. When World War I commenced in 1914, he strongly urged Greece to join on the side of the Allies, but King Constantine I, who was pro-German, pursued a neutral course. Venizélos tried to change his monarch's mind for two years, so in 1916, after German, Austrian, and Bulgarian forces invaded Macedonia, he led an insurrection against the king. The Greek rebels were assisted by French and British forces, who helped install Constantine's son, Alexander, on the throne. Venizélos then led Greece into war against the Central Powers and in 1919 he represented his country for two years during the Paris Peace Conference. In this capacity he managed to secure additional territorial gains in Thrace and the western Balkans. He returned home in 1920 to a hero's welcome. However, when King Alexander died suddenly, Constantine was recalled through a popular plebiscite. Rather than deal with his adversary, Venizélos resigned as prime minister and entered self-imposed exile in Paris.

Constantine pursued an unsuccessful war against KEMAL ATATÜRK in Anatolia, where his armies were badly defeated and 1.2 million refugees had to be absorbed. This led to a rebellion by the military and he was overthrown in 1920. Venizélos was then invited back to Greece and reinstalled as prime minister. He negotiated a peace treaty with the new Republic of Turkey in 1923 but quit his office the following year when several politicians tried to abolish the monarchy altogether. Venizélos moved briefly to Paris, but then returned to serve as head of the Liberal Party in the legislature. He was overwhelmingly elected prime minister

in 1928 for the third time and performed constructive work normalizing relations with Greece's Balkan neighbors. He also concluded an important series of territorial treaties with Turkey, Italy, and Yugoslavia. The onset of the Great Depression in 1929 greatly weakened his standing with the public, unfortunately, and in 1932 he was voted out of office. Venizélos continued on as head of the Liberals until 1935, when the monarchy was successfully reestablished. Because he now opposed a kingship for Greece, Venizélos resigned from office again. He was subsequently implicated in a plot against the throne and exiled again to Paris. He died there on March 18, 1936, widely acclaimed as Greece's outstanding international statesman of the early 20th century.

Further Reading

Gerolymatos, Andre. "Lloyd George and Eleuthérios Venizélos, 1912–1917." *Journal of the Hellenic Diaspora* 15, nos. 3–4 (1988): 37–50.

Kaloudis, George S. *Modern Greek Democracy: The End of a Long Journey?* Lanham, Md.: University Press of America, 2000.

Karamanlis, Konstantine A. "Venizélos and the External Relations of Greece from 1928 to 1932." Unpublished Ph.D. diss., Fletcher School of Law and Diplomacy, 1984.

Macrakis, Aglain Lily. "Cretan Rebel: Eleuthérios Venizélos in Ottoman Crete." Unpublished Ph.D. diss., Harvard University, 1983.

Mazower, Mark. "The Messiah and the Bourgeoisie: Venizélos and Politics in Greece, 1909–1912." *Historical Journal* 35 (December 1992): 885–904.

Vlavianos, Aristea A. "Venizélos, Constantine, the Great Powers and the Ethnikos Dichasmos." Unpublished master's thesis, James Madison University, 1994.

Verwoerd, Hendrik (1901–1966) *prime minister of South Africa*

Hendrik Frensch Verwoerd was born in Amsterdam, the Netherlands, on September 8, 1901, a son of Dutch Reformed Church (Calvinist) missionaries. As such he was raised in an intense religious atmosphere that strongly influenced his world view. His family relocated to Capetown, South Africa, while he was still a child, and he subsequently attended the University of Stellenbosch, an intellectual center of Afrikaner nationalism. Verwoerd performed brilliantly in college and went on to acquire advanced degrees in sociology from the Universities of Hamburg, Leipzig, and Berlin. While in Germany he was also impressed by the nascent National Socialist (Nazi) teachings of ADOLF HITLER. Verwoerd came home in 1927 and served as a professor of psychology and sociology at Stellenbosch. Already an ardent nationalist, in 1937 he was one of several Afrikaner professors who railed against the government's policy of granting German Jewish refugees asylum in South Africa. As Verwoerd's politics became gradually radicalized, he joined the race-supremacist National Party and the *Broederbond* (Brotherhood), a secret Afrikaner society. In 1937 he became editor of the influential newspaper *Die Transvaaler,* where his views of racial separation were crystallized in print. In addition to pro-Nazi views, he also scathingly denounced the British, black Africans, and Jews. Verwoerd unsuccessfully ran for the legislature in 1948, the year that the National Party was swept to power, but he later received an appointment to the senate.

In October 1950 Verwoerd was made minister of native affairs, an important post that he occupied for eight years. It was here that he served as the main architect of apartheid, the government's official policy of segregating citizens on the basis of race. No simple racist, Verwoerd strongly believed that white and black cultures were incompatible and ought to develop free of one another. To him God had ordained that people of differing backgrounds be permanently separated (apartheid means "apartness"). This entailed forcibly relocating the black majority from the cities and relegating them to various homelands (Bantustans) under traditional tribal chiefs. In practice this policy did no less than strip Africans of their political and civil rights. When required to serve as a source of cheap labor, they were beholden to the hated "pass system" in order to work and travel about. Furthermore, workers were not allowed to take their families, who remained behind in the homeland. It was a carefully contrived, strongly enforced system of racial oppression that would leave deep scars on South Africa's national psyche for decades to come.

Verwoerd was finally elected to the legislature in April 1958, where he became head of the National Party and prime minister. As head of state he was finally free to bring the full weight of the government upon erecting long desired racial barriers. In March 1960, when members of the Pan Africanist Congress sponsored a peaceful protest against apartheid in Sharpeville, they were brutally attacked by police forces. No less than 67 people were killed and more than 300 wounded, and the South African regime was intensely criticized by fellow members of the British Commonwealth. Verwoerd responded by sponsoring a referendum to make South Africa an independent republic. The measure passed narrowly, and on May 31, 1961, the Republic of South Africa was formally established. When member states continued objecting to the government's racial policies, Verwoerd pulled out of the Commonwealth altogether. Thereafter, antiapartheid groups successfully pressed for economic sanctions against the apartheid regime and South Africa grew increasingly isolated diplomatically. In light of increased guerrilla activity against the government, the republic stepped up counterinsurgency programs against blacks, outlawed the African National Congress, and began evolving into a repressive police state.

Verwoerd retained a good deal of popularity among his fellow Afrikaners and, with the onset of black guerrilla warfare, increasing numbers of English-speaking South Africans turned to him for security. On April 9, 1960, he miraculously survived an assassination attempt at the hands of a crazed white farmer, which only deepened his conviction of doing God's work. But on September 6, 1966, Verwoerd was stabbed to death in the legislature by a deranged messenger. Furthermore, the loathsome system of apartheid that he erected lasted 30 more years until the election of Nelson Mandela as South Africa's first black prime minister.

Further Reading

Alexander, Peter. *Workers, War, and the Origins of Apartheid: Labour and Politics in South Africa, 1939–48.* Athens: Ohio University Press, 2000.

Duffy, Joanne L. "Afrikaner Unity, the National Party, and the Afrikaner Nationalist Right in Stellenbosch, 1934–1938." Unpublished Ph.D. diss., University of Oxford, 2001.

Nesbitt, Francis N. "Race for Sanctions: The Movement against Apartheid, 1946–1994." Unpublished Ph.D. diss., University of Massachusetts–Amherst, 2002.

Roberts, Martin, and Josh Brooman. *South Africa, 1948–94: The Rise and Fall of Apartheid.* Harlow, England: Longman, 2001.

Van Woerden, Henk. *The Assassin: A Story of Race and Rage in the Land of Apartheid.* New York: Holt, 2001.

Waddy, Nicholas L. "The Growing Divide: British and South African Parliamentary Attitudes to Racial Policy, 1945–1948." Unpublished Ph.D. diss., University of Rochester, 2001.

Videela, Jorge (1925–) *president of Argentina*

Jorge Rafael Videla was born in Mercedes, Argentina, on August 2, 1925, the son of a high-ranking army officer. Like his father, he pursued a military career by attending the National Military College and being commissioned in 1944. Videla went on to compile an impressive service record, with diplomatic stints in Washington, D.C. By 1973 he was serving as the army's chief of staff, a position he retained until 1975, when President Isabel Perón (second wife of dictator JUAN PERÓN) appointed him commander in chief of the army. The Argentine military by now had a strong tradition of intervening in national politics during times of crisis. But Videla, a self-professed political moderate, was not viewed as a threat to the democratic order. Unfortunately the country was then racked by the twin evils of soaring inflation and a bloody left-wing insurgency in the cities. Perón, however well-intentioned, proved politically inept and could not restore either the economy or society. For this reason Videla, in concert with other senior military figures, bloodlessly toppled the civilian regime on March 24, 1976, and he was installed as acting president of a nine-man junta. In preparation, the legislature was dissolved, courts disbanded, and both unions and political parties were banned.

Argentina had known military governments before, but the thoroughness of Videla's handling of national affairs was unanticipated. The democratic process was completely suspended and supplanted by near despotic authority. Faced with widespread urban violence from guerrillas of the People's Revolutionary Army, Videla ordered the harshest crackdown upon left-wing dissidents and their suspected supporters that the nation ever knew. Upward of 30,000 guerrillas and their cohorts—including journalists, union leaders, and students—were arrested en masse and subjected to torture and interrogation. Worse, the majority were either murdered outright or simply categorized as "disappeared." The government's efforts were greatly facilitated by right-wing "death squads," which seemingly operated above the law with military approval. This period, known as the so-called Dirty War, was among the most repressive ever imposed in a Latin American country. Videla was fully intent upon crushing the communist insurgency and he succeeded, but at a terrible cost in human rights. The government also lent its energies and military intelligence in Operation Condor, a multinational effort throughout Latin America intending to target and eliminate guerrillas and leftists. The effort was largely successful, and political stability was restored—but the toll in lives proved immense.

Concurrent with the crackdown, Videla also sponsored economic reforms to reduce an annual inflation rate of 400 percent. He ordered the Peronist emphasis on government controls ended and substituted free-market principles and foreign investment. Some progress was made at improving Argentina's economy and balance of payments, but deep-seated structural problems remained. In 1978 Videla intended to surrender the presidency but he was persuaded by the junta to remain on another three years. He finally left office in March 1981, shortly before President LEOPOLDO GALTIERI led the nation into the disastrous Falkland Islands war. Defeat here paved the way for a return to civilian rule and in October 1983 RAÚL ALFONSÍN became the first civilian executive in seven years. After assuming office in 1984, one of his first acts was to have Videla and other military leaders arrested for human rights violations. Videla was tried, found guilty, and sentenced to life imprisonment. However, in 1991 President Carlos Saúl Menem, wishing to harmonize relations with the military, released Videla and others from jail. Videla remained unrepentant and defended his actions as being strictly in the interests of national security. But accusations of murder continued stalking the former general and in 1998 he was placed under house arrest while new charges were leveled against him. In September 2001 a federal judge ordered Videla to stand trial for the abduction of 72 foreigners in concert with Operation Condor—his trial remains pending.

Further Reading

Lewis, Daniel K. *The History of Argentina.* Westport, Conn.: Greenwood Press, 2001.

Lewis, Paul H. *Guerrillas and Generals: The "Dirty War" in Argentina.* Westport, Conn.: Praeger, 2002.

Marchak, Patricia. *God's Assassins: State Terrorism in Argentina in the 1970s.* Montreal: McGill-Queens University Press, 2002.

Munck, Geraldo L. *Authoritarianism and Democratization: Soldiers and Workers in Argentina, 1976–1983.* University Park: Pennsylvania State University, 1998.

Osiel, Mark. *Mass Atrocity, Ordinary Evil, and Hannah Arendt: Criminal Consciousness in Argentina's Dirty War.* New Haven, Conn.: Yale University Press, 2001.

Roehrig, Terence. *The Prosecution of Former Military Leaders in Newly Democratic Countries: The Cases of Argentina, Greece, and South Korea.* Jefferson, N.C.: McFarland, 2002.

Villeda Morales, Ramón (1909–1971) *president of Honduras*

Ramón Villeda Morales was born in Ocotepeque, Honduras, on November 26, 1909, and he studied medicine at the National University of Honduras. He pursued advanced studies in Germany and finally established a successful practice at Tegucigalpa in 1940. Shortly after, Villeda Morales became active in Liberal Party politics and, by dint of organizational prowess and speaking abilities, he emerged as party leader by 1949. He first ran for the Honduran presidency in October 1954 against National Party nominees Carias Andino and Abraham Williams, winning a plurality of votes. It then fell upon the legislature to resolve the election by a direct vote but National Party members boycotted the session to keep Villeda Morales from winning. On December 5, 1954, Vice President Julio Lozana declared himself constitutional dictator and, when Villeda Morales led a strike to protest the takeover in July 1956, he was exiled to Costa Rica. When Lozano was deposed in turn by the military five months later, Villeda Morales returned home and was installed as ambassador to the United States. In 1957 he again ran for the presidency and was elected by the constituent assembly. Villeda Morales thus became the first Liberal Party executive in several decades on December 21, 1957.

The new president had previously renounced radical reforms in a pact with the United Fruit Company, but he remained determined to effect change. In 1959, following an unsuccessful rebellion by the National Police, he dissolved them in favor of a new 2,000-man Civil Guard responsible to the Ministry of Government and Justice. This restored a sense of stability to the nation but it also angered the military, which felt that its autonomy was being violated. Villeda Morales next turned his attention to modernizing the Honduran national infrastructure. He initiated a concerted effort to develop new highways, ports, and air facilities, and also directed improvements in health programs and national education. He made a significant contribution to Honduras's economic well-being in July 1959 by signing into law the nation's first Labor Code. This document codified rights in terms of hours, wages, compensation, and the right to strike. The following month Villeda Morales directed adoption of the first social insurance law with increased benefits for unemployment, maternity leave, and disabilities. In 1960 he was among the first Central American leaders to endorse American president JOHN F. KENNEDY's Alliance for Progress, consisting of social reform legislation intending to preclude communist-style insurrections as in Cuba. Honduras consequently received large increases in economic and military aid, and Villeda Morales drew even closer to the United States in foreign policy. To facilitate trade he pushed Honduras along into the new Central American Common Market. In 1961 Honduras also broke relations with Cuba while the government cooperated closely with the Central Intelligence Agency to thwart communist guerrilla movements throughout the region.

In 1962, again at the behest of the United States, Villeda Morales signed a new and far-reaching agrarian reform law that brought idle acreage into production to ease the burden on overworked peasant organizations. This had the effect of alienating the powerful United Fruit Company and other conservative interest groups, who were wary of creeping socialism. By the time new elections were scheduled in 1963, neither the military nor the landed interests wished to see a continuation of Liberal Party rule. Moreover, once it appeared that the Liberals under Modesto Rodas Alvarado would win, the military suddenly seized control under Colonel Oswaldo López Arellano on October 3, 1963. Both Villeda Morales and Rodas Alvarano were then forced to flee the country. The military continued ruling Honduras until 1971, when Villeda Morales was finally allowed to go home. He then received an appointment as Honduran representative to the United Nations in New York but died shortly after arriving there on

October 8, 1971. Villeda Morales remains a significant national figure for his many reforms in labor, health, and education.

Further Reading

Echeverri-Gent, Elisavinda. "Labor, Class, and Political Representation: A Comparative Analysis of Honduras and Costa Rica," 2 vols. Unpublished Ph.D. diss., University of Chicago, 1988.

Euraque, Dario A. *Reinterpreting the Banana Republic: Region and State in Honduras, 1870–1972.* Chapel Hill: University of North Carolina Press, 1996.

Hammond, Tony. "The Role of the Honduran Armed Forces in the Transition to Democracy." Unpublished master's thesis, University of Florida, 1991.

MacCameron, Robert. *Bananas, Labor, and Politics in Honduras, 1954–1963.* Syracuse, N.Y.: Maxwell School of Citizenship and Public Affairs, Syracuse University, 1983.

Morris, James A. *Honduran Electoral Politics and Military Rule: The Geopolitics of Central America.* Albuquerque: University of New Mexico, Dept. of Political Science, 1982.

———. *Honduras: Caudillo Politics and Military Rulers.* Boulder, Colo.: Westview Press, 1984.

Vorster, Balthazar (1915–1983) *prime minister of South Africa*

Balthazar Johannes Vorster was born in Jamestown, South Africa, on December 13, 1915, the son of a wealthy sheep rancher. He attended the University of Stellenbosch, then a hotbed of Afrikaner (Dutch) nationalism, and befriended noted lecturer HENDRIK VERWOERD. Vorster quickly absorbed the notions of racial superiority and hatred for all things English, hallmarks of the Dutch-based National Party (NP). However, Vorster was quite given to extremes, and in 1938 he helped form the more militant Osewabrandwag (Ox wagon guard), which espoused anti-Semitic and pro-Nazi viewpoints. In 1939, when the government of JAN SMUTS led South Africa into World War II on the side of Great Britain, Vorster's followers strongly opposed the move. Pro-Nazi Afrikaners then launched a sabotage campaign to impede the war effort and Vorster was arrested and imprisoned for alleged complicity. After his release he resumed his political career by

attempting to rejoin the NP but was rejected as too extreme. He then unsuccessfully ran for office in 1948 as part of the right-wing Afrikaner Party and lost. It was not until 1953 that Vorster was allowed to rejoin the NP and he was finally elected to the legislature. He proved himself a skilled debater and an astute politician, so in 1958 Prime Minister Verwoerd appointed him minister of education. Vorster, who prided himself upon his toughness, implemented those aspects of apartheid (racial separation) intended to keep the black African majority subservient to whites. He performed up to hard-line expectations, so in 1961 Verwoerd made Vorster minister of justice and police. In this capacity he gained a degree of infamy by strengthening security forces and cracking down harshly on black dissent though the Sabotage Act of 1962. Through this expedient the African National Congress (ANC) was outlawed and its members, such as Nelson Mandela, could be subject to arrest and detention without trial. Vorster certainly reaffirmed his reputation for toughness, and following the assassination of Verwoerd in 1966, he succeeded him as prime minister.

Over the next 12 years Vorster headed up the South African apartheid regime, although with greater pragmatism than most right-wing extremists anticipated. At home he pursued a racial hard line, and in 1970 he created the first of the native homelands (Bantustans) intended to keep black tribes separated from white society. He also allowed security forces to arrest, harass, torture, and in some instances murder anti-apartheid Africans. This repression, in turn, had the effect of swelling the ranks of ANC guerrillas, who conducted a low-intensity urban war against the government. In 1976 hundreds of black demonstrators were killed by police and army forces during the Soweto uprising. In light of this oppression, South Africa faced sanctions and isolation from the rest of the world but Vorster, in concert with his defense minister P. W. Botha, made the nation self-sufficient in terms of modern weapons and economics. They also forged close relationships with the Jewish state of Israel to obtain the newest technology.

Vorster may have upheld the tenets of apartheid domestically but in the foreign policy arena he attempted a rapprochement with neighboring states. He met with leaders such as KENNETH KAUNDA of Zambia and SAMORA MACHEL of Mozambique to defuse regional tensions and, after the fall of Portugal's African empire in

1974, he urged Rhodesian prime minister IAN SMITH to seek accommodation with the black majority. Paradoxically, he singularly refused to contemplate such clear-eyed solutions to racial problems at home. In 1976, when South African forces were dispatched to fight Cuban mercenaries in AGOSTINO NETO's Angola, Vorster lost whatever goodwill he was able to cultivate among African heads of state. Poor health forced him to resign as prime minister in September 1978 and he assumed ceremonial tasks as state president. However, his role in covering up the so-called "Muldergate scandal" finally forced him from public life altogether on June 4, 1979, and he was succeeded by the even more reform-minded Botha. Vorster came out of retirement periodically to denounce his successor's liberal policies toward Coloreds and Asians before his death in Capetown on September 10, 1983. He is still regarded as among South Africa's most forceful and successful white politicians.

Further Reading

Chanock, Martin. *The Making of South African Legal Culture, 1902–1936: Fear, Favour, and Prejudice.* New York: Cambridge University Press, 2001.

Haynie, Stacia L. *Judging in Black and White: Decision Making in the South African Appellate Division, 1950–1990.* New York: P. Lang, 2003.

Hyam, Ronald. *The Lion and the Springbok: Britain and South Africa since the Boer War.* New York: Cambridge University Press, 2003.

Osada, Masako. *Sanctions and Honorary Whites: Diplomatic Policies and Economic Realities in Relations between Japan and South Africa.* Westport, Conn.: Greenwood Press, 2002.

Rhoodie, Eschel M. *The Real Information Scandal.* Atlanta, Ga.: Orbis, 1983.

Sanders, Mark. *Complicities: The Intellectual and Apartheid.* Durham, N.C.: Duke University Press, 2002.

W

Waldheim, Kurt (1918–) *secretary general of the United Nations and president of Austria*

Kurt Waldheim was born in St. Andrä-Wördern, Austria, on December 21, 1918, into a middle-class Catholic family. He studied law and diplomacy at the University of Vienna and, following the 1938 annexation of Austria by ADOLF HITLER, Waldheim joined a Nazi student group. When World War II erupted the following year, he was drafted into the army and saw active service on the eastern front. After being wounded he was transferred to the staff of General Alexander Lohr in the Balkans theater, where he remained until 1945. Once the war ended Waldheim worked in the foreign ministry as a secretary and performed diplomatic work in Paris. He also participated in negotiations that led to the end of Austria's military occupation by the Allied Powers in May 1955. Thereafter the country hewed closely to strict policies of neutrality. Waldheim then arrived in New York as part of the Austrian delegation to the United Nations, and he also served as ambassador to Canada. Back home in 1960, he next worked for the Ministry of Foreign Affairs before returning to the United Nations in 1964. Waldheim then became chairman of the Committee on Peaceful Uses of Outer Space until 1968, when he again joined the foreign ministry. After a third stint as UN ambassador in 1970 he returned home to run unsuccessfully for the presidency of Austria. He then resumed his work at the UN as a chairman within the Atomic Energy Committee in 1971. Waldheim had acquired a reputation as a professional, well-informed diplomat from a small neutral country. This made him an ideal compromise candidate to succeed U THANT as UN secretary general in December 1971.

Like his predecessor, Waldheim inherited a world in crisis. Over the next eight years he was forced to address lingering problems in Cyprus, the Middle East, and Southeast Asia. His biggest challenge was in helping to end the 1973 Arab-Israeli war, which threatened to engulf the entire region. Waldheim, an effective manager, easily won reelection as secretary general in December 1976, but he was confronted by escalating spirals of violence that UN efforts could not contain. Foremost of these were the Soviet invasion of Afghanistan in 1979 and the outbreak of the bloody Iran-Iraq war in 1980. Nor could he successfully resolve the dangerous Iranian hostage crisis between the United States and Iran that also threatened to expand into confrontation. Waldheim nonetheless handled his charge competently and in 1981 he sought to run for an unprecedented third term. He enjoyed backing from the United States and Russia, but China objected and his office was passed to the Peruvian JAVIER PÉREZ DE CUÉLLAR. After serving two years as a visiting professor of diplomacy at Georgetown University, Washington, D.C., he returned to Austria in 1984.

In 1986 Waldheim commenced his political career by running for the presidency of Austria with the conservative Austrian People's Party (OVP). This is a largely ceremonial post and his campaign proved lackluster until the World Jewish Congress produced evidence that Waldheim had been less than candid about his World War II activities. According to documentary sources, he belonged to units that committed atrocities against civilians in Yugoslavia and had also facilitated the deportation of 40,000 Jews to death camps. Waldheim stridently denied that he had anything to do with criminal behavior. He further insisted that his membership in Nazi-sponsored groups was taken only to protect his family. "I did what was necessary to survive the system, the war," he maintained,

"no more, no less." By portraying himself as a victim of Jewish extremists, Waldheim was elected president by a large margin, becoming Austria's first non-socialist president since 1945. In consequence Israel withdrew its ambassador from Austria, and the United States banned Waldheim from visiting. In February 1988 an international commission investigating the charges against Waldheim concluded that, while he did not actively participate in criminal activities, he had been less than forthcoming in admitting his past. The Austrian president thus became something of a pariah on the international scene while his nation endured diplomatic isolation. Waldheim served capably as always, but to spare his country additional grief he declined running for office in 1992. He has since served as a respected elder statesman and a private citizen at home.

Further Reading

Kille, Kent J. "Leadership and Influence in the United Nations: A Comparative Analysis of the Secretaries General." Unpublished Ph.D. diss., Ohio State University, 2000.

Linn, Andrew J. "The Careers of Adolph Eichmann, Dr. Joseph Mengele, and Kurt Waldheim." Unpublished master's thesis, University of Louisville, 2002.

Ryan, James D. *The United Nations under Kurt Waldheim, 1972–1981.* Lanham, Md.: Scarecrow Press, 2001.

Tittmann, Harold H. *The Waldheim Affair: Democracy Subverted.* Dunkirk, N.Y.: O. Frederick, 2000.

Vansant, Jacqueline. "Political Memoirs and Negative Rhetoric: Kurt Waldheim's In the Eye of the Storm and Im Glaspalast der Weltpolitik." *Biography* 25, no. 2 (2002): 343–362.

Waldheim, Kurt. *In the Eye of the Storm: A Memoir.* Bethesda, Md.: Alder and Alder, 1986.

Kurt Waldheim *(UN Photo/Y. Nagata)*

Weizmann, Chaim (1874–1952) *president of Israel*

Chaim Weizmann was born in Motol, in the Russian Empire (present day Belarus), on November 27, 1874, the son of a successful Jewish merchant. He was raised in a fervent Zionist atmosphere and was inculcated with beliefs that Jews should resurrect the ancient state of Israel as a homeland. Weizmann proved himself a brilliant student and, because Russian authorities restricted Jewish access to higher education, he enrolled at the University of Freiburg, Switzerland, and the University of Geneva. He graduated with the highest possible honors in 1900 and lectured on chemistry at his alma mater for several years. However, Weizmann also found time to join the World Zionist Organization to develop his political and religious views. Thereafter the twin themes of science and Zionism dominated his life. However, he disagreed with the cautious brand of leadership dominating Zionist thinking at that time and gradually formulated what he called synthetic Zionism to reconcile the competing schools of thought extant. In 1904 Weizmann arrived at the University of Manchester, England, to teach and research. While present he met and befriended Prime Minister ARTHUR BALFOUR, who seriously considered his suggestions for a Jewish state. He visited Palestine soon after and established a company to expedite the settlement of Jewish settlers there. By 1914 he was also de facto leader of the worldwide Zionist movement and intensified the push for a Jewish homeland. Weizmann greatly enhanced his career in World War I as a military researcher and was responsible for the invention of acetone in smokeless gunpowder.

Weizmann carefully used his friendship with the British elite to advocate his beliefs. These efforts culminated in the Balfour Declaration of November 1917, whereby Great Britain called for the eventual creation of a Jewish state in Palestine. The following year the British also introduced him to FAISAL I of Syria (later Iraq) with whom he reached an accord on Arab-Jewish cooperation. By 1920 Weizmann headed the World Zionist Organization and methodically pursued his nationalist goals by traveling worldwide to raise money and recruits. In 1934 he returned to Palestine to establish the Daniel Sieff Research Institute in Rehovot. Weizmann also continued cooperating closely with the English authorities who administered Palestine as a League of Nations mandate—although he railed against moves to curtail Jewish immigration in the face of mounting Arab violence. During World War II Weizmann performed useful research in both the United States and Great Britain and formulated a process for synthetic rubber. However, his long absence from the Zionist leadership led to the rise of other, more militant figures such as DAVID BEN-GURION and MENACHEM BEGIN, who proved willing to fight both the Arabs and England for a homeland. After the war Weizmann addressed the new United Nations assembly in 1947 and—in view of the Nazi holocaust against the Jews—pleaded for creation of a Jewish state. He finally succeeded and Great Britain agreed to partition Palestine into Jewish and Arab portions. Weizmann was also instrumental in convincing American president HARRY S. TRUMAN to supply the new nation with arms and financial assistance in order to survive. Consequently, the day after Israel was founded in 1948 it received American diplomatic recognition.

Once the brief but victorious Arab-Israeli war concluded, the Jewish state of Israel reemerged following an absence of nearly 19 centuries. Weizmann was appointed president of the new provisional government but real power was ultimately assumed by Ben-Gurion. On February 16, 1949, Weizmann was formally sworn in as the first official president, a largely ceremonial post. The restrictions of this office suited Weizmann perfectly for he was worn down by his exertions and devoted considerable time to publishing chemistry papers. Although his reputation as a Zionist leader had diminished with age, he was still a popular figure and easily won reelection in 1951. Weizmann died in Rehovot on November 9, 1952, a pivotal figure in the history of his nation. The world-famous Chaim Weizmann Research Institute in Rehovot has been named in his honor.

Further Reading

Avishal, Bernard. *The Tragedy of Zionism: How Its Revolutionary Past Haunts Israeli Democracy.* New York: Helios Press, 2002.

Miller, Rory. *Divided against Zion: Anti-Zionist Opposition in Britain to a Jewish State in Palestine, 1945–1948.* Portland, Ore.: Frank Cass, 2000.

Reinharz, Jehuda. *Chaim Weizmann: The Making of a Statesman.* New York: Oxford University Press, 1993.

———. "His Majesty's Zionist Emissary: Chaim Weizmann's Mission to Gibraltar in 1917." *Journal of Contemporary History* 27 (April 1992): 259–277.

Rose, Norman. *Chaim Weizmann: A Biography.* New York: Viking Press, 1986.

Weizmann, Chaim. *Trial and Error: The Autobiography of Chaim Weizmann.* New York: Harper, 1949.

———. *The Letters and Papers of Chaim Weizmann,* 23 vols. London: Oxford University Press, 1968–80.

Welensky, Roy (1907–1991) *prime minister of the Central African Federation*

Roy Welensky was born in Salisbury, Southern Rhodesia (Zimbabwe), on January 20, 1907, the son of a Lithuanian Jewish immigrant and a South African mother. Poorly educated, he worked many years with the railroads and became active in the railwaymen's trade union. Welensky, over six feet tall and 250 pounds in his prime, was also physically robust and became Rhodesia's heavyweight boxing champion between 1926 and 1928. In 1938 he was elected to the Northern Rhodesia (Zambia) legislative council and worked to protect the rights of white laborers in their disputes with cheaper black Africans. Intent upon preserving white racial privileges, he also founded the Labour Party in 1941. Throughout World War II Welensky was director of manpower in northwestern Rhodesia and fulfilled his assignment to the satisfaction of British authorities; he would be knighted for these efforts in 1953. Prior to that, Welensky expanded his political activities by advocating a stronger union between the two Rhodesias to cement white political and economic supremacy over the indigenous black population. In 1953 the British government allowed the new Central African Federation to be born, although it now included the region of Nyasaland (Malawi). The three regional governments closely coordinated their efforts to preserve their privileged positions, despite resounding opposition by local African leaders. Welensky, meanwhile, was admitted into the government as minister of transport under Prime Minister Sir Godfrey Huggins. Three years later he replaced Huggins and became the federation's second prime minister and head of the United Federal Party.

The Central African Federation was a dream come true for Welensky and others who embraced notions of white supremacy, but it was doomed from the start. White settlers, comprising only 5 percent of the population, controlled the land and the political process to the exclusion of the overwhelming black majority. Resentment was rife and occasioned numerous and bloody protests. In 1959 Welensky was forced to declare a state of emergency and cracked down harshly on the opposition. His excesses soon came to the attention of the British government. In 1960 Prime Minister HAROLD MACMILLAN questioned the efficacy of white rule and hoped some kind of multiracial democracy would emerge in the federation. Welensky, however, remained firmly wedded to white supremacy and adamantly opposed any form of power sharing. The hulking prime minister made several trips to London to defend his regime but the British remained unmoved. Welensky then made threatening noises about declaring independence and leaving the Commonwealth altogether, but he relented. In 1963 he reluctantly attended the Victoria Falls Conference, which granted independence to the new states of Zambia and Malawi, effectively breaking up the short-lived federation. Welensky angrily denounced Macmillan but ultimately determined that the last bastion of white rule in Central Africa, Southern Rhodesia, would at least remain part of the British Commonwealth. To his last days he was embittered over the demise of his new homeland.

Welensky stood for a seat in the Rhodesian parliament in 1964 but was defeated, and concluded his political career. The following year he bitterly opposed IAN D. SMITH's efforts to seek complete independence from Great Britain—the very act he himself had once proposed in 1960. For the next 15 years he lived as a private individual until 1980, when Rhodesia became the new nation of Zimbabwe under African majority rule. The following year Welensky and his family relocated to Britain where he died on December 5, 1991. He was an effective politician but his cherished federation proved so fraught with racism that it could not survive the challenge of rising African nationalism.

Further Reading

Allighan, Garry. *The Welensky Story.* London: Macdonald, 1962.

Clegg, Edward M. *Race and Politics: Partnership in the Federation of Rhodesia and Nyasaland.* New York: Oxford University Press, 1960.

Franklin, Henry. *Unholy Wedlock; the Failure of the Central African Federation.* London: G. Allen and Unwin, 1963.

Makaya, Peter. "Sir Roy Welensky and the Federation of Rhodesia and Nyasaland, 1907–1964." Unpublished master's thesis, Georgia State University, 1977.

Welensky, Roy. *Welensky's 4000 days: The Life and Death of the Federation of Rhodesia and Nyasaland.* New York: Roy Publishers, 1964.

Wood, J. R. T. *The Welensky Papers: A History of the Federation of Rhodesia and Nyasaland.* Durban, South Africa: Graham, 1983.

Whitlam, Gough (1916–) *prime minister of Australia*

Edward Gough Whitlam was born in Kew, Australia, on July 11, 1916, the son of a successful lawyer. After serving with the Royal Australian Air Force in World War II he attended the University of Sydney to study law and was admitted to the bar in 1947. In 1952 Whitlam successfully ran for a seat in Parliament as a Labor Party member and held it for the next 26 years. Labor was then politically marginalized owing to a strong resurgence by the Liberal (actually conservative) Party, but Whitlam determined to revamp it and increase its appeal to the rising middle class. In 1959 he became a member of the party's parliamentary board and the following year he rose to deputy leader. However, Whitlam's reforms caused great resentment among the traditional old guard of the left wing and he narrowly escaped being ejected from the party for his support for Catholic schools. The intraparty battle continued until February 1967 when Whitlam finally supplanted the more traditional Arthur Caldwell as head of Labor. He was now free to accelerate his efforts at bringing the party more toward the political center and dropping its procommunist orientation. His endeavors bore fruit in 1969 when Labor enlarged its parliamentary holdings by 7 percent, and in December 1972, while campaigning under the slogan of "It's time," Whitlam captured the prime ministership. He was the first Labor leader to hold high office since 1949. Labor also commanded a large majority in the House of Representatives, although it came short in controlling the Senate.

Now in power, Whitlam instituted changes on a number of fronts. In foreign policy he extended diplomatic recognition to Communist China in 1971 and the following year he ended conscription and brought Australian troops home from Vietnam. He also entered into talks with Papua New Guinea to establish a time frame for granting independence. Closer to home, Whitlam passed rules affording equal pay for women, greater recognition and rights for Australia's aboriginal peoples, and limits upon American and British influence in cultural matters. Furthermore, the government lowered the voting age to 18, introduced free college education for qualified candidates, expanded welfare benefits, and finally abandoned the traditionally race-oriented approach to non-white immigration. After two decades of conservative rule, Whitlam's social reforms forever altered the political landscape of Australia.

Despite his success at social engineering, Whitlam failed to greatly improve the national economy. Australia remained beset by protracted periods of stagnation and rising inflation brought on by the 1973 Arab oil embargo throughout his tenure in office. His major economic initiatives were also blocked by the Liberal-controlled Senate. In 1974 Whitlam scheduled early elections to try to break the legislative deadlock, but Labor actually lost seats in the House while the Senate remained unchanged. This defeat emboldened Conservatives under MALCOLM FRASER to be more confrontational and in 1975 the Senate resolutely refused to fund more of the government's social programs. Whitlam was further pummeled by the outbreak of numerous administration scandals that further weakened his public standing. He could have dissolved Parliament and called for new elections to resolve the issues, but he refused and settled upon a war of nerves with the Senate. The budget impasse continued for several weeks until Sir John Kerr, Australia's English-appointed governor general, dismissed Whitlam from office and allowed Fraser to head an interim government. This was the first instance in 200 years that the British Crown intervened to remove an Australian head of state. An angry Whitlam then barnstormed the country seeking to upset the Conservatives, but Labor lost in a landslide and Fraser continued as prime minister.

Whitlam resumed his role as head of the opposition in Parliament until 1977, when Labor lost another national election. He thereupon resigned as party chief and finally withdrew from politics in 1978. Whitlam enjoyed a very active retirement and variously served as a university lecturer, Australia's United Nations representative for UNESCO, and head of various constitutional commissions. He has also penned a number of highly regarded books on political science. Whitlam is regarded as a well-intentioned prime minister and critical to the rebirth of the Labor Party but unable to manage the economy that ultimately did him in. His dismissal from office remains one of the most controversial episodes in Australian political history.

Further Reading

Emy, Hugh, Owen Hughes, and Race Mathews, eds. *Whitlam Re-visited: Policy Development, Policies, and Outcomes.* Leichhardt, New South Wales: Pluto Press, 1993.

Monk, Paul M. "Secret Intelligence and Escape Clauses: Australia and the Indonesian Annexation of East Timor, 1963–76." *Critical Asian Studies* 33 (June 2001): 181–208.

Powell, Mike. "The Whitlam Labor Government: Barnard and Whitlam, a Significant Historical Dyad." *Australian Journal of Politics and History* 43, no. 2 (1997): 183–199.

Pusey, Michael. *The Experience of Middle Australia: The Dark Side of Economic Reform.* New York: Cambridge University Press, 2003.

Warhurst, John. "Transitional Hero: Gough Whitlam and the Australian Labor Party." *Australian Journal of Political Science* 31 (July 1996): 243–252.

Whitlam, Gough. *Abiding Interests.* St. Lucia, Qld.: University of Queensland Press, 1997.

Wilhelm II (1859–1941) *emperor of Germany*

Frederick Wilhelm Victor Albrecht von Hohenzollern was born in Potsdam, Prussia, on January 27, 1859, a son of Prince Frederick of Prussia and Victoria, eldest daughter of England's Queen Victoria. A difficult birth left him with a badly deformed left arm and throughout life the prince tended to overcompensate through arrogance and profanity. After passing through the University of Bonn, he was commissioned into the Prussian army and became extremely fond of military life and parades. More important, he absorbed the Prussian sense of martial superiority to other nations, a strident sense of duty to the kingdom, and intolerance toward any opinions but his own. To his peculiar mindset, he was invariably right and regarded differing attitudes as both treasonous and "un-German." With the defeat of France in 1871, Germany had been transformed from a collection of independent states to a single, unified empire under Prussian military and political leadership. In March 1888 the 29-year-old Wilhelm was suddenly thrust into leadership, following the death of his father, when he was enthroned as kaiser (emperor). The wily chancellor Otto von Bismarck and others believed that the young monarch would be more pliable than his father toward state policies, but the two leaders were soon at cross-purposes. Wilhelm, wishing to exercise his independence from Bismarck, suddenly dismissed him in 1890 and decided to personally lead Germany down a new path. In time his ascension had disastrous consequences for Germany—and Europe.

Wilhelm, possessing none of the diplomatic finesse of Bismarck, embarked on an ultranationalistic campaign of militarism and expansionism. Utterly contemptuous of France, he espoused similar views toward Russia and ended the long-standing treaty of friendship between the two countries. Wilhelm was also determined to establish a global colonial empire like other European nations and commenced construction of a large and powerful navy. This build-up earned him the ire of Great Britain, then the world's leading naval power, which felt that Wilhelm's imperialistic drive directly threatened its own empire. Moreover Wilhelm's arrogant behavior further insulted and alienated British public opinion. In 1898 he openly lauded the South Africa Boers in their ill-fated war for independence, and several years later, during an interview in England, he openly proclaimed his countrymen's dislike for that country. Wilhelm's *Weltpolitik* (world policy) thus remained bent on securing Germany's imperial place under the sun, regardless of the circumstances. Such thoughtless behavior drove France, Russia, and England into a grand military alliance against Germany—the Triple Entente. Germany, meanwhile, entered into a secret alliance with the Austro-Hungarian Empire. In July 1914, after Archduke Ferdinand was assassinated by a Serbian nationalist, the kaiser firmly supported Emperor FRANZ JOSEPH's ultimatum toward Serbia. This in turn brought on a rapid Russian mobilization by Czar NICHOLAS II and a German declaration of war. Furthermore, once German forces violated Belgian neutrality, England sided with France and the Russians. Germany was thus caught in the pincers of a two-front war. Over the next four years World War I unfolded with unparalleled ferocity and proved disastrous for all involved.

During the war years Wilhelm abrogated his responsibilities for leadership and slowly surrendered more and more political power to Generals Erich von Ludendorff and PAUL VON HINDENBERG. Consequently he had very little to say about the disastrous policy of resuming unrestricted submarine warfare at sea in 1917, despite the forebodings of Chancellor THEOBALD VON BETHMANN HOLLWEG. Consequently the United States was brought into the war on behalf of the Allies, and the infusion of 1 million American soldiers quickly tipped the scales against Germany. By the fall of 1918 the war was lost, yet President WOODROW WILSON, who considered Wilhelm an aggressor, refused to consider an armistice with the imperial government. After considerable maneuvering in Berlin, buttressed by the fact that the army was on the verge of mutiny and would no longer follow the kaiser, Wilhelm abdicated and fled to Holland on November 10, 1918. Wilson and other Allied leaders wanted him tried for war crimes but the Dutch government declined to extradite him. Wilhelm spent the rest of his life in luxurious exile at Doorn Castle, awaiting the day when the German people would depose the Weimar Republic and invite him back to the throne. After the rise of ADOLF HITLER in 1933, this became an impossibility and the former emperor continued living in isolation. When the Germans conquered Holland in May 1940, Hitler refused to acknowledge his presence and forbade ranking officers from even visiting him. Wilhelm died at Doorn on June 4, 1941, a symbolic anachronism from an imperial age. His erratic, bellicose behavior compounded Germany's strategic isolation and was a major cause of his own downfall.

Further Reading

Anderson, Margaret L. *Practicing Democracy: Elections and Political Culture in Imperial Germany.* Princeton, N.J.: Princeton University Press, 2000.

Clark, Christopher M. *Kaiser Wilhelm.* Harlow: Longman, 2000.

Eley, Geoff, and James Retallack, eds. *Wilhelminism and Its Legacies: German Modernities, Imperialism, and the Meanings of Reform, 1890–1930.* New York: Berghahn Books, 2003.

Feuchtwanger, E. J. *Imperial Germany, 1850–1918.* New York: Routledge, 2001.

Jefferies, Matthew. *Imperial Culture in Germany, 1871–1918.* Basingstoke: Palgrave Macmillan, 2003.

Macdonogh, Giles. *The Last Kaiser: The Life of William II.* New York: St. Martin's Press, 2000.

Seligman, Matthew S. *Germany from Reich to Republic, 1871–1918: Politics, Hierarchy, and Elites.* New York: St. Martin's Press, 2000.

Wilhelm II. *Wilhelm II: The Kaiser's Personal Monarchy, 1888–1900.* New York: Cambridge University Press, 2004.

Williams, Eric (1911–1981) *prime minister of Trinidad and Tobago*

Eric Eustace Williams was born in Trinidad on September 25, 1911, into a modest background. In concert with the small island of Tobago, Trinidad forms a small chain immediately north of the Venezuelan coastline. A distinguished student, Williams was admitted to Oxford University in 1932 and graduated six years later with a doctorate in Caribbean history. He subsequently joined the faculty at Howard University in Washington, D.C., and began a lifelong diatribe against British cultural superiority. Over the next several years Williams became a recognized authority on Caribbean slavery and published several books on the topic. He also joined the Caribbean Commission, established during World War II to better coordinate the colonial holdings of Great Britain, Holland, and the United States. However, he was extremely political in outlook and his professed leanings toward socialistic governance alienated him from members of the board. Williams then came home to found a militant cultural group, the Teachers Educational and Cultural Association (TECA) to foment anticolonial change. After teaching several years on Trinidad, Williams carried his politicizing one step further by founding the People's National Movement (PNM) in January 1956. His activism and unrelenting criticism of colonialism rendered him one of Trinidad and Tobago's most popular public figures. In 1956 the PNM won a round of legislative elections, and Williams was appointed chief minister at a time when negotiations for independence from Great Britain were in the offing. Williams also directed his nation's entry into the new West Indies Federation, although, when the PNM lost power in 1962, the federation was dissolved. Prior to this, the PNM adopted more leftist policies, swept the latest legislative elections, and Williams was appointed the first prime minister in August 1962. But having led Trinidad and Tobago to independence, he nonetheless decided to remain within the British Commonwealth for the economic benefits it offered.

Once in power, Williams enacted a policy he deemed "empirical socialism," with programs for free education and generous social services. He also pursued an independent foreign policy by establishing diplomatic relations with Communist Cuba, but Williams was careful to balance his ideological zeal with pragmatism and he maintained good relations with the United States. In economic terms, his government moderated its socialistic slant and invited foreign investment. He also instituted a series of carefully crafted five-year plans to enhance the island's economic growth and independence. This program, coupled with the rise in oil export prices, led Trinidad and Tobago to become the wealthiest nation among the British Caribbean islands.

Williams's success as a leader and his sound economic planning made him politically popular, and he easily won reelection in 1966 and 1971. However, in 1970 the islands were racked by a "black power" movement that painted Williams as overtly pro-European. When a radical-led rebellion erupted in the armed forces he declared a state of emergency to suppress it. After 1973 his position was buttressed by surging petroleum prices following the Arab oil boycott and in 1976 the PNM won another decisive election victory. Williams ultimately served 20 years as prime minister before dying in office on March 29, 1981. The final years of his tenure were marked by declining influence over island politics and growing detachment from public affairs in general. Nonetheless, his longevity, high scholarship, and economic success mark him as one of the most influential Caribbean leaders of recent history.

Further Reading

Cateau, Heather, and H. H. Selwyn. *Capitalism and Slavery Fifty Years Later: Eric Eustace Williams—a Reassessment of the Man and His Work.* New York: Peter Lang, 2000.

Darity, William A. "Eric Williams and Slavery: A West Indian Viewpoint?" *Callaloo* 20, no. 4 (1997): 801–816.

Douglas, Lincoln H. "A Pedagogy of the Public Square: The Story of Eric Williams's Adult Education Movement." Unpublished Ed.D., Northern Illinois University, 2000.

Feyno, Mario. "The Greatness Thrust upon Eric Williams." *Caribbean Quarterly* 47, no. 4 (2001): 49–57.

Henry, Ralph. "Eric Williams and the Reversal of the Unequal Legacy of Capitalism and Slavery." *Callaloo* 20, no. 4 (1997): 829–848.

Meighoo, Kirk P. *Politics in a 'Half Made Society': Trinidad and Tobago, 1925–2001.* Princeton, N.J.: M. Wiener Publishers, 2003.

Williams, Eric. *Inward Hunger: The Education of a Prime Minister.* Chicago: University of Chicago Press, 1971.

Wilson, Harold (baron of Rievaulx) (1916–1995)
prime minister of Great Britain

James Harold Wilson was born in Yorkshire, England, on March 11, 1916, the son of a government chemist. An exceptional student, he was admitted to Jesus College, Oxford University, and studied politics, philosophy, and economics. In 1938 he started a teaching career at Oxford and also worked with Lord Beaverbrook in drawing up plans for what became the British welfare state. Wilson began his political career in 1945 when he successfully ran for a seat in Parliament as a Labour Party member. His skills at politicking were impressive, and within two years Prime Minister CLEMENT ATTLEE assigned him a seat on his cabinet as president of the board of trade. Aged but 31 years, Wilson became the youngest sitting minister since William Pitt the Younger in the 18th century. He served the administration effectively until 1951, when he resigned over the charging of health care fees to fund British participation in the Korean War. After this act Wilson was closely identified with the left wing of his party, although he consistently displayed pragmatic streaks that infuriated party purists. He continued rising through the party hierarchy, and in 1960 unsuccessfully challenged Hugh Gaitskell for the mantle of party leadership. However, when Gaitskell died unexpectedly in 1963, Wilson was the overwhelming favorite to succeed him. He then astutely united the warring factions of his party behind a center-left agenda and in 1964 defeated Conservative ALEXANDER DOUGLAS-HOME to become the first Labour prime minister in 13 years. Plain-spoken and simply attired, Wilson reveled in his unpretentious middle-class background and sought to closely identify with the majority of British voters.

Wilson inherited a dispirited nation in economic straits. Great Britain had long ceased being a world military power, and its fundamental industrial and economic weaknesses served to underscore that reality. Previously, Wilson campaigned on a pledge to bring science and technology into the forefront of British modernization but he proceeded cautiously. He attempted limiting increases in wages and prices but to no avail, as the economy continued sinking. Many of the more radical elements in Labour railed against Wilson's refusal to embark on dramatic social programs, but his efforts were continually undercut by the weak economy. Conditions worsened in the face of major strikes and by 1967 Wilson was necessarily forced to devaluate the pound—a feat he had pledged himself against. It took a further two years to restore Britain's international balance of payments with a surplus.

Despite problems at home, Wilson remained determined to assert Britain's role abroad. In 1967 he applied for membership in the European Common Market to facilitate trade, but the effort stalled when French president CHARLES DE GAULLE vetoed the application. England's inability to influence foreign affairs, even within its own Commonwealth, became painfully apparent when Prime Minister IAN D. SMITH of Rhodesia unilaterally declared independence. Wilson could only respond ineffectively through the use of sanctions. During his tenure widespread violence in Northern Ireland also erupted and Britain deployed military troops and reimposed direct rule to restore order. On a more positive note, Wilson did pass useful social legislation touching upon race relations, abortion, and divorce. And, while giving verbal support to the American-led war in Vietnam, he flatly refused a request by President LYNDON B. JOHNSON to commit British troops to combat. He also withdrew the remaining British garrisons from the Far East as a cost-cutting measure. But by 1970 Labour had worn out its welcome with the British electorate, and that June Wilson was defeated and replaced by the Conservative EDWARD HEATH.

Wilson continued on in Parliament as head of the opposition, and the Conservatives proved no better at handling the economy than Labour. Elections held in February 1974 returned Wilson as prime minister with the smallest of majorities. Again, his tenure in office was beset by a declining economy, bitter strikes, inflation, and overall economic malaise. Worse yet, Britain had been brought into the EEC by Heath and its membership was up for renewal. The majority of Labour bitterly opposed its continuance but Wilson orchestrated a public referendum that confirmed British membership. This was the biggest accomplishment of his second term. After several more months of poor economic performance, Wilson suddenly resigned from office on March 16, 1976, and was replaced by JAMES CALLAGHAN. The announcement stunned the public, but Queen Elizabeth II responded by elevating him to the peerage as Baron Wilson of Rievaulx. He continued on in the House of Lords for several more years before retiring from public life in 1983. Wilson struggled with cancer for a decade before dying in London on May 24, 1995. Though little appreciated while in office, he compiled the longest tenure in office of any modern Labour leader (eight years) and performed effectively despite the economic problems he inherited.

Further Reading

Daddow, Oliver J. *Harold Wilson and European Integration: Britain's Second Application to Join the EEC.* Portland, Ore.: Frank Cass, 2003.

Dean, Dennis. "The Race Relations Policy of the First Wilson Government." *20th Century British History* 11, no. 3 (2000): 259–283.

Dockrill, Saki. "Forging the Anglo-American Global Defense Partnership: Harold Wilson, Lyndon Johnson, and the Washington Summit, December, 1964." *Journal of Strategic Studies* 23, no. 4 (2000): 107–130.

Rose, Peter. *How the Troubles Came to Northern Ireland.* New York: Palgrave in association with the Institute of Contemporary British History, 2000.

Seldon, Anthony, and Kevin Hickson, eds. *New Labour, Old Labour: The Wilson and Callaghan Governments, 1974–79.* New York: Routledge, 2004.

Wilson, Harold. *Memoirs: The Making of a Prime Minister, 1916–64.* London: Weidenfeld and Nicolson, 1986.

Young, John W. "The Wilson Government's Reform of Intelligence Coordination, 1967–68." *Intelligence and National Security* 16, no. 2 (2001): 133–151.

Wilson, Woodrow (1856–1924) *president of the United States*

Thomas Woodrow Wilson was born in Staunton, Virginia, on December 28, 1856, the son of a Presbyterian minister. He inherited from his father stern moral convictions and a personal sense of mission that defined his entire life. Wilson attended college intermittently due to poor health, but he finally graduated from Princeton University in 1879. He next studied law and briefly opened a legal practice in Atlanta, Georgia, before pursuing graduate studies at Johns Hopkins University, Baltimore. There Wilson found his niche as an outstanding historian, and he graduated with honors in 1886. He taught with distinction for many years and in 1902 was elevated to president of Princeton University. There he also acquired fame as a determined educational reformer and in 1910 he received the Democratic nomination for the governorship of New Jersey. The scholarly Wilson proved himself a surprisingly effective campaigner and won easily. Once in office, he pursued his personal credo of modernization and reform, securing such notable legislation as direct primaries, anticorruption laws, employers' liability, and regulation of public utilities. Success here made him a viable candidate for the Democratic presidential nomination for 1912, and he was finally chosen on the 46th ballot. The national election that year was thrown askew when former president THEODORE ROOSEVELT, having failed to dislodge Republican incumbent WILLIAM HOWARD TAFT, ran as an independent on the Bull Moose Party ticket. The conservative vote was therefore split, and Wilson managed to out-poll both opponents and gain the White House.

As president, Wilson subscribed to a notion of strong executive leadership and used it effectively to enact his reform-minded agenda. He quickly secured a number of historically important bills, including a revised tariff, the Federal Reserve Act, and the Federal Trade Commission Act, and imposition of the first income tax. But from the onset foreign affairs began dominating Wilson's attention and energies. In 1914 he refused to recognize the dictatorship of Mexico's VICTORIANO HUERTA, and ordered American naval forces to seal the port of Veracruz to prevent his regime from receiving arms supplies. Wilson subsequently ordered American troops into Mexico to pursue the guerrilla bandit Pancho Villa. Villa was never caught but the campaign was well conducted by General John J. Pershing, in whom Wilson explicitly confided. The tempo of international tensions had climaxed in August 1914 when World War I erupted in Europe. Wilson, strongly backed by public opinion, was committed to a policy of neutrality toward all belligerents. Unfortunately German hostility toward neutral shipping at sea was underscored by the new submarine warfare. In May 1915, when the British liner *Lusitania* was sunk with the loss of 128 American lives, Wilson sternly warned the Germans to refrain from U-boat warfare but otherwise remained neutral. The political wisdom of this move paid dividends in the 1916 presidential election when Wilson was narrowly reelected under the slogan, "He kept us out of war." The Germans refrained until the spring of 1917, when General PAUL VON HINDENBERG announced resumption of submarine warfare—regardless of the consequences. At this juncture, Wilson felt that United States intervention on behalf of France and Great Britain was all but inevitable. He therefore asked for and received a declaration of war against the Central Powers on April 6, 1917. "The world," he insisted, "must be made safe for democracy." This proved no small task, as the United States was

Woodrow Wilson *(Library of Congress)*

woefully unprepared for modern war and had to raise a gigantic army from scratch. But, assisted by the enlightened leadership of General Pershing, American forces arrived in Europe during the spring of 1918 and tipped the balance of the war against Germany on the western front. By November 1918 Kaiser WILHELM II was forced to abdicate, and the Germans concluded an armistice recognizing their defeat.

Wilson's entrenched idealism was never more apparent than during the peace negotiations at Paris in the spring of 1919. His overarching principles had been the defeat of imperial Germany and concrete measures to guarantee the peace afterward. Therefore, in January 1918 he had outlined his famous Fourteen Points, a set of political principles intended to enshrine self-determination and national boundaries. More important, it called for creation of an international body, the League of Nations, which would defuse world tensions, circumvent war, or carry out actions against aggressor nations. To emphasize the urgency of his beliefs, Wilson attended the Paris Peace Conference in person, becoming the first president to conduct foreign policy abroad. And, while he failed to limit reparations levied against Germany, he prevented France from detaching the Rhineland and other areas from that country. He also dissuaded the Italians from seizing Dalmatia, but could not convince Japan to relent from acquiring the Shantung peninsula in China. Happily, European leaders were also receptive to the League of Nations—although Wilson faced a much harder sell at home. Elections in 1918 had delivered Congress into the hands of the Republicans, who felt that commitments to the League of Nations would embroil America in commitments abroad and end its traditional isolationism.

Wilson came home in 1919 determined to force American acceptance of the League of Nations. With the best of intentions, he believed this was a moral responsibility that the nation must shoulder, but his puritanical stridency worked against him. From the onset Wilson made it clear to Congress that no compromise legislation would be acceptable to him—it was all or nothing. But the Republicans were equally adamant that American interests abroad should never be beholden to any international body. Undeterred, Wilson embarked on a strenuous national campaign to secure its passage, only to suffer a severe stroke en route. When political compromise proved impossible, the Senate rejected the League of Nations in November 1919. Wilson remained a near-invalid for the rest of his term in office, a mere shadow of the steely executive he had been. When Democratic candidate James Cox insisted on carrying the cause of the League of Nations into the 1920 elections, he was handily defeated by Republican WARREN G. HARDING. Wilson's idealistic dream of a mechanism to enforce world peace thus vanished, but for his efforts he received the 1919 Nobel Peace Prize. He died in Washington, D.C., on February 3, 1924, a headstrong, inflexible moralist but among the most accomplished executives in American history.

Further Reading

Ambrosius, Lloyd E. *Wilsonianism: Woodrow Wilson and His Legacy in American Foreign Relations.* New York: Palgrave Macmillan, 2002.

Auchincloss, Louis. *Woodrow Wilson.* New York: Viking, 2000.

Bucklin, Steven J. *Realism and American Foreign Policy: Wilsonians and the Kennan-Morganthau Thesis.* Westport, Conn.: Praeger, 2001.

Burton, David H. *Taft, Wilson, and World Order.* Madison, Wis.: Associated University Presses, 2003.

Cooper, John M. *Breaking the Heart of the World: Woodrow Wilson and the Fight for League of Nations.* New York: Cambridge University Press, 2001.

Davis, Donald E., and Eugene P. Trani. *The First Cold War: The Legacy of Woodrow Wilson in U.S.-Soviet Relations.* Columbia: University of Missouri Press, 2002.

Lynch, A. "Woodrow Wilson and the Principle of 'National Self-Determination': A Reconsideration." *Reviews of International Studies* 28 (April 2002): 419–436.

Macmillan, Margaret O. *Paris 1919: Six Months That Changed the World.* New York: Random House, 2002.

Pierce, Anne R. *Woodrow Wilson and Harry Truman: Missions and Power in American Foreign Policy.* Westport, Conn.: Praeger, 2003.

Startt, James D. *Woodrow Wilson and the Press: Prelude to the Presidency.* New York: Palgrave Macmillan, 2004.

Witte, Sergei (1849–1915) *prime minister of Russia*

Sergei Yulyevich Witte was born in Tiflis, Georgia (in czarist Russia), on June 17, 1849, the son of a senior government bureaucrat. He passed through the University of Odessa in 1871 and was admitted to the governor general's chancellery. In 1877 he opened a successful railroad company employing modern business practices and was subsequently tapped by the imperial government to develop the national railway system. Witte, an accomplished organizer, was tremendously successful in this role and he proved instrumental in helping develop and refine the famous trans-Siberian railway linking European and Asiatic Russia. He eventually promulgated what became known as the "Witte system," which utilized railroad construction, protectionism, and foreign investment to accelerate Russia's nascent drive toward industrialization. In 1892 Witte was appointed minister of ways of communication by Czar Alexander III, and shortly afterward he assumed his most important role, minister of finance. Again, he acted decisively to update Russia's struggling capitalistic system. He created a state bank to finance industry, placed the ruble on the gold standard to facilitate conversion into other currencies, and secured favorable long-terms loans from France, Germany, and Great Britain. Moreover, Witte proved amazingly free from the prevailing and deep-seated prejudices of his day. With few exceptions, he appointed talented Jews, Poles, Ukrainians, and Germans to positions of high authority.

But even a genius of Witte's caliber could not overcome the inherent autocracy and backwardness of Russia's political institutions. His policies, which gravitated toward creation of a large and stable middle class, mostly alienated the aristocracy, including the new czar, NICHOLAS II. And, more than many contemporaries, Witte also realized that Russia needed time and peace to complete its transition to modernity. Therefore he vociferously opposed the government's expansionist policies in the Far East, which threatened to embroil the country in hostilities with Japan. After a series of economic depressions and labor disputes, the czar finally dismissed Witte as minister in 1903, reducing him to a ceremonial role as chairman of the committee of members. But when Russia was badly defeated in the Russo-Japanese War of 1904–05, he was called back into service as a peace negotiator in Portsmouth, New Hampshire. Assisted by American president THEODORE ROOSEVELT, Witte secured favorable terms, considering the magnitude of the disaster, and returned home a national hero. However, he arrived in a nation riven by strikes, labor unrest, and revolution, as the old order unraveled under the weight of leftist agitation. It was during this period that Witte, now formally restored to government service, made his greatest contributions.

Witte was autocratic by nature and an exponent of strong, centralized government. However, he realized that a degree of democratization would be necessary to forestall revolutionary unrest. Thus in 1905 he promulgated the October Manifesto, which outlined basic civil rights for Russian citizens for the first time in 300 years. It also enshrined constitutional government by creating Russia's first elected legislature, the Duma. Witte then became the nation's first prime minister and he negotiated a series of emergency loans from abroad to stabilize the tottering Russian government. Yet even at this late date, Witte failed to secure the czar's trust. In April 1906 he was dismissed a sec-

ond time and replaced by PYOTR STOLYPIN. While in retirement Witte found the time to help reorganize the State Council, but his influence on state affairs waned. He strongly but futilely argued against Russian participation in World War I and undertook several private initiatives to secure a negotiated settlement with Germany. Witte's death in St. Petersburg on March 12, 1915, spared him the agony of watching the imperial system collapse in fire and ruin in 1917. He was a highly capable minister whose talents were unequal to the task of modernizing Russian politics and society.

Further Reading

Crankshaw, Edward. *The Shadow of the Winter Palace: The Drift to Revolution, 1825–1917.* New York: Da Capo, 2000.

Harcave, Sidney. *Count Sergei Witte and the Twilight of Imperial Russia: A Biography.* Armonk, N.Y.: M.E. Sharpe, 2004.

Sergei Witte *(Library of Congress)*

Hildebrandt, David E. "Reports from St. Petersburg: The British Embassy's Evaluation of Sergei Witte's Economic and Industrial Programs, 1900–1901." Unpublished master's thesis, South West Texas State University, 1995.

Marks, Steven G. *Road to Power: The Trans-Siberian Railroad and the Colonization of Asian Russia, 1850–1917.* London: I. B. Tauris, 1991.

Tomaszewski, Fiona K. *A Great Russia: Russia and the Triple Entente, 1905–1914.* Westport, Conn.: Praeger, 2002.

Witte, Sergei. *Memoirs of Count Witte.* Armonk, N.Y.: M. E. Sharpe, 1990.

Wood, Alan. *The Origins of the Russian Revolution, 1861–1917.* New York: Routledge, 2003.

Y

Yaméogo, Maurice (1921–1993) *president of Burkina Faso*

Maurice Yaméogo was born in Koudougor, French Upper Volta (Burkina Faso), in December 1921, a member of the influential Mossi tribe. He was trained locally at missionary schools before entering the French civil service. In 1932 Upper Volta was joined to nearby Cote d'Ivoire by the French for administrative purposes and did not emerge as a separate entity until 1948. Two years earlier Yaméogo had been elected to the new territorial legislature and the Grand Council of all West Africa as part of the Union Voltaic, a Catholic-dominated party that opposed political domination by the Cote d'Ivoire. Yaméogo was repeatedly elected to the legislature and in March 1957 Premier Ouezzin Coulibaly appointed him minister of agriculture and he joined the Parti Démocratique Unifié (PDF), Unified Democratic Party. After Coulibaly died in September 1958, Yaméogo replaced him as president of the PDF and premier. In this capacity he directed the colony to abandon the French-speaking federation structure proposed by LÉOPOLD SÉDAR SENGHOR, which ultimately caused its collapse. Upper Volta at that time was locked in deep discussion over its impending independence from France, and dissension arose within the ranks of the PDF. Yaméogo countered by establishing the Union Démocratique Voltaïque (UDV), Voltaic Democratic Union, in December 1959, which went on to capture the legislature in new elections. The following year, once Upper Volta became independent, Yaméogo was retained in high office as the new nation's first president. In 1965 he was reelected with 99.98 percent of votes cast in tightly controlled elections.

As president, Yaméogo instituted a draconian, authoritarian style of leadership. He outlawed the political opposition and was seconded by a rubber-stamp legislature. His country, then among the poorest in the world, was further beset by his extravagant lifestyle. In 1966 he wed a local beauty queen half his age and spent $100,000 on his ceremony and honeymoon. Such lavish excess greatly angered the citizenry and discontent rose. Once the burgeoning national deficit began ruining the economy, Yaméogo unilaterally imposed stringent austerity measures with reduced wages and higher taxes. Such measures were strongly resisted by organized labor, which inspired mass demonstrations against the regime. The spiraling escalation of violence induced the army to intervene on January 3, 1966, and Yaméogo was bloodlessly deposed. He was then arrested, charged with embezzlement, and detained over the next four years. Yaméogo was finally released under a general amnesty in 1970, although stripped of his civil rights.

Since 1970 Yaméogo vicariously resumed his political career through the activities of his son, Herman, a state minister. In 1977 he founded a new party, the Union Nationale pour la Démocratie et le Développement (UNDD), National Union for the Defense of Democracy, which scored heavily in elections, although he was not a candidate. To expedite his gradual rehabilitation, he was allowed to visit President Sangoule Lamizana and in 1980 he was allowed to serve as head of the UNDD's propaganda wing. However, his political rehabilitation was delayed several years following a coup in 1980, and his rights were not fully restored until 1991. At that time Yaméogo was living in Cote d'Ivoire and he died on a plane flight from there to Burkina Faso on September 15, 1993. He had ruled as a despot but his role as an architect of national independence was secure, and President Blaise Compaoré ordered three days of national mourning in his honor.

Further Reading

Boubacar, Diarra S. "Political Change, Rural Transformation and Development Administration: The Politics of Change and Development in Francophone Africa with Special Reference to the Upper Volta." Unpublished master's thesis, University of Minnesota, 1974.

Cordell, Dennis D., Joel W. Gregory, and Victor Piche. *Hoe and Wage: A Social History of a Circular Migration System in West Africa.* Boulder, Colo.: Westview Press, 1996.

Engberg-Pedersen, Lars. *Endangering Development: Politics, Projects, and Environment in Burkina Faso.* Westport, Conn.: Praeger, 2003.

Englebert, Pierre. *Burkina Faso: Unsteady Statehood in West Africa.* Boulder, Colo.: Westview Press, 1996.

McFarland, Daniel M., and Lawrence Rupley. *Historical Dictionary of Burkina Faso.* Lanham, Md.: Scarecrow Press, 1998.

Skinner, Elliott P. *The Mossi of Burkina Faso: Chiefs, Politicians, and Soldiers.* Prospect Heights, Ill.: Waveland Press, 1989.

Yoshida Shigeru (1878–1967) *prime minister of Japan*

Yoshida Shigeru was born in Tokyo on September 22, 1878, into a family of prominent politicians. He was subsequently adopted by a merchant whose wealth allowed him to obtain an elite education. Yoshida studied diplomacy at Tokyo Imperial University in 1906 and entered the diplomatic service. After holding numerous consular posts in China and Manchuria, he transferred to Washington, D.C., in 1919. That year he also represented Japan at the Paris Peace Conference before subsequently serving as ambassador in London. Yoshida proved himself a capable diplomat, and by 1928 he had served as minister to Sweden, Norway, and Denmark. However, by 1930 Japan itself was seized by a pervasive militant nationalism, which Yoshida decried. That year army officers in the government scuttled his nomination to serve as foreign minister on account of his liberal views. Yoshida then resumed his ambassadorship in Great Britain until 1939 when, disillusioned by Japan's drift toward war, he withdrew from diplomacy altogether and entered into business. Yoshida remained highly critical of Prime Minister TOJO HIDEKI's government throughout World War II, and in June 1945 he was imprisoned for suggesting surrender. Following the Japanese capitulation and Allied occupation of September 1945, Yoshida was released from jail. He was one of few senior officials untainted by wartime service.

Out of prison Yoshida was appointed foreign minister in an interim administration. In this capacity he

Yoshida Shigeru *(Library of Congress)*

met with General Douglas MacArthur, arranged for him to confer with Emperor HIROHITO, and also convinced him to allow the imperial system to be retained. In 1946 Yoshida became head of the Liberal Party and a major player in national politics. Japan was then governed by Prime Minister HATOYAMA ICHIRO, who was suddenly removed from power by Allied authorities, and on May 22, 1946, Yoshida took his place. His accession was a decisive moment in Japanese national and political history for it placed him in the forefront of occupation politics. Yoshida, a realist, submitted to the notion that Japan should remain closely meshed with the United States in defense and foreign policy matters while also pursuing modern industrialization. In time his policy became widely regarded as the "Yoshida Doctrine." He was also strongly anticommunist and pleased the Americans by purging the government and labor unions of leftists and their sympathizers. Yoshida nonetheless cooperated closely with occupation authorities and helped to craft a new constitution that granted women equal rights, enshrined freedom of expression, and made future Japanese military forces defensive in nature. He cultivated a strong personal following among allies in the Diet (legislature), which allowed him to rule in a near autocratic manner.

Under Yoshida's determined rule the Japanese economy rebounded and made its first strides toward world dominance. In 1951 he concluded a security pact with the United States that formalized existing defense arrangements, including the retention of American bases on Okinawa. His political fortunes crested in April 1952 when the Americans finally ended their military occupation, and Japan reacquired national sovereignty. That year he also declared Japan's intention—in concert with U.S. prerogatives—to recognize Taiwan's CHIANG KAI-SHEK as the sole legitimate leader of China. However, Yoshida resisted strong pressure by the United States to rearm Japan's military during the cold war, and also managed to limit the new National Defense Force to 150,000 men as planned. Despite his successes, Yoshida became increasingly unpopular due to his aloof manner and in December 1954 he was removed as both head of the Liberal Party and prime minister. He subsequently retired from politics and basked in his reputation as a highly respected elder statesman. Yoshida died in Osio on October 20, 1967, one of the most important Japanese politicians of the 20th century. He was largely responsible for Japan's reemergence into the community of nations, its acceptance of democratization, and its economic modernization. Consequently he received the first state funeral of the postwar period.

Further Reading

Beer, Lawrence W. *From Imperial Myth to Democracy: Japan's Two Constitutions, 1889–2001.* Boulder, Colo.: University Press of Colorado, 2002.

Finn, Richard B. *Winners in Peace: MacArthur, Yoshida, and Postwar Japan.* Berkeley: University of California Press, 1992.

Hellegers, Dale M. *We, the Japanese People: World War II and the Origins of the Japanese Constitution.* Stanford, Calif.: Stanford University Press, 2002.

Moore, Ray A. *Partners for Democracy: Crafting the New Japanese State under MacArthur.* New York: Oxford University Press, 2002.

Oinas-Kukkonen, Henry. *Tolerance, Suspicion, and Hostility: Changing U.S. Attitudes Toward the Japanese Communist Movement, 1944–1947.* Westport, Conn.: Greenwood Press, 2002.

Peaslee, Steven M. "Yoshida's Victory: Individual Roles and Greater Forces in Postwar Japanese Rearmament." Unpublished master's thesis, Harvard University, 1991.

Yoshida, Shigeru. *The Yoshida Memoirs: The Story of Japan in Crisis.* Westport, Conn.: Greenwood Press, 1973.

Yrigoyen, Hipólito (1850–1933) *president of Argentina*

Hipólito Yrigoyen was born in Buenos Aires, Argentina, on July 13, 1850, the son of a blacksmith. He briefly entered law school but quit to become police commissioner of a city neighborhood in 1879. Three years later he commenced his political career by acquiring a seat in the provincial legislature. Yrigoyen served briefly and taught at a girls' school for several years before finally returning to politics by joining the middle-class oriented Civic Union Party, Unión Cívica (UC). Following a failed revolt in 1891, the new Unión Cívica Radical (UCR), Radical Civic Union, split off from the UC, and Yrigoyen joined. In 1896 he assumed leadership of the UCR after the death of Leandro N. Alem. In this capacity he sought to mobilize the nation's rising middle class against the oligarchic interests traditionally dominating Argentine politics. Curiously, as a political figure,

Yrigoyen's public persona remained cloaked in obscurity. He rarely spoke in public, lived and dressed modestly in a run-down neighborhood, yet enjoyed a reputation for charismatic leadership. Part of his success lay in an uncanny ability to craft intricate political bargains behind the scenes. In 1912 the ruling Partido Autonomista Nacional (PAN), National Autonomous Party, sought to preempt rising discontent by expanding the voting franchise. However, rather than establishing a large conservative base, this played into Yrigoyen's extensive network of patronage. Elections held in 1916 established him as Argentina's first democratically elected president.

Yrigoyen presented himself as a champion of the middle class and continuing political reform, but he conducted his affairs conservatively. He did nothing to upset his patronage-based system and was also careful not to infringe upon traditional conservative interests. Internationally, he kept Argentina neutral during World War I, overhauled the university system, and nationalized the oil industry. Yet the nation was experiencing a deep economic depression that undermined the effect of his endeavors. The distress arising from rampant inflation occasioned numerous labor strikes that culminated in a bloody confrontation between workers and paramilitaries on January 9, 1919. Yrigoyen did nothing to assist his erstwhile allies and instead shored up his political base among moderates and conservatives. Consequently, by the time his first term ended in 1922, he had failed to implement the badly needed political reforms. That year his successor, Marcelo T. de Alvear, an aristocratic-leaning member of the UCR, succeeded him in office. Over the ensuing four years De Alvear managed to alienate moderate supporters by overtly catering to conservatives, and Yrigoyen, his former mentor, finally broke with him. The UCR was consequently split down the middle and Yrigoyen, running again for president, was decisively reelected with 60 percent of votes cast.

Yrigoyen's second term proved even more disruptive than his first. Verging on senility he had apparently lost his fine grasp of politics and failed to maintain his tangled alliances of patronage. Worse, after 1929 Argentina was beset by the Great Depression, which gutted the national economy. Yrigoyen was sensitive to the plight of the poor under such circumstances, but his open support for them incited the middle class and rich against the UCR. The military was also incensed by Yrigoyen's constant meddling in their affairs. On September 6, 1930, he was bloodlessly overthrown by the army and sent into exile. Yrigoyen was soon allowed back home but he never again held public office. He died in Buenos Aires on July 3, 1933, the most popular Argentine executive until JUAN PERÓN, but otherwise lacking a concrete political philosophy.

Further Reading

Hora, Roy. *The Landowners of the Argentine Pampas: A Social and Political History, 1860–1945.* New York: Oxford University Press, 2001.

Horowitz, Joel. "Argentina's Failed General Strike of 1921: A Critical Moment in the Radicals' Relations with Unions." *Hispanic American Historical Review* 75, no. 1 (1995): 57–79.

———. "Bosses and Clients: Municipal Employment in the Buenos Aires of the Radicals, 1916–30." *Journal of Latin American Studies* 31 (October 1999): 617–644.

Lewis, Daniel K. *The History of Argentina.* Westport, Conn.: Greenwood Press, 2001.

Potash, Robert A. *The Army and Politics in Argentina,* 3 vols. Stanford, Calif.: Stanford University Press, 1969–96.

Rock, David. *State Building and Political Movements in Argentina, 1860–1916.* Stanford, Calif.: Stanford University Press, 2002.

Yuan Shikai (Yuan Shih-K'ai) (1859–1916)
president of China

Yuan Shikai was born in Xiangcheng, Henan Province, China, on September 16, 1859, into an established aristocratic family. He received a classical Chinese education but failed the bureaucratic exams and opted instead for a military career. Yuan displayed considerable leadership abilities in 1882, when he rapidly suppressed a Japanese-inspired rebellion in Korea. During the unsuccessful Sino-Japanese War, 1894–95, he distinguished himself further for his logistical work, and subsequently led efforts to modernize the obsolete Chinese army with German advisers. Yuan returned to Beijing soon after and became an important player at the Qing (Manchu) imperial court. In 1889, when informed by conspirators of an impending rebellion against the Empress Ci Xi, he promptly betrayed them to the government and was promoted to governor of

Shandong. In 1900 he was responsible for suppressing the Boxer Rebellion against foreigners and greatly strengthened the forces under his command. He became one of the most powerful figures in northern China, and in 1901 he assumed duties as high commissioner of military and foreign affairs. A professional soldier, Yuan was painfully aware of China's growing military and economic backwardness, so he vigorously embraced reform and modernization. He pursued these policies to expand his military and political alliances and further enhance his national status. This fact did not go unnoticed by a wary Qing court, and by 1909 Yuan had been forced into retirement.

In October 1911 the Chinese revolution commenced, and the court urgently requested the previously disgraced Yuan to return to service. He did so coyly and on his own terms, more concerned with acting as a power broker than a general. The Qing dynasty was forced to abdicate, and the leading revolutionary, SUN YAT-SEN, was appointed provisional president. However, Yuan remained a force to reckon with and Sun was persuaded to step down and allow him to serve in his place. He assumed office in March 1912 and was immediately confronted by a nation bankrupt and verging on chaos. Yuan responded with plans to borrow enormous amounts of foreign money, a scheme widely resented by the Kuomintang (KMT) nationalists. Yuan then arranged for the KMT parliamentary leader to be murdered and banned his party. The result was a second revolution that Yuan easily crushed, and he consolidated his grip on power. He was formally sworn in on October 10, 1913, and three months later he dissolved the National Assembly. A new political council was then appointed, which granted Yuan dictatorial powers and made him president for life.

Yuan's momentary triumph was soon undermined by China's chronic military and political weakness. After World War I began in 1914, Japan eagerly annexed all German possessions in China, an act further whetting its appetite for aggression. Japan then presented Yuan's government with the notorious "Twenty-One Demands," which would have reduced the entire country to protectorate status. China's position was essentially hopeless, and by 1915 Yuan reluctantly accepted most of Japan's terms. Such subservience cost him his political credibility with most of the nation. He then blundered incredibly by renouncing the republic completely and establishing a

Yuan Shikai *(Library of Congress)*

new dynasty with himself as emperor. This move occasioned the outbreak of several rebellions and Yuan was summarily abandoned by most of his leading generals. After occupying the throne but a few days, he resigned. Yuan died a bitter and disillusioned man in Beijing on June 6, 1916. Many of his subordinates subsequently established themselves as regional warlords, which brought further chaos and disunity to China. Yuan was a talented soldier but overtly ambitious as a political figure. While reviled for his futile attempts to seize power, he remains one of the most effective national reformers of the late imperial period.

Further Reading

Esherick, Joseph. *Reform and the Revolution in China: The 1911 Revolution in Hunan and Hubei.* Ann Arbor: Center for Chinese Studies, University of Michigan, 1998.

Fung, Edmund S. K. *The Military Dimension of the Chinese Revolution: The New Army and Its Role in the Revolution of 1911.* Vancouver: University of British Columbia Press, 1980.

Hsueh, Chun-tu. *The Chinese Revolution of 1911.* Armonk, N.Y.: M. E. Sharpe, 1983.

Lin, Ming-te. "Yuan Shih-kai and the 1911 Revolution." *Chinese Studies in History* 15, nos. 3–4 (1982): 123–128.

MacKinnon, Stephen R. *Power and Politics in Late Imperial China: Yuan Shi-kai in Beijing and Tianji, 1901–1908.* Berkeley: University of California Press, 1980.

Reynolds, Douglas R. *China, 1895–1912: State-Sponsored Reforms and China's Late-Qing Revolution: Selected Essays from Zhongguo jindai shi (Modern Chinese History, 1840–1919).* Armonk, N.Y.: M. E. Sharpe, 1995.

Zarrow, Peter G. "Chinese Anarchists: Ideals and the Revolution of 1911." Unpublished Ph.D. diss., Columbia University, 1987.

Z

Zaghlūl, Sa'd (1857–1927) *prime minister of Egypt*

Sa'd Zaghlūl was born in Ibyanah, Egypt, in July 1857, into a family of modest means. After obtaining an Islamic education he attended Al-Azhar University in Cairo to study law and philosophy. It was there he absorbed the teachings of Jamal al-Din and Muhammad Abduh, two Islamic scholars with a pronounced modernizing, pro-Western bent. After graduation Zaghlūl passed through the Egyptian School of Law and in 1892 he was appointed judge in the Court of Appeals. By 1906 he was head of the Ministry of Education and advocated increased efforts to uplift the educational levels of all Egyptians. He also helped found the Hizb al-Ummah (People's Party) that stressed close cooperation with Great Britain. This was essential, as England had occupied Egypt and the Sudan since 1882 despite mounting resentment. Zaghlūl, meanwhile, also worked with the Ministry of Justice from 1910 to 1912, where he instituted many needed reforms. But in 1913 he resigned to protest the government's corrupt and shameless subservience to the British, after which he successfully stood for a seat in the Legislative Assembly. He was soon vice president of that body and reversed his previously pro-British stance in favor of independence. Zaghlūl was the first Egyptian figure of national standing to do so.

The onset of World War I in 1914 exacerbated tensions between Egypt and Great Britain. When the British imposed martial law and banned all political activity, riots broke out and the assembly was dissolved. Zaghlūl, like other nationalists, feared that England would reduce Egypt to a colony, and increased his political agitation for independence. In November 1918 he headed a Wafd (delegation) that approached the British High Commissioners to demand their immediate withdrawal. The British refused and responded to social unrest by arresting Zaghlūl in March 1919 and deporting him to Malta. He was released the following month and next ventured to the Paris Peace Conference to repeat his demands. He failed again to get results, and several months later, when the British dispatched Lord Milner to discuss possible independence, Zaghlūl instigated a boycott of the talks. In 1921 negotiations were again resumed but when Zaghlūl led large-scale disruptions, he was arrested a second time and exiled to Gibraltar. He was detained there two years while his reputation as Egypt's leading nationalist was enhanced. But this time his efforts proved successful, and in 1922 the British granted Egypt partial independence.

The British slowly relinquished control of Egypt, but when elections were allowed in December 1923, the Wafd Party won decisively and in January 1924

Zaghlūl became the country's first elected prime minister. However, nationalist resentment continued spilling out onto the street, and in November 1924 the British commander of the Egyptian army was assassinated. Zaghlūl then received an ultimatum from the British government demanding his resignation, and he left office after only 11 months. Nonetheless, the Wafd Party overwhelmingly won a new round of elections and, rather than have Zaghlūl reappointed prime minister, King Faud dissolved the parliament. In May 1926 the Wafd again carried the election, and Zaghlūl was allowed to serve as president of the Chamber of Deputies. He occupied this office until his death in Cairo on August 23, 1927. Zaghlūl is considered Egypt's first nationalist leader and a major force in the drive toward independence. Moreover, the Wafd Party he founded exerted tremendous influence upon political affairs for 30 years, until GAMAL ABDEL NASSER established a republic in 1952.

Further Reading

Badrawi, Malak. *Political Violence in Egypt, 1910–1925: Secret Societies, Plots, and Assassinations.* Richmond, England: Curzon, 2000.

Bishku, Michael B. "The British Empire and the Question of Egypt's Future, 1919–1922." Unpublished Ph.D. diss., New York University, 1981.

McIntyre, John D. *The Boycott of the Milner Mission: A Study in Egyptian Nationalism.* New York: P. Lang, 1985.

Pollard, Clarissa L. "Nurturing the Nation: The Family Politics of the 1919 Egyptian Revolution." Unpublished Ph.D. diss., University of California–Berkeley, 1997.

Smith, Russell Y. "The Making of an Egyptian Nationalist: The Political Career of Saad Zaghlūl Pasha to 1919." Unpublished Ph.D. diss., Ohio State University, 1972.

Terry, Janice J. *The Wafd, 1919–1952: Cornerstone of Egyptian Political Power.* London: Third World Centre for Research and Pub., 1982.

Zhao Ziyang (Chao Tzu-yang) (1919–   ) *general secretary, Communist Party of China*

Zhao Ziyang was born in Henan Province, China, on October 17, 1919, the son of a prosperous landlord. He joined the Communist Youth League in 1932 and two years later solicited membership in the Chinese Communist Party (CCP). Zhao functioned as a party propagandist against Japan throughout World War II and performed similar work as a prefectural leader during the civil war against CHIANG KAI-SHEK's Nationalists. When the People's Republic of China was proclaimed by MAO ZEDONG in 1949, Zhao transferred to the southern reaches of the country and occupied a succession of increasingly significant party posts. His career received a major boost in 1955 when he became part of the People's Council of Guangdong Province, where he specialized in agrarian and economic reforms at the expense of doctrinaire collectivization. Here Zhao pioneered the use of private plots and free rural markets to counter the disastrous effects of Mao's Great Leap Forward campaign in 1958. His efforts proved highly successful, and in 1965 he was rewarded with promotion to first party secretary of Guangdong Province. However, Zhao's willingness to question party orthodoxy led to his being branded a "capitalist roader" during the so-called Cultural Revolution, and in 1967 he was arrested and paraded through the streets as a criminal. Zhao was not politically rehabilitated until 1971 when he was reassigned party work in Inner Mongolia. But within years his career resumed its fast track when he became first party secretary of vitally important Szechwan Province and was encouraged to experiment with reforms again. This proved to be Zhao's finest hour, for his policy of decentralization and peasant empowerment led to dramatic increases in grain and industrial production. Hailed as a hero, Zhao was appointed to the Politburo by Deng Xiaoping in 1977, and three years later he supplanted HU YAOBANG as premier (prime minister).

As premier Zhao embarked on a program of radical economic and structural reforms bent on making the Chinese economy more productive and profitable—in a word, more capitalistic. He gave the industrial sector greater autonomy from the party apparatus and incorporated a more efficient tax system. He also incurred the wrath of hard-liners by attempting to streamline bureaucracy and reduce interference from the CCP but still managed to replace HUA GUOFENG as premier of the state council in 1980. The economy responded impressively but also brought a rise of inflation and corruption. Another unforeseen development was the push for greater democratization, principally among the large student population. Serious political destabilization resulted, and in 1986 Zhao was forced to dismiss his ally Hu and replace him with the more orthodox Li Peng.

In 1987 Zhao's good performance resulted in his becoming general secretary of the CCP, in effect, the head of China. He continued pursuing his reforms and liberalization policies against a storm of conservative criticism and mounting student demands for freedom. A crisis was reached in the spring of 1989 following the death of Hu, when spontaneous student demonstrations erupted across the length and breadth of China. The largest of these was in Tiananmen Square in Beijing. Zhao experienced tremendous pressure to use military force to end the demonstration, but he openly sided with the students and refused to interfere. An internecine party struggle ensued in which liberals were finally ousted by the hard-liners, and the Tiananmen Square demonstrations were repressed with deadly force on June 4, 1989. Zhao was arrested, accused of having made "mistakes," and removed from power. He consequently lost all his offices and titles and was placed under house arrest indefinitely. Once replaced by hard-liner Jiang Zemin, he also endured the ignominy of becoming an official "non-person." Zhao continues under house arrest to the present day, although he reputedly follows national politics closely. In August 2002 he issued a tersely worded statement to be read at the 16th Party Congress and attacked Jiang for his lack of progressive politics. He is still considered one of China's most successful economic reformers.

Further Reading

Fewsmith, J. *China since Tiananmen: The Politics of Transition*. New York: Cambridge University Press, 2001.

———. *Dilemmas of Reform in China: Political Conflict and Economic Debate*. Armonk, N.Y.: M. E. Sharpe, 1994.

Fincher, John. "Zhao's Fall, China's Loss." *Foreign Policy*, no. 76 (fall 1989): 3–25.

Goldman, M. *Sowing the Seeds of Democracy in China: Political Reforms in the Deng Xiaoping Era*. Cambridge, Mass.: Harvard University Press, 1994.

Shambaugh, David L. *The Making of a Premier: Zhao Ziyang's Provincial Career*. Epping, England, Bowker, 1984.

Woodruff, John. *China in Search of Its Future: Reform vs Repression, 1982 to 1987*. Secaucus, N.J.: Carole Pub. Group, 1990.

Zhelev, Zhelyu (1935–) *president of Bulgaria*

Zhelyu Zhelev was born in Vesselinovo, Bulgaria, on March 3, 1935, the son of poor farmers. Bulgaria was occupied by Soviet troops during World War II and they imposed a communist-style dictatorship upon the country under GEORGI DIMITROV. As a promising intellectual, Zhelev joined the Communist Party and was allowed to attend Sofia University to study philosophy. But even at this juncture he proved something of a maverick thinker for in 1958 his master's thesis openly criticized the ideology of VLADIMIR LENIN. Zhelev was consequently expelled from both the party and the university and he was forced to seek menial employment in his wife's village. He remained an outcast until 1972, when he was offered a sociologist position at the Center for Amateur Arts. Zhelev was eventually rehabilitated politically, readmitted to the university, and successfully defended his thesis in 1974. He then served in the Institute for Culture and published a landmark book entitled *Fascism* in 1982. This was superficially a critique of German, Italian, and Spanish fascism, but was in actuality a stinging rebuke of Bulgarian political institutions. The book was subsequently banned and Zhelev was dismissed from academe a second time. Fortunately, he did manage to complete and defend his doctorate on political philosophy in 1987.

By this time Bulgaria, like all communist-controlled states of Eastern Europe, was experiencing profound changes, thanks to the liberalization policies of Soviet premier MIKHAIL GORBACHEV. Zhelev, as one of the nation's leading dissidents, was actively organizing opposition to the Bulgarian Communist Party, and in 1988 he founded the Club in Support of Openness and Reform. The following year the hard-line communists renamed themselves the Bulgarian Socialist Party to retain a measure of political popularity. Zhelev countered by gathering various opposition groups into a single entity, the Union of Democratic Forces (UDF), in which he served as president of the Coordination Council. By 1990, in response to overwhelming popular pressure, the former Bulgarian communists agreed to allow the first free elections in 40 years. In the spring of 1990 Zhelev was elected to the new National Assembly and he also served as president of the UDF. That August his party, while winning fewer seats than the Socialists, managed a coalition arrangement with other parties and Zhelev became president of the new Bulgarian republic. Having succeeded long-time dictator TODOR ZHIVKOV, he became the first elected chief executive in Bulgarian history.

Under the Bulgarian system, the prime minister wields actual power of state while the presidency is more or less a unifying, ceremonial position. Nonetheless, Zhelev determined, for the sake of national unity, to forget the past and operate with magnanimity. He therefore pursued a policy of political reconciliation between communists and noncommunists, along with Bulgars and the Turkish minority. The result was a remarkable violence-free transition from totalitarianism to democracy and capitalism. Economically, Zhelev was committed to building a free market in Bulgaria, and he supported privatization of all state-owned industries. Furthermore, intent upon working Bulgaria into the fabric of the European Community, he met repeatedly with Western officials to better coordinate economic agendas. Impatient for results, he ordered an accelerated drive toward decollectivization of agriculture in 1992, while also instituting improved relations with neighboring Greece and Turkey. The transition to freedom proved politically difficult and in 1992 Zhelev was forced to endure a vote of "no confidence" in the National Assembly. He survived and remained in office another four years. But in June 1996 Zhelev lost the UDF presidential vote and five months later he stepped down in favor of Petar Stoyanov.

Considering that Bulgaria was one of the more hard-line communist regimes of Eastern Europe, Zhelev's tenure in office was surprisingly productive and peaceful. Since leaving public office he has continued on as something of a political sage, in the vein of Czechoslovakian playwright Václav Havel. He reemerged on the international scene in January 1998 by handing over top-secret Bulgarian documents pertaining to former dictator Todor Zhivkov and his role in suppression of ALEXANDER DUBČEK's "Prague Spring" in 1968. "Although it is only a piece of the puzzle of those events," he maintains, "I believe it will help to give a full picture of social and political life in 1968."

Further Reading

Baer, Josette. "Perspectives in Totalitarianism: Comparing the Theories of Zheliu Zhelev and Hannah Arendt." *East Central Europe* 27, no. 2 (2000): 69–85.

Bell, John D. *Bulgaria in Transition: Politics, Economics, Society, and Culture after Communism.* Boulder, Colo.: Westview Press, 1998.

Dimitrov, Vesselin. *Bulgaria: The Uneven Transition.* London: Routledge, 2001.

Ganev, Venelin I. "Preying on the State: Political Capitalism after Communism." Unpublished Ph.D. diss., University of Chicago, 2000.

Giatzidis, Emil. *An Introduction to Post-communist Bulgaria: Political, Economic, and Social Transformations.* New York: Manchester University Press, 2002.

Melone, Albert P. *Creating Parliamentary Government: The Transition to Democracy in Bulgaria.* Columbus: Ohio State University Press, 1998.

Zhivkov, Todor (1911–1998) *general secretary of the Bulgarian Communist Party*

Todor Zhivkov was born on September 7, 1911, in Pravets, Bulgaria, a son of poor peasants. He trained as an apprentice and was befriended by communist agitator GEORGI DIMITROV, who persuaded him to join the Bulgarian Communist Party in 1932. Zhivkov continued with his underground political efforts despite the fact that his faction was not particularly beholden to the Moscow line. However, when German forces invaded the Soviet Union in June 1941, the bickering communists finally unified themselves. Throughout the war Zhivkov was a guerrilla leader and he enjoyed considerable success in that role. On September 8, 1944, as the Red Army was approaching the capital of Sofia, he seized the city and arrested several leading ministers. He then was appointed head of the new militia force, consisting principally of former guerrillas, whose mission was to round up and execute thousands of suspected collaborators. In consequence of his newfound loyalty to the Soviet Union, Zhivkov was made a nonvoting member of the Communist Party Central Committee. Thereafter he made a rapid ascent up the party bureaucracy, filling a succession of increasingly important posts. After serving as first secretary of the capital committee in 1948 and becoming a full member of the Politburo in 1950, Zhivkov's rise was abetted by the death of JOSEPH STALIN in 1953. Stalin's successor, NIKITA KHRUSHCHEV, initiated a sweeping de-Stalinization of the Eastern Bloc, and Zhivkov immediately toed the new, more moderate line. With

Khrushchev's help, he toppled Stalinist prime minister Vulko Chervenkov in April 1956, and was appointed general secretary of the Bulgarian Communist Party. At that time, aged but 43 years, Zhivkov was the youngest leader of a Soviet Bloc nation.

Zhivkov ultimately retained power for 35 years, longer than any other Eastern leader. Part of his longevity can be traced to unswerving obedience toward Moscow in terms of both economic and foreign policy. In his pronouncements he often equated Bulgarian patriotism with loyalty to Russia. Consequently, the Soviets rewarded their faithful ally with ample supplies of weapons, credit, and food. Zhivkov also displayed a pragmatic streak in simply buying off the intelligentsia with patronage rather than oppressing them. After the 1964 coup in Moscow that deposed Khrushchev and installed LEONID BREZHNEV, he quickly reversed himself and supported the new orthodox line. He also became more reactionary by nature and developed a cult of personality around himself. But Zhivkov's unquestioning obedience toward Soviet leaders was a source of tension within his own party, and in 1965 he endured a coup attempt from disgruntled military and party leaders—the only such instance from within a Soviet Bloc nation. To further consolidate his hold on power, Zhivkov assumed the powers of the prime minister in 1962 and, once a new constitution was enacted, took on the title of president in 1971. All told he maintained an iron grip on Bulgaria and for over three decades functioned as the Soviet Union's most pliable ally.

By the late 1980s the East Bloc was being upended by the liberalizing policies of new Soviet premier MIKHAIL GORBACHEV. Loyal soldier that he was, Zhivkov publicly endorsed the changes even though they were slowly undermining his authority. But he was still a hard-line communist in other respects and could enact destructive policies. In 1984 he ordered the country's Turkish minority to adopt Bulgarian names, triggering a mass exodus of refugees. But by 1989 communist regimes throughout Eastern Europe were tottering and political change proved irrevocable. Zhivkov, unyielding and inflexible as ever, tried to resist and was bloodlessly deposed in a coup in December 1989. The following spring he was arrested and expelled from the party. In 1992 Zhivkov was convicted of embezzlement but the elderly leader was allowed to serve his seven years in house arrest. Six years later he was allowed to rejoin the communists' successors in the Bulgarian Socialist Party.

Zhivkov died in Sofia on August 6, 1998, still a respected father figure to the nation. When the new government refused to grant him a state funeral, thousands of former followers escorted his burial procession through the capital. In September 2001, 12 years after his downfall, Zhivkov was further honored in his hometown when residents erected a 10-foot bronze statue in his memory.

Further Reading

Anguelov, Zlatko. *Communism and the Remorse of an Innocent Victimizer.* College Station: Texas A & M University Press, 2002.

Bell, John D. *The Bulgarian Communist Party from Blagerov to Zhivkov.* Stanford, Calif.: Hoover Institution Press, 1986.

Genov, Nikolai, and Anna Krusteva. *Recent Social Trends in Bulgaria, 1960–1995.* Ithaca, N.Y.: McGill-Queen's University Press, 2001.

Glapinski, Adam. *The Origin, Development, and Collapse of Communism in Bulgaria, 1944–1990.* Boulder: University of Colorado Press, 1994.

Tchakarov, Kostadin. *The Second Floor: An Expose of the Backstage Politics in Bulgaria.* London: Macdonald, 1991.

Zhivkov, Todor. *Statesman and Builder of the New Bulgaria.* New York: Pergamon, 1982.

Zhou Enlai (Chou En-lai) (1898–1976) *prime minister of China*

Zhou Enlai was born in Huaian, Kiangsu Province, China, on March 5, 1898, into an affluent family of Mandarin bureaucrats. His parents died during his infancy and he was raised and educated by an uncle. In 1917 Zhou attended college in Japan and was introduced to Marxist political philosophy. Two years later he returned to Beijing to take part in revolutionary activities and edit a radical newspaper. He was subsequently arrested for protesting the ceding of land to Japan, and in 1920 he visited Paris, France, to continue his education. Zhou openly associated with French and Chinese socialists living there and joined a communist front organization. In 1922 he studied in Berlin and while there formally joined the Chinese Communist Party (CCP). Zhou returned to China in 1924 and found the nation beset by social and political ferment. In an attempt to suppress regional warlords, he next joined the Kuomintang (KMT, or Nationalist Party) of revolutionary SUN YAT-SEN, then in alliance with the communists. He was appointed deputy director of political affairs at the newly created Wampoa Military Academy under General CHIANG KAI-SHEK. However, in 1927 Chiang succeeded Sun as head of the KMT and he viciously turned on his erstwhile communist allies. Zhou fled from Shanghai and joined the main communist force under MAO ZEDONG in 1929. It proved a fateful alliance for, in contrast to the crude and boisterous Mao, Zhou cut a sophisticated figure who exuded urbanity and charm. Their careers became inextricably linked over the next 40 years.

Zhou functioned extremely well as a leading communist diplomat and spokesman throughout the formative decade of the 1930s and into World War II. His efforts proved instrumental in persuading Chiang and the KMT to present a united front against Japanese aggression after 1937. After 1945 Zhou continued meeting with Allied ambassadors in China, especially American secretary of state George C. Marshall, and received high marks for his acumen, courtesy, and skill. The long-anticipated showdown between the Nationalists and communists finally erupted in 1946 and ended three years later in a decisive victory for Mao's peasant-based guerrillas. When the People's Republic of China finally emerged in 1949, Zhou was simultaneously appointed prime minister (premier) and foreign minister, and tasked with expanding China's diplomatic contacts abroad. His efforts were largely stymied by a hostile United States, which refused to allow China a seat in the United Nations. When the Korean War broke out in 1950, it fell upon Zhou to issue the Americans a warning through the Indian ambassador that the presence of U.S. forces north of the 38th parallel would trigger Chinese intervention. General Douglas MacArthur blithely ignored the warning, and the Chinese struck suddenly in November 1950, ensuring that the war was stalemated by 1953. The following year Zhou became the first communist Chinese ambassador to work abroad when he appeared at the 1954 Geneva Convention. This was convened to end the First Indochina War between France and Vietnam's HO CHI MINH. Again, Zhou performed smoothly and even issued hints that diplomatic relations with the United States were possible. In 1955 he

appeared at the Bandung Conference, Indonesia, and asserted China's claim as leader of the developing nations. When tensions flared between the Chinese mainland and Chiang's forces sequestered on Taiwan in 1958, Zhou prevailed upon Mao not to invade the island of Matsu and risk a confrontation with the United States. He was also active in promoting close relations with the Soviet Union although, following the rise of reform-minded NIKITA KHRUSHCHEV, an ideological split between Russia and China proved inevitable. Still, Zhou did his best to contain hostility between the two communist superpowers despite skirmishing along their common border in 1969.

Domestically, Zhou was a useful ally of Mao and his sometimes erratic, radical policies such as the Great Leap Forward of 1958 and the Great Cultural Revolution of 1966. However, he always sought to steer a moderate ground to mitigate ideological excesses, and was frequently accused of harboring and protecting dissidents from radical forces. But by 1971 China was as diplomatically isolated as ever, and even Mao saw the need for a new and dramatic rapprochement with the United States to offset the growing military might of the Soviet Union. In 1971 Zhou initiated his famous "ping pong" diplomacy, when athletes from the United States were cordially invited to China for the first time. This paved the way for President RICHARD M. NIXON to visit China the following year, establish formal diplomatic relations, and allow China into the UN. He even managed to strike a friendly accord with Japan, long considered among China's most deadly enemies. After Mao died in 1975, Zhou was officially retained as prime minister but he was actually running China. His most important work was to rehabilitate the political career of arch reformer Deng Xiaoping and to disarm and discredit the radical "Gang of Four" who attempted to fill the vacuum left by Mao's death. Zhou himself died in Beijing on January 8, 1976. Like other revolutionary leaders of his generation, he was a truly beloved public figure and hailed as the "people's premier." His sagacity, tact, and consummate professionalism were instrumental in helping reestablish China's links to the rest of the world.

Further Reading

Bloodworth, Dennis. *The Chinese Machiavelli: 3,000 Years of Chinese Statecraft.* New Brunswick, N.J.: Transaction Publishers, 2004.

Chan, Adrian. *Chinese Marxism.* New York: Continuum, 2002.

Gregor, Anthony J. *A Place in the Sun: Marxism and Fascism in China's Long Revolution.* Boulder, Colo.: Westview Press, 2000.

Han, Suyin. *Eldest Son: Zhou Enlai and the Making of Modern China, 1898–1976.* New York: Kodansha International, 1995.

Lee, Chae-jin. *Zhou Enlai: The Early Years.* Stanford, Calif.: Stanford University Press, 1994.

Shao, Kuo-kang. *Zhou Enlai and the Foundations of Chinese Foreign Policy.* New York: St. Martin's Press, 1996.

Smith, Stephen A. *A Road Is Made: Communism in Shanghai, 1920–1927.* Honolulu: University of Hawaii, 2000.

Song, Yongyi. "The Role of Zhou Enlai in the Cultural Revolution: A Contradictory Image from Diverse Sources." *Issues and Studies* 37 (March–April 2001): 1–28.

Zia ul-Haq, Mohammad (1924–1988) *president of Pakistan*

Mohammad Zia ul-Haq was born in Jullander, East Punjab, India, on August 12, 1924, the son of an army clerk. Though Muslim, he was well educated at Christian missionary schools and subsequently attended the Royal Indian Military Academy in Dhehra Dun. Zia was then commissioned in the military and rendered distinguished service with the British in Burma during World War II. In 1947 Britain partitioned the subcontinent into two new nations, Hindu-dominated India and Muslim-dominated Pakistan. Zia sided with the latter and joined the Pakistani army. He proved himself a dedicated soldier and in 1955 was selected to attend the Command Staff College in Quetta. After several tours of military schools in the United States, Zia fought well in the 1965 Indo-Pakistani War and by 1969 had advanced to brigadier general. However, it was not until the administration of ZULFIKAR ALI BHUTTO in 1975 that Zia's career greatly accelerated. He was made lieutenant general in 1975, and the following year Bhutto elevated him to army chief of staff—over the objections of more senior officers. Clearly the prime minister wanted a high-ranking military commander with few political aspirations

and the pious, devout Zia seemed a perfect choice. But in March 1977 Bhutto's manipulation of elections backfired, when the opposition accused him of rigging the process. Pakistan then erupted into ceaseless demonstrations and disorder that threatened national stability. At this juncture Zia, nominally aloof from politics, decisively intervened on July 5, 1977, and toppled the Bhutto regime. He declared himself president on September 16, 1978.

Zia initially intended to restore civilian authority within 90 days, but this was not feasible due to widespread social unrest. He consequently clamped down on dissent by suspending the constitution, dissolving parliament, and outlawing political and labor activity. This had the effect of restoring a semblance of order to Pakistan but there remained the problem of Bhutto. Zia initially wanted to release the former prime minister but his popularity surged, and the general feared revenge. At length he arranged for Bhutto to be charged with the murder of a political opponent, for which he was hanged in April 1979. This act embittered members of the Pakistan People's Party (PPP) against the government and led to more instability. The economy was failing and political stability deteriorated once again, but Zia was succored by the December 1979 Soviet invasion of neighboring Afghanistan. Suddenly the United States, one of his biggest critics, became his staunchest ally. As a Muslim, Zia strongly opposed the Soviet occupation, and he allowed the Americans to supply clandestine military aid to freedom fighters using Pakistani soil. His cooperation proved essential in the containment of Soviet expansionism.

Buoyed by American financial aid, Zia was allowed to slowly restore the democratic process in a modified form. He introduced strict Islamic law that called for harsh punishments and sought to shore up support from fundamentalist Muslim groups. He also promoted regional cooperation by reestablishing good relations with India and China. Zia finally permitted elections in March 1985, but political parties were still forbidden. Zia had arranged his own elevation to the presidency of Pakistan, which was confirmed in a referendum in December 1984. He also authored specific constitutional changes allowing him to dissolve parliament at his discretion and enhanced the power of his office. Zia continued running Pakistani affairs smoothly and efficiently until August 17, 1988, when he was killed in an unexplained airplane crash. Two years earlier Benazir Bhutto, daughter of the late prime minister, had returned home to organize the PPP for upcoming elections. In November 1988 she was elected the first female prime minister of an Islamic country, fittingly avenging her father's death.

Further Reading

Ahmed, Mumtaz. "The Crescent and the Sword: Islam, the Military, and Political Legitimacy in Pakistan, 1977–1985." *Middle East Journal* 50, no. 3 (1996): 372–386.

Arif, Khalid M. *Working with Zia: Pakistan's Power Politics.* New York: Oxford University Press, 1995.

Burki, Shahid J., Craig Baxter, and Robert LaPorte. *Pakistan under the Military: Eleven Years of Zia ul-Haq.* Boulder, Colo.: Westview Press, 1991.

Hussain, Mushahid. *Pakistan's Politics: The Zia Years.* New York: Konark Pub., 1991.

Parveen, Shaukat Ali. *Politics of Conviction: The Life and Times of Muhammad Zia-ul-Haq.* London: London Centre for Pakistan Studies, 1997.

Wirsing, Robert G. *Pakistan's Security under Zia, 1977–1988: The Policy Imperatives of a Peripheral Asian State.* New York: St. Martin's Press, 1991.

Ziring, Lawrence. "Public Policy Dilemmas and Pakistan's Nationality Problem: The legacy of Zia ul-Haq." *Asian Survey* 28 (August 1986): 795–817.

BIBLIOGRAPHY

Current Biography. New York: H. W. Wilson Co., 1940– .

Eccleshall, Robert, and Graham Walker, eds. *Biographical Dictionary of British Prime Ministers.* New York: Routledge, 1998.

Encyclopedia of World Biography. Detroit. Gale Group, 1998– .

Fredriksen, John C. *Biographical Dictionary of Modern World Leaders, 1992 to the Present.* New York: Facts On File, 2003.

Glickman, Harvey, ed. *Political Leaders of Contemporary Africa South of the Sahara.* New York: Greenwood Press, 1992.

Hamilton, Neil A. *Founders of Modern Nations: A Biographical Dictionary.* Santa Barbara, Calif.: ABC-Clio, 1995.

———. *Presidents: A Biographical Dictionary.* New York: Facts On File, 2001.

Hutchinson Encyclopedia of Modern Political Biography. Boulder, Colo.: Westview Press, 1999.

Jackson-Laufer, Guida M. *Women Rulers through the Ages.* Santa Barbara, Calif.: ABC-Clio, 1999.

Kavanagh, Dennis, ed. *A Dictionary of Political Biography.* New York: Oxford University Press, 1998.

Laybourn, Keith. *British Political Leaders: A Biographical Dictionary.* Santa Barbara, Calif.: ABC-Clio, 2001.

Lentz, Harris M. *Encyclopedia of Heads of State and Governments, 1900 through 1945.* Jefferson, N.C.: McFarland, 1999.

Leung, Pak-Wah. *Political Leaders of Modern China: A Biographical Dictionary.* Westport, Conn.: Greenwood Press, 2002.

Magill, Frank N., and John Powell. *U.S. Government Leaders.* Pasadena, Calif.: Salem Press, 1997.

Newsmakers. Detroit: Gale Group, 1985– .

Palmer, Alan W. *Who's Who in Modern History.* London: Routledge, 2001.

———. *Who's Who in World Politics: From 1860 to the Present Day.* New York: Routledge, 1996.

Powell, John, ed. *Biographical Encyclopedia of the 20th Century World Leaders,* 5 vols. New York: Marshall Cavendish, 2000.

Rosen, Greg, ed. *Dictionary of Labour Biography.* London: Politico's, 2001.

Sobel, Robert, and David B. Sicilia, eds. *The United States Executive Branch: A Biographical Directory of Heads of State and Cabinet Officials.* Westport, Conn.: Greenwood Press, 2003.

Uwechue, Ralph. *Makers of Modern Africa: Profiles in History.* London: Africa Books, 1996.

Vazquez Gomez, Junita. *Dictionary of Mexican Rulers, 1325–1997.* Westport, Conn.: Greenwood Press, 1997.

Wilsford, David. *Political Leaders of Contemporary Western Europe: A Biographical Dictionary.* Westport, Conn.: Greenwood Press, 1995.

Young, Hugo, ed. *Political Lives.* New York: Oxford University Press, 2001.

INDEX BY COUNTRY

INDEX

Boldface numbers indicate main entries.
Italic numbers indicate photographs.